Lecture Notes in Computer Science 4338

Commenced Publication in 1973
Founding and Former Series Editors:
Gerhard Goos, Juris Hartmanis, and Jan van Leeuwen

Editorial Board

David Hutchison
Lancaster University, UK

Takeo Kanade
Carnegie Mellon University, Pittsburgh, PA, USA

Josef Kittler
University of Surrey, Guildford, UK

Jon M. Kleinberg
Cornell University, Ithaca, NY, USA

Friedemann Mattern
ETH Zurich, Switzerland

John C. Mitchell
Stanford University, CA, USA

Moni Naor
Weizmann Institute of Science, Rehovot, Israel

Oscar Nierstrasz
University of Bern, Switzerland

C. Pandu Rangan
Indian Institute of Technology, Madras, India

Bernhard Steffen
University of Dortmund, Germany

Madhu Sudan
Massachusetts Institute of Technology, MA, USA

Demetri Terzopoulos
University of California, Los Angeles, CA, USA

Doug Tygar
University of California, Berkeley, CA, USA

Moshe Y. Vardi
Rice University, Houston, TX, USA

Gerhard Weikum
Max-Planck Institute of Computer Science, Saarbruecken, Germany

Prem Kalra   Shmuel Peleg (Eds.)

Computer Vision, Graphics and Image Processing

5th Indian Conference, ICVGIP 2006
Madurai, India, December 13-16, 2006
Proceedings

 Springer

Volume Editors

Prem Kalra
Indian Institute of Technology Delhi
Department of Computer Science and Engineering
Hauz Khas, New Delhi 110016, India
E-mail: pkalra@cse.iitd.ac.in

Shmuel Peleg
The Hebrew University of Jerusalem
School of Computer Science and Engineering
91904, Jerusalem, Israel
E-mail: peleg@cs.huji.ac.il

Library of Congress Control Number: 2006938165

CR Subject Classification (1998): I.4, I.5, I.2.10, I.2.6, I.3.5, F.2.2

LNCS Sublibrary: SL 6 – Image Processing, Computer Vision, Pattern Recognition, and Graphics

ISSN   0302-9743
ISBN-10   3-540-68301-1 Springer Berlin Heidelberg New York
ISBN-13   978-3-540-68301-8 Springer Berlin Heidelberg New York

Springer is a part of Springer Science+Business Media

springer.com

© Springer-Verlag Berlin Heidelberg 2006
Printed in Germany

Typesetting: Camera-ready by author, data conversion by Scientific Publishing Services, Chennai, India
Printed on acid-free paper   SPIN: 11949619   06/3142   5 4 3 2 1 0

Preface

The Indian Conference on Computer Vision, Graphics and Image Processing (ICVGIP) is a forum bringing together researchers and practitioners in these related areas, coming from national and international academic institutes, from government research and development laboratories, and from industry. ICVGIP has been held biannually since its inception in 1998, attracting more participants every year, including international participants.

The proceedings of ICVGIP 2006, published in Springer's series *Lecture Notes in Computer Science*, comprise 85 papers that were selected for presentation from 284 papers, which were submitted from all over the world. Twenty-nine papers were oral presentations, and 56 papers were presented as posters. For the first time in ICVGIP, the review process was double-blind as common in the major international conferences. Each submitted paper was assigned at least three reviewers who are experts in the relevant area. It was difficult to select such a few papers, as there were many other deserving, but those could not be accommodated.

The support of the reviewers has been crucial, and we thank them for their valuable efforts and the time devoted for the conference. We would like to thank the team of IIIT Hyderabad, who developed and provided the online conference management software, which was used for ICVGIP 2006. Parag Kumar Chaudhuri of IIT Delhi helped greatly in the entire process and logistics, from the Call for Papers to the preparation of the proceedings. Siddharth Srinivasan, a MTech student at IIT Delhi, also contributed in the logistics. We would also like to thank the support of our sponsors, especially M/S Adobe India, M/S IBM India Research Lab, M/S Google India, M/S Yahoo! India Research and Development, M/S Tata Consultancy Services Ltd, and M/S HPL India.

We have no doubt that ICVGIP 2006 was another step towards making ICVGIP an important worldwide event to showcase research and development in the areas of computer vision, graphics and image processing.

Prem Kalra
Shmuel Peleg
(Program Chairs)

Organization

ICVGIP 2006 Team

General Chairs

Rangachar Kasturi
The University of South Florida

Subhashis Banerjee
IIT Delhi

Program Chairs

Shmuel Peleg
The Hebrew University of Jerusalem

Prem Kalra
IIT Delhi

Organizing Chairs

C. Muruganantham
Thiagarajar College of Engineering, Madurai

Santanu Chaudhury
IIT Delhi

Plenary Chair

P. Anandan
Microsoft Research India

Program Committee

Scott T. Acton	University of Virginia
Neeharika Adabala	Microsoft Research
Narendra Ahuja	UIUC/IIIT Hyderabad
P. Anandan	Microsoft Research
Gabriella Sanniti di Baja	Instituto di Cibernetica, Italy
Chandrajeet Bajaj	University of Texas, Austin
Subhashis Banerjee	IIT Delhi
Jayanta Basak	IBM India Research Lab
Kiran Bhat	Industrial Light and Magic

B.B. Bhattacharya	ISI Kolkata
Kanad Biswas	University of Central Florida
P.K. Biswas	IIT Kharagpur
Prabin Bora	IIT Guwahati
Ronan Boulic	EPFL, Switzerland
Bhabatosh Chanda	ISI Kolkata
Sharat Chandran	IIT Bombay
B.B. Chaudhuri	ISI Kolkata
Santanu Chaudhury	IIT Delhi
Subhasis Choudhury	IIT Bombay
Amit Roy-Chowdhury	University of California, Riverside
Sukhendu Das	IIT Madras
Larry Davis	University of Maryland, USA
Vito de Gesu	University of Palermo, Italy
U.B. Desai	IIT Bombay
Venu Govindaraju	University of Buffalo, USA
Venu Madhav Govindu	
Amarnath Gupta	USC, USA
Phalguni Gupta	IIT Kanpur
Sunil Hadap	PDI/DreamWorks, USA
C.V. Jawahar	IIIT Hyderabad, USA
S.D. Joshi	IIT Delhi
Prem Kalra	IIT Delhi
B. Kartikeyan	SAC Ahmedabad
Rangachar Kasturi	University of South Florida, USA
Ravi Kothari	IBM India Research Lab
Subodh Kumar	Nvidea, USA
M.K. Kundu	ISI Kolkata
Arvind Lakshmikumar	Sarnoff India
Zicheng Liu	Microsoft Research, Redmond, USA
Nadia Magnenat Thalmann	Miralab, University of Geneva, Switzerland
Dinesh Manocha	UNC, Chapel Hill, USA
Dimitri Metaxas	Rutgers University, USA
S.P. Mudur	Concordia University, Canada
Amitabh Mukherjee	IIT Kanpur
D.P. Mukherjee	ISI Kolkata
Jayanta Mukhopadhyay	IIT Kharagpur
C.A. Murthy	ISI Kolkata
Anoop Namboodiri	IIIT Hyderabad
P.J. Narayanan	IIIT Hyderabad
Srinivasa Narasimhan	CMU, USA
H. Niemann	University of Erlangen, Germany
Umapada Pal	ISI Kolkata
Ajay Kumar	IIT Delhi
Vladimir Pavlovic	Rutgers University, USA
Witold Pedrycz	University of Alberta, Canada
Shmuel Peleg	Hebrew University of Jerusalem, Isreal

Marc Pollefeys	UNC at Chapel Hill, USA
Arun Pujari	University of Hyderabad
A.N. Rajagopalan	IIT Madras
Subrata Rakshit	CAIR, Bangalore
K.R. Ramakrishnan	IISc, Bangalore
Ravi Ramamoorthi	Columbia University, USA
Visvanathan Ramesh	Siemens Research, USA
Anand Rangarajan	University of Florida, USA
S.V. Rao	IIT Guwahati
Ramesh Raskar	MERL, USA
Ajay K. Ray	IIT Kharagpur
Sumantra Dutta Roy	IIT Bombay
Konrad Schindler	Monash University, Australia
Steve Seitz	University of Washington, USA
S. Sengupta	IIT Kharagpur
Mubarak Shah	University of Central Florida, USA
P.S. Sastry	IISc, Bangalore
Sung Yong Shin	KAIST, South Korea
Kaleem Siddiqi	McGill University, Canada
Karan Singh	University of Toronto, Canada
Jayanthi Sivaswamy	IIIT Hyderabad
S.N. Srihari	University of Buffalo, USA
S.H. Srinivasan	Yahoo Software Development India
Peter Sturm	INRIA, Rhone Alpes, France
Srikanth Suryanarayananan	GE Global Research
Tanveer Syeda-Mahmood	IBM Almaden Research Center, USA
Daniel Thalmann	EPFL, Switzerland
Kentaro Toyama	Microsoft Research India
J. Udupa	University of Pennsylvania, USA
Amitabh Varshney	University of Maryland, USA
Namrata Vaswani	Iowa State University, USA
Manik Varma	Microsoft Research, India
Ragini Verma	University of Pennsylvania, USA
Yaser Yacoob	University of Maryland, College Park, USA
Andrew Zisserman	Oxford University, UK

Additional Reviewers

Chris Alvino	Saurav Basu	Ayesha Choudhary
Ankur Agarwal	Basabi Bhaumik	Lipika Dey
Nafiz Arica	Jay Bhatnagar	Matthew Flagg
Himanshu Arora	Ujjwal Bhattacharya	Yasutaka Furukawa
Karl Axnick	Matthew Boonstra	Bernhard Geiger
Yousuf Aytar	Parag Chaudhuri	Bernard Ghanem
Sajjad Baloch	Jatin Chhugani	Prithwijit Guha
Rajendar Bahl	Tat-Jun Chin	Anubha Gupta

Gaurav Harit
Gang Hua
Vardhman Jain
Parmeshwar Khurd
Valentina Korzhova
Gurunandan Krishnan
Arun Kumar
Avinash Kumar
Jingen Liu
Uma Mudenagudi
Atul Negi

Sangmin Park
Kolin Paul
Salil Prabhakar
P.V.Madhusudhan Rao
Imran Saleemi
Subhajit Sanyal
Geetika Sharma
Vinay Siddahanavalli
Pradip Sircar
Bong-Soo Sohn
Hari Sundar

Sinisa Todorovic
Himanshu Vajaria
Uday Kumar Visesh
Hanzi Wang
Jianguo Wang
Peng Wang
Binglong Xie
Shuntaro Yamazaki
Youngrock Yoon

Table of Contents

Image Restoration and Super-Resolution

Segmentation and Classification

Image Filtering/Processing

Graphics and Visualization

Video Analysis

Reducing False Positives in Video Shot Detection Using Learning
Techniques 421
   Nithya Manickam, Aman Parnami, and Sharat Chandran

Text Driven Temporal Segmentation of Cricket Videos 433
   K. Pramod Sankar, Saurabh Pandey, and C.V. Jawahar

Tracking and Surveillance

Recognition (Face/Gesture/Object)

Compression

Document Processing/OCR

Content Based Image Retrieval

Stereo/Camera Calibration

Biometrics

Edge Model Based High Resolution Image Generation[*]

Malay Kumar Nema[1], Subrata Rakshit[1], and Subhasis Chaudhuri[2]

[1] Centre for Artificial Intelligence and Robotics, Bangalore
[2] VIP Lab, Department of Electrical Engineering, IIT Bombay, Mumbai

Abstract. The present paper proposes a new method for high resolution image generation from a single image. Generation of high resolution (HR) images from lower resolution image(s) is achieved by either reconstruction-based methods or by learning-based methods. Reconstruction based methods use multiple images of the same scene to gather the extra information needed for the HR. The learning-based methods rely on the learning of characteristics of a specific image set to inject the extra information for HR generation. The proposed method is a variation of this strategy. It uses a generative model for sharp edges in images as well as descriptive models for edge representation. This prior information is injected using the Symmetric Residue Pyramid scheme. The advantages of this scheme are that it generates sharp edges with no ringing artefacts in the HR and that the models are universal enough to allow usage on wide variety of images without requirement of training and/or adaptation. Results have been generated and compared to actual high resolution images.

Index terms: Super-Resolution, edge modelling, Laplacian pyramids.

1   Introduction

Generation of high resolution (HR) images from low resolution (LR) images have been attempted through reconstruction based approaches and learning based approaches. Reconstruction based approaches require multiple images. They make use of subpixel shifts between images to pool in the extra information needed to create the HR image. Methods employed include sub-pixel registration, nonuniform interpolation [1][2] and frequency domain approaches [3][4]. An exhaustive list of methods can be found in [5], [6]. Learning based approaches build a relation between LR and HR images, based on the imaging process and/or description of corresponding edges between LR and HR. Multiresolution based mehods are a natural choice for this problem. The multiresolution representations seperate the information in images by frequency. The generation of HR is essentially the problem of generating the missing (hypothetical) level(-1) subband. Solutions have been proposed based on zoom [7][8], wavelet [9] and contourlet [10] coefficients. A detailed discussion can be obtained from [11]. The problem may be

---

[*] This work is supported by DRDO through project CAR-008.

P. Kalra and S. Peleg (Eds.): ICVGIP 2006, LNCS 4338, pp. 1–12, 2006.

decomposed into three parts: (i) formulating a model for predicting edges in HR based on edges in LR (ii) using the model for calculating the high frequency components to be added and (iii) injecting those (postulated) components in a manner consistent with the known lower frequency components as given in the LR image. This paper presents a new method for each of these, based on Laplacian pyramids and their variations. Laplacian pyramids [12] are chosen for the multiresolution representation as they provide the simplest and most regular representation of edges in the subbands. There is a single, non-directional subband at each level, unlike the three subbands for 2D wavelets. The 4/3 redundancy also leads to more regular structures in the subband.

Our model for predicting edges in the HR image is based on the observation that edges arising due to occlusion remain sharp at every resolution. Edges arising due to shading and surface patterns should become blurred when resolution is increased. Conversely, the majority of the sharp edges in an image may be assumed to be occlusion edges. For generating an HR image, these sharp edges must be identified in the LR and their sharpness must be restored in the HR image. Simple interpolation will blur all edges while increasing feature sizes. Our HR generation is limited to the objective of preserving sharpness of edges which are sharp in LR. (A single image method cannot, in any case, introduce new edges and features into the HR image.) The Laplacian pyramid, like all other multiresolution representations, creates a hierarchy of subbands encoding edges of decreasing sharpness. Thus the first subband, designated L_0, captures all the sharp edges in the image. This paper presents methods for interpolating L_{-1} from L_0, restoring the sharpness of the edge representations and ensuring consistency between this modified L_{-1} and the given LR image.

The current work makes use of two recent results related to Laplacian pyramids. It has been shown that Laplacian subbands can be represented using edge model elements [13]. (Note that these are descriptive models describing the patterns corresponding to edges of various sharpness and geometry, as opposed to the generative model for edges discussed earlier.) A model-based description is convenient for altering the sharpness of selected edges without affecting the resolution or frequency content of the image as a whole. Another result of relevance to the present work is the extension of Burt's Laplacian pyramids called Symmetric Residue pyramids [14] (SRP). It addresses the issue of consistency between pyramid subbands and the nature of independent information at each level. The methods given there are used in the present work to initially postulate an L_{-1} from given L_0 and then, after selective edge sharpening, to ensure consistency between modified L_{-1} and L_0.

The paper is organised as follows. We provide relevant details of edge modelling of Laplacian subbands in Section 2. Subsequently we briefly review SRP in Section 3. Section 4 discusses generation of L_{-1} using edge-model representation, including effect of subsampling on the modelling process. Section 4 ends with the algorithm for generation of L_{-1}. Section 5 provides results and performance evaluation and the paper concludes in Section 6.

2   Edge-Modelling

For purposes of interpolation for HR, we need a mechanism to model the dominant, sharp edges in the L_0 subband. As such, it is important to have a representation that is edge based rather than pixel or frequency based since it will allow edge specific modifications. As the SRP based interpolation (see Sec 3) can fill in the mid- and lower-frequency components later, the MSE of the modelling process is not that critical. The Laplacian subband edge-modelling process described in [13] provides such a model. The modelling elements shown in the Figure 1 are the ones which are called Primitive Set(PS)-28.

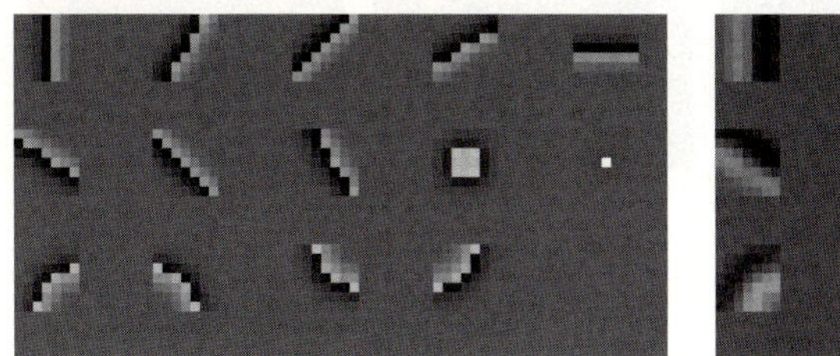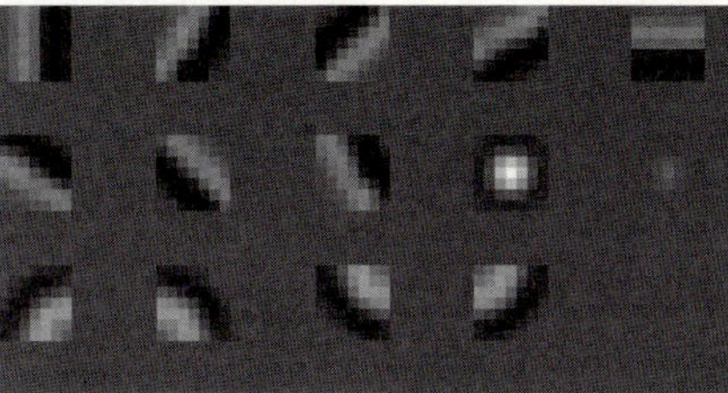

(a) The 14 elements based on sharp edges   (b)The 14 elements based on smoother edges

Fig. 1. The PS28 primitive set elements. The 7×7 elements, scaled for display.

The PS-28 elements are defined as 7×7 images. The PS is chosen to be a set of sharp and blur edge elements as represented in Laplacian subbands. Due to its band-pass nature, only edges of certain thickness can be dominant in any subband. As mentioned in [13], the problem simplifies if one opts for the task of selecting 7×7 blocks that can be represented using individual PS elements (the modelling approach) instead of representing arbitrary 7×7 blocks as a superposition of a given set (projection onto basis approach). Denote the PS elements as $\mathbf{p_i}$ and the block to be modelled as $\mathbf{x}$. For computing a representation using a basis set, the procedure would be to compute a set of coefficients, α_i, to best represent any given $\mathbf{x}$. For edge modelling in [13], the procedure adopted is to take each element $\mathbf{p_i}$ and see which part of the image it can best model. Various model fit criteria are used to determine in which order the Laplacian gets modelled by the various model elements. The objective is to find an $\mathbf{x}$, model element $\mathbf{p_i}$ and associated scalar α that minimises

$$J = \frac{\|(\mathbf{x} - \alpha.\mathbf{p_i})\|}{\|(\mathbf{x})\|}.$$ (1)

The edge-model element for a particular location was picked on the basis of energy and modelling error. For each 7×7 block extracted from the Laplacian image, the following were computed. The energy of the extract determines the amount of signal present. Laplacians, like all subbands, are zero-mean and sparse. The energy is concentrated in only a few areas. Only blocks having energy above a threshold were considered for modelling. The threshold was initially set high and reduced with each iteration till it reached a lower cut off. This cut off determined the termination of the iterative process, as errors below this threshold were not modelled further. Only blocks whose energy crosses the current threshold, were considered for modelling by elements of the primitive set. A sample result of the accuracy of modelling process is shown in Figure 2. It is seen that the modelling of Laplacian subbands can be done to a reasonable accuracy.

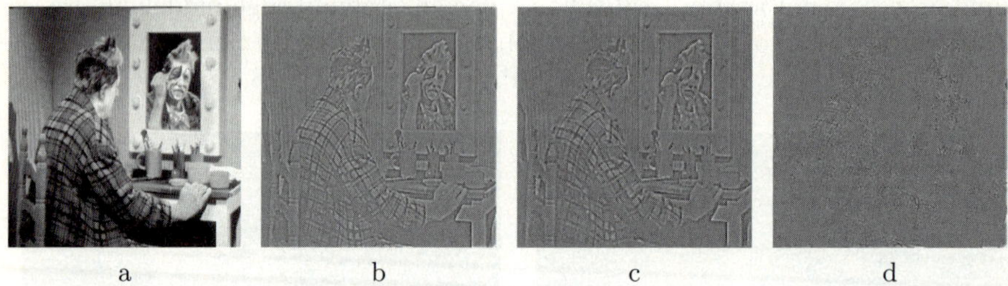

a   b   c   d

Fig. 2. Demonstration of modelling accuracy: (a) `Clown` image, (b) Laplacian of `Clown` image, (c) Modelled Laplacian (d) Modelling error

3   Symmetric Residue Pyramids

Symmetric Residue Pyramids [14] were proposed as an extension to Burt Laplacian pyramids. Initial aim of the SRP was to achieve better signal compaction. It makes use of the fact that the Laplacian subband at the level i, L_i and gaussian subband at next level $i+1$, G_{i+1} are related due to the redundancy in the Laplacian pyramids. The set of all possible L_i can be divided into equal sized cosets corresponding to each possible G_{i+1}. The process of generating an acceptable L_i given a G_i starts with an initial guess, which may even be a blank (zero) image. An iterative process is deployed to get one of the acceptable L_i: (exp is the expand/interpolation operation, ss is subsampling and lpf is low-pass filtering)

1. $L_i[0] = $ Initial guess (may even be 0 image)
2. $G_i[k] = exp(G_{i+1}) + L_i[k]$ (usual pyramid reconstruction)
3. $L_i[k+1] = G_i[k] - exp(ss(lpf(G_i[k])))$

The above process can be used to guess L_i to within an element in the correct coset. The reconstruction process only needs the difference between this element and the actual L_i, denoted as SL_i. The SRP is defined by $SL_i, i = 0...n$, G_{n+1}. Decomposition of **Lena** image using Burt Laplacian pyramid and SRP is shown in Figure 3(a) and 3(b) respectively.

    The above processes are of relevance to the current work for two reasons. The iterative scheme, initialzed with a blank L_{-1}, is a good way of interpolating an L_{-1} from L_0. It is certainly better than simple interpolation (essentially $L_{-1} = exp(L_0)$). More importantly, it highlights the need for, and the method of utilization, of additional information. The SRP subbands show that the missing information is with regards to high frequency informaion about the sharp edges.

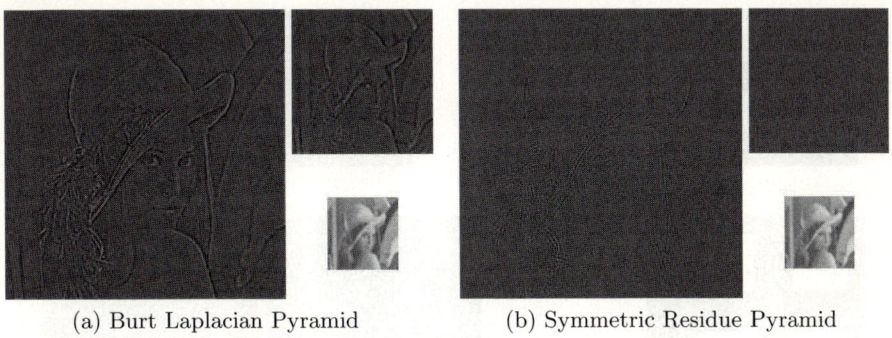

(a) Burt Laplacian Pyramid   (b) Symmetric Residue Pyramid

Fig. 3. Decompositions of **Lena** image

This is just the kind of information that could be provided by the edge model based interpolation or sharpenning of a Laplacian. Moreover, any information fed as a prior $(L_{-1}[0])$, can be considered as an addition of two components: one that is part of the L_{-1} coset corresponding to G_0 and one that is not. The former constitutes the part of the prior that is consistent with the LR and latter the inconsistent part. Once the iteration process is run, the latter is eliminated. This is of importance because it means that our generation of the prior need not be very accurate. A certain amount of error correction can be performed.

Having reviewed the necessary building blocks, the generation of L_{-1} is addressed next.

4 Generation of L_{-1} Using Edge-Model Representation

Given the edge-model based representation of the Laplacian subbands, it is intuitive to use direct method of placing them at calculated position in $2X$ (2 times) to get L_{-1}. We have done experiments which reveal that the modelling of subsampled images does suffer from errors while modelling any of the even or odd location. The even or odd location depends on the choice of pixels in subsampling process. The error becomes prominent when a $2X$ Laplacian image i.e. L_{-1} is generated using the description. Though the error could be suppressed by a choice of higher energy threshold for modelling, it would affect the modelling accuracy at the L_0 level itself. This is shown in Figure 4. The image consists of four 64×64 blocks. The left top pixel of the boxes is placed at even-even (block at left top), odd-even (block at right top), even-odd (box at bottom left), and odd-odd (block at bottom right) locations. Figure 4(d) shows the modelling error at LR only. It is clearly visible that the modelling error is more in case of the blocks placed at the location where one of the starting positions happens to be odd. The bottom right block suffers the most as it is placed at the odd-odd location.

The image formation process can be assumed to be modelled by the expression [15][16] $\mathbf{y} = \mathbf{DBMx} + \mathbf{n}$. Here $\mathbf{M}$ is a warp matrix, $\mathbf{B}$ represent a blur matrix and $\mathbf{D}$ is a subsampling matrix, and $\mathbf{n}$ is noise vector. $\mathbf{y}$ and $\mathbf{x}$ are the

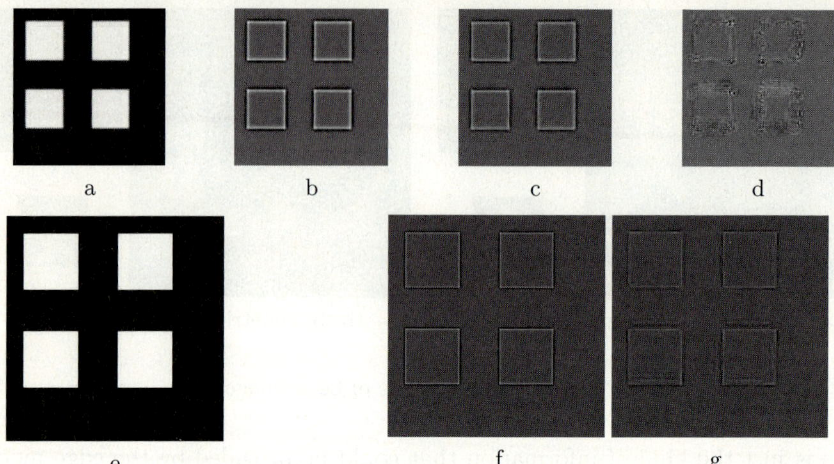

Fig. 4. Subsampling and grid positions. Top: (a) Low resolution (LR) image (b) L_0 of LR (c) Modelled L_0 of LR. (d) modelling error. Modelling errors after subsampling are more for odd grid positions. Bottom: (e) Original (HR) image (f) True L_0 of HR image (g) Estimate of HR's L_0, based on modelling description of L_0 of LR. The interpolation error also depends on position.

LR and HR respectively. **D** breaks the equivalence between even and odd grid points in the HR image. In the above example the modelling elements generated happened to be the ones which correspond to edges at even positions, *i.e.*, the positive peak corresponds to even row or column location in the image. It is not desirable to circumvent this problem by incorporating modelling elements for both even and odd location edges. It doubles the number of elements from PS-28 to PS-56 and increases the complexity of the modelling process. In practise, this approach does not lead to reduction in modelling error. For the specific case of interpolation and edge sharpening, an indirect solution is devised based on post-interpolation modelling.

4.1   Dealing with Modelling Error Due to Subsampling

Our final objective is to define an L_{-1} based on some model reconstruction. As such a model for L_0 itself is not a necessity. One solution is to interpolate L_0 to $\hat{L}_{-1}$ *before* performing the edge modelling. The quality of the interpolation method is clearly important. In our case we have used the symmetric residue process to get the $\hat{L}_{i-1}$, as explained earlier. After interpolation, we generate the edge-model description of the interpolated image's Laplacian subband. The variation in edge patterns due to even-odd positions is attenuated because the equivalence between various grid points gets restored when they are upsampled. As edge representation gets blurred during interpolation, the model is dominated by the elements corresponding to the thicker edges. These modelling elements are now replaced by sharp edge modelling elements. By doing so we undo the

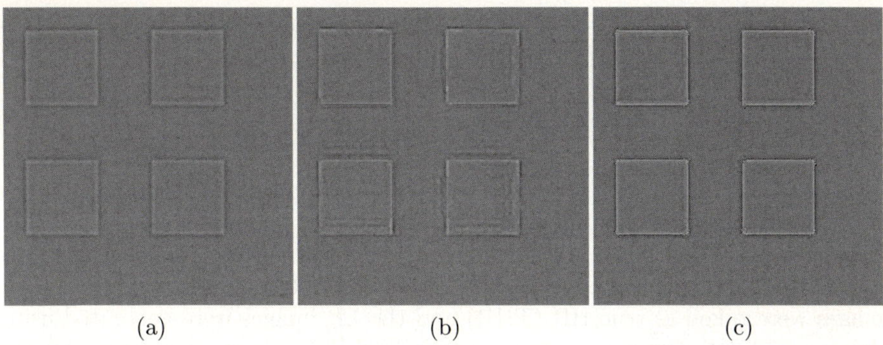

(a)   (b)   (c)

Fig. 5. Generation of sharp edges by post-interpolation model switch. (a) L_{-1} by interpolating L_0 has thick edges. (b) L_{-1} obtained from edge-model description of L_0 has errors (cf Fig 4 g). (c) L_{-1} obtained by modelling the left image and switching model elements before reconstruction has sharp edges with no ringing artefacts.

blurring caused by interpolation and restore the sharpness of edges at $2X$ also. The effect is shown in the Figure 5.

4.2 L_{-1} Generation Algorithm

The process of generating HR images from LR images, as developed in previous sections, is summarized here. The standard pyramid notations are used: initial image is G_0, its first subband is L_0, the HR image is denoted G_{-1} and its first subband is L_{-1}. Edges in Laplacians refer to the their representations as coupled positive-negetive linear structures.

1. Given a G_0 (LR image), generate $\hat{L}_{-1}$ using the iterative process used in SRP with the null prior (**0** image). This gives an estimate of L_{-1} with edges at correct locations but with wrong widths.
2. Generate an edge model description of $\hat{L}_{-1}$.
3. Switch the blur elements to corresponding sharp elements and reconstruct to get $\tilde{L}_{i-1}$. This version of L_{-1} should have sharp edges but may not have lower frequency details due to modelling errors.
4. Using G_0 (LR image), again generate L_{-1} using the iterative process used in SRP, but with $\tilde{L}_{-1}$ as the prior.
5. Genrate the HR image as $G_{-1} = exp(G_0) + L_{-1}$.

The above algorithm uses the SRP and Laplacian edge modelling processes in a way that allows them to complement each other. The SRP based interpolation is able to insert the correct mid- and low-frequency components in $\hat{L}_{-1}$, consistent with G_0. However, it can neither insert nor alter any high-frequency components $(\pi/2 \ldots \pi)$. This leads to blurring of sharp edges. By invoking the assumption that sharp edges arise due to occlusion, we proceed to sharpen all edges in the image that are sharp enough to be in L_0. This is done by modelling the initial estimate $(\hat{L}_{-1})$ and replacing thick edge models with sharp edge models. This revised estimate, $\tilde{L}_{-1}$, has high frequencies injected at the right places.

In order to minimize any errors introduced by the model-switch process, it is regularized by once again passing through the SRP process.

5   Results

In order to evaluate the proposed method, its performance was tested on a diverse set of five images and compared with the results for bicubic interpolation. The representative set is shown in Figure 6, consisting of an artificial image, a texture dominated image, a linear edge dominated image and two portraits. The available images were taken as true HR (THR) and the LR images were generated using blurring and subsampling of these images. The HR images generated from the LR for the proposed and bicubic methods were compared to the THR. The result is shown in Figure 7. The HR images generated by the proposed method has sharper edges. An analysis of the errors indicate that the proposed method does best for isolated edges. In regions having dense edges (as in Barbara texture regions), the errors are largest. This is mainly due to Laplacian edge modelling limitations. However, the errors are no larger than for bicubic interpolation. Thus the modelling step does not introduce instabilities at these regions.

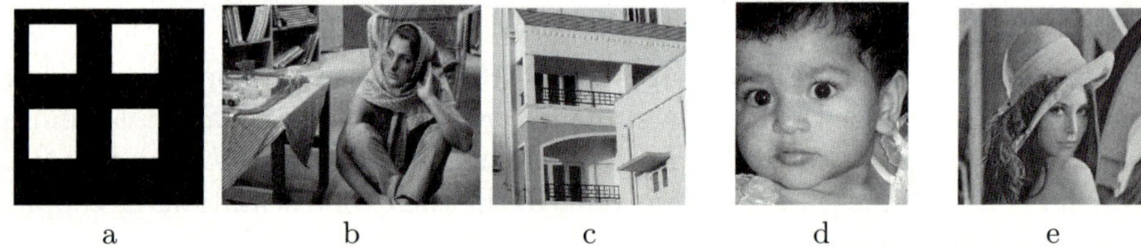

a   b   c   d   e

Fig. 6. Representative set (a) Box (b) Barbara (c) Building (d) Apoorva (e) Lena

5.1   Numerical Evaluation

Aside from visual inspection, it is desirable to have a numerical evaluation of performance. In the present case, availbility of ground truth allows for computation of error based SNR metrics. However, the standard SNR for images would be dominated by the energy present in low frequencies. In order to emphasize the accuracy of the finer details for HR generation, modified measures are used. We have defined HF PSNR (*High Frequency Proportional Signal to Noise Ratio*) where we consider only the HF noise and a proportional amount of the signal power (as actual HF signal is often very small and peak HF power unrealistic). The HF PSNR is thus defined as

$$\text{HF PSNR} = 10 \log \left[\frac{\text{NA} \times \sum |FT_{orig}[i,j]|^2}{\hat{\sum} |FT_{est}[i,j] - FT_{orig}[i,j]|^2} \right] \tag{2}$$

where $\sum$ is summation over all components,
$\hat{\sum}$ is summation over the HF components $[0.25\pi, \pi]$,
NA = fraction of spectral components summed over in the denominator,

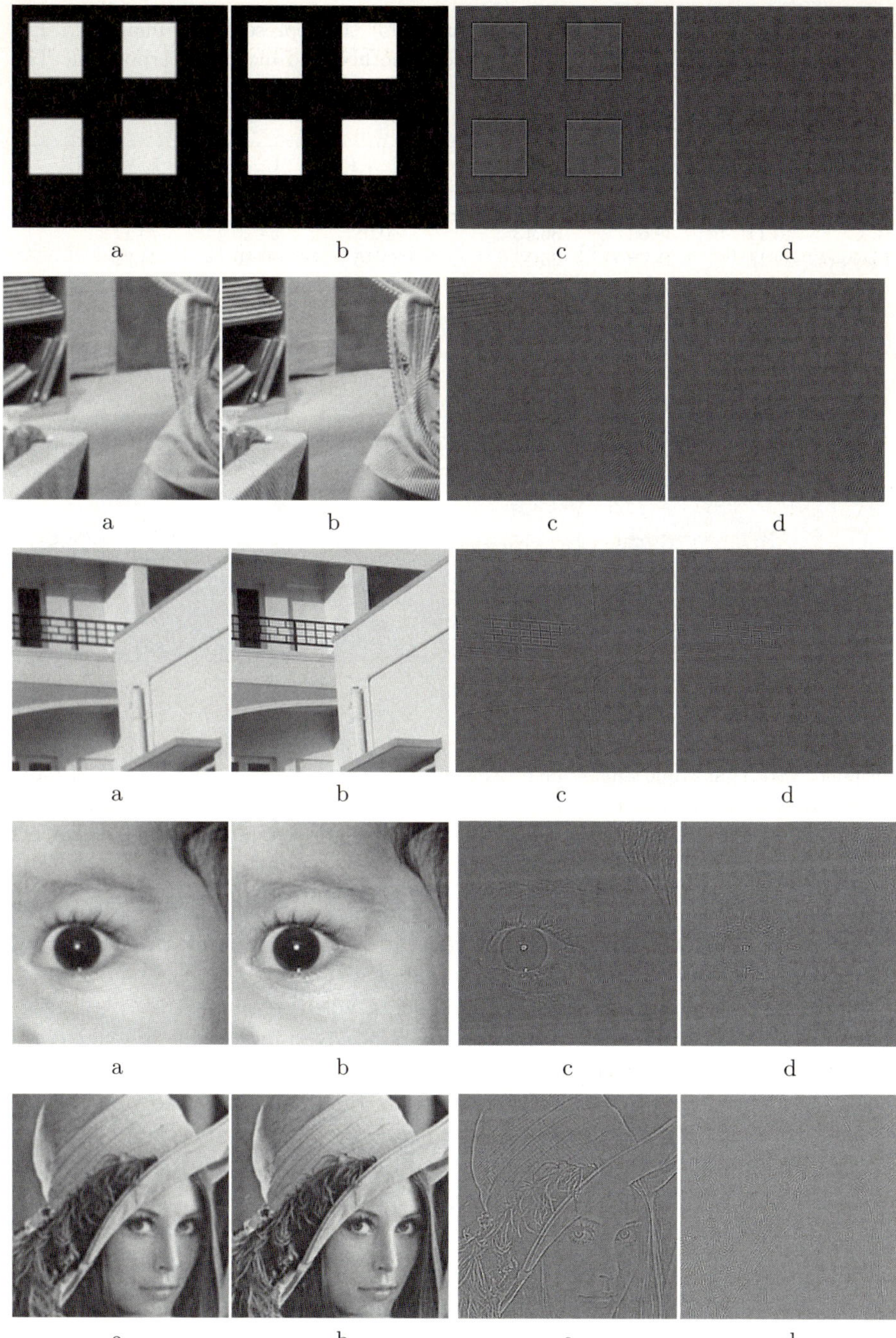

Fig. 7. Comparative results (selected areas magnified for display) : (a) Output of Bicubic interpolation (b) Output of our method (c) Error in bicubic interpolation, (d) Error in our method. Dynamic range of residual images are stretched to suit display.

Table 1. The HF PSNR and L_{-1}PSNR values for the representative image set. The calculation is done for SRP based method, our method and bicubic interpolation. The HF PSNR is calculated over 0.25π to π.

image	HF PSNR for bicubic	HF PSNR for SRP	HF PSNR for our method	L_{-1} PSNR for bicubic	L_{-1} PSNR for SRP	L_{-1} PSNR for our method
Box	19.11	33.65	36.13	30.98	44.20	46.11
Barbara	24.16	25.76	25.52	33.45	34.46	34.22
Building	24.86	26.58	26.64	32.20	33.42	33.52
Apoorva	34.95	34.94	34.66	37.41	37.20	37.05
Lena	30.68	31.84	31.45	34.17	34.87	34.50

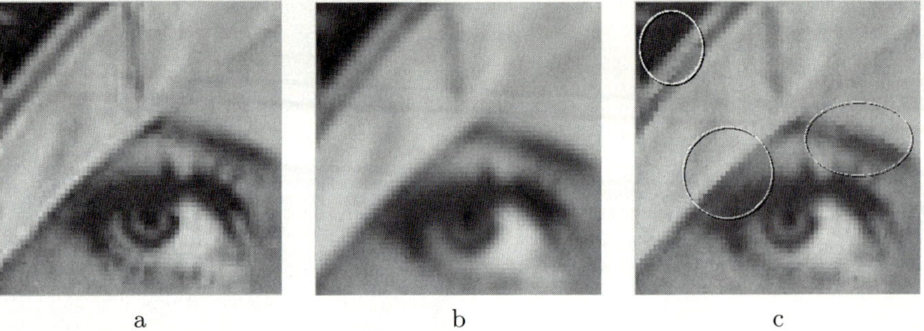

a   b   c

Fig. 8. Sharpening of edges (a) Original image (b) Bicubic interpolated (c) Proposed method. Note that some edges have been rendered even sharper than in the original HR image (marked by ovals). This happens due to our underlying model that all sharp edges are occlusion edges that should be rendered as step edges. These enhancements are visually acceptable though they degrade the SNR measures.

$FT_{est}[i,j]$ = Fourier Transform of the generated HR image and
$FT_{orig}[i,j]$ = Fourier Transform of the original HR image.

The HF-PSNR considers all high frequencies, whether or not they play a role in defining edges. Conversely, it ignores the role played by lower frequency components in edges. As the generation of HR was critically dependent on generation of the L_{-1}, we define L_{-1}-PSNR [1] where the PSNR is computed on the L_{-1} image rather than the G_{-1} image.

$$L_{-1}\text{PSNR} = 10\log\left[\frac{(2^B - 1)^2}{\text{MSE}_{L_{-1}}}\right]. \tag{3}$$

where $\text{MSE}_{L_{-1}}$ is mean squared error defined for L_{-1} subband as

$$\text{MSE}_{L_{-1}} = \frac{1}{m \times n}\sum_m \sum_n (L_{-1}[m,n] - \tilde{L}_{-1}[m,n])^2. \tag{4}$$

---

[1] For consistency with earlier sections, we continue to refer to the THR and HR as G_{-1} and the corresponding Laplacian level as L_{-1}.

The HF PSNR and L_{-1}-PSNR values calculated for the sample set is given in Table 1. In addition to bicubic, we have also compared the proposed method to interpolation by SRP using the **0** prior.

In Table 1 it is observed that the proposed method gives good results for all types of images, but its comparative advantage varies from image to image. For images with sharp straight edges (`Box, Building`) it is the best. For soft images (`Apoorva`) it scores less, though the output looks sharp in Figure 7. This discrepency is explained on detailed examination of the errors. The true high resolution image itself may not have perfectly sharp edges due to optics or processing. The proposed method makes them sharp by opting for the model element change. This is shown in Figure 8. While such sharpenning may be visually acceptable (or even be desirable), they degrade THR based SNR measures.

6   Conclusion and Future Work

A method of achieving HR image from a single LR image has been proposed. It is based on a generic generative edge model that removes the requirement for any training set and makes the method widely applicable. It exploits the model based description of Laplacian subbands and the Symmetric Residue pyramid techniques to generate a putative Laplacian subband corresponding to the desired HR image. The results of this method are good. At some places the edges are rendered sharper than in the original HR image. As no ringing artefacts are created by this over-compensation, it is not a major concern as far as Super-Resolution is concerned. Other errors are introduced due to modelling failures. Both the modelling and the SRP processes may need to be optimized for this method. Future direction of work will also focus on using this single image approach in association with reconstruction-based approaches to exploit multiple LR images optimally.

Acknowledgements

Authors wish to thank Director CAIR and collegues in CV Group CAIR and VIP lab. IITB for their support and encouragement. Autors also thank CAIR's internal reviewers and ICVGIP reviewers for their comments and suggestions.

References

1. Ur, H., Gross, D.:   Improved resolution from sub-pixel shifted pictures. CVGIP:Graphical Models and Image Processing **54** (1992) 181–186
2. Nguyen, N., Milanfar, P.: An efficient wavelet-based algorithm for imaqe superresolution. In: Proc. Int. Conf. Image Processing. Volume 2. (2000) 351–354
3. Tsai, R., Huang, T.: Multiple frame image restoration and registration. In: Advances in Computer and Image Processing, CT: JAI Press Inc. (1984) 317–339
4. Rhee, S., Kang, M.: Discrete cosine transform based regularized high-resolution image reconstruction algorithm. In: Opt. Eng. Volume 38. (1999) 1348–1356

5. Chaudhuri, S., ed.: Super-Resolution Imaging. Norwell,MA: Kluwer Academic (2001)
6. Park, S.C., Park, M.K., Kang, M.G.: Super-resolution image reconstruction: A technical overview. In: IEEE Signal Processing Magazine. (2003) 21–36
7. Joshi, M., Chaudhuri, S.: Super-resolution imaging: Use of zoom as a cue. In: Proc. ICVGIP, Ahmedabad, India. (2002)
8. Joshi, M., Chaudhuri, S.: Zoom based super-resolution through sar model fitting. In: Proc.Intl Conf. on Image Processing (ICIP), Singapore,. (Oct. 2004)
9. Jiji, C.V., Joshi, M.V., Chaudhuri, S.: Single frame image super-resolution using learnt wavelet coefficients. Intl. J. Imaging Science & Tech. (special issue on high resolution image reconstruction) **14** (Sep. 2004) 105–112
10. Jiji, C.V., Joshi, M.V., Chaudhuri, S.: Single frame image super-resolution through contourlet learning. EURASIP J. Applied Signal Processing (2006) 1–11
11. Chaudhuri, S., Joshi, M.: Motion-Free Super-Resolution. (Springer)
12. Burt, P., Adelson, E.: The laplacian pyramid as a compact image code. IEEE Trans. Commuication **31** (1983) 532–540
13. Nema, M.K., Rakshit, S.: Edge-model based representation of laplacian subbands. In: Proc. Seventh Asian Conf. on Computer Vision (ACCV 7), Hyderabad, India,. (Jan. 2006) 80–89
14. Rakshit, S., Nema, M.K.: Symmetric residue pyramids: An extension to burt laplacian pyramids. In: Proc. IEEE ICASSP, Hong Kong,. (2003) III–317–III–320
15. Elad, M., Feuer, A.: Restoration of a single superresolution image from several blurred, noisy and undersampled measured images. IEEE Trans. Image Processing **6** (1997) 1646–1658
16. Naguyen, N., Milanfar, P., Golub, G.: Efficient generalizd cross-validation with applications to parameteric image restortion and resolution enhancement. IEEE Trans. Image Processing **10** (2001) 1299–1308

Greyscale Photograph Geometry
Informed by Dodging and Burning

Carlos Phillips and Kaleem Siddiqi

School of Computer Science and Centre for Intelligent Machines, McGill University
{carlos, siddiqi}@cim.mcgill.ca

Abstract. Photographs are often used as input to image processing and computer vision tasks. Prints from the same negative may vary in intensity values due, in part, to the liberal use of dodging and burning in photography. Measurements which are invariant to these transformations can be used to extract information from photographs which is not sensitive to certain alterations in the development process. These measurements are explored through the construction of a differential geometry which is itself invariant to linear dodging and burning.

1   Introduction

Photographs are often used as test data in the computer vision literature. Properties of these photographs ranging from "Gaussian curvature" to edges, to statistical characterizations of the intensity values are commonly used to extract interpretations. In some cases, the method of acquisition of these photographs plays a central role. This is certainly the case in some of the work on the three-dimensional reconstruction of photographed scenes which is based on projective geometry (e.g. [1]). In other work, the mechanism by which the photograph is captured plays less of a role. It is sometimes overshadowed by the identification of features which are thought to be relevant to biological visual systems (e.g. [2]). Whether the camera optics are modeled or not, most approaches to computer vision ignore the variability of the prints resulting from identical scenes and optics. This observation also holds for digital photographs since their creation process closely mirrors that of photographs printed from film.

In this article we examine the process by which a black and white photograph is developed. This is followed by the construction of a geometry which is invariant to dodging and burning. We use this geometry to develop a set of invariant measures and illustrate their use in an example segmentation task.

1.1   Film

The active part of black and white film is an emulsion. It contains a uniform distribution of silver halide crystals suspended in a gelatin. Upon exposure to sufficient light, a small part of the crystal becomes reduced to metallic silver. The choice of a particular silver halide, such as silver bromide or silver iodide, together with the choice of gelatin determines the film's response to light. The

P. Kalra and S. Peleg (Eds.): ICVGIP 2006, LNCS 4338, pp. 13–24, 2006.

film development process reduces crystals which have been sufficiently exposed to light entirely into metallic silver which makes the negative visibly dark in areas. The silver halide crystals do not store an intensity value. Their state is almost binary. Thus grey tones are represented by different densities of metallic silver simply referred to as the density on the film.

During the development process, the film is placed in a developer liquid. The developer reacts with the crystals which were hit by light. Crystals which have absorbed less light tend to react slower thus the amount of time that the film spends in the developer influences how dark the negative will be. This will in turn influence how bright the print will be. The term exposure is used to represent how affected the film is by the oncoming light. The exposure of a region on the negative is given by the product the average light intensity hitting that region and the amount of time during which the light has hit it, also known as the exposure time:

$$E = T \times I. \tag{1}$$

1.2   Printing

A photograph is printed by projecting a light through the negative onto photo paper and then developing the paper. The process by which photo paper captures information about the light hitting it is quite similar to that for the film. Here, as with the film, there are choices to be made about the chemical makeup of the light capturing membrane which will have profound effects on the final product. One of the key differences between photo paper and film is the number of stops. An average sheet of photo paper has no more than five stops of sensitivity to light intensity compared to the 15 stops which some negatives can represent. Thus film can record a range of intensities which is around 2^{15} greater than photo paper. There is therefore a decision to be made about what intensity range will be expressed on the photo paper. This decision will affect the contrast of the produced print as well as what information will be clearly represented in the printing.

Denser regions of the negative will absorb more of the light projected onto the negative than areas where there are few metallic silver spots. However, the spots are never so tightly packed that no light will pass at all. Every part of the photo paper will therefore be hit by light. Thus increasing exposure time will increase the exposure of the entire photo paper proportionally to the density of the relevant region on the negative. This process does not simply change the contrast of the photograph, it alters what information will be present in the final print. Since denser regions of the negative allow less light through, it takes longer for a sufficient amount of lidght to cross those regions to represent photograph details than it does for bright regions. Thus, the simplest way to display this information is to increase the exposure time of the photo paper. However, this in turn can saturate the dark regions of the print where light flows freely through the negative. This demonstrates that the way in which various densities on the print relate to each other and to the negative is not fixed. Figure 1(a) illustrates this. Increasing the exposure time of the negative on the photo paper by a factor of k is equivalent to shifting the chemical reduction function to the left by $\ln(k)$. This follows directly from Equation 1.

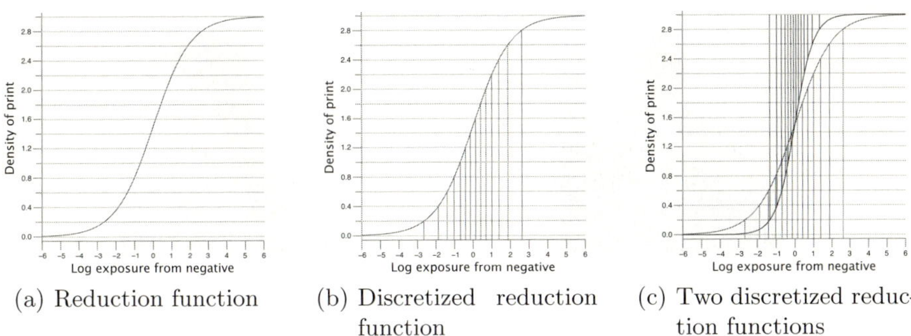

(a) Reduction function

(b) Discretized reduction function

(c) Two discretized reduction functions

Fig. 1. Figure (a) shows an example chemical reduction function which specifies how exposure through the negative affects the density on the photo paper. The numbers in the graph only serve to show that the grid is regularly spaced and the standard direction of increasing values. Figure (b) adds bins representing a regular discretization of the photo paper density. The vertical lines represent the borders of the bins. Notice that the induced discretization of log exposures is not necessarily regular and depends on the reduction function. The example reduction function illustrates how exposure values are better captured in the mid-exposure range. Figure (c) demonstrates how a different choice of reduction function can change how exposure information is encoded.

1.3   Dodging and Burning

The previous section discussed the process by which a print is made directly from a negative. Dodging and burning are two commonly used techniques used during the printing of photographs which alter the exposure time of specific regions of the final print. Dodging involves completely blocking light from contacting certain regions of the photo paper for a portion of the exposure time. Burning involves doing a complete exposure followed by another exposure during which the light is restricted to contacting only a particular region of the photo paper. The process is often carried out using pieces of cardboard to block out the light. For dodging, the cardboard is affixed to a thin rigid rod so that it may be held over any part of the photograph.

For esthetic reasons, the dodging and burning tools must be kept in motion during their use. This allows the exposure times to vary "smoothly" between the regions being worked on and the rest of the photograph. Without the motion, the silhouette of the tool being used would become visible on the print. As indicated in [3] and in [4], photographers feel that they can apply these techniques liberally on photographs, especially when significant motion is used. Adams claims that most photographs can benefit from some dodging or burning [3]. Further, it is clear that he does not present these alterations as tools to change the subject, but rather as tools to accentuate particular properties of the subject. Thus in processing photographs, we must be aware of the possibility that such transformations may have been applied and that they may be hard to detect or reverse. Figure 2 shows an extreme case of burning.

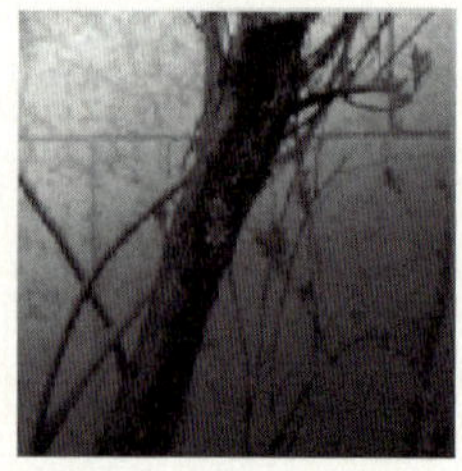

(a) Original photograph

(b) Transformed photograph

Fig. 2. Figure (a) shows a portion of the original photograph. Figure (b) shows the same photograph once burning has been applied. The burning is simulated using Adobe Photoshop^{TM}.

Dodging and burning selectively alter the exposure times of regions of the print. Their effect can therefore be explained using the standard notions of photographic development explored in §1.1 and §1.2. In particular, recall that changing exposure time is equivalent to shifting the chemical reduction function along the log exposure axis. This implies that dodging and burning can be seen as shifting the reduction function locally as long as every part of the print has a non-zero exposure time. In fact, assuming that when in motion the dodging or burning tool moves linearly and that the tool is close enough to the print so that the penumbra of the tool is not significant, this observation completely determines the impact of the techniques on the print. For example, a region which was hidden from exposure for exactly half the development time would have the same final development as if the chemical reduction function was shifted by $-\ln(2)$ for that region and there had been no dodging at all. Further, since dodging restricts the exposure time and burning increases it, the only difference between them is that burning shifts the reduction function to the left while dodging shifts it to the right.

2   Greyscale Photograph Geometry

As Florack argues in [5], we should not impose a topology or geometry directly on the space of photographs. Rather than impose properties on physical entities, we should instead impose them on the space of measurements and on measurement results. The measurements which we are interested in can be parameterized by their location, log-width and orientation. The log-width of a measurement distinguishes between the various scalings of a measurement while the orientation parameter destinguishes between its possible rotations. The set of measurements and results for a given photograph is therefore a subset of the space $\mathcal{I} = \mathbb{M} \times \mathcal{U}$ which we call the image space and where $\mathbb{M} = \mathbb{R}^2 \times \mathbb{R} \times S^1$ is the measurement space and S^1 is the one dimensional sphere. The space $\mathcal{U}$ contains all possible measurement results. A point in image space corresponds to a value being returned by a measurement at a given location, log-width and orientation. Throughout the rest of this article, we will refer to the set of image space points corresponding to a particular photograph as its *image*, or simply an image if the photograph is not specified.

Since $\mathbb{M}$ is a four-dimensional space and the measurement values are a function of points in $\mathbb{M}$, we can assume that an image is a four-dimensional differential manifold in $\mathcal{I}$. Now that images have a manifold structure, we can define a geometry for these images based on the relationships between the components of their ambient space. We will begin by establishing a geometry on the measurement space $\mathbb{M}$ and then proceed to extend it to the full image space $\mathcal{I}$.

2.1   Geometry of the Measurement Space

In the Riemannian geometry of a Euclidean space a (perhaps arbitrary) unit length is chosen. The notions of length and curvature are dependent on the chosen unit length in this situation. Our situation differs in that each measurement views its width as being of unit length. Thus if the locations of two measurements remain the same but their widths double, then their perceived distance will halve.

The measurement space with a fixed width, $\mathbb{M}^w$, looks like Euclidean space with the standard circle principal bundle. This has the effect of rotating the orientation values along with the location plane. Given the observations from this and the previous paragraph, we can define a Riemannian metric on $\mathbb{M}^w$ as $\langle \ , \ \rangle_{(x,\theta)} = g_1 \, dx^1 \otimes dx^1 + g_2 \, dx^2 \otimes dx^2$. Since distances are inversely proportional to width as expressed above, the g_i coefficients must be $1/w^2$. Thus we get the following metric for $\mathbb{M}^w$

$$\langle \ , \ \rangle_{(x,\theta)} = \frac{dx^1 \otimes dx^1 + dx^2 \otimes dx^2}{w^2}. \tag{2}$$

The orientation circle and location parameters are closely related since the orientation circle represents the direction in which the measurement is taken. So any curve in measurement space must have its orientations and location tangents aligned. This can be achieved by creating a sub-Riemannian geometry defined by a distribution on $\mathbb{M}^w$ using the following cotangent equation and then restricting curves to travel along this distribution:

$$\Omega = dx^2 - \tan\theta dx^1 = 0. \tag{3}$$

So far the proposed geometry is invariant to scaling of the visual signal since scaling the signal also scales measurements proportionally. However, in the full measurement space, width is allowed to vary. Since the width of a measurement can be seen as a length from another measurement's point of view, the measurement space metric must include a term to take into account variation in width which itself must be inversely proportional to current width:

$$\langle\ ,\ \rangle_{(x,\theta)} = \frac{dx^1 \otimes dx^1 + dx^2 \otimes dx^2 + dw \otimes dw}{w^2}. \tag{4}$$

This makes the measurement space fully invariant to scaling as well as to rotation and translation. The distribution defined for $\mathbb{M}^w$ can be used unchanged in $\mathbb{M}$ to represent the relationship between location and orientation.

The constructed metric is well known as the metric for the upper-half plane model of three-dimensional hyperbolic geometry [6].

2.2   Geometry of the Image Space

Much as was the case for orientation, we cannot introduce measurement values into the metric. To do so would be to establish intrinsic location related properties in measurement values. The measurements we choose will be based on brightness information. We will therefore start by defining the measurements to collect average brightness over a unit disc. Let's call these measurements $b_{x,\theta,w}$. We will examine how these measurements interact with a set of simple photographic transformations so as to derive better values to use when defining base measurements.

The image space $\mathcal{I}_b$ for this measurement can be expressed by adding a brightness line $\mathcal{B} = \mathbb{R}$ to the measurement space: $\mathcal{I}_b = \mathbb{M} \times \mathcal{B}$. The argument for excluding measurement values from the metric applies to brightness. However, excluding brightness from the metric does not exclude it from the geometrical description. On the contrary, it defines $\mathcal{I}$ geometrically up to acceptable transformations of the brightness line. We choose to include the linear dodging transformation, assuming linear reduction functions, introduced earlier along with varying exposure time in the set of transformations under which image content is invariant,

$$u \leftarrow u + a_1 x + a_2 y + t_u, \tag{5}$$

where a_1, a_2 and t_v are arbitrary constants, the last one representing a translation of v. In this equation, u is a coordinate for the brightness line. We have chosen this transformation since it is a basic image correction transformation. As desired, a difference of brightness values at two distinct measurement points is meaningless (i.e. not invariant to the transformation group).

Our analysis bears some resemblance to that of Koenderink and van Doorn's [4]. Our motivation is quite different. Most significantly, since measurements were not explicitly considered in [4] the notions of measurement width and orientation were not developed. In our work these ideas turn out to be key for the development of a methodology for hierarchical decomposition (moving from coarse measurement sizes to finer ones), which is the focus of §3. We note that in the context of metrics for greyscale photographs there is also related work by Eberly and his colleagues [7].

2.3   Invariant Measurements

It is clear from the previous section that average brightness is not an invariant measurement to the photographic transformations which we have discussed. There are many possible invariant measurements. In this section we focus on perhaps the simplest, a measurement type which is based on best fit planes.

For a given measurement point $v = (x_1, x_2, \theta, w)$, the associated measurement value for our example is a best fit plane p_v for the brightness of the photograph over a disk d described by location (x_1, x_2) and radius w. The fit minimizes the average integral of $(B(x, y) - p(x, y))^2$ over d, where B represents the brightness values while p represents the plane. The plane is recorded using three parameters. The first two are the slopes of the plane along orthonormal axes u_t and u_n where u_t is in line with θ and u_t forms a right-handed frame with u_n. The last parameter is simply the brightness value of the plane over point (x, y). Thus the space of measurement values $\mathcal{U}$ is composed of these planes p and for convenience we define functions $m_t, m_n, b : \mathcal{I} \to \mathbb{R}$ which return the u_t-slope, u_n-slope and elevation at a given image point respectively.

The plane parameters described above are clearly invariant to rotation and translation of the Euclidean plane. However, they are not invariant to transformations such as linear dodging or scaling. When a linear dodging is applied to a visual signal, it leaves the values collected by dm_t and dm_n along a curve invariant. The changes in plane elevations given by db, however, are not invariant to this subgroup of transformations as we have seen when examining average brightness measures. There we saw that though differences in brightness values were preserved along a brightness line, they are not preserved when taken across brightness lines. We can use this to define an invariant value given below, which is one way of representing how much the plane is increasing in height as you move along a curve:

$$\Omega_b = du - m\sqrt{dx_1^2 + dx_2^2}.$$

When a photograph is scaled by a scale factor s, all the slopes at corresponding points are scaled by $\frac{1}{s}$ and all the corresponding measurement widths are scaled by s. Therefore

$$\Omega_t = w \cdot dm_t \quad \text{and} \quad \Omega_n = w \cdot dm_n$$

are invariant under scaling of curves in $\mathcal{I}$. The values of $du - m\sqrt{dx_1^2 + dx_2^2}$ are also invariant for the same reasons. Thus we get three invariant values which represent the changes in slope and elevation of the planes along a given curve. In the next section, we use these measurements and relations to develop an algorithm for region grouping.

This concludes our construction of the geometric model and of our basic set of invariant measurements. This model can be used to create other measurement classes which are invariant to the photographic transformations covered in this paper. Further, expressions based on the values which are computed using the presented measurements can themselves be used as input into standard image processing algorithms. In the next section, we examine the properties which are represented in the model through an example task of segmentation.

3   Example Task

So as to illustrate aspects of the image space geometry, we define a naïve segmentation process based on the invariant measurements presented in §2.3. Algorithms 1 and 2 describe the two steps of the process in pseudo-code. First the invariant measurements are estimated so as to produce an image for the input photograph. The image manifold is collapsed into two-dimensional surfaces. Then the grouping algorithm segments the image points into separate surfaces based on local affinity. Note that the widths referred to in the algorithms are not scales as in [8] put simply widths of measurement discs. The presented algorithms are provided for the sole purpose of examining the structures created using the invariant measurements.

Figure 3(c) illustrates the level of detail collected at different measurement widths. Each layer image shows the averaging of approximation discs which have been kept after running the measurement algorithm. These layers can be

---

Algorithm 1. Measurement Algorithm

---

for $w = max\_width$ down to 1 **do**
  for q a pixel in the photograph **do**
    $d \leftarrow$ the disk of radius w centered at q
    $p_d \leftarrow$ plane fit to intensity over d
    $f_{(q,w)} \leftarrow$ the mean squared error of the fit
  end for
end for
for $w = max\_width$ down to 1 **do**
  for q a pixel in the photograph **do**
    if $\frac{f_{(q,w)}}{w} > \epsilon$
    or $\frac{f_{(q,w)}}{w} > \frac{f_{(q,w+1)}}{w}$
    or $\frac{f_{(q,w)}}{w} > \frac{f_{(q,w-1)}}{w}$ **then**
      delete p_d
    end if
  end for
end for
for $w = 1$ to max_width **do**
  for q a pixel in the photograph **do**
    for $v \in \{(1,0,0),(0,1,0),(0,0,1)\}$ where the components represent directions x_1, x_2 and w resp. **do**
      $\Delta_b(q,w) \leftarrow \Omega'_b(v)$
      $\Delta_t(q,w) \leftarrow \Omega'_t(v)$
      $\Delta_n(q,w) \leftarrow \Omega'_n(v)$
    end for
  end for
end for

This defines a discretized three-dimensional manifold in $\mathcal{I}$ which depends on parameter ϵ. For our experiments, we set $\epsilon = 0.1$. We use symbols Δ' instead of Δ to indicate that difference equations are used to approximate the infinitesimal measurements.

Algorithm 2. Grouping Algorithm

$\quad$ **for** $w = 1$ to max_radius **do**
$\quad\quad$ **for** q a pixel in the photograph **do**
$\quad\quad\quad$ **for** $v \in \{\gamma : \gamma \in \{-1, 0, 1\}^3\}$ **do**
$\quad\quad\quad\quad$ **for** $i \in \{1, 2, 3\}$ **do**
$\quad\quad\quad\quad\quad$ **if** $v_i = -1$ **then**
$\quad\quad\quad\quad\quad\quad$ $q_i \leftarrow q_i - 1$
$\quad\quad\quad\quad\quad$ **end if**
$\quad\quad\quad\quad$ **end for**
$\quad\quad\quad\quad$ $v = (|v_1|, |v_2|, |v_3|)$
$\quad\quad\quad\quad$ At location q with width w in direction v:
$\quad\quad\quad\quad$ **if** $\max(\Delta_b, k\Delta_t, k\Delta_n) < \delta w$ **then**
$\quad\quad\quad\quad\quad$ (q_1, q_2, d) is adjacent to $(q_1, q_2, d) + \gamma$
$\quad\quad\quad\quad$ **end if**
$\quad\quad\quad$ **end for**
$\quad\quad$ **end for**
$\quad$ **end for**

This produces a grouping across measurement points which is dependent on parameters k and δ given the output from the measurement algorithm. For our experiments, we set $k = 1$ and $\delta = 0.5$.

---

recombined by simply drawing one over the other, from greatest width to smallest. Pixels for which there is no measurement in a given layer are left unaltered when the layer is drawn. This is shown in Figure 3(d).The important thing to note is that structures in the photographs appear at reasonable widths. For example the trunk of the tree appears around widths of 10 pixels but is not present around widths of 20 pixels. Figure 4 shows that in fact the layers presented in Figure 3 form two-dimensional surfaces. The results of applying the naïve grouping algorithm, shown in Figure 5(b), show that structural information about the photograph can easily be extracted from the image structure. Figures 5(a) and 5(b) confirm that the measurements are indeed unchanged by the application of a Adobe Photoshop™ burning effect. Finally, Shi and Malik's graph-cut based algorithm [9] is applied on the original photograph and on the transformed photograph to show that this popular approach to segmentation is sensitive to dodging and burning transformations when intensity value measurements are used as inputs. This sensitivity can be problematic if the information from the original negative is being sought rather than information about the particular print being examined.

4   Conclusion

We have introduced a geometry which is invariant to certain forms of burning and dodging. We then used this geometry to create invariant measurements which represent information which would not change given a different development process.

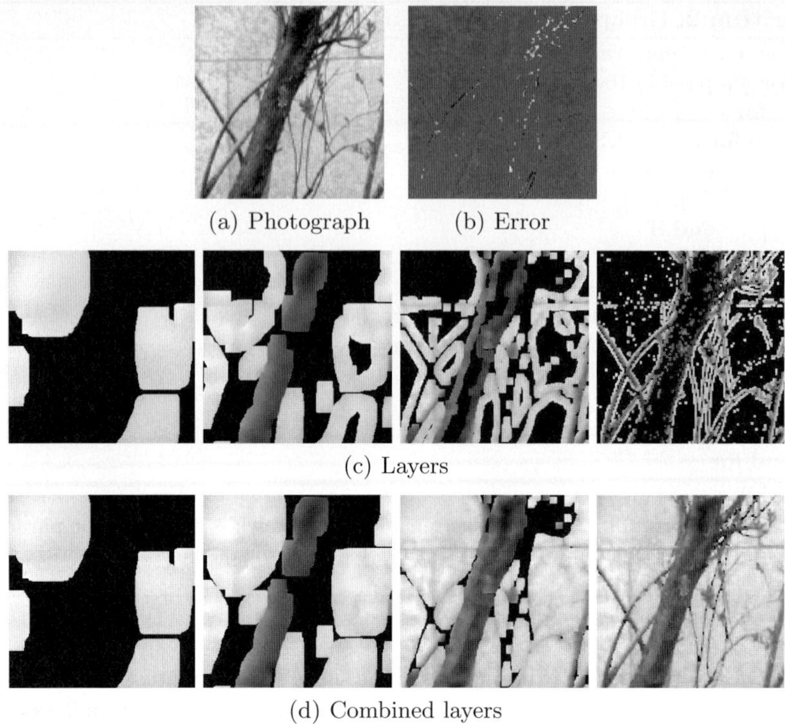

(a) Photograph   (b) Error

(c) Layers

(d) Combined layers

Fig. 3. (a): The original photograph. **(b)**: The difference between the original photograph and the photograph reconstructed from the layers. **(c)**: From left to right, the measurement size layers with widths 20, 10, 4 and 1 pixels, respectively. **(d)**: From left to right, the reconstructed photographs for measurement size layers with widths down to 20, 10, 4 and 1 pixels, respectively.

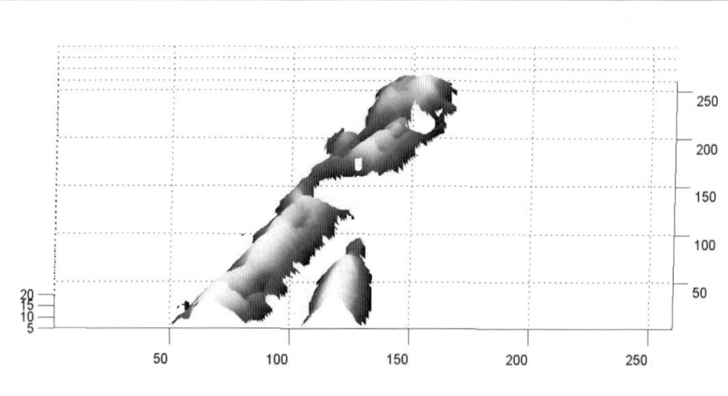

Fig. 4. Two of the surfaces obtained by the grouping algorithm, corresponding to the trunk of the tree and the region to its lower right. These surfaces are manifolds in 3D, which could in fact overlap when viewed from any fixed viewing direction.

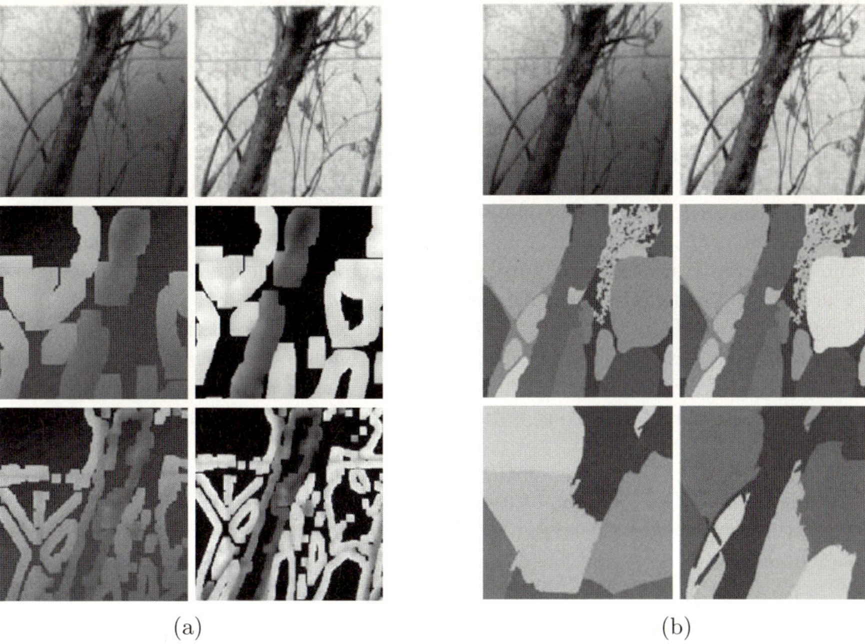

(a)   (b)

Fig. 5. These illustrations demonstrate that the presented approach is in fact invariant to the defined photographic transformations. (a): Left Column: from top to bottom, the original photograph and its layers with widths 10 and 4 pixels. Right Column: from top to bottom, the original photograph with a linear dodging transformation applied to it and its layers with widths 10 and 4 pixels. In fact the average grading is not represented in the image structure and both photographs are identically represented, as invariance to linear dodging requires. (b): Left Column: from top to bottom, the original photograph, our grouping and the grouping from [9]. Right Column: from top to bottom, the original photograph with a linear dodging transformation applied, our grouping of the transformed photograph and the grouping generated by [9]. The source code from http://www.cis.upenn.edu/~jshi with default parameters was used to compute the results of the algorithm presented in [9].

The presented algorithm used properties of best-fit planes to represent a photograph. There are many more possibilities for measurements which would fit this framework. Further, the photograph representation presented in this paper could be combined with existing vision algorithms for such tasks as object recognition within photographs for which we do not know the development process.

Acknowledgments

We would like to thank Jiambo Shi for making his source code available.

References

1. Faugeras, O.: Three-dimensional computer vision: a geometric viewpoint. MIT Press, Cambridge, MA, USA (1993)
2. Marr, D.: Vision: a computational investigation into the human representation and processing of visual information. W. H. Freeman, San Francisco (1982)
3. Adams, A.: The Print. Volume Book 3 of The New Ansel Adams Photography Series. Little, Brown and Company, Boston (1983)
4. Koenderink, J.J., van Doorn, A.J.: Image processing done right. European Conference On Computer Vision, Lecture Notes in Computer Science **2350** (2002) 158–172
5. Florack, L.: Image Structure. Kluwer Dorecht (1997)
6. Guggenheimer, H.W.: Differential Geometry. Dover Publications (1977)
7. Eberly, D.: Ridges In Image and Data Analysis. Kluwer Academic Publishers (1996)
8. Lindeberg, T.: Effective scale: A natural unit for measuring scale-space lifetime. IEEE Transactions On Pattern Analysis and Machine Intelligence **15** (1993) 1068–1074
9. Shi, J., Malik, J.: Normalized cuts and image segmentation. IEEE Transactions on Pattern Analysis and Machine Intelligence **22** (2000) 888–905

A Discontinuity Adaptive Method for Super-Resolution of License Plates

K.V. Suresh and A.N. Rajagopalan

Image Processing and Computer Vision Laboratory,
Department of Electrical Engineering,
Indian Institute of Technology Madras,
Chennai - 600 036, India
`sureshkvsit@yahoo.com, raju@ee.iitm.ac.in`

Abstract. In this paper, a super-resolution algorithm tailored to enhance license plate numbers of moving vehicles in real traffic videos is proposed. The algorithm uses the information available from multiple, sub-pixel shifted, and noisy low-resolution observations to reconstruct a high-resolution image of the number plate. The image to be super-resolved is modeled as a Markov random field and is estimated from the low-resolution observations by a graduated non-convexity optimization procedure. To preserve edges in the reconstructed number plate for better readability, a discontinuity adaptive regularizer is proposed. Experimental results are given on several real traffic sequences to demonstrate the edge preserving capability of the proposed method and its robustness to potential errors in motion and blur estimates. The method is computationally efficient as all operations are implemented locally in the image domain.

1   Introduction

Intelligent Transport Systems (ITS) that combine electronics, information, communication, and network technologies are being increasingly used to address traffic problems in developed as well as developing countries [1]. One of the important goals of ITS is to decipher the identity of vehicles to enable monitoring of offenses and crimes on public routes. If a low-resolution video surveillance system captures an untoward incident on the road, a post-facto analysis of the stored video may be required. However, due to image degradation, information about the identity of the vehicles involved in the incident may not be easily derivable. For improving the readability of license plate text, a method is suggested in [2] that enhances only the character pixels while de-emphasizing the background pixels. Cui et al. [3] have presented a multi-frame-based binarization scheme for the extraction and enhancement of characters in license plates. Sato et al. [4] present a sub-pixel interpolation-based video text enhancement scheme. But interpolation cannot restore the high frequency components lost during sampling.

The video quality degrades due to various reasons such as motion blur, distance to camera, and noise. Cost considerations also dictate the resolution of

P. Kalra and S. Peleg (Eds.): ICVGIP 2006, LNCS 4338, pp. 25–34, 2006.

surveillance cameras. Super-resolution is a process in which a high-resolution (HR) image is constructed from a set of sub-pixel shifted low-resolution (LR) images. Fundamentally, the task involves dealiasing and deblurring [5]. For the problem on hand, since there is relative motion between the camera and the vehicle, one can use sub-pixel motion information for enhancing the text in traffic videos. In [6], a Bayesian super-resolution algorithm based on the simultaneous autoregressive model developed for text image sequences is used to enhance license plates. In [7], a method for generating an HR slow-motion sequence from compressed video is suggested, in which an area of interest such as the license plate is slowed down and super-resolved. Miravet and Rodriguez [8] use neural networks to perform super-resolution of license plates. A learning-based framework has been proposed in [9] for zooming the digits in a license plate.

In this paper, our aim is to propose a super-resolution algorithm suitable for enhancing license plate text in real traffic videos. This is a challenging problem for several reasons. The distance of the camera to the vehicle is typically large rendering it difficult for even humans to decipher the text. The low-resolution images are quite noisy, and blurred. Motion and blur estimates derived from such degraded images will not be correct. It is well-known fact that the performance of super-resolution algorithms is good only when these parameters are known accurately. The high-resolution license plate image is modeled as a Markov Random Field (MRF) and a maximum *a posteriori* (MAP) estimate of the super-resolved image is obtained, given the low-quality observations. The purpose behind modeling by MRF which is a statistical characterization is to lend robustness to errors in motion and blur estimates during the reconstruction process. Since our objective is to improve readability of the license plate text, we propose a discontinuity adaptive MRF (DAMRF) prior in which the degree of interaction between pixels across edges is adjusted adaptively. Because this prior is non-convex, we use Graduated Non-Convexity (GNC) which is a deterministic annealing algorithm for performing optimization. All matrix operations are implemented as local image operations for computational speed-up. The performance of the proposed method is found to be quite good when tested on real traffic video sequences.

2   Problem Formulation

The relation between a lexicographically ordered low-resolution observation and the original high-resolution image can be expressed in matrix formulation as

$$\underline{y}_r = DH_r W_r \underline{x} + \underline{n}_r, \qquad\qquad 1 \leq r \leq m \qquad (1)$$

Here, $\underline{x}$ is the original HR image of dimension $N_1 N_2$ x 1, $\underline{y}_r$ is the rth LR image of dimension $M_1 M_2$ x 1, D is a down-sampling matrix of dimension $M_1 M_2$ x $N_1 N_2$. Matrix H_r is the camera defocus blur matrix, and W_r is the geometric warping matrix for the rth frame. Each of these matrices is of dimension $N_1 N_2$ x $N_1 N_2$. The term $\underline{n}_r$ is the noise in the rth frame. We assume that there are m number of LR observations i.e., $1 \leq r \leq m$.

Solving for $\underline{x}$ in Eq. (1) given the observations $\underline{y}_r$ is an ill-posed inverse problem. Because the blur operator may exhibit zeros in the frequency domain rendering the process non-invertible. At high frequencies, there will be excessive noise amplification since the transfer function of the blurring operator is low-pass in nature. Moreover, the presence of noise in the observation process can result in an observation sequence which is inconsistent with any scene. Hence, it is important to use *a priori* information about $\underline{x}$ that will reduce the space of solutions which conforms to the observed data. The Bayesian MAP formulation allows for incorporation of prior knowledge about $\underline{x}$ to improve robustness during the reconstruction process.

The MAP estimate of the super-resolved image $\underline{x}$ given m low-resolution images is given by

$$\hat{\underline{x}} = \arg\max_{\underline{x}} \left\{ P(\underline{x}|\underline{y}_1, \cdots \underline{y}_m) \right\} \tag{2}$$

Using Bayes' rule and taking the logarithm of the posterior probability, the MAP estimate of $\underline{x}$ is given by

$$\hat{\underline{x}} = \arg\max_{\underline{x}} \left\{ \log[P(\underline{y}_1, \cdots \underline{y}_m|\underline{x})] + \log P(\underline{x}) \right\} \tag{3}$$

We need to specify the prior image density $P(\underline{x})$ and the conditional density $P(\underline{y}_1, \cdots \underline{y}_m|\underline{x})$. Using the observation model in Eq. (1) and the fact that the noise fields are statistically independent of X and as well as each other, we have

$$P(\underline{y}_1, \cdots \underline{y}_m|\underline{x}) = \frac{1}{(2\pi\sigma^2)^{m\frac{M_1 M_2}{2}}} \exp\left\{ -\sum_{r=1}^{m} \frac{||\underline{y}_r - DH_r W_r \underline{x}||^2}{2\sigma^2} \right\} \tag{4}$$

where σ^2 is the variance of the observation noise.

Using Eq. (4) in Eq. (3) and neglecting constant terms, the MAP estimate can be equivalently written as

$$\hat{\underline{x}} = \arg\min_{\underline{x}} \left\{ \sum_{r=1}^{m} \frac{||\underline{y}_r - DH_r W_r \underline{x}||^2}{2\sigma^2} - \log P(\underline{x}) \right\} \tag{5}$$

3   Discontinuity Adaptive MRF (DAMRF) Prior

We model the super-resolved image to be estimated as a Markov random field because it provides a foundation for the characterization of contextual constraints and the densities of the probability distributions of interacting features in images.

MRF theory helps in analyzing the spatial dependencies of physical phenomena. Let F be a random field over an $N \times N$ lattice of sites $L = (i, j) : 1 \leq i, j \leq N$. The random field F is said to be an MRF on L with respect to a neighborhood system η if

1. $P(F = f) > 0, \forall f \in \mathcal{F}$
2. $P[F_{i,j} = f_{i,j} | F_{k,l} = f_{k,l}, \forall (k,l) \neq (i,j)] =$
$$P[F_{i,j} = f_{i,j} | F_{k,l} = f_{k,l}, (k,l) \in \eta_{i,j}]$$

where $\eta_{i,j}$ is the neighborhood of the site (i,j) and $\mathcal{F}$ denotes the configuration space. It is natural to expect that the image intensity at a pixel will not depend on the image data outside its neighborhood when the image data on its neighborhood are given. MRF image models even with first order neighborhood system are known to be powerful.

The practical use of MRF models can be largely ascribed to the equivalence between MRFs and Gibbs Random Field (GRF) established by Hammersely and Clifford [10]. The theorem states that F is an MRF on L with respect to neighborhood η if and only if F is a Gibbs random field on L. i.e.,

$$P[\underline{F} = \underline{f}] = \frac{1}{Z} \exp\{-U(\underline{f})\} \tag{6}$$

where Z is the partition function given by $Z = \sum_f \exp\{-U(\underline{f})\}$ and $U(\underline{f})$ is the energy function which is given by

$$U(\underline{f}) = \sum_{c \in C} V_c(\underline{f}) \tag{7}$$

Here, c is called the clique of the pair (L, η) which is a subset of sites in L in which all pairs of sites are mutual neighbors. The set C is the set of all cliques. Since we model the HR image X as an MRF, we can write

$$P[\underline{X} = \underline{x}] = \frac{1}{Z} \exp\{-U(\underline{x})\} \tag{8}$$

where

$$U(\underline{x}) = \sum_{c \in C} V_c(\underline{x}) \tag{9}$$

The choice of the clique potential $V_c(\underline{x})$ is crucial as it embeds important prior information about the image to be reconstructed. The prior model can be chosen as

$$\sum_{c \in C} V_c(\underline{x}) = \sum_{c \in C} g(d_c \underline{x})$$

where $d_c \underline{x}$ is a local spatial activity measure of the image and has a small value in smooth regions and a large value at edges. A common choice for the prior model is a Gauss-Markov random field model [11] which has the form

$$g(n) = n^2$$

However, this image model can result in a blurred estimate of the super-resolved license plate, particularly along edges due to over-smoothing. Geman and Geman [10] introduced the concept of line fields which helps in preserving edges. But the use of line fields makes the energy function non-differentiable. Schultz et al. [12] have used a discontinuity preserving model of the form

$$g(n) = \begin{cases} n^2, & |n| \leq T \\ 2T(|n| - T) + T^2, & |n| > T \end{cases}$$

where T is the threshold parameter separating the quadratic and linear regions. The threshold which is dependent on factors like image content and noise has to be appropriately tuned for every new case. This threshold when fixed at low values lets in noise and at high values penalizes weak edges.

To improve the readability of the license plate, we propose to use a discontinuity adaptive MRF (DAMRF) model in which the degree of interaction between pixels across edges is adjusted adaptively in order to preserve discontinuities. A necessary condition for any regularization model to be adaptive to discontinuities [13] is

$$\lim_{n \to \infty} |g'(n)| = \lim_{n \to \infty} |2nh(n)| = C \tag{10}$$

where n is the difference between neighboring pixel values and $C \in [0, \infty)$ is a constant. We propose to choose $g(n)$ as

$$g(n) = \gamma - \gamma e^{-n^2/\gamma} \tag{11}$$

Fig. 1 shows the function defined by Eq. (11). It is convex in the band $B_\gamma = \left(-\sqrt{\gamma/2}, \sqrt{\gamma/2}\right)$ and non-convex outside. The DA function allows the smoothing strength to increase monotonically as n increases within the band B_γ thus smoothing out noise. Outside this band, smoothing decreases as n increases thereby preserving the discontinuities.

Using the DA prior function and assuming a first-order neighborhood for MRF, we can write

$$\sum_{c \in C} V_c(\underline{x}) = \sum_{i=1}^{N_1} \sum_{j=1}^{N_2} 4 * \gamma - \gamma \exp\{-[x(i,j) - x(i, j-1)]^2/\gamma\}$$

$$-\gamma \exp\{-[x(i,j) - x(i, j+1)]^2/\gamma\} - \gamma \exp\{-[x(i,j) - x(i-1, j)]^2/\gamma\}$$

$$-\gamma \exp\{-[x(i,j) - x(i+1, j)]^2/\gamma\} \tag{12}$$

Using Eqs. (12), (9), and (8) in Eq. (5) and finding the gradient at the nth iteration, we get

$$\mathrm{grad}^{(n)} = \frac{1}{\sigma^2} \sum_{r=1}^{m} W_r^T H_r^T D^T (D H_r W_r \underline{x} - \underline{y}_r) + \lambda G^{(n)} \tag{13}$$

where λ is the regularization parameter and the gradient at (k, l) is given by

$$G^{(n)}(k,l) = 2[x(i,j) - x(i, j-1)] \exp\{-[x(i,j) - x(i, j-1)]^2/\gamma\} +$$
$$2[x(i,j) - x(i, j+1)] \exp\{-[x(i,j) - x(i, j+1)]^2/\gamma\} +$$
$$2[x(i,j) - x(i-1, j)] \exp\{-[x(i,j) - x(i-1, j)]^2/\gamma\} +$$
$$2[x(i,j) - x(i+1, j)] \exp\{-[x(i,j) - x(i+1, j)]^2/\gamma\} \tag{14}$$

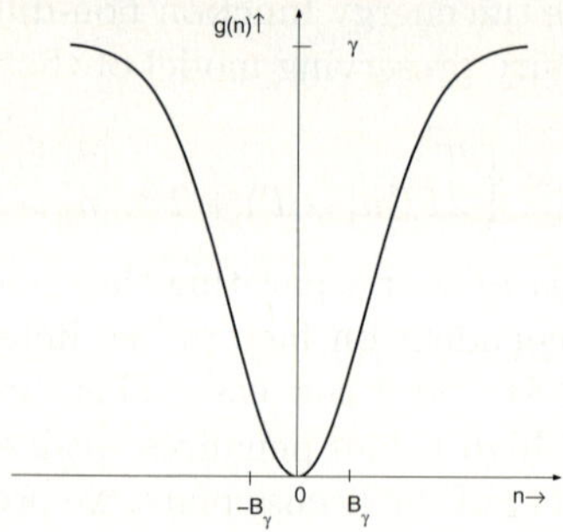

Fig. 1. A discontinuity adaptive function

4   Optimization Using Graduated Non-convexity

The DA function is non-convex and annealing can be used to overcome the problem of local minima. There are two types of annealing: deterministic and stochastic. We use a deterministic annealing method called Graduated Non-Convexity (GNC) algorithm for optimization [13]. The idea of GNC is to start with a strictly convex cost function by choosing a large value for γ and to find a unique minimum using gradient descent in the first phase. This value is then used as the initial value for the next phase of minimization with a smaller γ. These steps are repeated by lowering the value of γ until convergence. It finds a good solution with much less computational cost.

Algorithm. Super-resolution using GNC

Require: Observations $\{Y_i\}$, blur kernels, and motion parameters.
1: Calculate $X^{(0)}$ as the average of the bilinearly up-sampled and aligned images.
2: Choose a convex $\gamma^{(0)} = 2v$, where v is the maximum value of the gradient along the x and y directions in the initial estimate $X^{(0)}$.
3: $n = 0$
4: Do   a. Update $X^{(n)}$ using $X^{(n+1)} = X^{(n)} - \alpha \, \mathrm{grad}^{(n)}$
        b. Set $n = n + 1$;
        c. If $(\mathrm{norm}(X^{(n)} - X^{(n-1)}) < \epsilon)$ set $\gamma^{(n)} = \max\left[\gamma_{\text{target}}, k\gamma^{(n-1)}\right]$;
    UNTIL $(\mathrm{norm}(X^{(n)} - X^{(n-1)}) < \epsilon)$ and $(\gamma^{(n)} = \gamma_{\text{target}})$;
5: Set $\hat{X} = X^{(n)}$
    where α is the step size, ϵ is a constant for testing convergence, and k is a factor that takes $\gamma^{(n)}$ slowly towards γ_{target}.

Calculation of the gradient in Eq. (13) involves operations on large matrices which can be computationally very intensive. The matrices W_r, H_r, and D, and their transposes are implemented using only simple local image operations as follows thereby yielding a considerable speed-up.

- D is implemented by averaging q^2 pixels in the higher dimension to calculate each pixel in the lower dimension where q is the resolution factor.
- H_r is implemented by convolving the image with the respective blur kernels.
- W_r is implemented by warping the image using bilinear interpolation.
- D^T is implemented by spreading equally the intensity value in the lower dimension to the q^2 pixels in the higher dimension.
- H_r^T is implemented by convolution of the image with the flipped kernel. i.e., if $h(i,j)$ is the imaging blur kernel, then the flipped kernel $\hat{h}$ satisfies $\hat{h}(i,j) = h(-i,-j), \quad \forall (i,j)$.
- W_r^T is implemented by backward warping if W_r is implemented by forward warping.

Note that for implementation of matrix D in image domain, we need $(q^2 - 1)$ additions and one multiplication (by $\frac{1}{q^2}$) whereas D^T needs one multiplication (by $\frac{1}{q^2}$) to calculate each pixel. The warping operation is typically performed using bilinear interpolation. Each pixel value in the warped image is calculated from its four neighboring pixels using the interpolation coefficients. Hence to implement matrices W_r and W_r^T in image domain, we need 7 additions and 8 multiplications (except at the borders) to determine each pixel. The number of computations for blurring an image depends on the size of the blur kernel. If we denote the kernel size as bl_size, then we need bl_size^2 multiplications and $(bl\_size^2 - 1)$ additions to compute each pixel.

The overall computational advantage that can be derived by implementing the proposed algorithm using local image domain operations instead of large matrix multiplications is given in Table 1. The table gives comparisons for implementation of D, H_r, W_r, and their transposes. We assume the dimension of the HR image to be $N \times N$ and that of the LR image to be $M \times M$. The blur kernel size is denoted by bl_size and q is the resolution factor. Note that, there is a substantial gain in implementing using local image operations.

Table 1. Computations required for W_r, H_r, D, and their transposes

Operation	Matrix domain computations	Image domain computations
W_r, W_r^T	$N^2 \times N^2$ multiplications $N^2 \times (N^2 - 1)$ additions	$N^2 \times 8$ multiplications $N^2 \times 7$ additions
H_r, H_r^T	$N^2 \times N^2$ multiplications $N^2 \times (N^2 - 1)$ additions	$N^2 \times bl\_size^2$ multiplications $N^2 \times (bl\_size^2 - 1)$ additions
D	$M^2 \times N^2$ multiplications $M^2 \times (N^2 - 1)$ additions	$M^2 \times 1$ multiplications $M^2 \times (q^2 - 1)$ additions
D^T	$N^2 \times M^2$ multiplications $N^2 \times (M^2 - 1)$ additions	$M^2 \times 1$ multiplications -Nil-

5   Experimental Results

In this section, we demonstrate the performance of the proposed method for super-resolving license plates and also compare it with other techniques. In our experiments, we considered resolution improvement by a factor of 2. The values chosen for the various parameters were $\lambda = 0.005$, $\gamma^{(0)} = 300$, $\gamma_{target} = 10$, $k = 0.95$, and $\alpha = 6$. We considered real data for testing our method. For this purpose, video frames (25 frames/second) of a busy traffic way were captured using a SONY handycam. The data was gathered from a flyover of height about 20 feet. The viewing angle of the camera relative to the ground was about 45°. The movement of vehicles was away from the camera. Because we use successive frames, scaling is negligible and is ignored. Since the vehicles were moving away from the camera and roughly along a straight line there was no rotation. Our objective is to go beyond the resolution of the camera to enhance the license plate region by using the motion information in the captured observations.

In the first example, the license plate (of size 16×58 pixels) of a moving car was cropped from four consecutive frames of the traffic video and these low-quality frames are shown in Figs. 2(a)-2(d). The sub-pixel motion corresponding to LR frames was computed using [14]. The resultant motion estimates were fed as input to different super-resolution techniques, namely the LS method [15], the GMRF method [11], the HMRF method [12], and the proposed method. Note that these motion estimates are not accurate since they are computed from noisy, and aliased observations. The assumption of Gaussian PSF for the camera defocus blur is also an approximation. Results corresponding to each of the above methods is shown in Fig. 2. The reconstructed image using the LS technique (Fig. 2(e)) is poor as it is very sensitive to errors in motion and blur estimates. The output of the GMRF algorithm (Fig. 2(f)) is quite blurred and some of the numbers are not at all discernible. HMRF performs relatively better (Fig. 2(g)) but some of the numbers are not easily readable. For example, the second digit '3' can be confused with '9' while the last digit '4' can be misinterpreted as '6'. In comparison, the proposed DAMRF algorithm yields the best result with distinctly defined edges as shown in Fig. 2(h). The license plate number (K 8354) can be read clearly without any ambiguity.

In the next example, the license plate of another car was cropped from four consecutive frames (Figs. 3(a)-3(d)). Note that the visual quality of these plates is very poor. The output corresponding to different super-resolution methods is given in Figs. 3(e)-3(h). We again observe that the reconstructed image using DAMRF is significantly better compared to existing methods. The text on the

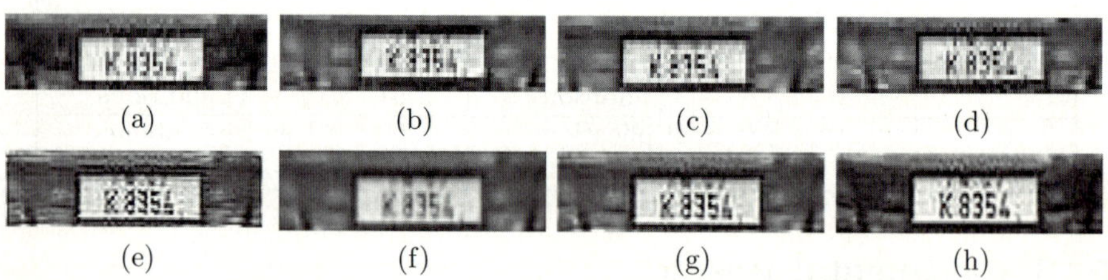

Fig. 2. (a)-(d) Cropped license plates. Super-resolved image using (e) LS, (f) GMRF, (g) HMRF, and (h) DAMRF.

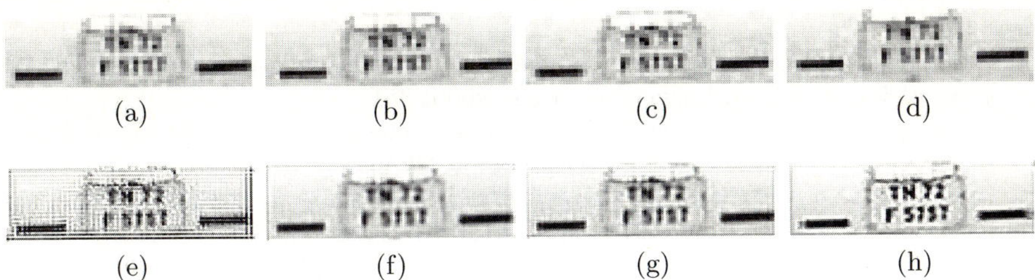

(a)   (b)   (c)   (d)

(e)   (f)   (g)   (h)

Fig. 3. (a)-(d) Cropped license plates. Super-resolved image using (e) LS, (f) GMRF, (g) HMRF, and (h) DAMRF.

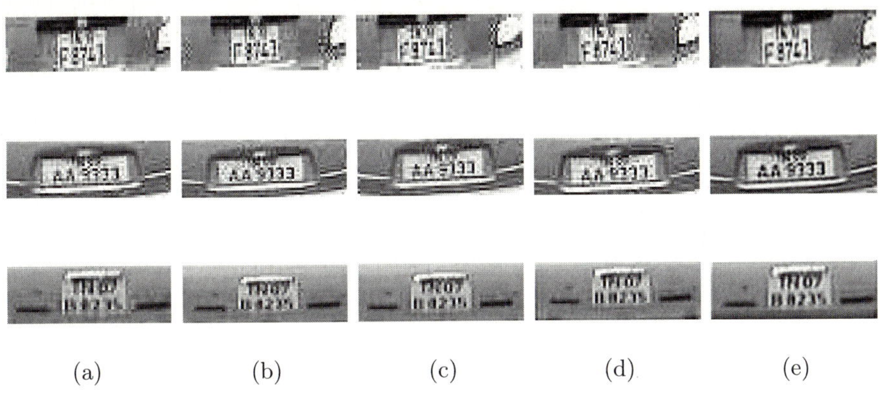

(a)   (b)   (c)   (d)   (e)

Fig. 4. (a)–(d) Low resolution observations. (e) Super-resolved images using the proposed method.

license plate comes out clearly in the super-resolved image using the proposed method.

In Fig. 4 we have given results corresponding to the license plates of some more cars. Note that in all the cases, the readability of the number plate improves significantly after performing super-resolution on the captured video frames using the proposed method.

6 Conclusions

A robust super-resolution algorithm using a discontinuity adaptive prior is proposed to enhance the license plate text of moving vehicles. The algorithm fuses the information available from multiple observations of a vehicle to obtain a high quality license plate image. The high-resolution image is modeled as an MRF and is estimated using graduated non-convexity. The effectiveness of the proposed method was demonstrated on many real traffic video sequences. The proposed DAMRF method is robust to errors in motion and blur estimates and preserves the edges in the reconstructed license plate text.

References

1. Rajagopalan, A.N., Chellappa, R.: Vehicle detection and tracking in video. In: Proc. of Intl. Conf. on Image Process. **1** (2000) 351–354
2. Zhang, Y., Zhang, C.: A new algorithm for character segmentation of license Plate. In: Proc. of IEEE Intelligent Vehicles Symp. (2003) 106–109
3. Cui, Y., Huang, Q.: Character extraction of license plates from video. In: Proc. of IEEE Conf. on Computer Vision and Pattern Recognition. (1997) 502–507
4. Sato, T., Kanade, T., Hughes, E., Smith, M., Satoh, S.: Video OCR: Indexing digital news libraries by recognition of superimposed caption. ACM Multimedia Systems Special Issue on Video Libraries. **7** (1999) 385–395
5. Chaudhuri, S.: Super-resolution imaging. Kluwer Academic, USA. (2001)
6. Cortijo, F.J., Villena, S., Molina, R., Katsaggelos, A.: Bayesian super-resolution of text image sequences from low-resolution observations. In: IEEE Intl. Symp. on Signal Process. and its Application. (2003) 421–424
7. Chaudhuri, S., Taur, D.R.: High-resolution slow-motion sequencing - How to generate a slow-motion sequence from a bit stream. IEEE Signal Process. Mag. **22** (2005) 16-24
8. Miravet, C., Rodriguez, F.B.: A hybrid MLP-PNN architecture for fast image super-resolution. In: Intl. Conf. on Neural Information Process. (2003) 417–424
9. Rajaram, S., Gupta, M.D., Petrovic, N., Huang, T.S.: Learning-based nonparametric image super-resolution. EURASIP Journal on Applied Signal Process. (2006)
10. Geman, S., Geman, D.: Stochastic relaxation, Gibbs distribution and the Bayesian restoration of images. IEEE Trans. on Pattern Anal. and Mach. Intell. **6** (1984) 721–741
11. Hardie, R.C., Barnard, K., Armstrong, E.E.: Joint MAP registration and high-resolution image estimation using a sequence of undersampled images. IEEE Trans. on Image Process. **6** (1997) 1621–1632
12. Schultz, R., Stevenson, R.L.: Extraction of high-resolution frames from video sequences. IEEE Trans. on Image Process. **5** (1996) 996-1011
13. Li, S.Z.: Markov random field modeling in computer vision. Springer-Verlag, Tokyo. (1995)
14. Irani, M., Peleg, S.: Improving resolution by image registration. CVGIP: Graph. Models and Image Process. **53** (1991) 231–239
15. Zomet, A., Peleg, S.: Super-resolution from multiple images having arbitrary mutual motion. Super-resolution Imaging. ed., Chaudhuri, S., Kluwer Academic. (2001) 195–209

Explicit Nonflat Time Evolution for PDE-Based Image Restoration

Seongjai Kim and Song-Hwa Kwon

Department of Mathematics & Statistics, Mississippi State University
Mississippi State, MS 39762 USA
`skim@math.msstate.edu`
IMA, University of Minnesota, 207 Church Street S.E.
Minneapolis, MN 55455
`shkwon@ima.umn.edu`

Abstract. This article is concerned with new strategies with which explicit time-stepping procedures of PDE-based restoration models converge with a similar efficiency to implicit algorithms. Conventional explicit algorithms often require hundreds of iterations to converge. In order to overcome the difficulty and to further improve image quality, the article introduces new spatially variable constraint term and timestep size, as a method of nonflat time evolution (MONTE). It has been verified that the explicit time-stepping scheme incorporating MONTE converges in only 4-15 iterations for all restoration examples we have tested. It has proved more effective than the additive operator splitting (AOS) method in both computation time and image quality (measured in PSNR), for most cases. Since the explicit MONTE procedure is efficient in computer memory, requiring only twice the image size, it can be applied particularly for huge data sets with a great efficiency in computer memory as well.

1 Introduction

Partial differential equation (PDE)-based image processing has been a popular tool for image restoration, since the first anisotropic diffusion model by Perona and Malik in 1990 [1]. A considerable amount of research has been carried out for the theoretical and computational understanding of various models; see e.g., [2,3,4,5,6,7,8,9] and [10,11,12]. It is now well understood that by choosing proper energy functionals in variational formulation and scaling their stationary Euler-Lagrange equations by appropriate factors, the resulting evolutionary models can restore important image features relatively well.

However, most of conventional PDE-based restoration models tend either to converge to a piecewise constant image or to lose fine structures of the given image, particularly unless they are both incorporating appropriate parameters and discretized by suitable numerical schemes. Although these results are important for understanding the current diffusion-like models, the resultant signals may not be desired in applications where the preservation of both slow transitions

P. Kalra and S. Peleg (Eds.): ICVGIP 2006, LNCS 4338, pp. 35–44, 2006.
© Springer-Verlag Berlin Heidelberg 2006

and fine structures is important. More advanced models are yet to be developed, along with effective strategies for the choice of appropriate parameters and numerical schemes.

It is often the case that conventional explicit algorithms for solving PDE-based restoration models require hundreds of iterations to converge. This article introduces numerical strategies for the selection of spatially variable constraint parameter and timestep size, as a *method of nonflat time evolution* (MONTE), with which explicit procedures can converge fast and restore images in a comparable quality with implicit algorithms. In MONTE, the constraint parameter is selected larger on fast transitions, which in turn can suppress undesired dissipation effectively there; the timestep size is set reversely proportional to the sum of the diffusion coefficient and the constraint parameter, which makes the explicit procedure stable. Note that the MONTE solution must be defined on a nonflat time surface.

The new strategies have been implemented, incorporating an anisotropic diffusion spatial scheme, for both *additive operator splitting* (AOS) method [13] and the explicit algorithm. The explicit algorithm incorporating MONTE turns out to converge in 4-15 iterations for all restoration examples we have tested. Furthermore, it has often restored better images (measured in PSNR) than the AOS algorithm. Since the new explicit MONTE procedure is efficient in computer memory, requiring only twice the image size, it can be applied, particularly for huge data sets (e.g., 3D images), with a great efficiency in both convergence and computer memory.

An outline of the paper is as follows. In the next section, we briefly review PDE-based restoration models and their linearized time-stepping methods, followed by an anisotropic diffusion spatial scheme. Section 3 contains new numerical strategies for variable constraint parameters, variable timestep sizes, and their applications to the explicit time-stepping method. In Section 4, we present numerical results to show efficiency (in computation time) and effectiveness (in the preservation of important image features) of the explicit MONTE procedure. Section 5 conclude our developments and experiments.

2   Preliminaries

This section reviews briefly PDE-based restoration models and their linearized time-stepping procedures, followed by an anisotropic diffusion spatial scheme.

2.1   PDE-Based Restoration Models

Let u_0 be an observed image of the form

$$u_0 = u + v, \tag{1}$$

where u is the desired image and v denotes a mean-zero noise of variance σ^2. Then, popular PDE-based restoration models can be written in the following general form:

$$\frac{\partial u}{\partial t} + S(u) = R(u_0 - u), \tag{2}$$

where S is a (nonlinear) diffusion operator and R denotes a nonnegative constraint term. For example, the Perona-Malik (PM) model [1], the total variation (TV) model [8], the improved TV (ITV) model [6,11], and the convex-concave anisotropic diffusion (CCAD) model [4,5] can be specified as follows:

$$\begin{aligned}
S(u) &= -\nabla \cdot (c(|\nabla u|)\nabla u), & R &= 0, & \text{(PM)} \\
S(u) &= -\kappa_1(u), & R &= \lambda, & \text{(TV)} \\
S(u) &= -|\nabla u|\,\kappa_1(u), & R &= \lambda\,|\nabla u|, & \text{(ITV)} \\
S(u) &= -|\nabla u|^q \kappa_q(u), & R &= \beta\,|u_0 - u|, & \text{(CCAD)}
\end{aligned} \tag{3}$$

where $\lambda,\ \beta \geq 0,\ 0 \leq q < 2$, and

$$c(x) = (1 + x^2/K^2)^{-1}, \quad \kappa_q(u) = \nabla \cdot \left(\frac{\nabla u}{|\nabla u|^q}\right),$$

for some $K > 0$.

The PM and TV models tend to converge to a piecewise constant image; such a phenomenon is called the *staircasing effect*. To suppress the staircasing effect, Marquina and Osher [6] suggested the ITV model, a scaling of the TV model by a factor of $|\nabla u|$. Since $|\nabla u|$ vanishes only on flat regions, its steady state is analytically the same as that of the TV model. The ITV model turns out to reduce the staircasing effect successfully; however, it is yet to be improved for a better preservation of fine structures. The CCAD model is a non-variational generalization of the ITV model and can be implemented as a stable numerical algorithm for $q \geq 0$; see [5] for details.

Note that the image is originally time-independent; the time in (2) has been introduced in order to deal with the corresponding steady-state PDEs conveniently. Thus the time is an artificial variable and can be considered as an algorithmic parameter for the solution, the restored image.

2.2 Linearized Time-Stepping Procedures

Let Δt^n be the nth timestep size and $t^n = \sum_{i=1}^n \Delta t^i$, $n \geq 1$, with $t^0 = 0$. Define $u^n = u(\cdot, t^n)$, $n \geq 0$, with $u^0 = u_0$. Given $u^0, \cdots, u^{n-1}$, we will try to compute u^n by linearized time-stepping procedures. For $\ell = 1, 2$, let $\mathcal{S}_\ell^{n-1}$ be diffusion matrices approximating directional operators of the diffusion term S; for example, for the CCAD model,

$$\mathcal{S}_\ell^{n-1}\, u^m \approx -|\nabla u^{n-1}|^q\, \partial_{x_\ell}\left(\frac{\partial_{x_\ell} u^m}{|\nabla u^{n-1}|^q}\right), \quad m = n-1,\, n. \tag{4}$$

(See Section 2.3 below for details of an anisotropic diffusion spatial scheme.) Define $\mathcal{A}^{n-1} = \mathcal{A}_1^{n-1} + \mathcal{A}_2^{n-1}$, where

$$\mathcal{A}_\ell^{n-1} = \mathcal{S}_\ell^{n-1} + \frac{1}{2}\,\mathcal{R}^n, \quad \ell = 1, 2. \tag{5}$$

Here $\mathcal{R}^n$ is an evaluation of the constraint term R for the nth time level, of which an effective strategy will be considered in Section 3.1. Then, a linearized θ-method for (2) can be formulated as follows: for $0 \leq \theta \leq 1$,

$$\frac{u^n - u^{n-1}}{\Delta t^n} + \mathcal{A}^{n-1}\left[\theta u^n + (1-\theta)u^{n-1})\right] = \mathcal{R}^n u_0. \tag{6}$$

For $\theta = 0$, the θ-method computes u^n *explicitly*; when Δt^n is constant spatially, it must be sufficiently small in order for the algorithm to be stable. On the other hand, for $\theta > 0$, one can solve the linear system (6) by applying an iterative algebraic solver or the *alternating direction implicit* (ADI) procedure [14,15,4].

Although the algebraic system (6) is often solved implicitly ($\theta = 1/2$ or 1) in the literature, the explicit procedure ($\theta = 0$) is still popular, due to simplicity in implementation and efficiency in computer memory. However, it requires to choose Δt^n sufficiently small for stability and therefore converges in a huge number of iterations, which is its major disadvantage. In Section 3.2, we will study a strategy for the choice of *spatially* variable Δt^n, i.e., $\Delta t^n = \Delta t^n(\mathbf{x})$; with which the explicit procedure can converge quickly, e.g., in about 10 iterations. In Section 4, the new explicit algorithm will be compared with the AOS method:

$$\frac{u^{n,k} - u^{n-1}}{\Delta t^n} + 2\mathcal{A}_k^{n-1}u^{n,k} = \mathcal{R}^n u_0, \quad k = 1,2,$$
$$u^n = (u^{n,1} + u^{n,2})/2, \tag{7}$$

which holds the maximum principle independently of the timestep size and involves a splitting error of $\mathcal{O}(\Delta t)$; see [13].

2.3 An Anisotropic Diffusion Spatial Scheme

For a completeness of the article, this subsection presents an anisotropic diffusion scheme for $\mathcal{S}_\ell^{n-1}$ utilized in (4), which was first introduced in [16]. We will show the construction of $\mathcal{S}_1^{n-1}$; the analogue can be applied to obtain $\mathcal{S}_2^{n-1}$. Let $\mathcal{D}u_{i-1/2,j}^{n-1}$ be a finite difference approximation of $|\nabla u^{n-1}|$ evaluated at $\mathbf{x}_{i-1/2,j}$, the mid point of $\mathbf{x}_{i-1,j}$ and $\mathbf{x}_{i,j}$. For example, a second-order scheme reads

$$\mathcal{D}u_{i-1/2,j}^{n-1} = \left((u_{i,j}^{n-1} - u_{i-1,j}^{n-1})^2 \right.$$
$$\left. + \left[\frac{1}{2}\left(\frac{u_{i-1,j+1}^{n-1} + u_{i,j+1}^{n-1}}{2} - \frac{u_{i-1,j-1}^{n-1} + u_{i,j-1}^{n-1}}{2}\right)\right]^2\right)^{1/2}. \tag{8}$$

Define

$$d_{ij,W}^{n-1} = [(\mathcal{D}u_{i-1/2,j}^{n-1})^2 + \varepsilon^2]^{q/2}, \quad d_{ij,E}^{n-1} = d_{i+1,j,W}^{n-1}, \tag{9}$$

where ε is a positive constant (small) introduced to prevent $d_{ij,W}^{n-1}$ from approaching zero. Then the differential operators in (4), $\ell = 1$, can be approximated as

$$-\partial_{x_1}\left(\frac{\partial_{x_1}u^m}{|\nabla u^{n-1}|^q}\right) \approx -\frac{1}{d_{ij,W}^{n-1}}u_{i-1,j}^m$$

$$+\left(\frac{1}{d_{ij,W}^{n-1}}+\frac{1}{d_{ij,E}^{n-1}}\right)u_{i,j}^m - \frac{1}{d_{ij,E}^{n-1}}u_{i+1,j}^m, \tag{10}$$

$$|\nabla u^{n-1}|^q \approx \frac{2\,d_{ij,W}^{n-1}\cdot d_{ij,E}^{n-1}}{d_{ij,W}^{n-1}+d_{ij,E}^{n-1}}.$$

Note that the last approximation is the harmonic average of $d_{ij,W}^{n-1}$ and $d_{ij,E}^{n-1}$ and first-order accurate. It follows from (4) and (10) that the three consecutive non-zero elements of the matrix $\mathcal{S}_1^{n-1}$ corresponding to the pixel $\mathbf{x}_{ij}$ read

$$[\mathcal{S}_1^{n-1}]_{ij} = (-s_{ij,W}^{n-1},\, 2,\, -s_{ij,E}^{n-1}), \tag{11}$$

where

$$s_{ij,W}^{n-1} = \frac{2\,d_{ij,E}^{n-1}}{d_{ij,W}^{n-1}+d_{ij,E}^{n-1}}, \qquad s_{ij,E}^{n-1} = \frac{2\,d_{ij,W}^{n-1}}{d_{ij,W}^{n-1}+d_{ij,E}^{n-1}}. \tag{12}$$

Note that $s_{ij,W}^{n-1}+s_{ij,E}^{n-1} = 2$. The above anisotropic diffusion numerical scheme has been successfully applied for image zooming of arbitrary magnification factors [17,16] and a simultaneous denoising and edge enhancement [5].

3   The Method of Nonflat Time Evolution (MONTE)

In this section, we will introduce an effective variable constraint parameter and an explicit scheme incorporating variable timestep size $\Delta t^n = \Delta t^n(\mathbf{x})$.

3.1   Constraint Parameters

For most PDE-based models, the constraint parameter has been chosen as constant, due to simplicity. However, constant constraint parameters can often be ineffective in the preservation of interesting image features such as edges and textures, because the diffusion operator may introduce an extra dissipation on fast transitions.

In order to overcome the difficulty, one consider a *variable* constraint parameter as follows: Multiply the stationary part of (2) by $(u_0 - u)$ and average the resulting equation *locally* to obtain

$$R(\mathbf{x}) \approx \frac{1}{\sigma_{\mathbf{x}}^2}\frac{1}{|\Omega_{\mathbf{x}}|}\int_{\Omega_{\mathbf{x}}} (u_0 - u)\,S(u)\,d\mathbf{x},$$

where $\Omega_{\mathbf{x}}$ is a neighborhood of $\mathbf{x}$ (e.g., the window of (3×3) pixels centered at $\mathbf{x}$) and $\sigma_{\mathbf{x}}^2$ denotes the local noise variance measured over $\Omega_{\mathbf{x}}$. Then, the right side of the above equation can be approximated as

$$R(\mathbf{x}) \approx \frac{1}{\sigma_{\mathbf{x}}^2}\,\|u_0 - u\|_{\mathbf{x}}\cdot\|S(u)\|_{\mathbf{x}}, \tag{13}$$

where $\|g\|_{\mathbf{x}}$ denotes a local average $|g|$ over $\Omega_{\mathbf{x}}$. The constraint parameter in (13) is proportional to both the absolute residual $|u_0 - u|$ and the diffusion magnitude $|S(u)|$, which may effectively suppress the extra dissipation arising on fast transitions. Note that the local noise variance $\sigma_{\mathbf{x}}^2$ must be estimated appropriately; see [18] for an effective estimation of $\sigma_{\mathbf{x}}^2$.

Let the neighborhood $\Omega_{\mathbf{x}}$ be chosen to include a single pixel $\mathbf{x}$. Then the constraint parameter in (13) related to a pixel (i, j) in the nth time level can be formulated as

$$R_{ij}^n = \eta_1 \cdot |u_{0,ij} - u_{ij}^{n-1}| \cdot |(\mathcal{S}^{n-1} u^{n-1})_{ij}|, \tag{14}$$

where η_1 is nonnegative constant and $\mathcal{S}^{n-1} = \mathcal{S}_1^{n-1} + \mathcal{S}_2^{n-1}$.

3.2   An Explicit Nonflat Time-Stepping Procedure

For $\theta = 0$, the θ-method (6) can be rewritten as

$$u^n = (1 - \Delta t^n \, \mathcal{S}^{n-1}) \, u^{n-1} + \Delta t^n \, \mathcal{R}^n (u_0 - u^{n-1}). \tag{15}$$

Let the diffusion matrix $\mathcal{S}^{n-1}$ incorporate a five-point stencil, i.e.,

$$\begin{aligned}
[\mathcal{S}^{n-1} u^{n-1}]_{ij} &= s_{ij,C}^{n-1} \, u_{ij}^{n-1} - s_{ij,W}^{n-1} \, u_{i-1,j}^{n-1} \\
&\quad - s_{ij,E}^{n-1} \, u_{i+1,j}^{n-1} - s_{ij,S}^{n-1} \, u_{i,j-1}^{n-1} - s_{ij,N}^{n-1} \, u_{i,j+1}^{n-1},
\end{aligned} \tag{16}$$

where $s_{ij,W}^{n-1}, \, s_{ij,E}^{n-1}, \, s_{ij,S}^{n-1}, \, s_{ij,N}^{n-1} \geq 0$ and $s_{ij,C}^{n-1} := s_{ij,W}^{n-1} + s_{ij,E}^{n-1} + s_{ij,S}^{n-1} + s_{ij,N}^{n-1}$. For the diffusion matrix $\mathcal{S}_1^{n-1}$ in (11) and its analogue $\mathcal{S}_2^{n-1}$, we have $s_{ij,C}^{n-1} = 4$.

When (16) and (14) are adopted respectively for the diffusion and constraint terms, the explicit procedure (15) can be written as

$$\begin{aligned}
u_{ij}^n &= [1 - \Delta t^n \, (s_{ij,C}^{n-1} + R_{ij}^n)] \, u_{ij}^{n-1} \\
&\quad + \Delta t^n \, (s_{ij,W}^{n-1} \, u_{i-1,j}^{n-1} + s_{ij,E}^{n-1} \, u_{i+1,j}^{n-1} \\
&\quad + s_{ij,S}^{n-1} \, u_{i,j-1}^{n-1} + s_{ij,N}^{n-1} \, u_{i,j+1}^{n-1}) + \Delta t^n \, R_{ij}^n \, u_{0,ij}.
\end{aligned} \tag{17}$$

The above iteration is stable when all coefficients in the right side are nonnegative. Thus the stability condition for (17) reads

$$\Delta t^n \leq \frac{1}{s_{ij,C}^{n-1} + R_{ij}^n}. \tag{18}$$

A common practice for the choice of Δt^n is

$$\Delta t^n = \min_{ij} \frac{1}{s_{ij,C}^{n-1} + R_{ij}^n}. \tag{19}$$

Recall that R_{ij}^n is proportional to both the absolute residual and the diffusion magnitude, while $s_{ij,C}^{n-1}$ is a multiple of the diffusion coefficient. Thus the timestep size Δt^n in (19) has been chosen as a constant, in order for the algorithm (17)

not to introduce nonphysical oscillations (instability) on regions of the fastest
transition. However, this choice can slow down evolution of the solution on other
regions, particularly on slow transitions. This is why conventional explicit methods have often required hundreds of iterations to converge.

As an alternative to (19), this article considers the following variable timestep
size $\Delta t^n = \Delta t^n(\mathbf{x})$:

$$\Delta t_{ij}^n = \frac{1}{s_{ij,C}^{n-1} + R_{ij}^n}. \tag{20}$$

The above choice of a variable timestep size deserves the following remarks:

- On slow transitions, the constraint parameter R_{ij}^n approaches zero and therefore a larger timestep must be set, which in turn makes the algorithm work
  faster in image restoration.
- Since PDE-based models often incorporate an extra (faster) diffusion on fast
  transitions, the choice in (20) can serve as a modulator which tries to equalize
  the speed of diffusion over the image domain.
- The computed solution u^n resides on a nonflat time surface, which causes no
  difficulties. Note that the time in PDE-based denoising models of interests
  has been introduced, as an artificial variable, in order to enhance convenience
  in numerical simulation. The variable timestep size in (20) can be viewed
  as a variable parameter of the algorithm (15) which is introduced to solve
  steady-state problems of the form

$$S(u) = R(u_0 - u).$$

  Here we have chosen Δt^n to enhance efficiency in algorithmic convergence.
  We will see in Section 4 that the choice is also effective in quality of image
  restoration.
- With (20), the algorithm (17) can be rewritten as

$$
\begin{aligned}
u_{ij}^n = \frac{1}{s_{ij,C}^{n-1} + R_{ij}^n} \Big(& s_{ij,W}^{n-1}\, u_{i-1,j}^{n-1} + s_{ij,E}^{n-1}\, u_{i+1,j}^{n-1} \\
& + s_{ij,S}^{n-1}\, u_{i,j-1}^{n-1} + s_{ij,N}^{n-1}\, u_{i,j+1}^{n-1} + R_{ij}^n\, u_{0,ij} \Big),
\end{aligned}
\tag{21}
$$

  which is an average of $u_{0,ij}$ and four neighboring pixel values of u^{n-1}; the
  weights are computed anisotropically, incorporating all the pixel values of
  u^{n-1} on the (3×3) window centered at (i,j), as presented in Section 2.3.

4   Numerical Experiments

In this section, we verify effectiveness of the explicit MONTE procedure, comparing with the AOS method (7). Both algorithms incorporates the same spatial
schemes in Section 2.3 and the same constraint parameter in Section 3.1. The
explicit MONTE procedure utilizes the variable timestep size (20), while the
AOS method is provided with the *constant* timestep size which experimentally

Fig. 1. Sample images: Lenna, Elaine, and Zebra

Table 1. A PSNR analysis: comparison between the AOS and the explicit MONTE

Noise		AOS				Explicit MONTE		
Image	PSNR	Δt	Iter	PSNR	Etime	Iter	PSNR	Etime
Lenna	27.27	0.44	6	32.14	0.47	4	32.83	0.32
	21.25	0.41	12	28.83	0.92	7	29.48	0.56
	16.81	0.42	15	26.22	1.20	9	26.95	0.72
Elaine	27.28	0.43	7	31.51	0.53	4	31.91	0.40
	16.82	0.41	19	27.34	1.40	9	27.50	0.89
Zebra	24.78	0.15	7	28.03	0.57	6	28.06	0.67
	16.82	0.15	15	23.01	1.28	11	23.34	1.22

results in the best PSNR among all constant timestep sizes. A personal computer of 2.66 GHz Celeron processor is utilized for the computation; the elapsed time (Etime) is the real time in second.

The input images are scaled by $1/255$ to have values between 0 and 1. Most algorithm parameters are chosen heuristically for the algorithms to perform their best. We set $\varepsilon = 0.01$ in (9); the iterations are stopped when $\max_{ij} |u_{ij}^n - u_{ij}^{n-1}| \leq 0.01$. The ITV model [6] is selected for the numerical experiment. For simplicity and a fair comparison, we have utilized the true value of noise variance σ^2 for the parameter η_1 in (14): $\eta_1 = 0.4/\sigma^2$. This choice of the parameter has been verified to be most effective (among all constant η_1) for both algorithms. See [18] for an effective estimation of $\sigma_{\mathbf{x}}^2$.

The algorithms have been tested various synthetic and natural images. Here we will present numerical results, obtained with the sample images in Figure 1.

Table 1 contains a PSNR analysis, comparing performances of the AOS and explicit procedures applied to the sample images. The variable Δt is the best constant timestep size we have experimentally found for the AOS, which tends to become small for texture images such as Zebra. As one can see from the table, the explicit MONTE can restore images better than the AOS method measured in PSNR for all cases. It should be noticed that the explicit scheme (17) converges in 4-11 iterations, while the AOS algorithm requires more iterations. Such a fast convergence for the explicit algorithm is due to the MONTE, the variable

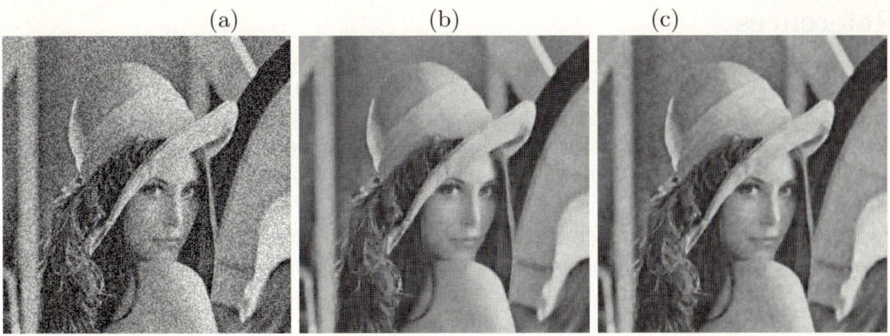

Fig. 2. Lenna image: (a) a noisy image (PSNR=21.25) and restored images by (b) the AOS method (PSNR=28.83) and (c) the explicit procedure (PSNR=29.48)

constraint term (14) and the variable timestep size (20), which tries to equalize the speed of diffusion over the image domain.

Figure 2 depicts a noisy image of Lenna (PSNR=21.25) and its restored images by the two algorithms. The AOS and explicit iterations converge in 12 and 7 iterations, respectively, as shown in Table 1. As one can see from the figure, image details are preserved satisfactorily by the AOS, while the new explicit method has resulted in a better restored image. The MONTE has proved efficient in computation time and effective in the preservation of interesting image features.

The explicit MONTE procedure has converged in 4-15 iterations for all tested cases (including those not presented in this article). One should notice that the explicit procedure is efficient in computer memory, requiring only twice the image size.

5   Conclusions

Conventional explicit algorithms for solving PDE-based restoration models often require hundreds of iterations to converge. In this article, we have introduced strategies for spatially variable constraint parameter and timestep size, as a method of nonflat time evolution (MONTE). The explicit MONTE has been compared with the additive operator splitting (AOS) method to prove its efficiency and effectiveness. It has been numerically verified that the explicit MONTE procedure converges in only 4-15 iterations for all tested cases of image denoising. The new explicit method has converged faster and produced better restored images (measured in PSNR) than the AOS algorithm, for most cases. Since the explicit MONTE procedure is efficient in computer memory, requiring only twice the image size, it can be applied particularly for huge data sets (e.g., 3D images) with a great efficiency in computer memory.

Acknowledgment

The work of S. Kim is supported in part by NSF grants DMS-0630798 and DMS-0609815.

References

1. Perona, P., Malik, J.: Scale-space and edge detection using anisotropic diffusion. IEEE Trans. on Pattern Anal. Mach. Intell. **12** (1990) 629–639
2. Alvarez, L., Lions, P., Morel, M.: Image selective smoothing and edge detection by nonlinear diffusion. II. SIAM J. Numer. Anal. **29** (1992) 845–866
3. Catte, F., Lions, P., Morel, M., Coll, T.: Image selective smoothing and edge detection by nonlinear diffusion. SIAM J. Numer. Anal. **29** (1992) 182–193
4. Kim, S.: PDE-based image restoration: A hybrid model and color image denoising. IEEE Trans. Image Processing **15** (2006) 1163–1170
5. Kim, S., Lim, H.: A non-convex diffusion model for simultaneous image denoising and edge enhancement. Electronic Journal of Differential Equations (2006) (accepted).
6. Marquina, A., Osher, S.: Explicit algorithms for a new time dependent model based on level set motion for nonlinear deblurring and noise removal. SIAM J. Sci. Comput. **22** (2000) 387–405
7. Nitzberg, M., Shiota, T.: Nonlinear image filtering with edge and corner enhancement. IEEE Trans. on Pattern Anal. Mach. Intell. **14** (1992) 826–833
8. Rudin, L., Osher, S., Fatemi, E.: Nonlinear total variation based noise removal algorithms. Physica D **60** (1992) 259–268
9. You, Y.L., Xu, W., Tannenbaum, A., Kaveh, M.: Behavioral analysis of anisotropic diffusion in image processing. IEEE Trans. Image Process. **5** (1996) 1539–1553
10. Chan, T., Shen, J.: Image Processing and Analysis. SIAM, Philadelphia (2005)
11. Osher, S., Fedkiw, R.: Level Set Methods and Dynamic Implicit Surfaces. Springer-Verlag, New York (2003)
12. Sapiro, G.: Geometric partial differential equations and image analysis. Cambridge University Press, Cambridge (2001)
13. Weickert, J., ter Haar Romeny, B., Viergever, M.: Efficient and reliable schemes for nonlinear diffusion filtering. IEEE Trans. on Image Processing **7** (1998) 398–410
14. Douglas, Jr., J., Gunn, J.: A general formulation of alternating direction methods Part I. Parabolic and hyperbolic problems. Numer. Math. **6** (1964) 428–453
15. Douglas, Jr., J., Kim, S.: Improved accuracy for locally one-dimensional methods for parabolic equations. Mathematical Models and Methods in Applied Sciences **11** (2001) 1563–1579
16. Cha, Y., Kim, S.: Edge-forming methods for image zooming. J. Mathematical Imaging and Vision (2006) (in press).
17. Cha, Y., Kim, S.: Edge-forming methods for color image zooming. IEEE Trans. Image Process. **15** (2006) 2315–2323
18. Kim, S., Kwon, S.H.: Efficiency and reliability in nonlinear diffusion filtering. (in preparation)

Decimation Estimation and Super-Resolution Using Zoomed Observations

Prakash P. Gajjar, Manjunath V. Joshi, Asim Banerjee, and Suman Mitra

Dhirubhai Ambani Institute of Information and Communication Technology,
Gandhinagar, India

Abstract. We propose a technique for super-resolving an image from several observations taken at different camera zooms. From the set of these images, a super-resolved image of the entire scene (least zoomed) is obtained at the resolution of the most zoomed one. We model the super-resolution image as a Markov Random Field (MRF). The cost function is derived using a Maximum a posteriori (MAP) estimation method and is optimized by using gradient descent technique. The novelty of our approach is that the decimation (aliasing) matrix is obtained from the given observations themselves. Results are illustrated with real data captured using a zoom camera. Application of our technique to multiresolution fusion in remotely sensed images is shown.

1   Introduction

In many of the imaging applications, images with high spatial resolution are desired and often required. The spatial resolution can be increased by using high density sensor for capturing the image. However, this is not possible as there exist a limit on pixel size. The resolution enhancement from a single observation using image interpolation is of limited application because of the aliasing present in the low resolution image. Super-resolution refers to the process of producing a high spatial resolution image from several low-resolution observations. When one captures the images with different zoom settings, the amount of aliasing is different in differently zoomed observations. This is because the least zoomed entire area of the scene is represented by a very limited number of pixels, i.e., it is sampled with a very low sampling rate and the most zoomed image with a higher sampling frequency. Therefore, larger scene coverage will have lower resolution with more aliasing effect. By varying the zoom level, one observes the scene at different levels of aliasing and blurring. Thus, one can use zoom as a cue for generating high-resolution images at the lesser zoomed area of a scene.

The super-resolution idea was first proposed by Tsai and Huang [1] using frequency domain approach and employing motion as a cue. In [2], the authors use a Maximum a posteriori framework for jointly estimating the registration parameters and the high-resolution image for severely aliased observations. A MAP estimator with Huber-MRF prior is described by Schultz and Stevenson in [3]. Lin and Shum determine the fundamental limits of reconstruction-based super-resolution algorithms using the motion cue and obtain the magnification limits

P. Kalra and S. Peleg (Eds.): ICVGIP 2006, LNCS 4338, pp. 45–57, 2006.

from the conditioning analysis of the coefficient matrix [4]. Capel and Zisserman [5] have proposed a technique for automated mosaicing with super-resolution zoom by fusing information from several views of a planar surface in order to estimate its texture. The authors in [6] integrate the tasks of super-resolution and recognition by directly computing a maximum likelihood parameter vector in high-resolution tensor space for face recognition.

Most of the methods of super-resolution proposed in literature use motion cue for estimating high resolution image. This requires registration of images with sub-pixel accuracy. The non-redundant information can also be obtained by using different camera parameters or different lighting conditions while capturing the scene. The authors in [7] describe an MAP-MRF based super-resolution technique using blur cue. They recover both the high-resolution scene intensity and the depth fields simultaneously using the defocus cue. The authors in [8] recover the super-resolution intensity field from a sequence of zoomed observations. The resolution of entire scene is obtained at the resolution of the most zoomed observed image which consists of only a portion of the actual scene. For more details refer to [9].

In this paper, we obtain super-resolution by using zoom as a cue. We model the super-resolution image as an MRF and assume that the high resolution image at the most zoom setting is super-resolved. In our image formation model, we learn the decimation (aliasing) matrix from the most zoomed observation and use MAP-MRF formulation to obtain super-resolved image for the entire scene. We are also assuming that the images are registered while zooming. However after registering the images we need to estimate the aliasing accurately so that the model fits well. It may be interesting to see that our approach generates a super-resolved image of the entire scene, although only a part of the observed scene has multiple observations.

2   Image Formation Model

The zoom based super-resolution problem can be cast in a restoration framework. There are p observed images Y_i, $i = 1$ to p, each captured with different zoom settings and are of size $M_1 \times M_2$ pixels each. Fig. 1 illustrates the block schematic of how the low-resolution observations of a scene at different zoom settings are related to the high-resolution image. Here we consider that the most zoomed observed image of the scene Y_p ($p = 3$) has the highest spatial resolution. We are assuming that there is no rotation about the optical axis between the observed images taken at different zooms. Since different zoom settings give rise to different resolutions, the least zoomed scene corresponding to entire scene needs to be upsampled to the size of $(q_1 q_2 \ldots q_{p-1}) \times (M_1 \times M_2)$ pixels ($= N_1 \times N_2$ pixels), where q_1, q_2, $\ldots$, q_{p-1} are the corresponding zoom factors between two successively observed images of the scene $Y_1 Y_2$, $Y_2 Y_3$, $\ldots$, $Y_{p-1} Y_p$ respectively. Given Y_p, the remaining $(p-1)$ observed images are then modeled as decimated and noisy versions of this single high-resolution image of the appropriate region in the scene. The most zoomed observed image will have no decimation. The low resolution image observation model is shown in Fig. 2.

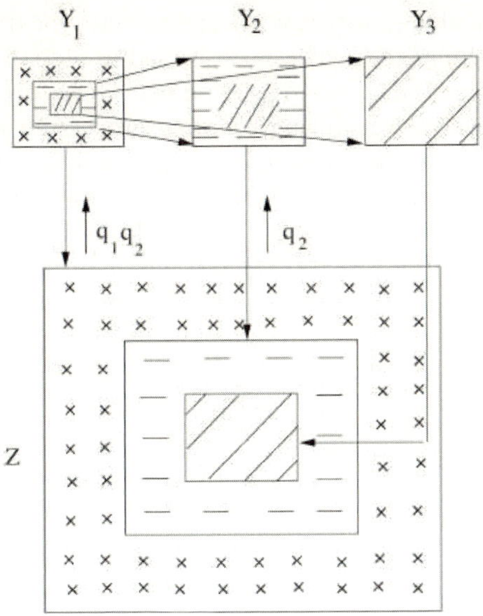

Fig. 1. Illustration of observations at different zoom levels, Y_1 corresponds to the least zoomed and Y_3 to the most zoomed images. Here z is the high resolution image of the scene.

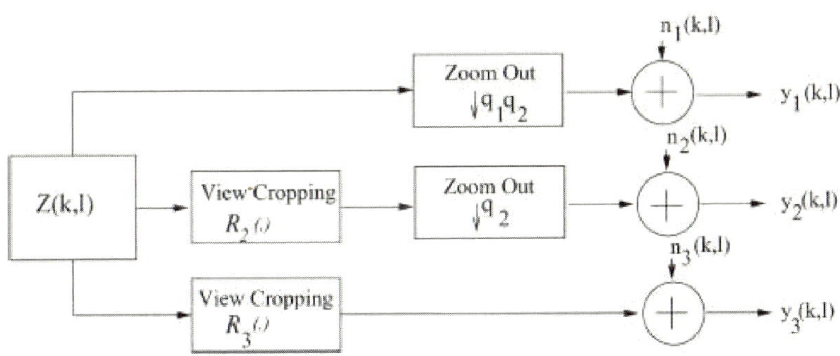

Fig. 2. Low-resolution image formation model for three different zoom levels. View cropping block just crops the relevant part of the high resolution image Z as the field of view shrinks with zooming.

Let $\mathbf{y}_m$ represent the lexicographically ordered vector of size $M_1 M_2 \times 1$, which contains the pixels from differently zoomed images Y_m and $\mathbf{z}$ be the super-resolved image. The observed images can be modeled as

$$\mathbf{y}_m = D_m \mathbf{C}_m (\mathbf{z} - z_{\alpha m}) + \mathbf{n}_m, \qquad m = 1, \cdots, p, \tag{1}$$

where D is the decimation matrix which takes care of aliasing present while zooming. The subscript m in D denotes that the amount of decimation depends on the amount of zoom for m^{th} observation, size of which depends on the zoom factor. For an integer zoom factor of q, the decimation matrix D consists of

q^2 non-zero elements along each row at appropriate locations. The procedure for estimating the decimation matrix is described in section 3. $\mathbf{C}_m$ is a cropping operator with $z_{\alpha_m} = z(x - \alpha_{m_x}, y - \alpha_{m_y})$ and $\alpha_m = (\alpha_{m_x}, \alpha_{m_y})$ representing the lateral shift of the optical shift during zooming process for the mth observation. The cropping operation is analogous to a characteristic function which crop outs the $\lfloor q_1 q_2 \ldots q_{m-1} N_1 \rfloor \times \lfloor q_1 q_2 \ldots q_{m-1} N_2 \rfloor$ pixel area from the high resolution image $\mathbf{z}$ at an appropriate position. $\mathbf{n}_m$ is the i.i.d noise vector with zero mean and variance σ_n^2. It is of the size, $M_1 M_2 \times 1$. The multivariate noise probability density is given by

$$P(\mathbf{n}_m) = \frac{1}{(2\pi\sigma_n^2)^{\frac{M_1 M_2}{2}}} e^{-\frac{1}{2\sigma_n^2} \mathbf{n}_m^T \mathbf{n}_m}. \tag{2}$$

Our problem is to estimate $\mathbf{z}$ given $\mathbf{y}_m$s, which is an ill-posed inverse problem. It may be mentioned here that the observations captured are not blurred. In other words, we assume identity matrix for blur.

3   Estimation of Decimation (Aliasing) Matrix

The general model for super-resolution based on motion cue is [10],

$$\mathbf{y} = DHW\mathbf{z} + \mathbf{n}, \tag{3}$$

where W is a warping matrix, H is a blur matrix, D is a decimation matrix and $\mathbf{n}$ is a noise vector. Here the decimation model to obtain the aliased pixel intensities from the high resolution pixels has the form [3]

$$D = \frac{1}{q^2} \begin{pmatrix} 1\ 1 \ldots 1 & & & \mathbf{0} \\ & 1\ 1 \ldots 1 & & \\ & & \ddots & \\ \mathbf{0} & & & 1\ 1 \ldots 1 \end{pmatrix}. \tag{4}$$

As an example, consider an observation of size 2×2. For the decimation factor of $q = 2$, the size of $\mathbf{z}$ becomes 4×4. $\mathbf{z}$ can be represented as lexicographically ordered vector having 16 elements. The Decimation matrix D is of size 4×16 and it can be expressed with reordering of $\mathbf{z}$ as

$$D = \frac{1}{4} \begin{pmatrix} 1\ 1\ 1\ 1\ 0\ 0\ 0\ 0\ 0\ 0\ 0\ 0\ 0\ 0\ 0\ 0 \\ 0\ 0\ 0\ 0\ 1\ 1\ 1\ 1\ 0\ 0\ 0\ 0\ 0\ 0\ 0\ 0 \\ 0\ 0\ 0\ 0\ 0\ 0\ 0\ 0\ 1\ 1\ 1\ 1\ 0\ 0\ 0\ 0 \\ 0\ 0\ 0\ 0\ 0\ 0\ 0\ 0\ 0\ 0\ 0\ 0\ 1\ 1\ 1\ 1 \end{pmatrix}. \tag{5}$$

In other words the aliased pixel intensity at a location (i, j) of a low resolution image for a zoom factor of $q = 2$ is given by

$$y(i, j) = \frac{1}{4} z(2i, 2j) + \frac{1}{4} z(2i, 2j+1) + \frac{1}{4} z(2i+1, 2j) + \frac{1}{4} z(2i+1, 2j+1) + n(i, j). \tag{6}$$

Here $(2i, 2j), (2i, 2j+1), (2i+1, 2j)$ and $(2i+1, 2j+1)$ are corresponding 4 (q^2) pixel locations in the higher resolution image and $n(i, j)$ is the noise at the pixel (i, j).

The decimation matrix in Eq. (4) indicates that a low resolution pixel intensity $y(i, j)$ is obtained by averaging the intensities of q^2 pixels corresponding to the same scene in the high resolution image and adding noise intensity $n(i, j)$ (refer to Eq.(1)). In other words, all q^2 high resolution intensities are weighted equally by $\frac{1}{q^2}$ ($\frac{1}{4}$ for $q = 2$) to obtain the distorted or aliased pixel. This decimation model simulates the integration of light intensity that falls on the high resolution detector. This assumes that the entire area of a pixel acts as the light sensing area and there is no space in the pixel area for wiring or insulation. In other words, fill factor for the CCD array is unity. However, in practice, the observed intensity at a pixel captured due to low resolution sampling depends on various factors such as camera gain, illumination condition, zoom factor, noise etc. Hence the aliased low resolution pixel intensity of an image point is not always equally weighted sum of the high resolution intensities. Since we capture the images at different resolutions using zoom camera and the most zoomed image is assumed to be alias free, we estimate the weights from the most zoomed region. These weights are obtained by considering the most zoomed image and corresponding portion in the lesser zoomed images. We estimate 4 weights for a zoom factor of 2 and 16 for a zoom factor of 4. The estimated weight vectors are then used in Eq.(1) for forming D matrix to get the observation model. It may be noted that for a given zoom factor, we are not estimating different weights for each location. Since the average brightness of each observation varies due to AGC of camera, we used mean correction to maintain average brightness of the captured images approximately the same and use these observations for the D matrix estimation as well as for experimentation. Mean correction for Y_2 is obtained by subtracting it's mean from each of its pixel and adding the mean of corresponding portion in Y_1. Similarly, for Y_3, it is obtained by subtracting from each pixel, its mean and adding the mean of corresponding portion in Y_1. (Refer to Fig.1.)

The decimation matrix of the form shown in Eq.(4), can now be modified as,

$$D = \begin{pmatrix} a_1 & a_2 & \dots & a_{q^2} & & & & & & & & \mathbf{0} \\ & & & & a_1 & a_2 & \dots & a_{q^2} & & & & \\ & & & & & & & & & & & \\ & \mathbf{0} & & & & & & & a_1 & a_2 & \dots & a_{q^2} \end{pmatrix}, \tag{7}$$

where $|a_i| \leq 1, i = 1, 2, \dots q^2$. The Decimation matrix D for the considered example of 2×2 observation can be expressed with reordering of $\mathbf{z}$ as

$$D = \begin{pmatrix} a_1 & a_2 & a_3 & a_4 & 0 & 0 & 0 & 0 & 0 & 0 & 0 & 0 & 0 & 0 & 0 & 0 \\ 0 & 0 & 0 & 0 & a_1 & a_2 & a_3 & a_4 & 0 & 0 & 0 & 0 & 0 & 0 & 0 & 0 \\ 0 & 0 & 0 & 0 & 0 & 0 & 0 & 0 & a_1 & a_2 & a_3 & a_4 & 0 & 0 & 0 & 0 \\ 0 & 0 & 0 & 0 & 0 & 0 & 0 & 0 & 0 & 0 & 0 & 0 & a_1 & a_2 & a_3 & a_4 \end{pmatrix}. \tag{8}$$

The aliased pixel intensity at a location (i, j) for a zoom factor of $q = 2$ is now given by

$$y(i, j) = a_1 z(2i, 2j) + a_2 z(2i, 2j+1) + a_3 z(2i+1, 2j) + a_4 z(2i+1, 2j+1) + n(i, j). \tag{9}$$

In [11], authors discuss the spatial interaction model and choice of neighbors and use the same for texture synthesis. They model every pixel in an image as a linear combination of neighboring pixels considering neighborhood system. They estimate the model parameters using the Least Squares (LS) estimation approach as the initial estimates. In this paper, we use their approach for estimating the weights in decimation matrices for different zoom factors.

4   Super-Resolving a Scene

4.1   MRF Prior Model for the Super-Resolved Image

In order to obtain a regularized estimate of the high-resolution image, we define an appropriate prior term using an MRF modeling of the field. The MRF provides a convenient and consistent way of modeling context dependent entities. This is achieved through characterizing mutual influence among such entities using conditional probabilities for a given neighborhood. The practical use of MRF models is largely ascribed to the equivalence between the MRF and the Gibbs Random Fields (GRF). We assume that the high-resolution image can be represented by an MRF. This is justified because the changes in intensities in a scene is gradual and hence there is a local dependency. Let Z be a random field over an regular $N \times N$ lattice of sites $L = \{(i, j) | 1 < i, j < N\}$. From the Hammersley-Clifford theorem for MRF-GRF equivalence, we have,

$$P(Z = z) = \frac{1}{Z_p} e^{-U(z)}, \tag{10}$$

where $\mathbf{z}$ is a realization of Z, Z_p is a partition function given by $Z_p = \sum_z e^{-U(z)}$ and $U(z)$ is energy function given by $U(z) = \sum_{c \in C} V_c(z)$. $V_c(z)$ denotes the potential function of clique c and $\mathbf{C}$ is the set of all cliques. The lexicographically ordered high resolution image $\mathbf{z}$ satisfying Gibbs density function is now written as

$$P(\mathbf{z}) = \frac{1}{Z_p} e^{-\sum_{c \in C} V_c(\mathbf{z})}. \tag{11}$$

We consider pair wise cliques on a first-order neighborhoods consisting of the four nearest neighbors for each pixel and impose a quadratic cost which is a function of finite difference approximations of the first order derivative at each pixel location. i.e.,

$$\sum_{c \in C} V_c(\mathbf{z}) = \lambda \sum_{k=1}^{N_1} \sum_{l=1}^{N_2} [(z_{k,l} - z_{k,l-1})^2 + (z_{k,l} - z_{k-1,l})^2], \tag{12}$$

where λ represents the penalty for departure from the smoothness in $\mathbf{z}$.

4.2 Maximum a Posteriori (MAP) Estimation

Having defined the MRF prior, we use the MAP estimator to restore the high-resolution field $\mathbf{z}$. Given the ensemble of images $\mathbf{y}_i$, $i = 1$ to p, at different resolutions, the MAP estimate $\hat{\mathbf{z}}$, using Bayesian rule, is given by

$$\hat{\mathbf{z}} = \operatorname*{argmax}_{\mathbf{z}} \; P(\mathbf{z}|\mathbf{y}_1, \mathbf{y}_2, \cdots, \mathbf{y}_p) = \operatorname*{argmax}_{\mathbf{z}} \; P(\mathbf{y}_1, \mathbf{y}_2, \cdots, \mathbf{y}_p|\mathbf{z})P(\mathbf{z}). \quad (13)$$

Taking the log of the posterior probability we can write,

$$\hat{\mathbf{z}} = \operatorname*{argmax}_{\mathbf{z}} \; [\sum_{m=1}^{p} \log P(\mathbf{y}_m|\mathbf{z}) + \log P(\mathbf{z})], \quad (14)$$

since n_m are independent. Now using Eqs. (1) and (2), we get

$$P(\mathbf{y}_m|\mathbf{z}) = \frac{1}{(2\pi\sigma_n^2)^{\frac{M_1 M_2}{2}}} e^{-\frac{\|\mathbf{Y}_m - D_m C_m (\mathbf{Z} - z_{\alpha m})\|^2}{2\sigma_n^2}}. \quad (15)$$

The final cost function is obtained as

$$\hat{\mathbf{z}} = \operatorname*{argmin}_{\mathbf{z}} \; [\sum_{m=1}^{p} \frac{\|\mathbf{y}_m - D_m C_m (\mathbf{z} - z_{\alpha m})\|^2}{2\sigma_n^2} + \sum_{c \in C} V_c(\mathbf{z})]. \quad (16)$$

The above cost function is convex and is minimized using the gradient descent technique. The initial estimate $\mathbf{z}^{(0)}$ is obtained as follows. Pixels in the zero order hold of the least zoomed observation corresponding to the entire scene is replaced successively at appropriate places with zero order hold of the other observed images with increasing zoom factors. Finally, the most zoomed observed image with the highest resolution is copied at the appropriate location (see Fig. 1.) with no interpolation.

5 Experimental Results

In this section, we present the results of the proposed method of obtaining super-resolution by estimating the decimation. All the experiments were conducted on real images taken by a zoom camera and known integer zoom factors. It assumed that the lateral shift during zooming is known. In each experiment, we consider three low resolution observations Y_1, Y_2, Y_3 of an image. Each observed image is of size 72×96. Zoom factor q between Y_1 and Y_2 is 2 and that between Y_1 and Y_3 is 4. The super-resolved images for the entire scene are of size 288×384. We obtain super-resolution and compare the results obtained using decimation matrix of the form in Eq. (4) consisting of equal weights. We used the quantitative measures Mean Square Error (MSE) and Mean Absolute Error (MAE) for comparison of the results. The MSE used here is

$$MSE = \frac{\sum_{i,j}[f(i,j) - \hat{f}(i,j)]^2}{\sum_{i,j}[f(i,j)]^2} \tag{17}$$

and MAE is

$$MAE = \frac{\sum_{i,j}|f(i,j) - \hat{f}(i,j)|}{\sum_{i,j}|f(i,j)|}, \tag{18}$$

where $f(i,j)$ is the original high resolution image and $\hat{f}(i,j)$ is estimated super-resolution image. In order to use high resolution image for the entire scene the most zoomed image was captured with entire scene content. However, while experimenting only a portion of it was used. The estimated D matrices are used in the cost function given by Eq. (16).

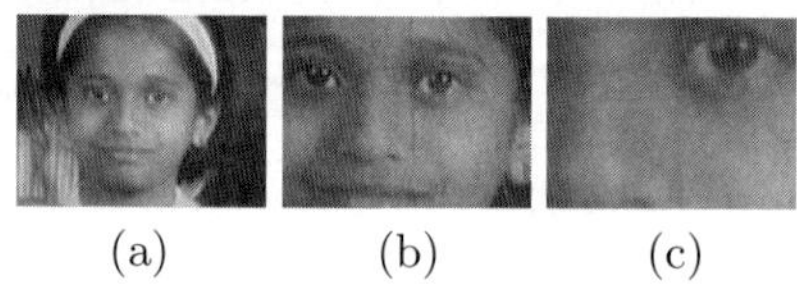

(a)   (b)   (c)

Fig. 3. Observed images of 'Nidhi' captured with three different integer zoom settings. The zoom factor between (a) and (b) is 2 and between (b) and (c) is also 2.

In the first experiment, we considered three low resolution observations of a girl image 'Nidhi' shown in Fig. 3, where the observed images have less intensity variations. Fig. 4(a) and (b) shows zoomed 'Nidhi' image obtained by successive pixel replication and successive bicubic interpolation respectively. In both the images the seam is clearly visible. Fig. 5(a) shows super-resolved 'Nidhi' image obtained by using the decimation matrix of the form in Eq. (4) and Fig. 5(b) shows super-resolved 'Nidhi' image obtained by proposed method by using the estimated decimation matrix of the form in Eq. (7). The comparison of the

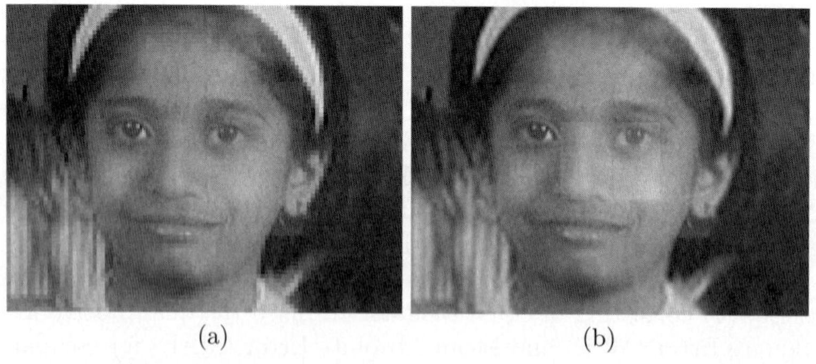

(a)   (b)

Fig. 4. Zoomed 'Nidhi' image (a) using successive pixel replication and (b) using successive bicubic interpolation

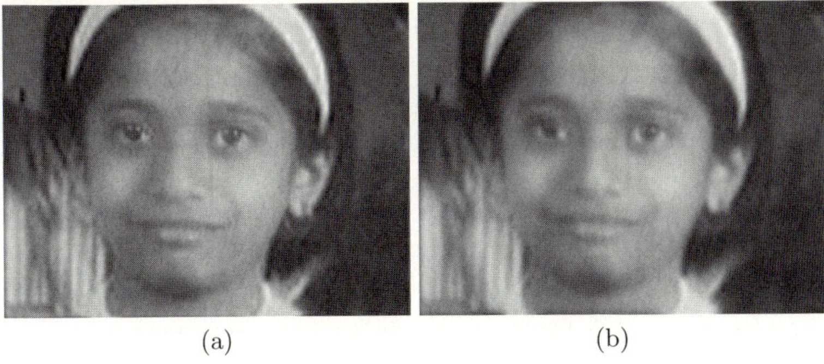

(a)   (b)

Fig. 5. Super-resolved 'Nidhi' image (a) using equal weights decimation matrix and (b) using estimated weights for decimation matrix.

images show more clear details in the regions like cheeks and forehead in the image obtained by the proposed method.

In the second experiment, we considered low resolution observations of a house shown in Fig. 6. Zoomed house images obtained by successive pixel replication and successive bicubic interpolation are shown in Fig. 7 (a) and (b) respectively. Fig. 8 shows super-resolved house images obtained using the two different methods. The comparison of the figures show that there is less blockiness in the super-resolved image obtained by the proposed method. Branches of trees opposite to windows are more clearly visible.

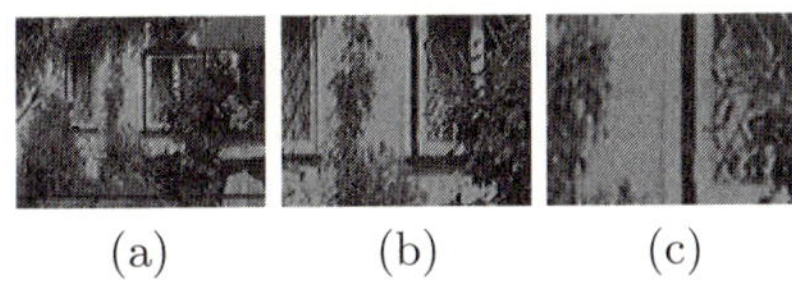

(a)   (b)   (c)

Fig. 6. Observed images of a house captured with three different integer zoom settings

(a)   (b)

Fig. 7. Zoomed house image (a) using successive pixel replication and (b) using successive bicubic interpolation

Fig. 8. Super-resolved house image. (a) using equal weights decimation matrix and (b) using estimated weights for decimation matrix.

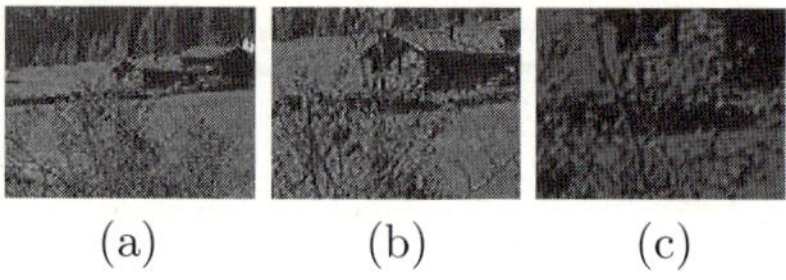

(a)   (b)   (c)

Fig. 9. Observed images of a scene captured with three different integer zoom settings

Fig. 10. Super-resolved scene image. (a) using equal weights decimation matrix and (b) using estimated weights for decimation matrix.

In order to consider images with significant texture, we experimented by capturing zoomed images of a natural scene. The observed images are displayed in Fig. 9. Fig. 10 shows super-resolved scene images. The small house near the center of image appear sharper in the image super-resolved using the proposed approach.

Table 1. shows the quantitative comparison of the our results with the one obtained using equal weights for decimation matrix. It can be seen that for all the three experiments, MSE and MAE of the super-resolved images obtained by using estimated decimation matrices is lower than those obtained by fixed decimation matrix entries showing improvement in the quantitative measures.

Table 1. Comparison of performance of the two methods of super-resolution

Image	MSE		MAE	
	Estimated decimation	Fixed decimation (Equal weights)	Estimated decimation	Fixed decimation (Equal weights)
Nidhi	0.0484	0.0514	0.0489	0.0525
House	0.6671	0.6733	0.6678	0.6751
Scene	0.2732	0.3056	0.2741	0.3082

6 Application of Zoom Based Super-Resolution to Multiresolution Fusion in Remotely Sensed Images

In this section we show the application of the proposed zoom based super-resolution to multiresolution fusion in remotely sensed images. The process of combining panchromatic (Pan) and multispectral (MS) data to produce images characterized by both high spatial and spectral resolutions is known as multiresolution fusion. Because of the technological limitations, MS images are generally acquired with a lower spatial resolution. With a fusion of different images, we can overcome the limitations of information obtained from individual sources and obtain a better understanding of the observed scene. Since the Pan image has high spatial resolution and MS images have lower spatial resolution, we estimate the aliasing on MS images by using the Pan image. The same Pan image is used to estimate the aliasing on each of MS images. Available Pan image can be used for estimating aliasing matrices for all the MS images as the aliasing depends on difference in spatial resolution between high resolution and low resolution images.For the experiment, we consider LANDSAT-7 Enhanced Thematic

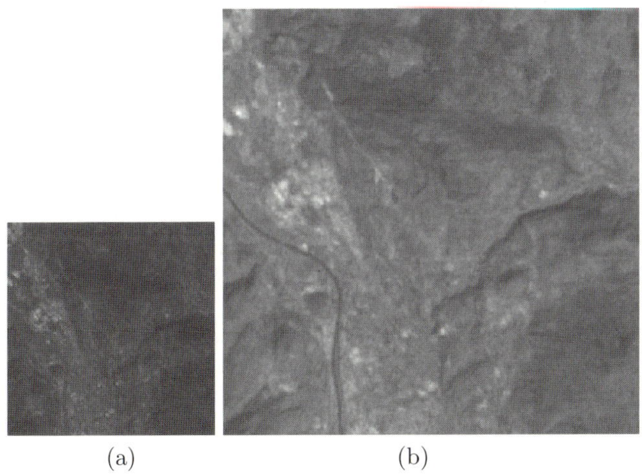

(a)   (b)

Fig. 11. (a) MS image (Band 1) and (b) fused image using estimated weights for decimation matrix

Mapper Plus (ETM+) images acquired over a city. We use available Pan image and six MS images having decimation factor of $q = 2$ between the Pan image and MS images. We learn the decimation matrix from the Pan image and minimize the cost function given by Eq. (16) for each of MS images separately. It may be noted that the $\mathbf{z}$ in the equations has to be replaced by $\mathbf{z}_m$, where $m = 1, 2, \ldots, 5$ (One of the MS images, Band 6, is not used.). Due to space limitation, we show results for only one MS image. Fig. 11(a) shows observed MS image (Band 1). The fused image obtained by using estimated weights is shown in in Fig. 11(b). From the figure it is clear that the fused image has high spatial resolution with negligible spectral distortion. It may be mentioned that we have not compared the performance of this method with other methods of fusion available in the literature due to space limitation.

7   Conclusion

We have presented a technique to recover the super-resolution intensity field from a sequence of zoomed observations by using decimation matrices derived from the observations. The resolution of the entire scene is obtained at the resolution of the most zoomed observed image that consists of only a small portion of the actual scene. The high-resolution image is modeled as an MRF and the decimation matrix entries are estimated using appropriate regions in the lesser zoomed image and the most zoomed image. Our future work involves incorporating the line fields in MRF model so that the discontinuities can be better preserved in the super-resolved image and also to extend the proposed approach for fractional zoom settings.

References

1. Tsai, R.Y., Huang, T.S.: Multiframe image restoration and registration. Advances in Computer Vision and Image Processsing. (1984) 317 – 339
2. Hardie, R.C., Barnard, K.J., Armstrong, E.E.: Joint map registration and high-resolution image estimation using a sequence of undersampled images. IEEE Trans. Image Process. **6** (1997) 1621 – 1633
3. Schultz, R.R., Stevenson, R.L.: A Bayesian approach to image expansion for improved definition. IEEE Trans. Image Process. **3** (1994) 233 – 242
4. Lin, Z., Shum, H.Y.: Fundamental limits of reconstruction-based super-resolution algorithms under local translation. IEEE Trans. Pattern Anal. Machine Intell. **26** (2004) 83 – 97
5. Capel, D., Zisserman, A.: Automated mosaicing with super-resolution zoom. Proc. IEEE Int. Conf. Comput. Vision Pattern Recogn. (1998) 885 – 891
6. Jia, K., Gong, S.: Multi-modal tensor face for simultaneous super-resolution and recognition. Proc. of IEEE Int. Conf. on Computer Vision **2** (2005) 1683 – 1690
7. Rajan, D., Chaudhuri, S.: Generation of super-resolution images from blurred observations using an MRF model. J. Math. Imag. Vision **16** (2002) 5 – 15
8. Joshi, M.V., Chaudhuri, S., Rajkiran, P.: Super-resolution imaging: Use of zoom as a cue. Image and Vision Computing **22** (2004) 1185 – 1196

9. Chaudhuri, S., Joshi, M.V.: Motion-free Super-resolution. Springer (2005)
10. Park, S.C., Park, M.K., Kang, M.G.: Super-resolution image reconstruction: A technical overview. IEEE Signal Processing Magazine **20** (2003) 21 – 36
11. Kashyap, R., Chellappa, R.: Estimation and choice of neighbors in spatial-interaction models of images. IEEE Trans. Inf. Theory **IT-29** (1983) 60 – 72

Description of Interest Regions with Center-Symmetric Local Binary Patterns

Marko Heikkilä[1], Matti Pietikäinen[1], and Cordelia Schmid[2]

[1] Machine Vision Group, Infotech Oulu and Department of Electrical and
Information Engineering, PO Box 4500, FI-90014, University of Oulu, Finland
[2] INRIA Rhône-Alpes, 655 Avenue de l'Europe, 38334 Montbonnot, France
`markot@ee.oulu.fi`, `mkp@ee.oulu.fi`, `cordelia.schmid@inrialpes.fr`

Abstract. Local feature detection and description have gained a lot of interest in recent years since photometric descriptors computed for interest regions have proven to be very successful in many applications. In this paper, we propose a novel interest region descriptor which combines the strengths of the well-known SIFT descriptor and the LBP texture operator. It is called the *center-symmetric local binary pattern (CS-LBP) descriptor*. This new descriptor has several advantages such as tolerance to illumination changes, robustness on flat image areas, and computational efficiency. We evaluate our descriptor using a recently presented test protocol. Experimental results show that the CS-LBP descriptor outperforms the SIFT descriptor for most of the test cases, especially for images with severe illumination variations.

1 Introduction

Local features extracted from images have performed very well in many applications, such as image retrieval [1], wide baseline matching [2], object recognition [3], texture recognition [4], and robot localization [5]. They have many advantages over the other methods. They can be made very distinctive, they do not require segmentation, and they are robust to occlusion. The idea is to first detect interest regions that are covariant to a class of transformations. Then, for each detected region, an invariant descriptor is built. In this paper, we focus on interest region description. For more information on interest region detection the reader is referred to [6].

A good region descriptor can tolerate illumination changes, image noise, image blur, image compression, and small perspective distortions, while preserving distinctiveness. In a recent comparative study the best results were reported for the SIFT-based descriptors [7]. For some interesting recent work on interest region description done after this study, see [8,9,10,11]. The local binary pattern (LBP) texture operator [12], on the other hand, has been highly successful for various problems, but it has so far not been used for describing interest regions. In this paper, we propose a novel interest region descriptor which combines the strengths of the SIFT descriptor [3] and the LBP operator [12]. Our descriptor is constructed similarly to SIFT, but the individual features are different. The

P. Kalra and S. Peleg (Eds.): ICVGIP 2006, LNCS 4338, pp. 58–69, 2006.

gradient features used by SIFT are replaced with features extracted by a *center-symmetric local binary pattern (CS-LBP) operator* similar to the LBP operator. The new features have many desirable properties such as tolerance to illumination changes, robustness on flat image areas, and computational simplicity. They also allow a simpler weighting scheme to be applied. For evaluating our approach, we use the same test protocol as in [7]. It is available on the Internet together with the test data [13]. The evaluation criterion is recall-precision, i.e., the number of correct and false matches between two images.

The rest of the paper is organized as follows. In Section 2, we first briefly describe the SIFT and LBP methods, and then introduce the proposed descriptor in detail. The experimental setup is described in Section 3, and Section 4 presents the experimental results. Finally, we conclude the paper in Section 5.

2   Interest Region Description

Our interest region descriptor is based on the SIFT descriptor [3] which has shown to give excellent results [7]. The basic idea is that the appearance of an interest region can be well characterized by the distribution of its local features. In order to incorporate spatial information into the representation, the region is divided into cells and for each cell a feature histogram is accumulated. The final representation is achieved by concatenating the histograms over the cells and normalizing the resulting descriptor vector. The major difference between the proposed descriptor and the SIFT descriptor is that they rely on different local features. Instead of the gradient magnitude and orientation used by the SIFT, we introduce novel center-symmetric local binary pattern (CS-LBP) features that are motivated by the well-known local binary patterns (LBP) [12]. Before presenting in detail the CS-LBP descriptor, we give a brief review of the SIFT descriptor and the LBP operator.

2.1   SIFT and LBP

SIFT Descriptor. The SIFT descriptor is a 3D histogram of gradient locations and orientations. Location is quantized into a 4×4 location grid and the gradient angle is quantized into 8 orientations, resulting in a 128-dimensional descriptor. First, the gradient magnitudes and orientations are computed within the interest region. The gradient magnitudes are then weighted with a Gaussian window overlaid over the region. To avoid boundary effects in the presence of small shifts of the interest region, a trilinear interpolation is used to distribute the value of each gradient sample into adjacent histogram bins. The final descriptor is obtained by concatenating the orientation histograms over all locations. To reduce the effects of illumination change the descriptor is first normalized to unit length. Then, the influence of large gradient magnitudes is reduced by thresholding the descriptor entries, such that each one is no larger than 0.2, and renormalizing to unit length.

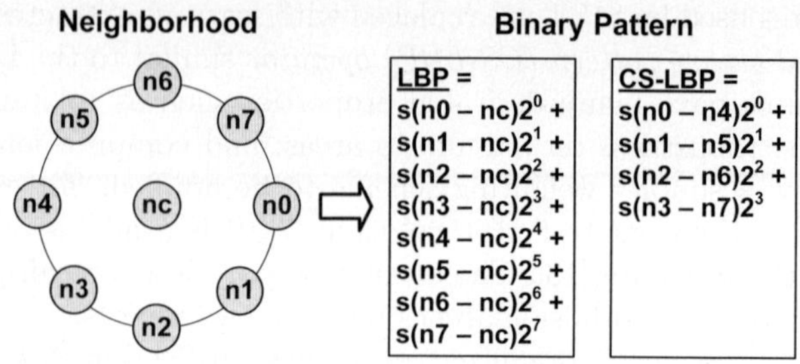

Fig. 1. LBP and CS-LBP features for a neighborhood of 8 pixels

LBP Operator. The local binary pattern is a powerful graylevel invariant texture primitive. The histogram of the binary patterns computed over a region is used for texture description [12]. The operator describes each pixel by the relative graylevels of its neighboring pixels, see Fig. 1 for an illustration with 8 neighbors. If the graylevel of the neighboring pixel is higher or equal, the value is set to one, otherwise to zero. The descriptor describes the result over the neighborhood as a binary number (binary pattern):

$$LBP_{R,N}(x,y) = \sum_{i=0}^{N-1} s(n_i - n_c)2^i, \quad s(x) = \begin{cases} 1 & x \geq 0 \\ 0 & otherwise \end{cases}, \tag{1}$$

where n_c corresponds to the graylevel of the center pixel of a local neighborhood and n_i to the graylevels of N equally spaced pixels on a circle of radius R. The values of neighbors that do not fall exactly on pixels are estimated by bilinear interpolation. Since correlation between pixels decreases with distance, a lot of the texture information can be obtained from local neighborhoods. Thus, the radius R is usually kept small. In practice, (1) means that the signs of the differences in a neighborhood are interpreted as an N-bit binary number, resulting in 2^N distinct values for the binary pattern. The LBP has several properties that favor its usage in interest region description. The features are robust against illumination changes, they are very fast to compute, do not require many parameters to be set, and have high discriminative power.

2.2   CS-LBP Descriptor

In the following, we provide details on our interest region descriptor which combines the strengths of the SIFT descriptor and the LBP texture operator.

Region Preprocessing. We first filter the region with an edge-preserving adaptive noise-removal filter (we used `wiener2` in Matlab). The edge-preserving nature of the filter is essential for good performance, since much of the information comes from edges and other high-frequency parts of a region. Our experiments have shown that this filtering improves the performance on average around 5 percent (depending on the test images), and therefore all the experiments presented in this paper are carried out with this kind of filtering. Furthermore, the region data is scaled between 0 and 1 such that 1% of the data is saturated at the low and high intensities of the region. This increases the contrast of the region.

Feature Extraction with Center-Symmetric Local Binary Patterns. After pre-processing, we extract a feature for each pixel of the region using the center-symmetric local binary pattern (CS-LBP) operator which was inspired by the local binary patterns (LBP). The LBP operator produces rather long histograms and is therefore difficult to use in the context of a region descriptor. To produce more compact binary patterns, we compare only center-symmetric pairs of pixels, see Fig. 1. We can see that for 8 neighbors, LBP produces 256 different binary patterns, whereas for CS-LBP this number is only 16. Furthermore, robustness on flat image regions is obtained by thresholding the graylevel differences with a small value T:

$$CS-LBP_{R,N,T}(x,y)= \sum_{i=0}^{(N/2)-1} s(n_i - n_{i+(N/2)})2^i, \ s(x) = \begin{cases} 1 & x > T \\ 0 & otherwise \end{cases}, \quad (2)$$

where n_i and $n_{i+(N/2)}$ correspond to the grayvalues of center-symmetric pairs of pixels of N equally spaced pixels on a circle of radius R. The value of the threshold T is 1% of the pixel value range in our experiments. Since the region data lies between 0 and 1, T is set to 0.01. The radius is set to 2 and the size of the neighborhood is 8. All the experiments presented in this paper, except the parameter evaluation, are carried out for these parameters ($CS-LBP_{2,8,0.01}$) which gave the best overall performance for the given test data. It should be noted that the gain of CS-LBP over LBP is not only due to the dimensionality reduction, but also to the fact that the CS-LBP captures better the gradient information than the basic LBP. Experiments with LBP and CS-LBP have shown the benefits of the CS-LBP over the LBP, in particular, significant reduction in dimensionality while preserving distinctiveness.

Feature Weighting. Different ways of weighting the features are possible. For example, in the case of SIFT, the bins of the gradient orientation histograms are incremented with Gaussian-weighted gradient magnitudes. A comparison of different weighting strategies, including the SIFT-like weighting, showed that simple uniform weighting is the most suitable choice for the CS-LBP features. This is, of course, good news, as it makes our descriptor computationally very simple.

Descriptor Construction. In order to incorporate spatial information into our descriptor, the region is divided into cells with a location grid. Our experiments showed that a Cartesian grid seems to be the most suitable choice. For the experiments presented in this paper, we selected a 4×4 Cartesian grid. For each cell a CS-LBP histogram is built. In order to avoid boundary effects in which the descriptor abruptly changes as a feature shifts from one histogram bin to another, a bilinear interpolation is used to distribute the weight of each feature

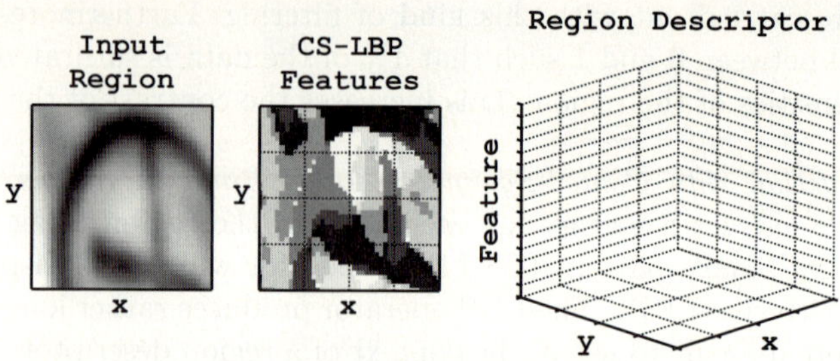

Fig. 2. The CS-LBP descriptor

into adjacent histogram bins. The resulting descriptor is a 3D histogram of CS-LBP feature locations and values, as illustrated in Fig. 2. As explained earlier, the number of different feature values depends on the neighborhood size of the chosen CS-LBP operator.

Descriptor Normalization. The final descriptor is built by concatenating the feature histograms computed for the cells to form a $(4 \times 4 \times 16)$ 256-dimensional vector. The descriptor is then normalized to unit length. The influence of very large descriptor elements is reduced by thresholding each element to be no larger than 0.2. This means that the distribution of CS-LBP features has greater emphasis than individual large values. Finally, the descriptor is renormalized to unit length.

3   Experimental Setup

For evaluating the proposed descriptor, we use the same test protocol as in [7]. The protocol is available on the Internet together with the test data [13]. The test data contains images with different geometric and photometric transformations and for different scene types. Six different transformations are evaluated: *viewpoint change, scale change, image rotation, image blur, illumination change,* and *JPEG compression.* The two different scene types are *structured* and *textured* scenes. These test images are shown on the left of Fig. 3. The images are either of planar scenes or the camera position was fixed during acquisition. The images are, therefore, always related by a homography (included in the test data). In order to study in more detail the tolerance of our descriptor to illumination changes, we captured two additional image pairs shown on the right of Fig. 3.

The evaluation criterion is based on the number of correct and false matches between a pair of images. The definition of a match depends on the matching strategy. As in [7], we declare two interest regions to be matched if the Euclidean distance between their descriptors is below a threshold. The number of correct matches is determined with the *overlap error* [14]. It measures how well the regions A and B correspond under a known homography H, and is defined by the ratio of the intersection and union of the regions: $\epsilon_S = 1 - (A \cap H^T B H)/(A \cup$

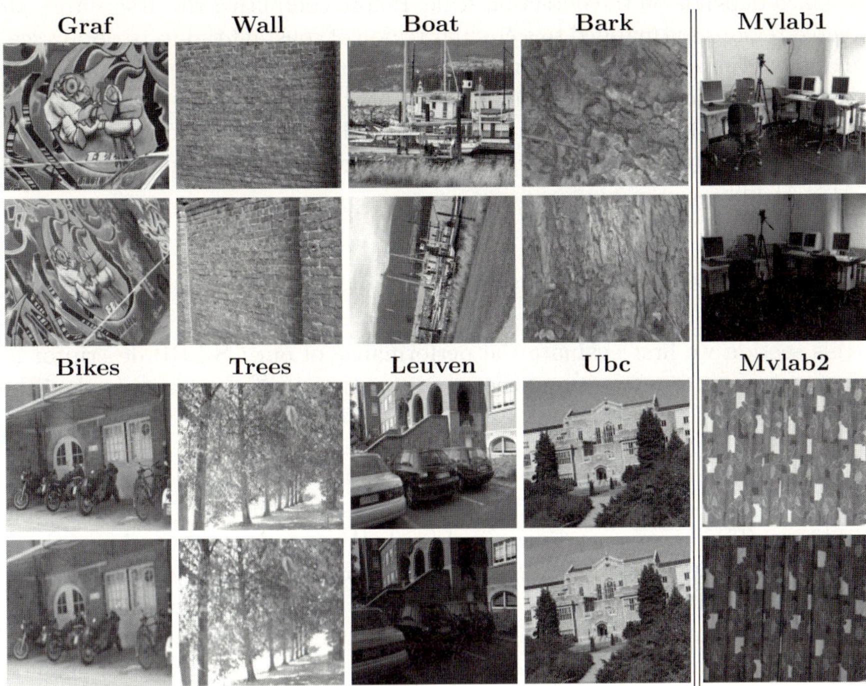

Fig. 3. Test images (left): **Graf** (viewpoint change, structured scene), **Wall** (viewpoint change, textured scene), **Boat** (scale change + image rotation, structured scene), **Bark** (scale change + image rotation, textured scene), **Bikes** (image blur, structured scene), **Trees** (image blur, textured scene), **Leuven** (illumination change, structured scene), and **Ubc** (JPEG compression, structured scene). Additional test images (right): **Mvlab1** (illumination change, structured scene) and **Mvlab2** (illumination change, textured scene).

$H^T BH$). A match is assumed to be correct if $\epsilon_S < 0.5$. A descriptor can have several matches and several of them may be correct. The results are presented with *recall* versus *1-precision*:

$$recall = \frac{\#correct\ matches}{\#correspondences}, \quad 1 - precision = \frac{\#false\ matches}{\#all\ matches}, \qquad (3)$$

where the *#correspondences* stands for the ground truth number of matching regions between the images. The curves are obtained by varying the distance threshold and a perfect descriptor would give a recall equal to 1 for any precision.

The interest region detectors provide the regions which are used to compute the descriptors. In the experiments, we use two different detectors: *Hessian-Affine* [6] and *Harris-Affine* [15]. The two detectors output different types of image structures. Hessian-Affine detects blob-like structures while Harris-Affine looks for corner-like structures. Both detectors output elliptic regions of varying size which depends on the detection scale. Before computing the descriptors, the detected regions are mapped to a circular region of constant radius to obtain scale and affine invariance. Rotation invariance is obtained by rotating the normalized regions in the direction of the dominant gradient orientation, as suggested in [3]. For region detection and normalization, we use the software routines provided by the evaluation protocol. In the experiments, the normalized region size is fixed to 41×41 pixels.

4   Experimental Results

In this section we first evaluate the performance of our CS-LBP descriptor for different parameter settings and then compare the resulting version to the SIFT descriptor.

Descriptor Parameter Evaluation. The evaluation of different parameter settings is carried out for a pair of images with a viewpoint change of more than 50 degrees. The images are shown in Fig. 4. We use the Hessian-Affine detector which extracts 2454 and 2296 interest regions in the left and right images, respectively. The performance is measured with nearest neighbor matching, i.e., a descriptor has only one match. We keep the 400 best matches and report the percentage of correct matches. Note that there are 503 possible nearest neighbor correspondences identified between the images.

We compare the matching performance (percentage of correct matches) for differently spaced location grids, different parameters of the CS-LBP operator, and two weighting schemes. Fig. 5 shows that a 4×4 Cartesian grid outperforms all the other grid spacings. The left graph clearly shows that a uniform weighting outperforms a SIFT-like one and that a neighborhood size 8 is better than 6 or 10. The graph on the right compares different values for the radius and the threshold and shows that a radius of 1 and a threshold of 0.01 give best results. In conclusion, the 4×4 Cartesian grid and the $CS - LBP_{1,8,0.01}$ with uniform weighting give the best performance. For the given image pair, the best results are obtained with a radius of 1. However, experiments with many other image pairs have shown that a radius of 2 actually gives better overall performance. Thus, in the comparison with SIFT, we set the radius to 2 instead of 1. The results also show that our descriptor is not very sensitive to small changes in its parameter values. Note that due to space constraints, Fig. 5 does not cover all

Image 1	Image 2		CS-LBP	SIFT
		Recall	0.386	0.316
		1 - Precision	0.515	0.603
		Correct Matches	194 / 400	159 / 400

Fig. 4. Left: Image pair with a viewpoint change of more than 50 degrees. Right: The matching results for the 400 nearest neighbor matches between the images.

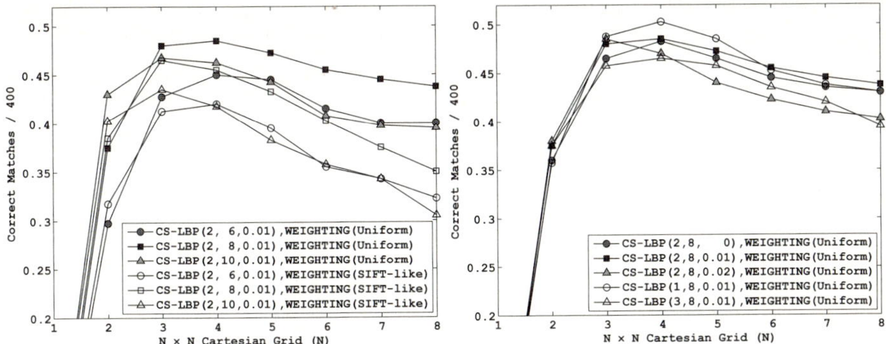

Fig. 5. Evaluation of different parameter settings. See text for details.

the tested parameter settings and that the omitted results are consistent with our conclusions.

The dimensionality of the CS-LBP descriptor can be reduced without loss in performance. When reducing the dimension from 256 to 128 with PCA, the results seemed to remain unchanged. The performance of the 64-dimensional descriptor is still very close to that of the original one. This property makes our descriptor applicable in systems where the matching speed is important. Note that a data set different from the test data was used to estimate the covariance matrices for PCA. The comparison experiments presented next are carried out without using dimension reduction.

Comparison with the SIFT Descriptor. Figures 6 and 7 show the comparison results for Hessian-Affine and Harris-Affine regions, respectively. For Hessian-Affine regions, our descriptor is better than SIFT for most of the test cases and performs about equally well for the remaining ones. A significant improvement of CS-LBP is obtained in the case of illumination changes. For example, for the *Leuven* images, our descriptor gives approximately 20% higher recall for 1-precision of 0.4. The difference is even larger for the additional two test pairs (*Mvlab1* and *Mvlab2*). Clearly better results are also obtained for the *Graf*, *Bikes*, and *Ubc* images which measure the tolerance to viewpoint change, image blur, and JPEG compression, respectively. As we can see, the CS-LBP descriptor performs significantly better than SIFT for structured scenes, while the difference for textured scenes is smaller. Similar results are achieved for Harris-Affine regions. Both descriptors give better overall results for Hessian-Affine regions than for Harris-Affine ones. This is consistent with the findings in [6] and can be explained by the fact that Laplacian scale selection used by the region detectors works better on blob-like structures than on corners [7]. In other words, the accuracy of interest region detection affects the descriptor performance.

Additional experiments were carried out for the scale invariant versions of the detectors, i.e., *Hessian-Laplace* and *Harris-Laplace* [7]. They differ from the affine invariant detectors in that they omit the *affine adaptation* step [15]. The results are not presented due to space limitation, but the ranking of the two

    M. Heikkilä, M. Pietikäinen, and C. Schmid

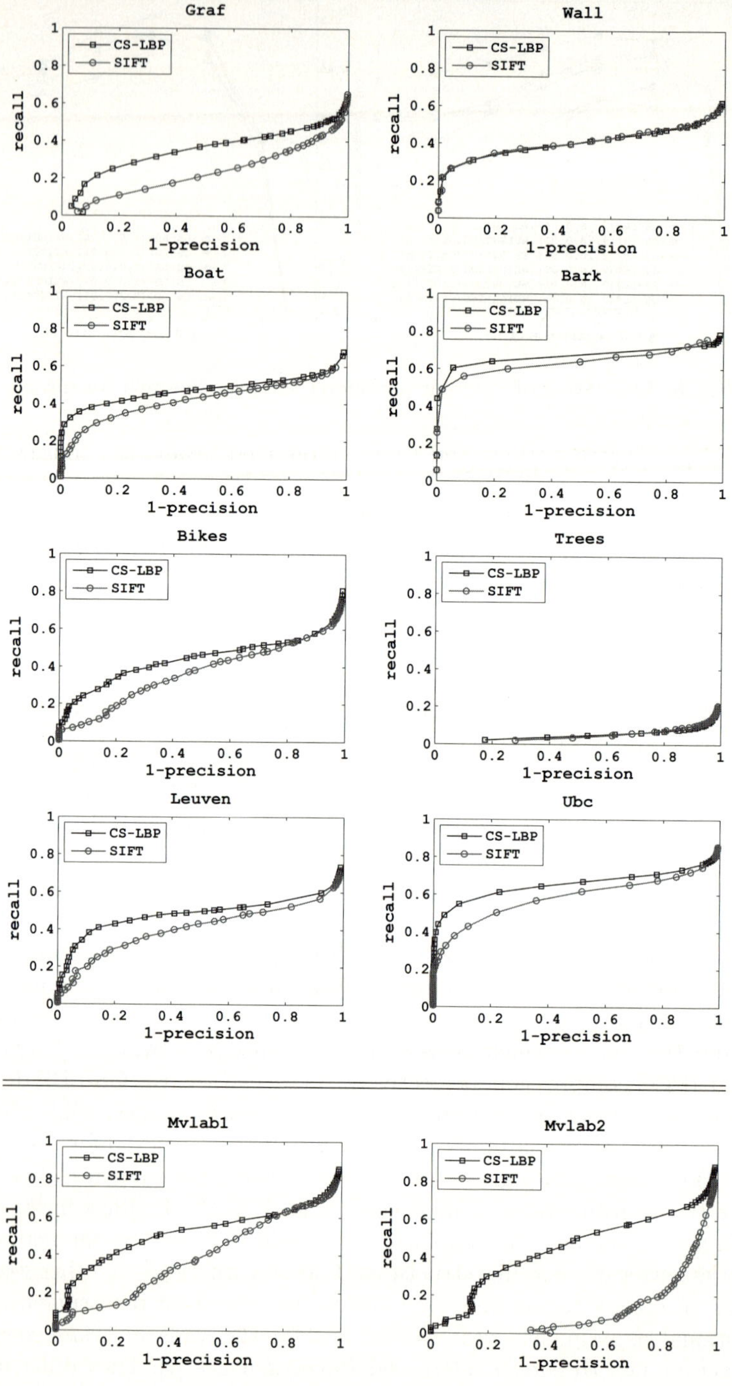

Fig. 6. Comparison results for Hessian-Affine regions

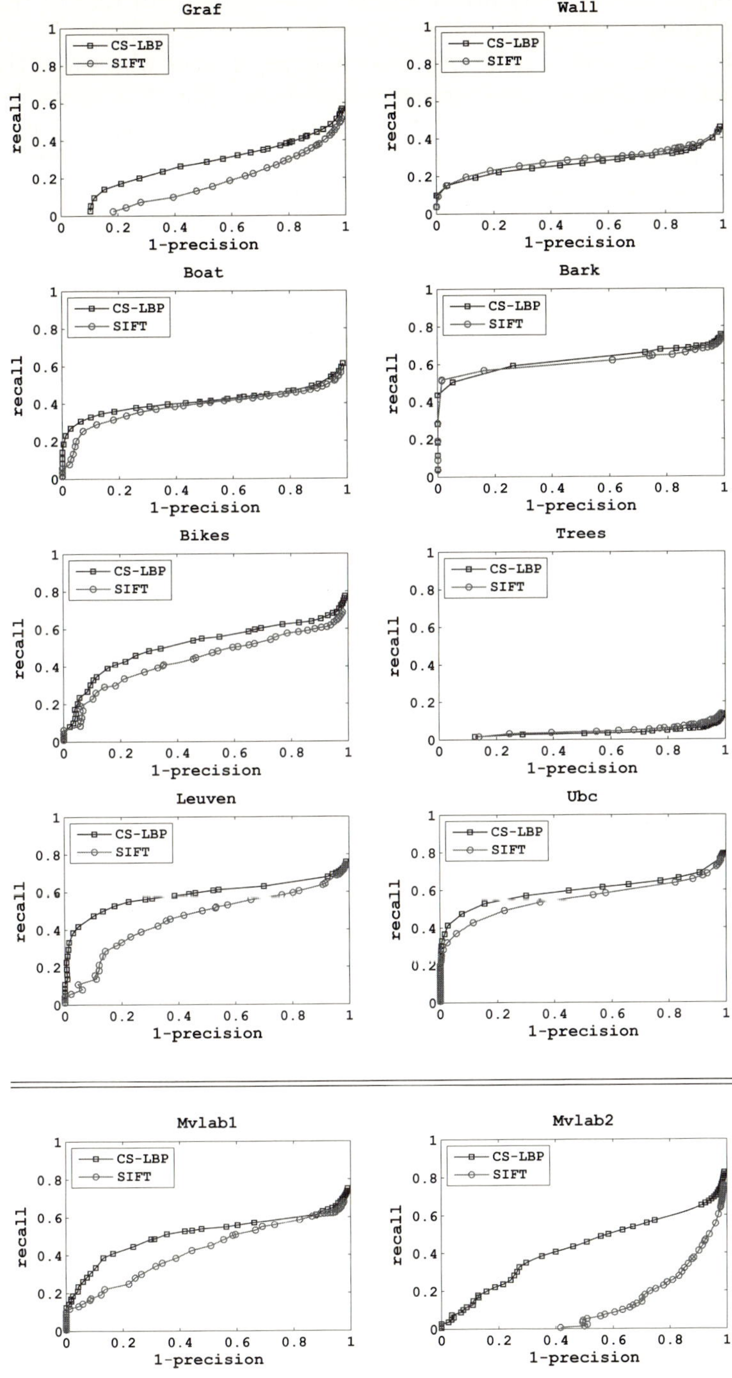

Fig. 7. Comparison results for Harris-Affine regions

descriptors for the scale invariant regions is comparable to that of the affine invariant regions.

We also performed an additional matching experiment which uses the same setup that was used in the parameter evaluation. Fig. 4 presents recall, 1-precision, and the number of correct matches obtained with the two descriptors for a fixed number of 400 nearest neighbor matches. As we can see, the CS-LBP descriptor clearly outperforms the SIFT descriptor.

5   Conclusions

A novel CS-LBP interest region descriptor which combines the strengths of the well-known SIFT descriptor and the LBP texture operator was proposed. Instead of the gradient orientation and magnitude based features used by SIFT, we proposed to use center-symmetric local binary pattern (CS-LBP) features introduced in this paper. The CS-LBP descriptor was evaluated against the SIFT descriptor using a recently presented test framework. Our descriptor performed clearly better than SIFT for most of the test cases and about equally well for the remaining ones. Especially, the tolerance of our descriptor to illumination changes is clearly demonstrated. Furthermore, our features are more robust on flat image areas, since the graylevel differences are allowed to vary close to zero without affecting the thresholded results. It should be also noted that the CS-LBP descriptor is computationally simpler than the SIFT descriptor. Future work includes applying the proposed descriptor to different computer vision problems such as object recognition and tracking.

Acknowledgment

The financial support provided by the Academy of Finland and the Infotech Oulu Graduate School is gratefully acknowledged.

References

1. Mikolajczyk, K., Schmid, C.: Indexing based on scale invariant interest points. In: 8th IEEE International Conference on Computer Vision. Volume 1. (2001) 525–531
2. Tuytelaars, T., Gool, L.V.: Matching widely separated views based on affine invariant regions. International Journal of Computer Vision **59** (2004) 61–85
3. Lowe, D.G.: Distinctive image features from scale-invariant keypoints. International Journal of Computer Vision **60** (2004) 91–110
4. Lazebnik, S., Schmid, C., Ponce, J.: A sparse texture representation using local affine regions. IEEE Transactions on Pattern Analysis and Machine Intelligence **27** (2005) 1265–1278
5. Se, S., Lowe, D., Little, J.: Global localization using distinctive visual features. In: IEEE/RSJ International Conference on Intelligent Robots and System. Volume 1. (2002) 226–231

6. Mikolajczyk, K., Tuytelaars, T., Schmid, C., Zisserman, A., Matas, J., Schaffalitzky, F., Kadir, T., Gool, L.V.: A comparison of affine region detectors. International Journal of Computer Vision **65** (2005) 43–72
7. Mikolajczyk, K., Schmid, C.: A performance evaluation of local descriptors. IEEE Transactions on Pattern Analysis and Machine Intelligence **27** (2005) 1615–1630
8. Bay, H., Tuytelaars, T., Gool, L.V.: SURF: Speeded up robust features. In: European Conference on Computer Vision. Volume 1. (2006) 404–417
9. Abdel-Hakim, A.E., Farag, A.A.: CSIFT: A SIFT descriptor with color invariant characteristics. In: IEEE Computer Society Conference on Computer Vision and Pattern Recognition. Volume 2. (2006) 1978–1983
10. Brown, M., Szeliski, R., Winder, S.: Multi-image matching using multi-scale oriented patches. In: IEEE Computer Society Conference on Computer Vision and Pattern Recognition. Volume 1. (2005) 510–517
11. Ling, H., Jacobs, D.W.: Deformation invariant image matching. In: 10th IEEE International Conference on Computer Vision. Volume 2. (2005) 1466–1473
12. Ojala, T., Pietikäinen, M., Mäenpää, T.: Multiresolution gray-scale and rotation invariant texture classification with local binary patterns. IEEE Transactions on Pattern Analysis and Machine Intelligence **24** (2002) 971–987
13. http://www.robots.ox.ac.uk/~vgg/research/affine/.
14. Mikolajczyk, K., Schmid, C.: An affine invariant interest point detector. In: European Conference on Computer Vision. Volume 1. (2002) 128–142
15. Mikolajczyk, K., Schmid, C.: Scale & affine invariant interest point detectors. International Journal of Computer Vision **60** (2004) 63–86

An Automatic Image Segmentation Technique Based on Pseudo-convex Hull

Sanjoy Kumar Saha[1], Amit Kumar Das[2], and Bhabatosh Chanda[3]

[1] Computer Science and Engineering Department
Jadavpur University, Kolkata, India
`sks_ju@yahoo.co.in`
[2] Computer Science and Technology Department
Bengal Engineering and Science University, Shibpur, Howrah, India
`amit@cs.becs.ac.in`
[3] Electronics and Communication Science Unit
Indian Statistical Institute, Kolkata, India
`chanda@isical.ac.in`

Abstract. This paper describes a novel method for image segmentation where image contains a dominant object. The method is applicable to a large class of images including noisy and poor quality images. It is fully automatic and has low computational cost. It may be noted that the proposed segmentation technique may not produce optimal result in some cases but it gives reasonably good result for almost all images of a large class. Hence, the method is found very useful for the applications where accuracy of the segmentation is not very critical, e.g., for global shape feature extraction, second generation coding etc.

1   Introduction

Today it is needless to mention the importance and necessity of image segmentation. Probably it is the most intensively researched topic in the field of image processing and understanding. Some major concepts include feature thresholding [1], region growing [2], change in feature detection [3], facet model [4], active contour [5], watershed [6], etc. In [7], a scheme is presented to find out the semantic objects in an image. But, it is applicable for colour images only. A multilevel hypergraph partitioning method has been discussed in [8]. The scheme suffers from prohibitive computational cost. Depending on the application domain as well as the quality of the image data many variations of these approaches have come up. Thus, hundreds of papers are available in the literature. All these segmentation algorithms may be classified into two groups: (i) Region extraction and (ii) Contour detection. However, these two groups have a strong correspondence between them. That means if region is available, contour can readily be found by applying boundary extraction method [1] and, on the other hand, if contour is available, region can be generated straightaway by filling [9]. Secondly, none of these algorithms are fully automatic; they always need some form of user intervention – in the form of threshold selection or markers selection or contour initialization etc.

P. Kalra and S. Peleg (Eds.): ICVGIP 2006, LNCS 4338, pp. 70–81, 2006.

In this paper, we present a fully automatic, low cost and robust segmentation algorithm. However, it should be noted that the proposed algorithm may not give the best result in many cases, but it gives reasonably good result for a really large class of images. By the term 'reasonably good result' here we mean that the outer-most contour of the segmented/extracted region approximates the actual contour closely. This kind of segmentation results is good enough in various types of applications, where exact segmentation may not be very crucial. For example, it may be suitable for extracting global shape features (like aspect ratio, circularity, etc.) that are used in CBIR, for second generation compression where different regions are coded differently, for supplying initial contour to snake algorithm, or may be used as a mask for selecting marker in watershed algorithm etc.

The paper is organized as follows. Section 2 elaborates the problem while section 3 presents fast algorithm for computing Pseudo-convex hull. Proposed segmentation algorithm is described in section 4 step by step. Experimental results are presented in section 5 and section 6 contains concluding remarks.

2   Problem Formulation

It is mentioned earlier that the proposed algorithm works for a class of images. So, first, we like to define that class. Depending on the contents, images may be grouped into three classes: (i) class of images containing a single dominant object (Class-1), (ii) class of images containing many objects of more or less equal significance (Class-2), and (iii) class of images containing no objects of specific interest, but their combination appears very picturesque (Class-3). The class-3 is exemplified by outdoor scenery consisting mostly of sky, water body (like, sea, river, lake etc.), grass-field, beach etc. none of which is particularly important, but surely the combination is. Images of a group of people, cluttered objects, busy area (e.g., railway station, departmental store, city street, etc.), business meeting and like belong to Class-2. Finally, Class-1 contains images of our child, friend, relative, home, car, pet, object of our interest (e.g., ancient building, monument, sculpture and statue, biomedical image, animal, bird, etc.), famous personality, and so on. These objects, in the image, occupy the major area mostly at the center and are sharply focused. There could be other objects too in the image, but those are given usually less emphasis while photographed and are treated as background. Hence, we say that Class-1 contains images of single dominant object. In any estimate, number of images belong to Class-1 is by far large than that of Class-2 and Class-3 together. It is also observed that dominant objects or the objects of interest in the Class-1 images are closely convex shaped. However, the term 'closely' is qualitative in nature and introduces ambiguity in decision. So an objective measure is in order.

An object A is said to be *convex* if its intersection with a line having any slope angle θ produces at most one line segment. However, in order to explain the working of our algorithm we describe convex object in a different way. Suppose an image contains an object A. If two distinct line segments, with an angle θ

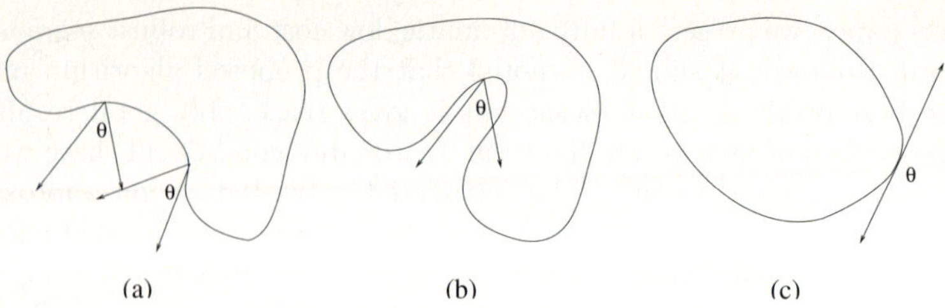

(a)   (b)   (c)

Fig. 1. Different types of objects: (a) pseudo-convex, (b) concave, and (c) convex

between them, starting from every point on the boundary of A can reach the image frame without intersecting any of the interior point of A [see Fig. 1], then we call A is n *pseudo-convex* object with respect to θ; It is readily evident that the objects we mostly deal with are neither strictly convex nor concave, but are of type pseudo-convex. Hence, in this work, we classify 2D objects into three groups: Convex, Pseudo-convex and Concave.

Since we work on discrete domain and it is known that digital straight line segment can uniquely defined only for the slope 0°, 45°, 90° and 135° [10], we confine our definition of pseudo-convex objects in terms line segment of said orientations only.

Fig. 2. Different types of objects (a) convex, (b) ramp-convex, (c) ortho-convex and (d) wedge-convex objects

Definition: A digital object A is said to be *pseudo-convex* if two line segments, with an angle θ between them and one of them is either horizontal (slope 0°) or vertical (slope 90°), starting from every point on the boundary of A can reach the image frame without intersecting any of the interior point of A.

A is a true convex object for $\theta \geq 180^o$ and it is taken as a concave object if $\theta < 45^o$. Otherwise, if $45^o \leq \theta < 180^o$ then the object is 'closely convex shaped' which can be further classified as follows. If $135^o \leq \theta < 180^o$ then the shape of A is called ramp-convex. It is ortho-convex if $90^o \leq \theta < 135^o$. A is wedge-convex for $45^o \leq \theta < 90^o$. Figure 2 shows some examples of convex, ortho-convex, ramp-convex and wedge-convex objects.

The proposed segmentation algorithm is based on the idea of obtaining a closely convex region corresponding to the dominant object in an image. It may be noted that this region is nothing but the pseudo-convex (ramp, ortho or wedge-convex) hull of the dominant object.

Now suppose a digital graylevel image $I(i,j)$ contains a dominant object and ideal segmentation of I produces a binary image containing a connected component A corresponding to the dominant object. Our segmentation algorithm tries to obtain a closely convex (e.g., convex, ortho-convex, ramp-convex or wedge-convex) region, say, R such that

$$error = \#\{(A \cap R^c) \cup (A^c \cap R)\} < t_a \tag{1}$$

The operator '#' stands for cardinality of a set and t_a is the threshold of tolerance. In the proposed method R is computed as pseudo-convex hull of the set of pixels obtained from initial processing (e.g., edge pixel extraction) of I for a given θ. Detail of the algorithm is described in the next section.

3 Fast Algorithm for Computing Pseudo-convex Hull

Since backbone of the proposed scheme is computing pseudo-convex (i.e., ramp-convex or ortho-convex or wedge-convex) hull. We first present an efficient algorithm for the same. To design the algorithm we adopt the definition of pseudo-convex except that the lines originate from image frame. And then it is examined whether pair of lines with given θ has reached the boundary before meeting any interior pixels.

Suppose a binary image $B(i,j)$ contains a set of points A whose pseudo-convex hull is to be determined. That means $B(i,j)$ may be represented as

$$B(i,j) = \begin{cases} 1 & (i,j) \in A \\ 0 & \text{otherwise} \end{cases}$$

An example of B is shown in Fig. 3(a)(i). Hence, the steps of the algorithm are:

Step 1: Take four other arrays $H(i,j)$, $V(i,j)$, $D1(i,j)$ and $D2(i,j)$ of same size as that of $B(i,j)$, and initialize them with 1's.

Step 2: Now for each row of $H(i,j)$ [An example is illustrated in Fig. 3(b & c)(i)]

    1. Start from first column, change its pixel value to zero and move right until $B(i,j) = 1$ or the last column is reached.

    2. If the last column is not reached then start from last column, change pixel values to zero, and move left ward until $B(i,j) = 1$.

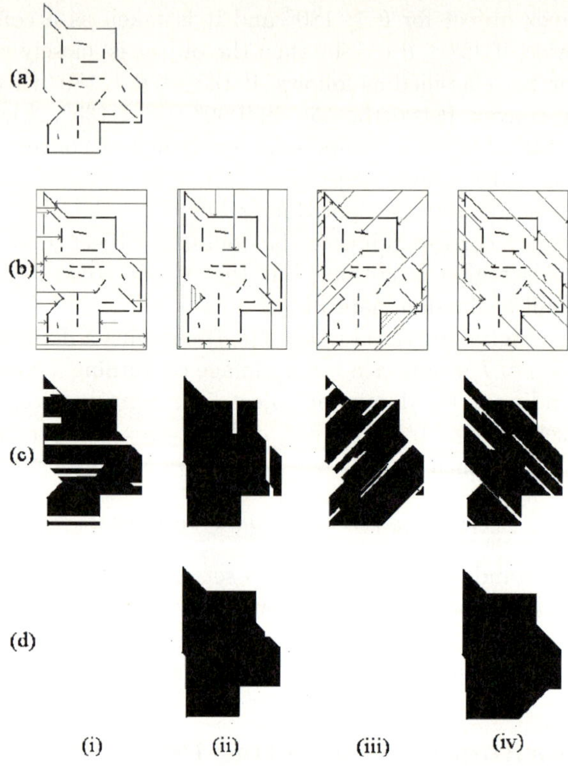

Fig. 3. Scanning directions and output of each step of pseudo-convex hull algorithm

Step 3: Now repeat sub-steps of 2 for $V(i,j)$, $D1(i,j)$ and $D2(i,j)$ with appropriate directions i.e., upward and downward for V and so on. [Results are illustrated in Fig. 3(b & c)(ii)-(iv).]

Step 4: Finally, produce a binary image $P(i,j)$ that contains the pseudo-convex hull of the given point set A as follows:

$$P(i,j) = \begin{cases} 1 & H(i,j) + V(i,j) + D1(i,j) + D2(i,j) \geq th \\ 0 & \text{otherwise} \end{cases}$$

1. $th = 1$ is equivalent to $\theta = 135^o$ and we have ramp-convex hull. [See Fig. 3(d)(iv).]
2. $th = 2$ is equivalent to $\theta = 90^o$ and if only $H(i,j)$ and $V(i,j)$ taken, we have ortho-convex hull. [See Fig. 3(d)(ii).]
3. $th = 3$ is equivalent to $\theta = 45^o$ and we have wedge-convex hull.

Finally, it may be noted that wedge-convex hull ($hull_w$) is the closest estimate of the object as

$$A \subseteq hull_{wedge}(A) \subseteq hull_{ortho}(A) \subseteq hull_{ramp}(A) \subseteq hull(A)$$

As the algorithm involves only the traversal of the pixels along a direction originating from the image frame, computational cost is quite low. The order of such complexity is $o(n)$, where, n is the number of pixels in the image.

4   Description of the Proposed Scheme

In this section we describe the details of the proposed segmentation algorithm. Note that the segmentation algorithm is fully automated and assumes that the image contains only one dominating object and other objects, if present, are small in comparison to the object of interest.

4.1   Segmentation Algorithm in Steps

Input to this step is a gray level image representing the intensity map of the scene. If the original image is in colour we convert it to HLS or HSV or any other similar triplet and take the L or V component as an intensity image. The segmentation is done in three steps, assuming that the image background does not have high contrast texture, as elaborated below:

   I. Noise removal.
  II. Initial Segmentation.
      (a) Formation of Gradient image.
      (b) Thresholding.
 III. Final Segmentation.
      (a) Approximate object area determination.
      (b) Removal of small objects by component labeling.
      (c) Final extraction of object region.

   Explanation of each steps are in order.

Noise removal. Smoothing filters are, in general, used for noise removal and blurring. Blurring is used as a preprocessing step to remove small details from the image prior to extraction of large objects as well as bridging of small gaps in lines and curves. In our case noise removal gets priority rather than blurring and we would like to keep edge sharpness intact. We used median filtering which is a suitable tool to get the desired effects. A 5×5 window is used over which the median filtering is done to remove noise.

Initial Segmentation a) Formation of Gradient image
   Here edges are detected on the basis of gray level discontinuities. To achieve this, gradient (i.e., the maximum rate of change of the gray level within a specified neighborhood) at every point of the filtered image is computed.
   The neighborhood around a pixel (i,j) within which the gradient is computed and the weights given to the neighboring pixels are shown below:

a	b	c		1	$\sqrt{2}$	1
d	(i,j)	e		$\sqrt{2}$	(i,j)	$\sqrt{2}$
f	g	h		1	$\sqrt{2}$	1

The gradient at the centre point (i, j) of the 3×3 mask is computed using the difference operator based on the concept of Weber ratio as follows.

$$m_0 = (c + \sqrt{2}e + h)/(2 + \sqrt{2})$$
$$m_1 = (a + \sqrt{2}d + f)/(2 + \sqrt{2})$$
$$g_0 = | m_0 - m_1 | /(m_0 + m_1 + 1)$$

Similarly, g_1 is computed considering the elements a, b, c and f, g, h. For g_2, the diagonal elements b, c, e and d, f, g are considered. And, g_3 is computed considering the elements a, b, d and g, h, e. The intensity gradient $g(i, j)$ at the point (i, j) is then defined as

$$g(i, j) = max\{g_0, \ g_1, \ g_2, \ g_3\} \tag{2}$$

The value of $g(i, j)$ ranges from -127 to 127 and is symmetrically distributed with zero mean. It is observed that the distribution of $g(i, j)$ closely follows Laplace density function [11].

$$f(x) = \frac{1}{2\sigma}e^{-|x-\mu|/\sigma} \quad \text{for } -\infty < x < \infty \tag{3}$$

where μ is the mean and σ is the standard deviation of the population. Secondly, $p\%$ of population lie in the range $[\mu - k\sigma, \ \mu + k\sigma]$ where

$$k = -ln(1 - \frac{p}{100}) \tag{4}$$

b) Thresholding
The gradient image is then subject to a threshold operation to get a binary image containing edge pixels. Suppose we assume that less than $q\%$ of all the image pixels are edge pixels and $p = 100 - q$. Then the threshold is $\mu + k\sigma$; μ and σ are computed from the gradient image. Edge image is given by

$$B(i, j) = \begin{cases} 1 & \text{if } |g(i, j)| > \mu + k\sigma \\ 0 & \text{otherwise} \end{cases} \tag{5}$$

In our experiment we have taken $q = 20$. Obviously, the threshold computed this way may not give optimum results for all kinds of images. The resulting edge images thus have *thick* or *broken* or *extraneous* edges or their combination. However, these edge pixels are sufficient to generate approximate pseudo-convex hull of the object of interest as will be seen below.

These steps are demonstrated by an example shown in Fig. 4. Fig. 4(a) is the input gray level image and Fig. 4(b) shows its edge pixels.

Final Segmentation a) Approximate object area determination
To find out the object, the edge image obtained in previous step undergoes the pseudo-convex hull algorithm as described in section 3. We determine wedge-convex hull of the set of edge pixels, i.e., use $th = 3$. We choose wedge-convex hull to ensure that the boundary of the computed hull be as close to the concave

region of the object as possible and also that the nearby small objects or extraneous edges due to background texture (if any) do not merge with the dominant object.

The result of approximate object area determination is shown in Fig. 4(c). This process may generate small objects due to presence of extraneous edge pixels as seen in figure Fig. 4(c). They may be removed through connected component analysis as described below.

b) Removal of small objects by component labeling
After computing the wedge-convex hull we get an initial estimate of the dominant object. We also get some small objects arising out of scattered extraneous edge pixels in the background. These can be isolated by component labeling and subsequently removed keeping only the biggest one.

Fig. 4(d) shows the result after removal of small objects by connected component analysis.

c) Final extraction of object region
After removal of small objects we finally determine the dominant object region by applying pseudo-convex hull algorithm with $th = 1$ on the point set of largest connected component obtained from previous step. This time we choose to compute ramp convex hull to remove undesired intrusion into the object region due to broken edges. However, this also fills up concave regions. Result of the final step is shown in Fig. 4(e).

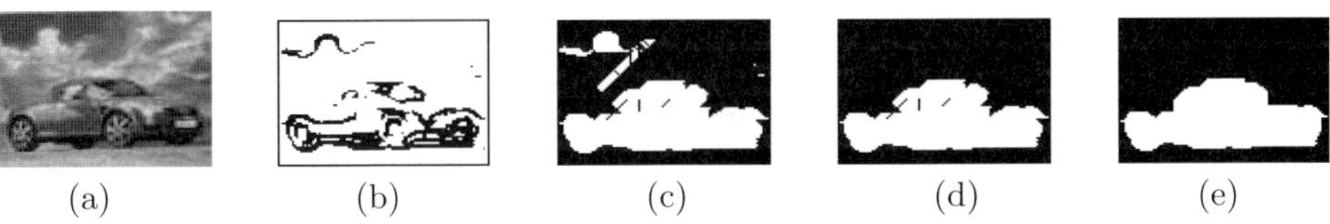

(a)   (b)   (c)   (d)   (e)

Fig. 4. Segmentation steps; (left to right) a) Original image; b) After threshold operation; c) After 1st level of segmentation; d) After removal of small component and e) Final segmentation

5   Experimental Results and Discussion

The segmentation algorithm proposed here are implemented on a Alphaserver DS 20E machine with UNIX OS. The average time taken (for image of size 200×320 approx.) is less than 10 msec. The algorithm can be made even faster by readily parallelizing various parts. We have tested the proposed algorithm on a large number (1000 approx.) of images of various types. A few results of the experiment are shown in Fig. 5 where the original image, segmented image and the contour superimposed original image are shown side by side.

To compare the performance of the proposed segmentation scheme, we have implemented the scheme proposed by Siebert [12]. The results are shown in figure 6.

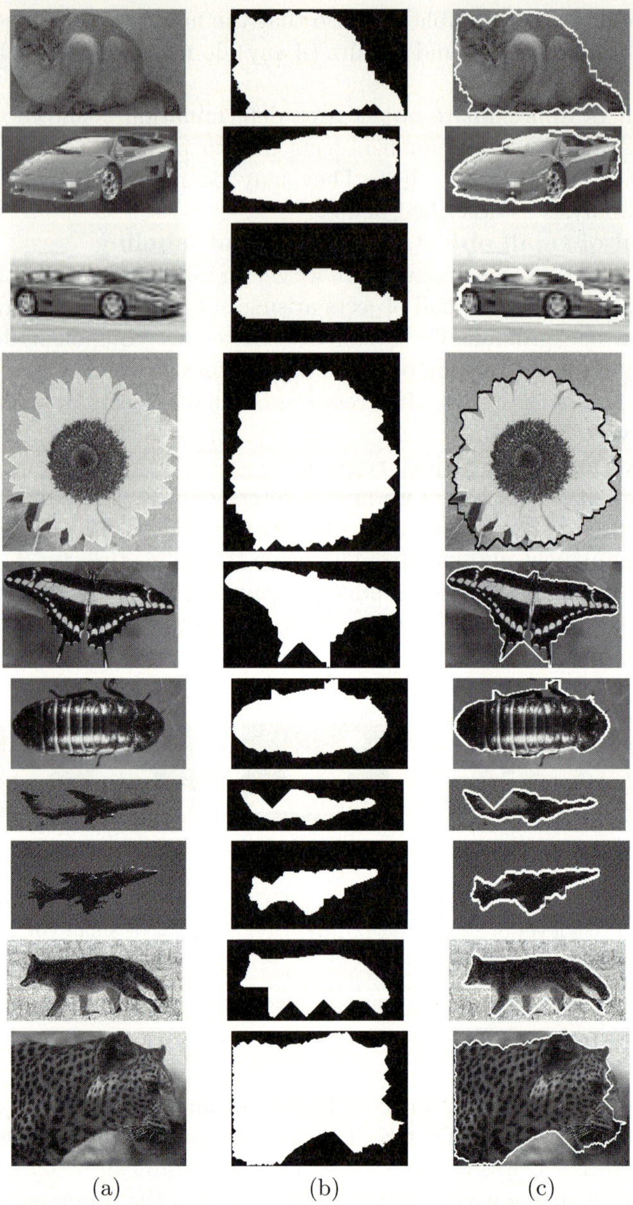

(a)   (b)   (c)

Fig. 5. Segmentation Results (left to right): (a) Original image; (b) Segmented image and (c) Superimposed image taking the original and the segmented image

To get the visually best possible result in case of Siebert's scheme, the parameters are set manually. It appears that Siebert's scheme suffers from various drawbacks. The algorithm depends on a number of parameters like θ_{cc}, *abrupt change* etc. setting of which cannot be automated. θ_{cc} is a fraction of strong point count

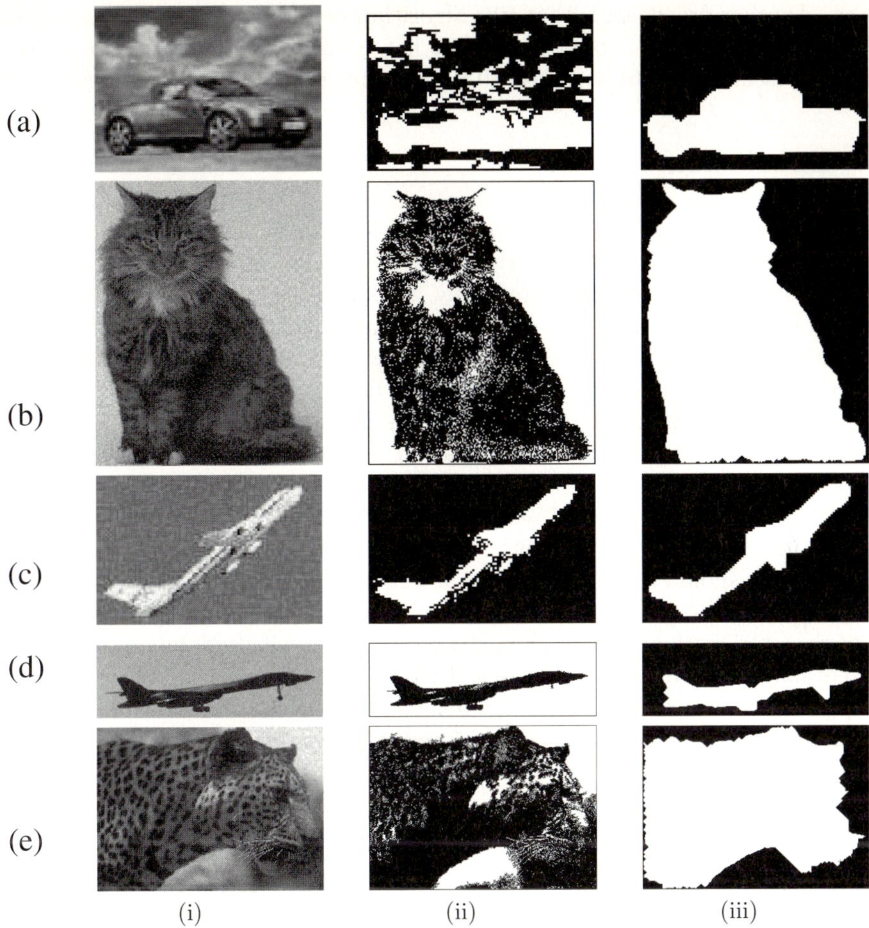

(i)   (ii)   (iii)

Fig. 6. Column (i) shows original image; (ii) and (iii) show corresponding segmented image by Siebert's scheme and our scheme respectively. In case of Siebert's
scheme (θ_{cc}, *abrupt change*) for the five images considered are (0.4, 0.4), (0.4, 0.5),
(0.1, 0.3),(0.4, 0.4) and (0.3, 0.4) respectively.

in the image and is a criterion to determine how far the region growing will
continue. A region growing may result into overspill. If the overspill results into
abrupt change in certain parameters (say, region size), then that overspill is discarded. The region growing starts from a seed region which is selected based on
the smoothness factor. Hence, sometimes the central object (figure 6(b),(d),(e))
and sometimes the encompassing background (figure 6(a),(c)) appear as output.
Moreover, the performance varies from image to image and fails if the background
contains texture. As figure 6 shows, the performance of Siebert's algorithm is
very good for (d) and moderate in case of (b) and (c). But, it fails in case of
(a) and (e). On the other hand, our scheme provides good output for all those

cases. Another drawback is that, the algorithm is very slow. Segmenting around 500 images using the two algorithms, it has been observed that on an average the proposed algorithm is almost 10 times faster than Siebert's algorithm.

6 Conclusion

In this paper we have presented a fast and robust image segmentation algorithm based on edge detection and determination of pseudo-convex hull of edge points. The algorithm may be considered fully automatic as the required parameters are set in the algorithm itself and no user intervention is needed during batch operation. Assigned value of the parameters are not claimed to be optimal, they together can do the job reasonably well in almost all the cases. For example, the threshold used to detect edge points is by no means the best, even then the detected edge points provide sufficient clue to estimate the object region through the pseudo-convex hull algorithm. The result of the proposed algorithm is compared with that of of a recent work and is found superior in most of the cases.

Finally, it should again be noted that emphasis is given to design simple and fully automated segmentation method that incurs very low computational cost. The proposed method may not give the best result in all cases, but it surely gives acceptable results in almost all cases. Thus the method is useful where accuracy of segmentation is not very critically demanded. The class for which the method would give good results is also defined and is found really large.

References

1. Rosenfeld, A., Kak, A.C.: Digital Picture Processing. Volume II. Academic Press, N.Y. (1982)
2. Pavlidis, T., Liow, Y.T.: Integrating region growing and edge detection. IEEE Trans. on PAMI **12(3)** (1990) 225–233
3. Canny, J.: A computational approach to edge detection. IEEE Trans. on PAMI **8(6)** (1986)
4. Haralick, R.M., Shapiro, G.L.: Computer and Robot Vision. Volume 2. Addison Wesley, Reading, MA (1992)
5. Williams, D.J., Shah, M.: A fast algorithm for active contours. CVGIP: Image Understanding **55(1)** (1990) 14–26
6. Beucher, S.: Watersheds of functions and picture segmentation. In: Proceedings of IEEE ICASSP-82. (1982)
7. Mezaris, V., Kompatsiaris, I., Strintzis, M.G.: Still image segmentation tools for object-based multimedia applications. Intl. Journal of Pattern Recognition and Artificial Intelligence **18(4)** (2004) 701–725
8. Rital, S., Cherifi, H., Miguet, S.: A segmentation algorithm for noisy images. In: Proceedings of 11th Intl. Conf. on Computer Analysis of Images and Patterns, France (2005)
9. Foley, J.D., Dam, A., Feiner, S.K., Hughes, J.D.: Computer Graphics - Principles and Practices. Addision - Wesley (1993)

10. Rosenfeld, A.: Digital straight line segments. IEEE Trans. on Computer **C-23** (1974) 1264–1269
11. Rao, C.R.: Linear Statistical Inference and Its applications, 2nd ed. Wiley Eastern, New Delhi (1973)
12. Siebert, A.: Segmentation based image retrieval. SPIE 3312 **SRIVD VI** (1998) 14–23

Single-Histogram Class Models for Image Segmentation

F. Schroff[1], A. Criminisi[2], and A. Zisserman[1]

[1] Dept. of Engineering Science, University of Oxford,
Parks Road, Oxford, OX1 3PJ, UK
{schroff, az}@robots.ox.ac.uk
[2] Microsoft Research Ltd, Cambridge, CB3 0FB, UK
antcrim@microsoft.com

Abstract. Histograms of visual words (or textons) have proved effective in tasks such as image classification and object class recognition. A common approach is to represent an object class by a set of histograms, each one corresponding to a training exemplar. Classification is then achieved by k-nearest neighbour search over the exemplars.

In this paper we introduce two novelties on this approach: (i) we show that new compact *single* histogram models estimated optimally from the entire training set achieve an equal or superior classification accuracy. The benefit of the single histograms is that they are much more efficient both in terms of memory and computational resources; and (ii) we show that bag of visual words histograms can provide an accurate pixel-wise segmentation of an image into object class regions. In this manner the compact models of visual object classes give simultaneous segmentation and recognition of image regions.

The approach is evaluated on the MSRC database [5] and it is shown that performance equals or is superior to previous publications on this database.

1 Introduction

Segmenting natural images automatically in a bottom up fashion has a long history but has not been that successful – see [16] for a recent example and earlier references. Two more recent and fruitful trends are *class driven segmentation*, where object class models propose object localisations that can then refine a more local (bottom up) image segmentation [1, 2, 9, 11, 12, 17], and *interactive segmentation* in which a human supplies approximate segmentations and then refines and groups automatically generated image based segmentations [4, 15]. For example, consider a colour based segmentation of a patchy cow – a purely bottom up segmentation will tend to separate the image into many different regions rather than recognising the cow as a single, coherent object – there is a clear need for segmentation and recognition to work together.

Many class driven recognition and segmentation algorithms represent the object class or texture using multiple exemplars [1, 2, 9, 11, 12, 20]. One contribution of this paper is to show that equal or superior recognition results can be

P. Kalra and S. Peleg (Eds.): ICVGIP 2006, LNCS 4338, pp. 82–93, 2006.
© Springer-Verlag Berlin Heidelberg 2006

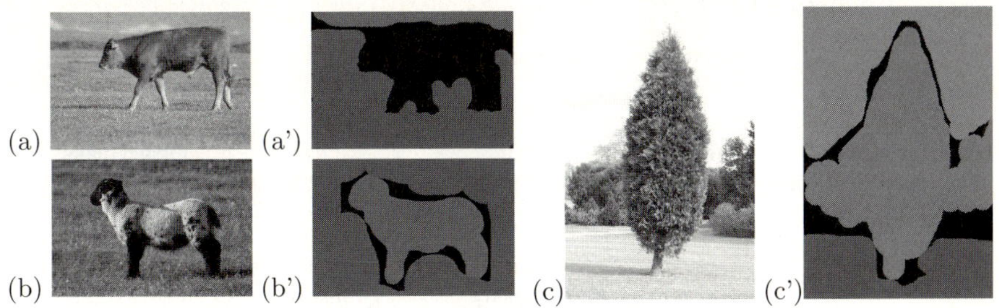

Fig. 1. The image database. (a–c) Example images from the MSRC database and (a'–c') their ground-truth class segmentation maps. The colour indicates the object class, with different kinds of grass, for example, associated with a common "grass" label. Note the presence of unlabelled (black) pixels.

obtained by a single class model if an appropriate distance measure is used, and also to explain why this result comes about. A second contribution of this paper is to show that pixel-wise *segmentations* can be obtained from sliding windows using class models.

In more detail we represent an object category by a single histogram of dense visual words, and investigate the effectiveness of this representation for segmentation. The advantage of a single class histogram is a very compact, and consequently computationally efficient, representation. Histograms of visual words have been used previously for region or image level classification [6, 8, 14, 18, 23], though for the most part based on sparse descriptors. Others that have used dense descriptors [3, 22, 8] have only considered soft segmentations based on the support of the visual words, rather than explicit pixel-wise classification.

Previous authors [22] have also investigated representing each class in a compact way using a single Gaussian model of each category. The class models explored here are even simpler and more efficient since they consist of simple histograms without a covariance. We compare the performance of our class models with those of [22] using the same data sets.

For the experiments in this paper we use the MSRC image database [5] (see figure 1). The database contains many classes including grass, trees, sheep, buildings, bicycles and others, seen from different viewpoints and under general illumination conditions. A coarse region level ground truth labelling is available, and this is used to learn the class histograms, and also to assess the pixel level and region level classifications during testing. For example, in the 120 training images there are 64 labelled grass regions and 22 labelled cow regions.

2   Background: Features, Visual Words and Histograms

This section illustrates the basic algorithms for estimating the object class models and the intermediate data representation necessary for classification. The training and testing steps have much in common and are briefly described next.

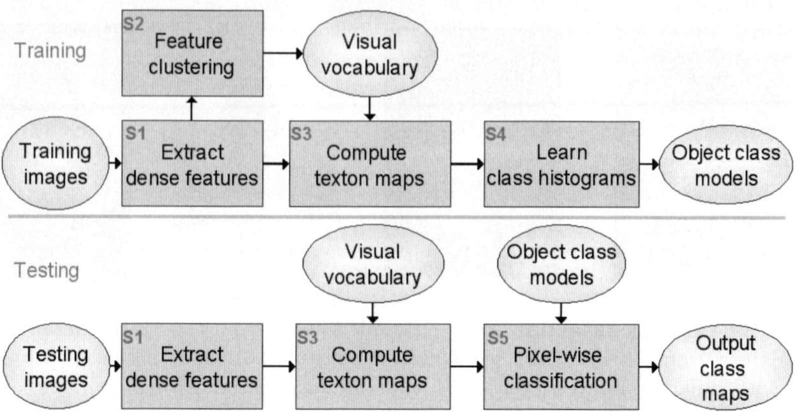

Fig. 2. Flow diagram for the training and testing algorithms

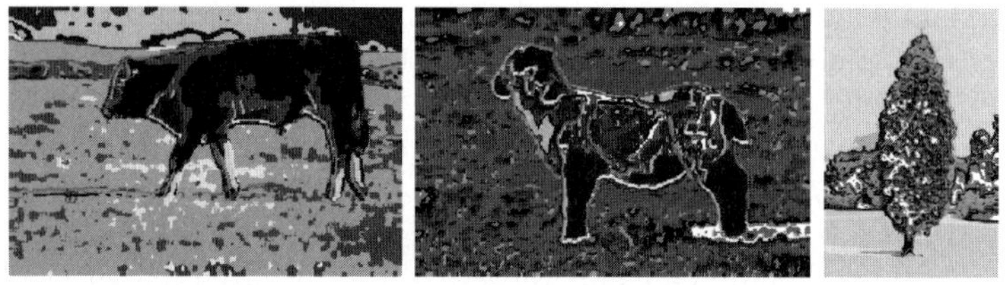

Fig. 3. Texton maps for the images of figure 1. Different colours uniquely identify different textons/visual words. A small visual vocabulary with only 50 words has been used here for illustration.

In this paper, feature vectors are estimated densely, i.e. at each pixel location. The actual feature vectors (step S1 in figure 2) are raw 3×3 or 5×5 colour patches [3, 20] in the *CIE-LAB* colour space. Thus, their dimensionality is 27 or 75, respectively.

During training a vocabulary of V visual words (also called textons, [13, 20, 21, 22]) is built by clustering the feature vectors extracted from many training images (step S2). Feature clustering is performed by K-means on a randomly sampled 25% subset of feature vectors using equal numbers from each training image. Note, a suitable degree of invariance (to lighting, rotations, scale etc) is learnt implicitly from the training images (since these provide examples of lighting changes etc), and no additional invariances are built in.

Given the set of cluster centres (these are the visual words or textons), it is now possible to associate each pixel in the training images with the closest visual word in the vocabulary (step S3). The result may be visualised by generating colour-coded word maps such as in figure 3.

Finally, we compute histograms of visual words for each of the training regions (step S4). Those histograms can then be (i) stored separately as training exemplars, or (ii) combined together to produce compact and yet discriminative models of object categories. Here we estimate such *single-histogram* class models and demonstrate classification accuracy comparable to standard k-nearest-neighbour classification (k-NN) on the exemplars.

During testing (step S5), an input image is converted into its corresponding texton map. Then, pixel-wise classification is obtained by means of a sliding window technique. A window of dimension $(2w + 1) \times (2w + 1)$ is slid across the image to generate a histogram of visual words for each position. The centre pixel is then classified according to the closest class histogram. In this manner an image can be segmented into the various classes it contains, for example into pixels arising from grass, trees or sheep.

3   Single-Histogram Models for Efficient Classification

This section describes details of our class model estimation algorithm (step S4 in figure 2). During training the histograms corresponding to different training regions (exemplars) belonging to the same class are combined together into a single, optimally estimated class histogram. During testing for pixel-wise classification, a histogram is computed for *each* pixel of the test image using a sliding window, and this histogram is then compared to each of the C (the number of classes) class histograms (as opposed to each of the (possibly many) training regions/exemplars in the case of k-NN classification). The use of single class histograms clearly reduces the classification cost. The class models are used both for the aforementioned pixel-wise classification, via a sliding window, and for region level classification, explained later on.

The key question then is how to compute such single-histogram models. Let **p** be one of the exemplar histograms and **q** the single histogram model that we seek. Histograms are represented as V-vectors, with V the vocabulary size. For a given class c, the "optimal" class histogram **q** is the one which minimises the overall distance to all the N_c exemplar histograms $\mathbf{p}^j$, as this minimises intra-class variability. Ideally, for best discrimination, one would also like to maximise the inter-class variability, and we return to this point later. The optimal solution $\hat{\mathbf{q}}$ depends on the histogram distance function used during classification. In this paper we analyse and compare the two most common alternatives: (i) a Kullback-Leibler divergence (D_{KL}), and (ii) a Euclidean distance (D_{L2}). The same framework may also be applied to other distance measures, such as histogram intersection, χ^2, Bhattacharyya or Alpha-Divergence.

Kullback-Leibler divergence: The KL divergence between the two normalised histograms **a** and **b** is defined as:

$$D_{KL}(\mathbf{a} \parallel \mathbf{b}) = \sum_i a_i \log \frac{a_i}{b_i} \quad .$$

The subscript i labels the bins (a_i or b_i), with $i = 1 \ldots V$.

Given a class c we seek the model histogram $\hat{\mathbf{q}}$ which minimises the following cost:

$$E_{KL} := \sum_{j=1}^{N_c} n^j D_{KL}(\mathbf{p}^j \parallel \mathbf{q}) \quad \text{subject to} \ \parallel \mathbf{q} \parallel_1 = 1, \ q_i \geq 0 \ \forall i \quad , \qquad (1)$$

where n^j denotes the number of pixels in the jth exemplar region, and is used as a weight to each exemplar histogram. N_c is the number of exemplar regions for the object category c. The normalised histogram for the jth exemplar image region in class c is denoted $\mathbf{p}^j$. Note that the weighting factors n^j could be set to one, thus treating all training exemplars equally. Both versions were explored and gave comparable results.

Standard manipulation yields the global minimum of (1) as:

$$\hat{\mathbf{q}} := \frac{\sum_j n^j \mathbf{p}^j}{\sum_j n^j} \quad . \qquad (2)$$

It can be shown [7] that $\hat{\mathbf{q}}$, with n^j as defined, corresponds to the maximum likelihood estimate of the visual word distribution for class c given its N_c training region visual words. In other words, $\hat{\mathbf{q}}$ describes the overall visual word distribution in all training regions.

During classification, given a query image sliding window, or region and its corresponding histogram $\mathbf{p}$, the closest class model $\tilde{\mathbf{q}} = \arg\min_{\mathbf{q}} D_{KL}(\mathbf{p} \parallel \mathbf{q})$ is chosen, i.e. $\tilde{\mathbf{q}}$ is the model that best explains $\mathbf{p}$ and the corresponding class the most likely one.

Euclidean Distance: The Euclidean distance between the two histograms $\mathbf{a}$ and $\mathbf{b}$ is defined as:

$$D_{L2}(\mathbf{a}, \mathbf{b}) = \sum_{i=1}(a_i - b_i)^2 \quad .$$

Once again, given the class c and its exemplar histograms $\mathbf{p}^j$ we seek the histogram $\hat{\mathbf{q}}$ which minimises the following cost:

$$E_{L2} := \sum_{j=1}^{N_c} n^j D_{L2}(\mathbf{p}^j, \mathbf{q}) \quad \text{subject to} \quad \parallel \mathbf{q} \parallel_1 = 1, \ q_i \geq 0 \ \forall i \quad . \qquad (3)$$

Standard manipulation leads to the same $\hat{\mathbf{q}}$ as obtained by minimising (1), i.e. as given in (2).

Next we assess the discrimination power of the learnt class models by measuring pixel-wise classification performance.

4　Results and Comparative Evaluation

In this section we assess the validity of our models by measuring accuracy of segmentation/recognition against two subsets of the MSRC database [5]: a six class subset, *6-class* = { *cow, sheep, dog, cat, bird, grass* }; and a nine class subset, *9-class* = { *building, grass, tree, cow, sky, aeroplane, face, car, bicycle* } [22].

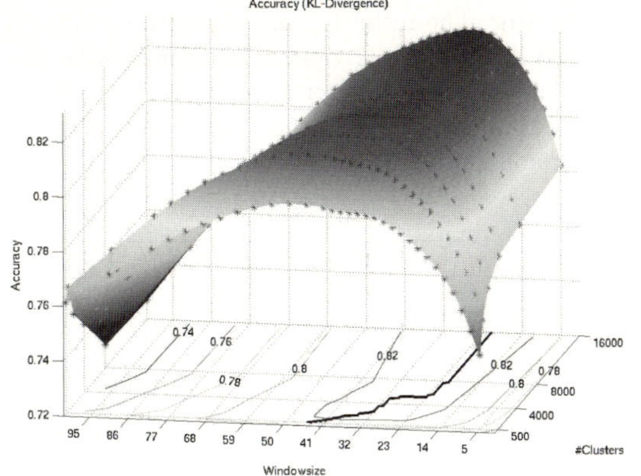

V	Acc.	w	Acc.
$(w = 11)$	(%)	$(V = 8000)$	(%)
500	79.1	5	80.3
1000	80.7	11	**82.4**
2000	81.7	15	**82.4**
4000	82.3	20	82.1
8000	82.4	26	81.1
16000	**83.0**	30	80

Fig. 4. Accuracy analysis on the 6-class set. Pixel-wise classification performance as a function of the size w of the sliding window and the size V of the visual vocabulary. The features are 27-dimensional 3×3 CIE-LAB patches. The vocabulary is learnt by K-means clustering run for 500 iterations. KL divergence is used for histogram comparisons.

The databases are split into 125 training and 50 test images for the *6-class* set, and 120 training and 120 test images for the *9-class* set. The visual vocabulary and class models are learnt from the training data only. As mentioned before, during testing a window of dimension $(2w + 1) \times (2w + 1)$ is slid across the image to generate a histogram of visual words for each pixel, and thereby classifying the centre pixel.

Accuracy of segmentation/recognition is measured by the proportion of test pixels correctly classified according to ground truth. Only the pixels belonging to one of the aforementioned classes are taken into consideration. In the remainder we refer to this accuracy as pixel-wise classification performance, as opposed to region-wise classification performance which is introduced later. In the following we first evaluate performance using the *6-class* set together with single class histograms over the system parameters: features $(3 \times 3, 5 \times 5)$; number of iterations in K-means; vocabulary size V; and window size w. We then compare the performance of the single class histogram to that of using k-NN over all the exemplars.

The effect of the window and vocabulary sizes: The first set of experiments are designed to evaluate optimal values for the size of the sliding window w, the vocabulary size V, and the best feature clustering technique.

Figure 4 plots the pixel-wise classification accuracy as a function of both the window size w and the vocabulary size V. Two cross-sections of the accuracy function through the maximum are shown in the table. The maximum performance is reached for $w = 11 - 15$ and $V = 16,000$. Accuracy does not vary much over the range $V = 8,000 - 128,000$, so from here on a vocabulary of size $V = 8,000$ is used to reduce computational cost. The optimal value $w = 12$

Table 1. Variations of K-means clustering. The mean ($\pm$ one standard deviation) pixel-wise classification accuracy computed over multiple runs of K-means; with the number of runs used in each case shown in brackets. Different numbers of iterations of K-means for constructing the visual vocabulary on the *6-class* and *9-class* sets are compared. KL divergence together with single class histograms on 5×5 patches was used.

	KM, 0 iters	KM, 1 iter	KM, 10 iters	KM, 500 iters
6-class	$81.96 \pm 0.20\%$ (50)	$82.24 \pm 0.20\%$ (10)	$82.54 \pm 0.15\%$ (5)	$\mathbf{82.56} \pm 0.13\%$ (5)
9-class	$74.72 \pm 0.22\%$ (10)	$74.92 \pm 0.17\%$ (10)	$\mathbf{75.07} \pm 0.15\%$ (10)	–

Table 2. k-NN vs. single-histograms. Comparing the *pixel*-wise classification performance obtained by our single-histogram class models with that obtained from conventional nearest neighbour. In this case we used $V = 8000$ and 5×5 patches as features. K-means with 10 iterations was used to construct the visual vocabulary. For the 6-class set the best performing k out of $k = 1 \ldots 100$ and for the 9-class the performance for k-NN with $k = 1$ is reported. Using single-histogram class models in conjunction with KL divergence produces the best results.

	D_{KL}(6-class)	D_{L2}(6-class)	D_{χ^2}(6-class)	D_{KL}(9-class)	D_{L2}(9-class)	D_{χ^2}(9-class)
k-NN	82.1%	76.6%	78.7%	71.6%	65.1%	72.0%
single hist.	**82.4%**	77.0%	–	**75.2%**	58.7%	–

is also used. The performance is found not to depend much on the size of the feature (i.e. size of colour patch), 5×5 colour patches are used from here on. *The effects of different clustering techniques:* In table 1 we compare the influence of different numbers of iterations in K-means clustering for the construction of the visual vocabulary. Zero iterations denote randomly sampled cluster centres from the feature space, which is how K-means is initialised in all cases. Interestingly the performance is only slightly affected by the number of iterations. In particular there is only a small gain in increasing from 10 to 500 iterations. From here on we use 10 iterations as a trade off between performance and computational time for the experiments.

Keeping all exemplar histograms vs. single-histogram class models: Next we compare the performance of single-histogram models with respect to conventional k-NN classification, and provide evidence for the main claim of the paper.

Table 2 summarises the results of applying a k-NN approach, i.e. maintaining all the exemplar histograms of each class separately, and our single-histogram class models. Classification performance is measured for both KL and L2 distance. In all cases the accuracy obtained by the proposed class models is comparable (if not superior) to that obtained by k-NN. Experiments were carried out for the 6-class and 9-class datasets, as shown (the optimal k in the k-NN was $k = 1$ for KL divergence, and $k = 3, 4$ for L2; for the 9-class set only $k = 1$ was used). Substituting L2 distance for KL divergence reduces the performance by nearly 6%. This confirms the better suitability of the KL divergence *for* single class histograms (see following discussion).

Table 3. Confusion matrices for the single class histogram method (see table 2). (a) for the 6-class set; achieving an overall pixel-wise classification accuracy of **82.4%**. (b) for the 9-class set; achieving a pixel-wise classification accuracy of **75.2%**. KL divergence is used in both cases.

GT\Cl	grass	cow	sheep	bird	cat	dog
grass	95.61	2.0	1.2	1.2		0.1
cow	3.8	71.9	6.4	1.0	5.4	11.5
sheep	3.2	12.0	62.7	4.3	4.9	13.0
bird	5.5	27.1	24.0	27.7	10.4	5.4
cat		5.5	12.4	6.9	69.8	5.5
dog	1.1	24.7	2.3	6.5	18.2	47.2

(a) conf. mat. for 6-class set

GT\Cl	build.	grass	tree	cow	sky	plane	face	car	bike
build.	56.7	0.0	4.8	3.0	2.2	12.8	1.4	11.6	7.5
grass	0.5	84.8	9.7	3.9		1.2			
tree	6.4	5.6	76.4	1.2	0.3	1.3		2.4	6.5
cow	1.9	2.4	2.7	83.8			0.2	4.5	3.7	0.8
sky	6.5		2.1		81.1	6.4		3.9	
plane	16.8	0.8	5.0	3.4	0.1	53.8		16.6	3.5
face	4.6	0.0	0.4	19.1			0.6	68.5	3.6	3.2
car	7.4		1.1	3.4	0.7	2.6	2.0	71.4	11.6
bike	9.9	0.1	4.8	2.9			1.5	0.1	8.8	72.0

(b) conf. mat. for 9-class set

Table 4. Region-wise classification. Comparing the *region*-wise classification performance obtained by our single-histogram class models with that obtained from conventional nearest neighbour. Shown are the *best* results if V is varied (V is shown in brackets). Results are comparable to previous published performances for this dataset [22].

	1-NN (χ^2)	cl-Hist (KL)	1-NN ([22])	1-NN T ([22])
9-class	92.34 (for V = 4000 and V =32000)	93.43 (V=64000)	93.4	92.7

Table 3 shows the confusion matrices for selected experiments of table 2. The matrices are row normalised (so that the percentages in each row sum to 100%). Only pixels belonging to one of the classes are considered. For the 6-class set, the grass class is recognised most reliably, followed by cows, cats and sheep. This provides us with an idea of the relative difficulty of modelling each class. At this point one may think that our models work well only with texture-defined objects (grass, woolly sheep...). However, we also include classification of man made (less texture-like) objects such as cars and bicycles in the 9-class database (as also used in [22]). Table 3b presents the confusion matrix. The performance is still well above 70%, thus confirming the modelling power of the proposed class histograms (see following discussion).

4.1   Region Level Classification

Next we compare the accuracy of discrimination of our models with that achieved by the Gaussian models proposed in Winn et al. [22]. Following their evaluation methodology, we classify each input test *region*[1] as belonging to one of the classes in the database and measure the error with respect to ground truth. Table 4 shows that the proposed, simpler class models perform comparably. For this comparison the exact training/test splits were provided by the authors of [22].

---

[1] The area of the region and its ground truth label is known

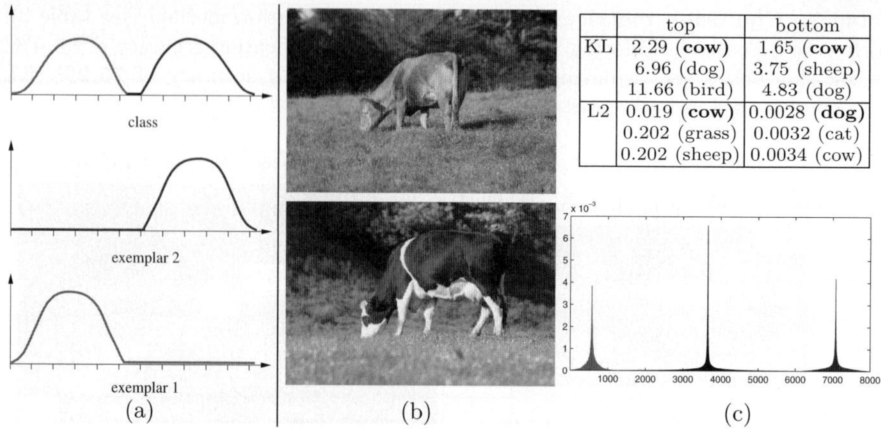

	top	bottom
KL	2.29 (**cow**)	1.65 (**cow**)
	6.96 (dog)	3.75 (sheep)
	11.66 (bird)	4.83 (dog)
L2	0.019 (**cow**)	0.0028 (**dog**)
	0.202 (grass)	0.0032 (cat)
	0.202 (sheep)	0.0034 (cow)

Fig. 5. Advantages of KL. Different instances of cows induce different proportions of visual words. A unified "cow" model histogram (c) will contain different "modes" for the different visual aspects and species of the instances. (a) provides a schematic visualisation. In (c) the mode corresponding to the top cow in (b) is shown in red (left), and for the bottom cow in blue (right). The remaining visual words of the *cow*-model are shown in black in the middle. Note that a simple sorting of the visual words has been employed to bring out the different modes. The table shows the distances of the cow exemplars in (b) to the class models (showing the nearest class in bold). KL divergence ignores zero bins in the query histograms and is thus better suited for this scenario (note the wrong classification with L2 for the bottom cow).

Each of the methods (k-NN using χ^2 on exemplars, and KL for single-class histograms) are optimised separately over the size of the vocabulary V, and the best result is reported. χ^2 is reported for k-NN as this gives superior results to L2 and it is the standard distance measure for region classification on exemplars [20]. In both cases the features are 5×5 patches and the visual vocabulary was constructed with K-means (10 iterations). In addition to the results given in the table we experimented on the 6-class database using $V = 8000$. The result is similar in that the 1-NN χ^2 performance was 79.5% and the single-class histogram reached 85.5%.

4.2   Discussion

As the experiments demonstrate, KL divergence is superior to both $L2$ and χ^2 distance when the single-histogram models are used ([19] uses KL for similar reasons). This observation can be explained by the fact that the KL divergence does not penalise zero bins in the query histogram (which are non-zero in the model) as much as the other two distances. As a result of the way our class models are learnt, they are likely to have many non-zero bins due to the contribution of all training images' visual words to the model histogram. Query histograms that stem from a very specific object instance are very likely to have many zero bins. Consider the three schematic histograms shown in figure 5a. If $L2$ (or χ^2)

Fig. 6. Class segmentation results. (a) Original photographs. (b) Ground-truth class labels. (c) Output class maps obtained with KL divergence. (d) Output class maps obtained with L2 distance. In most cases L2 gives less accurate segmentation. In all cases our single-histogram class models were used, together with 5×5 patch features, $V = 8000$ and K-means clustering.

distances are used then each exemplar histogram will have a large distance from the class histogram (due to bins q_i of the mode in the class histogram which are not present in each of the exemplars). However, the KL divergence ignores all the null bins of the exemplar histograms (as these are zero p_i values in $p_i \log \frac{p_i}{q_i}$), thus making it a better suited distance. Figure 5c provides an example of such a multi-modal class histogram (here the cow model), and two exemplar regions inducing modes in the class model. The table shows the actual distances of the two cow regions to the three closest class models. In this case the bottom cow would be classified incorrectly as dog if L2 was used.

The optimal estimation of a class histogram is related to the topic vectors of Probabilistic Latent Semantic Analysis (pLSA) used in statistical text analysis [10]. Using the common terminology, each exemplar region represents a document by its word frequencies, visual words in our case. In the pLSA "learning" stage each exemplar is modelled by a topic distribution and each topic by a visual word distribution. In our case we use the additional information provided by the training data and hence define the topics to correspond to the object categories. Furthermore, each exemplar is constrained to be modelled by one topic only – the class assigned to it by the training annotation. Consequently, our method directly corresponds to pLSA in that it also minimises the KL divergence of the modelled data to the given data. The model is just more constrained in our case.

As mentioned earlier it would be desirable to maximise the inter-class distance when building the single-histograms. Maximising the inter-class distance or generally merging the class histograms in a discriminative way is left for future research. See [7] for related approaches.

Finally, figure 6 shows results of class segmentations of images. Note that the (visual) accuracy of the L2 classification results is inferior to that obtained with KL divergence.

5   Conclusion

This paper has introduced a new technique for the estimation of compact and efficient, generative single-histogram models of object classes. The models are applied to simultaneously segment and recognise images.

Despite their simplicity, our single-histogram class models have proved as discriminative as keeping around *all* exemplar histograms (and classifying via nearest neighbour approaches). The main advantage being their storage economy, computational efficiency and scalability. Note, the computational efficiency is a significant advantage since methods for speeding up nearest neighbour search, such as k-D trees, do not perform well in high dimensions. Here the number of dimensions equals the number of histogram bins and is of the order of thousands. Thus, finding the closest exemplar (in k-NN classification) reduces to a linear search through all the exemplars, whilst for single class histograms the search is only linear in the number of classes.

Different histogram similarity functions have been compared. In the case of single-histogram class models, the KL divergence has been demonstrated to achieve higher accuracy than widely used alternatives such as L2 and χ^2 distances.

The pixel labelling results demonstrate that our class histograms can also be used to segment out objects. A natural next step is to combine such labellings with a contrast dependent prior MRF in the manner of [4] in order to obtain crisp segmentation boundaries. Alternatively the resulting pixelmaps can be used to initialise graph-cuts methods automatically rather than manually as in [15].

In future work we will compare performance of the single class histograms against other standard discriminative classifiers trained on the exemplars. For instance, an SVM could be trained on sliding-window histograms for pixel-wise classification or, as in the work of [17], weak classifiers can be built from histograms of visual words within sliding rectangular regions, and then combined into a discriminative classifier using boosting.

Bibliography

[1] E. Borenstein and S. Ullman. Class-specific, top-down segmentation. In *Proc. ECCV*, pages 109–124, 2002. 82

[2] E. Borenstein and S. Ullman. Learning to segment. *ECCV*, 2004. 82

[3] A. Bosch, A. Zisserman, and X. Munoz. Scene classification via pLSA. In *Proc. ECCV*, 2006. 83, 84

[4] Y. Y. Boykov and M. P. Jolly. Interactive graph cuts for optimal boundary and region segmentation of objects in N-D images. In *Proc. ICCV*, 2001. 82, 92

[5] A. Criminisi. Microsoft research cambridge object recognition image database. version 1.0, 2004. **http://research.microsoft.com/vision/cambridge/ recognition/**. 82, 83, 86

[6] G. Csurka, C. Bray, C. Dance, and L. Fan. Visual categorization with bags of keypoints. In *Workshop on Stat. Learning in CV, ECCV*, pages 1–22, 2004. 83

[7] I. Dhillon, S. Mallela, and R. Kumar. A divisive information-theoretic feature clustering algorithm for text classification. J. Machine Learning Research, 2003. 86, 92

[8] L. Fei-Fei and P. Perona. A Bayesian hierarchical model for learning natural scene categories. In *Proc. CVPR*, Jun 2005. 83

[9] X. He, R. S. Zemel, and M. Á. Carreira-Perpiñán. Multiscale conditional random fields for image labeling. *Proc. CVPR*, 2004. 82

[10] T. Hofmann. Unsupervised learning by probabilistic latent semantic analysis. *Machine Learning*, 43:177–196, 2001. 91

[11] M. P. Kumar, P. H. S. Torr, and A. Zisserman. OBJ CUT. In *Proc. CVPR*, 2005. 82

[12] B. Leibe and B. Schiele. Interleaved object categorization and segmentation. In *BMVC*, volume 2, pages 264–271, 2003. 82

[13] T. Leung and J. Malik. Representing and recognizing the visual appearance of materials using three-dimensional textons. *IJCV*, 43(1):29–44, Jun 2001. 84

[14] P. Quelhas, F. Monay, J.-M. Odobez, D. Gatica, T. Tuytelaars, and L. Van Gool. Modeling scenes with local descriptors and latent aspects. In *Proc. ICCV*, pages 883–890, 2005. 83

[15] C. Rother, V. Kolmogorov, and A. Blake. Grabcut: interactive foreground extraction using iterated graph cuts. *Proc. ACM SIGGRAPH*, 23(3):309–314, 2004. 82, 92

[16] E. Sharon, A. Brandt, and R. Basri. Segmentation and boundary detection using multiscale intensity measurements. In *Proc. CVPR*, volume 1, pages 469–476. IEEE Computer Society, 2001. 82

[17] J. Shotton, J. Winn, C. Rother, and A. Criminisi. TextonBoost: Joint Appearance, Shape and context Modeling for Multi-Class Object Recognition and Segmentation. *Proc. ECCV*, 2006. 82, 92

[18] J. Sivic, B. C. Russell, A. A. Efros, A. Zisserman, and W. T. Freeman. Discovering object categories in image collections. In *Proc. ICCV*, 2005. 83

[19] E. Spellman, B. C. Vemuri, and M. Rao. Using the KL-center for Efficient and Accurate Retrieval of Distributions Arising from Texture Images. In *Proc. CVPR*, 2005. 90

[20] M. Varma and A. Zisserman. Texture classification: Are filter banks necessary? In *Proc. CVPR*, volume 2, pages 691–698, Jun 2003. 82, 84, 90

[21] M. Varma and A. Zisserman. A statistical approach to texture classification from single images. *IJCV*, 62(1–2):61–81, Apr 2005. 84

[22] J. Winn, Criminisi, A., and T. Minka. Object Categorization by Learned Universal Visual Dictionary. *Proc. ICCV*, 2005. 83, 84, 86, 89

[23] J. Zhang, M. Marszalek, S. Lazebnik, and C. Schmid. Local features and kernels for classifcation of texture and object categories: An in-depth study. Technical Report RR-5737, INRIA Rhône-Alpes, Nov 2005. 83

Learning Class-Specific Edges for Object Detection and Segmentation

Mukta Prasad[1], Andrew Zisserman[1], Andrew Fitzgibbon[2],
M. Pawan Kumar[3], and P.H.S. Torr[3]

[1] University of Oxford, U.K.
[2] Microsoft Research, Cambridge, U.K.
[3] Oxford Brookes University, U.K.
http://www.robots.ox.ac.uk/~{mukta, vgg}

Abstract. Recent research into recognizing object classes (such as humans, cows and hands) has made use of edge features to hypothesize and localize class instances. However, for the most part, these edge-based methods operate solely on the geometric shape of edges, treating them equally and ignoring the fact that for certain object classes, the appearance of the object on the "inside" of the edge may provide valuable recognition cues.

We show how, for such object classes, small regions around edges can be used to classify the edge into object or non-object. This classifier may then be used to prune edges which are not relevant to the object class, and thereby improve the performance of subsequent processing. We demonstrate learning class specific edges for a number of object classes — oranges, bananas and bottles — under challenging scale and illumination variation.

Because class-specific edge classification provides a low-level analysis of the image it may be integrated into any edge-based recognition strategy without significant change in the high-level algorithms. We illustrate its application to two algorithms: (i) chamfer matching for object detection, and (ii) modulating contrast terms in MRF based object-specific segmentation. We show that performance of both algorithms (matching and segmentation) is considerably improved by the class-specific edge labelling.

1 Introduction

There is a long tradition of using edge features in object recognition: dating back to the 1980s edges were used for recognizing specific objects [7,11,15]; and more recently edges have been used for recognizing object *classes* such as humans (e.g. in Gavrila's combination of chamfer matching and a template tree [6] or by shape context [1,17]), hands [21,23], and animals such as cows and horses [9,14,19].

In algorithms such as [6], recognition is performed while treating image edges equally regardless of their context. However, all edges are not equal. The edges on the boundary of an object from a specific class have the characteristic local colour or texture of that object class on one side (and can have anything else

P. Kalra and S. Peleg (Eds.): ICVGIP 2006, LNCS 4338, pp. 94–105, 2006.
© Springer-Verlag Berlin Heidelberg 2006

on the other side). Similarly, class specific edges may also have a characteristic shape. The key idea of this paper is to learn a classifier for the object class of interest which can label an edge with the probability of it belonging to that object class or not.

Our objective is learn a classifier based on all the available local information around an edge – appearance, texture and shape. While conventional cue integration tends to occur later in the processing pathway, this "early vision" integration means that it is easy to modify existing applications to use our class-specific edges, offering the potential for improved performance across a range of applications.

Previous research has considered classifying edges: Carmichael *et al.* [3] learnt edge shape (but not appearance) for mugs; McHenry *et al.* [12,13] built a classifier by hand for recognizing glass by combining a number of cues (e.g. specularities and the similarity between the image regions on either side of the edge); and Sidenbladh and Black [20] learn edge likelihoods for limbs for human detection in video sequences. The methods most closely related to ours are those of Shahrokni *et al.* [18] and Dollar *et al.* [4]. Both these approaches consider each pixel of the image independently and obtain its probability of being an (object class specific) edge. Due to the variation in negative examples, which include regions with no edges, they are forced to employ a large set of features. In contrast, our method classifies only the edges (i.e. not all pixels) which are provided by a standard detector (e.g. canny). This significantly reduces the variability in negative examples. For instance, homogeneous background regions are pruned away by canny. Class-specific edge detection is then obtained using simple local features together with a standard classifier such as the SVM [16,8] which guarantees a global minimum.

The organization of this paper is as follows. In §2, we describe our method for edge classification. We then give two illustrative examples of its use. First for object detection based on chamfer matching in §3, and then for object segmentation in §4 using the OBJCUT algorithm of [10].

2   Classifying Edges for an Object Class

In this section we describe how local information can be learnt to classify detected edges into those arising from the boundaries of an object class or not. Our objective is to separate class-specific boundary edges from other image edges — those arising from internal discontinuities, specularities, and background clutter. We illustrate our method on two classes here, oranges and bottles.

We follow the standard machine learning procedure and assemble a set of images which are used to train and evaluate the classifier. We assemble a database for each class of about 100 images. Each dataset is split into half for training and testing. The images cover a wide range of scale, pose and illumination conditions, and include multiple object instances, partial occlusions, and background clutter. Examples are shown in figures 1–3. Edges are obtained using the Canny edge detector with hysteresis. To simplify ground truth annotation, edges are

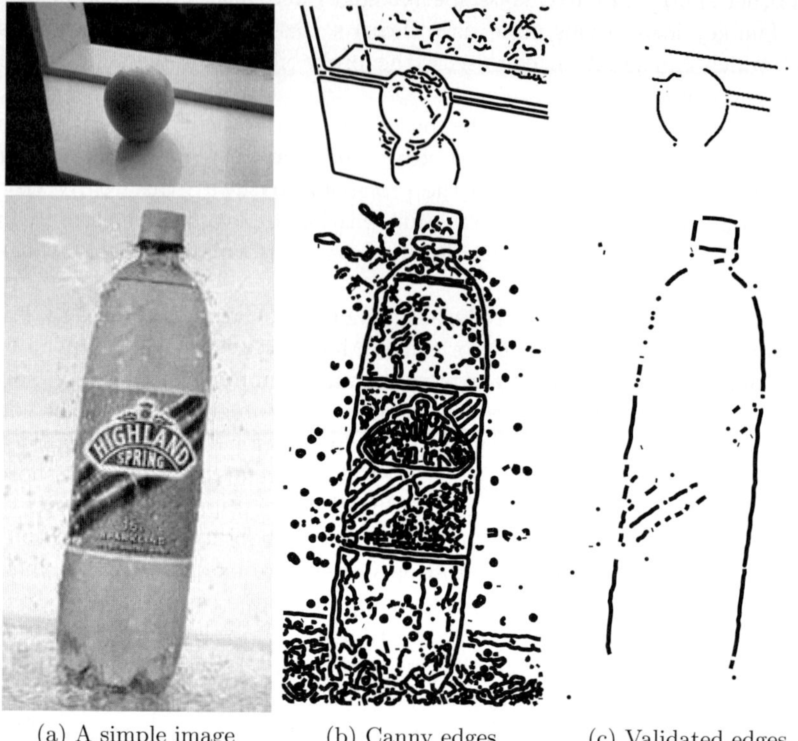

(a) A simple image   (b) Canny edges   (c) Validated edges

Fig. 1. Overview. The background and internal gradients in (b) throw off chamfer matching. (c) The class-specific validated edges help in removal of edges from clutter and internal gradients. Template matching works better on this edgemap. Note that most of the non-class edges have been suppressed, greatly simplifying subsequent processing such as object detection or class specific segmentation.

linked into chains automatically according to their spatial proximity as shown in figure 1(b), and all edge chains are manually annotated so they are positive if they lie on the boundary of an object instance; all other edge chains are negative.

There is then the question of how to represent the appearance (e.g. colour distribution), texture and shape of the edges. At the simplest level we could simply extract a patch around each edge point and use a feature vector consisting of the ordered colour pixels – this would implicitly capture the shape (since the edge boundary runs through the patch). It would also capture the texture since Varma and Zisserman [25] have shown that a simple patch feature is sufficient to classify texture in monochrome images. On the other hand, with such a simple representation we are not explicitly recording that the distributions on each side of the edge may be different. To deal with this point, we do use a simple patch centred on the edge, but rotate the patch so that its x-axis is aligned with the edge tangent (derived from the Canny operator and edge chains). In detail, we choose a $m \times n$ patch around the edge as our feature. This is rotated so that the edge chain runs horizontally through its centre, giving a rotationally invariant image descriptor. We also record the colour values of each pixel to represent the appearance ([25] only used grey values).

Classification. A Support Vector Machine (SVM) [16] is used to learn an edge classifier for the patch features. The parameters we need to learn are: the size of the patch; and for the SVM: the kernel type (we compare linear, RBF and

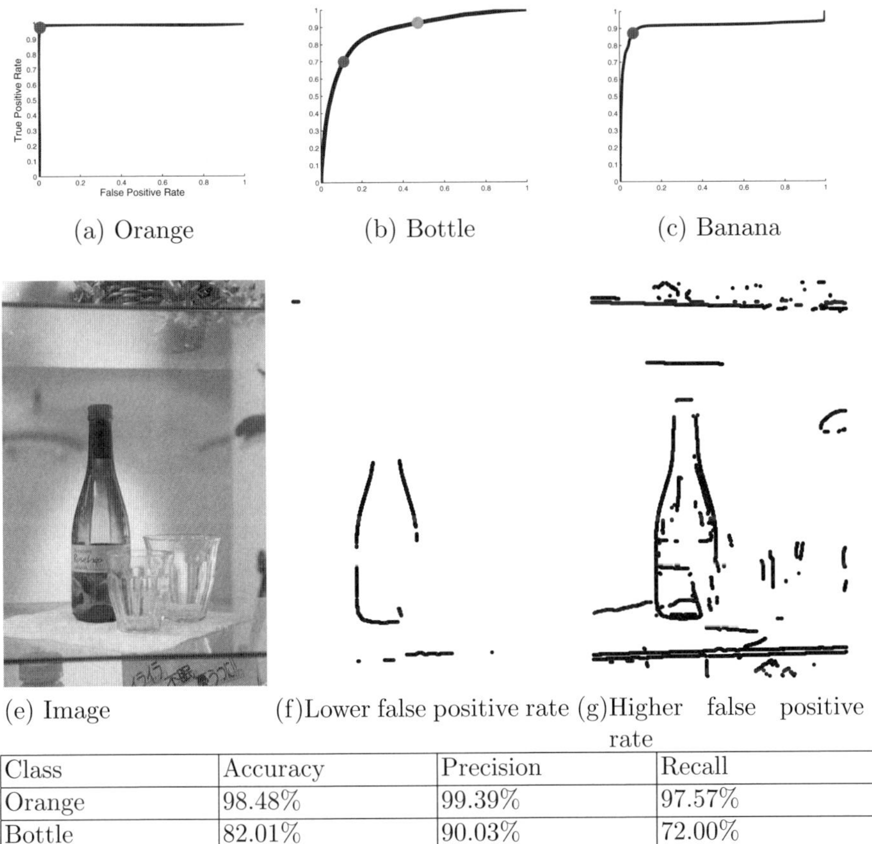

Class	Accuracy	Precision	Recall
Orange	98.48%	99.39%	97.57%
Bottle	82.01%	90.03%	72.00%
Banana	90.37%	92.79%	87.53%

Fig. 2. Edge Classification Results. The ROC curve plots the True Positive Rate against the False Positive Rate as the threshold is varied for classification between the minimum and maximum values of the SVM output. (f),(g) show edge classification with a variation in the operating point for the bottle image of (e). In (b) the operating point towards the left results in lower false positives as seen in (f) and a change to the green operating point on the right results in a higher false positive rate (g). The red points on (a),(b) and (c) show the operating point used for the datasets. The classification results at these operating points are given in the table.

polynomial kernels of degree $1, 2$ and 3) and the slack variables. Optimizing over the test data we find that the best performance for the orange and banana datasets is achieved with a polynomial kernel of degree 2, and with patches of size $m = 11$ (in the y direction) and $n = 11$ (in the x direction). For the bottle dataset, the RBF kernel shows superior performance, the size of the patches being the same.

Flip ambiguity. Our patches extracted from the images are rotationally invariant up to a flip factor. The object region can lie either on the top or bottom half of the patch. In the presence of dominant characteristics such as colour and texture, the patches can be flipped to remove this ambiguity. For the orange and banana classes, effective gaussian mixture models of colour characteristics are built from training data for this purpose.

For bottles the colour and texture is much more variable and hence gaussian mixture models for colour will not be helpful in disambiguation. For such categories the classifier will have to handle the ambiguity by choosing the appropriate support vectors and slack variables.

Alternatively, we can try to handle this ambiguity at the kernel level. We experimented with modifying the RBF kernels to internally flip the patches and choose the one which best optimizes the cost. For example, using the kernel

$$k(x, x') = \max\left(\exp\left(-\gamma\|x - x'\|^2\right), \exp\left(-\gamma\|x - \mathrm{flipud}(x')\|^2\right)\right)$$

where $\mathrm{flipud}(x)$ flips the patch vertically, with the intuition that the correct alignment of the patches (flipped or not) will have lower cost due to more consistency of the object region. However, upon experimentation, we find that this kernel (and similar modifications of linear kernels) have slightly inferior performance compared to the standard polynomial and RBF kernels. This difference is heightened if the category has a strong colour model.

For our three classes, the performance of the classifier is summarized in the table of figure 2. The accuracy, recall and precision are defined as

$$\begin{aligned}
\text{Accuracy} &= \left(\frac{tp+tn}{tp+fp+fn+tn}\right) & tp &= \text{True Positive} \\
\text{Precision} &= \left(\frac{tp}{tp+fp}\right) & tn &= \text{True Negative} \\
\text{Recall} &= \left(\frac{tp}{tp+fn}\right) & fp &= \text{False positive} \\
& & fn &= \text{False negative}
\end{aligned} \tag{1}$$

The models are fairly well learnt as can be seen from the receiver operator characteristic curves in the top row of figure 2. In the case of bottles, the lack of one distinctive colour or texture reduces our accuracy. For such object classes, (lacking distinctive colour or texture) other representations may be necessary. For example, texton distributions or separate local colour histograms for each side of the boundary. Other classifiers, such as Adaboost, may also be employed.

The veracity of classification on several example images is shown in figure 3. In subsequent sections we will use both the classification and also the distance from the decision boundary as a confidence measure. The occurrence of false positives and the degree of suppression of true negatives, can be controlled by

Edge labels: black: detected +ves, gray: detected −ves

Fig. 3. Edge classification. Example images and the class based edge classifications. A large number of edges from clutter, specularity and internal gradients that confuse template matching are discarded by this classification.

varying the operating point along the ROC curve. Figure 2 shows the varying result of suppression of false edges with the variation of the operating point.

3   Chamfer Matching

In this section we illustrate how edge specific classification can be used to improve the performance of an object detection algorithm based on chamfer matching. In chamfer matching a set of learnt object templates are matched to the detected edges in the image using a distance transform. The position at which the convolution of the template with the distance transform of the feature image (capped at a certain threshold for stability) is minimal, determines the match. Chamfer can be made more robust by taking orientation at edges into account.

In practice, an artificial template database is created by geometrical transformations of exemplar templates, and a hierarchical tree is built to enhance the search speed [6]. Given a test image, hierarchical chamfer matching is then used to fit the object model over the test image. With the occasional modification, this is a standard algorithm for object detection. However, this algorithm applied to the simple orange object class gives numerous and classic mismatches (figure 4 (a)).

3.1   Class Based Chamfer Matching

We use our edge classifier to determine the relevant edges for the current object of interest (see figure 3). Performing chamfer matching on only the positive edges from the classifier output results in a tremendous improvement (figure 4(b)) compared to the original truncated oriented chamfer matching (figure 4(a)) . This can be used to improve any algorithm that uses template matching, such as OBJCUT.

(a) Basic Chamfer   (b) Chamfer with   (c) Improved

class-specific edges   OBJCUT

Fig. 4. Improving Chamfer for object localization. (a) Chamfer Matching using all image edges. The matches latch on to irrelevant edges corresponding to internal gradients and specularities (first row), and clutter (circular lid, second and third row). **(b)** Matching on *class* edges and texture. This leads to better matching – compare with the confusions arising from the problems in (a). **(c)** Modified OBJCUT results are much more accurate.

4   Class Based Segmentation — OBJCUT

In this section we illustrate how edge specific classification can be used to improve the performance of an object segmentation algorithm. In particular we modify the OBJCUT algorithm of Kumar *et al.* [10]. OBJCUT is a Bayesian method for class based binary segmentation using Object Category Specific Markov Random Field (MRF) and Pictorial Structures. In practice it is implemented in two stages:

1. Initialization–the edges and texture features in the image are used to determine the object's position in the image (as in §3)
2. Segmentation–the match found is used to initialize the image segmentation. Graph cuts are used to optimize the energy over an Object Category Specific MRF.

We change this method to affect two terms in the OBJCUT energy function using class-based edge classification: (i) As in §3 we modify the initialization by chamfer matching to only use class specific edges; and, (ii) We modify the boundary term in the MRF to encourage segmentation along high contrast regions, *but* only if they are relevant to the object class. This is described in more detail below.

4.1   The Boundary Term

Following [2] the MRF used in OBJCUT has a contrast dependent prior. This means that a segmentation which introduces a change of state between pixels (i.e. a change from foreground to background in this case) adds a cost to the energy, *but* this cost is diminished if there is a strong gradient between the pixels (as measured in the image/data). The inclusion of data-dependent pairwise terms for pixels in a clique gives a substantial improvement in segmentation quality, and the resulting MRF can still be minimized using graph cuts as described in [2].

We are given an image $\mathbf{D}$ containing an instance of the object. The label at each pixel x is denoted by m_x. We want the algorithm to consider only those edges that are relevant to the object class. Therefore, only those edges of the MRF which coincide with object boundaries are weakened. Our edge classification (§2) gives us a likelihood $edge(x)$, for every pixel x (+ve for valid

Table 1. Average number of misclassified pixels per image

Object class	OBJCUT	OBJCUT + modified MRF	OBJCUT + modified MRF + chamfer matching
Orange	2947	2457	256
Bottle	8121	8064	4077

Fig. 5. More results. The performance of our method on some examples is shown on the banana, orange and bottle datasets. This dataset, has a wide range of challenges from pose, scale, clutter and lighting. In the presence of multiple instances, we use the best Chamfer match as shown in Row 1. The segmentation using the initialization from Row 1, 3 and 5, by the improved OBJCUT is shown on Row 2, 4 and 6.

boundary, $-$ve otherwise). A new boundary term is defined, which adds to the category specificity of the MRF:

$$\zeta(\mathbf{D}|m_x, m_y) = \begin{cases} \lambda * \exp(-edge(x)) & \text{if edge exists} \\ \text{constant} & \text{for no edge at } x \end{cases} \tag{2}$$

λ is the parameter controlling the influence of this boundary term.

4.2 Implementation

For OBJCUT with the modified category specific MRF and shape model, the optimal parameters must be found. A large number of parameters (around 20) are identified for the model to be learnt. $5-6$ control the relative weights between the colour likelihoods, shape likelihoods, prior and the boundary terms, and are most crucial for performance and strongly interrelated. A simple, gradient descent is performed to optimize performance on the ground truth labelling over this subset of important parameters. Subsequently, the other parameters can be individually optimized in a similar manner. We start with large step sizes for gradient descent and reduce them as we refine our estimates.

4.3 Results

The performance is measured by the number of misclassified pixels in the test data with respect to the manually segmented ground truth. Table 1 summarizes the results for two object classes.

We choose 23 images with single oranges for optimization with respect to ground truth. The basic OBJCUT (optimized for performance) yields segmentation over 22 out of the 23 images with an average misclassification of 2947.2 pixels per image. (Note: Each image has an average of 90, 000 pixels). OBJCUT with a modified MRF (with the boundary term using only relevant edges) yields segmentation over 22 images with an average misclassification of 2457.3 pixels per image. The final OBJCUT with modifications at both the Chamfer matching (top) and MRF (low) levels yields segmentations over all of the 23 images over which we are optimizing. The per image error reduces drastically to 255.5 pixels per image. Note: Each image has 90, 000 pixels on an average. For the orange class, we get visually correct segmentations for 47 out of 50 images. For the bottle class, we get 57 correct segmentations out of 90 images. The banana dataset is our most challenging dataset, owing to the wide shape variations and image clutter. We get good segmentations of around 37 out of 60 images. While both our edge based modifications improve OBJCUT, the use of relevant edges in chamfer matching makes the more significant difference (see figures 4,(c) and 5).

5 Conclusion

We have demonstrated the advantages in using class specific edges both for Chamfer matching and segmentation. However, the implications of such class specific edge labelling are many fold — since any algorithm for object classes using edges can now be improved. Examples include tracking, segmentation [22] and recognition [5,14,19]. Of course, the performance of the classifier can be improved and we are currently investigating other feature vectors and classifiers such as boosted trees [24]. We are also interested in finding efficient methods for parameter optimization. This is important for optimal results with algorithms like OBJCUT and for experimentation with new kernels.

References

1. S. Belongie, J. Malik, and J. Puzicha. Matching shapes. In *Proc. ICCV*, volume 1, pages 454–461, 2001.
2. Y. Boykov and M. Jolly. Interactive graph cuts for optimal boundary and region segmentation of objects in n-d images. In *ICCV*, pages 105–112, 2001.
3. O. Carmichael, S. Mahamud, and M. Hebert. Discriminant filters for object recognition. Technical Report CMU-RI-TR-02-09, Carnegie Mellon University, Mar 2002.
4. P. Dollar, T. Zhuowen, and S. Belongie. Supervised learning of edges and object boundaries. In *Proc. CVPR*, 2006.
5. V. Ferrari, T. Tuytelaars, and L.J. Van Gool. Object detection by contour segment networks. pages III: 14–28, 2006.
6. D. Gavrila. Pedestrian detection from a moving vehicle. In *Proc. ECCV*, pages II: 37–49, 2000.
7. D. P. Huttenlocher and S. Ullman. Object recognition using alignment. In *Proc. ICCV*, pages 102–111, 1987.
8. T. Joachims. Making large-scale support vector machine learning practical. In A. Smola B. Schölkopf, C. Burges, editor, *Advances in Kernel Methods: Support Vector Machines*. MIT Press, Cambridge, MA, 1998.
9. M. P. Kumar, P. H. S. Torr, and A. Zisserman. Extending pictorial structures for object recognition. In *Proc. BMVC.*, 2004.
10. M.P. Kumar, P.H.S. Torr, and A. Zisserman. OBJ CUT. In *Proc. CVPR*, pages I: 18–25, 2005.
11. D. G. Lowe. Three-dimensional object recognition from single two-dimensional images. *Artificial Intelligence*, 31(3):355–395, 1987.
12. K. McHenry and J. Ponce. A geodesic active contour framework for finding glass. In *Proc. CVPR*, 2006.
13. K. McHenry, J. Ponce, and D. A. Forsyth. Finding glass. In *Proc. CVPR*, pages 973–979, 2005.
14. A. Opelt, A. Pinz, and A. Zisserman. Incremental learning of object detectors using a visual alphabet. In *Proc. CVPR*, 2006.
15. C. Rothwell, A. Zisserman, D. Forsyth, and J. Mundy. Canonical frames for planar object recognition. In *Proc. ECCV*, LNCS 588. Springer-Verlag, 1992.
16. B. Scholkopf and A. Smola. *Learning with Kernels*. MIT Press, 2002.
17. E. Seemann, B. Leibe, K. Mikolajczyk, and B. Schiele. An evaluation of local shape-based features for pedestrian detection. In *Proc. BMVC.*, 2005.
18. A. Shahrokni, F. Fleuret, and P. Fua. Classifier-based contour tracking for rigid and deformable objects. In *Proc. BMVC.*, Oxford, UK, 2005.
19. J. Shotton, A. Blake, and R. Cipolla. Contour-based learning for object detection. In *Proc. ICCV*, pages I: 503–510, 2005.
20. H. Sidenbladh and M. Black. Learning image statistics for bayesian tracking. In *Proc. ECCV*, 2001.
21. B. Stenger, A. Thayananthan, P.H.S. Torr, and R. Cipolla. Hand pose estimation using hierarchical detection. In *CVHCI04*, pages 105–116, 2004.
22. J. Sun, W. Zhang, X. Tang, and H. Shum. Background cut. In *Proc. ECCV*, 2006.

23. A. Thayananthan, B. Stenger, P.H.S. Torr, and R. Cipolla. Shape context and chamfer matching in cluttered scenes. In *Proc. CVPR*, pages I: 127–133, 2003.
24. Z. Tu. Probabilistic boosting-tree: Learning discriminative models for classification, recognition, and clustering. In *Proc. ICCV*, pages II: 1589–1596, 2005.
25. M. Varma and A. Zisserman. Texture classification: Are filter banks necessary? In *Proc. CVPR*, volume 2, pages 691–698, Jun 2003.

Nonparametric Neural Network Model Based on Rough-Fuzzy Membership Function for Classification of Remotely Sensed Images

Niraj Kumar and Anupam Agrawal

Indian Institute of Information Technology, Allahabad – 211 011

Abstract. A nonparametric neural network model based on Rough-Fuzzy Membership function, multilayer perceptron, and back-propagation algorithm is described. The described model is capable to deal with rough uncertainty as well as fuzzy uncertainty associated with classification of remotely sensed multi-spectral images. The input vector consists of membership values to linguistic properties while the output vector is defined in terms of rough fuzzy class membership values. This allows efficient modeling of indiscernibility and fuzziness between patterns by appropriate weights being assigned to the back-propagated errors depending upon the Rough-Fuzzy Membership values at the corresponding outputs. The effectiveness of the model is demonstrated on classification problem of IRS-P6 LISS IV images of Allahabad area. The results are compared with statistical (Minimum Distance), conventional MLP, and FMLP models.

1 Introduction

Geospatial information, we gather through different sensors and from the concepts of the geographical objects, is generally vague, imprecise and uncertain. Also, the imprecision becomes obvious due to the multi-granular structure of the multi-sensor satellite images and that leads to error accumulation at every stage in geo-processing. It has been observed that the ground truth data, an essential ingredient for a supervised learning, may itself contain redundant, inconsistent, conflicting information.

The geospatial information is received in different windows of the electromagnetic spectrum and at different resolutions. This presents selective look of the geospatial objects under view of the satellite sensor. Therefore, the totality of capturing the truth or facets of the objects seems to be very difficult. This implies that at a given set of parameters of observation, we have limited capability to discern two objects. It is equivalent to say that the knowledge generated from the satellite image at a given resolution and spectrum band, is granular. It is, therefore, imperative to have more observational parameters to decompose this granule, i.e. to obtain finer view of the objects. The effect is that based on the observational parameters, any two objects, may appear same, whereas, the ground truths about the objects force us to have different opinion on them. This phenomenon introduces the rough uncertainty into the

P. Kalra and S. Peleg (Eds.): ICVGIP 2006, LNCS 4338, pp. 106–117, 2006.

information system due to imprecision inducted by the observation system. Since the boundaries of various land covers in satellite image are not precise, so fuzzy uncertainty is also associated here.

After the Fuzzy Set theory [4], the Rough Set theory proposed by Z. Pawlak [1], has emerged as another major mathematical approach for managing uncertainty that arises from inexact, noisy, or incomplete information. The focus of rough set theory is on the ambiguity caused by limited discenibility of objects in the domain of discourse.

In this paper, we have attempted to integrate rough sets, fuzzy sets, and artificial neural network (ANN) for designing a nonparametric rough fuzzy neural network model to deal with indiscernibility and fuzziness between patterns. Here we have used the generalized concept of rough membership function in pattern classification tasks to Rough-Fuzzy Membership functions to deal with rough uncertainty [9] in geospatial information gathered by satellites and in ground truth data. Unlike the rough membership value of a pattern, which is sensitive only towards the rough uncertainty associated with the pattern, the rough-fuzzy membership value of the pattern signifies the rough uncertainty as well as the fuzzy uncertainty associated with the pattern.

2 Background

2.1 Rough Sets

Let R be an equivalence relation on a universal set X. Moreover, let X/R denote the family of all equivalence classes introduced on X by R. One such equivalence class in X/R, that contains $x \in X$, is designed by $[x]_R$. For any output class $A \subseteq X$, we can define the lower $\underline{R}(A)$ and upper $\overline{R}(A)$ approximation which approaches A as closely as possibly from inside and outside respectively [9]. Here

$$R(A) = \cup \left\{ [x]_R \mid [x]_R \subseteq A, x \in X \right\} \qquad (1\text{-a})$$

is the union of all equivalence classes in X/R that are contained in A, and

$$\overline{R}(A) = \cup \left\{ [x]_R \mid [x]_R \cap A \neq \phi, x \in X \right\} \qquad (1\text{-b})$$

is the union of all equivalence classes in X/R that overlap with A. A rough set $R(A) = \langle \overline{R}(A), \underline{R}(A) \rangle$ is a representation of the given set A by $\overline{R}(A)$ and $\underline{R}(A)$. The set $BN(A) = \overline{R}(A) - \underline{R}(A)$ is a rough description of the boundary of A by the equivalence classes of X/R. The approximation is rough uncertainty free if $\overline{R}(A) = \underline{R}(A)$. Thus, when all the patterns from an equivalence class do not carry the same output class labels, rough ambiguity is generated as a manifestation of the one-to-many relationship between that equivalence class and the output class labels.

The rough membership function $r_A(x) : A \to [0,1]$ of a pattern $x \in X$ in the output class A is defined by

$$r_A(x) = \frac{\|[x]_R \cap A\|}{\|[x]_R\|}$$

(2)

where $\|A\|$ denotes the cardinality of the set A.

2.2 Fuzzy Sets

In traditional two-state classifiers, where a class A is defined as a subset of a universal set X, any input pattern $x \in X$ can either be a member or not be a member of the given class A. This property of whether or not a pattern x of the universal set belongs to the class A can be defined by a characteristic function $\mu_A(x): X \to \{0,1\}$ as follows

$$\mu_A(x) = \begin{cases} 1 & \text{if and only if } x \in A \\ 0 & \text{Otherwise} \end{cases}$$

(3)

In real life situations, however, boundaries between the classes may be overlapping. Hence, it is uncertain whether an input pattern belongs totally to the class A. To take care of such situations, in fuzzy sets the concept of characteristic function has been modified to membership function $\mu_A(x): X \to [0,1]$. This function is called membership function, because larger value of the function denotes more membership of the element to the set under consideration.

2.3 Rough Fuzzy Sets

Let X is a set, R is an equivalence relation defined on X and the output class $A \subseteq X$ is a fuzzy set. A rough-fuzzy set is a tuple $\langle \overline{R}(A), \underline{R}(A) \rangle$, where the lower approximation $\underline{R}(A)$ and the upper approximation $\overline{R}(A)$ of A are fuzzy sets of X/R, with membership functions defined by

$$\mu_{\underline{R}(A)}\left([x]_R\right) = \inf\left\{\mu_A(x) \mid x \in [x]_R\right\}$$

(4-a)

$$\mu_{\overline{R}(A)}\left([x]_R\right) = \sup\left\{\mu_A(x) \mid x \in [x]_R\right\}$$

(4-b)

Here, $\mu_{\underline{R}(A)}\left([x]_R\right)$ and $\mu_{\overline{R}(A)}\left([x]_R\right)$ are the membership values of $[x]_R$ in $\underline{R}(A)$ and $\overline{R}(A)$, respectively.

2.4 Rough-Fuzzy Membership Function

The rough-fuzzy membership function of a pattern $x \in X$ for the fuzzy output class $C_i = A \subseteq X$ is defined by [9]

$${}^{I}C_i = \frac{\|F \cap C_i\|}{\|F\|} \tag{5}$$

where $F = [x]_R$ and $\|C_i\|$ means the cardinality of the fuzzy set C_i. One possible way to determine the cardinality is to use: $\|C_i\| \overset{def}{=} \underset{x \in X}{\Sigma} \left(\mu_{C_c}(x) \right)$ For the '$\cap$' (intersection) operation, we can use

$$\mu_{A \cap B}(x) \overset{def}{=} \min \left\{ \mu_A(x), \mu_B(x) \right\} \forall x \in X \tag{6}$$

It must be noted that, the concept of rough-fuzzy set is necessary when dealing with ambiguous concepts, whereas rough-fuzzy membership function is needed when uncertain data are considered.

3   Related Work

The main approaches to classification of remote sensing images are statistical methods [10], Artificial Neural Network methods [11], Fuzzy methods [12], [16], Fuzzy neural networks [13], Multi-source classification methods [14] and Hybrid approaches [15]. Statistical methods like Parallelepiped method, Minimum distance classifier, and Maximum likelihood classifier are very much dependent on the distribution of classes.

There has been a spurt of activity to integrate different computing paradigms such as fuzzy set theory, neural networks, genetic algorithms, and rough set theory, for generating more efficient hybrid systems that can be classified as *soft computing* methodologies. The purpose is to provide flexible information processing systems that can exploit the tolerance for imprecision, uncertainty, approximate reasoning, and partial truth in order to achieve tractability, robustness, and low cost in real life ambiguous situations [2]. Neuro-fuzzy computing [3] captures the merits of fuzzy set theory [4] and artificial neural networks [5]. This integration promises to provide, to a great extent, more intelligent systems (in terms of parallelism, fault tolerance, adaptivity, and uncertainty management) to handle real-life recognition/decision making problems. But all these models only deal with fuzzy uncertainty.

Artificial Neural networks are generally described as nonparametric. The performance of the neural network depends to a significant extent on how well it has been trained and not on the adequacy of assumptions concerning the statistical distribution of the data. The most popular neural network classifier in remote sensing is the multi-layer perceptron. Classification can also be carried out by other main type of neural networks such as SOM and fuzzy ARTMAP [15].

A fuzzy classification is a soft classification, which is used to find out uncertainty in the boundary between classes and to extract the mixed pixel information. This is achieved by applying a function called "membership function" on remotely sensed images. Using "hard" classification methods, we cannot measure the uncertainty in an image whereas in a fuzzy classification technique, we can get more information from the data [12]. Fuzzy multilayer perceptron (FMLP) introduced by Pal and Mitra [13], is a fuzzy version of MLP having advantages of both neural network and fuzzy logic. It employs the supervised back propagation learning algorithm and incorporates fuzzy set-theoretic concepts in both input and output stages.

Many researchers have looked into the implementation of decision rules extracted from operation data using rough set formalism, especially in problems of machine learning from examples and control theory [6]. In the context of neural networks, an attempt of such implementation has been made by Yasdi [7]. The intention was to use rough sets as a tool for structuring the neural networks. The methodology consisted of generating rules from training examples by rough-set learning, and mapping the dependency factors of the rules into the connection weights of a four-layered neural network. Application of rough sets in neurocomputing has also been made in [8]. However, in this method, rough sets were used for knowledge discovery at the level of data acquisition, (*viz.*, in preprocessing of the feature vectors), and not for structuring the network.

4   Proposed Method

As explained in section 1 due the multi-granular structure of the multi-sensor satellite images, we have limited capability to discern two objects. The effect is that based on the observational parameters, any two objects, may appear same, whereas, the ground truths about the objects forces us to have different opinion on them, i.e. we must have to deal with rough uncertainty in association with fuzzy uncertainty to obtain better classification accuracy. The fuzzy MLP model explained in [13] and fuzzy classification model proposed by Farid [16] only deals with fuzzy uncertainty. Apart from that, extraction of class-conditional spectral parameters using mean and standard deviation from supervised training sites of pure pixels used in the FMLP is dependent on the distribution of the reflectance values. In [17] it is observed that Neural Network classifiers as compared to statistical classifiers are nonparametric (distribution free). Statistical classifiers give incorrect results when reflectance values of classes are very close.

The proposed method effectively copes up with these two problems and provides better classification accuracy. The steps of the proposed method are described below.

Step 1: Generating equivalence classes for M_1 pure labeled training vectors

Let U be the set of M_1 pure labeled pixels i.e. $U = \left\{ (x_1, y_1), ..., \left(x_{M_1}, y_{M_1} \right) \right\}$

where (x_i, y_i) represents a pure labeled pixel and $A = \left(U, A \cup \{d\} \right)$ be a decision system, where $A = \{a_1, a_2, ..., a_D\}$ is the set of conditional attributes such that $a_j(X_i) = f_{i,j}$, D is the dimensionality of the input feature, d is the decision attribute such that $d(X_i) = Y_i$ where $Y_i = (y_{i,1}, ... y_{i,L})$, L is the total number of land cover classes and $|U| = M_1$.

The equivalence relation $IND(A) = \left\{ (x_i, x_j) \in U \times U : \forall_{a \in A} \left(a(x_i) = a(x_j) \right) \right\}$ divides the set of objects U into equivalence classes and two objects belong to the same class if and only if they have the same values on attributes from A. It is to be noted that if each equivalence class generated by $IND(A)$ contains the objects belonging to same output class then there is no rough uncertainty. Here we can also use rough set to find the reduct $B \subseteq A$ (B is the reduced set of attributes while maintaining the decision capability of the decision table) and then generate the equivalence classes corresponding to $IND(B)$. Let $[x]_{IND(A)}$ represents the equivalence class to which x belongs. The equivalence class $[x]_{IND(A)}$ can be understood as a degenerated fuzzy set with those elements belonging to the class possessing a membership of one, and zero otherwise.

Step 2: Assigning fuzzy membership grade to each fuzzy output class for M_1 pure labeled pixels

The M_1 pixels under consideration are pure labeled pixels i.e. for them we are confirmed that to which class they belongs, so here we are taking the fuzzy membership value to the appropriate class as 0.9 and to others as 0.1/(L-1), where L is the number of land cover classes. Thus for this stage membership function can be defined as

$$\mu_{C_i}(x) = \begin{cases} 0.9 & \text{if Ci is the appropriate class of x} \\ 0.1/(L-1) & \text{Otherwise} \end{cases} \tag{7}$$

where C_i, i=1,2,.....,L is the fuzzy output class.

Step 3: Calculating Rough-Fuzzy membership grade to each fuzzy output class for M_1 pure labeled pixels

The Rough-Fuzzy membership value $^lC_i(x)$, to class C_i for input vector x =(f_1,...f_D) is calculated using the equation (5) described in section 2.4.

Step 4: Designing and training neural network for M_1 pure labeled pixels

A (H+1) layered MLP with D neurons in input and L neurons in output layer, consisting of H-1 hidden layers, is trained by clamping the input vector $X_i = \left(f_{i,1}, ... f_{i,D} \right)$ at input layer and the desired L-dimensional output vector with components $^lC_i(x)$ at the output layer.

Step 5: Computation of Rough-Fuzzy membership grades for M_1 pure and M_2 unlabeled mixed training vectors

In this step M_2 unlabeled mixed training samples are included in the training set. For (M_1+M_2) training vectors we calculate the rough-fuzzy membership grade to each class by clamping the input vector $X_i = \left(f_{i,1}, ... f_{i,D} \right)$ i=1, 2,...., M_1+M_2 at the input layer of neural network trained in the previous step. The output values of the training vectors are normalized such that all the membership values of the classes sum up to 1.

Normalization is done by first obtaining the total output sum and then all the output values are divided by the total sum. Obtaining membership values using Neural network makes the Rough Neuro-Fuzzy classifier independent of class reflectance distribution and inclusion of unlabeled pixels helps in increasing the classification accuracy.

Step 6: Input data fuzzification

The (M_1+M_2) labeled training vectors are fuzzified before being employed in the FMLP training session. This means that every non-normal component of input pattern $X_i = \left(f_{i,1}, \ldots f_{i,D} \right)$, i=1,........, M_1+M_2 is converted into normal degrees of membership to fuzzy linguistic sets low, medium, and high as explained in [13].

Step 7: Supervised training of final Rough Neuro-Fuzzy network via backpropagation algorithm

The complete training set, consisting of (M_1+M_2) training vectors, is employed by the traditional error backpropagation algorithm to train Rough Neuro Fuzzy Network. The proposed Rough Neuro Fuzzy Network is an (H+1)-layered MLP with $3 \times D$ neurons in the input layer and L neurons in output layer, such that there are H-1 hidden layers. The input vector, with components fuzzified as in [13], is clamped at the input layer while the desired L-dimension output vector obtained in step 5 is clamped during training at the output layer.

5   Results and Discussion

Two study areas from high resolution multi-spectral IRS-P6 LISS-IV satellite image of Allahabad region acquired in April 2004 are selected for classification purpose. The spatial resolution of the images is 5.8 m. Three bands available in IRS-P6 LISS-IV are taken into consideration for analysis. The two LISS-IV satellite images are first geo-referenced using 15 well distributed Ground control points (GCP) for each image collected using Leica GS5 GPS receiver and then the images were converted to Geo-tiff image format. This is just to make the analysis work easier. The first study area has a geographical extent of $81^{\circ}45'36.07''E$ to $81^{\circ}47'23.67''E$ and $25^{\circ}26'23.92''N$ to $25^{\circ}25'12.42''N$ and second study area has a geographical extent of $81^{\circ}51'49.53''E$ to $81^{\circ}53'17.57''E$ and $25^{\circ}26'30.63''N$ to $25^{\circ}27'27.37''N$.

For study area 1 there are totally seven predefined classes for three bands in the image which are used for analysis. For study area 2 there are totally six predefined classes for three bands in the image which are used for analysis.

MATLAB is used for writing program for classification. MATLAB Mapping toolbox is used to read shape files and geo registered images. A well distributed 90 ground truth pixels were collected using the GPS receiver for each class in each study area. Out of these 90 pixels, 50 pixels were used from training of ANN and remaining 40 were used for accuracy assessment. Pixels were collected as 2D point shapefiles. Overall accuracy, User's accuracy, Producer's accuracy and Kappa Coefficient [10] of the proposed methodology are compared with statistical, neural network, and FMLP models. Fig. 1(a) and Fig. 1(b) show the study area 1 and study area 2 respectively.

Fig. 2(a) and Fig. 2(b) show the classified images of study area 1 and study area 2 respectively, using statistical method (Minimum Distance).

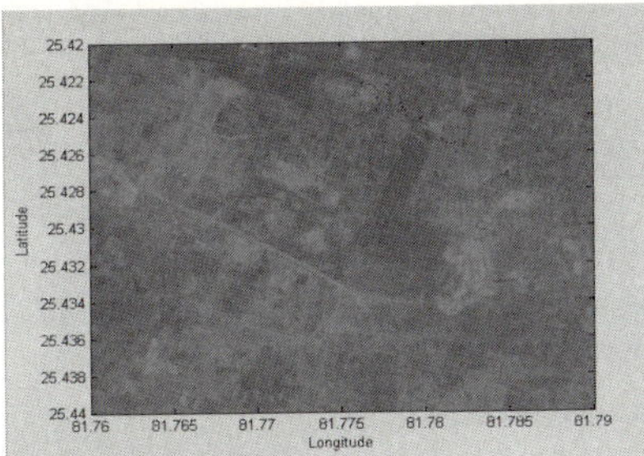

Fig. 1(a). Study area 1

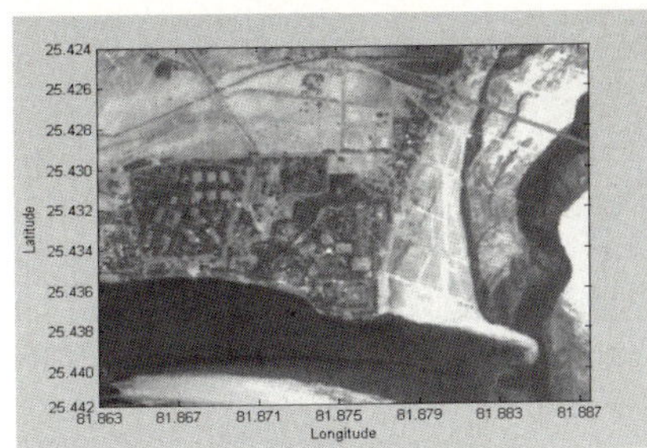

Fig. 1(b). Study area 2

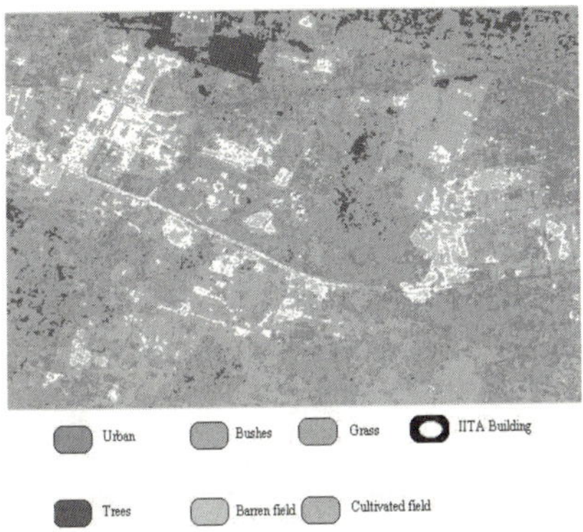

Fig. 2(a). Classified Study area 1 byStatistical method

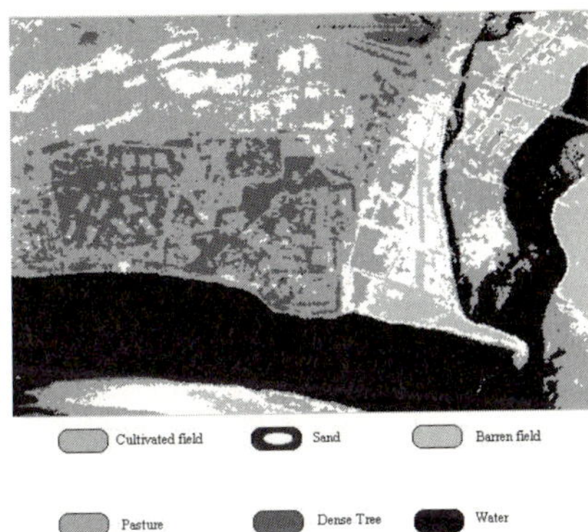

Fig. 2(b). Classified Study area 2 by Statistical method

Fig. 3(a) and Fig. 3(b) show the classified images of study area 1 and study area 2 respectively, using Neural Network method.

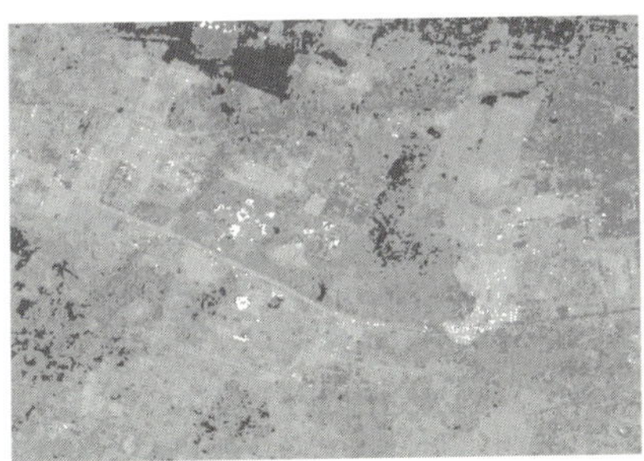

Fig. 3(a). Classified Study area 1 by Neural Network method

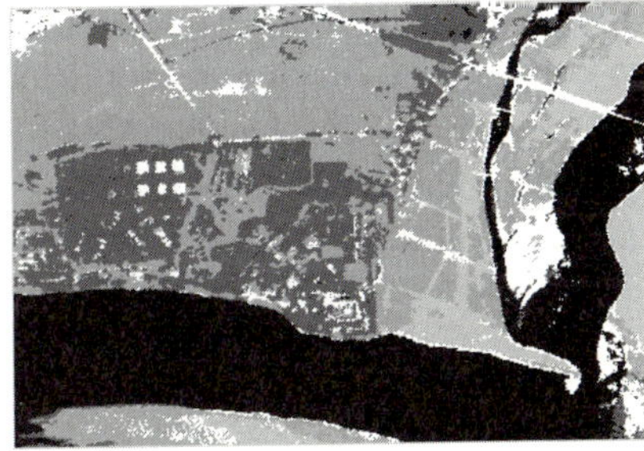

Fig. 3(b). Classified Study area 2 by Neural Network method

Fig. 4(a) and Fig. 4(b) show the classified images of study area 1 and study area 2 respectively, using the FMLP method.

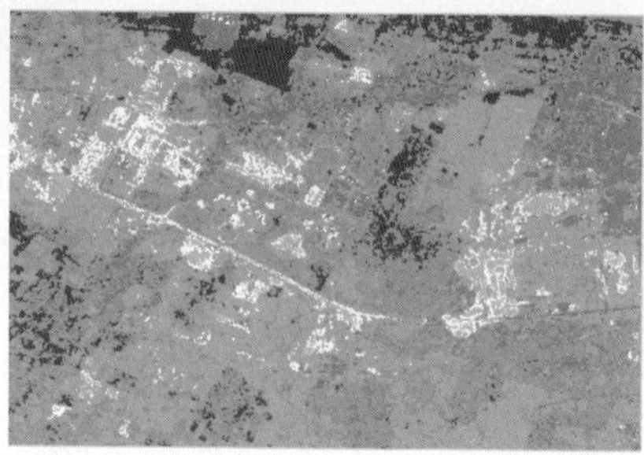

Fig. 4(a). Classified Study area 1 by FMLP method

Fig. 4(b). Classified Study area 2 by FMLP method

Fig. 5(a) and Fig. 5(b) show the classified images of study area 1 and study area 2 respectively, using the proposed method.

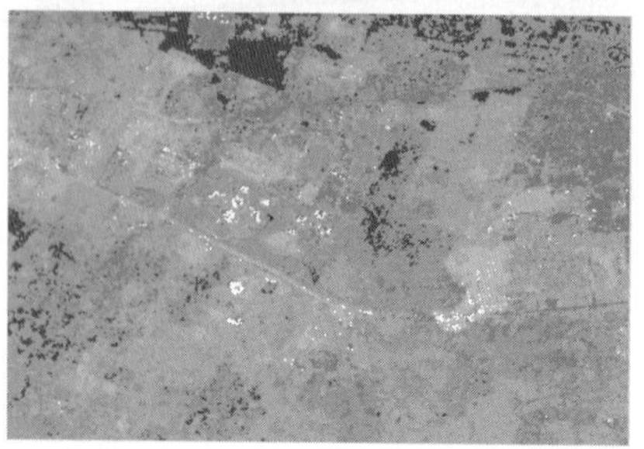

Fig. 5(a). Classified Study area 1 by proposed method

Fig. 5(b). Classified Study area 2 by proposed method

Table 1 briefly shows the overall accuracy and Kappa coefficients for the Statistical (Minimum Distance), Neural Network, FMLP, and the proposed method in cases of study area 1 and study area 2.

Fig. 6(a) and Fig. 6(b) show the plots of overall accuracy for study area 1 and study area 2 respectively, in case of various classifiers.

Table 1. Overall Accuracy and Kappa coefficients for study area 1 and study area 2

	Overall Accuracy	Kappa Coefficient	Overall Accuracy	Kappa Coefficient
	Study area 1		Study area 2	
Statistical	94.29%	93.31%	93.33%	92.04%
Neural Network	94.64%	93.68%	94.17%	92.99%
FMLP	92.86%	91.38%	86.67%	84.25%
Proposed	97.14%	96.61%	97.5%	96.95%

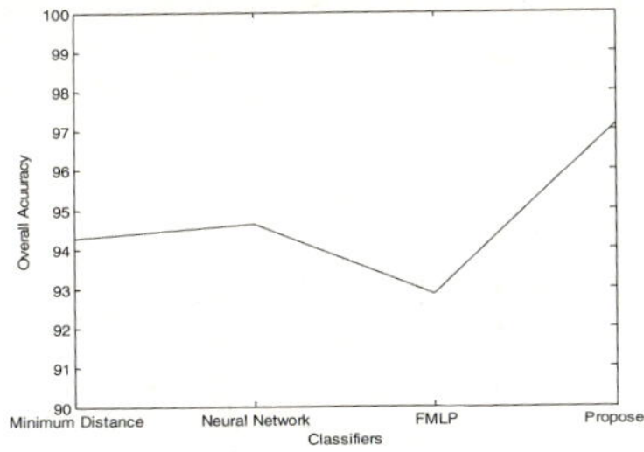

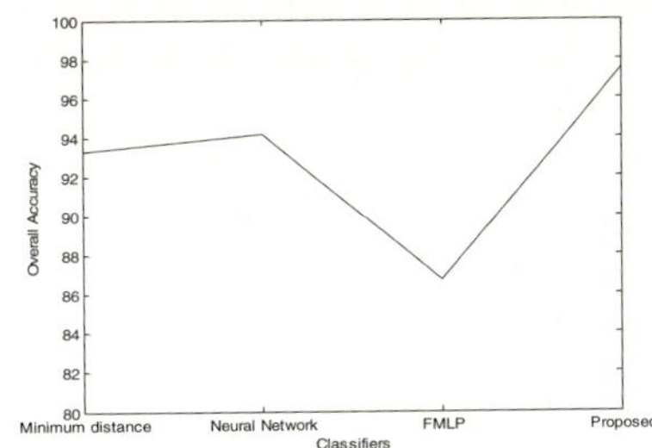

Fig. 6(a). Plot of Overall Accuracy for study area 1

Fig. 6(b). Plot of Overall Accuracy for study area 2

Fig. 7(a) and Fig. 7(b) show the plots of Kappa Coefficients for study area 1 and study area 2 respectively, in case of various classifiers.

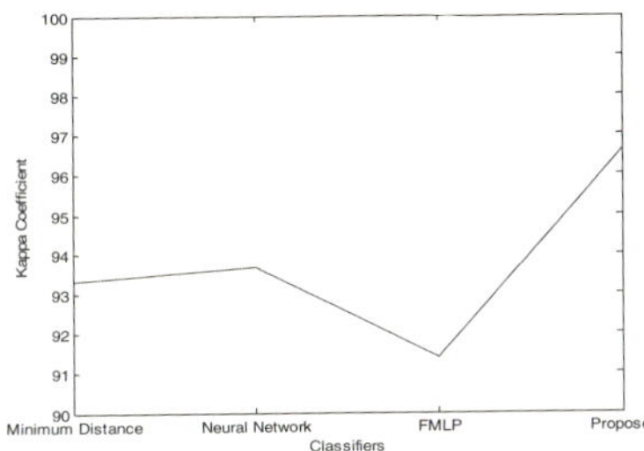

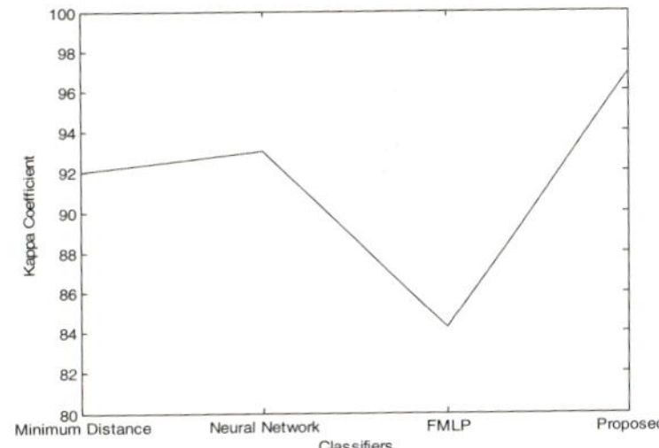

Fig. 7(a). Plot of Kappa Coefficient for study area 1

Fig. 7(b). Plot of Kappa Coefficient for study area 2

Fig. 8(a) and Fig. 8(b) show the bar charts of User's accuracy for study area 1 and study area 2 respectively, in case of various classifiers.

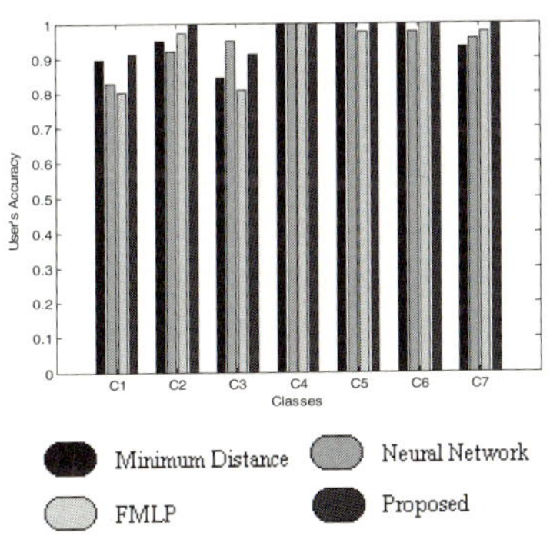

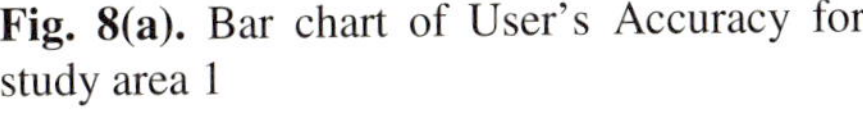

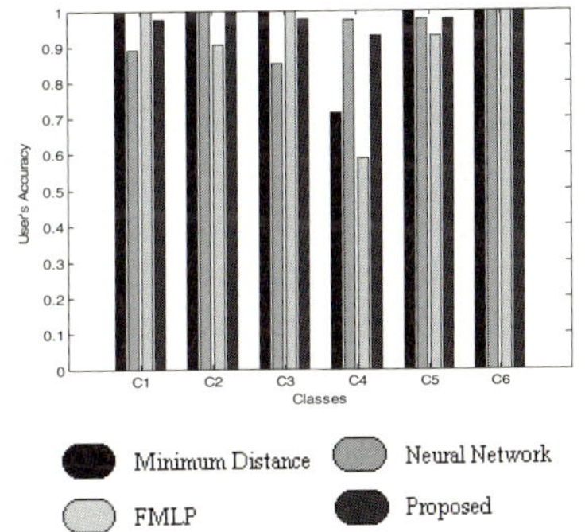

Fig. 8(a). Bar chart of User's Accuracy for study area 1

Fig. 8(b). Bar chart of User's Accuracy for study area 2

Fig. 9(a) and Fig. 9(b) show the bar charts of Producer's accuracy for study area 1 and study area 2 respectively, in case of various classifiers.

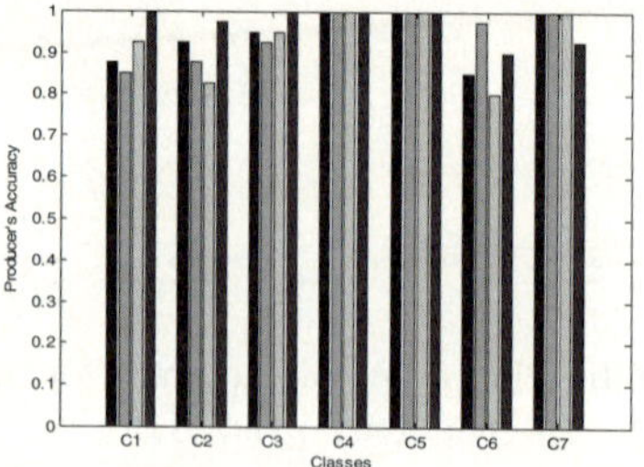

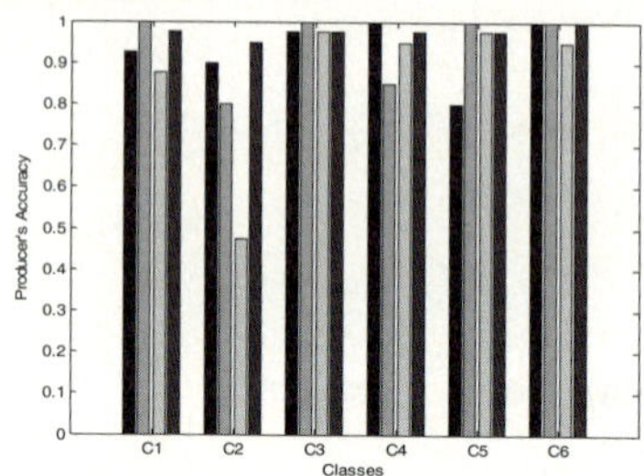

Fig. 9(a). Bar chart of Producer's Accuracy for study area 1

Fig. 9(b). Bar chart of Producer's Accuracy for study area 2

From the comparison of overall accuracy and Kappa Coefficients it becomes clear that the proposed method is giving better results in comparison to other ones. The proposed method also gives better User's and Producer's accuracy in case of most of the classes. The proposed method is distribution free, and is capable enough to handle fuzzy uncertainty as well as rough uncertainty associated with the satellite image classification process.

6 Conclusions and Future Scope

From this experimentation we found that the concept of rough set plays an important role for getting better accuracy in case of multispectral image classification. We see that the knowledge generated from the satellite image at a given resolution and spectrum band is granular, which generates rough uncertainty in data/information. This uncertainty can not be dealt with by simply considering the overlapness in terms of fuzzy logic. To deal with this situation, we have to consider the vagueness which is generated due to insufficiency of knowledge about the event, data or world. FMLP only considers the fuzzy uncertainty associated with data. Moreover, the initial fuzzy membership value calculation is also dependent on distribution of data. In the proposed Rough Neuro-Fuzzy method we tried to deal with both of these flaws. By the use of Rough-Fuzzy membership value in place of simple fuzzy membership value, we can effectively model rough uncertainty as well as fuzzy uncertainty. The use of neural network to generate Rough-Fuzzy Membership value for final training vectors makes the whole model distribution free. The experimental results shown in the previous section are supporting for the same.

As a further improvement in the proposed approach, instead of using classical equivalence classes we can use fuzzy equivalence classes based on weak fuzzy similarity relation. By using this we can model the fuzziness associated in multispectral image classification more effectively.

References

1. Pawlak, Z.: Rough Sets - Theoretical Aspects of Reasoning about Data. Kluwer Academic Publishers, Dordrecht (1991)
2. Zadeh L.A.: Fuzzy Logic, Neural Networks, and Soft Computing. Comm. ACM, 37 (1994), 77-84
3. Bezdek, J.C., Pal, S.K.: Fuzzy Models For Pattern Recognition: Methods that Search for Structures in Data. IEEE Press, New York (1992)
4. Zadeh, L.A.: Fuzzy sets. Inform. Contr., 8(1965) 338–353
5. Lippmann, R.P.: An Introduction to Computing with Neural Nets. IEEE Acoust., Speech, Signal Processing Mag., 4(1987) 4–22
6. Slowinski, R. (Eds.): Intelligent Decision Support - Handbook of Applications and Advances of the Rough Sets Theory. Kluwer Academic Publishers (1992)
7. Yasdi, R.: Combining Rough Sets Learning and Neural Learning Method to Deal with Uncertain and Imprecise Information. Neuro-Computing, 7(1995) 61-84
8. Czyzewski, A., Kaczmarek A.: Speech Recognition Systems Based on Rough Sets and Neural Networks. Proc. 3rd Wkshp. Rough Sets and Soft Computing (RSSC'94), San Jose, CA, (1994) 97–100
9. Sarkar, M., Yegnanarayana B.: Rough-Fuzzy Membership Functions. Proc. IEEE World Congress on Computational Intelligence, Alaska, USA, 1(1998) 796 – 801
10. Jensen, John R.: Introductory Digital Image Processing, a Remote Sensing Perspective. 2nd Edn. Prentice Hall series in Geographic Information Science (1995)
11. Gopal, S., Fischer, M.: A Comparison of Three Neural Network Classifiers for Remote Sensing Classification. IEEE Geoscience and Remote Sensing Symposium, 1(1996) 787-789
12. Wang, F.: Fuzzy Supervised Classification of Remote Sensing Images. IEEE Transactions on Geoscience and Remote Sensing, 28(1990) 194-201
13. Pal, S., Mitra, S.: Multi-layer Perceptron, Fuzzy Sets, and Classification. IEEE Transaction on Neural Networks, 3 (1992) 683–697
14. Bencdiktsson, J.A., Sveinsson, J.R.: Multisource Remote Sensing Data Classification Based on Consensus and Pruning. IEEE Transactions on Geoscience and Remote Sensing, 41 (2003), 932-936
15. Tso, B., Mather, P.M.: Classification Methods for Remotely Sensed Data. CRC Press (2001)
16. Melgani, F., Al Hashemy B.A.R., Taha, S.M.R.: An Explicit Fuzzy Supervised Classification Method for Multispectral Remote Sensing Images. IEEE Transactions on Geoscience and Remote Sensing, 38(2000) 287-295
17. Paola, J.D., Schowengerdt, R.A.: Detailed Comparison of Backpropagation Neural Network and Maximum-Likelihood Classifiers for Urban Land Use Classification. IEEE Transactions on Geoscience and Remote Sensing, 33(1995) 981-996

Aggregation Pheromone Density Based Image Segmentation

Susmita Ghosh[1], Megha Kothari[1], and Ashish Ghosh[2],*

[1] Department of Computer Science and Engineering
Jadavpur University, Kolkata 700032, India
[2] Machine Intelligence Unit and Center for Soft Computing Research
Indian Statistical Institute
203 B. T. Road, Kolkata 700108, India
ash@isical.ac.in

Abstract. Ants, bees and other social insects deposit pheromone (a type of chemical) in order to communicate between the members of their community. Pheromone that causes clumping or clustering behavior in a species and brings individuals into a closer proximity is called aggregation pheromone. This paper presents a novel method for image segmentation considering the aggregation behavior of ants. Image segmentation is viewed as a clustering problem which aims to partition a given set of pixels into a number of homogenous clusters/segments. At each location of data point representing a pixel an ant is placed; and the ants are allowed to move in the search space to find out the points with higher pheromone density. The movement of an ant is governed by the amount of pheromone deposited at different points of the search space. More the deposited pheromone, more is the aggregation of ants. This leads to the formation of homogenous groups of data. The proposed algorithm is evaluated on a number of images using different cluster validity measures. Results are compared with those obtained using *average linkage* and *k-means* clustering algorithms and are found to be better.

1   Introduction

Image segmentation plays a vital role in image processing and computer vision problems. Number of image segmentation techniques exist in the literature, which can be grouped into several categories such as edge based, region based, histogram thresholding and clustering [1] based. Several image segmentation techniques exist [2,3,4] where clustering is used to group the points in the characteristics feature space into segments. Features that are commonly used for image segmentation by clustering not only include the gray values, but also include textural features defined on local neighborhood [5].

Numerous abilities of ants have inspired researches for designing various clustering techniques [6,7]. Several species of ants cluster their corpses into "cemeteries" in an effort to clean up their nests. Experimental works illustrate that ants

---

* Corresponding author.

P. Kalra and S. Peleg (Eds.): ICVGIP 2006, LNCS 4338, pp. 118–127, 2006.
© Springer-Verlag Berlin Heidelberg 2006

group corpses, which are initially randomly distributed in space, into clusters within a few hours. It seems that some feedback mechanism (using local density or similarity of data items) determines the probability that an ant will pick up or drop a corpse. Such behavior is used as a model to design several algorithms for clustering data [6,7,8,9,10,11]. Besides nest cleaning, many functions of aggregation behavior have been observed in ants and ant like agents [12,13,14]. These include foraging-site marking and mating, finding shelter and defense. Tsutsui *et al.* [15,16] used aggregation pheromone systems for continuous function optimization where aggregation pheromone density is defined by a density function in the search space.

Inspired by the aforementioned aggregation behavior found in ants and ant like agents a clustering algorithm was proposed in [17]. In this paper the aggregation behavior of ants is used to perform image segmentation, viewing image segmentation as a clustering problem. The aim is to partition the image into clusters/segments such that pixels within a cluster are homogeneous, whereas pixels of different clusters are heterogeneous.

2   Aggregation Pheromone Based Image Segmentation

As mentioned in the introduction, aggregation pheromone brings individuals into closer proximity. This group formation nature of aggregation pheromone is being used as the basic idea of the proposed algorithm. Here each ant represents one data. The ants move with an aim to create homogenous groups of data. The amount of movement of an ant towards a point is governed by the intensity of aggregation pheromone deposited by all other ants at that point. This gradual movement of ants in due course of time will result in formation of groups or clusters. The proposed technique has two parts. In the first part, clusters are formed based on ants' property of depositing aggregation pheromone. The number of clusters thus formed might be more than the desired number. So, to obtain the desired number of clusters, in the second part, agglomerative *average linkage* clustering algorithm is applied on these already formed clusters.

2.1   Formation of Clusters

While performing image segmentation for a given image we group similar pixels together to form a set of coherent image regions. Similarity of the pixels can be measured based on intensity, color, texture and consistency of location of different pixels. Individual features or combination of them can be used to represent an image pixel. For each image pixel we associate a feature vector $\mathbf{x}$. Clustering is than performed on these set of feature vectors so as to group them. Finally, clustering result is mapped back to the original spatial domain to have segmented image.

Consider a data set of n patterns $(\mathbf{x_1}, \mathbf{x_2}, \mathbf{x_3}, ..., \mathbf{x_n})$ and a population of n-ants $(A_1, A_2, A_3, ..., A_n)$ where an ant A_i represents the data pattern $\mathbf{x_i}$. Each individual ant emits aggregation pheromone in its neighborhood. The intensity of aggregation pheromone emitted by an individual A, at $\mathbf{x}$ decreases with its distance from it. Thus the pheromone intensity at a point closer to $\mathbf{x}$ is more than those at other points that are farther from it. To achieve this, the pheromone intensity emitted by A is chosen to be a Gaussian function. The pheromone intensity deposited at $\mathbf{x}'$ by an ant A (located at $\mathbf{x}$) is given by

$$\triangle\tau'(A, \mathbf{x}') = \exp^{-\frac{d(\mathbf{x},\ \mathbf{x}')^2}{2\delta^2}}. \tag{1}$$

The total aggregation pheromone density deposited by the entire population of n ants at $\mathbf{x}'$ is then given by

$$\triangle\tau(\mathbf{x}') = \sum_{i=1}^{n} \exp^{-\frac{d(\mathbf{x_i},\ \mathbf{x}')^2}{2\delta^2}}, \tag{2}$$

where, δ denotes the spread of Gaussian function.

Now, an ant A' which is initially at location $\mathbf{x}'$ moves to the new location $\mathbf{x}''$ (computed using Eq. 3) if the total aggregation pheromone density at $\mathbf{x}''$ is greater than that of $\mathbf{x}'$. The movement of an ant is governed by the amount of pheromone deposited at different points in the search space. It is defined as

$$\mathbf{x}'' = \mathbf{x}' + \eta.\frac{Next(A')}{n}, \tag{3}$$

where,

$$Next(A') = \sum_{i=1}^{n} (\mathbf{x_i} - \mathbf{x}').\exp^{-\frac{d(\mathbf{x_i},\ \mathbf{x}')^2}{2\delta^2}}, \tag{4}$$

with, η as a step size. This process of finding a new location continues until an ant meets a location where the total aggregation pheromone density is more than its neighboring points. Once the ant A_i finds out such a point $\mathbf{x}'_i$ with greater pheromone density, then that point is assumed to be a new potential cluster center, say $\mathbf{Z_j}$ $(j = 1, 2, ..., C, C$ being number of clusters); and the data point with which the ant was associated earlier (*i.e.*, $\mathbf{x_i}$) is now assigned to the cluster so formed with center $\mathbf{Z_j}$. Also the data points that are within a distance $\delta/2$ from $\mathbf{Z_j}$ are assigned to the newly formed cluster. On the other hand, if the distance between $\mathbf{x}'_i$ and the existing cluster center $\mathbf{Z_j}$ is less than $\delta/2$ and the ratio of their densities is greater than *threshold_density* (a predefined parameter), then the data point $\mathbf{x_i}$ is allocated to the already existing cluster centering at $\mathbf{Z_j}$. Higher value of density ratio shows that the two points are of nearly similar density and hence should belong to the same cluster. The proposed algorithm for formation of clusters (APC) is given below using pseudo codes.

```
begin
Initialize σ, threshold_density, η
C = 0
for i = 1 to n do
if the data pattern xi is not already assigned to any cluster
```

```
Compute △τ(xᵢ) using Eq. 2
label 1: Compute new location x′ᵢ using Eq. 3
Compute △τ(x′ᵢ)
if (△τ(x′ᵢ) > △τ(xᵢ))
Update the location of ant Aᵢ to x′ᵢ and goto label 1
else continue
if (C == 0) //If no cluster exists
Consider x′ᵢ as cluster center Z₁ and increase C by one
else
for j = 1 to C
if (min(△τ(x′ᵢ), △τ(Zⱼ))/ max(△τ(x′ᵢ), △τ(Zⱼ))  >  threshold_density and
d(x′ᵢ, Zⱼ) < δ/2)
Assign x′ᵢ to Zⱼ
else
Assign x′ᵢ as a new cluster center say, Z_{C+1} and increase C by one
Assign all the data points that are at a distance of δ/2 from x′ᵢ to
the newly formed cluster Z_{C+1}
end of else
end of for
end of else
end of if (if the data pattern xᵢ ...)
end of for
end
```

2.2   Merging of Clusters

Number of clusters formed by the above algorithm may be more than the desired
number. In this stage, to obtain the desired number of clusters we apply *average
linkage* [18] algorithm. The algorithm starts by merging the two most similar
clusters until the desired number of clusters are obtained.

3   Objective Evaluation of Clustering Results

The clustering results obtained by the above described method are quantified
using following cluster validity measures.

• *Davies Bouldin Index*: This index is a function of the ratio of the sum of
within-cluster scatter to between-cluster separation [18]. The average scatter of
order q within the ith cluster $(S_{i,\,q})$ and the distance between i^{th} and j^{th} clusters
$(d_{ij,\,q})$ are computed as

$$S_{i,\,q} = \left(\frac{1}{|C_i|} \sum_{x \epsilon C_i} ||\mathbf{x} - \mathbf{Z_i}||^q \right)^{\frac{1}{q}}, \tag{5}$$

$$d_{ij,\,q} = ||\mathbf{Z_i} - \mathbf{Z_j}||_q. \tag{6}$$

where $\mathbf{x}$ is the data point belonging to cluster C_i, $\mathbf{Z_i}$ is the centroid of cluster C_i, $q \geq 1$ and $d_{ij,\,q}$ is the Minkowski distance of order q. Subsequently, we compute the index for the ith cluster as

$$R_{i,\,q} = \max_{j,\,i \neq j} \left\{ \frac{S_{i,\,q} + S_{j,\,q}}{d_{ij,\,q}} \right\}. \tag{7}$$

The *Davies-Bouldin (DB)* index for C clusters is defined as

$$DB = \frac{1}{C} \sum_{i=1}^{C} R_{i,\,q}. \tag{8}$$

The smaller the DB value, better is the clustering.

• *S_Dbw* : *S_Dbw* index with C number of clusters is based on the clusters' compactness in terms of intra-cluster variance and inter-cluster density [19]. It is defined as

$$S\_Dbw(C) = Scat(C) + Den(C), \tag{9}$$

where $Scat(C)$ represents the intra-cluster variance and is defined as

$$Scat(C) = \frac{1}{C} \sum_{i=1}^{C} ||\sigma(\mathbf{Z_i})||/\sigma(s); \tag{10}$$

the term $\sigma(s)$ is the variance of the data set and $\sigma(\mathbf{Z_i})$ is the variance of cluster C_i. Inter-cluster density, $Den(C)$, is defined as

$$Den(C) = \frac{1}{C-1} \sum_{i=1}^{C} \left(\sum_{i=1, i \neq j}^{C} \frac{den(\mathbf{u_{ij}})}{max\{den(\mathbf{Z_i}), den(\mathbf{Z_j})\}} \right) \tag{11}$$

where $\mathbf{Z_i}$ and $\mathbf{Z_j}$ are centers of clusters C_i and C_j, respectively and $\mathbf{u_{ij}}$ is the mid point of the line segment joining $\mathbf{Z_i}$ and $\mathbf{Z_j}$. The term $den(\mathbf{u})$ is defined as

$$den(\mathbf{u}) = \sum_{i=1}^{n_{ij}} f(\mathbf{x}, \mathbf{u}), \tag{12}$$

where n_{ij} is the total number of data points belong to clusters C_i and C_j ; the function $f(\mathbf{x}, \mathbf{u})$ is defined as

$$f(\mathbf{x}, \mathbf{u}) = \begin{cases} 0, \text{ if } d(\mathbf{x}, \mathbf{u}) > stdev; \\ 1, \text{ otherwise.} \end{cases} \tag{13}$$

where $stdev$ is the average standard deviation of C clusters and is defined as

$$stdev = \frac{1}{C} \sqrt{\sum_{i=1}^{C} ||\sigma(\mathbf{Z_i})||} \tag{14}$$

and $d(\mathbf{x}, \mathbf{u})$ is the Euclidean distance between $\mathbf{x}$ and $\mathbf{u}$.
   Lower the value of S_Dbw, better is the clustering.

Table 1. Comparison of results of the proposed aggregation pheromone based algorithm (APC) with *average linkage* and *k-means*

Data	APC			Average linkage			k-means		
set	*DB*	*S_Dbw*	*Time*	*DB*	*S_Dbw*	*Time*	*DB*	*S_Dbw*	*Time*
Tank	**0.3026**	**0.1576**	439.2	0.3887	0.2389	**435.4**	0.6337	1.0216	470.4
	(0.032)	(0.024)	(4.87)	(4.9E-09)	(0)	(11.80)	(0.002)	(0.056)	(5.14)
Lena	0.5330	**0.5508**	506.3	**0.4814**	0.5560	602.6	0.5556	0.6411	528
	(0.018)	(0.029)	(8.13)	(7.0E-09)	(1.4E-08)	(8.26)	(0.002)	(0.034)	(9.84)
Brain	**0.4307**	**0.1567**	**43.7**	0.4797	0.1798	134	0.5089	0.2122	53.2
	(0.078)	(0.044)	(9.91)	(0)	(0)	(7.74)	(0.005)	(0.003)	(8.01)

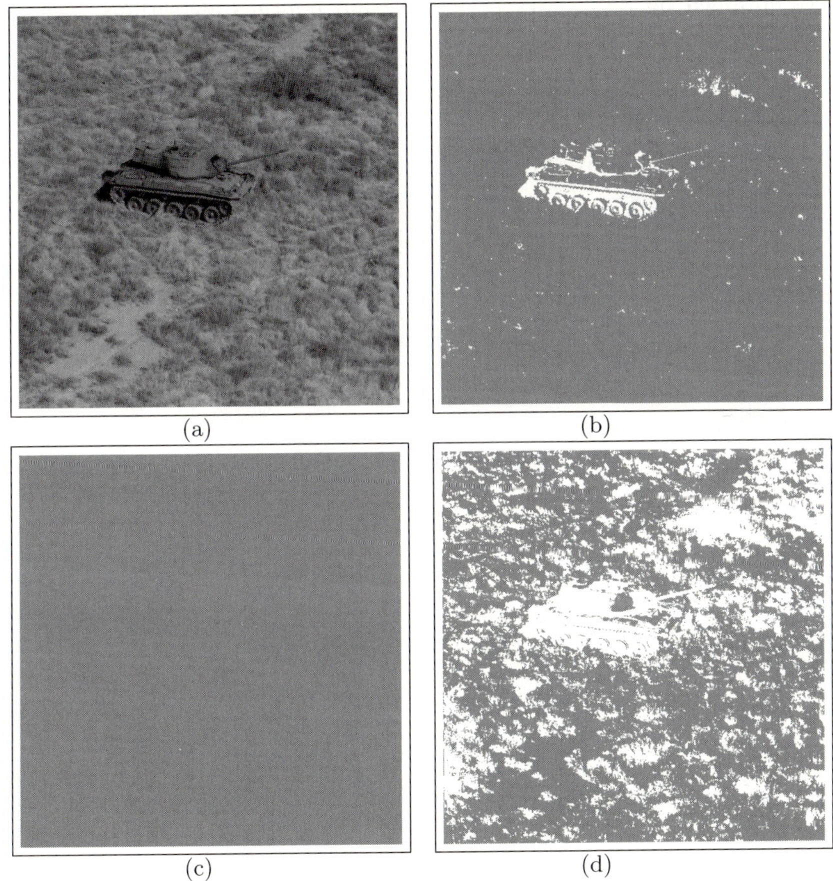

Fig. 1. a) original image, b) *APC* segmentation result, c) *Average link* result and d) *k-means* result with k=2

4 Experimental Results

4.1 Results

To evaluate the effectiveness of the proposed algorithm, we have considered only gray value of pixels as a feature. Experiments were carried out on three images (Tank, Lena and Brain). Values of η and *threshold_density* were kept to 1 and 0.9, respectively; and different values of δ in the range [0, 1] were considered. Results obtained are validated using two different cluster validity indices as described in Section 3. The results obtained by the proposed *APC* algorithm are compared with those of *average linkage* and *k-means* clustering algorithms. Table 1 gives the mean values (over 10 runs) of different performance indices and their corresponding standard deviations (shown in bracket) for each of the images obtained by *APC*, *average linkage* and *k-means* algorithms. The CPU

Fig. 2. a) original image, b) *APC* segmentation result, c) *Average link* result and d) *k-means* result with k=3

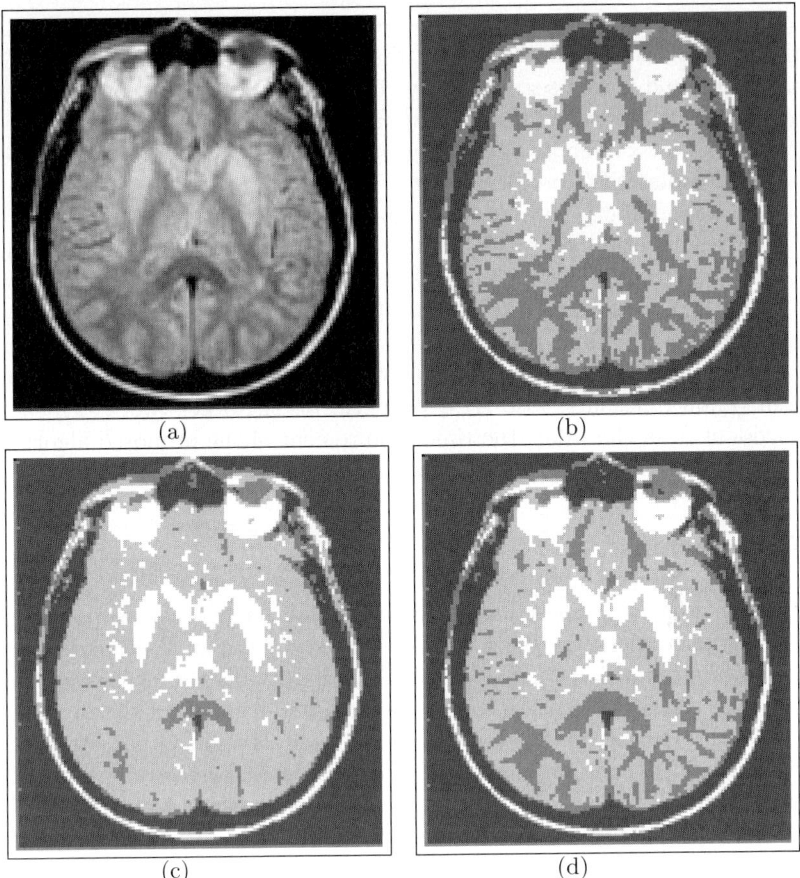

Fig. 3. a) original image, b) *APC* segmentation result, c) *Average link* result and d) *k-means* result with k=4

time (in milliseconds) needed for all the algorithms are also given in the table for comparison. Results in bold face indicate the best ones.

Fig. 1 shows the segmentation result obtained on the Tank image by all the three algorithms. As may be seen, *average linkage* algorithm fails completely to segregate the tank (Fig. 1c); *k-means* algorithm segmented out the tank but the amount of false classification was very high; but the proposed *APC* algorithm successfully segmented out the tank with very less false classification (Fig. 1b). In terms of validity measures also the performance of the proposed *APC* algorithm is found to be better (Table 1) than those of other two.

Original Lena image is shown in Fig. 2a and the segmentation results obtained for the Lena image by *APC*, *average linkage* and *k-means* are shown in Figs. 2b-2d. From the results one can see that the background is not clearly separated out in case of *average linkage*, whereas with the *APC* and *k-means* it is well done. The shade on the face of Lena is well segmented with the proposed *APC* algorithm which is not obtained with that of *k-means*. Also, the top left part of the background is well segmented by the *APC* algorithm in comparison with the other two. When validity measures are taken into consideration it is found that with *DB* index *average linkage* algorithm performs well on Lena image but with *S_Dbw* index *APC* performs better.

Another image that is considered for our experiments is Brain image. The segmentation results obtained by all the three algorithms for this image are shown in Figs. 3b-3d. Original Brain image is shown in Fig. 3a. From the results one can see that the fine structures in the Brain image are very well segmented by the proposed *APC* algorithm; *average linkage* fails to identify these fine structures and *k-means* identifies these fine structures but with higher misclassification. In terms of validity measures also *APC* outperforms the other two.

As evident from the table, the time requirement of the proposed algorithm is mostly less compared to the other two algorithms.

5   Conclusions

In this paper we have proposed a new algorithm for image segmentation based on aggregation pheromone density, which is inspired by the ants' property to accumulate around points with higher pheromone density. Experiments were carried out with three different images to evaluate the performance of the proposed algorithm both qualitatively as well as quantitatively. In this paper segmentation is viewed as a clustering problem and hence for comparative evaluation we have used cluster validity measures; and comparative study is made with two clustering algorithms namely, *average linkage* and *k-means* algorithms. Future study should involve more number of features and object extraction from noisy images.

Acknowledgements

Authors would like to acknowledge the Department of Science and Technology, Government of India and University of Trento, Italy, the sponsors of the India-Trento Program on Advanced Research (ITPAR), under which a project titled **"Advanced Techniques for Remote Sensing Image Processing"** is being carried out at Department of Computer Science and Engineering, Jadavpur University, Kolkata.

References

1. Gonzalez, R.C., Woods, R.E.: Digital Image Processing. Second edn. Pearson education (2003)
2. Pal, N., Pal, S.: A review on image segmentation techniques. Pattern Recognition **26(9)** (1993) 1277–1294
3. Kettaf, F.Z., Bi, D., de Beauville, J.P.A.: A comparision study of image segmentation by clustering techniques. In: Proceedings of ICSP'96. (1996) 1280–1283

4. Saatchi, S., Hung, C.C.: Hybridization of the ant colony optimization with the k-means algorithm for clustering. In Kalviainen, H., ed.: SCIA 2005. Volume 3540 of LNCS., Springer- Verlag, Berlin Heidelberg (2005) 511–520

5. Chanda, B., Majumder, D.D.: Digital Image Processing and Image Analysis. Prentice Hall of India, New Delhi (2003)

6. Deneubourg, J.L., Goss, S., Franks, N., Sendova-Franks, A., Detrain, C., Chretien, L.: The dynamics of collective sorting: Robot-like ants and ant-like robots. In Meyer, J.A., Wilson, S.W., eds.: Proceedings of the 1st Conference on Simulation of Adaptive Behavior: From Animals to Animats 1, MIT press/Bradford Books (1991) 356–365

7. Lumer, E.D., Faieta, B.: Diversity and adaptation in populations of clustering ants. In Cliff, D., Husbands, P., Meyer, J.A., Wilson, S.W., eds.: Proceedings of the 3rd International Conference on Simulation of Adaptive Behaviour:From Animals to Animats 3. (1994) 501–508

8. Monmarché, N., Slimane, M., Venturini, G.: On improving clustering in numerical database with artificial ants. In Floreano, D., Nicoud, J.D., Mondala, F., eds.: Advances in Artificial Life, 5th European Conference ECAL'99, Lecture Notes in Artificial Intelligence 1974, Swiss Federal Institute of Technology, Lausanne, Switzerland, Springer-Verlag (1999) 626–635

9. Handl, J., Knowles, J., Dorigo, M.: On the performance of ant-based clustering. In: Proceedings of the 3rd International Conference on Hybrid Intelligent Systems, Design and Application of Hybrid Intelligent Systems, IOS press (2003) 204–213

10. Liu, S., Dou, Z.T., Li, F., Huang, Y.L.: A new ant colony clustering algorithm based on DBSCAN. In: Proceedings of the 3rd International Conference on Machine Learning and Cybernetics, Shanghai (2004) 1491–1496

11. Vizine, A.L., de Castro, L.N., Hruschka, E.R., Gudwin, R.R.: Towards improving clustering ants: an adaptive ant clustering algorithm. Informatica **29** (2005) 143–154

12. Bell, W.J.: Chemo-orientation in walking insects. In Bell, W.J., Carde, R.T., eds.: Chemical Ecology of Insects. (1984) 93–109

13. Ono, M., Igarashi, T., Ohno, F., Sasaki, M.: Unusual thermal defence by a honeybee against mass attack by hornets. Nature **377** (1995) 334–336

14. Sukama, M., Fukami, H.: Aggregation arrestant pheromone of the German cockroach, Blattella germanica (L.) (Dictyoptera: Blattellidae): isolation and structure elucidation of blasttellastanoside-A and B. Journal of Chemical Ecology **19** (1993) 2521–2541

15. Tsutsui, S.: Ant colony optimization for continuous domains with aggregation pheromones metaphor. In: Proceedings of the 5th International Conference on Recent Advances in Soft Computing (RASC'04), United Kingdom (2004) 207–212

16. Tsutsui, S., Ghosh, A.: An extension of ant colony optimization for function optimization. In: Proceedings of the 5th Asia Pacific Conference on Simulated Evolution and Learning (SEAL04), Pusan, Korea (2004)

17. Kothari, M., Ghosh, S., Ghosh, A.: Aggregation pheromone density based clustering. In: Proceedings of 9th International conference on Information Technology, Bhubaneswar, India, IEEE Computer Society press (2006)

18. Theodoridis, S., Koutroumbas, K.: Pattern Recognition. Second edn. Elsevier Academic Press, Amsterdam (2003)

19. Halkidi, M., Vazirgiannis, M.: Clustering validity assessment: finding the optimal partitioning of a data set. In: Proceedings of ICDM, California, USA (2001)

Remote Sensing Image Classification: A Neuro-fuzzy MCS Approach

B. Uma Shankar, Saroj K. Meher, Ashish Ghosh*, and Lorenzo Bruzzone[1]

Machine Intelligence Unit, Indian Statistical Institute
203 B. T. Road, Kolkata 700108, India
[1] Department of Information and Communication Technologies
University of Trento, Via Sommarive, 14, I-38050, Trento, Italy

Abstract. The present article proposes a new neuro-fuzzy-fusion (NFF) method for combining the output of a set of fuzzy classifiers in a multiple classifier system (MCS) framework. In the proposed method the output of a set of classifiers (i.e., fuzzy class labels) are fed as input to a neural network, which performs the fusion task. The proposed fusion technique is tested on a set of remote sensing images and compared with existing techniques. Experimental study revealed the improved classification capability of the NFF based MCS as it yielded consistently better results.

1 Introduction

The objective of designing a pattern classification system is to achieve the best possible performance for the problems at hand. This leads to the development of different classification schemes with different performance levels, and hence they may offer complementary information about the patterns to be classified. This motivated fusing/combing classifiers' outputs for improved performance. The idea is not to rely on a single classifier, rather to use all or some of them for consensus decision making by combining their individual performance. Recently many efforts aimed at it have become popular [1,2,3,4,5,6,7,8,9]. Moreover, the multiple classifier systems (MCSs) are found to be successful with the combination of diverse classifiers. i.e., the classifiers should not commit the same mistake. Further, the performance of an MCS is highly dependent on the combination scheme. Many studies have been published in this area of research, e.g., if only class labels are available a majority voting [10,11] or label ranking [12,13] is used. If continuous outputs like posteriori probabilities are available, an average or some other linear combination can be used [14,15]. If the classifier outputs are interpreted as fuzzy membership values then fuzzy rules [16,17], belief functions and Dempster-Shafer techniques [14,18] can be used for combination.

Classification of land cover regions of remote sensing images is essential for efficient interpretation of them [19,20]. This task is very complex because of low illumination quality and low spatial resolution of remotely placed sensors and

---

* Corresponding author. `ash@isical.ac.in`

P. Kalra and S. Peleg (Eds.): ICVGIP 2006, LNCS 4338, pp. 128–139, 2006.
© Springer-Verlag Berlin Heidelberg 2006

rapid changes in environmental conditions. Various regions like vegetation, soil, water bodies etc. of a natural scene are often not well separated. Moreover, the gray value assigned to a pixel is an average reflectance of different types of land covers present in the corresponding pixel area. Therefore, a pixel may represent more than one class with varying degree of belonging. Thus assigning unique class label to a pixel with certainty is one of the major problems. Conventional methods cannot deal with this imprecise representation of geological information. Fuzzy set theory introduced in [21] provides a useful technique to allow a pixel to be a member of more than one category or class with graded membership [22]. Many attempts have been made for remote sensing image analysis and classification using fuzzy logic [19,23,24,25,26,27].

We have considered a set of fuzzy classifiers in the design of MCSs in this article. Various existing fuzzy and non-fuzzy fusion methods for combination of classifiers' output are considered and found that the performances are varying with the input data sets and fusion methods. We propose a neuro-fuzzy (NF) fusion method to overcome the risk of selecting a fusion method as neural networks can do this in an adaptive way. The performance is demonstrated on a set of remote sensing images. Experimental study revealed that the MCS with the proposed NF fusion method provided consistently better classification.

2   Fuzzy Classifiers and Combination Methods

A brief description of the four fuzzy classifiers and six existing combination schemes used for the present study is made in the following sections.

Fuzzy k-nearest neighbor (Fk-NN): k-NN is based on the determination of k number of nearest neighbors of a test pattern and assigning it the class label that majority of the neighbors have. Keller *et al.* [28] incorporated the concepts of fuzzy set theory [21] into the k-NN voting procedure and proposed a fuzzy version of k-NN rule. The membership degree of a test pattern $\mathbf{x}$ to class c is calculated as

$$\mu_i(\mathbf{x}) = \frac{\sum_{j=1}^{k} \mu_{ij} \left(\frac{1}{\|\mathbf{x} - \mathbf{x}_j\|^{2/(m_f-1)}} \right)}{\sum_{j=1}^{k} \left(\frac{1}{\|\mathbf{x} - \mathbf{x}_j\|^{2/(m_f-1)}} \right)} \tag{1}$$

where $i = 1, 2, ...C$ (number of classes), and $j = 1, 2, ..., k$ (number of nearest neighbors). μ_{ij} is the membership degree of the pattern $\mathbf{x}_j$ from the training set to class i, among the k nearest neighbors of $\mathbf{x}$. For this study, the algorithm was implemented with $m_f = 2$ and $k = 5$ (selected on the basis of performance).

Fuzzy maximum likelihood (FML): The FML [23] is a fuzzy evaluation of the conventional ML parameters. The mean and variance-covariance matrix estimated using the fuzzy membership values for each pattern are called *fuzzy mean* and *fuzzy variance-covariance* matrix. The membership function (MF) for class c of a pattern $\mathbf{x}$ can be expressed as

$$f_c(\mathbf{x}) = p_c(\mathbf{x}) \ / \ \sum_{j=1}^{C} p_j(\mathbf{x}) \tag{2}$$

where $p_j(\mathbf{x})$ can be computed as

$$p_j(\mathbf{x}) = \frac{1}{(2\pi)^{D/2}|\Sigma_j|^{1/2}} exp\left[-\frac{1}{2}(\mathbf{x}-\mu_j)^T \Sigma_j^{-1}(\mathbf{x}-\mu_j)\right] \tag{3}$$

with $j = 1, 2, ...C$ and D is the dimension of the feature space, assuming a Gaussian distribution for the input data. The fuzzy mean can then be defined as

$$\mu_c = \left(\sum_{i=1}^{N} f_c(\mathbf{x}_i)\mathbf{x}_i\right) \ / \ \left(\sum_{i=1}^{N} f_c(\mathbf{x}_i)\right) \tag{4}$$

where N is the total number of patterns, f_c is the MF of class c, and $\mathbf{x}_i$ is the ith pattern. The fuzzy variance-covariance matrix can be defined as

$$\Sigma_c = \frac{\sum_{i=1}^{N} f_c(\mathbf{x}_i)(\mathbf{x}_i - \mu_c)(\mathbf{x}_i - \mu_c)^T}{\sum_{i=1}^{N} f_c(\mathbf{x}_i)}. \tag{5}$$

For the estimation of the MF in FML, the parameters mean and variance-covariance matrix require the fuzzy representation of the patterns to different classes. Chen [27] described a suitable method which estimates the fuzzy representation of the land covers in an *iterative* manner and does not require the prior information. In this work we have adopted this procedure.

Fuzzy product aggregation reasoning rule (FPARR): The FPARR classification process is performed in three steps [29]. In the first step, it fuzzifies the input feature vector using a π-type MF [30] to get the feature-wise degree of support of a pattern ($\mathbf{x} = [x_1, x_2, ...x_d, ...x_D]^T$) to all classes. The membership values ($f_{d,c}(x_d)$) thus generated expresses the degree of support of dth feature to c^{th} class. Thus for a pattern $\mathbf{x}$ the membership matrix after the fuzzification process can be expressed as

$$F(\mathbf{x}) = \begin{bmatrix} f_{1,1}(x_1) & f_{1,2}(x_1) & ... & f_{1,C}(x_1) \\ f_{2,1}(x_2) & f_{2,2}(x_2) & ... & f_{2,C}(x_2) \\ ... & ... & ... & ... \\ f_{D,1}(x_D) & f_{D,2}(x_D) & ... & f_{D,C}(x_D) \end{bmatrix} \tag{6}$$

In the second step, the fuzzified feature values are aggregated using *product* reasoning rule (RR). The RR is operated on the membership matrix column-wise to get the combined membership grade of features to various classes. The resultant vector thus generated represents the fuzzy classification showing the class belonging.

Fuzzy explicit (FE): The FE classification method [26] also uses three steps. In the first step, it finds the membership matrix for each of the pixels/patterns with a Gaussian MF [26]. Thus a fuzzy membership matrix can be evaluated as in the case of FPARR. The membership matrix is then processed using a *MIN* reasoning rule (RR) in the second step. A rescaling operation is also performed on the output membership values (after applying RR) for all classes.

2.1   Classifier Combination Methods

The fuzzy classifiers' output are combined using a suitable fusion method. For the present study we have considered some of the popular existing techniques. At first the output of the fuzzy classifiers that provide the class belongingness of an input pattern to different classes are arranged in a matrix form defined as decision profile (DP) matrix [31]. It is to be noted that the element of DP matrix need not be fuzzy output only. It could be the labels obtained from the methods providing posterior probability or certainty or possibility values [8]. Mathematically the DP matrix for L classifiers and C classes is defines as

$$DP(\mathbf{x}) = \begin{bmatrix} d_{1,1}(\mathbf{x}) & \dots & d_{1,c}(\mathbf{x}) & \dots & d_{1,C}(\mathbf{x}) \\ \dots & \dots & \dots & \dots & \dots \\ d_{l,1}(\mathbf{x}) & \dots & d_{l,c}(\mathbf{x}) & \dots & d_{l,C}(\mathbf{x}) \\ \dots & \dots & \dots & \dots & \dots \\ d_{L,1}(\mathbf{x}) & \dots & d_{L,c}(\mathbf{x}) & \dots & d_{L,C}(\mathbf{x}) \end{bmatrix}, \tag{7}$$

where $d_{l,c}$ represent the degree of belonging of the pattern assigned by the lth classifier to the cth class.

In the classifier fusion systems, some methods calculate the support for different classes using the corresponding column of DP matrix, regardless of the support for the other classes. This type of fusion methods that use the DP matrix in a class-by-class manner is called class-conscious (CC) combiners. The alternative group is known as class-indifferent (CI). The former uses the context of the DP matrix, i.e., recognizing that a column corresponds to a class, but disregard part of the information with respect to rest of the classes; whereas the CI methods use the whole DP matrix but disregard its context. In the CC group various fuzzy aggregation reasoning rules like *maximum, minimum, product, sum, mean* etc. can be applied on each column of the DP matrix. This operation provides a combined output obtained from the aggregation of the classifiers' output for a particular class. Two popular fuzzy combination methods named as *decision template (DT)* and *Dempster-Shafer (DS)* normally work on the DP matrix coming under the CI group. A brief description of the above mentioned fusion methods are given below.

Existing fusion methods: Among the various fusion methods majority voting is the simplest one. In fuzzy aggregation based fusion methods, each column of the DP matrix is separately combined using various fuzzy aggregation rules like *maximum, minimum, product, sum* and *mean* to get a total support for one class. Maximum of these values for C classes represent the class label for the input pattern [8]. Mathematically the support $\bar{D}_j$ for the class j is defined as

$$\bar{D}_j(\mathbf{x}) = G((d_{1,j}(\mathbf{x}), ...d_{l,j}(\mathbf{x}), ..., d_{L,j}(\mathbf{x})),$$

where $\mathbf{x}$ is the input pattern, $d_{l,j}(\mathbf{x})$ is the membership value of $\mathbf{x}$ obtained by l^{th} classifier for j^{th} class and G is the fuzzy aggregation rule.

The probabilistic product aggregation rule performs fusion using continuous-valued outputs [8]. Let $d_{l,c}(\mathbf{x})$ be the degree of "support" given by classifier l for the class c. Let the feature space be partitioned into L non overlapping subsets which are conditionally independent. Let $P(c)$ denote the prior probability for class c. Then the set of discriminant values proportional to the true posterior probabilities is given by

$$\mu_c(\mathbf{x}) = \frac{\prod_{l=1}^{L} d_{l,c}(\mathbf{x})}{P(c)^{L-1}}, \quad c = 1, 2, ..., C. \tag{8}$$

The class label assigned to $\mathbf{x}$ is the highest of $\mu_c(\mathbf{x})$. In this fusion method the fuzzy membership values are assumed to be the probability of a pattern for different classes. Similarly, the fuzzy integral method is performed on each column of the DP matrix to obtain the degree of belonging of each pattern for all classes. In this fusion method, for an input $\mathbf{x}$, C vectors (of length L) of fuzzy densities are calculated. These values are sorted according to the cth column of the DP matrix. The sorted values are changed iteratively and the final degree of support for class c for an input pattern is calculated.

The next group of fusion methods is known as CI, e.g., DT and DS. The idea of the DT model is to "remember" the most typical DP matrix for each class and then compare it with the current $DP(\mathbf{x})$ matrix. The closest match will label $\mathbf{x}$. The $DT_c(\mathbf{x})$ for class c is the average of the DP matrices of the elements of the training set Z in class c. Any kind of similarity measures can be applied for this purpose. A detail description of the method can be found in [31]. In *DS* based fusion method the classifiers' output are possibility/membership values. Instead of calculating the similarity between the DT_c and $DP(\mathbf{x})$ matrix, the *DS* algorithm computes the proximity between the DT_c for a class and the output of a classifier, and from this proximity values belief degrees are computed. Based on the belief degrees membership degree for each class is computed for a pattern. The details are available in [14,18].

3   Neuro-fuzzy Combiner

It is well understood that the fuzzy classifiers are suitable for the classification of different ill-defined classes with overlapping boundaries [22]. For remote sensing

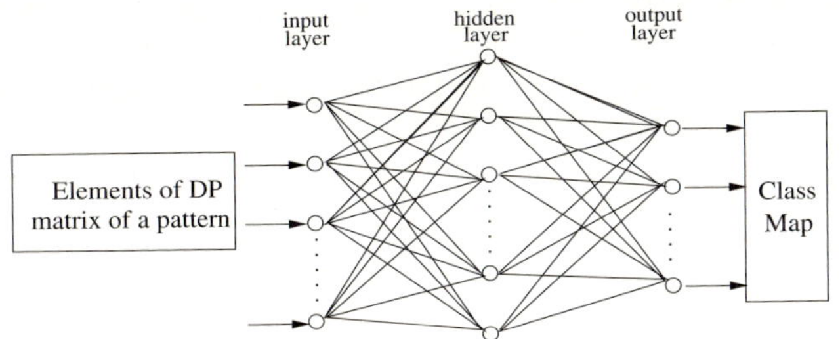

Fig. 1. A three-layer feed-forward neural network

images, classes are normally ill-defined and overlapping. Thus we have used only fuzzy classifiers in the present investigation. We propose a neuro-fuzzy fusion method based MCS that works with fuzzy classifiers, where the output of the classifiers are combined using a neural network (NN) to learn the classes in an iterative way. The activation value of the output neurons show the degree of class labels of the input pattern.

The scheme proposed in the present article falls under the CI category. The elements of the DP matrix are used as input to a three-layered feed forward multi-layer perceptron (MLP) (Fig. 1) which acts as a combiner. Number of input nodes of the NN is equal to the product of number of classifiers used in the MCS and classes present in the data set. Number of output nodes of the NN is equal to the number of classes present in the data set.

Each processing node of MLP, except the input-layer nodes, calculates a weighted sum of the outputs from the nodes in the preceding layer to which it is connected. This weighted sum then passes through a transfer function to derive its own output which is then fed to the nodes in the next layer. Thus, the input and output to node v are obtained as $net_v = \sum_u W_{uv} O_u + bias_v$ and $O_v - S(net_v)$, where w_{uv} is the weight for the connection linking node u to node v, $bias_v$ is the bias value for node v, O_u is the output of node u, and S stands for the activation function (AF) (sigmoid function [32,33]). MLP uses back-propagation (BP) learning algorithm [32,33] for weight updating. The BP algorithm reduce the sum of square error called as cost function (CF), between the actual and desired output of output-layer neurons in a gradient descent manner. The weights are corrected using the following equation:

$$\Delta W_{vu}(n+1) = \alpha \Delta W_{vu}(n) + \eta \delta_v O_u, \tag{9}$$

where n, α, η and δ are the iteration number, momentum parameter, learning rate and node error, respectively. The details of BP algorithm including derivation of the equations can be obtained from [32,33].

The last step of the proposed NFF based MCS system is a hard classification by performing a *MAX* operation to defuzzify the output of the NN. Here the pattern is classified to a class corresponding to the highest node value obtained at output of the NN.

4   Results and Discussion

The proposed scheme has been evaluated using a set of remote sensing images (due to space scarcity we report here results on only two images). Training samples are selected according to a prior assumption of the land cover regions and are used to estimate the parameters of the classifiers. After learning the classifier, it is used to classify the land covers of the whole image.

4.1   Performance Measurement Parameters

Two performance measures described below have been used in the present study.

β index: β is defined [25] as the ratio of the total variation and within-class variation. For a given image and given number of classes, *the higher the homogeneity within the classes, the higher would be the β value.* Mathematically β can be represented as

$$\beta = \left(\sum_{i=1}^{C} \sum_{j=1}^{M_i} (\mathbf{x}_{ij} - \overline{\mathbf{x}})^2 \right) \Big/ \left(\sum_{i=1}^{C} \sum_{j=1}^{M_i} (\mathbf{x}_{ij} - \overline{\mathbf{x}}_i)^2 \right), \tag{10}$$

where $\overline{\mathbf{x}}$ is the mean grey value of all the pixels of an image (pattern vector), M_i is the number of pixels in the ith (i = 1,2,...C) class, x_{ij} is the grey value of the jth pixel ($j = 1, 2, ...M_i$) in class i, and $\overline{\mathbf{x}}_i$ is the mean of M_i pixel values of the ith class.

Xie-Beni index: The XB index [34] provides a validity criterion based on a function that identifies overall compactness and separation of partition without any assumption to the number of substructures inherent in the data. It is mathematically expressed as the ratio of compactness (θ) and separation (ξ), i.e.,

$$XB = \frac{1}{Z} \frac{\sum_{c=1}^{C} \sum_{z=1}^{Z} \mu_{cz}^2 \|V_c - \mathbf{x}_z\|^2}{\min_{c \neq j} \|V_c - V_j\|^2}, \tag{11}$$

where V_c is the centroid of the cth class and $\mathbf{x}_z$ is z^{th} pattern in the data set. Z is the total number of data points in the data set and μ_{cz} is the membership value of the zth pattern to c^{th} class. The *smaller* the XB value, the better is the classification.

4.2   Description of Images

IRS-1A image: The IRS-1A image is obtained from Indian Remote Sensing Satellite [35]. We have used the image taken from the Linear Imaging Self Scanner with spatial resolution of 36.25m x 36.25m and wavelength range of 0.45-0.86μm.

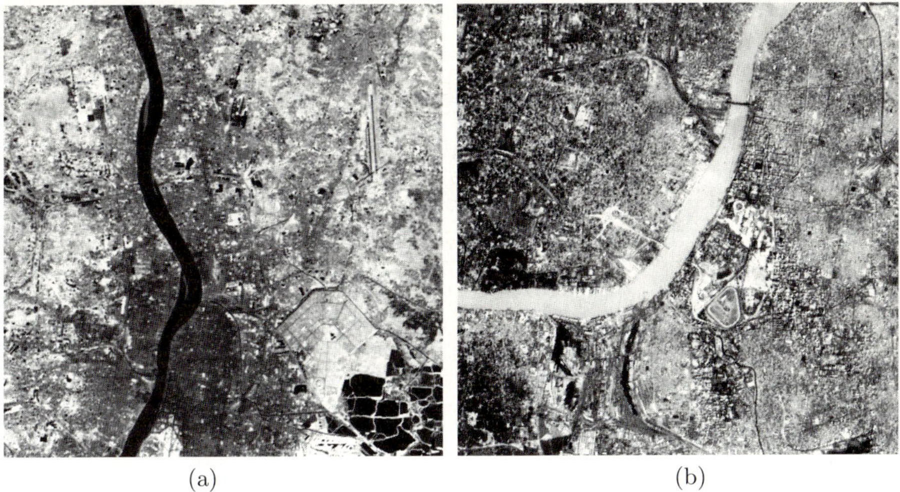

(a)   (b)

Fig. 2. Original (a) IRS-1A (band-4), and (b) SPOT (band-3) image

The whole spectrum range is decomposed into four spectral bands, namely, blue
(band1), green (band2), red (band3) and near infrared (band4) of wavelengths
0.45-0.52μm, 0.52-0.59μm, 0.62-0.68μm, and 0.77-0.86μm, respectively. Since the
image is poorly illumination, we have presented the enhanced image (band4) in
Fig. 2. However, the algorithms are implemented on actual (original) image. The
image in Fig. 2a covers an area around the city of Calcutta in the near infrared
band having six major land cover classes: *pure water* (PW), *turbid water* (TW),
concrete area (CA), *habitation* (HAB), *vegetation* (VEG) and *open spaces* (OS).
PW class contains pond water, fisheries etc. River water where the soil content is
more belong to TW class. CA class consists of buildings, runways, roads, bridges
etc. Suburban and rural habitation, where concrete structure are comparatively
less come under HAB class. VEG class represents crop and forest areas. OS class
contains the barren land.

SPOT image: The SPOT image shown in Fig. 2b is obtained from SPOT
satellite (Systeme Pour d'Observation de la Terre) [20]. The Calcutta image
used here has been acquired in the wavelength range of 0.50-0.89μm. The whole
spectrum range is decomposed into three spectral bands namely, green (band1),
red (band2) and near infrared (band3) of wavelengths 0.50-0.59μm, 0.61-0.68μm,
and 0.79-0.89μm, respectively. This image has a higher spatial resolution of 20m
x 20m. We have considered the same six classes as in case of IRS-1A image.

4.3   Classification of Remote Sensing Images

Selection of the training samples for all classes are made according to a prior
assumption of the land cover regions. These training samples are used to estimate
the parameters of the classifiers. After learning the classifier, it is used to classify
the land covers of the whole image.

Table 1. β and XB values of individual classification methods

Sl. No.	Classification method	Image			
		IRS-1A		SPOT	
		β	XB	β	XB
1	Fk-NN (k=5)	7.0121	0.9594	6.9212	2.5004
2	FMLC	7.0523	0.9356	6.9896	2.4231
3	FE	7.1312	0.9112	7.0137	2.3031
4	FPARR	**8.1717**	**0.8310**	**8.1078**	**2.1021**

Table 2. β and XB values for different combination schemes

Classifiers for fusion	Fusion method used		β index		XB index	
			IRS-1A image	SPOT image	IRS-1A image	SPOT image
Fk-NN (k=5) FMLC FE FPARR	Voting		8.3134	8.2314	0.8211	2.1005
	Fuzzy Aggregation reasoning rule	MAX	0.7903	2.1000	0.7903	2.1000
		MIN	8.3213	8.5134	0.7879	1.9733
		PROD	8.6217	*8.6321*	0.8003	2.0178
		SUM	8.4312	8.3781	0.8202	2.0013
		MEAN	8.2013	8.2011	0.8201	1.9010
	Probabilistic product		8.5011	8.6005	0.7983	1.9334
	Fuzzy integral		8.5078	8.5017	*0.7710*	1.9768
	Decision template		8.4032	8.5712	0.7801	*1.9001*
	Dempster-Shafer		*8.6421*	8.5312	0.7781	1.9783
	Neuro-fuzzy		**8.8012**	**8.7763**	**0.7697**	**1.8738**

Initially the individual performance of fuzzy classifiers are tested on these images using β and XB indices and depicted in Table 1. It is found that among the four classifiers the FPARR based method is providing the best result.

Further, the validation results (β and XB) produced by MCSs with different combination techniques are provided in Table 2. It is observed that all MCSs with existing fusion methods are providing better results compared to any of the individual classifiers. However, this improvement is not consistent for any of the images. For example, with IRS-1A image, better results are obtained for Dempster-Shafer fusion based MCS with β as a validity measure; whereas fuzzy integral fusion based MCS showed improved performance with XB measure (Table 2). Results are completely different for SPOT image which provided better result with PROD aggregation reasoning rule based MCS in terms of β measure, and DT fusion based MCS in terms of XB measure. Hence, there is a risk in selecting any of these six fusion methods for a particular data set. The performance of the proposed NFF based MCS is then evaluated. The results revealed that the performance is further improved consistently for both the images with respect to the validity measures used here (Table 2). The classified images with this method are shown in Figs. 3a and 3b. It can be seen from these images that all

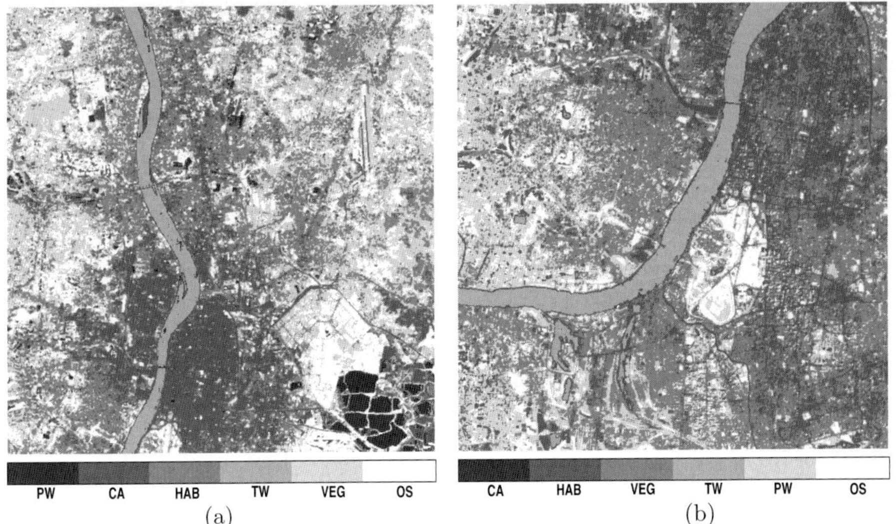

Fig. 3. Classified (a) IRS-1A and (b) SPOT image using proposed fusion based MCS

the classes (PW, TW, CA, HAB, VEG and OS) have come out clearly. Also various structures (like rivers, canals, lakes, roads, bridges, airport runways) present in the images are segregated out properly.

5   Conclusion

A new neuro-fuzzy multiple classifier system (MCS) is presented in this article. Here output of fuzzy classifiers are fed as input to a neural network that acts as a combiner. Performance of the proposed scheme is successfully demonstrated on two remote sensing images, and compared with six existing combination techniques. It is seen that for both the images considered here, the proposed model works well and the improvement is consistent; whereas the results are different for different fusion methods and highly dependent on input data sets.

References

1. Drucker, H., Cortes, C., Jackel, L.D., LeCun, Y., Vapnik, V.: Boosting and other ensamble methods. Neural Computation **6** (1994) 1289–1301
2. Bertolami, R., Bunke, H.: Ensemble methods for handwritten text line recognition systems. In: Proceedings of the 2005 IEEE International Conference on Systems, Man and Cybernetics. (2005) 2334–2339
3. Kittler, J., Hatef, M., Duin, R.P.W., Matas, J.: On combining classifiers. IEEE Transactions on Pattern Analysis and Machine Intelligence **20** (1998) 226–239
4. Fumera, G., Roli, F.: A theoretical and experimental analysis of linear combiners for multiple classifier systems. IEEE Transactions on Pattern Analysis and Machine Intelligence **27** (2005) 942–956

5. Gutta, S., Huang, J.R.J., Jonathon, P., Wechsler, H.: Mixture of experts for classification of gender, ethnic origin, and pose of human faces. IEEE Transactions on Neural Networks **11** (2000) 948–960

6. Moonasar, V., Venayagamoorthy, G.K.: A committee of neural networks for automatic speaker recognition ASR systems. In: Proceedings of the IJCNN '01. International Joint Conference on Neural Networks. Volume 4. (2001) 2936–2940

7. Chee, L.P., Harrison, R.F.: Online pattern classification with multiple neural network systems: an experimental study. IEEE Transactions on Neural Networks **23** (2003) 235–247

8. Kuncheva, L.I.: Combining Pattern Classifiers: Methods and Algorithms. Wiley-Interscience (2004)

9. Multiple Classifier Systems, International Workshop on MCS. Volume 1857, 2096, 2364, 2709, 3077 and 3541 of LNCS., Springer (2000-2005)

10. Kimura, F., Shridhar, M.: Handwritten numerical recognition based on multiple algorithms. Pattern Recognition **24** (1991) 969–983

11. Franke, J., Mandler, E.: A comparison of two approaches for combining the votes of cooperating classifiers. In: Proceedings of 11th IAPR International Conference on Pattern Recognition systems. (1992) 611–614

12. Ho, T.K., Hull, J.J., Srihari, S.N.: Decision combination in multiple classifier systems. IEEE Transactions on Pattern Analysis and Machine Intelligence **16** (1994) 66–75

13. Bagui, S.C., Pal, N.R.: A multistage generalization of the rank nearest neighbor classification rule. Pattern Recognition Letters **16** (1995) 601–614

14. Xu, L., Krzyzak, A., Suen, C.Y.: Methods of combining multiple classifiers and their applications to handwriting recognition. IEEE Transactions on Systems, Man, and Cybernetics **22** (1992) 418–435

15. Hashem, Schmeiser, B.: Improving model accuracy using optimal linear combinations of trained neural networks. IEEE Transactions on Neural Networks **6** (1995) 792–794

16. Cho, S.B., Kim, J.H.: Combining multiple neural networks by fuzzy integral and robust classification. IEEE Transactions on Systems, Man, and Cybernetics, **25** (1995) 380–384

17. Cho, S.B., Kim, J.H.: Multiple network fusion using fuzzy logic. IEEE Transactions on Neural Networks **6** (1995) 497–501

18. Rogova, G.: Combining the results of several neural network classifiers. Neural Networks **7** (1994) 777–781

19. Tso, B., Mather, P.M.: Classification Methods for Remotely Sensed Data. Taylor and Francis, London (2001)

20. Richards, J.A., Jia, X.: Remote Sensing Digital Image Analysis: An Introduction. 3rd edn. New York: Springer Verlag (1999)

21. Zadeh, L.A.: Fuzzy sets. Information Control **8** (1965) 338–353

22. Kuncheva, L.I.: Fuzzy Classifier Design. Springer-Verlag (2000)

23. Wang, F.: Fuzzy supervised classification of remote sensing images. IEEE Transactions on Geoscience and Remote Sensing **28** (1990) 194–201

24. Maselli, F., Rodolfi, A., Copnese, C.: Fuzzy classification of spatially degraded thematic mapper data for the estimation of sub-pixel components. International Journal of Remote Sensing **17** (1996) 537–551

25. Pal, S.K., Ghosh, A., Shankar, B.U.: Segmentation of remotely sensed images with fuzzy thresholding, and quatitative evaluation. International Jounal of Remote Sensing **21** (2000) 2269–2300

26. Melgani, F., Al Hashemy, B.A.R., Taha, S.M.R.: An explicit fuzzy supervised classification method for multispectral remote sensing images. IEEE Transaction on Geoscience and Remote Sensing **38** (2000) 287–295
27. Chen, C.F.: Fuzzy training data for fuzzy supervised classification of remotely sensed images. In: Asian Conference on Remote Sening (ACRS 1999). (1999)
28. Keller, J.M., Gray, M., Givens, J.: A fuzzy k-nearest neighbor algorithm. IEEE Transactions on Systems, Man and Cybernatics **15** (1985) 580–585
29. Ghosh, A., Meher, S.K., Shankar, B.U.: Fuzzy supervised classification using aggregation of features. Technical report, MIU/TR-02/2005, Indian Statistical Institute (2005)
30. Pal, S.K., Majumder, D.D.: Fuzzy sets and decision making approaches in vowel and speaker recognition. IEEE Transactions on Systems, Man and Cybernetics **7** (1977) 625–629
31. Kuncheva, L.I., Bezdek, J.C., Duin, R.P.W.: Decision templates for multiple classifier fusion: An experimental comparison. Pattern Recognition **34** (2001) 299–314
32. Haykin, S.: Neural Networks: A Comprehensive Foundation. 2nd edn. Prentice Hall (1998)
33. Lippmann, R.P.: An introduction to computing with neural nets. IEEE ASSP Magazine (1987) 4–22
34. Xie, X.L., Beni, G.: A validity measure for fuzzy clustering. IEEE Transactions on Pattern Analysis and Machine Intelligence **13** (1991) 841–847
35. NRSA: IRS data users hand book. Technical report (1989) Document No. IRS/NRSA/NDC/HB-02/89.

A Hierarchical Approach to Landform Classification of Satellite Images Using a Fusion Strategy

Aakanksha Gagrani[1], Lalit Gupta[1], B. Ravindran[1], Sukhendu Das[1,*],
Pinaki Roychowdhury[2], and V.K. Panchal[2]

[1] Department of Computer Science and Engineering, IIT Madras
[2] Defence Terrain Research Labortory, DRDO, India
*sdas@iitm.ac.in

Abstract. There is increasing need for effective delineation of meaningfully different landforms due to the decreasing availability of experienced landform interpreters. Any procedure for automating the process of landform segmentation from satellite images offer the promise of improved consistency and reliality. We propose a hierarchical method for landform classification for classifying a wide variety of landforms. At stage 1 an image is classified as one of the three broad categories of terrain types in terms of its geomorphology, and these are: desertic/rann of kutch, coastal or fluvial. At stage 2, all different landforms within either desertic/rann of kutch , coastal or fluvial areas are identified using suitable processing. At the final stage, all outputs are fused together to obtain a final segmented output. The proposed technique is evaluated on large number of optical band satellite images that belong to aforementioned terrain types.

1 Introduction

Landform Classification is a problem of identifying the predefined class of landforms, given a satellite image of the area. In order to explore the navigable areas, identification of the exact landform becomes a crucial task. Due to the varying geographic nature of landforms and existence of large number of classes, landform segmentation is very much different from a conventional image segmentation problem. Geographical definitions give only a very theoretical aspect of the size, shape and several other features of the landforms. For e.g. "Barchan dunes" are caused by highly uniform environmental conditions and wind blowing only in one direction. Barchans can become aligned together along a plane perpendicular to the wind. If the line becomes somewhat straight, dune scientists refer to these forward marching ridges as "transverse dunes". For such kind of landforms shape is an important feature. However the definitions do not clarify the type of shape features to be used for processing. Another category is the coastal bar. Coastal bars have no specific color, shape or size. Formulation of these abstract geographical definitions into a single set of features and rules is

P. Kalra and S. Peleg (Eds.): ICVGIP 2006, LNCS 4338, pp. 140–151, 2006.

a difficult task for the purpose of segmentation or classification. Hence a single classifier or a single set of features cannot efficiently handle various types of landforms from a satellite image, we propose a hierarchy of classifiers in a unified framework.

A few approaches have dealt with the problem of landform identification in the past. However, only a limited set of landforms were used for classification. Pennock et al. [1] has dealt with the problem by using self organizing feature map. They calculate the DEM (Digital Elevation Model) and the land cover map as features. The DEM map normally divides the area into rectangular pixels and store the elevation of each pixel. These features are then fed to the SOM for further classification. The method is used to classify the landform of Kobe city in Japan into hill, plateau, fan and reclaimed land. These classified landforms were adopted for an earthquake damage evaluation of the 1995 Hyogoken Nanbu earthquake in Kobe. Gorsevski et al. [2] proposed a method to assign digital terrain attributes into continuous classes. They used fuzzy k-means for classifying the continuous landforms. The method finds its usefulness in overcoming the problem of class overlap. The aim is to describe landslide hazard in roaded and road less areas of a forest. As the size of the data increases and when there are artifacts introduced by the derivation of landform attributes from DEM, the performance of the fuzzy k-means suffers. Burrough et al. [3] proposed a method to overcome the limitations of the above given model by using spatial sampling, statistical modeling of the derived stream topology and fuzzy k-means using the distance metric. Results are shown on images obtained from Alberta, Canada, and the French pre-Alps.

SVMs is a state-of-art pattern recognition technique whose foundations stem from statistical learning theory [4]. They have widely been used in literature for image segmentation and classification. Chen et al. [5] presented an algorithm for image segmentation using support vector machines. They used two different sets of features for image segmentation - first, the gray levels of 5x5 neighboring pixels and second, the gray level and grad orientation of 9x9 neighboring pixels. They concluded that to obtain good segmentation results feature set should be chosen appropriately, for instance they achieved superior results using second feature set. Results on these two different set of features using SVM as classifier, are shown on two images in their work. Kim et al. [6] proposed an algorithm for texture classification using multi-class SVM. The gray levels in a window of 17x17 were used as features and multi-class SVM based on one-against-others decomposition is used for classification. They have compared the results with different kernels and by varying window sizes. They concluded that polynomial kernel with degree 5 gives superior results than other kernels. Results are shown on images composed of two-five textures.

In the work presented in this paper, we have employed hierarchical feature-based methods using image pixel intensity and shape, for the classification of different types of landforms. The flowchart for the complete methodology is shown in Fig. 1. The hierarchical approach used in this paper has enabled us to process a large variety of landforms with varying features. The rest of the paper is

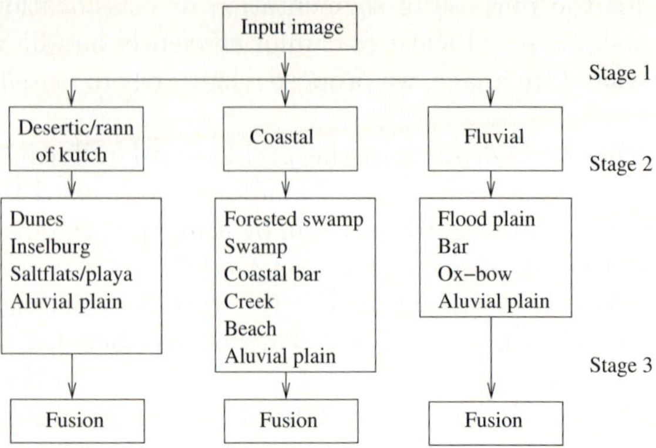

Fig. 1. Flowchart of the proposed hierarchical landform classification scheme

organized as follows. Section 2 gives overview of landform classification. Section 3 describes the proposed methodology. Section 4 discusses the experimental results obtained. Section 5 concludes the paper with the discussion on contribution.

2 Overview of Landform Classification

We attempt to solve the problem of landform classification from satellite images using a hierarchical method of segmentation. This is a divide-and-conquer strategy, which divides the complex problem into smaller solvable units. We have obtained training and testing samples of about 20 different landforms. The complexity lies in the fact that the rules governing a decision to obtain a landform widely varies from one to another. For example, some landform such as, dunes, inselberg, flood-plains have very distinct texture features, whereas water bodies, salt flats/playas have distinct band signatures, and others have very distinct shapes (OX-Bow, Meanders and Parabolic dunes) and sizes (swamps, plains etc.). The signatures, adjacency and association rules of these landforms are also fuzzy (uncertain), according to geo-morphologists who provide us with this ground truth.

The task is complex, as no classifier would be able to handle the wide variety of features (texture, color, size and shape), rules of association across all different landforms, and in some cases even for a particular landform. A large set of features extracted based on certain features will confuse a classifier, which will suffer from the following major disadvantages: correct and weighted combination of features, curse of dimensionality and lack of adequate training samples to capture the large variability within a class/landform.

The complete methodology for Landform classification can now be divided into three stages, which is depicted in Fig. 1. At the first stage, a SVM is used to classify an image belonging to either one of the three major terrains types found in the bed of earth (at least in India). These are Desertic/Rann of kutch

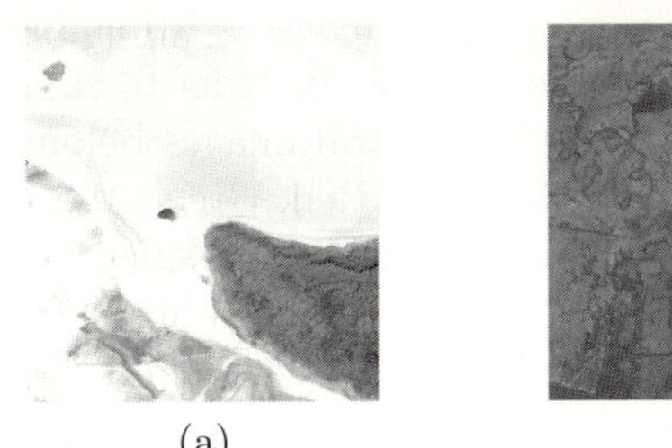
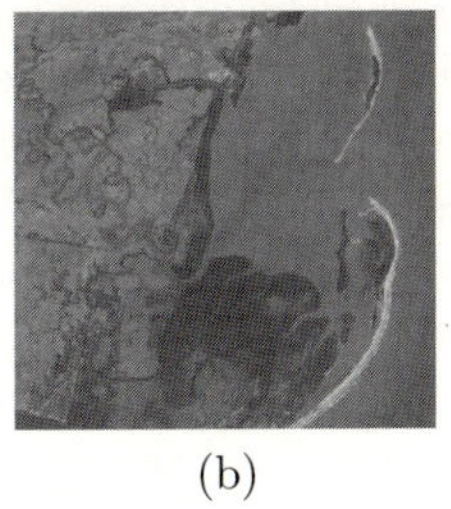
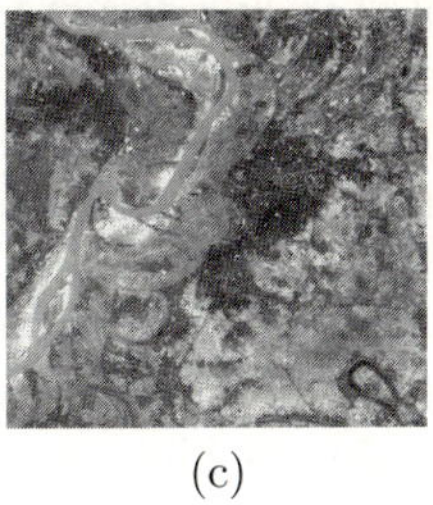

(a)   (b)   (c)

Fig. 2. Examples of a few set of satellite images for the three major terrains (a) Desertic terrian/Rann of kutch; (b) Coastal terrian; (c) Fluvial (river side) terrian

(we are considering rann of kutch and the desertic in a single category), Fluvial (river side) and Coastal landforms. This is a fundamental assumption in our approach and it works well for certain application, such as trafficability and disaster management for defense, GIS and resource mapping. As we are not interested in land-use patterns, urban areas are not considered. Examples of a few set of satellite images for the three major terrains are given in Fig. 2. We have assumed that coastal, fluvial and desertic are non-overlapping classes, which we typically found to be true in practical scenarios. For example, dunes can only occur in a desertic area, and coastal bars can only be found in a coastal area. Similarly, OX-BOW patterns can occur only in fluvial zones. This enables us to identify the probable set of landforms occurring in the input image, only under a particular super-group that has been determined at the first stage. Once the image is classified as desertic, fluvial or coastal, each pixel of the image is classified into the actual landforms with SVM, trained using mean of intensity features, computed as:

$$\mathbf{x}_{i,j} = \{\mu(I^r_{i,j}) \quad \mu(I^g_{i,j}) \quad \mu(I^n_{i,j})\} \tag{1}$$

where, $\mathbf{x}_{i,j}$ represents a 3D feature vector corresponding to $(i,j)^{th}$ pixel. $I^r_{i,j}$, $I^g_{i,j}$ and $I^n_{i,j}$ represent intensity values of $(i,j)^{th}$ pixel in Red, Green and NIR bands (the three spectral bands used for processing) of the input image, respectively and $\mu(h)$ represents mean of h in a 3x3 window. Other methods such as moments for shape matching [7] and pixel connectivity [8] are used to obtain other major landforms. Finally, outputs of different landforms are fused using a criteria to obtain final classification result. The complete methodology to obtain all landforms and fusion strategy employed to obtain final classification results is described in the following sections.

3   Description of the Methods Used for Classification

3.1   Supergroup Classification

This is the topmost stage of the proposed hierarchical classification as shown in Fig. 1. A Support Vector Machine (SVM) based classification technique has been adopted in our design for the task of identifying an input image as belonging to one of the desertic, coastal or fluvial landform super-groups. In order to capture and exploit the variability among the different multi-spectral images belonging to each of the super-groups, histograms of all the 3 bands: Red, Green and NIR bands are used as features for classification. Thus, the SVM-classifier in our case has been trained using histograms of all the three bands of multi-spectral training samples belonging to each one of the three: Desertic, Coastal and Fluvial categories. A high degree of success has been achieved at this stage which will be discussed in Sec. 4.

3.2 Desertic/Rann of Kutch Landform Classification

The flowchart of proposed methodology for the classification of landforms in a desertic/rann of kutch area is shown in Fig. 3. It can be observed from image shown in Fig. 8 that saltflats/playas (barren areas with highly saline and alkaline soils, formed through the concentration of mineral residues in salt water) appear bright and inselberg/rocky exposure (a steep ridge or hill left when a mountain has eroded and found in an otherwise flat, typically desert plain) appear dark as compared to dunes/sandy plains (mounds of loose sand grains shaped up by the wind). We exploit this property to differentiate between these three landforms. The steps of processing used for classification are as follows:

1. A multi-class SVM (using one-against others decomposition [6]) trained using mean of pixel intensity values of all three spectral bands, is used to differentiate between dunes/sandy plains, rocky exposure and saltflats/playas.
2. The output obtained is fused using algorithm described in Sec. 3.5.

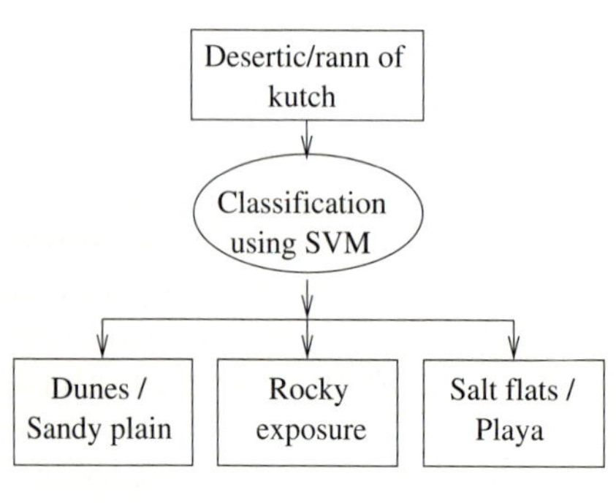

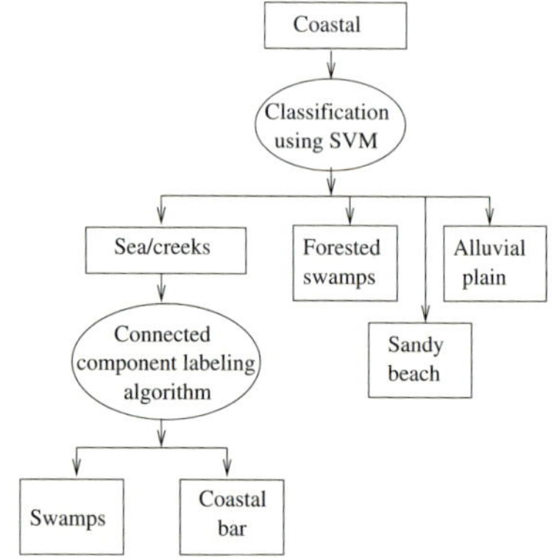

Fig. 3. Flowchart showing stages of classification of desertic landforms. Features used for SVM are mean of pixel intensity values of all three spectral bands.

Fig. 4. Flowchart showing stages of classification of coastal landforms. Features used for SVM are mean of pixel intensity values of all three spectral bands.

3.3   Coastal Landform Classification

The flowchart of proposed methodology for the classification of landforms in a coastal area is shown in Fig. 4. It can be observed from the image shown in Fig. 9(a) that intensity-based features have a major role to play for extraction of coastal landforms. Association rules have also been employed in order to encode human-knowledge in observing certain key characteristics of coastal landforms within the system. The steps of processing for identification of landform in coastal images are as follows:

1. A multi-class SVM (using one-against others decomposition [6]) trained using mean of pixel intensity values of all three spectral bands, is used to differentiate between sea, forested swamp (a wetland containing trees), sandy beach and alluvial plain.
2. Since coastal bars are landforms that possess unique characteristic property of being enclosed by sea on all sides, a connected component [8] labeling algorithm is employed to determine all connected components surrounded by sea.
3. Similarly, swamps (a wetland that features permanent inundation of large areas of land by shallow bodies of water) are patches of land that possess high water-content and have been obtained by identifying segments classified as sea in step 1 surrounded by land.
4. The outputs obtained in steps 1,2 and 3 are fused using the algorithm described in Sec. 3.5, to obtain final classification results.

3.4   Fluvial Landform Classification

The flowchart of methodology followed for the classification of landforms in a fluvial area is shown in Fig. 5. An example of fluvial image is shown in Fig. 10(a) Since fluvial landforms are produced by the action of river or an active channel, a satellite image taken of a fluvial area mostly contain an active channel within it. The steps of processing for identification of landfroms in fluvial images are as follows:

1. A multi-class SVM (using one-against others decomposition) trained using mean of pixel intensity values of all three spectral bands, is used to differentiate between active channel, flood plain (the low area along a stream or river channel into which water spreads during floods) and alluvial plain.
2. Flood plains in general occur adjacent to active channel, a connected component [8] labeling algorithm is employed to confirm that all segments identified as flood plains in step 1 are connected to active channel. The segments that are not connected to active channels (river) are classified as alluvial plains.
3. A SVM trained using moment features [7] (shape) is used to distinguish oxbow (a U-shaped bend in a river or stream) and active channel among the segments which are classified as active channel in step 1.

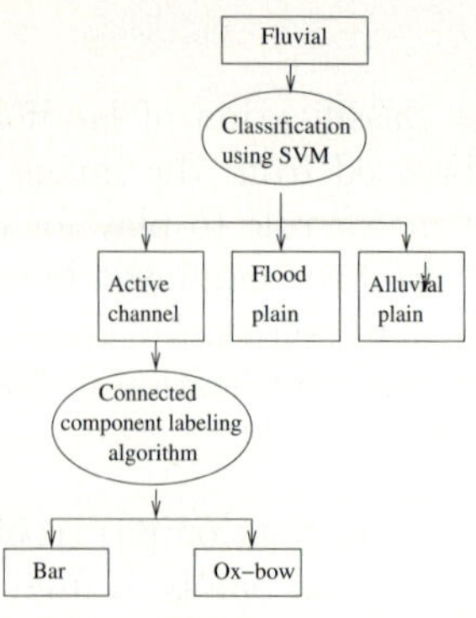

Fig. 5. Flowchart showing stages of classification of fluvial landforms. Features used for SVM are mean of pixel intensity values of all three spectral bands.

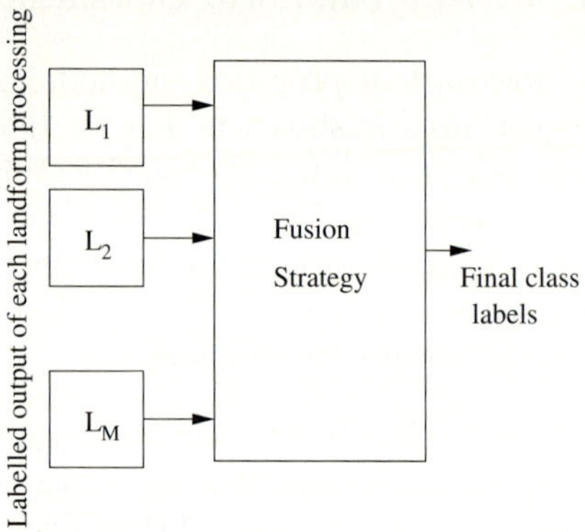

Fig. 6. Block diagram of the fusion strategy

4. Since bars are landforms that possess unique characteristic property of being enclosed by active channel on all sides, a connected component labeling algorithm is employed to determine all connected components surrounded by active channel.
5. The outputs obtained in steps 1,2,3 and 4 are fused using algorithm described in Sec. 3.5 to obtain final classification results.

3.5   Fusion

As mentioned in Sec. 2, an input image may contain multiple landforms within it. However, due to the diverse characteristics (properties) possessed by different landforms, specific processing algorithms have been designed and implemented for extraction of a few landforms. As mentioned above, all segmentation results produced from the different processing algorithms, need to be merged and combined appropriately. We need an efficient process of merging or fusing the outputs of different classifier, as a perticular pixel may be assigned to two or more number of classes by different classifiers.

The strategy adopted by the current system design, attempts to fuse segmentation results of individual landforms on the basis of their association and adjacency phenomena to occur together in nature. Using knowledge acquired from domain experts in geomorphology three adjacency Tables 1 - 3 have been built in order to encode the adjacency relationships that exist among different landforms under each super-group. Before fusing results of two different landforms under the same super-group, their corresponding entry in the adjacency table is checked. In case their association is invalid (as indicated by 'NA'), there is no chance whatsoever for the two candidate landforms to occur together and therefore cause an uncertainty. In the other case when their association is valid (as indicated by a landform index with higher precedence), the two landforms under consideration may have a pixel overlap and in such cases their fusion is

Table 1. Adjacency table for desertic/rann of kutch landforms

	Dunes (L_1)	Rocky exposure (L_2)	Saltflats (L_3)
Dunes (L_1)	-	L_2	L_3
Rocky exposure (L_2)	L_2	-	L_2
Salfflats (L_3)	L_3	L_2	-

Table 2. Adjacency table for coastal landforms

	Swamp (L_1)	Forested swamp (L_2)	Coastal bar (L_3)	Beach (L_4)	Creek/ sea(L_5)	Alluvial plain (L_6)
Swamp (L_1)	-	NA	L_3	L_4	NA	L_1
Forested swamp (L_2)	NA	-	Both	L_4	NA	L_2
Coastal bar (L_3)	L_3	Both	-	L_4	L_3	L_3
Beach (L_4)	L_4	L_4	L_4	-	L_4	L_4
Creek/Sea (L_5)	NA	NA	L_3	L_4	-	L_5
Alluvial plain (L_6)	L_1	L_2	L_3	L_4	L_5	-

Table 3. Adjacency table for fluvial landforms

	Ox-bow (L_1)	Active channel (L_2)	Bar (L_3)	Flood plain (L_4)	Alluvial plain (L_5)
Ox-bow (L_1)	-	NA	NA	L_1	L_1
Active channel (L_2)	NA	-	L_3	L_2	L_2
Bar (L_3)	NA	L_3	-	L_3	L_3
Flood plain (L_4)	L_1	L_2	L_3	-	L_4
Alluvial plain (L_5)	L_1	L_2	L_3	L_4	-

done by assigning the area of overlap to the landform with higher precedence. The block diagram of the fusion stage has been shown in Fig. 6.

The fusion strategy adopted for combination of labeled outputs of each landform processing is given below. For combination of two labeled outputs $L_k(X, Y)$ and $L_j(X, Y)$ to form the combined output $O(X, Y)$, (where k and j are the highest labels in precedence among all the class labels assigned before fusion, $1 \le k, j \le M$). M being the number of possible landform classes with in that super-class (desertic, fluvial or coastal).

Algorithm for Fusion

1. If landforms k and j do not occur together then output $O(X, Y)$ is given as:

$$O(X, Y) = \operatorname*{argmax}_{1 \le j \le M} c_j(X, Y) \qquad (2)$$

where, c_j is the number of times label j appears in the neighborhood of point (X, Y).

2. If landforms k and j may occur together then output $O(X,Y)$ is given as:

$$O(X,Y) = \begin{cases} L_k(X,Y) & if \quad prec(k) > prec(j) \\ L_j(X,Y) & if \quad prec(j) > prec(k) \\ \Psi(X,Y) & if \quad prec(j) = prec(k) \end{cases} \tag{3}$$

where, the function $prec()$ is encoded in the adjacency table and $\Psi(X,Y)$ is the new label assigned to the pixel (X,Y).

The adjacency table for all super-group classes (types of terrains) are shown in Tables 1 - 3. Each adjacency table is a symmetric matrix of size $N * N$, where N is the total number of landforms within that super-group. The entries in any adjacency matrix are:

L_i - Landform number with higher precedence among the two adjacent landforms.

N/A - Invalid (not possible).

Both - If both landform occur with equal precedence.

Knowledge of geoscientists is encoded in the table. Experts opinion is conseiderd to form the adjacency matrix.

4   Experimental Results

To verify the effectiveness of the proposed method, experiments were performed on several test images of size 300x300. The SVM used for super group classification was trained using 180 training samples (60 for each class) and tested

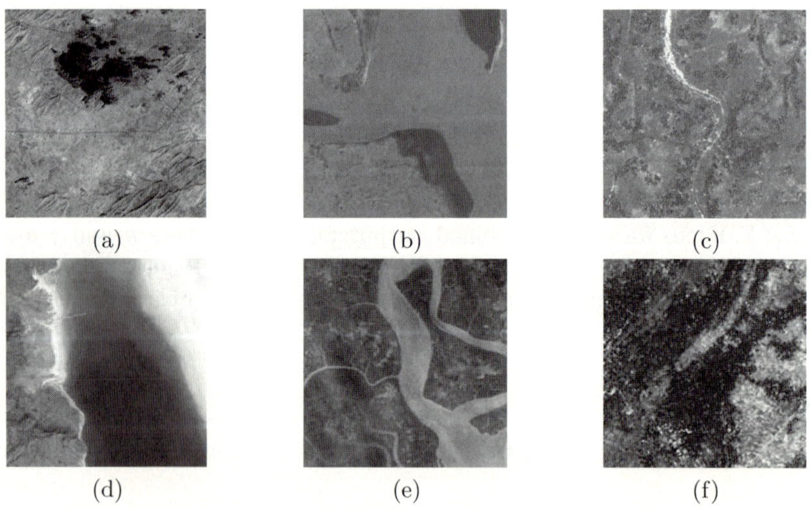

(a)   (b)   (c)

(d)   (e)   (f)

Fig. 7. Examples of classified ((a)-(c)) and missclassified ((d)-(f)) images at stage 1 (supergroup classification): (a) Desertic Image; (b) Coastal Image; (c) Fluvial Image; (d) Rann of kutch image misclassified as coastal; (e) Coastal image misclassified as fluvial; (f) Fluvial image misclassified as coastal

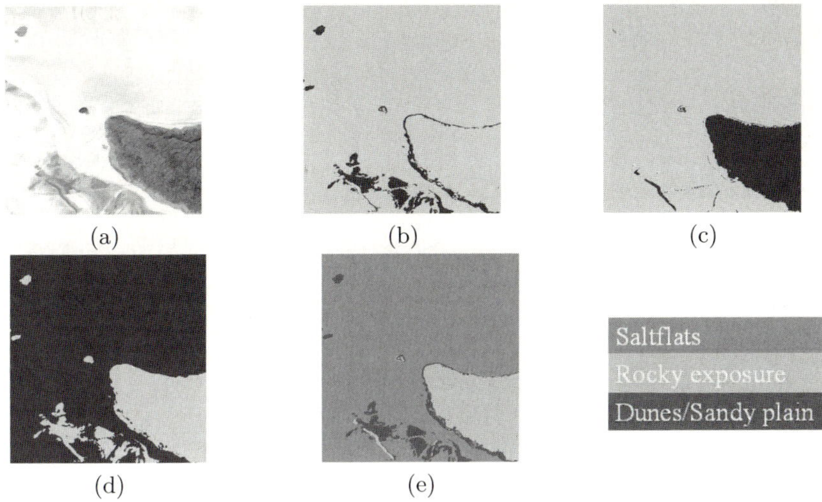

(a)   (b)   (c)

(d)   (e)

Fig. 8. (a) Input image consists of desertic landforms (b) Dunes/Sandy plains; (c) Inselburg/rocky exposure; (d) Saltflats/playa; (e) Fused Result

using 600 samples (200 each class). We obtained 99.2% of classfication accuracy, with a SVM using polynomial kernel of degree 2. Figs. 7(a)-(c) show examples of correctly classified images of desertic, coastal and fluvial terrians, respectively at stage 1 (supergroup classification). Figs. 7(d)-(f) show examples of a rann of kutch, coastal, fluvial terrians misclassfied as coastal, fluvial, coastal terrians, respectively at stage 1 (supergroup classification).

Results obtained at stages 2 and 3 using our proposed methodology are shown in Figs. 8 - 10. Fig. 8(a) shows input image of a desertic/rann of kutch area. The corresponding landfroms obtained after classification are shown in: (b) dunes/sandy plains; (c) rocky exposure; and (d) saltflats/playas. Result obtained after fusing the individual outputs is shown in Fig. 8(e). Fig. 9(a) shows input image of a coastal area. The corresponding landforms obtained after classification are shown in: (b) coastal bar; (c) forested swamp; (d) swamp; (e) beach; (f) sea/creek and (g) alluvial plain. Result obtained after fusing the individual outputs is shown in Fig. 9(h). Fig. 10(a) shows input image of a fluvial area. The corresponding landforms obtained after classification are shown in: (b) active channel; (c) flood plain; (d) bar; (e) ox-bow; and (f) alluvial plain Result obtained after fusing the hidividual outputs is shown in Fig. 10(g). Although active channel is not a landform but it is shown because other landforms are associated with the active channel. It can be observed from Figs.8-10, that each landform has been identified correctly in the final output.

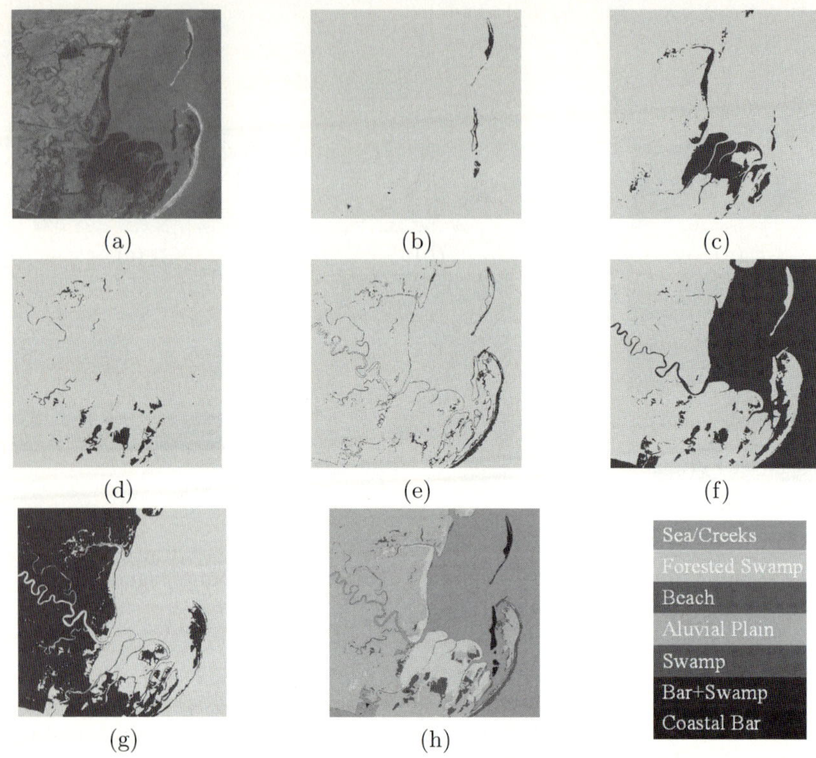

Fig. 9. (a) Input image consists of coastal landforms; (b) Coastal bar; (c) Forested swamp; (d) Swamp; (e) Beach; (f) Creeks/sea; (g) Alluvial plain; (h) Fused result

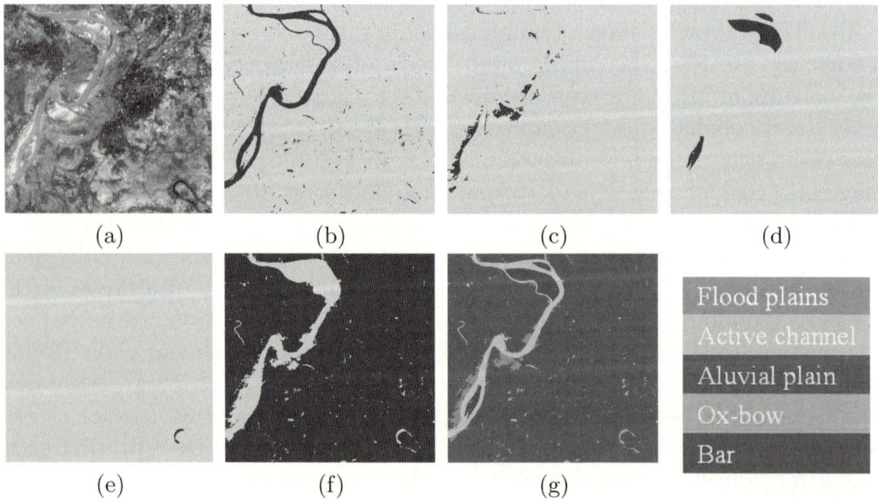

Fig. 10. (a) Input image consists of fluvial landforms; (b) Active channel; (c) Flood plain; (d) Bar; (e) Ox-bow; (f) Alluvial plain; (g) Fused Result

5   Conclusion

A hierarchical approach for landform classification has been proposed in the paper. The proposed hierarchical framework enables us to consider large number of landform classes for segmentation of satellite images. The proposed methodology has been tested on a large number of images. Results show that all major landforms have been identified correctly. With the increase in the number of landforms the complexity of the adjacency table will also increase, as well as the super-classes in Fig. 1. However the performance of the system has yet to be analysed for such situations. Future work includes expanding the system to handle more set of landforms, for instance, a method to discriminate among different dunes.

References

1. Pennock, D.J., Zebarth, B.J., Dejong, W.: Landform classification and soil distribution in hummocky terrain, saskatchewan, canada. In: In Proceedings of British Machine Vision Conference, Norwich, UK (1987) 297–315
2. Gorsevski, P.V., Gessler, P.E., Jankowski, P.: Integrating a fuzzy k-means classification and a bayesian approach for spatial prediction of landslide hazard. Journal of Geographical Systems **5** (2003) 223–251
3. Burrough, P.A., van Ganns, P.F.M., MacMillan, R.A.: High-resolution landform classification using fuzzy k-means. Fuzzy sets and systems **113** (2000) 37–52
4. Vladimir N. Vapnik: An overview of statistical learning theory. IEEE Trans. on Neural Networks **10** (1999) 988–999
5. ying Chen, Q., Yang, Q.: Segmentation of images using support vector machines. In: Proceedings of the third international conference on machine learning and cybernetics, Shanghai (2004) 3304–3306
6. Kim, K.I., Jung, K., Park, S.H., Kim, H.J.: Support vector machines for texture classification. IEEE Tran. on Pattern Analysis and Machine Intelligence **24** (2002) 1542–1550
7. Alt, F.L.: Digital pattern recognition by moments. Journal of the Association for Computing Machinery **9** (1962) 240–258
8. Haralick, Robert, M., Shapiro, G.L.: Computer and Robot Vision. Addison-wesley (1992)

An Improved 'Gas of Circles' Higher-Order Active Contour Model and Its Application to Tree Crown Extraction*

Péter Horváth[1,2], Ian H. Jermyn[2], Zoltan Kato[1], and Josiane Zerubia[2]

[1] University of Szeged, Institute of Informatics, P.O. Box 652,
H-6701 Szeged, Hungary
Fax:+36 62 546 397
{hp, kato}@inf.u-szeged.hu

[2] Ariana (joint research group CNRS/INRIA/UNSA), Inria,
B.P. 93, 06902 Sophia Antipolis, France
Fax:+33 4 92 38 76 43
{Ian.Jermyn, Josiane.Zerubia}@sophia.inria.fr

Abstract. A central task in image processing is to find the region in the image corresponding to an entity. In a number of problems, the region takes the form of a collection of circles, *e.g.* tree crowns in remote sensing imagery; cells in biological and medical imagery. In [1], a model of such regions, the 'gas of circles' model, was developed based on higher-order active contours, a recently developed framework for the inclusion of prior knowledge in active contour energies. However, the model suffers from a defect. In [1], the model parameters were adjusted so that the circles were local energy minima. Gradient descent can become stuck in these minima, producing phantom circles even with no supporting data. We solve this problem by calculating, via a Taylor expansion of the energy, parameter values that make circles into energy inflection points rather than minima. As a bonus, the constraint halves the number of model parameters, and severely constrains one of the two that remain, a major advantage for an energy-based model. We use the model for tree crown extraction from aerial images. Experiments show that despite the lack of parametric freedom, the new model performs better than the old, and much better than a classical active contour.

1 Introduction

A central problem in image understanding is to find the region R in the image domain corresponding to a particular entity. The crucial quantity is $P(R|I, K)$, the probability that region R corresponds to the entity given the image data I and any prior knowledge K we may choose to include. Typically, to solve such problems automatically, a significant amount of prior knowledge specific to the entity must be included, in particular about region geometry. Generic assumptions, *e.g.* about boundary smoothness, do not suffice.

* This work was partially supported by EU project IMAVIS (FP5 IHP-MCHT99), EU project MUSCLE (FP6-507752), Egide PAI Balaton, OTKA T-046805, and a HAS Janos Bolyai Research Fellowship. We thank the French National Forest Inventory (IFN) for the data.

P. Kalra and S. Peleg (Eds.): ICVGIP 2006, LNCS 4338, pp. 152–161, 2006.

The tree crown extraction problem provides an example. Submetre resolution remote sensing images in principle permit the automatic extraction of the region R corresponding to tree crowns, and the subsequent evaluation of various parameters of importance in forestry and conservation. Particularly in plantations, R takes the form of a collection of approximately circular connected components of similar size. We thus have a great deal of prior knowledge about R, without which trees that are close together or that do not differ much in intensity from the background cannot be extracted correctly. The question is then how to incorporate such prior knowledge into a model for R?

We focus on 'active contour' models [2]. In this context, a region R is represented by its boundary ∂R. $P(R|I, K)$ is constructed implicitly, via an energy functional $E(\partial R) = E_{\mathrm{g}}(\partial R) + E_{\mathrm{i}}(\partial R, I)$, where E_{g} and E_{i} correspond to prior and likelihood. In classical active contours, prior energies E_{g} are constructed from single integrals over the contour. E_{g} includes only local, differential interactions between boundary points, and thus only very simple prior knowledge, *e.g.* boundary smoothness.

To include more complex prior knowledge, longer-range interactions are needed. There is a large body of work that does this implicitly, via a template region or regions to which R is compared, *e.g.* [3,4,5,6]. However, such energies effectively limit R to a bounded subset of region space close to the template(s), which excludes, *inter alia*, cases like tree crown extraction in which R has an unknown number of connected components. 'Higher-order active contours' (HOACs) [7] provide a complementary approach. HOACs generalize classical active contours to include multiple integrals over ∂R. Thus HOAC energies explicitly model long-range interactions between boundary points without using a template. This allows the inclusion of complex prior knowledge while permitting the region to have an arbitrary number of connected components, which furthermore may interact amongst themselves. The approach is very general: classical energies are linear functionals on the space of regions; HOACs include all polynomial functionals.

In [1], a HOAC energy E_{g} was used for tree crown extraction. In this 'gas of circles' model, collections of mutually repelling circles of given radius r_0 are local minima of E_{g}. The model has many potential applications in varied domains, but it suffers from a drawback: such local minima can trap the gradient descent algorithm used to minimize the energy, thus producing phantom circles even with no supporting data. The model as such is not at fault: an algorithm capable of finding the global minimum would not produce phantom circles. This suggests two approaches to tackling the difficulty. One is to find a better algorithm. The other is to compromise with the existing algorithm by changing the model to avoid the creation of local minima, while keeping intact the prior knowledge contained in the model. In this paper, we take this second approach. We solve the problem of phantom circles in [1]'s model by calculating, via a Taylor expansion of the energy, parameter values that make the circles into inflection points rather than minima. In addition, we find that this constraint halves the number of model parameters, and severely constrains one of the two that remain, while improving the empirical success of the model.

In section 2 we present the 'gas of circles' model E_{g}. In section 3, we introduce the inflection point constraint and show how it fixes some of the parameters. In section 4, we apply the model to tree crown extraction. We briefly review previous work, describe our likelihood energy E_{i} and the gradient descent algorithm used to minimize $E = E_{\mathrm{i}} + E_{\mathrm{g}}$, and present experimental results. In section 5, we sum up.

2 The 'Gas of Circles' HOAC Model

A region boundary[1], ∂R, is a map $\gamma : S^1 \to \mathbb{R}^2$ modulo orientation-preserving diffeomorphisms of S^1. The HOAC energy E_g used by [1] is then given by[2]

$$E_g(\partial R) = \lambda L(\partial R) + \alpha A(R) - \frac{\beta}{2} \iint dp\, dp'\, \mathbf{t}(p) \cdot \mathbf{t}(p')\, \Psi(r(p, p')) , \qquad (2.1)$$

where p is a coordinate on S^1; L is the boundary length functional; A is the region area functional; $r(p, p') = |\gamma(p) - \gamma(p')|$; $\mathbf{t} = \partial_p \gamma$; and Ψ is an interaction function that determines the geometric content of the model. In [1],

$$\Psi(z) = \begin{cases} \frac{1}{2}\left(2 - \frac{z}{d} + \frac{1}{\pi} \sin \frac{\pi z}{d}\right) & z < 2d , \\ 0 & z \geq 2d . \end{cases} \qquad (2.2)$$

With this Ψ, the last term in (2.1) creates a repulsion between antiparallel tangent vectors. This has two effects. First, for particular ranges of α, β, and d ($\lambda = 1$ wlog), circular structures, with a radius r_0 dependent on the parameter values, are stable to perturbations of their boundary. Second, such circles repel one another if they approach closer than $2d$. Regions consisting of collections of circles of radius r_0 separated by distances greater than $2d$ are thus local energy minima. In [1], this was called the 'gas of circles' model.

In order to determine parameter values so that a circle of radius r_0 be an energy minimum, [1] conducted a stability analysis. The energy was Taylor expanded around a circle, and the result was expressed in the Fourier basis. This is the natural basis to use because it diagonalizes (2.1): Fourier components do not interact. The parameters were chosen so that, for a circle of radius r_0, the first derivative of the functional (2.1) was zero (energy extremum) and the second derivative of (2.1) was positive definite (energy minimum). The first constraint determines β in terms of α and d, while the second places constraints on the ranges of the latter two parameters. The values of α and d can further be adjusted so that the energy of the circle is positive (to avoid circle creation everywhere), but not too high. In more detail: if γ_r is a circle of radius r, and $\delta\gamma$ is a small variation of the circle with Fourier components a_k, the energy to second order is

$$E_g(\gamma_r + \delta\gamma) = E_0(r) + a_0 E_1(r) + \frac{1}{2} \sum_k |a_k|^2 E_2(k, r) ,$$

where

$$E_0(r) = 2\pi\lambda r + \pi\alpha r^2 - \pi\beta G_{00}(r) , \qquad (2.3a)$$

$$E_1(r) = 2\pi\lambda + 2\pi\alpha r - 2\pi\beta G_{10}(r) , \qquad (2.3b)$$

$$E_2(k, r) = 2\pi\lambda r k^2 + 2\pi\alpha$$

$$- 2\pi\beta\left[2G_{20}(r) + G_{21}(k, r) + 2irkG_{23}(k, r) + k^2 r^2 G_{24}(k, r)\right] . \qquad (2.3c)$$

---

[1] We describe the case of one simply-connected connected component. The generalization to multiple multiply-connected connected components is trivial.

[2] The same HOAC energy was first used, but with different parameter values, by Rochery *et al.* [7], to model network shapes.

The G_{ij} are also functions of d. Note that $E_1 = \partial_r E_0$ and $E_2(0, r) = \partial_r E_1$.

Equations (2.3) have the following consequences. First, since the large r behaviour of E_0 is dominated by the α term, we must have $\alpha \geq 0$ for the energy to be bounded below. Second, the condition $E_1(r_0) = 0$ determines β in terms of the other parameters:

$$\beta(r_0) = \frac{\lambda + \alpha r_0}{G_{10}(r_0)} \ . \tag{2.4}$$

Third, because $G_{10} > 0$, $\beta > 0$ is necessary for an extremum. Fourth, although $E_2(k, r_0) > 0$ can only be checked numerically, when $k = 0$, it implies

$$\alpha(r_0) > \beta(r_0)(2G_{20}(r_0) + G_{21}(0, r_0)) = \beta(r_0)\tilde{G}(r_0) \ .$$

3   Monotonic Energy Function

The left of figure 2 shows a plot of the energy of a circle versus radius for parameter values selected according to the above criteria. Viewed as a Gibbs energy, this curve has just the form we require: circles of radius r_0 are metastable (*i.e.* local minima), with an energy that is low but nevertheless higher than that of the empty region. In the absence of supporting data, the global minimum will thus be the empty region, the correct behaviour. A gradient descent algorithm, however, cannot escape from these local minima, meaning that circles of radius r_0, once formed during gradient descent, cannot disappear, even if the data does not support their existence. In practice such circles sometimes do form, which is clearly undesirable. The best solution to this problem would be an algorithm capable of finding the global minimum of the energy. A slightly less ambitious approach, which we take here, involves making a compromise with the algorithm, changing the model to avoid the creation of these local minima, while preserving as much of the prior knowledge as possible.

The idea we will pursue is to adjust the parameters so that the minimum of the curve on the left in figure 2 is replaced by a broad, approximately flat area, as shown in the three rightmost plots in figure 2. Such an energy means that in the absence of image data, a circle will shrink and disappear, whereas small amounts of image data will be sufficient to create a minimum in the flat area, thus producing a stable circle. The natural method to achieve such a broad flat region is to create an energy function that has a single inflection point. If necessary the parameters can then be tweaked to ensure that the gradient of energy wrt radius is positive rather than simply non-negative. It is, however, a nontrivial exercise to find parameter values that result in inflection points. We address this problem via further analysis of the energy (2.1).

We still require that a circle of radius r_0 be stable to sinusoidal perturbations with $k > 0$, but now we also require that such a circle be an inflection point with respect to perturbations with $k = 0$, that is, changes of radius. We will see that these demands are sufficient to fix the prior energy E_{g} up to an overall multiplicative constant and a small range of values for d. More precisely, we still require that $E_1(r_0) = 0$ and $E_2(k, r_0) > 0$ for $k > 0$, but we now require that $E_2(0, r_0) = 0$ too. The first condition gives equation (2.4). The second condition, which follows from equation (2.3c), also relates α and β:

$$\alpha(r_0) = \beta(r_0)\tilde{G}(r_0) \ . \tag{3.1}$$

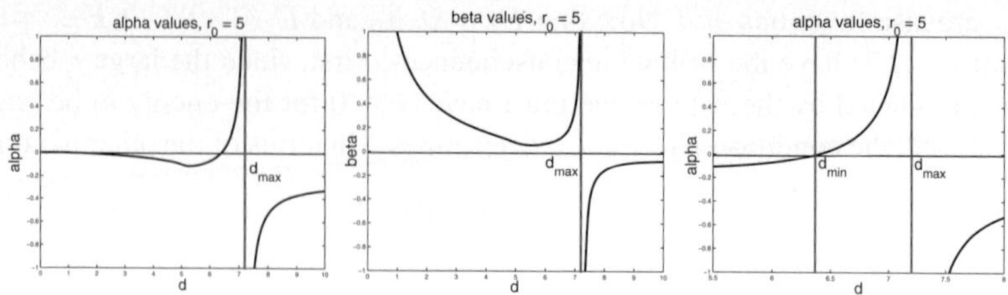

Fig. 1. From left to right ($r_0 = 5.0$ throughout): α plotted against d; β plotted against d; enlarged plot of α near the critical domain

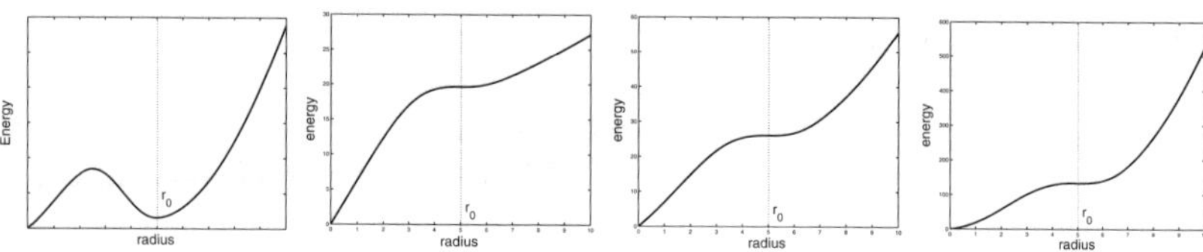

Fig. 2. Plot of E_0 against r for $r_0 = 5.0$. Left: model in [1], with a local energy minimum. Right three: new model, with α and β determined by equations (3.2). Second from left, $d = 6.4$; second from right, $d = 6.8$; far right, $d = 7.2$. For this value of r_0, $d_{\min} = 6.3880$, $d_{\max} = 7.2495$.

We can solve equations (2.4) and (3.1) for α and β, giving

$$\alpha(r_0) = \frac{\lambda \tilde{G}(r_0)}{G_{10}(r_0) - r_0 \tilde{G}(r_0)} \quad \text{and} \quad \beta(r_0) = \frac{\lambda}{G_{10}(r_0) - r_0 \tilde{G}(r_0)} . \tag{3.2}$$

These equations fix α and β as functions of r_0 and d. Since r_0 is fixed by the application, the only remaining parametric degrees of freedom are the value of d, and the overall strength of the prior term, represented by λ. Recall, however, that we also require α and β to be positive. The question is then how to find values of d for a given r_0 so that $\alpha(r_0) > 0$ and $\beta(r_0) > 0$.

3.1   Determination of d

To illustrate the behaviour we want to understand, figure 1 shows plots of α and β against d for fixed r_0, in this case $r_0 = 5$. There are two critical points, $d_{\min}$ and $d_{\max}$. Only for the range $d_{\min} < d < d_{\max}$ are both α and β positive. Our goal is therefore to find $d_{\min}$ and $d_{\max}$ as functions of r_0.

From equations (3.2), it can be seen that $d_{\max}$ arises from a zero in the denominator, while $d_{\min}$ arises from a zero in the numerator. It is therefore sufficient to find these zeros in order to find $d_{\min}$ and $d_{\max}$. To proceed, we first note a scaling property of G_{00}. The function G_{00} is given by the following integral [1]:

$$G_{00}(r) = \int_{-\pi}^{\pi} dp \, \cos(p) \, r^2 \, \Psi\left(2r \left|\sin \frac{p}{2}\right|\right) . \tag{3.3}$$

Since $\Psi(z)$ is a function of z/d only, by pulling d^2 out of the integral we can write G_{00} as $G_{00}(r) = d^2 \hat{G}_{00}(r/d)$. Now recall that $G_{10} = \frac{1}{2}\partial_r G_{00}$ and $\tilde{G} = \partial_r G_{10}$. We then find that

$$\tilde{G}(r_0) = \hat{\tilde{G}}(r_0/d) \quad \text{and} \quad G_{10}(r_0) - r_0\tilde{G}(r_0) = d\big(\hat{G}_{10}(r_0/d) - \frac{r_0}{d}\hat{\tilde{G}}(r_0/d)\big) ,$$

$$(3.4)$$

where $\hat{G}_{10}(z) = \frac{1}{2}\partial_z \hat{G}_{00}(z)$ and $\hat{\tilde{G}}(z) = \partial_z \hat{G}_{10}(z)$. Thus both numerator and denominator of equations (3.2) can be written, up to multiplication by positive coefficients, as functions of r_0/d. Now, $f(r, d) = \hat{f}(r/d)$ and $f(r, d_0) = 0$ imply $f(ar, ad_0) = 0$ for all $a \in \mathbb{R}$; thus if we determine $d_{\min}$ and $d_{\max}$ for one value of r_0, we know their values for any r_0.

To determine $d_{\min}$ and $d_{\max}$ while avoiding iterative numerical procedures to find these points, we use a polynomial approximation to G_{00}:

$$G_{00}(r) = \sum_{n=0}^{\infty} b_n r^n .$$

It is easy to show that

$$b_m = \begin{cases} 0 & m < 2 , \\ \frac{1}{(m-2)!} \int_{-\pi}^{\pi} dp \, \cos(p) \, Y^{(m-2)}(0) & m \geq 2 , \end{cases} \qquad (3.5)$$

where $Y(r) = \Psi(2r|\sin(p/2)|)$. The derivatives of Y evaluated at zero are

$$\frac{Y^{(m)}(0)}{(2|\sin(p/2)|)^m} = \Psi^{(m)}(0) = \begin{cases} 1 & m = 0 , \\ 0 & m = 1 \text{ or } m \text{ even} , \\ (-1)^{\frac{m-1}{2}} \frac{1}{2d}\left(\frac{\pi}{d}\right)^{m-1} & m \geq 3 \text{ and } m \text{ odd} . \end{cases}$$

Substituting into equation (3.5) gives b_m:

$$b_m = \begin{cases} 0 & m < 5 \text{ or } m \text{ even} , \\ (-1)^{\frac{m-1}{2}} \frac{4(2\pi)^{m-3}}{m!!(m-4)!!} \frac{1}{d^{m-2}} & m \geq 5 \text{ and } m \text{ odd} . \end{cases}$$

We can then derive expressions for $\tilde{G}$ and $G_{10} - r\tilde{G}$:

$$\tilde{G}(r) = 2 \sum_{\substack{m \geq 3 \\ m \text{ odd}}} \frac{(-1)^{\frac{m+1}{2}} (2\pi)^{m-1}(m+1)}{m!!(m-2)!!} \left(\frac{r}{d}\right)^m$$

$$G_{10}(r) - r\tilde{G}(r) = 2d \sum_{\substack{m \geq 4 \\ m \text{ even}}} \frac{(-1)^{\frac{m-2}{2}} (2\pi)^{m-2}}{[(m-3)!!]^2} \left(\frac{r}{d}\right)^m .$$

We computed the roots of these polynomials including terms up to $m = 49$. The smallest positive roots furnish the values of $d_{\min}$ and $d_{\max}$. The result is that $d_{\min} \simeq 1.2776r_0$ and $d_{\max} \simeq 1.4499r_0$. The rightmost three graphs in figure 2 show plots of E_0 against r for $r_0 = 5$, with d values chosen from the domain $d_{\min} < d < d_{\max}$.

4 Tree Crown Extraction

The tree crown extraction problem is important in forestry, and has been much studied. Gougeon [8] uses an automatic valley following method to delineate tree crowns. Larsen [9] uses a template matching method based on a 3D model to find spruce trees. This works well, but requires knowledge of image acquisition and illumination parameters to construct the template. Neither of these methods model the spatial distribution of trees. Perrin *et al.* [10] model a forest as a marked point process with ellipses as marks, thereby including inter-tree interactions. The method in this paper is similar in spirit, although expressed in a very different language. It has the advantage that the tree shape is not hard-constrained, but the disadvantage that it is difficult to apply to dense forest.

4.1 Likelihood Energy and Energy Minimization

We use E_g, with parameters fixed as described above, as a prior model for the region R of the image domain corresponding to trees. We also need a likelihood energy $E_\mathrm{i}(I, R)$. We will model the image in R, and in the background $\bar{R}$, using Gaussian distributions.[3] We add a term that predicts high gradients along the boundary ∂R:

$$E_\mathrm{i}(I, R) = \lambda_i \int dp\,\mathbf{n}(p)\cdot\partial I(\gamma(p)) + \alpha_i \left[\int_R d^2x\,\frac{(I(x) - \mu)^2}{2\sigma^2} + \int_{\bar{R}} d^2x\,\frac{(I(x) - \bar{\mu})^2}{2\bar{\sigma}^2} \right] ,$$

where $\mathbf{n}$ is the (unnormalized) outward facing normal. Note that to facilitate comparison of parameters in the prior energy, we set $\lambda = 1$ in E_g and introduce a weight α_i in E_i. The parameters μ, σ, $\bar{\mu}$, and $\bar{\sigma}$ are learned from examples using maximum likelihood, and then fixed.

The energy $E = E_\mathrm{g} + E_\mathrm{i}$ is minimized using gradient descent. The descent equation is

$$\hat{\mathbf{n}} \cdot \partial_t \gamma(p) = -\lambda_i \partial^2 I(\gamma(p)) + \alpha_i \left[\frac{(I(\gamma(p)) - \bar{\mu})^2}{2\bar{\sigma}^2} - \frac{(I(\gamma(p)) - \mu)^2}{2\sigma^2} \right]$$

$$- \kappa(p) - \alpha + \beta \int dp'\,\hat{\mathbf{r}}(p, p') \cdot \mathbf{n}(p')\,\Psi^{(1)}(r(p, p')) ,$$

where κ is the curvature of the contour, $\mathbf{r}(p, p') = \gamma(p) - \gamma(p')$, and $\hat{\mathbf{r}} = \mathbf{r}/r$. In the algorithm, it is convenient to represent the boundary by the zero level set of its signed distance function [11]. We use the extended level set framework described in [7] to cope with the nonlocal forces arising from HOAC energies.

4.2 Experimental Results

We tested the model on colour infrared aerial images of poplar stands located in the 'Saône et Loire' region in France, provided by the French National Forest Inventory

---

[3] We ignore the normalization constant $Z(R) = \int DI\,e^{-E_\mathrm{i}(I,R)}$ since in our case it merely changes λ and α, and we are interested in stability of the posterior in the absence of image-dependent terms.

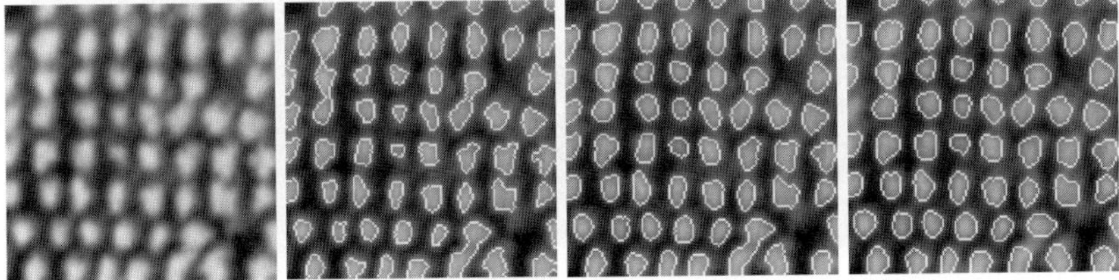

Fig. 3. From left to right: image of poplars ©IFN; the best result with a classical active contour $(70, 0.08, 5.8)$; result with model in [1] $(150, 0.15, 5.8, 4.67, 4.16, 4.16)$; result with new model $(90, 0.08, 5.47, 2.61, 6, 4.16)$.

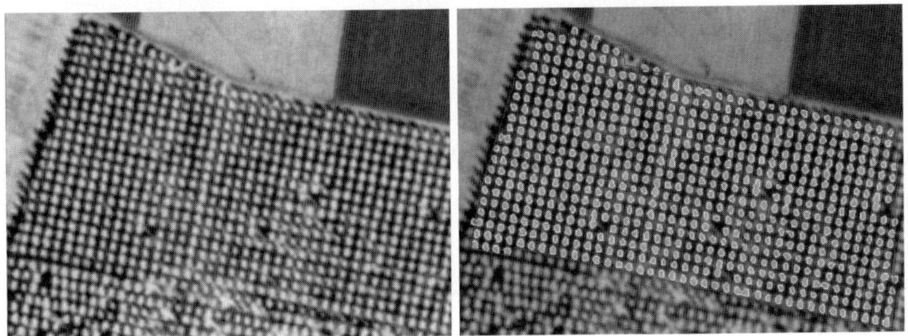

Fig. 4. Left: bigger slice of planted forest ©IFN; right: result using new model $(90, 0.04, 5.49, 2.65, 5, 3.47)$. The contour was initialized to the red line.

(IFN). We compare our new model to a classical active contour ($\beta = 0$), and the model in [1] containing an energy minimum. Note that the new model has three free parameters, λ_i, α_i and d, since the other likelihood parameters are fixed by training, while the other prior parameters are fixed once r_0 is known. The classical active contour also has three free parameters (λ_i, α_i, and α), while the model used in [1] has four (λ_i, α_i, α, and d). The initial contour in all experiments, except that in figure 4, was a rounded rectangle slightly bigger than the image domain. The image values in the region exterior to the image domain were set to $\bar{\mu}$ to ensure that the contour would shrink inwards.

Figure 3 shows four images.[4] On the left is the data. Next comes the best result we could obtain using the same likelihood but setting $\beta = 0$, *i.e.* using a classical active contour. Note how the absence of the quadratic term, which includes the prior shape knowledge, prevents trees from being separated. Next is the result we obtain with the model in [1], while on the right is the result obtained with the new model. Note that the parameter values for the new model, although fixed, nevertheless produce a comparable result. One tree on the border is missing, but on the other hand, two trees are separated that were merged by the old model.

---

[4] Parameter values in image captions are written in the form $(\lambda_i, \alpha_i, \alpha, \beta, d, r_0)$, truncated if the parameters are not present.

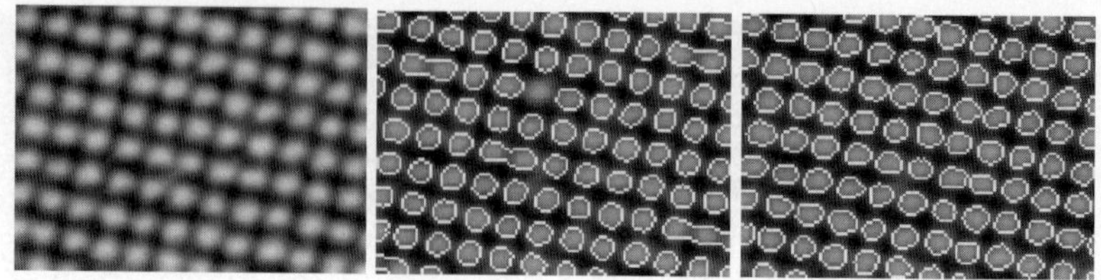

Fig. 5. Left to right: regularly planted poplars ©IFN; result with model in [1] $(40, 0.05, 5, 4.08, 3.47, 3.47)$; result with the new model $(90, 0.07, 5.49, 2.65, 5, 3.47)$.

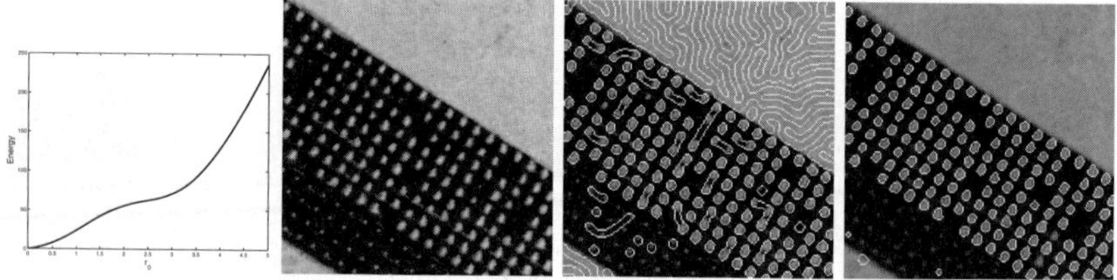

Fig. 6. Left to right: energy of a circle with α slightly greater than the value given by equation (3.2), to create slightly positive gradient everywhere; regularly planted poplars ©IFN; result with model in [1] $(15, 0.008, 4.5, 3.73, 2.51, 2.51)$; result with new model $(40, 0, 6 > 5.40, 2.65, 3.6, 2.51)$.

Figure 4 shows two images. On the left is the data, while on the right is the result obtained using the new model. The initial contour in this experiment was the red line. With a couple of exceptions, the trees are separated and the extraction is accurate.

Figure 5 shows three images. On the left is the data; in the middle is the result obtained with the model in [1]; on the right is the result obtained with the new model. Despite its fixed parameters, the new model produces a better result, finding a tree missed by the old model, and again separating trees that were merged by the old model.

For the experiment in figure 6, we used an α value slightly larger than that given by equations (3.2), in order make E_1 slightly positive for all r. This ensures that in the absence of image data, circles will disappear. The resulting E_0 is shown on the left in the figure. Next comes the data. The aim of the experiment is to detect the older, larger radius trees in the upper part of the plantation area. Third from left is the best result using the model in [1]. Note the phantom regions generated as the contour becomes trapped in local energy minima (the phantom regions in the bright exterior area are also reinforced by the image term). On the right is the result using the new model. With one exception, the phantom regions are eliminated, while the level of error elsewhere is comparable to the old model.

5 Conclusion

The 'gas of circles' model developed by [1] has numerous potential applications in image processing, *e.g.* tree crown extraction from remote sensing images and cell extraction from biological and medical images. The model in [1] suffers, however, from phantom circles created by the fact that circles of a given radius are local energy minima. The requirement that regions consisting of collections of circles of a given radius be inflection points rather than local minima solves this problem. In addition, the requirement halves the number of model parameters, and severely constrains one of the two that remain, a major advantage for an energy-based model. Despite the small remaining freedom to adjust the parameters, experiments on the tree crown detection problem show that the new model performs comparably or better than the old local minimum model, and much better than a classical active contour.

References

1. Horváth, P., Jermyn, I.H., Kato, Z., Zerubia, J.: A higher-order active contour model for tree detection. In: Proc. International Conference on Pattern Recognition (ICPR), Hong Kong, China (2006)
2. Kass, M., Witkin, A., Terzopoulos, D.: Snakes: Active contour models. International Journal of Computer Vision **1** (1988) 321–331
3. Cremers, D., Kohlberger, T., Schnörr, C.: Shape statistics in kernel space for variational image segmentation. Pattern Recognition **36** (2003) 1929–1943
4. Foulonneau, A., Charbonnier, P., Heitz, F.: Geometric shape priors for region-based active contours. Proc. IEEE International Conference on Image Processing (ICIP) **3** (2003) 413–416
5. Paragios, N., Rousson, M.: Shape priors for level set representations. In: Proc. European Conference on Computer Vision (ECCV), Copenhague, Danemark (2002) 78–92
6. Leventon, M., Grimson, W., Faugeras, O.: Statistical shape influence in geodesic active contours. In: Proc. IEEE Computer Vision and Pattern Recognition (CVPR). Volume 1., Hilton Head Island, South Carolina, USA (2000) 316–322
7. Rochery, M., Jermyn, I.H., Zerubia, J.: Higher order active contours and their application to the detection of line networks in satellite imagery. In: Proc. IEEE Workshop Variational, Geometric and Level Set Methods in Computer Vision, at ICCV, Nice, France (2003)
8. Gougeon, F.A.: Automatic individual tree crown delineation using a valley-following algorithm and rule-based system. In Hill, D., Leckie, D., eds.: Proc. Int'l Forum on Automated Interpretation of High Spatial Resolution Digital Imagery for Forestry, Victoria, British Columbia, Canada (1998) 11–23
9. Larsen, M.: Finding an optimal match window for Spruce top detection based on an optical tree model. In Hill, D., Leckie, D., eds.: Proc. of the International Forum on Automated Interpretation of High Spatial Resolution Digital Imagery for Forestry, Victoria, British Columbia, Canada (1998) 55–66
10. Perrin, G., Descombes, X., Zerubia, J.: A marked point process model for tree crown extraction in plantations. In: Proc. IEEE International Conference on Image Processing (ICIP), Genova, Italy (2005)
11. Osher, S., Sethian, J.A.: Fronts propagating with curvature dependent speed: Algorithms based on Hamilton-Jacobi formulations. Journal of Computational Physics **79** (1988) 12–49

A New Extension of Kalman Filter to Non-Gaussian Priors

G.R.K.S. Subrahmanyam, A.N. Rajagopalan, and R. Aravind

IIT Madras, India

Abstract. In the Kalman filter, the state dynamics is specified by the state equation while the measurement equation characterizes the likelihood. In this paper, we propose a generalized methodology of specifying state dynamics using the conditional density of the states given its neighbors without explicitly defining the state equation. In other words, the typically strict linear constraint on the state dynamics imposed by the state equation is relaxed by specifying the conditional density function and using it as the prior in predicting the state. Based on the above idea, we propose a sampling-based Kalman Filter (KF) for the image estimation problem. The novelty in our approach lies in the fact that we compute the mean and covariance of the prior (possibly non-Gaussian) by importance sampling. These apriori mean and covariance are fed to the update equations of the KF to estimate the aposteriori estimates of the state. We show that the estimates obtained by the proposed strategy are superior to those obtained by the traditional Kalman filter that uses the auto-regressive state model.

Keywords: Dynamic state space models, Kalman filter, Auto-regressive models, Importance sampling, Markov random fields.

1   Introduction

The problem of image estimation involves recovering the original image from its noisy version. The image estimation problem can be cast in to a state estimation from noisy measurements in state space representation of the image. When the state transition and measurement equations are both linear, and the state and measurement noises are independent and additive Gaussian, the Kalman filter gives the minimum mean square error (MMSE) estimate of the state. Extension of the 1-D KF to 2-D was first proposed by Woods and Radewan [7]. They considered the local neighborhood in updation of the state vector and arrived at a suboptimal filter known as the reduced update Kalman filter (RUKF) [8]. The reduced order model Kalman filter (ROMKF) proposed in [9] includes only local states in its state vector, but performs on par with RUKF. Effects of any distortion resulting from blur and noise can be removed by Kalman filtering, provided the appropriate image and blur parameters are completely known. In general, however, such parameters are apriori unknown, and furthermore can vary spatially as a function of the image coordinates. Hence, adaptive identification/filtering procedures are necessary for satisfactory restoration. A rapid

P. Kalra and S. Peleg (Eds.): ICVGIP 2006, LNCS 4338, pp. 162–171, 2006.

edge adaptive filter for restoration of noisy and blurred images based on multiple models has been presented in [12].

A primary issue with all image estimation methods is about how they handle noise smoothing versus preservation of edges since the two requirements are contradictory. Geman and Geman [13] approach the edge preservation problem using line fields. The smoothness constraint is switched off at points where the magnitude of the signal derivative exceeds certain thresholds. For a thorough survey of techniques for image estimation, we refer the reader to [11].

To preserve edges, one must look beyond Gaussianity. Increasingly, for many application areas, it is becoming important to include elements of non-linearity and non-Gaussianity, in order to model accurately the underlying dynamics of a physical system. In this paper, we propose an interesting extension to the traditional Kalman filter to tackle discontinuities by incorporating non-Gaussianity within the Kalman filtering framework. This is achieved by modeling the prior as a discontinuity adaptive Markov random field and proposing sampling-based approaches to derive necessary statistical parameters required for the update stage of the Kalman filter. If the state transition equation is not known but an assumption on the state transition density (possibly non-Gaussian) can be made we can still use the Kalman filter update equations in the proposed frame work. The edge preservation capability is implicitly incorporated using the discontinuity adaptive state conditional density. Importance sampling is used to obtain the statistics of this PDF and the Kalman filter is used to update the prior estimates.

We use the discontinuity adaptive function given by Li [2] to construct the prior conditional density and show how the edges are better retained in our method. This is in addition to obtaining better overall estimates of the entire image. It may be noted that the proposed approach is different from the Ensemble Kalman filter [6,5] which is based on Monte Carlo simulation of the state probability distribution. It works by creating and propagating the ensemble through model operator. The mean and the error covariance are obtained by the analysis of the ensemble. In contrast, we use the Monte Carlo approach only to determine the mean and covariance of the conditional PDF. It is possible to extend the proposed approach to nonlinear filtering problem.

2   The Kalman Filter

The Kalman filter, rooted in the state-space formulation of linear dynamical systems, provides a recursive solution to the linear optimal filtering problem [10]. It applies to stationary as well as non-stationary environments. The solution is recursive in that each updated estimate of the state is computed from the previous estimate and the new input data.

2.1   Dynamic State-Space Model

The general state space model can be broken down into a state transition model and measurement model. In linear Gaussian regression, the state space representation is as follows:

$$\mathbf{x}_{k+1} = \mathbf{F}_k \mathbf{x}_k + \mathbf{w}_k \tag{1}$$

$$\mathbf{y}_k = \mathbf{H}_k \mathbf{x}_k + \mathbf{v}_k \tag{2}$$

where $\mathbf{y}_k \in \mathrm{R}^{n_y}$ denotes the output observations, $\mathbf{x}_k \in \mathrm{R}^{n_x}$ is the state of the system, $\mathbf{w}_k \in \mathrm{R}^{n_w}$ is the process noise and $\mathbf{v}_k \in \mathrm{R}^{n_v}$ is the measurement noise. The mappings $\mathbf{F}_k : \mathrm{R}^{n_x} \rightarrow \mathrm{R}^{n_x}$ and $\mathbf{H}_k : \mathrm{R}^{n_x} \rightarrow \mathrm{R}^{n_y}$ represent the deterministic process and measurement models. To complete the specification of the model, the prior distribution is denoted by $p(\mathbf{x}_0)$. The process noise $\mathbf{w}_k$ is assumed to be additive white Gaussian, with zero mean and with covariance matrix defined by $\mathbf{Q}_k$. The measurement noise $\mathbf{v}_k$ is additive white Gaussian with covariance matrix $\mathbf{R}_k$. The process and measurement noise are assumed to be uncorrelated. The states are assumed to follow a first-order Markov model and the observations are assumed to be independent given the states.

For the state space model given above, the minimum mean squared error (MMSE) estimate of the state $\mathbf{x}_k$ can be derived using the following Kalman recursive equations [3]:

State estimate propagation:-
$$\widehat{\mathbf{x}}_{k/k-1} = \mathbf{F}_k \widehat{\mathbf{x}}_{k-1}$$

Error covariance propagation:-
$$\mathbf{C}_{k/k-1} = \mathbf{F}_k \mathbf{C}_{k-1} \mathbf{F}_k^T + \mathbf{Q}_{k-1}$$

Kalman gain matrix:-
$$\mathbf{K}_k = \mathbf{C}_{k/k-1} \mathbf{H}_k^T \left[\mathbf{H}_k \mathbf{C}_{k/k-1} \mathbf{H}_k^T + \mathbf{R}_k \right]^{-1}$$

State estimate update:-
$$\widehat{\mathbf{x}}_k = \widehat{\mathbf{x}}_{k/k-1} + \mathbf{K}_k (\mathbf{y}_k - \mathbf{H}_k \widehat{\mathbf{x}}_{k/k-1})$$

Error covariance update:-
$$\mathbf{C}_k = (\mathbf{I} - \mathbf{K}_k \mathbf{H}_k) \mathbf{C}_{k/k-1}$$

Here, $\widehat{\mathbf{x}}_{k-1}$ and $\mathbf{C}_{k-1}$ are the posteriori estimates of the state and error covariance of the previous step available at time k, $\widehat{\mathbf{x}}_{k/k-1}$ and $\mathbf{C}_{k/k-1}$ are the apriori estimates of the state and error covariance at time k, $\mathbf{y}_k$ is the new measurement at time k, $\mathbf{F}_k$ and $\mathbf{H}_k$ are the state transition and measurement matrices at time k, $\mathbf{K}_k$ is the Kalman gain, and the $\widehat{\mathbf{x}}_k$ and $\mathbf{C}_k$ are the posterior state and error covariance of the present step.

For the image estimation problem, $\mathbf{x}_k$ corresponds to the true image pixels and $\mathbf{y}_k$ are the observations of the degraded image pixel. Matrix $\mathbf{F}_k$ contains the auto-regressive (AR) coefficients of the image. For example, if a_1, a_2, a_3 are the AR coefficients of the original image (i.e., coefficients of a three pixel neighborhood with non-symmetric half plane support (NSHP)), then $\mathbf{F}_k = \begin{bmatrix} a_1 & a_2 & a_3 \\ 1 & 0 & 0 \\ 0 & 1 & 0 \end{bmatrix}$.

Since we do not assume any blurring, we have $\mathbf{H}_k = [1\ 0\ 0]$. The above filter is referred to as the Auto-Regressive Kalman Filter (ARKF). Note that the filter imposes a strong (linear) constraint on the state equation. It is important to observe that linear dependence implies statistical dependence but not vice-versa. Our idea is to arrive at a more general framework wherein pixel dependencies can be expressed statistically.

3   Discontinuity Adaptive Prior

A realization of a random field is generated when we perform a random experiment at each spatial location and assigns the outcome of the random experiment to that location. A Markov random field (MRF) possesses Markovian property: i.e., the value of a pixel depends only on the values of its neighboring pixels and on no other pixel [4,2]. More details of MRF can be found in Li [2].

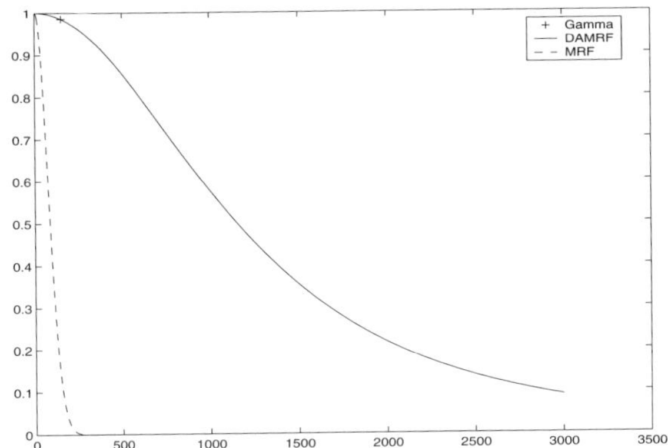

Fig. 1. Plot shows how MRF and DAMRF differ in the weighing with respect to η

Smoothness is a property that underlies a wide range of physical phenomena. However, it is not valid at discontinuities. How to apply the smoothness constraint while preserving edges has been an active research area within the MRF framework. Li [2] identifies that the fundamental difference among different models for dealing with discontinuities lies in the manner of controlling the interaction among neighboring points. Li then proposes a discontinuity adaptive (DA) model based on the principle that whenever a discontinuity occurs, the interaction should diminish. One such interaction function is $h_\gamma(\eta) = \frac{1}{1+\frac{\eta^2}{\gamma}}$

and its corresponding adaptive potential function is $g_\gamma(\eta) = \gamma \log(1 + \frac{\eta^2}{\gamma})$. The function is such that the smoothing strength $|\eta h_\gamma(\eta)|$ increases monotonically as η increases [2] within a band $B_\gamma = (-\sqrt{\gamma}, \sqrt{\gamma})$. Outside the band, smoothing decreases as η increases and becomes zero as $\eta \to \infty$. This enables it to preserve image discontinuities. It differs from the quadratic (Gaussian) regularizer which smoothes edges as $\eta \to \infty$. In Fig. 1 we show that for large η the Gaussian MRF assigns zero weight while the discontinuity adaptive MRF (DAMRF) allows edges with finite weight.

In the case of a simple GMRF model, the state conditional probability density function (PDF) is given by $\exp(-\eta^2)$ where $\eta^2(x) = ((x - c_1)^2 + (x - c_2)^2 + (x - c_3)^2)/2\beta^2$. Pixels c_1, c_2, c_3 denote the previously (estimated) pixels in the NSHP support. This can be shown to be equivalent to a Gaussian (PDF) with mean $(c_1+c_2+c_3)/3$ and variance $\Gamma = \beta^2/3$. We assume the state conditional density to be non-Gaussian and of the form $\exp(-g_\gamma(\eta))$ where $g_\gamma(\eta) = \gamma \log(1 + \frac{\eta^2}{\gamma})$ and η is as defined in the simple MRF case which leads to the DAMRF model [2].

4   Importance Sampling

It is not analytically possible to compute the mean and covariance of the non-Gaussian DAMRF distribution. Hence, we resort to Monte Carlo techniques. An efficient way of doing this is to adopt the importance sampling method. Our aim is to obtain the conditional mean and variance of the distribution corresponding to the DAMRF at every pixel, using importance sampling.

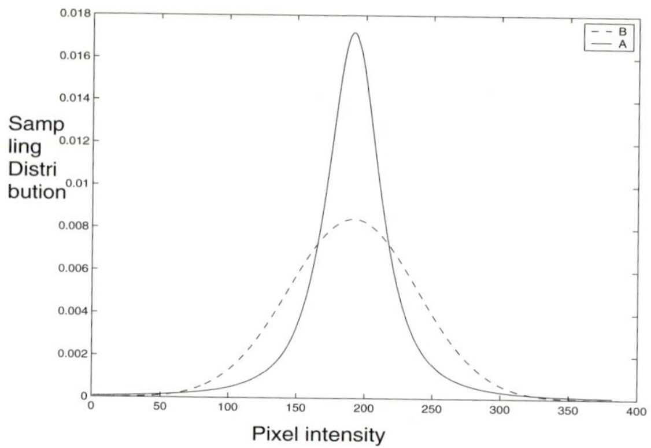

Fig. 2. Importance sampling: A is the PDF whose moments are to be estimated, while B is the sampler density

Importance Sampling (IS) is a Monte Carlo method to determine the estimates of a (non-Gaussian) target PDF, provided its functional form is known up to a multiplication constant [1]. Let us consider a PDF $A(s)$ which is known up to a multiplicative constant but it is very difficult to make any estimates of its moments. However, from the functional form, we can estimate its support (region where it is non-zero). Consider a different distribution $B(s)$ which is known up to a multiplicative constant, is easy to sample, and is such that the (non-zero) support of $B(s)$ includes the support of $A(s)$. Such a density $B(s)$ is called a sampler density. A typical plot showing the PDFs of B (solid line) and A (dashed line) is given in Fig. 2.

Our aim is to determine the first two central moments of the PDF A. Since it is difficult to draw samples from the non-Gaussian PDF A, we draw L samples, $\{s^{(l)}\}_{l=1}^{L}$ from the sampler PDF B. If these were under A, we can determine the moments of A with these samples. In order to use these samples to determine the estimates of the moments of A, we proceed as follows.

When we use samples from B to determine any estimates under A, in the regions where B is greater than A, these estimates are over-represented. In the regions where B is less than A, they are under-represented. To account for this,

we use correction weights $w^l = \frac{A(s^{(l)})}{B(s^{(l)})}$ in determining the estimates under A.
For example, to determine the mean of the distribution A we use $\widehat{\mu}_a = \frac{\sum_l w^l s^{(l)}}{\sum_l w^l}$.
If $L \to \infty$ the estimate $\widehat{\mu}_a$ tends to the actual mean of A. This methodology of
estimating moments of A by sampling from an importance function B forms the
core of importance sampling.

5   The Proposed Kalman Filter

In this section, we present a new algorithm for estimating an image from its
degraded version using the state conditional PDF and Kalman filter update
equations. In section 3, we showed how to construct a DAMRF PDF using a
discontinuity adaptivity MRF function. In section 4, we explained how to determine the estimates of a PDF using importance sampling. We now present a novel
strategy which integrates the above steps within the Kalman filter framework
to restore images degraded by additive white Gaussian noise. In the proposed
strategy, only the assumption on the conditional PDF needs to be made. The
parameters of the PDF are a function of the already estimated pixels and the
values of Γ and γ. This implicitly generalizes the state transition equation. The
steps involved in the proposed method are as follows:

1. At each pixel, construct the state conditional PDF using the past three pixels
   from its NSHP support, and the values of Γ and γ in the DAMRF model
   (section 3) . Using the DAMRF function given by [2] we construct the state
   conditional PDF as

$$P(X(m,n)/\widehat{X}(m-i,n-j)) = \exp\left(-\gamma \log(1 + \frac{\eta^2(X(m,n))}{\gamma})\right); \quad (3)$$

   where $(i,j) = (0,1),(1,0),(1,1)$ and
   $$\eta^2(X(m,n)) = ((X(m,n) - \widehat{X}(m,n-1))^2 + (X(m,n) - \widehat{X}(m-1,n))^2$$
   $$+ (X(m,n) - \widehat{X}(m-1,n-1))^2)/(2\beta^2), \text{ and } \beta^2 = 3\Gamma.$$
   Here, X and $\widehat{X}$ refers to the original image and the estimated image, respectively. The pixels $\widehat{X}(m,n-1),\widehat{X}(m-1,n)$ and $\widehat{X}(m-1,n-1)$ are the
   (estimated) past three pixels of the NSHP support.
2. Obtain the mean and covariance of the above PDF using importance sampling as described in section 4. Explicitly, we draw samples $\{s^l\}$ from a
   Gaussian sampler [1] The sampler $B(s)$ has mean $\mu_b = (\widehat{X}(m,n-1) +$
   $\widehat{X}(m-1,n)+\widehat{X}(m-1,n-1))/3$ and variance $\sigma_b^2 = 15\beta^2$. We weight these
   samples through the importance weights $w^l = \frac{A(s^l)}{B(s^l)}$. The mean $\widehat{\mu}_a$ and variance $\widehat{\sigma}_a^2$ of A are computed as

$$\widehat{\mu}_a = \frac{\sum_l w_l s^{(l)}}{\sum_l w_l} \qquad\qquad \widehat{\sigma}_a^2 = \frac{\sum_l w_l(s^{(l)} - \mu_a)^2}{\sum_l w_l} \qquad (4)$$

---

[1] The idea is to have the support of the target density A included in the support of
the sampler density B so that the mean 'μ_b' is near to the actual mean of the MRF,
and the variance 'σ_b^2' is high enough.

3. The predicted mean and error covariance are fed to the update stage of the Kalman filter as follows:

$$\widehat{\mathbf{x}}_{k/k-1} = \widehat{\mu}_a; \quad \mathbf{C}_{k/k-1} = \widehat{\sigma}_a^2;$$

Kalman gain matrix:- $\mathbf{K}_k = \mathbf{C}_{k/k-1}\mathbf{H}_k^T \left[\mathbf{H}_k\mathbf{C}_{k/k-1}\mathbf{H}_k^T + \mathbf{R}_k\right]^{-1}$

State estimate update:- $\widehat{\mathbf{x}}_k = \widehat{\mathbf{x}}_{k/k-1} + \mathbf{K}_k(\mathbf{y}_k - \mathbf{H}_k\widehat{\mathbf{x}}_{k/k-1})$

This gives the estimated mean $\widehat{X}(m,n) = \widehat{\mathbf{x}}_k$; go to step 1 and repeat.

Finally, the filtered image is $\widehat{X}$.

We note that in this case the state becomes a scalar, the matrix $\mathbf{H}_n = 1$, and $\mathbf{y}_n$ is the scalar observation pixel. This approach does not need the state equation (1).

In the proposed approach, based on the past three pixels of the NSHP support, the prior is constructed. Importance sampling is used to estimate the mean and covariance of the non-Gaussian prior. These estimates are effectively used by the Kalman filter update equations (Kalman gain and mean updation equations), to arrive at the posterior mean (the estimated pixel intensity). Note that in the proposed formulation, the prior is not restricted to be Gaussian. In other words, the process noise can have any distribution but with a known functional form.

6   Experimental Results

In this section, we compare the proposed importance sampling based Kalman Filter (ISKF) with the auto-regressive Kalman Filter (ARKF). In an AR based Kalman filter, the original image is used to determine the AR coefficients and the process noise. An alternative is to use the AR coefficients obtained from images of the same class or to use the observed image itself. But this will in general, degrade the performance of the algorithm. In contrast for the proposed algorithm, the image model parameters are not required. Since the conditional PDF has all the information. The proposed algorithm has two parameters γ and Γ which depend on the image. We have found that the optimum γ for most images is in the range of 1 to 2 while the required value of Γ is in the range of 50 to 150. For low values of γ and high values of Γ the estimated image will be noisy, and for high values of γ and low values of Γ the estimated image will be blurred. For a quantitative comparesion of ARKF and the proposed method we use the improvement-in-signal-to-noise-ratio (ISNR) which is defined as $ISNR = 10\log_{10}\left(\frac{\sum_{m,n}(Y(m,n)-X(m,n))^2}{\sum_{m,n}(\widehat{X}(m,n)-X(m,n))^2}\right) dB$. Here, (m,n) are over entair image. X, Y and $\widehat{X}$ represent the original image, degraded observation, and the estimated image, respectively.

Fig. 3(a) shows the "daisy" image. The image after degradation by additive white Gaussian noise of $SNR = 10$ dB is shown in Fig. 4(a). The images estimated by ARKF and the proposed importance sampling-based Kalman filter, are given in Figs. 4(b) and 4(c), respectively. Note that the image estimated by the proposed approach has sharp petals. At the same time, it is less noisy in

(a)　　　　　　　　(b)　　　　　　　　(c)

Fig. 3. Original images (a) Daisy image, (b) Flowers image and (c) Bric image

(a)　　　　　　　　(b)　　　　　　　　(c)

Fig. 4. Daisy (a) Image degraded by additive white Gaussian noise ($SNR = 10$ dB). Image estimated using (b) AR based KF ($ISNR = 3.42$ dB) and (c) Proposed method ($ISNR = 4.25$ dB, $\Gamma = 50$, $\gamma = 1.5$).

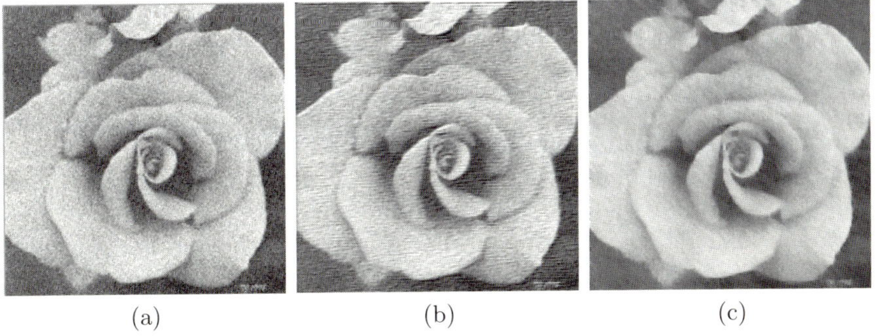

(a)　　　　　　　　(b)　　　　　　　　(c)

Fig. 5. Flower (a) Degraded image ($SNR = 10$ dB). Image estimated by (b) AR based KF ($ISNR = -1.39$ dB) (c) Proposed method ($ISNR = 3.73$ dB, $\Gamma = 50$, $\gamma = 1.5$).

homogeneous regions compared to the ARKF output. It has a superior improvement-in-signal-to-noise-ratio (ISNR) value over ARKF.

Next, we show in Fig. 3(b) a flower image. It is degraded by additive white Gaussian noise of $SNR = 10$ dB (Fig. 5 (a)). The image estimated by ARKF and the proposed approach are shown in Figs. 5(b) and 5 (c), respectively. The image estimated by the proposed approach has very little noise, retains the edges, and has higher ISNR value. Note the ringing-like artifact in the image estimated by ARKF. For the proposed method, the overall appearance of the estimated image is quite good.

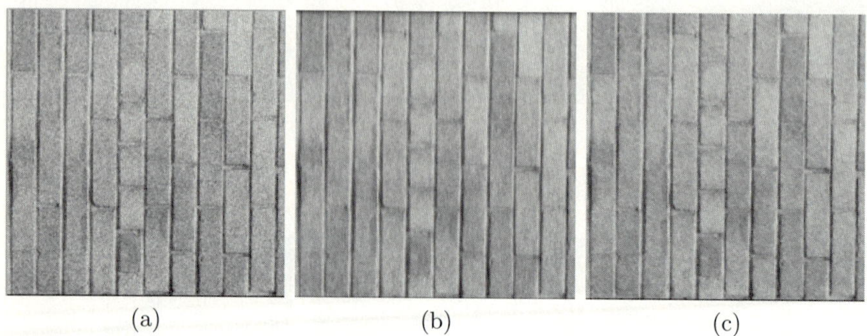

(a)   (b)   (c)

Fig. 6. Brick (a) Degraded image ($SNR = 10$ dB). Image estimated using (b) AR based KF ($ISNR = -1.3$ dB) (c) Proposed method ($ISNR = 1.96$ dB, $\Gamma = 50$, $\gamma = 2$).

Fig. 3(c) shows a brick image while its degraded version is given in Fig. 6(a). The images estimated by ARKF and the proposed method are shown in Figs. 6(b) and Fig. 6(c), respectively. The proposed sampling-based Kalman filter again outperforms ARKF. The image retains the horizontal edges quite well and is much closer to the original image as compared to ARKF.

The above results show that the proposed approach is superior to ARKF in reducing noise, preserving edges, and yelding better ISNR values. Fixing the parameters for the proposed scheme is also quite simple as discussed in the beginning of this section.

7   Conclusions

We have proposed a novel importance sampling-based discontinuity adaptive Kalman filter. Instead of using the state transition equation to predict the mean and error covariance (as in traditional Kalman filter formulation), we use a DA non-Gaussian state conditional density function for prediction. Importance sampling is used to determine the apriori mean and covariance of a DAMRF model. These are then used in the Kalman filter update equations to obtain the a posteriori mean. The image estimates obtained by the proposed approach are superior to those obtained with the auto-regressive Kalman filter.

References

1. D. J. C. Mackay, "Introduction to Monte Carlo methods", In M. I. Jordan, editor, "Learning in graphical models", NATO Science Series, pp. 175–204. *Kluwer Academic Press*, 1998.

2. S. Z. Li, "Markov random field modeling in computer vision", *Springer Verlag*, 1995.
3. S. Haykin, "Kalman filtering and neural networks", *John Wiley and Sons*, 2001.
4. M. Petrou and P. G. Sevilla, "Image processing dealing with texture", *John Wiley and Sons*, 2006.
5. J. Drecourt, "Kalman filtering in hydrological modeling", *Technical report* (2003).
6. G. Evensen, "The ensemble Kalman filter: theoretical formulation and practical implementation", *Ocean Dynamics*, vol. 53, pp. 343-367, 2003.
7. J. W. Woods and C. H. Radewan, "Kalman filter in two dimensions", *IEEE Trans. on Information Theory*, vol. 23, pp. 473-482, 1977.
8. J. W. Woods and V. K. Ingle, "Kalman filtering in two dimensions-Further results", *IEEE Trans. Acoustics Speech and Signal Proc.*, vol. 29, pp. 188-197, 1981.
9. D. Angwin and H. Kaufman, "Image restoration using a reduced order model Kalman filter", *IEEE Trans. on Signal Processing*, vol. 16, pp. 21-28, 1989.
10. http://www.cs.unc.edu/~welch/kalman/
11. H. Kaufman and A. M. Tekalp, "Survey of estimation techniques in image restoration", *IEEE Control Systems Magazine*, vol. 11, pp. 16 - 24, 1991.
12. A. M. Tekalp, H. Kaufman and J. Woods, "Edge-adaptive image restoration with ringing suppression", *IEEE Trans. Acoustics Speech and Signal Proc.* vol. 37, pp. 892-899, 1989.
13. S. Geman and D. Geman, "Stochastic relaxation, gibbs distributions, and the bayesian restoration of images", *IEEE Trans. Pattern Anal. Machine Intell.*, vol. 6, pp. 721-741, 1984.

A Computational Model for Boundary Detection

Gopal Datt Joshi and Jayanthi Sivaswamy

Centre for Visual Information Technology,
IIIT Hyderabad, Andhra Pradesh
India, 500032
`gopal@research.iiit.ac.in`, `jsivaswamy@iiit.ac.in`

Abstract. Boundary detection in natural images is a fundamental problem in many computer vision tasks. In this paper, we argue that early stages in primary visual cortex provide ample information to address the boundary detection problem. In other words, *global visual primitives* such as object and region boundaries can be extracted using *local features* captured by the receptive fields. The anatomy of visual cortex and psychological evidences are studied to identify some of the important underlying computational principles for the boundary detection task. A scheme for boundary detection based on these principles is developed and presented. Results of testing the scheme on a benchmark set of natural images, with associated human marked boundaries, show the performance to be quantitatively competitive with existing computer vision approaches.

1 Introduction

Boundary detection constitutes a crucial step in many computer vision tasks. A boundary map of an image can provide valuable information for further image analysis and interpretation tasks such as segmentation, object description etc. Fig. 1 shows an image and the associated boundary map as marked by human observers. It can be noted that the map essentially retains gross but important details in the image. It is hence sparse yet rich in information from the point of scene understanding. Extracting a similar boundary map is of interest in computer vision.

The problem of boundary detection is different from the classical problem of edge detection. A boundary is a contour in the image plane that represents a change in pixel's ownership from one object or surface to another [2]. In contrast, an edge is defined as a significant change in image features such as brightness or color. Edge detection is thus a low-level technique that is commonly applied toward the goal of boundary detection. In general, it is desirable to be able to accurately extract all types of boundaries: for instance those formed between two luminance regions, two textured regions and texture-luminance regions as shown in Fig. 2. There are some attempts in computer vision to address all these attributes completely [2] [3] [4] [5] using complex and computationally intensive schemes. In contrast, humans have an outstanding ability to detect boundaries pre-attentively (fast in nature). This means that the human visual system (HVS)

P. Kalra and S. Peleg (Eds.): ICVGIP 2006, LNCS 4338, pp. 172–183, 2006.

(a)

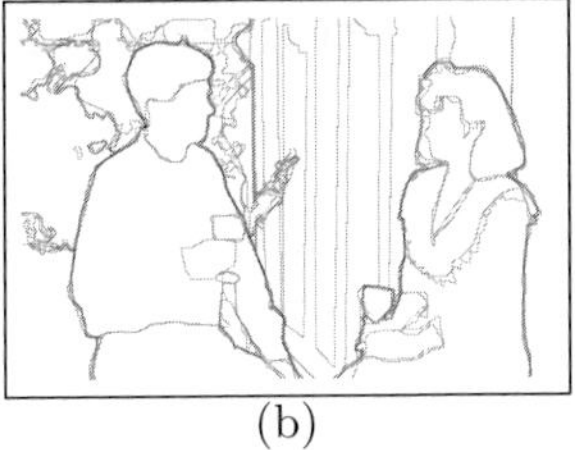
(b)

Fig. 1. (a) Example image (b) Human-marked segment boundaries. Image shows boundaries marked by 4-8 observers. The pixels are darker where more observers marked a boundary [1].

is capable of extracting all important boundary information in its *early* stages of processing. Studying the visual mechanisms underlying these tasks can provide an alternative solution to the boundary detection problem. It may also lead to simple and fast scheme for boundary detection in computer vision.

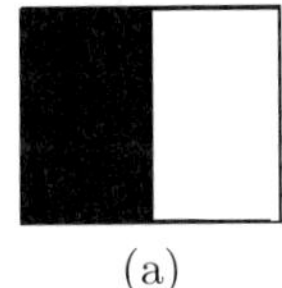
(a)

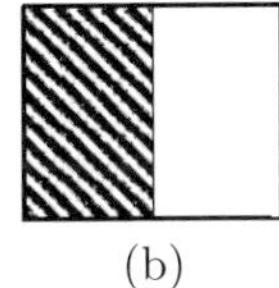
(b)

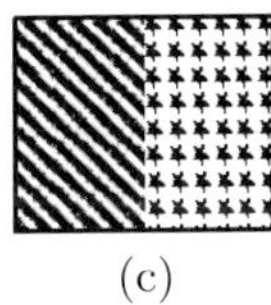
(c)

Fig. 2. Types of boundaries

Some attempts have been made to model boundary detection in HVS. One such model assumes that saliency of boundaries arise from long-range interaction between orientation-selective cortical cells [6]. This model accounts for a number of experimental findings from psychophysics but its performance is unsatisfactory on natural images and it is computationally intensive. Another model emphasises the role of local information and focuses on cortical cells which are tuned to bar type features [7] [8]. It extracts edge information which is followed by an assessment based on the local context. These models have been shown to perform well on natural images but are incapable of detecting boundaries formed by texture regions (shown in Fig. 2(b), 2(c)). In this paper, we present a computational model for the boundary detection functionality of the HVS which can extract all types of boundaries. We present results of testing this model on a set of benchmarked images where boundaries are marked by human observers.

The presentation in this paper is organised as follows. In the next section, we review the relevant neurophysiological and psychophysical findings in early stages of the HVS and end with a proposal for a computational model for boundary detection. In section 3, a computational scheme is developed based on the proposed computational model. In section 4, the performance of the proposed scheme is compared against human marked boundaries followed by some concluding remarks.

2   Computation Model for Boundary Detection

Real world images are processed in our visual system to produce boundaries. These images are characterised by colour, texture [1] and non-texture (only regular luminance/colour based) regions. Thus, boundaries can arise due to the adjacency of any of these regions in natural images. Some of these that can occur in grey scale images (which is the focus of this paper) are shown in figure 2: luminance-luminance or LL boundary, texture-luminance or TL boundary, and texture-texture or TT boundary.

Any image point can be declared as a boundary only after understanding its local context. By context is meant a characterisation of the local surround in terms of luminance and texture. In the early stages of HVS, there is evidence that the derived representation provides enough texture and non-texture information to address boundary detection effectively. At the retinal level, visual input (image) is filtered by ganglion cells whose local classical receptive field's (CRF's)[2] are a close fit to a Laplacian of Gaussian [9]. Thus the representation derived at the retinal level is an edge map. The results of this processing form direct input to Lateral Geniculate Nucleus (LGN) in the mid-brain. This area has no known filter function but serves mainly to project binocular visual input to various sites, especially to the visual cortex. The cells found in this area have a functional role similar to that of the retinal ganglion cells except that they also perform binocular mapping. In our work, we ignore binocular details associated with the LGN cells.

The Ganglion and LGN cells are classified into two classes, known as P and M-cells [10] [11] [12]. The P-cells have smaller receptive fields and signal high spatial frequencies in the image while the M-cells have (2-3 times) larger receptive fields and they cannot resolve high spatial frequencies [10] [12] [13]. We can infer that P-cells strongly respond to fine and coarse edges whereas M-cells respond to coarse edges and quite poorly to fine edges. At this stage of HVS, there is not much information associated with any detected edge to declare it as a boundary point. When we consider a texture patch for example, the M-cells respond to its contour while the P cells respond to its contour as well as any edges arising from the texture elements within the patch. Hence, there is an ambiguity in determining if an edge belongs to a texture region or not based on the cell responses. Thus, it is difficult to separate out texture and non-texture information effectively at this stage of HVS. Such a situation however, gets resolved in the cortical level which is the next stage of the HVS, called as area V1.

The cortical cells in area V1 are sensitive to some new attributes like orientation. Furthermore, their sensitivity to edge features becomes more specialised compared to the LGN cells. Hubel and Wiesel [14] distinguished between *simple* and *complex cells* in cat primary visual cortex (area $V1$) that are selective to

---

[1] It is a spatial structure characterising, apart from colour and the gray level, the visual homogeneity of a given zone of an image.

[2] The receptive field is, by definition, the visual area within which one can activate an individual neuron.

intensity changes in specific orientation (oriented edge features). Although complex cells have many properties in common with simple cells, including orientation selectivity, their defining feature is that a suitably oriented pattern will elicit a response no matter where it lies in the receptive field [14] [15]. This property is known as "phase invariance". Although, simple and complex cells bring orientation selectivity in feature detection, their response to texture and non-texture patterns is ambiguous, similar to LGN cells. There are some other cells in area V1 having more specialised behavior like *bar cells*, *grating cells* and *end- stopped cells.* [16] [17] [18]. These cells are more specialised forms of complex cells.

The bar and grating cells play an important role in boundary detection [18] [19]. It is important to know their characteristics and inter-connections with the previous stages. These cells mostly get their input from the M- cells of area LGN [10] [11] [20] [21]. The grating cell responds only to a texture edge and not to any isolated edge or line [18] [19]. On the other hand, a bar cell responds only to an isolated edge or line but does not respond to any texture edge [7]. Hence, it is possible to disambiguate between an edge belonging to a textured region and a non-textured region.

To summarise, the HVS appears to use a principle of increasing functional specialisation to enable certain features of the visual pattern to become more explicit in successive stages of processing [9]. Such functional specialisation serves to resolve the ambiguity present in the previous stages.

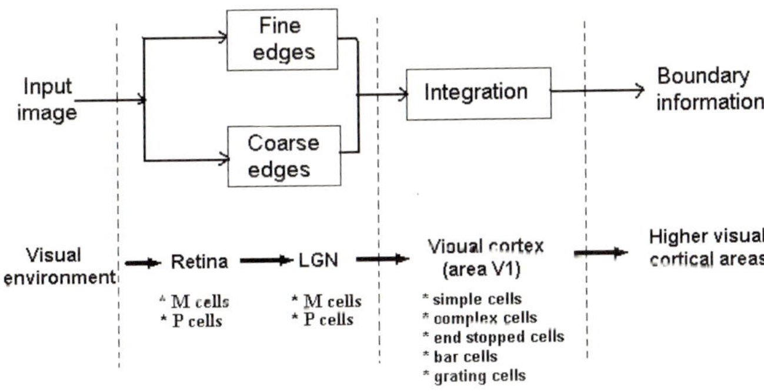

Fig. 3. Computational model for boundary detection and corresponding processing stages in HVS

Based on the above findings, we propose a computational model for boundary detection (given in Fig. 3): The visual input (or an image) is processed by P and M types of ganglion and LGN cells in order to extract redundant subsets of fine and coarse edges. This information is passed to the next stage (area V1) where the bar and grating cell operators help extract texture and non-texture information. The boundaries that are formed by texture and non-texture regions are extracted via an integration process that combines the outputs of the bar and grating cells. The output of integration is usable in any high level task. Next, we present an implementation scheme based on the proposed model.

3 Implementation

3.1 Image Representation at LGN Level

At the retinal level, *ganglion cells* signal the spatial difference in the light intensity falling upon adjacent locations in the retina. At the output of this stage (retina), the visual system provides an efficient representation in terms of fine edge locations. This *fine* edge map can be computed using any standard gradient-based edge detector. Assuming the gradient is computed in two orthogonal directions x and y. The gradient map G be for a given input image I is:

$$G(x, y) = \sqrt{(I_x^2 + I_y^2)} \tag{1}$$

where I_i is partial derivative of image in i direction. The P-type cells produce a response similar to the gradient map and extract fine edges in the image whereas, M-cells are tuned for coarse edge features. We derive such characteristics by using local surround. For every point p in an image, we consider its surround and associate with the point a histogram of the surround which we call as the *Photoreceptor Histogram* (h_p). For computational purpose, the surround is taken to be be a window of fixed size. The Photoreceptor Histogram (h) is a K-long vector where K is the maximum no. of grey levels in the image. The histogram operation ignores spatial details and captures coarse details within a local surround which is actually relevant to get a boundary details. Such details can lead to the detection of coarse edges similar to the M-type cells. Here, we do not present the detection of such edges (as it is not of use) but it can be easily obtained by a sum of gradient values computed at every element of the transformed vector (h_p).

3.2 Image Representation at Area V1

In area V1, cells gain orientation selectivity and exhibit more specialised behavior towards texture and non-texture patterns. In the context of boundary detection, bar and grating cells are more useful as they provide unambiguous information about such patterns.

Bar Cells. A bar cell responds most strongly to a single bar stimulus, such as a line or edge, in its receptive field and it has a reduced response when more bars are present in the surrounding region of the stimulus. In natural images, it is equivalent to a detector which responds only to isolated edges and not to edges which belong to a texture region [7]. Such a characteristic can be achieved by a surround (local) assessment of P-type LGN cell response. This notion is called *surround inhibition* which models intra-cortical interaction among cells.

For a given point in the image, the inhibition term is computed in an annular area around it. Let a filter function $g_\sigma(x, y)$ be defined as follows (inverse of $g_\sigma(x, y)$ is shown in Fig. 4):

$$g_\sigma(x, y) = \frac{1}{||P(DoG)||} P(DoG(x, y)) \tag{2}$$

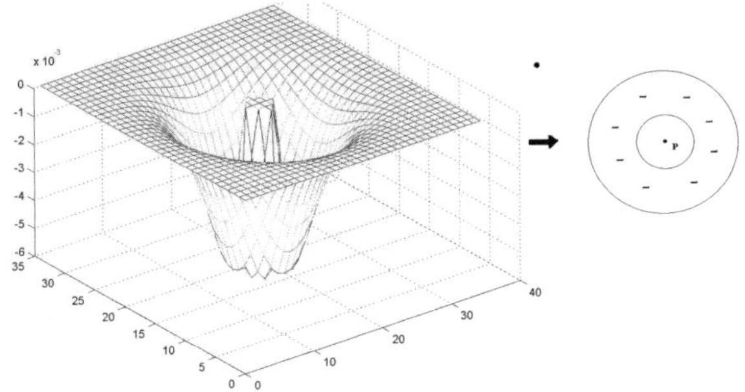

Fig. 4. Inhibition function which models the contribution of the surround (2D and 1D profile)

where $P(x) = \frac{x+|x|}{2}$ is a rectification operator, $|.|$ denotes modulus, $DoG(x,y)$ is a difference of Gaussian functions with standard deviations σ in the ratio of $n : 1$ for some integer n; and $||.||$ denotes the L_1 norm. The surround influence is applied to the gradient image G (obtained from equation 1) as follows:

$$S(x, y) = (G * g_\sigma)(x, y) \tag{3}$$

A bar cell response E_α at a location (x, y) is then obtained as:

$$E_\alpha(G(x, y)) = P(G(x, y) - \alpha.S(x, y)) \tag{4}$$

where the factor α controls the strength of the influence by the surround inhibition. If there is no texture surrounding (i.e., there is an isolated edge) a given image point, the response at that point will be equal to the gradient value as there will be no inhibition. However, if there are other edges in the surrounding region, the inhibition term $S(x, y)$ will become strong enough to cancel completely, the contribution of the gradient term. This model for bar cells provides a contour representation for any given input by discarding irrelevant edges within texture regions. In the later stages of our boundary detection scheme, we will use this functional model by the name *surround inhibition*.

Grating Cells. The grating cells are responsible for texture processing in the early stages of HVS. These cells respond strongly to a grating (periodic pattern of edges) of specific orientation, periodicity and position and not to isolated edges [18]. The role of the grating cells as a texture operator has been established in [19]. Texture regions are distinguishable based on the distribution of the edges within. Using this fact, we can define a similarity measure between two texture regions. Such a measure is useful to determine any boundary between two texture regions. For instance, any point which lies in between two texture regions which are dissimilar can be declared as a boundary point. A measure of such similarity is therefore of interest. Given two photoreceptor histograms h_{p1} and h_{p2}, we use the χ^2-statistic [22] to define a (dis-)similarity measure:

$$\chi^2(h_{p1}, h_{p2}) = \sum_{k=1}^{K} \frac{[h_{p1}(k) - h_{p2}(k)]^2}{[h_{p1}(k) + h_{p2}(k)]} \tag{5}$$

where $k \in [1, K]$ is the intensity level. Two similar texture regions will cause the numerator of the above expression to diminish, and hence the similarity measure to be low. In natural images, the diverse nature of the texture regions results in a wide range of variability in the above measure. To address this problem we transform these values to fit in the range of $0 - 1$ in such a way as to emphasise only low values as follows.

$$R(\chi^2) = e^{-\frac{(\chi^2)^2}{2\tau^2}} \tag{6}$$

where τ is a parameter that controls the level of penalty. The similarity measure can be used to determine if a point lies on TL and TT types of boundaries by considering the histograms of points located to its left and right. Next, we integrate the information extracted up to this point in order to obtain boundaries.

3.3   Integration: A Scheme for Boundary Detection

This stage integrates information gathered from the P and M cells of LGN as well as the bar and grating cells of V1. Let $\chi^2 = [(\chi_x^2)^2 + (\chi_y^2)^2]^{\frac{1}{2}}$ where, χ_x^2 and χ_y^2 are computed along the x and y-axis, respectively. The integration is achieved as follows:

$$\tilde{B}(x, y) = \gamma.G(x, y) + \beta.\chi^2(x, y) \tag{7}$$

where, γ and β are appropriate weights. The integration scheme has two sub-parts with each part contributing to the extraction of specific types of boundaries: the first part will be a maximum at the location of a LL boundary whereas the second part will be a maximum at TL and TT boundaries. To determine how the weights are to be assigned, let us re-examine the first part. This term will also be significant within the texture regions of TL and TT boundary which needs to be suppressed. This can be partially achieved by choosing the weight γ to be dependent on the texture measure χ^2 as follows: $\gamma = 1.0 - R(\chi^2)$. This choice of weight ensures that the first term nearly vanishes in equation 7 when edges are formed due to sub-patterns in a texture region. The weight β can simply be a scalar.

In principle, equation 7 signals (with a maximum) texture boundaries and edges. Of these, to extract only boundary points due to all types of boundaries, we need to further suppress the response for edges within texture regions. This is accomplished by applying *surround inhibition* (E_α) as found in bar cells.

$$B(x, y) = E_\alpha(\tilde{B}(x, y)) \tag{8}$$

Next, we present the results of testing the proposed scheme on natural images and evaluate the same against human-marked boundaries.

4   Performance Evaluation and Results

Most of the methods for the evaluation of edge and boundary detectors use natural images with associated desired output that is subjectively specified by the human observer [1] [4] [7]. We tested the performance of the proposed scheme by applying a *precision-recall (PR)* framework using human-marked boundaries from the Berkeley segmentation dataset [1] as ground truth. The segmentation dataset contains 5-10 segmentations for each image. The dataset has training images and testing images. The training images were not used as there is no training involved in our scheme and hence the evaluation was done only on the test image set (100 images) which consisted of both indoor and outdoor scenes.

The precision-recall curve is a parametric curve that captures the trade off between accuracy and noise as the detector's threshold varies. *Precision* is the fraction of detections that are true positives rather than the false positives, while *recall* is the fraction of true positives that are detected rather than missed. The PR curves are hence appropriate for quantifying boundary detection. The PR measures are particularly meaningful in the context of boundary detection when we consider applications that make use of boundary maps, such as stereo or object recognition. It is useful to characterise a detector in terms of how much true signal is required to succeed R (recall), and how much noise can be tolerated P (precision). A method to determine the relative cost μ between these quantities for a given application is given in [2]. We follow the same and use the *F-measure* (proposed therein) which is defined as

$$F = PR/(\mu R + (1 - \mu)P) \qquad (9)$$

The location of the maximum F-measure along the curve provides the optimal threshold for an application for a desired μ, which we set to be 0.5 in our experiments When a single performance measure is required or is sufficient, precision and recall can be combined with the F-measure. The F-measure curve is usually unimodal, so the maximal F-measure may be reported as a summary of the detectors performance.

Precision and recall are appealing measures, but to compute them we must determine which true positives are correctly detected, and which detections are false. We have used the correspondence algorithm presented in [2] to compute true and false detection using output boundary map and available ground truths. In summary, given the computed boundary map, we compute the points on the precision-recall curve independently by first thresholding the output image to produce a binary boundary map and then matching this computed boundary map against each of the human boundary maps in the ground truth segmentation data set.

In our scheme, the following parameter values were empirically chosen to obtain best results. Once chosen, they were fixed to remain constant for all 100 test images. The window sizes in bar and grating cells' functional modelling were 7×7 and 15×15, respectively. The value for β was chosen to be 0.6 and value of α was 0.1. In equation 5, the intensity level was quantised from 256 to

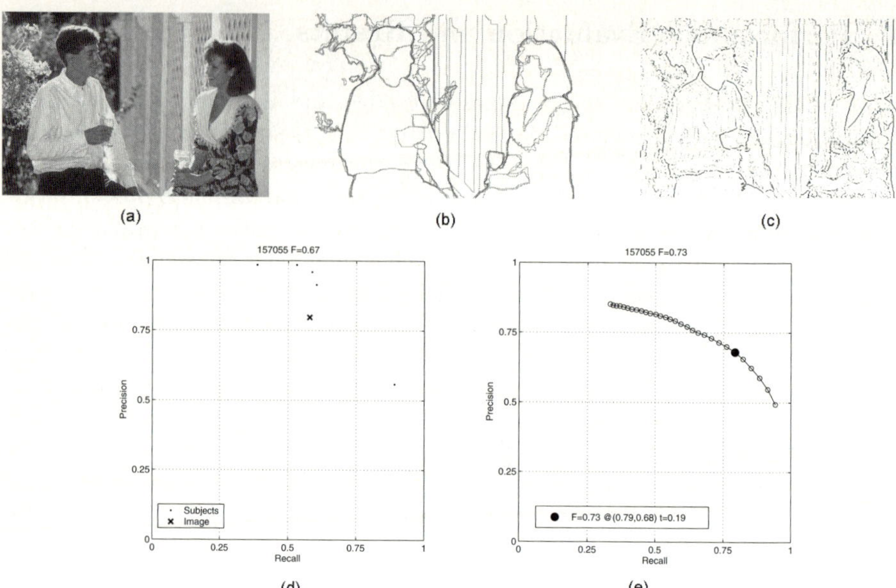

Fig. 5. (a) Sample test image, (b) Associated observer-segmented results, (c) Extracted boundary map, (d) PR curves for each observer relative to the rest.(e) PR curve for the proposed scheme. The curve is scored by its maximal F-measure, the value and location of which are shown in the legend.

Table 1. Comparison of proposed scheme with other schemes

Method	Performance
Brightness and texture gradient	0.63
Brightness gradient	0.60
Proposed scheme	**0.59**
Texture gradient	0.58
Multi-scale gradient magnitude	0.58
Second moment matrix	0.57
Gradient magnitude	0.56

32 as it had no effect on the value of χ^2 while it helped greatly minimise the computation. Fig. 5 shows the performance of the proposed scheme on a sample test image. It provides a comparison of the scheme against human observers. The points marked by a dot on the figure 5(d) show the precision and recall of segmentation by each human observer relative to other observers(a total of five). The median F-measure for the observers is 0.67 while the maximum obtained value using the proposed scheme is 0.73 indicated by a big dot in the PR curve (in fig 5(e)). The scheme was tested on a test dataset of 100 images and the overall performance was computed using a bench-marked algorithm [2] which gives a score based on the obtained results. The obtained score is 0.59 (shown in table. 1). Some of obtained soft boundary maps are shown in the Fig. 6.

Fig. 6. Sample test images, their corresponding ground truth and obtained results from the presented boundary detection scheme. First row shows the original images; second row shows the corresponding ground truth images; third row shows obtained soft boundary map. In the soft boundary map, intensity of the boundaries varies from 0-1.

Our scheme was also assessed against the existing boundary detection approaches reported in [2] using the same Berkeley dataset. Table 1 shows the relatives scores. The top two methods differ from the proposed scheme in the types of texture and non-texture features used and in the complex manner in which they are processed to compute boundary maps. In general, all the reported methods use training images for tuning parameters to obtain the best boundary map. In contrast, our scheme is simpler and the reported performance was achieved without any training. The latter is an attractive feature. In short, the performance of the proposed scheme is reasonably good.

5   Discussion and Conclusion

Evidence that complex cells receive direct input from the LGN cells in addition to simple cells [10] [11] [20] [21] is significant in terms of understanding the computations performed in V1. However, this has generally not received much attention in the computational modelling literature. It appears that the early stages in primary visual cortex provide ample information to address the boundary detection problem. The richness of information emerges from the capability of the HVS to extract global visual primitives from local features with no top-down influence.

A model for boundary detection based on these principles has been developed and presented. The model is useful for computing boundary points in images with performance which is competitive with existing computer vision approaches. It is also computationally simpler than most of the existing approaches to boundary extraction.

The functions of individual cells found in HVS have been modelled at a fixed single scale. However, evidence for multi-scale processing exists in the form of cortical cells of different sizes. Our initial attempt has been limited to understand the kind of processing and interaction carried out by the cells of fixed size. The model can be enhanced by extending it to a multi-scale framework and by including colour information.

References

1. Martin, D., Fowlkes, C., Tal, D., Malik, J.: A database of human segmented natural images and its application to evaluating segmentation algorithms and measuring ecological statistics. Proc. of International Conference on Computer Vision (2001)
2. Martin, D., Fowlkes, C., Malik, J.: Learning to detect natural image boundaries using brightness and texture. IEEE Transactions on Pattern Analysis and Machine Intelligence **26 (5)** (2004) 530–549
3. Ma, W.Y., Manjunath, B.S.: Edgeflow: A technique for boundary detection and segmentation. IEEE Transactions on Image Processing **9 (8)** (2000) 1375–1388
4. Malik, J., Belongie, S., Leung, T., Shi, J.: Contour and texture analysis for image segmentation. International Journal of Computer Vision **42 (1)** (2001) 7–27
5. Shi, J., Malik, J.: Normalized cuts and image segmentation. IEEE Transactions on Pattern Analysis and Machine Intelligence **22 (8)** (2000) 888–905

6. Yen, S., Finkel, L.: Extraction of perceptually salient contours by striate cortical networks. Vision Research **38 (5)** (1998) 719–741

7. Grigorescu, C., Petkov, N., Westenberg, M.: Contour detection based on nonclassical receptive field inhibition. IEEE Transactions on Image Processing **12 (7)** (2003) 729–739

8. Joshi, G.D., Sivaswamy, J.: A simple scheme for contour detection. Proc. of the Conference on Computer Vision Theory and Applications (2006) 236–242

9. Marr, D., Hildreth, E.: Theory of edge detection. Proceedings of the Royal Society of London, Series B **207** (1980) 187–217

10. Hoffmann, K.P., Stone, J.: Conduction velocity of afferents to cat visual cortex: a correlation with cortical receptive field properties. Brain Research **34** (1971) 460–466

11. Martinez, L., Alonso, J.M.: Complex receptive fields in primary visual cortex. The Neuroscientist **9(5)** (2003) 317–331

12. V.Bruce, Green, P.R., Georgeson, M.A.: Visual Perception: physiology, psychology and ecology. Fourth edition, Psychology Press (2004)

13. Lennie, P., Trevarthen, C., Essen, D.V., Wassle, H.: Parallel processing of visual information. Visual Perception-The Neurophysiological Foundations, Academic Press, San Diego **92** (1990)

14. Hubel, D.H., Wiesel, T.N.: Receptive fields, binocular interaction and functional architecture in the cats visual cortex. Journal of Psychology **160** (1962) 106–154

15. Alonso, J.M., Martinez, L.M.: Functional connectivity between simple cells and complex cells in cat striate cortex. Nature Neuroscience **1(5)** (1998) 395–403

16. Baumann, R., van der Zwan, R., Peterhans, E.: Figure-ground segregation at contours: a neural mechanism in the visual cortex of the alert monkey. European Journal of Neuroscience **9 (6)** (1997) 1290–1303

17. Dobbins, A., Zucker, S.W., Cynader, M.S.: Endstopped neurons in the visual cortex as a substrate for calculating curvature. Nature **329 (6138)** (1987) 438–441

18. von der Heydt, R., Peterhans, E., Drsteler, M.R.: Grating cells in monkey visual cortex: coding texture? Channels in the Visual Nervous System: Neurophysiology, Psychophysics and Models (Blum B, ed) (1991) 53–73

19. Kruizinga, P., Petkov, N.: Nonlinear operator for oriented texture IEEE Transactions on Image Processing **8 (10)** (1999) 1395–1407

20. Alonso, J.M.: The microcircuitry of complex cells in cat striate cortex. Society for Neuroscience **22(198.1)** (1996) 489

21. Mel, B.W., Ruderman, D.L., Archie, K.A.: Translation-invariant orientation tuning in visual *Complex Cells* could derive from intradendritic computations. The Journal of Neuroscience **18(11)** (1998) 4325–4334

22. Liu, X., Wang, D.: A spectral histogram model for textons and texture discrimination. Vision Research **42 (23)** (2002) 2617–2634

Speckle Reduction in Images with WEAD and WECD

Jeny Rajan[1] and M.R. Kaimal[2]

[1] NeST, Technopark, Trivandrum, India
[2] Department of Computer Science, University of Kerala, Trivandrum, India
jenyrajan@rediffmail.com, mrkaimal@yahoo.com

Abstract. In this paper we discuss the speckle reduction in images with the recently proposed Wavelet Embedded Anisotropic Diffusion (WEAD) and Wavelet Embedded Complex Diffusion (WECD). Both these methods are improvements over anisotropic and complex diffusion by adding wavelet based bayes shrink in its second stage. Both WEAD and WECD produces excellent results when compared with the existing speckle reduction filters. The comparative analysis with other methods were mainly done on the basis of Structural Similarity Index Matrix (SSIM) and Peak Signal to Noise Ratio (PSNR). The visual appearance of the image is also considered.

1   Introduction

Speckle noise is a common phenomenon in all coherent imaging systems like laser, acoustic, SAR and medical ultrasound imagery [1]. For images that contain speckle, the goal of enhancement is to remove the speckle without destroying important image features [2]. Synthetic Aperture Radar (SAR) images are corrupted by speckle noise due to the interference between waves reflected from microscopic scattering through the terrain. Because of its undesirable effect, speckle noise reduction turns out to be a key pre-processing step in order to interpret SAR images efficiently [3]. In medical imaging, the grainy appearance of 2D ultrasound images is due mainly to speckle. Here the speckle phenomenon results from the constructive-destructive interference of the coherent ultrasound pulses back scattered from the tiny multiple reflector that constitute biological materials. Speckle typically has the unfortunate aspect of falling into the high sensitivity region of human vision to spatial frequency. The frequency spectrum of speckle is also similar to the imaging system modulation transfer function. Speckle can therefore obscure the diagnostically important information.[4]. In certain applications, however the removal of speckle may be counter productive. Examples in which speckle preservation is important include feature tracking in ultrasonic imaging [5] and detection of features that are the same scale as the speckle patterns (e.g., coagulation damage) [6]. The source of speckle noise is attributed to random interference between the coherent returns. Fully developed speckle noise has the characteristic of multiplicative noise [7]. Speckle noise follows a gamma distribution and is given as

P. Kalra and S. Peleg (Eds.): ICVGIP 2006, LNCS 4338, pp. 184–193, 2006.

$$F(g) = \frac{g^{\alpha-1}}{(\alpha-1)!a^{\alpha}} e^{\frac{-g}{a}}$$ (1)

where g is the gray level and α is the variance. Below figure shows the plot of speckle noise distribution.

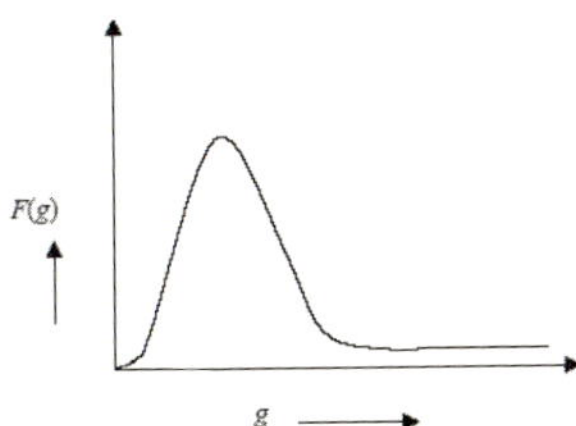

Fig. 1. Plot of speckle noise distribution

A number of methods are proposed in the literature for removing speckle from ul-trasound images. Popular methods among them are Lee, Frost, Kuan, Gamma and SRAD filters. The Lee and Kuan filters have the same formation, although the signal model assumptions and the derivations are different. Essentially, both the Lee and Kuan filters form an output image by computing a linear combination of the center pixel intensity in a filter window with the average intensity of the window. So, the filter achieves a balance between straightforward averaging (in homogeneous regions) and the identity filter (where edges and point features exist). This balance depends on the coefficient of variation inside the moving window[2].

The Frost filter also strikes a balance between averaging and the all-pass filter. In this case, the balance is achieved by forming an exponentially shaped filter kernel that can vary from a basic average filter to an identity filter on a point wise, adaptive ba-sis. Again, the response of the filter varies locally with the coefficient of variation. In case of low coefficient of variation, the filter is more average-like, and in cases of high coefficient of variation, the filter attempts to preserve sharp features by not aver-aging. The Gamma filter is a Maximum A Posteriori (MAP) filter based on a Bayes-ian analysis of the image statistics [1]. Speckle Reducing Anisotropic Diffusion (SRAD) is an edge sensitive diffusion method for speckled images [2].

Wavelet Embedded Anisotropic Diffusion (WEAD) [8] and Wavelet Embedded Complex Diffusion (WECD)[9] are extensions of non linear Anisotropic and Com-plex diffusion by adding Bayesian shrinkage at its second stage. The methods increase the speed of processing and improve the quality of images than their parent methods.

The paper is organized as follows. Section 2 deals with diffusion techniques for removing noise from images. It mainly discusses anisotropic and complex diffusion. Section 3 explains the recently proposed WEAD and WECD and its capability to remove speckle noises. Experimental results and comparative analysis with other popular methods is shown in Section 4. Finally conclusion and remarks are added in Section 5.

2 Noise Removal with Diffusion Techniques

Diffusion is a physical process that equilibrates concentration differences without creating or destroying mass [10]. This physical observation, the equilibrium property can be expressed by Fick's law

$$j = -D.\nabla u \tag{2}$$

This equation states that a concentration gradient ∇u causes a flux j, which aims to compensate for this gradient. The relation between ∇u and j is described by the diffusion tensor D, a positive definite symmetric matrix. The case where j and ∇u are parallel is called isotropic. Then we may replace the diffusion tensor by a positive scalar valued diffusivity g. In the general case i.e., anisotropic case, j and ∇u are not parallel. The observation that diffusion does only transport mass without destroying it or creating new mass is expressed by the continuity equation

$$d_t u = -\text{div } j \tag{3}$$

where t denotes the time. If we apply the Fick's law into the continuity equation we will get the diffusion equation. i.e.,

$$\frac{\partial u}{\partial t} = Div(D \cdot \nabla u) \tag{4}$$

This equation appears in many physical transport process. In the context of heat transfer, it is called the heat equation [10]. When applied to an image, the linear diffusion will generate scale space images. Each image will be more smoothed than the previous one. By smoothing an image, to some extend noise can be removed. This is why linear diffusion is used for noise removal. But one problem with this method is its inability to preserve image structures.

2.1 Anisotropic Diffusion

To avoid the defects of linear diffusion (especially the inability to preserve edges and to impel inter region smoothing before intra region smoothing) non-linear partial differential equations can be used. In [11] Perona and Malik has given 3 necessary conditions for generating multiscale *semantically meaningful* images

1. Causality : Scale space representation should have the property that no spurious detail should be generated passing from finer to coarser scale.
2. Immediate Localization : At each resolution, the region boundaries should be sharp and coincide with the semantically meaningful boundaries at that resolution.
3. Piecewise Smoothing : At all scales, intra region smoothing should occur preferentially over inter region smoothing.

Linear diffusion is especially not satisfying the third condition, which can be overcome by using a non linear one. Among the non linear diffusion , the one proposed by

Perona and Malik [11] and its variants are the most popular. They proposed a nonlinear diffusion method for avoiding the blurring and localization problems of linear diffusion filtering. There has been a great deal of interest in this anisotropic diffusion as a useful tool for multiscale description of images, image segmentation, edge detection and image enhancement [12]. The basic idea behind anisotropic diffusion is to evolve from an original image $u_0(x, y)$, defined in a convex domain $\Omega \subset R \times R$, a family of increasingly smooth images $u(x,y,t)$ derived from the solution of the following partial differential equation [11] :

$$\frac{\partial u}{\partial t} = div\left[c(\nabla u)\nabla u\right] \;,u(x, y)\big|_{t=0} = u_0(x, y) \tag{5}$$

where ∇u is the gradient of the image u, *div* is the divergence operator and c is the diffusion coefficient. The desirable diffusion coefficient $c(.)$ should be such that equation (5) diffuses more in smooth areas and less around less intensity transitions, so that small variations in image intensity such as noise and unwanted texture are smoothed and edges are preserved. Another objective for the selection of $c(.)$ is to incur backward diffusion around intensity transitions so that edges are sharpened, and to assure forward diffusion in smooth areas for noise removal [12]. Here are some of the previously employed diffusivity functions[13] :

A. Linear diffusivity [14]:
$$c(s) = 1, \tag{6}$$

B. Charbonnier diffusivity [15]:
$$c(s) = \frac{1}{\sqrt{1 + \dfrac{s^2}{k^2}}} \tag{7}$$

C. Perona−Malik diffusivity [11] :
$$c(s) = \frac{1}{1 + \left(\dfrac{s}{k}\right)^2} \tag{8}$$

$$c(s) = \exp\left[-\left(\frac{s}{k}\right)^2\right] \tag{9}$$

D. Weickert diffusivity[10] :
$$c(s) = \begin{cases} 1 & s = 0 \\ 1 - \exp\left(\dfrac{-3.31488}{\left(s/k\right)^8}\right) & s > 0 \end{cases} \tag{10}$$

E. TV diffusivity [16] :
$$c(s) = \frac{1}{s} \tag{11}$$

F. BFB diffusivity [17]:
$$c(s) = \frac{1}{s^2} \tag{12}$$

2.2 Complex Diffusion

In 1931 Schrodinger explored the possibility that one might use diffusion theory as a starting point for the derivation of the equations of quantum theory. These ideas were developed by *Fuerth* who indicated that the Schrodinger equation could be derived from the diffusion equation by introducing a relation between the diffusion coefficient and Planck's constant, and stipulating that the probability amplitude of quantum theory should be given by the resulting differential equation [18]. It has been the goal of a variety of subsequent approaches to derive the probabilistic equations of quantum mechanics from equations involving probabilistic or stochastic processes. The time dependent Schrodinger equation is the fundamental equation of quantum mechanics. In the simplest case for a particle without spin in an external field it has the form [19]

$$i\hbar \frac{\partial \psi}{\partial t} = -\frac{\hbar^2}{2m}\Delta \psi + V(x)\psi \tag{13}$$

where $\psi = \psi(t, x)$ is the wave function of a quantum particle, m is the mass of the particle, $\hbar$ is Planck's constant, $V(x)$ is the external field potential, Δ is the Laplacian and $i = \sqrt{-1}$. With an initial condition $\psi|_{t=0} = \psi_0(x)$, requiring that $\psi(t,\cdot) \in L_2$ for each fixed t, the solution is $\psi(t,\cdot) = e^{\frac{-i}{\hbar}tH}\psi_0$, where the exponent is shorthand for the corresponding power series, and the higher order terms are defined recursively by $H^n\psi = H(H^{n-1}\psi)$. The operator

$$H = -\frac{\hbar^2}{2m}\Delta + V(x) \tag{14}$$

called the Schrodinger operator, is interpreted as the energy operator of the particle under consideration. The first term is the kinetic energy and the second is the potential energy. The duality relations that exist between the Schrodinger equation and the diffusion theory have been studied in [9]. The standard linear diffusion equation is as in (4). From (13) and (4) we can derive the following two equations.

$$I_{RT} = C_R I_{Rxx} - C_I I_{Ixx} \;,\; I_{R|t=0} = I_0 \tag{15}$$

$$I_{IT} = C_I I_{Rxx} + C_R I_{Ixx} \;,\; I_{I|t=0} = 0 \tag{16}$$

where I_{RT} is the image obtained at real plane and I_{IT} is the image obtained at imaginary plane at time T and $C_R = \cos(\theta)$, $C_I = \sin(\theta)$. The relation $I_{Rxx} \gg \theta I_{Ixx}$ holds for small theta approximation[8]:

$$I_{RT} \approx I_{Rxx} ; \quad I_{It} \approx I_{Ixx} + \theta I_{Rxx} \tag{17}$$

In (17) I_R is controlled by a linear forward diffusion equation, whereas I_I is affected by both the real and imaginary equations. The above said method is linear complex diffusion equation.

A more efficient nonlinear complex diffusion can be written as in eqn. (18) [19]

$$I_t = \nabla \cdot (c(\mathrm{Im}(I)\nabla I)$$
(18)

where

$$c(\mathrm{Im}(I)) = \frac{e^{i\theta}}{1 + \left(\dfrac{\mathrm{Im}(I)}{k\theta}\right)^2}$$
(19)

where k is the threshold parameter Non linear complex diffusion seems to be more efficient than linear complex diffusion in terms of preserving edges.

3 WEAD and WECD

Both WEAD and WECD are improvements of anisotropic and complex diffusion by adding BayesShrink [20] at the second stage. In the case of WEAD, Bayesian Shrinkage of the non-linearly diffused signal is taken. The equation can be written as

$$I_n = B_s(I'_{n-1})$$
(20)

and in the case of WECD the Bayesian Shrinkage of the real part of the non-linearly complex diffused signal is taken. The equation can be written as

$$I_n = B_s(R_c(I'_{n-1}))$$
(21)

where B_s is the bayesian shrink and I'_{n-1} is anisotropic diffusion as shown in (5) at $(n-1)^{th}$ time and $R_c(I'_{n-1})$ is the real part of the non linearly diffused complex diffusion.

Numerically (20) and (21) can be written as

$$I_n = B_s\left(I_{n-1} + \Delta t d_n\right)$$
(22)

and

$$I_n = B_s(R_c(I_{n-1} + \Delta t d_n))$$
(23)

respectively.

The intention behind these two methods is to decrease the convergence time of the anisotropic diffusion and complex diffusion respectively. It is understood that the convergence time for denoising is directionally proportional to the image noise level. In the case of diffusion, as iteration continues, the noise level in image decreases (till it reaches the convergence point), but in a slow manner. But in the case of Bayesian Shrinkage, it just cut the frequencies above the threshold and that in a single step. An iterative Bayesian Shrinkage will not incur any change in the detail coefficients from

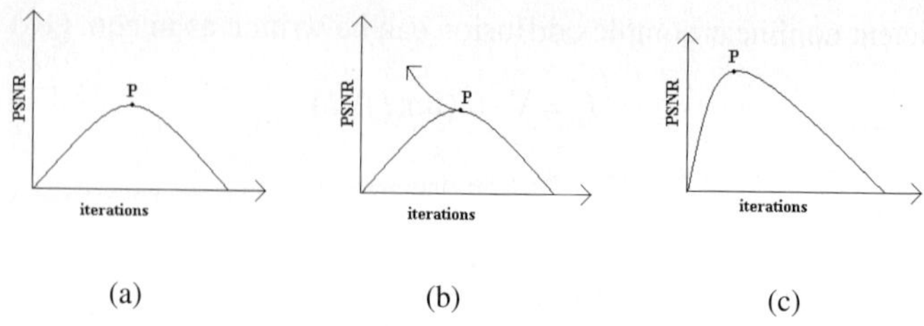

Fig. 2. Working of WEAD & WECD (a) Shows the convergence of a noisy image (convergence at P). If this P can be shifted towards left, image quality can be increased and time complexity can be reduced. Illustrated in (b). (c) shows the signal processed by WEAD & WECD. It can be seen that the convergence point is shifted to left and moved upwards.

the first one. Now consider the case of WEAD and WECD, here the threshold for Bayesian shrinkage is recalculated each time after diffusion, and since as a result of two successive noise reduction step, it approaches the convergence point much faster than anisotropic diffusion or complex diffusion.

As the convergence time decreases, image blurring can be restricted, and as a result image quality increases. The whole process is illustrated in Fig. 2. Fig. 2(a) shows the convergence of the image processed by diffusion methods. The convergence point is at **P**. i.e. at **P** we will get the better image, with the assumption that the input image is a noisy one. If this convergence point **P** can be shifted towards y-axis, its movement will be as in the figure shown in Fig 2 (b).i.e. if we pull the point **P** towards y-axis, it will move in a left-top fashion. Here the Bayesian shrinkage is the catalyst, which pulls the convergence point **P** of the anisotropic or complex diffusion towards a better place.

4   Experimental Results and Comparative Analysis

Experiments were carried out on various types of standard images. Comparisons and analysis were done on the basis of MSSIM (Mean Structural Similarity Index Matrix) [21] and PSNR (Peak Signal to Noise Ratio). SSIM is used to evaluate the overall image quality and is in the range 0 to 1. The SSIM works as follows, suppose x and y be two non negative image signals, one of the signals to have perfect quality, then the similarity measure can serve as a quantitative measure of the quality of the second signal. The system separates the task of similarity measurement into three comparisons: luminance, contrast and structure. The PSNR is given in decibel units (dB), which measure the ratio of the peak signal and the difference between two images.

Fig.3 shows the performance of various filters against speckle noise. It can be seen that the image processed by WEAD and WECD given a better result than the other three speckle filters. Table 1 shows a comparative analysis of popular speckle filters with WEAD and WECD. Various levels of noise are added to image for testing its capability. In all the cases the performance of WEAD and WECD was superior to others.

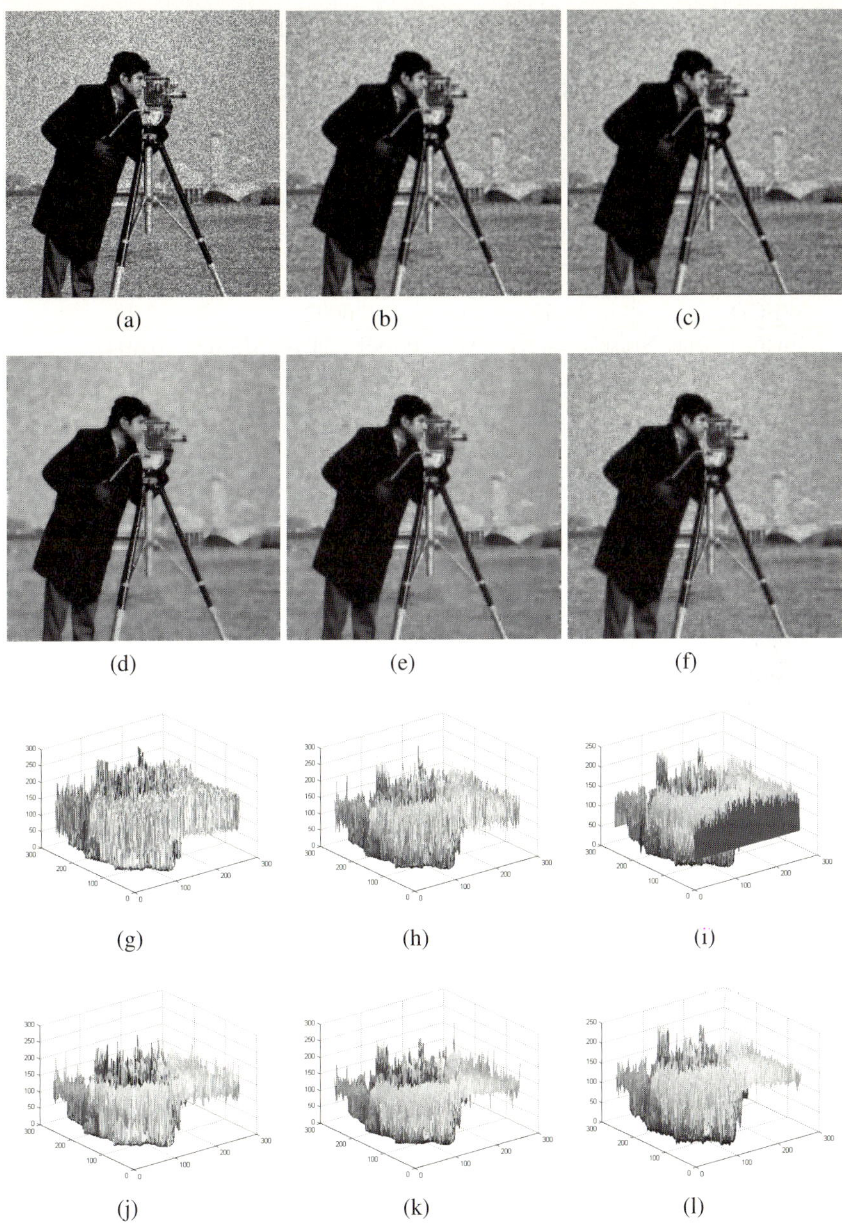

Fig. 3. Speckle affected image processed with various filters (a) Image with speckle noise (PSNR 18.85), (b) Image processed with Frost Filter (PSNR : 22.37), (c) Image Processed with Kuan Filter (PSNR : 23.12), (d) Image processed with SRAD (PSNR: 23.91), (e) Image processed with WEAD (PSNR : 25.40), (f) Image Processed with WECD (PSNR :24.52), (g), (h),(i), (j),(k),(l) shows the 3D plot of (a),(b),(c),(d),(e),(f)

Table 1. Comparative analysis of various speckle filters

Method	PSNR	MSSIM	Time Taken (in seconds)
Image : Cameraman, Noise variance : 0.04, PSNR : 18.85, MSSIM : 0.4311			
Frost	22.37	0.4885	5.75
Kuan	23.12	0.5846	10.00
SRAD	23.91	0.5923	0.68
WEAD	25.40	0.6835	31.00
WECD	24.52	0.6092	7.23
Image : Lena, Noise variance : 0.02 , PSNR : 24.16, MSSIM : 0.6047			
Frost	26.77	0.7027	5.81
Kuan	25.59	0.7916	9.96
SRAD	27.42	0.7750	0.75
WEAD	29.08	0.8208	18.56
WECD	28.56	0.7941	3.48
Image : Bird, Noise variance : 0.04, PSNR : 18.66 , MSSIM : 0.2421			
Frost	24.2604	0.4221	5.84
Kuan	25.78	0.5817	10.00
SRAD	27.65	0.6792	0.99
WEAD	29.98	0.8318	49.45
WECD	28.38	0.7117	17.59

5   Conclusion

In this paper a comparative analysis of Wavelet Embedded Anisotropic Diffusion (WEAD) and Wavelet Embedded Complex Diffusion (WECD) with other methods is done. When compared with other methods it can be seen that the complexity and processing time of WEAD and WECD is slightly more but the performance is superior. The hybrid concept used in WEAD and WECD can be extended to other PDE based methods.

References

1. L Gagnon, A Jouan, Speckle Filtering of SAR Images – A Comparative Study between Complex-Wavelet-Based and Standard Filters, Wavelet Applications in Signal and Image Processing : Proceedings of SPIE, Vol. 3169, (1997) 80-91
2. Yongjian Yu, Scott T Acton, Speckle Reducing Anisotropic Diffusion, IEEE Trans. on Image Processing, Vol. 11 (2002) 1260–1270
3. Zhao Hui Zhang, Veronique Prinet, SongDe MA, A New Method for SAR Speckle Reduction, IEEE (2002)
4. R.N Rohling, A.H. Gee, Issues in 3-D Free-Hand Medical Ultrasound Imaging, Technical Report, Cambridge University Engineering Department (1996)

5. G.E Trahey, S.M. Hubbard, O.T von Ramm, Angle Independent Ultrasonic Blood Flow Dtection by Frame-to-Frame Correlation of B-mode Images, Ultrasonics, Vol 26, (1988) 271 – 276

6. Z. Sun, H. Ying, J. Lu, A Noninvasive Cross-Correlation Ultrasound Technique for Detecting Spatial Profile of Laser – Induced Coagulation Damage – An *in vitro* Study, IEEE Trans. on Biomed. Engg., Vol. 48, (2001) 223-229

7. Sarita Dangeti, Denoising Techniques – A Comparison, Thesis Report, Submitted to the Dept. of Electrical and Computer Engineering, Louisiana State University and Agricultural and Mechanical College, (2003)

8. Jeny Rajan, M.R. Kaimal, Image Denoising using Wavelet Embedded Anisotropic Diffusion (WEAD), Proceedings of IEE International Conference on Visual Information Engineering, (2006)

9. Jeny Rajan, Image Denoising using Partial Differential Equations, M.Tech. Thesis, Submitted to Department of Computer Science, University of Kerala (INDIA), (2005).

10. Joachim Weickert, Anisotropic Diffusion in Image Processing, ECMI Series, Teubner – Verlag (1998)

11. P. Perona, J. Malik, Scale Space and Edge Detection using Anisotropic Diffusion, IEEE Trans. on Pattern Analysis and Machine Intelligence, Vol. 12. (1990) 629-639

12. Yu-Li You, Wenguan Xu, Allen Tannenbaum, Mostafa Kaveh, Behavioral Analysis of Analysis of Anisotropic Diffusion, IEEE Trans. on Image Processing, Vol. 5, (1996)

13. Pavel Mrazek, Joachim Weickert, Gabriele Steidl, Correspondence between Wavelet Shrinkage and Non linear Diffusion, Scale Space 2003, LNCS 2695, (2003) 101-116

14. T. Lijima, Basic Theory on Normalization of Pattern, Bulletin of the Electrotechnical Laboratory, Vol. 26, (1962) 368-388

15. P. Charbonnier, G. Aubert, L. Blanc-Feraud and M. Barlaud, Two deterministic half-quadratic regularization algorithms for computed imaging, In Proc. 1994 IEEE International Conference on Image Processing, Vol. 2, (1994) 168–172

16. F. Andreu, C. Ballester, V. Caselles, and J. M. Mazn, Minimizing total variation flow, Differential and Integral Equations, Vol 14, (2001) 321 – 360

17. S. L. Keeling and R. Stollberger, Nonlinear anisotropic diffusion filters for wide range edge sharpening, Inverse Problems, Vol 18, (2002) 175-190

18. M.D. Kostin, Schrodinger-Fuerth quantum diffusion theory: Generalized complex diffusion equation, J. Math. Phys, (1992)

19. Guy Gilboa, Nir Sochen and Yehoshua Y Zeevi, Image Enhancement and Denoising by Complex Diffusion Processes, IEEE Trans. On Pattern Analysis and Machine Imtelligence, Vol. 26, (2004).

20. S. Grace Chang, Bin Yu and Martin Vetterli, Adaptive Wavelet Thresholding for Image Denoising and Compression, IEEE Trans. Image Processing, Vol 9, (2000)

21. Zhou Wang, Alan Conard Bovik, Hamid Rahim Sheik and Erno P Simoncelli, Image Quality Assessment : From Error Visibility to Structural Similarity, IEEE Trans. Image Processing, Vol. 13, (2004)

Image Filtering in the Compressed Domain

Jayanta Mukherjee[1] and Sanjit K. Mitra[2]

[1] Dept. of Computer Science and Engineering
Indian Institute of Technology, Kharagpur, India
[2] Dept. of Electrical and Computer Engineering
University of California, Santa Barbara, USA
jay@cse.iitkgp.ernet.in, mitra@ece.ucsb.edu

Abstract. Linear filtering of images is usually performed in the spatial domain using the linear convolution operation. In the case of images stored in the block DCT space, the linear filtering is usually performed on the sub-image obtained by applying an inverse DCT to the block DCT data. However, this results in severe blocking artifacts caused by the boundary conditions of individual blocks as pixel values outside the boundaries of the blocks are assumed to be zeros. To get around this problem, we propose to use the symmetric convolution operation in such a way that the operation becomes equivalent to the linear convolution operation in the spatial domain. This is achieved by operating on larger block sizes in the transform domain. We demonstrate its applications in image sharpening and removal of blocking artifacts directly in the compressed domain.

1 Introduction

Filtering of images is required in various applications of image processing, such as noise removal, sharpening and edge extraction, anti-aliasing operations in image resizing, etc. These operations are usually performed in the spatial domain. As in many cases the images are stored in a compressed format, it is of interest to perform these operations directly in the compressed domain. This reduces the computational overhead associated with decompression and compression operations with the compressed stream. As DCT based JPEG standard is widely used for image compression, a number of algorithms have been advanced to perform various image processing operations in the DCT space [1]-[8].

In a classic work [9], Martucci has shown how the *convolution-multiplication* property of the *Fourier transform* could be extended to the class of *trigonometric transforms*, namely the *discrete cosine* and *sine transforms*. He has pointed out that like the *discrete Fourier transform* where *circular convolution* holds the convolution-multiplication property, in trigonometric transforms *symmetric convolutions* have similar properties. Hence, a class of linear filtering operations which could be mapped to symmetric convolutions of images, could be easily performed in the transform domain. In our work, we restrict our discussion to images in the *type-II block DCT* format. We demonstrate here that the *Gaussian filtering* could be performed in this domain and show its application in various

P. Kalra and S. Peleg (Eds.): ICVGIP 2006, LNCS 4338, pp. 194–205, 2006.

image processing applications such as smoothing of the blocking artifacts of highly compressed data, image sharpening, edge extraction, etc.

In the case of images stored in the block DCT space, linear filtering is usually performed on the sub-image obtained by applying an inverse DCT to the block DCT data. However, this results in severe blocking artifacts caused by the boundary conditions of individual blocks as pixel values outside the boundaries of the blocks are assumed to be zeros. On the other hand, the symmetric convolution has an advantage over the linear convolution operation in this regard, as in this case due to smooth transitions in the boundaries, the strength of blocking artifacts is reduced in the processed image. Moreover it does not provide similar boundary conditions of individual blocks what would have been there in the case of linear convolution of images in the spatial domain. Our objective in this work is to perform filtering with the blocks in the compressed domain in such a way that the symmetric convolution operation becomes equivalent to the linear convolution in the spatial domain. This has been achieved by operating on larger block sizes in the transform domain. To this end, we have used composition and decomposition of the DCT blocks using the spatial relationship of the DCT coefficients developed by Jiang and Feng [10]. It may be noted that in [8], Shin and Kang used the convolution-multiplication property of the DCT for designing anti-aliasing low pass filters for the purpose of image resizing. However, the approach was restricted for *image halving* and *image doubling* operations with the filtered output in the *type-I DCT* space. On the other hand, in our work *given an image in the type-II block-DCT space, the output is also of the same type.*

2   Symmetric Convolution and Convolution-Multiplication Properties in the DCT Domain

In this section we briefly review the concept of symmetric convolution and its equivalent operation in the DCT domain [9]. For the sake of brevity, we restrict our discussion to the 1-D case, as the concepts are trivially extended to 2-D.

Let $h(n), 0 \leq n \leq N$, be a sequence of length $N + 1$. Its N-point 1-D *type-I* DCT is defined by

$$C_{1e}\{h(n)\} = H_I^{(N)}(k) = \sqrt{\tfrac{2}{N}}\alpha(k) \sum_{n=0}^{N} h(n) \cos(\tfrac{n\pi k}{N}), \qquad (1)$$
$$0 \leq k \leq N.$$

Likewise, $x(n), 0 \leq n \leq N - 1$, be a sequence of length N. Its N-point 1-D *type-II* DCT is defined by

$$C_{2e}\{x(n)\} = X_{II}^{(N)}(k) = \sqrt{\tfrac{2}{N}}\alpha(k) \sum_{n=0}^{N-1} x(n) \cos(\tfrac{(2n+1)\pi k}{2N}), \qquad (2)$$
$$0 \leq k \leq N - 1.$$

In Eqs. (1) and (2), $\alpha(k)$ is $\sqrt{\tfrac{1}{2}}$ for $k = 0$, otherwise its value is 1.

It should be noted that the type-I $N-$point DCT is defined with $(N + 1)$ samples, whereas, the type-II DCT is defined with N samples. They can be considered as *generalized discrete Fourier transforms* (GDFT's) [9] of *symmetrically extended sequences*. After symmetric extensions, the resulting periods in both the cases are $2N$. For the type-I DCT, the *symmetric extension* of the $(N+1)$ samples is carried out as follows:

$$\hat{h}(n) = \begin{cases} h(n), 0 \leq n \leq N, \\ h(2N-n), N+1 \leq n \leq 2N-1, \end{cases} \tag{3}$$

whereas, for the type-II DCT the symmetric extension of the length-N input sequence is carried out as follows (before applying GDFT to it):

$$\hat{x}(n) = \begin{cases} x(n), 0 \leq n \leq N-1, \\ x(2N-1-n), N \leq n \leq 2N-1. \end{cases} \tag{4}$$

In this paper we refer the symmetric extensions of Eqs. (3) and (4) as *type-I* and *type-II symmetric extensions*, respectively.

The *symmetric convolution* of two finite-length sequences of appropriate lengths is nothing but the *periodic convolution* of their *symmetrically extended sequences* (having the same periods). The output resulting from this operation is observed for a specific interval. This operation is illustrated below.

Let $x(n), 0 \leq n \leq N-1$, and $h(n), 0 \leq n \leq N$, be two sequences. Denote the *type-II symmetric extension* of $x(n)$ as $\hat{x}(n)$ and the *type-I symmetric extension* of $h(n)$ as $\hat{h}(n)$. *Symmetric convolution* of $x(n)$ and $h(n)$, denoted by the operator Ⓢ is then defined as follows.

$$\begin{aligned} y(n) &= x(n)\text{Ⓢ}h(n) \\ &= \hat{x}(n) \circledast^{2N} \hat{h}(n) \\ &= \Sigma_{k=0}^{n}\hat{x}(k)\hat{h}(n-k) + \Sigma_{k=n+1}^{2N-1}\hat{x}(k)\hat{h}(n-k+2N), \\ &\qquad 0 \leq n \leq N-1, \end{aligned} \tag{5}$$

where the operator $\circledast^{2N}$ denotes the $2N$-point *circular* convolution.

In [9] Martucci has discussed how *convolution-multiplication properties* hold for trigonometric transforms with symmetric convolution. In particular, with respect to Eq. (5) this property is given by:

$$C_{2e}\{x(n)\text{Ⓢ}h(n)\} = C_{2e}\{x(n)\}C_{1e}\{h(n)\}. \tag{6}$$

It should be noted that as the N-th coefficient of type-II DCT of $x(n)$ (denoted by $X_{II}^{(N)}(N)$) is zero, only N multiplications are involved in Eq. (6).

The above concepts could easily be extended to 2-D. Here, the $M \times N$-point type-I 2-D DCT is defined over $(M+1) \times (N+1)$ samples and the type-II 2-D DCT is defined over $M \times N$ samples. These can also be derived from the *2-D GDFT* defined over symmetrically extended sequences as discussed earlier. We denote the type-I and type-II DCTs of $x(m,n)$ by $C_{1e}\{x(m,n)\}$ and $C_{2e}\{x(m,n)\}$, respectively. Similar convolution multiplication properties hold also in 2-D and a trivial extension of Eq. (6) to 2-D is as follows:

$$C_{2e}\{x(m,n)\text{Ⓢ}h(m,n)\} = C_{2e}\{x(m,n)\}C_{1e}\{h(m,n)\} \tag{7}$$

It should be noted here that Eq. (7) involves $M \times N$ multiplications.

3   Filtering in the Block DCT Space

The convolution-multiplication property as expressed by Eq. (7) has a particular significance in its application to filtering of images represented in the *type-II block DCT* space. Given the *type-I DCT* of the *impulse response* of a filter, one can easily compute the filtered output using Eq. (7). In such a situation both the input (image) and the output (filtered image) remain in the type-II DCT space. As different compression schemes such as JPEG and MPEG have adopted the type-II DCT representation of images and videos, filtering in the transform domain itself can be performed directly using Eq. (7). However, this filtering operation in the transform domain is equivalent to symmetric convolution in the spatial (time) domain of an image (signal). Hence, only filters with impulse responses that are even functions can be supported by this operation. For performing the symmetric convolution (in this case), specifications for the first (positive) quadrant (half) of the spatial (time) domain are only required. This also reduces the storage requirement of the filter.

A Filtering Example. We illustrate next the implementation of a Gaussian filter in the block DCT domain. A *Gaussian filter* has an impulse response that is an *even* function and performs *low-pass filtering*. For a symmetric convolution in 2-D, specifications in the first quadrant of the discretized image space are required. The 2-D Gaussian impulse response in the first quadrant of the spatial domain is given by

$$h(m, n) = \frac{1}{2\pi\sigma_x\sigma_y}e^{-\frac{1}{2}\left(\frac{m^2}{\sigma_x^2} + \frac{n^2}{\sigma_y^2}\right)},$$
$$0 \leq m \leq M, 0 \leq n \leq N. \tag{8}$$

Let $H_I(k, l), 0 \leq k \leq M, 0 \leq l \leq N$, denote the type-I DCT of $h(m, n)$. Given a $M \times N$ type-II DCT block $\mathbb{B} = \{B_{II}(k, l), 0 \leq k < M, 0 \leq l < N\}$, the output $\mathbb{F}$ in the transform domain is then computed as follows:

$$\mathbb{F} = \{F_{II}(k, l) = B_{II}(k, l).H_I(k, l), 0 \leq k < M, 0 \leq l < N\}. \tag{9}$$

In our work we have assumed $\sigma_x = \sigma_y$, and henceforth both are referred to as σ.

Boundary Conditions. Filtering in the spatial domain is implemented by a linear convolution of an image with a finite length impulse response with the boundaries of the image zero-padded. Because of the sharp transitions at the boundaries, blocking artifacts occur at the boundaries. In a symmetric convolution, symmetric extensions at the boundaries of a block results in smoother transitions at the boundaries. As a result, the symmetric convolution results in better boundary conditions than that obtained using the linear convolution. To arrive at a smoother transition at the boundaries, with the help of Eq. (9), the symmetric convolution is applied to an independent block (of size 8×8 in the present case). It is of interest to compare its performances to that of a linear convolution operation. In Table 1 the PSNR values of the images obtained using the symmetric convolution operation have been computed by considering the images obtained via a linear convolution as the reference. It is observed that the quality of the filtered images obtained by symmetric convolution of 8×8 blocks suffer heavily due to blocking artifacts. This is also reflected by the low PSNR values in Table 1. One of the objectives of the present work is to outline

Table 1. PSNR Values of Gaussian Filtered Images

	PSNR (dB)		
σ	Pepper	Mandrill	Lena
2.0	28.73	28.89	28.65
3.0	26.10	27.12	26.43
4.0	24.91	26.17	25.41
5.0	24.85	26.09	25.40

filtering in the block DCT domain so that the operation becomes equivalent to filtering of the whole image by a linear convolution with the impulse response of the filter. Consider a block of size N in 1-D. Let the *effective length of the impulse response*[1] be K (beyond $(K-1)$-th position sample values are zero). Hence, the convolved output response (through symmetric or circular convolution) between the sample positions K and $(N-1-K)$ will be the as same as those obtained from linear convolution with the complete input sequence. This implies that the smaller the value of K, the closer the result is to that of linearly convolved output. This may be observed from the PSNR values in Table 1. Increasing values of σ make the *effective length* of the filter longer. For example, *effective half length* of a Gaussian impulse response with σ will be around 2σ. As can be seen in Table 1, PSNR values get degraded with increasing σ. Hence, one should keep *effective half length* small to get performance similar to that of the corresponding linear convolution operation. However, small value of N (e.g. 8) places a severe restriction on the filter design. In addition, filter response also deviates largely from its desirable characteristics due to the truncation errors. As a result, one should consider larger block sizes for this purpose. One could form blocks of larger sizes from smaller sizes directly in the transform domain following the technique of Jiang and Feng [10]. After performing filtering operation with larger blocks, the filtered blocks are decomposed into their original sizes to get back the results in the specified block DCT domain.

Composition and Decomposition of the DCT Blocks. For convenience, we discuss the spatial relationships of the DCT blocks in 1-D. Let $C_i^{(N)}, 0 \leq i \geq M - 1$, the i-th N-point DCT block of a sequence $\{x(n)\}, n = 0, 1, ..., M \times N - 1$. Jiang and Feng [10] showed that a block DCT transformation is nothing but an orthonormal expansion of the sequence $\{x(n)\}$ with a set of $M \times N$ basis vectors, each of which is derived from the basis vectors of N-point DCT. Hence, there exists

---

[1] For symmetric convolution, impulse response is defined for positive half only. In this case we refer K as the *effective half filter length*.

an invertible linear transformation from M blocks of N-point DCT transform to the usual MN-point DCT transform. In other words, for a sequence of N-point DCT blocks $\{C_i^{(N)}\}, i = 0, 1, ...M - 1$, the corresponding composite DCT $C^{(MN)}$ (MN-point DCT), there exists a matrix $A_{(M,N)}$ of size $MN \times MN$ such that[2]

$$C^{(M.N)} = A_{(M,N)}.[C_0^{(N)} C_1^{(N)} ......C_{M-1}^{(N)}]^T \tag{10}$$

The above analysis in 1-D can also be extended to 2-D. For details one may refer the discussion made in [6]. It should be noted that the conversion matrices and their inverses are sparse [10]. Hence, lesser number of multiplications and additions of two matrices is required than those required in usual matrix multiplications.

4   Filtering with Block Composition and Decomposition

In our technique $L \times M$ number of 8×8 blocks are merged into a single block (say, $\mathbb{B}^{(LN \times MN)}$). Then, the resulting block is subjected to the filtering operation. Let $h(m, n), 0 \leq m \leq 8L, 0 \leq n \leq 8M$, be the filter response specified in the first quadrant of the image space. Let $H_I(k, l), 0 \leq k \leq 8L, 0 \leq l \leq 8M$, denote the type-I DCT of $h(m, n)$ (i.e., $C_{1e}(h(m, n)) = H_I(k, l)$). The filtered response (say, $\mathbb{B}_f^{(LN \times MN)}$)is computed by multiplying an element of $\mathbb{B}^{(LN \times MN)}$ with the corresponding element of $\mathbb{H}$ (refer Eq. (9)). Finally, $\mathbb{B}_f^{(LN \times MN)}$ is decomposed into $L \times M$ blocks (of size 8×8). We refer this algorithm in our work as the *Block_Filtering_on_Composition_Decomposition* (BFCD) algorithm.

We have performed the same Gaussian filtering given by Eq. (9) using the BFCD algorithm. Table 2 lists the PSNR values of the images obtained using the BFCD algorithm with the Gaussian filtered image obtained via linear convolution in the spatial domain as the reference for different values of L and M. In our simulations we have kept the values of L and M same. It can be seen that the PSNR values increases with increasing block sizes. It is also observed that blocking artifacts are also less visible in the filtered images. One may interestingly note that it is expected that the larger the block size, the closer the result is to that obtained using the convolution. However, in Table 2 it can be seen that for $L(= M) = 4$, the PSNR values are lower for all values of σ compared to that obtained in the case of neighboring L and M values. In fact, the degradation in the PSNR values happens when the block sizes are integral multiples of the image size. In that case, a block at the right and bottom boundaries gets totally fitted within the image. Hence the boundary effect of symmetric convolution is felt from all sides of the block. When the block sizes are not integral multiple of image sizes, a boundary block (containing right and bottom margin of the image) contains a fraction of the image pixel data and the rest are assumed to be zeros. In such a case, the distortion due to the boundary conditions of symmetric convolution is less.

---

[2] The transpose of a matrix X is denoted here by X^T.

Table 2. PSNR values obtained using Gaussian filtering with BFCD

L(=M)	σ	PSNR (dB)			Per pixel	Equivalent number
		Pepper	Mandrill	Lena	Computational cost	of additions per pixel
2	2.0	29.68	29.65	29.72	28 M + 32 A	116
	3.0	27.46	28.10	27.93		
	4.0	27.00	27.94	27.67		
3	2.0	34.44	32.50	32.59	46.17 M + 53.33 A	191.84
	3.0	31.45	31.01	30.70		
	4.0	30.70	30.87	30.38		
4	2.0	30.56	30.08	30.32	71.5 M + 96 A	310.5
	3.0	28.55	28.48	28.64		
	4.0	28.20	28.32	28.47		

4.1   Computational Costs

In this section we compare the computational costs of the transform domain technique with that of the spatial domain technique. If the costs of a single multiplication and a single addition are $\mathcal{M}$ and $\mathcal{A}$, respectively, then the total cost for an operation requiring a number of multiplications and b number of additions is $a\mathcal{M} + b\mathcal{A}$. We have also considered the cost of a multiplication operations is *three times* of the cost of addition for providing a combined cost measure following the similar practice used in an earlier work [13].

Computational Cost with Spatial Domain Operations. Costs associated with spatial domain operation are due to computations involved in: (i) IDCT of individual blocks, (ii) Convolution of the image with a $(2K - 1) \times (2K - 1)$ mask, and (iii) DCT of individual blocks. It should be noted that the effective filter size is $(2K - 1) \times (2K - 1)$. Outside this support, the filter's impulse response samples are taken as zeros. As a result, per pixel, one has to perform $(2K - 1)^2$ multiplications and $((2K - 1)^2 - 1)$ additions. However, exploiting the symmetry in the impulse response in the spatial domain (for the class of filters under consideration of this paper), the number of multiplications could be reduced to K^2. In addition there are costs involved due to DCT and IDCT. We make use of the computationally efficient algorithm developed by Loeffer et al which computes 8×8 DCT (as well as IDCT) with 176 multiplications and 464 additions [11]. Additionally 5.5 multiplications and 14.5 additions per pixel are needed for performing the 8×8 DCT and IDCT. Typically for $K = 8$, numbers of multiplications and additions per pixel are 69.5 and 238.5, respectively.

Computational Cost with BFCD. Costs associated with BFCD are due to computations involved in: (i) Composition of $L \times M$ blocks into a single block, (ii) Element to element multiplications between DCT coefficients of composed block and type-I DCT coefficient of the impulse response, and (iii) Decomposition of the filtered block into $L \times M$ blocks of 8 size.

Following a similar approach for efficient computation of block composition and decomposition of type-II DCT as discussed in [6], numbers of per pixel operations for the BFCD algorithm are presented in Table 2 for different values

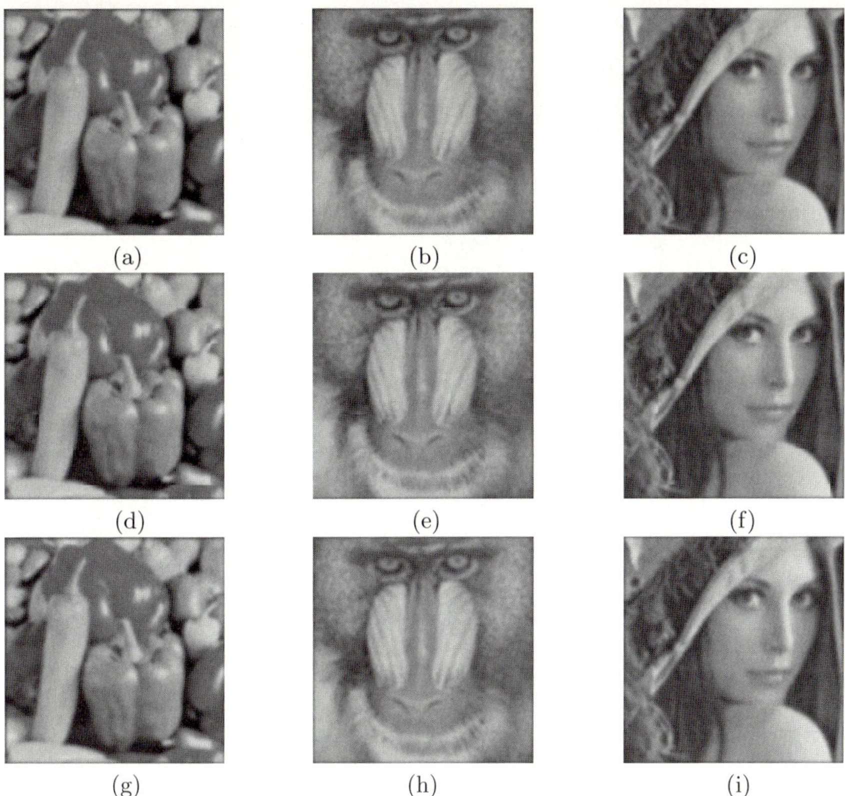

Fig. 1. Gaussian filtering with $\sigma = 2.0$: (a)-(c): Filtering in the spatial domain using linear convolution, (d)-(f) Filtering in the DCT domain using the BFCD algorithm for $L = M = 5$ and (g)-(i): Filtering in the DCT domain using the OBFCD algorithm

of L (or M). Comparing the computational cost of the BFCD algorithm with the corresponding spatial domain operation, it is evident that the BFCD is a faster operation. For example for $L = M = 5$, the number of equivalent addition operations for the BFCD algorithm is 393.45, while the requirement for spatial domain approach (for $K = 8$) is 447. It may be noted however that the BFCD algorithm provides an approximate solution. For $L = M = 5$, the approximate Gaussian filtered image with $\sigma = 2.0$ maintains quite high PSNR values (typically 35.56 dB, 33 dB and 33.14 dB for the images *Pepper*, *Mandrill*, and *Lena*, respectively and refer Figures 1(d)-(f)) with respect to the filtered image obtained through spatial convolution. For obtaining the exact solution, we outline an overlapping block filtering approach in the compressed domain as described in the following subsection.

4.2 Filtering with Overlapping Blocks

One way of removing the boundary effects is to apply BFCD in overlapping set of blocks and retain the results of those blocks which are not affected by

Table 3. Performances of Gaussian Filtering with OBFCD

L(=M)	$\sigma_x(=\sigma_y)$	PSNR (dB)			Per pixel computational cost	Equivalent number of additions per pixel
		Pepper	Mandrill	Lena		
3	2.0	301.42	300.99	301.71	103.88 M + 120 A	431.64
	3.0	301.85	301.31	302.03		
	4.0	302.69	302.10	302.91		
4	2.0	294.23	293.56	294.40	127.11 M + 170.67 A	552
	3.0	294.43	293.75	294.61		
	4.0	295.33	294.61	295.47		
5	2.0	293.18	292.51	293.39	144.92 M + 180 A	614.76
	3.0	293.37	292.66	293.56		
	4.0	294.28	293.56	294.47		

the boundary conditions due to the symmetric extension. For example, if the effective half filter size is $K \times K$ (in spatial domain), BFCD could be applied to $L \times M$ number of blocks producing only the $(L - 2\lceil \frac{K}{8} \rceil) \times (M - 2\lceil \frac{K}{8} \rceil)$ central blocks as the output. Naturally, this will increase the redundancy in the computation and there will be an increase in the number of multiplications and additions as a consequence. We refer this algorithm as *Overlapping_Block_Filtering_on_Composition_Decomposition* (OBFCD). Figures 1(g)-(i) show the results using OBFCD for $L = 3$ and $M = 3$. It can be seen that the filtered images are almost the same as those obtained by the linear convolution (Figures 1(a)-(c)). Table 3 presents the PSNR values obtained by OBFCD. In this case, PSNR values are significantly higher (around 300 dB). This implies that the OBFCD operation is equivalent to the spatial domain convolution. Table 3 also includes the computational cost associated with OBFCD. In this case, it can be seen that as OBFCD requires more computations than BFCD, it is marginally faster than the corresponding spatial domain operation. Typically, for $L = M = 3$, OBFCD requires 431.64 equivalent number of addition operations per pixel of the image, whereas for the spatial domain approach for $K = 8$, the required number is 447. It is also observed from Table 3 that it is not necessary to increase the value of $L(= M)$ beyond 3. Output response does not vary significantly with increasing $L(\geq 3)$. It remains close to the spatially convolved output. However this depends upon the effective half filter size ($K \times K$). We summarize our observations in the following lemma:

Lemma 1: The minimum value of L for *effective half filter size $K \times K$* is given by $L_{min} = 2\lceil \frac{K}{8} \rceil + 1$.

Proof: As $(L - 2\lceil \frac{K}{8} \rceil) > 0$, $L > 2\lceil \frac{K}{8} \rceil$. Hence, $L_{min} = 2\lceil \frac{K}{8} \rceil + 1$.   □

5   Applications of Image Filtering

In this section we demonstrate two specific image processing applications of the proposed image filtering.

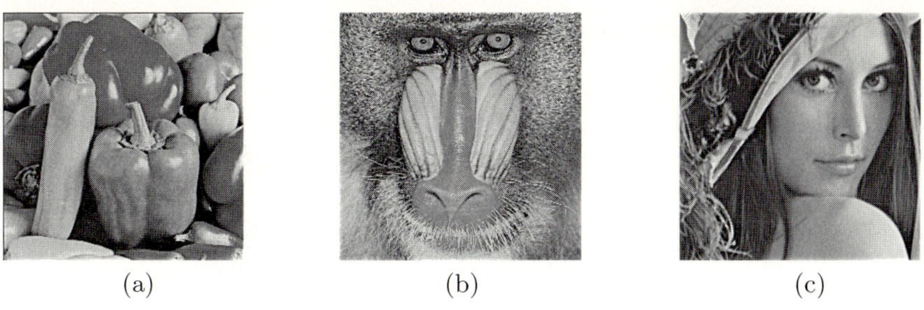

(a)   (b)   (c)

Fig. 2. Image sharpening using OBFCD filtering with $\lambda = 0.7$, $\sigma = 2.0$, $L = M = 3$ and $K = 8$: (a) Peppers, (b) Mandrill, and (c) Lena.

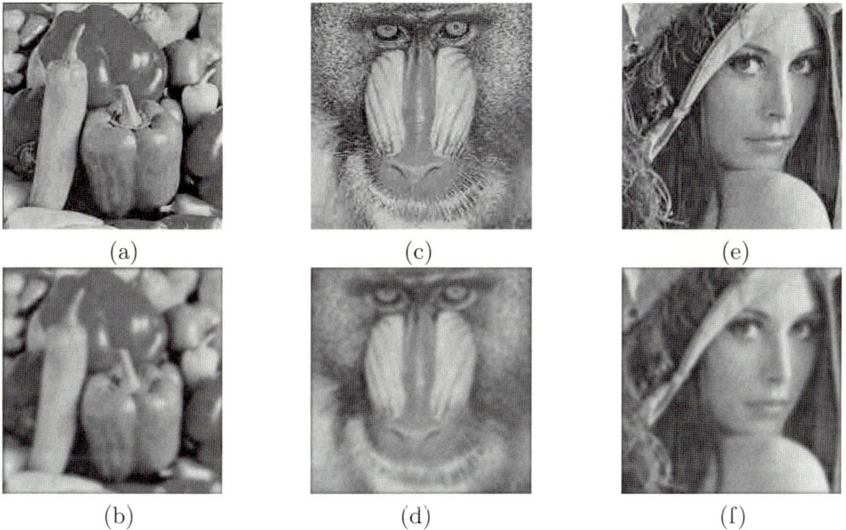

(a)   (c)   (e)
(b)   (d)   (f)

Fig. 3. Removal of blocking artifacts of highly compressed JPEG images using OBFCD filtering with $\sigma = 2.0$, $L = M = 3$ and $K = 8$. Images are compressed with JPEG compression scheme with the quality factor 10.0:(a) Peppers: JPEG compressed, (b) Peppers: After OBFCD filtering, (c) Mandrill: JPEG compressed, (d) Mandrill: After OBFCD filtering, (e) Lena: JPEG compressed, and (f) Lena: After OBFCD filtering.

5.1   Image Sharpening

One approach to image sharpening operation is carried out by adding a fraction of the high-pass filtered output to the original image. Let B_f be the low-pass filtered block using BFCD or OBFCD in the transform domain. Let B be its corresponding original block in the transform domain. Hence the sharpened block in the transform domain is computed as follows:

$$B_s = B + \lambda(B - B_f). \tag{11}$$

In Eq. (11) $\lambda \, (> 0)$ is the parameter controlling the amount of image sharpening. Figure 2 shows the sharpened images for $\lambda = 0.7$.

5.2 Blocking Artifacts Removal

Blocking artifacts are often visible in images reconstructed from highly compressed data. These blocking artifacts can be masked by applying low pass filtering directly in the compressed domain. We present here examples of such filtering of JPEG compressed images (with *quality factor* =10.0). Blocking artifacts are clearly visible in Figures 3(a), (c), and (e), respectively. Their visibility has been substantially reduced in the filtered images shown in Figures 3(b), (d), and (f), respectively.

6 Concluding Remarks

In this paper we have described filtering in the block DCT space using the convolution-multiplication properties of trigonometric transforms [9]. We have made use of the block composition and decomposition methods of [10] for satisfying the boundary conditions as in the case of linear convolution. We have demonstrated the application of the proposed algorithm in performing two specific image processing operations such as enhancement, and removal of blocking artifacts, in the transform domain.

Acknowledgment

This work was supported in part by a University of California MICRO grant with matching support from Intel Corporation, Qualcomm Corporation and Xerox Corporation.

References

1. B.C. Smith and L. Rowe, "Algorithms for manipulating compressed images," *IEEE Comput. Graph. Applicat. Mag.*, vol. 13, pp. 34–42, September 1993.
2. A. Neri, G. Russo, and P. Talone, "Inter-block filtering and downsampling in DCT domain," *Signal Processing: Image Commun.*, vol. 6, pp. 303–317, August 1994.
3. H.W. Park, Y.S. Park, and S.K. Oh, "L/M-image folding in block DCT domain using symmetric convolution," *IEEE Trans. on Image Processing*, vol. 12, pp. 1016–1034, September 2003.
4. J. Tang and E. Peli, "Image enhancement using a contrast measure in the compressed domain," *IEEE Signal Processing Letters*, vol. 10, pp. 289–292, October 2003.
5. B. Shen, I.K. Sethi, and V. Bhaskaran, "DCT convolution and its application in compressed domain," *IEEE Trans. on Circuits and Systems for Video Technology*, vol. 8, pp. 947–952, December 1998.
6. J. Mukherjee and S.K. Mitra, "Arbitrary resizing of images in the DCT space," *IEE Proc.: Vision, Image and Signal Processing*, vol. 152, no. 2, pp. 152-164.
7. Y.S. Park and H.W. Park, "Design and analysis of an image resizing filter in the block-DCT domain," *IEEE Trans. on Circuits and Systems for Video Technology*, vol. 14, pp. 274–279, February 2004.

8. G.S. Shin and M.G. Kang, "Transform domain enhanced resizing for a discrete-cosine-transform-based codec," *Optical Engineerring.*, vol. 42, pp. 3204–3214, November 2003.
9. S.A. Martucci, "Symmetric convolution and the discrete sine and cosine transforms," *IEEE Trans. on Signal Processing*, vol. 42, pp. 1038–1051, May 1994.
10. J. Jiang and G. Feng, "The spatial relationships of DCT coefficients between a block and its sub-blocks," *IEEE Trans. on Signal Processing*, vol. 50, pp. 1160–1169, May 2002.
11. C. Loeffer, A. Ligtenberg, and G.S. Moschytz, "Practical fast 1-D DCT algorithms with 11 multiplications," *Proc. IEEE Int. Conf. Accoustics, Speech and Signal Processing*, vol. 2, pp. 988–991, May 1989.
12. R. Dugad and N. Ahuja, "A fast scheme for image size change in the compressed domain," *IEEE Trans. on Circuits and Systems for Video Technology*, vol. 11, pp. 461–474, April 2001.
13. B. Shen, I.K. Sethi, and V. Bhaskaran, "Adaptive motion vector resampling for compressed video downscaling, " *IEEE Trans. on Circuits and Systems for Video Technology*, vol. 9, pp. 929-936, September, 1999.

Significant Pixel Watermarking Using Human Visual System Model in Wavelet Domain

Jayalakshmi M., S.N. Merchant, and U.B. Desai

SPANN Lab, Electrical Engineering Department
Indian Institute of Technology, Bombay, Powai, Mumbai-76
{jlakshmi, merchant, ubdesai}@ee.iitb.ac.in

Abstract. In this paper, we propose a novel algorithm for robust image watermarking by inserting a single copy of the watermark. Usually, robustness is achieved by embedding multiple copies of the watermark. The proposed method locates and watermarks 'significant pixels' of the image in the wavelet domain. Here, the amount of distortion at every pixel is kept within the threshold of perception by adopting ideas from Human Visual System (HVS) model. The robustness of the proposed method was verified under six different attacks. To verify the advantage of selecting the significant pixels over the highest absolute coefficients, simulations were performed under both cases with quantization of pixels as per HVS model. Simulation results show the advantage of selecting the 'significant pixels' for watermarking gray images as well as color images.

1   Introduction

Recent years have witnessed an outgrowth in the volume of digital data which can be easily manipulated and reproduced. Digital watermarking has been proposed as a means for owner verification, content authentication, broadcast monitoring etc. A number of watermarking algorithms in spatial domain [1], [2] as well as transform domain have been proposed. A major disadvantage of spatial domain techniques is the low robustness of the watermark. The robustness of the watermark could be improved if the properties of the cover image could be exploited. The most commonly used transforms for digital watermarking are Discrete Fourier Transform (DFT), Discrete Cosine Transform (DCT) and Discrete Wavelet Transform (DWT) [3], [4], [5], [6], [7], [8].

Given its suitability to model the HVS behavior, the DWT has gained interest among watermarking researchers. In [9] a blind watermarking algorithm which embeds the watermark in the DWT domain by exploiting the characteristics of the HVS is presented. Here, watermark strength modulation is accomplished through a mask giving a pixel by pixel measure of the sensibility of the human eye to local image perturbations. Mask construction relies on a work by Lewis and Knowles [10]. Some modifications to the method by Lewis and Knowles are proposed in [9] to make it suitable to the computation of the maximum visibly tolerable watermark energy that can be used for each DWT coefficient.

We propose a wavelet based non-blind watermarking scheme for images with a comparatively larger size than the watermark. Usually robustness is achieved

P. Kalra and S. Peleg (Eds.): ICVGIP 2006, LNCS 4338, pp. 206–215, 2006.

by inserting multiple copies of the watermark, whereas we have inserted a single copy of the watermark and still robustness is maintained by selecting the coefficients with respect to their interband dependencies [11]. Wavelet transform allows us to study the image at different space-frequency resolutions and making use of this property, we locate some important feature points in images. These pixels are referred as 'significant pixels'. Generally watermarking schemes embed information only in the high frequency components or in a selected subclass of them. But in our proposed scheme the pixels are so chosen that they have significant magnitude in high frequency as well as low frequency regions. This should in turn provide better robustness.

Transparency is one of the important criteria in digital watermarking. Since the significant pixels bear a very important role in the perceptual quality of the image, the distortion at these pixels are kept below the threshold of perception as per HVS model [9].

To test the resilience of the proposed method to different signal processing operations, we have selected mainly six different attacks in the case of gray images and color images. The attacks considered are salt-pepper noise with median filtering, Gaussian noise addition, mean filtering, quantization of watermarked pixels, JPEG compression and cropping. On color images, color palette filtering using Adobe Photoshop software was also experimented. The simulation results show the added advantage of selecting significant pixels compared to high absolute coefficients.

The rest of the paper is organized as follows. Section 2 illustrates the proposed algorithm. Section 3 and Section 4 give the experimental results and conclusion respectively.

2   Proposed Algorithm

Wavelet representation of any data gives information about the variations of the data at different scales. Wavelet detail image is obtained as the convolution of the image with the wavelet function dilated at different scales. We know from which signal points each wavelet coefficient at a particular scale is computed. We can further study the wavelet coefficients for the same points at a finer scale. These coefficients are called children coefficients.

We have used three level wavelet decomposition using Haar wavelet to locate significant pixels [12]. The three level wavelet decomposition is shown in Fig. 1. In the proposed algorithm watermark is embedded only in the significant pixels in bands V_2, D_2 and H_2. But for calculating the significance factor 'S' we have considered all the bands except L_2.

2.1   Watermark Embedding

Let us denote the bands by $B_i{}^\theta$ where 'B' can be replaced by V, H or D as 'θ' varies. The suffix 'i' denotes the level of wavelet decomposition in which that particular band is present. To locate the significant pixels, choose every pixel in third level, say $B_2{}^\theta$ and its corresponding children coefficients at all finer

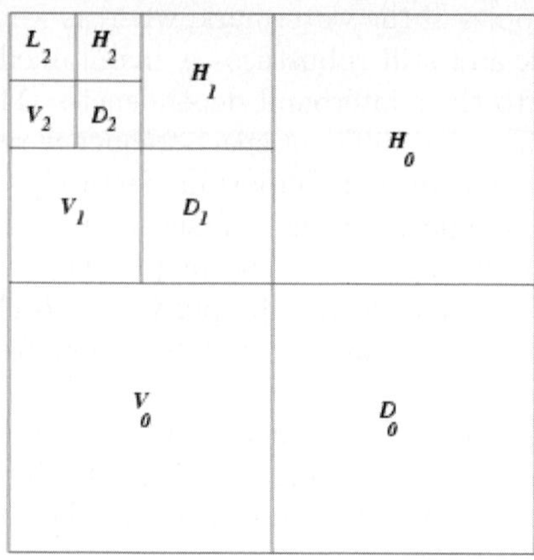

Fig. 1. Three level wavelet decomposition with different bands

resolutions namely $B_1{}^\theta$ and $B_0{}^\theta$. The significance factor (S) of every pixel in band $B_2{}^\theta$ is defined as follows.

$$S(i,j) = |B_2{}^\theta(i,j)| + \max_{l,k=0,1} |B_1{}^\theta(2i-k, 2j-l)| \tag{1}$$

$$+ \max_{m,n=0,1,2,3} |B_0{}^\theta(4i-n, 4j-m)|,$$

$$\forall\, (i,j)\, \epsilon\, B_2$$

After calculating significance factor(S) at every pixel in bands V_2, H_2 and D_2, these values are sorted. In our method only the highest significant pixels will be watermarked. Let the watermark be represented by a column vector w of size $K \times 1$, obtained after randomizing. The watermark is embedded at every significant pixel in band $B_2(i,j)$ as follows.

$$B_2'{}^\theta(i,j) = B_2{}^\theta(i,j) + \alpha w_k q_2^\theta(i,j) \qquad k = 1, 2, ...K \tag{2}$$

Here $B_2'{}^\theta$ is the watermarked pixel and α is the multiplication factor to keep the watermark below the level of perception. The value of α is unity if the watermark is binary. The value of q, which is the maximum quantization at every pixel below the level of perception, is calculated using HVS model as given in [9].

The model presented in this paper is with reference to the four level decomposed image, where band L_2 in Fig. 1 is further decomposed into V_3, H_3, D_3 and L_3. According to this model maximum allowable distortion at every pixel is estimated as the weighted product of three different parameters.

$$q_l^\theta(i,j) = \hat{q}_l^\theta(i,j)/2 \tag{3}$$

$$\hat{q}_l^\theta(i,j) = \Theta(l,\theta)\Lambda(l,i,j)\Xi(l,i,j)^{0.2} \tag{4}$$

Each term in the above equation is explained below. Here $'l'$ and $'\theta'$ denote the level of decomposition and the orientation of the selected band respectively. The first term $\Theta(l,\theta)$ takes into account the sensitivity to noise depending on the band. Eyes are less sensitive to noise in high resolution bands and bands having orientation of 45°.

$$\Theta(l,\theta) = \left\{ \begin{array}{ll} \sqrt{2}, & if\theta = 1 \\ 1, & \text{otherwise} \end{array} \right\} \cdot \left\{ \begin{array}{l} 1.00, \text{ if l=0} \\ 0.32, \text{ if l=1} \\ 0.16, \text{ if l=2} \\ 0.10, \text{ if l=3} \end{array} \right\}$$

The second term takes into account the local brightness based on the gray-level values of the low pass version of the image. Also it considers the fact that eyes are less sensitive to very dark and very bright regions of the image. In [10], this factor is computed in the following way.

$$\Lambda(l,i,j) = 1 + L(l,i,j) \tag{5}$$

where

$$L(l,i,j) = \frac{L_3}{256}(1 + \lfloor \frac{i}{2^{3-l}} \rfloor, 1 + \lfloor \frac{j}{2^{3-l}} \rfloor) \tag{6}$$

Since eye is less sensitive to very dark regions as in the case of bright regions, in [9], this factor is modified as in the following equation.

$$\hat{L}'(l,i,j) = 1 - L(l,i,j), \qquad if L(i,j) \leq 0.5 \tag{7}$$
$$L(l,i,j), \qquad otherwise$$

The third term takes care of the fact that eye is less sensitive to noise in highly textured areas but more sensitive near edges.

$$\Xi(l,i,j) = \sum_{k=0}^{3-l} \frac{1}{16^k} \sum_{\theta=0}^{2} \sum_{x=0}^{1} \sum_{y=0}^{1} [B_{k+l}^{\theta}(y + \frac{i}{2^k}, x + \frac{j}{2^k})]^2 \tag{8}$$
$$.Var\{L_3(1 + y + \frac{i}{2^{3-l}}, 1 + x + \frac{j}{2^{3-l}})\}$$

where the first term gives the local mean square value and Var gives the variance around the 2x2 neighborhood of each pixel. After embedding the watermark, inverse transformation is performed to get the watermarked image.

2.2   Watermark Detection and Evaluation

For extracting the watermark from a possibly tampered image we need to use the original image and hence our algorithm is non-blind. Since watermark bits are embedded only at the significant pixels, we need to locate these pixels on the possibly attacked image and then get the quantization at those pixels. We have used Peak Signal-to-Noise Ratio ($PSNR$) as measure of perceptual quality of the watermarked image. Normalized correlation coefficient(γ) is defined as a measure of similarity between the original watermark (w) and retrieved watermark (w').

Suppose there are K pixels in the watermark, then normalized correlation coefficient is defined as follows.

$$\gamma = \frac{\sum_{i=1}^{K} w_i w_i'}{\sqrt{\sum_{i=1}^{K} w_i^2 \sum_{i=1}^{K} w'_i{}^2}}. \tag{9}$$

3 Experimental Results

The proposed algorithm was tested on both gray and color images of size 512×512. The binary watermark of size 16×16, shown in Fig. 2a, is embedded only once in the image. We have proposed to use the third decomposed level for embedding. But for the purpose of comparison, results of embedding and retrieval with second and fourth level decompositions are also included. Since the watermark is embedded only once and the quantization to each coefficient is as per HVS model, as a fair means of comparison, simulations were performed with highest absolute coefficients in second, third and fourth level decomposition, quantized as per HVS model given in [9].

The significant pixels of color images were located by considering the luminance component of the images in YCbCR representation. We have chosen four gray level images and two color images for experimentation. The watermarked images of Lena and Peppers are shown in Fig. 2b and 2c. We have not included all the test images in the paper due to space limitations. The PSNR of the watermarked images under all the considered cases are tabulated in Table 1.

(a) Watermark   (b) Watermarked Lena   (c)Watermarked Peppers

Fig. 2. Original watermark and watermarked images

3.1 Resilience to Attacks

Any watermarking scheme should be able to withstand both intentional and non-intentional signal processing operations. We have considered six different attacks, namely, salt-pepper noise with median filter, Gaussian noise addition, mean filter, quantization of the watermarked pixels, JPEG compression and

Table 1. PSNR(dB) of watermarked images

Images	Lena	Barbara	Baboon	Airplane	Peppers(color)	Airplane(color)
Significant pixels{2-level}	49.56	51.37	50.43	47.84	50.30	49.45
Significant pixels{3-level}	47.46	47.93	48.83	45.21	47.95	46.39
Significant pixels{4-level}	42.25	43.05	44.02	39.10	42.06	40.32
High absolute coeff{2-level}	50.04	50.76	51.63	47.43	49.98	48.50
High absolute coeff{3-level}	47.38	47.28	49.50	44.77	47.81	45.87
High absolute coeff{4-level}	42.30	42.14	44.29	39.27	41.87	40.40

cropping. The results discussed below are of third decomposed level unless otherwise specified. Also, only a few results are included in the paper due to lack of space. Nevertheless, simulations were carried out on all images and results were tabulated.

Salt- pepper noise with zero mean and 0.01 variance was added to the watermarked images and were then median filtered to get an output image that closely matched the original. Fig. 3a and Fig. 3b show the attacked images by salt-pepper noise and median filter and Fig. 3c and Fig. 3d show the retrieved watermarks from them. The correlation coefficient and visual similarity of the retrieved watermarks emphasize the advantage of selecting significant pixels for watermarking over highest absolute pixels. It can be seen from the results that the significant pixels in third decomposed level gave better performance than the highest absolute coefficients with salt pepper noise addition with median filtering.

Digital images may be corrupted due to Gaussian noise while transmission. Therefore, we have considered Gaussian noise addition as another attack. The

(a) Significant pixels

(b) High absolute pixels

(c) From a, $\gamma = 0.9063$

(d) From b, $\gamma = 0.8828$

Fig. 3. Salt-pepper noise with median filtered images and retrieved watermarks

(a) Significant pixels   (b) High absolute pixels

(c) From a, $\gamma = 0.7578$ (d) From b, $\gamma = 0.6094$

Fig. 4. Gaussian noise added images and retrieved watermarks

noise considered has mean zero and variance 0.001. The attacked images of Lena and the retrieved watermarks from them are shown in Fig. 4. The results for all the cases were considered and the significant pixels outperformed the highest absolute coefficients. The results with noise were averaged over 100 sample runs.

Mean filtering was performed with a 3×3 mask and the averaged image had very good visual similarity with the original image. The mean filtered images and the retrieved watermarks are shown in Fig 5. The advantage of selecting significant pixels instead of highest absolute coefficients is obvious in case of averaging.

Quantization of the watermarked images were performed by quantizing the watermarked pixels to multiples of 10, 20 and 40. Fig. 6 shows the quantized images to multiples of 40 and the retrieved watermarks from them.

JPEG compression is one of the attacks to which all image watermarking methods should be resistant to. We have tabulated the correlation coefficients for all the test images for quality factors varying from 10 to 100. The correlation coefficients obtained were very close to unity in most cases, the lowest being 0.8594 and 0.7812, with quality factor 10, for Lena watermarked using significant pixels and high absolute coefficients respectively.

We have also tried to retrieve the watermark after cropping the watermarked image. The simulation results show that the method proposed works satisfactorily, provided cropping does not remove any significant part of the image. For example, cropped baboon image along with the retrieved watermark is shown in Fig. 8. The coefficients watermarked are the significant pixels from third and fourth levels of decomposition. Here 62.5% of the watermarked image is retained after cropping. The correlation coefficient obtained is 0.8906 and 0.8672 from the

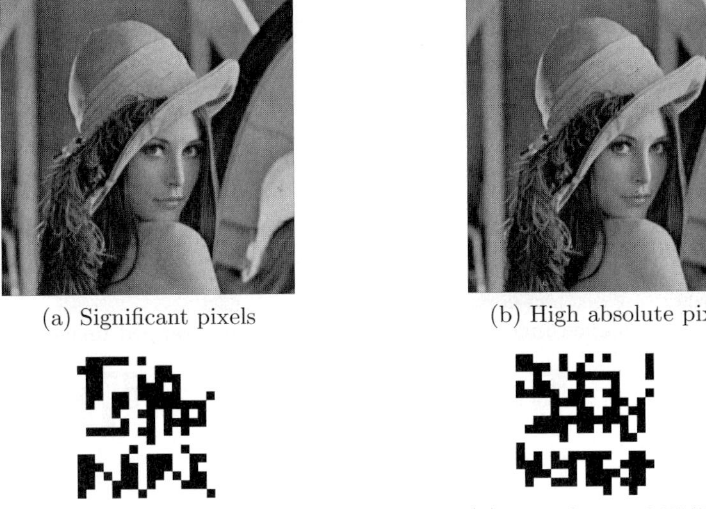

(a) Significant pixels

(b) High absolute pixels

(c) From a, $\gamma = 0.7813$

(d) From b, $\gamma = 0.5547$

Fig. 5. Mean filtered images and retrieved watermarks

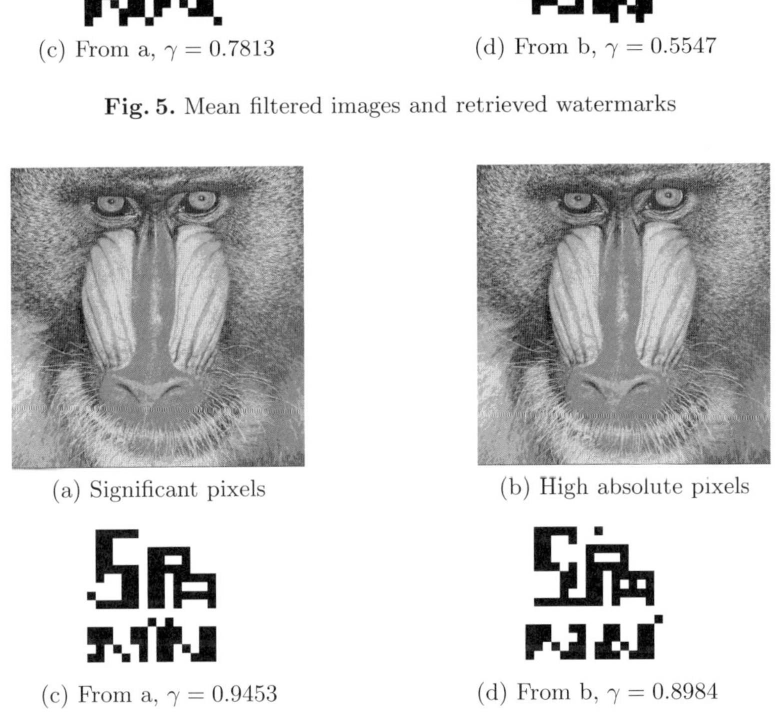

(a) Significant pixels

(b) High absolute pixels

(c) From a, $\gamma = 0.9453$

(d) From b, $\gamma = 0.8984$

Fig. 6. Quantized images to multiples of 40 and retrieved watermarks

fourth and third levels respectively. For the purpose of comparison the retrieved watermark from the highest absolute coefficients of fourth and third levels of decomposition are also shown.

Another attack that was specifically performed on color images was color palette filter using Adobe Photoshop software. The selected filter had stroke size 2, stroke detail 3 and softness 5 so that the attacked image was not perceptually

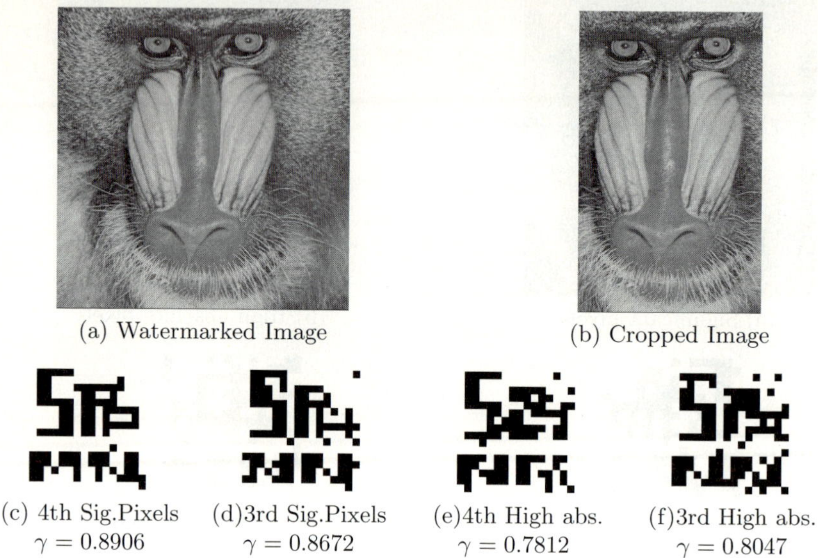

(a) Watermarked Image   (b) Cropped Image

(c) 4th Sig.Pixels   (d)3rd Sig.Pixels   (e)4th High abs.   (f)3rd High abs.
$\gamma = 0.8906$ $\gamma = 0.8672$ $\gamma = 0.7812$ $\gamma = 0.8047$

Fig. 7. Retrieved Watermarks from cropped image

much distorted. Table 2 shows the correlation coefficients of the retrieved watermarks from three different color images, with the original watermark and the values show the superior performance of the significant pixels over highest absolute pixels.

Table 2. Color palette filtering

Images	Sailboat	Peppers	Airplane
Significant pixels{2-level}	0.3984	0.4688	0.5859
Significant pixels{3-level}	0.5703	0.6250	0.5703
Significant pixels{4-level}	0.7188	0.8594	0.8594
High absolute coeff{2-level}	0.2188	0.2500	0.2891
High absolute coeff{3-level}	0.4375	0.5469	0.3906
High absolute coeff{4-level}	0.6641	0.7656	0.8125

4   Conclusion

We have introduced significant pixels in wavelet domain for robust watermarking. Moreover, every selected pixel was quantized to the maximum using HVS model. The scheme worked well without losing robustness and transparency. The simulation results show that the significant pixel would be a better choice for watermarking compared to high absolute coefficients. Also the simulation results prove that, higher the level of decomposition better the robustness. But the transparency may be crucial and difficult to maintain as higher bands are selected. Obviously, as we move from one band to the next higher band, larger number of pixels are distorted in the original image and the number of available pixels for watermarking becomes comparable with the number of watermark bits.

References

1. Wolfgang, R.B., Delp, E.J.: A watermark for digital images. Proceedings of IEEE Int. Conf. Image proc. **3** (1996) 219–222
2. Wolfgang, R., Delp, E.J.: Fragile watermarking using the vw2d watermark. Proceedings of SPIE **3228** (1997) 297–308
3. Ruanaidh, J.J.K.O., Dowling, W.J., Boland, F.M.: Phase watermarking of digital images. Proc. Int. Conf. Image Processing **3** (1996) 239–242
4. Hsu, C.T., Wu, J.L.: Hidden signatures in images. Proc. Int. Conf. Image Processing **3** (1996) 223–226
5. Kundur, D., Hatzinakos, D.: A robust digital image watermarking scheme using wavelet based fusion. Proceedings of IEEE Int. Conf. Image proc. (1997) 544–547
6. Inoue, H., Miyazaki, A., Yamamoto, A., Katsura, T.: A digital watermark based on wavelet transform and its robustness on image compression and transformation. IEICE Trans. Fund. Electron., Commun., Comput. Sci., **E82-A** (1999) 2–10
7. Xia, X., Boncelet, C.J., Arce, G.R.: A multiresolution watermark for digital images. Proceedings of IEEE Int. Conf. Image Proc. (1997) 548–551
8. Alghoniemy, M., Tewfik, A.H.: Geometric invariance in image watermarking. IEEE Trans. Image Proc. **13** (2004) 145–153
9. Barnii, M., Bartolini, F., Piva, A.: Improved wavelet based watermarking through pixel-wise masking. IEEE Trans. Image Proc. **10** (2001) 470–477
10. Lewis, A.S., Knowles, G.: Image compression using 2-d wavelet transform. IEEE Trans. Image Proc. **1** (1992) 244–250
11. Kundur, D., Hatzinakos, D.: Towards robust logo watermarking using multiresolution image fusion principles. IEEE Trans. Multimedia **6** (2004) 185–198
12. Tian, Q., Sebe, N., Lew, M.S., Loupias, E., Huang, T.S.: Content-based image retrieval using wavelet based salient points. Proceedings of SPIE **4315** (2000) 425–436.

Early Vision and Image Processing: Evidences Favouring a Dynamic Receptive Field Model

Kuntal Ghosh[1], Sandip Sarkar[1], and Kamales Bhaumik[2]

[1] Saha Institute of Nuclear Physics, 1/AF Bidhannagar, Kolkata-64, India
`kuntal.ghosh@saha.ac.in`
[2] West Bengal University of Technology, BF-142 Bidhannagar, Kolkata-64, India
`kamales_bhaumik@yahoo.com`

Abstract. Evidences favouring a dynamic receptive field model of retinal ganglion cells and the cells of Lateral Geniculate Nucleus (LGN) have been presented based on the perception of some brightness-contrast illusions. Of the different kinds of such stimuli, four, namely the Simultaneous Brightness-contrast, the White effect, the DeValois and DeValois checkerboard illusion and the Howe stimulus have been chosen to establish this model. The present approach attempts to carry forward the works that look upon visual perception as a step-by-step information processing task rather than a rule-based Gestalt approach and provides a new biologically inspired tool for simultaneous smoothing and edge enhancement in image processing.

1   Introduction

The present work is aimed at understanding and explaining some of the aspects of visual signal processing mainly at the retinal level and in the simple cells of primary visual cortex. The topic may be initiated by recalling a memorable observation of J. B. Barlow [1] :

A description of that activity of a single nerve cell which is transformed to and influences other nerve cells and of a nerve cell's response to such influences from other cells, is a complete enough description for functional understanding of the nervous system. There is nothing else " looking at " or controlling this activity, which must therefore provide a basis for understanding how the brain controls behaviour.

Assumption of such a position was no doubt a great leap forward in unfurling the " mysteries " of the functioning of the nervous system, probably the first straightforward physical and materialistic approach to achieve an understanding of it in contrast to the Gestalt or holistic approach. Yet in spite of being essentially objective in its spirit, it could not but finally surrender itself amidst the relics of anti-science subjectivism. This resulted from its mechanical mode of relying upon the attempts to provide perceptual explanations by means of single cell recordings only. The "part" alone thus assumed importance and the "whole" lost its legitimate role. It was forgotten that the part and the whole are only

P. Kalra and S. Peleg (Eds.): ICVGIP 2006, LNCS 4338, pp. 216–227, 2006.

interrelated concepts and truth always emerges from a dialectical synthesis of the two. The success of Hubel-Wiesel's work [2,3], wherein they could model the activity of a deep-seated neuron of layer VI as an output of a summation circuit having inputs from neurons of outer plexiform layer, led to an over-emphasis in the study of the details of the neuronal circuits in the understanding of the functions of brain, completely ignoring the role of emergent behaviours of complex systems. A faith was spread that for any conceivable complicated human perception, one would be able to identify a type of neurons in the brain leading to the final output of the perception and the study of the circuits connected with that cell would lead to a complete understanding of the mechanism of that perception. What therefore started as a beginning of a new direction in neuroscience that was trying to rid itself of its mystical cloaks, led to unnecessary new mysticisms through the so-called *discoveries* like the grandmother detecting cell. Yet the basic point on which this approach initiated by Barlow [1] tried to emphasize, was that it is only neurons and neurons alone that are responsible for the entire information processing in nervous system. Like, for example in vision, starting from the two dimensional intensity array formation on the retina to the three dimensional object reconstruction and recognition in higher regions of the brain, the entire process is controlled and executed by networks of neurons of different types. This pro-materialistic approach, ushered in the radical thought process that there is no " soul " sitting anywhere and interpreting things from the neuronal outputs, but rather it is a collective, step-by-step synchronization of the outputs at various stages in the eye and the brain, no matter how complex that process is, that ultimately creates a perception of the world around us. It was this approach that generated vigor and excitement among the science community which needs to be carried forward in the proper perspective by eliminating all remnants of subjectivism.

The most likely approach in this direction would be to initially consider primary visual processing and start with gray scale scenario only. To get an insight into this, the methodology that we are going to adopt in the present work, is to study the brightness perception in case of some select brightness-contrast illusions. We shall first consider the well-known low-level illusion namely the Simultaneous Brightness-contrast stimulus, which is easily explainable with the well acclaimed Difference of Gaussian (DoG) model of the receptive field of retinal ganglion cells and the cells of lateral geniculate nucleus (LGN)[4]. Then we shall consider the more complex stimuli like the White effect [5], and the DeValois and DeValois checkerboard illusion [6] which are often thought to be inexplainable without a Gestalt approach [7]. We shall explain these effects by extending the DoG model that serves to support a dynamic model of the receptive field based on a linear combination of three Gaussians. Finally we shall consider a very interesting variant of the White effect stimulus called the Howe stimulus [8], that itself challenges the Gestalt school explanation and apply the above dynamic model of the receptive field to provide a considerably satisfactory explanation to this phenomenon as well. Finally, as a corollary, we shall also see how this model may provide a new approach to edge enhancement in images.

2   The Proposed Model

2.1   The Classical Model

It is well-known that the brightness of a region of visual space is not related to the luminance of that region alone, but also depend on the luminance of its adjacent regions. When the brightness of a test region shifts away from the brightness of the surround region the phenomenon is termed as a brightness-contrast event. Such events, like the Mach band, the Simultaneous Brightness-contrast, the Hermann grid illusion or the grating induction effect can be more or less explained with the help of the isotropic DoG model of primary visual processing [4], even though there are still many subtle aspects of these stimuli that require a deeper understanding of how even these low-level brightness-contrast illusions are actually processed [9,10]. Let us first consider the Simultaneous Brightness-contrast (SBC) illusion shown in Figure 1. This is a well-studied textbook example where a gray patch on a white background looks darker than an equiluminant gray patch on a black background. This model is well-explained by the classical DoG model. If Figure 1 is convoluted with a DoG filter given by:

Fig. 1. The Simultaneous Brightness-Contrast illusion

$$DOG(\sigma_1, \sigma_2) = A_1 \frac{1}{\sqrt{2\pi}\sigma_1} \exp(-\frac{x^2}{2\sigma_1{}^2}) - A_2 \frac{1}{\sqrt{2\pi}\sigma_2} \exp(-\frac{x^2}{2\sigma_2{}^2}) \qquad (1)$$

then the convoluted image clearly bears the signature of our illusory perception. Such a convoluted image has been shown in Figure 2 (a). That the convoluted image is no illusion again has easily been confirmed by drawing two horizontal line profiles through the two test patches as shown in Figure 2(b). The result is easily understandable because the inhibition for the upper test patch from its dark surrounding makes it look brighter than that of the lower test patch with its bright surrounding.

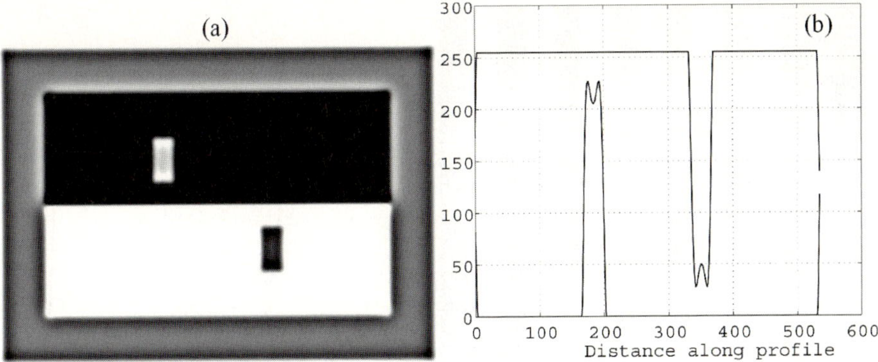

Fig. 2. (a) The Simultaneous Brightness-contrast stimulus when convoluted with DoG (b) Horizontal line profiles through the two test patches in (a). Clearly the test patch in brighter neighbourhood has become darker.

Fig. 3. The White Effect

2.2   The Classical Model Modified

We now consider the case of the White effect [5] which has caused much hype among the Gestalt theorists since it totally contradicts the lateral inhibition based theory of primary visual processing. Let us take a look at the White effect stimulus shown in Figure 3. In this effect, the direction of brightness change does not consistently correlate with the amount of black or white border in contact with the gray test patch or in its general vicinity. It can easily be seen from Figure 3 that the same vertically oriented rectangle that we used in the SBC

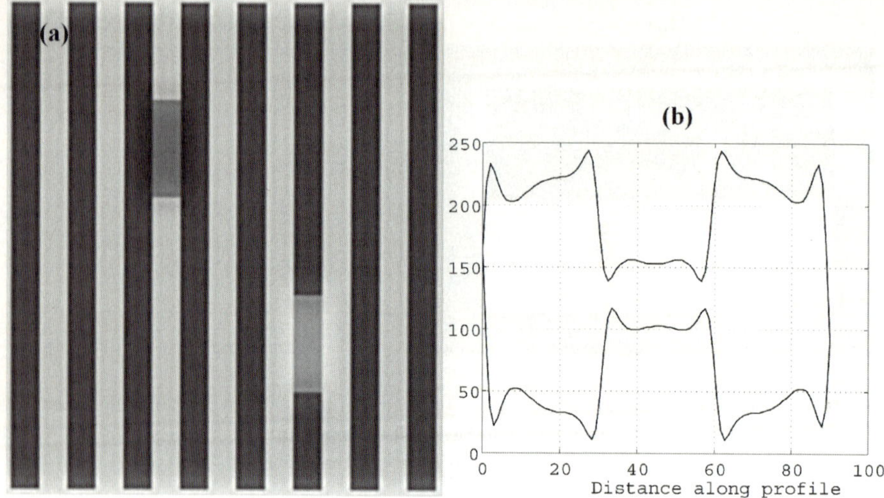

Fig. 4. (a) The White effect stimulus when convoluted with MDoG. (b) Horizontal line profiles through the two test patches in (a). Here unlike in Figure 2(b), the test patch in brighter neighbourhood has become brighter.

Fig. 5. The DeValois and DeValois Checkerboard stimulus

(Figure 1), when sitting on the white stripe of a vertical grating, appears darker than an identical test patch sitting on a black stripe. Because the later test patch has more border contact with the black flanking bars and yet appears darker, the effect is opposite to the SBC and hence cannot be explained by lateral inhibition. Most of the explanations of White effect provided so far are not computational models, except that of Ross and Pessoa [11]. But the White effect can also be explained in the light of a simple modification of the classical DoG model, that takes into consideration a disinhibitory contribution from the amacrine cells [12]. This model is based on the existence of an extended surround beyond the classical receptive field. Such an extra-classical receptive field is reported both for LGN cells as well as the retinal ganglion cells [13,14]. The proposed Modified DoG model is:

$$MDOG(\sigma_1, \sigma_2, \sigma_3) = A_1 \frac{1}{\sqrt{2\pi}\sigma_1} \exp(-\frac{x^2}{2\sigma_1{}^2}) - A_2 \frac{1}{\sqrt{2\pi}\sigma_2} \exp(-\frac{x^2}{2\sigma_2{}^2})$$

$$+ A_3 \frac{1}{\sqrt{2\pi}\sigma_3} \exp(-\frac{x^2}{2\sigma_3{}^2}) \tag{2}$$

This simple computational model is capable of explaining the White effect. If we convolve Figure 3 with this model, we find that the convoluted image bears

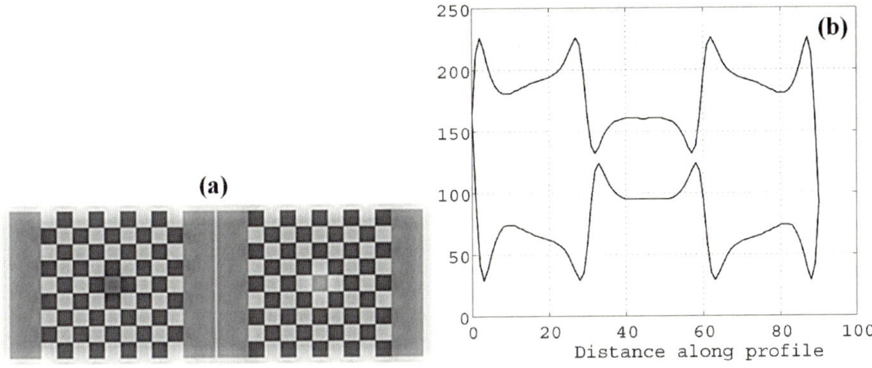

Fig. 6. (a) The Checkerboard stimulus when convoluted with MDoG. (b) Horizontal line profiles through the two test patches in (a). Here again the test patch in brighter neighbourhood has become brighter.

Fig. 7. The Howe stimulus

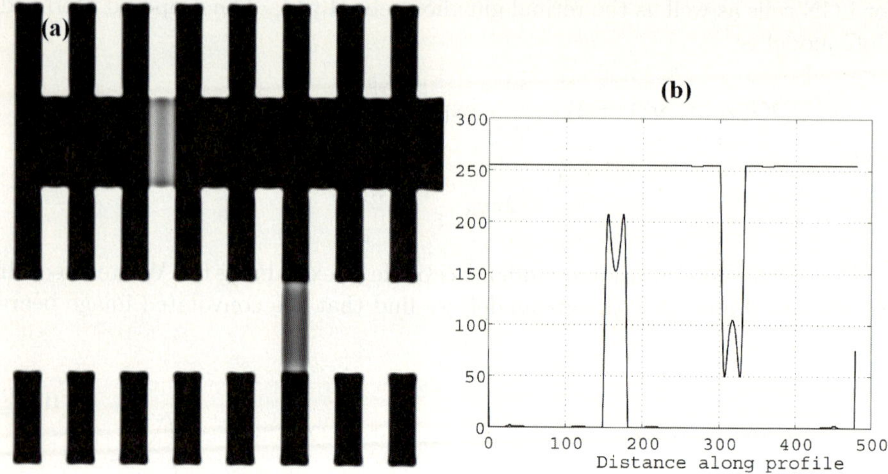

Fig. 8. (a) The Howe stimulus when convoluted with MDoG. (b) Horizontal line profiles through the two test patches in (a). Here again, unlike the White effect the test patch in brighter neighbourhood has become darker.

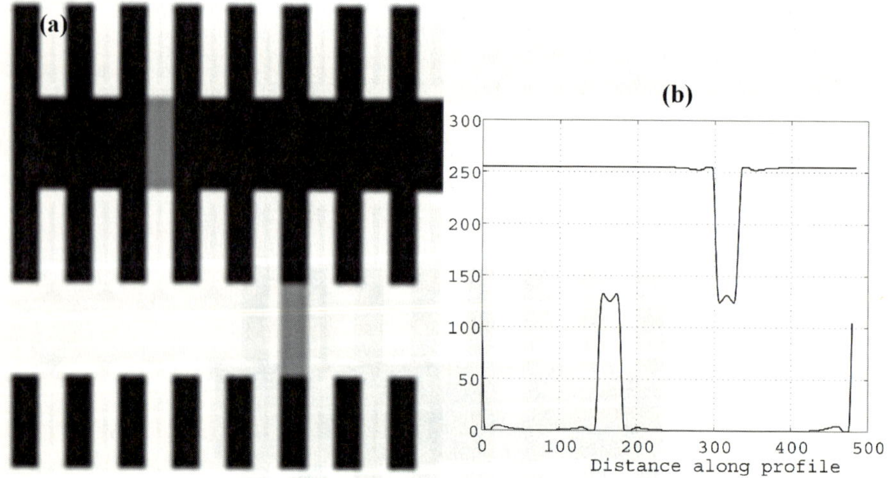

Fig. 9. (a) The Howe stimulus when convoluted with MDoG for the alternative settings. (b) Horizontal line profiles through the two test patches in (a). Here neighbourhood has no effect on the luminance of the test patches.

signature of the illusory perception in Figure 4 (a). This can again be verified by drawing horizontal profiles through the two test patches, with two neighbouring stripes on either side of each, as shown in Figure 4(b). A similar stimulus is the checkerboard illusion [6], shown in Figure 5. This is also inexplainable with the isotropic DoG model, since the test patch with darker neighbourhood on the left, appears less bright than the one with brighter neighbourhood on the right. This

Gaussian Filtered Image

(a) CD AB (b) (c)

Fig. 10. (a) The benchmark image of egg-on-plate. (b) The resultant image when (a) is convoluted with a Gaussian function. (c) The resultant image when (a) is convoluted with the MDoG function.

illusion can also be explained with the help of the modified model for exactly the same parameter values as for explaining the White effect. This can be seen in Figure 6(a) and 6(b).

2.3   The Gestalt Theories and Their Limitations

The White effect and checkerboard illusions have led many investigators to abandon spatial filtering and receptive field based explanations, not only for these particular cases, but for brightness perception in general. Consequently, three explanations of the White effect that have been put forward are all certain rule based theories. For example Todorovic [15] put forward a T-junction rule and Anderson [16] also suggested a lightness rule. The computational model based

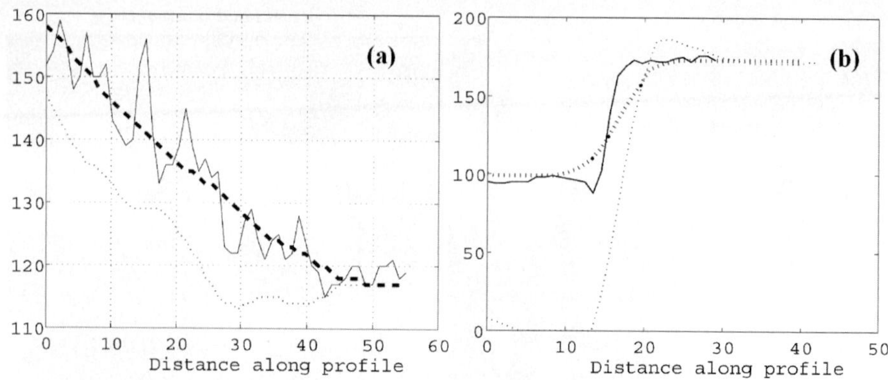

Fig. 11. (a) The intensity profile of AB marked in Figure 10(a) has been plotted with a solid line. The thicker dotted line represents the same line profile in Figure 10(b) and the thinner dotted line, that in Figure 10(c). Clearly, the MDoG function can behave as a smoothing function, like the Gaussian. (b) The intensity profile of CD marked in Figure 10(a) has been plotted with a solid line. The coarser dotted line represents the same line profile in Figure 10(b) and the finer dotted line, that in Figure 10(c). Clearly, the MDoG function can also behave as an edge enhancing function, like any derivative operator and unlike the Gaussian.

on higher level groupings that was forwarded by Ross and Pessoa [11] in its simplified form, also segments visual scenes by means of T-junctions. However, all the three explanations are incomplete if we consider the Howe effect, a novel variation of White's display [8] shown in Figure 7, where the T-junctions remain exactly the same compared to Figure 3 and yet the image perception changes. It was reported by Howe [8], that when this stimulus was observed by thirty-three naive observers, almost all of them reported either an opposite perception of brightness compared to White effect or no illusory perception at all. None of the three Gestalt explanations mentioned above, can explain these perceptions.

3   Results with the Proposed Dynamic Model

The modified DoG model proposed in the previous section has been found to be very effective in explaining many brightness-contrast illusions [9]. From this work, we find that the model is actually a dynamic one that operates at practically three different sets of amplitudes (A_1, A_2 and A_3) and sampling intervals depending upon the illusory stimulus. If we apply the set of values used for explaining SBC by the proposed bhaumodel [9], then convoluting Figure 7 with this model we achieve an explanation of the perception of those seventeen observers who reported an opposite perception of brightness compared to White effect. This has been shown in Figure 8 (a) and in its horizontal line profiles in Figure 8 (b).

If on the other hand, we apply the settings for explaining Mach band and Hermann grid illusion [9] when convoluting, we arrive at the explanation of

Fig. 12. (a) The benchmark image of Lena. (b) The resultant image when (a) is convoluted with a Gaussian function. (c) The resultant image when (a) is convoluted with the MDoG function.

those thirteen observers who reported equiluminance for both the patches. The convolution result and its corresponding line profiles are shown in Figure 9 (a) and 9 (b).

Finally, we apply the proposed filter on benchmark images and analyse the results. We find that the proposed filter behaves simultaneously as a smoothing function and an edge enhancer, in contrast to a normal Gaussian function that can only act as a smoothing function. This is clear from Figures 10 and 11 using the benchmark image egg-on-plate. Thus unlike the Laplacian of Gaussian function [17], which is an equivalent to the DoG, even without applying a derivative filter, we have achieved an enhancement of edges, together with smoothing

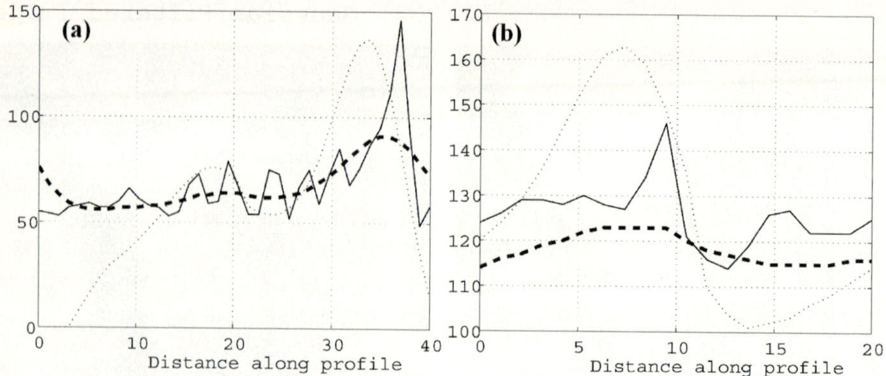

Fig. 13. (a) The intensity profile of AB marked in Figure 12(a) has been plotted with a solid line. The thicker dotted line represents the same line profile in Figure 12(b) and the thinner dotted line, that in Figure 12(c). Clearly, we find again that the MDoG function can behave as a smoothing function, like the Gaussian. (b) The intensity profile of CD marked in Figure 12(a) has been plotted with a solid line. The thicker dotted line represents the same line profile in Figure 12(b) and the thinner dotted line, that in Figure 12(c). So we find again that the MDoG function can also behave as an edge enhancing function, like any derivative operator and unlike the Gaussian.

using a linear combination of three Gaussian functions at different scales. For the benchmark image (Figure 10(a)) we have selected two horizontal line profiles AB and CD in two different regions of the image and compared the effects along these two profiles, after applying the Gaussian filter (Figure 10(b)) and the proposed filter (Figure 10(c)) respectively. The corresponding line profiles in Figure 11(a), show that like with the Gaussian, a smoothing has been achieved along the profile AB, with the proposed filter as well. On the other hand, the line profiles in Figure 11(b), show that unlike the Gaussian the proposed filter at the same time enhances the edge along the profile CD. Another benchmark image of Lena has similarly been processed and analyzed in Figures 12 and 13, yielding similar results.

4   Conclusion

Evidences in favour of a dynamic model of primary visual processing is presented here, based on a step-by-step information processing approach in contrast to the rule-based Gestalt approach. The model is able to explain not only the low-level brightness-contrast illusions, but also those, which were so far supposedly totally outside the purview of low-level vision. It is also capable of enhancing image edges without direct differentiation. Hence smoothing and edge enhancement may simultaneously be achieved in this new biologically inspired approach.

References

1. Barlow, H. B.: Single units and sensation: a neuron doctrine for perceptual psychology? Perception **1** (1972) 371-394
2. Hubel D. H. and Wiesel T. N.: Receptive fields of single neurons in the cat's striate cortex. Journal of Physiology **148** (1959) 574-591
3. Hubel D. H. and Wiesel T. N.: Receptive fields, binocular interaction and functional architecture in the cat's visual cortex.Journal of Physiology **166** (1962) 106-154
4. Palmer, S. E.: Vision Science: Photons to Phenomenology, MIT Press, Cambridge, Massachusetts (1999)
5. White, M: The effect of the nature of the surround on the perceived lightness of gray bars within square-wave test gratings. Perception **10** (1981) 215-230
6. DeValois, R. L. and DeValois, K. K.: Spatial Vision, Oxford University Press, New York (1988)
7. Agostini, T. and Proffitt D. R.: Perceptual organization evokes simultaneous lightness contrast. Perception **22** (1993) 263-272
8. Howe, P. D. L.: A comment on the Anderson (1997), the Todorovic (1997), and the Ross and Pessoa (2000) explanation of White's effect. Perception **30** (2001) 1023-1026
9. Ghosh, K., Sarkar, S. and Bhaumik, K.: A possible explanation of the low-level brightness-contrast illusions in the light of an extended classical receptive field model of retinal ganglion cells. Biological Cybernetics **94** (2006) 89-96
10. Ghosh, K., Sarkar, S. and Bhaumik, K.: Proposing new methods in low-level vision from the Mach band illusion in retrospect. Pattern Recognition **39** (2006) 726-730
11. Ross, W. D. and Pessoa, L.: Lightness from contrast: A selective integration model. Perception and Psychophysics **62** (2000) 1160-1181
12. Ghosh, K., Sarkar, S. and Bhaumik, K.: A possible mechanism of zero-crossing detection using the concept of extended classical receptive field of retinal ganglion cells. Biological Cybernetics **93** (2005) 1-5
13. Sun, C., Chen, X., Huang, L. and Shou, T.: Orientation bias of the extraclassical re-ceptive field of the relay cells in the cat's dorsal lateral geniculate nucleus. Neuroscience **125** (2004) 495-505
14. Passaglia, L., Enroth-Cugell C. and Troy, J. B.: Effects of remote stimulation on the mean firing rate of cat retinal ganglion cells. Journal of Neuroscience **21** (2001) 5794-5803.
15. Todorovic, D.: Lightness and junctions. Perception **26** (1997) 379-395
16. Anderson, B. L.: A theory of illusory lightness and transparency in monocular and binocular images: the role of computer junctions. Perception **26** (1997) 419-453
17. Marr, D., Hildreth, E.: Theory of edge detection. Proceedings of Royal Society of London B **207** (1980) 187–217.

An Alternative Curvature Measure for Topographic Feature Detection

Jayanthi Sivaswamy, Gopal Datt Joshi, and Siva Chandra

Centre for Visual Information Technology,
IIIT Hyderabad, Andhra Pradesh
India, 500032
jsivaswamy@iiit.ac.in, gopal@research.iiit.ac.in

Abstract. The notion of topographic features like ridges, trenches, hills, etc. is formed by visualising the 2D image function as a surface in 3D space. Hence, properties of such a surface can be used to detect features from images. One such property, the curvature of the image surface, can be used to detect features characterised by a sharp bend in the surface. Curvature based feature detection requires an efficient technique to estimate/calculate the surface curvature. In this paper, we present an alternative measure for curvature and provide an analysis of the same to determine its scope. Feature detection algorithms using this measure are formulated and two applications are chosen to demonstrate their performance. The results show good potential of the proposed measure in terms of efficiency and scope.

1 Introduction

A feature detection system for 2D digital images is a part of the back-end of computer vision systems. It is commonly preceded by an image enhancement system and operates on the intensity values of the image pixels. The detected features which are used by a higher level system for further processing and understanding of the scene, are of two types: (a) perceptual features such as edges, corners, contours, boundaries etc., and (b) topographic features such as ridges, valleys, watersheds etc.

The notion of topographic features, such as ridges, valleys, watersheds etc., is formed by visualising the 2D image function as a surface in 3D space. Features of this kind are detected by exploiting the properties of the image surface. One such useful property, which can be used to detect image features, is the curvature of the image surface. It has been successfully used to detect ridges, valleys, thin nets and crest lines from digital images [1] [2]. In general, curvature can be used to detect features where the image surface bends sharply. Such features are characterised by points of maximal curvature on the image surface.

Detection of features using curvature information requires efficient techniques to calculate the curvature of image surfaces. A common approach to curvature based feature detection is based on the differential geometry of image surfaces

P. Kalra and S. Peleg (Eds.): ICVGIP 2006, LNCS 4338, pp. 228–239, 2006.

[3] [4]. For every point (m, n) on an image, a surface $f(m, n)$ is fit to the 'neighborhood' of the point prior to computing the first and second partial derivatives. There exist two curvature measures, namely, the maximum and minimum principal curvatures along two orthogonal principal directions which measure the bend in the surface and are typically used to detect ridges and valleys from digital images. A pixel is defined as a ridge pixel if the magnitude of the maximum principal curvature (MPC) at that pixel is a local maximum in some direction. Depending on the reference coordinate system, a high negative curvature indicates a strong ridge strength while a high positive curvature indicates a strong valley strength, or vice versa. The direction along which the MPC is a maximum is the direction perpendicular to the orientation of the ridge (or valley) at that pixel. An algorithm for the curvature-based feature detection approach described above can be found in [4]. The algorithm involves four steps: Fit a surface $I(m, n)$ to the neighborhood of the point of interest (a local graph representation); compute the first and second partial derivatives of the image function; determine the principle curvatures of the surface; and finally evaluate curvature measures to find desired features.

Curvature can also be estimated without the knowledge of a local graph representation [5] [6]. Such methods calculate the principle curvatures of the surface numerically from an ensemble of directional curvature estimates. Estimation of curvature using these methods seem to perform about as accurately as the analytic techniques [7]. Furthermore, lack of need for a local graph representation reduces the computational load relative to the analytic techniques.

In this paper, we define a curvature measure, called the Surface Tangent Derivative (STD), as an estimate of the curvature of image surfaces. Though slightly different from the true curvature measure, STD lends itself for a computationally efficient implementation. This ability makes it a superior measure than the standard curvature for use in *real time* feature detection applications.

The paper is organised as follows. The proposed curvature measure (STD) is derived in section 2. An analysis of the same is presented in section 3 and an efficient implementation of the measure is presented in section 4; algorithms for detecting two different kinds of topographical features are presented in section 5; and section 6 presents validation of STD on two different applications followed by concluding remarks.

2 The Surface Tangent Derivative (STD)

The curvature at a point on the image surface is a measure of the bend in the surface along a particular direction. Because of this direction-specific nature of curvature, one can define the curvature of the image surface along a particular direction, in terms the curvature of the 1D profile of the image intensity values along that direction. In this section, we present an alternative measure of surface curvature of 2D digital images using such an approach. Before presenting the new measure, we shall first review the definition for curvature of a 1D function.

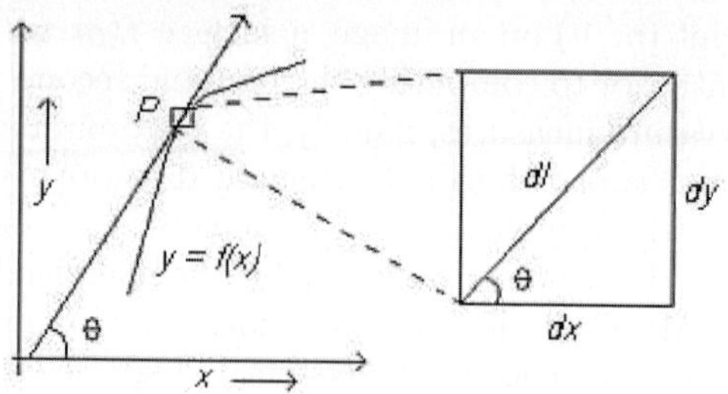

Fig. 1. Illustration of curvature of a 1D function

Let $y = f(x)$ be a 1D function. Let the tangent at a point $P : x$ on this function make an angle θ with the x-axis as shown in Figure 1. If dl is the differential arc length at the point P, then the extrinsic curvature of the function $f(x)$ at this point is defined as:

$$k(x) = \frac{d\theta}{dl} = \frac{d\theta}{\sqrt{dx^2 + dy^2}} = \frac{\frac{d\theta}{dx}}{\sqrt{1 + \left(\frac{dy}{dx}\right)^2}} \tag{1}$$

Since, θ is the angle made by the tangent with the x-axis, it can be computed as:

$$\theta = tan^{-1}\left(\frac{dy}{dx}\right) \tag{2}$$

Hence, the numerator term $\frac{d\theta}{dx}$ can be computed as:

$$\Upsilon(x) = \frac{d\theta}{dx} = \frac{d}{dx}\left[tan^{-1}\left(\frac{dy}{dx}\right)\right] = \frac{\frac{d^2y}{dx^2}}{1 + \left(\frac{dy}{dx}\right)^2} \tag{3}$$

Substituting the above expression in equation 1, we get:

$$k(x) = \frac{\frac{d^2y}{dx^2}}{\left(1 + \left(\frac{dy}{dx}\right)^2\right)^{\frac{3}{2}}} \tag{4}$$

which is the true curvature measure. As the point P moves on the curve $y = f(x)$, the tangent angle θ changes. This change over a given arc length dl is the true curvature measure $k(x)$. On a closer examination of equation 1, we can see that the numerator term $\Upsilon(x)$ represents the rate of change the tangent angle with respect to the projection of the arc length over the x axis. Comparing the equations 3 and 4, we see that the two expressions differ only by the power of the denominator. Significantly, $\Upsilon(x)$ will peak sharply at the locations of medial points of ridge profiles (as does $k(x)$), where the first derivative of the profile function vanishes and the second derivative is a negative maximum. We propose using $\Upsilon(x)$ as an alternative to the true curvature measure $k(x)$ since it also provides information about the rate of change the tangent angle as a point moves along a curve. In the case of 2D images, $\Upsilon(x)$ corresponds to a derivative of the angle made by a surface tangent line with the image plane, in some direction. Accordingly, we distinguish it from the true curvature measure, by calling it as the Surface Tangent Derivative (STD). We will now analyse STD as a curvature measure. The analysis is aimed at providing information about the of STD as a feature detector, specifically for ridges/valleys. A theoretical analysis of the scope of STD is also useful to determine its limits as compared to the true curvature measure. A 1D profile-based analysis of the for true curvature measure has been reported in [8]. We follow a similar analysis for STD to assess its scope relative that of true curvature.

3   The Scope of Proposed STD Curvature Measure

A ridge/valley detection technique detects the medial lines of surface structures using their curvature information. Medial lines are loci of 'medial points' of the cross section profiles of ridges/valleys. Therefore, it has been shown [8] that 1D profile functions can be used to perform an analysis of curvature based ridge/valley detection, by reformulating the original 2D framework to detect medial points of 1D profile functions. We begin with some definitions. Let $f : \Re \to \Re$ be a 1D function. If a point $x = a$ is a point of local maximum of the function $y = |f(x)|$, then it is a point of magnitude maximum (PMMAX) of the function $y = f(x)$. Similarly, if a point $x = a$ is a point of local minimum of the function $y = |f(x)|$, then it is a point of magnitude minimum of the function (PMMIN) $y = f(x)$.

Lemma 1: Let $f : \Re \to \Re$ be a 1D function for which derivatives upto the second order exist. If

$$(a) \left[\frac{dy}{dx}\right]_{x=a} = 0 \ \ and, (b) \left[y\frac{d^2y}{dx^2}\right]_{x=a} < 0$$

then, x=a is a PMMAX of the function $y = f(x)$.

Proof: Follows from definition of derivatives. See [8] for details.

   We shall now state the criterion for curvature based medial point detection using the STD.

Definition 1: Let $f : \Re \to \Re$ be a 1D function for which derivatives up to the second order exist. A point $x = a$ is a medial point of the function $y = f(x)$ if it is a PMMAX of $\Upsilon(x)$.

The PMMAX of the curvature is where the first derivative of the curvature vanishes. The derivative of the curvature is found by differentiating the expression in equation 3.

$$\frac{d\Upsilon}{dx} = \frac{\frac{d^3y}{dx^3}\left(1+\left(\frac{dy}{dx}\right)^2\right) - 2\frac{dy}{dx}\left(\frac{d^2y}{dx^2}\right)^2}{\left(1+\left(\frac{dy}{dx}\right)^2\right)^2} \tag{5}$$

Considering equation 5, it is clear that the first derivative of the curvature can vanish under four different conditions. These are:

$$\mathbf{C1} \ :: \ \frac{dy}{dx} = 0, \frac{d^2y}{dx^2} \neq 0, \frac{d^3y}{dx^3} = 0; \quad \mathbf{C2} \ :: \ \frac{dy}{dx} = 0, \frac{d^2y}{dx^2} = 0, \frac{d^3y}{dx^3} = 0$$

$$\mathbf{C3} \ :: \ \frac{dy}{dx} \neq 0, \frac{d^2y}{dx^2} = 0, \frac{d^3y}{dx^3} = 0; \quad \mathbf{C4} \ :: \ \frac{dy}{dx} \neq 0, \frac{d^2y}{dx^2} \neq 0, \frac{d^3y}{dx^3} \neq 0$$

In C4, the numerator as a whole, of the expression on the right hand side of equation 5 goes to zero.

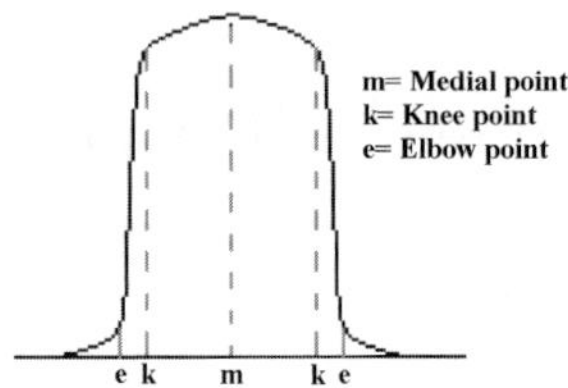

Fig. 2. Cross- section of a ridge and the various points of extremal curvature

The second derivative of the profile function is zero in C2 and C3. Hence, by equation 3, the STD measure of the profile function also goes to zero at such points. Therefore, a point satisfying C2 or C3 cannot be a PMMAX of the STD function. A medial point is either the top of a ridge profile, or the bottom of a valley profile. In other words, the medial points are points of the extremal image intensities. Hence, a PMMAX which satisfies C4 cannot be a medial point of a ridge/valley profile. Such PMMAX occur as 'knee/elbow' points of the ridge profiles as shown in fig. 2. In practice, it is either rejected by setting a threshold or in few rare cases, is wrongly classified as a ridge/valley pixel. Therefore, medial points which satisfy the criterion in Definition 1 should satisfy only C1. However, a point satisfying C1 need not satisfy the criterion in Definition 1. The condition under which a point satisfies C1 is also a PMMAX of the STD function can be found by applying Lemma 1 to the STD expression in 3. This condition is:

$$\left[\frac{d^2y}{dx^2} \left\{ \frac{d^4y}{dx^4} - 4\left(\frac{d^2y}{dx^2}\right)^3 \right\} \right]_{x=a} < 0 \tag{6}$$

If at some points on the profile, the fourth-derivative is non-zero in addition to C1 being satisfied and the curvature function has a PMMAX, then, the profile function has to satisfy the inequality in 6. This can be proven by expanding the STD expression using the Taylor's series. A detailed proof is given in [8].

We can now identify the classes of ridge/valley profiles detectable using the STD. C1 requires the third-derivative to be zero while the second-derivative is non-zero. There are five different possibilities for the second derivative function:

Class 1: It has a PMMAX where the first derivative vanishes.

Class 2: It is non-zero and is a point of inflection where the first-derivative vanishes.

Class 3: It is a non-zero constant function and there exists a point where the first-derivative vanishes.

Class 4: It has a non-zero PMMIN where the first and fourth-derivatives vanish.

Class 5: It has a PMMIN where the fourth-derivative is nonzero, and condition C1 and the inequality 6 are satisfied at that point.

These correspond to five classes of ridge/valley profiles that can be detected using the STD. The STD measure rejects PMMINs of the curvature function and non-extrema which have also been shown to be rejected by the true curvature measure $k(x)$ [8]. Thus in terms of scope, the STD is identical to the true curvature measure. However, due to the difference (lower for STD) in the power of the denominator of $\Upsilon(x)$ and $k(x)$ we can expect a lower specificity for the STD, which is not a serious problem in many applications. In the next section, we present a efficient method for computing the proposed STD measure.

4   Calculation of STD

The proposed scheme calculates the STD measure at a pixel location (which corresponds to a point on the image surface) for a particular direction α. Let the STD measure at a pixel location (n, m), along a direction α, be denoted by $\Gamma(n, m, \alpha)$. Using equation 3, the angle made by the surface tangent with the image plane at a pixel (n, m), along the direction α in the base-plane, is calculated as:

$$\Psi(n, m, \alpha) = tan^{-1}[I_\alpha(n, m)] \tag{7}$$

where $I(n, m)$ is the image function, $I_\alpha(n, m)$ is the first directional derivative along the direction α. The STD is the derivative of the angle Ψ and given as:

$$\Gamma(n, m, \alpha) = \Psi(n, m, \alpha) \tag{8}$$

In the above equation, $\Psi(n, m, \alpha)$ is the directional derivative of the surface tangent angle Ψ, in the direction α. We can use an efficient numerical technique to estimate these derivatives. In theory, at any given point on the surface, an STD measure can be obtained for every possible direction measuring the bend in the surface along that particular direction. However, for a function defined over a discrete grid (such as digital images), it is possible to evaluate the STD measure only along a finite number of directions. Thus, the STD can be calculated in four directions at each point, and the results be combined to obtain the two principle curvatures. The four different directions correspond to the 8 neighbours of a pixel. These four directions are specified in the set $\Omega = \{-45°, 0°, 45°, 90°\}$.

5   Topographical Feature Detection Using STD

Topographical features are characterised by high values of STD measure. In this section, we present algorithms for detection of two different kinds of features namely ridges/valleys which are characterised by points of maximum curvature in a *particular* direction and hills/craters which are characterised by maximum curvature in *all* directions.

5.1   Ridge Detection Algorithm

Let $I(n,m)$ be the image function. Calculate the STD for four different directions as $\Gamma(n,m,a)$, $\alpha \in \Omega$. Let t_Γ be the threshold for ridge strength. For every pixel location (n,m), do the following:

1. *Evaluate $|\Gamma_{max}| = max\{\Gamma(n,m,\alpha); \alpha \in \Omega\}$ and the corresponding orientation α_{max}.*
2. *If $|\Gamma_{max}| > t_\Gamma$ and $\Gamma(n,m,\alpha_{max}) < 0$, then:*
   – Check if $|\Gamma_{max}|$ is greater than $|\Gamma(n,m,\alpha)|$ of the neighbouring pixels corresponding to the direction α_{max}. If yes, then mark the pixel (n,m) as a ridge pixel. Else, do nothing.
   Else: Do nothing.

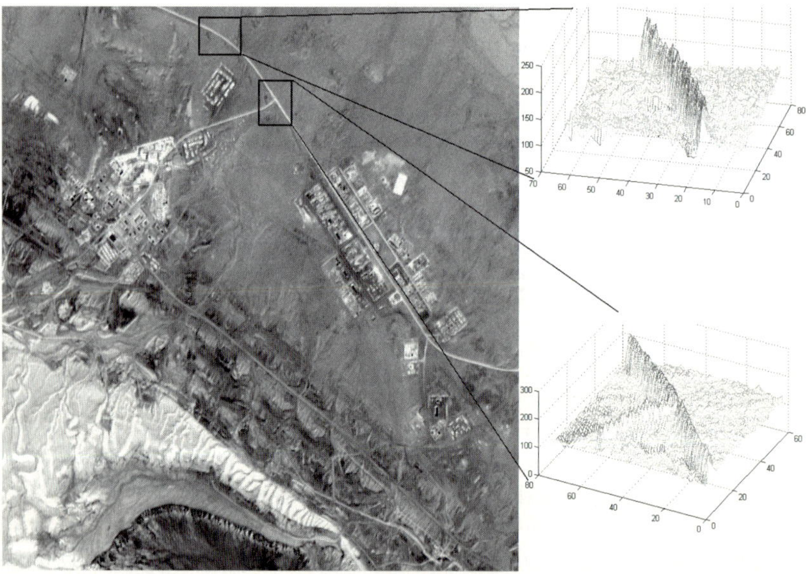

Fig. 3. Satellite test image and 3D profiles of ridges within sub regions

5.2   Hill Detection Algorithm

The ridge detection algorithm can be modified to label a pixel as a hill pixel if the value of $|\Gamma(n,m)|$ is a maximum in *all* directions.

6   Case Studies

We have chosen two different applications to test feature (ridges and hills) detection using the STD. The purpose of these case studies is to validate the working of STD measure and not to evaluate it against existing solutions to these problems.

6.1   Road Detection in Satellite Images

Roads in satellite images can be seen as narrow ridges or valleys in the intensity plane (shown in fig. 3). Curvature-based approaches have been used to extract road structures [9]. The ridge detection algorithm was used to extract roads from the satellite image using the STD measure computed using a fixed sized mask of 5×5. Fig. 4 shows the obtained output image.

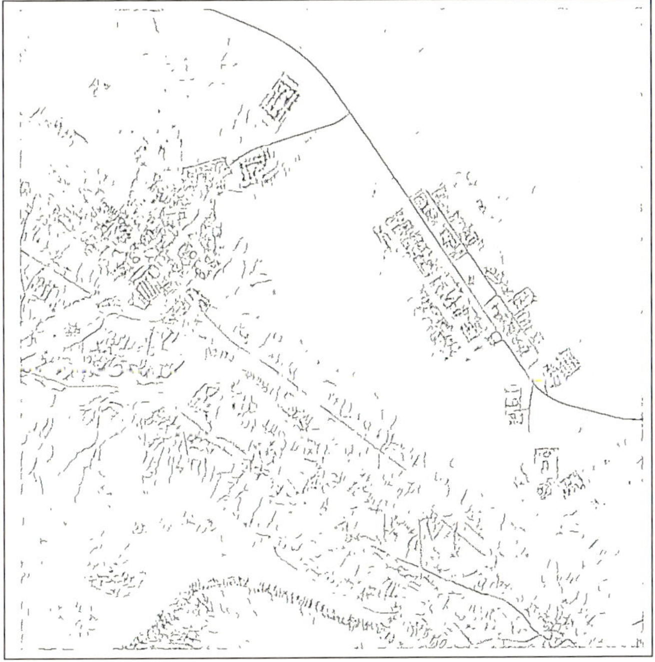

Fig. 4. Output image showing ridges (in white)

The presented scheme for ridge detection is able to extract all ridge profiles in the given input image. The image contains different profiles of the ridges which vary in their shape and intensity. The shape of a ridge is more important in extraction rather than the intensity values. In general, road detection methods involve two processes: road detection, post-processing. Post-processing uses domain knowledge to reduce the outliers from the road extraction module. In our result, we only present the results of road extraction process. Standard criteria to evaluate any road detection method include continuity in roads' structure, no under- and over-detection. The presented detection result appear to meet the given criteria. The medial lines of the salient roads are continuous in the output image. The profiles which are similar to ridges are extracted very well. STD's capability to extract different types of ridges profiles (in equation 3) are well illustrated in this case. However, the result seems to be noisy which is due to the presence of structures whose profiles are similar to the ridge profiles. As of now, our scheme does not use any domain knowledge of the structures such as their location, surround regions, characteristics of roads, etc. These information can be used to improve the results.

6.2   Detection of Micro-Aneurysms (MAs) in Fundus Fluorescein Angiograms (FFA)

Most diseases of the retina alter the structure and the functionality of the vasculature in the retina. One such disease, the Diabetic Retinopathy (DR), leads to the occurance of neo-vascularisation. Neo-vascularisation is the growth of new blood vessels branching out of the existing vessels. The early sprouts of these new vessels are called microaneurysms (MA). They are bulb-like microscopic structures occuring as small and bright circular disks in FFA images. MAs are therefore an important lesion in any retinopathy screening programme. Computer automated detection of MAs offers a fast, objective and reproducible method for quantifying DR, which also reduces the manual workload.

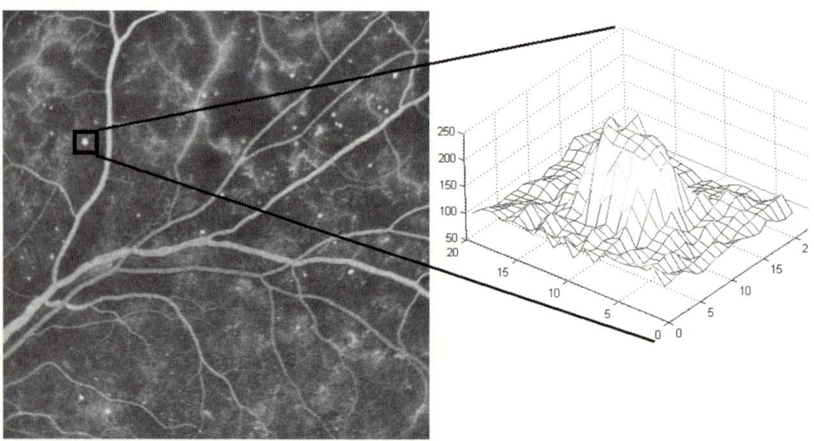

Fig. 5. A sample FFA image and the 3D profile of an MA

MAs appear as bright tiny spots in FFA images. If the image is visualised as a surface in 3D space, MAs form hill-like features (shown in Fig. 5). Hence, a hill detection algorithm can be used to detect MAs. A typical cross-sectional profile of a hill-like feature along some direction, is similar to profile shown in Fig. 2. The medial point of such a profile is a hill point and characterised by maximum curvature in *all* directions.

The algorithm given in section 5.2 is used to extract hill-like features (MAs). A threshold t_r for the strength of the hill-ness of a pixel is set so that the hills detected have a certain minimum strength. This helps in filtering out noise pixels which are otherwise prone to detection as hill pixels. Noise is further reduced by smoothing the image using 5×5 gaussian mask before the STD computation. The MAs vary in their size and appear as hills of different shapes (narrow to wide). As a fixed size mask is inadequate to capture all these features, we used multiple scales to compute the STD measures and collated (using a simple logical *OR* operation) the results across scales. Computation at 4 scales was used with Sobel masks of sizes (from 5×5 to 11×11) were used.

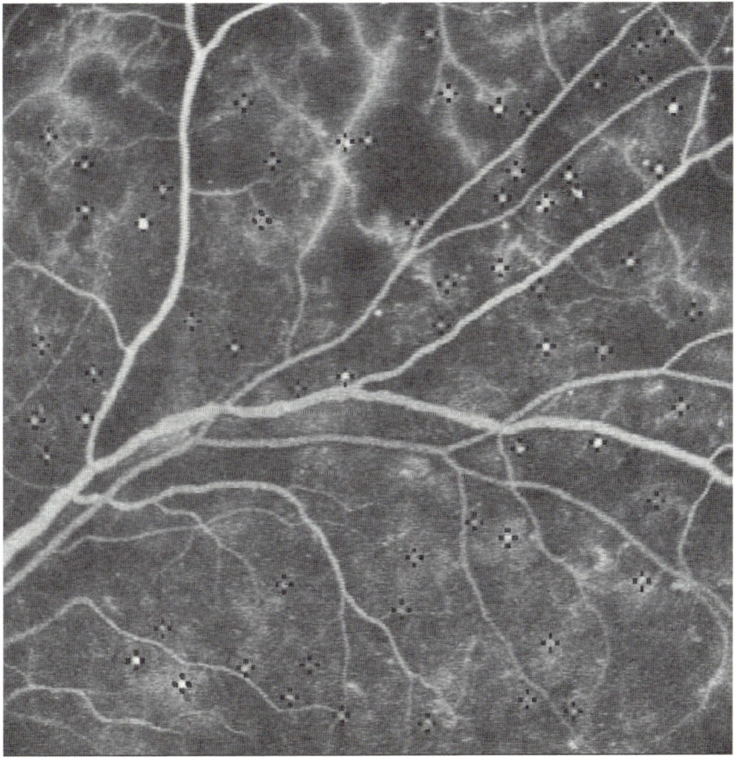

Fig. 6. Output of multi-scale detection of MAs shown superimposed on the original image

The results of MA detection are shown in Figure. 6 superimposed on the original image for convenience. MAs are indicated by enclosing with 4 small lines. The STD-based hill detection algorithm is able to detect all MAs present in the given

FFA image. However, it also gives false responses close to the veins which have similar characteristics as MAs. It is difficult to avoid such false responses in the detection process. These false responses can be removed using post-processing steps. It is noteworthy that our tests done over 25 FFA images (and visually verified by a medical expert) have shown that the detection rarely resulted in any false negatives [10]. In summary, we can state that STD based method provides a reliable extraction of hill profiles which helps to develop solutions for various image analysis problems.

7   Discussion and Conclusion

Topographical feature detection using curvature information is a widely used technique. We have re-examined the definition for extrinsic curvature and proposed a simpler curvature measure (STD) based on the derivative of the surface tangent to an image surface. A theoretical analysis of the the proposed measure has also been presented which shows its scope to be equal to that of the true curvature measure. STD-based algorithms were used to detect roads and MAs and the obtained results demonstrated the ability of STD to capture a variety of ridge/hill profiles. The results also illustrated that continuous ridge lines can be obtained using the STD-based approach. Theoretically, the STD has a lower specificity compared to the true curvature measure. The conducted experiments on ridge/hill detection using the STD did not focus on this point. Analytical and empirical determination of the degree of specificity of STD vs. true curvature is currently being investigated.

References

1. Lopez, A., Lumbreras, F., Serrat, J., Villanueva, J.: Evaluation of methods for ridge and valley detection. IEEE Transactions on Pattern Analysis and Machine Intelligence **21(4)** (1999) 327–335
2. Maintz, J.B.A., van den Elsen, P.A., Viergever, M.A.: Evaluation of ridge seeking operators for multimodality medical image matching. IEEE Transactions on Pattern Analysis and Machine Intelligence **18(4)** (1996) 353–356
3. Eberly, D., Gardner, R., Morse, B., Pizer, S., Scharlach, C.: Ridges for image analysis. Journal of Mathematical Imaging and Vision **4** (1994) 353–373
4. Monga, O., Armande, N., Montesinos, P.: Thin nets and crest lines: Applications to satellite data and medical images. Proc. IEEE Conference of Image Processing **2** (1995) 468–471
5. Fan, T., Medioni, G., Nevatia, R.: Description of surfaces from range data using curvature properties. Proc. IEEE Conference on Computer Vision and Pattern Recognition (1986) 86–91
6. Hoffman, R., Jain, A.K.: Segmentation and classification of range images. IEEE Transactions on Pattern Analysis and Machine Intelligence **9(5)** (1987) 608–620
7. Flynn, P.J., Jain, A.K.: On reliable curvature estimation. Proc. of the International Conference on Computer Vision and Pattern Recognition (1989) 110–116

8. Chandra, S., Sivaswamy, J.: An analysis of curvature based ridge and valley detection. Proc. of International conference on Acoustics speech and signal processing (ICASSP) (2006)
9. Tupin, F., Maitre, H., Margin, J.F., Nicolars, J.M., Pechersky, E.: Detection of linear features in sar images: Application to road network extraction. IEEE Transactions on Geoscience and Remote Sensing **36** (1998) 434–453
10. Chandra, S.: Analysis of retinal angiogram images. M.S. Thesis, Centre for Visual Information Technology, IIIT Hyderabad, India (2005).

Nonlinear Enhancement of Extremely High Contrast Images for Visibility Improvement

K. Vijayan Asari, Ender Oguslu, and Saibabu Arigela

Computational Intelligence and Machine Vision Laboratory
Department of Electrical and Computer Engineering
Old Dominion University, Norfolk, Virginia, USA

Abstract. This paper presents a novel image enhancement algorithm using a multilevel windowed inverse sigmoid (MWIS) function for rendering images captured under extremely non uniform lighting conditions. MWIS based image enhancement is a combination of three processes viz. adaptive intensity enhancement, contrast enhancement and color restoration. Adaptive intensity enhancement uses the non linear transfer function to pull up the intensity of underexposed pixels and to pull down the intensity of overexposed pixels of the input image. Contrast enhancement tunes the intensity of each pixel's magnitude with respect to its surrounding pixels. A color restoration process based on relationship between spectral bands and the luminance of the original image is applied to convert the enhanced intensity image back to a color image.

1 Introduction

A human observer can clearly see individual objects both in the sunlight and shadowed areas, since the eye locally adapts while scanning different regions of the scene. The size of pupil is variable to accommodate different levels of radiance from different regions in a scene, while the camera aperture is fixed when capturing the scene. Current imaging and display devices such as CRT monitors (100:1) and printers are limited dynamic range devices. The best photographic prints can provide contrasts up to 10^3:1. But the real world scenes can reach a dynamic range of six orders of magnitude (10^6:1). When attempting to display high dynamic range images into low dynamic range devices, either the low intensity areas, which are underexposed, or the high intensity areas, which are overexposed, cannot be seen. To handle this problem, various image processing techniques such as histogram equalization, gamma correction, logarithmic compression and levels/curves method were developed. They are usually based on global processing, so they have some limitations such as loosing some features during processing, and not enhancing some features. More advanced image enhancement techniques have been developed to obtain better performance. These techniques are able to compress the dynamic range while maintaining or improving local contrast to achieve high visual quality.

Various techniques were developed to deal with images captured in non uniform lighting conditions. Retinex based algorithms developed from E.Land's theory [1] are effective techniques dealing with dynamic range compression and color constancy.

P. Kalra and S. Peleg (Eds.): ICVGIP 2006, LNCS 4338, pp. 240–251, 2006.

Rahman *et al.* [2-4] modified the Retinex theory with another center/surround method (Multi Scale Retinex with Color Restoration - MSRCR) which computes the new pixel by a ratio of the treated pixel to the weighted average of the surrounding pixels. The drawback of MSRCR is that the color restoration function changes image chromatics in an unpredictable fashion. To treat this problem dynamic range and color constancy are computed independently. The MSR is only applied to the luminance channel to preserve the chromatics of the original image. Luma dependent nonlinear enhancement (LDNE) [5] processes only the luminance information of the color images instead of all three spectral bands to reduce the processing time. Color noise in shadow/dark areas are suppressed by adding the convolution results instead of multiplying them. In MSRCR and LDNE, dynamic range compression and contrast enhancement are implemented jointly but AINDANE (Adaptive Integrated Neighborhood Dependent Approach for Nonlinear Enhancement) [6] and IRME (Illuminance-Reflectance Model for Nonlinear Enhancement) [7] use separate processes for dynamic range compression and contrast enhancement.

In computer graphics, the tone mapping solves the problem of reproducing the HDR images on LDR devices [8-9]. Larson *et al.* [10] developed a tone-mapping operator based on iterative histogram adjustment and spatial filtering process. The aim of this operator is to produce images that preserve visibility in high dynamic range scenes. Chiu *et al.* [11] considered that tone mapping should be neighborhood dependent. Schlik [12] developed the Chiu's algorithm by using a first-degree rational polynomial function to map high-contrast scene luminance to display system values. This function is not adaptive enough for contrast enhancement for all images. Pattanaik et al. [13] presented a tone-mapping algorithm that represents the pattern, luminance and color processing in the Human Visual System. This algorithm allows not only chromatic adaptation, but also luminance adaptation. However, as other local processing algorithms, it is sensitive to strong halo effects. To eliminate the halo effects, Tumblin and Turk [14] developed a Low Curvature Image Simplifier (LCIS) method. This method can accept inputs from real world image maps and produces necessary output for any device. LCIS separates the input scene into large features and fine details, compressing the former and preserving the latter. This method drastically reduces the dynamic range, but tends to overemphasize fine details. Raanan Fattal [15] used the gradient field of the luminance image for HDR compression by attenuating the magnitudes of large gradients.

A new image enhancement technique named MWISE (Multilevel Windowed Inverse Sigmoid for Enhancement) is proposed in this paper for enhancing the images captured in extremely non-uniform lighting conditions. MWISE is capable of compressing bright regions and at the same time enhancing the dark regions by preserving the main structure of the illuminance - reflectance modality.

2 The MWISE Algorithm

The MWISE algorithm for the enhancement of color images consists of three major constituents, namely adaptive intensity enhancement, contrast enhancement and color restoration. The structure of MWISE is shown in Fig.1.

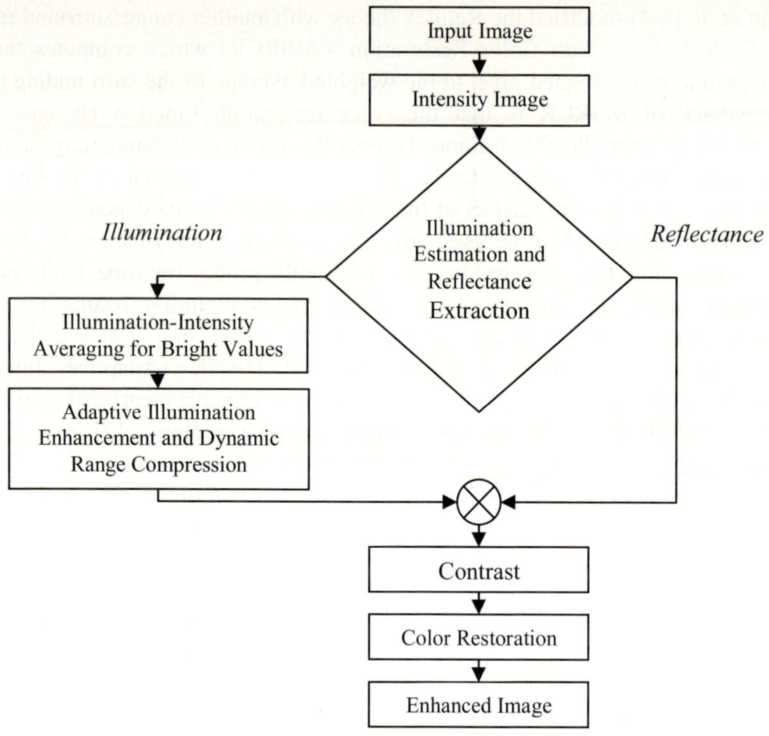

Fig. 1. Structure of the MWISE algorithm for color image enhancement

2.1 Adaptive Intensity Enhancement

First, Color images in RGB color space are converted to intensity (grayscale) images using NTSC standard method defined as

$$I(x, y) = 0.2989 \times R + 0.587 \times G + 0.114 \times B \tag{1}$$

where R, G, B are the red, green and blue components of a color image.

Illumination Estimation. Illumination in an image is characterized by two components: illumination $L(x, y)$ and reflectance $R(x, y)$, and is defined as:

$$I(x, y) = R(x, y).L(x, y) \tag{2}$$

Illumination represents the low frequency components of the image and reflectance represents the high frequency components. Hence a Gaussian low-pass filtered result of the intensity image is considered as illumination, which is obtained as:

$$L(x, y) = \sum_{m=0}^{M-1} \sum_{n=0}^{N-1} I(m, n) F(m + x, n + y) \tag{3}$$

where F is the 2D Gaussian function with size M×N and can be defined as:

$$F(x, y) = K \exp\left(-\frac{(x+y)^2}{c^2}\right) \tag{4}$$

where $K = \sum_x \sum_y F(x, y) = 1$ and c is the size of the neighborhood.

Averaging Illumination and Intensity for Bright Pixels. The estimated illumination is smooth in the parts of the image illuminated from the same luminous source, but however, it can also present abrupt variation when the scene is illuminated by different light sources in the case of background lights. So, the illumination estimation: for less than 80% of the highest gray scale value (i.e. 255 for 8-bit image) is the illumination which is obtained in (3) and for the other gray scale values, a weighted averaging of illumination and intensity values are given by:

$$L'(x, y) = \frac{I(x, y) - 204}{51} I(x, y) + \left(1 - \frac{I(x, y) - 204}{51}\right) L(x, y) \tag{5}$$

This averaging produces minimum halo effect in bright regions by reducing the influence of dark neighboring pixels. After obtaining new illumination estimation, the reflectance estimation can be obtained by (2).

Enhancing Dark Illumination and Compressing Bright Illumination. The new illumination value $L'(x, y)$ is normalized to the range [0 10] using (6) and then treated by an enhancement and compression process to increase the illumination values of low-illumination (dark) pixels, and to reduce the illumination values of high-illumination (bright) pixels using the MWIS transfer function.

$$L''(x, y) = \frac{L'(x, y)}{25.5} \quad \text{for 8-bit depth images} \tag{6}$$

Then normalized illumination values are treated by this process also normalizes the illumination values to the range [0 1]. This transfer function can be defined as

$$L''_{enh} = \frac{1}{1 + e^{(-\alpha \times L'')}} + \frac{1}{1 + e^{(-\beta \times (L'' - 10))}} - 0.5 \tag{7}$$

where α is a parameter to adjust the curve for dark pixels and β is a parameter to adjust the curve for bright pixels. For adaptive-ness of MWIS transfer function, intensity image is divided into sub images of sizes based on the image enhancement experiments and can be expressed as:

$$m = 0.0625 \times M \qquad n = 0.0625 \times N \tag{8}$$

where m and n define the size of the sub image, M and N define the size of the intensity image. The parameters α and β can be determined based on the mean of the darkest sub-image L_{m_min} and mean of the brightest sub image L_{m_max} as:

$$\alpha = \begin{cases} \dfrac{76.5 - L_{m\_min}}{51} & \text{for} & 0 \leq L_{m\_min} \leq 51 \\ 0.5 & \text{for} & 51 < L_{m\_min} \leq 127 \end{cases} \qquad (9)$$

$$\beta = \begin{cases} \dfrac{L_{m\_max} - 255}{51} + 1.5 & \text{for } 204 \leq L_{m\_max} \leq 255 \\ 0.5 & \text{for } 128 \leq L_{m\_min} < 204 \end{cases} \qquad (10)$$

A dark image can be determined as an image which has no bright sub image (i.e. L_{m_max} is less than 127) and a bright image can be determined as an image which has no dark sub-image (i.e. L_{m_min} is more than 127) For these images the shapes of the curves are adjusted according to the value of the image's global mean as:

$$\alpha = \frac{127 - I_m}{63.5} + 1.5 \qquad \text{for } L_{m\_max} < 127 \qquad (11)$$

$$\beta = \frac{I_m - 128}{63.5} + 1.5 \qquad \text{for } L_{m\_min} > 127 \qquad (12)$$

Where I_m is the global mean of the image. For some type of images, it is desired to pull up and pull down the illuminations very much at the same time, but at the expense of color consistency. In this situation, the shapes of the curves can be adjusted manually. In Fig.2, the shape of the curve for very dark images obtained by $\beta = 0.5$ and α is tuned with respect to the global mean of the image, and shape of the curve for very bright image with $\alpha = 0.5$ and β is tuned according to the global mean of the image.

Combination of Enhanced-Illumination and Reflectance. The visually significant image features (high frequency components) are combined with enhanced

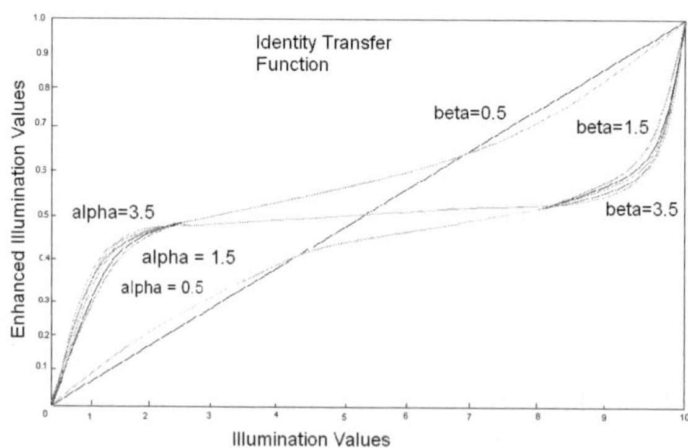

Fig. 2. Various curves of MWIS transfer function

illumination to obtain illumination and reflectance components during contrast enhancement.

$$I_{enh}(x, y) = L''_{enh}(x, y)R(x, y) \qquad (13)$$

During this process, a few bright pixels which are surrounded by dark pixels leave out the range [0 1].

2.2 Contrast Enhancement

A surrounding pixel-dependent contrast enhancement technique is used to obtain sufficient contrast, even higher than that of the original image.

Obtaining Intensity Information of Surrounding Pixels. For a $M{\times}N$ intensity image, 2D discrete spatial convolution with a Gaussian kernel is used to obtain the intensity information of surrounding pixels and is expressed as

$$I_{conv}(x, y) = \sum_{m=0}^{M-1} \sum_{n=0}^{N-1} I(m, n)F(m + x, n + y) \qquad (14)$$

Where Gaussian function can be obtained as

$$F(x, y) = K \exp\left(-\frac{(x + y)^2}{c^2}\right) \qquad (15)$$

Where $K = \iint F(x, y)dxdy = 1$ and c is the scale or Gaussian surround space constant which determines the size of the neighborhood.

Intensity Transformation Process. Surrounding intensity information is compared with the intensity value of the center pixel and the result is used to identify the value of corresponding enhanced intensity pixel by

$$S(x, y) = 255{\times}I_{enh}(x, y)^{E(x, y)} \qquad (16)$$

where $S(x, y)$ is the pixel intensity value after contrast enhancement and $E(x, y)$ is the ratio of the surrounding intensity information over input image,

$$E(x, y) = \left[\frac{I_{conv}(x, y)}{I(x, y)}\right]^P \qquad (17)$$

2.3 Color Restoration

In the MWISE algorithm, a basic linear color restoration process based on the chromatic information of the input image is applied. This process can be expressed as

$$S_j(x, y) = S(x, y)\frac{I_j(x, y)}{I(x, y)} \qquad (18)$$

where $j = $ r, g, b represents red, green, blue spectral band respectively.

3 Experimental Results and Discussion

The MWIS algorithm was applied to process a large number of images consisting of very dark and bright parts. The main beneficial point of the MWISE algorithm over MSRCR, LDNE, AINDANE and IRME is the enhancement of the overexposed regions. In Fig.3 the image is composed of only bright regions. For this type of images, curvature of the second inverse sigmoid is large. In Fig.4 the image is composed of only dark regions. For this type of images, curvature of first inverse sigmoid is large. MWISE is also tested on daylight images (Fig.5) that do not have extremely dark and bright regions. While most of the images are well enhanced, some type of images that have mostly blue-sky turns to gray. The brightness of the sky misguides the parameter β, so the curve of the second inverse sigmoid function shapes more than required.

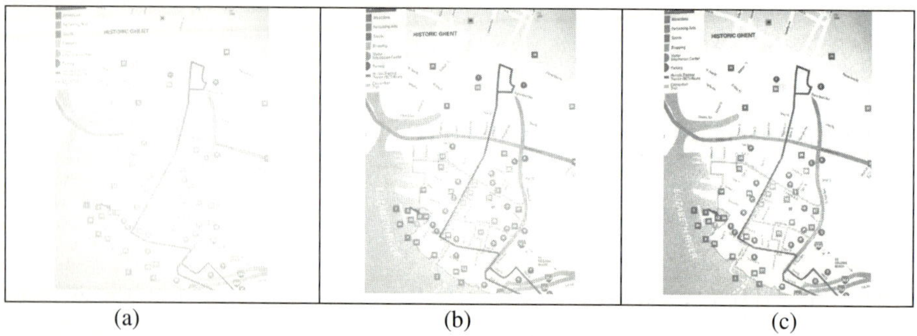

(a)   (b)   (c)

Fig. 3. Image under "over illumination"; (a)Original image; (b) Enhanced image with $\alpha = 0.5$ and $\beta = 1.5$; (c) Enhanced image with $\alpha = 0.5$ and $\beta = 3.5$

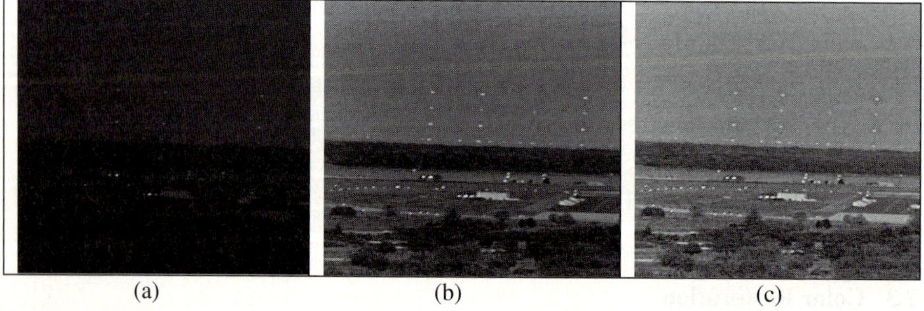

(a)   (b)   (c)

Fig. 4. Image under "low illumination"; (a) Original image; (b) Enhanced image with $\alpha = 1.4020$ and $\beta = 0.5$; (c) Enhanced image with $\alpha = 3.5$ and $\beta = 0.5$

In Figure 6, a sample image is processed for comparison among the performancesof the MWISE, MSRCR, AINDANE, and IRME techniques. The original image in Fig. 6(a) has some overexposed regions near the lamp and some

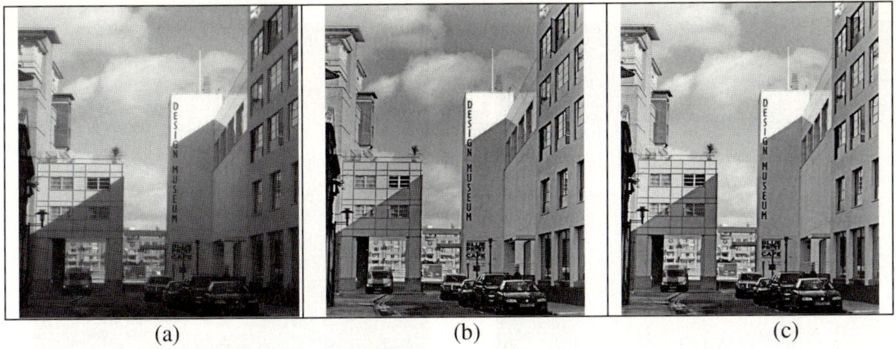

Fig. 5. Image on "daylight";   (a) Original image; (b) Enhanced image with $\alpha = 1.28$ and $\beta = 1.3627$; (c) Enhanced image with $\alpha = 1.28$ and $\beta = 0.5$

dark regions at the corners. The enhancement result with MSRCR introduced unnatural color or artifacts in dark areas as illustrated in Fig. 6(b). Also, the bright region near the lamp still cannot be seen. It can be observed that the images processed with AINDANE (Fig. 6(c)) and IRME (Fig. 6(d)) have a higher visual quality than those processed by MSRCR. They yield higher color accuracy and a better balance between the luminance and the contrast across the whole image. But, they are not sufficient to enhance overexposed regions. The result of the proposed algorithm is illustrated in Fig. 6(e). MWISE produced sufficient luminance enhancement in both dark and bright regions and also demonstrate high contrast, since it has flexibility and adaptiveness of AINDANE and IRME. Another comparison among these algorithms is also performed on different sample image shown in Fig. 7(a). Figures 7(b), 7(c), 7(d) and 7(e) illustrate the enhancement results of MSRCR, AINDANE, IRME and MWISE algorithms, respectively. All of the algorithms performed well for dark regions. MSRCR has lack of good contrast for this image. MSRCR and AINDANE did not perform well on overexposed regions (middle region of the hurricane). For this image, although IRME has the capability to enhance bright region due to the shape of the transfer function, the contrast of bright region is not sufficient.

3.1 Quantitative Evaluation

The visibility in original images and enhanced images are evaluated by using a statistical method [16], which is a connection between numerical and visual representations. A large number of images are tested over this statistical method. The evaluation of different images and their corresponding enhanced images are plotted (in Fig.8). The points, which are expressed with squares, represent the original images and the points, which are expressed with circles, represent the enhanced images.

Effects of the MWISE algorithm are depicted by transferring images towards the visually optimal region (rectangle). Since the original images had very dark and/or very bright properties, the enhanced images have not moved inside the visually optimal region, but they are moving towards this region.

(a) Original image   (b) Enhanced image with MSRCR

(c) Enhanced image with AINDANE   (d) Enhanced image with IRME

(e) Enhanced image with MWIS algorithm ($\alpha = 0.8$, $\beta = 2$)

Fig. 6. Performance comparisons of the proposed technique

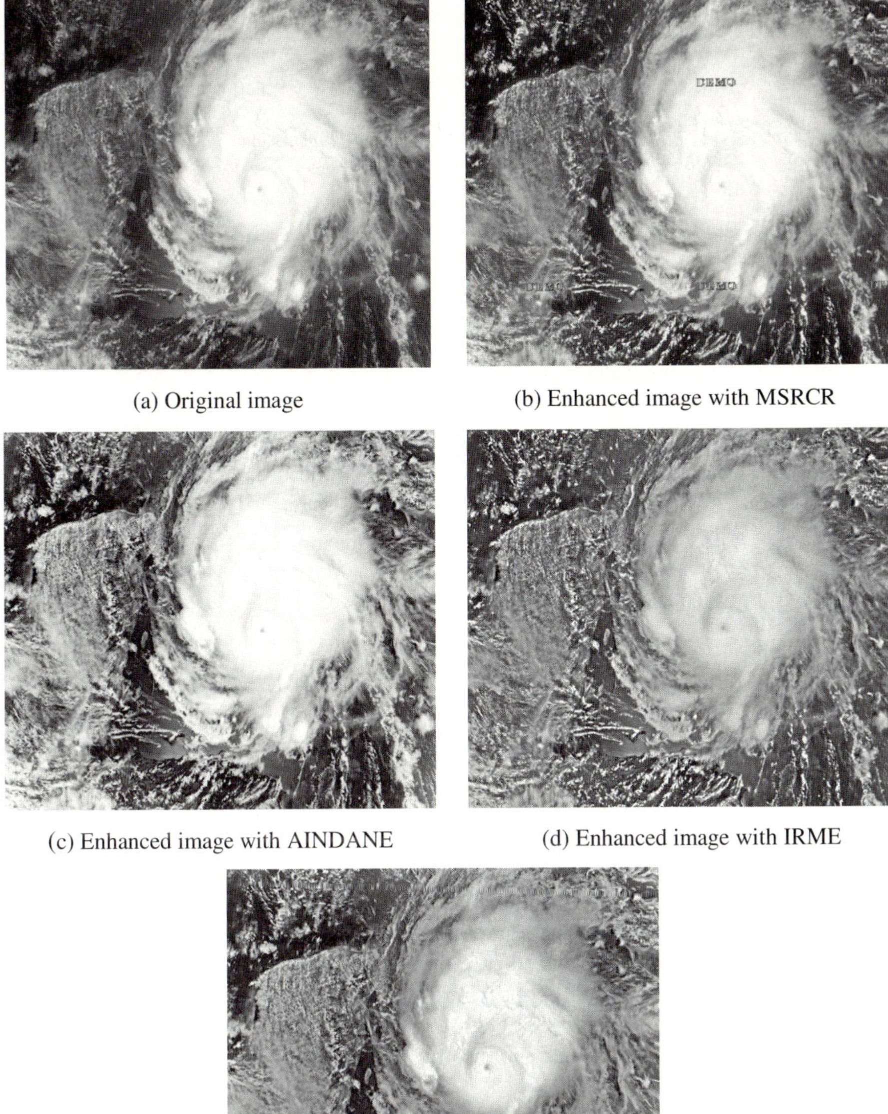

(a) Original image   (b) Enhanced image with MSRCR

(c) Enhanced image with AINDANE   (d) Enhanced image with IRME

(e) Enhanced image with MWIS algorithm(($\alpha =1$, $\beta=1.5$)

Fig. 7. Performance comparisons of the proposed technique

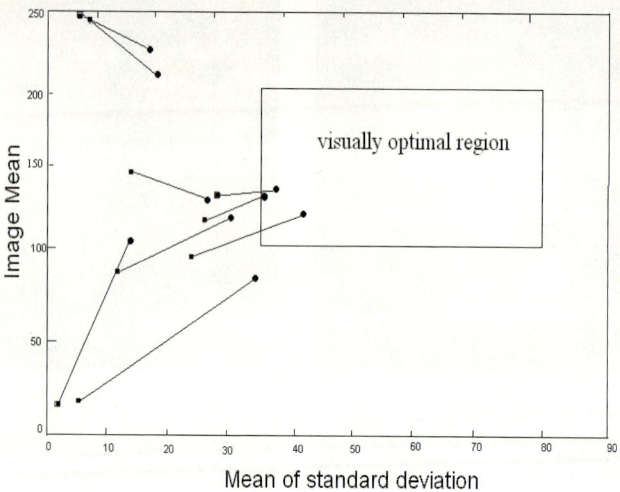

Fig. 8. Image quality evaluations

4 Conclusion

A new image enhancement algorithm for extremely non- uniform lighting images based on a multilevel windowed inverse sigmoid transfer function has been presented in this paper. The intensity enhancement, contrast enhancement and color restoration issues were considered separately to make the algorithm more adaptable to image characteristics. The input intensity image was separated into the illumination and reflectance components preserving the important features of the image. The adaptive ness of the transfer function, depending on the statistical information of the input image and its sub images, makes the algorithm more flexible and easier to control. To reduce the halo effects in bright regions, neighborhood average of illumination and intensity for bright regions was used as estimated illumination. It is observed that the MWISE algorithm yields visually optimal results on images captured under extremely non uniform lighting conditions. This algorithm would be a promising image enhancement technique that can be useful in further image analysis for pattern recognition applications.

References

1. E. Land, "Recent advances in retinex theory," *Vision Res.,* vol.16, pp.445-458, 1976.
2. D. Jabson, Z. Rahman, and G. A. Woodel, "Properties and performance of a center/surround retinex," *IEEE Trans. on Image Processing: Special Issue on Color Processing 6,* pp.451-462, March 1997.
3. Z. Rahman, D. Jabson, and G. A. Woodel, "Multiscale retinex for color image enhancement," *Proc.IEEE Int. Conf. on Image Processing,* 1996

4. Z. Rahman, D. Jabson, and G. A. Woodel, "Multiscale retinex for color rendition and dynamic range compression," *Applications of Digital Image Processing XIX*, A.G.Tescher, Ed., *Proc.SPIE* 2847, pp.183-191, 1996.
5. L. Tao and V. K. Asari, "Modified luminance based MSR for fast and efficient image enhancement," Proc. *IEEE Int. Workshop on Applied Imagery and Pattern Recognition, AIPR - 2003*, pp. 174-179, October 2003.
6. L. Tao and K. V. Asari, "An adaptive and integrated neighborhood dependent approach for nonlinear enhancement of color images," *SPIE Journal of Electronic Imaging,* vol. 14, no. 4, pp. 1.1-1.14, October 2005.
7. L. Tao, R. C. Tompkins, and K. V. Asari, "An illuminance-reflectance model for nonlinear enhancement of video stream for homeland security applications," Proc. *IEEE Int. Workshop on Applied Imagery and Pattern Recognition, AIPR - 2005*, Washington DC, October 19 - 21, 2005.
8. M. Ashikhmin, "A tone mapping algorithm for high contrast images," *Proc. Eurographics Workshop on Rendering*, pp. 145-156, 2002.
9. F. Drago, K. Martens, T. Annen, and N. Chiba, "Adaptive logarithmic mapping for displaying high contrast scenes," *Proc. Eurographics*, 2003.
10. G. W. Larson, H. Rushmeier, and C. Piatko, "A visibility matching tone reproduction operator for high dynamic range scenes," *IEEE Trans. Visualization and Computer Graphics,* 3(4), pp.291-306, 1997.
11. K. Chiu, M. Herf, P. Shirley, S. Swamy, C. Wang, and K. Zimmerman, "Spatially nonuniform scaling functions for high contrast images," *Graphics Interface*, pp.245-255, May 1993.
12. C. Schlick, "Quantization techniques for visualization of high dynamic range pictures," *5th Eurographics Workshop on Rendering*, June 1994.
13. S. N. Pattanaik, J. A. Ferwarda, M. D. Fairchild, and D. P. Greenberg, "A multiscale model of adaptation and spatial vision for realistic image display," *Proc. SIGGRAPH 98, Computer Graphics Proc., Annual Conference Series,* pp.287-298, July 1998.
14. J. Tumblin, G. Turk, "LCIS: A boundary hierarchy for detail-preserving contrast reduction," *Proc. SIGGRAPH 99*, pp.83-90, 1999.
15. R. Fattal, D. Lischinski, and M. Werman, "Gradient domain high dynamic range compression," *Proc. ACM SIGGRAPH 02*, ACM Press, pp. 249-256, 2002.
16. D. J. Jabson, Z. Rahman, G. A. Woodell, "Statistics of visual representation," *Proc. SPIE*, vol. 4736, pp. 25-35, 2002.

Culling an Object Hierarchy to a Frustum Hierarchy

Nirnimesh, Pawan Harish, and P.J. Narayanan

Center for Visual Information Technology
International Institute of Information Technology
Hyderabad, India
{nirnimesh@research., harishpk@research., pjn@}iiit.ac.in

Abstract. Visibility culling of a scene is a crucial stage for interactive graphics applications, particularly for scenes with thousands of objects. The culling time must be small for it to be effective. A hierarchical representation of the scene is used for efficient culling tests. However, when there are multiple view frustums (as in a tiled display wall), visibility culling time becomes substantial and cannot be hidden by pipelining it with other stages of rendering. In this paper, we address the problem of culling an object to a hierarchically organized set of frustums, such as those found in tiled displays and shadow volume computation. We present an adaptive algorithm to unfold the twin hierarchies at every stage in the culling procedure. Our algorithm computes from-point visibility and is conservative. The precomputation required is minimal, allowing our approach to be applied for dynamic scenes as well. We show performance of our technique over different variants of culling a scene to multiple frustums. We also show results for dynamic scenes.

1   Introduction

Visibility culling of a scene is central to any interactive graphics application. The idea is to limit the geometry sent down the rendering pipeline to only the geometry with a fair chance of finally becoming visible. It is important for the culling stage to be fast for it to be effective; otherwise the performance gain achieved will be overshadowed. Hierarchical scene structures are commonly used to speed up the process. Hierarchical culling of bounding boxes to a view frustum is fast and sufficient in most applications. Assarsson et al. [1] described several optimizations for view frustum culling. Bittner et al. [2] exploited temporal coherence to minimize the number of occlusion queries for occlusion culling to a view frustum.

Fast frustum culling is particularly crucial for rendering to multiple frustums simultaneously. (1) CAVE [3] is a multi-display virtual-reality environment which requires visibility culling to multiple frustums. (2) Another application using multiple frustums involves occlusion culling of a scene by eliminating objects in the frustum shadows formed by all principal occluders, as proposed by Hudson et al. [4]. (3) Cluster-based tiled displays require fast culling to multiple frustums corresponding to each tile in the display (Figure 7). (4) Multi-projector

P. Kalra and S. Peleg (Eds.): ICVGIP 2006, LNCS 4338, pp. 252–263, 2006.
© Springer-Verlag Berlin Heidelberg 2006

display systems [5] use several overlapping frustums corresponding to each of the projectors. (5) Multiple frustums are also required to compute visibility for architectural environments [6,7,8].

Any real-world interactive visualization application typically deals with scenes with millions of triangles. An effective way of arranging the scene involves scene graphs. The spatial hierarchy of a scene graph greatly reduces the number of checks for visibility culling. Similarly, when the number of frustums is large, it is natural to also treat them hierarchically. In the most general case, we would want to cull any general object hierarchy to any general frustum hierarchy.

In this paper, we use a hierarchical representation of view frustums to cull the scene to all the frustums coherently. Our method adaptively merges the two hierarchies – the scene hierarchy and the frustum hierarchy – for visibility culling. To this end, we present an algorithm which determines which hierarchy to traverse and when. To our knowledge, this is the first work which considers this decision to be important and effective for coherent culling to multiple frustums. Here, we address the specific problem of culling an object hierarchy to a frustum hierarchy for a tiled display wall (Figure 7). Our tiled display wall system [9] uses a number of commodity systems in a cluster, each powering a tile. The system uses a scene graph (Open Scene Graph [10]) representation of a massive scene. The network resources limit the amount of data that can be transmitted, thereby making efficient visibility culling an important requirement. The individual frustums in the display wall have a fixed arrangement with respect to each other and have a common viewpoint. Such a tight arrangement of frustums motivates our visibility culling algorithm to perform coherent computations which are both fast and scalable. We are able to bring down the culling time for a hierarchical version of UNC's power plant model for a 4×4 tiled display from about 14 ms using the traditional approach to about 5 ms using our adaptive algorithm.

Our visibility culling approach performs *from-point* visibility as opposed to *from-region* visibility performed by several other culling techniques [11,12]. Besides, our culling approach is conservative, as opposed to other probabilistic or approximate culling techniques [13,14,15], which can lead to serious rendering artifacts. This is critical for the kind of applications in which the multiple frustums come into use. For a cluster-based tiled display wall, for instance, the load on the network needs to be minimized and the interactivity needs to be preserved. Culling determines the geometry that will be cached on the rendering nodes. Approximate culling techniques lead to probabilistic prefetching, often leading to freezes during rendering.

We present experimental results from our visibility culling algorithm for the Fatehpur Sikri model and UNC's Power plant model. We have focused only on fast culling to multiple frustums, and have therefore not discussed the later stages in the rendering pipeline. We compare the results with different variants for culling to multiple frustums. We also investigate the performance of our culling technique for a dynamic scene, when many objects change position. This involves additional overheads in updating the bounding boxes at many nodes before the culling can be performed.

2   Related Work

Visibility determination has been a fundamental problem in computer graphics [16] since the scene is typically much larger than the graphics rendering capabilities. Cláudio et al. [17] and Durand et al. [18] have presented comprehensive visibility surveys. View-frustum culling algorithms avoid rendering geometry that is outside the viewing frustum. Hierarchical techniques have been developed [19], as well as other optimizations [1,14]. Funkhouser et al. [20] described the first published system that could support models larger than main memory, based on the from-region visibility algorithm of Teller and Sequin [6]. Aliaga et al. [12] described MMR, the first published system to handle models with tens of millions of polygons at interactive frame rates, although it did require an expensive high-end multi-processor graphics workstation.

Assarsson et al. [1] presented several optimizations for fast view frustum culling, using different kinds of bounding boxes and bounding sphere. For their octant test, they split the view frustum in half along each axes, resulting in eight parts, like the first subdivision of an octree. Using bounding sphere for objects, it is sufficient to test for culling against the outer three planes of the octant in which the center of the bounding sphere lies. This can be extended to general bounding volumes as well [21]. Our frustum hierarchy approach is inspired by this idea of subdividing the view-frustum into octants. However, Assarsson et al. divide the view-frustum only once, whereas we complete this procedure to construct a full frustum hierarchy. Bittner et al. [2] used hardware occlusion query techniques to exploit temporal coherence and reduce CPU-GPU stalls for occlusion culling. Since the occlusion culling information holds good for all frustums for our specific case of tiled display walls, separate occlusion culling for each frustum is not necessary.

Another way to look at occlusion relationships is to use the fact that a viewer cannot see the occludee if it is inside the shadow generated by the occluder. Hudson et al. [4] proposed an approach based on dynamically choosing a set of occluders, and computing their shadow frusta, which is used for culling the bounding boxes of a hierarchy of objects. Bittner et al. [22] improved this method by combining the shadow frusta of the occluders into an occlusion tree. This method has an advantage over Hudson et al. as the comparison in the latter is done on a single tree as opposed to each of the m frustums individually, hence improving the time complexity from $O(m)$ to $O(\log m)$. Our approach of constructing a tree of view frustums resembles this technique of handling frustums. We go even further to combine the frustum hierarchy with object hierarchy.

3   Object Hierarchy and Frustum Hierarchy

We work with two hierarchies in our culling technique. The first is the spatial hierarchy of the scene, represented using a scene graph (OpenGL Performer [23], Open Scene Graph [10]). In the Object Hierarchy (OH), each node has a bounding volume such that the bounding volume of an internal node entirely encloses the bounding volumes of all its children. Only leaf nodes contain actual geometry. A well-formed scene graph would have compact geometry nodes so that bounding volumes can be used to provide accurate visibility tests.

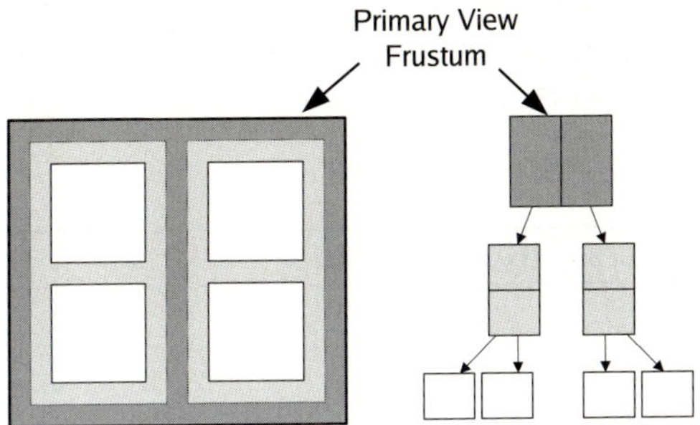

Fig. 1. Frustum Hierarchy (FH). White boxes represent view frustums. Their hierarchical grouping for 3 levels is shown on the right. The bisection plane at each internal node is also shown. Note that near and far planes are not shown.

The second hierarchy we deal with is that of view frustums (Figure 1). Our frustum Hierarchy (FH) is analogous to a BSP-like division. In the most general scenario, a number of independent view frustums in 3D are grouped together hierarchically. Every internal node's bounding volume encloses that of its children. A plane bisects each internal node's volume into half-spaces containing its children. The leaf nodes in the hierarchy correspond to individual view frustums. For a tiled display wall application, each rendering node corresponds to one view-frustum. The root node in the frustum hierarchy corresponds to the primary view-frustum (shown in Figure 1). The case of overlapping view frustums, commonly used for multi-projector displays, is easily handled by treating the overlapping regions as additional independent frustums.

4   Adaptive Traversal of Object and Frustum Hierarchies

Ideal traversal through OH and FH is crucial for optimal performance. The preprocessing step required is discussed in Section 4.1. In Section 4.2, we first discuss several schemes for traversing these hierarchies, and then present our adaptive algorithm.

4.1   Preprocessing

Oriented bounding boxes (OBB) give a compact representation of object's geometry and orientation in space. It is desirable that culling be performed to OBBs only as opposed to the whole geometry since it is fast and conservative. During the preprocessing stage, the scene graph is loaded into main memory. For a set of 3D points, their eigen vectors represent their orientation. Therefore, at the leaf nodes of OH, the eigen vectors of the geometry points provide oriented bounding boxes. However, at the internal nodes, we compute the eigen vectors using just the children's bounding box vertices. This is a fast approximation of an oriented bounding box for the internal node.

A Frustum hierarchy, FH, is constructed, with each internal node having a bisection plane. Beginning at the root node, `root` in OH, call Algorithm 1 as `preprocess(root)`. Preprocessing takes place in a bottom-up fashion. The bounding box information thereby computed is stored with each of the nodes in the scene graph.

Algorithm 1. preprocess(OH_Node)

1: $G \Leftarrow \phi$
2: **if** not leaf(OH_Node) **then**
3:     **for all** child c of OH_Node **do**
4:         preprocess(c)
5:         $G \Leftarrow G+$ bounding box vertices of c
6:     **end for**
7: **else**
8:     $G \Leftarrow G+$ OH_Node.getGeometry()
9: **end if**
10: $e \Leftarrow$ compute eigen vectors of G
11: $BBOX \Leftarrow$ compute OBB from e
12: OH_Node.save_bbox($BBOX$)

4.2   Frustum Culling Approaches

Our culling procedure involves a first level culling to the primary view frustum, so as to eliminate objects completely outside the view. The next step involves classifying these n objects to m view frustums. A *naive approach* involves testing each of these objects with all the view frustums. The expected time complexity for this approach is $O(mn)$. We now discuss several other hierarchical variations to this approach, followed by our adaptive algorithm.

OH without FH: This is a commonly used approach, wherein the scene graph is culled to all the view frustums one by one. It does not exploit any hierarchical arrangement of frustums, and therefore performs poorly with large number of view frustums. This approach has a average time complexity of $O(m \log n)$.

FH without OH: If the frustum hierarchy only is utilized, each object has to be tested against it, beginning from the root. For every internal node in the FH, if an object is present entirely on one side of its bisection plane, its visibility can be safely eliminated from all frustums lying in the other half-space. Therefore, we can potentially eliminate half the number of frustums at each node in the hierarchy. Hence, the average case time complexity is $O(n \log m)$.

Adaptive OH and FH: In both the above cases, the two hierarchies (OH and FH) are used independent of each other, i.e. when the OH is traversed, frustums are treated non-hierarchically and when FH is traversed, objects are treated non-hierarchically. Hence, adaptive merging of the two hierarchies leads to substantial reduction in computations. Consider the different cases:

- At leaf nodes in OH, only FH traversal remains.
- At leaf nodes in FH, only OH traversal remains.
- At all internal nodes, decide whether to further traverse FH or OH.

The precomputed data stored during preprocessing stage (Section 4.1) is utilized to arrive at the above decision. If an OH-node is not intersected by an FH-node's bisection plane, the frustum hierarchy should be unfolded further, keeping the OH intact. Unfolding OH here leads to a large number of OH-nodes to deal with in the next iteration. If the bisection plane of an FH-node intersects the bounding box of an OH-node, OH should be unfolded, thereby breaking the object to its constituents. We classify the children into three groups (L=Left, C=Cuts, R=Right) depending on their position with respect to the FH-node's bisection plane. The group L contains all the children lying completely in negative half-space, R contains those lying in the positive and C contains the rest (the objects that cut the plane).

For each node `OH_Node` determined to be visible in the primary frustum, the algorithm `adaptive_OHandFH_Cull(OH_Node, FH_root)` (Algorithm 2) is called, where `FH_root` is the FH root. `ClassifyLCR()` is an accessory function which categorizes `OH_Node`'s children into the sets L, C and R according to their position with respect to an FH node's current bisection plane. The algorithm recurses for the members in L and R to the corresponding child-frustum (Algorithm 2: lines 11, 14) while the members of C is recursed for both the child-frustums (Algorithm 2: lines 7–8). When the FH is exhausted, the remaining objects are marked to be visible in the corresponding view frustum. The objects in set C need to be checked with both the half-spaces. However, the number of frustums under consideration get reduced by half for objects in set L and R, thereby potentially halving the computations. The number of children to deal with might increase because `classifyLCR()` breaks up an OH node into its children. At this stage, there are two options. We can carry on with each object independently or can regroup the objects in sets L and R into pseudo-groups. This involves re-computing the bounding box for the pseudo-group. Pseudo-groups do not really exist in the scene graph but can reduce the computations required for further stages. Our experiments show that this regrouping is advantageous only for scene graphs with very high branching factor. Otherwise, the overhead of forming the pseudo-group overshadow the gain achieved. Note that pseudo regrouping is not shown in Algorithm 2.

Our adaptive algorithm follows an $O(m\, n^{\log_p q} + (p-q)\log m)$ time complexity, on a quick analysis, where p is the average branching factor of OH and q is the average number of nodes in set C. Exact analysis is difficult as it depends on the goodness of the branching and the spatial separation of child nodes at each level. Hence, p and q depend heavily on the scene structure, the view frustums arrangement and the viewpoint. The average case time complexity follows a sublinear pattern. In the worst case, the complexity becomes $O(m\,n)$ when $q = p$, when all OH leaves fall in all FH leaves, and the hierarchy is inconsequential. In the best cast, the complexity is $O(\log m)$ when $q = 0$. This is the situation when only one FH leaf contains the entire OH. In practice, the algorithm is able to adapt to variations in complexity of the visible scene, which is very common during interactive walkthroughs.

Algorithm 2. adaptive_OHandFH_Cull(OH_Node, FH_Node)

1: **if** leaf(FH_Node) **then**
2:     Mark OH_Node as visible to FH_Node
3:     return
4: **end if**
5: $[L, C, R] \Leftarrow$ ClassifyLCR(OH_Node, FH_Node.plane)
6: **for all** c in set C **do**
7:     adaptive_OHandFH_Cull(c, FH_Node.neg)
8:     adaptive_OHandFH_Cull(c, FH_Node.pos)
9: **end for**
10: **for all** l in set L **do**
11:     adaptive_OHandFH_Cull(l, FH_Node.neg)
12: **end for**
13: **for all** r in set R **do**
14:     adaptive_OHandFH_Cull(r, FH_Node.pos)
15: **end for**

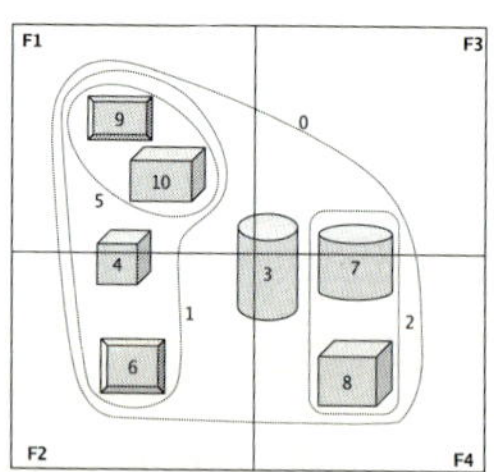

Fig. 2. Hierarchy of objects as visible to a 2×2 tiled arrangement of view frustums. The grouping of objects is shown. F1, F2, F3 and F4 represent view frustums. Their adaptive culling is shown in Figure 3.

Line 2 of Algorithm 2 marks the `OH_node` as visible to the `FH_node`. Line 5 performs the classification of the object node to L, C and R. Lines 7, 8 recurses for every child in C, the set of objects cut by the plane. Lines 11 and 14 recurse to the next stage of FH.

The algorithm can easily deal with dynamic scenes as well, since the preprocessing stage involves cheap eigen-vector calculations only. The visibility determination remains unchanged. Besides, very little extra data is stored for the algorithm execution. Note that bisection using a plane is possible in Algorithm 2

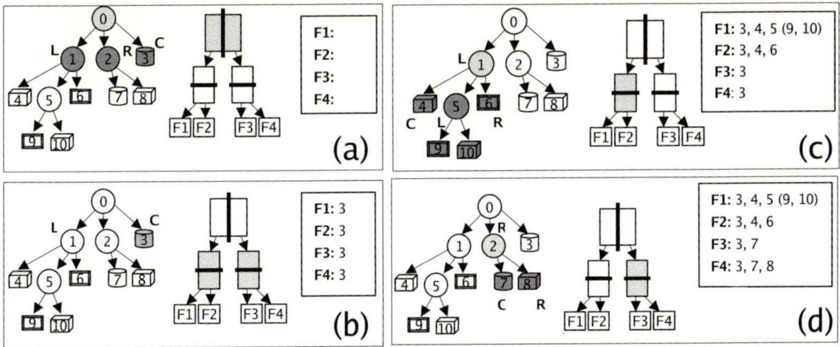

Fig. 3. Adaptive culling of the scene structure in Figure 2. The object and frustum hierarchies are shown along with already determined visibility list. Working nodes are shown as light-gray. Dark gray objects are the ones that need to be recursed further. (a) OH root is classified as per the bisection plane of the FH root. L, C, R classification is shown. (b) Continuing culling for set C. (c) Continuing culling for set L. (d) Continuing culling for set R.

for an application such as tiled display walls because the tile sizes are uniform and the frustum space ultimately divides to form the individual tile frustums. This might not be true for non-uniform frustums. However, a hierarchy of frustums can still be built. Only, in such a case, the terminal frustum in line 2 of Algorithm 2 will further involve a check for visibility before marking an object as visible.

5   Experimental Results

We perform several walkthrough experiments on models of different scene complexities to test the performance of the adaptive algorithm. We used a hierarchical model of Fatehpur Sikri, which has 1.6 M triangles spread over 770 nodes (288 internal + 482 leaf), with an average branching factor of 2.67. We also used a hierarchical model of UNC's power plant, which has geometry spread over 5037 nodes (1118 internal + 3919 leaf), with an average branching factor of 4.5.

Figure 4(a) shows a logarithmic plot of culling time taken by various algorithms discussed in Section 4.2 for a 4000 frame walkthrough on the Fatehpur model. The walkthrough is such that the entire scene is visible. This is a worst-case situation; typical walkthroughs perform better. Our adaptive algorithm (Algorithm 2) takes the least time almost throughout the walkthrough. This is followed by the *FH without OH* approach. The *OH without FH* approach performs worse than both these two.

Figure 4(b) shows the culling time for a walkthrough on the power plant model. The plots for *OH without FH* and *FH without OH* approaches coincide, as opposed to lagging performance by *OH without FH* approach in Figure 4(a). This is because the high branching factor in OH makes the *OH without FH* approach more significant. However, the adaptive algorithm performs significantly better than all the other approaches.

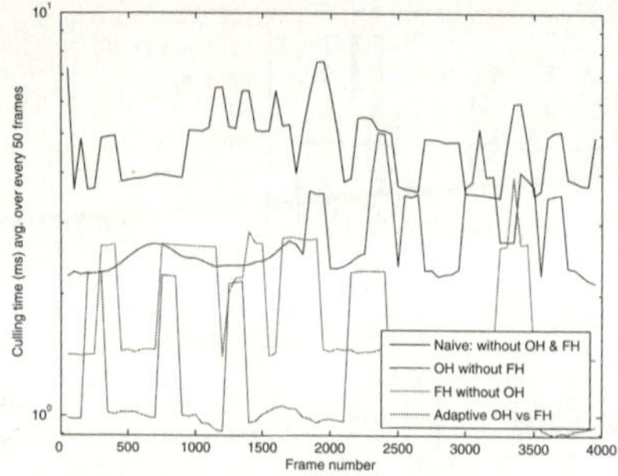

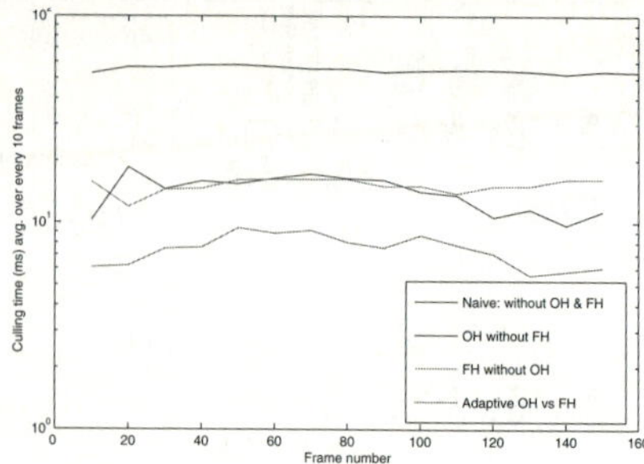

(a) A 4000 frame walkthrough on the Fatehpur Sikri model

(b) Walkthrough on the power plant model

Fig. 4. Culling performance for various approaches. The lower the time, the better. Our adaptive algorithm outperforms others almost throughout the walkthrough.

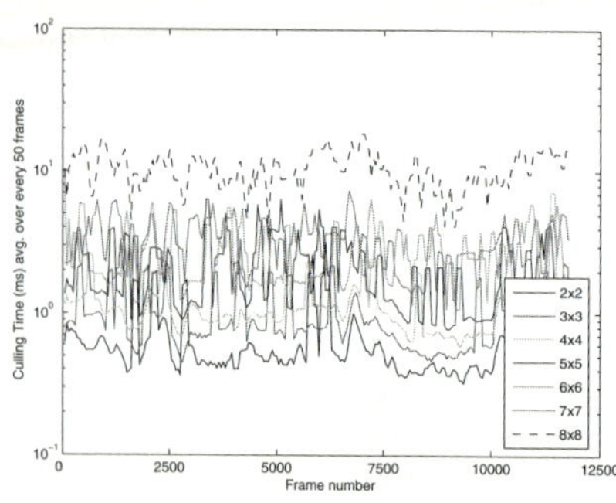

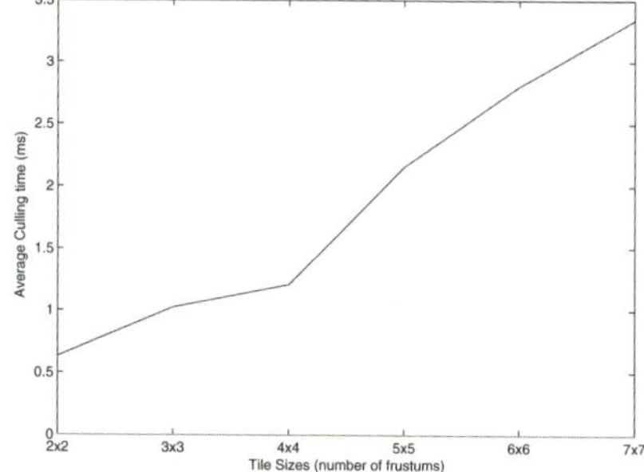

(a) Culling scalability plot for a 11000 frame walkthrough

(b) Plot showing average culling time against different tile configurations

Fig. 5. Culling scalability performance on the Fatehpur Sikri model

We conducted scalability tests with respect to the tile size for different configurations of tiled displays. Figure 5 shows the plots for our adaptive algorithm for an 11000 frame walkthrough of the Fatehpur Sikri model. The algorithm takes about 11 ms, on an average, for culling to an 8×8 configuration, thereby making the culling applicable for setting up display walls of such configuration. Otherwise culling time limits the overall frame rate achievable on a server-managed display wall such as ours(Figure 7, [9]), where the rendering is done by client machines and data-transmission can be performed in parallel with the culling of the next frame.

Figure 6 shows the performance of our adaptive algorithm for a dynamic scene. Different percentages of the scene is changed prior to every update. Dynamic scenes have objects moving in space. The bounding boxes of these objects and their parents till the OH root need to be recomputed. Fast OBB computations (Section 4.1) permit dynamic scenes to be culled at interactive frame rates. Although speed can be further increased with axis-aligned bounding boxes (AABB), it comes at the cost of poor visibility culling. In an optimal situation,

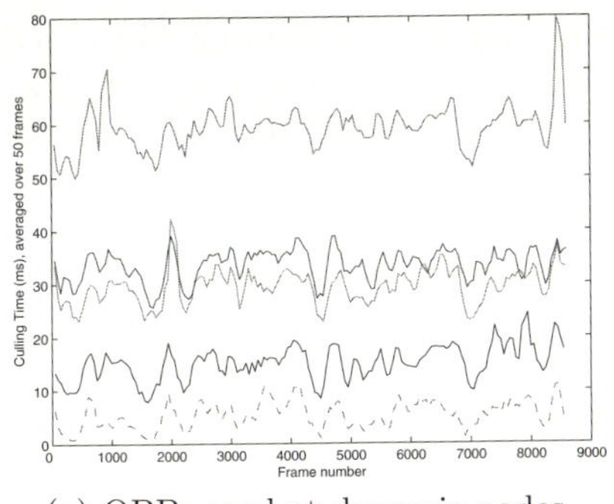

(a) OBBs used at dynamic nodes

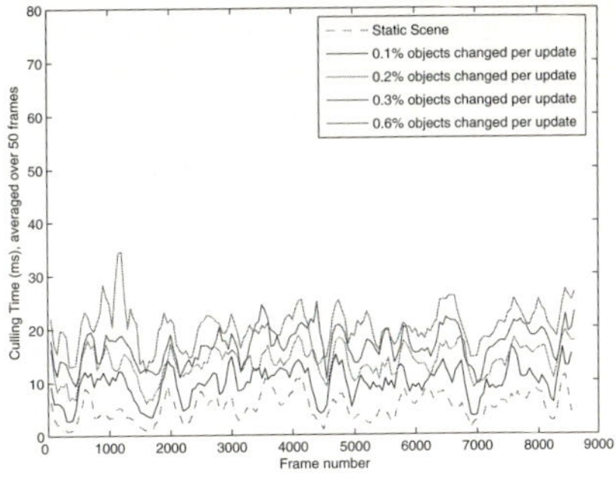

(b) AABBs used at dynamic nodes

Fig. 6. Culling performance on the power plant scene for different percentages of dynamic objects. The model has a total of 5037 objects. The performance with AABB is better than with OBB but at the cost of over-conservative visibility culling.

Fig. 7. A 4×4 display wall rendering of UNC's Powerplant. The combined resolution is 12 MPixels. Efficient rendering to a display wall requires fast visibility culling of the scene to all the frustums. Adaptive culling by merging of the object and frustum hierarchies makes this possible for even bigger tile configurations.

a hybrid of both OBBs and AABBs should be used. It is beneficial to compute AABBs for dynamic portions of the scene. Note that the percentage of dynamic objects shown in Figure 6 are extreme case situations. In practice, the scenes are less dynamic and so the adaptive algorithm performs even better.

6   Conclusions and Future Work

We presented a conservative, from-point visibility culling approach for culling a large scene to a hierarchy of view-frustums. We presented an adaptive algorithm which determines the optimal path, merging object and frustum hierarchies. The algorithm performs logarithmically in practice. Due to this, it can scale well for large number of frustums which is critical for the application scenario of a tiled display wall. The performance gain by our algorithm is shown on several walkthrough experiments. The algorithm makes culling for very large tile display setups feasible. Huge models can be handled at interactive frame rates. We also showed that the adaptive algorithm is applicable for dynamic scenes as well.

Though we showed the performance on a two-dimensional, tight-fit array of frustums, the results can be extended to other hierarchies of frustums. We are currently extending it to other typical situations like a 2D array of frustums with small overlap used in multi-projector displays. We are also working on culling to general frustum hierarchies needed for applications like shadow volume computations. A BSP-tree like partitioning of the frustums, very similar to our current approach, will be needed in such cases.

Acknowledgements. This work was partially funded by Microsoft Research through their University Relations, India.

References

1. Assarsson, U., Möller, T.: Optimized View Frustum Culling Algorithms for Bounding Boxes. Journal of Graphics Tools: JGT **5** (2000) 9–22
2. Bittner, J., Wimmer, M., Piringer, H., Purgathofer, W.: Coherent Hierarchical Culling: Hardware Occlusion Queries Made Useful. Comput. Graph. Forum **23** (2004) 615–624
3. Cruz-Neira, C., Sandin, D.J., DeFanti, T.A.: Surround-screen projection-based virtual reality: the design and implementation of the CAVE. In: SIGGRAPH. (1993)
4. Hudson, T., Manocha, D., Cohen, J., Lin, M., Hoff, K., Zhang, H.: Accelerated occlusion culling using shadow frusta. In: Symposium on Computational geometry. (1997)
5. Raskar, R., Brown, M.S., Yang, R., Chen, W.C., Welch, G., Towles, H., Seales, W.B., Fuchs, H.: Multi-projector displays using camera-based registration. In: IEEE Visualization. (1999) 161–168
6. Teller, S.J., Sequin, C.H.: Visibility preprocessing for interactive walkthroughs. In: SIGGRAPH. (1991)
7. Airey, J.M.: Increasing update rates in the building walkthrough system with automatic model-space subdivision and potentially visible set calculations. PhD thesis (1990) Director-Frederick P. Brooks, Jr.
8. Airey, J.M., Rohlf, J.H., Frederick P. Brooks, J.: Towards image realism with interactive update rates in complex virtual building environments. In: Symposium on Interactive 3D graphics. (1990)
9. Nirnimesh, Narayanan, P.J.: Scalable, Tiled Display Wall for Graphics using a Coordinated Cluster of PCs. In: 14th Pacific Conference on Computer Graphics and Applications (Pacific Graphics). (2006)
10. Burns, D., Osfield, R.: OpenSceneGraph A: Introduction, B: Examples and Applications. In: IEEE Virtual Reality Conference. (2004)

11. Funkhouser, T.A.: Database Management for Interactive Display of Large Architectural Models. In: Graphics Interface. (1996)
12. Aliaga, D.G., Cohen, J., Wilson, A., Baker, E., Zhang, H., Erikson, C., III, K.E.H., Hudson, T., Stürzlinger, W., Bastos, R., Whitton, M.C., Jr., F.P.B., Manocha, D.: MMR: an interactive massive model rendering system using geometric and image-based acceleration. In: Symposium on Interactive 3D Graphics. (1999)
13. Corrêa, W.T., Klosowski, J.T., Silva, C.T.: Visibility-Based Prefetching for Interactive Out-Of-Core Rendering. In: IEEE Symposium on Parallel and Large-Data Visualization and Graphics. (2003)
14. Klosowski, J.T., Silva, C.T.: The Prioritized-Layered Projection Algorithm for Visible Set Estimation. IEEE Trans. Vis. Comput. Graph. **6** (2000) 108–123
15. Slater, M., Chrysanthou, Y.: View volume culling using a probabilistic caching scheme. In: Virtual Reality Software and Technology. (1997)
16. Sutherland, I.E., Sproull, R.F., Schumacker, R.A.: A characterization of ten hidden-surface algorithms. ACM Comput. Surv. **6** (1974) 1–55
17. Cohen-Or, D., Chrysanthou, Y., Silva, C.T., Durand, F.: A survey of visibility for walkthrough applications. IEEE Trans. Vis. Comput. Graph. **9** (2003) 412–431
18. Durand, F.: 3D Visibility: analytical study and applications. PhD thesis, Université Joseph Fourier, Grenoble I (1999)
19. Clark, J.H.: Hierarchical Geometric Models for Visible Surface Algorithms. Commun. ACM **19** (1976) 547–554
20. Funkhouser, T.A., Séquin, C.H., Teller, S.J.: Management of large amounts of data in interactive building walkthroughs. In: Symposium on Interactive 3D Graphics. (1992)
21. Assarsson, U., Möller, T.: Optimized View Frustum Culling Algorithms. Technical Report 99–3, Department of Computer Engineering, Chalmers University of Technology (1999)
22. Zhang, H., Manocha, D., Hudson, T., Kenneth E. Hoff, I.: Visibility culling using hierarchical occlusion maps. In: SIGGRAPH. (1997)
23 Rohlf, J., Helman, J.: IRIS Performer: a high performance multiprocessing toolkit for real-time 3D graphics. In: SIGGRAPH. (1994)

Secondary and Tertiary Structural Fold Elucidation from 3D EM Maps of Macromolecules

Chandrajit Bajaj and Samrat Goswami

Department of Computer Sciences,
Computational Visualization Center,
Institute of Computational Engineering and Sciences,
University of Texas at Austin,
Austin, Texas 78712

Abstract. Recent advances in three dimensional Electron Microscopy (3D EM) have given an opportunity to look at the structural building blocks of proteins (and nucleic acids) at varying resolutions. In this paper, we provide algorithms to detect the secondary structural motifs (α-helices and β-sheets) from proteins for which the volumetric maps are reconstructed at $5 - 10\mathring{A}$ resolution. Additionally, we show that when the resolution is coarser than $10\mathring{A}$, some of the tertiary structural motifs can be detected from 3D EM. For both these algorithms, we employ the tools from computational geometry and differential topology, specifically the computation of stable/unstable manifolds of certain critical points of the distance function induced by the molecular surface. With the results in this paper, we thus draw a connection between the mathematically well-defined concepts with the bio-chemical structural folds of proteins.

1 Introduction

Three dimensional Electron Microscopy reconstruction(3D EM) and in particular single particle cryo-EM reconstruction [1], has advanced rapidly over recent years, such that several macromolecules (complexes of proteins and ribo-nucleic acids or RNA) can be resolved routinely at low resolution (10-20 $\mathring{A}$) and in some cases at sub-nanometer (intermediate) resolution (7-10 $\mathring{A}$) [2]. The ultra-structure of these complexes once elucidated from the 3D EM (henceforth 3D Maps), provide not only insights into individual protein and RNA folds and structural motifs, but even more importantly provide information about how the various structural components interact. In addition, with the increasing capability of determining multiple structural folds and conformers (secondary structures and tertiary arrangements) of a complex [3], there is the promise of studying the dynamics of such interacting systems.

Proteins are polypeptide chains of amino acids, (and nucleic acids are sugar-phosphate chains of acidic bases). The secondary structure of proteins are made up of a set of helical (or crudely, cylindrical) arrangement of sub-chains called α-helices and mostly planar arrangement of sub-chains called β-sheets. The various

P. Kalra and S. Peleg (Eds.): ICVGIP 2006, LNCS 4338, pp. 264–275, 2006.

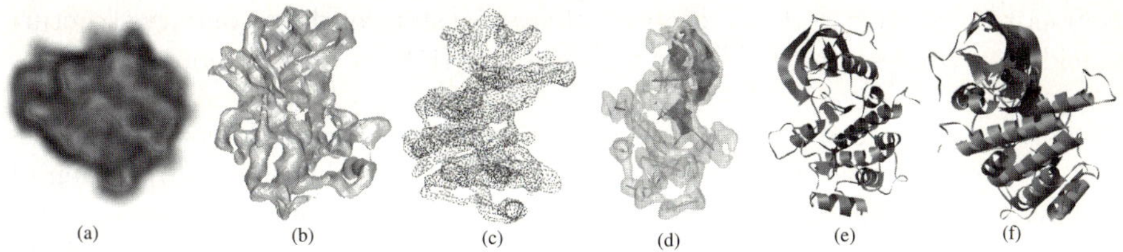

Fig. 1. Secondary structure elucidation algorithm for Insulin Receptor Tyrosine Kinase Domain with pdbid: 1IRK. (a) volume rendering of its blurred 3D Map at $8\mathring{A}$ resolution (b) surface rendering of the protein's molecular surface (c) pointset sampling of the molecular surface (d) The red patch inside the transparent surface depicts the β-sheet while the straight lines designate the axes of the cylinders which correspond to the α-helices (e) The secondary structural motifs, documented in the Protein Data Bank, where the helices are shown as ribbon coils and the sheets are sets of ribbon strands. (f) combined display of (d) and (e).

structural conformations of sub-groups of helices and sheets, yield the various different tertiary folds [4]. Relatively similar configuration of secondary and tertiary folds arise also in RNA [5].

In this paper, we provide a solution to the problem of automatically elucidating the structural secondary and tertiary folds of proteins (and nucleic acids) from 3D Maps of macromolecular complexes. A 3D Map is akin to a 3D spatial matrix of electron density values. With the improved reconstruction resolution of 3D Maps of macromolecules via 3D EM, the secondary and tertiary structural folds of proteins and RNA can be fully elucidated. Often (as evidenced by structures in the PDB), the atomic resolution structures of individual proteins or RNA, that make up the macromolecule are also discerned via X-ray diffraction and/or Nuclear Magnetic Resonance techniques, allowing us to validate our 3D EM secondary/tertiary structure elucidation algorithms [6]. Depending on the resolution of the 3D Map (in $\mathring{A}$), our goals here are to either detect the secondary structural motifs, or segment the molecule into significant components that can be associated with different tertiary structural folds.

Our processing pipeline has three macro steps, namely, (i) segmentation of the macromolecular 3D Map into individual protein (or RNA), subvolumes using the techniques of [7] and implemented in the publicly available VolRover tool [8]. (ii) computation of a "distance function" to a suitable molecular surface approximation of the individual protein (or RNA) using the methods detailed in [9,10] (iii) medial axis computation, classification, and construction of stable and unstable manifolds of the critical points of different indices. We skip a description of the first step, as the most recent developments are summarized in [7]. Step (ii) is sketched in Section 3, for completeness. The main contributions of this paper are: (a) Elucidation of secondary structural motifs (α-helices and β-sheets) from relatively higher resolution ($5-10\mathring{A}$) 3D Map of individual protein or RNA molecules, (b) Decomposition of the molecular surface of individual proteins or RNA, into its tertiary structural motifs, for 3D Maps at relatively coarser resolution $(10-15\mathring{A})$. Figure 1 shows the steps of the secondary structure elucidation process on the 3D Map of protein 1IRK at a resolution 8 $\mathring{A}$.

Prior Work. There are relatively few published algorithms that detect α-helices and β-sheets of proteins from 3D Maps at coarse resolution ($> 6\mathring{A}$). Wen et al have devised an algorithm called *Helix Hunter* [11] for detecting α-helices in a low resolution map where they modeled the helices as cylinders and the density function of the cylinder is convolved with the original map to detect the peaks of the cross-correlation. The main disadvantage of this technique is that it searches exhaustively over the space of all rigid-body transformations and therefore is very slow. A similar approach for detection of β-sheets was adopted by Kong and Ma [12,13] who modeled it as a disk like primitive and searched through the input map to find the possible positions of the disk that yielded high cross-correlation. This work, due to its exhaustive search paradigm, is also extremely compute intensive. Recently, Yu and Bajaj [14] have developed a secondary structure elucidation algorithm based on the relative magnitudes of the eigenvalues of the structure tensor computed at various select groups of voxels.

Given a compact surface Σ smoothly embedded in $\mathbb{R}^3$, a distance function h_Σ can be assigned over $\mathbb{R}^3$ that assigns to each point its distance to Σ. $h_\Sigma : \mathbb{R}^3 \rightarrow \mathbb{R}$, $x \mapsto \inf_{p \in \Sigma} \|x - p\|$ In applications, Σ is often known via a finite set of sample points P of Σ. Therefore it is quite natural to approximate the function h_Σ by the function $h_P : \mathbb{R}^3 \rightarrow \mathbb{R}$, $x \mapsto \min_{p \in P} \|x - p\|$ which assigns to each point in $\mathbb{R}^3$ the distance to the nearest sample point in P. Distance functions have found use in surface reconstruction [9,15,16,17], Medial axis approximation [18,19], shape segmentation and feature analysis [20]. Recently, Goswami et al [21] have presented an algorithm to compute the unstable manifolds of the index 1 and index 2 saddle points of this distance function and demonstrated its use in detecting flat and tubular features of any shape.

2   Preliminaries

Voronoi-Delaunay Diagram: We do not to go over the detail about this well-known datastructure due to space limitation and encourage reader to consult a standard computational geometry textbook [22]. In this work, we primarily use the duality of Voronoi and Delaunay diagram which states that every $k \leq 3$ dimensional Voronoi element is dual to a $3 - k$ dimensional Delaunay simplex.

Critical Points of h_P: The critical points of h_P are the points in $\mathbb{R}^3$ which lie within the convex hull of its closest points from P. It turns out that the critical points of h_P are the intersection points of the Voronoi objects with their dual Delaunay objects [23].

- *Maxima* are the Voronoi vertices contained in their dual tetrahedra,
- *Index 2 saddles* lie at the intersection of Voronoi edges with their dual Delaunay triangles,

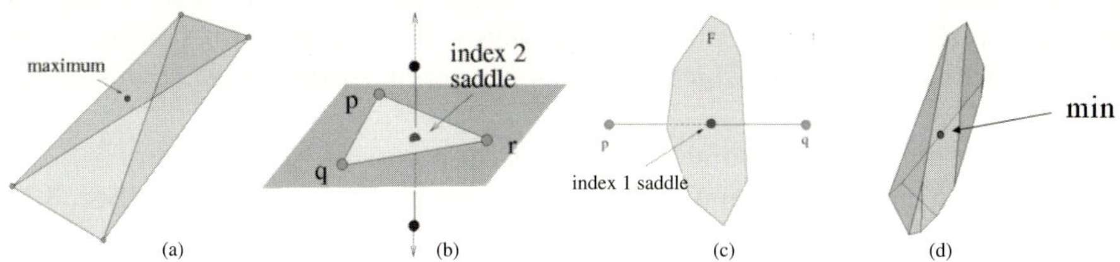

Fig. 2. The relative position of Voronoi and their dual Delaunay objects that results in the generation of critical points

- *Index 1 saddles* lie at the intersection of Voronoi facets with their dual Delaunay edges, and
- *Minima* are the sample points themselves as they are always contained in their Voronoi cells.

An illustration of the four types of critical points and the relative position of the Voronoi/Delaunay objects resulting these four types is shown in Figure 2.

At any point $x \in \mathbb{R}^3$, one can assign a vector field which is the direction of the steepest ascent of the distance function. The critical points are assigned zero vectors. This vector field induces a *flow*. If a point is allowed to move following the vector field, it traces an *orbit* and ends at a critical point. The set of points whose orbits end at a critical point c is called the *stable manifold* of c. Similarly, a point traces an *inverted orbit* when it follows the steepest descent of the distance function, and ends at a critical point c'. The set of points whose inverted orbits end at c' is called *unstable manifold* of c'.

The stable manifold of a maximum is a three dimensional polytope which is bounded by the stable manifold of critical points of lower indices. Similarly, the unstable manifold of a minimum is a three dimensional polytope which is bounded by the unstable manifold of critical points of higher indices. In this paper, our focus is on stable manifold of maxima and unstable manifold of the index 1 and 2 saddle points.

3   Secondary Structure Identification

The processing pipeline of α-helix and β-sheet identification from 3D Maps, consists of the following steps:

(a) Molecular Surface Extraction and Sampling: Starting with a 3D EM map of a protein (or RNA), a molecular surface is extracted via contouring [24]. For robust contouring, we use the implementation in the publicly available software TexMol [25]. Although several possible isosurfaces can be computed from the 3D Map, we select an isovalue using contour trees [26] (also implemented in TexMol), and topological curation wherein the isosurface is a single connected component, after removal of smaller completely nested surface components (i.e. voids). We call this extracted and curated surface component the molecular surface S of the protein (or RNA). Further, a sufficiently dense set of points are sampled from S. We call this poinset P which becomes the input to the latter stages of our algorithm.

(b) Detection of index 1 and index 2 critical points of h_P (Sec. 2).

(c) Computing unstable manifold of a subset of those critical points (Sec. 3.1).

(d) Detection of α-helix and β-sheets from the unstable manifolds (Sec. 3.2).

3.1   Computing U_1 and U_2 from P

Structure and computation of the unstable manifold of an index 1 saddle point (U_1) and an index 2 saddle point (U_2) have been described in detail in [21]. For completeness, we describe it briefly here.

U_1: Unstable Manifolds of index 1 saddle points are two dimensional. An index 1 saddle point, c lies at the intersection of a Voronoi facet F and a Delaunay edge. For any point $x \in F \setminus c$, h_P increases radially outward from c. Therefore the orbit of one such x hits the Voronoi edges bounding F. Thus F is in $U(c)$. Once the flow hits a Voronoi edge, if the dual Delaunay triangle is acute angled, the flow is along the Voronoi edge, and otherwise, the flow enters the Voronoi facet dual the Delaunay edge opposite to the largest angle of the dual Delaunay triangle. This iterative process computes the unstable manifold of c. The exact computation and its approximation have been described in [21]. Figure 3(a) illustrates an intermediate stage of this computation where the blue facet contains c, yellow facets are currently in $U(c)$ and pink facets are to be included in the subsequent iterations.

U_2: An index 2 saddle point is generated by the intersection of a Voronoi edge and a Delaunay triangle. The unstable manifold of an index 2 saddle point is one dimensional. It is a polyline with one endpoint at the saddle point and the other endpoint at a local maximum. The polyline consists of segments that are either subsets of Voronoi edges or lie in the Voronoi facets. Due to the later case, the polyline may not be a subcomplex of Vor P. Again, the exact computation and its approximation have been described in [21]. Figure 3(b) illustrates an example. Figure 3(c) shows the unstable manifolds of index 1 and index 2 saddle points on the interior medial axis of the 3D map of molecule 1IRK.

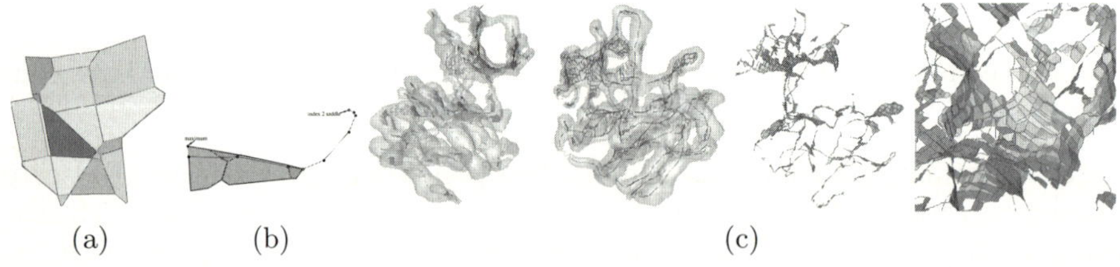

(a)   (b)   (c)

Fig. 3. General structure of U_1 and U_2 is shown in (a,b). (c) A collage of U_1 (yellow) and U_2 (red) of the molecule 1IRK. Note U_2 bounds U_1.

3.2 α-Helix and β-Sheet Selection

The unstable manifold of index 1 and index 2 saddle points restricted to the medial axis of the molecular surface decomposes the medial axis into linear (U_2) and planar (U_1) portions. We call the linear subset M_L and the planar subset M_F. The next task is to select a subset of M_L and M_F that gives the α-helices and β-sheets of the protein. Typically, an α-helix is a cylindrical subvolume of the molecule which is of width approximately 2.5Å. Also the subvolume does not deviate much from a straight cylinder for proteins [4,11]. These two conditions, dictate the following computational steps.

The unstable manifold of every index 2 saddle on the medial axis is a polyline with Voronoi vertices at the joints. Every Voronoi vertex has h_P value which can be computed by the circumradius of the dual Delaunay tetrahedron. Locally this gives the radius of the cylinder that best fits the molecular surface in the cylindrical regions. We first populate the set H with the Voronoi vertices whose h_P values fall within 2Å and 3Å. A 3Å neighborhood graph is then computed over H that clusters the points. The choice of 3Å is dictated by the fact that pitch of the helices is 1.5Å and usually there is more than 2 turns in every helix. The diametrical point pair in every cluster is then computed. The maximum deviation of any intermediate point from the straight line joining the point pair decided how straight the fitted cylinder to the cluster is. This way we select those clusters from H and the cylinders fitted to these clusters produce the detected α helices. The process is shown in 4(b).

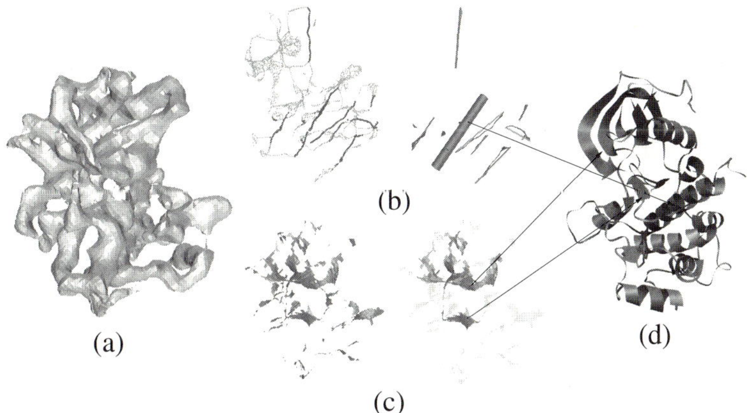

Fig. 4. (a) The molecular surface of 1IRK. (b) The selected Voronoi vertices on U_2 and the fitted cylinder. (c) Filtering out subsets of U_1 which are small (green) or do not satisfy the width test (magenta). (d) shows the secondary structures obtained from the PDB and its correspondence with the computed structure (b,c).

The selection of β-sheets is similar. U_1 gives the possible candidates for β-sheets. First we notice that there are some tiny components that are created due to sampling artifacts, and they do not correspond to real planar substructures of the molecule. We first filter these small clusters out (green patches in

Figure 4(c)). After this first stage of filtering, we are left with the planar subsets of the medial axis (cyan in Figure 4(c)). At this point we apply the knowledge, that β-sheets are of width roughly 1.5Å [4,12] and we filter out the planar patches which do not satisfy this "thickness" criterion. The width of a facet in U_1 is easy to check as they are the Voronoi facets and therefore have an 1-1 correspondence with their dual Delaunay edges which cross the medial axis. Therefore, we select only those Voronoi facets from U_1 whose dual Delaunay edges are of length between 1Å and 2Å. The portions of U_1 which are filtered out by this test are shown in magenta in Figure 4(c). The rest of U_1, which qualify for β-sheets, are shown in cyan. The sheets detected in are shown to correspond well with the β-sheets of the molecule 1IRK obtained from Protein Data Bank.

4   Tertiary Fold Elucidation

Tertiary structural folds (or motifs) provide useful information about the conformational and packing arrangement of a protein molecule. Such tertiary folds can be discerned when a coarser resolution 3D Map of the molecule is available. In this section, we show how such information can be gleaned again by looking at the distance function h_P induced by the set of points P sampled on an approximation of the molecular surface S extracted from a coarse resolution 3D Map. Our main focus is on the maxima of h_P. We have already seen that the maxima are the intersection of the Delaunay tetrahedra with their dual Voronoi vertices. In other words, these are the circumcenters of only those Delaunay tetrahedra whose circumcenters lie inside them. As a first step of the tertiary fold detection, we collect the maxima which are the circumcenters of the interior Delaunay tetrahedra.

Once the set of interior maxima is populated, we use their stable manifolds to decompose the volume bounded by S into a set of bio-chemically meaningful segments. These stable manifolds are three dimensional solid subsets of the interior of the molecular surface S. Such techniques have been proved useful earlier in segmentation and matching of free-form objects [20]. We follow the algorithm for computing the stable manifold of a maximum approximately, as described in [20].

Given two Delaunay tetrahedra σ and σ' which share a common triangle t, we say $\sigma < \sigma'$, if the circumcenter of σ lies in the half-space defined by t that does not contain the fourth vertex of σ. Figure 5(a) describes this case. Note that σ' is not always unique (Figure 5(b)). However, this can be proved that, a Delaunay tetrahedron σ can have at most two neighbors σ_1 and σ_2, for which $\sigma < \sigma_1$ and $\sigma < \sigma_2$. Also, it is to be noted, that the Delaunay tetrahedron σ_{max} whose dual Voronoi vertex is a maximum, has none of its neighbors σ' for which $\sigma_{max} < \sigma'$.

Following the above observation the stable manifold of the maxima are approximated. The set of maxima is sorted according to h_P. Starting from the biggest maximum, the algorithm collects all σ which falls under the transitive closure of the relation '$<$'. A subtle problem remains. The stable manifolds of the maxima are often numerous, and therefore they need to be clubbed carefully to bring out the underlying features of the molecule. To this goal, we apply a

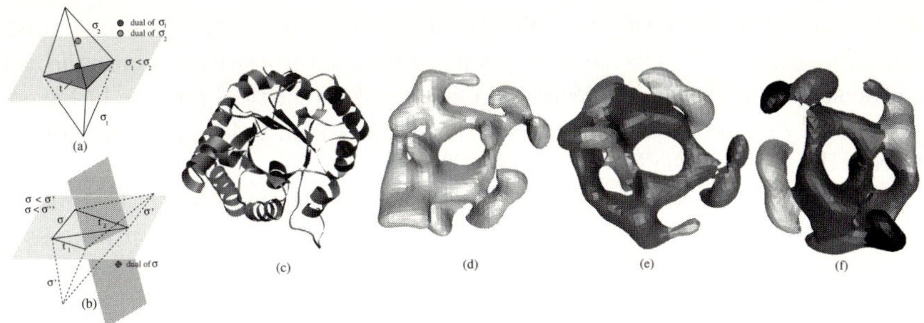

Fig. 5. (a) $\sigma_1 < \sigma_2$. (b) The situation when σ has two neighbors σ' and σ'' for both of which $\sigma < \sigma'$ and $\sigma < \sigma''$. (c) 1TIM: Helices surround the sheets to form the tertiary structure called α/β-*barrel*. (d) Molecular surface of 1TIM at 15Å resolution. (e,f) The initial segmentation and further refinement to bring out the β-fold of the *barrel* from the surrounding helices (yellow, magenta and blue).

merging step, which adjoins two stable manifolds of two maxima sharing a common boundary when the h_P function values at the maxima as well as at a point on the common boundary are comparable to each other.

Figure 5(c-f) shows an example of the stable manifolds and the tertiary folds that they correspond to. It is worth mentioning that, in our experience, tertiary motifs are not always readily decomposable using this algorithm. Nevertheless, we observe that the decomposition algorithm successfully detects the helical region and separates them from the beta regions. The beta regions are sometimes decomposed into more than one component which need to be associated separately to reflect a single fold.

5   Implementation and Results

For calibrating our structure elucidation algorithms, we downloaded atomic level descriptions of proteins from the Protein Data Bank [27]. For each protein, we first "blurred" them into a 3D map (to correspond to a reconstructed 3D EM map) at varying resolutions (5 to 15 Å), using publicly available software EMAN [28]. From these volumetric maps, we extracted the proteins molecular surface using TEXMOL [25]. Next we collected a pointset sampling of the molecular

Table 1. Name and PDBID of the proteins used in the calibration process

PDBID	Protein	PDBID	Protein
1IRK	Insulin Receptor Tyrosin Kinase Domain	1TIM	Triose Phosphate Isomerase
1PLQ	Proliferating Cell Nuclear Antigen	1RIE	Rieske Iron-sulphur Protein
1CID	T Cell Surface Glycoprotein CD4	1MBN	Myoglobin
1VDF	Cartilage Oligomeric Matrix Protein	1JPC	Agglutinin
1AOR	Aldehyde Ferrodoxin Oxydoreductase	1BBH	Cytochrome C'

surface, and used the Cocone software for surface reconstruction and medial axis computation [29]. The next step was to detect the critical points and compute the stable/unstable manifolds of a subset of the critical points. These computations rely on the Voronoi Diagram - Delaunay triangulation of the pointset, and were done using the CGAL library [30].

The calibration process is essential before we apply them to 3D EM maps of unknown atomic descriptions. The datasets used in the calibration process are summarized in Table 1. Details of the molecules are available from the Protein Data Bank (PDB) via the pdbid. Figure 6 shows the snapshots of the key steps of the algorithm. Figure 6(a) shows the U_1 (green) and U_2 (red) of 1BBH. The clusters of points lying on U_2, selected by the width criterion of α-helix, and the

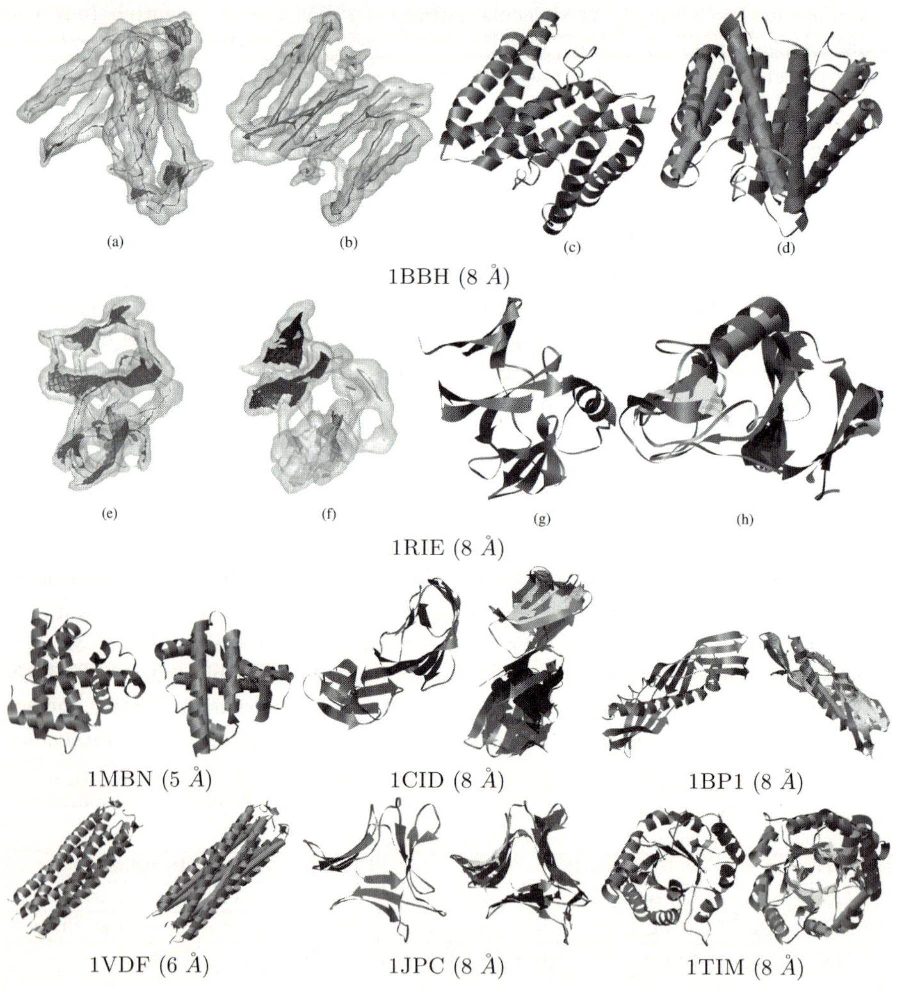

Fig. 6. Performance of our α-helix and β-sheet detection algorithm

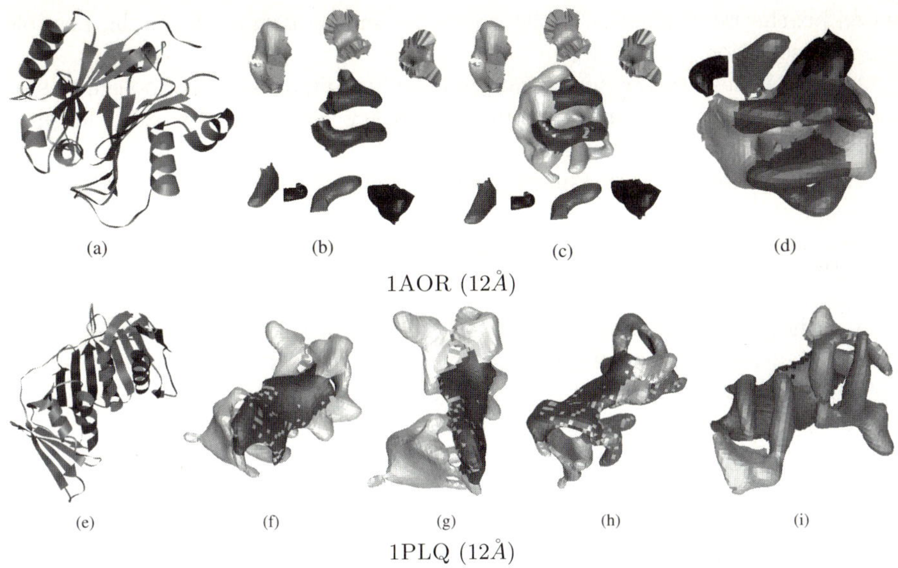

1AOR (12Å)

1PLQ (12Å)

Fig. 7. Performance of the tertiary fold elucidation algorithm

axis of the cylinders to be fitted to the clusters are shown in Figure 6(b). Figure 6(c) shows the secondary structure of 1BBH documented in the PDB. It has total 8 helices and all of them are detected correctly (green cylinders) by our algorithm (Figure 6(d)). The second row in Figure 6 shows similar set of pictures for 1RIE. It has three β-sheets which are identified correctly (red, yellow and blue patches). Third and fourth row show the performance of the algorithm on six more molecules at varying resolutions.

Figure 7 shows the performance of our tertiary fold detection algorithm. Top row shows the secondary structure of 1AOR as provided by PDB along with the ensemble of the segments of the protein at 12 Å. The tertiary structure of 1AOR is named as β *sandwich*. The two red segments (in c) correspond to the two β-sheets. The bottom row shows similar results for 1PLQ (at 12 Å). The tertiary fold elucidation can successfully separate the three sheets (red, yellow, green) from the helices (blue).

6   Conclusions

We have presented an algorithm for secondary and tertiary fold elucidation of a protein from 3D EM maps at varying resolutions. Similar constructions are applicable for ultra-structure elucidation of RNA's. The algorithms work by analyzing the stable and unstable manifolds of a subset of the critical points of the distance function, computed from the molecular surface pointset sampling of the protein.

The algorithm presented in this paper relies on a suitable approximation of the molecular surface. We plan to further investigate the choice of such surfaces based on the bond lengths of the atoms present to narrow down the possible range of selection.

Also we believe the critical points of h_P which lie outside the molecular surface, carry useful information about the tertiary structure. For example, presence of α/β barrels accommodate a through hole in protein surface which can be characterized by exterior index-2 saddle points.

Acknowledgments

The authors are supported in part by NSF grants ITR-EIA-0325550, CNS-0540033 and NIH grants P20 RR020647, R01 GM074258-021 and R01-GM0 73087. We thank the Jyamiti group at The Ohio State University for providing the Cocone software for surface reconstruction and medial axis approximation. We also thank Dr. Zeyun Yu for valuable discussion on secondary structure elucidation of virus proteins.

References

1. Frank, J.: Three-Dimensional Electron Microscope of Macromolecular Assemblies. San Diego: Academic Press (1996)
2. Baker, T.S., Olson, N.H., Fuller, S.D.: Adding the third dimension to virus life cycles: three-dimensional reconstruction of icosahedral viruses from cryo-electron micrographs. Microbio. and Mol. Bio. Reviews **63**(4) (1999) 862–922
3. Zhou, Z.H., Baker, M.L., Jiang, W., Dougherty, M., Jakana, J., Dong, G., Lu, G., Chiu, W.: Electron cryomicroscopy and bioinformatics suggest protein fold models for rice dwarf virus. Nature Structural Biology **8**(10) (2001) 868–873
4. Branden, C., Tooze, J.: An Introduction to Protein Structure. Garland Publishing Inc., New York (1999)
5. Schneider, B., Morveki, Z., Berman, H.: RNA conformational classes. Nucleic Acids Research **32, 5** (2004) 1666–1677
6. Bajaj, C., Yu, Z.: Geometric processing of reconstructed 3D maps of macromolecular complexes. In Aluru, S., ed.: Handbook of Computational Molecular Biology. Chapman and Hall, CRC Press (2005) Chap 45
7. Yu, Z., Bajaj, C.: Automatic ultra-structure segmentation of reconstructed cryo-em maps of icosahedral viruses. IEEE Transactions on Image Processing **14, 9** (2005) 1324–1337
8. CVC, UT Austin: Volrover. (http://cvcweb.ices.utexas.edu/software/guides.php)
9. Bajaj, C., Bernardini, F., Xu, G.: Automatic reconstruction of surfaces and scalar fields from 3D scans. In: ACM SIGGRAPH. (1995) 109–118
10. Bajaj, C., Lee, H., Merkert, R., Pascucci, V.: Nurbs based b-rep models from macromolecules and their properties. In: Proc. 4th Sympos. on Solid Modeling and Applications. (1997) 217–228
11. Wen, J., Baker, M., Ludtke, S., Chiu, W.: Bridging the information gap: computational tools for intermediate resolution structure interpretation. J. of Mol. Bio. **308** (2001) 1033–1044
12. Kong, Y., Ma, J.: A structural-informatics approach for mining β- sheets: locating sheets in intermediate-resolution density maps. J. of Mol. Bio **332** (2003) 399–413

13. Kong, Y., X.Zhang, T.S.Baker, Ma, J.: A structural-informatics approach for tracing β-sheets: building pseudo-Ca traces for β-strands in intermediate-resolution density maps. J. of Mol. Bio. **339** (2004) 117–130
14. Yu, Z., Bajaj, C.: Computational approaches for automatic structural analysis of large bio-molecular complexes. Technical Report TR-06-05, Department of Computer Sciences, UT Austin (2006)
15. Edelsbrunner, H.: Surface reconstruction by wrapping finite point sets in space. In Aronov, B., Basu, S., Pach, J., Sharir, M., eds.: Ricky Pollack and Eli Goodman Festschrift. Springer-Verlag (2002) 379–404
16. Chaine, R.: A geometric convection approach of 3-d reconstruction. In: Proc. Eurographics Sympos. on Geometry Processing. (2003) 218–229
17. Giesen, J., John, M.: The flow complex: a data structure for geometric modeling. In: Proc. 14th ACM-SIAM Sympos. Discrete Algorithms. (2003) 285–294
18. Chazal, F., Lieutier, A.: Stability and homotopy of a subset of the medial axis. In: Proc. 9th ACM Sympos. Solid Modeling and Applications. (2004) 243–248
19. Siddiqi, K., Shokoufandeh, A., Dickinson, J., Zucker, S.: Shock graphs and shape matching. Computer Vision (1998) 222–229
20. Dey, T.K., Giesen, J., Goswami, S.: Shape segmentation and matching with flow discretization. In Dehne, F., Sack, J.R., Smid, M., eds.: Proc. Workshop Algorithms Data Strucutres (WADS 03). LNCS 2748, Berlin, Germany (2003) 25–36
21. Goswami, S., Dey, T.K., Bajaj, C.L.: Identifying flat and tubular regions of a shape by unstable manifolds. In: Proc. 11th Sympos. Solid and Physical Modeling. (2006) 27–37
22. de Berg, M., van Kreveld, M., Overmars, M., Schwarzkopf, O.: Computational Geometry: Algorithms and Applications. Springer-Verlag, Berlin (1997)
23. Siersma, D.: Voronoi diagrams and morse theory of the distance function (1999)
24. Lorensen, W., Cline, H.: Marching Cubes: A High Resolution 3D Surface Construction Algorithm. In: SIGGRAPH. (1987) 163–169
25. Bajaj, C., Djeu, P., Siddavanahalli, V., Thane, A.: Interactive visual exploration of large flexible multi-component molecular complexes. In: Proc. of the Annual IEEE Visualization Conference. (2004) 243–250
26. van Kreveld, M., van Oostrum, R., Bajaj, C., Pascucci, V., Schikore, D.: Contour trees and small seed sets for isosurface generation. In Rana, S., ed.: Topological Data Structures for Surfaces. John Wiley & Sons (2004) Chap 5, pg 71 –86
27. Berman, H.M., Westbrook, J., Feng, Z., Gilliland, G., Bhat, T., Weissig, H., Shindyalov, I., Bourne, P.: The Protein Data Bank. Nucleic Acids Research (2000) 235–242
28. Ludtke, S., Baldwin, P., Chiu, W.: EMAN: semiautomated software for high-resolution single-particle reconstructions. J. of Struct. Bio. (**128**) 82–97
29. Cocone: Tight Cocone Software for surface reconstruction and medial axis approximation. (http://www.cse.ohio-state.edu/~tamaldey/cocone.html)
30. CGAL Consortium: CGAL: Computational Geometry Algorithms Library. (http://www.cgal.org)

Real-Time Streaming and Rendering of Terrains

Soumyajit Deb[1,2], Shiben Bhattacharjee[1], Suryakant Patidar[1],
and P.J. Narayanan[1]

[1] Centre for Visual Information Technology
International Institute of Information Technology Hyderabad
[2] Microsoft Research India, Banglore
sdeb@microsoft.com, {shiben@research., skp@research., pjn@}iiit.ac.in

Abstract. Terrains and other geometric models have been traditionally stored locally. Their remote access presents the characteristics that are a combination of file serving and realtime streaming like audio-visual media. This paper presents a terrain streaming system based upon a client server architecture to handle heterogeneous clients over low-bandwidth networks. We present an efficient representation for handling terrains streaming. We design a client-server system that utilizes this representation to stream virtual environments containing terrains and overlayed geometry efficiently. We handle dynamic entities in environment and the synchronization of the same between multiple clients. We also present a method of sharing and storing terrain annotations for collaboration between multiple users. We conclude by presenting preliminary performance data for the streaming system.

1   Introduction

Traditional graphics applications store all geometry locally in the main memory itself. Geometry can also be stored remotely and received progressively when needed and rendered on the fly. Streaming of geometry of large virtual environments can be beneficial and difficult if the network bandwidth is low. Such systems find applications when data cannot be replicated easily. Dynamic environments such as those used for battlefield visualization involving real terrains and multiple players is an example. Different users may read/update parts of the virtual environment while maintaining a collaborative and consistent system across heterogeneous users connected from client machines with different capabilities and network bandwidths. A similar situation is presented by massive, multi-player online games consisting of dynamic persistent worlds.

Geometry cannot be split into frames or chunks unlike media like audio and video. Some parts of a model cannot be lost unlike video where the loss of a frame may be acceptable. A complete model is necessary to render geometry. Each may be used for rendering several frames and hence need to be stored at the client. In this sense, geometry should be served like files from a file-server. On the other hand, geometric model should reach in time for real-time rendering of the final rendered video. Delay can result in the undesirable effects like the freezing and popping. The real-time constraint makes it possible for us to talk

P. Kalra and S. Peleg (Eds.): ICVGIP 2006, LNCS 4338, pp. 276–288, 2006.
© Springer-Verlag Berlin Heidelberg 2006

about streaming geometry. The parallel in geometry to the reduced bit-rate encoding of audio and video is *level of detail (LOD)*, which is the representation of the shape at different levels of approximations. The server can send a lower detail model to the client to reduce various resource requirements. Thus, remote access of geometry is an interesting mix of data serving and content streaming.

In this paper, we address the issue of streaming terrain data over networks. Real terrain datasets can span multiple gigabytes in size and are difficult to render interactively using brute force methods. Level of detail methods must be used to reduce the amount of detail to be rendered. However, if we are to render terrains remotely, the biggest bottleneck is the available network bandwidth between the server and the client. We need to optimize the transmitted terrain data accordingly depending upon client type and and available bandwidth. This is a hard problem as the system must achieve performance akin to local rendering at the client end. This is compounded by the fact that the system must keep track of any dynamic entities that exist in the environment and update the clients accordingly. This work extends to terrains an earlier work on geometry streaming [1]. We propose an optimized terrain representation based upon tiles for efficient transmission and rendering in Section 3. In Section 4 we look at the basic requirements of a geometry streaming system and our design and implementation of the same. Section 5 presents efficient ways of adapting these techniques for a terrain rendering system including performance improvements for the system using the ideas of prefetching and caching. Methods to synchronize and render multiple dynamic entities in the environment are discussed in 6 followed by experimental results in 7 and conclusions 8.

2   Related Work

Media streaming over the web has been popular and several standards exist. Most media streamers allow a specific bitrate to be chosen based upon available bandwidth and dynamic changing of bitrate to adjust accurately to client parameters. Google Earth/Maps streams maps and satellite imagery in real-time over the internet. However it does not address individual client characteristics which may lead to lags and freezes.

Djurcilov and Earnshaw added compression of models to VRML and developed an integrated visualization system, where the basic selection of data is done by the user [2,3]. However even after revisions of VRML which included geometry compression (Li et al.) [4], it is not usable for web-based serving since data needs to be transmitted before rendering can begin. Commercial products for remote visualization includes VisServer software from Silicon Graphics which allows rendering of any OpenGL application on remote clients by transmission of individual frames. Funkhouser describes a system based upon client server architecture for multi-user virtual environments [5]. The WireGL/Chromium project is a system that provides the familiar OpenGL API to each node in a cluster, virtualizing multiple graphics accelerators into a sort-first parallel renderer with a parallel interface [6]. [7] uses a crude model at the client for navigation and streams actual high quality views from the server using viewing parameters to protect high detail content.

Among geometry based approaches, Schneider and Martin describe a framework which adapts to the client characteristics including network bandwidth and the client's graphics capabilities [8]. Martin describes an Adaptive Rendering and Transmission Environment (ARTE) framework that facilitates the delivery of 3D models while monitoring the resources available [9]. This uses MPEG4 stream compression which may lead to lag in response to user input. Teler describes a remote rendering system utilizing path prediction and bandwidth based level of detail reduction [10]. This system fails to dynamically change/adapt parameters during the course of the walk-through which may lead to suboptimal performance. Deb and Narayanan develop a system to stream general polygonal models between a server and client in [1]. However this approach is suitable for only tessellated models and may not be the optimal for terrains.

In recent terrain rendering approaches, Lossaso and Hoppe[11] describe how terrains can be broken into geometric clipmaps of varying metric sizes and that these clipmaps can be used as Level of Details. This is however not the most optimal representation for streaming. Their method also calculates the blend/morph factor on a per vertex basis because of inhomoegeneous tile sizes which may slow down lower end clients. Wagner [12] divides the terrain into regular square tiles for rendering. However the view frustum culling approach used by [12] fails in cases when the terrain has large variations in heights. The ground plane is unable to include the projection of tiles, which are near to the camera looking at horizon, since they are out of that projection but inside the view frustum. Pouderoux and Marvie [13] design an out of core terrain rendering system based upon a heuristic metric. However they do not address the problem of network streaming.

In our system, we follow a technique similar to Wagner [12] for dividing the terrain into square tiles to make it easy for the geometry streaming system to select regular data to be transmitted to the client. We can calculate blending factors on a per tile basis because of the use of a regular tile structure thus reducing the amount of computation. Given the tile indices, their object space location is easily computable making query systems on the terrain efficient. However regular tiles become very small at the extremities of the viewing frustum. We take care of this problem by using very low levels of detail for such tiles in view. We tweak Wagner's frustum culling technique by having the projection on realtime average height of terrain in the view and not simply the ground plane.

3   Terrain Rendering

We describe the various steps involved in first creating our terrain representation and then rendering it. Before rendering the tiles, we must store them in a data structure that is suitable for both rendering and also for transmission. View frustum culling is required to select only the necessary entities in the view frustum. VFC is very useful for streaming as it allows us to select only a small portion of the entire terrain for transmission.

3.1   Data Organization

Terrain data consists of a height value for every point x, y on a rectangular grid. We divide it into **tiles** of equal size for rendering. By equal we mean they cover the same rectangular area on the heightmap. To handle levels of detail, we arrange the data in a specific way. For a tile with size $2^n \times 2^n$ height values, we store m number of LODs, $m \le n$, m is a user defined number based upon characteristics and size of the terrain. We also keep the distance between adjacent heights in x, y as s_x, s_y Fig 1. For an LOD l we have $2^{n-l+1}+1 \times 2^{n-l+1}+1$ $(l > 0)$ number of height values and $2^n + 1 \times 2^n + 1$ for $l = 0$. Note the extra heights at the end corners of the tiles, they are the height values at the starting corners of the next tile; kept as they help in stitching (see Section 3.5). This means $l = 0$ holds highest detail and $l = m$ holds lowest detail as illustrated in Fig. 1. For $l > 0$ we keep original height values h at $(2i, 2j)$ locations, $0 \le i, j \le 2^{n-l}$. We replace the height values at $(2i, 2j + 1)$ locations with $avg(h_{2i,2j}, h_{2i,2j+2})$, at $(2i + 1, 2j)$ locations with $avg(h_{2i,2j}, h_{2i+2,2j})$, at $(2i + 1, 2j + 1)$ locations with $avg(h_{2i,2j}, h_{2i+2,2j+2})$; where i, j vary as bounded. This is done so that while rendering when LOD l with alternate height values dropped, we don't see any change in the structure.

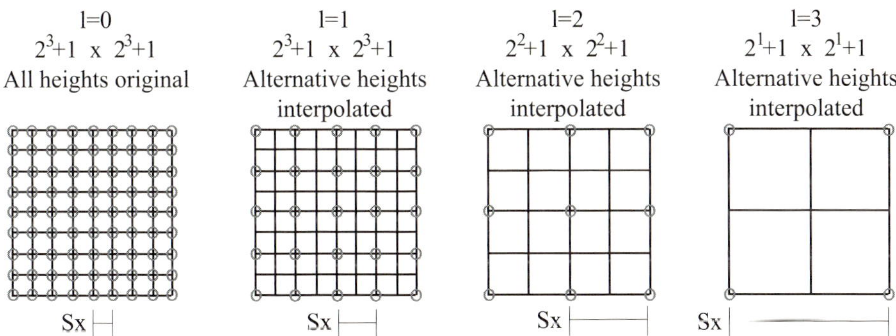

Fig. 1. Data organization: An e.g. with $n = 3$ and $m = 3$, blue circled height values are original, rest are interpolated. Note that, they occupy the same area on ground.

3.2   View Frustum Culling

In each frame, we query the graphics API for view frustum equations and calculate the projection P of the frustum (generally a trapezoid) on the base plain. This base plain is $z = a_h$, a_h is the approximated average height of the terrain in view of previous frame. This is because we haven't accessed the terrain data yet and thus will be using the data from previous frame assuming that the view hasn't changed much. We then calculate orthogonal bounding rectangle of P. We can directly map the coordinates of the bounding rectangle to tile indices. Using these tile indices, we find other tiles that are inside P (Fig.2). We keep the indices that return positive in a tile buffer B_t for use in rendering. We do not

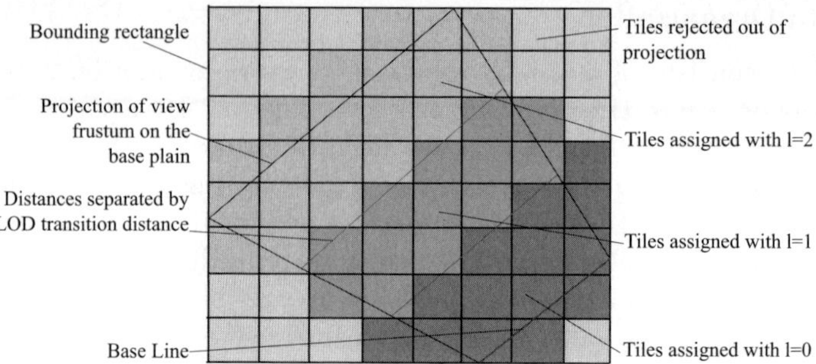

Fig. 2. View frustum culling and LOD assignment

need to do 3D view frustum culling as terrains are injective functions on x, y, and thus can be reduced to 2D in turn to reduce number of required calculations.

3.3   LOD and Blending Factor Calculation

Using the camera parameters we calculate a base line, that is perpendicular to the view vector and parallel to the ground plane. For each tile in B_t, we calculate the perpendicular distance d of its mid point from this line (Fig.2). This distance d is used to calculate LOD l as $\lfloor d/l_t \rfloor$ where l_t is the LOD transition distance. We choose this distance d instead of the direct distance of the tile from the camera because if the field of view of the camera is high, we shall end up rendering tiles at the corner of screen that are actually close to camera in screen space but far in object space in very low level of detail. The value $frac(d/l_t)$ is the blending factor α. α is used for smooth level of detail changes of tiles as explained in Section 3.4. We save l and α in B_t along with the tile indices.

3.4   Rendering

With all data in place, the tiles can be rendered from B_t. For all tile indices in B_t, we load the level l and $l+1$ of that tile. The index is clamped to m to avoid memory exceptions. The distance between adjacent heights for l can be calculated as $(s_{x_l}, s_{y_l}) = (s_x, s_y)2^l$ Fig 1. We calculate the heights h for $l > 0$ as

$$h = h_{(2i,2j)_l}(1 - \alpha) + h_{(i,j)_{(l+1)}}\alpha$$

$l = 0$ is a special case: $h = h_{(i,j)_0}(1 - \alpha) + h_{(i,j)_1}\alpha$, i, j vary as bounded. We can now see that when α is 0, $h = h_{(2i,2j)_l}$, and when α is 1, $h = h_{(i,j)_{(l+1)}}$. Thus this blending factor is able to smoothly change between the two height values of 2 different LODs of the same tile as we move the camera. On the fly, we also calculate the average of the heights at the mid point of these tiles, a_h, which will be used in the next frame for view frustum culling (See Section 3.2).

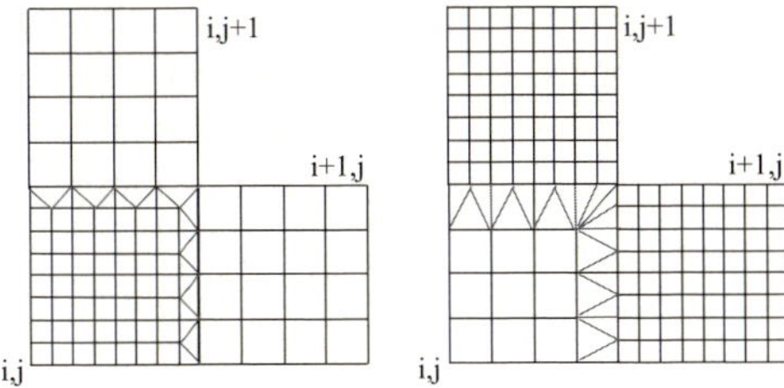

Fig. 3. Tile Stitching: tile i, j is stitched only to $i, j + 1$ and $i + 1, j$

3.5   Tile Stitching

Since every tile is getting assigned l and α independently, we find un-tessellated areas near the corner of each of the tiles. We assume that a tile on the ground with LOD l can have a nearby tile whose LOD can be only $l - 1$ or $l + 1$. This makes tile stitching easy and smooth blending of LODs works perfectly. Our assumption remains true iff l_t is always more than the maximum distance a tile can extend on the ground, i.e., the tile is never able to skip an LOD in between. So for a tile index t_i, t_j in B_t, we get the l and α of $t_{(i+1)}, t_j$ and $t_i, t_{(j+1)}$, and use them for the corner heights of t_i, t_j Fig 3. Note that we are not looking at $(i - 1, j), (i, j - 1)$ indices of tiles since those corners are already stitched by earlier tiles.

4   General Geometry Streaming

The basic objective of a geometry streamer is to provide each client with data appropriate to it as quickly and efficiently as possible. The server must allow the highest quality rendered output possible for the client and transmit geometry and assets that allow the client to maintain an acceptable frame-rate. Changing latencies should not cause the system to freeze or hang for long durations during the walkthrough. The server should adapt to the different client parameters such as graphics capability, network bandwidth and connection latency. Ideally, these must be met strictly. We briefly outline the basic requirements of a Client-Server geometry streaming system. The basic architecture of the system is similar to the system in [1] which may be referred to for further information.

Transparency: A transparent streaming system treats remote and local objects without distinction. The architecture of the system allows a user program to include remote models from multiple servers into its local virtual environment. The client API will handle the necessary tasks such as server interaction, data caching and management etc., transparently. The streamed data will match with the client machine's capabilities and the network properties.

Support for varying clients and networks: No client should receive a model that it cannot handle at interactive rates. A suitable level of detail is sent to each client based on capabilities of rendering hardware. Multiple levels of detail may be used for improved performance on low-end clients. The heightmap and model detail can be reduced to handle different connection speeds to avoid freezing. A model matching the client's capabilities may be sent subsequently by progressively refining the original heightmap or model. Frequent updates to the model at the client can be avoided by sending the client more information than immediately necessary. Continuous connection monitoring and adjustment of detail is essential for good streaming performance.

Support for dynamic objects and local modifications: The server module should keep track of the static and dynamic objects transmitted to the client for each of the connected clients. Changes to an existing model in the virtual environment are notified to all clients possessing the same. All clients must have access to dynamic objects and their state information. User programs can have local control of transmitted model. It can mix and match remote models with local models, and can modify local copies of remote models.

The system consists of the Server Module, the Client Module and the Terrain Renderer (User Program) as shown in shown in Fig 4.

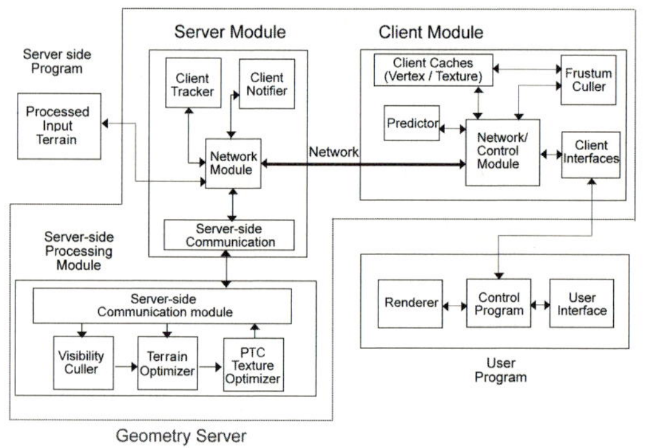

Fig. 4. Geometry Streaming System Block Diagram

The basic functions of the server module include managing a database of heightmaps and models, accepting incoming connections from different clients, serving the clients appropriately and quickly and handling dynamic objects in the virtual environment. Server receives requests for transmission from clients. In response, it generates and transmits a representation of the model suitable for the client. Each client request is translated into a model optimized based on available bandwidth, client capabilities and viewer speed. Low quality models will suffice when the user is moving fast, which may be progressively refined when the user slows down.

The client module interfaces with the user program on one side and the server module on the other. It provides a client API to the user program through which, the user program communicates with the client module, provides an initial set of client parameters and receives data. The amount of data transmitted is to be minimized by the system to avoid wasteful use of available bandwidth.

A local model and a remotely served heightmap/model should appear the same to the user for transparent streaming. A handle to the remote heightmap or model is returned to the user program by the client module. This is used by the Terrain Renderer (User Program) directly. The user program is responsible for the interaction with the user and the navigation control in the virtual environment. The user program passes the motion parameters to the client module on user movement in the virtual environment.

5   Terrain Streaming

In our system, the terrain data exists on the server and must be transmitted to the client on demand. The renderer described in Section 3 is completely based on the client side. Instead of loading the data from local storage, the renderer issues an API call *LoadRemoteTile()* to the client module. This call requests for a particular tile in the terrain at a desired level of detail. The client module maintains a local cache of tiles which is typically much larger than the number of tiles in the viewing frustum. The cache maintains tiles at varying levels of detail depending upon initially negotiated client parameters and available network bandwidth. If the tile does not exist in the client cache, the client module streams it from the server. Until the tile is actually received, an upsampled version of the existing data for the same location in the heightmap is used if available.

Tile Transmission: At the start of the walkthrough, the system transmits a very low resolution heightmap for the entire terrain dataset. As the viewer moves around over the terrain, higher quality data is streamed to the client depending upon viewer position. The renderer will have a bare minimum representation of the entire terrain available to it. The renderer requests for newer data as and when required. To transmit the tile, the last transmitted resolution of the tile is checked and only the residue between the high resolution tile and the supersam pled version of the low resolution tile is transmitted to the client by the server. The residue is compressed using the wavelet based PTC codec [14] before transmission. At the client end, the client module decompresses the representation and generates the high resolution tile. We use geomorphing to smoothly blend across tiles without any visible artifacts.

Tile Selection: Selecting the optimal set of tiles to be streamed is difficult problem. We need to not only select the tiles to stream but also the level of detail of the tiles to be streamed. We only need to stream tiles that are visible or would become potentially visible in the near future. This is done by taking multiple square sets of tiles around the viewing frustum. The inner squares have the higher levels of detail than the outer squares. Once the frustum moves, newer higher resolution tiles must be streamed to the client.

Object Selection: Objects present on the tiles are selected in a similar manner as the tiles. The objects are anchored to a particular point on the terrain. The discrete levels of detail of the object are precomputed. When selecting a particular level of detail of an object, we check the level of detail of the underlying tile and select the LOD of the object accordingly. The entire model must be transmitted as there is no easy way of creating a general polygonal model from a residue and lower level of detail in real-time. We maintain a list of transmitted objects on the server and never retransmit the same or lower level of detail.

The client module performs caching and prediction needed for better performance and interfaces with the server. The client module prefetches data based on predicted motion depending on the latency between the server and the client. The client caches already transmitted data so that requests can be avoided when the viewer retraces the navigation path. A balance is established so that the amount of data prefetched is enough to cover the potential areas in the virtual environment that the viewer might visit until the time of the next request. Caching and prefetching are transparent to the renderer. The organization of the cache is important as a cache miss is extremely expensive as data must be fetched from the remote server before it can be rendered in full detail. Each heightmap and its corresponding geometry is timestamped when the cache is updated. The object tracker logs the objects moving in and out of the cache along with their LOD.

Using the positions of the viewer in the past, the motion parameters are extracted. These are then used to estimate future motion This method of prediction works when the motion of the user in the world is smooth and continuous. Good performance from the prefetching algorithm is absolutely necessary to maintain a smooth walkthrough. Formally, we average the motion in the last 5 frames to generate the motion parameters for the next frame. We use a prediction scheme similar to [15]. However we assume that the rate of change of acceleration is constant. Assuming a constant acceleration may not be the right thing in case an object is experiencing rotational motion. If a_i is the acceleration, v_i the velocity and P_i the position vector in the ith frame which takes t_i time to render, assuming that the change in acceleration is smooth, we get the following relationships: $a_i - a_{i-1} = a_{i+1} - a_i$ or $a_{i+1} = 2a_i - a_{i-1}$. Knowing that $a_i = \frac{v_i - v_{i-1}}{t_i - t_{i-1}}$ and $v_i = \frac{P_i - P_{i-1}}{t_i - t_{i-1}}$, this reduces to $v_{i+1} = v_i + (t_{i+1} - t_i)(2a_i - a_{i-1})$ and finally to $P_{i+1} = P_i + c_1(t_{i+1} - t_i)v_i + c_2(t_{i+1} - t_i)^2(2a_i - a_{i-1})$, for some constants c_1 and c_2. The right hand side of this equation consists of known quantities other than t_{i+1}. P_{i+1} can be written completely in terms of earlier samples of P and frame time t. We do not reproduce the same here for the sake of brevity. Normalizing P_{i+1} will yield us the position vector of the point for which data needs to be prefetched. Since we do not know the value of t_{i+1}, we must estimate it from older known values of frame times. Once we know the future position of the viewer, we can prefetch data corresponding to that particular position. The amount of data prefetched depends directly on the size of the cache. We can control the bounds of the area of the terrain to be prefetched depending upon the cache size.

6   Dynamic Entities and Collaborative Environments

An environment or mode is defined as dynamic if its objects can change in form, position or appearance or if there is any addition or deletion of objects.

Synchronization of the state of a dynamic object in all clients is essential to avoid inconsistencies. The magnitude of the amount of data to be transmitted depends upon the type of change occurring in the dynamic environment. The different types of dynamic events that may occur in the VE are:

- Change in the position of an object in the VE: This is the simplest case as only the new position needs to be sent. If motion is parametric, the positions can be computed by the user if initialized properly. No data needs to be transmitted since the position of the object maybe calculated by the client provided such a motion model is known to the client.
- Change in form/shape of the object: The model of the newly changed shape needs to be streamed.
- Addition of a new object to the VE: The server needs to calculate which clients need the object based on the view frustums and notify the clients accordingly.
- Deletion of an object from the VE: Notify the clients who possess the object. They in turn can delete the object from their client cache.

To handle dynamic data efficiently, the client must be notified of the changes immediately. There are two ways in which this can done. One way is to send the changed data directly. The other way is to inform the clients about the change and allow them to initiate data transmission. The approach of lazy updates is preferable since data need not be sent unless needed. When the dynamic object comes into view at the client's end, data can be requested for and transmitted. The difference in this scenario over a typical static VE is that the server needs to initiate the transmission of individual objects in the VE without applying visibility calculations. This is an additional requirement to handle dynamic environments. A typical sequence of events during a walk-through of an environment with dynamic objects is as follows: (1) Dynamic Object is introduced into the VE or an existing object changes form. (2) Server Module checks the type of change and the clients affected by it. (3) Server notifies the affected clients of the change. (4) Clients request and download the required information when they need it.

Online mapping applications are becoming all pervasive. We have witnessed web based mapping applications such as *Windows Live Local* and *Google Maps* gain popularity over the past few years. The next step in evolution of such applications is a real 3D interface with community editing and sharing features. Our current system allows annotations of the terrain as basic collaborative features. Once a user annotates a particular position in the heightmap, the renderer passes this information to the server. Henceforth these annotations are treated in the same manner as dynamic objects. The only difference is that we allow serialization of the annotations at the server side in a database. The entry for each annotation includes the coordinates of anchor point in the heightmap as an index for retrieval. Currently we use flat text files but extending it to a real database instead is easy. The data is preserved across sessions of work. We intend to improve upon this feature and allow multiple options.

7   Results

Our test client system consisted of a Pentium M 2GHz laptop with 2GB of memory and 6800 Ultra graphics. For the low end test, we used a Pentium 4 1.5GHz machine with 256MB memory and onboard Intel 845G graphics. The server was an AMD Opteron CPU running at 2.8GHz with 2GB of main memory. Please do note that the clock speeds of the CPUs are not comparable. The laptop CPU is significantly faster than the low end client because of a better architecture. The client and server were connected over a 100BaseT LAN. The lower bandwidth conditions were simulated over this network by limiting network traffic. The terrain was a 10000x10000 heightmap which was around 300MB of data. We use the *Quality factor* metric from [1] to measure the performance of the system. This metric is 1.0 when the client is rendering at its best LOD.

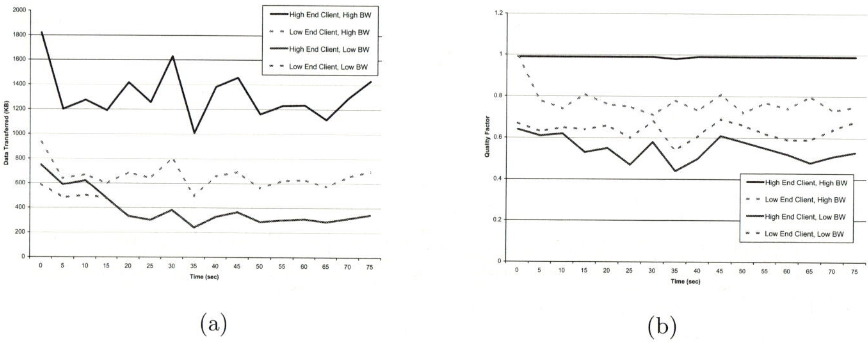

(a)   (b)

Fig. 5. (a) Data transferred during Walkthrough and (b) Achieved Quality Factor

The data transfer graph is indicated in Fig.5. We find that the data transfer graph is especially smooth. This implies that the walkthrough is free of hitches and popping. Fig 6 shows the number of high resolution tiles submitted compared to lower resolution tiles. We find that the high resolution tiles account for the majority of the data transmitted to the client. This is because we use a lower compression ratio for high resolution tiles as they are close to the viewer. We find the quality factor 5 to be extremely high as expected with the system achieving a high framerate 6. The quality factor seems to degrade with client type and available bandwidth. The higher end client is worse affected by lower available bandwidth than the lower end client as a larger amount of data needs to be transmitted in case of the higher end client. The low end client, we find that the system is initially unable to cope with the amount of data causing poor frame rates. The system consequently reduces the highest level of detail transmitted to the client and henceforth the walkthrough experience is acceptably smooth. The amount of data transmitted also flattens to a plateau indicating a smooth walkthrough experience without hitches. The quality factor

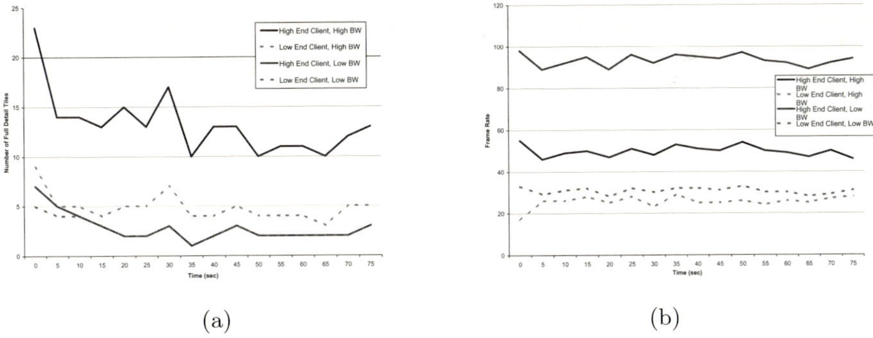

(a)   (b)

Fig. 6. (a) Number of Highest LOD tiles transferred and (b) Achieved Framerate of Walkthrough

Fig. 7. (a)Output on Real Dataset (b)Dynamic Objects (c) High LOD terrain (d) Low LOD terrain

is lower for the low-end client than the high end client but still quite acceptable. From the low bandwidth tests, we cap the maximum available bandwidth to 100 KB/s. We observe that the network bandwidth is always utilized for progressive refinement.

8   Conclusions and Future Work

We presented a Terrain Streaming and Rendering system which renders data received from a remote server and appropriately adapts to client characteristics and network bandwidth. The system utilizes a tile representation for efficient transmission. It uses a combination of visibility culling, clientside caching, speculative prefetching, motion prediction and deep compression to achieve perfomance similar akin to local rendering. The system supports dynamic entities in the environment allowing the content developer to create collaborative 3D virtual environments. It also supports shared annotations as a preliminary collaborative feature. We intend to include support for realistic terrain deformations at the client end in future versions along with more collaboration support. Streaming systems that serve terrains are especially suitable for applications like Virtual Earth which must transmit large amounts of terrain information. Multiplayer games and flight simulators shall also benefit by utilizing streaming to incorporate new content.

References

1. Deb, S., Narayanan, P.: Design of a geometry streaming system. In: ICVGIP. (2004) 296–301
2. Djurcilov, S., Pang, A.: Visualization products on-demand through the web. In: VRML. (1998) 7–13
3. Earnshaw, R.: The Internet in 3D Information, Images and Interaction. Academic Press (1997)
4. Li, J.: Progressive Compression of 3D graphics. Ph.D Dissertation, USC (1998)
5. Funkhouser, T.A.: Ring: A client-server system for multi-user virtual environments. I3D (1995) 85–92
6. Humphreys, G., Eldridge, M., Buck, I., Stoll, G., Everett, M., Hanrahan, P.: WireGL: A scalable graphics system for clusters. In: SIGGRAPH. (2001) 129–140
7. Koller, D., Turitzin, M., et al, M.L.: Protected interactive 3d graphics via remote rendering. In: SIGGRAPH. (2004) 695–703
8. Schneider, B., Martin., I.M.: An adaptive framework for 3D graphics over networks. Computers and Graphics (1999) 867–874
9. Martin, I.M.: Arte - an adaptive rendering and transmission environment for 3d graphics. In: Eighth ACM international conference on Multimedia. (2000) 413–415
10. Teler, E., Lischinski, D.: Streaming of Complex 3D Scenes for Remote Walkthroughs. EuroGraphics (2001) 17–25
11. Losasso, F., Hoppe, H.: Geometry clipmaps: terrain rendering using nested regular grids. ACM Trans. Graph. **23** (2004) 769–776
12. Wagner, D.: Terrain geomorphing in the vertex shader. ShaderX2, Shader Programming Tips and Tricks with DirectX 9, Wordware Publishing (2003)
13. Pouderoux, J., Marvie, J.E.: Adaptive streaming and rendering of large terrains using strip masks. In: Proceedings of ACM GRAPHITE 2005. (2005) 299–306
14. Malvar, H.S.: Fast progressive image coding without wavelets. In: DCC '00: Proceedings of the Conference on Data Compression, Washington, DC, USA, IEEE Computer Society (2000) 243–252
15. Guthe, M., Borodin, P., Klein, R.: Real-time out-of-core rendering. To appear in the International Journal of Image and Graphics (IJIG) (2006)

Ad-Hoc Multi-planar Projector Displays

Kashyap Paidimarri and Sharat Chandran

Indian Institute of Technology Bombay
http://www.cse.iitb.ac.in/~{kashyapp, sharat}

Abstract. High-resolution portable projectors have become commodity items now to own – but not to use. It is not always possible to find a display area where the camera can be properly aligned so that an undistorted image be seen. We present a method to project an undistorted image using a digital projector on a piecewise-planar display area.

We use uncalibrated structured light ranging to segment the unknown projection area and further compute the homographies that map the projector space to the camera space through each of the planes. The edge detection and point-correspondences are subpixel precise. Finally, we use these computed homographies to pre-warp the display image so that a distortion-free image is visible. Our results show a seamless and correct rectification with accurate segmentation of the planes.

1   Introduction

Increasingly digital projectors have become commonplace. But using a projector requires that a good display area be available. This is not always the case. The costs and maintenance, not to speak of the inconvenience suggests that "it would be nice to project on an arbitrary wall or desk corner." Manual calibration of such a configuration is painstaking and error-prone, and give less than desirable

Fig. 1. Cluttered working environment precludes casual use of projectors. In this figure, the projection polygon has been demarcated for clarity. All images in this paper are best seen in color on a monitor.

P. Kalra and S. Peleg (Eds.): ICVGIP 2006, LNCS 4338, pp. 289–298, 2006.

experience. Fig. 1 shows a cluttered office environment where there is no available area of projection apart from the wall corner. In such an environment it is imperative that a method be devised to remove the distortion so that the user sees a rectangular and correct image.

1.1 Projector Camera Systems

Of late, there have been a variety of solutions to this problem and most often, a camera is used to provide visual feedback to the system (hence the field, called 'Projector Camera systems.'). These systems range from a simple one-projector one-camera configuration to clusters of projectors and cameras intended to enlarge the available display area. The primary ideas in this field come from multiple view geometry of cameras [1]. An LCD (or DLP) projector, unlike older CRT projectors, can be modeled as a pinhole camera. Thus the projector becomes a dual of the camera and hence, both the capture and the display process can be represented as perspective transforms.

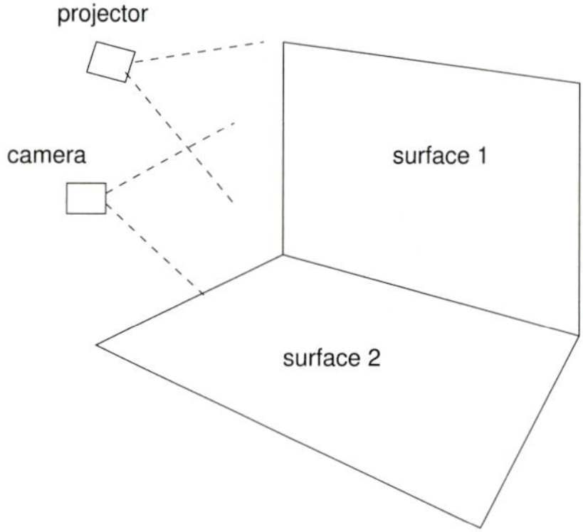

Fig. 2. Projector-Camera systems

Problem Definition: The primary components of such a system are a digital projector, an arbitrary display surface, and a digital camera. We are working with a model of the system where we have a single projector and camera projecting on a display surface formed from the juxtaposition of two or more planes as in Fig. 2. A minimal assumption is that the region of interest is covered in the field of view of both the camera and the projector.

Related Work: Given a calibrated projector-camera pair, conventional structure-light ranging can be used to reconstruct a complete 3D model of the display environment [2,3]. However, such methods are overkill because recovery of the complete geometry of the scene, the projector, and the camera is not necessary for rectification. In [4], the projection area is divided into a rectangular mesh and planar homographies are calculated from each rectangle of projection to the display. These homographies are then stitched together and the image is pre-warped to achieve the correction. This method is applicable to any arbitrary continuous surface. A similar method [5] uses affine transforms rather than homographies followed by texture-mapping. However, these methods suffer from artifacts at sharp edges because they do not explicitly identify the planes. The work most resembling ours appears in [6]; planar homographies are estimated from projected points and metric rectification is achieved under the constraint that the display surface contains a rectangle of known aspect ratio whose boundaries are visible.

This paper: In this work, we present a method to automatically correct an ad-hoc projector display using a camera. Correction is achieved in the sense that the camera position is a 'sweet spot' from where the display is guaranteed to be geometrically identical to what was intended to be displayed by the projector. Regions around the camera center look acceptable (see Fig. 9). Our method can be combined with a head tracking system to further correct the display to any new position the user might move to. The techniques we contribute in putting together a working system include:

- Automatic segmentation of planar regions. This is the key challenge in ad-hoc projector usage.
- Use of lines as features instead of points or blobs in the intermediate process of homography calculation, and the use of point-line duality. The advantage is that lines are easier to detect and to a greater accuracy using voting mechanism. Thus, our system is tolerant to clutter even on the display surface (see, for example, the white board in Fig. 1).

The rest of this paper is organized as follows. Sec. 2 briefly reviews the theory of projective transforms and their application in projector-camera systems. The system design is presented in Sec. 3 followed by implementation details and results in chapter 4. We conclude in the last section.

2   Homographies for Projector Camera Systems

At the very heart of projector camera systems are planar *homographies* or *projective transforms*. A mapping $h : \mathbb{P}^2 \rightarrow \mathbb{P}^2$ is a *projectivity* [1] iff there exists a non-singular 3×3 matrix H such that for any point in $\mathbb{P}^2$ represented by a vector x, $h(x) = Hx$. $\mathbb{P}^2$ is the projective plane and points are represented in their homogeneous 3-vector representation. Projectivities form a group since the inverse of a projectivity is also a projectivity and so is the composition of two projectivities. Since in homogeneous coordinates lines are the dual of points, for $l \in \mathbb{P}$ we have $l' \in \mathbb{P}'$

$$l' = H^{-T}l$$

where we have been given a projectivity H from plane $\mathbb{P}$ to $\mathbb{P}'$, and points on the line related by $x' = Hx$.

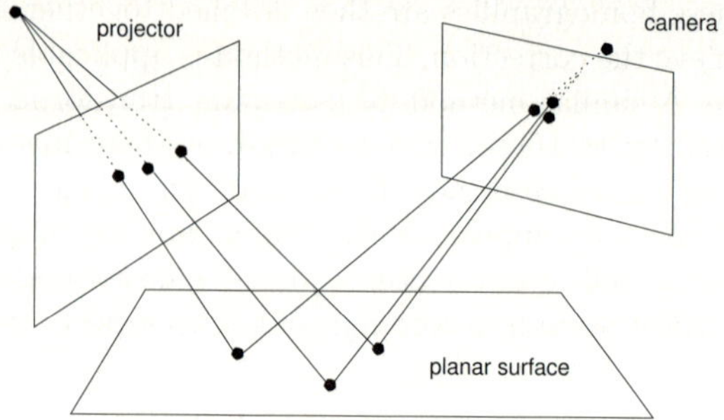

Fig. 3. Projective transform from projector to camera through a plane

Since the camera is the element that can observe images that the projector generates, albeit through the screen, it is critical to compute the homographies between these planes. A homography $_pH_s$ maps points from the projector plane to the planar display surface, and another homography $_sH_c$ maps from the surface to the camera plane. Composing these two we get the transformation from projector to camera $_pH_c = {_pH_s} \circ {_sH_c}$. Thus a point $\mathbf{x}$ in the projector plane P is transformed to point $\mathbf{x}'$ in the camera plane C. Finally $_cH_p$ is used to pre-warp the input image

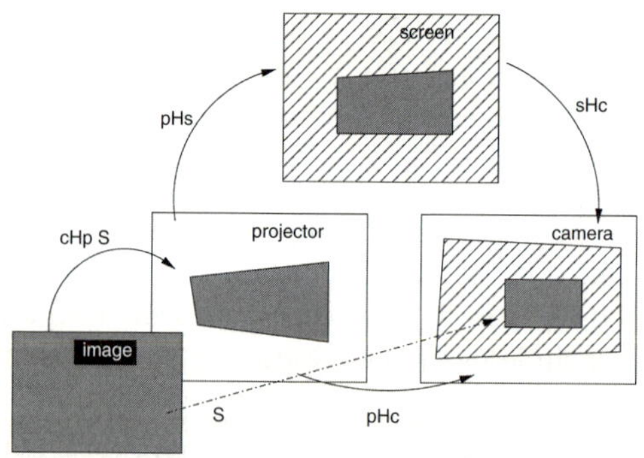

Fig. 4. Projective transforms between the camera, projector and the screen. Correction happens by applying an inverse map to the projected image.

from the application before projection. The image should now appear rectilinear in the final camera image except for the scaled rigid-body transform S that preserves shape. It is necessary to apply a correct S to ensure that the pre-warped image sent to the projector is not clipped to the projector's resolution.

3   System Design

We now present our system. For simplicity, we assume in the description below that we are dealing with two planar surfaces, and divide the steps into three stages.

Structured light: This is the data-collection stage where we use uncalibrated structured light in the form of lines to identify kinks caused by the intersection of the planes. Further, we also identify the line segments that are formed due to multiple planar regions.

Homography: We determine the line of separation between planes, followed by a determination of the partitioning of the data. Finally point correspondences are evaluated from the data and the projective transforms from the projector plane to the camera plane through each of the surfaces of projection are found.

Image Correction: The partitioning edge is now identified in the projector space (rather than the camera space) by using each of the homographies. Then appropriate inverse homographies are applied to each partitioned region of the projected image. Finally a stitching is applied.

We now describe details of our system.

3.1   Structured Light

Our structured light registration is run in two phases with different angles for each of the phases. Common choice of angles for the two phases are $0°$ and $90°$. For each angle we iteratively create lines and scan the entire projection space. The corresponding camera images are retrieved and a kink-detection algorithm is run to find the kink introduced in the line due to the wall corner. This facilities the breaking of the input lines into line subsegments.

Fig. 5 shows a captured image during the structured light registration phase. A white line is projected against black background and an image of the display area is captured by the camera. The following steps are needed to identify the kink and the individual segments.

Binarize the image: Convert the image to gray-scale and apply a fixed threshold to segment the white projected line from the background. We have seen that this is quite robust to general ambient lighting. Adaptive thresholds and other techniques from the image processing literature can be used to counter the effect of unpredictable lighting.

Line fitting: We use the Hough transform to fit lines to the binary image. The Hough transform returns all identified lines and we discard lines that lie too close to each other. Effectively, this ignores clutter on the display area. The standard Hough transform however identifies only the lines and not the line-segments and further processing is required.

Kink detection: The detected lines are now intersected to find the kink. We then sample points in the original image along each line on opposite directions of the detected kink to partition the line.

Using lines over points/blobs has the advantage that lines are easier to detect and to a greater accuracy. Blobs tend to get distorted due to perspective distortion.

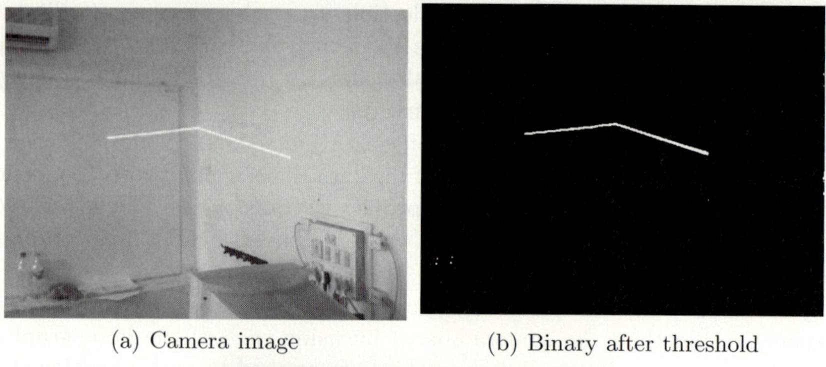

(a) Camera image   (b) Binary after threshold

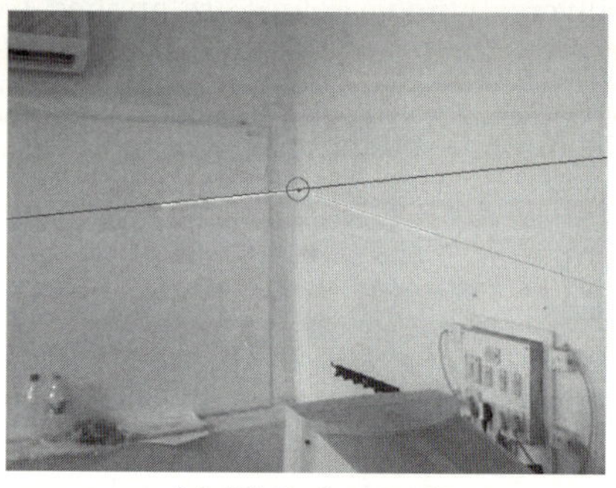

(c) Kink detected

Fig. 5. Kink detection in the structured light image

3.2   Point Correspondences and Homographies

Recall that at this stage, we have individual kinks but no line of separation. We also have false positives in the kinks. We do not know which points belong to which plane and their relationship.

Line fitting: The structured light registration returns the detected kinks and the corresponding lines and line-segments in the captured camera image. Least-squares line-fitting is applied on the detected kinks and an initial estimate is found. This is further refined by removing outliers from among the detected kinks by measuring the distance to the fitted line from each kink. Experiments have proven this to be quite robust because the data tends to have low noise except for a few random outliers. Fig. 6 shows a line fitted to the detected kink points after outliers have been removed. The edge detection is highly accurate with sub-pixel precision and this shows in the results where even a low-resolution camera is sufficient to correct a high-resolution display.

Partitioning the segments: Now that the intersection of the two planes has been identified in the camera image, the previously detected segments can be partitioned onto the each of the planes. Lines that haven't been broken into

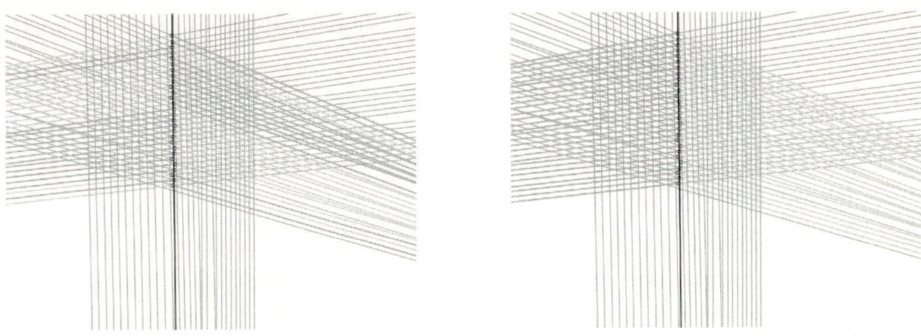

Fig. 6. (a) Fitting a line to the detected kinks, and (b) after cleaning up and reordering

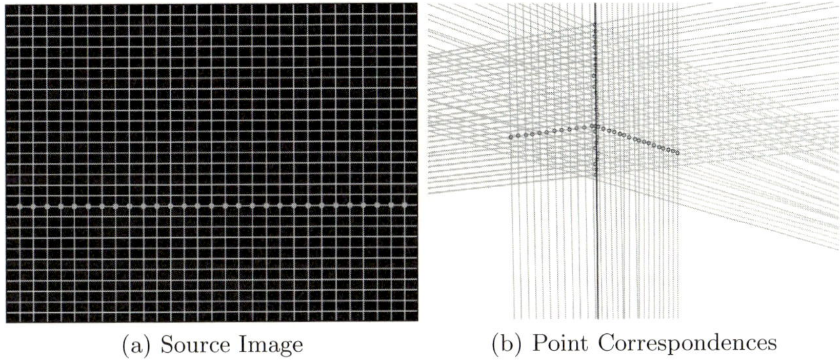

(a) Source Image   (b) Point Correspondences

Fig. 7. Point correspondences between projector and camera image

segments because they do not cross the edge are left as such. Fig. 6 shows the plotted lines color coded to identify the partition they are in.

Correspondence: The structured light registration was run at two orthogonal angles. We now find pairwise intersections between lines from each of the first and second phase respectively. Points of intersection in the source image are unambiguous, however the calculated point of intersection in the camera captured image, needs to be again tested for sanity. The point correspondences are also partitioned onto each of the planes depending on where they occur in the captured image. Fig. 7 shows a row of corresponding points between the projected image and the captured data.

Partitioning the image space: We now use the point correspondence data for each of the planes to evaluate a homography from the projector to the camera. Homographies $_p^1H_c$ and $_p^2H_c$ map points on the projector plane to the camera plane through each of the two planes of the display surface respectively. An important property of the homographies is that they must agree on the common intersecting lines of two planes, which was previously found. If L_c is the partitioning line in the camera image, then

$$L_p = {}^1_pH_c^{-T}L_c = {}^2_pH_c^{-T}L_c$$

3.3   Image Correction

We need to compute the inverse transformations corresponding to ${}^1_pH_c$ and ${}^2_pH_c$ to pre-warp the input image. Let us denote ${}^1_cH_p$ and ${}^1_cH_p$ as the corresponding inverse transforms. Now given an input image I, the warp H gives an image P to be projected, where $P(H * x) = I(x)$. However, the standard method for applying a warp is to once again find the inverse of the warping transform and use a linear (or bilinear or cubic) filtering to fill pixels in the destination image. For each pixel x' in the target image P, $P(x') = I(H^{-1} * x')$.

In our method, it reduces to using ${}^1_pH_c$ and ${}^2_pH_c$ for the warping. We thus generate images P_1 and P_2 from image I where $P_1(x') = I({}^1_pH_c * x')$, and $P_2(x') = I({}^2_pH_c * x')$.

All that remains is to composite together the two warped images at the partitioning line to generate the final image to be projected. In order to do this we generate a mask M where $M(x) = 1$, if x lies on the first plane in the projector coordinate frame; else $M(x) = 0$. So, in order to generate the final image P we do a masked copy of P_1 and P_2 using the mask M.

$$P(x') = P_1(x'), \text{ if } M(x') = 1 \quad P(x') = P_2(x'), \text{ if } M(x') = 0.$$

4   Implementation and Results

We have implemented the system in C++ using the OpenCV [7] libraries. OpenCV is a cross-platform library targeted towards work in computer vision and image processing. The following are the details of the hardware and the software:

Projector. Sharp XR-1S DLP projector with a native resolution of 800x600.
Camera. A 'Creative Live!' webcam with a maximum resolution of 640x480. Note that it does not match the projector resolution.
Platform. Linux 2.6 with Video4Linux, spca5xx usb-webcam drivers and ffmpeg. We have also tested the system on Microsoft Windows XP.

4.1   Results

Fig. 8 shows the image projected from the projector and that which is seen by the camera. The camera image is rectilinear with complete agreement at the seam of the two planes (seen in magenta). The seamlessness is a measure of the correctness of the edge-detection method and the homography estimation because the partitioning edge in the projector image can only be inferred using the two computed homographies. When the two homographies do not agree, we see a pair of lines instead of one. In addition the grid lines running across the two planes stay truly

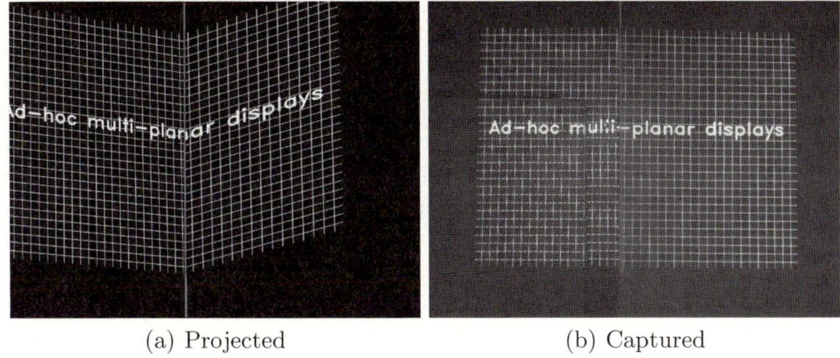

(a) Projected   (b) Captured

Fig. 8. The projected image and the image as seen from the camera

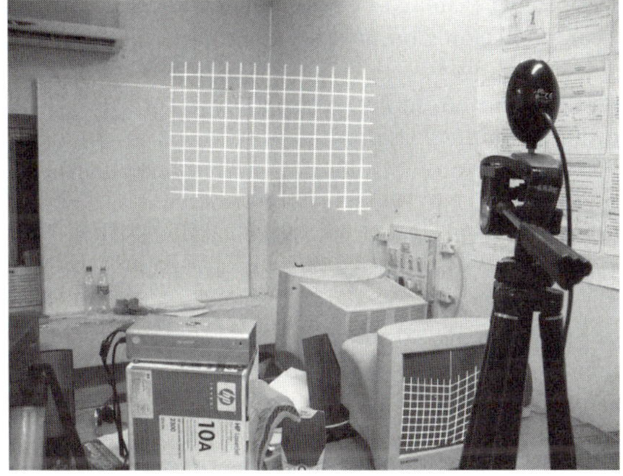

Fig. 9. The corrected scene

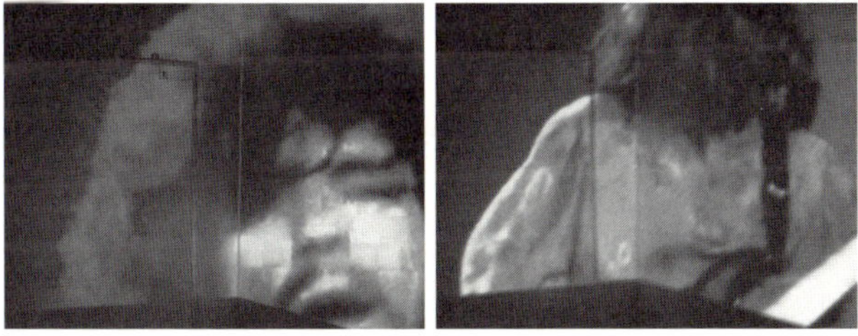

Fig. 10. Video excerpts on the wall corner

parallel. We have also demonstrated the system with video (Fig. 10) as input. Our experiments indicate a high degree of robustness and accuracy.

For completeness, we show (see Fig. 9) the motivating example of Fig. 1. The wall corner is now more usable as a projection area and for watching videos!

5 Conclusion

We have developed and implemented a method to display distortion free rectilinear images on wall corners and other multi-planar display surfaces. Results
show high accuracy and the method is robust to environmental factors apart
from high ambient lighting. A low-end usb-webcam is sufficient to correct a
high-resolution display and previously unusable display room areas now become
usable as display surfaces.

References

1. Hartley, R., Zisserman, A.: Multiple View Geometry in Computer Vision. Cambridge University Press (2000)
2. Raskar, R., Welch, G., Cutts, M., Lake, A., Stesin, L., Fuchs, H.: The office of the
   future: a unified approach to image-based modeling and spatially immersive displays.
   In: 25th annual conference on Computer graphics and interactive techniques. (1998)
   179–188
3. Raskar, R., Beardsley, P.: A self-correcting projector. In: Computer Vision and
   Pattern Recognition. Volume 2. (2001) 504–508
4. Heda, N.: Correcting projector display for multi planar surfaces. Master's thesis,
   Indian Institute of Technology, Bombay (2005)
5. Raskar, R., van Baar, J., Beardsley, P., Willwacher, T., Rao, S., Forlines, C.: iL-
   amps: geometrically aware and self-configuring projectors. In: ACM Trans. Graph.
   Volume 22. (2003) 809–818
6. Sukthankar, R., Stockton, R., Mullin, M.: Smarter presentations: Exploiting homography in camera-projector systems. In: International Conference on Computer
   Vision. Volume 1. (2001) 247–253
7. Intel: OpenCV: Open   Source   Computer   Vision   Library.
   `www.intel.com/research/mrl/research/opencv` (2004)

PACE: Polygonal Approximation of Thick Digital Curves Using Cellular Envelope

Partha Bhowmick[1], Arindam Biswas[1], and Bhargab B. Bhattacharya[2]

[1] Computer Science and Technology Department
Bengal Engineering and Science University, Shibpur, Howrah, India
{partha, abiswas}@becs.ac.in
[2] Advanced Computing and Microelectronics Unit
Indian Statistical Institute, Kolkata, India
bhargab@isical.ac.in

Abstract. A novel algorithm to derive an approximate cellular envelope of an arbitrarily thick digital curve on a 2D grid is proposed in this paper. The concept of "cellular envelope" is newly introduced in this paper, which is defined as the smallest set of cells containing the given curve, and hence bounded by two tightest (inner and outer) isothetic polygons on the grid. Contrary to the existing algorithms that use thinning as preprocessing for a digital curve with changing thickness, in our work, an optimal cellular envelope (smallest in the number of constituent cells) that entirely contains the given curve is constructed based on a combinatorial technique. The envelope, in turn, is further analyzed to determine polygonal approximation of the curve as a sequence of cells using certain attributes of digital straightness. Since a real-world curve/curve-shaped object with varying thickness and unexpected disconnectedness is unsuitable for the existing algorithms on polygonal approximation, the curve is encapsulated by the cellular envelope to enable the polygonal approximation. Owing to the implicit Euclidean-free metrics and combinatorial properties prevailing in the cellular plane, implementation of the proposed algorithm involves primitive integer operations only, leading to fast execution of the algorithm. Experimental results including CPU time reinforce the elegance and efficacy of the proposed algorithm.

1 Introduction

The subject on properties, characterizations, and representations of digital curves (DC) has been researched continuously since the debut of digitization of graphical objects and visual imageries [1], [2]. Nevertheless, in the abundance of various problems and their algorithms related with digital objects, polygonal approximation of a digital curve/object has received special attention for its efficient representation and for its potential applications in connection with analysis of digital images [3], [4], [5]. The set of straight edges of the concerned polygon carries a strong geometric property of the underlying objects, which can be used

P. Kalra and S. Peleg (Eds.): ICVGIP 2006, LNCS 4338, pp. 299–310, 2006.

for efficient high level description of the objects and for finding the similarity among different objects in the digital plane.

Since an optimal solution of polygonal approximation targeted to minimize the number of vertices, and space thereof, is computationally intensive, several heuristic and meta-heuristic approaches based on certain optimality criterion have been proposed over the last few decades, and some of these that have come up in recent times may be seen in [6], [7], [8], [9], [10], [11], etc. Further, there also exist various studies and comparisons of the proposed techniques, e.g., [12], [10], [13], to cite a few. This entire collection of polygonal approximation algorithms, however, consider the input digital curve to be strictly "irreducible"[1] (and connected thereof), failing which the algorithm may produce undesired results pertaining to polygonal approximation.

Hence, in case of a thick DC, thinning is required to ensure the property of "irreducibility" to the input DC so that it can qualify for the subsequent process of polygonal approximation. A thinning procedure, being plagued by asymmetric erosion in thick regions and shifting of junction/end points, and being liable to slow down the overall run time of the approximation process, is susceptible to deteriorate the results of approximation. Furthermore, the result goes on worsening if there occurs some missing grid points (pixels) in the input DC — which splits, therefore, into multiple DC's — producing several approximate polygons instead of a single polygon, thereby giving rise to misleading impression, and more specifically, posing severe problems in the subsequent applications. These problems have been tackled in our method using the novel concept of cellular envelope of an arbitrary digital curve whose thickness may vary non-uniformly. In our method, we consider that all possible thicknesses — including 0 (missing pixel) and 1 (one pixel thick) — may occur in a DC^2 when it is subject to polygonal approximation. The idea of outer and inner boundaries of polygonal regions is also present in rounding the intersection of two polygonal regions [14] and simplification envelopes [15].

A brief outline of the paper is as follows. In Sec. 2, we present a combinatorial algorithm to derive the cellular envelope of an arbitrary DC (stage I) using its inner and outer isothetic polygons [16], [17], [18], [19]. Sec. 3 enumerates some digital geometric properties of cellular straight segments (CSS), followed by the motivation and underlying principle for their extraction (stage II) from the cellular envelope of the input DC obtained in stage I. In Sec. 4, we present our method **PACE** and the two algorithms corresponding to stage I and stage II. Sec. 5 exhibits some test results on a curve-shaped object with varying curve thickness. Finally in Sec. 6, we summarize its strength and point out the future scope of improvements.

---

[1] A digital curve C is said to be "irreducible" if and only if removal of any grid point p in C makes C disconnected.

[2] Henceforth, in this paper, we use the term "DC" to denote a digital curve (reducible or irreducible) as well as a curve-shaped object that may contain multiple disconnected segments producing the *impression* of a single object.

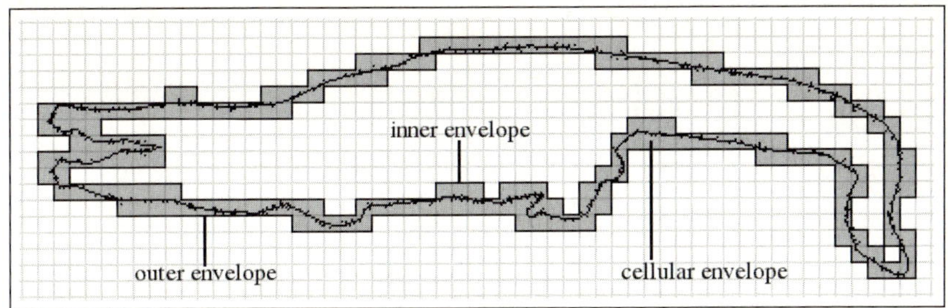

Fig. 1. Cellular envelope $\mathcal{E}(\mathcal{C},\mathcal{G})$ of a real-world (thick, rough, and reducible) curve-shaped object $\mathcal{C}$ for cell size $g = 8$

2   Cellular Envelope

If $\mathcal{C}$ be a given DC, and $\mathcal{G} = (\mathcal{H},\mathcal{V},g)$ be a set of uniformly spaced horizontal grid lines ($\mathcal{H}$) and vertical grid lines ($\mathcal{V}$) with spacing g, then the cellular envelope of $\mathcal{C}$, corresponding to the cellular plane defined by $\mathcal{G}$, is given by

$$
\begin{aligned}
\mathcal{E}(\mathcal{C},\mathcal{G}) &= \mathcal{E}_{out}(\mathcal{C},\mathcal{G}) \setminus \mathcal{E}_{in}(\mathcal{C},\mathcal{G}) \text{ if } \mathcal{C} \text{ is closed or contains a closed part,} \\
&= \mathcal{E}_{out}(\mathcal{C},\mathcal{G}) \text{ if } \mathcal{C} \text{ is open,}
\end{aligned}
\tag{1}
$$

where $\mathcal{E}_{out}(\mathcal{C},\mathcal{G})$ and $\mathcal{E}_{in}(\mathcal{C},\mathcal{G})$ represent the respective outer and inner envelopes of $\mathcal{C}$ w.r.t. $\mathcal{G}$, such that (i) each point $p \in \mathcal{C}$ should lie inside $\mathcal{E}_{out}(\mathcal{C},\mathcal{G})$ and outside $\mathcal{E}_{in}(\mathcal{C},\mathcal{G})$; (ii) each vertex of $\mathcal{E}(\mathcal{C},\mathcal{G})$ (and of $\mathcal{E}_{out}(\mathcal{C},\mathcal{G})$ and $\mathcal{E}_{in}(\mathcal{C},\mathcal{G})$, thereof) is in $\mathcal{G}$; and (iii) area of $\mathcal{E}(\mathcal{C},\mathcal{G})$ is minimized.

The cellular envelope of a DC (curve-shaped object) $\mathcal{C}$, which is rough, not irreducible, and disconnected (since it has uneven thickness and stray pixels) has been shown in Fig. 1. Note that, the cellular envelope $\mathcal{E}(\mathcal{C},\mathcal{G})$ shown in this figure is for cell size $g = 8$, and the envelope "tightly encloses" all the points of $\mathcal{C}$ with no points lying outside $\mathcal{E}(\mathcal{C},\mathcal{G})$.

2.1   Combinatorial Properties of a Cellular Envelope

Let $\mathcal{I}$ be the 2D image plane having height h and width w, and containing the entire object $\mathcal{C}$. Let $\alpha(i,j)$ be the point of intersection of the horizontal grid line $l_H : x = i \in \mathcal{H}$ and the vertical grid line $l_V : y = j \in \mathcal{V}$. Let $\mathcal{S}_{LT}$, $\mathcal{S}_{RT}$, $\mathcal{S}_{LB}$, and $\mathcal{S}_{RB}$ be the respective left-top, right-top, left-bottom, and right-bottom square cells with the common grid point $\alpha(i,j)$, and let $\alpha'(i, j + g)$ and $\alpha''(i + g, j)$ be the respective grid points lying immediate right and lying immediate below α, as shown in Fig. 2. We construct a binary matrix A_e (*edge matrix*) that contains $((w/g)(h/g + 1)) \times ((h/g)(w/g + 1))$ entries, each entry being in one-to-one correspondence with a particular edge of a particular cell. If an edge $e(\alpha,\beta)$ connecting two neighbor grid points α and β is intersected by the object $\mathcal{C}$, then the corresponding entry in A_e is '1', otherwise '0'.

Now, from A_e, we construct another binary matrix A_c (*cell matrix*) of size $(h/g) \times (w/g)$, in which each entry corresponds to a unique cell — the entry is

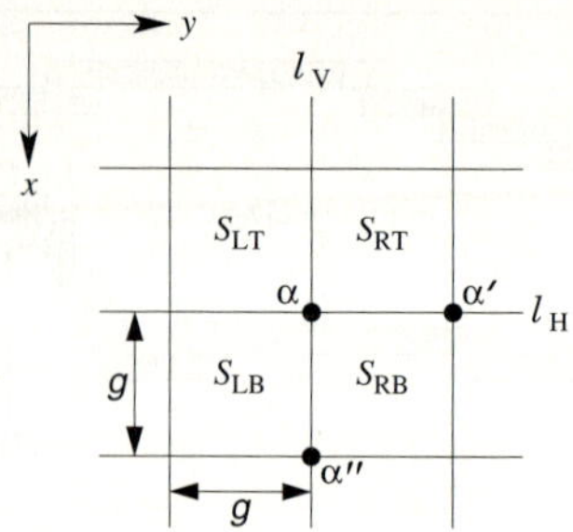

Fig. 2. Four cells with common vertex α

'1' if at least one of the four edges of the concerned cell is intersected by the object C, and is '0' otherwise — which is checked from the correspondence of its edge information in A_e.

Next, the candidature of α as a vertex of the (inner or outer) envelope is checked by looking at the combinatorial arrangements (w.r.t. object containments) of the four cells having common vertex α. There exist $2^4 = 16$ different arrangements of these four cells, since each cell has 2 possibilities ('0'/'1'). These 16 arrangements can be further reduced to 5 cases, where, a particular case $\mathbf{C}_q$, $q = 0, 1, \ldots, 4$, includes all the arrangements where exactly q out of these four cells has/have object containments (i.e., contain(s) parts of the object C), and the remaining (i.e., $4 - q$) ones have not. That is, the case in which the sum of the 4 bits in the corresponding entries in A_c is equal to q is represented by $\mathbf{C}_q$. Further, out of these 5 cases, cases $\mathbf{C}_1$ and $\mathbf{C}_3$ *always* and case $\mathbf{C}_2$ *conditionally* produce vertices of the inner/outer envelope, as explained below.

Case $\mathbf{C}_1$. $\binom{4}{1} = 4$ arrangements are possible where only one cell with vertex α contains C, i.e., exactly one of the corresponding four entries in A_c is '1' and each other is '0'. The envelope will have its one edge ending at α and the next edge starting from α. Hence, if α lies inside C, then it is a 270^0 vertex of $\mathcal{E}_{in}(C, \mathcal{G})$, and if α lies outside C, then it is a 90^0 vertex of $\mathcal{E}_{out}(C, \mathcal{G})$ (the angle $90^0/270^0$ of a vertex means its internal angle in the corresponding envelope).

Case $\mathbf{C}_2$. $\binom{4}{2} = 6$ arrangements are possible in which exactly two of the four cells contain C. If the cells containing C are diagonally opposite (2 out of 6 arrangements), then α is a vertex (90^0 for $\mathcal{E}_{in}(C, \mathcal{G})$ and 270^0 for $\mathcal{E}_{out}(C, \mathcal{G})$); otherwise α is an ordinary point on the envelope perimeter.

Case $\mathbf{C}_3$. $\binom{4}{3} = 4$ arrangements are possible for $q = 3$, where, out of the four cells, only one cell is free. In each such arrangement, α would be a 90^0 vertex for $\mathcal{E}_{in}(C, \mathcal{G})$) and a 270^0 vertex for $\mathcal{E}_{out}(C, \mathcal{G})$).

For case $\mathbf{C}_0$: $\binom{4}{0} = 1$ arrangement, α is just an ordinary grid point lying outside $\mathcal{E}_{out}(C, \mathcal{G})$ or inside $\mathcal{E}_{in}(C, \mathcal{G})$), whereas for case $\mathbf{C}_4$: $\binom{4}{4} = 1$ arrangement, α is a grid point included in C (since no two traversable edges are incident on it).

3   Cellular Straight Segments

There exist several works on constructs, properties, and applications of cell complexes and cellular straight segments (CSS), e.g., [20], [21], [22], [2], [23], in which the primal as well as many alternative definitions of CSS are found. For example, as indicated in [2], a CSS $\mathbf{C}$ can be defined as the minimal set of cells c specified by a real straight line segment $\mathbf{L}$ such that

$$\mathbf{L} \cap c \neq \emptyset, \ \forall \ c \in \mathbf{C}; \tag{2}$$

$$\text{and } \mathbf{L} \subset \mathbf{C}, \tag{3}$$

which makes its primal definition.

Another definition of CSS involving the Euclidean metric space is given in [20], in which it has been shown that a cellular curve $\mathbf{C}$ is a CSS if and only if there exists a direction θ and a pair of (parallel) lines in the real plane (tangential to and) containing $\mathbf{C}$, such that the distance between, and measured in the direction (say, $\theta_\perp$) perpendicular to, this pair of lines does not exceed the distance (along $\theta_\perp$) between the closest pair of parallel lines containing the square formed by $(2 \times 2 =) 4$ cells sharing a common vertex.

In a recent work [21], an Euclidean-free definition of CSS has been given in terms of "fully partitioned (finite) strings" $(S^{(0)})$ and "higher order derived strings" $(S^{(j)} : j \geq 1)$, the latter being derived iteratively from the preceding string (i.e., $S^{(j-1)}$) by replacing the majority symbol substrings of $S^{(j-1)}$ by its length, and by deleting the minority symbols of $S^{(j-1)}$. Subsequently, it has been shown that a string $S (= S^{(0)})$ represents a CSS, provided the jth order derived string of S exists for all $j \geq 0$.

Alternatively, in the perspective of digital straightness, if we consider the center points of these edge-connected cells as grid points, then it follows that a family of cells is edge-connected if and only if the set of center points of these cells is 4-connected. Thus CSS provides a suitable option — apart from that provided by digital straight line segments (DSS) [24] — for adjudging the straightness of a curve in the digital plane, as indicated in a contemporary work [2]. A linear off-line algorithm for CSS recognition, based on convex hull construction, is briefly sketched in [22]. In our work, we have designed an on-line algorithm to derive the set of CSS's from the cellular envelope of a curve-shaped object, which cannot be subject to direct DSS extraction/polygonal approximation due to its inherent nature of possessing varying thickness, as mentioned in Sec. 1.

We have considered the center of each cell for extracting the longest line segment iteratively in (a part of) a cellular envelope $\mathcal{E}(\mathcal{C}, \mathcal{G})$ corresponding to the given curve $\mathcal{C}$ and given cell size g imposed by the grid $\mathcal{G}$. We have used some digital geometric properties of DSS formulated and explained in [2], [24]. Before explaining our algorithm, the DSS properties (defined w.r.t. chain codes [25]) relevant to our work, which were established in [24], and later (see [2]) correlated with the other straightness options such as cellular straightness, are mentioned below.

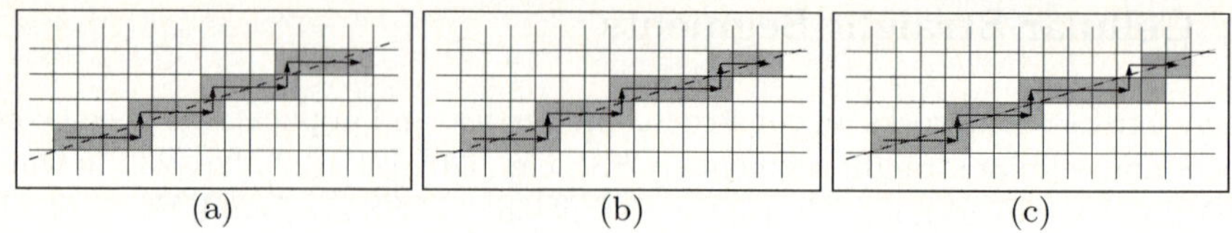

(a)   (b)   (c)

Fig. 3. Examples of cellular curves considered to explain the significance of straightness properties (R1)–(R4). Note that the directed path that traces the ordered set of centers of the cells shows the digital curve (DC) corresponding to a cellular curve. The curves in (a) and (b) are CSS's (the dashed lines show the corresponding real lines); but the curve in (c) is not, since there does not exist any real line that can pass through the set of cells defining this curve (see text for explanation).

(R1) The runs have at most two directions, differing by 90^0,[3] and for one of these directions, the run length must be 1.

(R2) The runs can have only two lengths, which are consecutive integers.

(R3) One of the run lengths can occur only once at a time.

(R4) For the run length that occurs in runs, these runs can themselves have only two lengths, which are consecutive integers; and so on.

Few examples of cellular curves/envelopes are shown in Fig. 3 to explain the significance of properties (R1)–(R4). For the curve in (a), if we consider the center of each cell as a grid point, as mentioned earlier, then its chain code is $000200020002000 = 0^3 2 0^3 2 0^3 2 0^3$, which consists of codes 0 and 2 only, and contains consecutive 0's but no two consecutive 2's, thereby satisfying property (R1). Regarding (R2), (R3), and (R4), since there is only one run length (of 0's), this curve trivially satisfies these three properties, and becomes a CSS. Similarly, since the curve in (b) has chain code $0^3 2 0^3 2 0^3 2 0^2$, which obeys (R1)–(R4), it is a CSS. On the contrary, the curve in (c) has chain code $0^3 2 0^3 2 0^5 2 0^1$, which satisfies (R1), but violates (R2) as 0 has non-consecutive run lengths (3 and 5) — even if we do not consider the leftmost and the rightmost run lengths (which are 3 and 1, respectively), and so it is not a CSS.

In our method for extraction of CSS from the cellular envelope $\mathcal{E}(\mathcal{C},\mathcal{G})$, we have adhered to the properties (R1–R4). In addition, we have considered that also the leftmost and the rightmost run lengths of a CSS should follow property (R2) (which is not mandatory as suggested in [24]).

4   Proposed Method (PACE)

The method on finding the (cellular) polygonal approximation of an object $\mathcal{C}$ consists of stage I and stage II. In stage I, we construct the cellular envelope $\mathcal{E}(\mathcal{C},\mathcal{G})$ based on the combinatorial arrangement of the cells containing $\mathcal{C}$ (Sec. 2).

---

[3] In our work, we have considered 4-connectivity of a DSS, i.e., having chain codes lying in the set $\{0, 2, 4, 6\}$, since the cells in the cellular envelope $\mathcal{E}(\mathcal{C},\mathcal{G})$ obtained for the curve $\mathcal{C}$ (Sec. 2) are connected in 4-neighborhood. In a DSS with 8-connectivity, however, the runs would have directions differing by 45^0 as stated in [24].

STEP 1.   Initialize each entry in A_e and each entry in A_c with '0'.

STEP 2.   DFS-VISIT on C starting from p using 8-connectivity to reach the nearest cell edge e_p of G.

STEP 3.   DFS-VISIT on A_e starting from the entry $A_e(e_p)$ corresponding to e_p in A_e using 4-connectivity (of '1's in A_e) to assign:
'1' to the entry in A_e corresponding to each cell edge e intersected by C, and
'1' to the entry in A_c corresponding to each of the two cells with e as the common edge.

STEP 4.   DFS-VISIT on A_c starting from some cell (e.g., c_p, the left adjacent cell of e_p) of the cellular envelope formed by the '1's obtained in step 3 using 4-connectivity (of '1's in A_c); and check whether the entry $A_c(c)$ corresponding to the cell c currently under DFS-VISIT satisfies at least one of the following two conditions:
(i) both the left and the right adjacent entries of $A_c(c)$ are '1's;
(ii) both the bottom and the top adjacent entries of $A_c(c)$ are '1's.
If (i) or/and (ii) is/are true, then terminate the DFS-VISIT, since the current cell c lies either on a horizontal edge/part (when (i) satisfies) or on a vertical edge/part (when (ii) satisfies) of the cellular envelope of C; and declare c as the seed cell c_0 for stage II.

STEP 5.   If no seed cell c_0 is found in step 4, then the cell size is not sufficiently large compared to the (minimum) thickness of the input curve C. Hence the user may be asked to increase the cell size (i.e., grid separation g); alternatively, an arbitrary cell of the envelope may be considered to be the seed cell c_0.

Fig. 4. Algorithm FIND-CELLULAR-ENVELOPE(C, G, p) in stage I

In stage II, we analyze the cells of $\mathcal{E}(C, G)$ to extract the straight pieces from $\mathcal{E}(C, G)$, considering the center of each cell of $\mathcal{E}(C, G)$ as a grid point and using the straightness properties (Sec. 3).

4.1   Stage I: Finding the Cellular Envelope

We consider any point $p \in C$ as the start point defining the object C. For the time being, consider that C is connected in 8-neighborhood. Then using DFS-VISIT (Depth First Search algorithm [26]), we can reach the nearest edge e_p of a cell that intersects C. Starting from e_p, using DFS-VISIT on the edges of the cells, we visit those cell edges that are intersected by $\mathcal{E}$; this procedure helps us in constructing the edge matrix A_e and the cell matrix A_c (Sec. 2), which are finally used to obtain $\mathcal{E}(C, G)$. The major steps of the algorithm FIND-CELLULAR-ENVELOPE(C, G, p) to find the cellular envelope of a connected (and of uniform or non-uniform thickness) object C w.r.t. the cellular array imposed by the grid G is given in Fig. 4.

In case C has some missing points/pixels, i.e., possesses disconnectedness, then it may happen that none of the edges of a cell is intersected by C, although C is

---

STEP 1. Traverse (cell-wise) towards left and towards right from c_0 to extract all possible pairs of CSS starting from c_0, such that
(i) the chain code of each CSS, and
(ii) the combined chain code of the two CSS's
in each pair are in conformity with properties (R1)–(R4);

STEP 2. Find a/the pair of CSS that has maximum sum of lengths; merge this pair into a single CSS, namely C_1;
declare c_0 and c_1 as the left and the right terminal cells of C_1;
store (the centers of) c_0 and c_1 in the ordered set T.

STEP 3. Start from c_1 to extract the next (longest) CSS, $C_2 := (c_1, c_2)$, with terminal cells c_1 and c_2;
store c_2 in T; and mark the cells defining C_2 as VISITED.

STEP 4. Repeat STEP 3 starting from the last entry (i.e., terminal cell) in T to get the CSS's defining $\mathcal{E}$ until all cells of $\mathcal{E}$ are VISITED (using DFS-VISIT).
Note: (i) If a CSS has both its terminal cells in the 4-neighborhood of another (longer) CSS, then the former (shorter) CSS is not included in T (Fig. 6(a)). (ii) For a bifurcating/branching CSS, we store both its terminal cells in T (Fig. 6(b)).

STEP 5. Declare T as the polygonal approximation of the cellular envelope $\mathcal{E}$.

Fig. 5. Algorithm FIND-CSS$(\mathcal{E}, c_0)$ in stage II

contained in that cell. To circumvent this problem, we have to directly construct the cell matrix A_c, without constructing A_e, which would, however, increase the time complexity (and the run time, thereof) of stage I. Further, if the curve possesses too much gap/disconnectedness, so that the gap is even larger than the cell size, then this may result to gap (in the edge-connectivity) of the cells constituting the envelope $\mathcal{E}(\mathcal{C}, \mathcal{G})$, which gets fragmented into two or more pieces, thereby producing faulty results. Choosing an appropriate cell size is, therefore, necessary to obtain the desired cellular envelope of a disconnected DC in stage I.

4.2 Stage II: Finding the Cellular Straight Segments

In stage II, the algorithm FIND-CSS$(\mathcal{E}, c_0)$[4], given in Fig. 5, extracts the ordered set of CSS's from the cellular envelope $\mathcal{E}$ as follows. W.l.o.g., since in stage I, the seed cell c_0 lies on a horizontal part (or on a vertical part, or on a thick part) of $\mathcal{E}$, we negotiate two traversals (STEP 1) — one towards left and the other towards right of c_0 — to obtain two CSSs with complying straightness such that the sum of their lengths is maximal, and merge these two to get the first CSS, C_1, to be included in the ordered set T of terminal cells (STEP 2). The starting cell for extracting the next CSS (STEP 3) from the cellular envelope is, therefore, considered to be the right terminal cell c_1 of C_1. We use the algorithm DFS-VISIT [26] to explore the cells constituting the envelope and to extract the CSSs, whose terminal cells are finally reported in T.

---

[4] Now onwards, we denote the cellular envelope of $\mathcal{C}$ by $\mathcal{E}$ for simplicity.

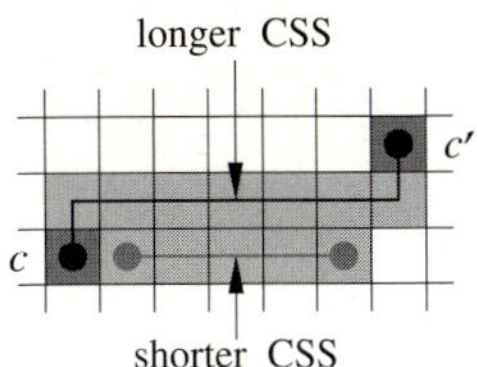
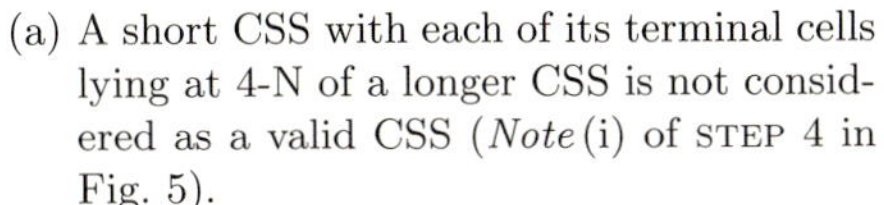
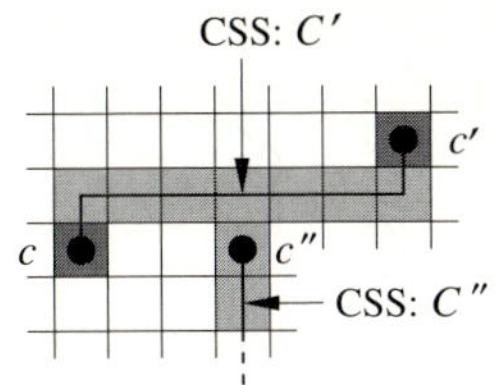

(a) A short CSS with each of its terminal cells lying at 4-N of a longer CSS is not considered as a valid CSS (*Note* (i) of STEP 4 in Fig. 5).

(b) For a branching CSS, C'', each of its terminal cells (one is c'' and the other not shown) is stored in T (*Note* (ii) of STEP 4 in Fig. 5).

Fig. 6. Inclusion and exclusion of terminal cell(s) of CSS in T

Time complexity. If N be the number of points defining the curve $\mathcal{C}$, then its envelope $\mathcal{E}$ consists of $O(N/g)$ cells. Due to DFS-VISITs, therefore, the time complexity in stage I is bounded by $O(N/g)$. In stage II, extraction of each CSS C_i takes $O(|C_i|)$ time, where $|C_i|$ is the number of cells defining C_i. Hence, the time complexity to extract all CSS's in step II is $O(\sum |C_i|) = O(N/g)$, which gives the total time complexity of **PACE** as $O(N/g)$.

5   Experiments and Results

We have implemented the two algorithms, namely FIND-CELLULAR-ENVELOPE and FIND-CSS, that make the proposed method **PACE** for polygonal approximation of an arbitrarily thick DC, in C in SunOS Release 5.7 Generic of Sun_Ultra 5_10, Sparc, 233 MHz, and have tested various digital curves of arbitrary shape, changing thickness, and irregular connectedness. It may be mentioned here that, since the concept of a cellular polygon introduced in this work is entirely new, and no other work on cellular polygon exists at present, we could not have a comparative study of our method in this paper.

The result for an (non-thinned) edge map of a "duck" is shown in Fig. 7, which testifies the elegance of **PACE** in deriving the cellular polygon corresponding to a DC. It may may be noticed in this figure that, some of the cells in the envelope $\mathcal{E}$ have not been included in any CSS; because in the algorithm FIND-CSS, we have considered the (terminal cells of) each locally longest CSS to be included in P (see the *Note* in STEP 4). But when there is a bifurcation/self-intersection (e.g., in and around the root of its tail) or a sharp bend (e.g., at the tip of its beak), the cellular envelope (Fig. 7(b)) contains several cells across its thickness, which may cause error in the polygonal approximation as manifested in Fig. 7(d) in the part of the polygon corresponding to the region in and around the tail root. Hence a proper value of the cell size, g, is mandatory to ensure a good cellular envelope corresponding to a DC, and a good polygonal approximation thereof.

The major strength of the proposed method is the inherent nature of Euclidean-free metrics and operations involved in both the stages. This imparts high

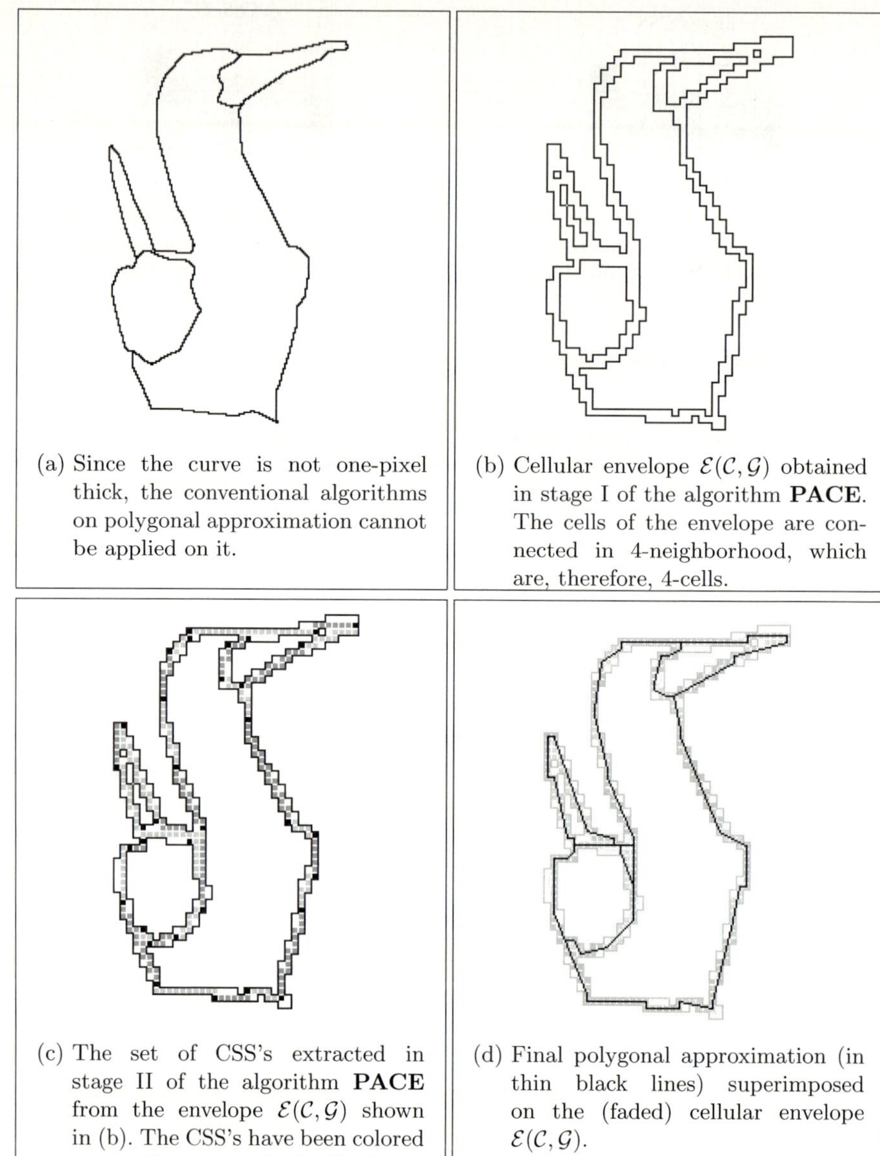

(a) Since the curve is not one-pixel thick, the conventional algorithms on polygonal approximation cannot be applied on it.

(b) Cellular envelope $\mathcal{E}(\mathcal{C}, \mathcal{G})$ obtained in stage I of the algorithm **PACE**. The cells of the envelope are connected in 4-neighborhood, which are, therefore, 4-cells.

(c) The set of CSS's extracted in stage II of the algorithm **PACE** from the envelope $\mathcal{E}(\mathcal{C}, \mathcal{G})$ shown in (b). The CSS's have been colored gray with the terminal cell of each CSS shown in black.

(d) Final polygonal approximation (in thin black lines) superimposed on the (faded) cellular envelope $\mathcal{E}(\mathcal{C}, \mathcal{G})$.

Fig. 7. Results of algorithm **PACE** for cell size $g = 4$ on a curve-shaped digital object $\mathcal{C}$ of nonuniform thickness representing the edge map of a "duck"

execution speed to the implementation of **PACE**, which is reflected in the respective CPU times presented in Table 1. Further, with increase in the cell size g, the compression ratio (CR) improves consistently, but the quality of approximation deteriorates, as evidenced by the average errors (measured w.r.t. both

Table 1. Results of **PACE** on the "duck" image (1748 pixels), shown in Fig. 7, for different grid sizes (g)

g	$|\mathcal{E}|$	$|P|$	CR	avg. error		CPU time (secs.)		
				$d_\perp^{(\mathcal{E})}$	$d_\perp^{(P)}$	$\mathcal{E}$	P	total
2	703	130	0.074	0.87	0.92	0.026	0.227	0.253
3	445	93	0.053	1.25	1.34	0.019	0.142	0.161
4	382	53	0.030	1.49	1.97	0.014	0.129	0.143
8	191	22	0.013	2.85	3.36	0.006	0.108	0.114
12	125	18	0.010	4.03	5.58	0.004	0.071	0.075

$|\mathcal{E}|$ = number of cells in $\mathcal{E}$; $|P|$ = number of terminal cells in P; CR $(= |P|/|\mathcal{C}|)$ = compression ratio; $d_\perp^{(\mathcal{E})}$ = isothetic error averaged over (centers of) all cells of $\mathcal{E}$ from (their corresponding nearest points of) $\mathcal{C}$; $d_\perp^{(P)}$ = isothetic error averaged over all terminal cells in P from $\mathcal{C}$, where $\max\{|x_1 - x_2|, |x_2, y_2|\}$ is the isothetic distance between two points (x_1, y_1) and (x_2, y_2).

$\mathcal{E}$ and P) of the curve $\mathcal{C}$ in this table. This again indicates that the cell size g should be suitably chosen to get an acceptable tradeoff in the approximation.

6 Conclusion and Future Work

We have presented here the novel concept of approximating a curve-shaped digital object by a cellular polygon. The algorithm is marked by its **(i)** indifference to change in thickness of the input DC, **(ii)** innovative combinatorial approach to construct the optimum cellular envelope for the given DC, **(iii)** use of straightness properties inherited from digital geometry, **(iv)** independency to Euclidean paradigm, and **(v)** realization without any floating point operation, which collectively make it robust, speedy, and efficient. Presently, we are experimenting on the nature of variation of the cellular envelope and the resulting polygon of a DC with its registration (both translation and rotation) w.r.t. grid, which will be reported shortly.

References

1. Klette, R., Rosenfeld, A.: Digital Geometry: Geometric Methods for Digital Image Analysis. Morgan Kaufmann (2004)
2. Klette, R., Rosenfeld, A.: Digital straightness: A review. Discrete Applied Mathematics **139** (2004) 197–230
3. Aken, J.R.V., Novak, M.: Curve-drawing algorithms for raster display. ACM Trans. Graphics **4** (1985) 147–169
4. Attneave, F.: Some informational aspects of visual perception. Psychological Review **61** (1954) 183–193
5. Imai, H., Iri, M.: Computational geometric methods for polygonal approximations of a curve. CVGIP **36** (1986) 31–41

6. Perez, J.C., Vidal, E.: Optimum polygonal approximation of digitized curves. PRL **15** (1994) 743–750
7. Schröder, K., Laurent, P.: Efficient polygon approximations for shape signatures. In: Proc. ICIP. (1999) 811–814
8. Schuster, G.M., Katsaggelos, A.K.: An optimal polygonal boundary encoding scheme in the rate distortion sense. IEEE Trans. Circuits and Systems for Video Technology **7** (1998) 13–26
9. Tanigawa, S., Katoh, N.: Polygonal curve approximation using grid points with application to a triangular mesh generation with small number of different edge lengths. In: Proc. AAIM 2006. (2006) 161–172
10. Teh, C.H., Chin, R.T.: On the detection of dominant points on digital curves. IEEE Trans. PAMI **2** (1989) 859–872
11. Yin, P.Y.: Ant colony search algorithms for optimal polygonal approximation of plane curves. Pattern Recognition **36** (2003) 1783–1797
12. Rosin, P.L.: Techniques for assessing polygonal approximation of curves. IEEE Trans. PAMI **19** (1997) 659–666
13. Yin, P.Y.: A new method for polygonal approximation using genetic algorithms. PRL **19** (1998) 1017–1026
14. Devillers, O.: Inner and outer rounding of set operations on lattice polygonal regions. In: Proc. 20th Ann. Symp. Computational Geometry (2004) 429–437
15. Cohen, J., et al.: Simplification Envelopes. In: Proc. SIGGRAPH (1996) 119–128
16. Bhattacharya, P., Rosenfeld, A.: Contour codes of isothetic polygons. CVGIP **50** (1990) 353–363
17. Bhowmick, P., Biswas, A., Bhattacharya, B.B.: Isothetic polygons of a 2D object on generalized grid. In: Proc. PReMI 2005. LNCS **3776**. 407-412
18. Biswas, A., Bhowmick, P., Bhattacharya, B.B.: **TIPS**: On finding a **T**ight **I**sothetic **P**olygonal **S**hape covering a 2d object. In: Proc. SCIA 2005. LNCS **3540**. 930–939
19. Yu, B., Lin, X., Wu, Y., Yuan, B.: Isothetic polygon representation for contours. CVGIP **56** (1992) 264–268
20. Fam, A., Sklansky, J.: Cellularly straight images and the hausdorff metric. In: Proc. Conf. on Pattern Recognition and Image Processing. (1977) 242–247
21. Geer, P., McLaughlin, H.W.: Cellular lines: An introduction. Discrete Mathematics and Theoretical Computer Science (2003) 167–178
22. Kim, C.E.: On cellular straight line segments. Computer Graphics Image Processing **18** (1982) 369–391
23. Klette, R.: Cell complexes through time. In: Proc. Vision Geometry. Volume IX of SPIE 4117. (2000) 134–145
24. Rosenfeld, A.: Digital straight line segments. IEEE Transactions on Computers **23** (1974) 1264–1268
25. Freeman, H.: On the encoding of arbitrary geometric configurations. IRE Trans. Electronic Computers **EC-10** (1961) 260–268
26. Cormen, T.H., Leiserson, C.E., Rivest, R.L.: Introduction to Algorithms. Prentice Hall of India Pvt. Ltd. (2000)

Texture Guided Realtime Painterly Rendering of Geometric Models

Shiben Bhattacharjee[1],[*] and Neeharika Adabala[2]

[1] CVIT, International Institute of Information Technology Hyderabad
[2] Microsoft Research India

Abstract. We present a real-time painterly rendering technique for geometric models. The painterly appearance and the impression of geometric detail is created by effectively rendering several brush strokes. Unlike existing techniques, we use the textures of the models to come up with the features and the positions of strokes in 3D object space. The strokes have fixed locations on the surfaces of the models during animation, this enables frame to frame coherence. We use vertex and fragment shaders to render strokes for real-time performance. The strokes are rendered as sprites in two-dimensions, analogous to the way artists paint on canvas. While animating, strokes may get cluttered since they are closely located on screen. Existing techniques ignore this issue; we address it by developing a level of detail scheme that maintains a uniform stroke density in screen space. We achieve painterly rendering in real-time with a combination of object space positioning and image space rendering of strokes. We also maintain consistency of rendering between frames . We illustrate our method with images and performance results.

Keywords: Non-Photo-realistic Rendering, Real-time Painterly Rendering, Stroke Based Rendering, Texture Guided Strokes, Levels of Detail of Strokes.

1   Introduction

Paintings are often used to depict ideas. The aesthetics and expressiveness of paintings enables effective capture of the intentions of the artist. Animations are therefore often created in painterly style. In recent times computers are often used to generate the environments in cartoon based entertainment. (Eg. Titan A.E., Transformers etc.) Use of computers saves artists from the tedious need to create various views of the same static environment, but it leads to a visual disparity between the hand drawn objects and the environment as computer generated images appear synthetic and lack abstraction. Painterly rendering, a non-photorealistic rendering technique, can harmonize the composition of hand drawn elements and the computer modeled environment. Therefore, painterly rendering has been the focus of several graphics researchers.

More recently games depicting cartoon like appearance based upon cartoon serials/movies (Eg. Teenage Mutant Ninja Turtles, 2004) have been made. These

---

[*] This work was done while being an intern in Microsoft Research India.

P. Kalra and S. Peleg (Eds.): ICVGIP 2006, LNCS 4338, pp. 311–320, 2006.

games could benefit from real-time painterly rendering. When painterly rendering is applied in gaming scenarios one has to address two key issues namely, frame to frame coherence, and level of detail management. In this paper we present a real-time painterly rendering algorithm that addresses theses issues. Existing painterly rendering techniques for animations employ geometry alone for placement of strokes and ignore textures that are a crucial part of models. They also do not address the issue of cluttered strokes. We present a painterly rendering technique that uses texture guided stroke placement on models and handles problems due to cluttering of strokes.

The organization of the rest of the paper is as follows: We briefly describe related work in the following section. We outline our technique in the section 3 and give details on stroke position computation, classification of strokes and rendering of strokes. We also describe a technique to address problem of stroke cluttering. Illustrations of our results and the performance of our system are discussed in section 4. We conclude with a discussion on the aesthetic considerations and technical aspects in section 5.

2   Related Work

Abstract representation of still images was introduced by Haeberli [1], he uses image color gradient and user interactivity for painting. Hertzmann [2] places curved brush strokes of multiple sizes on images for painterly rendering. The technique fills color by using big strokes in the middle of a region and uses progressively smaller strokes as one approaches the edges of the region. Shiraishi and Yamaguchi [3] improves the performance of above method by approximating the continuous strokes by placement of rectangular strokes discreetly along the edges to create painterly appearance. Santella and DeCarlo[4] used eye tracking data to get points of focus on images and create painterly rendering with focus information. All these techniques work well on single images but they usually involve iterative (optimization) techniques that make them cumbersome for real-time applications (see [5]). Also if they are applied on each frame of an animation independently, it often leads to flickering of strokes due to incoherence of strokes between frames.

Painterly rendering for animation was introduced in Meier's work [6] which focuses on eliminating shower door effect and achieve frame to frame coherence. Non existence of programmable graphics hardware, however, made the technique non-realtime. Also the method was limited to fetch stroke properties from geometry. Klein et al. [7] used realtime creation of painterly textures for painterly rendering using image based rendering algorithms for simple geometric models. Their algorithm lacks frame to frame coherence. Haller and Sperl [8] describes a realtime painterly process inspired by Meier [6]. Their approach makes the painterly rendering process work in real-time with the help of programmable graphics hardware. The method extracts stroke properties from geometry alone, and it does not address the problem of cluttering of strokes with changes in viewpoint.

3   Our Approach

A painting is created by placing several brush strokes of various shapes at specific
locations on the canvas. In our approach we use the textures of models to enable
us to select the number, location and shape of strokes to render. The position
of the strokes are defined by the image space coordinates of a pixel in a texture
and property of the stroke is stored as the pixel value at that location. We
call the resulting image as a **feature image**. The stroke locations are in the
image/texture space; we transform the 2D positions of stroke locations to 3D
object space coordinates for painterly rendering.

The outline of the algorithm is as follows:

```
Start:
  Load various stroke textures;
  Load Model Information;
  Extract features from Model's textures;
  Transform features from Image to 3D space;
  For each frame:
    PASS1:
      Draw the object;
      Save the screen as a texture;
      Save the depth information as a texture;
    PASS2:
      Draw Edge strokes;
      Draw Filling strokes;
      Draw Feature strokes;
End
```

In each frame we render the object/scene and save it as a **reference image**. We
also save the depth information as a **depth texture**. In the next pass, we render
sprites at the stroke locations using vertex and fragment shaders. These brush-
strokes are categorized based on the details given in section 3.1. The sprites are
texture mapped with brush stroke textures, alpha blended and associated with
color information from the reference image. The depth texture is used to decide
the visibility of sprites/strokes. When a face of the object occupies less area in
the screen space, the strokes in that region become cluttered and overlap. We use
levels of detail to overcome the cluttering. The level of detail scheme, however,
has a popping artifact during transitions. We develop an approach for smooth
level of detail change, the details of which are presented in section 3.3.

3.1   Feature Extraction from Textures

This section describes the technique we use to obtain features from textures.
When painting, one has to decide locations of strokes, number of strokes, shapes
of strokes and orientations of strokes. These properties are gathered from the
textures associated with the model. For each texture, example figure 1(a), we
use a simple Sobel's edge detector [9] to get the edges and store them in the
gray-scale feature image. Then this edge map is used to get another set of edges

running parallel along the detected edges. These parallel edges store the angle along which the edge is oriented at each pixel as the pixel value as shown in figure 1(b). The angles in the range $[0, \pi]$, are discretized and scaled in the range $[100, 200]$ as the pixel value in the feature image. We then stipple the lines by running a mask on the lines and nullifying a number of surrounding pixels. The size of the mask is a parameter that decides the concentration of strokes while rendering since each non-null pixel location represents a stroke. A smaller size implies a greater concentration of stroke locations, which in turn implies a larger number of strokes. The generated points on the original edges have pixel value 255. Strokes at these locations are called **edge strokes**. Strokes on the points, which are on the lines parallel to the edges, are called **feature strokes**. In the remaining empty area we distribute points with a pixel value 64, with random spacing as shown in figure 1(c). These strokes are called **filling strokes**.

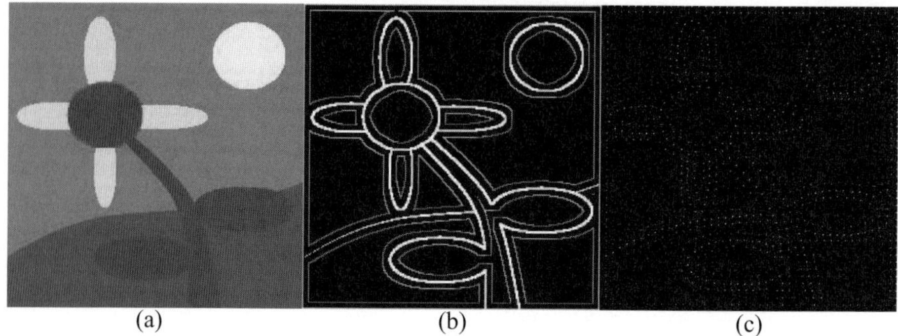

Fig. 1. (a) Example texture; (b) Detected Edges and parallel edges storing the orientation; (c) Final **feature image** giving stroke locations; here different pixel values indicate whether the strokes are edge, feature or filling strokes

3.2   Stroke Location Transfer from Image to Object Space

As a pre-processing step we transform the positions of pixels in the feature image to object space depending upon which face the strokes are stuck to. We use simple geometric transformation equations to solve this issue. We find the 3D points (x, y, z) for any pixel (X, Y) as

$$aX + bY + k = x$$

$$cX + dY + k = y$$

$$eX + fY + k = z$$

For any 3 pixels in the texture $(X_1, Y_1), (X_2, Y_2), (X_3, Y_3)$, if we know 3 object coordinates $(x_1, y_1, z_1), (x_2, y_2, z_2), (x_3, y_3, z_3)$ (Eg. 3 corners of a triangular face), we can solve the equations for a, b, c, d, e, f. We save stroke positions and their properties for each face.

3.3   Rendering

Rendering consists of two passes; the first pass renders the object and saves it on a texture as the reference image. The second pass involves calculation of a Level of Detail (LOD) factor and a blending factor for each face depending upon its screen occupancy. Less the occupancy, lower the level of detail associated with the face during rendering. The order of rendering strokes is based on their category. Rendering of some strokes is skipped based on the LOD.

Creation of Reference Image. We render the textured geometric model, and copy the output to a texture example figure 2(a). The depth information is copied to a depth texture.

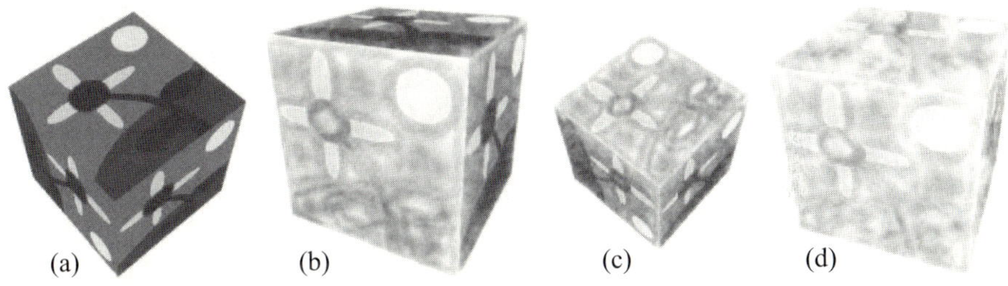

Fig. 2. (a) Reference Image; (b) Cluttered strokes of oblique faces; (c) Cluttered strokes when far; (d) No clutter when with LOD scheme

Calculation of Levels of Detail. We see a cluttering of strokes, in figure 2(c), when the geometric model is distant. We calculate the distance of the camera from each face. This distance d is used to calculate LOD indicator l_d which is the level of detail due to distance, as $N(d - min)/(max - min)$ where max and min are the maximum and minimum distance respectively the object travels from the eye position, and N is the number of LODs available. When the face is at min distance to camera, l_d equals 0 and when the face is at max distance to camera, l_d equals N.

However, faces also cover less screen space when they are nearly parallel to the viewing direction as shown in figure 2(b). To address this issue, we calculate another LOD indicator, level of detail due to orientation l_o, as $l_o = (1 - |n.v|)N$, where n is the normal of the face and v is the unit view vector. As per dot product's nature, $l_o = N$ when n and v are perpendicular to each other i.e. face is completely out of view, and $l_o = 0$ when n and v are equal i.e. face completely faces you.

Thus we use $l_d = 0, l_o = 0$ as the highest LOD indicators and $l_d = N, l_o = N$ as the lowest LOD indicators. We take the weighted mean of the two and use the value for assigning an LOD factor l and blending factor α to the face as follows:

$$l = [w_o l_o + w_d l_d], \alpha = 1 - \{w_o l_o + w_d l_d\}$$

where w_d and w_o are user decided weights for farness and orientation respectively. We skip 2^l number of strokes while drawing stokes for a face. For a stroke with index i in a face, if the expression $mod(i, 2^{(l+1)})$ returns a non null value, means that this stroke is skipped when LOD changes for this face. We multiply α with this stroke's opacity, so that it gradually becomes transparent as the face approaches the next LOD transition. When the face shifts to the next LOD, this stroke is dropped but we do not see any popping artifact since it gradually becomes totally transparent. Ours strokes do not clutter, example figure 2(d). The calculations involving assignment of blending factor is done on the GPU with the help of vertex shaders explained in more detail in the next section.

Rendering of Strokes. We render the edge strokes first. For each edge stroke we pass on the edge stroke location to the vertex shader 4 times with 4 texture coordinates of a randomly chosen perturber texture. Sample edge stroke textures are shown in figure 3(a). This randomness is pre-computed to avoid inconsis-

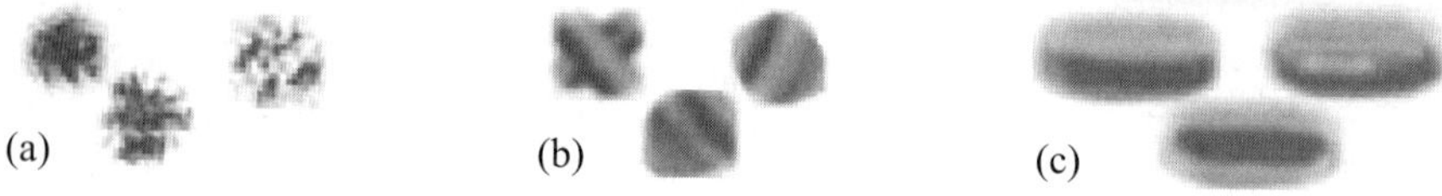

(a)   (b)   (c)

Fig. 3. (a) Edge Stroke textures; (b) Filling Stroke textures; (c) Feature Stroke textures

tency between frames. A vertex shader, which we call **VS1** for future reference, calculates the sprite coordinates using the texture coordinates. We calculate the sprite coordinates after we have applied the model-view transformation to the stroke location. To maintain constant sprites size, we calculate the sprite coordinates after we have projected the stroke location. A fragment shader, which we call **FS1** for future reference, picks color information from the edge stroke texture; uses the red stream as the amount of perturbation in x axis direction and blue stream as the amount of perturbation in y axis direction, of the location of pixel of reference image (see figure 4(b)).

$$p_x = 2C_r - 1, p_y = 2C_b - 1$$

$$O_c = I_c T_{x+kp_x, y+kp_y}$$

where p is the disturbance with a scale k in the reference texture's T coordinates x, y at that fragment location, C is the color of the stroke texture at that fragment location and I_c is the optional input color for the whole stroke. O_c is output fragment color of the **FS1**. Also we use the blending factor and multiply it with the opacity of the stroke as explained in the previous section. Now using the filling stroke coordinates and filling stroke textures randomly chosen from available ones as show in figure 3(b). We render the filling strokes as sprites. We use the same vertex shader **VS1** but a different fragment shader, which we call **FS2** for future reference, since we want to perturb the color picked up from the reference texture. **FS2** uses the filling stroke texture's color streams to

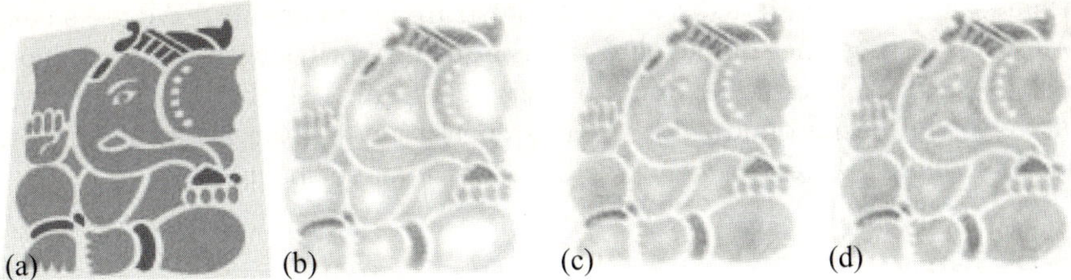

(a)   (b)   (c)   (d)

Fig. 4. Lord Ganesha; Using (a) Reference texture, (b) Rendering of edge strokes followed by (c) Rendering of filling strokes and then (d) Finally rendering of feature strokes to get the final output

change the color of the background reference texture at that fragment location (see figure 4(c)).

$$p = 2C - 1$$

$$O_c = I_c(T_{x,y} + kp)$$

where the notations mean the same as explained earlier. **FS2** does the same job as **FS1** regarding the blending factor. Next we use feature stroke coordinates and feature stroke textures randomly chosen from available ones to render the feature strokes as sprites. Sample feature strokes are shown in figure 3(c). We use a different vertex shader, which we call **VS2** for future reference. **VS2** incorporates not only calculation of sprite coordinates but also rotation of the sprite in the image space according to feature information stored along with the stroke coordinate. The rotated strokes are rotated by another angle which is due to the animation of the model. We use **FS2** for the later part of the processing of this stroke. Figure 4(d), is a example of the output when all the strokes are rendered. The strokes are alpha blended, therefore order of blending is important. This is where depth texture comes in picture. An example depth texture is shown in figure 5(a). In **FS1** and **FS2** we test the depth of the pixel to be less than or equal to the depth value at that location in the depth texture, if the pixel does

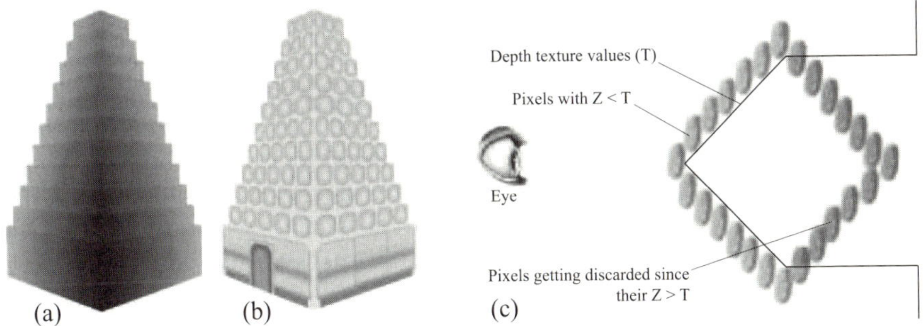

(a)   (b)   (c)

Fig. 5. (a) A sample depth texture for (b) A reference image; (c) Only pixels of strokes with depth less than depth texture value pass

not pass the condition, it is discarded as illustrated in figure 5(c). We use a small offset when testing since our strokes are front facing sprites with constant depth. All strokes drawn have a maximum opacity less than 1, so that the rendering is relative to the background color. This is consistent with an artist using water colors, the painting has a tone of the color of the paper being used.

4   Results

We use a system with the following specifications: Intel Pentium 4 3.4 GHz, 2.00 GB RAM, nVIDIA 6800 Ultra. We implement the algorithm in C++, with libraries OpenGL, SDL and CGgl along with Nvidia CG for shaders. We render simple models: cube with 6 faces, building with 15 faces, a South-Indian Style temple with 55 faces and a tall building with 1000 faces. The results are given

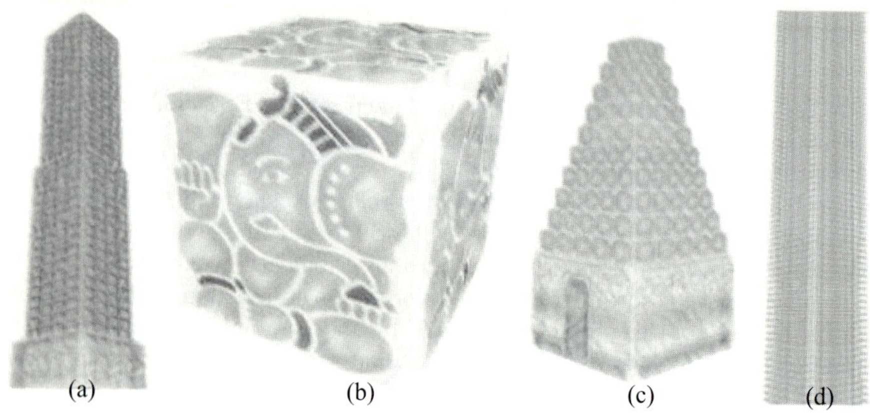

Fig. 6. Various Painterly Rendered Objects: (a) Building; (b) Cube; (c) Temple; (d) Tall building

in table 1 and outputs are shown in figure 6. The cube with LOD system gives a frame rate of 150 to 200 as the model oscillates between the near and far plane of the camera respectively. The performance of the system is dependent on the type of strokes that are rendered as the shaders have different calculations for different category of strokes. The speed of the system is mainly influenced by the number of strokes. Example as given in table 1, the cube with 6 faces and 4266 stroke count gives similar frame rates as the Tall Building with 1000 faces and 4400 stroke count. We do most of the calculations on the GPU. Only the calculations for LOD are done on the CPU as they decide the primitives that are getting rendered rather than computations that are performed on the primitives.

Table 1. Frame Rates for Model: Building

Model	No. of faces	No. of Strokes	FPS
Building	15	7455	107
Building	15	3727	185
Building	15	1863	357
Temple	55	7170	89
Temple	55	3585	170
Temple	55	1797	402
Cube	6	8532	60
Cube	6	4266	120
Cube	6	2133	232
Tall Building	1000	51200	16
Tall Building	1000	25600	30
Tall Building	1000	12800	50
Tall Building	1000	17600	51
Tall Building	1000	8800	81
Tall Building	1000	4400	140

5   Conclusions and Future Work

We presented a system which produces a painterly rendering of simple geometric models. Its a combination of stroke based rendering of still 2D images and
painterly rendering in 3D. The visual appearance depends on the number of
strokes used, the stroke textures, the size of strokes. In some scenes, when less
strokes are used, it gives a nice visual appearance of a light water color drawing. Large strokes bring abstract effect whereas small strokes bring accuracy to
the object. Stroke texture used should have a smooth gradient content, high
frequency stroke textures create discreteness between adjacent strokes and spoil
the hand drawn appearance.

As future work, we will explore making technical improvements to our implementation at various places. Copying the scene and depth texture after PASS1
as explained in section 3.3 are done by the `glCopyTexImage2D()` function. We
can improve the implementation by rendering directly to textures with the help
of `pbuffers`. The visibility testing of strokes is done on a fragment shader, i.e.
on all of it's pixels. This can be done even more efficiently if we can access the
depth texture at the vertex shader level (we want a stroke to be visible as a
whole or not). Vertex texture fetch is a possibility, however vertex textures are
slow and are limited to vendor and specific data types. We are studying vertex
texture fetch improvements.

References

1. Haeberli, P.: Paint by numbers: abstract image representations. In: SIGGRAPH
   '90: Proceedings of the 17th annual conference on Computer graphics and interactive techniques, New York, NY, USA, ACM Press (1990) 207–214

2. Hertzmann, A.: Painterly rendering with curved brush strokes of multiple sizes. Computer Graphics **32** (1998) 453–460

3. Shiraishi, M., Yamaguchi, Y.: An algorithm for automatic painterly rendering based on local source image approximation. In: NPAR '00: Proceedings of the 1st international symposium on Non-photorealistic animation and rendering, New York, NY, USA, ACM Press (2000) 53–58

4. Santella, A., DeCarlo, D.: Abstracted painterly renderings using eye-tracking data. In: NPAR '02: Proceedings of the 2nd international symposium on Non-photorealistic animation and rendering, New York, NY, USA, ACM Press (2002) 75–ff

5. Hertzmann, A.: Tutorial: A survey of stroke-based rendering. IEEE Comput. Graph. Appl. **23** (2003) 70–81

6. Meier, B.J.: Painterly rendering for animation. Computer Graphics **30** (1996) 477–484

7. Klein, A.W., Li, W.W., Kazhdan, M.M., Correa, W.T., Finkelstein, A., Funkhouser, T.A.: Non-photorealistic virtual environments. In Akeley, K., ed.: Siggraph 2000, Computer Graphics Proceedings, ACM Press / ACM SIGGRAPH / Addison Wesley Longman (2000) 527–534

8. Haller, M., Sperl, D.: Real-time painterly rendering for mr applications. In: GRAPHITE '04: Proceedings of the 2nd international conference on Computer graphics and interactive techniques in Australasia and South East Asia, New York, NY, USA, ACM Press (2004) 30–38

9. Gonzalez, R.C., Woods, R.: Digital Image processing. (Addison-Wesley)

10. Hertzmann, A., Perlin, K.: Painterly rendering for video and interaction. (2000)

11. Hertzmann, A., Jacobs, C.E., Oliver, N., Curless, B., Salesin, D.H.: Image analogies. In Fiume, E., ed.: SIGGRAPH 2001, Computer Graphics Proceedings, ACM Press / ACM SIGGRAPH (2001) 327–340

12. Hertzmann, A.: Fast paint texture (2002)

13. Strothotte, T., Masuch, M., Isenberg, T.: Visualizing Knowledge about Virtual Reconstructions of Ancient Architecture. In: Proceedings Computer Graphics International, The Computer Graphics Society, IEEE Computer Society (1999) 36–43

14. Freudenberg, B., Masuch, M., Strothotte, T.: (Walk-through illustrations: Frame-coherent pen-and-ink style in a game engine)

15. Lee, H., Kwon, S., Lee, S.: Real-time pencil rendering. In: NPAR '06: Proceedings of the 3rd international symposium on Non-photorealistic animation and rendering, New York, NY, USA, ACM Press (2006) 37–45

16. DeCarlo, D., Santella, A.: Stylization and abstraction of photographs. In: SIGGRAPH '02: Proceedings of the 29th annual conference on Computer graphics and interactive techniques, New York, NY, USA, ACM Press (2002) 769–776

17. Santella, A., DeCarlo, D.: Visual interest and npr: an evaluation and manifesto. In: NPAR '04: Proceedings of the 3rd international symposium on Non-photorealistic animation and rendering, New York, NY, USA, ACM Press (2004) 71–150

18. Nienhaus, M., Dollner, J.: Sketchy drawings. In: AFRIGRAPH '04: Proceedings of the 3rd international conference on Computer graphics, virtual reality, visualisation and interaction in Africa, New York, NY, USA, ACM Press (2004) 73–81

Real-Time Camera Walks Using Light Fields

Biswarup Choudhury, Deepali Singla, and Sharat Chandran

Indian Institute of Technology Bombay
http://www.cse.iitb.ac.in/~{biswarup, deepali, sharat}

Abstract. An interesting alternative to traditional geometry based rendering is Light Field Rendering [1,2]. A camera gantry is used to acquire authentic imagery and detailed novel views are synthetically generated from unknown viewpoints. The drawback is the significant data on disk.

Moving from static images, a walkthrough or a *camera walk* through the implied virtual world is often desirable but the repeated access of the large data makes the task increasingly difficult. We note that although potentially infinite walkthroughs are possible, for any given path, only a subset of the previously stored light field is required. Our prior work [3] exploited this and reduced the main memory requirement. However, considerable computational burden is encountered in processing even this reduced subset. This negatively impacts real-time rendering.

In this paper, we subdivide the image projection plane into "cells," each of which gets all its radiance information from the cached portions of the light field at select "nodal points." Once these cells are defined, the cache is visited *systematically* to find the radiance efficiently. The net result is *real-time* camera walks.

1   Introduction

In contrast with traditional geometry based rendering, a somewhat recent approach for "flying" through scenes is Image-Based Rendering (IBR) ([4], [5], [6]) which uses a confluence of methods from computer graphics and vision. The IBR approach is to generate novel views from virtual camera locations from pre-acquired imagery ([7], [8]). Synthetic realism is achieved, so to speak, using real cameras.

Light Field Rendering [1] (or Lumigraphs [2],[9],[10]) is an example of IBR. The approach is to store samples of the plenoptic function [11] which describe the directional radiance distribution for every point in space. The subset of this function in an occlusion-free space outside the scene can be represented in the form of a four-dimensional function. The parameterization scheme is shown in Fig. 1(a). Every viewing ray, computed using a *ray-shooting* technique, from the novel camera location C passing through the scene is characterized by a pair of points (s, t) and (u, v) on two planes. By accessing the previously acquired radiance associated with this four tuple, the view from C is generated.

In the general case, C can be anywhere in three-dimensions. So six light slabs are combined so that the entire scene is covered (Fig. 1(b)). An unfortunate consequence of this scheme is the huge datasize of the lightfield. The authors in

P. Kalra and S. Peleg (Eds.): ICVGIP 2006, LNCS 4338, pp. 321–332, 2006.
© Springer-Verlag Berlin Heidelberg 2006

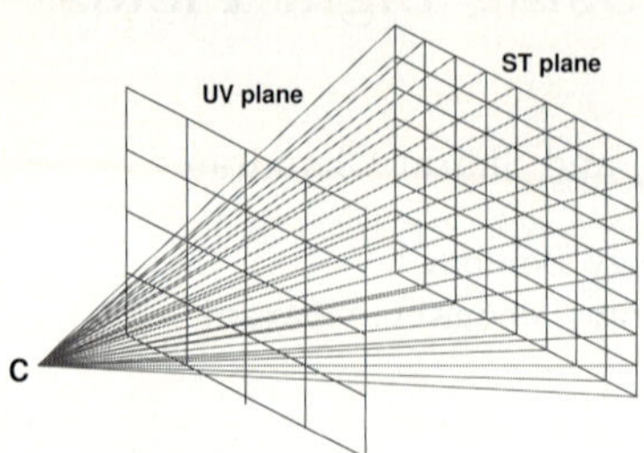

(a) Two-Plane Parametrization.

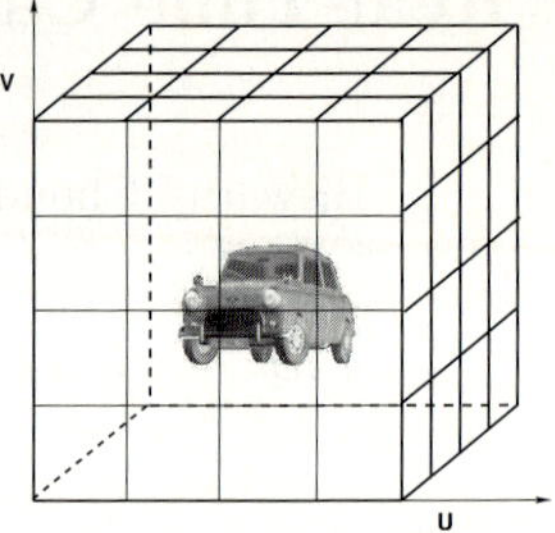

(b) Complete Lightfield: Six slabs of two-plane lightfields.

Fig. 1. The light field is a description of all light rays in a region of interest

[12] propose an interactive rendering based on Lumigraphs [2], by either using a smaller set of textures (with compromise in quality) or by storing the reconstructed image as a new texture for subsequent nearby images (with additional geometric information).

1.1   Problem Statement and Contributions

The beauty of image based rendering lies in re-sampling and combining the pre-acquired imagery. In a typical walkthrough situation, a person is expected to walk along a trajectory in three space and "suitably" sample the input images (in our case, light field). The problem we pose in this paper is *"Given the huge light field on disk, and a camera walk, how efficiently can the scene as seen by the camera be rendered?"*

In interactive walkthroughs, light field rendering is impacted by the sampling density of acquired images. For example, lightfield generated in [1] is sampled at 0.125 units; for a 512x512 image, the size of the lightfield is about 4.8GB. With increase in the resolution and density of acquired images, the size of the light field increases dramatically. For *interactive* rendering of the scene, one needs to store the complete light field in volatile memory, and perform computationally heavy [13] ray shooting operations.

Earlier in [3], we observed that for a camera walk, only a subset of the complete lightfield is needed. We computed the *optimal* location of a sparse set of "nodal points," suitable for the camera walk. The *lightweight* light field stored at these nodal points is enough to render the scene from any of the infinite points — termed *query* points — on the camera path. The advantage of this was that at the time of camera walk, accesses to the hard disk were reduced or absent. However, considerable computational burden was encountered in processing the input light field to obtain this subset. In addition, the number of ray shooting operations required for rendering an image from a query point on the camera walk was a function of the resolution of the rendered image size. Thus, rendering time increases considerably with increase in image size. In this paper, we show that efficiently caching the subset of light field, appropriate for the camera walk, and further *dividing the image plane into "cells"* results in rendering an image from a query point in real-time. Specifically,

1. We partition the image plane into "cells," each of which gets all the information (radiance values) from a specific nodal point, thereby avoiding the necessity to perform ray-plane intersections. Further, we show that for unknown, on-line camera walks, the nodal points once used can be discarded paving the way for memory efficient real-time implementation.
2. The correctness of our scheme is shown using a mathematical characterization of the geometry of the light field.
3. A new light field dataset, using a Mini Cooper car model, has been generated and experiments have been performed on it. Results validate our technique.

2   Our Approach

As in the original work [1], the field of view of the query camera is expected to be identical to the cameras that generated the light field. Likewise, sheared perspective projection handles the problem of aligning the plane of projection with the lightfield-slab. The center of projection of the camera moves along a plane parallel to the UV and the ST plane. For brevity, consider a setup similar to the **two slab setup** (Fig. 1(a)) where planes, UV and ST are replaced by lines U and S. We call this as the **two-line setup** (Fig. 2(a)). The query points q lie on line C, which in turn replaces the camera plane. As in [1], nearest neighbor approximation is employed for determining the radiance corresponding to q. We provide the complete mathematical framework with respect to this setup.

The rest of this paper is organized as follows. Section 2.1 and Section 2.2 summarize [3] for coherence (If proofs are not desired, this paper is self-contained). Section 2.3 develops the mathematical framework for our new algorithm. In Section 3 and Section 4, we give details of our approach and present our algorithm. Experimental results and analysis are discussed in Section 5. Finally in Section 6, we provide our concluding remarks.

2.1   Fixed-Direction Algorithm

In this section, we provide a brief summary of the concept of nodal points for a query point q. Later, we use these concepts in the mathematical characterization of the rest of the paper.

Denote Δl to be the constant distance $d[G_i, G_{i+1}]$ between two consecutive grid points on the U line, i.e., the distance between the input lightfield camera locations. For a specific s, denote $\texttt{assoc}(q)$, where q is a point on C, to be the closest grid vertex G (on U) to the ray $\overline{qs}$. In Fig. 2(a), $\texttt{assoc}(q) = G_1$. Given q, we use Algorithm 2.1 to compute nodal points N_1 and N_2. The radiance $L[q]$, in the direction of s, is obtained from these nodal points (presumably cached).

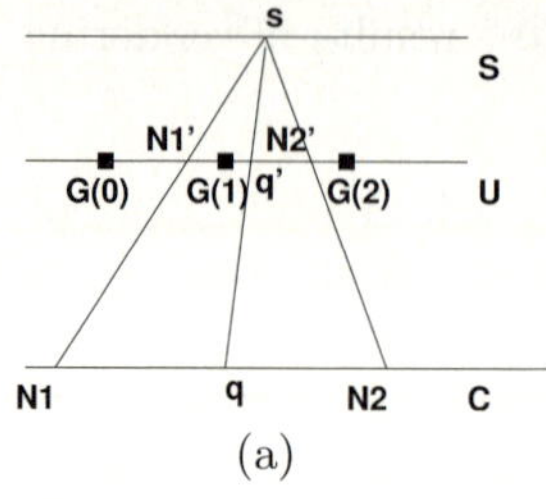

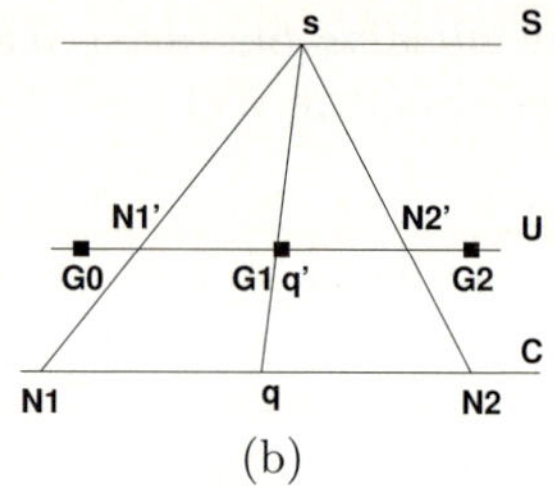

Fig. 2. (a): N_1 and N_2, the nodal points for q are marked such that $d[q'N_1'] = d[q'N_2'] = \frac{\Delta l}{2}$. (b): `assoc`$(N_1)$ is G_0 and `assoc`(N_2) is G_2.

Algorithm 2.1. Fixed-Direction (q, s)

Shoot a ray from q to s to obtain q' on U. Mark points N_1' and N_2' on U at a distance $d = \frac{\Delta l}{2}$ apart on either side of q'. This determines the nodal points N_1 and N_2 on C.
if `assoc`$(N_1) == G_1$ **then**
    $L[q] = L[N_1]$
else
    $L[q] = L[N_2]$
end if

In the case of two-plane parametrization, given q, one may compute four nodal points N_1, N_2, N_3 and N_4. Shoot the ray from q to s for a given s to obtain q' on UV. Now, mark four points $(q'.u \pm \frac{\Delta l}{2}, q'.v \pm \frac{\Delta l}{2}, z_{uv})$, where $q'.u$ and $q'.v$ represent the component of q' along u and v respectively, and z_{uv} is the z coordinate of the UV plane. These four points correspond to four nodal points on the camera COP (center of projection) plane. We use `assoc` of these nodal points to determine $L[q]$.

Notice that if the distance d in Algorithm 2.1 is more than $\frac{\Delta l}{2}$, as in Fig. 2(b), an incorrect value of $L[q]$ is computed. When d is as specified in Algorithm 2.1, it is easy to observe that either `assoc`$(N_1) = G_1$ or `assoc`$(N_2) = G_1$; it cannot be the case that `assoc`$(N_1) = G_0$ and `assoc`$(N_2) = G_2$. A choice less than $\frac{\Delta l}{2}$ might be suitable to maintain correctness, but will increase the number of nodal points, and hence decrease our efficiency. *Also note that the* `if` *condition in* Algorithm 2.1 *cannot be dispensed with. We cannot simply pick the nearest nodal point.*

2.2   All-Directions Algorithm

Algorithm 2.1 is "backward" in that it computes nodal points given a query point; in a sense it appears useless. However using this algorithm as the basis, in [3] we proved that,

- The nodal points N_1, N_2 corresponding to a query point q are sufficient for determining the radiance of *any query point* in the interval $[N_1, N_2]$. This generalizes to three dimensions.
- Choice of nodal points is independent of the direction (of s).

Using the above results, we use Algorithm 2.2 to compute the radiance corresponding to any query point q in the interval $[N_1, N_2]$. For simplicity, the algorithm has been presented for the two line setup.

Algorithm 2.2. All-Directions (q)

Determine nodal points N_1, N_2 bounding q.
for all $s \in$ S **do**
   Shoot a ray from query point q to s.
   if assoc(N_1) $==$ assoc(q) **then**
     $L[q] = L[N_1]$
   else
     $L[q] = L[N_2]$
   end if
end for

2.3   Image Plane Intervals

In Algorithm 2.2, the scene as rendered from a query point q is determined expensively by shooting N rays (to the N sample points on S), followed by a lookup of assoc for each of the N rays. This computational burden increases dramatically with the increase in query points on a camera walk. Expectedly, the situation for the two-plane setup is worse. (The number of shot rays are $N \times N$ for a query point.) With an independent increase in the number of query points, the computational requirements prohibit real-time rendering.

In this section, we show how to subdivide the image plane into cells and thereby derive a deterministic "square wave" pattern of using nodal points for each cell. For the sake of exposition, we consider the two-line setup wherein cells degenerate to intervals. The following lemma depends on *mid grid points*, which are defined as the points lying in the middle of any two adjacent grid points. For a query point q bounded by nodal points $[N_j, N_{j+1}]$, consider (respectively) rays from q, N_j and N_{j+1} through the mid grid points on U. These divide S into intervals $[S_i, S_{i+1}]$ (i is a whole number) (see, for example, Fig. 3(a)).

Lemma 1. Range Lemma: *The radiance values corresponding to all s points in an interval $[S_i, S_{i+1}]$ can be determined from a single nodal point.*

Proof: Without loss of generality, let the interval under consideration be $[S_2, S_3]$ (Fig. 3(a)). Let s_p be any point in the interval $[S_2, S_3]$. Observe that for s_p, assoc(q)=G_2. By construction, $\forall s \in [S_2, S_4]$, assoc(N_1)=G_2. Since $[S_2, S_3]$ is a subset of $[S_2, S_4]$, so $\forall s \in [S_2, S_3]$, assoc(N_1)=G_2. Thus, for s_p, assoc(q)=assoc (N_1) and therefore $L(q)=L(N_1)$. $\qquad\qquad\square$

Thus, in general, we can avoid ray shooting for a range of s values in any interval since the radiance $L(q)$ will come from *some* fixed nodal point. The next lemma tells us that even the choice of nodal point is deterministic.

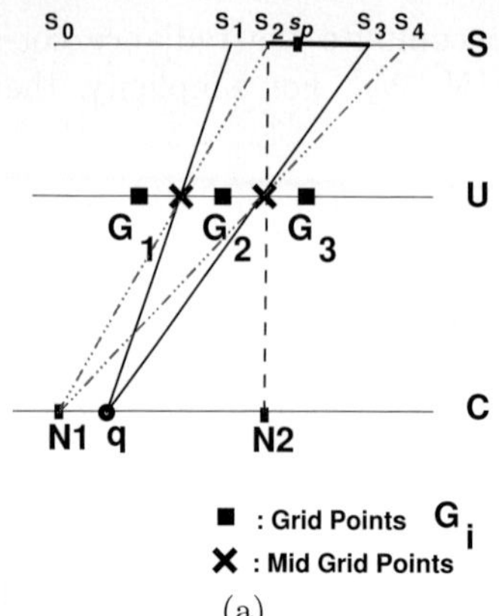

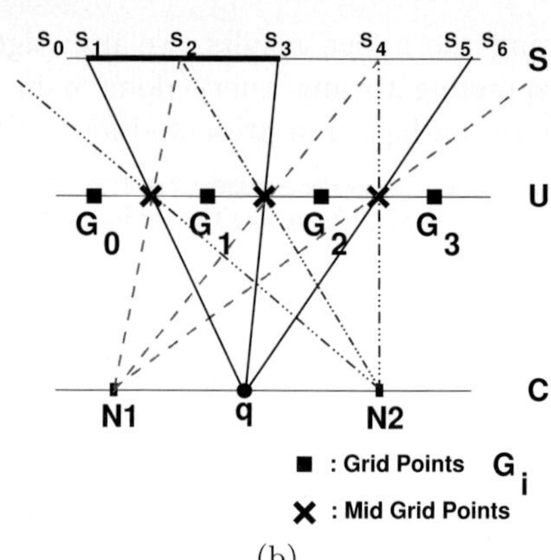

Fig. 3. (a): Radiance $L(q,s)$ for $\forall s \in [S_2, S_3]$ can be determined from N_1. (b): $\forall s \in [S_1, S_2], L(q)=L(N_2)$; $\forall s \in [S_2, S_3], L(q)=L(N_1)$.

Lemma 2. Toggle Lemma: *If $L(q)=L[N_j]$ for some $s \in [S_i, S_{i+1}]$, then $\forall s \in [S_{i+1}, S_{i+2}]$, $L(q)=L[N_{j+1}]$ and vice-versa.*

Proof: Without loss of generality, let $[S_1, S_2]$ and $[S_2, S_3]$ be the two intervals under consideration (Fig. 3(b)). By construction, we observe that $\forall s \in [S_1, S_2]$, $\mathtt{assoc}(q)=G_1$ and $\mathtt{assoc}(N_2)=G_1$. So $\forall s \in [S_1, S_2]$, $L(q)=L[N_2]$. The lemma claims that $\forall s \in [S_2, S_3]$, $L(q)=L[N_1]$.

By construction, $\mathtt{assoc}(q)=G_1, \forall s \in [S_1, S_3]$. Also, $\mathtt{assoc}(N_1)=G_1, \forall s \in [S_2, S_4]$. The intersection of intervals $[S_1, S_3]$ and $[S_2, S_4]$ is $[S_2, S_3]$. Hence, $\forall s \in [S_2, S_3]$, $\mathtt{assoc}(q)=\mathtt{assoc}(N1)$, or, $L(q)=L[N_1]$.

The situation when we consider the intervals $[S_2, S_3]$ and $[S_3, S_4]$ is similar; we find that $\forall s \in [S_3, S_4]$, $L(q)=L[N_2]$. □

Thus the lemma asserts that, for a query point, the radiance corresponding to each interval in S, is deterministic as a toggle between bounding nodal points. This is best visualized as a square wave (Fig. 4) and is exploited in our algorithm (Algorithm 2.3).

Algorithm 2.3. **Interval Algorithm** (q)

Determine the nodal points N_j, N_{j+1}, bounding q.
Determine all intervals $[S_i, S_{i+1}]$ on S using q, N_j and N_{j+1}.
Shoot a ray from query point q to the first s in $[S_0, S_1]$.
$\mathtt{Toggle} = (\mathtt{assoc}(N_j) == \mathtt{assoc}(q))\ ?\ N_j : N_{j+1}$
for all intervals **do**
  for all $s \in [S_i, S_{i+1}]$ **do**
    $L[q] = L[\mathtt{Toggle}]$
  end for
  $\mathtt{Toggle} = (\mathtt{Toggle}==N_j)\ ?\ N_{j+1} : N_j$
end for

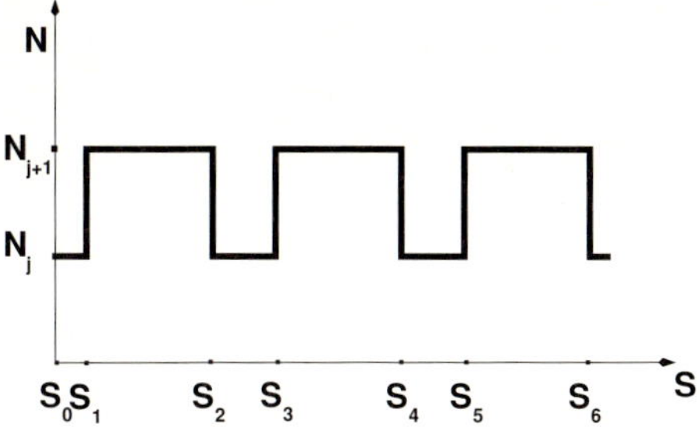

Fig. 4. Nodal points are accessed in a "toggle" manner for any query point. The duty cycle of the square wave is dependent on which query point is used. Size of the image plane determines the end conditions.

3   The Algorithm

We now have the apparatus to select the nodal points and divide the image plane into cells, given a query point. For the sake of exposition, we consider two types of cases (Fig. 5). In the first case, the input is an unrestricted camera walk and nodal points are computed on the fly (Fig. 5(a)). As we traverse along the camera walk, nodal points "used" can be discarded. In the second case, the first input is a domain, and nodal points are computed after the domain is given (Fig. 5(b)). The second input are camera walks restricted to be in the domain. In this case, multiple walks can be rendered efficiently without recomputing new nodal points, and in parallel.

3.1   Case 1

<table>
<tr><td>Algorithm 3.1. Incremental-Camera Walk (<code>walk</code>)</td></tr>
<tr><td>

1. Starting from the initial query point on the camera walk, mark four nodal points at a distance $\Delta x = \Delta l \times R$, where R is the ratio of the distance between the camera plane and the ST plane, and the distance between the UV and ST plane. For simplicity, the nodal points are selected parallel to the u and v directions as shown in Fig. 5(a). A cell thus is created.
2. The light field is cached at four nodal points in the grid enclosing the query point (The precise computation of the light field at the nodal points can take advantage of the methods suggested in Section 4, instead of the method in [1].)
3. Apply Algorithm 2.3 iteratively to calculate the radiance at all query points (along the camera walk) inside the cell.
4. As the walk exits the cell, update the nodal points and go to Step 2.

</td></tr>
</table>

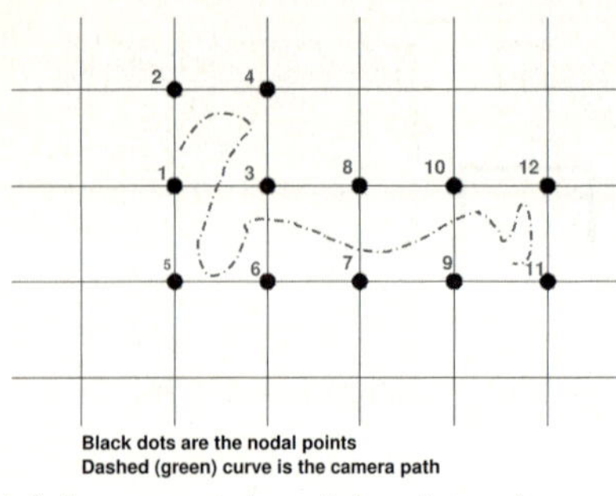

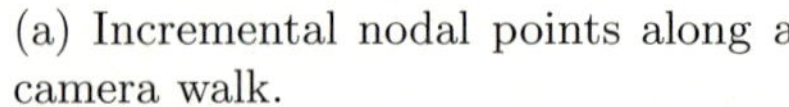

Black dots are the nodal points
Dashed (green) curve is the camera path

(a) Incremental nodal points along a camera walk.

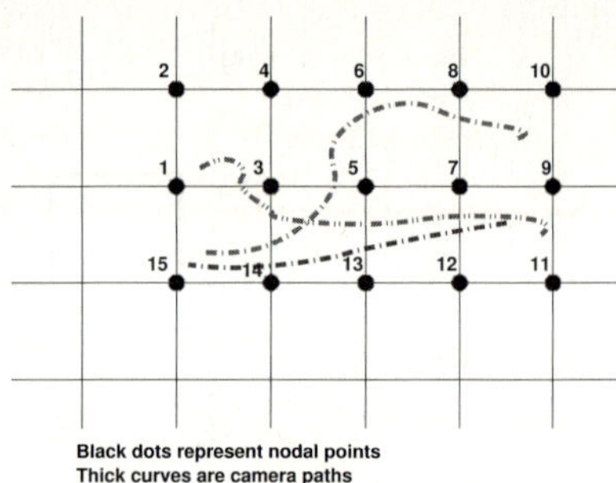

Black dots represent nodal points
Thick curves are camera paths

(b) Domain-based nodal points.

Fig. 5. Rendered scene as viewed from a camerawalk can be computed from nodal points

3.2   Case 2

Next, if we are given several camera walks lying in a domain, we pick domain-based nodal points, as shown in Fig. 5(b). Scene from any query point, on any camera walk, or even at random, in the rectangular region defined by the bounding box of the nodal points can be rendered efficiently as shown below.

Algorithm 3.2. Domain-Camera Walk (domain)

1. Determine the bounding box of the domain specified.
2. Mark nodal points at a distance $\Delta x = \Delta l \times R$, where R is the ratio of the distance between the camera plane and the ST plane, and the distance between the UV and ST plane along the complete bounding box. For simplicity, the nodal points are selected parallel to the u and v directions as shown in Fig. 5(b). A grid is thus created.
3. The light field is cached at all the nodal points in the grid (The precise computation of the light field at the nodal points can take advantage of the methods suggested in Section 4, instead of the method in [1].)
4. Apply Algorithm 2.3 to calculate the radiance at any query point inside any cell of the grid.

In summary, the incremental algorithm is more suitable when the user does not want to specify the camera walk in advance. The domain-based algorithm, on the other hand, is useful when the user has a number of camera walks, or random query points in a domain.

4   Caching Radiance at Nodal Points

In Algorithm 2.2, the radiance computation for nodal points was done using the method in [1]. Caching of nodal points can be less expensive by using the ideas in

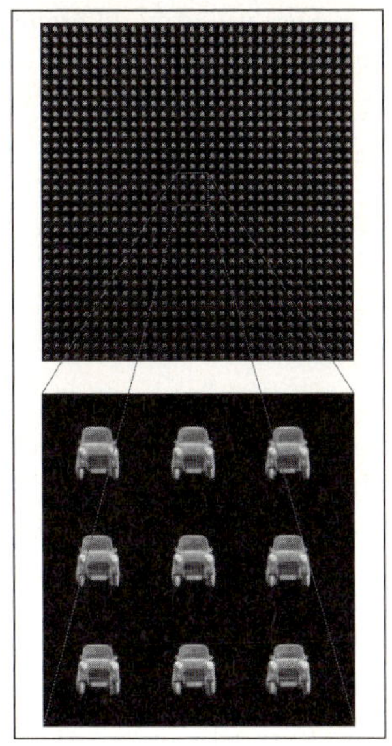

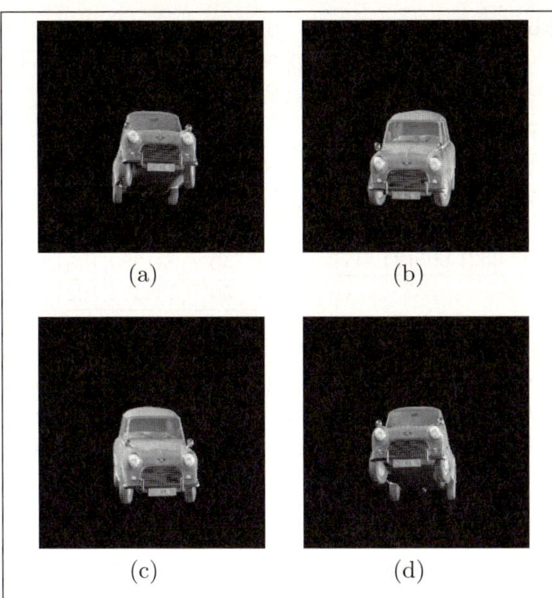

Fig. 6. Lightfield for the MiniCooper

Fig. 7. Rendered novel images (best seen in color)

Lemma 1, i.e., by dividing S into intervals (or the image plane ST into cells). The radiance values for a number of image pixels is computed from a fixed camera grid point. Further, the relationship between the intervals and the camera grid points can be easily determined. As a result, in our method for nodal points, ray shooting has to be done only *once* to find the intervals and their corresponding grid points.

5   Experiments and Results

In this section, we first describe the implementation details and then show the significant computational advantage. For baseline comparisons, and since it is a standard, and freely available, we use [1] to contrast our method. Various simulations on different paths confirm our claims to superiority.

Mini Cooper Dataset: We have generated a new lightfield dataset for purposes of our experimentation (Fig. 6). It consists of images of a Mini Cooper car model captured from cameras placed on a 32x32 grid. The Mini Cooper, a CSG model, was rendered by performing radiosity computation with 3 different light sources using Povray. Some features of the Mini Cooper include specular metal body, reflective window glasses, inner details of the car (car seats, rear-view mirror). Resolution of the images is 256 x 256.

Table 1. Time in seconds for different camera walks

$|q|$	[1]	§3.1
164	82.617	5.020
335	165.015	10.468
550	281.126	14.640
741	376.040	17.997
1023	521.605	24.417

Table 2. Number of disk accesses for camera walks on different planes

zCam	[1]	§3.1
10	160338	23244
20	211730	20640
30	222284	15360
40	231329	12512
50	238442	10240

Table 3. Time in seconds for camera walks on different planes

zCam	$|p|$	[1]	§3.1
10	170	317.424	30.349
20	86	413.178	27.141
30	60	432.255	20.717
40	46	444.092	17.173
50	40	462.085	14.764

Quality: We downloaded the reference implementation [1], obtained the input lightfield dataset after the decompression stage, and then "hooked" our modification. The rendered images (Fig. 7) using our method are identical to those generated in [1]. The output is devoid of any artifacts — `diff` under Gnu-Linux reports the null set.

Theoretical Analysis: The advantages of our technique arise due to efficient nodal light field caching, and division of the image plane into cells. For a path with q query points, let the number of nodal points needed be p. Note that for a camerawalk, the number of query points is much larger than the number of nodal points, i.e., $q \gg p$ (e.g., for $|q| =886$, $|p|=40$ on a plane at **zCam**=50). Let the average number of grid points required for generating an image from a query point be g. We penalize disk access to the lightfield data (densely sampled and at a high resolution) by a factor of d.

In [1], the number of rays shot is of the order of the resolution of an image (NxN). Theoretically, the total time taken is $q(k_1 N^2 + dg)$, where k_1 is the time taken by each ray shooting operation and corresponding computations. In our method, time taken for caching each nodal point is less than that taken by a query point in [1] (Section 4). For each nodal point, the initial computation of determining cells is constant (c_1) but again, the time taken for disk accesses is dg. For a query point, computation of cells takes constant time (c_2). So the theoretical computational gain is

$$\frac{q(k_1 N^2 + dg)}{p(c_1 + dg) + qc_2} = \frac{\mathsf{O}(q(N^2 + dg))}{\mathsf{O}(pdg + q)} \tag{1}$$

Computational Advantage: All our experimentation was performed on an Intel Pentium IV 2.4GHz, 1 GB RAM Linux based computer. Our results confirm the theoretical computational advantage in Equation 1.

1. Table 1 depicts the results we obtained using different camera walks. The two techniques compared are [1] and Algorithm 3.1 (with caching of nodal points as in Section 4). The distance between two successive query points on the camera walk is constant for all the experiments. With increase in the number of query points, the rate of increase of time taken in [1] is more than

Table 4. Total time in seconds for loading light field into a domain and rendering from random query points. The rendering time after loading is nominal.

$|q|$	[1]	§3.2
64	29.949	12.35
130	61.294	12.587
212	99.255	12.682
300	140.166	13.019
464	215.86	13.44

Table 5. Number of disk accesses for random query points on a plane

$|q|$	[1]	§3.2
64	15987	9968
130	32229	9968
212	52400	9968
300	74360	9968
464	114707	9968

that of our method. Note that the number of frames rendered per second ranges from 30 to 40.

2. In Table 2 and Table 3, we show the results using camera walks on parallel planes at varying distances from the lightfield setup. The total number of query points was kept constant, in this case it happened to be 886. The computational gain increases with increase in the value of **zCam**, because the number of nodal points decrease with increase in **zCam**.

3. Table 4 and Table 5 compares the results of Algorithm 3.2 (with caching of nodal points as in Section 4) with [1]. The experiments have been performed on a fixed domain (42 nodal points) and with random number of query points. The rate of increase in the time taken by our algorithm, as the number of query points increases is very low, because most of the computational time is spent generating the (fixed number of) nodal point images. Rendering of images from the query points takes nominal computational time.

4. We also compared our method with the technique in our previous work [3] and observed a significant computational gain. For instance, on a camera walk with $|q|$=370 (and **zCam** ranging from 10 to 50), our method was on an average 10 orders of magnitude faster.

6   Conclusion

In this paper, we have looked at the problem of reducing the computational burden in dealing with the rich and densely sampled light field when a user walks through a virtual world. We have achieved this by recognizing that instead of considering the complete light field, it is enough to consider a sparse set of nodal points. We have proved that the division of the image plane into cells and thereafter, deriving a deterministic pattern of the use of the nodal points for each of these cells, has increased the computational efficiency significantly. The proofs of the mathematical characterizations of these concepts have been provided. A new lightfield dataset for purposes of experimentation has been generated and experimental results have been shown to validate our technique.

Our description does not explicitly deal with decompression issues (indeed, in the first stage [1] of rendering, the entire light field is decompressed as it is read into memory from disk). However, there is no conceptual blockade in applying the general caching strategy and the mathematical elements even in these cases.

Acknowledgements. This work was funded by an Infosys Ph.D. fellowship grant. The base Light field code was downloaded from `graphics.stanford.edu` The Mini Cooper model was taken from `www.oyonale.com` and the lightfield generated with Povray. We thank the members of ViGIL, IIT Bombay for useful discussions.

References

1. Levoy, M., Hanrahan, P.: Light field rendering. In: SIGGRAPH 1996: Proceedings of the 23rd annual conference on Computer graphics and interactive techniques, New York, NY, USA, ACM Press (1996) 31–42
2. Gortler, S.J., Grzeszczuk, R., Szeliski, R., Cohen, M.F.: The lumigraph. In: SIGGRAPH 1996: Proceedings of the 23rd annual conference on Computer graphics and interactive techniques, New York, NY, USA, ACM Press (1996) 43–54
3. Pandey, A., Choudhury, B., Chandran, S.: Efficient lightfield based camera walk. In: Fourth Indian Conference on Computer Vision, Graphics and Image Processing ICVGIP. (2004) 302–307
4. Debevec, P., Gortler, S.: Image-based modeling and rendering. In: SIGGRAPH 98 Course Notes. ACM SIGGRAPH, Addison Wesley, July. (1998)
5. Shum, H.Y., Wang, L., Chai, J.X., Tong, X.: Rendering by Manifold Hopping. International Journal of Computer Vision **50** (2002) 185–201
6. Chen, S.E.: Quicktime VR: an image-based approach to virtual environment navigation. In: SIGGRAPH 1995: Proceedings of the 22nd annual conference on Computer graphics and interactive techniques, New York, NY, USA, ACM Press (1995) 29–38
7. Unger, J., Wenger, A., Hawkins, T., Gardner, A., Debevec, P.: Capturing and rendering with incident light fields. In: EGRW '03: Proceedings of the 14th Eurographics workshop on Rendering, Aire-la-Ville, Switzerland, Switzerland, Eurographics Association (2003) 141–149
8. Shum, H.Y., He, L.W.: Rendering with concentric mosaics. In: SIGGRAPH 1999: Proceedings of the 26th annual conference on Computer graphics and interactive techniques, New York, NY, USA, ACM Press (1999) 299–306
9. Isaksen, A., McMillan, L., Gortler, S.J.: Dynamically reparameterized light fields. In: SIGGRAPH 2000: Proceedings of the 27th annual conference on Computer graphics and interactive techniques, New York, NY, USA, ACM Press (2000) 297–306
10. Buehler, C., Bosse, M., McMillan, L., Gortler, S.J., Cohen, M.F.: Unstructured lumigraph rendering. In: SIGGRAPH 2001: Proceedings of the 28th annual conference on Computer graphics and interactive techniques, ACM Press (2001) 425–432
11. Adelson, E.H., Bergen, J.R.: The Plenoptic Function and the Elements of Early Vision. In: Computational Modeling of Vision Processing. MIT Press (1991)
12. Sloan, P.P., Cohen, M.F., Gortler, S.J.: Time critical lumigraph rendering. In: SI3D '97: Proceedings of the 1997 symposium on Interactive 3D graphics, New York, NY, USA, ACM Press (1997) 17–ff.
13. Sharma, P., Parashar, A., Banerjee, S., Kalra, P.: An Uncalibrated Lightfield Acquisition System. In: Third Indian Conference on Computer Vision, Graphics and Image Processing ICVGIP. (2002) 25–30

Massive Autonomous Characters:
Animation and Interaction

Ingu Kang[1,2] and JungHyun Han[1,*]

[1] Game Research Center, College of Information and Communications
Korea University, Seoul, Korea
[2] Nexon Co., Ltd.

Abstract. This article reports the result of an experiment which integrates GPU-accelerated skinning, sprite animation, and character behavior control. The experiment shows that the existing techniques can be neatly integrated: thousands of characters are animated at real-time and the overall motion is natural like fluid. The result is attractive for games, especially where a huge number of non-player characters such as animals or monsters should be animated.

Keywords: game, character animation, skinning, impostor, behavior control, GPU.

1   Introduction

Animation of large crowds is an area of research that has been receiving an increased amount of interest. Especially, it is becoming essential in multi-player online games that can accommodate a huge number of simultaneous players or non-player characters (NPCs). A good example of NPCs is a herd of land animals. Such a herd is made up of autonomous discrete animals, but the overall motion seems fluid. Reynolds observed that the motion is the aggregate result of the actions of individual animals, each acting solely on the basis of its own local perception of the world[1].

This article reports an experiment result for real-time interaction with autonomous discrete NPCs. For rendering a large number of NPCs, the multi-resolution technique proposed by Kang *et al.*[2] is used. The group of NPCs responds to the player character's interaction, as well as to each other and their environment. For controlling the group behavior, the mental models proposed by Reynolds[1,3] have been adopted, which mediate between several conflicting behavioral goals.

The experiment results show that the two existing techniques can be neatly integrated. Such integration is attractive for real-time graphics applications such as games, especially where a huge number of NPCs including animals or monsters should be rendered.

---

* Corresponding author.

P. Kalra and S. Peleg (Eds.): ICVGIP 2006, LNCS 4338, pp. 333–338, 2006.

2   Rendering of Large Crowds

This section summarizes the multi-resolution rendering technique for large crowds, proposed by Kang *et al.*[2]. Note that an NPC in close proximity with a player character can interact with the player, and the interaction may cause various actions of the NPC. However, an NPC at a distance does not interact with the player character, and performs a limited set of actions. Therefore, different levels of detail in NPC animation are used: *skinning animation*[4] for NPCs at close proximity as well as all player characters, and *impostors* (animated sprites)[6,7] for distant NPCs.

Skinning has been the dominant approach to character animation in real-time applications. The skinning algorithm is based on a hierarchy of bones, and each vertex in the mesh is assigned a set of influencing bones and a blending *weight* for each influence. Then, the deformed vertex position v_c for a configuration c is computed as follows:

$$v_c = \sum_{i=1}^{n} w_i M_{i,c} M_{i,d}^{-1} v_d \tag{1}$$

where w_i is the weight, v_d is dress-pose location of the vertex, $M_{i,c}$ is the transformation matrix associated with the i-th influence in configuration c, and $M_{i,d}^{-1}$ is the inverse of the dress-pose matrix associated with the i-th influence.

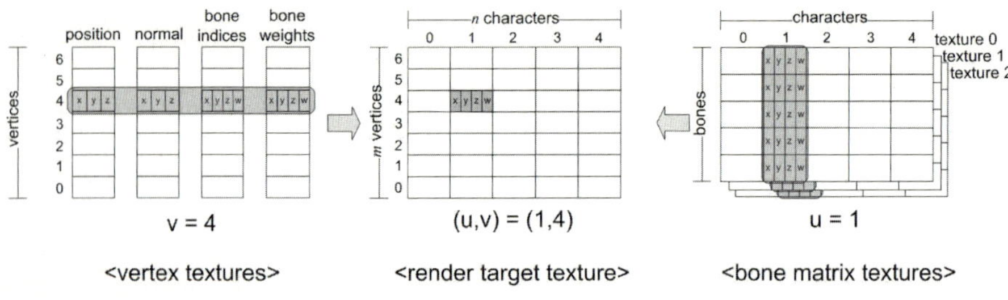

Fig. 1. Skinning and render target texture (from [2])

The four 1D textures in the left side of Fig. 1 show the skinning data for a vertex. A vertex is influenced by 4 bones, and the bone matrices are computed every frame. As shown in the right side of Fig. 1, each row of the 3×4 matrix is recorded in a separate texture. Through a single drawcall, all vertices of all characters are transformed, and written into the *render target texture*, as shown in the middle of Fig. 1. In implementation, the vertex shader renders a quad covering the render target, and the pixel shader fills each texel of the render target texture, where a texel corresponds to a vertex of a character. Then, the render target texture is copied to a vertex buffer object (VBO)[5], and then each character is rendered by the vertex shader using a given index buffer.

The GPU-based skinning algorithm is integrated with sprite animation. A sprite's size is 32×32. For each keyframe, sprites are captured from 256 viewpoints in the spherical coordinates: 8 along the longitude in the range $[0,\pi/2]$, and 32 along the latitude in the range $[0,2\pi]$. The set of 256 sprites is stored in a 512×512 texture. For a character, 11 keyframes are used. The impostors are rendered through hardware-accelerated *point sprites*, for rendering of which both OpenGL and DirectX have standard interfaces.

3   Behavior Control

Reynolds[1] suggested a flocking algorithm which takes a bird as a particle. Three steering behaviors are considered: *separation* for avoiding local flock-mates, *alignment* towards the average heading of local flock-mates, and *cohesion* to move towards the average position of local flock-mates. In addition, *avoidance* behavior is included to avoid obstacles or enemies. In his later work[3], Reynolds also suggested to use *lattices* as spatial directories for the speedup purpose.

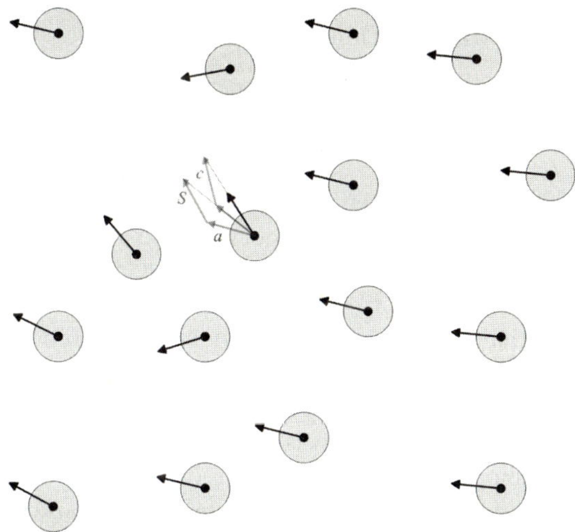

Fig. 2. Vectors for behavior control

In order to control the massive animated NPCs discussed in the previous section, the behavior control algorithm of [1,3] has been adopted. Three steering behaviors (separation, alignment, and cohesion) are used to define the path of each NPC, and the avoidance behavior makes the NPCs flee from the player character and get away from the fences. The four behaviors lead to specific velocity vectors for an NPC, and summed through user-defined weight values. The summed vector determines the combined velocity of an NPC. See Fig. 2 where s, a, and c stand for separation, alignment, and cohesion, respectively.

An NPC's steering behaviors are determined by considering the neighboring NPCs in close proximity. For the sake of the real-time performance, the entire terrain is partitioned into lattices, and only the NPCs in a lattice and neighboring lattices are considered.

In the current experiments, the horses move following the terrain surface, and therefore the moves are restricted basically to 2D. The behavior control algorithm is applicable to 3D space, for example, to determine the behaviors of a flock of birds. Note that, however, behavior control in 2D surface is more difficult than that of 3D space. It is because collisions among the NPCs are harder to handle in the 2D surface. Imagine hundreds of animals in a cage. In the current implementations, the maximum velocity has been set to be high enough for efficient handling of collisions. However, such a high velocity may cause unnatural change of moving directions such as abrupt rotation. The maximum velocity should be properly set according to the features of specific NPCs. For example, the maximum velocity of horses should be greater than that of sheep.

Better performances can be achieved by applying the behavior control algorithm only to the NPCs in close proximity, i.e. the skinning-animated characters. In FPS (first-person shooting) games, for example, the NPCs interacting with the player are those in close proximity, and therefore it is a reasonable choice to apply the behavior control algorithm only to them.

4   Implementation and Result

The algorithms have been implemented in C++, OpenGL and Cg on a PC with 3.2 GHz Intel Pentium4 CPU, 2GB memory, and NVIDIA Geforce 7800GTX 256MB. For experiments, a horse character is used, which is composed of 38 bones, 555 vertices and 1,084 polygons. Table 1 shows how the performance changes in FPS on the ratio of skinning and impostor rendering when 1,000 horses are rendered. Obviously, the rendering performance is improved as the ratio of impostor rendering to skinning is increased. When the behavior control algorithm is executed, the overall FPS is decreased.

Fig. 3 shows snapshots of animating hundreds of horses with behavior control. The three steering behaviors (separation, alignment and cohesion) are implemented. In addition, the human player character is working as an enemy, and causes avoidance behavior of the NPCs (horses). Fig. 4 shows snapshots of

Table 1. Performances

# skinning	# impostor	FPS (no behavior control)	FPS (behavior control)
1000	0	57	52
800	200	70	63
600	400	91	79.5
400	600	124	103.5
200	800	207	155.5

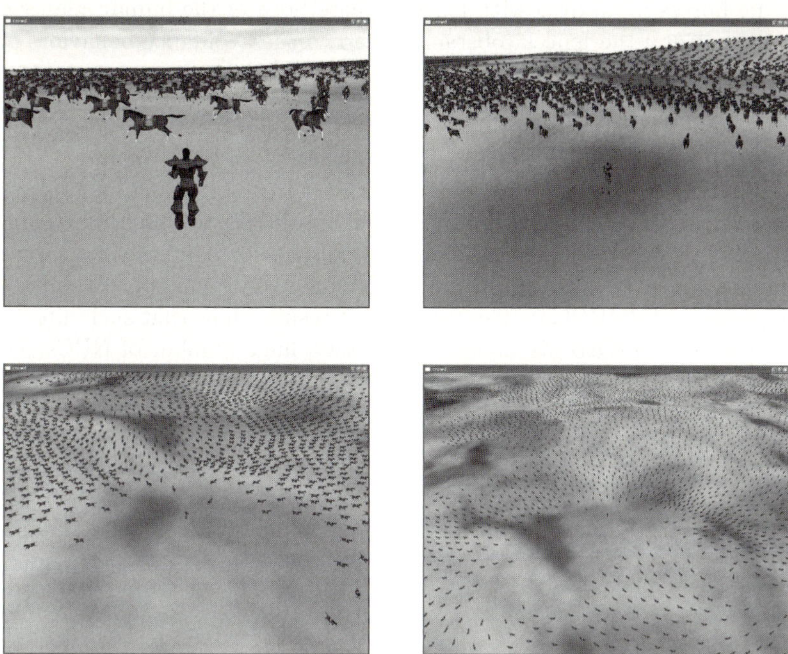

Fig. 3. Large crowd rendering with behavior control

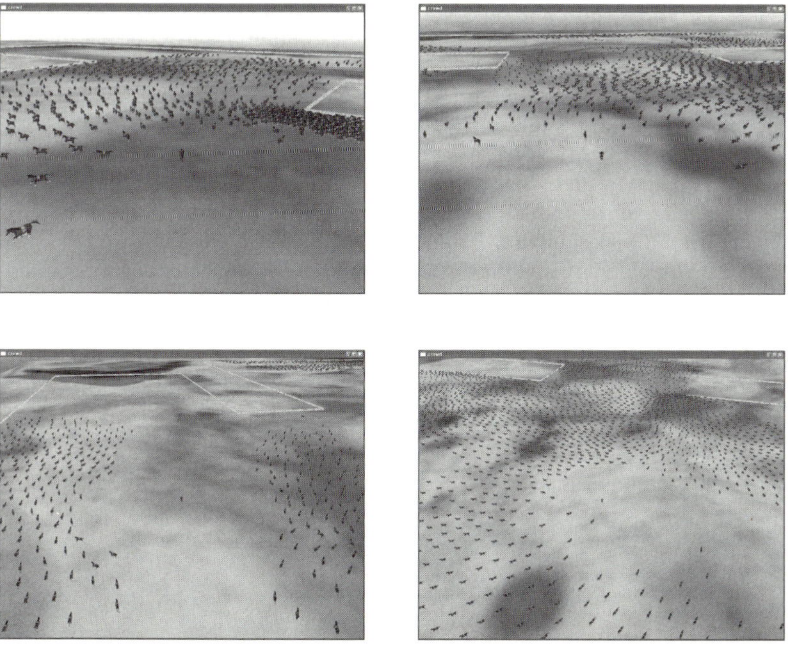

Fig. 4. Large crowd rendering in a scene of fences with behavior control

animating horses in an area with fences, where both of the human player character (enemy) and the fences (obstacles) lead to the avoidance behaviors of the horses.

5   Conclusion

This article presented integration of a multi-resolution technique for real-time animation of large crowds and the character behavior control. The target application of the presented approach is the massively multi-player online role playing games (MMORPGs). The experiment results show that such integration is attractive for MMORPGs, especially where a huge number of NPCs such as animals or monsters should be animated.

Acknowledgements

This research was supported by MIC, Korea under ITRC IITA-2005-(C1090-0501-0019).

References

1. Reynolds, C.: Flocks, Herds, and Schools: A Distributed Behavioral Model. SIG-GRAPH87 (1987) 25-34.
2. Kang, I., Eom. Y., Han, J.: A Multi-resolution Technique for Real-time Animation of Large Crowds. International Symposium on Computer and Information Sciences. (2006).
3. Reynolds, C.: Interaction with Groups of Autonomous Characters. Game Developers Conference (2000).
4. Lewis, J.P., Cordner, M., Fong, N.: Pose space deformations: A unified approach to shape interpoalation and skeleton-driven deformation. SIGGRAPH2000 165–172.
5. NVIDIA: Using vertex buffer objects. NVIDIA White Paper. October 2003.
6. Guymon, M.: Pyro-techniques: Playing with fire. Game Developer **7** (2000) 23-27.
7. Maciel, P., Shirley, P.: Visual navigation of large environments using textured clusters. Proc. Symposium of Interactive 3D Graphics(1995).

Clickstream Visualization Based on Usage Patterns

Srinidhi Kannappady, Sudhir P. Mudur, and Nematollaah Shiri

Dept. of Computer Science and Software Engineering
Concordia University, Montreal, Quebec, Canada
{s_kannap,mudur, shiri}@cse.concordia.ca

Abstract. Most clickstream visualization techniques display web users' clicks by highlighting paths in a graph of the underlying web site structure. These techniques do not scale to handle high volume web usage data. Further, historical usage data is not considered. The work described in this paper differs from other work in the following aspect. Fuzzy clustering is applied to historical usage data and the result imaged in the form of a point cloud. Web navigation data from active users are shown as animated paths in this point cloud. It is clear that when many paths get attracted to one of the clusters, that particular cluster is currently "hot." Further as sessions terminate, new sessions are incrementally incorporated into the point cloud. The complete process is closely coupled to the fuzzy clustering technique and makes effective use of clustering results. The method is demonstrated on a very large set of web log records consisting of over half a million page clicks.

1 Introduction

Web usage analysis of large and popular websites can provide vital information about online business transactions that can be used by business administrators to improve the services provided through their websites. Web usage data has normally been analyzed either in the form of user sessions or in the form of clickstream data. A session is typically the set of pages (URLS) visited by a user from the moment the user enters a web site to the moment the same user leaves it [19]. Clickstream is a generic term to describe visitors' paths through one or more web sites [13]. Analysis of clickstream data can show how visitors navigate and use the web site over time.

Visualization techniques are claimed to be among the best ways to analyze and understand web usage data [17]. Through visualization one can discover interesting patterns more easily than by looking at raw usage logs. In addition, there is also the possibility of generating recommendations from these patterns [18]. As user interests are not fixed and change over time, web usage data for a popular web site is very large, sparse, and fuzzy. The most basic way to visualize web usage data is by using the spanning tree technique to convert a log file into the users' browsing map. This technique is not robust and does not scale well enough to construct a users' browsing map when the web site is complex and the volume of clickstream data is large.

Our approach differs from earlier work in that we show dynamic web usage trends by overlaying clickstream data for every active user in the form of an animated

P. Kalra and S. Peleg (Eds.): ICVGIP 2006, LNCS 4338, pp. 339–351, 2006.

particle moving within a clustered visual representation of historical web usage data.Visual analysis of the paths followed by these active users can provide insight into the current online interests and trends. Our visualization process can be briefly described as follows: In the first phase, we create a three dimensional (3D) point cloud visual representation of historical web log data. For this, the large volume of web usage data available is first organized into sessions. Fuzzy clustering is then carried out on these sessions. This identifies a small number of the sessions as cluster centers. And for all other sessions, we get fuzzy membership values with respect to these clusters. Using a combination of Multi Dimensional Scaling (MDS) and Sammon Mapping (SM), the cluster centers are assigned positions in 3D space to optimally reflect the dissimilarity interrelationships amongst them. Next we render all the user sessions as a point cloud by direct use of the fuzzy membership values of these sessions with the cluster centers. This yields a 3D visual representation of the web usage pattern. The second phase involves real time visualization of clickstream data. An active user is defined as the one whose most recent web page visit was initiated within a period, say, 45 minutes. The web pages visited by each active user are maintained as a dynamically updated session. When an active session is updated by addition of the new web page he/she visited, the dissimilarities between this updated session and the current cluster centers are used to obtain the fuzzy membership values into the clusters; these values are then used to update the position of the session within the point cloud.

Given that a popular website will have a large number of new page clicks per second, the positions of active sessions are updated frequently. Periodically, as active sessions terminate (i.e., no new page visited by the active user within the last 45 minutes), we dynamically update the web usage profiles using an incremental version of the fuzzy clustering technique. When a session is incrementally added to the current clustering of the web usage data, it could be designated as a new cluster center or just be like other sessions with different membership values to the existing clusters. In the latter case, it is rendered in the usual manner into the point cloud. In the former case, we have devised an incremental version of Sammon Mapping which yields a new 3D position for this session. All subsequent visuals of user sessions and clickstream data then make use of the newly added cluster centers as well. We have experimented with our department's website with over 10,000 pages and web log data gathered over a period of a few months consisting of over half a million web page clicks. For simulating real time web page click, we divided the web log records into a historical data set and a click stream data set (the last 5,000 records).

The rest of this paper is organized as follows. Section 2 is a review of related work on web usage visualization. Section 3 briefly describes the fuzzy clustering technique and also the metric MDS and SM technique used for projecting high dimensional data into low dimension. In Section 4 we explain the process of rendering the web usage data as a point cloud with the active sessions animated as they are incrementally updated with web page click data. We also show results of our experiments on large web usage data. In section 5, we describe the use of incremental fuzzy clustering algorithm for updating the point cloud image to accommodate new usage sessions. Section 6 concludes with some observations and potential future work.

2 Related Work

Most web usage visualizations highlight paths traversed by users in a graph of the website structure. Hence results from research on the general problem of visualizing graph structures become applicable [23]. Further, the near hierarchical structures of the web make visualizing them slightly easier than visualizing a general graph. Cone trees [8], Hyperbolic tree maps [15], and Landscape [1] are typical examples of web structure visualization approaches. SiteLens, from Inxight Software (www.inxight.com), used the hyperbolic tree technique to visualize Web site structure, while NicheWorks [21] used an angular layout similar to disk trees [4]. In most of these visualizations, the main goal is to help users navigate more effectively by visually representing the non-linear information access structure. On the other hand, it is very important for web usage analysis to get insight into usage patterns, current interests, and trends based on web clicks, particularly for large websites with high volume usage. There is considerably less attention on clickstream visualization. Unfortunately, it is hard, if not impossible, to visualize sparse voluminous data of a large number of dimensions of numerous items in a workable manner, as comprehension decreases with the amount of data displayed [8].

WebQuilt [9] is a tool that uses a proxy server to log the user's clickstream. It uses directed graphs to construct a visualization of the user's browsing path. The thickness and the color of the arrows indicate the user's browsing behavior. The thicker arrows denote a more heavily traversed path, and darker arrows mean that more time is spent. Vividence Clickstream [22] and ClickViz [3] use a similar approach to visualize the user's click stream data. Some visualization tools use 3D or multidimensional graphics, which can incorporate more features in one graph. Examples of tools using this kind of technology include Disk tree [4], VISIP [6], Parallel Coordinate [10], and Scalable Framework [14]. However, none of these scale up to be able to handle clickstream data consisting of millions of records. Further, none of them keep any visual record of usage history, thus making it difficult to gage patterns and trends. Our work differs from all the above mainly in the following aspect: we closely couple our visualization technique with a data mining technique that discovers usage patterns in the form of user profiles and then animates active users' click data by overlaying it on a point cloud rendering of clustered historical usage data.

3 Fuzzy Clustering and Dimensionality Reduction

In what follows, we describe the techniques of fuzzy clustering, dimensionality reduction, and graphic mapping used in this work.

3.1 Relational Fuzzy Subtractive Clustering (RFSC)

For discovering usage patterns, we have used Relational Fuzzy Subtractive Clustering algorithm (RFSC) [19]. We have chosen this over other fuzzy clustering techniques for its distinct advantages, namely scalability to large usage data, efficiency, ability to handle noise, and most importantly the existence of an incremental version [20] which we use to maintain up to date usage profiles. RFSC works on web log data organized into sessions and dissimilarity values between sessions defined using the measure given in [16]. We briefly describe the core algorithm to provide a flavor of the RFSC technique. A detailed exposition can be found in [19, 20].

The RFSC algorithm starts by considering each session x_i as a potential cluster center. The potential P_i of each session x_i is calculated as follows:

$$P_i = \sum_{j=1}^{N_U} e^{-\alpha R_{ij}^2} , \text{ where } \alpha = 4/\gamma^2$$

R_{ij} is the dissimilarity between sessions x_i and x_j, N_U is the total number of objects to be clustered, and γ is essentially the neighborhood calculated from the relational matrix R. It also true that $R_{ij} \geq 0$, $R_{ij} = R_{ji}$, and $R_{ii} = 0$.

The session with highest potential (P_1^*) is selected as the first cluster center. Next, the potential of every other session is reduced proportional to the degree of similarity with this previous cluster center. Thus there is larger subtraction in potential of sessions that are closer to this cluster center compared to those which are farther away. After this subtractive step, a session (x_t) with the next highest potential (P_t) is selected as the next candidate cluster center. Now to determine whether this can be accepted as an actual cluster center or not, two threshold values are used, $\overline{\in}$ (accept ratio) and $\underline{\in}$ (reject ratio), where we have that $0 < \overline{\in}$, $\underline{\in} < 1$, and $\underline{\in} < \overline{\in}$. If $P_t > \overline{\in} P_1^*$, then x_t is selected as the next cluster center, and this is followed by the subtractive step described above. If $P_t < \underline{\in} P_1^*$, then x_t is rejected, and the clustering algorithm terminates. If the potential P_t lies between $\overline{\in} P_1^*$ and $\underline{\in} P_1^*$, then we say that potential has fallen in the gray region, in which case we check whether x_t provides a good trade-off between having a sufficient potential and being sufficiently far from existing cluster centers. If this holds, then x_t is selected as the next cluster center. This process of subtraction and selection continues until $P_t < \underline{\in} P_1^*$, which is the termination condition. After finding C cluster centers, the membership degree of different x_j to each cluster c_i is calculated using the formula: $u_{ij} = e^{-\alpha R_{c_i j}^2}$, $i = [1..C]$ & $j = [1..N_U]$, in which $R_{c_i j}$ is the dissimilarity of the ith cluster center x_{c_i} with the jth session x_j. When $x_j = x_{c_i}$, we have $R_{c_i j} = 0$ and that the membership $u_{ij} = 1$. When $x_j = x_{c_i}$, we have $R_{c_i j} = 0$ and the membership $u_{ij} = 1$. While most other fuzzy clustering algorithms impose the condition $\sum_{i=1}^{C} u_{ij} = 1$, RFSC does not. This effectively makes RFSC algorithm less sensitive to noise. Noise sessions are easily identified as their membership values will always lie on the asymptote of each of the clusters.

We have used a point cloud representation in 3D for visualizing usage patterns. Hence, in the next step we need to assign 3D coordinates to each of the sessions. For this, we make use of a dimensionality reduction technique. However, as we shall soon see, our experimental web log data of over half a million page clicks gets organized into 64,529 sessions. Dimensionality reduction for this large data can be computationally prohibitive, as it would involve Eigen value analysis using a matrix of this size iteratively. In particular, convergence can be a major problem as there are many near equal dissimilarity values in the dataset. Fortunately, RFSC provides us with a much smaller number of cluster centers. Therefore, we first map these cluster centers into 3D and then use the fuzzy membership values to render the rest of the sessions.

3.2 Metric Multidimensional Scaling

Metric MDS begins with an n×n dissimilarity matrix R with elements r_{ij}, where $1 \leq i,j \leq n$. The objective of metric MDS is to find a configuration of points in p-dimensional space ($p=3$, in our case) from the dissimilarities between the data points such that the coordinates of the n points in p dimensions yield an Euclidean distance matrix whose elements are as close as possible to the elements of R. Using the metric MDS, we obtain the initial configuration. Since this is quite standard, we refer the reader to [21] for details. However, fidelity to the original distance relationship is poor due to low dimensional projection. To minimize this loss, we use Sammon Mapping, with suitable modifications to be able to handle the special characteristics of web usage data, described next.

3.3 Sammon Mapping

Sammon Mapping (SM) [17] is an unsupervised, nonlinear method that tries to preserve relative distances. The algorithm that generates a Sammon map employs a nonlinear transformation of the observed distances among data items when mapping data items from a high-dimensional space onto a low-dimensional space. Let r^{*}_{ij} denote the dissimilarity (usually Euclidean distance) between two different data items i and j in the original dimensional space, and r_{ij} denote the distance in the required projected space. Then the error function of SM is defined as follows:

$$E = \frac{1}{\displaystyle\sum_{i=1}^{n}\sum_{j=i+1}^{n} r^{*}_{ij}} \sum_{i=1}^{n} \sum_{j=i+1}^{n} \frac{(r^{*}_{ij} - r_{ij})^2}{r^{*}_{ij}} \qquad (1)$$

Here, smaller the error value E, the better is the map we obtain. However, in practice, we are often unlikely to obtain perfect maps especially when the dataset is large and in high-dimensional space. Therefore, approximate preservation is what we can expect.

Let $E(m)$ be the mapping error after the iteration step m, i.e.,

$$E(m) = (1/c)\sum_{i<j}^{n}[r^{*}_{ij} - r_{ij}(m)]^2 / r^{*}_{ij} \qquad (2)$$

where $c = \displaystyle\sum_{i<j}^{n} r^{*}_{ij}$, $r_{ij} = \sqrt{\displaystyle\sum_{k=1}^{p}[y_{ik}(m) - y_{jk}(m)]^2}$, and r_{ij}^{*} is the original distance matrix.

The new d-space configuration at iteration step $m+1$ is given by:

$$y_{pq}(m+1) = y_{pq}(m) - (MF) \times \Delta_{pq}(m) \qquad (3)$$

where $\Delta_{pq}(m) = \dfrac{\partial E(m)}{\partial y_{pq}(m)} \Bigg/ \left| \dfrac{\partial^2 E(m)}{\partial y_{pq}(m)^2} \right|$

and MF is the "magic factor" determined empirically to be about 0.3 or 0.4.

$$\frac{\partial E(m)}{\partial y_{pq}} = \frac{-2}{c} \sum_{j=1}^{n} \left[\frac{r_{pj}^* - r_{pj}}{r_{pj} r_{pj}^*} \right] (y_{pq} - y_{jq}) \qquad (4)$$

$$\frac{\partial^2 E}{\partial y_{pq}^2} = \frac{-2}{c} \sum_{j=1}^{n} \frac{1}{r_{pj}^* r_{pj}} \left[\left(r_{pj}^* - r_{pj} \right) - \frac{(y_{pq} - y_{jq})^2}{r_{pj}} \left(1 + \frac{r_{pj}^* - r_{pj}}{r_{pj}} \right) \right] \qquad (5)$$

This is an iterative process which terminates when the Sammon stress value E cannot be decreased anymore. The guidelines for best stress values suggested by Kruskal [12] are given in the following table:

Table 1. Stress guidelines suggested by Kruskal [12]

Stress	0.3	0.2	0.1	0.025	0.0
Goodness of fit	Poor	Fair	Good	Excellent	Perfect

3.3.1 Modified Sammon Mapping

We can observe that if any two points in the d-space have identical values, then the Sammon stress E will go beyond 1, which is not desirable. When going through the Sammon Mapping iterations for web usage data, we observed that quite often, the distance between some pair of clusters reaches close to zero, thus blowing up the stress value disproportionately. To overcome this problem, we modified equations (4) and (5) above so that even though the d-space has identical values, the stress E does not blow up. This is done by observing that r_{pj} in the denominator of these equations essentially provides a scale factor which can be avoided. The corresponding modified equations are as follows:

$$\frac{\partial E(m)}{\partial y_{pq}} = \frac{-2}{c} \sum_{j=1}^{n} \left[\frac{r_{pj}^* - r_{pj}}{r_{pj}^*} \right] (y_{pq} - y_{jq}) \qquad (6)$$

$$\frac{\partial^2 E}{\partial y_{pq}^2} = \frac{-2}{c} \sum_{j=1}^{n} \frac{1}{r_{pj}^*} \left[\left(r_{pj}^* - r_{pj} \right) - (y_{pq} - y_{jq})^2 \left(1 + r_{pj}^* - r_{pj} \right) \right] \qquad (7)$$

If we consider the mapping error in equation (5), we note that it is not necessary to maintain c in equations (6) and (7) for a successful solution of the optimization problem, since minimization of $(1/c)\sum_{i<j}^{n} [r_{ij}^* - r_{ij}(m)]^2 / r_{ij}^*$ and $\sum_{i<j}^{n} [r_{ij}^* - r_{ij}(m)]^2 / r_{ij}^*$ yield the same result.

We tested the modified SM algorithm using some benchmark datasets such as *iris* and *wine* [2] and confirmed that the results were the same as those obtained using the original SM algorithm. We use this modified SM algorithm in our work.

4 Rendering Fuzzy Clustering of Usage Sessions

We have chosen a simple 3D point cloud visual representation for reflecting the web usage patterns discovered by RFSC. Keeping in mind scalability requirements given the huge volume of web usage data, its sparseness, the inherent fuzziness and noise, and our need for dynamic update to handle clickstream data in real time, we feel that a point cloud, though very simple, is quite adequate. This was based on the following observations.

Choice of 3D over 2D: When clustering web usage sessions, the number of clusters for large data could lie in the range of few hundreds. The added dimension of "depth" in 3D provides the ability to better reflect the distance relationships. With the current trends in 3D graphics hardware, it becomes possible to use a simple metaphor of navigating in space and looking around a collection of clusters (clouds, in our case) to visually inspect the dataset and gain more insight.

Choice of Point cloud: The point cloud can easily handle the fuzziness captured by the clustering technique and visually depict this fuzziness with considerable fidelity.

Scalability of the Visual Mapping Technique: Sessions represented as particles in 3D space is a simple mapping computation and intensity can be varied to reflect closeness of association with a cluster. Large volumes of data can be handled efficiently and more importantly without undue computational overhead.

Noise Visualization: Noise sessions are easily detected in RFSC, as their membership values lie on the asymptotes of each of the clusters. Noise sessions are therefore assigned random positions in the 3D visual space. The effectiveness of this visual mapping is discussed in [11].

Close Integration with Clustering Method: Lastly, it was desired to have a simple method integral to clustering, so that one could show the navigational path in real time to help the web administrator get insight into current trends and interests.

We have the 3D positions of cluster centers from MDS and modified SM. Every point in the dataset has a membership value with every cluster center, which we use to assign 3D positions. The method is simple and described below.

4.1 Assigning 3D Position to Click Data Received from Active User Sessions

Every session (other than cluster centers and noise) is classified into one of following categories:

i) The first category consists of sessions having large affinity towards only one cluster center. The sessions that belong to this category will have one high membership value and all other membership values will be much lower.

ii) In the second category, sessions will have high affinity towards two cluster centers, and much lower membership values for all other clusters.

iii) In the third category, sessions will have high affinity towards three cluster centers, and much lower membership values for all other clusters.

iv) All other sessions are treated as noise.

For each session, cluster centers are addressed in the order of their membership values $(m_1, m_2, m_3 \ldots)$ say, C_1, C_2, C_3, etc. Let a be the average distance between clusters, and R be any random 3D vector.

Steps for rendering sessions that belong to the first category:

1) We consider Polar coordinates, i.e., (r, Θ, Φ), where the radius $r = 0.3a(1 - m_1)$.

2) The values Θ, Φ are chosen randomly to account for the fuzziness.

3) Then we convert these spherical coordinates to Cartesian coordinates, which gives a position (dx, dy, dz) in 3D space relative to the position of C_1.

4) These points are assigned full intensity.

Steps for rendering sessions that belong to the second category:

1) Multiply vector difference, $C_2 - C_1$ by $(1 - m_1)$ to get the vector P.
2) Carry out cross product of $C_2 - C_1$ with random vector R to get vector N.
3) Multiply vector N with $0.5a(1 - m_2)$.
4) Obtain the desired point coordinates by adding the vectors C_1, P, and N.
5) Lastly, assign intensity values reduced in proportion to the distance from the cluster centre.

Steps for rendering sessions that belong to the third category:

1) Multiply vector difference, $C_2 - C_1$ by $(1 - m_1)$ to get the vector P.
2) Carry out cross product of $C_2 - C_1$ with random vector R to get vector N.
3) Multiply vector N by $0.5a(1 - m_2)$.
4) Obtain point coordinates by adding the vectors C_1, P, and N.
5) Follow steps 1 to 4 for the first and third cluster centers.
6) Take the weighted average of the two points (step 4) to get the final point.
7) Assign intensity values reduced in proportion to the summed distances from the cluster centers.

The above procedure yields a computationally efficient method for assigning 3D positions to sessions. Use of dominant membership values results in preserving the inherent relationships much better. We have used the user access logs from our department server during January 15, 2004 to May 5, 2004. This file is cleaned in a preprocessing phase, organized into session data and then a relational data (dissimilarity) matrix is computed using all but the last 5000 log records. This relational matrix is then input to the RFSC algorithm. The total number of user sessions obtained was 64,529 and the number of cluster centers identified by RFSC was 46. Dissimilarity values between cluster centers are extracted from the relational data matrix and used as the input to the dimensionality reduction technique (partially shown in left table in Fig. 1). The result of applying MDS to this dissimilarity matrix is shown in the middle table in Fig. 1. The reader may note some of the zero distances, illustrating the importance of the proposed modification to Sammon Mapping for this kind of data. The Sammon stress value E obtained for this dataset using our method was 0.11 and the much improved result is shown in the right most table in Fig. 1.

	C#1	C#2	C#3	C#4	C#5	C#6
C#1	0.0	1.0	1.0	1.0	1.0	1.0
C#2	1.0	0.0	1.0	1.0	1.0	1.0
C#3	1.0	1.0	0.0	1.0	0.889	1.0
C#4	1.0	1.0	1.0	0.0	1.0	1.0
C#5	1.0	0.889	1.0	1.0	0.0	1.0
C#6	1.0	1.0	1.0	1.0	1.0	0.0

	C#1	C#2	C#3	C#4	C#5	C#6
C#1	0.0	0.0	0.086	0.342	0.167	0.158
C#2	0.0	0.0	0.086	0.342	0.167	0.158
C#3	0.086	0.086	0.0	0.324	0.109	0.232
C#4	0.342	0.342	0.342	0.0	0.420	0.232
C#5	0.167	0.167	0.109	0.420	0.0	0.310
C#6	0.158	0.158	0.232	0.379	0.310	0.0

	C#1	C#2	C#3	C#4	C#5	C#6
C#1	0.0	0.291	0.321	0.545	0.644	0.587
C#2	0.291	0.0	0.252	0.523	0.845	0.718
C#3	0.321	0.252	0.0	0.725	0.841	0.752
C#4	0.545	0.523	0.725	0.0	0.702	0.532
C#5	0.644	0.845	0.841	0.702	0.0	0.226
C#6	0.587	0.718	0.752	0.532	0.226	0.0

Fig. 1. Dissimilarity values: original (left), after MDS (middle), after Sammon Mapping (right)

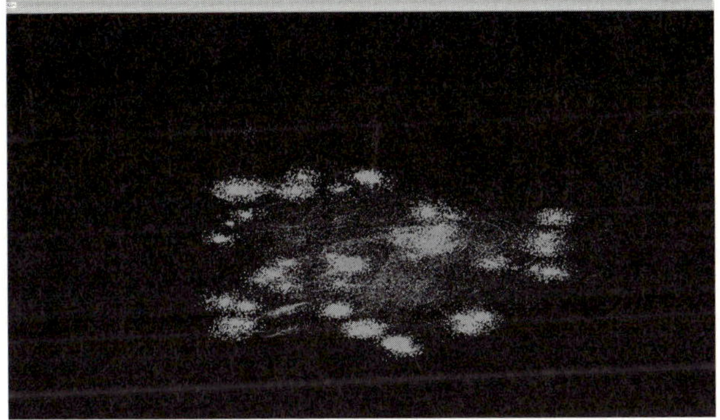

Fig. 2a. Point cloud image of fuzzy clustering of web usage sessions

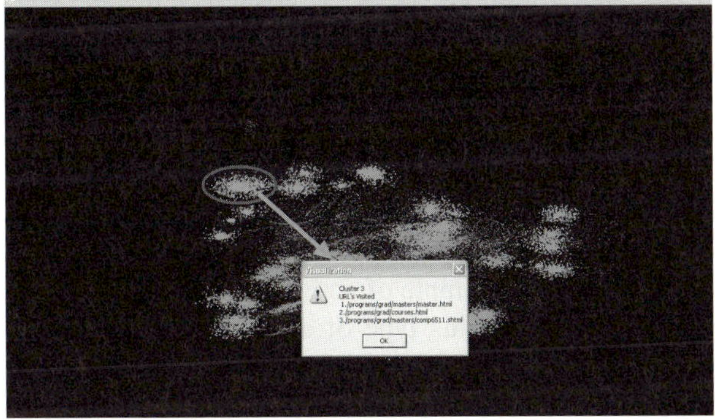

Fig. 2b. Representation of profile details of clicked cluster

The time needed to determine the coordinate values using our method was around 1 hour. This was because the distances between any pair of these 46 cluster centers were almost the same (close to 1), as can be seen in the left table in Fig. 1. In comparison, the time it took to find the coordinates for the *iris* dataset with 150 elements was less than a second since the distances were far more distinct. Fig. 2a shows a point cloud visual representing this usage data. Clicking on any point on this image will yield the preferences of the associated user profile (Fig. 2b).

4.2   Animating Clickstream Data Received from Active User Sessions

As mentioned earlier, once we have the historical web usage data imaged as a point cloud, we consider the currently active sessions. As each active user navigates through different web pages in the website, we animate this as a linear path in 3D overlaid on the 3D point cloud model. This is done as follows: The web page clicks are retrieved every frame and analyzed. This could create a new active session or update the pages visited by an active user session. We first calculate the session dissimilarity of each updated active user session with the current cluster centers. Then we obtain the fuzzy memberships with all existing cluster centers. Lastly, we assign a new position to each updated user session by the method described in section 4 and render it in a distinct color.

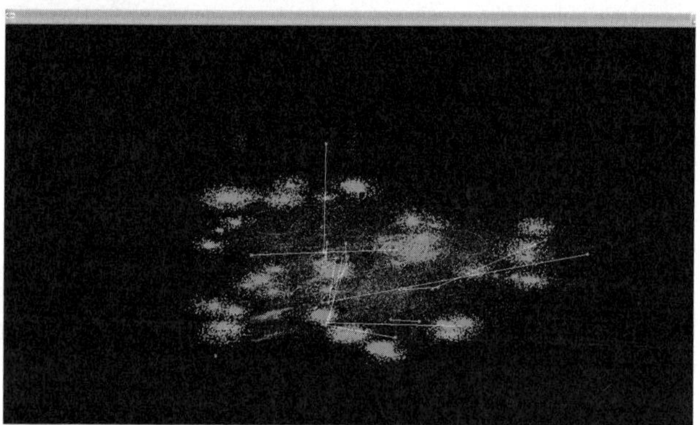

Fig. 3. Active user path visualization from clickstream data

For experimental purposes, we analyzed the last 5000 records of our web log and extracted the updates to active user sessions in an incremental fashion. Fig. 3 shows a screenshot which illustrates a sample of active user sessions as darker dots and the paths followed until this time. This type of animation enables one to visually get deeper insight into current trends and interests. For example, when an existing cluster is the attractor for many active user paths, it indicates that this is a "hot" usage profile.

5   Incremental RFSC and Visualization

Over a period of time, active sessions are terminated; in our case when there is no activity from that user for 45 minutes. The paths of terminated active sessions are removed from the display. However, as the number of such sessions increases, for correct visual depiction of the web site usage history, these must be reflected in the point cloud. For high volume usage, the over head is quite high if we have to carry out complete reclustering of the entire usage data (old clustered sessions plus newly completed sessions). Instead, we make use of the Incremental RFSC algorithm [20]. Whenever a new session is added, this algorithm either makes it a new cluster center or assigns fuzzy membership values to existing clusters.

As new clusters are discovered, it becomes essential to add the new clusters into the point cloud without changing the position of the existing clusters, to avoid any visual confusion to the viewer. We have again devised a method for plotting the new cluster without having to run the MDS and SM methods for the whole data again. We first obtain an initial coordinate value using the distance between the new cluster center and the existing cluster centers. Then we use the SM method described in section 3 to decrease the error in distance between the newly found cluster center and the existing cluster centers. When the Sammon stress goes beyond a pre-defined threshold, we need to perform the MDS and SM for the entire data set. We have experimented by removing the sessions belonging to a cluster and then found that Incremental RFSC does add that new cluster and this method assigns a new 3D position to the cluster center, sufficiently distinguishable from the rest.

6   Conclusions and Future Work

Historical data of web usage must be used in any visualization of clickstream data, if the web administrators have to gain insight into changes in trends and interests over time. Web usage data is however, very large, sparse, noisy, non-Euclidean and fuzzily classified, making its visualization a difficult task. In this paper, we have proposed using a combination of techniques: (i) RFSC for fuzzy clustering, (ii) a combination of Multidimensional Scaling followed by modified Sammon Mapping, we introduced, for dimensionality reduction to enable point cloud like visual rendering of the usage data, and (iii) incremental RFSC for continued update of the point cloud and (iv) animation of active user paths to get insight into trends and interests. By cleverly using the membership values assigned by RFSC to the other sessions, we developed a fast method for rendering the large data.

Future work is primarily on improvements to the current technique. First, we plan to provide another window which displays the structure of the website and highlights any usage profile, selected by user clicking on the point cloud. This will obviate the need for the message box which we currently display over the point cloud. Second, we plan to provide interrogation facility in the form of "if then" queries. For example, the web administrator can change the structure by editing one or more links, and the system would react by illustrating the effect of this change on usage profiles, for instance, in terms of the number of links to be traversed.

Acknowledgements

This work was supported in part by NSERC (Canada) and ENCS, Concordia University. We thank B.S. Suryavanshi for his contribution in the development of the RFSC algorithm used in this work. We also thank the CSE Department at Concordia for providing us with the web log records used as part of our experiments.

References

1. Andrews, K.: Visualizing Cyberspace: information visualization in the harmony internet browser. In Proc. 1st IEEE Symp. On Information Visualization, (1995), pp. 90-96.
2. Blake, C.L., Merz, C.J.: UCI Repository of Machine Learning Databases. (1998)
3. Brainerd, J., Becker, B.: Case Study: E-commerce Clickstream Visualization. In Proc. of the IEEE Symp. On Information Visualization, (2001), pp. 153-156.
4. Chi, E.H.: Improving Web Usability through Visualization. Internet Computing, 6(2), (2002), pp. 64-71.
5. Chi, E.H.: WebSpace Visualizations. In Proc. 2nd Int'l World Wide Consortium (W3C), IEEE Internet Computing, 6(2), (1994), pp. 64-71.
6. Cugini, J., Scholtz, J.: VISIP: 3D Visualization of Paths through Websites. In Proc. Int'l workshop on Web-Based Information Visualization, Florence, Italy, (1999), pp. 259-263.
7. Han, J., Kamber, M.: Data Mining: Concepts and Techniques. Morgan Kaufmann, (2000).
8. Herman, I., Melancon, G., Marshall, M.S.: Graph Visualization and Navigation in Information Visualization: a survey. IEEE TVCG, 6(1), (2000), pp. 24-43.
9. Hong, J.I. Landay, J.A.: WebQuilt: A Framework for Capturing and Visualizing the Web Experience, In Proc. 10th Int'l World Wide Web Conference, Hong Kong, China, (2001), pp. 717-724.
10. Inselberg, A., Dimsdale, B.: Parallel coordinates: A tool for visualizing multi-dimensional geometry. In Proc. Visualization 90, San Francisco, CA, USA, (1999), pp. 361-370.
11. Kannappady, S., Mudur, S.P., Shiri, N.: Visualization of Web Usage Patterns. In Proc. 10th Int'l Database Engineering & Applications Symposium (IDEAS), New Delhi, India, (2006).
12. Kruskal, J.B.: Multidimensional Scaling by optimizing goodness of fit to a nonmetric hypothesis. Psychometrika, 29(1), (1964), pp. 1-27.
13. Lee, J., Podlaseck, M., Schonberg, E., Hoch, R.: Visualization and Analysis of Clickstream Data of Online Stores for Understanding Web Merchandising. Int'l Journal of Data Mining and Knowledge Discovery, 5(1), (20001), Kluwer Academic Publishers.
14. Lopez, N., Kreuseler, Schumann, H.: A scalable framework for information visualization, Trans. on Visualization and Computer Graphics, (2001).
15. Munzner, T.: Drawing Large Graphs with H3Viewer and Site Manager. In Proc. Graph Drawing 98, Springer-Verlag, New York, (1998), pp. 384-393.
16. Nasraoui, O., Krishnapuram, R., Joshi, A., Kamdar, T.: Automatic Web User Profiling and Personalization using Robust Fuzzy Relational Clustering, in E-commerce and Intelligent Methods Ed., Springer-Verlag, (2002).

17. Sammon, J.W. Jr.: A non-linear mapping for data structure analysis, IEEE Trans. on Computers, 18, (1969), pp. 401-409.
18. Simonson, J., Fuller, G., Tiwari, A.: A Survey of Web History Data Analysis and Visualization, In http://www.math.grinnell.edu/~lindseyd/ResearchState.html
19. Suryavanshi, B.S., Shiri, N., Mudur, S.P.: An Efficient Technique for Mining Usage Profiles Using Relation Fuzzy Subtractive Clustering. In Proc. Int'l workshop on Challenges in Web Information retrieval and Integration, (2005), pp.23-29.
20. Suryavanshi, B.S., Shiri, N., Mudur, S.P.: Incremental Relational Fuzzy Subtractive Clustering for Dynamic Web Usage Profiling. In Proc. WEBKDD Workshop on Training Evolving, Expanding and Multi-faceted Web Clickstreams, Chicago, Illinois, USA, (2005).
21. Trevor, F.C., Michael A.A.C.: Multidimensional Scaling, 2nd Edition, Chapman & Hall/CRC, (2001).
22. Vivince Clickstreams, In http://www.vivdince.com/resources/public/solutions/demo/demo-print.htm
23. Wills, G.J.: Nicheworks-Interactive Visualization of Very Large Graphs. In proc. Graph Drawing 97, Lecture Notes in Computer Science, Springer-Verlag, Berlin, (1997).

GPU Objects

Sunil Mohan Ranta, Jag Mohan Singh, and P.J. Narayanan

Center for Visual Information Technology
International Institute of Information Technology
Hyderabad, India
{smr@research., jagmohan@research., pjn@}iiit.ac.in

Abstract. Points, lines, and polygons have been the fundamental primitives in graphics. Graphics hardware is optimized to handle them in a pipeline. Other objects are converted to these primitives before rendering. Programmable GPUs have made it possible to introduce a wide class of computations on each vertex and on each fragment. In this paper, we outline a procedure to accurately draw high-level procedural elements efficiently using the GPU. The CPU and the vertex shader setup the drawing area on screen and pass the required parameters. The pixel shader uses ray-casting to compute the 3D point that projects to it and shades it using a general shading model. We demonstrate the fast rendering of 2D and 3D primitives like circle, conic, triangle, sphere, quadric, box, etc., with a combination of specularity, refraction, and environment mapping. We also show combination of objects, like Constructive Solid Geometry (CSG) objects, can be rendered fast on the GPU. We believe customized GPU programs for a new set of high-level primitives – which we call *GPU Objects* – is a way to exploit the power of GPUs and to provide interactive rendering of scenes otherwise considered too complex.

1   Introduction

Points, lines, and polygons are the basic primitives in conventional graphics. Acceleration hardware is optimized to process them quickly in a pipeline. Complex shapes are converted to these primitives before rendering. Procedural geometry, on the other hand, involves on-the-fly creation of arbitrarily accurate shape from compact descriptions, usually in the form of implicit equations. The graphics display pipeline cannot render procedural geometry directly. Procedural objects are converted to piecewise linear models using polygons and lines before rendering. This results in a loss in resolution and incurs computational overhead. Ray-tracing methods can handle procedural geometry to produce high-quality renderings. These methods have very high computational complexity and are not suitable for interactive applications.

The Graphics Processor Units (GPUs) have seen very steep growth in processing capabilities. They deliver highest computation power per unit cost today and have been improving at a quick pace. Introduction of programmability in GPUs at the vertex and the fragment levels has brought novel uses of the graphics hardware. We present several examples of fast and accurate rendering of

P. Kalra and S. Peleg (Eds.): ICVGIP 2006, LNCS 4338, pp. 352–363, 2006.

procedural objects on the GPUs in this paper. The equations of the objects are evaluated exactly at each pixel it projects to in a way similar to the ray-tracing techniques. This results in high quality rendering at all resolution levels and exact, per pixel lighting. We also apply the technique to objects that are traditionally not considered to be procedural. All of this is performed at interactive frame rates.

Procedural geometry has many benefits over polygonal geometry. In the latter, the surface is approximated by a triangle mesh. Triangulation in itself is an overhead, which requires time consuming preprocessing of the geometry. Triangulated mesh requires high memory bandwidth from the CPU to the GPU and huge video memory for storage. Procedural geometry can save both bandwidth and memory requirements drastically. Resolution independent rendering of curved surfaces [1] was achieved using procedural geometry on GPU. Resolution independence results in the curved surfaces appearing exactly curved at all magnification levels. Procedural geometry finds its application in Constructive Solid Geometry (CSG), which is used in solid modeling to create complex shapes by combining simple shapes primitives with boolean operators on sets [2]. The primitives used in CSG are ground set of shapes such as box, sphere, cylinder, cone, torus, prism, etc.

In this paper, we outline a general procedure for rendering a wide class of objects using ray-casting from a GPU. We also show how high-quality lighting options can be computed exactly for these objects. We demonstrate the procedure to interactively render several generic objects very fast on the GPU. These include triangle, quadrilateral, circle, conic, sphere, box, tetrahedron, quadric, etc. We also show how different lighting models can be incorporated into the rendering. We then extend the basic procedure to render a combination of objects together and demonstrate it on various CSG objects. We believe this is the first time high-quality ray-casting of CSG objects has been performed at interactive rates. Our work lays the foundation for a class of *GPU Objects* that can be rendered interactively in high quality. We show overview of our results in

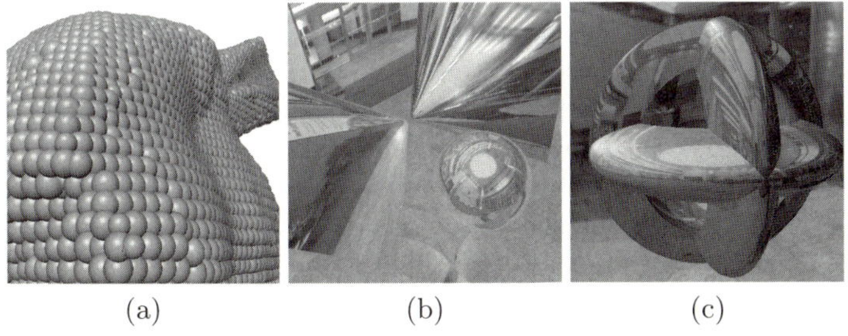

(a)   (b)   (c)

Fig. 1. GPU Objects: (a) Bunny with 36K spheres at 57 fps. (b) Hyperboloid with reflection and sphere with reflection and refraction at 300 fps. (c) Four-primitive CSG at 22 fps.

Figure 1. A GPU Object consists of program fragments for the CPU, the vertex shader and the pixel shader and can be called like a function by an application program with the parameters for the objects. As the limitations of today's GPUs go away and the architecture evolves to include more memory, longer programs, and more flexible shaders, customized GPU Objects will be a way to exploit their compute power to provide interactive rates to rich scenes.

2   Prior Work

Graphics hardware is getting faster which helps rasterization to produce good rendering effects. The effects generated by ray tracing are the most realistic. Programmable graphics hardware is able to deliver the promise of realistic rendering effects using ray tracing. Ray tracing of procedural objects [3] transforms the three dimensional ray-surface intersection into a two dimensional ray-curve intersection problem, which is solved by using strip trees. It was demonstrated on procedural objects such as fractal surface, prisms and surfaces of revolutions. Ray tracing of complex scenes [4] incorporated several new schemes such as bounding box being a good convex hull of the object, division of the object into hierarchies and efficient data structure for traversing this hierarchy. These techniques were used for speeding up ray tracing. Ray-tracing on GPU [5] with different methods such as Whitted ray tracing, path tracing, and hybrid rendering algorithms showed that it runs faster on GPU than on CPU. Ray Engine [6] does a ray-triangle intersection on GPU and achieves effects such as recursive ray tracing, path tracing, form factor computation, photon mapping, subsurface scattering, and visibility processing. Ray tracing of ellipses with EWA filtering which results in anti-aliased splats was done by Botsch et. al [7]. Ray tracing of perspectively correct ellipsoids on GPU [8] render ellipsoid by transformation of a unit sphere. GPU accelerated primitives [9] presents a framework for rendering of quadric surfaces on GPU. They use a different Ray Tracing Area for each type of quadric to minimize the load on pixel shader. Ray tracing of quadrics on GPU [10] which uses efficient bounding box computation has been done recently. Fully Procedural Graphics [11] proposes the extension of graphics hardware so that it may be able to support procedural rendering of objects.

CSG has already been a well explored area using CPU based algorithms. Initial methods included the generalization of scanline algorithm using ray tracing for rendering of intersecting objects [12]. CSG graph representation is optimized into Convex Difference Aggregates for efficient CSG of convex objects [13]. Normalization and bounding box pruning for CSG [14] demonstrated on the pixel planes architecture and surface intersection using bounding box optimization [15] achieve faster CSG. The use of stencil buffer and depth peeling techniques was done for CSG by Guha et. al [16]. Blister [17] evaluates Blist representation of CSG expression directly on GPU and is able to render large number of primitives in real-time.

3   Rendering Geometric Objects

The fundamental operation used by our rendering method is the intersection of a ray with an object. The intersection is computed in the pixel shader for each pixel, given the parameters of the object being rendered. This step is essentially the conventional ray casting implemented on the pixel shader. The points on the ray in parametric form can be represented as $P = O + tD$, where t is the parameter along the ray, O the camera center and D the direction of the ray. The intersection of the ray with an object given by $f(P) = 0$ can be calculated by substituting the parametric form for P and solving the resulting equations for the smallest value of t. Polynomial forms of $f()$ span a range of useful objects and are easy to solve. Many non-linear forms of $f()$ can also be solved for analytically. Representations such as triangle, quadrilateral, box, tetrahedron, etc., are not procedural, but can be intersected with a ray efficiently on the pixel shader.

We now give a generic procedure to draw a general object using an appropriate shader. The object is given by the implicit form $f(P) = 0$.

Algorithm 1. renderGeomObject(f)

CPU: An OpenGL program performs the following.

1: Pass the parameters of $f()$ to the graphics pipeline as graphics bindings such as texture coordinates, color and position. A texture can be used if more data needs to be sent.

2: Draw an OpenGL primitive such that the screen-space area of the object is covered by it. This ensures that all pixels will be drawn and the corresponding shaders will be executed. The primitive used could be a dummy one with the right number of vertices.

Vertex Shader: A vertex shader performs the following.

3: Pass the parameters from the CPU to the pixel shader.

4: Transform the OpenGL primitive drawn by the CPU to cover the screen-space area of the object using the object parameters.

5: Perform other pixel independent calculations required for the pixel shader and passes on the results.

Pixel Shader: A pixel shader performs the following.

6: Receive the parameters of the object and own pixel coordinates (i, j) from the pipeline.

7: Perform an acceptance test for (i, j) based on the parameters of $f()$. This involves computing exactly if the pixel will be on the projected region of the object. This may require the parameters of $f()$, the Modelview, Projection, Viewport matrices, etc. The acceptability can be computed in a 2D texture space in some cases.

8: Compute the ray-object intersection for accepted pixels. This involves solving an equation in t that is based on $f()$.

9: Compute the 3D point corresponding to the smallest t among the intersecting points. Also compute the depth and normal at that point using $f()$.

10: Shade the pixel using the lighting, material, normal, and viewing information that is available to the shader. The reflected ray at the intersection point can be pursued to apply environment mapping, refraction etc.

It is important to setup the screen-space bounding area as compactly as possible as it affects the computation time. A compact bounding polygon is a good option. The CPU and the vertex shader set this up in combination. The interpolation of texture coordinates performed by the primitive assembly unit can be exploited to send values to all pixels, if suitable. This would be useful for data like the 3D position, depth, etc., that may be needed at the pixel shader. It is also possible to draw a single point-primitive with appropriate point-size [10]. This can involve extra calculations performed at the pixel shader. The pixel shaders code memory and computation time could be stretched by this, while the task of the CPU and the vertex shader are simplified. Every pixel in the bounding area need to check if it is part of the actual object. The ray-object intersection will give imaginary results for pixels that are outside the object. Easier acceptance tests may be available for some shapes. The intersection point for the accepted rays has 3D position (from the ray equation), a normal vector (from derivatives of $f()$), and a view direction (from the camera position). Every pixel can be lit accurately using these. The reflected and refracted rays can be computed and used for effects like environment mapping and refraction. Recursive ray tracing is, however, not possible as the pixel shaders don't support recursion or deep iteration due to the SIMD programming model available at the fragment units.

We now explain how the above generic procedure can be used to render several different 2D and 3D objects.

3.1   Planar Shapes

We consider the shapes circle, conic, triangle, and parallelogram. For planar shapes, the pixel acceptance can be performed in two ways: in the 3D space and in the texture space. In the former, the ray-plane intersection and the acceptance tests are performed in 3D space. In the latter, the vertex shader converts the coordinates to in-plane coordinates and passes them as texture coordinates. These values are interpolated by the rasterizer. The pixel shader performs the acceptance test using the 2D equations using the interpolated texture coordinates. Texture space acceptance test is more efficient but requires a dedicated bounding area. This means only one primitive can be rendered at a time.

Circle: A square is used as the bounding area for the circle. A more close fitting regular polygon can also be used, but at the cost of increasing the vertex shader time. The parameters for the circle are its center, radius and the plane normal. These values are passed using texture coordinates to the shaders. A dummy square with coordinates $(\pm 1, \pm 1)$ is passed by the CPU and are transformed by the vertex shader to a square with length twice the radius. The implicit equation $|P - C| - r \leq 0$ is evaluated in world coordinates to check validity in 3D space. For texture space calculations, the in-plane coordinates of the square corners are sent by the vertex shader as a texture coordinate. This is interpolated by the rasterizer and the interpolated value is available to the pixel shader. The circle equation can be evaluated in 2D using the texture coordinates. We illustrate the algorithm for rendering of a circle with environment mapping below :

Algorithm 2. CircleRender(Center, Radius and Normal)

1: **CPU** Send a dummy quad with coordinates $(\pm 1, \pm 1)$.
2: **Vertex Shader** Convert the corner coordinates of the quad to in-plane coordinates and set them as texcoord.
3: **Pixel Shader** receive center and in-plane coordinates
4: **if** distance of current pixel from center $>$ radius **then**
5:    discard
6: **else**
7:    use normal for lighting.
8:    use reflected ray for environment mapping. reflected ray is obtained by reflecting the ray from camera center to current pixel about the normal
9:    return color and depth of accepted pixel
10: **end if**

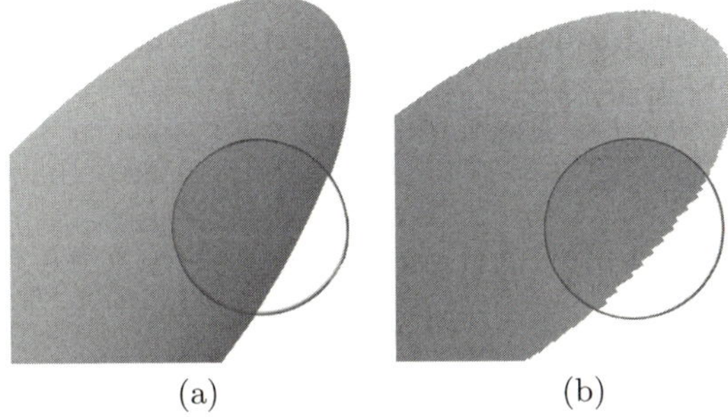

(a)   (b)

Fig. 2. (a)Ellipse rendered procedurally on GPU (b) Ellipse rendered using a texture of 512x512 resolution. GPU based rendering is resolution independent and has no aliasing artifacts where circle shows the zoomed view.

Conic: Conic is a curve formed by intersecting a cone with a plane. Shapes such as hyperbola, ellipse, circle, and parabola can be represented using conics. Conics are represented in matrix notation as $PCP^T = 0$ where C is a symmetric matrix. A conic is described using 6 parameters for C, and the base plane normal. The bounding area for a conic is computed by finding orthogonal lines tangent to the conic. The bounding area thus formed is a rectangle. The dummy square from the CPU is aligned to this rectangle by the pixel shader. The shader also computes the in-plane coordinates of the rectangle vertices as texture coordinates, which are interpolated before reaching the pixel shader. Pixel shader evaluates PCP^T for the in-plane coordinates and its sign is used for acceptance.

In fragment shader we first compute intersection of the ray with plane. Equation of plane with normal n and passing through point p is given by $n \cdot (p - x) = 0$ and its intersection with ray is given by $t = n \cdot (p - O)/n \cdot D$. The traced point is converted to 2D point and then checked with equation of the conic. For texture space test, the ray-plane intersection and conversion to 2D point is computed in vertex shader and interpolated values are used in pixel shader for acceptance test using sign of PCP^T.

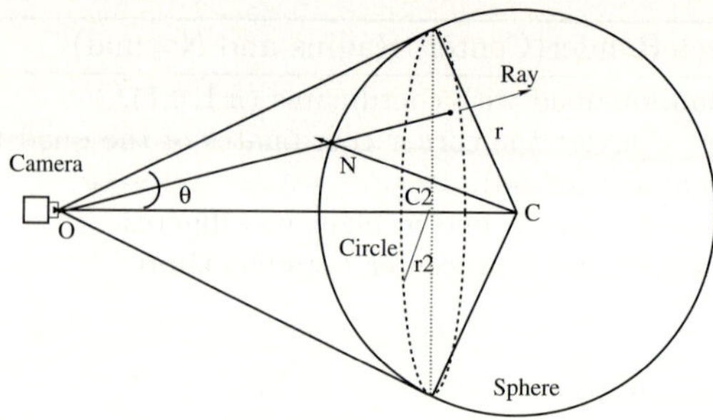

Fig. 3. The sphere is converted into a circle normal to camera view vector

Triangle and Parallelogram: Triangle is strictly not a procedural object. However, the interior of the triangle is given by $0 \leq u, v \leq 1$, where u, v are the barycentric coordinates calculated using the vertices. The bounding area for triangle is a one pixel wider triangle in screen space. Three points are sent from the CPU which are converted to the barycentric coordinates by the vertex shader using Möller et al. algorithm [18]. Triangle bound checking on barycentric coordinates is used for acceptance test. For 3D space test the coordinates are evaluated in pixel shader and then used for bound checking. The same can be achieved in texture space, by evaluating the barycentric coordinates on the vertex shader and interpolating it to the pixel shader.

A parallelogram can be handled in a similar way. The condition for acceptance is $0 \leq u, v \leq 1$. As for triangle, this acceptance test can be done either in 3D space or in texture space.

3.2   3D Shapes

We consider the following 3D shapes: sphere, quadric, cylinder, cone, parallelepiped, and tetrahedron. For 3D objects, the bounding area is either a bounding box for the object in 3D space or bounding rectangle in projected space. 3D shapes can have one or more intersections with ray. Nearest intersection is used for calculating depth and shading. For use as CSG primitive all intersections are important.

Sphere: A sphere can be represented using a quadric. It is handled more efficiently than a general quadric by Toledo et al. [9]. We use a different approach in order to render it even more efficiently by reducing the problem to rendering of a circle of appropriate radius and orientation. Figure 3 shows a sphere with center C and radius r and its projected circle with center $C2$, radius $r2$, and oriented along the ray from sphere center to camera center. The procedure for rendering a sphere, SphereRender(C, r) is described in Algorithm 3.

Thus, we reduce the bounding area for sphere to bounding area of the circle, which in general is a camera facing regular polygon. It can be drawn using a polygon with optimal edges or even as a single point with proper size. Figure

---

Algorithm 3. SphereRender(C, r)

1: **CPU** Send a dummy quad
2: **Vertex Shader** $r2 = r\cos(\sin^{-1} r/d)$; $C2 = (1 - \frac{r^2}{d^2})C + \frac{r^2}{d^2}O$.
   Convert to in-plane coordinates using [18] and send corner points as texcoord.
3: **Pixel Shader** receive $C, C2, r$ and $r2$ and in-plane coordinates $P : (u, v)$
4: **if** $|P - C2| > r2$ **then**
5:    discard
6: **else**
7:    solve quadratic equation for ray-sphere intersection and use smaller t.
8:    light using 3D point, normal, and view vector.
9:    use reflected ray for environment mapping if enabled.
10:    **if** refraction **then**
11:       intersect refracted ray again with sphere,
12:       refract it once more and use it for environment mapping.
13:    **end if**
14:    set color of pixel as linear combination of above colors.
15:    return color and depth of accepted pixel
16: **end if**

Fig. 4. Top: Bunny Model with 35,947 spheres is rendered at 57 fps at 512x512 viewport and its zoomed view. Bottom: Ribosome molecule with 99,130 spheres is rendered at 30 fps at 512x512 viewport and its zoomed view.

4 shows rendering of large datasets represented as collection of spheres at interactive frame rates. We used NVIDIA GeForce 6600 GT in our experiments.

Cylinder and Cone: The bounding area for cylinder is billboard rectangle along cylinder axis and a square at end of the cylinder facing the camera. The bounding area for cone is billboard triangle along cone axis and a square at the base of the cone. Ray intersection involves solving quadratic equation, and real roots producing pixels are accepted.

Fig. 5. Sphere and Ellipsoid with environment mapping and refraction at 300 fps

General Quadric: Quadric surfaces are second order algebraic surfaces represented in matrix notation as $PQP^T = 0$ where Q is a symmetric matrix and P is a point. Bounding area for the quadric is computed from its conic projection defined as $C = PQP^T$ where P is projection matrix. The base plane of the conic is QC. Ray intersection of quadric is given by roots of quadratic equation in t and pixels resulting in complex values of t are discarded. For texture space acceptance test, ray is intersected with base plane of conic in vertex shader and texture space values of intersections are used in pixel shader for inside-conic test. Quadrics with reflection, refraction and environment mapping are shown in Figure 5.

Parallelepiped and Tetrahedron: Parallelepiped is formed by three pairs of parallel parallelograms. A parallelepiped can be represented using four vertices. The six parallelograms can be described using these vertices and the intersection with each is computed. Bounding area for parallelepiped is given by three parallelogram faces. 3D space ray-parallelogram intersection is computed for every face, and the nearest intersection point is considered for lighting. For CSG both intersection are of importance.

Tetrahedron is formed by four triangles and can be represented using its four vertices. The four triangles can be described using these vertices. A regular tetrahedron is represented using apex position, direction vector and side length. Bounding box for tetrahedron is formed by four triangles of it and the intersection with each triangle is computed using ray-triangle intersection in 3D space.

4   Rendering CSG Objects

We showed how different objects can be rendered fast using special shaders on the GPU. The object is rendered with correct depth and color values. Thus, the GPU rendering can be mixed with normal polygonal rendering and the picture will have correct occlusions and visibility. We now see how a combination of objects can be drawn together by the GPU. The motivation is to draw CSG objects, which are formed using union, intersection, and subtraction of other objects. CSG objects are represented using CSG trees of primitives and are popular in CAD to describe objects exactly. Procedural objects are commonly used in CSG.

We show the rendering of CSG objects that are boolean combinations of the objects we have seen earlier. Ray casting at the pixel shader is used for this.

Algorithm 4. renderCSGObject()

CPU:

1: Write the primitives of the CSG tree into the texture memory with appropriate descriptions.
2: Calculate the screen-space bounding area for the positive primitives in the scene and draw it using OpenGL.

Pixel Shader:

1: Read the CSG tree and information about the primitives from the texture.
2: Calculate all ray intersection for every primitive.
3: Sort the intersections by t. Preserve primitive id for each intersection point. Set toi as +1 for entry intersections (smaller t) and -1 for exit intersections (larger t).
4: Create two counters: $plus$ for positive and $minus$ for negative primitives and initialize both to zero.
5: Examine each intersection point. Add its toi to the $plus$ counter if the corresponding primitive is a positive one. Add toi to the $minus$ counter otherwise. The counters contains the number of positive and negative objects encountered by the ray from beginning.
6: Stop when the $minus$ counter is zero and $plus$ counter is positive. This is the first visible point along the ray. The primitive for this intersection is the visible primitive.
7: Compute depth and normal using the visible primitive. Reverse normal direction if the visible primitive is negative.
8: Light the point using the normal material properties etc.

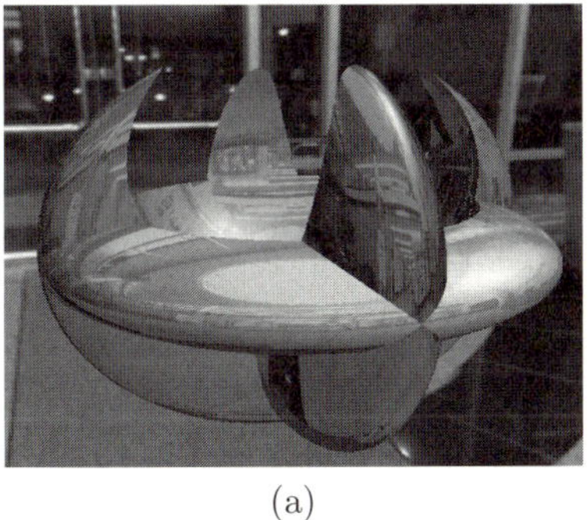
(a)

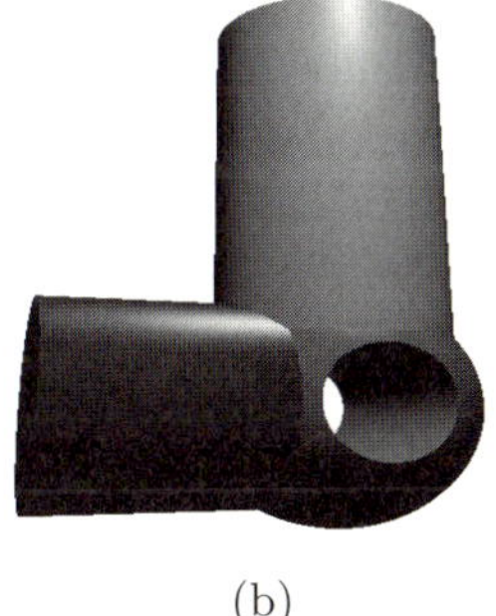
(b)

Fig. 6. (a) CSG of four quadrics with reflection and environment mapping at 20 fps. (b) CSG of cylinders and spheres with phong shading at 20 fps.

However, the ray could intersect multiple objects and the boolean combination between them decides what actually gets drawn. Thus, all objects in the CSG tree need to be rendered *together* to generate the correct image at each pixel. Points are evaluated for being on the boundary of composite object for drawing [17].

Our scheme stores the CSG tree in texture memory and its reference is made available to the shaders. Each primitive is represented using an id for its type, the parameters for that type of primitive, and a flag to indicate if the primitive is used in an additive or subtractive sense. We outline a procedure renderCSGObject() (Algorithm 4), to draw a simple CSG object, consisting of a set of positive primitives and a set of negative ones.

The above procedure can render complex CSG objects. Rendering many primitives together is a challenge on today's GPUs with its limitations on the shader length. We are able to render CSG objects shown in Figure 6 containing upto 5 quadric primitives on the NVidia 6600GT system. This will improve with newer generation cards and very complex CSG objects will be possible in the future. We show some of our results in the accompanying video.

5   Conclusions and Future Work

In this paper, we presented a scheme for rendering several high-level objects using appropriate shaders on programmable GPUs. We showed interactive rendering of several geometric and CSG objects with sophisticated, per pixel, lighting. The figures and accompanying video demonstrate the effectiveness and speed of our method in rendering many high level objects.

The GPUs are getting more powerful and more programmable with every generation. While they speed up the rendering of conventional geometry, their impact can be felt more in rendering higher level primitives that are slow to render today. This can be made possible using specialized shader packages that can draw certain types of objects quickly. These packages – which we call *GPU Objects* – could be parametrized to generate a class of objects and a class of rendering effects. These GPU Objects can be invoked by a rendering program as they do with OpenGL primitives. They can be mixed freely with one another and with conventional geometry rendering and will produce the correct visibility and lighting effects. We are currently devising generic GPU Objects that can be parametrized to get a variety of objects. Such objects will be possible to render at high speeds on the future GPUs as they get more flexible.

References

1. Loop, C.T., Blinn, J.F.:   Resolution independent curve rendering using programmable graphics hardware. ACM Trans. Graph. **24** (2005) 1000–1009
2. Requicha, A.A.G.: Representations for rigid solids: Theory, methods, and systems. ACM Comput. Surv. **12** (1980) 437–464
3. Kajiya, J.T.: New techniques for ray tracing procedurally defined objects. ACM Trans. Graph. **2** (1983) 161–181

4. Kay, T.L., Kajiya, J.T.: Ray tracing complex scenes. In: SIGGRAPH '86. (1986) 269–278
5. Purcell, T.J., Buck, I., Mark, W.R., Hanrahan, P.: Ray tracing on programmable graphics hardware. In: SIGGRAPH '02. (2002) 703–712
6. Carr, N.A., Hall, J.D., Hart, J.C.: The ray engine. In: HWWS '02: Proceedings of the ACM SIGGRAPH/EUROGRAPHICS conference on Graphics hardware, Eurographics Association (2002) 37–46
7. Botsch, M., Hornung, A., Zwicker, M., Kobbelt, L.: High quality surface splatting on today's gpus. In: Proc. of symposium on Point-Based Graphics '05. (2005) 17–24
8. Gumhold, S.: Splatting illuminated ellipsoids with depth correction. In: VMV. (2003) 245–252
9. Toledo, R., Levy, B.: Extending the graphic pipeline with new gpu-accelerated primitives. Tech report, INRIA (2004)
10. Christian Sigg, Tim Weyrich, M.B., Gross, M.: Gpu-based ray-casting of quadratic surfaces. In: Proceedings of Eurographics Symposium on Point-Based Graphics 2006 (to appear). (2006)
11. Whitted, T., Kajiya, J.: Fully procedural graphics. In: HWWS '05: Proceedings of the ACM SIGGRAPH/EUROGRAPHICS conference on Graphics hardware. (2005) 81–90
12. Atherton, P.R.: A scan-line hidden surface removal procedure for constructive solid geometry. In: SIGGRAPH '83. (1983) 73–82
13. Rappoport, A., Spitz, S.: Interactive boolean operations for conceptual design of 3-d solids. In: SIGGRAPH '97. (1997) 269–278
14. Goldfeather, J., Monar, S., Turk, G., Fuchs, H.: Near real-time csg rendering using tree normalization and geometric pruning. IEEE Comput. Graph. Appl. **9** (1989) 20–28
15. Mazzetti, M., Ciminiera, L.: Computing csg tree boundaries as algebraic expressions. In: SMA '93: Proceedings on the ACM symposium on Solid modeling and applications. (1993) 155–162
16. Guha, S., Mungala, K., Shankar, K., Venkatasubramanian, S.: Application of the two-sided depth test to csg rendering. In: I3D, ACM Interactive 3D graphics. (2003)
17. Hable, J., Rossignac, J.: Blister: Gpu-based rendering of boolean combinations of free-form triangulated shapes. ACM Trans. Graph. **24** (2005) 1024–1031
18. Moller, T., Trumbore, B.: Fast, minimum storage ray-triangle intersection. J. Graph. Tools **2** (1997) 21–28

Progressive Decomposition of Point Clouds Without Local Planes*

Jag Mohan Singh and P.J. Narayanan

Center for Visual Information Technology
International Institute of Information Technology
Hyderabad, India
{jagmohan@research., pjn@}iiit.ac.in

Abstract. We present a reordering-based procedure for the multiresolution decomposition of a point cloud in this paper. The points are first reordered recursively based on an optimal pairing. Each level of reordering induces a division of the points into approximation and detail values. A balanced quantization at each level results in further compression. The original point cloud can be reconstructed without loss from the decomposition. Our scheme does not require local reference planes for encoding or decoding and is progressive. The points also lie on the original manifold at all levels of decomposition. The scheme can be used to generate different discrete LODs of the point set with fewer points in each at low BPP numbers. We also present a scheme for the progressive representation of the point set by adding the detail values selectively. This results in the progressive approximation of the original shape with dense points even at low BPP numbers. The shape gets refined as more details are added and can reproduce the original point set. This scheme uses a wavelet decomposition of the detail coefficients of the multiresolution decomposition. Progressiveness is achieved by including different levels of the DWT decomposition at all multiresolution representation levels. We show that this scheme can generate much better approximations at equivalent BPP numbers for the point set.

1   Introduction

Polygon-based graphics is useful when the properties – such as color, normals, depth – can be interpolated linearly along a plane, from their values at the vertices. This results in the approximation of the shape for many natural objects. As the graphics capability improves, they get represented using finer and finer polygons. Recently, points have attracted renewed attention as the basic graphics representation primitives [1]. The interest in point-based representations is due to the increase in the resolution of polygon models. The polygons in the graphics models have been shrinking in size for greater accuracy and visual fidelity. Per pixel calculations are made in the graphics hardware in most cases to improve the shading

* This research was carried out with partial funding from the Naval Research Board, India.

P. Kalra and S. Peleg (Eds.): ICVGIP 2006, LNCS 4338, pp. 364–375, 2006.
© Springer-Verlag Berlin Heidelberg 2006

effects. The display resolution has, on the other hand, been saturating. Thus, it is common for the polygons of a model to be of the same order as a screen pixel in many situations. This makes polygons cumbersome and inefficient to handle. Point-based representations could be more natural and efficient in such situations.

Point based models contain a very large number of points often running into the millions. Representing them in a compressed manner is therefore essential. Multiresolution representation and progressive decoding are important to point based models even more than geometric models. Methods proposed for that typically compute a local plane of support to induce a regular grid to the points [2,3]. This facilitates the application of many standard signal and image compression algorithms to points. These local planes are computationally intensive to find and can cause approximation errors. Since points have no connectivity, they are conceptually independent of one another and can be reordered with no loss in information.

In this paper, we present a simple multiresolution decomposition of a point set based on their proximity without the need for a local plane. Our scheme is based on the reordering of the points that naturally provides multiresolution representation and progressive decoding. Our method reorders and decomposes points successively into approximation and detail sets, loosely similar to the wavelet decomposition. The approximation results in representation of the point set in a different levels of decreasing detail. The detail sets are vector differences between point-pairs. We further reduce the representational complexity of the approximations by changing the quantization based on the sampling rate, keeping a fine balance between sampling and quantization. We provide a progressive representation for the point set. This is done by decomposing the details using DWT up to a certain number of levels and is used to obtain an approximation of the detail. While reconstructing the point set we use the approximated details instead of the original details. This scheme is used for generating an approximation of the point set with given number of bits.

We survey the literature related to the compression of point-based representations in Section 2. Section 3 presents the details of our multiresolution decomposition scheme and decompression. Section 4 shows results and is followed by a few concluding remarks in Section 5.

2   Related Work

Compression techniques have mainly focused on triangle meshes. Triangle based mesh compression mainly focuses on encoding connectivity [4,5,6]. Vertex positions are obtained by quantization followed by predictive coding. Progressive coders allow for better prediction of positions which allow for reconstruction of intermediate shapes by using a prefix of encoded bit stream. These include progressive meshes [7] which uses greedy edge collapses to arrive at lower resolution mesh. Progressive geometry compression [8] eliminates the need for connectivity compression by using semi-regular meshes, wavelet transforms, and zero-tree encoding.

Point based representations allow us to work directly on point data without worrying about connectivity. QSplat [9] uses a multiresolution data structure based on a bounding volume hierarchy. This is optimized for rendering of large point based models such as those obtained through the Digital Michelangelo Project [10]. The preprocessing allows dynamic level of detail selection on the fly. Layered Point Clouds [11] handles large point based models and adjust their sampling according to their projected size on the screen. The sampling technique [12] used is able to handle complex and procedural geometry. Point set surfaces [3] use Moving Least Square (MLS) which is a projection operator which can be used both for upsampling and downsampling of the surface. MLS operator can be used for generating multiresolution point sets [13]. They use a polynomial and a local plane and generate multiple resolutions by varying the degree of the polynomial. The number of choices available for encoding between two consecutive levels are however limited. MLS is a smoothing operator and it smooths the sharp features of the point set surface. Efficient Simplification of Point Sampled Surfaces [14] estimates the curvature of points using local planes. They use curvature and quadric error metric for simplification which is computationally expensive. Progressive compression of point sampled models [15] finds an optimal pairing of points and replace them by their average at lower level of approximation. This is followed by differential coding where the residues are decreased further by the use of local planes and a prediction operator. The residues are coded using a zerotree coder which gives a progressive stream and finally using arithmetic coding. This scheme can be used for generating progressive levels from a given point set at a fixed rate and progressive rate. This scheme is able to handle point attributes such as geometry, color and normals. However, averaging sends the points to outside the manifold and local plane computation which is needed is expensive. Predictive point-cloud compression [16] uses a prediction tree, which is a spanning tree over the vertices. Rooting of the tree defines a partial order. The tree is built greedily by adding those nodes that predicts the new point with smallest residue such as constant and linear. The residues are then encoded by arithmetic coding. This generates multiresolution hierarchy of the original point set. This scheme handles only geometry.

3   Multiresolution Decomposition Using Reordering

We propose a lossless, multiresolution decomposition of the geometry of the point set. Our scheme is based on a reordering of the points. Points are first paired up optimally such that the sum of distances between the pairs is minimum. The pairing induces a partitioning of the points into Odd and Even halves. The Odd half provides a lower resolution representation of the model. This process is repeated recursively with successive Odd sets to get a lossless multiresolution decomposition of the point set. We also adjust the quantization at the lower levels to match the sampling. Detail and quantized approximation are encoded by arithmetic encoding. The multiple resolutions of the representation provide discrete LODs of the original point cloud with decreasing number of points.

3.1   Reordering of Points

Our algorithm uses the minimum weighted perfect matching [17] for pairing up the points. A perfect matching in a graph G is a subset of edges such that each node in G is met by exactly one edge in the subset. Given a real weight c_e for each edge e of G, the minimum-weight perfect-matching problem is to find a perfect matching M of minimum weight $\Sigma(c_e : e \in M)$. An implementation of Edmond's original algorithm will run in time $O(n^2 m)$ where n is the number of nodes in the graph and m is the number of edges. Minimum weighted perfect matching uses an improved version of Edmond's algorithm and is bounded by $O(nm \log(n))$. The pairing at each level minimizes the total Euclidean distance between all pairs. The edge weights can additionally include distances between colors and normals if those attributes are also being compressed. We do not construct the complete graph but only an adjacency graph connecting each vertex with its $k = 16$ nearest neighbours.

After applying perfect matching we get odd and even point sets.While choosing the odd point set and even point set after perfect matching we enhance coherence in the even point set. The odd point is chosen such that the vector from the odd point to the even point has positive X, Y, and Z components in that order of priority. This will increase the correlation between the pairing vectors since our intention is to replace the even points with them. The perfect matching would reorder the point sets such that the total distance between the odd and even point sets. After, getting the lowermost odd point set by repeatedly applying perfect matching. We would reorder the point sets such that odd points are in positions $(1, \cdots, N/2)$ and the corresponding even points are in the positions $(N/2 + 1, \cdots, N)$. This reordering is applied recursively to the odd half of the points so that after reordering the points remain matched. When a point in the odd section is reordered its matching even point should also be reordered to maintain the pairing. If only one level of decomposition is done then the even point set has to be reordered only once. However, if k levels of decomposition is done or perfect matching is applied k times, then the movement of a point at the lowest level can result in reordering of 2^{k-1} points.

3.2   Approximation and Detail

The even point can be replaced by a vector from the matching odd point. If the pairing is done well, these vectors will have similar values and can compress well.

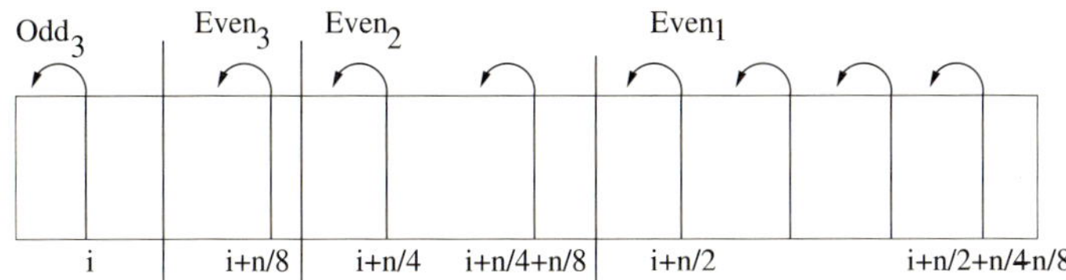

Fig. 1. Point set reordering with three levels of decomposition arrows show the movement of matching points. The positions show where the matched points appear after reordering.

This is performed in all hierarchical decomposition levels. The approximation point set is same as the odd point set. The detail point set is obtained by taking vector difference between the matched even point and the odd point for every point in the even point set. Thus, after k levels of decomposition the approximation is A_k and the detail is D_k. We denote j^{th} point of detail D_i as $D_i[j]$ and j^{th} point of approximation A_i as $A_i[j]$. Note that the lower resolution approximations have the larger index among A_is and D_is. The approximation and detail are shown after three levels of decomposition Figure 1.

A3	D3	D2	D1

Fig. 2. Approximation and detail after decomposition. $A3$ is the lowest resolution level. $A3$ and $D3$ make up $A2$ in a lossless manner and so on recursively.

If each even point $i + N/2^j$ at level j is replaced by the vector from its odd counterpart i at each step, the decomposition divides the original point set successively into $A_k, D_k, D_{k-1}, D_{k-1}, \cdots D_1$.

The approach used by [15] is similar to the full edge collapse used in triangle meshes. Our approach is similar to the half-edge collapse used in triangle meshes. In triangle meshes the full edge collapse might result in converting a manifold mesh to a non-manifold mesh [18]. The same can happen in point sampled models as the average position is not expected to lie on the manifold. Figure 3 shows the back part of the of the bunny model with positions as average on the left one and retained on the right. The edge weight of the graph constructed in both the cases is the Euclidean distance and attributes are averaged in one case and retained in another. The averaged representation appears more regular, but has the points that are clearly away from the original manifold. This problem is more serious at lower levels of approximation.

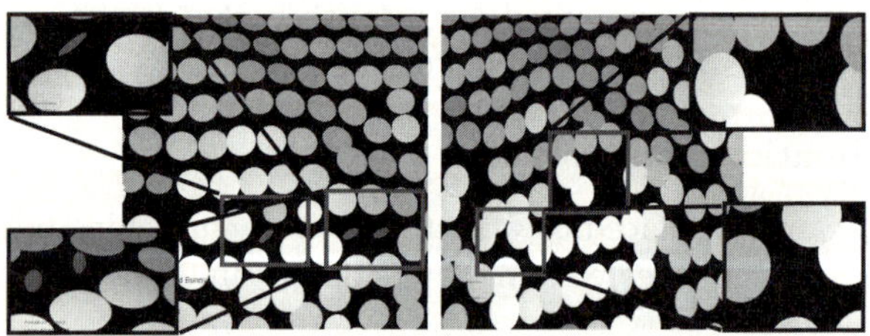

Fig. 3. Comparison between averaging the pairs and retaining one of them. The averaged Bunny (left) have points that move away from the manifold (as shown in the inset), but the retained Bunny (right) has all the points on the original manifold.

3.3   Balanced Quantization and Sampling

It has been established that the quantization and sampling should be matched to each other in point-sampled representations [19]. It is fruitless to represent coordinates with precision when they are sparsely sampled. Conversely, the quality will be poor if a densely sampled set of points is represented using only a few bits. This can be exploited to gain greater compression ratios at higher levels of decomposition.

The point coordinates are represented using fixed precision integers. The number of bits used should depend on the sampling rate at that level. Twelve to fifteen bits per coordinate will suffice for most practical models used today. Thereafter, when approximation A_{i-1} is split into A_i and D_i, the coordinates of A_i are stripped off the least significant bit. Thus, the coordinates at level i are represented using $p - i$ bits if the original points are represented using p bits. The least significant bits that are collected as an $(N/2^i)$-bit entity E_i of extra information Figure 4.

Hence, our k-level decomposition of points consists of $A_k, D_k, E_k, D_{k-1}, E_{k-1}$ $D_{k-1}, E_{k-2}, \cdots, D_1$, and E_1. The computation of approximation and detail from the point set in our case does not involve the use of local coordinate frames as done in [15].

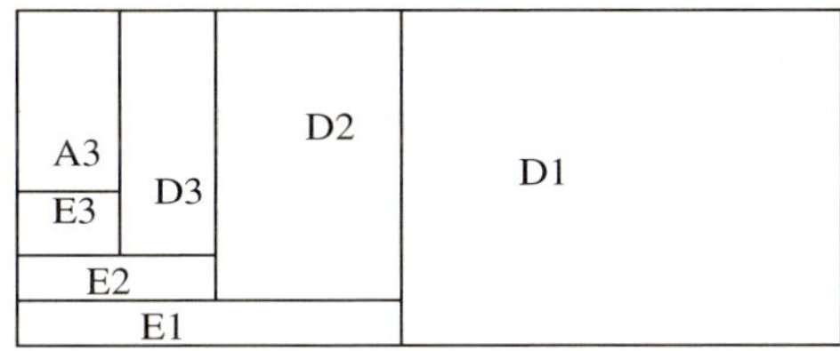

Fig. 4. Point Set after reordering and quantization

3.4   Compressed Representation

The approximation and detail are encoded using arithmetic encoding [20]. The extra detail, obtained during quantization, is packed into a stream of bytes and no encoding is applied as they do not compress much. The encoding is lossless. Given the lower level approximation, detail and extra-detail we can compute the higher level approximation exactly.

3.5   Decompression

The original point set has been reordered so that approximation and detail are matched. Thus decompression is simple and the level up to which we need lossless reconstruction is computed from the same. Hence, in our scheme the data size needed to store the complete progressive point set is same as the original point set. In order to obtain a better approximation, we use the coarsest level of approximation and the encoded detail levels and extra detail levels till we get the required level of approximation. We achieve high compression this way as details and approximation after encoding require less space than the encoded higher approximation level.

Table 1. PSNR and BPP for Different Models. Compression ratio is inversely proportional to BPP.

Level	Bunny(35k)	Santa(75k)	GolfBall(122k)	Venus(134k)	Armadillo(172k)
0	∞/30.84	∞/41.71	∞/41.29	∞/31.17	∞/42.82
1	45.60/7.65	66.41/12.8	62.38/13.05	49.69/6.96	80.15/12.24
2	44.16/3.74	53.53/5.79	61.30/6.72	48.18/2.99	66.19/5.79
3	43.18/1.74	51.19/2.86	60.68/3.27	47.18/1.41	55.61/2.56
4	42.30/0.91	49.81/1.39	50.17/1.50	46.29/0.67	53.12/1.28
5	41.54/0.47	48.76/0.65	47.46/0.75	45.52/0.30	51.6/0.63
6	40.87/0.23	47.91/0.31	45.86/0.37	44.84/0.16	50.48/0.27
7	40.29/0.14	47.22/0.18	44.71/0.18	44.23/0.08	49.61/0.14
8	-	46.62/0.09	43.74/0.09	43.7/0.04	48.88/0.08
9	-	-	42.93/0.05	43.2/0.02	48.28/0.04

Level	Lion(183k)	Lucy(262k)	Heptoroid(286k)	Brain(294k)	Octopus(465k)
0	∞/31.57	∞/41.19	∞/22.59	∞/43.01	∞/41.79
1	53.7/8.11	66.26/12.06	65.66/15.03	65.69/13.94	60.33/9.98
2	52.94/3.11	63.37/5.82	61.22/7.05	61.98/6.38	59.36/4.41
3	51.99/1.67	58.11/2.8	56.59/3.27	54.57/3.29	58.35/1.69
4	51.13/0.96	56/1.32	49.5/1.59	50.67/1.56	57.5/0.87
5	50.38/0.47	54.64/0.61	44/0.78	48.82/0.71	56.74/0.48
6	49.72/0.22	53.62/0.27	41.71/0.38	47.60/0.35	56.08/0.21
7	49.15/0.11	52.81/0.13	33.51/0.19	46.72/0.17	55.51/0.10
8	48.65/0.063	52.16/0.07	28.18/0.09	46/0.07	55.02/0.05
9	48.23/0.032	51.65/0.039	25.87/0.04	45.41/0.044	54.57/0.02
10	47.84/0.018	51.22/0.02	24.36/0.021	44.94/0.024	54.19/0.014

3.6   Results

Table 1 shows the PSNR and bits per pixel (BPP) for different point based models after our decomposition. Some of the models at different resolutions are shown in Figure 6. The figure shows the model using a surfel radius that is higher for lower resolution models.

We also give the rate distortion curves for different models (see Figure 5). The compression is lossless hence the reconstructed model from the coarsest approximation and details will match exactly. PSNR is calculated by considering the error induced in the geometry as we go down the levels. The peak signal is the diameter of the bounding sphere of the point set. The mean square error is the cumulative magnitude of the details and the extra-details as we go down the levels. The BPP at a level is calculated as a ratio of the total number of bits in its representation to the total number of points.

We are able to achieve high levels of compression and low BPP values using the scheme. Each lower level has approximately half the number of points as the next higher model. Thus, the levels represent successive approximations using fewer points but at very low bpp numbers. Our method can be thought of as retaining the high level information as we down the lower levels which is more important

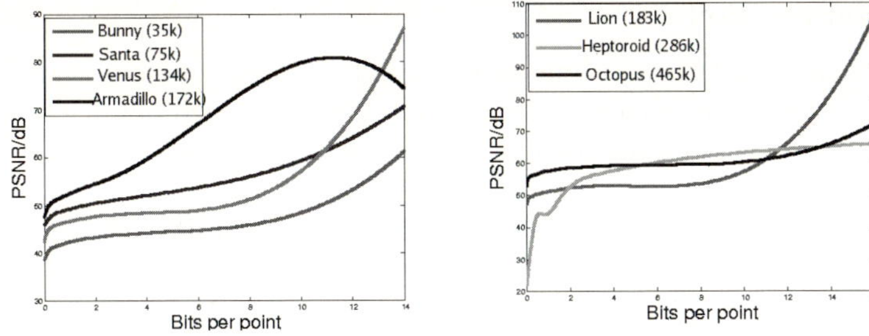

Fig. 5. PSNR/BPP for Bunny, Santa, Venus, Armadillo, Lion, Heptoroid, and Octopus Models

Fig. 6. Left to Right, Top to Bottom: Lucy model at Levels 7 (0.13 BPP), 4 (1.32 BPP) and 2 (5.82 BPP) , Venus at Levels 8 (0.04 BPP), 5 (0.30 BPP) and 3 (1.41 BPP). Octopus at Levels 9 (0.02 BPP), 5 (0.48 BPP) and 2 (4.41 BPP).

for perception and approximating the shape than the low level information which is a result of averaging process. Thus, averaging will lead to low pass version of the signal which is not a true approximation of the original shape. However, retaining the high pass information will give us the important features in the shape and the rest can be filled by changing the surfel radii accordingly.

4 Progressive Representation of the Point Set

The multiresolution decomposition given above differs from a standard wavelet decomposition critically, though there are structural similarities. In a wavelet decomposition, if the detail coefficients are set to zero, an averaged version of the signal is reproduced. This version is approximate but dense, covering the whole domain. In our decomposition, if the detail coefficients are set to zero, the points are repeated. The higher levels do not contain any additional information if a detail value is 0. We need a scheme in which different approximations of D_is can be generated. While a 0 value for D_i repeats points, approximation of D_i can generate a dense representation of the original point set. One way to do this is to approximate the detail values as a $1D$ signal. Different approximations of this signal will contain different details.

4.1   Decomposition

We treat each detail D_i as a one dimensional sequence of slow varying numbers and compress the sequence using DWT. Thus, for each detail D_i, DWT is applied k_i times. k_i is chosen such that the last level has about M points. We used a simple 7 -tap Daubechies wavelet for decomposition and set M as 25. A representation of this is shown in Figure 7 where k_i is $5, 10$, and 15 for D_3, D_2 and D_1 respectively. Let $\mathcal{D}_i$ be the DWT decomposition of D_i.

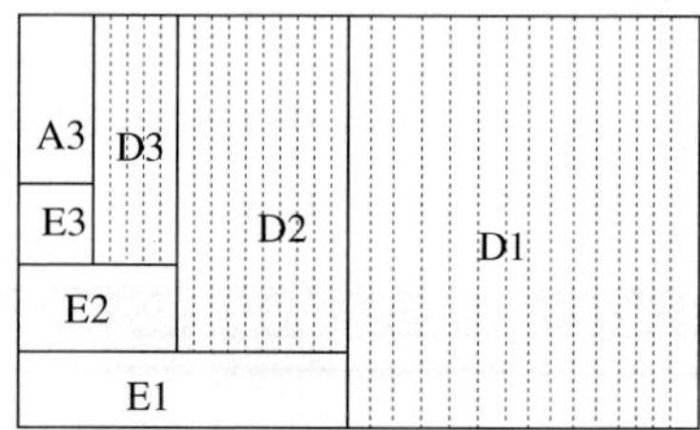

Fig. 7. Point set after reordering, quantization and wavelet decomposition of detail values. This is obtained by decomposing D_3, D_2 and D_1 into $5, 10$, and 15 levels respectively.

4.2   Progressive Representation

Each D_i can be approximated by including only a number of its DWT levels resulting in a smooth version of the D_i sequence. Since, each $D_i[j]$ value acts as a displacement on a point $A_i[j]$, it generates another point in the representation. This results in a better approximation of the point set. A dense representation of the point set with as many points as the original point set can be obtained if we include some of all D_is in the representation. If we set all D_is to 0 for $i < j$, a representation with as many points as the approximation level A_j can be obtained. We give a procedure to generate an approximation of the point set with M points and S number of bits given a model with N original points and k multiresolution decomposition levels.

The above algorithm can produce approximations of the point set with different number of points and total size. The combination of A_k and $\mathcal{D}'_i, E'_i, \ k \leq i < j$ is a compact representation of the point set. They can be used to reconstruct the model in two steps. First, approximate D'_is for each level is found by applying IDWT on each $\mathcal{D}_i$, setting the missing coefficients to 0. Next, an approximation A'_j of the point set is generated using the decompression technique given in Section 3.5 using A_k and D'_is and E_is. In our experiments, we allocate 80% of the bits at every level to $\mathcal{D}_i$ and the rest to E_i.

4.3   Results

We give the rate distortion curves for different models (see Figure 8) using progressive representation. Since the decomposed model has exactly the same

---

Algorithm 1. Progressive Representation(M, S)

1: Find level $j = \lceil \log_2 N/M \rceil$ with more than M points. Skip D_is for all $i < j$.
2: Include the lowest level A_k. Subtract its size from S. This is the number of bits available for D_is and E_is.
3: Allocate these bits equally among the levels from k to j.
4: **for** $i = k$ to j **do**
5:     Let S_i be the size allocated to level i. A fraction r of it is used for D_i and rest for E_i.
6:     If S_i is greater than the combined size of $\mathcal{D}_i$ and E_i, set $\mathcal{D}'_i \leftarrow \mathcal{D}_i$ and $E'_i \leftarrow E_i$.
7:     Otherwise, construct $\mathcal{D}'_i$ with as many DWT coefficients of $\mathcal{D}_i$, starting with the most approximate level, such that the combined size is rS_i and construct E'_i with $(1 - r)S_i$ bits of E_i
8: **end for**
9: Return A_k and $\mathcal{D}'_i, E'_i$ for $i= k$ to j

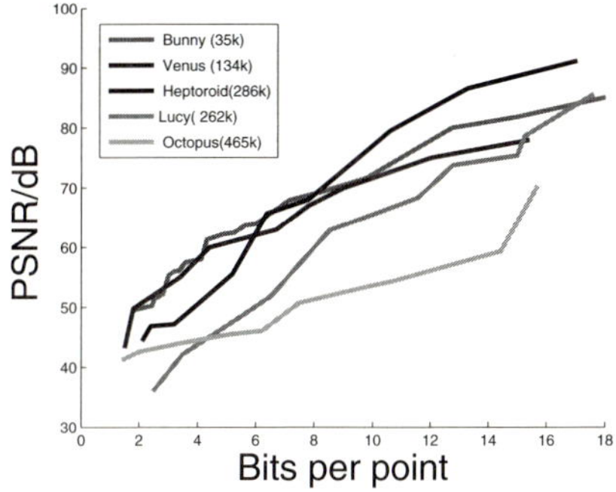

Fig. 8. Rate distortion curve for Bunny, Venus, Heptoroid, Lucy and Octopus models for the progressive representation. These cannot be directly compared directly with Figure 5 as the PSNR is calculated in a different way here as explained in the text.

number of points as the reordered original point-set, the PSNR can be calculated by taking from the error between the corresponding points. This is a better measure of quality unlike those used in Section 3 or by Waschbüsch et al. [15] The peak signal is the diameter of the bounding sphere of the point set. BPP is calculated by taking into account number of bits used to go till the higher most level of approximation using the approximation and reconstructed details. Lucy Model at different BPP is shown in Figure 9 with increased radius for hole free appearance. We compare the quality of models achieved by progressive representation and multiresolution decomposition Figure 10. Note that higher BPP are required in progressive representation but the model has fewer holes. We use the procedure progressive representation for to generate any number of points.

Fig. 9. Lucy Model at 2.27 BPP, 3.16 BPP, and 8.24 BPP respectively using the progressive representation

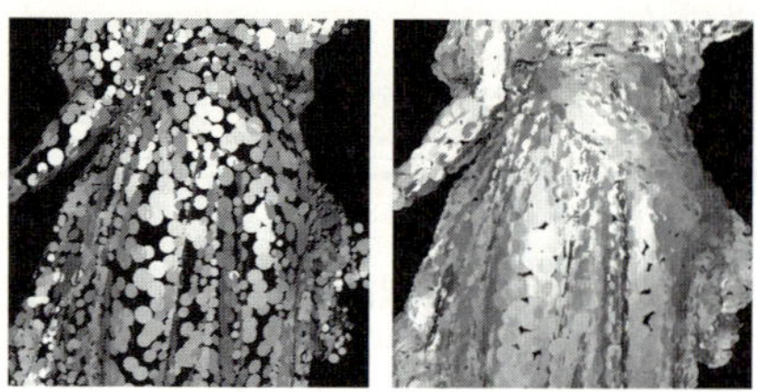

Fig. 10. Lucy Model at 3.11 BPP from the multiresolution decomposition (left) and progressive representation (right) with same radius for both. Progressive representation is visually superior.

5   Conclusions and Future Work

We presented a simple, reordering based algorithm to decompose a point set into multiple resolutions. The algorithm is based on optimal pairing and decomposes the points into a low resolution approximation and a series of detail vectors. The points of all approximation levels fall on the original manifold. We are able to get further compression using balanced quantization at every sampling level. The multiresolution decomposition provides discrete levels of detail to the point set. We also present a progressive representation of the point set by compressing the detail vectors using wavelets. By selectively including different numbers of coefficients of the wavelet decomposition at each detail level, we are able to get a wide range of representations for the point set, ranging from the lowest approximation to a totally lossless representation. The progressive representation scheme can be used to generate a model with the given number of points and a given BPP. Progressive representation results in better visual appearance compared to the multiresolution decomposition.

Currently, the decomposition is performed on the whole point set. This decreases the coherence of the detail vectors. Partitioning the points into different parts of the model and treating each part independently will perform better. The detail vectors will be more coherent and will compress well using DWT. We can also select different progressive levels for different parts of the point set based on proximity or importance. We are exploring these ideas currently.

References

1. Kobbelt, L., Botsch, M.: A survey of point-based techniques in computer graphics. Computer and Graphics **28** (2004) 801–814
2. Pauly, M., Gross, M.: Spectral processing of point-sampled geometry. In: SIGGRAPH '01. (2001) 379–386
3. Alexa, M., Behr, J., Cohen-Or, D., Fleishman, S., Levin, D., Silva, C.T.: Computing and rendering point set surfaces. IEEE Transactions on Visualization and Computer Graphics **9** (2003) 3–15
4. Gumhold, S., Strasser, W.: Real time compression of triangle mesh connectivity. In: SIGGRAPH '98. (1998) 133–140
5. Rossignac, J.: Edgebreaker: Connectivity compression for triangle meshes. In: IEEE Transactions on Visualization and Computer Graphics. Volume 5. (1999) 133–140
6. Touma, C., Gotsman, C.: Triangle mesh compression. In: Graphics Interface. (1998) 26–34
7. Hoppe, H.: Progressive meshes. In: SIGGRAPH '96. (1996) 99–108
8. Khodakovsky, A., Schroder, P., Sweldens, W.: Progressive geometry compression. In: SIGGRAPH '00. (2000) 271–278
9. Rusinkiewicz, S., Levoy, M.: Qsplat: a multiresolution point rendering system for large meshes. In: SIGGRAPH '00. (2000) 343–352
10. Levoy, M., Pulli, K., Curless, B., Rusinkiewicz, S., Koller, D., Pereira, L., Ginzton, M., Anderson, S., Davis, J., Ginsberg, J., Shade, J., Fulk, D.: The digital michelangelo project: 3d scanning of large statues. In: SIGGRAPH '00. (2000) 131–144
11. Gobbetti, E., Marton, F.: Layered point clouds. In: Eurographics Symposium on Point Based Graphics. (2004) 113–120, 227
12. Stamminger, M., Drettakis, G.: Interactive sampling and rendering for complex and procedural geometry. In: Rendering Techniques 2001 (Proceedings of the Eurographics Workshop on Rendering 01). (2001)
13. Fleishman, S., Cohen Or, D., Alexa, M., Silva, C.T.: Progressive point set surfaces. ACM Trans. Graph. **22** (2003) 997–1011
14. Pauly, M., Gross, M., Kobbelt, L.P.: Efficient simplification of point-sampled surfaces. In: VIS '02: Proceedings of the conference on Visualization '02. (2002) 163–170
15. Waschbüsch, M., Gross, M., Eberhard, F., Lamboray, E., Wurmlin., S.: Progressive compression of point-sampled models. In: Proceedings of the Eurographics Symposium on Point-Based Graphics. (2004) 95–102
16. Gumhold, S., Karni, Z., Isenburg, M., Seidel, H.P.: Predictive point-cloud compression. In: Proceedings of the Sixth Israel-Korea Bi-National Conference. (2005) 125–129
17. Cook, W., Rohe, A.: Computing minimum-weight perfect matchings. INFORMS Journal on Computing **11** (1999) 138–148
18. Luebke, D., Reddy, M., Cohen, J.D., Varshney, A., Watson, B., Huebner, R.: Level of Detail for 3D Graphics. Morgan Kaufmann (2003)
19. Botsch, M., Wiratanaya, A., Kobbelt, L.: Efficient high quality rendering of point sampled geometry. In: EGRW '02: Proceedings of the 13th Eurographics workshop on Rendering. (2002) 53–64
20. Moffat, A., Neal, R.M., Witten, I.H.: Arithmetic coding revisited. ACM Trans. Inf. Syst. **16** (1998) 256–294

Task Specific Factors for Video Characterization

Ranjeeth Kumar, S. Manikandan, and C.V. Jawahar

Center for Visual Information Technology
International Institute of Information Technology
Gachibowli, Hyderabad - 500032, India
jawahar@iiit.ac.in

Abstract. Factorization methods are used extensively in computer vision for a wide variety of tasks. Existing factorization techniques extract factors that meet requirements such as compact representation, interpretability, efficiency, dimensionality reduction *etc.* However, when the extracted factors lack interpretability and are large in number, identification of factors that cause the data to exhibit certain properties of interest is useful in solving a variety of problems. Identification of such factors or *factor selection* has interesting applications in data synthesis and recognition. In this paper simple and efficient methods are proposed, for identification of factors of interest from a pool of factors obtained by decomposing videos represented as tensors into their constituent low rank factors. The method is used to select factors that enable appearance based facial expression transfer and facial expression recognition. Experimental results demonstrate that the factor selection facilitates efficient solutions to these problems with promising results.

1   Introduction

Factorization methods are popular in computer vision [1,2,3,4,5]. Applications of factorization methods include recovery of structure from motion(SfM) [1], separation of style and content [3], decomposition of facial expressions [4] and local parts decomposition [2,5]. The use of factorization techniques differs in aspects like the manner in which factors are extracted, interpreted and modeled. Tomasi and Kanade [1] recover the scene structure and the camera motion from a sequence of images taken with a moving camera by factorizing a measurement matrix into shape and motion factors using Singular Value Decomposition(SVD). The factors are interpretable, and they characterize the generative process. The model of image formation assumed therein is valid. The factors extracted i.e. the scene structure and the camera motion are useful for several other tasks. Tenenbaum and Freeman [3] use a bilinear model to characterize the interaction between style and content parameters. They use SVD and Expectation Maximization(EM) algorithms to carry out the tasks of classification, extrapolation and translation which require inferring the model, and one or both of the factors. The style and content factors in [3] are interchangeable and the generative model assumed (a simple bilinear model) is rich enough to capture the interaction between the factors although it lacks formal evidence. Moreover, their

P. Kalra and S. Peleg (Eds.): ICVGIP 2006, LNCS 4338, pp. 376–387, 2006.
© Springer-Verlag Berlin Heidelberg 2006

goal is not the extraction of the factors alone but to solve related tasks that require simultaneous learning of one or both of the factors and the factor model. Both these algorithms fall into the class of algorithms where the factors are fixed in number, interpretable and the factor model corresponds to the underlying generative model. Another class of algorithms attempt to identify sets of latent variables that aid in elimination of redundancies in the data. The small set of variables along with the factor model explain the structure in the data and result in compact representation. Ghahramani and Hinton [6] model the covariance structure of data assuming a simple factor model that is linear in the factors. A mixture of such models has been used for simultaneous dimensionality reduction and clustering. Techniques like Principal Component Analysis and Positive Tensor Factorization [7] extract factors that enable dimensionality reduction or compression. Tensor representation based methods are gaining wide attention in computer vision [8,9] as tensor representation is more suitable for image collections or videos. The observation that positive factorization of matrices results in local parts decomposition of objects [2] resulted in similar factorization methods for tensors [7,10]. Such factorization results in sparse encoding [5] of the data. The sparse and separable factors obtained using positive factorization are used for a variety of tasks like image encoding, model selection and face recognition [10]. The factors obtained by this latter class of techniques usually lack meaningful interpretations and do not necessarily correspond to the properties of the generative process but aid in reducing the bulkiness of data.

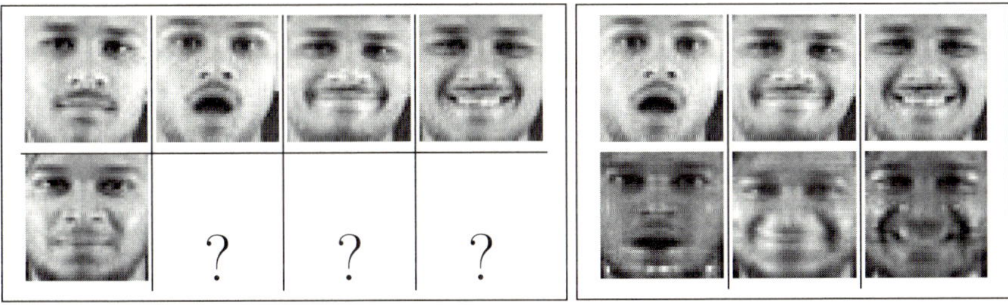

Fig. 1. The facial expression transfer problem : Given the videos of a person with different expressions the goal is to synthesize the videos of a second person with the same expressions (marked by ?'s in the left table). The right table (second row) shows the results using our method.

Orthogonal to the requirements of compact representations and interpretable factors, is the need for identification of factors (interpretable or otherwise) that cause the data to exhibit certain properties of interest. The performance of computer vision algorithms at tasks such as object classification, object detection is significantly enhanced by using a set of features that are relevant to the task rather than a full set of features representing the data. For instance, detecting a face needs features that characterize the holistic appearance of face while discriminating between two face classes would require filters capturing finer variations in the appearance of the faces. Similarly, identification of factors that give rise to properties of interest in the observed data has interesting applications such as data synthesis and recognition. For instance, given two sets of data with different desirable properties, identifying the relevant constituent factors and the factor model enables synthesis of a third collection with both of these properties. In this paper simple and efficient methods are proposed to perform such factor selection from a pool of factors obtained by decomposing a collection of images or a video represented as a tensor. The factors are selected so as to enable efficient appearance based solutions for two challenging tasks: facial expression transfer (explained pictorially in Figure 1), and facial expression recognition. The non-negative tensor factorization proposed in [10] is used to obtain the factors. Experimental results demonstrate that the selected factors enable both of the tasks with satisfactory results despite the use of appearance information alone.

2   Factor Selection for Videos

The expression transfer problem will be our running example. The solution proposed in the current work is based on decomposing the appearance of the face video represented as tensor using the non-negative tensor factorization(NTF) [10] technique and then selecting appropriate factors to be used in the synthesis. An N-valent tensor G of dimensions $[d_1] \times \cdots \times [d_N]$ has rank k if k is the smallest number such that G can be expressed as sum of k rank-1 tensors i.e.,

$$G = \sum_{j=1}^{k} \otimes_{i=1}^{N} \mathbf{u}_i^j \tag{1}$$

where the vectors $\mathbf{u}_i^j \in \mathcal{R}^{d_i}$. The NTF approximates the tensor G with a rank-k tensor $\hat{G} = \sum_{j=1}^{k} \otimes_{i=1}^{N} \mathbf{u}_i^j$ where $\mathbf{u}_i^j$s are all positive. The Nk vectors $\mathbf{u}_i^j$ are iteratively estimated using a gradient descent scheme such that the reconstruction error

$$\frac{1}{2} \left\| G - \sum_{j=1}^{k} \otimes_{i=1}^{N} \mathbf{u}_i^j \right\|^2 \tag{2}$$

is minimized. Given positive initial estimates of the vectors the method results in a non-negative decomposition of the tensor.

2.1   Video Factorization

A collection of images of an object or a video of an object can naturally be represented as a tensor by stacking the 2-D images as slices of a tensor. An alternative interpretation of the decomposition of a video provides insight into the selection of factors that best characterize the expression. Figure 2 shows the factorization of a video into constituent low-rank factors. The t-th $2D$ slice of the tensor G is given by $G_t = \sum_{j=1}^{k} u_{3,t}^j (\mathbf{u}_1^j \otimes \mathbf{u}_2^j)$ which is a linear combination of the matrices $\mathbf{u}_1^j \otimes \mathbf{u}_2^j$ weighted by the t-th coefficients of $\mathbf{u}_3^j$. The matrices $\mathbf{u}_1^j \otimes \mathbf{u}_2^j$

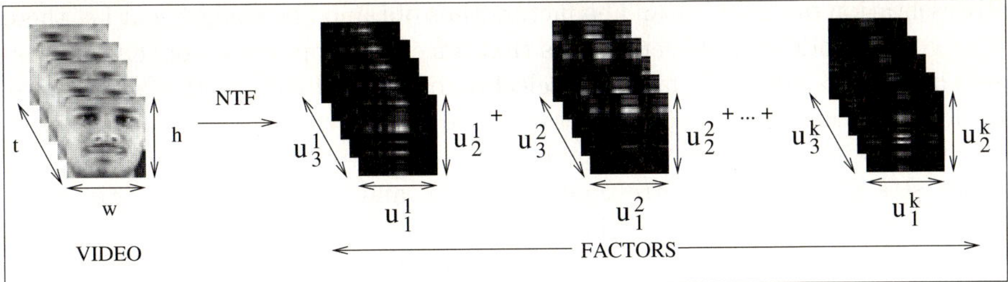

Fig. 2. Tensor Factorization of a video. Each frame of the video is sum of the corresponding frames from the low rank factors. Each low rank factor is formed by stacking weighted versions of a basis image.em Each basis image is a rank-1 matrix i.e outer product of two vectors.

can be viewed as basis images which which capture the appearance of the object. The positivity and sparseness imply that these images loosely correspond to parts of the object in the video. Figure 3 shows the factors obtained on factorization of a face video and the factors obtained. It can be seen that the energy in these images is located near the regions corresponding to various parts of the face like nose, eye etc.

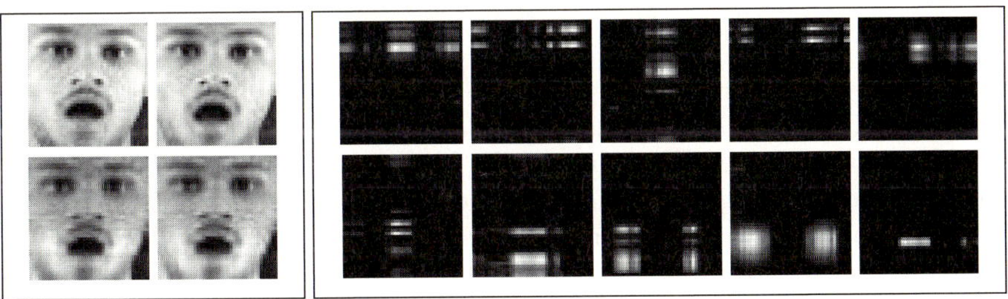

Fig. 3. Basis images corresponding to factors obtained by tensorial factorization of a face video (with the expression *surprise*). The first table shows the representative frames of the original video (top row) and the reconstructed video (second row). The second table shows a subset of the basis-image set. It can be seen that the energy in these images is concentrated near the regions which correspond to location of parts like cheeks, mouth, nose etc.

2.2   Basis Image Based Method

The identification of factors that best represent an expression requires the knowledge of the appearance of a neutral face. A neutral face video of the same subject as in the expression video is used for this purpose. Identification of the relevant factors is done by factorizing both the expression video and the neutral face video. Let V_E and V_N be the expression and neutral face videos and the $\mathbf{U}_E = \{\mathbf{u}_j^i\}$ and $\mathbf{U}_N = \{\mathbf{v}_j^i\}$ be the factors obtained by decomposing the tensor representation of V_E and V_N. The factors thus obtained lack alignment i.e. there is no correspondence between factors that affect the appearance of the same region in the two videos. To facilitate selection of relevant factors, the factors must be aligned. The correspondence between the factors can be established using a greedy algorithm that uses the similarity score between elements of the basis image sets $\mathbf{B}_E$ and $\mathbf{B}_N$ corresponding to $\mathbf{U}_E$ and $\mathbf{U}_N$ respectively. Since the basis images are all positive and sparse with local patches rudimentary metrics like sum of squared difference capture the similarity well. For the current work a similarity score based on the distance between the centroids of the local patches in the two images and the distribution of pixels around the centroid is used. The correspondence between the factors belonging to the two sets can be established by selecting the best matching pair of factors, eliminating them and then repeating the process for the remaining factors. Algorithm 1 gives the complete description of alignment of factors.

Algorithm 1. AlignFactors($\mathbf{U}_E, \mathbf{U}_N, k$)

1: Build basis image sets : $\mathbf{B}_E \leftarrow \mathbf{U}_E$, $\mathbf{B}_N \leftarrow \mathbf{U}_N$
2: Compute similarity scores : $S_{ij} \leftarrow similarity(\mathbf{B}_E^i, \mathbf{B}_N^j)$
3: $I \leftarrow \phi$
4: **for** $i = 1$ to k **do**
5:     Find p,q such that S_{pq} is maximum where $\mathbf{B}_E^p \in \mathbf{B}_E$, $\mathbf{B}_N^q \in \mathbf{B}_N$
6:     $I = I \cup \{(p,q)\}$
7:     $\mathbf{B}_E \leftarrow \mathbf{B}_E - \{\mathbf{B}_E^p\}$, $\mathbf{B}_N \leftarrow \mathbf{B}_N - \{\mathbf{B}_N^q\}$
8: **end for**
9: **return** I

Figure 4 shows the results of aligning the factors using the proposed algorithm. Once the corresponding factors have been identified the factors in the expression video corresponding to the maximally dissimilar pairs of factors are more likely to cause the expression appearance. Figure 5 shows the factors identified in this manner. It is evident that the factors that are maximally dissimilar have energy centered around the mouth region where the appearance differs drastically from that of a neutral face. The factors thus identified can now be used to transfer the expression. Besides the expression transfer problem, the factors can be used as cues for recognition of expressions. Sections 3 and 4 discuss these applications.

2.3   Factorization of the Difference Tensor

An alternative scheme for identification of factors that are useful for recognition arises from the Fisher-like criterion for discriminant analysis. Given two videos V_1 and V_2 represented as tensors $\mathbf{G}_1$ and $\mathbf{G}_2$ the objective is to find a rank-k tensor $\mathbf{W} = \sum_{j=1}^{k} \otimes_{i=1}^{3} \mathbf{w}_i^j$ such that projections of $\mathbf{G}_1$ and $\mathbf{G}_2$ on to this tensor differ the most. The objective is to optimize the quantity

$$\langle \sum_{j=1}^{k} \otimes_{i=1}^{3} \mathbf{w}_i^j, \mathbf{G}_1 \rangle - \langle \sum_{j=1}^{k} \otimes_{i=1}^{3} \mathbf{w}_i^j, \mathbf{G}_2 \rangle \tag{3}$$

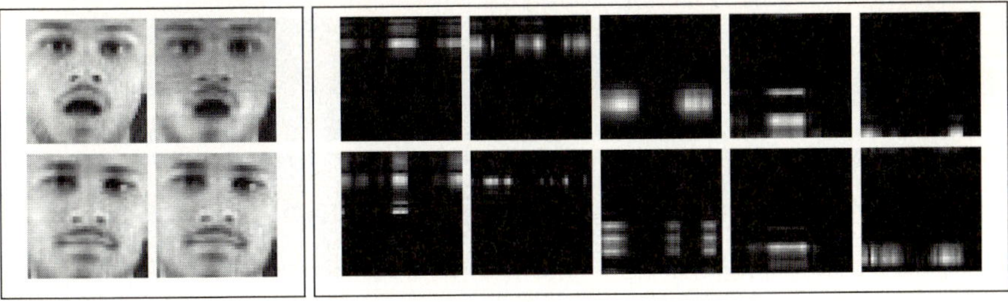

Fig. 4. Alignment of factors corresponding to a facial expression video and a neutral face video. The first table shows frames from both the videos and their reconstructions. The second table shows the aligned factors. The factors of the first video are shown in the top row and the corresponding factors are shown in the next row.

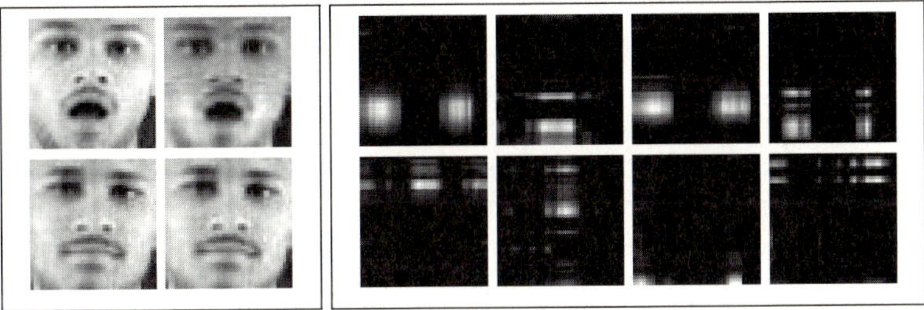

Fig. 5. Identification of expression-specific factors using basis images. The first table shows representative frames from two videos and their reconstructions from the factors : a *surprise* expression video (top row) and a neutral face video of the same subject (second row) . The second table (top row) shows the basis images corresponding to the factors chosen by the method. Note that the energy in these images is centered around the mouth region where the appearance differs significantly. The result of transferring these factors to the neutral video is shown in Figure 7. The second row shows the basis that are least preferred. These images resemble the invariant parts like nose and eyes.

which is equivalent to optimizing $\langle \sum_{j=1}^{k} \otimes_{i=1}^{3} \mathbf{w}_i^j, \Delta\mathbf{G} \rangle$ where $\Delta\mathbf{G} = \mathbf{G}_1 - \mathbf{G}_2$ captures the changes in the appearance of the video. Although the tensor $\Delta\mathbf{G}$ is not guaranteed to be positive, it can be normalized such that the elements are all non-negative and $\mathbf{W}$ is estimated as the rank-k approximation of $\Delta\mathbf{G}$. The factors $\mathbf{w}_i^j$ are not useful for the problem of expression transfer but when the basis images corresponding to these factors are used as filters, the frames of the two videos give rise to markedly different responses to those filters. Thus the factors provide a bank of highly discriminative filters that can be used effectively for classification tasks. Figure 6 shows the factors obtained by factorizing the difference tensor. It can be seen that the basis images corresponding to the resulting factors are useful for discriminating between the two expressions (*neutral* and *surprise*).

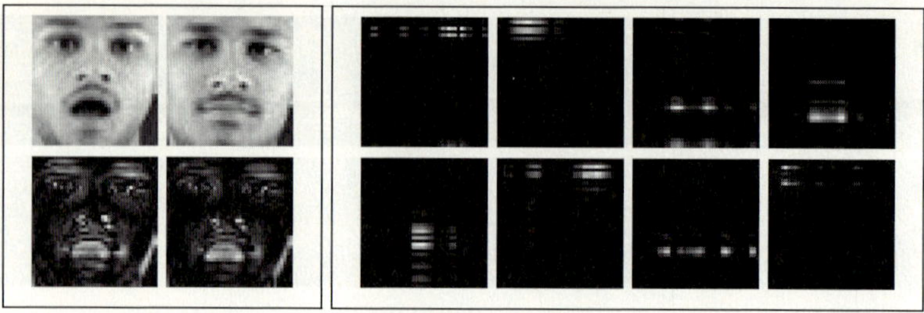

Fig. 6. Identification of discriminative filters by factorizing the difference tensor. The first table (top row) shows representative frames from both the videos. The next row shows frames from the difference tensor and reconstructions. The next table shows the basis images corresponding to the factors chosen by the algorithm obtained by factorizing the difference tensor. The energy in the images is centered around the mouth and the eyebrows where the appearance differs from the neutral face.

3   Facial Expression Transfer

The problem of expression transfer has a the flavor of style and content separation problem where the expression can be thought of as style and the underlying face as content and the appearance as a result of interaction between these two. An alternative pair of factors that cause the appearance of a face are the shape and texture characteristics of the face. However, the interaction between such factors may not be amenable to simple models like linear or bilinear models. As a simple and useful alternative the appearance factors obtained by decomposition of the facial expression video are be used to transfer the expression. As observed above the knowledge of appearance of the neutral face is a prerequisite for identification of the expression-specific factors as well as for transfer of the expression. The expression transfer problem considered in the current work is posed as follows: Given a video V_{1E} of a subject P_1 with certain expression E, the neutral face videos of the subject P_1 and another subject P_2, synthesize the video V_{2E} of subject P_2 with the same expression E.

The expression specific factors can be identified by using the algorithm described in Section 2. Once the factors are aligned and the relevant factors are identified the transfer is achieved by simply transferring the expression-specific factors in the source video to the target neutral video. Figure 7 shows the reconstructed video after the expression-specific factors are transfered to the neutral faces of the same subject and a second subject. Algorithm 2 summarizes the algorithm for expression transfer. The appearance based solution here transfers the appearance factors alone and might appear like a *cut and paste* method that results in discontinuities in the frames of synthesized videos. However experiments have shown that the synthesized videos are visually satisfactory with little or no discontinuities. However, the quality of synthesized video depends on the source video i.e. how close the shape of the source face is to the target face, differences in facial features like complexion, how well the expression is articulated in the source video etc.

Algorithm 2. TransferExpression($V_{1E}, V_{1N}, V_{2N}, k$)

1: $\mathbf{U}_{1E} \leftarrow NTF(V_{1E})$; $\mathbf{U}_{1N} \leftarrow NTF(V_{1N})$; $\mathbf{U}_{2N} \leftarrow NTF(V_{2N})$
2: $I = AlignFactors(\mathbf{U}_{1E}, \mathbf{U}_{1N})$
3: $J = AlignFactors(\mathbf{U}_{1N}, \mathbf{U}_{2N})$
4: Choose $\mathbf{U}_{1E}^* \subset \mathbf{U}_{1E}$ such that elements of $\mathbf{U}_{1E}^*$ are maximally dissimilar to corresponding factors in $\mathbf{U}_{1N}$, $\mathbf{U}_{1N}^*$ be the corresponding factors in $\mathbf{U}_{1N}$
5: Find $\mathbf{U}_{2N}^* \subset \mathbf{U}_{2N}$ the factors corresponding to $\mathbf{U}_{1E}^*$ using I, J and $\mathbf{U}_{1N}^*$
6: $\mathbf{U}_{2E} \leftarrow \mathbf{U}_{2N} \cup \mathbf{U}_{1E}^* - \mathbf{U}_{2N}^*$
7: $V_{2E} \leftarrow NTFReconstruct(\mathbf{U}_{2N})$

Experimental Results. Experiments were conducted on a dataset that was collected in-house. An OLYMPUS C7000 camera was used to capture the videos at 30fps under controlled settings with minimal illumination or pose variation. The videos were preprocessed to segment the faces and scale them to a fixed size. The algorithms proposed here work best in presence of a good degree of alignment of faces in the videos. The dataset consisted of 13 subjects in 8 different expressions including a neutral face video for each subject. The frame count in the videos was equalized (to 60), for the ease of implementation, by deleting frames where there was no change in appearance. The frames were all scaled to fixed dimensions. Figure 7 shows representative results of the experiments on this dataset. It can be seen that the results are visually satisfactory despite appearance information alone being made use of. The minor discontinuities and artifacts are due to the erroneous transfer of some rank-1 factors which come out as horizontal/vertical lines. Further, large variations in complexion and face shape also result in discontinuities. Low-pass filtering and contrast enhancement were applied on the frames of the synthesized video as a post-processing step.

4   Facial Expression Recognition

The second application considered is the recognition of facial expressions. Recognition of facial expression is a challenging task as the appearance of expressions varies drastically for different subjects. We explore the possibility of solving this problem using appearance based features alone by using the factors obtained by tensorial factorization. We used the neutral face video during training for identification of expression-specific factors. The recognition is done by comparing the constituent factors of the test video with the expression specific factors of the samples in the training set. For each expression-specific factor set in the training data a maximally similar subset of the factors of the test video is found. The matching score is computed as the mean similarity score between the matched factors. The test video is assigned the label of the training sample which results in maximum matching score.

A second method for recognition of expressions uses the factors obtained by decomposition of the difference tensor. First a classifier that can discriminate between two expressions is built and the the DDAG architecture [11] is used to

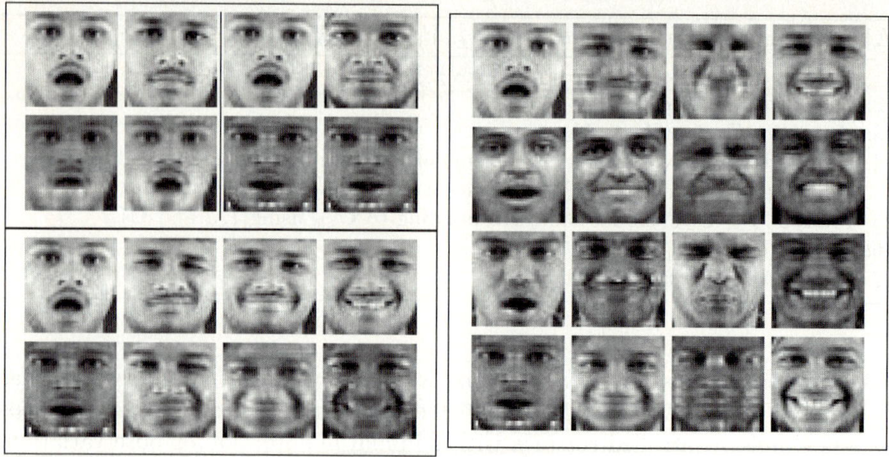

Fig. 7. Results of expression transfer using the algorithm described in section 3. First table : The top row shows frames from the facial expression video and the neutral face video considered for expression transfer (The first neutral face corresponds to the same subject). The second row shows the frames of the synthesized video using the algorithm. The third and fourth rows show four expressions (surprise, wink, smile, giggle) transferred to the neutral face of another subject. Second table : the expression transfer algorithm on a set of four subjects where the expression in the videos along the diagonal were transfered to other subjects (the columns show the same expression for different subjects and the rows show the same subject in different expressions). Only the diagonal videos were originally available.

extend it to multiple expressions. The basis images corresponding to the factors of the difference tensors are used as filters and the mean response to each filter over the entire video is taken as a feature. Feature vectors built in this manner are compared to training samples using Euclidean distance as the metric.

Experimental results. The dataset used for expression recognition is same as the dataset used for the expression transfer experiments. Excluding the neutral video there were 7 expressions of 13 subjects. Since the sample size was small leave-one out mode testing was used for testing both the algorithms. The Hinton diagrams corresponding to the confusion matrices for both the methods table 1. The leading diagonal elements show that the recognition accuracy is quite satisfactory despite the use of appearance information alone. The accuracy improved when the images of the faces of different persons are further aligned by manually selecting the control points such the centers of eyes and tip of the nose. The overall accuracy is around 51% comparable to the state of the art methods which use feature correspondences and muscular motion models [12]. The size of the dataset that is used for the experiments precludes any definite conclusion. However, as the nature of information used by the current technique differs from that of existing ones, they are complementary and development of a hybrid solution with improved recognition rate is a promising direction.

Fig. 8. Expressions used for the expression recognition experiment : *Smile, Left wink, Surprise, Giggle, Mock, Right wink, Disgust*

Table 1. The Hinton diagram of the confusion matrix for the expression recognition task. The squares along the diagonal represent fraction of correctly recognized samples. It can be seen that the accuracy is reasonable despite the absence the of feature correspondences or complex modeling schemes.

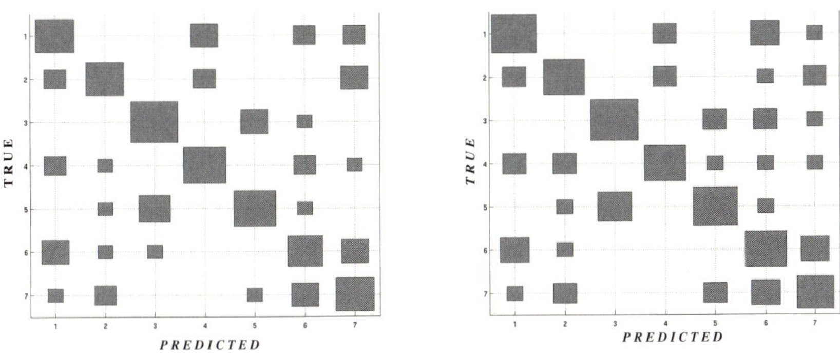

5   Relationship to Past Work

Expression transfer in face videos has number of applications in gaming, virtual worlds, interactive systems etc. It has been studied extensively both in computer vision and graphics. A method based on ratio images is presented in [13] which can transfer expression as well as capture illumination variation. Du and Lin [14] attempt to learn a linear mapping between parameters representing expression and appearance. Wang and Ahuja [4] use Higher-Order SVD (*HOSVD*) to decompose a collection of face expression images into two separate expression and person subspaces and use them to map expression on to a new face. Existing methods use feature point correspondences or complex motion models for expression transfer. The method that proposed in the current work is purely appearance based and is sensitive to various sources of differences in appearance such as the complexion, face shape etc. However, it does not use correspondences or complex modeling schemes for the task and is widely applicable. Moreover the current method is computationally efficient since the algorithm is dominated by the factorization step which has good convergence properties [10]. Facial Expression Recognition is a complex problem since the facial appearance corresponding to the same expression varies widely across different subjects. Previous methods use facial muscle motion models like FACS [15] and employ complex classifiers [12].

The method proposed here recognizes expressions using appearance cues alone and is complementary to the existing methods.

6 Conclusion

We have proposed methods for identification of task-specific factors that are useful for a range of tasks like video manipulation and recognition. To the best of our knowledge, a purely appearance based approach to expression transfer and expression recognition has not been attempted so far. The task-specific factor selection scheme provides efficient solutions for the tasks of expression transfer and recognition. The contributions of the current work are:

- Simple and efficient methods for selection of task-specific factors from the set of factors obtained by tensorial factorization of videos.
- An efficient technique to perform facial expression transfer without requiring feature correspondences or muscular motion models.
- A novel technique complementary to existing methods for recognition of expressions using expression-specific factor in facial expression videos.

The methods based on tensor representation of videos are more natural, simpler and insightful. Multilinear techniques offer new insights into analysis and processing of video information. The factors obtained by factorization of videos can be used for a number of other purposes like dynamic event analysis and background modeling. The appearance and dynamics separation achieved by tensorial factorization provides valuable cues for analysis of dynamic events in videos and we are actively pursuing this problem. In summary, task-specific factor selection makes it possible to solve a wide range of problems using tensorial factorization of videos/image-cubes and is a promising direction for future research.

Acknowledgments

One of the authors, Ranjeeth Kumar, would like to acknowledge the financial support provided by GE (through the GE Foundation Scholar-Leaders Program 2004-06) while carrying out this work.

References

1. Carlo Tomasi, Takeo Kanade: Shape and motion without depth. In: Proc. of the Third IEEE International Conf. on Computer Vision. (1990) 91–95
2. D. D. Lee, H. S. Seung: Learning the parts of objects by non-negative matrix factorization. Nature **401** (1999) 788–791
3. Joshua B. Tenenbaum, William T. Freeman: Separating style and content with bilinear models. Neural Computation **12** (2000) 1247–1283
4. Hongcheng Wang, Narendra Ahuja: Facial expression decomposition. In: Proc. of the Ninth IEEE International Conf. on Computer Vision. (2003) 958–965

5. Tamir Hazan, Simon Polak, Amnon Shashua: Sparse image coding using a 3d non-negative tensor factorization. Proc. of the Tenth IEEE International Conf. on Computer Vision (2005) 50–57
6. Zoubin Ghahramani, Geoffrey E. Hinton: The EM algorithm for mixtures of factor analyzers. Technical Report CRG-TR-96-1 (1996)
7. Max Welling, Markus Weber: Positive tensor factorization. Pattern Recognition Letters **22** (2001) 1255–1261
8. M. Alex, O. Vasilescu, Demetri Terzopoulos: Multilinear analysis of image ensembles: Tensorfaces. In: Proc. of the Seventh European Conf. on Computer Vision. Volume 1. (2002) 447–460
9. A. Shashua, A. Levin: Linear image coding for regression and classification using the tensor-rank principle. In: Proc. of the IEEE Conf. on Computer Vision and Pattern Recognition. (2001) 42–49
10. Amnon Shashua, Tamir Hazan: Non-negative tensor factorization with applications to statistics and computer vision. Proc. of the International Conf. on Machine Learning (2005) 792–799
11. John Platt, Nello Cristianini, John Shawe-Taylor: Large margin dags for multiclass classification. In Solla, S., Leen, T., Mueller, K.R., eds.: Advances in Neural Information Processing Systems 12. (2000) 547–553
12. Nicu Sebe, Michael S. Lew, Ira Cohen, Ashutosh Garg, Thomas S. Huang: Emotion recognition using a cauchy naive bayes classifier. In: Proc. of the 16 th International Conf. on Pattern Recognition. Volume 1. (2002) 17–20
13. Zicheng Liu, Ying Shan, Zhengyou Zhang: Expressive expression mapping with ratio images. In: Proc. of the 28th Annual Conf. on Computer Graphics and Interactive Techniques (SIGGRAPH). (2001) 271–276
14. Du Y., Lin X.: Mapping emotional status to facial expressions. In: Proc. of the International Conf. on Pattern Recognition. Volume II. (2002) 524–527
15. P. Ekman, W. V. Friesen: Facial Action Coding System : Investigator's Guide. Consulting Pshycologists Press, Palo Alto, CA (1978)

Video Shot Boundary Detection Algorithm

Kyong-Cheol Ko[1], Young- Min Cheon[1], Gye-Young Kim[1], Hyung –Il Choi[1],
Seong-Yoon Shin[2], and Yang-Won Rhee [2]

[1,*] Information Media Technology Research Institute, Soongsil University
1-1, Sangdo-Dong, Dongjak-Gu, Seoul 156-743, South Korea
{hic, gykim11}@ssu.ac.kr
[2] Department of Computer Information Science, Kunsan National University
68, Miryong-dong, Kunsan, Chonbuk 573-701, South Korea
{roadkkc, ywrhee}@kunsan.ac.kr

Abstract. We present a newly developed algorithm for automatically segmenting videos into basic shot units. A basic shot unit can be understood as an unbroken sequence of frames taken from one camera. At first we calculate the frame difference by using the local histogram comparison, and then we dynamically scale the frame difference by Log-formula to compress and enhance the frame difference. Finally we detect the shot boundaries by the newly proposed shot boundary detection algorithm which it is more robust to camera or object motion, and many flashlight events. The proposed algorithms are tested on the various video types and experimental results show that the proposed algorithm are effective and reliably detects shot boundaries.

1 Introduction

There are many shot detection methods already proposed in past decades [1], [2]. The common way for shot detection is to evaluate the difference value between consecutive frames represented by a given feature. Although reasonable accuracy can be achieved, there are still problem that limit the robustness of these algorithms [4].

One of the common problems in robust shot detection results from the fact there are many flashlights in news video, which often introduce false detection of shot boundaries. Only some simple solutions to this problem have been proposed in [2], [3]. There are main limitations are that they assume the flashlights just occur during one frame or limited window region. In real world, such as news video, there are many flashlight events occur during a period of time and influence multiple consecutive frames.

Another problem that has not been solved very effectively well is threshold selection when comparison changes between two frames. Most of the existing methods use global pre-defined thresholds, or simple local window based adaptive threshold.

Global threshold is definitely not efficient since the video property could change dramatically when content changes, and it is often impossible to find a universal optimal threshold method also has its limitation because in some situation the local statistics are polluted by strong noises such as big motions or flashlights.

---

[*] This work was supported by the Korea research Foundation Grant (KRF-2006-005-J03801).

P. Kalra and S. Peleg (Eds.): ICVGIP 2006, LNCS 4338, pp. 388 – 396, 2006.

The objective of this paper are: 1) to provide the metrics that are robust to camera and object motion, and enough spatial information is retained, 2) to provide the scaled frame difference that are dynamically compressed by log formula and it is more convenient to decide the threshold, 3) to propose a new shot boundary detection algorithm that are robust to camera operation or fast object movement, flashlight events.

The rest of this paper is organized as follows. In the next section 2, we provide a proposed algorithm that gives a detail description of the three new algorithms. Section 3 presents experimental results, and we conclude this paper and discuss the future work in Section 4.

2   The Proposed Algorithm

Firstly, we denote the metrics to extract the frame difference from consecutive frames. And we scale the frame difference by log formula which makes more dynamically robust to any camera or object motion, and many flashlight events. Finally we propose the new shot boundary detection algorithm. Our proposed algorithm works in real time video stream and not sensitive to various video types.

Throughout this paper, we shall treat a shot, defined as a continuous sequence of frames recorded from a single camera, as a fundamental unit in a video sequence.

2.1   Metrics in Shot Detection

To segment the video into shot units, we should first define suitable metrics to extract frame difference; so that a shot boundary is declared whenever that metric exceed a given threshold.

We use the local histogram comparison that are more robust to camera and object motion, and enough spatial information is retained to produce more accurate results [5], [6].

The local histogram comparison metrics are defined as:

$$d(f_i, f_j) = \sum_{bl=1}^{m} d_{x^2}(f_i, f_j, bl) \tag{1}$$

$$d_{x^2}(f_i, f_j, bl) = \sum_{k=1}^{N-1} (\frac{(H_i^r(k) - H_j^r(k))^2}{\max(H_i^r(k), H_j^r(k))} \times \alpha$$
$$+ \frac{(H_i^g(k) - H_j^g(k))^2}{\max(H_i^g(k), H_j^g(k))} \times \beta \tag{2}$$
$$+ \frac{(H_i^b(k) - H_j^b(k))^2}{\max(H_i^b(k), H_j^b(k))} \times \gamma),$$

where m is the total number of the blocks, and $H_i^r(k)$ denotes the histogram difference at gray level k for the block bl of i'th frame in red channels. α, β and γ are constants and, according to NTSC standard, we set these constants to 0.299, 0.587, and 0.114, respectively.

The best frame difference can be obtained by breaking the frame into 16 equal sized regions, using weighted x^2-test on color histograms for these regions and discarding the largest differences to reduce the effects of noise, object and camera movements.

2.2 Scaled Frame Difference

Most of video segmentation algorithms rely on suitable threshold of similarities between consecutive frames. However, the thresholds are highly sensitive to the type of input video. This drawback can be overcome by the scaled frame difference.

The scale of frame difference is performed by Log-formula which makes more dynamically compressed frame difference and Log-formula was referenced by digital image processing which was used to image enhancement.

The proposed Log –formula defined as:

$$d_{\log} = c \times \log(1 + d^2)$$

$$c = \frac{\max(d_{\log})}{\max(\log(1 + d^2))} \tag{3}$$

Where d is the frame difference extracted from equation (1) and c is the constant calculated from d.

Figure 1 shows the distribution of total frame differences extracted from news video.

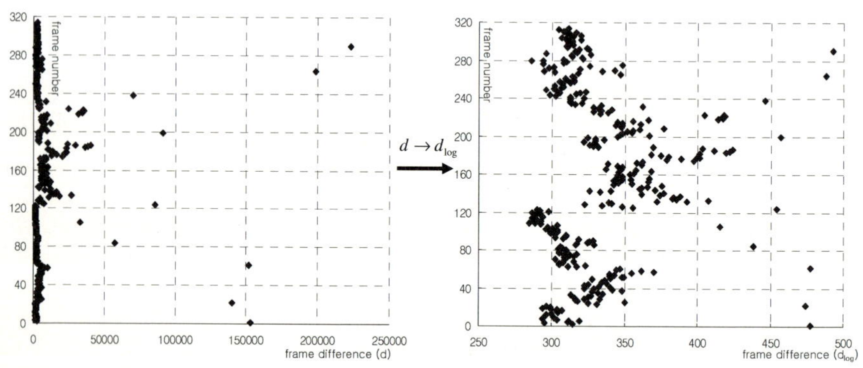

Fig. 1. Distribution of all frame difference 'd' and 'd_{log}'

Distribution of all frame differences d_{log} has widely spread difference values in a scaled region than d and each difference values are enhanced and concatenated each other more closely. So if we apply the simple shot cut rules, we can detect the shot boundaries only using the frame difference.

Table 1 shows the max (maximum), min (minimum), ave (average), and stdev (standard-deviation) represented from three video types(news, sports, adv.). Each of the frame differences d and d_{log} are calculated from the given equations (1) and equation (2).

Table 1. Comparison of difference values 'd' and 'd_{log}'

videos	Max.		Min.		Ave.		Stdev.	
	d	d_{log}	d	d_{log}	d	d_{log}	d	d_{log}
News	223057.9	492.6	1234.2	284.7	9191.3	334.2	23778	38.2
Sports	212168.3	490.6	703.2	262.2	3740.2	308.1	13380.3	25.1
Adv.	216088.1	491.3	3993.2	331.7	26494.2	391.6	30614.5	33.3

As mentioned above it, scaled difference values are more robust and reliable to detect the shot boundaries and are convenient to select the global threshold.

Figure 2 shows the normal graph of Table 1. Scaled frame difference d_{log} are dynamically compressed and more normally distributed under the scaled region than d.

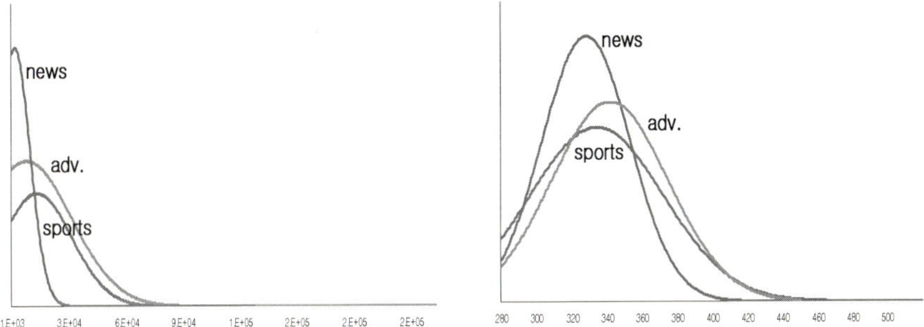

Fig. 2. Normal Distribution of frame difference 'd' and scaled frame difference 'd_{log}'

2.3   Shot Boundary Detection Algorithm

Shot boundary detection is usually the first step in generic video processing. A shot represents a sequence of frames captured from a unique and continuous record from a camera. Therefore adjacent frames of the same shot exhibit temporal continuity. Both the real shot cut and the abrupt cut could cause a great change in frame difference because of the special situations such as flashlight events, sudden lightening variances, and fast camera motion, or large object movements. So each shot corresponds to a single continuous action and no change of content can be detected inside a shot. Change of contents always happen at the boundary between two shots. Partitioning a video sequence into shots is also useful for video summarization and indexing.

We define shot boundary detection algorithm based on the temporal property of shot cut and abrupt cut. If the scaled frame difference of consecutive frames is larger than a max-threshold (th_{max}), and its neighboring difference value of frame difference is larger than a k-threshold (k_{gloval}), and also its Euclidian distance is satisfied with global-threshold (th_{gloval}) , then the shot cut is detected by shot boundary detection algorithm.

Figure 3 shows the proposed shot boundary detection algorithm more details.

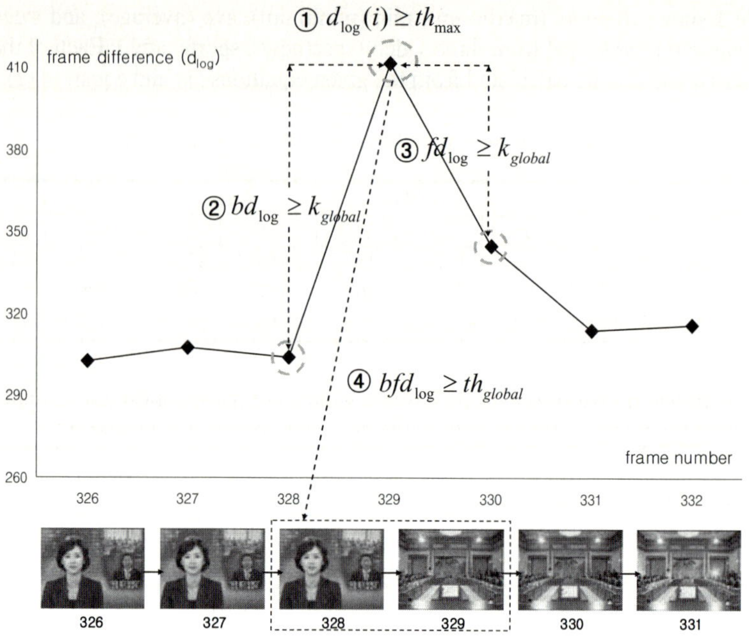

Fig. 3. The illustration graph of proposed shot boundary detection algorithm

As shown in Figure 3, the shot boundary detection algorithm can be summarized as follows:

Step 1. At first, if the scaled frame difference $d_{log}(i)$ is larger than a max-threshold th_{max} then the current frame is selected to candidate shot frame,

$$d_{\log}(i) \geq th_{max}$$

Step 2. And we calculate the newly defined difference value $bd_{log}(i)$, $fd_{log}(i)$ as follows:

$$bd_{\log}(i) = \left| d_{\log}(i) - d_{\log}(i-1) \right|,$$
$$fd_{\log}(i) = \left| d_{\log}(i+1) - d_{\log}(i) \right|$$

(4)

The calculated difference value $bd_{log}(i)$, $fd_{log}(i)$ must be larger than a k-threshold k_{gloval} .

$$bd_{\log}(i) \geq k_{global} \ \&\& \ fd_{\log}(i) \geq k_{global}$$

Setp 3. Finally, the Euclidean distance of each calculated frame difference value bfd_{log} is defined as:

$$bfd_{\log}(i) = \sqrt{(bd_{\log}(i))^2 + (fd_{\log}(i))^2}$$

(5)

And it must larger than a global-threshold th_{gloval} .

$$bfd_{\log}(i) \geq th_{global}$$

Step 1 is the basic step to check the candidate shot frame. Most of shot frame has a big difference value and we heuristically determine the max-threshold th_{max} from scaled frame difference. In experiments results, the determined max-threshold th_{max} was reliable and robust than previous approaches.

Step 2 is to check whether the current frame is shot cut or abrupt cut. A real shot cut has enough distance between bd_{log} and fd_{log} but abrupt cut has small distance each other. If the distance bd_{log} and fd_{log} is smaller than k-threshold k_{gloval}, then current frame is classified as abrupt cut.

Step 3 is to check the sensibility over the set of threshold bd_{log} and $fd_{log.}$.

Figure 4 shows the illustration of the proposed shot boundary detection algorithm.

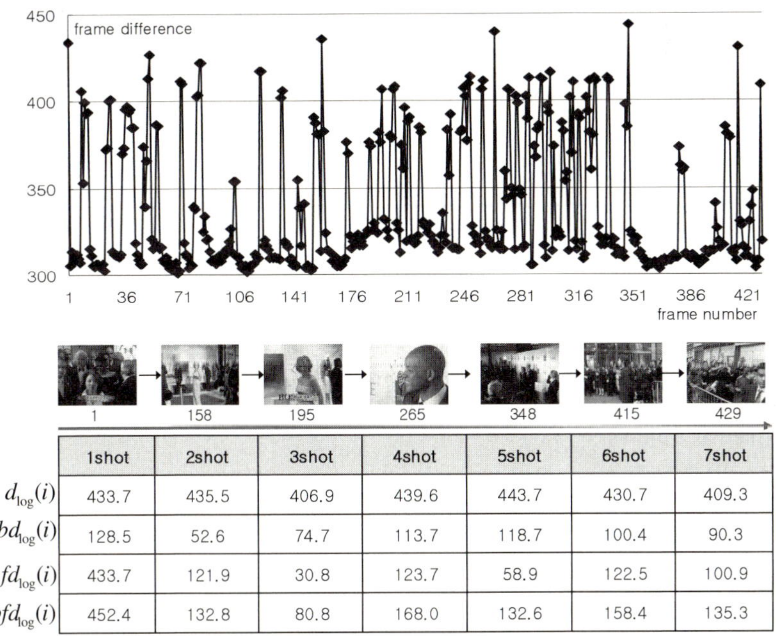

	1shot	2shot	3shot	4shot	5shot	6shot	7shot
$d_{\log}(i)$	433.7	435.5	406.9	439.6	443.7	430.7	409.3
$bd_{\log}(i)$	128.5	52.6	74.7	113.7	118.7	100.4	90.3
$fd_{\log}(i)$	433.7	121.9	30.8	123.7	58.9	122.5	100.9
$bfd_{\log}(i)$	452.4	132.8	80.8	168.0	132.6	158.4	135.3

Fig. 4. Distribution of remaining number of frames by the proposed algorithm

As shown in Figure 4, the diagram is the scaled frame difference of consecutive frames in sequence 'interview videos' which has a lot of flashlight events. Detected shot cut frame, and used difference value of each frame difference is shown in Figure 4.

All possible shot cut is detected and flashlight is eliminated in reliable.

3 Experimental Results

We evaluate the performance of our proposed method with DirectX 8.1 SDK, MS-Visual C++ 6.0 on Windows XP.

The proposed method has been tested on several video sequences such as news, interviews, and commercials videos that have a lot of scene changes occurs, as shown in table1. Each video sequence has the various types digitized in 320*240 resolutions at 30frames/sec.

Table 2. Description of the Videos in the experiment dataset

Videos	# of frames	# of abrupt cuts		# of shot cuts (ground truth)
		fast object and camera motion or etc.	flashlights	
news1	2772	2	31	26
news2	2665	2	55	19
Choice	2975	1	14	21
soccer	2167	3	6	22
Flash1	2578	1	52	15
Movie1	1175	2	25	11
Golf	665	12	0	19
Wine	3096	10	0	30

In table 2, 'News2' or 'Flash1' videos contain many flashlights events and 'Golf' or 'Wine' videos contain fast object and camera motions.

We manually identify the ground truth by a user with frame accuracy. In our experiments, the shot cut detection results are compared with the ground truth in terms of precision and recall. Assume N is the ground truth number of shot cuts, M is the number of missed cuts and F is the number of false alarms, the recall and precision are defined as follows:

$$\mathrm{Re}\,call = \frac{N - M}{N}$$

$$\mathrm{Pr}\,ecision = \frac{N - M}{N - M + F}$$

(3)

These two measures are both important. We certainly do not want to miss any critical shot changes. On the other hand, too many false alarms will compromise the efficiency of video segmentation.

Table 3 indicates that proposed algorithm can detect not only abrupt cuts but also shot cut with satisfactory accuracy. Approximately 97% of fast camera transitions, fast object motions and flashlight events are detected. The missed abrupt cuts mainly results from the fact that the frame differences between consecutive frames are lower than the given threshold.

Table 3. Experiment Results

Videos	# of abrupt cuts				# of shot cuts			
	# of false	# of missed	recall	preci-sion	# of false	# of missed	recall	precision
news1	0	2	94%	100%	2	0	100%	93%
news2	2	0	100%	97%	0	1	94%	100%
Choice	0	0	100%	100%	0	0	100%	100%
soccer	0	0	100%	100%	0	0	100%	100%
Flash1	0	0	100%	100%	1	1	93%	93%
Movie1	0	3	89%	100%	1	2	82%	90%
Golf	0	1	92%	100%	0	1	95%	100%
Wine	0	0	100%	100%	0	1	97%	100%
TOTAL	2	6	97%	99%	3	5	95%	97%

4 Conclusion

This paper has presented an effective shot boundary detection algorithm, which focus on three difficult problems solutions: To provide the metrics that are robust to camera and object motion, and enough spatial information is retained. To provide the scaled frame difference that are dynamically compressed by log formula and it is more convenient to decide the threshold. To propose a new shot boundary detection algorithm that are robust to camera operation or fast object movement, flashlight events. Experiments show that the proposed algorithm is promising.

However the automatic video partition is still a very challenging research problem especially for detecting gradual transitions or camera fabrication, special events and so on. Further work is still needed.

References

1. I. Koprinska and S. Carrato, "Temporal Video Segmentation: A Survey," Signal Processing Image Communication, Elsevier Science 2001.
2. G. Ananger, T.D.C. Little, "A survey of technologies for parsing and indexing digital video," Journal of Visual Communication and Image Representation, 1996, pp. 28-43.
3. D. Zhang, W. Qi, H. J. Zhang, "A News Shot Boundary Detection Algorithm," IEEE Pacific Rim Conference on Multimedia, pp. 63-70, 2001.
4. U. Gargi, R. Kasturi, and S. H. Strayer, "Performance Characterization of Video-Shot-Change Detection Methods," IEEE transaction on circuits and systems for video technology, Vol. 10, No. 1, Feb. 2000.
5. A. Nagasaka, Y. Tanaka, "Automatic video indexing and full-video search for object appearances," in Visual Database Systems II, pp. 113-127, Elsevier, 1995.
6. K. C. Ko, Y. W. Rhee, "Scene Change Detection using the Chi-test and Automated Threshold Decision Algorithm," ICCSA06, Vol. 3983, pp. 1060-1069, 2006.

7. C. L. Huang and B. Y. Liao, "A Robust Scene Change Detection Method for Video Segmentation," IEEE Trans on CSVT, Vol. 11. No. 12, pp. 1281-1288, December 2001.
8. H. Zhang, A. Kankamhalli, and S. Smoliar, "Automatic partitioning of full-motion video," ACM Multimedia Systems, New York: ACM Press, Vol. 1, 1993, pp. 10-28.
9. U. Gragi, R. Kasturi, S. Antani, "Evaluation of video sequence indexing and hierarchical video indexing," in: Proc. SPIE Conf. Storage and Retrieval in Image and Video Databases, 1995, pp. 1522-1530.
10. Gonzalez, "Digital Image Processing 2/E," Prentice-Hall, 2002.
11. R. M. Ford, C. Robson, D. Temple, M. Gerlach, "Metrics for shot boundary detection in digital video sequences," Multimedia Systems 8: 37-46, 2000.
12. A. Ekin, A. M. Tekalp, and R. Mehrotra, "Automatic soccer video analysis and summarization," IEEE Trans. On Image Processing, Vol. 12, No. 7, pp. 796-807, July 2003.
13. C. L. Huang and B. Y. Liao, "A Robust Scene Change Detection Method for Video Segmentation," IEEE Trans. Circuit System. Video Technology, Vol. 11, No. 12, December 2001.

Modeling of Echocardiogram Video Based on Views and States

Aditi Roy[1], Shamik Sural[1], J. Mukherjee[2], and A.K. Majumdar[2]

[1] School of Information Technology
[2] Department of Computer Science & Engineering
Indian Institute of Technology, Kharagpur, India
{aditi.roy@sit, shamik@sit, joy@cse, akmj@cse}.iitkgp.ernet.in

Abstract. In this work we propose a hierarchical state-based model for representing an echocardiogram video using objects present and their dynamic behavior. The modeling is done on the basis of the different types of views like short axis view, long axis view, apical view, etc. For view classification, an artificial neural network is trained with the histogram of a *'region of interest'* of each video frame. A state transition diagram is used to represent the states of objects in different views and corresponding transition from one state to another. States are detected with the help of synthetic M-mode images. In contrast to traditional single M-mode approach, we propose a new approach named as *'Sweep M-mode'* for the detection of states.

1   Introduction

In the last few decades, medical imaging research has seen a rapid progress. Echocardiography is a common diagnostic imaging technique that uses ultrasound to analyze cardiac structures and function [1]. Present work is motivated by the grow-ing interest in managing medical image/video collections based on their content.

Some systems and standards such as PACS [2] and DICOM [3] are used in medical imaging centers to digitize, view, communicate and store medical images. How-ever, these do not take into account the characteristics of the content of the medical images or videos. In recent past, advances have been made in content based retrieval of medical images [4]. Research has also been done on the extraction of cardiac object boundaries from sequences of echocardiographic images [5]. Work on echo-cardiographic video summarization, temporal segmentation for interpretation, storage and content based retrieval of echo video has been reported [6]. This process is heavily dependent on the available domain knowledge which includes spatial structure of the echo video frames in terms of the *'Region of Interest' (ROI)*, where an ROI is the region in a frame containing only the echo image of heart. On the other hand, an approach towards semantic content based retrieval of video data using object state transition data model has been put forward in [7][8]. In these articles, the echo videos are segmented based on states of the heart object. A view-based model-ing approach has been reported in

P. Kalra and S. Peleg (Eds.): ICVGIP 2006, LNCS 4338, pp. 397–408, 2006.
© Springer-Verlag Berlin Heidelberg 2006

[9], which uses parts based representation for automatic view recognition. They represent the structure of heart by a constellation of its parts (chambers) under the different views. Statistical variations of the parts in the constellation and their spatial relationships are modeled using Markov Random Field. Support Vector Machine [SVM] is used for view recognition which fuses the assessments of a test image by all the view-models. A state based modeling approach [10] measures the relative changes in left ventricular cavity in echo video sequences to identify end diastolic and end systolic frames. This information is then used in conjunction with the statistical correlation between echo video frames to extract information about systole and diastole states of heart. Thus, view-based modeling and state-based modeling of echo video are done separately. But hierarchical state-based modeling, combining views and states, is a new problem which has not been addressed till now, to the best of our knowledge.

In our work, we segment an echo video hierarchically based on views and states of the heart object by exploiting specific structures of the video. The advantage of using this approach is that it allows storage and indexing of the echo video at different levels of abstraction based on semantic features of video objects.

For hierarchical state-based modeling we first segment the video based on views. To detect view boundary, we use traditional color histogram based comparison [11] and edge change ratio [12]. After detecting shot boundary, we apply a novel technique for automatic view classification of each shot which is based on the signal properties and their statistical variations for each view in echo video. We train an artificial neural network [17] with the histogram of 'region of interest' of each video frame for classification. For state detection, we propose a new method using single and sweep M-Mode.

The rest of the paper is organized as follows. In Section 2, we discuss echo video segmentation techniques based on views. First, we give a brief description of the shot detection techniques used for detecting various views. Then we introduce our method for view classification. In Section 3, we discuss state detection using single and sweep M-mode and finally, we conclude in Section 4 of the paper.

2 Echocardiogram Video Segmentation Based on View

For browsing and content based manipulations of echo video, the visual information must be structured and broken down into meaningful components. Shots are the basic structural building blocks for this and shot boundaries need to be determined without user intervention. In Figure 1, we show the basic block diagram of the system. After detecting each shot, we classify them using our classifier. Then, each view is further segmented based on the states of the heart, as specified by its state transition diagram.

2.1 Shot Detection

As mentioned above, the first step of video processing for hierarchical state-based modeling is segmentation of the input video into shots. A shot can be defined as a sequence of interrelated frames captured from the same camera

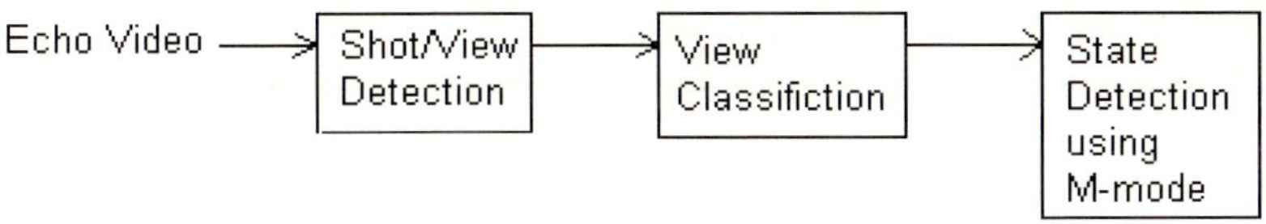

Fig. 1. Block diagram of the system for hierarchical state-based modeling of echo video

location that represents a continuous action in time and space. In echo video segmentation, traditional definition of shot is not applicable. An echo video is obtained by scanning the cardiac structure with an ultrasound device. Hence, depending on the location of the transducer, different views of echocardiogram video are obtained.

Echocardiogram Shot Definition. Echocardiogram images are used by cardiologists to analyze physiological and functional behaviors of cardiovascular components, e.g. heart chambers, valves, arteries, etc. In this process, the heart chamber can be viewed through different angles by changing the transducer position. Accordingly, the same chamber can be seen in different perspectives, known as *views*. In [6], four modes of echocardiography are identified i.e. two dimensional, Doppler, color Doppler, zoom-in. They define '*view*' as the sequence of frames corresponding to a single transducer location and mode of imaging.

But in this paper we use a different definition of view as mentioned in [1]. The views considered are:

1) Parasternal Long Axis View (LAX): Transducer placed parallel to the long axis of left ventricle and the ultrasound wave passes through the center of left ventricle chamber.
2) Parasternal Short Axis view (SAX): Transducer is rotated 90 in clockwise direction from the parasternal long axis view position.
3) Apical View: Transducer is placed in the cardiac apex.
4) Color Doppler: This uses color overlays on the reference frame sequence to show the blood flow in the heart based on the Doppler effect.
5) One dimensional: This is the gray-scale reference frame sequence of one dimensional signal locating anatomic structures from their echoes along a fixed axis of emission.

In this paper, we use the terms '*view*' and '*shot*' interchangeably. Transition from one view to another is always sharp.

Echocardiogram Shot Detection. Various automatic shot boundary detection algorithms for videos like movie, news, sports, etc., have been proposed in the literature. Due to the presence of high speckle noise in echo video, it is difficult to detect views in echo videos by applying these algorithms. We explore two methods to detect shot boundary, namely, histogram based comparison and edge change ratio. The main idea of these techniques is that if the difference between two consecutive frames is larger than a threshold value, then a shot transition is assumed to exist at that frame position.

The first approach is global histogram based comparison method [14][15]. Here we compute color histogram for each frame using 192 color bins, where each bin contains the percentage of pixels from the whole frame. Color histograms of two consecutive frames are compared using a cosine similarity metric. When the similarity value is below the threshold, a shot boundary is detected. The main drawback of this method is that, if two image frames belonging to different shots have similar histograms, then the shot boundary may not get detected.

The second approach is based on edge change ratio. Here each frame is first turned into gray scale image and then the edges are detected. We use Sobel operator due to its smoothing effect which is important for noisy echocardiogram video. Then for two consecutive frames, edge ratio is computed in terms of the number of new edge pixels entering the frame and the number of old edge pixels leaving the frame[12][16]. Exit-ing pixels are identified by keeping pixels in the first frame but not the second, and the entering pixels are identified by keeping pixels in the second frame and not in the first. Using these results, the edge change ratio (ECR) is determined as follows.

$$ECR_i = MAX(\frac{E_i^{in}}{E_i}, \frac{E_{i-1}^{out}}{E_{i-1}}) \tag{1}$$

Here for the ith frame, E_i^{in} is the number of entering edge pixels, E_i^{out} is the number of exiting edge pixels, and is E_i the total number of edge pixels. When the edge change ratio exceeds a threshold, a shot boundary is considered to exist. A global motion compensation based on Hausdroff distance is performed before the calculation of the ECR.

Between the two techniques described above, edge based method outperforms histogram based approach. The only drawback is that it cannot detect shot transition between apical view and color Doppler. In such situation, color histogram based comparison gives desired result. We combine these two methods using majority voting to detect shots in echocardiogram video and obtain 98% accuracy.

2.2   View Recognition

Automatic view recognition in echo video is a challenging task due to the presence of multiplicative noise and structural similarity among the constellations of the different views. Variations in the images captured under the same view but for different patients, make the problem even more difficult.

Here we classify three types of views i.e., long axis view, short axis view and apical view. Color Doppler view is classified at the time of detecting shots by the presence of color. One dimensional view is also identified during shot detection from their static nature.

For view classification we use the fact that, for each view, different sets of cardiac chambers are visible. The number of chambers present, their orientation and the presence of heart muscles in each view, gives different patterns of histogram. We identify the views based on their unique histogram patterns. In our approach, we first define a *'region of interest'* for each frame to minimize the effect of noisy background. The ROI region is selected after performing experiments on a large number of different types of echo videos containing all the view types. The ROIs marked on three representative frames, one from each view, are shown in Figure 2. Next we generate a gray scale histogram for this ROI using 64 bins. For each view, the histogram pattern is unique as shown in Figure 3. We use a neural network [17] for classifying the views from the 64-dimensional normalized histogram vector of each frame.

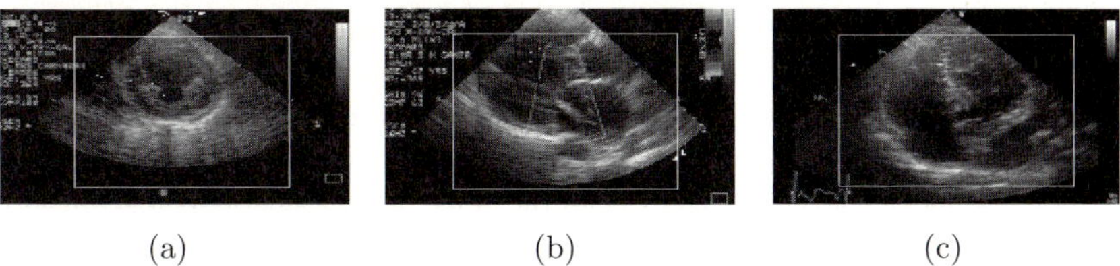

(a)   (b)   (c)

Fig. 2. Frames with ROI: (a) Short Axis View; (b) Long Axis View; (c) Apical View

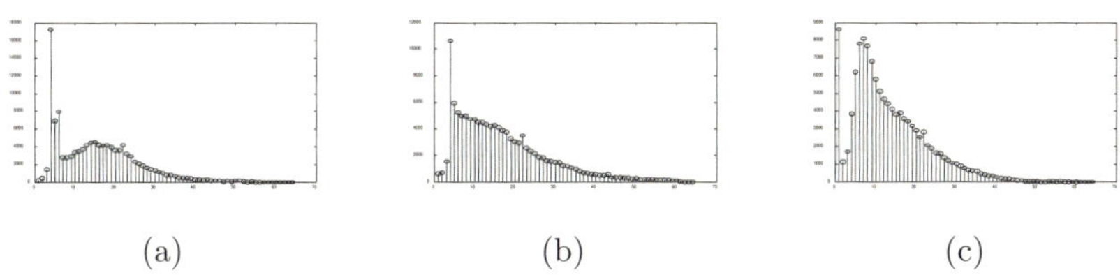

(a)   (b)   (c)

Fig. 3. Histogram of (a) Short Axis View, (b) Long Axis View, (c) Apical View for Fig. 2

We train the neural network with a total of 1260 frames, 400 each of short axis view and long axis view, and 460 of apical view. Every frame in the data set is manually labeled. We use a multilayer perceptron (MLP) with one input layer, one hidden layer and one output layer. The number of units in the input layer is 64, one for each histogram component. The number of units in the output layer is 3, one to represent long axis view, one for short axis view and one for apical view. The number of units in the hidden layer is empirically chosen as 80.

Table 1. View recognition results

True Class	Predicted Class		
	Short Axis View (no.of frames)	Long Axis View (no. of frames)	Apical View (no. of frames)
Short Axis View	128	2	1
Long Axis View	1	80	1
Apical View	3	12	140

We evaluated the performance of the classifier on a test data set of 365 frames. Table 1 shows view classification result in the form of a confusion matrix. An overall precision of 95.34% is obtained. The main source of misclassification is incorrect recognition of apical view frames as long axis view frames.

3   State Based Modeling of Echocardiogram Video

A state based video model is a means for extracting information contained in an un-structured video data and representing this information in order to support users' queries. A state stores information about the past, i.e. it reflects the input changes from the system start to the present moment. A transition indicates a state change and is described by a condition that needs to be fulfilled to enable transition. Action is an activity that is to be performed at a given moment. State transition diagram describes all the states that an object can have, the events or conditions under which an object changes state (transitions) and the activities undertaken during the life of an object (actions). In an echocardiogram video, the two states are *systole* and *diastole*.

Systole: During systole, the ventricles contract. The aortic and pulmonary valves open and blood is forcibly ejected from the ventricles into the pulmonary artery to be re-oxygenated in the lungs, and into the aorta for systemic distribution of oxygenated blood. At the same time, the mitral and tricuspid valves close to prevent backflow and the atria start to fill with blood again.

Diastole: During diastole, the ventricles relax. The pulmonary and aortic valves close and the mitral and tricuspid valves open. The ventricles then start to fill with blood again.

Figure 4 shows the state transition diagram of heart, where the two states are systole and diastole. When ventricles start expanding, transition from systole to diastole occurs. Similarly, transition occurs from diastole to systole with ventricular contraction.

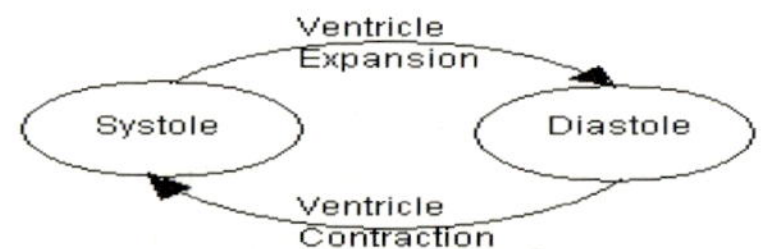

Fig. 4. State transition diagram of heart

3.1   Identification of States Using Single M-Mode

The signal in M-mode or motion mode echocardiography is obtained from the time sequence of a one-dimensional signal locating anatomic structures from their echoes along a fixed axis of emission. These measurements are usually represented as an image (see Figure 5(b)) in which the abscissa and the ordinate represent time and depth (or distance), respectively. The intensity of each pixel is a function of the reflected ultrasound energy. The cardiac borders have a periodic translational movement with time. Due to high level of noise, automated detection of these borders is not a trivial task to be solved by standard image processing techniques.

To obtain synthetic M-mode from 2-D echocardiogram, we use short axis view. User draws a straight line perpendicular to the walls of left ventricle where the wall motion is maximum. M-mode can be of different types depending on the position of the straight line. If the line is vertical, then the generated M-mode is termed as vertical M-mode. If the line is horizontal or diagonal, the M-mode is named accordingly. In general, only vertical M-modes are computed for diagnosis. But it is observed that for some views, horizontal M-mode gives more useful information than vertical M-mode. We, therefore, compute horizontal M-mode to get state information more accurately. Figure 5(a) shows the horizontal line drawn on a short axis view frame. To compute M-mode image, we scan along this line for each frame in the short axis view segment of the video. The intensity value along the straight line is taken as ordinate and frame number is taken as abscissa as shown in Figure 5(b).

Pre-processing. Most echocardiograms have a relatively high noise level because of intrinsic limitation in the measurement device. Substantial noise reduction with minimal information loss is achieved by smoothing the image. We first use Gaussian filtering to remove noise from M-mode images and then apply Sobel operator for edge detection.

1) *Smoothing:* We use a convolution kernel that approximates a Gaussian with of 0.45. To compute a Gaussian smoothing with a large standard deviation, we convolve the image three times with a smaller Gaussian kernel [77]. The Gaussian outputs a 'weighted average' of each pixel's neighborhood, with the average weighted more towards the value of the central pixels. Because of this, a Gaussian provides gentler smoothing and preserves edges better than other types of smoothing filter. Thus it helps in getting better edge detection result.

2) *Edge Detection:* For edge detection, we use Sobel operator mask because of its higher noise suppression characteristics than other edge detection operators.

The resulting M-mode image after applying Gaussian and Sobel operator on the M-mode image of Figure 5(b) is shown in Figure 5(c).

Border Extraction. Border extraction is one of the most important steps in processing an echo video. Difficulties arise from the fact that the observed time

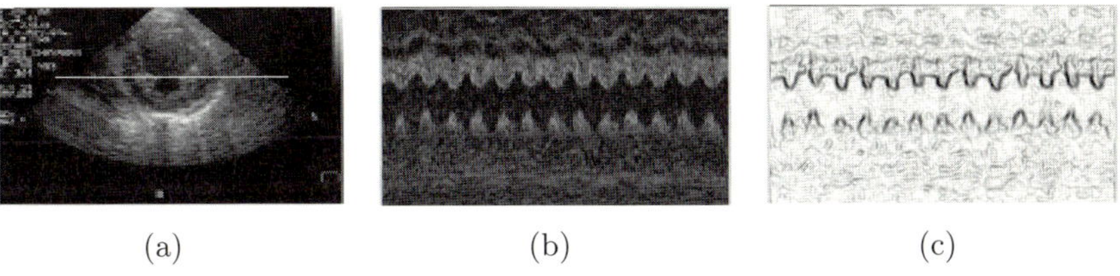

<table>
<tr><td align="center">(a)</td><td align="center">(b)</td><td align="center">(c)</td></tr>
</table>

Fig. 5. (a) User drawn line on a chosen frame of video, (b) M-mode image, (c) Edge detected smoothed M-mode image

trajectories of cardiac borders sometimes present discontinuities and may not always correspond to well-defined edges. Here we extract the border by searching for optimal path along time axis. We use a maximum tracking procedure [13] whose performance is improved by using a local model to predict the position of the next border point.

The system described by Unser *et al.*[13] is based on a search algorithm that traces gray-scale maxima corresponding to each relevant cardiac internal structure along the horizontal time axis. Although this algorithm was initially designed to be applied to the data directly, it can also be used in our system in which tracking of cardiac border is based on the position of *minimum intensity* pixel on the edge detected M-mode image. A digitized M-mode echocardiogram is represented as a two dimensional image $\{X_{k,l}\}$, where 'k' represents the time variable and 'l' represents the distance along the axis of the straight line drawn on the view. A brief review of the algorithms is presented here.

1) *Basic Algorithm:* The basic procedure is based on the fact that the movement of cardiac borders from one time frame to another is restricted to a relatively narrow region. A starting point is first determined by the user. Then, assuming the present position of the cardiac border to be l, the algorithm searches for the point with mini-mal intensity in the next vertical line in a window centered around the previous position $(l \pm w)$, where w is the window size. This point is then taken as the next position of the border. The procedure is iterated until all the frames have been considered. This simple approach follows a single path guided by locally optimizing the sum of the signal values along the trajectory. It usually detects the posterior wall epicardium satisfactorily, but generally fails in detecting the endocardium or the boundaries of the interventricular septum. We use this algorithm to detect the lower border, having lesser movement, shown in Figure 6(a).

2) *Kuwahara Algorithm (KMTA):* Kuwahara *et al.* suggest searching for the cardiac borders by reference to the border that has already been detected. Their algorithm uses the same principle as the basic algorithm except that the position and extent of the search window at a given time k is also a function of the relative displacement of the reference structure $\triangle l_r(K) = l_r(K) - l_r(K-1)$, where l_r is the reference cardiac border position. The reference position is now given by $l(K-1) + \triangle l_r(K)$, where $l(K-1)$ denotes the previously detected position of the structure. Furthermore, the width of the search window is increased in an asymmetric way, depending on the sign of $\triangle l(K)$. Broadening the search window in the expected direction of movement is designed to compensate for the greater velocity of the endocardium in systole and early diastole. We use this algorithm to detect the upper border in Figure 6(a).

State Identification. For identifying the states we first compute the distance between the two endocardium borders in each frame, as shown in Figure 6(a). Figure 6(b) shows the variation of cardiac border distance with respect to time.

In order to obtain state information, we use the cardiac border distance. The bottom end points of Figure 6(b) indicate end systole points and the top points indicate the end diastole points. During the time elapsed between end systole point to end diastole point, the heart is in diastole state and is in systole state from end diastole point to end systole point. In the diastole state left ventricle expands, thus the distance between the endocardium borders increases. Hence, the slope is positive. Similarly, in diastole, left ventricle contracts and the distance between the endocardium borders decreases which results in negative slope in the distance graph.

Using the distance information, we classify the echocardiogram video frames into two classes, namely, systole and diastole. In the echocardiogram video, the frames corresponding to positive slope are classified as diastolic state frames, while those corresponding to negative slope are classified as systolic. This completes the process of state detection from an echocardiogram video. The state transition graph obtained from Figure 6(b) is shown in Figure 6(c).

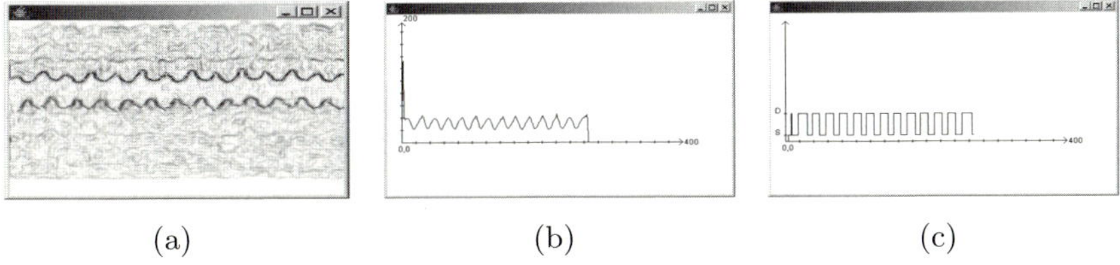

<table>
<tr><td align="center">(a)</td><td align="center">(b)</td><td align="center">(c)</td></tr>
</table>

Fig. 6. (a) Border extracted M-mode image, (b) Variation cardiac border distance with time, (c) State transition graph

Table 2 shows the detailed result of state identification from 267 frames in short axis view using single M-mode. This method gives total misclassification error of 26.22%. Most of the misclassified or unclassified frames are those during which state transition occurs. The table also shows Sweep M-mode results as explained in the next sub-section.

3.2 State Identification Using Sweep M-Mode

In order to further improve the state detection accuracy, we propose a multiple M-mode generation method termed as '*Sweep M-mode*'. It is so named because multiple M-modes are generated by scanning the intensity value along a straight line as before, while the straight line is continuously swept by a specified interval in a direction normal to a fixed axis.

To obtain sweep M-mode, user draws a line perpendicular to the direction of left ventricular wall motion (see straight line in Figure 7). Sweep M-modes are created by scanning the intensity value along the straight line perpendicular to this vertical line, taking it as Y-axis, for each frame of the video considered as X-axis. The Sweep M-modes are generated along the horizontal broken straight lines as shown in Figure 7. Now, as explained in Section 3.1, tracking of the cardiac borders is done for each M-mode individually.

To start tracking, initial border points need to be determined. For this user draws the left ventricle cavity border freehand at the same time when he draws the straight line in order to obtain sweep M-mode (freehand line in Figure 7). The intersection points of the cavity border and perpendicular straight lines are considered as the start-ing points for tracking the cardiac borders. Since border tracking of all the M-modes is not perfect due to inherent noise, we need to select only those few which are meaningful. It has been observed that in M-modes where tracking is perfect, the distance between the two cardiac borders never exceeds a threshold value. But if it does, the M-modes are surely mistracked. We use this as a heuristic to identify the proper M-modes. Thus, we select the most perfectly tracked M-modes as shown in Figure 8(a). The same method is followed for each individual M-mode to extract state information from a single M-mode.

The plot of the distance between two endocardium borders with respect to time for the selected M-modes is shown in Figure 8(b) and the state transition plot is shown in Figure 8(c). It is seen that the individual plots have many false state transitions. So we combine them using majority voting to identify the state information of each frame.

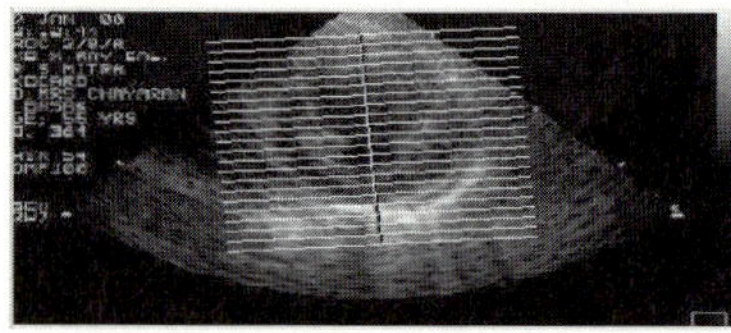

Fig. 7. User drawn straight line and cavity on a chosen frame of video

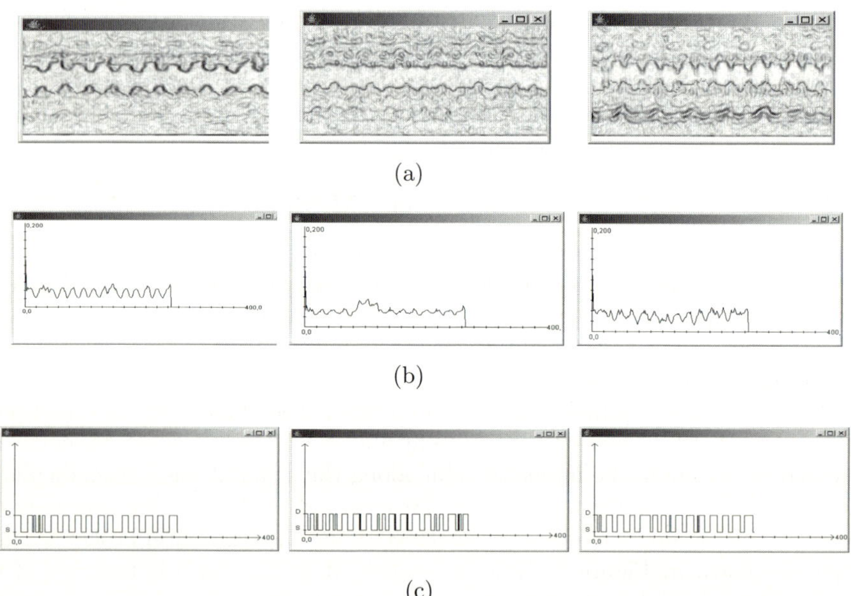

Fig. 8. Three selected M-modes: (a) Border extracted M-mode images, (b) Corresponding cardiac distance graph with time, (c) Corresponding state transition graph

We carried out experiments with the same echocardiogram video as before. The right hand part of Table 2 shows the detailed result obtained using sweep M-mode. It is seen that the misclassification error has come down to about 12.36%. Thus, use of sweep M-mode reduces the misclassification error as compared to single M-mode described in the previous section.

Table 2. Results of state identification using M-mode

True Class	Predicted Class					
	Single M-mode			Sweep M-mode		
	Systole	Diastole	Undetected	Systole	Diastole	Undetected
Systole	96	5	21	111	10	2
Diastole	26	101	18	18	123	3

4 Conclusion

In this paper we have proposed a new approach for hierarchical state-based modeling of echo video data by identifying the views and states of objects. We first detect the view boundaries using histogram based comparison and edge change ratio. Then we classify the views by considering signal properties of different views. Our technique gives a precision rate of 95.34%. To extract state information from each view, we use synthetic M-modes. At first, we apply single M-mode. But the misclassification error in identifying the states with the help of single M-mode is quite high (around 27%). So we introduce a new type of M-mode generation method named as sweep M-mode. Application of sweep M-mode reduces the misclassification error to about 13%. We have used this approach of hierarchical state-based modeling to develop an object relational video database for storage and retrieval of echocardiogram video segments. The proposed scheme is now being extended for finer (sub state) segmentation.

Acknowledgments. This work is partially supported by the Department of Science and Technology (DST), India, under Research Grant No. SR/S3/EECE/ 024/ 2003-SERC-Engg.

References

1. Feigenbaum, H.: *Echocardiography*, LEA & FEBIGER, 1997
2. Huang, H.K.: PACS: *Basic Principles and Applications*, Wiley, New York, 1999
3. DICOM: Http://Medical.nema.org/dicom.html
4. Shyu, C.R., Brodely, C.E., Kak, A.C, Osaka, A.: ASSERT: A physician-in-the loop content-based retrieval system for HRCT image databases. *Computer Vision and Image Understanding*, Vol. 75, July/August, pp. 111-132, 1999
5. Duncan, J.S., Ayache, N.: Medical image analysis: progress over two decades and the challenges ahead. *IEEE Trans. Pattern Analysis and Machine Intelli-gence*, Vol. 22, No. 1, January 2000, pp. 95-105, 2000

6. Ebadollahi, S., Chang, S.F., Wu, H.: Echocardiogram videos: summarization, temporal segmentation and browsing. *Proc. IEEE Int'l Conference on Image Processing*, (ICIP'02), Vol. 1, pp. 613-616, September 2002

7. Sing, P.K., Majumdar, A.K.: Semantic content based retrieval in a video data-base. *Proc. Int'l Workshop on Multimedia Data Mining*, (MDM/KDD'2001), pp. 50-57, August 2001

8. Acharya, B., Mukherjee, J., Majumdar, A.K.: Modeling dynamic objects in databases: a logic based approach. *ER 2001, LNCS 2224*, Springer Verlag, pp. 449-512

9. Ebadollahi, S., Chang, S.F., Wu, H.: Automatic view recognition in echocardiogram videos using parts-based representation. Proc. *IEEE Computer Society Conference on Computer Vision and Pattern Recognition*, (CVPR'04), Vol. 2, pp. II-II-9, June 2004

10. Acharya, B., Mukherjee, J., Majumdar, A.K.: An object state transition model for echocardiogram video data. *Proc. Conference of Multimedia Processing Systems*, pp. 103-106, 2000

11. Yu, H., Wolf, W.: A visual search system for video and image database. *Proc. IEEE Int'l Conference on Multimedia Computing and Systems*, pp. 517-524, June1997

12. Zabin, R., Miller, J., Mai, K.: A feature-based algorithm for detecting and classifying scene breaks. *Proc. ACM Multimedia*, pp. 189-200, 1995

13. Unser, M., Palle, G., Braun, P., Eden, M.: Automated extraction of serial myocardial borders from M-mode echocardiograms. I*EEE Trans. Medical Imaging*, Vol. 8, pp. 96-103, March 1989

14. Murphy, N., Marlows, S., O'Toole, C., Smeaton, A.: Evaluation of automatic shot boundary detection on a large video test suite. *The Challenges of Image Re-trieval - 2nd UK Conference on Image Retrieval*, 1999

15. Mas, J., Fernandez, G.: Video shot boundary detection based on color histogram. TREC 2003

16. Lienhart, P.: Reliable transition detection in videos: a survey and practioners guide. *Int'l Journal of Image and graphics*, Vol. 1, No. 3, pp. 469-486, 2001

17. Bishop, C.M.: *Neural networks for pattern recognition*. Oxford: Oxford Univer-sity Press.1997

Video Completion for Indoor Scenes

Vardhman Jain and P.J. Narayanan

Center for Visual Information Technology
International Institute of Information Technology
Hyderabad, India
{vardhman@research., pjn@}iiit.ac.in

Abstract. In this paper, we present a new approach for object removal and video completion of indoor scenes. In indoor images, the frames are not affine related. The region near the object to be removed can have multiple planes with sharply different motions. Dense motion estimation may fail for such scenes due to missing pixels. We use feature tracking to find dominant motion between two frames. The geometry of the motion of multiple planes is used to segment the motion layers into component planes. The homography corresponding to each hole pixel is used to warp a frame in the future or past for filling it. We show the application of our technique on some typical indoor videos.

1   Introduction

Segmenting and removing objects from images or videos is of much current interest. Object removal leaves the image or video with unknown information where the object was earlier placed. Missing information recovery in images is called *inpainting*. This is accomplished by inferring or guessing the missing information from the surrounding regions. For videos, the process is termed as *completion*. Video completion uses the information from the past and the future frames to fill the pixels in the missing region. When no information is available for some pixels, inpainting algorithms are used to fill them. Video completion has many applications. Post-production editing of professional videos in creative ways is possible with effective video completion techniques. Video completion is perhaps most effective with home videos. Video can be cleaned up by removing unnecessary parts of the scene. Inpainting and video completion is often interactive and involve the users as the objective is to provide desirable and appealing output.

Image inpainting inevitably requires approximation as there is no way of obtaining the missing information. For videos, the missing information in the current frame may be available from nearby frames. Significant work has been done on inpainting and professional image manipulation applications and tools exist to accomplish the task to various degrees. The solution to the problem of object removal in video depends also on the scene complexity. Most video completion work has focused on scenes in which a single background motion is present such as an outdoor scene. In scenes with multiple large motion, motion layer segmentation methods are used to obtain different motions layers. A particular layer can be removed by filling the information with the background layers. Scenes with multiple motion, such as indoor scenes, are challenging to these algorithms. For scenes with many planes, motion model fitting may not be suitable as the boundaries between the layers are not exact. This is especially problematic for video completion as the region being filled could straddle these boundaries. Periodicity of motion is also often used by techniques which fill the holes by patching from some other part of the video.

In this paper, we present a technique for video completion for indoor scenes. We concentrate on scenes where the background motion consists of two or three planes in the neighborhood of the object to be removed. The main contribution of this paper is the use of the geometry of intersecting planes in multiple views for motion segmentation, without applying a dense motion segmentation in the image. We also show that segmentation of only the nearby background around the missing region is sufficient for the task of video completion. Full-frame motion segmentation can thus be avoided. The geometric nature of the method ensures accurate and unique background assignment to the pixels in the unknown region, which to the best of our knowledge is not possible with other video completion methods. We particularly concentrate on scenes where the neighborhood around the object to be removed is planar in nature.

The rest of the paper is organized as follows. In Section 2, we describe relevant previous work. Section 3 discusses various stages of our algorithm in detail. Results are shown in Section 4. Conclusions and ideas for future work follow in Section 5.

2   Previous Work

The work presented here is closely related to a few well studied problems. *Image inpainting* fills-in the unknown regions (or holes) in an image based on the surrounding pixels. Structure propagation and texture synthesis are the two basic approaches for image inpainting. Structure propagation methods propagate the structure around the unknown region progressively to inside it. Bertalmio *et al* [1] proposed a method for filling-in of the image holes by automatic propagation of the isophotes (lines of similar intensity) in the image. Texture synthesis [2,3] methods assume the existence of a pattern in the image and fill the pixels in the missing region by finding a patch matching the neighboring texture in the whole image. Texture synthesis has been done at pixel level [2] as well as block level [3,4]. Structure propagation methods work well only on small holes, whereas texture synthesis methods require texture in the image. Methods combining both structure propagation and texture synthesis have been proposed in recent years and show impressive results [5,6]. These image inpainting methods calculate the values of unknown regions. These can only be an approximation of original data, however.

Kang *et al* [7] proposed a technique for inpainting or region filling using multiple views of a scene. Their technique is based on finding the appropriate region in the second view and then mapping the pixels back to the first view using the affine projection calculated using the correspondence in the two views. Similar methods are used in video completion as discussed below.

Object removal in videos has received attention in recent years. Two types of techniques have been proposed. The first type finds out the missing data by searching for a patch matching the neighborhood of the hole in the video. The match is defined in terms of spatial and temporal feature similarity. Periodicity in motion is a common assumption for these techniques. Space time video completion [8] uses a five dimensional sum of squared differences to find the appropriate patch for filling the holes where the matrices include the three color values and velocity along x and y direction. *Video Repairing* proposed by Jia *et al* [9] recovers the missing part of foreground objects by *movel* sampling and alignment using tensor voting to generate loops of motion by connecting the last frame to the first frame. Motion field interpolation based methods have also been developed recently. Kokaram *et al* [10] perform object removal by using the motion information to reconstruct the missing data by recursively propagating data from the surrounding regions. Matsushita *et al* [11] proposed *motion inpainting* where the inference of the unknown pixels information is based on the optical flow vectors which are in turn interpolated based on the flow of the surrounding pixels.

In the second scenario, explicit use of the geometry of multiple views is made to infer the information missing in the current frame from the nearby frames. This is directly related to the problem of disocclusion in computer vision. The fact that two views of a plane are related by a perspective transformation defined using a Homography matrix, forms the basis of most such approaches. Jia *et al* [9] proposed the repairing of the static background by the use of planar layered mosaics. The layers are assumed to be available from initial manual segmentation followed by tracking using the mean shift algorithm. Similar approach has been demonstrated by Zhang *et al* [12]. They use an automatic layer extraction approach followed by layered mosaicing. If some holes still remain an image inpainting approach is used in frame-wise manner based on a graph cuts formulation.

When the camera is far from the background, the nearby frames of the background can be approximated to be related by an affine or projective transformation. This approximation is used by some methods [9]. Such methods will fail for indoor scenes where multiple background motion exists. In general, it would be impossible to identify every single plane in the scene and apply layer mosaicing on each of them individually, automatically and accurately.

Structure from motion problems employ some techniques that are relevant to this problem. Vincent and Laganire [13] discuss the problem of dividing the image into planes. They start with a set of point correspondence and apply the RANSAC algorithm with an optimal selection of the four initial points to maximize the chance that the points are on same plane. All the other points in the image are declared to belong to the plane whose homography gives least reprojection error. Fraundorfer *et al* [14] find the interest regions in the two views on which affine region matching is performed. The affine matching is helpful in removing the non-planar regions from considerations. On the matched region the homography is determined and a region growing is performed around the region to include regions which match the homography well. During the region growing step the homography is updated to include the new interest points inside the region for the estimation. At the termination of the region growing, the scene is segmented into a set of planar regions. Wills *et al* [15] proposed a graph cuts formulation for motion segmentation. First a set of dominant motions in the two views is obtained. The energy terms in the graph are based on the re-projection error due to each motion model and the smoothness term is defined based on color similarity between the pixels.

The work presented in this paper combines many of these ideas to perform video completion indoor scenes with multiple background motions.

3   Video Completion for Indoor Scenes

In this paper, we address the problem of object removal and video completion for indoor scenes where the transformation of the background is non trivial and variable. An overview of the process is shown in Figure 1. We track the foreground (the object to be removed) interactively using our earlier work [16] to

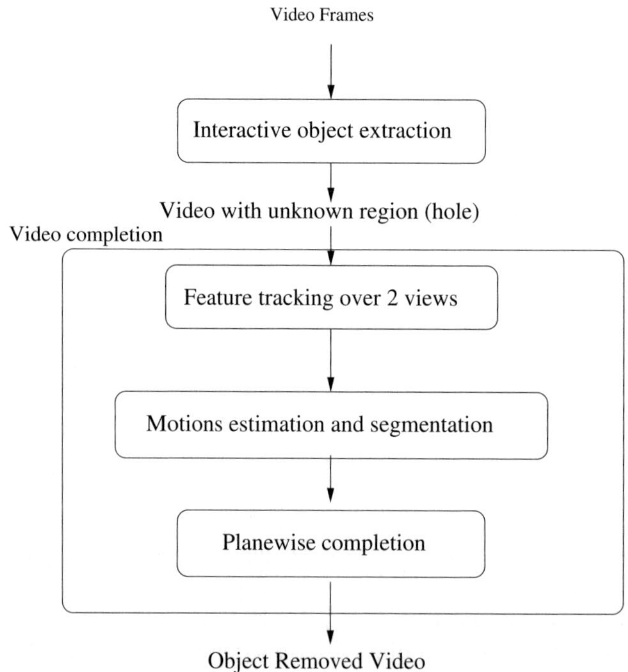

Fig. 1. The overview of the various steps of our system

track the objects across the video. For this paper, we assume that the background has a maximum of 2 planes around the object to be removed in two adjacent views. The region around the object is segmented into one or two planes, using dominant motion model estimation followed by an optimal boundary detection algorithm. We then apply the respective homography to recover the unknown pixels from the neighboring frames. These steps are explained below.

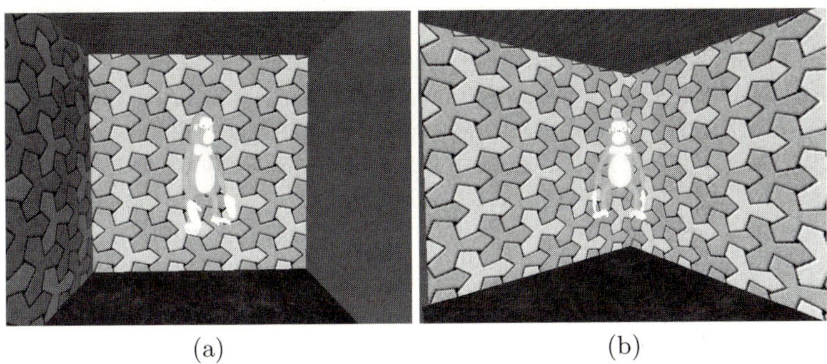

(a)   (b)

Fig. 2. Two different cases of object removal (a) The local background around the object is a single plane (b) The local background around the object is spread over more than 1 plane. Due to the local nature of the plane segmentation technique the first case (a) doesn't need any motion segmentation. Motion segmentation in the second case (b) is also local in nature and even though there are more planes in the image only the two planes which constitute the object's background would be segmented.

3.1   Object Segmentation

The segmentation step provides the masks of the object to be removed across the video frames. Unlike image inpainting techniques, getting this mask from the user in each frame is not feasible. We use an interactive method of object extraction using graph cuts and feature tracking to generate the mask across the video sequence.

The user gives a binary segmentation of the first frame, marking the foreground and the background. We track features points in the segmented frame to the current frame (unsegmented) and set them as seed points in the 3D graph constructed with the two frames. A graph cuts optimization on the graph gives the segmentation for the current frame. The user can mark extra stroke and run the iterative graph cut to improve the segmentation before proceeding to next frame. Our method has the advantage of being fast and interactively driven. This allows us to have complex object or object with complex motion segmented across the video. This method is similar to Video object cut and paste [17].

After running through the frames of video, we get the object mask in each frame. This mask defines the region to be filled in using the video completion algorithm.

3.2 Video Completion

Our algorithm's basic assumption is the existence of a piecewise planar background in local neighborhood of the object to be removed. Our video completion algorithm can be divided into following major sub-steps.

Feature tracking in two views: The first step is finding the corresponding feature points in the two frames of the video. We use the KLT tracking for tracking point features across the frames. The method involves finding trackable features in the first image, which are then matched in the second image. We find the features selectively in only local neighborhood of the hole, this is to ensure that we only consider useful correspondences for our motion estimation and completion steps. We call the region around the hole where we do the selective matching as the Region of Interest (ROI). Figure 3 (b) shows the optical flow vectors calculated in the ROI. The ROI can be obtained by dilating the object mask with an appropriate thickness.

Motion Segmentation: Given the point correspondences in the two images, our aim is to find the planar segmentation of the ROIs. Figure 2 shows the two possible scenarios. In Figure 2(a) the ROI around the object is a single plane, while in Figure 2 (b) the ROI includes two different planes. We use a combination of two approaches to robustly estimate the segmentation of the points inside the ROI into multiple planes. The algorithm proceeds by finding the dominant motions in the ROI using the set of correspondences. We use the RANSAC [18] algorithm to determine the dominant motion. RANSAC algorithm has the advantage of being robust to outliers, which are indeed present in our correspondence pairs due to the existence of multiple planes.

To begin with, we use all the correspondence pairs to determine the dominant motion. The features which are inliers for the current dominant motion are then removed from the set and the step is repeated to find the next dominant motion. To avoid RANSAC algorithm from choosing wrong set of initial four points, we modify the selection phase to accept the set of points only if they are within a set threshold distance. The points which are declared inliers to the RANSAC algorithm are then used for a least square error fitting estimate of the homography using the normalized DLT algorithm [19]. This fitting gives us the final homography for the set of points. Figure 3 (c,d) shows the automatically determined first and second dominant motions as cluster of optical flow vectors which are their inliers.

Optimal boundary estimation: Optimal boundary estimation is needed to actually separate the ROI into two different planes. This information is later used during the filling-in process. Note that unlike other methods [13,14] we cannot depend on the region growing method to give us the boundaries of the planes because we can not estimate these boundaries in the unknown region. We assume the intersection of the two planar regions to be a line. Let H_1 and

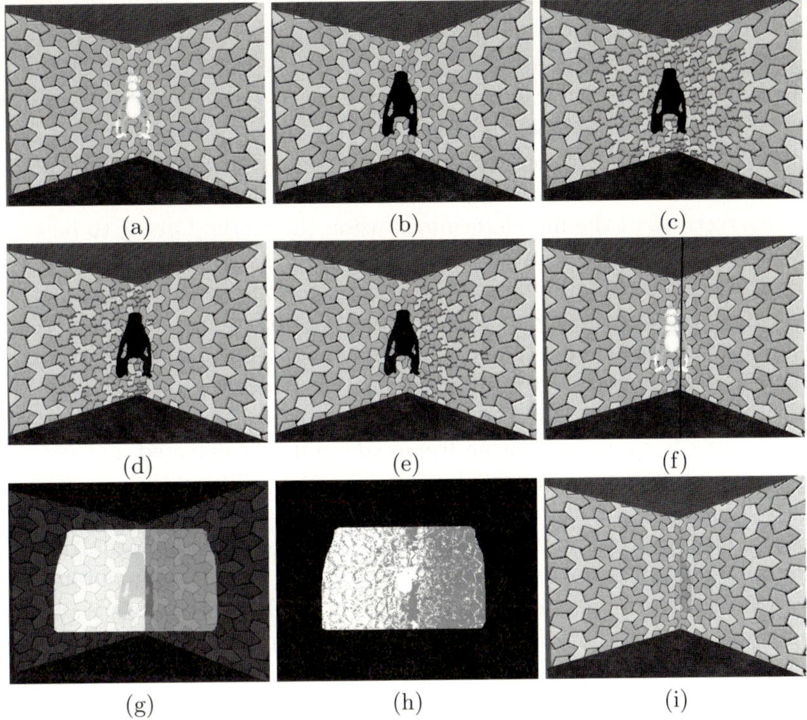

Fig. 3. Intermediate outputs at the various stages of the algorithm (a) Input image (second frame is not shown) (b) The object to be removed is masked out and region is shown in black (c) Sparse optical flow vectors on the image (shown in red, in twice the original size to make them visible) (d,e) First and Second dominant motion vectors clustered respectively (f) Line of intersection of the two planes calculated as detailed in Section 3.2. (g) The surrounding background of the region is segmented into two planes (h) Output of graph cuts based binary partitioning of the segments, shown for comparison (i) The results of the completion on this frame.

H_2 be the homography due to π_1 and π_2 between the two views. We find the *generalized eigenvectors* of the pair (H_1, H_2) by solving the equation,

$$H_1 v = \lambda H_2 v.$$

The eigenvectors obtained have the property that two of them are the projections of two points on the line of intersection of the two planes π_1, π_2 on to the image plane I_1 and third one is the epipole in the image I_1. The two eigenvectors corresponding to the points on the plane can be identified due to the equality of their corresponding eigenvalues. The reader is referred to Johansson [20] for a proof of this fact.

Using the homogeneous coordinates of the two points on the image plane, we can obtain the exact line of intersection in the image. In fact we need this line only over the ROI. Thus, we have the planar layers for the ROI. We warp these layers in the neighboring frame to the frame to be fill-in the unknown region. The correspondence between layers obtained in two views is established by measuring the percentage of the tracked points that are part of the layer in previous frame. In the ongoing discussion we use the word *label* of a pixel to refer to the layer assigned it. Figure 3. (f) shows a line obtained by this method, (g) shows the plane segmentation in the ROI which is defined by the line.

The correctness of the line determined using the method needs to be ensured as small errors in homography calculation can lead to high errors in line determination. In fact the homography pair may have complex generalized eigenvalues and eigenvectors and may not yield a valid pair of points to obtain the line. We validate the correctness of the boundary line by ensuring that it partitions the correspondence pairs into different clusters depending on the homography to which they belong. In case the line is not determinable or validation fails we obtain the line from a neighboring frame where it was detected and verified by applying the underlying homography.

It should be noted that the methods which give good results for dense motion segmentation from multiple views are not suitable for segmentation of the frames with the missing region. Graph cuts based motion segmentation techniques [15,21] determine the dominant motion models in the scene and assign each pixel to one of the motion model based on an optimal graph cuts segmentation. The unknown pixel can never be accurately assigned to any particular label in these approaches due to lack of both color and motion information, which are used for determining the weights in the graph. We show the result of applying binary graph cuts partitioning in Figure 3(f), to illustrate this fact. We only apply a binary labeling in the graph, the white region shows points supporting first dominant motion and gray region shows points supporting second dominant region. Grey region of the image was not considered for the segmentation stage. Similarly methods like [14,13] which assign the pixels to the motion model or planes based on re-projection error measure can not assign the unknown pixels to any particular layer accurately.

3.3   Layer-Wise Video Completion

The line dividing the two planes gives a single confident label to each pixel in the ROI. Once the label is determined we can fill the hole by warping the nearby frames according to the homography related to the label. We build the mosaic of each plane using the neighboring frames. The missing pixels are assigned the color from the mosaic of the plane correspondence to their label. This method is in principle similar to the layered mosaic approaches [9,12]. The difference is that we have exact knowledge of which plane an unknown pixel belongs to and use only that corresponding plane (layer). The blending of homographies of multiple layers is not needed. As in case of layered mosaic approaches the intensity mismatch might occur due to combination of various frames, simple blending methods could be applied to circumvent the error due to this.

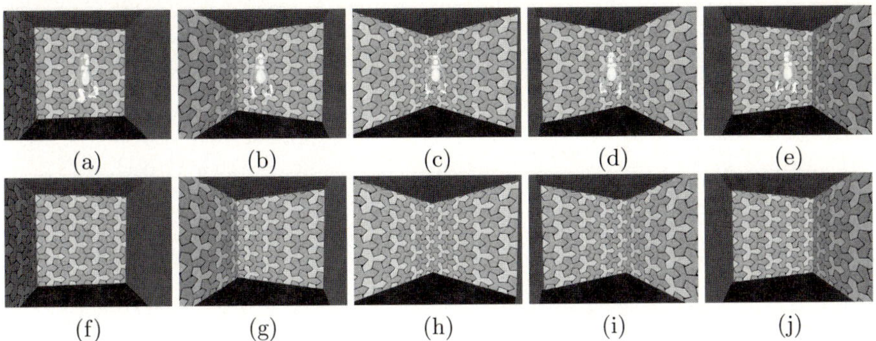

Fig. 4. The process applied on a synthetic sequence. (a-d) show the five frames of the sequence. (e-h) show the frames after completion. The monkey is removed from the original video. (a,e) have only one background plane, while in (b,c,d) two planes are present in the background.

3.4   Inpainting

Some pixels may remain unknown after the layer-wise video completion due to absence of the information in the video. Pixels which are always covered by the object to removed belong to this set. As in case of image inpainting techniques we can only approximate the values of these pixels based on the surrounding information. The extra information however is the knowledge of which plane the pixel belongs to. We can restrict the filling algorithm to use values only from the corresponding plane.

4   Results

We demonstrate the application of our approach on two sequences. Figure 4 shows the results of our algorithm on a synthetic sequence. The sequence is set in a room with two wall, a roof and a ceiling i.e. four planes. Our approach removes the monkey as shown in the figure. Due to intensity difference on the wall during the motion the mosaicing of the wall over the views generate some intensity seams. Simple blending applied during the mosaic construction gives much better results. No application of inpainting was needed in this sequence.

Figure 5 demonstrate the result of the technique applied to a real sequence. Some black holes are present in the output due to unavailability of data. Inpainting is not being applied on the sequence as it is neither structure rich nor texture rich. Seams which are visible in the results can be removed by applying some blending approach.

The algorithm takes around 2 seconds per frame for the motion segmentation and plane matching step the completion step is dependent on number of neighboring frames used for creating the mosaic and takes around 1-2 seconds when 12 (6 forward and 6 backward) frames are used.

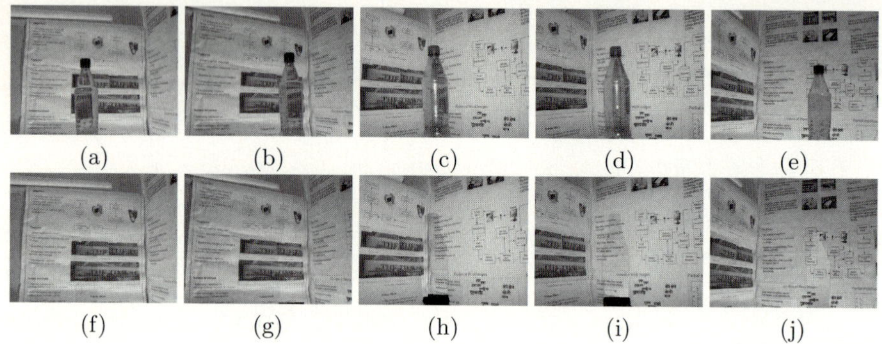

(a) (b) (c) (d) (e)

(f) (g) (h) (i) (j)

Fig. 5. The process applied on a real sequence, we remove the bottle from the video (a-e) shows five frames of the sequence. (f-j) shows the results of video completion algorithm on each input frame. Initial and final frames have only one background while frames in the middle have two background planes. The output has visible seams at the junction of the removed object due to very high intensity change in the scene.

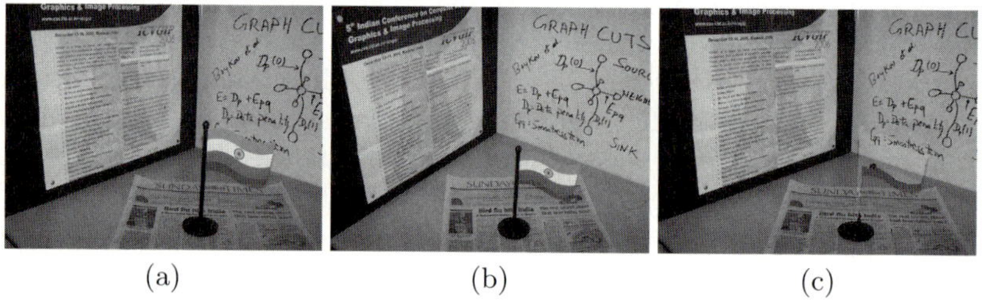

(a) (b) (c)

Fig. 6. Application of our approach to images. (a,b) two views of the scene containing 3 different background planes. (c) Image (a) is filled-in using information from image (b) to remove the hole created due to the removed flag. Note that the shadow of the flag is present in the completed image as shadow region was not selected for removal.

Our method can also be used for object removal in pairs of images. We demonstrate a simple example of this in Figure 6. The background of the flag object has three planes. Motion estimation gives us three different motion models. The intersection line is obtained for each pair of planes and used in same way as described as for videos for layer-wise completion of the unknown region. We used an affine region matching to determine the point correspondences as the inter-frame motion was large in this case. There is also significant change in illumination between the views, which is apparent after the flag is removed and the image is completed. Both images didn't see table in the region near the flag and in the region containing the flag's shadow. Thus, that information could not be filled in.

5   Conclusions and Future Work

In this paper, we address the problem of video object removal and completion for indoor scenes. Our method involves user interaction only for object selection and performs the rest of the operations without any user interaction. Ours is an attempt to use multiview information for scene inference and video completion. We showed results on scenes with piecewise planar background near the object to be removed. The technique can be easily extended to more planes as long as the dominant motion segmentation can be achieved.

The geometric information we used give better segmentation of multiple motions. The motions are segmented at the pixel level without region growing or interpolation, unlike the motion segmentation performed in the image space. Motion inpainting methods can work well for scenes with a multiple planes or non-textured surfaces. Combining the geometric information with motion inpainting will be the most promising one for scenes with multiple planes. We propose to investigate the problem further in that direction.

References

1. Bertalmio, M., Sapiro, G., Caselles, V., Ballester, C.: Image inpainting. In: SIGGRAPH '00: Proceedings of the 27th annual conference on Computer graphics and interactive techniques, New York, NY, USA, ACM Press/Addison-Wesley Publishing Co. (2000) 417–424
2. Efros, A., Leung, T.: Texture synthesis by non-parametric sampling. In: IEEE International Conference on Computer Vision, Corfu, Greece (1999) 1033–1038
3. Efros, A., Freeman, W.: Image quilting for texture synthesis and transfer. Proceedings of SIGGRAPH 2001 (2001) 341–346
4. Rother, C., Kolmogorov, V., Blake, A.: "grabcut": Interactive foreground extraction using iterated graph cuts. ACM Trans. Graph. **23** (2004) 309–314
5. Bertalmio, M., Vese, L., Sapiro, G., Osher, S.: Simultaneous structure and texture image inpainting. In: CVPR03. (2003) II: 707–712
6. Criminisi, A., Perez, P., Toyama, K.: Region filling and object removal by exemplar-based image inpainting. IEEE transactions on Image Processing **13** (2004) 1200–1212
7. Kang, S., Chan, T., Soatto, S.: Landmark based inpainting from multiple views. Technical report, UCLA Math CAM (2002)
8. Wexler, Y., Shechtman, E., Irani, M.: Space-time video completion. In: CVPR04. (2004) I: 120–127
9. Jia, J., Wu, T., Tai, Y., Tang, C.: Video repairing: Inference of foreground and background under severe occlusion. In: CVPR04. Volume 1. (2004)
10. Kokaram, A., Collis, B., Robinson, S.: A bayesian framework for recursive object removal in movie post-production. In: ICIP03. (2003) I: 937–940
11. Matsushita, Y., Ofek, E., Tang.X., Shum, H.: Full frame video stabilization. In: CVPR05. (2005)
12. Zhang, Y., Xiao, J., Shah, M.: Motion layer based object removal in videos. WACV/Motion **01** (2005) 516–521
13. Vincent, E., Laganiere, R.: Detecting planar homographies in an image pair. In: Symposium on Image and Signal Processing and Analysis (ISPA01). (2001)

14. Fraundorfer, F., Schindler, K., Bischof, H.: Piecewise planar scene reconstruction from sparse correspondences. Image and Vision Computing (2006)
15. Wills, J., Agarwal, S., Belongie, S.: What went where. In: Proceedings of IEEE Conference on Computer Vision and Pattern Recognition. (2003) 37–44
16. Jain, V., Narayanan, P.: Layer extraction using graph cuts and feature tracking. In: In Proceedings of the third, International Conference on Visual Information Engineering. (2006) 292–297
17. Li, Y., Sun, J., Shum, H.: Video object cut and paste. ACM Trans. Graph. **24** (2005) 595–600
18. Fischler, M., Bolles, R.: Random sample consensus: a paradigm for model fitting with applications to image analysis and automated cartography. Communication of the ACM **24** (1981) 381–395
19. Hartley, R.: In defence of the 8-point algorithm. In: ICCV '95: Proceedings of the Fifth International Conference on Computer Vision, Washington, DC, USA, IEEE Computer Society (1995) 1064
20. Johansson, B.: View synthesis and 3d reconstruction of piecewise planar scenes using intersection lines between the planes. IEEE International Conference on Computer Vision **1** (1999) 54–59
21. Bhat, P., Zheng, K., Snavely, N., Agarwala, A., Agrawala, M., Cohen, M., Curless, B.: Piecewise image registration in the presence of multiple large motions. In: CVPR06. (2006) II: 2491–2497

Reducing False Positives in Video Shot Detection Using Learning Techniques

Nithya Manickam, Aman Parnami, and Sharat Chandran

Department of Computer Science and Engineering
Indian Institute of Technology Bombay
`http://www.cse.iitb.ac.in/~{mnitya, nsaaman, sharat}`

Abstract. Video has become an interactive medium of daily use today. However, the sheer volume of the data makes it extremely difficult to browse and find required information. Organizing the video and locating required information effectively and efficiently presents a great challenge to the video retrieval community. This demands a tool which would break down the video into smaller and manageable units called shots.

Traditional shot detection methods use pixel difference, histograms, or temporal slice analysis to detect hard-cuts and gradual transitions. However, systems need to be robust to sequences that contain dramatic illumination changes, shaky camera effects, and special effects such as fire, explosion, and synthetic screen split manipulations. Traditional systems produce false positives for these cases; i.e., they claim a shot break when there is none.

We propose a shot detection system which reduces false positives even if all the above effects are *cumulatively* present in one sequence. Similarities between successive frames are computed by finding the correlation and is further analyzed using a wavelet transformation. A final filtering step is to use a trained Support Vector Machine (SVM). As a result, we achieve better accuracy (while retaining speed) in detecting shot-breaks when compared with other techniques.

1   Introduction

In recent times, the demand for a tool for searching and browsing videos is growing noticeably. This has led to computer systems internally reorganizing the video into a hierarchical structure of frames, shots, scenes and story. A frame at the lowest level in the hierarchy, is the basic unit in a video, representing a still image. *Shot detection techniques* are used to group frames into shots. Thus, a shot designates a *contiguous sequence of video frames recorded by an uninterrupted camera operation*. A scene is a collection of shots which presents different views of the same event and contain the same object of interest. A story is a collection of scenes that defines an unbroken event. Fig. 1 illustrates this paradigm.

Video shot detection forms the first step in organizing video into a hierarchical structure. Intuitively, a shot captures the notion of a single semantic entity. A *shot break* signifies a transition from one shot to the subsequent one, and may be

P. Kalra and S. Peleg (Eds.): ICVGIP 2006, LNCS 4338, pp. 421–432, 2006.

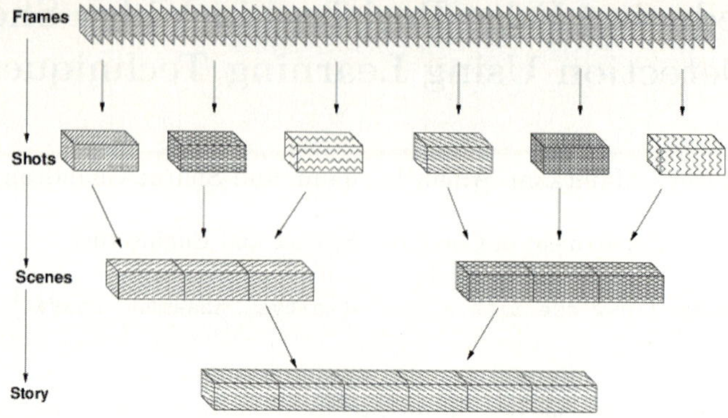

Fig. 1. Hierarchical structure of video

of many types (for example, fade, dissolve, wipe and hard (or immediate)). Our primary interest lies in improving hard cut detection by *reducing the number of places erroneously declared* as shot breaks (false positives).

A wide range of approaches have been investigated for shot detection but the accuracies have remained low. The simplest method for shot detection is *pairwise pixel similarity* [1,2], where the intensity or color values of corresponding pixels in successive frames are compared to detect shot-breaks. This method is very sensitive to object and camera movements and noise. A *block-based approach* [3,4] divides each frame into a number of blocks that are compared against their counterparts in the next frame. Block based comparison is often more robust to small movements falsely declared as shot-break. Sensitivity to camera and object motion, is further reduced by *histogram comparison* [4,5,6,7,8]. For example, a 16 bin normalized HSV color histogram is used in [6] to perform histogram intersection. In [7] a combination of local and global histogram is used to detect shot-breaks. However, all these methods perform less than satisfactorily when there are deliberate or inadvertent lighting variations. [9] uses a statistical distribution of color histogram of the shot to refine shot-breaks.

At the cost of more processing, the *edge change ratio method* [10,11] handles slow transitions by looking for similar edges in the adjacent frames and their ratios. [11] addresses the problem with illumination changes. Three-dimensional *temporal-space methods* [12,13] are better, but still sensitive to sudden changes in illumination. *Cue Video* [14] is a graph based approach, which uses a sampled three-dimensional RGB color histogram to measure the distance between pairs of contiguous frames. This method can handle special issues such as false positives from flash photography.

1.1   Problem Statement

As mentioned earlier, our main interest is in reducing false positives in challenging situations enumerated below.

1. *Illumination changes*: An example of this situation (inter-reflections, user-driven light changes, flash photography) is illustrated in Fig. 2. In the movie excerpt, lighting causes the actress to appear different. It is natural to the human, but confuses shot detection algorithms and even the camera as seen in the third frame!
2. *Camera effects*: These include effects such as zooming and tilting of objects of interest, shaky handling of amateur video, fast object motion, and fast camera motion. An example is illustrated in Fig. 3.
3. *Special effects*: An example of this situation (explosion) is illustrated in Fig. 4. Split screen is another possibility shown in the last figure.

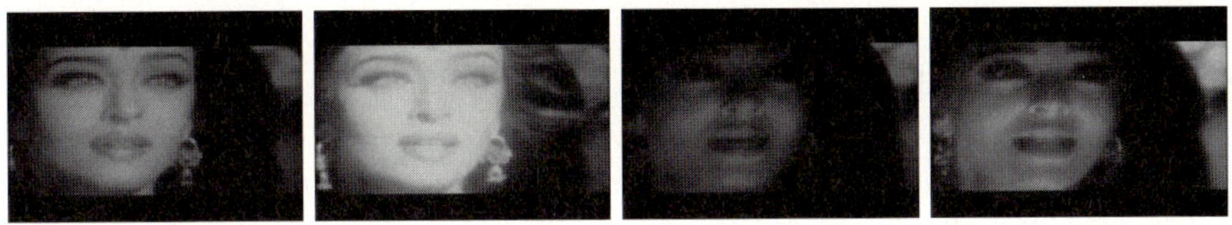

Fig. 2. A movie excerpt featuring Aishwarya Rai. Lightning creates unpredictable lighting changes.

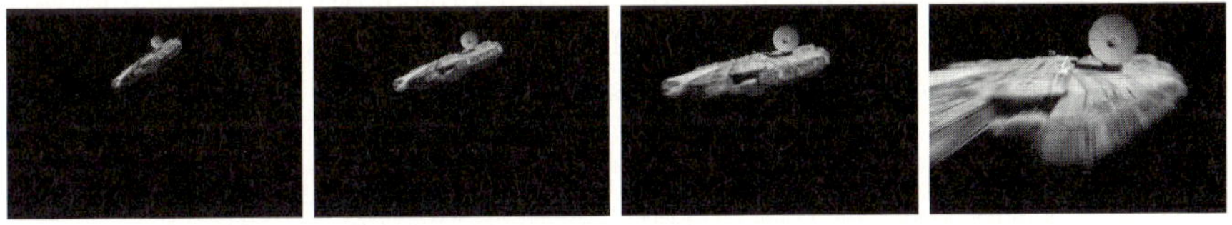

Fig. 3. Fast camera motion makes individual frames undecipherable

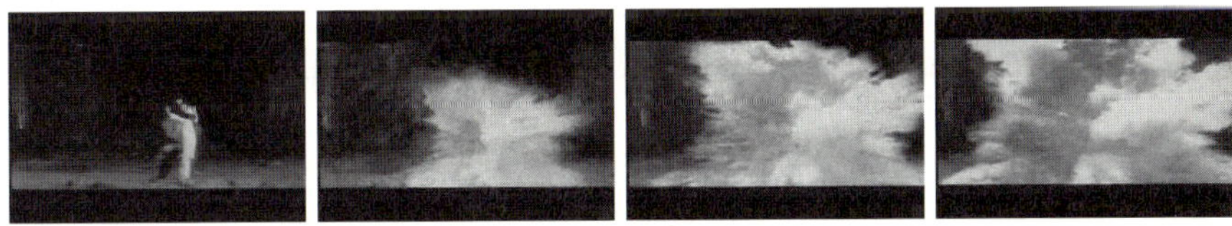

Fig. 4. Explosion in a dimly lit scene causes considerable change in color and intensity

Fig. 5. Two different scenes are displayed simultaneously using split-screen methods. However, a shot break may be observed in only one of them.

1.2   This Paper and Our Contributions

Our first attempt of detecting shot-breaks only from correlation value resulted in many false positives as the correlation value, when used as is, is unreliable. Therefore, *a multi layer filtering framework* as described in Section 2 is necessary. Based on a large number of experiments, we decided on the use of a Morlet wavelet based feature and a SVM to reduce false positives. It is significant to note that any framework should not increase errors if all unusual effects are cumulatively present in one sequence, or when gradual transitions are present. Our machine learning based scheme avoids this problem. Results of our experiments are given in Section 3 and we end with some concluding remarks in the last section.

2   Proposed Method

We propose a shot detection system which reduces errors even if all the above effects are cumulatively present in one sequence. Similarities between successive frames are computed by finding intensity-compensated correlation using ideas similar to the ones in [15]. We depart, by further analyzing these similarities using wavelet methods to locate the shot breaks and reduce false positives by analyzing the frames around the predicted shot-breaks. We further use learning techniques to refine our shot-breaks. The method is summarized in Fig. 6 and essentially consists of the following three steps.

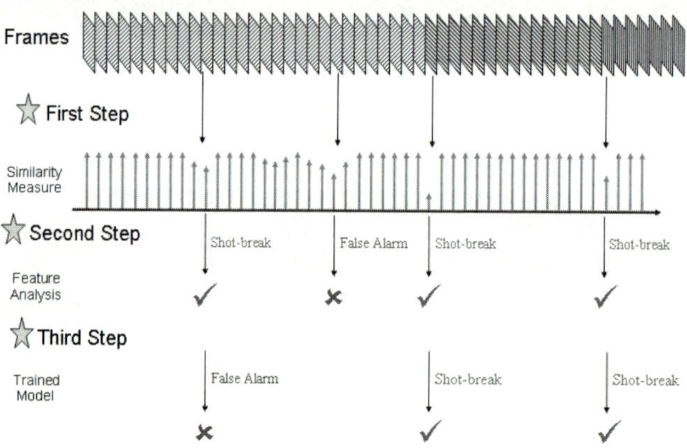

Fig. 6. Our filtering approach

1. Extracting features representing the similarity between the successive frames helps to determine candidate points for shot breaks. Candidate points for shot breaks are where similarity is low; four frames are indicated in the portion marked in Fig. 6 (First Step). This is further elaborated in Section 2.1 (for hard cuts) and Section 2.4 (for gradual transitions).

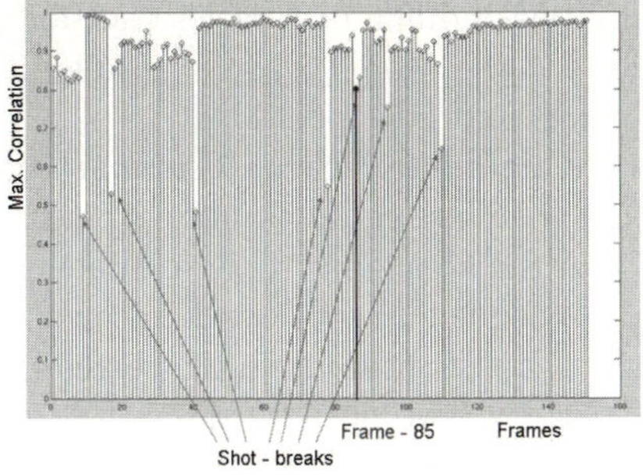

(a) A sample correlation sequence. Low values might indicate shot breaks.

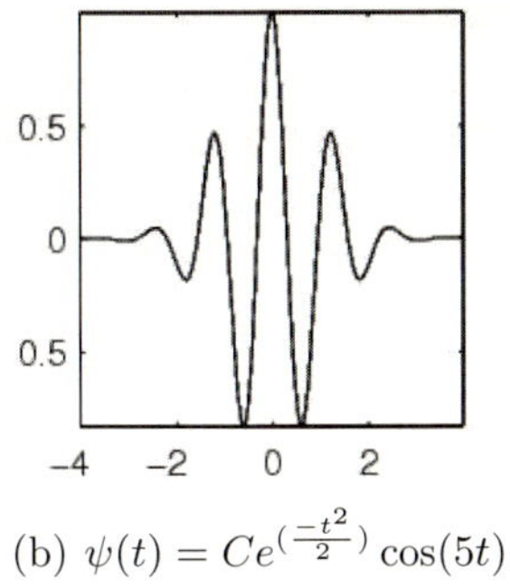

(b) $\psi(t) = Ce^{(\frac{-t^2}{2})}\cos(5t)$.

Fig. 7. Similarity features and the Morlet mother wavelet

2. Analyzing features to detect plausible shot breaks. As shown in Fig. 6 (Second Step) the second predicted shot break is dropped because it is a false alarm. This is further elaborated in Section 2.2 (for hard cut) and Section 2.5 (for gradual transitions). We then refine the detected shot breaks using more involved techniques to further reduce the false positives.
3. Training the system using a support vector machine to further improve the accuracy. In Fig. 6 (Third Step), the first candidate is now dropped. This technique is elaborated in Section 2.3 (for hard cuts) and Section 2.6 (for gradual transitions).

2.1 Hard Cut Feature Extraction

The similarity between two consecutive frames is computed using a normalized mean centered correlation. The correlation between two frames f and g is computed as

$$\frac{\sum_{i,j}(f(i,j) - m_f)(g(i,j) - m_g)}{\sqrt{\sum_{i,j}(f(i,j) - m_f)^2}\sqrt{\sum_{i,j}(g(i,j) - m_g)^2}} \tag{1}$$

where m_f and m_g are the mean intensity values of frame f and g respectively. A high correlation signifies similar frames, probably belonging to the same shot; a low value is an indication of an ensuing shot break.

The correlation values between successive frames are plotted as in Fig. 7(a). The locations of shot breaks as identified by a human annotator are also indicated. From this diagram, it is also clear that placing an ad-hoc value as threshold to detect shot breaks will not work. A delicate shot break, like the one at frame 85 is missed if a hard threshold is placed.

2.2 Hard Cut Shot Prediction

To overcome this difficulty, we consider the continuity of correlation values rather than the correlation values themselves, as an indicator of a shot. We achieve this using wavelet analysis. We have experimented with different wavelet transforms to detect this continuity and have observed that the Morlet wavelet results in a good discrimination between actual shot breaks and false positives.

The Morlet wavelet is a complex sine wave modulated with a Gaussian (bell shaped) envelope as shown in Fig. 7(b) . Note there are equal number of positive and negative values in the mother wavelet and the area sums to zero. Whenever there is no or little change in the correlation sequence, the wavelet transform returns zero value. If there is a hard cut, there is a discontinuity in the correlation value, which results in a distinctive PPNN pattern (two positive values followed by two negative values) in the lowest scale. At high scales the coefficient values are quite large. Hence hard cuts can be obtained by observing this pattern.

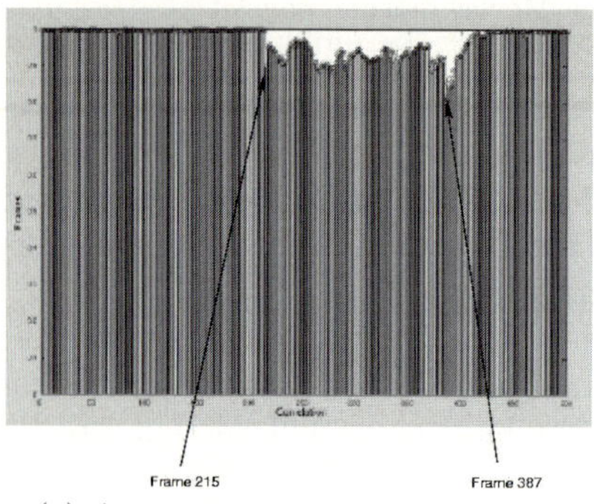

(a) A sample correlation sequence.

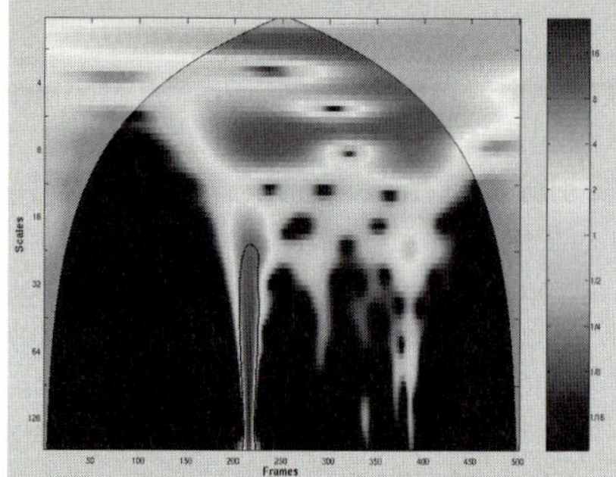

(b) A visualization of the relevant wavelet transform

Fig. 8. Using the Morlet wavelet

We graphically illustrate the power of the wavelet in Fig. 8. Fig. 8(a) shows a fluctuation in the correlation values from frames 215 up to 420. Out of these, frames 215 and 387 look like possible candidates for shot breaks. However, only frame 215 is an actual cut and frame 387 is a false positive (if reported as a cut).

In contrast, observe the corresponding Morlet wavelet transform in Fig. 8(b). The wavelet coefficients are high in all the scales around the frame 215, whereas the wavelet coefficients value around the frame 387 is not high at all the scales. Thus frame 215 is detected correctly as shot-break and frame 387 is dropped.

Filtering: After detecting possible locations of shot breaks, we improve the accuracy by analyzing the frames around predicted shot breaks in greater detail. The following measures are used.

1. Due to random lighting variations, the gray-scale value of successive frames in a shot might differ considerably resulting in a low correlation value. We pass potential shot break frames through a median filter. As a result, false positives are decreased without increasing false negatives.

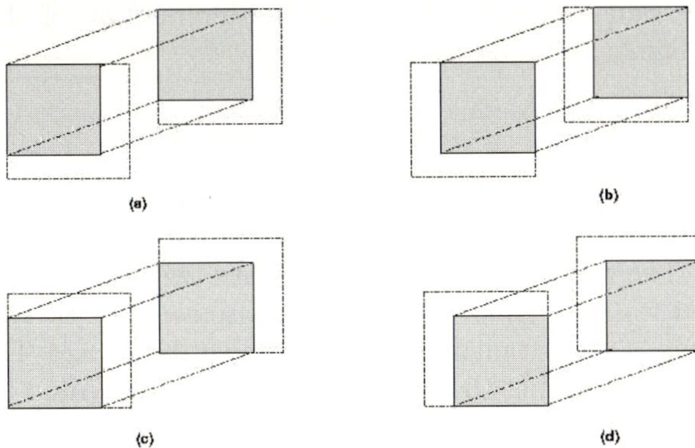

Fig. 9. Computing correlation of corresponding sub-windows

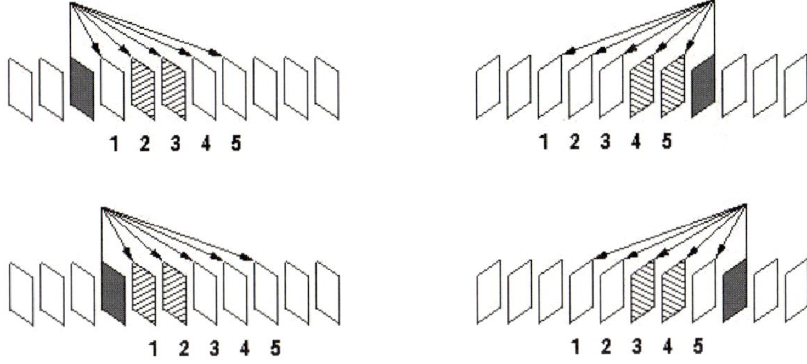

Fig. 10. Recomputing correlation in the frames around the shot-break. The dashed window indicates a shot break and the frame under focus is darkened. The correlation between the dark frame and other frames indicated by arrows is computed. The maximum of these values replaces the value computed earlier.

2. Synthetic manipulations such as animations or screen-split cause the correlation coefficient to become low resulting in false positives. We divide the frame into four overlapping sub-frames as shown in Fig. 9 and compute the correlation of corresponding sub-frames. One of these four correlation values reflect the desired relation. As a result, false positives are decreased.

3. MPEG errors and noise in the neighboring frame in low quality video can cause false positives in spite of recomputing the correlation value at shot-breaks. The correlation of the frames around the shot-break is recomputed in a window size as shown in Fig. 10. This measure helps in reducing false positives due to noise in the subsequent frames from the same shot.

4. Camera or object motion may cause low correlation value resulting in false positives. For the predicted frames only, *cross-correlation* is computed.

We select the best correlation values generated using the above measures and rerun the process of computing wavelet coefficients and detecting discontinuities with these new values. Finally, by taking the intersection of the two sets of predicted shot breaks, we produce a pruned set.

2.3 Training

We now describe how to train a SVM to further improve our accuracy. As the features play an important role in the training, we mainly focus on the features used in this process. The features extracted in previous two steps contribute correlation and wavelet features. Apart from this, we also compute traditional features like pixel differences, histogram differences, and edge differences. The training set consists of videos containing the challenging problem presented in Section 1.1, news videos, and movie clips. The features used in training the SVM are

1. Pixel differences which includes average pixel difference and Euclidean pixel difference
2. Histogram differences: Average histogram difference, histogram intersection, thresholded chi-square distance
3. Edge difference
4. Average intensity value
5. Correlation, Cross-correlation and maximum of the correlation values computed in the previous step
6. Presence of PPNN pattern in the lowest level of wavelet transform computed in the previous step
7. Lowest wavelet coefficient

Though our feature set contains some duplication, we use standard machine learning methods to select relevant features.

2.4 Gradual Transitions

Gradual transitions (or *graduals*) are shot transitions which occur over multiple frames resulting in smooth transition from one shot to another. As a result, gradual transitions are comparatively difficult to detect when compared to hard-cuts. The problem is increased with issues like uncertain camera motion common among amateurs resulting in false positives. Unfortunately, imposing more constraints to eliminate these false positives can eliminate the actual graduals as well. Most of the gradual detection algorithms [16,1,17,18,19] use a hard threshold to detect the shot transitions. Tuning these thresholds to improve the accuracy of the gradual detection system is a critical and important task. We use machine learning algorithms to solve this task.

A primary feature used in gradual detection is in the change in the brightness value of frames. The total brightness of a frame f is computed as

$$\sum_i \sum_j [f(i,j)]^2 \tag{2}$$

Within a shot, the total brightness remains predictable by and large. Upon encountering a gradual, we see a cone-like pattern. Fig. 11(a) shows a sample situation.

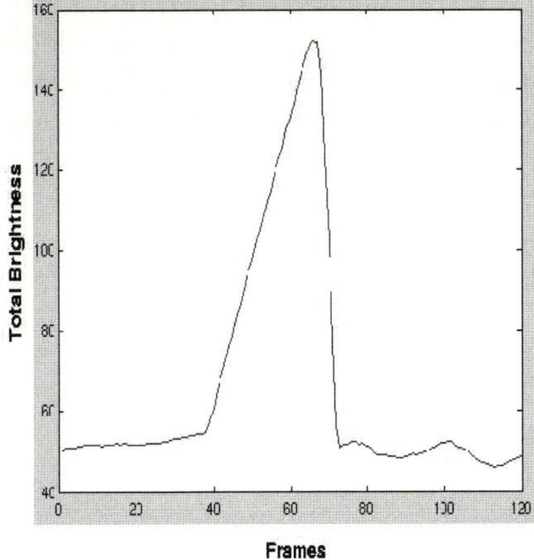

(a) A fade-out from frame 40 to 65 results in increasing brightness and a fade-in from frame 65 to 75 results in decreasing brightness value.

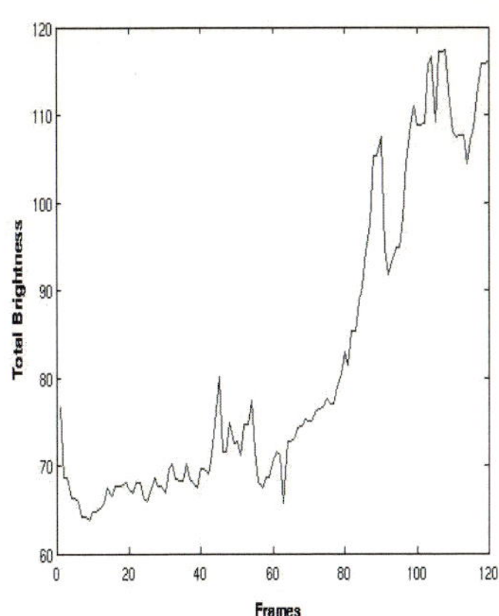

(b) Multiple "cones" can be found even when there is no shot break. In this example, a moving object has caused the changes.

Fig. 11. Sample brightness values around a gradual transition (a) can sometimes be predictable. At other times, the pattern can result in false positives.

2.5   Gradual Shot Prediction

The possible gradual transitions are predicted by detecting steady increase or decrease in the brightness values of the image sequence. Unfortunately, as exemplified in Fig. 11(b), false positives are produced. We improve the accuracy by analyzing the frames around predicted shot breaks in greater detail. The following measures are used.

1. Analysis by synthesis: The detected gradual transitions are checked for the dissolve linear property [17] thereby eliminating some of the false positives.
2. Edge Energy: Sequences containing illumination changes affects the total brightness value but do not affect the edge energy computed as

$$\sum_i \sum_j [\text{edge}(f(i,j))]^2 \tag{3}$$

As a result, a few false positives are eliminated.

2.6   Training

The following features are used for classifying gradual transitions. The videos in the training set are rife with characteristics mentioned in Section 1.1.

1. The normalized brightness difference between the start and end of the gradual transition.

2. The differences of brightness value between starting and middle point of the gradual transition and the difference between the brightness value of middle and end value is computed. The sum of these two differences is calculated.
3. The difference between the minimum value and the maximum value in the pixel difference sequence computed in the previous step.
4. Average edge energy value of the dissolve interval.

By this training process, we eliminate most of the hard-coded thresholds and make our system more flexible to use.

3   Experimental Results and Discussion

Our training data consists of a large number of videos. These involving the challenging problems stated in our problem statement and other videos which do not have too many unusual situations. Normal videos are included in the training set to avoid the over fitting problem in SVM.

We have tested our system on the data comprising of

- News videos each having around 500 hard cuts, containing different types of events. These are in multiple languages (notably Chinese and English).
- Short videos taken from motion pictures and from NASA. These involve some of the challenging problems mentioned in Section 1.1.
- Low-quality home video with varying lighting conditions and fast, shaky motion.
- Clips from motion picture containing illumination changes, fast camera motion, and object intrusion.

The ground truth for these experiments is from Trecvid 2005 [20].

Table 1 shows the experimental results on a news video which is a synthetically combined video of various challenging problems like fast camera motion, illumination change, flash light, explosion, and low video quality. We present results which shows the efficacy of our filtering approach. In the first attempt, we detect shot-breaks using only the first step (see Section 2). In the second attempt, we imposed the constraints to remove false positives as noted earlier, but do not use any learning methods. We note that the precision improves, but the recall drops. Many of the true positives were also eliminated. The third row shows our result on cross-validation with a split of 33% training data and 66% test data. The precision and recall go up.

Table 1. Result from a news video

Method	Precision	Recall	F-Measure
Without training, without filtering	0.686	1.0	0.814
Without training, with filtering	0.761	0.768	0.764
Cross-validation(33-training, 66-test)	0.892	0.992	0.939

Table 2. Result from an unseen video containing fast camera motion, object intrusion, and unpredictable illumination changes

Method	Precision	Recall	F-measure
Pixel Difference	0.926	0.571	0.707
Histogram Comparison	0.259	0.195	0.222
Correlation Value	0.785	0.734	0.759
Temporal Slice	0.750	0.604	0.669
Our Method	0.923	1.000	0.960

Table 2 shows the experimental results on unseen test data from motion video containing problems like fast camera motion, shaky handling of camera, object intrusion and illumination changes. The ground truth for these experiments was generated manually. As the results reflect, our system is successful in reducing the false positives considerably.

4   Conclusions

We have discussed in this paper the characteristics of videos that make shot detection a challenging problem. We have presented our framework that improves the accuracy of shot detection in such cases. In summary, we use mean-centered correlation as the similarity measure and use Morlet wavelet to predict shot-breaks by capturing the discontinuity in the correlation sequence. We further improve our accuracy by using a support vector machine.

Our shot detection system achieves the following:

1. Reduces false positives in the event of challenging problems like unpredictable illumination changes, camera effect & special effects.
2. Processes more than 30 frames per second with the accuracy required for the normal usage.
3. Presents a unique solution to solve all the problems, instead of combining different problem specific solutions.
4. Introduces a new wavelet based feature based on extensive experiments.

References

1. Zhang, H., Kankanhalli, A., Smoliar, S.: Automatic partitioning of full-motion video. ACM Multimedia Systems **1** (1993) 10–28
2. Bang, C., Chenl, S.C., Shyu, M.L.: Pixso: a system for video shot detection. Fourth International Conference on Information, Communications and Signal Processing (2003) 1320–1324
3. Shahraray, S.: Scene change detection and content-based sampling of video sequence. In: SPIE Storage and Retrieval for Image and Video Databases. (1995) 2–13
4. Swanberg, D., Shu, C., Jain, R.: Knowledge guided parsing in video database. In: SPIE Storage and Retrieval for Image and Video Databases. (1993) 13–24

5. Funt, B., Finlayson, G.: Color constant color indexing. Pattern Analysis and Machine Intelligence, IEEE **17** (1995) 522–529
6. Rasheed, Z., Shah, M.: Scene detection in Hollywood movies and TV shows. In: IEEE Conference on Computer Vision and Pattern Recognition. (2003) II: 343–348
7. Patel, N., Sethi, I.: Video shot detection and characterization for video databases. Pattern Recognition **30** (1997) 583–592
8. Li, D., Lu, H.: Avoiding false alarms due to illumination variation in shot detection. IEEE Workshop on Signal Processing Systems (2000) 828–836
9. Lu, H., Tan, Y.: An effective post-refinement method for shot boundary detection. CirSysVideo **15** (2005) 1407–1421
10. Zabih, R., Miller, J., Mai, K.: Feature-based algorithms for detecting and classifying scene breaks. Technical report, Cornell University (1995)
11. Yuliang, G., De, X.: A solution to illumination variation problem in shot detection. TENCON 2004. IEEE Region 10 Conference (2004) 81–84
12. Ngo, C., Pong, T., Chin, R.: Detection of gradual transitions through temporal slice analysis. In: IEEE Conference on Computer Vision and Pattern Recognition. (1999) I: 36–41
13. Yeo, C., Zhu, Y.W., Sun, Q., Chang, S.F.: A framework for sub-window shot detection. In: MMM '05: Eleventh International Multimedia Modelling Conference (MMM'05). (2005) 84–91
14. et. al., A.A.: IBM Research TRECVID-2005 Video Retrieval System. In: TREC Proc. (2005)
15. Vlachos, T.: Cut detection in video sequences using phase correlation. Signal Processing Letters **7** (2000) 173–175
16. Yoo, H.W., Ryoo, H.J., Jang, D.S.: Gradual shot boundary detection using localized edge blocks. Multimedia Tools and Applications **28** (2006) 283–300
17. Petersohn, C.: Fraunhofer HHI at TRECVID 2004: Shot boundary detection system. In: TREC Proc. (2004)
18. Covell, M., Ahmad, S.: Analysis by synthesis dissolve detection. In: International Conference on Image Processing. (2002) 425–428
19. Lienhart, R., Zaccarin, A.: A system for reliable dissolve detection in videos. In: International Conference on Image Processing. (2001) III: 406–409
20. NIST: TREC Video Retrieval Evaluation. `www-nlpir.nist.gov/projects/trecvid` (2005)

Text Driven Temporal Segmentation of Cricket Videos

Pramod Sankar K., Saurabh Pandey, and C.V. Jawahar

Centre for Visual Information Technology,
International Institute of Information Technology, Hyderabad, India
jawahar@iiit.ac.in

Abstract. In this paper we address the problem of temporal segmentation of videos. We present a multi-modal approach where clues from different information sources are merged to perform the segmentation. Specifically, we segment videos based on textual descriptions or commentaries of the action in the video. Such a parallel information is available for cricket videos, a class of videos where visual feature based (*bottom-up*) scene segmentation algorithms generally fail, due to lack of visual dissimilarity across space and time. With additional *top-down* information from textual domain, these ambiguities could be resolved to a large extent. The video is segmented to meaningful entities or scenes, using the scene level descriptions provided by the commentary. These segments can then be automatically annotated with the respective descriptions. This allows for a semantic access and retrieval of video segments, which is difficult to obtain from existing visual feature based approaches. We also present techniques for automatic highlight generation using our scheme.

1   Introduction

The significance and challenge of temporal segmentation of videos into meaningful entities, is parallelled only by its spatial counterpart. Much of the previous work in video segmentation has focused on shot-cut detection. Contiguous frames in the video, which have little change in visual content are generally grouped into a *video shot*. A shot change or a *cut* is detected, whenever the camera shifts, or the scene being captured changes significantly. However, our work focuses on obtaining a *scene segmentation*, which is a meaningful entity of a video [1]. This work is motivated by the following facts:

- Shot-Cut detection, using visual features, has been well addressed in literature [2,3,4]. However, the video shot obtained from cut detection is not generally a meaningful entity. Shots are a low-level or syntactic representation of the video content, while for the purpose of recognition, annotation and retrieval, a higher level semantic representation such as a "scene", is required.
- Semantic access to content, has met with much success in the text retrieval domain. Much work exists on mining and retrieving semantic concepts from document collections.
- A parallel text is available for many videos such as closed captions for news videos, subtitles for movies, lyrics for music videos, commentary for sports videos, etc. This text is a reliable source of information regarding the content of the video.

P. Kalra and S. Peleg (Eds.): ICVGIP 2006, LNCS 4338, pp. 433–444, 2006.

- With a synchronisation between the text and the video, the video segments would correspond to a textual description of the video. This allows for automatic annotation of video segments with the associated text. The videos could then be accessed at the semantic level and retrieved using human-understandable textual queries.

Segmenting a video into meaningful entities is very challenging since there is a lack of correspondence between the meaning of the scene and the visual features. Previous work that segments a video into scenes [1,5] using visual features [6,7] or scene dynamism [8], fail in many cases where there is no significant visual change across space and time. This is especially true for the class of sports videos. However, this class of videos have the advantage of being associated with a textual description in the form of a commentary that is generally available in parallel. This text provides ample information regarding the scene content and where and how it changes.

The Problem: In this paper we address the problem of segmenting a video into meaningful scenes, using the text that describes the video. Specifically, we use the commentaries available for sports videos, to segment a cricket video into its constituent scenes, called *balls*. Once segmented, the video could be automatically annotated by the text for higher-level content access.

The Challenges: The scene changes in a sports video are highly ambiguous, since there is no fixed point where one event ends and another begins. The videos are characterised by diverse visuals within the scene and very similar visuals across scenes (at the scene boundaries). This makes it difficult to find scene changes, using purely visual domain techniques. To complicate things further, during broadcast, a large number of *replays* are shown, which are not synchronous with the flow of the match. Moreover, the broadcast contains a large number of scenes, videos, graphics etc. that closely resemble the actual match. They also contain a large number of advertisements that overlap in visual content with the match scenes.

Apriori Knowledge Used: The ambiguities in the visual domain could be resolved by using parallel information for the video. The parallel information could be obtained form two sources: i) audio and ii) text. The audio in a sports video would consist of the commentators' running commentary and the audiences' reaction. The audio is available only in a feature space, which needs to be converted to a more meaningful domain (such as text) by using various speech recognition modules (which are inherently complex and not totally accurate). Moreover the information from the audio domain is as ambiguous as the visual domain (for very similar reasons). On the other hand, textual commentaries, as available from websites such as Cricinfo.com(TM), are meaningful, reliable, accurate, and complete, with regards to conveying the proceedings of the event. Textual descriptions are accurate and meaningful, and immediately correspond to a semantic representation. The semantics provide clues regarding the visual content, when described using visual scene categories. By identifying the scene category from text, the visual content could be estimated.

The Semantic Gap: The top-down information from text and the bottom-up information from visual features has to be synchronized and merged. The top-down information defines the approximate *content* of a video segment and the bottom-up techniques should be used to segment the video such that it *appears* similar to the model defined for the segment. However, the commentaries are a high level conceptual description of the scene, which cannot be directly represented using visual domain features, the so-called *Semantic Gap*. A mechanism is required to bridge the semantic gap by finding correspondences between scene changes and the scene descriptions. This is achieved by building approximate scene models for each of the scene categories.

In other words, the top-down (textual) and bottom-up (visual) information needs to be effectively merged to solve the problem on hand (segmentation). The visual clues are used to estimate a scene segmentation, which is refined by constraining the segmentation to look similar to the model defined. The optimization of this estimation is performed using the Maximum Likelihood (ML) framework. Though explained in the context of cricket videos, our techniques can be directly extended to any class of videos where the events occur from a given set of categories.

Automatic Annotation: Following the segmentation, the textual description is directly synchronized with the video segments. Thus, the segments could be automatically annotated. Automatic annotation of multimedia is of immense interest in the information retrieval community. Existing content based retrieval systems are computationally expensive and few approaches can robustly retrieve from large video collections. Text annotations of video allow us to build a text based retrieval system for videos, which is very quick and efficient.

2   Visual Domain Processing of Videos

It is common to use the domain knowledge of the class of videos for processing them, such as [9] for baseball, [10] for American football, [11] for tennis, and [12,13] for cricket etc. We use the domain knowledge of the videos to build scene categories and approximate scene models. The scene in cricket, is called the "ball" (similar to a "pitch" in baseball). The ball is defined to begin with the bowler running to deliver the ball, and end at the start of either i) the next ball, ii) a replay or iii) an advertisement. A ball consists of the bowler running to deliver the ball, the ball being delivered, played, fielded and returned. There are a minimum of six balls per *over*, and 50 overs for each side to play. Between consecutive overs there is a lengthy break which is typically filled with advertisements in the broadcast. A large number of replays are generally shown between the balls. A conceptual description of the broadcast cricket video is given in Figure 1.

In this section we describe the visual domain processing of the videos. We first detect shot changes in the video and categorise the shots into one of several classes. These shot classes and shot class transitions are used to model the scene categories as described in Section 3.

Shot Detection. Much work exists in shot-cut detection [2,3]. Popular techniques that use image features [7], optical flow [14] etc., are not applicable due to the heavy noise that is common in broadcast videos. In such cases, a histogram based descriptor is well suited [4]. To ensure invariance to minor changes in RGB values and to noise, the RGB axes are binned, and each pixel is assigned to the cube that the bins describe. To enforce

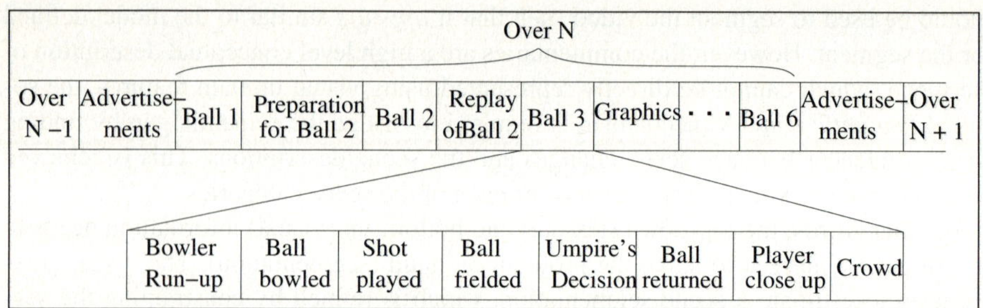

Fig. 1. Depiction of a generic cricket video. Each *over* has 6 (or more) *balls*, each scene consisting of the ball being delivered, played, fielded and returned. In a broadcast, replays and graphics are shown between the scenes and advertisements between the overs.

spatial consistence, we divide the frame to N blocks and build the binned histograms for each block. For cut detection, the histograms of consecutive frames are compared and a cut is detected if the difference is above a particular threshold. The threshold for the given video is found using the technique described in [15].

Soft Classification of Shots. The detected shots are classified into one of the shot categories. For cricket videos, these are the set $C = \{pitch\ view,\ run\text{-}up\ view,\ player\ close\text{-}up,\ crowd,\ advertisement,\ replay\}$. The different shot classes are shown in Figure 2. Though these classes exhibit wide disparity over different matches, the features from the video for a given cricket match (or in many cases a given tournament of matches) are very similar. The representative histogram feature vector $C_i = f_{C_i1}, f_{C_i2}, ..., f_{C_in}$ for each shot class is learnt from training data. Each shot $S = f_{S1}, f_{S2}, ..., f_{Sn}$ is compared with the class-representative feature vector C_i, using the L1-Norm to obtain $d(S, C_i) = \sum_{k=1}^{n}(f_{C_ik} - f_{Sk})$. The shots are classified using the maximum likelihood estimate as

$$Class(f_{S1}, f_{S2}, ..., f_{Sn}) = arg \max_i \frac{d(S, C_i)}{\sum_k(d(S, C_k))}$$

The accuracy of shot classification is presented in Figure 3 (a).

Another class of shots that we need to handle are the advertisements and replays. Previous advertisement detection methods [16] rely on the intensity in activity from the large variations in the video frames. However, this is also valid for action sequences in a sports video. Replay detection techniques [17] have used a replay transition detection, or slow motion as a clue, which are not applicable for our case. Instead, it was observed that for advertisements and replays, the video production removes the scoreboard at the bottom, that is generally present for the match play, as can be seen in Figure 2. The scoreboard could be detected to distinguish between match play and advertisement/replay. Our method provides a detection accuracy of 82.44% for the class advertisemnts/replays.

Segmenting using Visual Features. Scene segmentation in visual domain could be performed by using the pitch views as *canonical* scenes [18] that bound the action. However, due to the large number of replays, and the inaccuracy of shot classification, the

Fig. 2. Example frames from the shot classes, from left to right: Ground view, West Indies player, Crowd, Pitch view, Indian player and Advertisement. Note that the scoreboard present in the bottom of the screen for the shot classes, is absent for the advertisement.

identified pitch views are more than the number of balls, consequently, yielding poor segmentation. It was observed that over a duration of 8 hours of a match with 629 balls, 945 segments were obtained, where the extra segments come from repeated pitch view shots. Moreover, a large number of balls (52) were missed due to inaccurate shot classification. By enforcing a minimum time duration for each segment, a large number of false positives were eliminated, but many outliers still remained. Also the segmentation tends to favour segments of the same size, while the duration of the scenes would actually depend on the scene category.

3   Modelling the Scene Categories

In cases where the visual domain techniques are insufficient for scene segmentation, a parallel textual description could be used to provide additional information. Such parallel text is available for sports videos in the form of online commentaries. For. eg., the commentary of a cricket game is given below:

13.1 Smith to Sehwag, FOUR, short of a good length and outside the off, driven on the up superbly through cover, the timing and placement are excellent, Bravo dives desperately but can't quite pull it back

13.2 Smith to Sehwag, 1 run, played away for a single

13.3 Smith to Yuvraj Singh, FOUR, short of a length and outside the off, Yuvraj stands tall and times that magnificently through cover point. That is a good shot from Yuvraj!

It can be seen that the commentaries contain heavy usage of the domain specific vocabulary, which is a highly conceptual representation. Mapping such semantic concepts

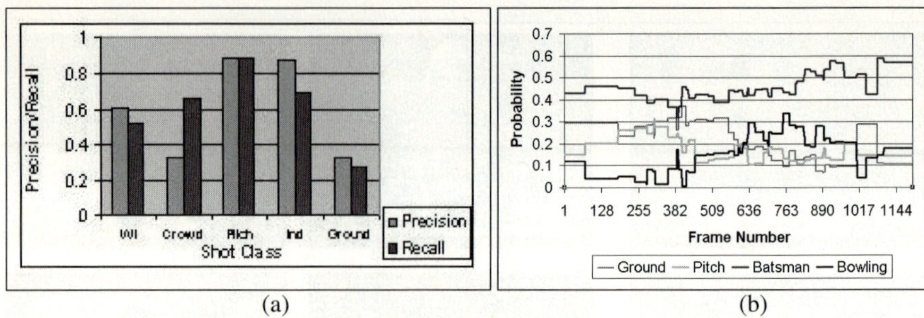

Fig. 3. (a) Precision-Recall of the shot classification (b) Scene model for the outcome FOUR

to lower level features from images/video is a major challenge corresponding to bridging the *semantic gap*. We model the scenes by finding an approximate map between the shot and scene classes. We assume that each scene class could be characterized by the shot classes it consists of, along with their durations and transitions. The scene building is described in Algorithm 1. The input to build the scene model are the training example scenes $< V_1, V_2, ..., V_n >$ of the scene S_s. Let L_{V_i} be the length of the video V_i. The text commentary is used to generate a hypothetical video's representation that is used as the model for the entire match.

The average duration of a given scene is computed from the examples and used to build a descriptor for the scene. The scene descriptor is the set of probabilities for a given frame to belong to each of the shot classes. These probabilities model the scene to a large extent. For example, in case of the outcome *four*, the pitch view would generally be followed by the ground view for some time, and the camera would then shift to the players. Such probabilities are computed for each frame and normalized to the average length of the scene. The scene model for the outcome FOUR is shown in Figure 3(b).

Algorithm 1. Train_Model(S_s, $< V_1, V_2, ..., V_n >$)

1: Find average length L_{Si} of the videos $< V_1, V_2, ..., V_n >$
2: Set S_s = NULL
3: **for** $V_i = V_1$ to V_n **do**
4:     Identify shots, $C_{i_1}, C_{i_2}, ..., C_{i_m}$ in V_i
5:     **for** each shot j = 1 to m and each shot-class k = 1 to l **do**
6:         Find probability $P_k(C_{i_j})$, of shot C_{i_j} belonging to the k th shot-class
7:     **end for**
        /*Build scene representation S_{s_i} as */
8:     **for** j = 1 to L_{V_i}, and each shot-class k = 1 to l **do**
9:         Append $P_k(C_{i_j})$ to $S_{s_{i_k}}$
10:    **end for**
11:    Scale $S_{s_{i_k}}$ to average length L_{Si}
12:    For each k = 1 to l, Append $S_{s_{i_k}}$ to S_{s_i}
13: **end for**
14: Average S_{s_i} over $i = 1$ to n to obtain S_s
15: **return** S_s

The above representation builds a model for the intra scene shot changes. To describe the video completely, an inter-scene model is required. The inter scene model describes the probabilities of a particular scene following a given scene. This is modelled for the purpose of handling advertisements and replays. The model learns the probability of an advertisement or replay to follow a given scene. Generally a replay follows a scene belonging to *four* or *six* etc., and advertisements follow an *out* scene. The intra-scene and inter-scene models are used to provide a model for the video to be matched against.

4   Text Driven Segmentation of the Video

4.1   Maximum Likelihood Formulation of Scene Segmentation

The segmentation procedure should identify the begin and end frames of the scenes, over the entire video. The real scene boundary Z_i is assumed to be fixed but unknown. The estimate z_i of the scene boundary, is assumed to be found near the real boundary Z_i with a probability distribution that follows a Gaussian. The Gaussian is centered around Z_i, with a variance σ. The estimate z_i is obtained from visual-temporal information. Let such an observation of the beginning and end of a scene S_i be z_{i_1} and z_{i_2} respectively. The likelihood that shot S_i bounded by z_{i_1} and z_{i_2} actually corresponds to a real scene X is given by $P(S_i|X) = P(z_{i_1}, z_{i_2}|X)$. This likelihood corresponds to a local cost of corresponding S_i to X. The global cost of matching scene estimate set γ with real scene boundaries is given by

$$L(\gamma) = p(Z_1, Z_2|\gamma) = \prod_{0<i<n} P(z_{i_1}, z_{i_2}|X)$$

where n is the number of shots in the video. The maximization of the global likelihood function corresponds to minimizing its negative logarithm. In cases where the scenes are not represented by a known model, the optimization of this function could be done using an Expectation Maximization approach, where both the segmentation and scene parameters are learnt simultaneously. However, using the textual information, the appropriate scene models could be plugged into the likelihood computation. The minimization in such a situation would correspond to a simple weighted matching or assignment problem, which could be solved in polynomial time using dynamic programming. The derivation of local cost between a scene estimate and a scene model is derived following the building of scene models in Section 4.2.

The Generative Video Model. In an ML framework, the observed data, D, or the given video, needs to be compared with an assumed model for the data M. In a general model fitting problem, there are two unknowns: i) the model parameters and ii) the mapping of the data to the model. These unknowns are estimated using an Expectation Maximization procedure. This would be a bottom-up approach. The results of a purely bottom up approach would be poor, due to the ambiguities present in the observed data and the absence of an appropriate scene model. Top-down information in the form of textual descriptions, could be used to identify the scene models and parameters. With such

---

Algorithm 2. Generate_Video_Representation($Match\_Commentary$)

1: Set G = NULL
2: Parse $Match\_Commentary$ and identify the ball B_i and their corresponding Outcomes O_i
3: **for** each ball i = 1 to n **do**
4:     Identify scene model S_s for O_i
5:     Append S_s to G
6: **end for**
7: Return G

---

information, the only unknown that remains, is the mapping of the observed data to the assumed model. The model M is built from the $Match\_Commentary$ using Algorithm 2.

4.2   Segmenting Using the Video Model

The model M, would be a hypothetical video, generated from the scene descriptions. For each ball in the match, the scene category is identified and the corresponding scene model is appended to the generated video. Advertisements and replay shots are added based on the probability of their occurrence following a given scene. The generated model provides an approximation of the shot and scene changes in the video for the given scene description. The mapping of D to M, can be computed using a Dynamic Programming (DP) technique [19]. Assuming that the distance array in the DP procedure is given as D, we use the DP cost computation:

$$D(i, j) = \min \begin{cases} D(i - 1, j) + c(i, 0) \\ D(i - 1, j - 1) + d(i, j) \\ D(i, j - 1) + c(0, j) \end{cases}$$

where the local distance between two frames, i and j is given by

$$d(i, j) = \sum_{s \in shotclasses} P(i_s).P(j_s)$$

$P(i_s)$ being the probability that the ith frame belongs to the s shot class; and $c(i, 0)$ is the cost of occlusion. The cost of occlusion is lesser if one of the frames belongs to an advertisement scene, and more otherwise. The optimal path of the match is found by backtracking the DP matrix. With this match, the observed scenes from D are warped onto the generated model M. The segments of a scene is the segment that maps to the scene in the generated model. The procedure is depicted in Figure 4. The procedure is given in Algorithm 3. In Algorithm 3, the Dynamic_Programming and Back_Track are standard dynamic programming and backtracking algorithms.

The scenes obtained from the text driven segmentation, were evaluated manually over a 20 minute video. The segments were found to be satisfactory. Out of 124 balls, the segmentation was able to identify about 98 balls correctly. The errors in identification are due to the overlap with replays and advertisements. The presence of large number of replays and advertisements, especially back to back, causes the estimation to perform poorly. It was also found that the segments generally follow the length of the

---

Algorithm 3. Segment_Video(V, G)

1: Set S = NULL
2: Identify shots, $C_1, C_2, ..., C_m$ in V
3: **for** each shot j = 1 to m and each shot-class k = 1 to l **do**
4:    Find probability $P_k(C_j)$, of shot C_j belonging to the k th shot-class
5: **end for**
   /*Build video representation S as */
6: **for** j = 1 to L_{V_i}, and each shot-class k = 1 to l **do**
7:    Append $P_k(C_j)$ to S_k
8: **end for**
9: Compute D = Dynamic_Programming(S, G)
10: Find optimal path using P = Back_Track(D)
   /*Segment Video*/
11: **for** each scene s = 1 to n **do**
12:    Find the scene segment G_s corresponding to s in generated video G
13:    Find correspondence of G_s in P
14:    Output V_s corresponding to G_s in P
15:    Annotate V_s with the scene description of s
16: **end for**

---

scene model, in the absence of other discrimination. The scene model, thus, constraints the accuracy of segments obtained.

5 Automatic Annotation of Scenes

Following the text driven segmentation of video, the balls are synchronized with their commentary. This enables automatic annotations of the video scenes with their respective description. Such an annotation could be used for retrieval and summarization. It should be noted that automatic annotation of videos using visual features alone is a very difficult task using existing techniques. It is in cases like these that cross-modal techniques are highly relevant.

5.1 Retrieval

From the process of annotation, each ball has an associated textual description, which allows us to build a text based search engine over the videos. The video segments are indexed by the keywords associated with them. The keywords are obtained from the uni-gram frequencies of the words in the entire commentary. The most commonly occurring words are removed as stop-words. For each keyword, the associated video segments are found and indexed to it. Given a query, the index is searched for the query word, and the matched index is retrieved for the user. The user can then click on the search results and view the video segment. A screenshot of the retrieval tool is shown in Figure 5.

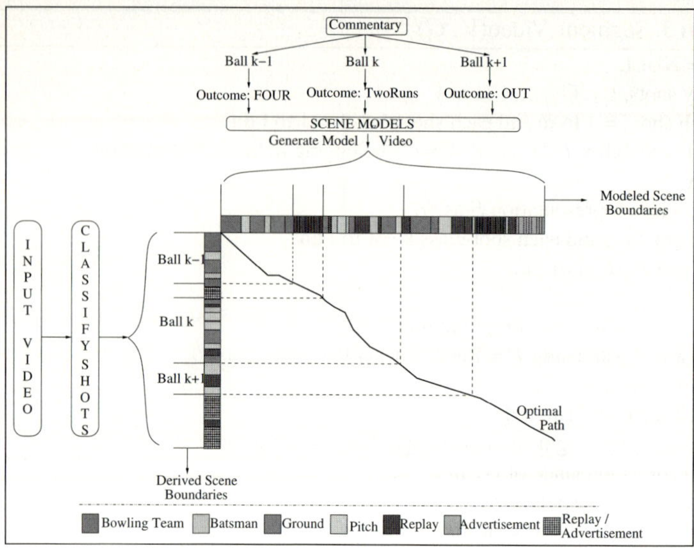

Fig. 4. The merging of visual, bottom-up and conceptual, top-down information for video segmentation using our framework

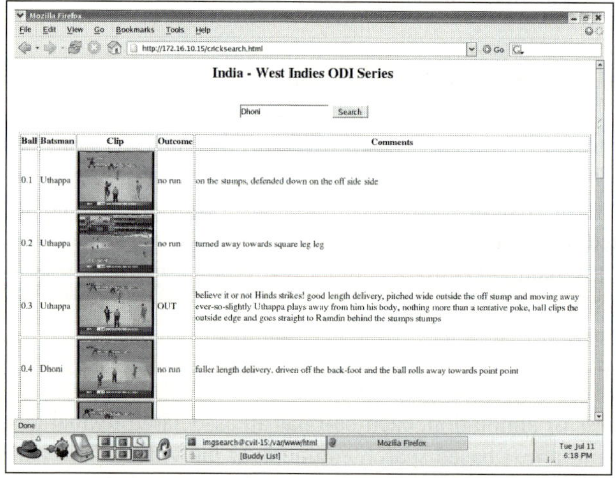

Ball	Batsman	Clip	Outcome	Comments
0.1	Uthappa		no run	on the stumps, defended down on the off side side
0.2	Uthappa		no run	turned away towards square leg leg
0.3	Uthappa		OUT	believe it or not Hinds strikes! good length delivery, pitched wide outside the off stump and moving away ever-so-slightly Uthappa plays away from him his body, nothing more than a tentative poke, ball clips the outside edge and goes straight to Ramdin behind the stumps stumps
0.4	Dhoni		no run	fuller length delivery, driven off the back-foot and the ball rolls away towards point point

Fig. 5. Snapshot of the "Cricket Browser", the tool that allows to browse through the matches and allows for searching the annotation, thereby providing semantic access to cricket videos

The retrieval of videos using our scheme is interactive, with a retrieval time of about 0.01 seconds. This is because the search is performed in the text domain, and no image or video feature comparisons are necessary (as in general CBIR). The user can search for popular outcomes such as *four, six, out* etc., or for scenes involving his favourite player. The user could also search in the descriptions, which means he could search for semantic concepts like an *out swinger*. Learning and identifying such subtle concepts using purely visual domain practises, is highly involved, which is circumvented by our approach. However, the accuracy of the search system is affected by the errors from the scene segmentation phase. With accurate scene segmentation, the search could provide accurate retrieval of video scenes.

5.2   Summarization

Highlights of the match are generated by finding *interesting* events from the commentary. An exciting ball is generally described in detail, with many adjectives in the sentences. These are identified using text processing schemes and the exciting balls are extracted for the highlights. We compared our highlights with those shown on TV for two matches. The evaluation measure was the number of highlights missed during the entire match. The results of the evaluations are shown in Table 1. The large disparity between the durations between the TV highlights and those generated by us is due to the fact that we have not incorporated replays into the highlights. The missed highlights are those which were not classified as *exciting* due to lack of detailed description in the commentary of some of the balls.

Table 1. Comparison of generated highlights with those created manually

Match	Input Duration	Highlights' Duration	TV Highlights' Duration	Missed Highlights
Ind Vs. WI 1	4.00	32 min	48 min	13
Ind Vs. WI 2	3.26 hr	37 min	45 min	16

6   Conclusions and Future Directions

The major contributions of our work are:

- A novel framework that performs temporal segmentation of videos into scenes by effectively merging the scene description information with visual features
- A formulation to partially bridge the semantic gap between the descriptions and the video shots they correspond to
- Automatic annotation of multimedia with text
- Search and retrieval, summarization and highlight generation of videos

One application of the results of our work is in learning semantic concepts such as a *poor shot* or a *good ball*. We have, in this work, modelled distinctive concepts for the scene models, but more robust representations are required to model concepts over shorter sequences. User preferences for highlights could be learnt using relevance feedback and customized match summaries could be generated. With an annotated corpus many video processing algorithms could be built and tested on this platform. Activity recognition systems could be reliably trained and evaluated using our corpus.

References

1. Rui, Y., Huang, T.S., Mehrotra, S.: Constructing table-of-content for videos. Multimedia Syst. **7** (1999) 359–368
2. Jiang, H., Helal, A., Elmagarmid, A.K., Joshi, A.: Scene change detection techniques for video database systems. Multimedia Syst. **6** (1998) 186–195
3. Koprinska, I., Carrato, S.: Temporal video segmentation: A survey. Signal Processing: Image Communication (2001) 477–500
4. Lefevre, S., Holler, J., Vincent, N.: A review of real-time segmentation of uncompressed video sequences for content-based search and retrieval. Real-Time Imaging **9** (2003) 73–98
5. Hanjalic, A., Lagendijk, R.L., Biemond, J.: Automated high-level movie segmentation for advanced video retrieval systems. IEEE Trans. Circuits Syst. Video Technol. **9** (1999) 580
6. Demarty, C., Beucher, S.: Morphological tools for indexing video documents. In: Proc. IEEE Intl. Conf. Multimedia Computing and Systems. (1999) 991
7. Zabih, R., Miller, J., Mai, K.: A feature-based algorithm for detecting and classifying production effects. Multimedia Syst. **7** (1999) 119–128
8. Rasheed, Z., Shah, M.: Scene detection in hollywood movies and tv shows. In: Proc. Computer Vision and Pattern Recognition. Volume 2. (June 2003) II – 343–8
9. Rui, Y., Gupta, A., Acero, A.: Automatically extracting highlights for tv baseball programs. In: ACM Multimedia, New York, NY, USA, ACM Press (2000) 105–115
10. Babaguchi, N., Kawai, Y., Kitahashi, T.: Event based indexing of broadcast sports video by intermodal collaboration. IEEE Trans. Multimedia **4** (2002) 68–75
11. Sudhir, G., Lee, J.C.M., Jain, A.K.: Automatic classification of tennis video for high-level content-based retrieval. In: Proc. International Workshop on Content-Based Access of Image and Video Databases. (1998) 81–90
12. Kolekar, M.H., Sengupta, S.: A hierarchical framework for generic sports video classification. In: ACCV (2). (2006) 633–642
13. Jadon, R.S., Chaudhury, S., Biswas, K.K.: Sports video characterization using scene dynamics. In: ICVGIP. (2004) 545–549
14. Fatemi, O., Zhang, S., Panchanathan, S.: Optical flow based model for scene cut detection. In: Canadian Conf. on Electrical and Computer Engineering. Volume 1. (1996) 470–473
15. Gunsel, B., Ferman, A., Tekalp, A.: Temporal video segmentation using unsupervised clustering and semantic object tracking. Journal of Electronic Imaging **7** (1998) 592–604
16. Lienhart, R., Kuhmunch, C., Effelsberg, W.: On the detection and recognition of television commercials. In: International Conference on Multimedia Computing and Systems. (1997) 509–516
17. Wang, L., Liu, X., Lin, S., Xu, G., Shum, H.Y.: Generic slow-motion replay detection in sports video. In: ICIP. (2004) 1585–1588
18. Li, B., Errico, J.H., Pan, H., Sezan, I.: Bridging the semantic gap in sports video retrieval and summarization. J. Vis. Commun. Image R. **15** (2004) 393–424
19. Cox, I.J., Hingorani, S.L., Rao, S.B., Maggs, B.M.: A maximum likelihood stereo algorithm. Comput. Vis. Image Underst. **63** (1996) 542–567

Learning Efficient Linear Predictors for Motion Estimation

Jiří Matas[1,2], Karel Zimmermann[1], Tomáš Svoboda[1], and Adrian Hilton[2]

[1] Center for Machine Perception Czech Technical University Prague, Czech Republic
[2] Centre for Vision, Speech and Signal Proc.
University of Surrey Guildford, England

Abstract. A novel object representation for tracking is proposed. The tracked object is represented as a constellation of spatially localised linear predictors which are learned on a single training image. In the learning stage, sets of pixels whose intensities allow for optimal least square predictions of the transformations are selected as a support of the linear predictor.

The approach comprises three contributions: learning object specific linear predictors, explicitly dealing with the predictor precision – computational complexity trade-off and selecting a view-specific set of predictors suitable for global object motion estimate. Robustness to occlusion is achieved by RANSAC procedure.

The learned tracker is very efficient, achieving frame rate generally higher than 30 frames per second despite the Matlab implementation.

1 Introduction

We formulate real-time object or camera tracking as establishing correspondence in a short-baseline pair of images followed by robust motion estimation. In real-time tracking, computation time together with the relative object camera veloc ity determine the maximum displacement for which features must be matched. Local features (corners, edges, lines) or appearance templates have both been widely used to estimate narrow baseline correspondences [1,2,3].

Recently more discriminative features have been introduced to increase robustness to changes in viewpoint, illumination and partial occlusion allowing wide-baseline matching but their are too computationally expensive for tracking applications since their include combinatorial search [4,5,6,7].

We propose a novel object representation for tracking. The tracked object is represented as a constellation of spatially localised linear predictors. The predictors are learned using a set of transformed versions of a single training image. In a learning stage, sets of pixels whose intensities allow for optimal prediction of the transformations are selected as a support of the linear predictor.

The approach comprises three contributions: learning object specific linear predictors which allow optimal local motion estimation; explicitly defining the trade-off between linear predictor complexity (i.e. size of linear predictor support) and computational cost; and selecting an view-specific set of predictors suitable for global object motion estimate. We introduce a novel approach to

P. Kalra and S. Peleg (Eds.): ICVGIP 2006, LNCS 4338, pp. 445–456, 2006.

learn a linear predictor from a circular region around the reference point which gives the best local estimation, in the least square sense, of the object motion for a predefined range of object velocities. Spatial localisation robust to occlusions is obtained from predicted reference points motions by RANSAC. The approach makes explicit the trade-off between tracker complexity and frame-rate.

Tracking by detection [8,9] establishes the correspondences between distinguished regions [6,4] detected in successive images. This approach relies on the presence of strong, unique features allowing robust estimation of large motions by matching across wide-baseline views. Detection approaches also allow automatic initialisation and re-initialisation during tracking. Methods dependent on distinguished regions are not able to track fast, saccadic motions with acceptable accuracy due to their low frame-rate.

Displacement estimation methods achieve higher frame rates but are not able to reliably estimate large inter-frame motions. The methods usually utilise gradient-base optimization algorithms minimising a criteria function. The method of Lucas and Kanade [2,1] minimise color dissimilarity. They assume that total intensity difference (dissimilarity) is a convex function in some neighbourhood. Thus, the motion is estimated by a few iterations of the Newton-Raphson method, where the difference image is multiplied by the pseudo-inverse of the image gradient covariance matrix. Black and Jepson [10] robustifies this idea by tracking in eigen-space. Jepson et al. [11] extend tracking by online adaptation to non-rigid changes using EM-algorithm.

The method of Lucas and Kanade [2,1] was also extended by Cootes [12] and applied to tracking by Jurie [13,14] who learn a linear approximation of the relationship between the local dissimilarity image and displacement. Assuming that there exists a neighbourhood where displacement can be found directly from gradients of image intensities, online tracking is performed by multiplying the difference image by a matrix representing the linear function. This is computationally efficient because no gradient or pseudo-inversion are required. Recently this approach [15] has been extended to more general regression functions, where displacements are estimated by RVM. Such methods can learn a larger range of pose changes but tracking is more complex resulting in a lower frame-rate. Since we believe that the computational cost grows faster than the region of convergence, the main attention is focused on Jurie's [13] linear predictor. Although, all proposed methods are simply extendible to an arbitrary motion predictor.

The computation cost of tracking is a trade-off between the time required for displacement estimation and the distance moved between successive frames. Therefore, we propose a tracking method which explicitly models the trade-off between tracker complexity and frame-rate. Given the expected maximum velocity of the object we learn the optimal support of linear predictors for frame-rate tracking.

It is desirable to have efficient tracking and motion estimation to limit the object movement between successive estimates. In this paper, we extend the computationally efficient tracking using linear models of motion proposed by Jurie et al. [13], whose linear predictors use a support around pixels with high gradient values. Instead, our approach learns the support suitable for estimation of the linear motion model. Given a circular region around a reference point we learn the k best pixels to estimate the linear motion from synthesized training images with known motion giving the optimal linear predictor support. Selection of predictors, suitable for the global object motion is performed online. This approach tracks a view-specific set of reference points using the optimal supports for efficient tracking with a known relationship between maximum object-camera velocity, motion estimation accuracy and computation time.

The rest of the paper is organised as follows. Section 2 introduces learning of linear predictors templates and reference points set, respectively. Section 3 describes tracking and the optimal size of the template neighbourhood. Following Section 4 shows the experiments and the last Section 5 summarises the results and conclusions.

2 Motion Estimation

In this section we introduce a method for learning a linear predictor as well as a subset of a given size from a circular region around the reference point, which minimise a training error. This subset is called a *linear predictor support* and the size is called *complexity of linear predictor*.

The input to our system is a single image of the object to be tracked. This image is used to synthesise a set of training images under the motion model to be tracked. In this work we assume planar object surfaces giving a homography for object motion estimation. The local linear approximation of the motion model for each image neighbourhood allows more general non-planar surfaces and perspective projection. Combining particular motion of regions into a global motion estimate imposes constraints on the object surface shape and motion model. Section 2.1 presents the learning of object specific linear predictors for local motion estimation. Section 2.2 describes predictor complexity estimation optimal with respect to the maximum object velocity.

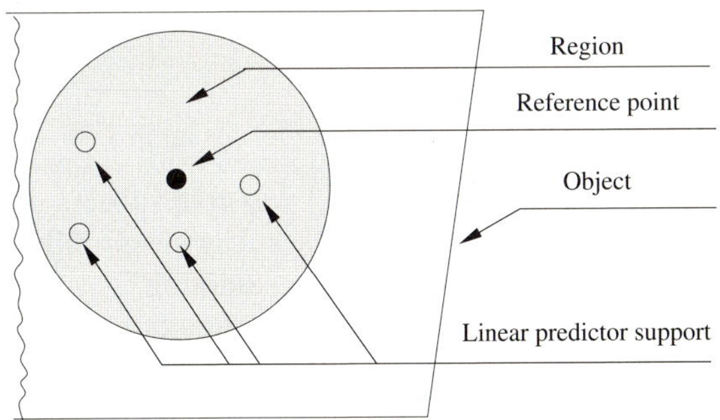

Fig. 1. Terminology: Reference point and a circular region around it. The linear predictor support is a learned set of pixels from the region.

2.1 Learning of Linear Predictors

In this section we present a method for learning a reference point specific linear predictor of a given complexity for estimation of the local motion. The set of pixels sampled in the predicted region is optimised to give the best k pixel predictor support for estimating the object motion using a linear approximation [1]. Optimisation is performed with respect to a set of synthesised training examples (i.e. perturbations) of the predicted region under known motion. The resulting subset gives efficient motion computation.

We are looking for a linear mapping $H : \mathcal{R}^k \to \mathcal{R}^2$, from which we can estimate the displacement $\mathbf{t}$ (2-vector) from the difference $\mathbf{d}$ (k-vector) between the template and observation on the support,

$$\mathbf{t} = H\mathbf{d}. \tag{1}$$

The ($2 \times k$ matrix) matrix H is estimated by the least squares method. A set of training examples are generated from a single input image by perturbing the observed object surface with random affine deformation. The range of possible affine deformations considered is given by the expected maximum relative velocity between the camera and object together with the camera frame-rate. Given m training examples, represented by $2 \times m$ matrix T and $k \times m$ matrix D such that columns are the corresponding pairs of displacements and intensity differences, the least-squares solution is:

$$H = TD^+ = TD^\top (DD^\top)^{-1} \tag{2}$$

The supporting set need not include all the pixels from a predicted region. For example in uniform image areas pixels will add no additional information to the transformation estimation whereas pixels representing distinct features (edges, corners, texture) will be important for localisation. We therefore want to select the subset of k pixels for a predicted region which provides the best local estimate of the motion according to the linear model defined in equation (1). The quality of a given subset of the pixels can be measured by the residual error of the transform estimated on the training data:

$$e = \|HD - T\|_F \tag{3}$$

For k pixels from the radius s we have $\binom{\pi s^2}{k}$ possible subsets of pixels. Explicit evaluation of the training error for all possible subsets is prohibitively expensive, we therefore subset is selected by randomised sampling.

The above analysis considers a single linear function H approximating the relationship between the observed image difference and object motion for a predicted region. This allows motion estimation upto a known residual error. For a given region of radius R the linear model gives an approximation error $r << R$

---

[1] Estimation of the optimal k with respect to the object maximum velocity is described in Section 2.2.

such that 95% of the estimated motions are within r of the known true value. Typically in this work $R \approx 20 - 30$ pixels and the resulting $r \approx 2 - 5$ pixels for a planar homography. Given a set of local motion estimates for different regions a robust estimate of the global object motion is obtained using RANSAC to eliminate the remaining 5% of outliers Section 3.

To increase the range across which we can reliably estimate the object motion we can approximate the non-linear relationship between image displacement and motion by a piece-wise linear approximation of increasing accuracy. For a given region we learn a series of linear functions $H_0, \ldots, H_q$ giving successive 95% approximation errors $r_0, \ldots, r_q$ where $r_0 > r_1 > \ldots > r_q$. This increases the maximum object velocity without a significant increase in computational cost.

2.2   Learning of Predictor Complexity

In this section we analyse the complexity of motion predictor in order to maximize framerate. To achieve real-time tracking, we generally want to utilise the observations at each frame to obtain a new estimate of the motion. This requires a trade-off between tracking complexity and estimation error due to object motion. Here we assume a maximum object velocity and optimise the motion estimation for tracking at frame-rate.

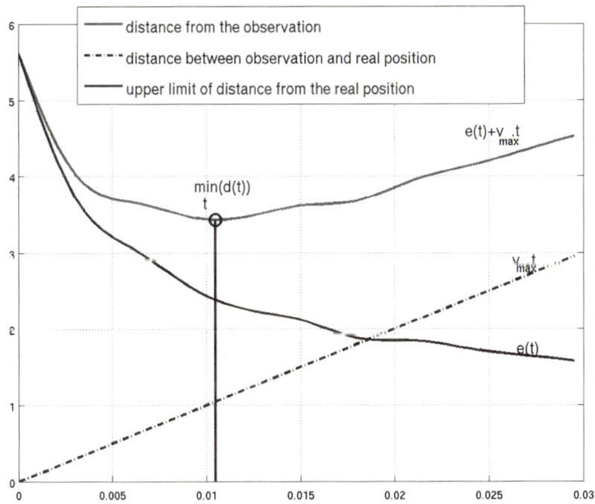

Fig. 2. Distance $d(t)$ from the real position of the object and its minimum

For a single linear predictor the error of displacement estimation decreases with its complexity (i.e. the number of pixels k selected from the predicted region). However, as k increases the error converges to a constant value with decreasing negative gradient. The error will only decrease when new structural information about the local variation in surface appearance is added. In uniform regions the variation is due to image noise and will not decrease localisation error. The computation cost increases linearly with the number of pixels used,

k. Therefore, we seek to define an optimal trade-off between computation time and motion estimation error.

Since the time needed for displacement estimation is a linear function of the number of pixels $t = ak$, the displacement error $e(t)$ is also a decreasing function of time. During the displacement estimation, the object moves away from the observation. The distance $d(t)$ from the real position of the object in the worst case is

$$d_{max}(t) = e(t) + v_{max}t, \tag{4}$$

where v_{max} is the maximum velocity of the object in pixels. Figure 2 shows the characteristic of the maximum distance and the motion estimation error $e(t)$ with increasing number of pixels k or time.

Assuming $\dot{e}(t) = \frac{de(t)}{dt}$ is a monotonically decreasing function, equation (4) has a unique solution given by:

$$t^* = \arg\min_t(d(t)) = \dot{e}^{-1}(-v_{max}) \tag{5}$$

The complexity of the tracker which minimises motion estimation error for real-time tracing is $k^* = \frac{t^*}{a}$. The worst expected accuracy error is $e(t^*) + v_{max}t^*$. Similarly, given the required accuracy, the maximum speed of the object could be estimated.

3   Tracking

Motion estimation for each individual prediction support requires a single matrix multiplication using equation (1). The cost of this operation is proportional to the number k of pixels in the regions. Matrix H is estimated offline in a pre-processing stage using synthesised training examples. Iterative refinement of the linear approximation using a hierarchy of q linear approximations $\mathsf{H}_0, ..., \mathsf{H}_q$ requires $\mathcal{O}(pkq)$ operations, where p is the number of regions and k is the predictor complexity.

Global motion estimation for a set of p regions is estimated using RANSAC to provide robustness to errors in local motion estimates and partial occlusion. In this work we assume planar object surfaces giving image motion defined by a homography with eight degrees-of-freedom. Once the motion of each region is estimated, we use 4-point RANSAC to filter out outliers and compute the correct motion of the object. Note, that this homography is applied to both the reference point positions and the supporting sets.

3.1   Active Region Set

Robust motion estimation in the presence of occlusion requires regions to be distributed across the object surface. It is not possible to find the set of regions suitable for object tracking independently on the object position, because if the object gets closer to the camera some regions can disappear and the global motion estimation can easily become ill-conditioned. In this section we present an online method which automatically selects a subset of p regions, called *active region set*, from all visible regions which provide the most accurate motion estimate and is sufficiently robust.

To optimise the distribution of regions across the surface, we define a coverage measure of the region reference points set X,

$$c(X) = \sum_{\mathbf{x} \in X} d(\mathbf{x}, X \setminus \mathbf{x}), \tag{6}$$

where distance between point $\mathbf{x}$ and set X is defined as the distance from the closest element of the set

$$d(\mathbf{x}, X) = \min_{\mathbf{y} \in X} \|\mathbf{x} - \mathbf{y}\|. \tag{7}$$

Ideally for optimal robustness to occlusion the coverage measure would be maximised. In practice, individual regions have an associated localisation error which must be taken into account. The quality $q(\mathbf{x})$ of individual regions is measured by their mean error $e(\mathbf{x})$ on the training data.

$$q(\mathbf{x}) = \max_{\mathbf{y} \in X} \big(e(\mathbf{y}) \big) - e(\mathbf{x}). \tag{8}$$

To find a suitable subset X of regions from all visible regions $\overline{X}$ we seek to optimise the weighted combination of the coverage and quality:

$$f(X) = w \frac{c(X)}{c(\overline{X})} + (1 - w) \frac{q(X)}{q(\overline{X})}, \tag{9}$$

where $w \in [0; 1]$ is the coverage weight. Given the maximum number of regions p we search for the optimal set of regions using the greedy search strategy presented in Algorithm 1.

Figure 3 shows example results obtained for $w = 0, 0.5, \text{and} 1$. In the case of $w = 0$ the p regions with the minimum error are selected resulting in clustering of regions in one part of the image. Conversely, $w = 1$ results in regions spread across the object with some having a relatively high motion estimation error. Intermediate values of w result in a compromise between region distribution and quality.

1. Let $\overline{X}$ be the set of possible regions and $X = \emptyset$ a subset of selected regions.
2. Select $\mathbf{x}^* \in \overline{X}$ holds $\mathbf{x}^* = \arg\max_{\mathbf{x} \in \overline{X} \setminus X} f(\mathbf{x} \cup X)$
3. $X = \mathbf{x}^* \cup X$ and $\overline{X} = \overline{X} \setminus \mathbf{x}^*$
4. if $|X| = p$ end, else goto 2

Algorithm 1. Active region set estimation

4 Experiments

The proposed method was tested on several different sequences of planar objects. We demonstrate robustness to large scaling and strong occlusions as well as

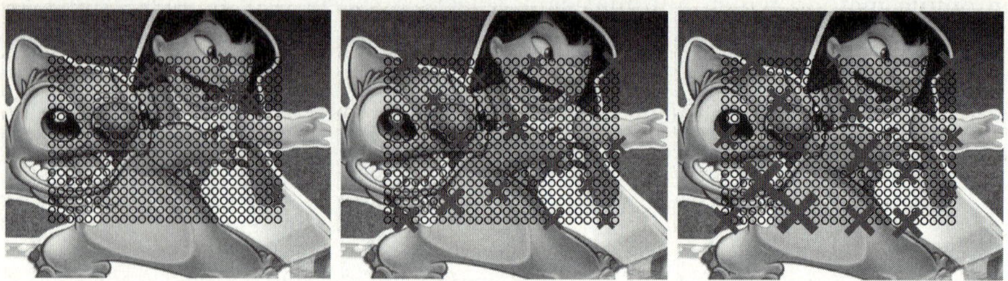

Fig. 3. Object coverage by regions for $w = 0, 0.5, 1$. Blue circles correspond to the all possible regions, red crosses to the selected regions. Size of crosses corresponds to the training error.

saccadic motions (e.g. like shaking), where object motion is faster than 30 pixels per frame. Section 4.1 investigates region suitability and influence of the coverage weight. We show that even the regions which are strong features, in the sense of Shi and Kanade [3] definition, may not be suitable for tracking. Section 4.2 summaries advantages and drawbacks of methods for linear predictor support estimation and Section 4.3 shows real experiments and discuss very low time complexity.

4.1   Active Region Set Estimation

In this experiment, we show influence of coverage weight on active region set and discuss region suitability for tracking. Different region sets selected for different weights are shown at Figure 3. The set of all possible regions is depicted by blue circles. Active region set of the most suitable 17 regions is labeled by red crosses, where size of the cross corresponds to the training error of the particular region. The weight defines the compromise between coverage and quality of the regions. The higher is the weight, the more uniform is the object coverage.

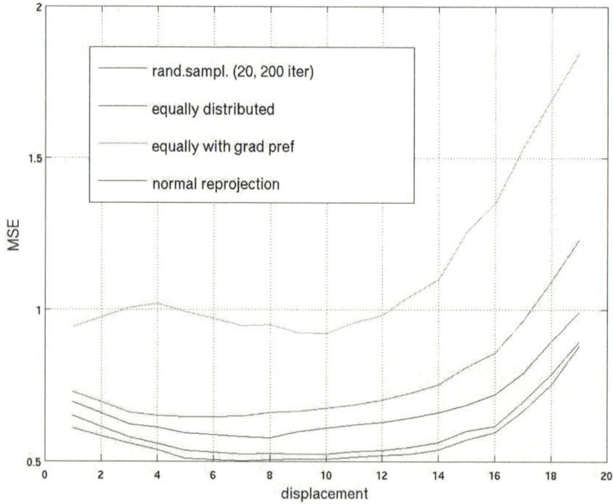

Fig. 4. Comparison of different methods for linear predictor support estimation

In the last case ($w = 1$), we can see that the teeth provide very high tracking error, although they are one of the strongest features due to the high values of gradient in their neighbourhood. The repetitive structure of teeth causes that different displacements correspond to the almost same observations. If the range of displacement had been smaller than teeth period, the training error would have been probably significantly smaller. In this sense, region quality is depends on the expected object velocity (or machine performance).

4.2 Comparison of Different Methods for Linear Predictor Support Estimation

In this experiment we compare several different methods for linear predictor support selection. The experiment was conducted on approximately 100 regions.

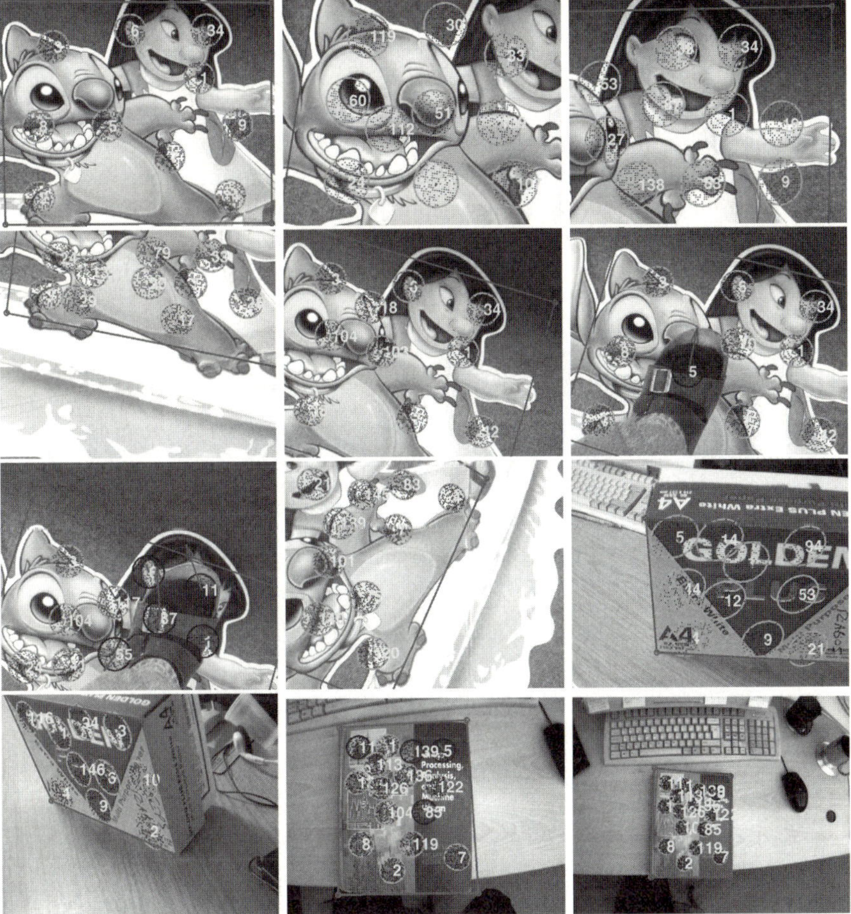

Fig. 5. Different sequences: Blue points represent support set, green circles highlight inliers, red arrows outline particular motion

From each region of 30-pixel radius a subset of 63 pixels was selected supporting by different methods.

Figure 4 compares average errors of tracking on artificial testing examples for different ranges of displacements of the following methods:

- Equally distributed pixels over the region - the support consists of pixels lying on a regular grid.
- Equally distributed with gradient based selection - pixels are divided into the grid-bins. The pixels with the highest gradient from each bin forms the support.
- Normal re-projection - First the least square solution is found for the whole n-pixel region. Each row of the obtained matrix H corresponds to the normal vector of n-dimensional hyper-plane. Particular components provide an information about pixel significance. The pixels corresponding to the highest components are utilised.
- Randomised sampling - Random subsets are repetitively selected from the region. Those which provide the lowest training error are utilised..

Since the global minimum seems for practical region sizes unreachble, it is necessary to use a heuristic method. Randomized sampling seems as the best choice, because even as few as 20 iterations provide very good results. The more iterations is performed, the closer to the global minimum we can get. In the other hand, randomised sampling requires as many estimation of least square problem

Fig. 6. 3D tracking: Robustness to motion blur achieved by learning

as iterations. If someone looks for a fast heuristic (e.g. for online learning) then normal re-projection method is a natural compromise.

4.3   Tracking

Figure 5 shows tracking of different planar objects including views from the acute angles, partial occlusion, shaking and large range of scales [2]. Figure 6 shows 3D tracking and robustness to the motion blur due to assured in learning stage.

Our slightly optimized matlab implementation runs at $30-140$ frames/second. The frame-rate is mainly dependent on the number of tracked regions and the sizes of their complexity. Time required for the particular motion estimation, pose estimation and the active region set selection is approximately the same.

5   Conclusions

We proposed a very efficient tracking method based on linear predictors of displacement. The predictors, learned from a randomly perturbed sample image, predict displacement of reference points from image intensities. The set of predictors changes during the tracking depending on the object pose. The dynamic selection makes the procedure robust against occlusions. The achieved frame rate depends on the object complexity, and it is generally higher than 30 frames per second despite the Matlab implementation.

Perhaps surprisingly, the reference points of the predictors do not often correspond to classical feature points which are mostly anchored at points with high gradient. The strength of method lies in the learning stage. The predictors are learned from the expected maximum velocity. The predictors are linear but strong enough to cover wide range of motions. The linearity allows for efficient learning.

Acknowledgement

Jiří Matas ackowledges support of Grant Agency of Czech Republic Project 201/06/1821 and EC project FP6-IST-004176 COSPAL. Karel Zimmermann and Tomáš Svoboda ackonwledge support of Czech Academy of Sciences Project 1ET101210407. Adrian Hilton acknowledges support EPSRC Platform Grant GR/S46543 at the Centre for Vision, Speech and Signal Processing, University of Surrey and by the EC project FP6-IST-004176 COSPAL.

References

1. Baker, S., Matthews, I.: Lucas-kanade 20 years on: A unifying framework. International Journal of Computer Vision **56** (2004) 221–255
2. Lucas, B., Kanade, T.: An iterative image registration technique with an application to stereo vision. In: IJCAI. (1981) 674–679

---

[2] We encourage readers to look at the additional material for whole sequences.

3. Shi, J., Tomasi, C.: Good features to track. In: Computer Vision and Pattern Recognition (CVPR'94). (1994) 593 – 600
4. Lowe, D.: Object recognition from local scale-invariant features. In: International Conference on Computer Vision. (1999) 1150–1157
5. Lowe, D.: Distinctive image features from scale-invariant keypoints. IJCV **60** (2004) 91-110.
6. Matas, J., Chum, O., Urban, M., Pajdla, T.: Robust wide-baseline stereo from maximally stable extremal regions. Image and Vision Computing **22** (2004) 761–767
7. Mikolajczyk, K., Tuytelaars, T., Schmid, C., Zisserman, A., Matas, J., Schaffalitzky, F., Kadir, T., van Gool, L.: A comparison of affine region detectors. IJCV **65** (2005) 43–72
8. Gordon, I., Lowe, D.: Scene modelling, recognition and tracking with invariant image features. In: International Symposium on Mixed and Augmented Reality (ISMAR). (2004) 110–119
9. Lepetit, V., Lagger, P., Fua, P.: Randomized trees for real-time keypoint recognition. In: Computer Vision and Pattern Recognition. (2005) 775–781
10. Black, M.J., Jepson, A.D.: Eigentracking: Robust matching and tracking of articulated objects using a view-based representation. In: European Conference on Computer Vision. (1996) 329–342
11. Jepson, A.D., Fleet, D.J., El-Maraghi, T.F.: Robust online appearance models for visual tracking. IEEE Transactions on Pattern Analysis and Machine Intelligence **25** (2003) 1296–1311
12. Cootes, T., Edwards, G., Taylor, C.: Active appearance models. PAMI **23** (2001) 681–685
13. Jurie, F., Dhome, M.: Real time robust template matching. In: British Machine Vision Conference. (2002) 123–131
14. Masson, L., Dhome, M., Jurie, F.: Robust real time tracking of 3d objects. In: International Conference on Pattern Recognition. (2004)
15. Williams, O., Blake, A., Cipolla, R.: Sparse bayesian learning for efficient visual tracking. Pattern Analysis and Machine Intelligence **27** (2005) 1292–1304

Object Localization by Subspace Clustering
of Local Descriptors

C. Bouveyron[1], J. Kannala[2], C. Schmid[1], and S. Girard[1]

[1] INRIA Rhône-Alpes, 655 avenue de l'Europe, 38300 Saint-Ismier, France
[2] Machine Vision Group, dept. of Electrical and Information Engineering,
90014 University of Oulu, Finland

Abstract. This paper presents a probabilistic approach for object localization which combines subspace clustering with the selection of discriminative clusters. Clustering is often a key step in object recognition and is penalized by the high dimensionality of the descriptors. Indeed, local descriptors, such as SIFT, which have shown excellent results in recognition, are high-dimensional and live in different low-dimensional subspaces. We therefore use a subspace clustering method called High-Dimensional Data Clustering (HDDC) which overcomes the curse of dimensionality. Furthermore, in many cases only a few of the clusters are useful to discriminate the object. We, thus, evaluate the discriminative capacity of clusters and use it to compute the probability that a local descriptor belongs to the object. Experimental results demonstrate the effectiveness of our probabilistic approach for object localization and show that subspace clustering gives better results compared to standard clustering methods. Furthermore, our approach outperforms existing results for the Pascal 2005 dataset.

1 Introduction

Object localization is one of the most challenging problems in computer vision. Earlier approaches characterize the objects by their global appearance and are not robust to occlusion, clutter and geometric transformations. To avoid these problems, recent methods use local image descriptors. Many of these approaches form clusters of local descriptors as an initial step; in most cases clustering is achieved with k-means or EM-based clustering methods. Agarwal and Roth [1] determine the spatial relations between clusters and use a Sparse Network of Windows classifier. Dorko and Schmid [2] select discriminant clusters based on the likelihood ratio and use the most discriminative ones for recognition. Leibe and Schiele [3] learn the spatial distribution of the clusters and use voting for recognition. Bag-of-keypoint methods [4,5] represent an image by a histogram of cluster labels and learn a Support Vector Machine classifier. Sivic *et al.* [6] combine a bag-of-keypoint representation with probabilistic latent semantic analysis to discover topics in an unlabeled dataset. Opelt *et al.* [7] use AdaBoost to select the most discriminant features.

However, visual descriptors used in object recognition are often high-dimensional and this penalizes classification methods and consequently recognition. Indeed, clustering methods based on the Gaussian Mixture Model (GMM) [8] show a disappointing behavior when the size of the training dataset is too small compared to the number

P. Kalra and S. Peleg (Eds.): ICVGIP 2006, LNCS 4338, pp. 457–467, 2006.

of parameters to estimate. To avoid overfitting, it is therefore necessary to find a balance between the number of parameters to estimate and the generality of the model. Many methods use global dimensionality reduction and then apply a standard clustering method. Dimension reduction techniques are either based on *feature extraction* or *feature selection*. Feature extraction builds new variables which carry a large part of the global information. The most popular method is Principal Component Analysis (PCA) [9], a linear technique. Recently, many non-linear methods have been proposed, such as Kernel PCA [10]. Feature selection, on the other hand, finds an appropriate subset of the original variables to represent the data [11]. Global dimension reduction is often advantageous in terms of performance, but loses information which could be discriminant, *i.e.*, clusters often lie in different subspaces of the original feature space and a global approach cannot capture this. It is also possible to use a parsimonious model [12] which reduces the number of parameters to estimate by fixing some parameters to be common within or between classes. These methods do not solve the problem of high dimensionality because clusters usually lie in different subspaces and many dimensions are irrelevant. Recent methods determine the subspaces for each cluster. Many subspace clustering methods use heuristic search techniques to find the subspaces. They are usually based on grid search methods and find dense clusterable subspaces [13]. The approach "mixture of Probabilistic Principal Component Analyzers" [14] proposes a latent variable model and derives an EM based method to cluster high-dimensional data. A similar model is used in [15] in the supervised framework. The model of these methods can be viewed as a mixture of constrained Gaussian densities with class-specific subspaces. An unified approach for subspace clustering in the Gaussian mixture model framework was proposed in [16]. This method, called High Dimensional Data Clustering (HDDC), includes the previous approaches and involves additional regularizations as in parsimonious models.

In this paper, we propose a probabilistic framework for object localization combining subspace clustering with the selection of the discriminative clusters. The first step of our approach is to cluster the local descriptors using HDDC [16] which is not penalized by the high-dimensionality of the descriptors. Since only a few of the learned clusters are useful to discriminate the object, we then determine the discriminative score of each cluster with positive and negative examples of the category. This score is based on a maximum likelihood formulation. By combining this information with the posterior probabilities of the clusters, we finally compute the object probability for each visual descriptor. These probabilities are then used for object localization, *i.e.*, localization assumes that points with higher probabilities are more likely to belong to the object. We evaluate our approach on two recently proposed object datasets [7,17]. We first compare HDDC to standard clustering methods within our probabilistic recognition framework. Experiments show that results with HDDC are consistently better than with other clustering methods. We then compare our probabilistic approach to the state of the art results and show that it outperforms existing results for object localization.

This paper is organized as follows. Section 2 presents the EM-based clustering method HDDC, *i.e.*, the estimation of the parameters and of the intrinsic dimensions of the subspaces. In Section 3, we describe the probabilistic object localization framework.

Experimental results for our approach are presented in Section 4. We conclude the paper in Section 5.

2 High-Dimensional Data Clustering

This section presents the clustering method HDDC [16]. Clustering divides a given dataset $\{x_1, ..., x_n\}$ of n data points into k homogeneous groups. Popular clustering techniques use Gaussian Mixture Models (GMM). The data $\{x_1, ..., x_n\} \in \mathbb{R}^p$ are then modeled with the density $f(x, \theta) = \sum_{i=1}^{k} \pi_i \phi(x, \theta_i)$, where ϕ is a multi-variate normal density with parameter $\theta_i = \{\mu_i, \Sigma_i\}$ and π_i are mixing proportions. This model estimates the full covariance matrices and therefore the number of parameters is very large in high dimensions. However, due to the *empty space* phenomenon we can assume that high-dimensional data live in subspaces with a dimensionality lower than the dimensionality of the original space. We therefore propose to work in low-dimensional class-specific subspaces in order to adapt classification to high-dimensional data and to limit the number of parameters to estimate. Here, we will present the parameterization of GMM designed for high-dimensional data and then detail the EM-based technique HDDC.

2.1 Gaussian Mixture Models for High-Dimensional Data

We assume that class conditional densities are Gaussian $\mathcal{N}(\mu_i, \Sigma_i)$ with means μ_i and covariance matrices Σ_i, $i = 1, ..., k$. Let Q_i be the orthogonal matrix of eigenvectors of Σ_i, then $\Delta_i = Q_i^t \Sigma_i Q_i$ is a diagonal matrix containing the eigenvalues of Σ_i. We further assume that Δ_i is divided into two blocks:

$$\Delta_i = \left. \left(\begin{array}{ccc|ccc} a_{i1} & & 0 & & & \\ & \ddots & & & \mathbf{0} & \\ 0 & & a_{id_i} & & & \\ \hline & & & b_i & & 0 \\ & \mathbf{0} & & & \ddots & \\ & & & 0 & & b_i \end{array} \right) \begin{array}{l} \left. \vphantom{\begin{array}{c} a \\ b \\ c \end{array}} \right\} d_i \\[2em] \left. \vphantom{\begin{array}{c} a \\ b \\ c \end{array}} \right\} (p - d_i) \end{array} \right.$$

where $a_{ij} > b_i, \forall j = 1, ..., d_i$. The class specific subspace $\mathbb{E}_i$ is generated by the d_i first eigenvectors corresponding to the eigenvalues a_{ij} with $\mu_i \in \mathbb{E}_i$. Outside this subspace, the variance is modeled by a single parameter b_i. Finally, let $P_i(x) = \tilde{Q}_i \tilde{Q}_i^t (x - \mu_i) + \mu_i$ be the projection of x on $\mathbb{E}_i$, where $\tilde{Q}_i$ is made of the d_i first columns of Q_i supplemented by zeros. Figure 1 summarizes these notations.

The mixture model presented above will be in the following referred to by $[a_{ij}b_i Q_i d_i]$. By fixing some parameters to be common within or between classes, we obtain particular models which correspond to different regularizations. For example, if we fix the first d_i eigenvalues to be common within each class, we obtain the more restricted model $[a_i b_i Q_i d_i]$. This model is in many cases more robust, *i.e.*, the assumption that the matrix Δ_i contains only two eigenvalues a_i and b_i seems to be an efficient way to regularize the estimation of Δ_i. In this paper, we focus on the models $[a_{ij}b_i Q_i d_i]$, $[a_{ij}b Q_i d_i]$, $[a_i b_i Q_i d_i]$, $[a_i b Q_i d_i]$ and $[ab Q_i d_i]$.

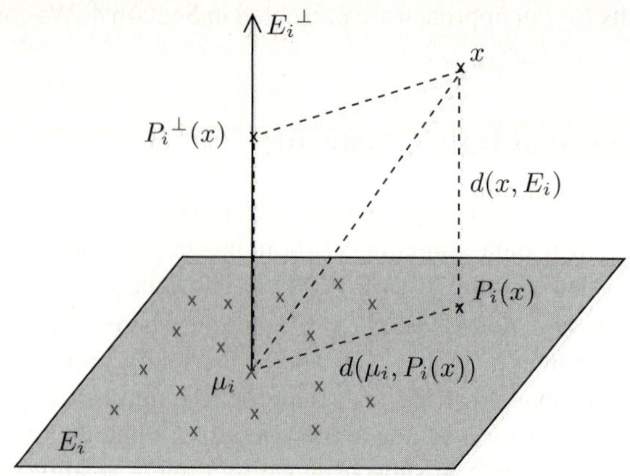

Fig. 1. The specific subspace $\mathbb{E}_i$ of the ith mixture component

2.2 EM Estimation of the Model Parameters

The parameters of a GMM are usually estimated by the EM algorithm which repeats iteratively expectation (E) and maximization (M) steps. In this section, we present the EM estimation of the parameters for the subspace GMM.

The **E-step** computes, at iteration q, for each component $i = 1, ..., k$ and for each data point $j = 1, ..., n$, the conditional probability $t_{ij}^{(q)} = P(x_j \in C_i^{(q-1)}|x_j)$. Using the Bayes formula and the parameterization of the model $[a_{ij}b_iQ_id_i]$, the probability $t_{ij}^{(q)}$ can be expressed as follows (the proof of the following result is available in [16]):

$$
t_{ij}^{(q)} = \frac{\pi_i^{(q-1)}\phi(x_j, \theta_i^{(q-1)})}{\sum_{\ell=1}^{k}\pi_\ell^{(q-1)}\phi(x_j, \theta_\ell^{(q-1)})} = 1/\sum_{\ell=1}^{k}\exp\left(\frac{1}{2}(K_i(x_j) - K_\ell(x_j))\right),
$$

where $K_i(x) = -2\log(\pi_i\phi(x, \theta_i))$ is called the cost function and is defined by:

$$
K_i(x) = \|\mu_i - P_i(x)\|_{\mathcal{A}_i}^2 + \frac{1}{b_i}\|x - P_i(x)\|^2 + \sum_{j=1}^{d_i}\log(a_{ij}) + (p-d_i)\log(b_i) - 2\log(\pi_i),
$$

where $\|.\|_{\mathcal{A}_i}$ is a norm on $\mathbb{E}_i$ such that $\|x\|_{\mathcal{A}_i}^2 = x^t\mathcal{A}_ix$ with $\mathcal{A}_i = \tilde{Q}_i\Delta_i^{-1}\tilde{Q}_i^{t}$. We can observe that $K_i(x)$ is mainly based on two distances: the distance between the projection of x on $\mathbb{E}_i$ and the mean of the class and the distance between the observation and the subspace $\mathbb{E}_i$. This cost function favours the assignment of a new observation to the class for which it is close to the subspace and for which its projection on the class subspace is close to the mean of the class. The variance terms a_{ij} and b_i balance the importance of both distances. For example, if the data are very noisy, $i.e.$, b_i is large, it is natural to weight the distance $\|x - P_i(x)\|^2$ by $1/b_i$ in order to take into account the large variance in $\mathbb{E}_i^\perp$.

The **M-step** maximizes at iteration q the conditional likelihood and uses the following update formulas. The proportions, the means and the covariance matrices of the mixture are classically estimated by:

$$\hat{\pi}_i^{(q)} = \frac{n_i^{(q)}}{n}, \quad \hat{\mu}_i^{(q)} = \frac{\sum_{j=1}^n t_{ij}^{(q)} x_j}{n_i^{(q)}}, \quad \hat{\Sigma}_i^{(q)} = \frac{1}{n_i^{(q)}} \sum_{j=1}^n t_{ij}^{(q)} (x_j - \hat{\mu}_i^{(q)})(x_j - \hat{\mu}_i^{(q)})^t.$$

where $n_i^{(q)} = \sum_{j=1}^n t_{ij}^{(q)}$. The ML estimators of model parameters are in closed form for the models considered in this paper. Proofs of the following results are given in [16].

– Subspace $\mathbb{E}_i$: the d_i first columns of Q_i are estimated by the eigenvectors associated with the d_i largest eigenvalues λ_{ij} of $\hat{\Sigma}_i$.
– Model $[a_{ij}b_iQ_id_i]$: the estimator of a_{ij} is $\hat{a}_{ij} = \lambda_{ij}$ and the estimator of b_i is:

$$\hat{b}_i = \frac{1}{(p - d_i)} \left(\mathrm{Tr}(\hat{\Sigma}_i) - \sum_{j=1}^{d_i} \lambda_{ij} \right). \tag{1}$$

– Model $[a_{ij}bQ_id_i]$: the estimator of a_{ij} is $\hat{a}_{ij} = \lambda_{ij}$ and the estimator of b is:

$$\hat{b} = \frac{1}{(p - \xi)} \left(\mathrm{Tr}(\hat{W}) - \sum_{i=1}^{k} \hat{\pi}_i \sum_{j=1}^{d_i} \lambda_{ij} \right), \tag{2}$$

where $\xi = \sum_{i=1}^{k} \hat{\pi}_i d_i$ and $\hat{W} = \sum_{i=1}^{k} \hat{\pi}_i \hat{\Sigma}_i$ is the estimated within-covariance matrix.
– Model $[a_i b_i Q_i d_i]$: the estimator of b_i is given by (1) and the estimator of a_i is:

$$\hat{a}_i = \frac{1}{d_i} \sum_{j=1}^{d_i} \lambda_{ij}. \tag{3}$$

– Model $[a_i b Q_i d_i]$: the estimators of a_i and b are respectively given by (3) and (2).
– Model $[abQ_id_i]$: the estimator of b is given by (2) and the estimator of a is:

$$\hat{a} = \frac{1}{\xi} \sum_{i=1}^{k} \hat{\pi}_i \sum_{j=1}^{d_i} \lambda_{ij}. \tag{4}$$

2.3   Intrinsic Dimension Estimation

Within the M step, we also have to estimate the intrinsic dimension of each class-specific subspace. This is a difficult problem with no exact solution. Our approach is based on the eigenvalues of the class conditional covariance matrix Σ_i of the class C_i. The jth eigenvalue of Σ_i corresponds to the fraction of the full variance carried by the jth eigenvector of Σ_i. We estimate the class specific dimension d_i, $i = 1, ..., k$, with the empirical method scree-test of Cattell [18] which analyzes the differences between successive eigenvalues in order to find a break in the scree. The selected dimension is the one for which the subsequent differences are smaller than a threshold. In our experiments the value used for this threshold was 0.2 times the maximum difference. The resulting average value for dimensions d_i was approximately 10 in the experiments presented in Section 4.

3   A Probabilistic Framework for Object Localization

In this section, we present a probabilistic framework for object localization which computes for each local descriptor x_j of an image the probability $P(x_j \in O|x_j)$ that x_j belongs to a given object O. It is then easy to precisely locate the object by considering only the local descriptors with high probabilities $P(x_j \in O|x_j)$. We first extract a set of local invariant descriptors using the Harris-Laplace detector [19] and the SIFT descriptor [20]. The dimension of the obtained SIFT features is 128. An interest point and its corresponding descriptor are in the following referred to by x_j.

3.1   Training

During training we determine the discriminative clusters of local descriptors. We first cluster local features and then identify discriminative clusters. Training can be either supervised or weakly supervised. In the weakly supervised scenario the positive descriptors include descriptors from the background, as only the image is labeled as positive.

Clustering.   Descriptors of the training images are organized in k groups using the clustering method HDDC. From a theoretical point of view, the descriptors x_j of an image are realizations of a random variable $X \in \mathbb{R}^p$ with the following density $f(x) = \sum_{i=1}^{k} \pi_i \phi(x, \theta_i) = \tau f^O(x) + (1 - \tau)f^B(x)$, where f^O and f^B are respectively the densities of descriptors of the object and of the background and τ denotes the prior probability $P(O)$. The parameter τ is equal to $\sum_{i=1}^{k} R_i \pi_i$, where $R_i = P(C_i \in O)$. The density f can thus be rewritten as follows:

$$f(x) = \underbrace{\sum_{i=1}^{k} R_i \pi_i \phi(x, \theta_i)}_{\text{Object}} + \underbrace{\sum_{i=1}^{k} (1 - R_i)\pi_i \phi(x, \theta_i)}_{\text{Background}} .$$

The clustering method HDDC provides the estimators of parameters π_i and θ_i, $\forall i = 1, ..., k$ and it thus remains to estimate parameters R_i, $\forall i = 1, ..., k$.

Identification of discriminative clusters.   This step aims to identify discriminative clusters by computing estimators of parameters R_i. Positive descriptors are denoted by P and negative ones by N. The conditional ML estimate of $R = \{R_1, ..., R_k\}$ satisfies:

$$\hat{R} = \underset{R}{\text{argmax}} \left\{ \prod_{x_j \in P} P(x_j \in O|x_j) \prod_{x_j \in N} P(x_j \in B|x_j) \right\} .$$

The expression of the gradient is:

$$\nabla_R = \sum_{x_j \in P} \frac{\Psi_j}{< R, \Psi_j >} - \sum_{x_j \in N} \frac{\Psi_j}{1 - < R, \Psi_j >},$$

where $\Psi_j = \{\Psi_{ji}\}_{i=1,...,k}$ and $\Psi_{ji} = P(x_j \in C_i|x_j)$ which are provided by HDDC. The ML estimate of R does not have an explicit formulation and it requires an iterative optimization method to find $\hat{R}$. We observed that the classical gradient method converges towards a solution very close to the least square estimator $\hat{R}_{LS} = (\Psi^t\Psi)^{-1}\Psi^t\Phi$, where $\Phi_j = P(x_j \in O|x_j)$. In our experiments, we use this least square estimator of R in order to reduce computation time. We assume for this estimation that $\forall x_j \in P$, $P(x_j \in O|x_j) = 1$ and $\forall x_j \in N$, $P(x_j \in O|x_j) = 0$. Thus, R_i is a measure for the discriminative capacity of the class C_i for the object O.

3.2   Object Localization

During recognition we compute the probability for each local descriptor of a test image to belong to the object. Using these probabilities, it is then possible to locate the object in a test image, *i.e.*, the descriptors of an image with a high probability to belong to the object give a strong indication for the presence of an object. Using the Bayes formula we obtain the posterior probability of an descriptor x_j to belongs to the object O:

$$P(x_j \in O|x_j) = \sum_{i=1}^{k} R_i P(x_j \in C_i|x_j), \tag{5}$$

where the posterior probability $P(x_j \in C_i|x_j)$ is given by HDDC. The object can then be located in a test image by using the points with the highest probabilities $P(x_j \in O|x_j)$. For comparison with existing methods we determine the bounding box with a very simple technique. We compute the mean and variance of the point coordinates weighted by their posterior probabilities given by (5). The mean is then the center of the box and a default bounding box is scaled by the variance.

4   Experiments and Comparisons

In this section, we first compare HDDC to standard clustering techniques within our probabilistic localization framework on the *Graz* dataset [7]. We then compare our approach to the results on the *Pascal 2005* dataset [17].

4.1   Evaluation of the Clustering Approach

In the following, we compare HDDC to the several standard clustering methods within our probabilistic localization framework: diagonal Gaussian mixture model (Diagonal GMM), spherical Gaussian mixture model (Spherical GMM), and data reduction with PCA combined with a diagonal Gaussian mixture model (PCA + diag. GMM). The diagonal GMM has a covariance matrix defined by $\Sigma_i = \text{diag}(\sigma_{i1}, ..., \sigma_{ip})$ and the spherical GMM is characterized by $\Sigma_i = \sigma_i Id$. In all cases, the parameters are estimated with the EM algorithm. The initialization of the EM estimation was obtained using k-means and was exactly the same for both HDDC and the standard methods. For this evaluation, we use the bicycle category of the *Graz* dataset which is consists of 200

Table 1. Object localization on *Graz*: comparison between HDDC and other methods. Precision is computed on segmented images with on average 10 detections per image (*i.e.*, detections such that $P(x_j \in O|x_j) > 0.9$).

Clustering method	HDDC $[**Q_id_i]$					Classical GMM			Result of [2]
	$[a_{ij}b_i]$	$[a_{ij}b]$	$[a_ib_i]$	$[a_ib]$	$[ab]$	PCA+diag	Diag.	Sphe.	
Precision	0.85	0.83	**0.92**	0.89	0.88	0.63	0.70	0.76	0.62

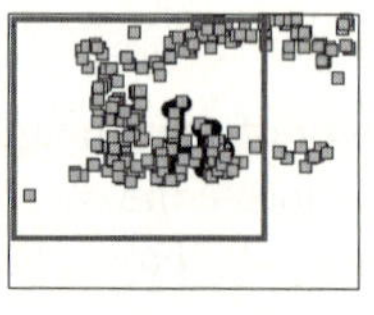  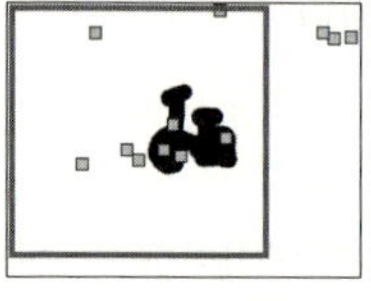 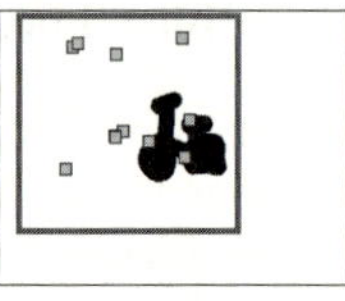

All detections   HDDC   PCA+diag. GMM   Diag. GMM

Fig. 2. Object localization on *Graz*: localization results displayed on groundtruth segmentations. We display the points with highest probabilities $P(x_j \in O|x_j)$. The same number of points is displayed for all models (5% of all detections which is equal to 12 detections per image).

training images and 100 test images. We determined 40 clusters with each clustering method in a weakly supervised setting.

The localization performance was evaluated using segmented images [7]. Table 1 summarizes localization performance of the compared methods as well as results presented in [2]. Precision is the number of points within the object region with respect to the total number of selected points. We can observe that the HDDC models give better localization results than the other methods. In particular, the model $[a_ib_iQ_id_i]$ obtains best results, *i.e.*, a precision of 92% when considering points with $P(x_j \in O|x_j) > 0.9$. We also observe that a global dimension reduction with PCA does not improve the results compared to diagonal GMM. This confirms our initial assumption that data of different clusters live in different low-dimensional subspaces and that a global dimension reduction technique is not able to take this into account. Figure 2 shows localization results on segmented test images with the different methods. The left image shows all interest points detected on the test images. The bounding boxes are computed with the displayed points, *i.e.*, the points with the highest probabilities in the case of the three right most images. It appears that our localization method identifies precisely the points belonging to the object and consequently is able to locate small objects in different positions, poses and scales whereas other methods do not give an efficient localization.

Table 2. Average precision (AP) for supervised and weakly-supervised localization on *Pascal test2*. The result in italic is the average result of the best method of the Pascal challenge [17].

Clustering method	Supervised					Weakly-supervised				
	Moto	Bike	People	Car	Aver.	Moto	Bike	People	Car	Aver.
HDDC	0.315	**0.172**	**0.091**	0.155	**0.183**	0.311	**0.161**	**0.046**	0.049	**0.142**
Best of [17]	**0.341**	0.113	0.021	**0.304**	*0.112*	/	/	/	/	/

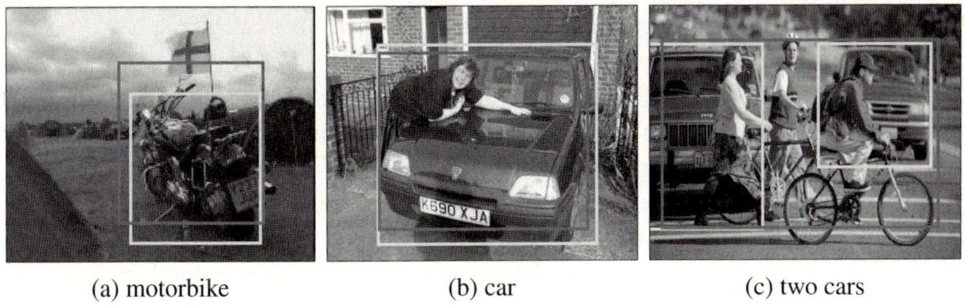

| (a) motorbike | (b) car | (c) two cars |

Fig. 3. Supervised localization on *Pascal test2*: predicted bounding boxes are in magenta and true boxes in yellow

4.2   Comparison to the State of the Art

For this second experiment, we compare our approach to the results on the Pascal visual object class 2005 dataset [17]. It contains four categories: motorbikes, bicycles, people and cars. It is made of 684 training images and two test sets: test1 and test2. We chose to evaluate our method on the set test2, which is the more difficult one and contains 956 images. Since the bounding boxes of the objects are available for all categories we evaluate our method with supervised as well as a weakly supervised training data. In the supervised case only the descriptors located inside the bounding boxes are labeled as positive during training. Here we use 50 clusters for each of the four categories. We use the model $[a_i b_i Q_i d_i]$ for HDDC, since the previous experiment has shown that it is the most efficient model. To compare with the results of Pascal Challenge [17], we use the localization measure "average precision" (AP) which is the arithmetic mean of 11 values on the precision-recall curves computed with ground-truth bounding boxes (see [17] for more details).

The localization results on *Pascal test2* are presented in Table 2 for supervised and weakly supervised training data. In the supervised case, Table 2 shows that our probabilistic recognition approach performs well compared to the results in the Pascal competition. In particular, our approach wins two "competitions" (bicycle and people) and is on average more efficient than the methods of the Pascal challenge. This is despite the fact that our approach detects only one bounding box per image for each category and this reduces the performance when multiple objects are present, as shown in the right part of Figure 3. Notice that our approach has the best overall performance although we do not have any model for the spatial relationships of the local features.

We can also observe that our weakly-supervised localization results are only slightly lower than the ones in the supervised case and on average better than the Pascal results in the supervised case. This means that our approach efficiently identifies discriminative clusters of each object category and this even in the case of weak supervision. There are no corresponding results for the Pascal Challenge, since all competing methods used supervised data. It is promising that the weakly supervised approach obtains good localization results because the manual annotation of training images is time consuming.

5   Conclusion

The main contribution of this paper is the introduction of a probabilistic approach for object localization which combines subspace clustering with the selection of discriminative clusters. This approach has the advantage of using posterior probabilities to weight interest points. We proposed to use the subspace clustering method called HDDC designed for high-dimensional data. Experimental results show that HDDC performs better than other Gaussian models for locating objects in natural images. This is due to the fact that HDDC correctly models the groups in their subspaces and thus forms more homogeneous groups. In addition, our method performs well also in the weakly-supervised framework which is promising. Finally, our approach provides better results than the state of the art methods and that using only one type of detector and descriptor (Harris-Laplace+Sift). We believe that the results could be further improved using a combination of descriptors as in [2,5]. Also, the localization results presented here are based on a very simple spatial model which can be easily improved to further increase the performance of our approach.

References

1. Agarwal, S., Roth, D.: Learning a sparse representation for object detection. In: 7th European Conference on Computer Vision. Volume 4. (2002) 113–130
2. Dorko, G., Schmid, C.: Object class recognition using discriminative local features. Technical Report 5497, INRIA (2004)
3. Leibe, B., Schiele, B.: Interleaved object categorization and segmentation. In: British Machine Vision Conference, Norwich, England (2003)
4. Willamowski, J., Arregui, D., Csurka, G., Dance, C., Fan, L.: Coategorizing nine visual classes using local appareance descriptors. In: International Workshop on Learning for Adaptable Visual Systems, Cambridge, UK (2004)
5. Zhang, J., Marszalek, M., Lazebnik, S., Schmid, C.: Local features and kernels for classification of texture and object categories. Technical report, INRIA (2005)
6. Sivic, J., Russell, B., Efros, A., Zisserman, A., Freeman, W.: Discovering objects and their location in images. In: International Conference on Computer Vision. (2005)
7. Opelt, A., Fussenegger, M., Pinz, A., Auer, P.: Weak hypotheses and boosting for generic object detection and recognition. In: European Conference on Computer Vision. Volume 2. (2004) 71–84
8. McLachlan, G., Peel, D.: Finite Mixture Models. Wiley Interscience, New York (2000)
9. Jolliffe, I.: Principal Component Analysis. Springer-Verlag, New York (1986)
10. Schölkopf, B., Smola, A., Müller, K.: Nonlinear component analysis as a kernel eigenvalue problem. Neural Computation **10** (1998) 1299–1319
11. Guyon, I., Elisseeff, A.: An introduction to variable and feature selection. Journal of Machine Learning Research **3** (2003) 1157–1182
12. Fraley, C., Raftery, A.: Model-based clustering, discriminant analysis and density estimation. Journal of American Statistical Association **97** (2002) 611–631
13. Parsons, L., Haque, E., Liu, H.: Subspace clustering for high dimensional data: a review. SIGKDD Explor. Newsl. **6** (2004) 90–105
14. Tipping, M., Bishop, C.: Mixtures of probabilistic principal component analysers. Neural Computation **11** (1999) 443–482

15. Moghaddam, B.: Principal Manifolds and Probabilistic Subspaces for Visual Recognition. IEEE Trans. on Pattern Analysis and Machine Intelligence **24** (2002) 780–788
16. Bouveyron, C., Girard, S., Schmid, C.: High-Dimensional Data Clustering. Technical Report 1083M, LMC-IMAG, Université J. Fourier Grenoble 1 (2006)
17. Everingham, M., Zisserman, A., Williams, C., Gool, L.V., et al.: The 2005 PASCAL visual object classes challenge. In: First PASCAL Challenge Workshop. Springer (2006)
18. Cattell, R.: The scree test for the number of factors. Multivariate Behavioral Research **1** (1966) 245–276
19. Mikolajczyk, K., Schmid, C.: Scale and affine invariant interest point detectors. International Journal of Computer Vision **60** (2004) 63–86
20. Lowe, D.: Distinctive image features from scale-invariant keypoints. International Journal of Computer Vision **60** (2004) 91–110

Integrated Tracking and Recognition of Human Activities in Shape Space

Bi Song, Amit K. Roy-Chowdhury, and N. Vaswani

University of California, Riverside, USA and
Iowa State University, USA

Abstract. Activity recognition consists of two fundamental tasks: tracking the features/objects of interest, and recognizing the activities. In this paper, we show that these two tasks can be integrated within the framework of a dynamical feedback system. In our proposed method, the recognized activity is continuously adapted based on the output of the tracking algorithm, which in turn is driven by the identity of the recognized activity. A non-linear, non-stationary stochastic dynamical model on the "shape" of the objects participating in the activities is used to represent their motion, and forms the basis of the tracking algorithm. The tracked observations are used to recognize the activities by comparing against a prior database. Measures designed to evaluate the performance of the tracking algorithm serve as a feedback signal. The method is able to automatically detect changes and switch between activities happening one after another, which is akin to segmenting a long sequence into homogeneous parts. The entire process of tracking, recognition, change detection and model switching happens recursively as new video frames become available. We demonstrate the effectiveness of the method on real-life video and analyze its performance based on such metrics as detection delay and false alarm.

1   Introduction

The problem of event analysis from video consists of the related issues of recognizing different activities and keeping track of the objects participating in the activities. In many practical applications, all we have is a video sequence consisting of a number of activities, and we have to track, *as well as* recognize, the various events taking place in the video. Often we have time critical applications where the option of first completing the tracking and then recognizing is not available. Thus it is important to design methods that can *simultaneously* track and recognize a sequence of human activities from a video sequence.

In this paper, we present a novel framework for *integrated* tracking and recognition of human activities consisting of the following steps which take place in a loop: (i) modeling the appearance and motion of single activity sequences and tracking them, (ii) detecting a change from one sequence to the next, and (iii) classifying which is the next activity to change to and start tracking it. This is achieved in a recursive manner as new video frames become available. Human activities are represented by non-linear, non-stationary dynamical models,

P. Kalra and S. Peleg (Eds.): ICVGIP 2006, LNCS 4338, pp. 468–479, 2006.

learned from training data. These models represent the change in the *shape* of
the human body in the course of the activity. Given a video sequence, the model
parameters are used for recognition, with the recognized parameters then driving the tracking algorithm. The method is able to automatically detect changes
from one activity to another and switch accordingly. Switching between models
occurs when the tracking error [1], which serves as a feedback signal, exceeds
a certain threshold. Thus our proposed system is able to persistently track and
recognize a *sequence* of multiple activities. A diagrammatic representation of this
framework is shown in Fig. 1. We present experimental results on real life video
of different activities and analyze the issues of recognition delay and tracking
accuracy.

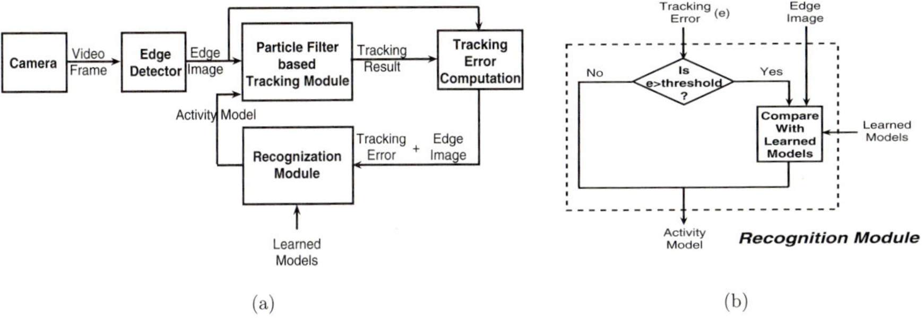

Fig. 1. (a): Framework of dynamical feedback system for simultaneous tracking
and recognition. (b): Recognition module incorporating change detection and model
switching.

1.1   Relation to Previous Work

A review of recent work is given in [7]. Based on the conclusions of [7], we
find that most existing methods handle events of short duration with moderate
changes in illumination, scene clutter and occlusion. In most video surveillance
methods, the tracks are obtained first followed by recognition [10,5,18]. Integrated tracking and recognition is very promising becasue of its ability to track
and recognize activities in a long video seuqnece, where switching between different activities will usually occur.

A few techniques have studied the problem of simultaneous tracking and recognition, though not always in the context of activity recognition. In [20,21], the
authors presented methods whereby the identity of a person, based on face recognition, is obtained after tracking the face over the whole sequence. However,
the identity of a face in a video sequence is a static parameter which can be
estimated by integrating over the entire sequence, whereas activities are inherently dynamic and hence the recognition needs to evolve in time. In [15,13], the
idea of integrated tracking and recognition of activities was proposed. However,
their method requires a-priori knowledge of the transition probability matrix
for switching between different activity models. While this is feasible in some

applications, designing such a transition matrix for uncontrolled environments like video surveillance may be difficult (since the class of possible activities is large and can change arbitrarily from one to another) and the process has to repeat for each application scenario. In contrast to this open-loop approach, we propose to use change detection measures to detect slow or sudden transitions between activities, and use these as a feedback signal in a closed-loop system.

Simultaneous tracking and recognition was also the theme in [6], but here the authors used color and depth information to create a "plan-view" map based on which tracking is done, and activity recognition was carried out using pose estimates; they did not consider the dynamics inherent in any activity. Simultaneous tracking of moving people and recognition of their activities has been performed in many applications using a Dynamic Bayesian Network (DBN) model tracked by a Rao-Blackwellized particle filter [11,3,2]. In [2], the authors perform figure tracking by defining a DBN to switch between various linear dynamical systems (also called Switched Linear Dynamical System (SLDS)). However, these methods also require knowledge of a state transition pdf for a seqeuence of changes, which implies learning what sequences are likely to occur. Key-frame segmentation methods [19] can achieve some of the goals of this research (i.e., find the switching instances), but they usually require the entire video to be available a-priori rather than simultaneously tracking, recognizing and detecting changes.

We use a discrete shape representation of the human body which is different from level set representations of shapes such as those described in [14,9,12]. The level set approach is theoretically infinite (and in practice large time varying finite) dimensional, and hence defining dynamics on and sampling from such a large dimensional space is computationally expensive. This is overcome through the use of various approximate tracking solutions. Level sets, however, have the advantage that they can adjust to large changes in the shape and topology, which is usually problematic for discrete representations. For large changes in shape, we show that it is possible to overcome this problem for many activity recognition applications by using a piecewise stationary dynamical model. We do not encounter topology changes in our application. Moreover, a discrete representation allows adoption of the overall framework to different descriptions of human body structure, like stick figures, cylindrical models, etc.

2   State Space Model for Shape Dynamics

We model the motion/deformation of a deforming shape as scaled Euclidean motion of a "mean shape" (i.e., translation, rotation, isotropic scaling) plus its non-rigid deformation. The term "shape activity" is used to denote a particular stochastic model for shape deformation. We define a "stationary shape activity" (SSA) as one for which the mean shape remains constant with time and the deformation model is stationary. We define a piecewise stationary shape activity (PSSA) model [17] as one that models a shape activity with slowly varying "mean shape" (approximated as piecewise constant). The SSA model is accurate for activities where the shape of the body does not change significantly in the course of the activity. The PSSA model deals with the case where the shape changes appreciably in the course of the activity. This allows us to handle large shape deformation using a discrete shape descriptor.

2.1   Shape Representation

We briefly review Kendall's statistical shape theory, details of which can be found in [4]. We use a discrete representation of shape for a group of k **landmarks**. The **configuration** is the set of landmarks: in the 2D case it is the x and y coordinates of the landmarks which can be represented as a k dimensional complex vector, Y_{raw}. This raw configuration can be normalized for translation and then for scale to yield the **pre-shape**, denoted by w. A configuration of k points after translation normalization, denoted by Y, lies in $\mathcal{C}^{k-1}$ (a (k-1)-dimensional complex space), while the pre-shape, w, lies on a hyper-sphere in $\mathcal{C}^{k-1}$. A pre-shape w_1 can be aligned with another pre-shape w_0 by finding the rotation angle for the best fit (minimum mean square error fit) and this gives the **Procrustes fit** of w_1 onto w_0. This is the **shape** of w_1 with respect to w_0. The **Procrustes distance** between preshapes w_1 and w_0 is the Euclidean distance between the Procrustes fit of w_1 onto w_0. The **Procrustes mean** of a set of preshapes $\{w_i\}$ is the minimizer of the sum of squares of Procrustes distances from each w_i to an unknown unit size mean configuration μ. Any pre-shape of the set can then be aligned with respect to this Procrustes mean to return the **shape** (denoted by z) with respect to the mean shape, μ.

The shape space, $\mathcal{M}$, is a manifold in $\mathcal{C}^{k-1}$ and hence its actual dimension is $\mathcal{C}^{k-2}$. Thus the tangent plane at any point of the shape space is a $\mathcal{C}^{k-2}$ dimensional hyperplane in $\mathcal{C}^k$. The tangent coordinate (denoted by v) with respect to μ, of a configuration, Y_{raw}, is evaluated as follows:

$$Y = CY_{raw}, \quad \text{where } C \triangleq I_k - 1_k 1_k^T / k$$

$$s \triangleq s(Y) = ||Y||, \quad w = Y/s,$$

$$\theta \triangleq \theta(Y, \mu) = -\arg(w^T \mu), \qquad z(Y, \mu) = w e^{j\theta}, \tag{1}$$

$$v \triangleq v(Y, \mu) = [I_k - \mu\mu^T] z = [I_k - \mu\mu^T] \frac{Y e^{j\theta}}{s}. \tag{2}$$

s is the scale of the centered configuration and θ is the rotation of the scaled configuration with respect to the mean shape.

The inverse mapping of (2) (tangent space to centered configuration space) is:

$$z(v, \mu) = (1 - v^* v)^{1/2} \mu + v, \tag{3}$$

$$Y(v, \theta, s, \mu) = zse^{-j\theta} = [(1 - v^* v)^{1/2} \mu + v] s e^{-j\theta}.$$

2.2   System Model

The observed configuration of landmarks, in a single frame at time t, after translation normalization, is defined by Y_t, and forms the observation vector. Let μ_t

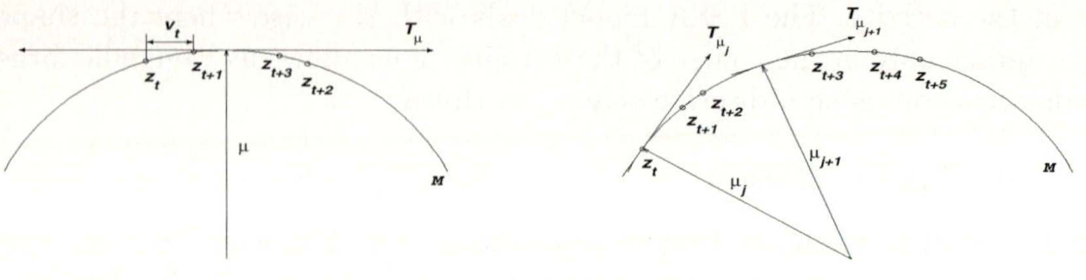

Fig. 2. Stationary and "Piecewise-Stationary" Shape Sequences on the shape manifold which is depicted using a circle ($\mathcal{M}$), instead of a complex $\mathcal{C}^{k-1}$ sphere. In (a), we show a stationary sequence of shapes; at all times the shapes are close to the mean shape and hence the dynamics can be approximated in T_μ (tangent space at μ). In (b), we show a piecewise-stationary sequence of shapes; the shapes move on the shape manifold.

denote mean shape associated with this frame. Denote the tangent space at μ_t by T_{μ_t}. Since the tangent plane is a $(k-2)$-dim hyperplane in $\mathcal{C}^k$, a tangent vector has only $(k-2)$ independent (complex) coefficients. We perform an SVD (Singular Value Decomposition) of the tangent projection matrix, $[I_k - \mu_t \mu_t^T]C$ (from (1), to obtain a $(k-2)$-dim orthogonal basis for T_{μ_t}. The basis vectors of the SVD, $\{\underline{u}_{t,i}\}_{i=1}^{k-2}$, are arranged as column vectors of a matrix, $U_t(\mu_t)$, i.e., $U_t^{\,k\times(k-2)} = [\underline{u}_{t,1}, \underline{u}_{t,2}...\underline{u}_{t,k-2}]$. The vector of coefficients $((k-2)$-dim) along these basis directions, $c_t(z_t, \mu_t)$, is thus a canonical representation of the tangent coordinate of z_t in T_{μ_t}. The tangent coordinate is given by $v_t(z_t, \mu_t) = U_t c_t$. The coefficients vector of the tangent coordinate of shape with respect to the current mean shape, c_t, and the motion parameters (scale s_t, rotation θ_t) form the state vector, i.e., $X_t = [c_t, s_t, \theta_t]$.

For a stationary shape activity, the "mean shape" is constant with time, i.e., $\mu_t = \mu_0$, and the shape sequence is clustered around the "mean shape" (see figure 2(a)). Hence the shape deformation dynamics can be defined in a single tangent space at the mean (which can be learnt as the Procrustes mean of the training data). The dynamics on c_t is defined by the autoregression model, $c_t = A_c c_{t-1} + n_t$.

PSSA Model for Shape Deformation. When the shape is not stationary but is slowly varying, one could model the "mean shape" as being piecewise constant [17]. Thus unlike SSA, the dynamics can be described in a single tangent space. Let the "mean shape" change times be $t_{\mu_1}, t_{\mu_2}, t_{\mu_3}, ...$ and the corresponding means be $\mu_1, \mu_2, \mu_3, ...$ Then we have the following dynamics: between $t_{\mu_{j-1}} \leq t < t_{\mu_j}$, $\mu_t = \mu_{j-1}$ and so $c_{t-1}(z_{t-1}, \mu_t) = c_{t-1}(z_{t-1}, \mu_{j-1})$. Hence in this interval, the dynamics is similar to that for an SSA, i.e.,

$$c_t(z_t, \mu_{j-1}) = A_{c,j-1} c_{t-1}(z_{t-1}, \mu_{j-1}) + n_t, \quad n_t \sim \mathcal{N}(0, \Sigma_{c,t})$$

$$v_t = U(\mu_{j-1})c_t,$$

$$z_t = (1 - v_t^* v_t)^{1/2} \mu_{j-1} + v_t. \quad \text{(from (3))} \qquad (4)$$

At the change time instant, $t = t_{\mu_j}$, $\mu_t = \mu_j$ and so the tangent coefficient c_{t-1} needs to be recalculated in the new tangent space with respect to $\mu_t = \mu_j$. This is achieved as follows[17]:

$$c_{t-1}(z_{t-1}, \mu_{j-1}) = U(\mu_t)^* z_{t-1} e^{j\theta(z_{t-1}, \mu_{j-1})}$$
$$c_t(z_t, \mu_{j-1}) = A_{c,j} c_{t-1}(z_{t-1}, \mu_{j-1}) + n_t,$$
$$v_t = U(\mu_{j-1}) c_t,$$
$$z_t = (1 - v_t^* v_t)^{1/2} \mu_{j-1} + v_t. \tag{5}$$

Global Motion Dynamics. We use the same global motion model as in [18] to represent the Euclidean motion of the mean shape. We use a Gauss-Markov model for log-scale, $\log s_t$, and a Markov uniform model for θ_t, i.e.,

$$\log s_t = \alpha_s \log s_{t-1} + (1 - \alpha_s)\mu_s + n_{s,t}$$
$$\log s_0 \sim \mathcal{N}(\mu_s, \sigma_s^2), \quad n_{s,t} \sim \mathcal{N}(0, \sigma_r^2)$$
$$\theta_t = \alpha_\theta \theta_{t-1} + n_{\theta,t}, \quad n_{\theta,t} \sim Unif(-a, a) \tag{6}$$

Training. Given a training sequence of centered (translation normalized) configurations, $\{Y_t\}_{t=1}^T$, for a particular activity, we first evaluate $\{c_t, v_t, s_t, \theta_t\}_{t=1}^T$ for each stationary sub-model (i.e., $t_{\mu_{j-1}} \le t < t_{\mu_j}$) as follows [1] :

$$\mu_{j-1} = \text{Procrustes mean of } Y_t, t_{\mu_{j-1}} \le t < t_{\mu_j}$$
$$s_t = ||Y_t||, \quad w_t = Y_t/s_t,$$
$$\theta_t(Y_t, \mu_{j-1}) = -angle(w_t^T \mu_{j-1}), \quad z_t(Y_t, \mu_{j-1}) = w_t e^{j\theta_t},$$
$$v_t(Y_t, \mu_{j-1}) = [I_k - z_{t-1} z_{t-1}^T] z_t,$$
$$c_t(Y_t, \mu_{j-1}) = U_l(z_{l-1})^T z_l. \tag{7}$$

If we assume a time invariant Markov model on c_t, we can use $\{c_t\}_{t=1}^T$ to learn its parameters [18].

2.3   Observation Model

In practice, the landmarks are not easy to extract directly from a given image, while an edge image is convenient to obtain by edge detection algorithms (e.g. Canny detector). Our observation is the edge image, $G_t = \Upsilon(I_t)$, (where Υ denotes the edge extraction operator) and I_t is the image at t. The observation likelihood describes the probability of a set of landmark points, Γ_t, on the edge image with $\Gamma_t \subset G_t$, given the predicted state vector, X_t. Let $\hat{Y}_t = h(X_t) = s_t z_t e^{-j\theta_t}$ be the predicted configuration of landmarks. It is assumed that a mapping, f, is known that associates each predicted landmark of $\hat{Y}_t$ with a point on the edges.

---

[1] Note, the last equation, $c_t = U_t^T z_t$, holds because $c_t = U_t^T v_t = U_t^T[I - \mu_{j-1}\mu_{j-1}^T]z_t = U_t^T[I - \mu_{j-1}\mu_{j-1}^T]C z_t = U_t^T U_t U_t^T z_t = U_t^T z_t$.

In practice this mapping is set up by searching for the closest edge along the normal of the predicted configuration (as in [8]) and this is treated as the observed landmark, Γ_t. Thus the observation likelihood is

$$p(\Gamma_t|X_t) \propto exp\{-\sum_{k=1}^{K} \frac{1}{2r_k K}||q_k - f(q_k, G_t)||^2\}, \tag{8}$$

where K is the shape vector dimension, r_k is the variance of the kth component, q_k is the kth predicted landmark, i.e., $q_k = \hat{Y}_{t,k}$ and $f(q_k, G_t) = \Gamma_t$ is the nearest edge point of q_k along its norm direction.

3   Tracking, Change Point Detection and Recognition

3.1   Tracking Using Particle Filters

In this paper, we use a particle filter for "tracking", i.e., for obtaining observations on the fly by tracing along the normals of the predicted configuration, $\hat{Y}_t$, to search for the closest edge (as described in Section 2.3). The particle filter is a sequential Monte Carlo method (sequential importance sampling plus resampling) which provides at each t, an N sample Monte Carlo approximation to the prediction distribution, $\pi_{t|t-1}(dx) = Pr(X_t \in dx|Y_{1:t-1})$, which is used to search for new observed landmarks. These are then used to update $\pi_{t|t-1}$ to get the filtering (posterior) distribution, $\pi_{t|t}(dx) = Pr(X_t \in dx|Y_{1:t})$. We use a particle filter because the observation model is nonlinear and the posterior can temporarily become multi-model when there are false edges due to background clutter.

3.2   Change Point Detection

Activities will change in the course of a long video sequence. The activity changes will cause the PF, with a large enough number of particles, and tuned to the dynamical model of a particular activity, to lose track when the activity changes. This is because under the existing activity model with which the particle filter operates, the new observations would appear to have very large observation noise. Thus the tracking error will increase when the activity changes and this can be used to detect the change times. The tracking error or prediction error is the distance between the current observation and its prediction based on past observations. When observation is an edge image, TE is calculated by

$$TE = \sum_{k=1}^{K} ||q_k - f(q_k, G_t)||^2.$$

For the case when the switch from one activity to another is a slow one, the PF dose not lose track very quickly (the tracking error increases slowly). The tracking error will take long to detect the change, and then we use the *Expected (negative) Log Likelihood (ELL)*, i.e., $ELL = E[-\log p(v_t)]$ [16]. *ELL* is approximated by

$$ELL^N = \frac{1}{N} \sum_{i=1}^{N} v_t^{(i)^T} \Sigma_v^{-1} v_t^{(i)} + K,$$

$$\text{where} \quad K \triangleq -\log \sqrt{(2\pi)^{2k-4}|\Sigma_v|},$$

and N is the number of particles, Σ_v is the covariance matrix of v.

3.3   Model Switching to a New Activity

Once the change time detection has happened successfully, the next problem is to determine the correct activity from the class of previously learned activity models. This is known as the problem of *model switching*. This is done by projecting the observed shape in a frame onto the mean shape for each of the learned activities and choosing the one with the largest projection. In practice, this is done for a few frames before a final decision is made, since individual frames of different activities may be similar. In order to initialize the shape after a model-switch, we use motion segmentation to isolate the person and re-estimate the scale and translation parameters (note that background information is not required). The autoregression matrix, A_c, is extremely sensitive to the training data, and is not used in the recognition experiments.

3.4   Simultaneous Tracking, Change Detection and Recognition (Simul-TraCR) Algorithm

We now outline the main steps of the simultaneous tracking and recognition algorithm, incorporating change detection and model switching. For simplicity, let us assume that there are two activities in the sequence, A_1 and A_2. For the first frame in A_1, the region of interest (a person or a group of people) is detected based on the application requirements (not part of this paper) and the corresponding model for the activity is determined as in Section 3.3. After this initialization, the algorithm now proceeds as follows.

Track. Based on the detected region and the chosen dynamical model, the particle filter is used to track the activity. Measures for determining the accuracy of the tracking algorithm (TE and ELL) are computed for each frame.

Change Detection. When the fidelity measures exceed a certain threshold (details in Section 4.1) for a few consecutive frames, a change is detected.

Model Switching. Once the change is detected, the new shape vector is obtained from the edge map of image frame and a search is initiated for the correct activity model. Given an observed image I_t, we label this frame as the activity that minimizes $||\Gamma_t - se^{j\theta}\mu_m + (a+jb)||^2, m = 1, ..., M$, where s, θ and $a + jb$ are the scale, rotation and translation parameters respectively, M is the number of all candidate activities, and Γ_t is obtained from I_t as explained in Section 2.3. If the distance is above a certain threshold for all m, we decide that the activity is not within the learned database and this is also indicated. Once the correct activity model is identified, we use this and go back to Track.

Note that change detection and switching may be between different portions of the same activity, specifically, for those activities in which a non-stationary dynamical model is needed.

4   Experimental Results

4.1   Indoor Activity Sequence

We now show examples of our Simul-TraCR algorithm on 10 different activities captured in video. The training and testing sequences were captured separately on different days. The binarized silhouette denoting the contour of the person in every frame of the *training* sequence is obtained using background subtraction. We extracted the shape from this binary image by uniformly sampling on the edge of the silhouette. Once the landmarks are obtained, the shape is extracted using the procedure described in Section 2.1. Using the training data, the parameters of the dynamical models for each activity were learnt using these shape sequences and as explained in Section 2.2. In the *testing* sequence, the silhouette is pre-computed only in the first frame if the background information is available; otherwise we use motion segmentation over a few initial frames to obtain the siluhouette. Thereafter it is obtained as the output of the tracking algorithm, as explained above. The database we collected consists of 10 activities (whose composition make up a number of normal everyday activities), bending across, walking towards camera and bending down, leaning forward and backward, leaning sideward, looking around, turning head, turning upper body, squatting, bending with hands outstretched, and walking. We will refer to the n_{th} activity as Act$n$.

Figure 3 shows the tracking results of several activities, along with the edge image observations for each of them. Activiies 1 and 2 are tracked with PSSA model composed of three and two "stationary" sub-models respectively. Activities 3-10 are tracked with the "stationary shape activity" model.

Figure 4 shows a plot of the tracking error of a multi-activity sequence which includes one slow change and some sudden changes. The order of activities is Act3, Act4, Act8, Act9 and Act7. From Act3 to Act4 the change happens slowly, other changes happen suddenly. There is a delay involved in detecting this change, which should not be confused with the one mentioned above for switching to the correct model. The total delay is the sum of the delays due to change detection and model switching. There is a long delay in the case of slowly changing activities, because the tracking error increases slowly, while for other changes, the delays for change detection are very short.

4.2   Experiments with Outdoor Data

The sequence on which we show our results consists of activities of two people: Person 1 walking with a package in hand and doing this multiple times, and Person 2 first walking towards the camera, and then walking parallel to the camera. There are three activities in this case: walking towards camera, walking

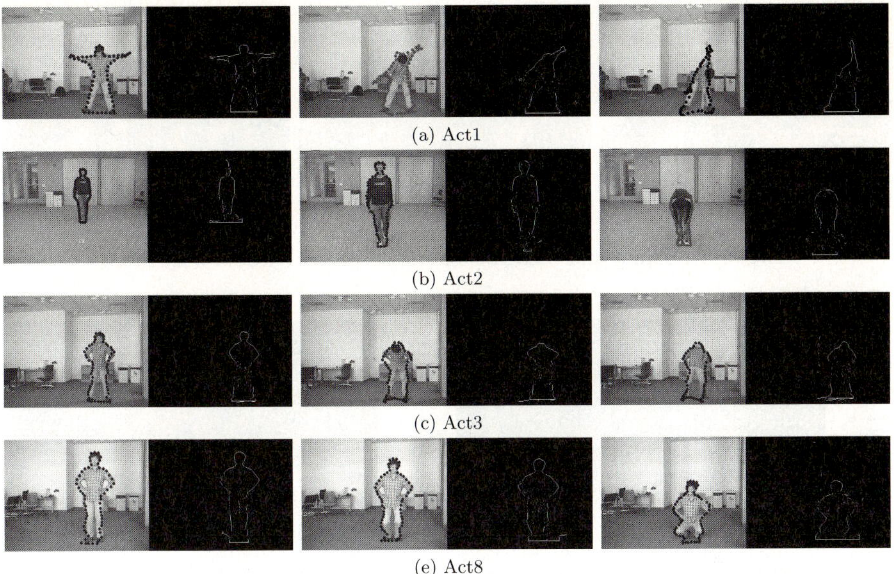

(a) Act1

(b) Act2

(c) Act3

(e) Act8

Fig. 3. Tracking results on video data. On the right is the edge image which is used as the observation.

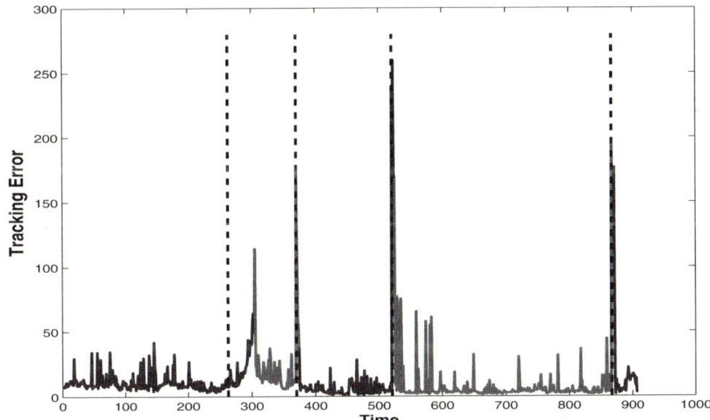

Fig. 4. Tracking error of multi-activity sequence which includes slow and sudden change. The order of activities is Act3, Act4, Act8, Act9 and Act7. From Act3 to Act4, the change happens slowly, other changes happen suddenly. The tracking error increases when an activity transition happens. Once the model switch occurs and the new model is able to track properly, the tracking error goes down.

parallel to camera, walking with small package in hand. The tracking results, along with the recognized activity, is shown in Figure 5. The recognition results for each frame for the two different people are shown in Fig. 6.

Fig. 5. Tracking and recognition results on an outdoor sequence

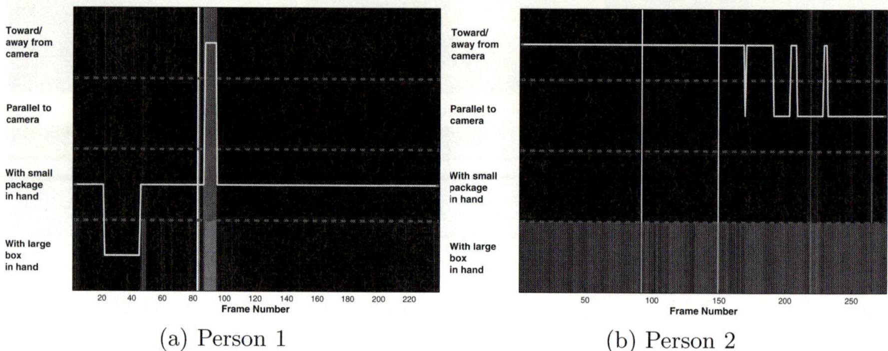

(a) Person 1   (b) Person 2

Fig. 6. Similarity Matrices, shown for the activities of of Person 1 in Figure 5(a), and Person 2 in Figure 5(b)-(c), respectively. The thick yellow line represents recognized activity for each frame.

5   Conclusion and Future Work

In this paper, we proposed a novel dynamical feedback system for simultaneous and persistent tracking, recognition and segmentation of human activities from video sequences. We use a non-linear, non-stationary model defined on the shape of human body contour to represent activities. The activities are recognized by comparing the tracked observations against a prior database. At the same time, the performance of our tracking algorithm is analyzed using feedback signals and this helps in segmenting the shots of different activities. We demonstrate the effectiveness of our system by showing experimental results on real life video of different activities. As a part of future work, we will address the problems of recognizing complex multi-person activities in networks of video cameras.

References

1. Y. Bar-Shalom and T. E. Fortmann. *Tracking and Data Association*. Academic Press, 1988.
2. T.-J. Cham and J. M. Rehg. A multiple hypothesis approach to figure tracking. In *Computer Vision and Pattern Recognition*, 1999.

3. A. Doucet, N. Freitas, and N. Gordon. *Sequential Monte Carlo Methods in Practice*. Springer, 2001.

4. I. Dryden and K. Mardia. *Statistical Shape Analysis*. John Wiley and Sons, 1998.

5. W. Grimson, L. Lee, R. Romano, and C. Stauffer. Using Adaptive Tracking to Classify and Monitor Activities in a Site. In *Computer Vision and Pattern Recognition*, pages 22–31, 1998.

6. M. Harville and D. Li. Fast, integrated person tracking and activity recognition with plan-view templates from a single stereo camera. In *Computer Vision and Pattern Recognition*, pages II: 398–405, 2004.

7. W. Hu, T. Tan, L. Wang, and S. Maybank. A survey on visual surveillance of object motion and behaviors. *IEEE Trans. on Systems, Man, Cybernetics - Part C: Applications and Reviews*, 34(3), 2004.

8. M. Isard and A. Blake. Condensation: Conditional Density Propagation for Visual Tracking. *International Journal of Computer Vision*, pages 5–28, 1998.

9. J. Jackson, A. Yezzi, and S. Soatto. Tracking deformable moving objects under severe occlusions. In *IEEE Conference on Decision and control*, Dec, 2004.

10. Y. Li and T. Boult. Understanding Images of Graphical User Interfaces: A new approach to activity recognition for visual surveillance. In *ACM UIST*, 2003.

11. L. Liao, D. Fox, and H. Kautz. Location-based activity recognition using relational markov networks. In *Proc. of the International Joint Conference on Artificial Intelligence*, 2005.

12. M. Niethammer and A. Tannenbaum. Dynamic level sets for visual tracking. In *IEEE Conference on Decision and Control*, 2004.

13. B. North, A. Blake, M. Isard, and J. Rittscher. Learning and classification of complex dynamics. *IEEE Trans. on Pattern Analysis and Machine Intelligence*, 22(9):1016–1034, 2000.

14. Y. Rathi, N. Vaswani, A. Tannenbaum, and A. Yezzi. Particle Filtering for Geometric Active Contours with Application to Tracking Moving and Deforming Objects. In *Computer Vision and Pattern Recognition*, 2005.

15. J. Rittscher and A. Blake. Classification of human body motion. In *International Conf. on Computer Vision*, volume 2, pages 634–639, 1999.

16. N. Vaswani. Change Detection in Partially Observed Nonlinear Dynamic Systems with Unknown Change Parameters. In *American Control Conference*, 2004.

17. N. Vaswani and R. Chellappa. NonStationary Shape Activities. In *Proc. of IEEE Conf. on Decision and Control*, 2005.

18. N. Vaswani, A. Roy-Chowdhury, and R. Chellappa. Shape Activities: A Continuous State HMM for Moving/Deforming Shapes with Application to Abnormal Activity Detection. *IEEE Trans. on Image Processing*, October 2005.

19. Y. Zhai and M. Shah. A general framework for temporal video scene segmentation. In *International Conf. on Computer Vision*, 2005.

20. S. Zhou, R. Chellappa, and B. Moghaddam. Visual Tracking and Recognition Using Appearance-Adaptive Models in Particle Filters. *IEEE Trans. on Image Processing*, 13(11):1491–1506, November 2004.

21. S. Zhou, V. Krueger, and R. Chellappa. Probabilistic recognition of human faces from video. *Computer Vision and Image Understanding*, 91:214–245, July-August 2003.

Inverse Composition for Multi-kernel Tracking

Rémi Megret, Mounia Mikram, and Yannick Berthoumieu

UMR 5131, Laboratoire d'Automatique, Productique et Signal,
Université Bordeaux 1/ENSEIRB, Talence, France
{megret, mikram, berthoum}@enseirb.fr

Abstract. Existing multi-kernel tracking methods are based on a forwards additive motion model formulation. However this approach suffers from the need to estimate an update matrix for each iteration. This paper presents a general framework that extends the existing approach and that allows to introduce a new inverse compositional formulation which shifts the computation of the update matrix to a one time initialisation step. The proposed approach thus reduces the computational complexity of each iteration, compared to the existing forwards approach. The approaches are compared both in terms of algorithmic complexity and quality of the estimation.

1   Introduction

Tracking based on color distributions [1,2,3,4] has drawn increasing interest recently, as it offers a flexible and generic framework for object tracking in videos. It is especially useful for non rigid objects, for which the integration of the information over spatially extended regions offers more allowance to slight misalignment compared to pixel based template matching [5].

The basic kernel tracking method associates a single color distribution to an object, and maximises the color similarity with a reference model using Mean-Shift [1]. Alternative approaches such as particle filters may be involved in order to take into account tracking ambiguities [6].

The parameter estimation of higher order motion models such as affine or homographic motion involves the use of an extended representation, which incorporates more information than just color. This was experimented with spatial-color distribution [7] [8] as well as with multi-kernel color distributions, where each spatial kernel is associated to a distinct color model [3,4]. An intermediate approach was recently proposed in [9] where a "texture of blobs" is used that is constituted of many overlapping kernels covering the surface of the object to track.

One of the difficulty with such multi-kernel tracking is the increased complexity introduced by the additional parameters to estimate. Previous works adopted an iterative optimisation framework based on Gauss-Newton optimisation [3,4], on quasi-Newton optimisation [9], or on the trust-region approach [10]. These methods are all based on an additive approach, where the motion parameters are incrementally refined by adding a correcting parameter until convergence.

P. Kalra and S. Peleg (Eds.): ICVGIP 2006, LNCS 4338, pp. 480–491, 2006.
© Springer-Verlag Berlin Heidelberg 2006

The goal of this paper is to propose a new framework for multi-kernel tracking, similar to the approach Baker and Matthews [11] introduced in image template based tracking. It covers the existing multi-kernel tracking approach, while allowing to derive a new efficient technique : the inverse compositional approach allows to use a fixed Jacobian for gradient based optimisation, which shifts a computationally costly part of the algorithm to the initialisation step and decreases the complexity of online computations.

The rest of the paper is organised as follows. In section 2, multi-kernel color distribution tracking will be exposed and the compositional framework introduced. This will serve as a global framework to present, in section 3, the classical forwards additive approach and, in section 4, the proposed inverse compositional approach. Finally, the techniques will be experimented and compared in section 5.

2   Tracking Using Color Distributions

This section presents the compositional framework for multi-kernel color distribution tracking. After formalising the notion of a multi-kernel color distribution, the framework will be exposed, and be shown to cover both the existing forwards additive approach, and a new inverse compositional approach.

2.1   Motion Model

The tracking occurs between two images I_{ref} and I related by an unknown 2D transformation $\mathbf{f}$ of parameter $\boldsymbol{\theta}^*$,

$$\forall \mathbf{x} \in \mathcal{D} \quad I_{\mathrm{ref}}(\mathbf{x}) = I(\mathbf{f}^{-1}(\mathbf{x}, \boldsymbol{\theta}^*)) \tag{1}$$

where $\mathcal{D}$ represents a region of interest in image I_{ref}.

In the sequel, the motion model is assumed to exhibit a group property. This is the case for most models of interest, and in particular non degenerate homographies or affine motion [11]. The latter will be exploited in this paper. For the sake of notational convenience, the group property is extended to the parameters using the following notations:

$$\mathbf{f}(\,\cdot\,, \boldsymbol{\theta}^{-1}) = \mathbf{f}^{-1}(\,\cdot\,, \boldsymbol{\theta}) \tag{2}$$

$$\mathbf{f}(\,\cdot\,, \Delta\boldsymbol{\theta} \circ \boldsymbol{\theta}) = \mathbf{f}(\,\cdot\,, \Delta\boldsymbol{\theta}) \circ \mathbf{f}(\,\cdot\,, \boldsymbol{\theta}) = \mathbf{f}(\mathbf{f}(\,\cdot\,, \boldsymbol{\theta}), \Delta\boldsymbol{\theta}) \tag{3}$$

and $\boldsymbol{\theta} = 0$ represents the parameters of the identity transformation.

2.2   Multi-Kernel Color Distribution

Color distribution tracking is based on the computation of the color distribution of an image region. In the sequel, this region is defined using real valued kernels, that associate a weight to each pixel. In order to estimate non-translational movements, a general multi-kernel approach is used, that is now presented. The reader interested in a discussion on the choice of the kernels is refered to [3].

Given
- a set of κ spatial kernels $(K_1, \ldots K_\kappa)$ defined as piecewise differentiable weighting functions $K_k(\mathbf{x})$ expressed in the reference coordinates $\mathbf{x}$,
- a parametric motion model $\mathbf{f}(\cdot, \boldsymbol{\theta})$ with parameter vector $\boldsymbol{\theta}$, which transforms each point $\mathbf{m}$ in the current image coordinates into a point $\mathbf{x} = \mathbf{f}(\mathbf{m}, \boldsymbol{\theta})$ in the reference coordinates, and its inverse transformation $\mathbf{m} = \mathbf{f}^{-1}(\mathbf{x}, \boldsymbol{\theta})$,
- a quantification indicative function $\delta_u(\cdot)$ whose value is 1 for colors belonging to color bin u and null otherwise,

the *multi-kernel color distribution* of image I with parameters $\boldsymbol{\theta}$ is defined as a vector $\mathbf{q}(I, \boldsymbol{\theta}) = (q_{k,u}(I, \boldsymbol{\theta}))_{k,u}$, where

$$q_{k,u}(I, \boldsymbol{\theta}) = C_k \iint_{\mathbf{x} \in \mathbb{R}^2} K_k(\mathbf{x})\, \delta_u(I(\mathbf{f}^{-1}(\mathbf{x}, \boldsymbol{\theta})))d\mathbf{x} \qquad (4)$$

The normalisation constant C_k is chosen such that $\sum_u q_{k,u}(I, \boldsymbol{\theta}) = 1$ for all k.

The subvector $(q_{u,k}(I, \boldsymbol{\theta}))_u$ represents the local color distribution, over the spatial kernel K_k, of image I after it has been aligned onto the reference coordinates according to parameters $\boldsymbol{\theta}$. The relationship of (4) with expressions used in previous works [3,4,9] will be discussed in section 4.2. The choice of this expression is motivated by its invariance with respect to any 2D motion model group, even non-affine ones. Indeed

$$\mathbf{q}(I, \boldsymbol{\theta}) = \mathbf{q}(I(\mathbf{f}(\cdot, \boldsymbol{\theta}^{-1})), 0) \qquad (5)$$

or more generally

$$\mathbf{q}(I, \Delta\boldsymbol{\theta} \circ \boldsymbol{\theta}) = \mathbf{q}(I(\mathbf{f}(\cdot, \boldsymbol{\theta}^{-1})), \Delta\boldsymbol{\theta}) \qquad (6)$$

2.3   Compositional Framework for Multi-Kernel Tracking

Let us now consider two images related by equation (1). In the following, $\mathbf{p}$ will be used for the reference image I_{ref} and $\mathbf{q}$ for the current image I

$$\mathbf{p}(\boldsymbol{\theta}) = \mathbf{q}(I_{\text{ref}}, \boldsymbol{\theta}) \qquad \text{and} \qquad \mathbf{q}(\boldsymbol{\theta}) = \mathbf{q}(I, \boldsymbol{\theta}) \qquad (7)$$

Because of (6) the following holds for any $\boldsymbol{\theta}_p$:

$$\mathbf{p}(\boldsymbol{\theta}_p) = \mathbf{q}(\boldsymbol{\theta}_p \circ \boldsymbol{\theta}^*) \qquad (8)$$

Multi-kernel image alignment can be formalised as finding $\boldsymbol{\theta}_p$ and $\boldsymbol{\theta}_q$ that minimise the dissimilarity between $\mathbf{p}(\boldsymbol{\theta}_p)$ and $\mathbf{q}(\boldsymbol{\theta}_q)$.

The actual matching relies on the minimisation of an error measure $E(\boldsymbol{\theta}_q, \boldsymbol{\theta}_p)$. Several error functions can be used, such as the Bhattacharyya distance or the Kullback-Leibler divergence. Following [4] and [3], the Matusita's metric will be used in this work:

$$E(\boldsymbol{\theta}_q, \boldsymbol{\theta}_p) = \sum_{k,u} e_{k,u}(\boldsymbol{\theta}_q, \boldsymbol{\theta}_p)^2 \qquad (9)$$

with a bin specific error vector $\mathbf{e}_{k,u}(\boldsymbol{\theta}_q, \boldsymbol{\theta}_p)$

$$e_{k,u}(\boldsymbol{\theta}_q, \boldsymbol{\theta}_p) = \sqrt{q_{k,u}(\boldsymbol{\theta}_q)} - \sqrt{p_{k,u}(\boldsymbol{\theta}_p)} \tag{10}$$

By equating $\boldsymbol{\theta}_q$ and $\boldsymbol{\theta}_p \circ \boldsymbol{\theta}^*$ in equation 8, the estimated alignment parameter is then

$$\boldsymbol{\theta}^* = \boldsymbol{\theta}_p^{-1} \circ \boldsymbol{\theta}_q \tag{11}$$

This formalisation shows the central role that composition plays for the image alignment problem using multi-kernel distributions. We call it the compositional framework, as the effective parameter estimation $\boldsymbol{\theta}^*$ is obtained by composing the estimates $\boldsymbol{\theta}_q$ and $\boldsymbol{\theta}_p$.

This framework covers existing *forwards additive* multi-kernel tracking methods [3,4,9], which optimise the error criterion with respect to $\boldsymbol{\theta}_q = \hat{\boldsymbol{\theta}} + \Delta\boldsymbol{\theta}$. We propose to optimise with respect to $\boldsymbol{\theta}_p = \Delta\boldsymbol{\theta}$ instead, which leads to *inverse compositional* multi-kernel tracking.

The terms forward additive and inverse compositional come from the analogy with the classification Baker and Matthews [11] proposed in the context of image template tracking. The framework we introduced formalises the adaptation of this classification to the context of multi-kernel histogram based representation. In particular, a more complex error function has to be taken into account, which is a distance between histograms derived from the images, instead of direct pixelwise compensated image difference. This will play a role in the gradient based optimisation.

The forwards additive approach will be briefly presented in section 3, in order to compare its structure to the proposed inverse compositional approach, which will be presented in section 4.

3   Forwards Additive Optimisation

The forwards additive approach used in [3] relies on the Gauss-Newton optimisation of the error $E(\hat{\boldsymbol{\theta}} + \Delta\boldsymbol{\theta}, 0)$ with respect to $\Delta\boldsymbol{\theta}$, where a single iteration is estimated using

$$\Delta\boldsymbol{\theta} = A(\hat{\boldsymbol{\theta}}) \, \mathbf{e}(\hat{\boldsymbol{\theta}}, 0) \tag{12}$$

where $A(\hat{\boldsymbol{\theta}})$ is an update matrix

$$A(\hat{\boldsymbol{\theta}}) = -\left(\mathbf{J}_{\mathbf{e}|\hat{\theta}}{}^{t} \mathbf{J}_{\mathbf{e}|\hat{\theta}}\right)^{-1} \mathbf{J}_{\mathbf{e}|\hat{\theta}}{}^{t} \tag{13}$$

and $\mathbf{J}_{\mathbf{e}|\hat{\theta}}$ represents the Jacobian of the error vector $\mathbf{e}(\boldsymbol{\theta}, 0)$ with respect to $\boldsymbol{\theta}$, computed at $\boldsymbol{\theta} = \hat{\boldsymbol{\theta}}$. It can be expressed by using the gradient of $e_{u,k}$ with respect to $\boldsymbol{\theta}$, as well as the partial derivative of $\mathbf{e}$ according to each coefficient θ_m of $\boldsymbol{\theta}$

$$\mathbf{J}_{\mathbf{e}|\hat{\theta}} = \begin{bmatrix} \vdots \\ \nabla_{e_{u,k}(\theta)|\hat{\theta}} \\ \vdots \end{bmatrix} = \begin{bmatrix} \cdots & \left.\dfrac{\partial\mathbf{e}(\boldsymbol{\theta})}{\partial\theta_m}\right|_{\hat{\theta}} & \cdots \end{bmatrix} \tag{14}$$

A robust estimator version of this approach is used in [4]. In [9], a quasi-Newton optimisation was used instead, based on $J_{E|\hat{\theta}}$ which also depends on $\hat{\theta}$.

The parameter update follows the forwards additive scheme of (15), and the whole process is repeated until convergence

$$\hat{\theta} \leftarrow \hat{\theta} + \Delta\theta \tag{15}$$

The expression of $J_{e|\hat{\theta}}$ depends on the error metric used. In particular, when using the Matusita's objective function of equation (10),

$$\mathbf{J}_{\mathbf{e}|\hat{\theta}} = \frac{1}{2}\mathrm{diag}(\mathbf{q}(\hat{\theta}))^{-1/2}\mathbf{J}_{\mathbf{q}|\hat{\theta}} \tag{16}$$

where $\mathbf{J}_{\mathbf{q}|\theta}$, the Jacobian of $\mathbf{q}(\theta)$, will be studied in more details in section 4.2.

4   Inverse Compositional Optimisation

In the previous approach, the computation of equations (12) and (13) is the bottleneck of the algorithm. Indeed, the update matrix $A(\hat{\theta})$ needs to be computed for each new iteration, which involves in particular the computation of $\mathbf{J}_{e|\theta}{}^{t}\mathbf{J}_{e|\theta}$.

An alternative approach is now proposed, that takes advantage of the general framework introduced in section 2.3 and allows to use a constant update matrix A, which can be pre-computed once during the model initialisation.

4.1   Principle

In a similar way as the forwards approach, a Gauss-Newton iteration is computed, but the parameter correction now applies to the kernel position in the reference image. The Gauss-Newton parameter update of $E(\hat{\theta}, \Delta\theta)$ with respect to $\Delta\theta$ satisfies:

$$\Delta\theta = A\ \mathbf{e}(\hat{\theta}, 0) \tag{17}$$

The update matrix A is now a constant matrix

$$A = -\left(\mathbf{J}_{\hat{\mathbf{e}}|0}{}^{t}\mathbf{J}_{\hat{\mathbf{e}}|0}\right)^{-1}\mathbf{J}_{\hat{\mathbf{e}}|0}{}^{t} \tag{18}$$

where $\mathbf{J}_{\hat{\mathbf{e}}|0}$ represents the Jacobian of $\mathbf{e}(\hat{\theta}, \Delta\theta)$ with respect to $\Delta\theta$ computed at $\Delta\theta = 0$. When using the Matusita metric, $\mathbf{J}_{\hat{\mathbf{e}}|0}$ does not depend on $\hat{\theta}$.

$$\mathbf{J}_{\hat{\mathbf{e}}|0} = -\frac{1}{2}\mathrm{diag}(\mathbf{p}(0))^{-1/2}\mathbf{J}_{\mathbf{p}|0} \tag{19}$$

The estimation rule (17) can be compared to the analogous rule (12) in the forwards approach, as it has the same structure. The main difference is that in the inverse approach, the A matrix does not depend on $\hat{\theta}$ anymore, which allows to pre-compute it offline, thus removing most of the online complexity.

In this approach, the correction parameter $\Delta\boldsymbol{\theta}$ represents an update on the kernel locations in the reference image. In order to convert it into an updated parameter vector for the motion between the two images, the compositional framework is invoked through equation (11), which corresponds to the update rule:

$$\hat{\boldsymbol{\theta}} \leftarrow \Delta\boldsymbol{\theta}^{-1} \circ \hat{\boldsymbol{\theta}} \tag{20}$$

The estimate $\hat{\boldsymbol{\theta}}$ is iteratively updated while it corresponds to a decrease of the error $E(\hat{\boldsymbol{\theta}}, 0)$ and until convergence.

4.2 Jacobian Computation

The computation of the Jacobian $\mathbf{J}_{\mathbf{p},0}$ or its more general form $\mathbf{J}_{\mathbf{q},\boldsymbol{\theta}}$ is not direct from equation (4), as δ_u is not easily differentiable. This part is detailed in the current section through the computation of the gradient of $q_{k,u}$.

An equivalent formulation of $q_{k,u}$ is used in [9], which is based on the coordinates $\mathbf{m}$ in the current image :

$$q_{k,u}(I, \boldsymbol{\theta}) = C_k \iint_{\mathbf{m}} K_k(\mathbf{f}(\mathbf{m}, \boldsymbol{\theta}))\, \delta_u(I(\mathbf{m}))\, j(\mathbf{m}, \boldsymbol{\theta})\, d\mathbf{m} \tag{21}$$

where $j(\mathbf{m}, \boldsymbol{\theta}) = \left|\mathbf{J}_{\mathbf{f}(\mathbf{m},\boldsymbol{\theta})|\mathbf{m}}\right|$ is the absolute value of the determinant of the Jacobian of $\mathbf{f}$ with respect to $\mathbf{m}$.

For affine transformations, $j(\mathbf{m}, \boldsymbol{\theta})$ is constant with respect to $\mathbf{m}$, which leads to a simplified expression

$$q_{k,u}(I, \boldsymbol{\theta}) = C_{k,\boldsymbol{\theta}} \iint_{\mathbf{m}} K_k(\mathbf{f}(\mathbf{m}, \boldsymbol{\theta}))\, \delta_u(I(\mathbf{m}))\, d\mathbf{m} \tag{22}$$

with $C_{k,\boldsymbol{\theta}} = C_k j(\mathbf{m}, \boldsymbol{\theta})$ corresponding to the kernel normalisation parameter that now depends on $\boldsymbol{\theta}$. This equation is very similar to the definitions of $q_{k,u}$ used in [4,3]. Note that for non-affine motion this equivalence does not hold, so that the computation of the Jacobian for more complex models should instead use the full expression (21).

By differentiating (22) and after taking into account the kernel normalisation $\sum_u q_{k,u} = 1$, the gradient can be simplified as (23).

$$\nabla_{q_{u,k}|\hat{\boldsymbol{\theta}}} = C_{k,\boldsymbol{\theta}} \iint_{\mathbf{m}} \nabla_{K_k(\mathbf{x})|\mathbf{f}(\mathbf{m},\hat{\boldsymbol{\theta}})}\, \mathbf{J}_{\mathbf{f}(\mathbf{m},\boldsymbol{\theta})|\hat{\boldsymbol{\theta}}}\, (\delta_u(I(\mathbf{m})) - q_{k,u}(\hat{\boldsymbol{\theta}})) d\mathbf{m} \tag{23}$$

In the simpler case of inverse composition, the Jacobian is

$$\nabla_{p_{u,k}|0} = C_k \iint_{\mathbf{x}} \nabla_{K_k(\mathbf{x})|\mathbf{x}}\, \mathbf{J}_{\mathbf{f}(\mathbf{x},\Delta\boldsymbol{\theta})|0}\, (\delta_u(I_{\mathrm{ref}}(\mathbf{x})) - p_{k,u}(0))\, d\mathbf{x} \tag{24}$$

The $-q_{k,u}(\hat{\boldsymbol{\theta}})$ term in the previous equations is related to the gradient of the normalisation constant $C_{k,\boldsymbol{\theta}}$ with respect to $\boldsymbol{\theta}$. Its influence is null for translation and rotation components, but should be taken into account when considering scale. Neglecting this term, as was done in [4], results in a biased estimation of the Jacobian. This is illustrated for the scale estimation in figure 3(d), where it leads to the under-estimation of the motion parameters.

From a practical point of view, the integrals must be replaced by discrete sums, on either the integer pixels $\{\mathbf{m}_i\}$ of the current image for (23) and (24), or on a regular grid $\{\mathbf{x}_j\}$ in the reference coordinates for (23). In order to improve the running time, this sampling was done on $\mathbf{x}$, which allows to pre-compute the kernel values and gradients at the sampling points.

A large choice of kernel functions can be used in this framework in the same way as with the forwards approach [3]. In this paper, Epanechnikov kernels are used. The kernel K_k, with centre $\mathbf{x}_k$ and covariance matrix B_k is defined by

$$K_k(\mathbf{x}) = \max(0, 1 - (\mathbf{x} - \mathbf{x}_k)^t B_k^{-1}(\mathbf{x} - \mathbf{x}_k)) \tag{25}$$

$$\nabla_{K_k(\mathbf{x})|\mathbf{x}} = -2(\mathbf{x} - \mathbf{x}_k)^t B_k^{-1} \quad \text{where } K_k(\mathbf{x}) > 0 \tag{26}$$

5   Experiments and Discussion

The properties of the forwards additive multi-kernel tracking approach have been experimentally studied and compared to the image template based approach in [4]. It was shown that the kernel approach allows for a larger region of convergence, thanks to the integration of the kernels. This comes at the cost of a slightly less precise alignment, which was resolved by combining the two approaches. As the inverse compositional approach proposed in this paper uses the same multi-kernel representation as the forwards approach, these experiments will not be duplicated here. The proposed method is expected to be faster to compute than the forwards method because of its algorithmic structure, while bearing similar tracking performances. This section will therefore be devoted to checking this hypothesis.

5.1   Computational Performance

The algorithmic structures of both the forwards additive and the inverse compositional are summed up and compared in figure 1.

For the complexity analysis, the following notations will be used : κ is the number of kernels, P the mean number of pixels for which a kernel is non null, U the number of color bins in each color histogram and T the number of degrees of freedom in $\boldsymbol{\theta}$. The cost of each step is of the order of $\mathcal{O}(\kappa P)$ for $\{1\}$ and $\{3\}$, $\mathcal{O}(\kappa U)$ for $\{4\}$, $\mathcal{O}(\kappa P T)$ for $\{5\}$, $\mathcal{O}(\kappa U T^2)$ for the computation of $\mathbf{J}_{e|\hat{\boldsymbol{\theta}}}{}^t \mathbf{J}_{e|\hat{\boldsymbol{\theta}}}$ and $\mathcal{O}(T^3)$ for its inversion in $\{6\}$, and $\mathcal{O}(\kappa U T)$ for $\{7\}$.

Given that U and P are large compared to the other parameters (of the order of 100 to 1000), steps $\{5\}$ and $\{6\}$ are the two most costly steps in the algorithm. Therefore, moving them to a pre-computation phase decreases the overall complexity of each iteration significantly.

In particular, with our current Matlab implementation, one iteration for $\kappa = 9$ kernels each covering $P = 150$ pixels and with the color quantised into $U = 64$

Forwards Additive	Inverse Compositional
Pre-computations	Pre-computations
{1} Reference distribution $\mathbf{p}$ (7)	**{1}** Reference distribution $\mathbf{p}$ (7) **{5}** Jacobian $\mathbf{J}_{\mathbf{e}\vert 0}$ (19) (24) **{6}** Update matrix A (18)
For each new frame	For each new frame
{2} Initial estimate $\hat{\boldsymbol{\theta}}$	**{2}** Initial estimate $\hat{\boldsymbol{\theta}}$
Iterate until convergence:	Iterate until convergence:
{3} Current distribution $\mathbf{q}(\hat{\boldsymbol{\theta}})$ (7) **{4}** Current error $\mathbf{e}(\hat{\boldsymbol{\theta}},0)$ (10) **{5}** Jacobian $\mathbf{J}_{\mathbf{e}\vert\hat{\boldsymbol{\theta}}}$ (16) (23) **{6}** Update matrix $A(\hat{\boldsymbol{\theta}})$ (13) **{7}** Step $\Delta\boldsymbol{\theta}$ (12) **{8}** New estimate : $\hat{\boldsymbol{\theta}} \leftarrow \hat{\boldsymbol{\theta}} + \Delta\boldsymbol{\theta}$	**{3}** Current distribution $\mathbf{q}(\hat{\boldsymbol{\theta}})$ (7) **{4}** Current error $\mathbf{e}(\hat{\boldsymbol{\theta}},0)$ (10) **{7}** Step $\Delta\boldsymbol{\theta}$ (17) **{8}** New estimate : $\hat{\boldsymbol{\theta}} \leftarrow \Delta\boldsymbol{\theta}^{-1} \circ \hat{\boldsymbol{\theta}}$

Fig. 1. Algorithm comparison. The pre-computations occur only during the model initialisation, and is not repeated for a new frame. For each step, the equation that defines the related computation is shown at the right.

color bins with an affine motion model ($T = 6$) requires 168 ms with the inverse compositional approach, instead of 359 ms with the classical forwards additive approach.

5.2 Convergence Properties

The forwards additive approach is a typical Gauss-Newton optimisation of the error $E(\boldsymbol{\theta},0)$. The inverse compositional approach adopts an hybrid scheme. Indeed, the general optimisation criterion is still $E(\hat{\boldsymbol{\theta}},0)$, but each iteration uses the $E(\hat{\boldsymbol{\theta}}, \Delta\boldsymbol{\theta})$ criterion. These functions both express the matching error as was shown in section 2.3. They are not identical when the error is large, which is why the convergence properties of the two approaches are now compared.

Figure 3(a-d) shows the return map of the two methods (forwards additive from section 3, inverse compositional from section 4), when perturbated with a pure translation (b), a pure rotation (c), and a pure scale (d). Nine Epanechnikov kernels centred on a regular 3×3 grid were used, as shown[1] in (a).

Overall, both approaches yield similar results. Indeed, both the forwards and the inverse methods approximate well the correction for small perturbations, and tend to under-estimate the correction for larger perturbations. This observation reflect the fact that both are based on a linearisation of the error around the initial parameters, which is valid for small perturbations.

---

[1] Test image courtesy of Krystian Mikolajczyk, `http://www.robots.ox.ac.uk/~vgg`.

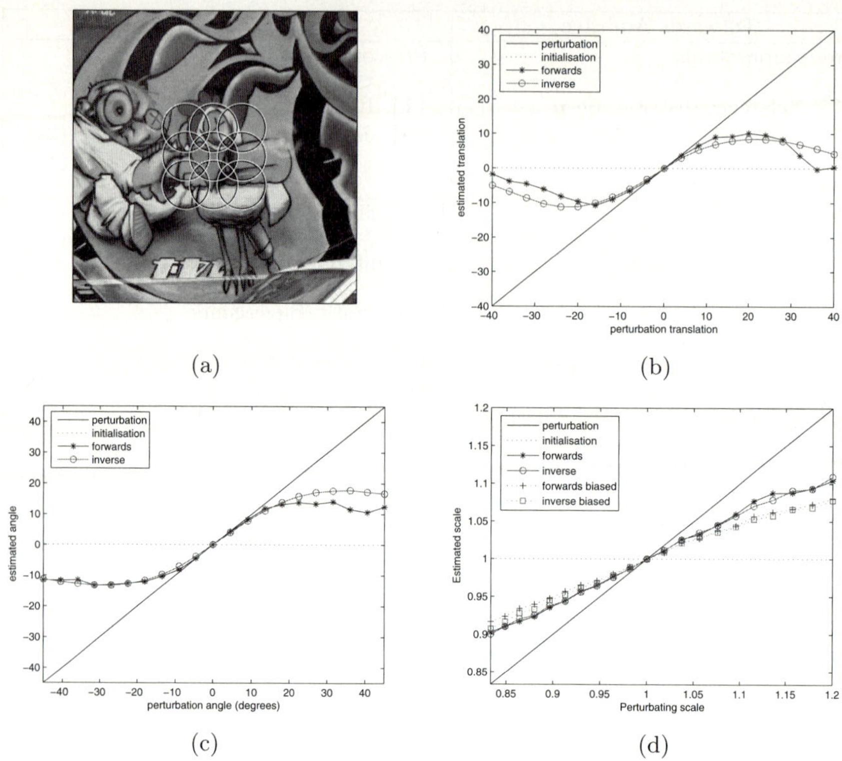

(a)   (b)

(c)   (d)

Fig. 2. Comparison of the parameter estimation of a single iteration for controled affine perturbations (see section 5.2). (a) Test image, with the supports of the nine Epanechnikov kernels overlayed. Return maps (corrected parameters depending on the perturbated parameters: the closer to the perturbation the better) for (b) an horizontal shift, (c) a rotation around the centre of the image.

The scale estimation exhibits a systematic under-estimation on this example. This is observed with other classical kernel configurations, but not when using a totally unambiguous image made of squares with unique colors. Although the unbiased approach presented in section 4.2 slightly improves the estimation, further work is needed to explain this behaviour. The estimations are nevertheless in the correct direction even for large perturbations, which make the iterative optimisation eventually converge to the correct parameters even in that case.

The quality of the parameter estimartion is also evaluated in more general conditions in figure 3(e-f), for one single iteration. The perturbations are a combination of random translations within $[-20, 20]$ pixels, rotations within $[-20, 20]$ degrees and scale within $[1.2^{-1}, 1.2]$.

The mean spatial error D corresponds to the average of the spatial error of the kernel centers, evaluated in the reference coordinates. These two measures allow to evaluate translation, rotation and scale errors in an unified manner.

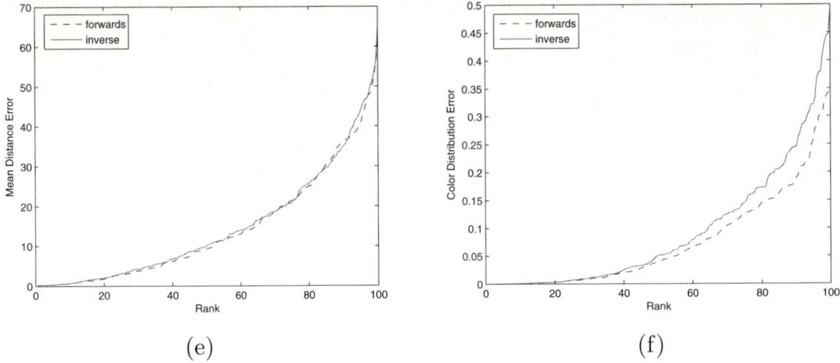

(e)   (f)

Fig. 3. Comparison of the parameter estimation quality of a single iteration for random affine perturbations (see section 5.2). Ranked mean spatial error (e) and color distribution error (f).

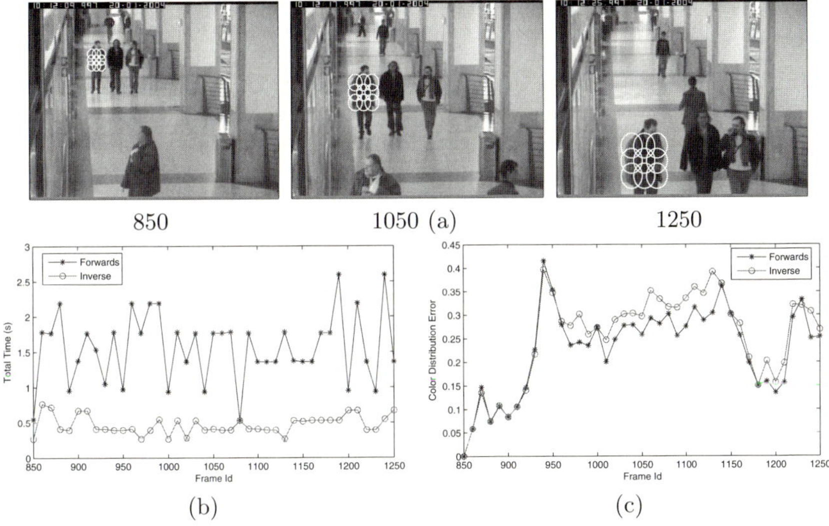

(b)   (c)

Fig. 4. Tracking example with scale change on CAVIAR video for the inverse compositional approach (a). Comparison of the computational time (b) and the color distribution error $E(\boldsymbol{\theta}, 0)$ after convergence (c) for each frame on the same video, with both approaches.

Results are sorted by increasing error. These results show that the inverse approach has a slightly larger color distribution error than the forwards approach (f), which can be explained by the fact that it does not operate directly on the optimisation criterion $E(\hat{\boldsymbol{\theta}}, 0)$. This difference do not seem to impact the parameter estimation, though, as the corrected parameter appear to be equally good from a spatial point of view (e).

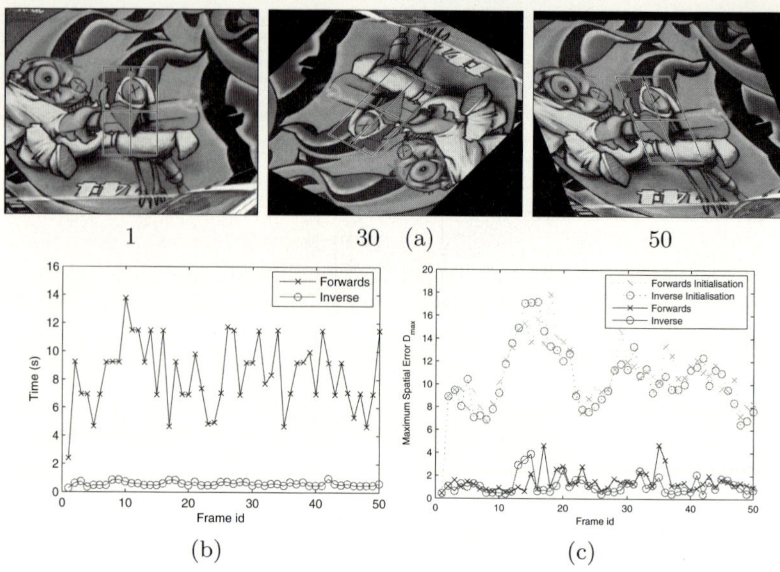

Fig. 5. Tracking example for a video with affine distortions, with the parameter estimation overlayed for the inverse approach (a). Comparison of the computational time (b). Comparison of the mean spatial error (c); the error for the initialisation at each frame is plotted to show the amount of correction needed on this sequence.

5.3   Tracking

In this section the computational performance and the quality of estimation are compared in tracking conditions: a person with scale change[2] in figure 4 and an image part with affine distortions in figure 5. Both trackings use 9 Epanechnikov kernels centred on a regular 3×3 grid. The parameters obtained with the forwards and the inverse approach are very similar, which is supported by similar mean spatial errors D with respect to the ground truth in figure 5-c, and comparable color distribution errors E in figure 5-c. In the last case, a slightly lower error is observed for the forwards approach, which was discussed in section 5.2. The computational time is in both cases significantly reduced by using the inverse approach instead of the forwards approach.

6   Conclusion

This paper presented the adaptation and the application of inverse composition, which is already used in image template tracking, to tracking with multi-kernel color distributions. The multi-kernel tracking paradigm was reformalised in order to cover both the existing forwards additive approach and a new inverse

---

[2] Video produced by the EC Funded CAVIAR project/IST 2001 37540.
`http://homepages.inf.ed.ac.uk/rbf/CAVIAR/`

compositional approach. The quality of the parameter estimation of the new technique is similar to the multi-kernel forwards additive approach, while shifting the computational burden from each iteration to a one-time initialisation step.

The structure of the proposed approach relies on an iterative optimisation with a constant update matrix A, which is estimated by inverting the Jacobian of the error function. This structure offers the possibility to introduce alternative forms for A, such as the hyperplane approximation [12], in a multi-kernel context.

Other interesting problems for future research would be to study how illumination changes, which can be taken into account in the forwards approach [4,9], could be handled in an inverse compositional approach, and how the choice of the kernel configuration impacts the performances of the method.

References

1. Comaniciu, D., Ramesh, V., Meer, P.: Kernel-based object tracking. IEEE Transactions on Pattern Analysis and Machine Intelligence **25** (2003) 564–575
2. Fan, Z., Wu, Y., Yang, M.: Multiple collaborative kernel tracking. In: IEEE Conference on Computer Vision and Pattern Recognition, San Diego, CA, USA (2005) 502–509
3. Hager, G.D., Dewan, M., Stewart, C.V.: Multiple kernel tracking with SSD. In: IEEE Conference on Computer Vision and Pattern Recognition, Washington, DC, USA (2004) 790–797
4. Georgescu, B., Meer, P.: Point matching under large image deformations and illumination changes. IEEE Transactions on Pattern Analysis and Machine Intelligence **26** (2004) 674–688
5. Baker, S., Matthews, I.: Lucas-kanade 20 years on: A unifying framework. International Journal of Computer Vision **56** (2004) 221–255
6. Pérez, P., Hue, C., Vermaak, J., Gangnet, M.: Color-based probabilistic tracking. In: European Conference on Computer Vision, ECCV'2002, LNCS 2350, Copenhaguen, Denmark (2002) 661–675
7. Elgammal, A.M., Duraiswami, R., Davis, L.S.: Probabilistic tracking in joint feature-spatial spaces. In: IEEE Conference on Computer Vision and Pattern Recognition, Madison, WI, USA (2003) 781–788
8. Zhang, H., Huang, W., Huang, Z., Li, L.: Affine object tracking with kernel-based spatial-color representation. In: IEEE Conference on Computer Vision and Pattern Recognition, San Diego, CA, USA (2005) 293–300
9. Guskov, I.: Kernel-based template alignment. In: IEEE Conference on Computer Vision and Pattern Recognition, New-York, USA (2006) 610–617
10. Liu, T.L., Chen, H.T.: Real-time tracking using trust-region methods. IEEE Transactions on Pattern Analysis and Machine Intelligence **26** (2003) 397–402
11. Baker, S., Matthews, I.: Equivalence and efficiency of image alignment algorithms. In: IEEE Conference on Computer Vision and Pattern Recognition, Kauai, HI, USA (2001) 1090–1097
12. Jurie, F., Dhome, M.: Hyperplane approximation for template matching. IEEE Transactions on Pattern Analysis and Machine Intelligence **24** (2002) 996–1000

Tracking Facial Features Using Mixture of Point Distribution Models

Atul Kanaujia, Yuchi Huang, and Dimitris Metaxas

Department of Computer Science, Rutgers University

Abstract. We present a generic framework to track shapes across large variations by learning non-linear shape manifold as overlapping, piecewise linear subspaces. We use landmark based shape analysis to train a Gaussian mixture model over the aligned shapes and learn a Point Distribution Model(PDM) for each of the mixture components. The target shape is searched by first maximizing the mixture probability density for the local feature intensity profiles along the normal followed by constraining the global shape using the most probable PDM cluster. The feature shapes are robustly tracked across multiple frames by dynamically switching between the PDMs. Our contribution is to apply ASM to the task of tracking shapes involving wide aspect changes and generic movements. This is achieved by incorporating shape priors that are learned over non-linear shape space and using them to learn the plausible shape space. We demonstrate the results on tracking facial features and provide several empirical results to validate our approach. Our framework runs close to real time at 25 frames per second and can be extended to predict pose angles using Mixture of Experts.

1   Introduction

Tracking deformable shapes across multiple viewpoints is an active area of research and has many applications in biometrics, facial expressions analysis and synthesis. Accurate reconstruction and tracking of 3D objects require well defined delineation of the object boundaries across multiple views.

Landmark based deformable models like Active Shape Models(ASM)[1]have proved effective for object shape interpretation in 2D images and have lead to advanced tools for statistical shape analysis. ASM detects features in the image by combining prior shape information with the observed image data. A major limitation of ASM is that it ignores the non-linear geometry of the shape manifold. Aspect changes of 3D objects causes shapes to vary non-linearly on a hyperspherical manifold. During tracking, the shape change is mostly smooth but in certain cases there may be discontinuities. For example, during a head rotation to the full profile face, some of the facial features may get occluded causing a drastic change in the shape. Besides the shape, the correspondences between the local 2D structures and the 3D object structures changes for the landmark based deformable models. The local grey level profiles at these landmarks also exhibit dramatic variations.

P. Kalra and S. Peleg (Eds.): ICVGIP 2006, LNCS 4338, pp. 492–503, 2006.
© Springer-Verlag Berlin Heidelberg 2006

There have been several efforts in the past to represent non-linear shape variations using kernel PCA and multi-layer perceptron[2,3]. The results from non-linear approaches largely depend on whether all the shape variations have been adequately represented in the training data. Discontinuities in the shape space may cause these models to generate implausible shapes. Kernel methods suffer from a major drawback to learn pre-image function for mapping shape in the feature space to the original space.

In this work we present a generic framework to learn non-linear shape space as overlapping piecewise linear subspaces. Our objective is to accurately track facial features across large head rotations. We use the Point Distribution Models(PDM) to represent the facial feature shapes and use ASM to detect them in the 2D image. The contribution of our work is: (1) Improve the specificity of ASM to handle large shape variations by learning non-linear shape manifold. (2)Real time framework to track shapes, and (3) Learning non-linearities for accurate prediction of 3D pose angles from 2D shapes. Our generic framework enables large scale automated training of different shapes from multiple viewpoints. The model can handle larger amount of variability and can be used to learn non-linear continuous shape manifold.

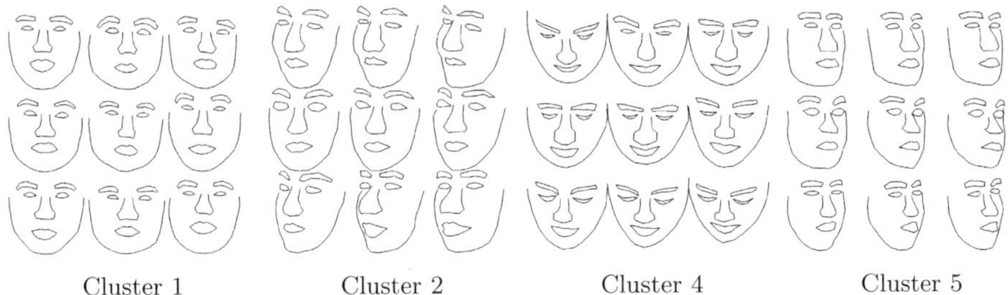

Cluster 1   Cluster 2   Cluster 4   Cluster 5

Fig. 1. Shapes from 4 different clusters of the training data set. Cluster 1 contains primarily frontal poses whereas Cluster 5 contains pose with head rotated to right.

2   Related Work

A large segment of research in the past decade focused on incorporating non-linear statistical models for learning shape manifold. Murase et. al. [4] showed that pose from multiple viewpoint when projected onto eigenspaces generates a 2D hypersphere manifold. Gong et. al [5] used non-linear projections onto the eigenspace to track and estimate pose from multiple viewpoints. Romdhani et al. [6] proposed an ASM based on Kernel PCA to learn shape variation of face due to yaw. More recently [7] has proposed a multi-view face alignment algorithm to infer visibilty of feature points across large rotations. The work stresses more on Bayesian estimation to learn shape parameters without providing insight into the shape space. Moreover their EM algorithm is impractical for real time shape fitting applications. Several prominent work exist on facial feature registration and tracking use appearance based models(AAM)[8,9]. [8] uses multiple independent 2D AAM models to learn correspondences between features of different viewpoints. We prefer ASM model over more accurate AAM model as shape based models can be easily generalized to a specific class of objects and is more robust to variations occurring due to changes in appearance and illumination compared to AAM. Most notable work in improving ASM to learn non-linearities in the training data is by Cootes et. al[3] in which large variation is shapes is captured by parametric Gaussian mixture density, learned in the principal subspace. In order to constrain the shape to lie within plausible shape subspace, the probability density is increased using gradient ascent. Our work differs from it in 2 aspects. Firstly we learn multivariate gaussian mixture density on the original shape space and not the parameteric subspace. Consequently the shape non-linearities are preserved across the clusters. We learn PDM within each cluster by projecting shapes of the clusters onto independent tangent spaces. Secondly we explicitly ensure that the learned sub-spaces are overlapping. This is required for efficient search and tracking of the shapes. In this respect our work follows from [10,11] although they primarily focus on shape analysis and surface learning. Unlike [8], our framework does not require explicit modeling of head pose angles. Although we use multivariate gaussian mixture model to learn initial clusters of the shape distribution, our subspaces are obtained by explicitly overlapping the clusters. ASM can be easily generalized to a specific class of objects and is more robust to variations occurring due to changes in appearance and illumination compared to Active Appearance Model(AAM). The faster convergence of ASM gives significant advantage over other shape analysis methods based on level sets and snakes.

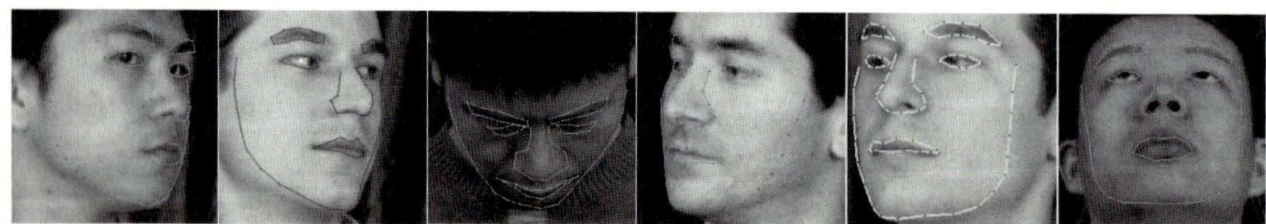

Fig. 2. *(Best Viewed in Color)*Shape fitting results on multiple Subjects across large head movement. The model recovers the pose irrespective of the initial cluster.

3   Learning Shape Manifold

Active Shape Model(ASM) is a landmark based model that tries to learn a statistical distribution over variations in shapes for a given class of objects. Changes in viewpoint causes the object shapes to lie on a hyper-sphere and cannot be accurately modeled using linear statistical tools. Face shape variation across multiple aspects is different across human subjects. A 30° head rotation will produce more distinctive shape variation for the face with raised features(eyes and nose) as compared to face with flat features. Hence learning independent ASM models and switching the models based on the learned pose, tends to generate abrupt shape changes and inaccurate fitting. Tracking shapes across multiple aspects requires modeling and synthesis of paths between the source and target shapes lying on a non-linear manifold. A complex, non-linear region can be approximated as a combination of multiple smaller linear subregions. Each subregion defines a hyper-ellipsoid within which a shape instance is constrained to lie. The search iteratively modify the shape by searching along the normals of the landmark points and simultaneously constraining it to lie on the shape manifold. The path between the source shape and the target shape is traversed by searching across multiple subspaces that constitute the non-linear shape surface. Tracking of features can be successfully leveraged by taking advantage of the heterogeneous nature of shape variations due to pose changes thereby causing these subregions overlap. The extent of overlap can be improved by having a fixed minimum mahalanobis radius for each subregion and including points across the cluster boundaries to learn the principal subspace. As a pre-requisite for shape analysis, all the 2D planar shapes are aligned to the common co-ordinate system using Generalized Procrustes Analysis[12]. The aligned shapes obtained from Procrustes analysis lie on a hyper-sphere. The tangent space approximation $\mathbf{T_s}$ projects the shapes on a hyper-plane normal to the mean vector and passing through it. Tangent space is a linear approximation of the general shape space so that the Procrustes distance can be approximated as euclidean distance be-

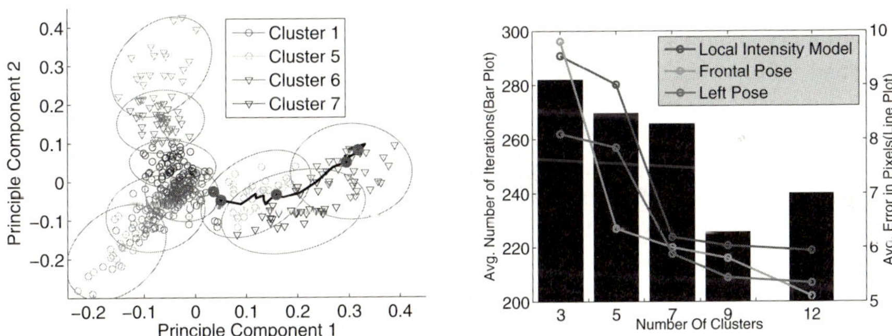

Fig. 3. *(Best Viewed in Color)***(Left)**The 9 overlapping subspaces (projected onto 2 Principal components) learned using GMM. The red cluster in the center is for the frontal pose. The other clusters corresponds to right, left and down movement. Iterative ASM search in fig.4 is shown as black path.**(Right***(Line Plot)***)** Increasing the number of clusters increases the accuracy of ASM for both the frontal and left head pose images. This is due to more accurate representation of the non-linear surface by piecewise linear regions. Increasing the number of gaussian components for the local intensity profile models(IPM) also improves the accuracy(red plot). **(Right***(Bar Plot)***)** The average ASM iterations(over 4 levels of gaussian pyramid) also improves with more gaussian components of the local intensity models but shows erratic increase for more than 10 components due to noise.

tween the planar shapes. The cluster analysis of shape is done in the global tangent space.

We assume a generative multivariate Gaussian mixture distribution for both the global shapes and the intensity profile models(IPMs). The conditional density of the shape $\mathbf{S_i}$ belonging to an N-class model $p(\mathbf{S_i}|\text{Cluster}) =$

$$\sum_{j=1}^{N} \gamma_j (2\pi)^{-\left(\frac{N}{2}\right)} \|\mathbf{C_j}\|^{-1/2} \exp\{-\frac{1}{2}(S_i - (\mu_j + P_j b_j))^T \mathbf{C_j}^{-1}(S_i - (\mu_j + P_j b_j))\} \quad (1)$$

We assume diagonal covariance matrix $\mathbf{C_j}$. γ_j are the cluster weights and (μ_j, P_j, b_j) are the mean, eigen matrix and eigen coefficients respectively for the principle subspace defined for each cluster. The clustering can be achieved by EM algorithm with variance flooring to ensure sufficient overlapping between the clusters. For each of the N clusters we learn a locally linear PDM using PCA and using the eigenvectors to capture significant variance in the cluster(98%). Unlike the method proposed in [3] where clustering is done in the PCA subspace, we use clustering in the global tangent space to decide class membership of the original shapes. Consequently the shape non-linearities are preserved across the clusters. We learn independent PDM within each cluster. Our algorithm allows more accurate modeling of the non-linear shape manifold using piecewise linear hyper-ellipsoid subspaces. The intensity profiles for the landmark points also exhibit large variation when trained over multiple head poses. The change in face aspects causes the profiles to vary considerably for the feature points that are occluded. The multivariate Gaussian mixture distribution(1) is learned for the local intensity profiles model(IPM) in order to capture variations that cannot be learned using a single PCA model.

Overlapping between Clusters: It is important that the adjacent clusters overlap sufficiently to ensure switching between subspaces during image search and tracking. The amount of overlap can be controlled by variance flooring during EM algorithm for clustering the data set. Setting minimum variance to a fixed value $\mathbf{V_{floor}}$ during the Maximization step, enables clusters to have larger expanse. Eventually the mahalanobis distance is used as a classification cost. The number of clusters also affect the degree of overlap. We can ensure subspace overlap by using boundary points between adjacent clusters to learn the subspace for both the clusters. These points can be obtained as nearest to the cluster center but not belonging to that cluster.

4   Image Search in the Clustered Shape Space

The search is done over 4 levels of Gaussian image pyramid. Conventional ASM uses Alternating Optimization(AO) technique to fit the shape by searching for

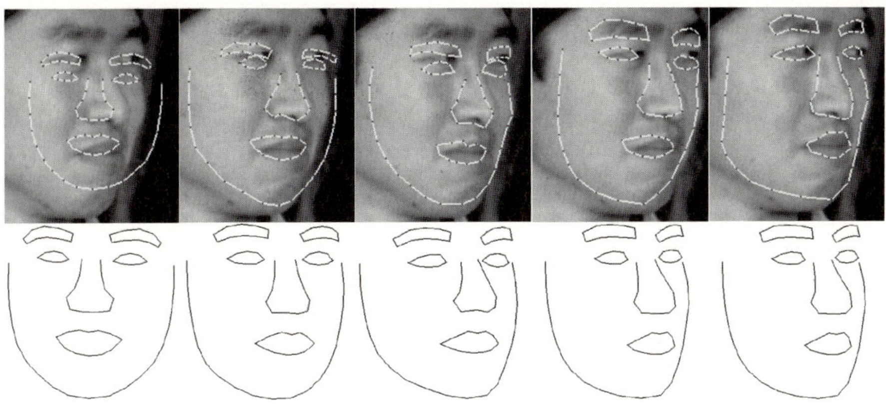

Fig. 4. Iterative search across multiple clusters to fit the face.The frames correspond to iteration 1(Cluster 1), iter. 3(Cluster 5), iter. 17(Cluster 7), iter. 23(Cluster 6) and final fit at iter. 33(Cluster 6) for level 4 of the Gaussian pyramid. The lower row shows the shapes of the cluster centers. Cluster 5 and Cluster 7 contain smaller head rotations while Cluster 6 contains extreme right pose. Fig. 3 shows the corresponding path of the iterative search.

the best matched profile along the normal followed by constraining the shape to lie within the learned subspace. The initial average shape is assumed to be in a region near to the target object. We use robust Viola-Jones face detector to extract a bounding box around the face and use its dimensions to initialize the search shape. The face detector has 99% detection rate for faces with off-plane and in-plane rotation angles $\pm 30^o$. We assign the nearest $Cluster_i$ to the average shape based on mahalanobis distance between the average shape and the cluster centers in the global tangent space. The image search is initiated at the top most level of the pyramid by searching IPM along normals and maximizing the mixture probability density (1) of the intensity gradient along the profile. The model update step shifts the shape to the current cluster subspace by truncating the eigen coefficients to lie within the allowable variance as $\pm 2\sqrt{\lambda_i}$. The shape is re-assigned the nearest cluster based on the mahalanobis distance and the shape coeficients are re-computed if the current subspace is different from the previous.

The truncation function to regularize the shapes usually generates discontinuous shape estimates. Bregler et. al. [11,3] suggests a continuous constrain function that can be maximized using gradient ascent to ensure that the shape lies within the subspace of the nearest cluster. A major limitation of their approach is the use of thresholding to discriminate a valid shape from an invalid shape. We use the truncation approach, due to its low computational requirement and faster convergence. The above steps are performed iteratively and converges irrespective of the initial cluster of the average shape. We present the algorithm steps below:

ASM Train in Clustered Shape Space

1. Align all the shapes $\mathbf{Y_i}$ to the average shape $\overline{\mathbf{X}}$ using procrustes analysis as $\mathbf{Y_{i,a}}$
2. Project the aligned shapes $\mathbf{Y_{i,a}}$ in the common tangent space of $\overline{\mathbf{X}}$ by scaling as $\mathbf{Y'_{i,a}} = \mathbf{Y_{i,a}}/(\mathbf{Y_{i,a}}.\overline{\mathbf{X}})$. This ensures that procrustes distance can be approximated as euclidean distance.
3. Cluster the rescaled shapes $\mathbf{Y'_{i,a}}$ to N Clusters using EM algorithm with minimum covariance $\mathbf{V_{floor}}$ to ensure overlapping clusters.
4. Generate the subregions from the original shapes using the cluster membership. Realign the shapes locally and project the shapes to tangent space of the cluster mean as $\mathbf{Y_{i,a,c}}$
5. Learn locally linear PCA models within each cluster as $\mathbf{Y_{i,a,c}} = \overline{\mathbf{X}}_\mathbf{c} + \mathbf{P_c}\mathbf{b_{c,i}}$
6. Learn Gaussian mixture density for the Intensity Profile Model(IPM) for each landmark.

ASM Search in Clustered Shape Space

1. Assign initial cluster $Cluster_{init}$ to the global average shape $\overline{\mathbf{X}}$ based on Mahalanobis Distance.
2. Search IPM along normal for the intensity profile that maximizes the mixture density probability (eqn. 1) to get new shape $\mathbf{Y_s}$
3. Constrain the shape $\mathbf{Y_s} = \overline{\mathbf{X}}_\mathbf{init} + \mathbf{P_{init}}\mathbf{b_{init,s}}$ by truncating $\mathbf{b_{init,s}}$ within the subspace of the current cluster to get new shape $\mathbf{Y'_s}$.
4. Re-assign $Cluster_i$ by projecting the new shape $\mathbf{Y'_s}$ onto global tangent space and finding the nearest cluster based on mahalanobis distance.
5. Re-estimate the parameter $\mathbf{b'_{i,s}}$ for the new cluster $Cluster_i$ by projecting the new shape $\mathbf{Y'_s}$ onto cluster mean shape tangent space.
6. Iterate until convergence.

---

5   Tracking Framework

Running ASM at every frame is computationally expensive and causes feature points to jitter strongly. We track the features using Sum of Squared Intensity Difference(SSID) tracker across consecutive frames[13]. The SSID tracker is a method for registering two images and computes the displacement of the feature by minimizing the intensity matching cost, computed over a fixed sized window around the feature. Over a small inter-frame motion, a linear translation model can be accurately assumed. For an intensity surface at image location $\mathbf{I}(\mathbf{x_i}, \mathbf{y_i}, \mathbf{t_k})$, the tracker estimates the displacement vector $\mathbf{d} = (\delta\mathbf{x_i}, \delta\mathbf{y_i})$ from new image $\mathbf{I}(\mathbf{x_i} + \delta\mathbf{x}, \mathbf{y_i} + \delta\mathbf{y}, \mathbf{t_{k+1}})$ by minimizing the residual error over a window $\mathcal{W}$ around $(\mathbf{x_i}, \mathbf{y_i})$ [13]

$$\int_{\mathcal{W}} [\mathbf{I}(\mathbf{x_i} + \delta\mathbf{x}, \mathbf{y_i} + \delta\mathbf{y}, \mathbf{t_{k+1}}) - \mathbf{g}.\mathbf{d} - \mathbf{I}(\mathbf{x_i}, \mathbf{y_i}, \mathbf{t_k})]\, d\mathcal{W} \qquad (2)$$

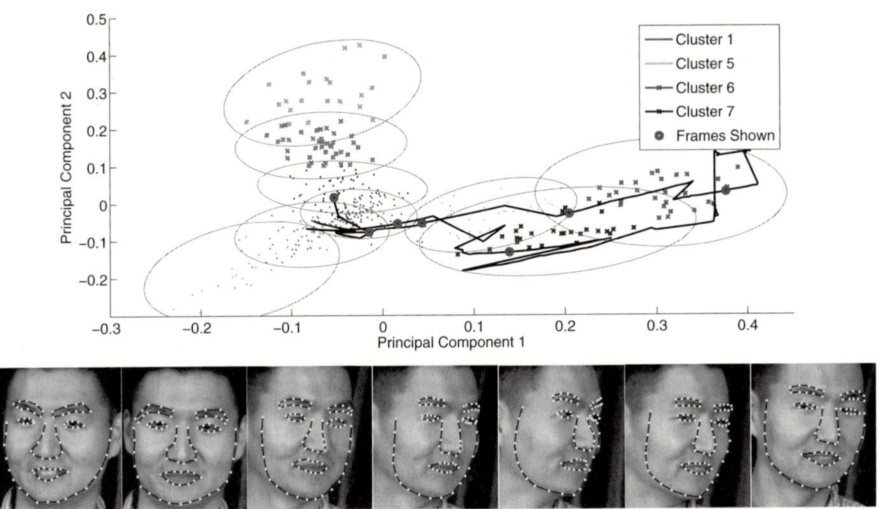

Fig. 5. *(Best Viewed in Color)*Tracking the shapes across right head rotation.**(Top)** The cluster projections on 2D space using 2 principal modes(for visualization)and the bounded by hyper-ellipsoid subspace. The right head rotation causes the shape to vary across the clusters. The red circles corresponds to the frames 1, 49, 68, 76, 114, 262 and 281. The entire tracking path lies within the subspace spanned by the hyper-ellipsoids.**(Bottom)** The images of the tracking result for the frames shown as red markers in the plot.

The inter-frame image warping model assumes that for small displacements of intensity surface of image window W, the horizontal and vertical displacement of the surface at a point (x_i, y_i) is a function of gradient vector g at that point. During tracking, some features(ASM landmarks) eventually lose track due to blurring or illumination changes. To avoid this, at every frame we re-initialize the points which have lost track by searching along the normal and maximizing the intensity profile mixture density1). At every frame we ensure that the shape Y_t obtained from tracking is a plausible shape by constraining the shape to lie on the shape manifold. We align the new shape Y_t to the global average shape $\overline{X}_{init}$ and re-assign it to the nearest Cluster$_i$ based on mahalanobis distance. The new shape Y_t is constrained to the subspace of the assigned Cluster$_i$. This ensures switching between the overlapping subspaces that form the non-linear shape manifold. Fig. 5 shows the path (projection on 2 principal components) of a shape for a tracking sequence when the subject rotates the head from frontal to full right profile view and back. The figure also illustrates the cluster switching as the person rotates the head. The entire path remains within the plausible shape manifold spanned by the 9 hyper-ellipsoid subspaces.

6   Pose Angle Estimation

The proposed framework does not use head pose angles for tracking features across large head rotations. In order to deal with discontinuities in shape space and adapting ASM model according to pose change, it may be required to predict pose angles. The current tracking framework can be extended to support pose angle prediction using mixture of experts(ME).

The mapping from 2D shape to 3D pose angle is intrinsically non linear. Inverse mappings from observations to 3D states cannot be functionally approximated due to ambiguities caused by perspective projection and the lost degree of freedom. Mixture of Experts(ME) provide a modular framework for learning non-linear mappings by clustering the dataset and simultaneously learning function approximators locally in the cluster. The EM algorithm for training ME decouples the optimization task into regressor fittng and multi-way classifier learning. In order to learn point distribution models for the shape $\mathbf{X}$, and the corresponding pose angles $\mathbf{A}$, ME formulates the problem as likelihood maximization. The Expectation step involves soft clustering:

$$P(\text{Cluster} = i | \mathbf{X}, \mathbf{A}) = \frac{p(\mathbf{A}|\mathbf{X}, \mathbf{F_i}(\mathbf{X}))P(\text{Cluster} = i|\mathbf{X})}{\sum_j^N p(\mathbf{A}|\mathbf{X}, \mathbf{F_j}(\mathbf{X}))P(\text{Cluster} = j|\mathbf{X})} \tag{3}$$

The density $P(\text{Cluster} = i|\mathbf{X})$ is the gate distribution for classifying shapes to the ith Cluster. The gate distribution is a multi-category classifier learned using softmax function. The pose angle predictions is done by the function approximators $\mathbf{F_i}(\mathbf{X})$ fitted locally to each cluster and are represented using Gaussian distribution $p(\mathbf{A}|\mathbf{X}, \mathbf{F_i}(\mathbf{X}))$. The likelihood is a binomial distribution $\prod_j^N \{p(\mathbf{A}|\mathbf{X}, \mathbf{F_i}(\mathbf{X}))P(\text{Cluster} = i|\mathbf{X})\}^{I(\text{Cluster}=j)}$ where $I(\text{Cluster} = j)$ is the indicator function for the class to which shape $\mathbf{X}$ belongs. The EM iteratively learns the parameters by independently maximizing the gate and the regressor distributions in the log likelihood $\mathcal{L}$ as the Maximization step.

$$\textbf{Log Likelihood:}\ \ \sum_i^M \sum_j^N \mathbb{E}[I(\text{Cluster} = j)]\log(P(\text{Cluster} = j|\mathbf{X_i})) \\ + \mathbb{E}[I(\text{Cluster} = j)]\log(p(\mathbf{A}|\mathbf{X_i}, \mathbf{F_j}(\mathbf{X_i}))) \tag{4}$$

Where $\mathbb{E}$ denotes the expected value. In effect the EM algorithm does soft clustering of the shapes $\mathbf{X}$ at each step and learns a pose predictor $\mathbf{F_j}$ locally in the cluster. We used linear regressors with softmax gate distribution in our framework. We experimented on the data set containing large shape variations due to yaw with pose angles varying from -90° to $+90^o$. The pose angles for the training set were estimated within an error of $\pm 5^o$ by linear interpolation between the full profile $\pm 90^o$ and frontal 0° poses and assuming constant angular velocity during the head rotation. The use of ME gave an average improvement in the prediction accuracy by $\mathbf{8.34^o}$ over single regressor on our data set. More number of experts usually improves the prediction accuracy. However they need to be regularized to avoid overfitting the training dataset. Fig.6 illustrates the ME fitting to the non-linear data. Mixture of Experts incorporates pose angles

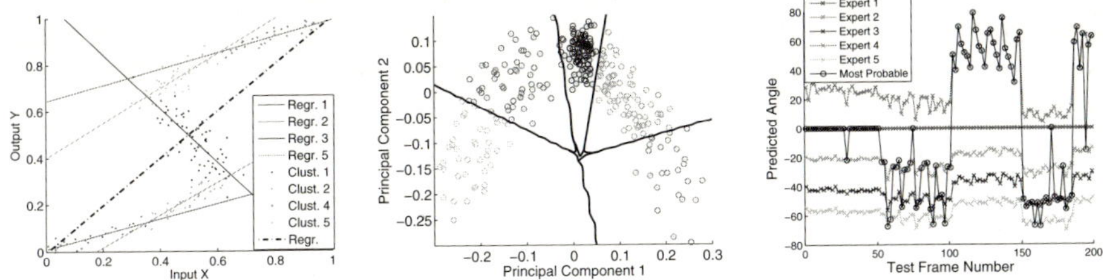

Fig. 6. *(Best Viewed in Color)*(**Left**) A non-linear toy dataset generated from the inverse mapping $x = y + 0.3\sin(2\pi y) + \epsilon$ where ϵ is zero mean Gaussian noise. Multiple locally learned linear regressors(shown in color) gives better predictions compared to single regressor(shown as black). (**Middle**) 5 Shape clusters(projected on 2 principle components) obtained from the learned gate distribution using Mixture of Experts. The data set contained right, frontal(blue points) and left head poses. (**Right**)Pose angle prediction on test data set using 5 Experts. The plot in black indicates the most probable expert. Notice how the most probable expert switch between different experts. The experts predict different range of pose angles and fit well locally.

information to cluster the shapes based on similarity between the aligned shapes and generates meaningful clusters that are based on pose variations. The gating network discriminatively classifies the data set into multiple classes. The overlapping subspaces are learned directly from the clusters.

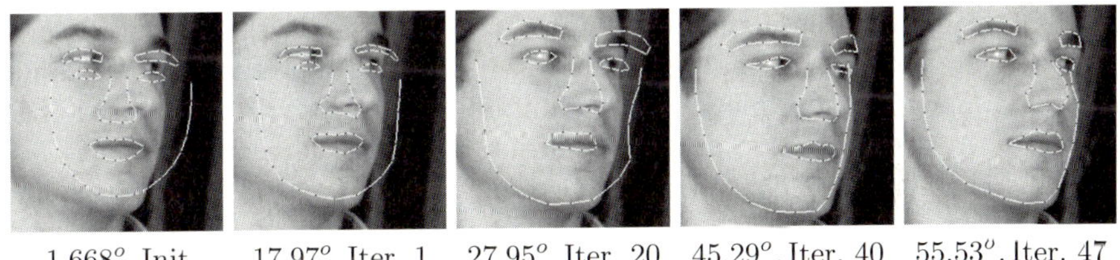

Fig. 7. Iteratively fitting ASM using clusters obtained from the Mixture of Experts. The lower row indicates the predicted angles at each of the iteration.

Full Profile and Self Occlusion: The case of full profile has been loosely handled in the past. Zhou et al. [7] presents a model for handling self occlusion and demonstrates the results only on the head poses with yaw $\sim 40^{o} - 50^{o}$. Romdhani et al. [6] does not discuss about the self occlusion. Unlike appearance based approaches, the shape undergoes drastic change during full profile head movement. The correspondence between face features and landmark points changes for the outer contour, the eyes and the eyebrows. Depending upon the targeted application the full profile has to be handled by either turn off the visibility of the landmark points which are occluded, or allowing the landmark points to lie along the boundary of the features of the face. Former approach induces discontinuities in the shape space and has to be handled by discrete model switching using stochastic methods [10]. We adopt the latter approach in our framework. The plausible shape space remains continuous in this case. The pose angle prediction enables us to identify the clusters which are full profile (clusters with pose angle in the range $90^o \pm 10^o$). For the full profile image search, we do not match local intensity along the normals for the occluded landmarks. Fig. 8 shows the results obtained from our framework. Occluded landmarks are shown as points.

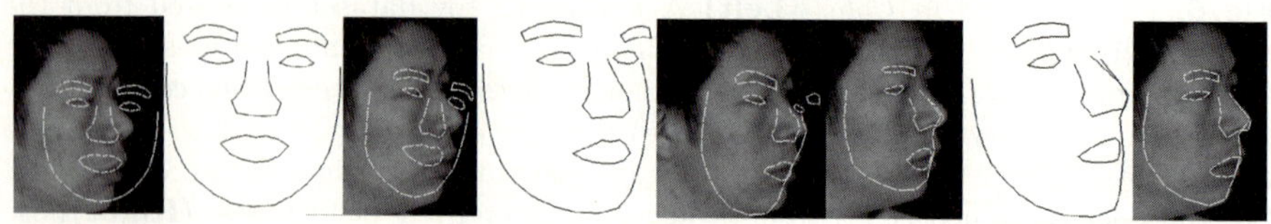

Fig. 8. Shape fitting results on a full profile pose initialized with the average frontal shape. The above frames correspond to iterations 1, 16, 74, 94 and 114 of level 4 of the gaussian pyramid. The initial average shape is in Cluster 1(cluster center shown as the 2nd image). The cluster switch during iteration 74 to Cluster 4(cluster center shown as the 4th image). The cluster switches to the profile cluster (cluster center shown as the 7th image)during iteration 94.

7   Conclusion

In this work we have presented a generic real time framework for detecting and tracking the deformable shapes across non-linear variations arising due to aspect changes. Detailed analysis and empirical results have been presented about issues related to modeling non-linear shape manifold using piecewise linear models. A composite method for pose angle estimation using Mixture of Experts is also proposed. The full profile shape is handled in a special way to ensure continuous shape space modeling.

Acknowledgement

The authors would like to thank Zhiguo Li and Gabriel Tsechpenakis for many insightful discussions. This research was supported in part by Department of Homeland Security, DARPA and NSF Grant.

Patent Pending

References

1. Cootes, T.: An Introduction to Active Shape Models. Oxford University Press (2000)
2. Sozou, P., Cootes, T., Taylor, C., Dimauro, E.: Non-linear point distribution modelling using a multi-layer perceptron. BMVC (1995)
3. Cootes, T., Taylor, C.: A mixture model for representing shape variation. BMVC (1997)
4. Murase, H., Nayar, S.: Learning and recognition of 3D Objects from appearance. IJCV (1995)
5. Gong, S., Ong, E.J., McKenna, S.: Learning to associate faces across views in vector space of similarities to prototypes. BMVC (1998)
6. Romdhani, S., Gong, S., Psarrou, A.: A Multi-View Nonlinear Active Shape Model Using Kernel PCA. BMVC (1999)
7. Zhou, Y., Zhang, W., Tang, X., Shum, H.: A Bayesian Mixture Model for Multi-view Face Alignment. CVPR (2005)
8. Cootes, T., Wheeler, G., Walker, K., Taylor, C.: View-Based Active Appearance Models. BMVC (2001)
9. Edwards, G.J., Taylor, C.J., Cootes, T.F.: Learning to Identify and Track Faces in Image Sequences. BMVC (1997)
10. Heap, T., Hogg, D.: Improving specificity in pdms using a hierarchical approach. BMVC (1997)
11. Bregler, C., Omohundro, S.: Surface Learning with Applications to Lipreading. NIPS (1994)
12. Goodall, C.: Procrustes methods in the statistical analysis of shape. Journal of the Royal Statistical Society (1991)
13. Tomasi, C., Kanade, T.: Detection and Tracking of Point Features. Technical Report CMU-CS-91-132 (1997)

Improved Kernel-Based Object Tracking Under Occluded Scenarios

Vinay P. Namboodiri, Amit Ghorawat, and Subhasis Chaudhuri

Department of Electrical Engineering
Indian Institute of Technology, Bombay
Mumbai, India
{vinaypn, sc}@ee.iitb.ac.in, amit.ghorawat@gmail.com

Abstract. A successful approach for object tracking has been kernel based object tracking [1] by Comaniciu *et al.*. The method provides an effective solution to the problems of representation and localization in tracking. The method involves representation of an object by a feature histogram with an isotropic kernel and performing a gradient based mean shift optimization for localizing the kernel. Though robust, this technique fails under cases of occlusion. We improve the kernel based object tracking by performing the localization using a *generalized (bidirectional) mean shift* based optimization. This makes the method resilient to occlusions. Another aspect related to the localization step is handling of scale changes by varying the bandwidth of the kernel. Here, we suggest a technique based on SIFT features [2] by Lowe to enable change of bandwidth of the kernel even in the presence of occlusion. We demonstrate the effectiveness of the techniques proposed through extensive experimentation on a number of challenging data sets.

1   Introduction

Real-time object tracking is indispensable to a vast number of computer vision applications like video surveillance and security, driver assistance, video abstraction, traffic management and video editing. Segmenting and tracking objects accurately with low computational complexity is a challenge.

A method which has been quite successful in handling this task is the kernel based object tracking algorithm [1]. In this method the target is spatially masked with an isotropic kernel. A spatially-smooth similarity function is defined and the target localization problem is then done by a gradient based optimization method, based on mean shift filter [3]. This method has been demonstrated to successfully work for non-rigid motion and in the presence of significant clutter. While in some cases it does handle partial occlusion, it unfortunately fails in a large number of cases. The reason for this can be traced to the mean shift based approach used for target localization. It is an effective method for clustering when the modes are distinct. However if there are multiple modes which are nearby then the gradient based optimization step can often converge to a local mode which is not necessarily the "true" mode. In this paper we address this issue effectively by considering a *generalized mean shift* based approach. This

P. Kalra and S. Peleg (Eds.): ICVGIP 2006, LNCS 4338, pp. 504–515, 2006.

method effectively handles the problem of partial occlusion and in some cases total occlusion in a more robust manner. A recent work which addresses the same problem is by Babu *et al.* [4] in which they consider the problem of improving the kernel object tracker. However, they address this problem by considering multiple tracking systems, that is they combine the mean shift filter with an SSD based tracking system. This affects the real time performance of the system and besides it does not actually address the core issue of the mean shift procedure which we have considered. Another approach [5], has been based on combination of particle filtering with blob tracking and is very successful in handling the occlusion problem, however, the method is computationally expensive.

The other aspect which is of interest has been that of adapting the bandwidth of the kernel to account for a change in scale of the object of interest. There have been a few approaches for data driven bandwidth selection [6,7] and a scale space based approach [8] for the mean shift procedure to account for the scale as well. However, while these approaches work well to account for a scale change when there is no occlusion, they fail when the scale changes with partial occlusion. To handle this aspect we consider a approach where we compute the SIFT [2] based features and compute the matches of key-points over the frames. Using this technique we are able to handle scale change even in the presence of occlusion.

In the next section we discuss the original kernel object tracker. In section 3 we discuss the procedure of generalized mean shift. Next, in section 4 we formulate a tracker based on generalized mean shift. The technique for scale change is presented in section 5. The experimental results are presented in section 6 and we conclude in section. 7.

2   Kernel-Based Object Tracking

The main contribution of the kernel based object tracking algorithm [1] has been in the target representation and localization aspects of tracking. The other aspects of tracking like initial object segmentation can be addressed using methods like background subtraction. Further, to make it more robust it can be associated with a prediction filter like Kalman filter. The target representation and localization is a bottom up process and has to handle changes in the appearance of the object. We now briefly discuss these aspects of the object tracker.

2.1   Target Representation

The reference *target model* is represented by its probability distribution function (p.d.f.) q in the feature space. Here the p.d.f.s are represented using m-bin histograms due to the low computational cost involved and the real-time processing restrictions. A target is represented by an ellipsoidal region in the image. Let $x_i^*, i = 1 \ldots n$ be the normalized pixel locations in the region defined as the target model. The region is locally centered at 0. An isotropic kernel with a convex and monotonic decreasing kernel profile $k(x)$, assigns smaller weights to pixels farther from the center. The function b associates to the pixel at location x_i^*

the index $b(x_i^*)$ of its bin in the quantized feature space. The probability of the feature $u = 1 \ldots m$ in the target model is then computed as

$$\hat{q}_u = C \sum_{i=1}^{n} k(||x_i^*||^2)\delta[b(x_i^*) - u] \tag{1}$$

where δ is the Kronecker delta function and C is the normalization constant and is given by

$$C = \frac{1}{\sum_{i=1}^{n} k(||x_i^*||^2)}. \tag{2}$$

The target model can be considered as centered at the spatial location 0. In the subsequent frame, a *target candidate* is defined at location y and is characterized by the pdf $p(y)$. Let $x_i, i = 1 \ldots n_h$ be the normalized pixel locations of the target candidate, centered at y in the current frame. Using the same kernel profile $k(x)$, but with bandwidth h, the probability of the feature $u = 1 \ldots m$ in the target candidate is given by

$$\hat{p}_u(y) = C_h \sum_{i=1}^{n_h} k(||\frac{y - x_i}{h}||^2)\delta[b(x_i) - u], \tag{3}$$

where

$$C_h = \frac{1}{\sum_{i=1}^{n_h} k(||\frac{y-x_i}{h}||^2)}. \tag{4}$$

A similarity function is defined that defines the distance among target model and candidates as

$$d(y) = \sqrt{1 - \rho|\hat{p}(y), \hat{q}|}, \tag{5}$$

where

$$\hat{\rho}(y) = \rho|\hat{p}(y), \hat{q}| = \sum_{u=1}^{m} \sqrt{\hat{p}_u(y)\hat{q}_u}, \tag{6}$$

is the sample estimate of the Bhattacharyya coefficient between p and q.

2.2   Localization

In the localization phase the distance measure between the target model and target candidates is minimized. Minimizing the distance given in eqn.(5) is equivalent to maximizing the Bhattacharyya coefficient $\hat{\rho}(y)$. The search for the new target location in the current frame starts at the location $\hat{y}_0$ of the target in the previous frame. The linear approximation of the Bhattacharyya coefficient in eqn.(6) is

$$\hat{\rho}(y) \approx \frac{1}{2} \sum_{u=1}^{m} \sqrt{\hat{p}_u(\hat{y}_0)\hat{q}_u} + \frac{1}{2} \sum_{u=1}^{m} \hat{p}_u(y)\sqrt{\frac{\hat{q}_u}{\hat{p}_u(\hat{y}}} \tag{7}$$

The resultant expression considering eqn.(3) is

$$\hat{\rho}(y) \approx \frac{1}{2} \sum_{u=1}^{m} \sqrt{\hat{p}_u(\hat{y}_0)\hat{q}_u} + \frac{C_h}{2} \sum_{u=1}^{n_h} w_i k(||\frac{y - x_i}{h}||^2), \tag{8}$$

where

$$w_i = \sum u = 1^m \sqrt{\frac{\hat{q}_u}{\hat{p}_u(\hat{y}_0)}} \delta[b(x_i) - u].$$ (9)

To minimize the distance, the second term in eqn.(8) has to be maximized. The second term represents the density estimate with kernel profile $k(x)$ at y in the current frame. The mode of this density in the neighborhood is the sought maximum that can be found employing the mean shift procedure. In this procedure, the kernel is recursively moved from the current location $\hat{y}_0$ to the new location $\hat{y}_1$ according to the mean shift procedure with the relation being

$$\hat{\mathbf{y}}_1 = \frac{\sum_{i=1}^{n_h} \mathbf{x}_i w_i g(||\frac{\hat{y}_0 - x_i}{h}||^2)}{\sum_{i=1}^{n_k} w_i g(||\frac{\hat{y}_0 . - x_i}{h}||^2)}$$ (10)

where $g(x) = -k'(x)$. In the next section we discuss the generalized mean shift procedure which can be used to find the modes more robustly.

3   Generalized Mean Shift

The mean shift procedure ([3,9]) when applied on a set of points explicitly moves the points towards their modes. The mean shift procedure has been extended in [10] to perform reverse mean shift which moves the points away from their modes. The generalized mean shift procedure combines forward and reverse mean shift methods so as to move the points to their correct modes without getting stuck in the local mode.

3.1   Generalized Mean Shift

The forward and reverse mean shift based methods move the points towards and away from the mode of the cluster respectively. However, when there are multiple modes close by it is possible that the point may be clustered to an incorrect mode away from its "true" mode. In order to handle this case, we formulate the notion of generalized mean shift where the points are perturbed away from their mode by the reverse mean shift and then clustered again using forward mean shift. This is not a purely convex optimization and hence it is able to move away from local minima and converge to the global minima provided that the global minima is near. The threshold for the global minima being nearer is decided by a dissimilarity factor and is discussed in section 6. The process of generalized mean shift is illustrated in fig. 1. It involves combining the forward and reverse mean shift procedures in an iterative manner with the switching between forward and reverse mean shift being decided using an automatic switching criterion. The reverse mean shift is a divergent procedure and tends to move the cluster values away from their mode in the direction of the gradient and the forward mean shift is a convergent procedure. Hence, in case of mixed clusters (that correspond to occluded scenarios), the generalized mean shift mixes the forward and reverse mean shift, ensuring that it is a convergent procedure, by switching the direction based on the dissimilarity factor.

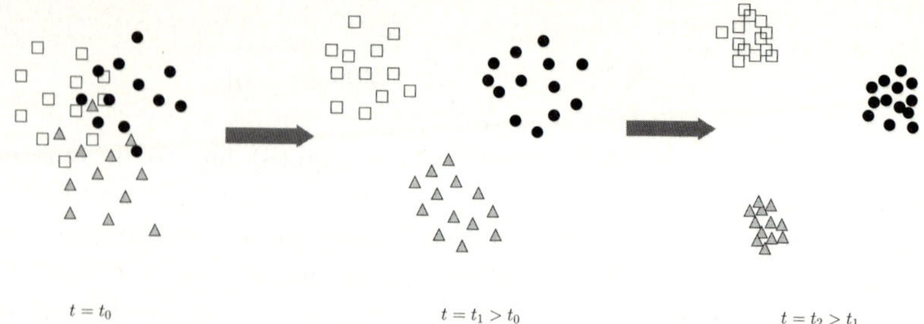

Fig. 1. Illustration of mixed diffusion in the feature space. The inverse diffusion results in the mixed clusters being separated and the individual elements of clusters coming closer together due to forward diffusion.

4   Tracking Using Generalized Mean Shift

The application of generalized mean shift optimization for tracking becomes relevant in the case of partial or total occlusion of tracked objects. In this case the modes of the histogram are affected and the kernel tends to be attached to the false mode, i.e. the occluding object. By using adaptive forward and reverse mean shift, i.e. the generalized mean shift, one can recover the true mode even after partial or total occlusion. The generalized mean shift is then given by:

$$\hat{\mathbf{y}}_1 = \mathrm{sgn(y)} \frac{\sum_{i=1}^{n_h} \mathbf{x}_i w_i g(|| \frac{\hat{y}_0 - x_i}{h} ||^2)}{\sum_{i=1}^{n_k} w_i g(|| \frac{\hat{y}_0. - x_i}{h} ||^2)} \tag{11}$$

where sgn(y) is a sign function and is determined by a dissimilarity factor threshold θ.

$$d(y) > \theta \Rightarrow \mathrm{sgn(y)} = -\gamma$$
$$d(y) <= \theta \Rightarrow \mathrm{sgn(y)} = +1. \tag{12}$$

Here γ is the reverse mean shift coefficient such that $0 < \gamma < 1$. The value of γ is generally less than 1 since the reverse mean shift procedure is divergent and hence it is required to dampen the divergent procedure. The value of θ is determined based on the distance measure between the target model and the candidate model and is fixed for a wide class of tracking scenarios. However, since the reverse mean shift is a divergent procedure, if the distance function during reverse mean shift increases beyond the value θ, then the sgn function is again made positive and the forward mean shift procedure is used. Thereby, one ensures that the generalized mean shift procedure is always convergent. The algorithm for the generalized mean shift procedure for Bhattacharyya coefficient is given in Algorithm 1.

Algorithm 1. Bhattacharyya Coefficient Maximization using **Generalized mean shift**

Input: The target model $\{\hat{q}_u\}_{u=1\ldots m}$ and its location $\hat{y}_0$ in the previous frame

1: Initialize the location of the target in the current frame with $\hat{y}_0$, compute $\{\hat{p}_u(\hat{y}_0)\}_{u=1\ldots m}$, and evaluate

$$\rho[\hat{p}(y_0), \hat{q}] = \sum_{u=1}^{m} \sqrt{\hat{p}_u(\hat{y}_0)\hat{q}_u}.$$

2: Derive the weights $\{w_i\}_{1=1\ldots n_h}$.
3: **if** $d[\hat{p}(y_0), \hat{q}] > \theta$ **then**
4:     $\text{sgn}(y) = -\gamma, 0 < r < 1$ and $a = 0$.
5: **end if**
6: Find the next location of the target candidate according to eqn.(11).
7: Compute $d(\hat{y}_1)$
8: **if** $d(\hat{y}_1) < d(\hat{y}_0)$ **then**
9:     $\hat{y}_1 \leftarrow \frac{1}{2}(\hat{y}_0 + \hat{y}_1)$
10:     Evaluate $\rho[\hat{p}(\hat{y}_1), \hat{q}]$
11: **else**
12:     reinitialize $\text{sgn}(y) = 1$ and go to Step 6.
13: **end if**
14: **if** $||\hat{y}_1 - \hat{y}_0|| < \epsilon$ **then**
15:     Stop.
16: **else**
17:     Set $\hat{y}_0 \leftarrow \hat{y}_1$
18:     go to Step 2.
19: **end if**

---

5   Scale Adaptation

While there have been works related to adapting the kernel bandwidth h based on the scale [6,7,8], the methods assume that there will be no occlusion during scale change or relatively no occlusion. In order to consider real world scenarios where there may be scale change while there is occlusion we consider a different approach based on Scale Invariant Feature Transform (SIFT) based features [2] proposed by Lowe.

5.1   SIFT Features

The SIFT features [2] are highly robust and are invariant to image scale and rotation and provide robust matching across a substantial range of affine distortion, change in 3D viewpoint and change in illumination which are pervasive in tracking. The scale of the key-points are computed by a search over all scales and image locations using a difference of Gaussian function and the interest points selected are invariant to scale and orientation. At each key-point location a detailed model is fit to determine the location and scale and it is ensured that the key-points selected are stable.

5.2   Scale Adaptation Using SIFT

Given a kernel at the current location and a kernel from an earlier location, the key-points are selected using the SIFT operator and key-point matches are calculated between the key-points in the kernels from the selected frames. Then the average change in the matched key-points is calculated. The scale of the kernel, i.e. the bandwidth factor h is then resized using the change in the scale as indicated by the matched key-points. Let S_m be the average scale of the matched key-points in the target model and S_c be the average scale of the matched key-points in the target candidate. Then we obtain the new value for the bandwidth parameter h as

$$\hat{h} = h * \frac{S_c + \alpha S_m}{(1 + \alpha) S_m} \tag{13}$$

where α is a weight factor which denotes the weight given to the scale of the target model key-points as compared to the scale of the target candidate key-points. We have used a value of $\alpha = 4$ in our experiments. Since even matches of a few key-points are sufficient to indicate the scale change, this method is able to adaptively change the size of the kernel even under severe partial occlusion thus making the kernel tracker more robust. In case there are no matches between the kernels as can happen in certain cases of total occlusion, the scale of the kernel is chosen to be the same as in the previous frame. This method of adapting to scale is more robust as compared to the scale space based approach advocated in [8] where the author proposes a scale space based mean shift approach. While, the idea of Gaussian scale space is similar, since these are considered for key-points instead of the whole kernel they are more resilient in case of occlusion.

6   Experimental Results

The proposed algorithm has been extensively tested on numerous videos from the Caviar [11], Jojic [12], and Karl-Wilhelm-Strasse [13] datasets. The generalized mean-shift tracker performed well for almost all the test cases under partial as well as full occlusion and in real time.

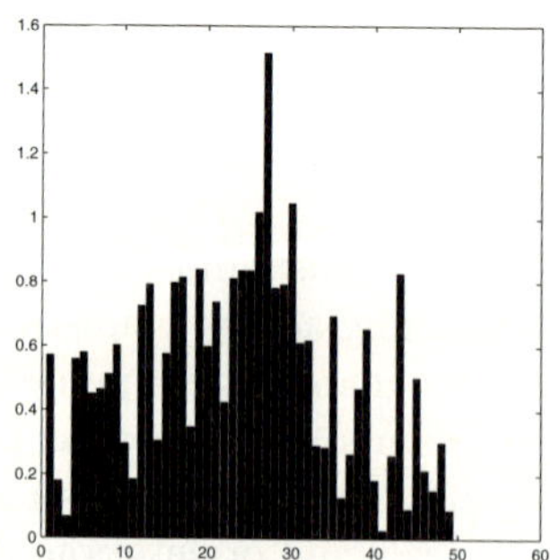

Fig. 2. Plot of Dissimilarity Factor (Y-axis) vs image frames (X-axis)

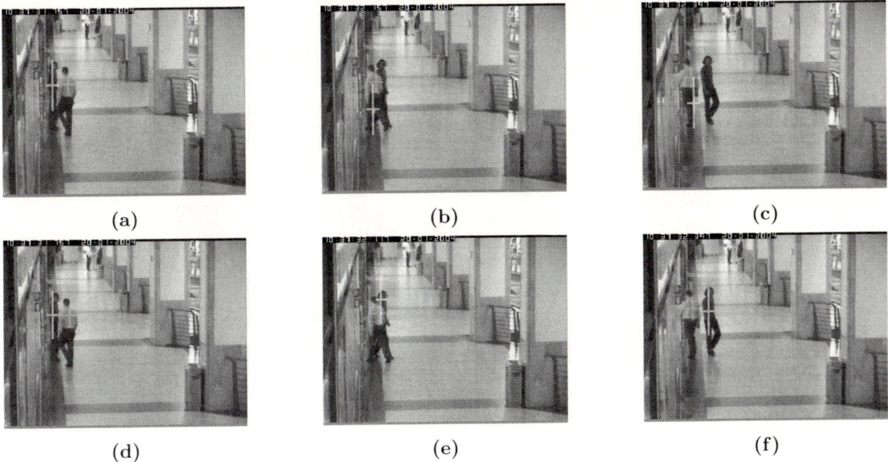

Fig. 3. *EnterExit* sequence: Tracking with occlusion.(a), (b), (c) show the results of the plain kernel tracker while (d), (e), and (f) show that of the proposed method on the Caviar data set.

The targets have been initialized by a manually chosen ellipse in all the video sequences. However, colored crosses have been used to indicate the kernel positions, they represent the minor and major axes of the tracking ellipse. We now discuss the results.

The *EnterExit* sequence is a set of 50, 384 x 288 pixel frames taken from the Caviar dataset [11]. It is a scene from a mall where one person enters a shop and another person exits it resulting in the two people crossing each other. Thus one observes partial occlusion. When we use the forward mean shift tracker [1], then the tracker fails to track the person entering the shop correctly and latches onto the person leaving the shop. This is due to the partial occlusion. However, as can be seen in Fig. 3, the proposed method is able to successfully track the person entering as well as the person leaving correctly even in case of partial occlusion.

Next we consider a close range sequence used by Jojic and Frey in [12]. The sequence consists of 40 frames with each frame 320x240 pixels in size. Here one can observe that there is full occlusion present. The results for the forward mean shift tracker and the proposed method are presented in Fig. 6. The interesting part is that the two close range observations are quite similar in terms of skin color. The forward mean shift tracker fails to track the two persons when there is full occlusion. However, due to the improvements proposed in terms of generalized mean shift optimization we are able to track the two persons even in case of full occlusion.

The algorithm presented is scalable and hence can be extended to higher number of objects being tracked simultaneously with occlusion. It has been tested on three objects and can be scaled up with ease. For this purpose another Caviar sequence has been used: *ThreePastShop* sequences (Fig. 4) which consists of 100

Fig. 4. *ThreePastShop* sequence: Tracking 3 targets with occlusion on the Caviar data set

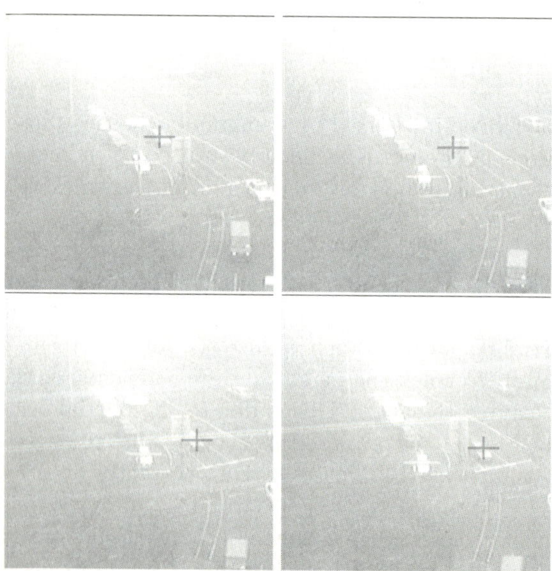

Fig. 5. *Karl-Wilhelm-Strass* sequence: Tracking vehicle targets with occlusion and fog

384 x 288 pixel frames shot at a corridor of a shopping mall. In this case we are able to successfully track three people and multiple occlusions. The results shown in Fig. 4 demonstrates this.

The proposed method has also been successfully tested on traffic videos. We ran experiments on the Karl-Wilhelm-Strass data set [13] (60 frames 350 x 350 pixels) with considerable fog and occlusion (Figure 5). Here we are able to track a car under severe fog and also occlusion when it passes under a billboard. This demonstrates the robustness of our approach.

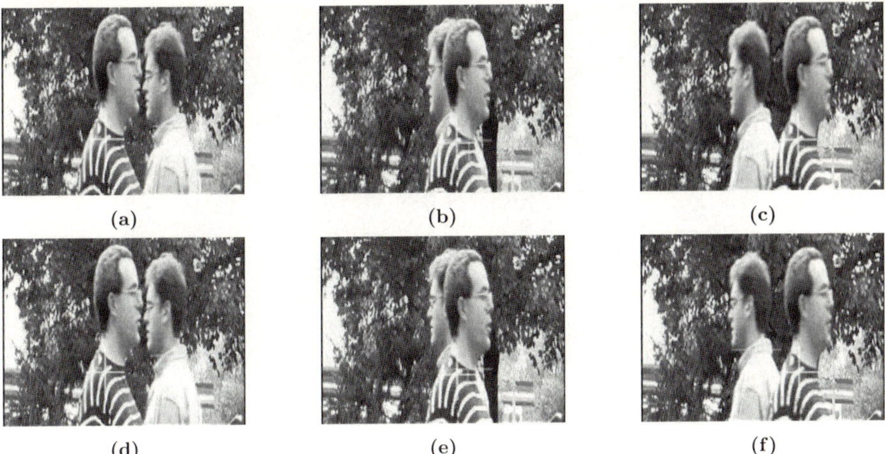

Fig. 6. *Jojic* sequence: Tracking with occlusion.(a), (b), (c) show the results of the plain kernel tracker while (d), (e), and (f) show that of the proposed method on the Jojic data set.

Further, we have demonstrated the effectiveness of the SIFT based technique to handle scale change in tracking videos. The results of the same are shown on a video clip from the movie "Breakfast at Tiffany's", which shows a scene where two persons are climbing down while being occluded by a passing motor-vehicle. The SIFT based technique enables effective handling of scale change as can be seen from the results in Fig. 7. The results can be better considered from the result videos available at *http://vinaypn.googlepages.com/tracking*. We now discuss the parameters used in our experiments. The generalized mean-shift approach has two parameters that need to be initialized manually. The first is a similarity factor threshold θ in eqn. (12) which is used to determine the sign of the sgn function. It can be seen from Figure 2 that at areas of partial or total occlusion the distance factor $d(y)$ is quite high and this can be used to determine a threshold value θ. In the Caviar, Karl-Wilhelm-Strass, "Breakfast at Tiffany's"sequences we used a threshold value of 0.4. While, in the sequence of Jojic we had to use a value of 0.15. This change can be attributed to the fact that this sequence was a close range video while all the others were shot from a considerable distance. Hence, we believe that if the range of the scene is known approximately, we need to initialize these parameters just once.

The other coefficient we used is the reverse mean-shift weight γ in eqn. (12) and we used a value of 0.4 for all the test cases. We found that these parameters are fairly global and were not changed in most of the test sequences.

There are a few areas where the tracker might fail. Whenever the foreground object is considerably bigger than the tracking kernel of the background object, the tracker will not be able to locate the object once the occlusion frames are over. This situation may be handled by using a much wider search window when the tracker fails to locate a match after a certain number of iterations.

Fig. 7. *Breakfast at Tiffany's* sequence: Tracking target with occlusion and scale change in a clip from the movie

The SIFT based technique to handle scale change requires relatively high resolution videos to be able to generate adequate number of match points to work effectively. Often, the tracked object's orientation changes in a video sequence. We have taken care to update our matching image to take care of these situations.

7   Conclusion

In this paper we address the problem of occlusion while tracking multiple objects using a kernel based tracker. We identify the problem as incorrect mode estimation due to the convex optimization method of mean shift based optimization used for localization. Hence, we suggest a modification based on generalized mean shift based optimization which is able to escape problems of local minima in a neighborhood. We further consider the problem of scale adaptation and propose a solution based on identifying scale change in key-points computed using SIFT. This method of scale change works well even in case of occlusion. The improved kernel tracker thus developed is robust and also processes the data in real time. The tracker's efficiency has been proved by extensive testing on various popular data sets.

There are certain cases where in case there is prolonged total occlusion, the errors are propagated. We intend to explore solutions based on a global search paradigm in such cases to handle the problems which are inherent due to the local nature of the approach considered.

Acknowledgments

Financial assistantship under the *Swarnajayanti* fellowship scheme from the Department of Science and Technology, India is gratefully acknowledged.

References

1. Comaniciu, D., Ramesh, V., Meer, P.: Kernel-based object tracking. IEEE Transactions on Pattern Analysis and Machine Intelligence **25** (2003) 564–575
2. Lowe, D.G.: Distinctive image features from scale-invariant keypoints. International Journal of Computer Vision **60** (2004) 91–110
3. Comaniciu, D., Meer, P.: Mean Shift: A Robust Approach toward Feature Space Analysis. IEEE Transactions on Pattern Analysis and Machine Intelligence **24** (2002) 603–619
4. Babu, V., Perez, P., Bouthemy, P.: Kernel-based robust tracking for objects. In: Proc. Asian Conference on Computer Vision, Hyderabad India, Part II. (2006) 353–362
5. Isard, M., MacCormick, J.: Bramble: A bayesian multiple-blob tracker. In: Proc.IEEE International Conf. on Computer Vision (ICCV), vol. 2. (2001) 34–41
6. Comaniciu, D., Ramesh, V., Meer, P.: The variable bandwidth mean shift and data-driven scale selection. In: Proceedings of IEEE International Conference on Computer Vision, Vol. 1. (2001) 438–445 held in Vancouver, Canada.
7. Comaniciu, D.: An algorithm for data-driven bandwidth selection. IEEE Transactions on Pattern Analysis and Machine Intelligence **25** (2003) 281–288
8. Collins, R.T.: Mean shift blob tracking through scale space. In: CVPR 2003 Conference Proceedings. (2003) 234–240 held in Madison, Wisconsin, June.
9. Fukunaga, K., Hostetler, L.D.: The estimation of the gradient of a density function, with applications in pattern recognition. IEEE Transactions on Information Theory **21** (1975) 32–40
10. Namboodiri, V.P., Chaudhuri, S.: Shock filters based on implicit cluster separation. In: Proc. Conference on Computer Vision and Pattern Recognition (CVPR 2005),20-26 June 2005, San Diego, CA, USA. (2005) 82–87
11. Fisher, R.B.: Pets04 surveillance ground truth data set. In: Proc. Sixth IEEE Int. Work. on Performance Evaluation of Tracking and Surveillance. (2004) 1–5
12. Jojic, N., Frey, B.: Learning flexible sprites in video layers. In: Proc.IEEE Conf. on Computer Vision and Pattern Recognition (CVPR), vol. 1. (2001) 199–206
13. Haag, M., Nagel, H.H.: Tracking of complex driving manoeuvres in traffic image sequences. Image and Vision Computing **16** (1998) 517–527

Spatio-temporal Discovery: Appearance + Behavior = Agent

Prithwijit Guha[1], Amitabha Mukerjee[2], and K.S. Venkatesh[1]

[1] Department of Electrical Engineering,
Indian Institute of Technology, Kanpur,
Kanpur - 208016, Uttar Pradesh
{pguha, venkats}@iitk.ac.in
[2] Department of Computer Science & Engineering,
Indian Institute of Technology, Kanpur,
Kanpur - 208016, Uttar Pradesh
amit@cse.iitk.ac.in

Abstract. Experiments in infant category formation indicate a strong role for temporal continuity and change in perceptual categorization. Computational approaches to model discovery in vision have traditionally focused on static images, with appearance features such as shape playing an important role. In this work, we consider integrating agent behaviors with shape for the purpose of agent discovery. Improved algorithms for video segmentation and tracking under occlusion enable us to construct models that characterize agents in terms of motion and interaction with other objects. We present a preliminary approach for discovering agents based on a combination of appearance and motion histories. Using uncalibrated camera images, we characterize objects discovered in the scene by their shape and motion attributes, and cluster these using agglomerative hierarchical clustering. Even with very simple feature sets, initial results suggest that the approach forms reasonable clusters for diverse categories such as people, and for very distinct clusters (animals), and performs above average on other classes.

1   Introduction

Our concepts carve nature into chunks that form more compact and efficient representations of the world. It is possible that much of our early categories are learned from a single system of knowledge, based ultimately on perception [1]. If so, how does one go about discovering these categories from the *passing show*? This is clearly one of the central problems of perception, and we attempt to approach this problem from a computational standpoint.

Temporal continuity and change plays a strong role in category formation. By three months, infants begin to pay attention to coherently moving blobs (Spelke objects [2]), and by six months they are sensitive to the spatio-temporal dynamics of occlusion [3]. Indeed, in significant respects, the behavior of objects may constitute a more important hallmark of their categorization (e.g. animacy) than appearance alone [4].

Computational models of object categorization and object recognition, on the other hand, have focused traditionally on clustering based on appearance attributes in static images [5]. While appearance attributes may be prior (e.g. faces), category formation seems to be strongly tied to dynamic scenes.

P. Kalra and S. Peleg (Eds.): ICVGIP 2006, LNCS 4338, pp. 516–527, 2006.

In this work, we consider dynamic image sequences and use improved algorithms for video segmentation and tracking under occlusion to construct coherent motion histories and occlusion relations simulating these cognitive aspects of infant category formation. The aspects of the scene that characterize agents may involve motion, shape and their interactions with other objects, and we present an attempt to form clusters based on the first two elements, and to form a set of features for the third. Thus, we obtain shape and motion characteristic for each agent instance and use an average-link hierarchical clustering algorithm to cluster agents in this combined-feature scenario. Comparing our results with those obtained based on appearance alone shows significant improvements in recognizing certain heterogeneous groups such as People. Thus, through this work, we present an initial approach for discovering agents based on a combination of appearance and motion histories.

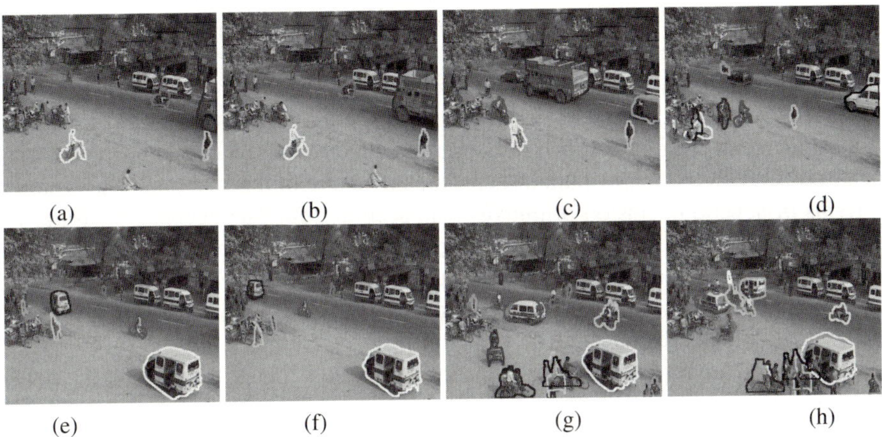

Fig. 1. Image sequence showing multi-agent activity in a traffic surveillance scenario. Vehicles, people, and animals are tracked across partial and complete occlusions and identified as agent instances. Frames (a)-(h) shows a crowd of people embarking a static tempo (marked as an erstwhile moving object) in the foreground, while a truck, motorcycles, rickshaws, bicycles and pedestrians are seen interacting along the main road.

1.1 Dynamic Image Characterization

We use an image sequence (acquired with a static camera) involving simultaneous interactions of tens of agents in a traffic scene, interacting with and occluding each other (figure 1). Agents are identified as connected blobs that are capable of motion, including those that are currently at rest. Agents constitute 3-manifolds in the $\{image \times time\}$ space, which is reduced to a set of features covering appearance and behavior.

Behavior of an agent can involve many aspects. Here we distinguish solitary behaviors (motions) from multi-agent behaviors (interactions). Based on the assumption that interaction involving proximity in $3D$ space may result in visual occlusion, we use occlusion, as one of the indicators of interaction. These three sets of features, then, are central to agent recognition:

- Appearance: attributes include shape, which is captured via the summary attributes of area, aspect ratio, and dispersedness (Perimeter^2 / Area).
- Motion : attributes include speed, direction change sequences, velocity change, as well as the quadratic-splined curve of the trajectory.
- Interactions: These are computed based on occlusion primitives (sub-section 2.3) such as isolation, crowding, fragmentation and disappearance.

Next we highlight our approach to multi-agent tracking in crowded scenarios. Since these algorithms have already been presented elsewhere [6] only a minimal summary is presented below.

2   Multiple Agent Tracking

Connected regions in the foreground (sub-section 2.1) that are seen to persist coherently over time constitute agents. Agents are tracked across multiple frames, and partial or complete occlusions are handled. The part of the image corresponding to an agent (called its support region) is tracked across frames by associating the predicted agent regions to foreground blobs obtained from figure-ground segmentation (2.1).

Several agents may correspond to the same blob (crowding), or a single agent may map to several blobs (fragmentation), etc; and the nature of this mapping is also stored in terms of several occlusion primitives (sub-section 2.3). The agents are further localized by an iterative centroid update algorithm, where their appearance (position and color) features are used to re-estimate the agent centroids (2.2). For the purpose of prediction, agent-blob associations are re-computed and agent models updated only for those agents which are unoccluded by others.

Agents which have been successfully tracked at the tth instant comprise the *active* set of agents $\mathcal{A}_{active}(t)$, whereas agents which have disappeared (occluded by others, etc.) constitute the set $\mathcal{A}_{disapp}(t)$ - which are matched with new agents when they arise in the scene. The system initializes itself with empty sets and agent instances are added (removed) as they appear (disappear) in the field of view.

2.1   Foreground Extraction

Agents are identified as foreground regions based on one of two kinds of evidence: first, as regions of change with respect to a learned background model; and second, as regions exhibiting motion. The background model is learned as a pixel-wise mixture of Gaussians [7] only for those pixels which exhibit no image motion. Inter-frame motion information [8] along with the higher level multi-agent tracking feedback (sub-section 2.2) is used further to disambiguate objects that come to a stop or objects that suddenly start moving [6]. The detected foreground pixels are further subjected to neighborhood-voting based corrections followed by connected component analysis to obtain a set of disjoint foreground blobs $\mathcal{F}(t) = \{f_i(t) : i = 1, \ldots, n_t\}$.

2.2   Agent Localization

Tracking multiple agents involve the use of their appearance models along with the trajectory information. The appearance of the jth agent having region of support consisting of $n_j(t)$ pixels at the tth instant is represented by an appearance model $\mathbf{a}_j(t) = \{\alpha_{jk}(t) : k = 1, \ldots, n_j(t)\}$, where $\alpha_{jk}(t) = [r_{jk}(t), g_{jk}(t), b_{jk}(t), \tilde{x}_{jk}(t), \tilde{y}_{jk}(t)]^T$ characterizes the kth component pixel of the jth agent. Here, the appearance is a collection of pixel positions $(\tilde{x}_{jk}(t), \tilde{y}_{jk}(t))$ relative to the centroid $\mathbf{c}_j(t)$ of the agent pixel set and the corresponding colors $(r_{jk}(t), g_{jk}(t), b_{jk}(t))$ in the RGB color space.

The agent-blob association is performed among the members of the active set $\mathcal{A}_{active}(t)$ and the set of foreground blobs $\mathcal{F}(t)$. If at least one pixel of $\mathbf{a}_j(t)$ overlaps $f_i(t) : |\{(\tilde{x}_{jk}(t), \tilde{y}_{jk}(t)) + \mathbf{c}*_j(t)\} \cap f_i(t)| \neq 0$, where $\mathbf{c}*_j(t)$ is the predicted agent centroid obtained at the tth instant from the motion history.

We consider the general case where the agents $\{A_p(t) : p = 1, \ldots, P_t\}$ are associated with the foreground blobs $\{f_q(t) : q = 1, \ldots, Q_t\}$. Let, $\mathbf{u}_l(t)$ be a foreground pixel characterized by color and position as $\mathbf{u}_l(t) = [r_l(t), g_l(t), b_l(t), x_l(t), y_l(t)]^T$. We consider $\mathbf{u}_l(t)$ to be the best match of the k^* pixel of the j^* associated agent, if the following are satisfied.

$$\tilde{\mathbf{u}}_{lj}(t) = [r_l(t), g_l(t), b_l(t), (x_l(t), y_l(t)) - \mathbf{c}_j^{(s)}(t)]^T \tag{1}$$

$$\lambda_{jkl}^{(s)}(t) = exp(-\|\alpha_{jk}(t) - \tilde{\mathbf{u}}_{lj}(t)\|_\Sigma) \tag{2}$$

$$v_l^{(s)}(t) = (j^*, k^*) = argmax_{j,k}\lambda_{jkl}^{(s)}(t) \tag{3}$$

where Σ is a weighing matrix and $\mathbf{c}_j^{(s)}(t)$ is the iteratively re-estimated centroid of the support of the jth agent in the sth iteration for the tth frame. The best match agent-pixel index two tuple for $\mathbf{u}_l(t)$ is given by $v_l^{(s)}(t) = (j^*, k^*)$, which indicates the visibility of the k^* pixel of the j^* agent as $\mathbf{u}_l(t)$. Thus, with respect to $\mathbf{u}_l(t)$, the centroid of $A_{j^*}(t)$ can be expected to be at $\hat{\mathbf{c}}_{j^*k^*l}^{(s)}(t) = (x_l(t), y_l(t)) - (\tilde{x}_{j^*k^*}(t), \tilde{y}_{j^*k^*}(t))$ with a certain weighted belief $\lambda_{jkl}^{(s)}(t)$. We re-estimate the agent centroid in the $(s+1)^{th}$ iteration as the weighted average of such expected centroid positions derived in s^{th} iteration as shown in equation 5.

$$V_j^{(s)}(t) = \{l, k : v_l^{(s)}(t) - (j, k)\} \tag{4}$$

$$\mathbf{c}_j^{(s+1)}(t) = \frac{\sum_{l,k \in V_j^{(s)}(t)} \hat{\mathbf{c}}_{jkl}^{(s)}(t)\lambda_{jkl}^{(s)}(t)}{\sum_{l,k \in V_j^{(s)}(t)} \lambda_{jkl}^{(s)}(t)} \tag{5}$$

The agent localization iterations are initialized with $\mathbf{c}_j^{(0)}(t) = \mathbf{c}*_j(t)$ and are terminated, when $max_j\|\mathbf{c}_j^{(s+1)}(t) - \mathbf{c}_j^{(s)}(t)\| \leq \epsilon_c$ is satisfied. The experiments are performed on 5000 frames of a traffic surveillance video, acquired with a static camera under almost constant ambient illumination conditions. We have used a diagonal weighing matrix (equation 2) of $\Sigma = [0.25, 0.25, 0.25, 1, 1]$ and obtained a tracking accuracy of 61%. The results of multiple agent tracking on the traffic video are shown in figure 1.

2.3 Interactions: Occlusion Primitives

Interactions between objects in $3D$ cannot be dealt with, but one may assume that objects in close proximity are likely to occlude one another (given a supra-horizon view).

The nature of this occlusion and its transitions constitute a partial signature of the interaction. Four types of occlusion situations are distinguished:

– Isolation ($\mathcal{O}(I)$): Single agent associated to single foreground blob (No occlusion).
– Crowding ($\mathcal{O}(C)$): More than one agents are associated to a single foreground blob (Occluding or occluded by other agents).
– Fragmentation ($\mathcal{O}(P)$): Agent appears as fragmented, being associated to multiple foreground blobs (partial occlusions).
– Disappearance ($\mathbf{O}(D)$): Agent unassociated to any foreground blob (Complete occlusion by background objects).

In *crowding / fragmentation* situations, only the agent trajectory is updated. Appearance models are updated only for those agents which are unoccluded by other agents/background objects. *Disappeared* agents are moved from $\mathcal{A}_{active}$ to $\mathcal{A}_{disapp}$. Foreground blobs (or fragments) unassociated to any agent in $\mathcal{A}_{active}$, are compared against those in $\mathcal{A}_{disapp}$ - if a match is not found, an entrance of a new agent is declared, otherwise the matched agent is reinstated in $\mathcal{A}_{active}$. Clearly, since our recognition is $2D$, many agents which re-emerge after near-complete occlusion may not be recognized - and indeed this is the case in approximately half of such situations.

3   Agent Characterization

An agent instance $A_j(t_s(j), t_e(j))$ is a space-time manifold characterized by the time indexed set of appearances (a collection of position (XY) and corresponding color (RGB) vectors) and the centroid-trajectory $\{c_j(t) : t = t_s(j), \ldots, t_e(j)\}$ during its scene presence $[t_s(j), t_e(j))$. This agent model encodes both the appearance and motion and constitutes part of the cognitive percept of the agent; the other aspects being its interactions with other objects.

This work focuses on unsupervised agent categorization based on low level features derived from the shape and the motion. As shape features, we consider the area (number of pixels in the support region), aspect ratio (vertical to horizontal length ratio of the minimum bounding box of the agent) and dispersedness (ratio of perimeter squared to area). Collins et al. [9] have successfully classified people and vehicles using this simple set of features, albeit in a supervised learning framework. The motion features include the set of speeds, directions of motion and the form (e.g. linear versus quadratic) of the trajectory in the image space. Such features can assist us in handling queries such as *"List all high speed vehicles"*, *"List all agents moving in a straight path from left to right"* or *"Group agents of similar size"* etc. The distributions of the shape and motion features of all the agents are shown in figure 2. Categorizing agents with respect to their low level features are described in further details in sub-section 3.1.

Motion and interactions together constitute the behavior model of an agent. Interactions in the real world often leave their imprints in terms of image space occlusions. Thus, the interactions with other objects in the scene can be represented by the occlusion primitive transition sequences of the concerned agents. This might lead to behavioral descriptions like *"The agent that walked across the tree"*.

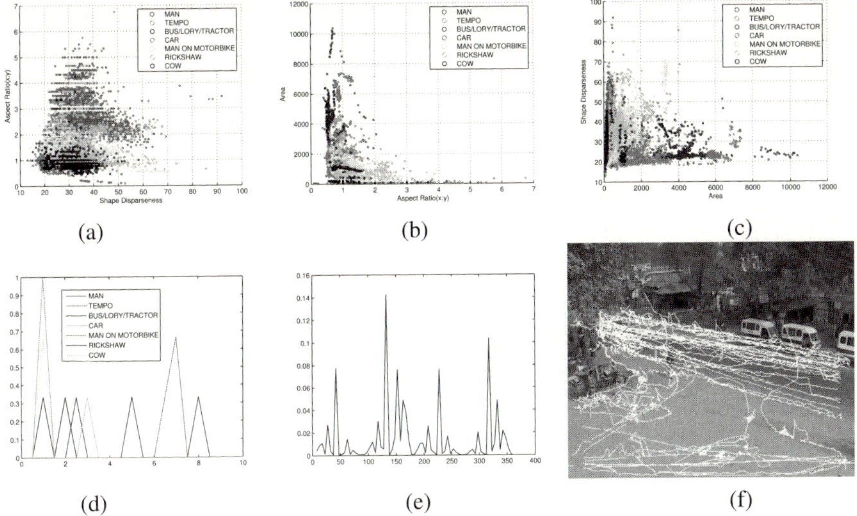

Fig. 2. Low level shape features projected on the (a) aspect ratio - dispersedness plane, (b) area - aspect ratio plane and (c) dispersedness - area plane; (d) Agent speed distribution in image plane; (e) Distribution of directions of motion in image plane; (f) Agent trajectories obtained till the first 2500 frames

3.1 Agent Categorization

The scene presence of the agents vary leading to the formation of variable length shape and motion feature sets. Here, the agent A_r is represented as a set of certain features q as $A_r^{(q)} = \{\mathbf{q}_{rj} : j = 1,\ldots,n_r^{(q)}\}$. Such forms of agent characterizations can't be efficiently handled by the usual approach of learning mixtures of Gaussians. Thus, we opt for *"agglomerative hierarchical clustering algorithms"* [10] which only require a definition of a distance measure between two such sets. Consider two Agents A_r and A_s characterized by their respective feature sets $A_r^{(q)}$ and $A_s^{(q)}$. We define the distance $\mathcal{D}_a(A_r^{(q)}, A_s^{(q)})$ between these two agent feature sets as,

$$\mathcal{D}_a(A_r^{(q)}, A_s^{(q)}) = \frac{1}{n_r^{(q)} n_s^{(q)}} \sum_{j=1}^{n_r^{(q)}} \sum_{k=1}^{n_s^{(q)}} \|\mathbf{q}_{rj} - \mathbf{q}_{sk}\| \tag{6}$$

We employ the *average-link clustering algorithm* as it offers a compromise between the single-link and complete-link ones and is more robust to outliers [10]. The algorithm initializes by assigning a cluster label to each of the agents. Thus, for a collection of agent feature sets $\{A_i\}_{i=1}^n$, the initial collection of clusters is given by $\{C_i = \{A_i\}\}_{i=1}^n$. A dendogram is formed in a bottom-up approach, where each iteration reduces the cluster number by one while merging two clusters, until finally, at the nth iteration, all the agents are assigned to a single cluster.

Consider the kth iteration, where we merge two of the $(n - k + 2)$ clusters obtained from the $(k - 1)^{th}$ step. The diameters of all possible 2-cluster mergers are computed and the pair minimizing the same is considered for merging. We select the cluster index pair (i^*, j^*) for merging in the kth iteration, if $(i^*, j^*) = argmin \mathcal{D}_c(C_i, C_j), \forall i, j = 1 \ldots (n - k + 2)$ and $i \neq j$, where $\mathcal{D}_c(C_i, C_j)$ is the distance between two clusters given by,

$$\mathcal{D}_c(C_i, C_j) = \frac{1}{|C_i||C_j|} \sum_{A \in C_i} \sum_{A' \in C_j} \mathcal{D}_a(A, A') \tag{7}$$

3.2   Categorizing with Shape and Motion Features

The multiple agent tracking performed on the aforementioned traffic surveillance video yielded the discovery of $n = 376$ agents. The appearances of the discovered agents are manually inspected for generating ground-truth data, from which we observe the existence of 10 distinct categories along with outliers (formed from track losses and spurious foreground detection) - $\Gamma(\text{SHAPE}) = \{$ OUTLIERS (62) PEOPLE (130), TEMPO (18), BUS (3), TRUCK (1), TRACTOR (3), CAR (18), MOTORBIKE (55), CYCLE (44), RICKSHAW (25), COW (17) $\}$.

We form the collection of agent shape feature (area, aspect ratio and dispersedness) sets $\{A_i^{(shape)}\}_{i=1}^n$, which are subjected to the average link clustering algorithm. A certain cluster $C_i^{(k)}$ in the kth iteration is declared to host a certain agent category Γ_j, if the agents of that class occur with the highest frequency in $C_i^{(k)}$. The sensitivity $\mathcal{S}_j(k)$ of categorizing the agent category Γ_j in the kth iteration is thus defined as,

$$\mathcal{S}_j(k) = \frac{1}{|\Gamma_j|} \sum_{i=1}^{n-k+1} |C_i^{(k)}| \delta(\beta(i) - j) \tag{8}$$

Where, $|\Gamma_j|$ is the total number of instances of the jth category, $\beta(i)$ denotes the category of an agent (from groundtruthed data), $| \bullet |$ determines the cardinality of a cluster and $\delta(\bullet)$ is the Kronecker Delta function. The sensitivities of clustering with up to 25 clusters for shape features and instances of the appearances of the discovered agents are shown in figure 3.

In a similar manner, we construct the agent trajectory feature sets of direction $\{A_i^{(direction)}\}_{i=1}^n$ and form $\{A_i^{(form)}\}_{i=1}^n$ which are subjected to hierarchical clustering. Manual inspection of the ground-truth data shows the existence of 6 different kinds of trajectories along with outliers (on account of track losses) - $\Gamma(\text{TRAJECTORY}) = \{$ OUTLIERS (205) LEFT TO RIGHT (77), FROM BOTTOM TURN LEFT (5), MOVE UP (4), RIGHT TO LEFT (76), U-TURN (3), MOVE TO BOTTOM (6) $\}$. Among these, there were only 163 LINEAR TRAJECTORIES. The sensitivities of detecting trajectories up to 100 clusters and the three distinctly discovered trajectories (LEFT TO RIGHT , FROM BOTTOM TURN LEFT and RIGHT TO LEFT)are shown in figure 4.

The high sensitivities (figures 3 and 4) in grouping the appearances of PEOPLE, TRUCK , CAR and the LINEAR TRAJECTORIES of agents moving LEFT TO RIGHT and RIGHT TO LEFT is indicative of the satisfactory performance of the proposed approach.

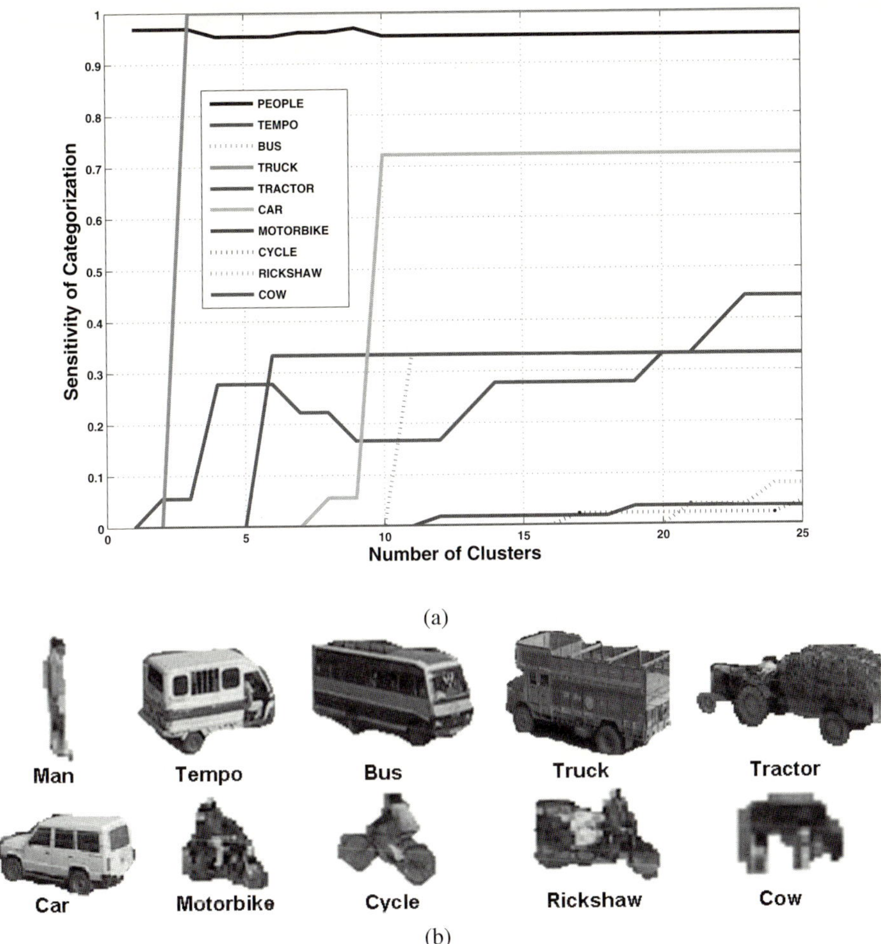

Fig. 3. Results of agent appearance discovery. Area, aspect ratio and dispersedness constitute the appearance features of an agent. However, the cardinalities of the appearance feature sets of the discovered agents vary due to their different frame presence. Here, we only have a measure of distance between two such sets and thus the average link clustering algorithm is executed on a collection of 376 (discovered) agent shape feature sets. (a) Detection rates achieved by the average link clustering algorithm computed by Cross-validating with ground-truth data. (b) Instances of appearances of discovered agents (appearances are scaled for better viewing purposes).

3.3   Behavior as Variable Length Occlusion Sequences

Models of single-agent behaviors are mainly characterized by their state space trajectories. Agent categorization in a surveillance scenario in terms of its motion features have already been discussed in sub-section 3.2. Agent-object interactions exhibit several different modes - the actions may involve actual contact (e.g. riding a bike, boarding or

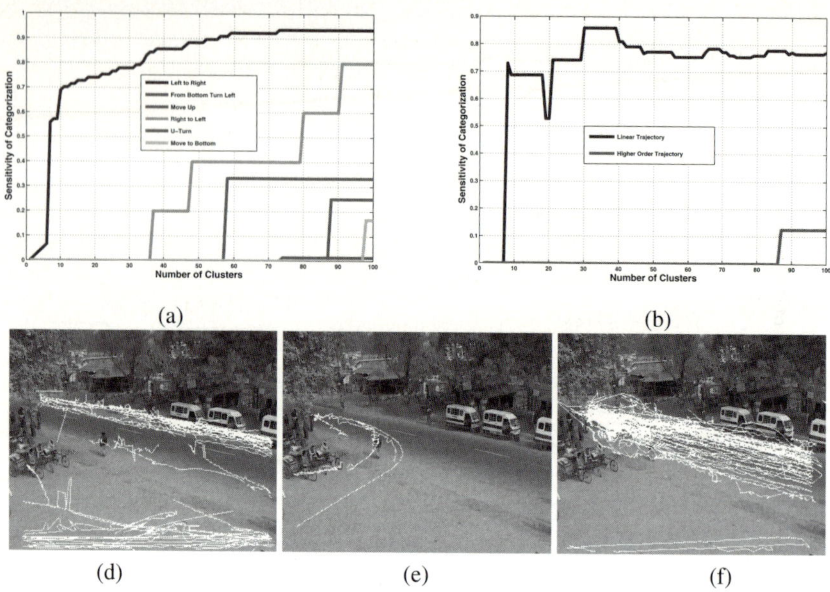

Fig. 4. Detection rates achieved by the average link clustering algorithm computed by cross-validating with ground-truth data. Sensitivity of categorization of agents by (a) *Trajectory direction* and (b) *Trajectory form* (linear versus higher order); Plotting discovered trajectories with respect to form and direction. Linear trajectories (in image plane) of agents moving (d) *Left to Right*, (e) *Right to Left* and (f) higher order trajectories of *Turning Left coming from Bottom*.

disembarking a vehicle, grouping etc.) or may involve interactions at a distance (e.g. following, chasing, overtaking, etc.). In terms of image space, actual contacts are necessarily reflected in terms of occlusions, but non-contact situations do not necessarily lead to non-overlap. Thus, we believe that occlusion sequences exhibited by an agent form visual signatures for the underlying interactions. More so, we identify that the occlusion state transition sequences form a more significant interaction description than the occlusion state sequences themselves. In this work, we aim to discover the interactions arising out of agents moving in complex environments undergoing both static and dynamic occlusions with background objects and other agents respectively.

A number of methodologies employing hidden Markov models, time-delay neural networks, recurrent networks etc. have been proposed for modeling and recognition of action/interaction sequences in a supervised learning framework. On the other hand, unsupervised learning of activity patterns have also been proposed by trajectory clustering [11] or variable length Markov model learning [12]. A good overview of such techniques can be found in [13].

Supervised activity modeling techniques are mostly task oriented and hence fail to capture the corpus of events from the time-series data provided to the system. Unsupervised data mining algorithms, on the other hand, discover the modes of spatio-temporal patterns thereby leading to the identification of a larger class of events. The use of VLMMs in the domain of activity analysis was introduced for automatic modeling of the actions in exercise sequences [14] and interactions like handshaking [12] or overtaking of vehicles [15] in a traffic scenario. These approaches propose to perform a vector quantization over the agent feature and motion space to generate temporally indexed agent-state sequences from video data. These sequences are parsed further to learn VLMMs leading to the discovery of behavioral models of varying temporal durations.

Incremental Transition Sequence Learning. In this work, we employ *"Incremental Transition Sequence Learning"* to capture the variable length sequences of occlusion primitives which describe different behavior patterns. The atomic event primitives (here, the occlusion primitives) ϵ constitute the set $\mathcal{E}$. Our approach to mining in this space involves the construction of an *activity tree* $\mathcal{T}_\alpha$ whose branches represent variable length event primitive sequences.

An empty (first in first out) buffer β_j (of length L, the maximum sequence length) and the null activity tree $\mathcal{T}_\alpha(j)$ (containing only the root node ρ_j) are initialized at the very first appearance of every j^{th} agent $\mathcal{A}_j$. Each node of $\mathcal{T}_\alpha(j)$ is a two tuple $\mathcal{T}_n \equiv (\epsilon, \pi)$ containing the primitive $\epsilon \in \mathcal{E}$ and a real number $\pi \in (0, 1]$ signifying the probability of occurrence of the path $\{\rho_j, \ldots, \mathcal{T}_n\}$ among the set of all possible paths of the same length.

Let, $\epsilon(j, t)$ be the event primitive observed for $\mathcal{A}_j$ at time t. If there is a transition in this event primitive, i.e. if $\epsilon(j, t) \neq \epsilon(j, t - 1)$, then $\epsilon(j, t)$ is pushed to β_j. Let the set of l-length paths (originating from ρ_j) of $\mathcal{T}_\alpha(j, t)$, be $B^{(l)}(j, t) = \{\alpha_u^{(l)}(j, t)\}_{u=1}^{b_l}$, where b_l is the number of l-length branches in the tree. More so, if the sequence $\{\beta_j[l - k](t)\}_{k=1}^{l}$ signify the bth path of $B^{(l)}(j, t)$, then the probabilities $\{\pi_u^{(l)}(j, t)\}_{u=1}^{b_l}$ of the nodes of $\mathcal{T}_\alpha(j, t)$ at the lth depth are updated as,

$$\pi_u^{(l)}(j, t) = (1 - \eta_l(t))\pi_u^{(l)}(j, t - 1) + \eta_l(t)\delta(u - b) \tag{9}$$

Where, $\eta_l(t)$ is the rate of learning l-length sequences at the tth instant and δ is the Kronecker delta function. However, in the current implementation a fixed learning rate η is employed such that $\eta_l(t) = max\left(\frac{1}{t}, \eta\right) \forall l$.

Occurrence of a new event primitive results in the formation of newer variable length sequences in the buffer. Thus, new nodes signifying this event primtive are added at different levels of the tree thereby growing newer branches. Each new node is initialized with an initial probability of $\eta_l(t)$, whereas the older node probabilities in the same levels are penalized by multiplying with a factor of $(1 - \eta_l(t))$. This ensures the self-normalizing nature of node probability updates (as in equation 9) such that they add up to unity at each depth.

3.4   Occlusion Interaction: Learning from O-Transitions

Consider a short video sequence where a person walks across a tree from left to right in the image space from which we sample 18 frames to illustrate the process of agent-background object interaction discovery. Key frames from this sequence are shown in figure 5(a)-(e). Incremental transition sequence learning is performed with a maximum depth of $L = 10$ and a learning rate η inversely proportional to the frame number. The growth of the activity tree is shown in figure 5(f).

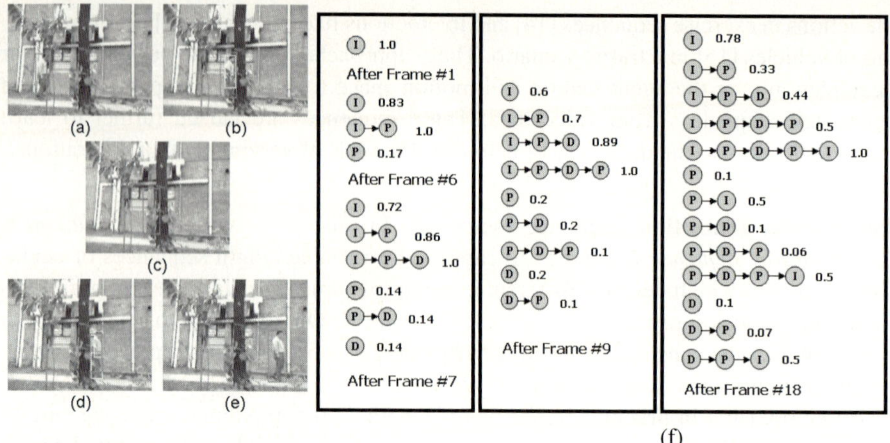

Fig. 5. Example video sequence: Man walks left to right behind a tree. Frames and Agent states: (a) 1-5: *isolated*; (b) 6: *partially occluded*, (c) 7-8: *disappeared*, (d) 9: *partially occluded* (e) 10-18: *isolated*. (f) Learning **Activity Tree**. The left-most nodes are just below the root of the growing tree. Results of incremental transition sequence learning are shown after frames 1, 6, 7, 9 and 18. Branches encode different variable length event sequences along with relative frequencies. Thus, in column 2 (after Frame 9), the sequence $\{(I \rightarrow P \rightarrow D), 0.89\}$ corresponds to the event primitive sequence $\{\mathcal{O}(I) \rightarrow \mathcal{O}(P) \rightarrow \mathcal{O}(D)\}$; i.e. the event sequence "coming from the left and getting hidden" occurs with relative frequency 89% among observed 3-length sequences.

Semantic labels can be assigned to the sequences in the occlusion-primitive space to denote different activities, and subsequences may constitute sub-activities. For example, consider the longest path $\{\mathcal{O}(I) \rightarrow \mathcal{O}(P) \rightarrow \mathcal{O}(D) \rightarrow \mathcal{O}(P) \rightarrow \mathcal{O}(I)\}$ learned in the activity tree from the aforementioned video that correspond to the activity of **walking across a tree from left to right**. Subsequences of this path viz. $\{\mathcal{O}(I) \rightarrow \mathcal{O}(P) \rightarrow \mathcal{O}(D)\}$ and $\{\mathcal{O}(D) \rightarrow \mathcal{O}(P) \rightarrow \mathcal{O}(I)\}$ also correspond to the visually significant events of **going to hide from left to right** and **reappearing and moving to the right**.

4 Conclusion

In this work we have attempted to capture some cognitive notions of perceptual category learning and attempted to devise computational analogs of this process. While our results in terms of category discovery are clearly preliminary, we believe that the high correlations obtained in terms of sensitivity matches (figures 3 and 4) do indeed provide some justification for such an approach, especially given that the system operates in completely unsupervised mode, without any information about the complex scene that is being observed.

Clearly, the results are indicative, and much work remains. In particular, characterizing the interactions between objects is a very rich area, of which the occlusion models used here only scratch the surface. In cognitive terms, the behavior of agents can be described compactly in terms of landmarks - and currently we are exploring the emergence of scene landmarks with which to characterize such interaction.

References

1. Quinn, P., Eimas, P.: The emergence of category representations during infancy: Are separate perceptual and conceptual processes required? Journal of Cognition and Development **1** (2000) 55–61
2. Spelke, E.S.: Principles of object perception. Cognitive Science **14** (1990) 29–56
3. Gredebaeck, G., von Hofsten, C.: Infants evolving representations of object motion during occlusion: A longitudinal study of 6- to 12-month-old infants. Infancy **6** (2004) 165–184
4. Mandler, J.M.: Foundations of Mind. Oxford University Press, New York (2004)
5. Mareschal, D., French, R.M., Quinn, P.: A connectionist account of asymmetric category learning in early infancy. Developmental Psychology **36** (2000) 635–645
6. Blind1: Details withheld. In: for Blind Review. (2006)
7. Zivkovic, Z.: Improved adaptive gaussian mixture model for background subtraction. In: Proceedings of the 17th International Conference on Pattern Recognition. Volume 2. (2004) 28–31
8. Proesmans, M., Gool, L.V., Pauwels, E., Osterlinck, A.: Determination of optical flow and its discontinuities using non-linear diffusion. In: The 3rd Eurpoean Conference on Computer Vision. Volume 2. (1994) 295–304
9. Collins, Lipton, Kanade, Fujiyoshi, Duggins, Tsin, Tolliver, Enomoto, Hasegawa: A system for video surveillance and monitoring: Vsam final report. Technical Report CMU-RI-TR-00-12, Robotics Institute, Carnegie Mellon University (2000)
10. Duda, R., Hart, P., Stork, D.: Pattern Recognition. 2nd Edition, John Wiley and Sons (2003)
11. Johnson, N., Hogg, D.: Learning the distribution of object trajectories for event recognition. In: Proceedings of the 6th British conference on Machine vision (Vol. 2), BMVA Press (1995) 583–592
12. Galata, A., Johnson, N., Hogg, D.: Learning variable-length markov models of behavior. Computer Vision and Image Understanding **81** (2001) 398–413
13. Buxton, H.: Learning and understanding dynamic scene activity: a review. Image and Vision Computing **21** (2003) 125–136
14. Johnson, N., Galata, A., Hogg, D.: The acquisition and use of interaction behavior models. In: Proceedings of IEEE Conference on Computer Vision and Pattern Recognition, IEEE Computer Society (1998) 866–871
15. Galata, A., Cohn, A.G., Magee, D., Hogg, D.: Modeling interaction using learnt qualitative spatio-temporal relations and variable length markov models. In van Harmelen, F., ed.: Proceedings of European Conference on Artificial Intelligence. (2002) 741–745

Fusion of Thermal Infrared and Visible Spectrum Video for Robust Surveillance

Praveen Kumar, Ankush Mittal, and Padam Kumar

Department of Electronics and Computer Engineering,
Indian Institute of Technology, Roorkee,
India 247667
`praveen.kverma@gmail.com, {ankumfec, padamfec}@iitr.ernet.in`

Abstract. This paper presents an approach of fusing the information provided by visible spectrum video with that of thermal infrared video to tackle video processing challenges such as object detection and tracking for increasing the performance and robustness of the surveillance system. An enhanced object detection strategy using gradient information along with background subtraction is implemented with efficient fusion based approach to handle typical problems in both the domains. An intelligent fusion approach using Fuzzy logic and Kalman filtering technique is proposed to track objects and obtain fused estimate according to the reliability of the sensors. Appropriate measurement parameters are identified to determine the measurement accuracy of each sensor. Experimental results are shown on some typical scenarios of detection and tracking of pedestrians.

1 Introduction

With the advances in sensor and computing technologies, new generation video surveillance and security system will be required to be *persistent* (ability to function continuously for 24 hours and in a variety of scenarios) and *intelligent* in combining multimedia information for robust operation. Color and grayscale video cameras have an obvious limitation of daytime operation only, whereas Infrared media are more informative in dark environment (especially in night). Traditional approaches analyze video only in a single modality; either using the visible spectrum or using another modality such as mid-wave or long-wave infrared images [1]. Since, the visible spectrum and thermal infrared are inherently complementary; having their own unique characteristics, combining them can be advantageous in many scenarios, when either may perform poorly. For example, in foggy weather condition and in night, IR sensor will outperform visible range camera. Sudden lighting changes, shadows and camouflage, in visible spectrum, can often cause the foreground detection to incorrectly classify pixels. Combining the visible analysis with infrared imaging seems very beneficial, as it is very robust to the above mentioned problems. However, in good lighting and stable background conditions, visible spectrum video would give better results because of containing strong edges, robust color and other features with comparatively low noise. Although humans and other hot objects usually appear as areas

P. Kalra and S. Peleg (Eds.): ICVGIP 2006, LNCS 4338, pp. 528–539, 2006.
© Springer-Verlag Berlin Heidelberg 2006

of high contrast and are more distinctive in infrared but well insulated clothing can cause the torso to have very low contrast and appear as background noise. Sudden temperature change, heat diffusion through objects in contact and "Halo effect" produced by some infrared sensors, which appears as a dark or bright halo surrounding very hot or cold objects respectively, are some additional difficulties that cause incorrect segmentation of object region. The challenge therefore is to determine the best approach to combine both modalities so that typical problems in both the domains can be addressed. This is made more challenging by the fact that some sources of data may give misleading or incorrect information. For example, changes in lighting, such as those caused by clouds blocking the sun's light during the daytime, can cause incorrect change detection in the visible spectrum. In a recent review on surveillance research [2], Hu et al. conclude in their section on Future Developments in Surveillance that *"Surveillance using multiple different sensors seems to be a very interesting subject. The main problem is how to make use of their respective merits and fuse information from such kinds of sensors"*. In another review of video surveillance and sensor networks research [3], Cucchiara argues that the integration of video technology with sensors and other media streams will constitute the fundamental infrastructure for new generations of multimedia surveillance systems.

This paper presents an approach of fusing the information provided by thermal infrared video and that of visible spectrum video for robust object detection and accurate object tracking thereby increasing the performance and robustness of the surveillance system. An enhanced object detection strategy is implemented with efficient fusion based approach. We collected a database of known scenarios in indoor and outdoor situations captured simultaneously by video and IR cameras. These image sequences (video and IR) are time synchronized and geometrically corrected to co-register them with their counterparts. For both sensor sequences, we apply our enhanced background subtraction algorithm using gradient information, to identify region of interests (ROI) and extract blobs corresponding to the objects in the scene. For individual sensor sequence, blobs have to be matched with the objects (tracked at fusion level) present in the previous frame and some measurement parameters are computed. For tracking purpose, track-to-track fusion scheme is used, where a separate Kalman Filter is used for each track to obtain a filtered estimate. An intelligent fusion algorithm subsequently proceeds to obtain fused measurement data for each object according to the reliability of the sensors. A Fuzzy Inference System (FIS) is employed to assign suitable weights to each sensors filtered estimate, based on the value of two parameters called '*Confidence*' and '*Appearance Ratio*', computed for all the objects in each sensor output. Finally, a defuzzificator obtains the fused estimated measurement based on the weightage values. The Experimental results are done to demonstrate the effectiveness of fusing visible and IR in some typical scenarios of detection and tracking of pedestrians.

2 Literature Review and Background

Object Detection and Tracking beyond Visible Spectrum: Recent literature on the exploitation of near-infrared information to track humans generally deals only with the face of observed people and a few are concerned with the whole body [4] but these approach rely on the highly limiting assumption that the person region always has a much brighter (hotter) appearance than the background. In [5], the author proposes a novel contour based background subtraction strategy to detect people in thermal imagery, which is robust across a wide range of environmental conditions. First of all, a standard background-subtraction technique is used to identify local region-of interest (ROI), each containing the person and surrounding thermal halo. The foreground and background gradient information within each region are then combined into a contour saliency map (highlighting the person boundary). Using a watershed-based algorithm, the gradients are thinned and thresholded into contour fragments and A* search algorithm is used to connect any contour gaps. However use of highly computational techniques, makes their approach inappropriate for use in real time surveillance settings.

Modality Fusion: Multi modal fusion is the process of combining data from multiple sources (of different spectrum) such that the resulting entity or decision is in some sense better than that provided by any of the individual sources [6]. Data fusion techniques have had a long history in radar and vision based military applications to enhance the information content of the scene by combining multispectral images in one image. However, only recently data fusion is being considered for enhancing the capabilities of automatic video-based detection and tracking system for surveillance purpose. In [7], the fusion of thermal infrared with visible spectrum video, in the context of surveillance and security, is done at the object level. Detection and tracking of blobs (regions) are performed separately in the visible and thermal modality. An object is made up of one or more blobs, which are inherited or removed as time passes. Correspondences are obtained between objects in each modality, forming a master-slave relationship, so that the master (the object with the better detection or confidence) assists the tracking of the slave in the other modality. In a recent work, Davis et al. [8] propose a new contour-based background-subtraction technique using thermal and visible imagery for persistent object detection in urban settings. Their algorithm requires co-registered image from two streams. Statistical background subtraction in the thermal domain is used to identify the initial regions-of-interest. Color and intensity information are used within these areas to obtain the corresponding regions of-interest in the visible domain. Within each image region (thermal and visible treated independently), the input and background gradient information are combined as to highlight only the boundaries of the foreground object. The boundaries are then thinned and thresholded to form binary contour fragments. Contour fragments belonging to corresponding regions in the thermal and visible domains are then fused using the combined input gradient information from both sensors.

Multi-Sensor Fusion: The determination of the target's position and velocity from a noisy time-series of measurements constitute a classical statistical estimation problem and it involves the use of sequential estimation techniques such as the Kalman filter or its variants. Observational data may be combined, or fused, at a variety of levels from the raw data (or observation) level to feature level, or at the decision level. In the fusion process, it is essential to asses the reliability of sensor data because the results could be seriously affected in the case of malfunctioning sensor. Therefore for fusing data collected from different sensors requires the determination of measurements' accuracy so that they can be fused in a weighted manner. In [9], the authors propose a multi-sensor data fusion method for video surveillance, and demonstrated the results by using optical and infrared sensors. The measurements coming from different sensors were weighted by adjusting measurement error covariance matrix by a metric called Appearance Ratio (AR), whose value is proportional to the strength of the segmented blobs. In [10], the authors propose a hybrid multi-sensor data fusion architecture using Kalman filtering and fuzzy logic techniques. They feed the measurement coming from each sensor to separate fuzzy–adaptive kalman filters (FKF), working in parallel. Based on the value of a variable called Degree of Matching (D0M) and the measurement noise covariance matrix R coming from each FKF, a fuzzy inference system (FIS) assigns a degree of confidence to each one of the FKFs output. Finally, a defuzzificator obtains the fused estimated measurement based on the confidence values. They demonstrated the result on a simulated dataset, by taking example of four noisy inputs.

3 Object Detection

Simple background subtraction and Thresholding is ineffective in detecting the objects in various situations because of typical problems (as noted before) in both the domains. We employ a fusion based enhanced and efficient detection strategy using both visible and thermal imagery, which is well suited to handle typical problems in both the domains. Our approach is based on the use of gradient information along with background subtraction, as proposed and demonstrated in [5] but differs in the sense that we don't use computational intensive techniques for real timeliness. Additionally we take a fusion approach with visible spectrum video based on mutual agreement between the two modalities.

Since the algorithm requires registered imagery from the two sensors, we initialize the system by manually selecting four corresponding feature points from a pair of thermal and visible images. A homography matrix created from these points is used to register the thermal and visible images. First of all, localized regions of-interest (ROIs) are identified in both domains by applying standard gaussian background-subtraction, which generally produces regions that encompass the entire foreground object with surrounding halo in IR and shadows in visible, if present. The statistical background model for each pixel (in thermal or visible intensity) is created by computing *weighted* means and variances and the foreground pixels in the ROI then obtained using the squared Mahalanobis Distance by using following equation:

$$ROI(x, y) = \begin{cases} 1 & \dfrac{\left(I(x, y) - \mu(x, y)\right)^2}{\sigma(x, y)^2} \succ 100 \\ 0 & \text{otherwise} \end{cases} \qquad (1)$$

Now, at this step we examine the ROI's from both the domains, to get fused ROI that will be used to cue further processing in both the domains. Since the ROIs will include shadow in visible and halo in IR (if present) along with the foreground objects, taking intersection of both ROIs, will eliminate regions that are not present in both the modalities (like shadows, noise, etc.). However, if either of the sensor is performing poorly, either due to malfunctioning or environmental conditions, taking intersection will degrade the output of other sensor as well. Hence, we take the intersection only when both the ROIs have reasonable amount of mutual agreement in detecting foreground regions. Otherwise, we continue processing with the original ROIs separately for each domain and leave the detection of noise region at later stage. For determining the mutual agreement in both modalities, we use the following ratio (R), defined as:

$$R = \frac{P_{(1,1)}}{P_{(1,0)} + P_{(0,1)}} \tag{2}$$

where $P(x,y)$ is the total sum of pixels whose visible classification is x and whose infrared classification is y. Therefore, R is the ratio of the agreed foreground pixels to the total disagreed pixels. Now if R is greater than a predefined threshold, we assume that there is a high degree of mutual agreement in both the modalities, and we choose the fused ROI for further processing.

We again examine the difference image in each domain within resultant ROI in an attempt to extract gradient information corresponding only to the foreground object. Sobel operator is applied to calculate foreground gradient magnitudes from difference image and background gradient magnitudes. As proposed in [5] a gradient map is formed by taking pixel wise minimum of the normalized foreground gradient magnitudes and the normalized foreground-background gradient-difference magnitudes (as shown in equation 3), preserving the foreground object gradients that are both strong and significantly different from the background.

$$GradientMap = \min\left(\frac{\| \langle Ix, Iy \rangle \|}{\max}, \frac{\| \left(\langle Ix - BGx \rangle, \langle Iy - BGy \rangle \right) \|}{\max} \right) \tag{3}$$

By Thresholding the gradient map and applying morphological operations like closing and dilation, we obtain blobs corresponding to actual foreground objects (without halo or diffused shadows). The approach is equally applicable to both thermal and visible imagery. Figure 1 shows the output of the various steps of object segmentation applied to an infrared image having halo effect.

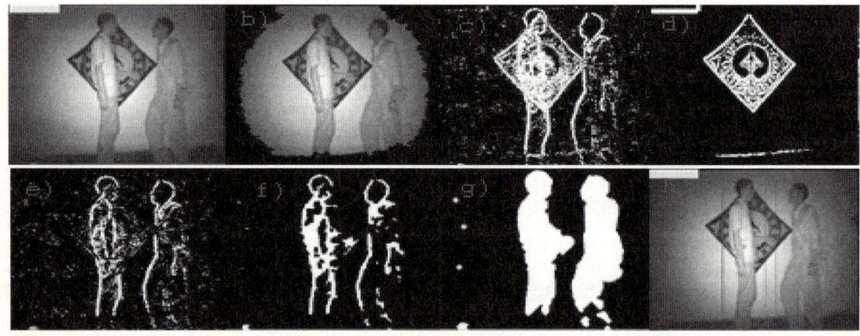

Fig. 1. Segmentation Output shown for infrared image with halo effect a) original image b) ROI c) Foreground gradient d) Background gradient e) Gradient map f) after Thresholding g) blobs h) objects detected

4 Target Tracking

Achieving better trajectory accuracy and continuity is of great importance for the successive steps of behavior understanding performed by a surveillance system. In particular, the trajectories of the objects in the scene have to be analyzed to detect suspicious events [11]. Tracking takes place at two levels. In the first level of the tracking procedure the system matches the blobs detected in the current frame with those extracted in the previous frame. Second level of tracking takes place at fusion level, where the objects (combination of one or more blobs) are tracked, using a fusion filter to obtain fused estimate of the object state. For getting an estimate of segmentation output and reliability, we compute certain measurement parameters for blobs, which are defined as follows:

1. "**Appearance Ratio (AR)**": Let D be the *difference map obtained as the absolute difference between the current frame and a reference image with T as threshold to binarize D , and let B_j be the j-th blob extracted from the sensor, then the Appearance Ratio for that blob is defined as*

$$AR(B_j) = \frac{\sum_{x,y \in B_j} D(x, y)}{|B_j| \times T} \tag{4}$$

where $|B_j|$ is the number of pixels of the blob B_j. The value of AR is proportional to the strength of the segmented blobs from each sensor. A low AR value indicates that the pixel intensity in the blob region has barely crossed the threshold. Thus AR value can be compared to determine which sensor is more informative
2. "**Overlapping**": *Overlapping O(a,b), between blobs a and b, is defined as:*

$$Omax(a,b) = Maximum(\ IA(a,b) / A(a),\ IA(a,b) / A(b))$$
$$Omin(a,b) = Minimum(\ IA(a,b) / A(a),\ IA(a,b) / A(b)) \tag{5}$$

where A(i) is the area of the ith blob's bounding box, and *IA(a,b)* is the intersection area between them. These two factors are used in matching blobs.
3. "**Resemblance**": between two blobs is estimated with respect to the degree of match between two blobs (using *Omin*) and similarity factor. R(a,b) is defined as:

$$R(a,b) = Omin(a,b)\ \times [\ 1 - [Abs(Aa-Ab) / Maximum(Aa,\ Ab)] \tag{6}$$

4. "**Confidence (C)**": It gives the persistence of a blob over time and is defined by the following equation:

$$C(a) = (\sum_{b=0}^{n} R(a,b) \times C(b)) + 1 \tag{7}$$

where *a* is the new blob, *b is* the preceding blob, and *n* the number of preceding blobs that matched to the present one. As seen from the equation, the confidence on matching from *t-1* to *t* increases if the blob has been tracked for a long time and the resemblance from two time steps is large. Note that the minimum value of confidence of any blob is 1, which is in case of its first appearance in the scene.

Initially an object can be made up from an isolated blob or many closer blobs. The system first of all matches the current set of blobs with the objects detected in the previous frames by simple spatial occupancy overlap tests between the predicted locations of objects and the locations of blobs in current frame. The maximum overlapping factor (*Omax*) is used for this purpose. The system then establishes correspondence between the individual blobs (of current and previous frames) that correspond to same object. This is done by maintaining a list of blobs in the previous frames that correspond to each object. Subsequently, specific parameters like resemblance and confidence factor are calculated for each blob. The object's confidence is computed as the average of the confidence of individual blobs comprising the object. The appearance ratio for an object is calculated by summing up the numerator and denominator for each individual blobs and then dividing. The confidence C and appearance ratio AR is used in the fusion process to estimate the measurement accuracy of each sensor for extracted objects.

5   Fusion Process

We employ second order Kalman filter to model the motion of each object in the scene. The fusion procedure maintains its own list of targets. In the fusion process, the fused estimate should be more biased by accurate measurements and almost unaffected by inaccurate or malfunctioning ones. An intelligent fusion algorithm based on fuzzy logic techniques is designed to obtain fused measurement data (for each object). The main advantages derived from the use of fuzzy logic techniques with respect to traditional schemes are the simplicity of the approach, the capability of fuzzy systems to deal with imprecise information, and the possibility of including heuristic knowledge about the phenomenon under consideration [10].

The reliability of the sensors is estimated by two input parameters, the Appearance Ratio (AR) and Confidence (C). AR value reflects the strength of segmentation output from each sensor at current instance. The value of C also reflects on the temporal consistency of the sensor in maintaining good detection of a particular object. Also the confidence for an object detected as a single blob will be more than the object detected in fragemented parts (blobs).

Figure 2 shows the Hybrid Fuzzy logic-Kalman Fusion filter. A separate fuzzy inference system (FIS) is employed to monitor each channel and assigns suitable weights to each sensor's filtered estimate. Based on the values of the variables *C* and *AR,* the FIS assigns a weightage *w*, on the interval [0,1], to each of the KF's outputs. This value reflects the reliability of the sensor's measurement and it acts as a weight that tells the defuzzifactor, the confidence level at which it should take each KF's output value.

Each FIS was implemented using two inputs, the current value of *C* and *AR*; and one output, the weight *w*. For *C* and *AR*, we consider three fuzzy sets: ZE=zero, S=small, L=large. The membership function for C and AR are shown in figure 3. For

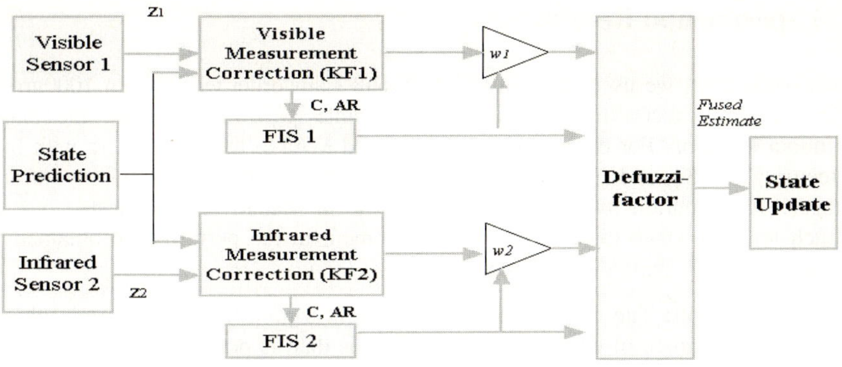

Fig. 2. A Hybrid Fuzzy logic-Kalman Fusion Filter

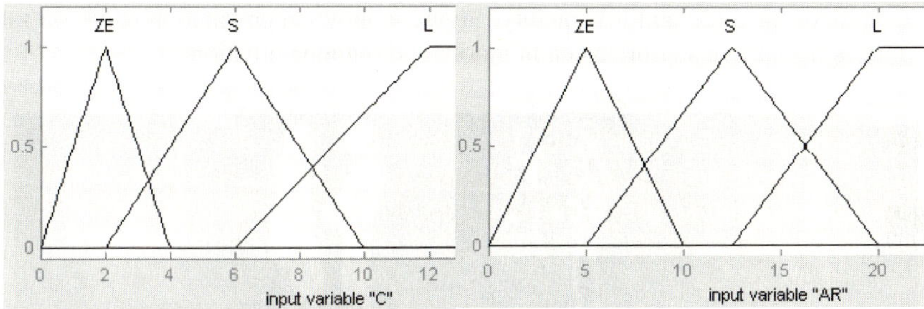

Fig. 3. Membership function for C and AR

the output w, three fuzzy singletons were defined with the labels: G=1=good, AV=0.5=average and P=0=poor. Thus the fuzzy rule base of each FIS comprises of following nine rules:

1. If $C=ZE$, and $AR=ZE$, then $w=P$
2. If $C=ZE$, and $AR=S$, then $w=P$
3. If $C=S$, and $AR=ZE$, then $w=P$
4. If $C=ZE$, and $AR=L$, then $w=AV$
5. If $C=S$, and $AR=S$, then $w=AV$
6. If $C=L$, and $AR=ZE$, then $w=AV$
7. If $C=S$, and $AR=L$, then $w=G$
8. If $C=L$, and $AR=S$, then $w=G$
9. If $C=L$, and $AR=L$, then $w=G$

The above rules are based on two simple heuristic considerations. First, if both C and AR are large for an extracted object from a sensor, it implies that the sensor's filtered estimate is highly reliable. Second, if both of these values are near to minimum, the output is unreliable. Thus, using the compositional rule of inference sum-prod, the FIS calculates the weight, which tells the defuzzifactor at what confidence level it should take each output. Note that this method of fusion is suitable for any number of sensors.

6 Experimental Results

For experiments, we used the Sony TRV65 Hi8 Camcorder with 37mm 1000nm IR filter that allows recording of daytime video (visible spectrum) and nighttime images in indoor situation. For outdoor situation we used MATIS thermal camera with InSb detector (320x284) and spectral range of 3-5 μm, for capturing good quality infrared images. The program implementation was done in Matlab 7.0. We tested our approach at every stage to analyze the improvement in the performance obtained by combining visible and infrared imagery.

Object Detection: The object detection approach is robustly able to detect objects across a wider range of environmental conditions than is possible with standard approaches as demonstrated in [5]. Here we have also tested the method over different ranges of IR sensors (with varying degree of noise, halo effect etc) suitable for indoor and outdoor surveillance. We collected samples of IR images from three sensors ranging from high, medium and low quality. Figure 4 shows segmentation result on sample images from these sensors taken in indoor and outdoor situations.

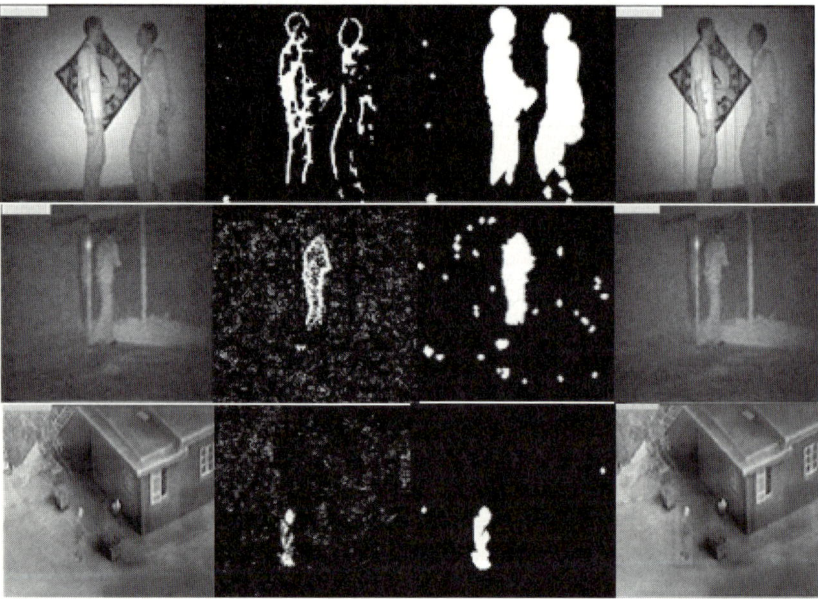

Fig. 4. First column shows the original IR images, second column shows the corresponding gradient map, third column shows the blobs extracted and the fourth one show the objects detected in the images

The IR images in the first and second row are night shot images (from Sony Camcorder) taken in indoor situations. The IR image in first row contains Halo around people and the second row image is extremely noisy. The third row shows an outdoor situation where the person's body is quite insulated by clothing and only the head portion appears as hot spot. In spite of these challenges, the output shows properly

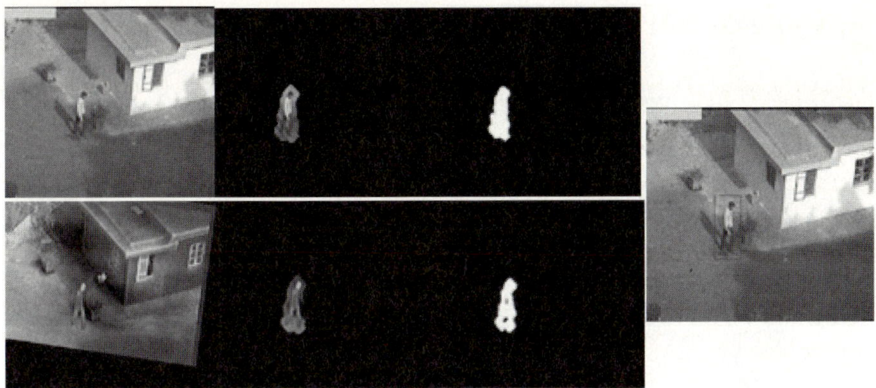

Fig. 5. First row shows the image in visible domain having shadow and the second row shows the corresponding IR image, after registration. The second column shows the Fused ROI in both domain and the third column shows the blob extracted. Finally the detected object region (shown in visible image) does not contain shadow.

segmented out objects. In Figure 5, an outdoor situation of one pedestrian walking near a building is presented and it shows that the IR image can be helpful in removing shadows from the visible image.

Object Tracking: For comparison of accuracy in tracking the trajectory, the following performance measures were adopted:

$$J_{zv} = \sqrt{\frac{1}{n}\sum_{k=1}^{n}\left(za_k - z_k\right)^2} \tag{8}$$

$$J_{ze} = \sqrt{\frac{1}{n}\sum_{k=1}^{n}\left(za_k - \hat{z}_k\right)^2} \tag{9}$$

Where za_k is the actual value of the position; z_k is the measured position; and $\hat{z}_k$ is the estimated position at an instant of time k. Figure 6 (appendix) shows a pedestrian being tracked with fused measurement of centroid position (shown with red cross) and fused estimate (with green cross) is shown in visible imagery. Actual position was calculated by manually segmenting the pedestrian. Table 1 shows the performance measures obtained by using only visible, only thermal and using both modalities.

Table 1. Comparison of tracking accuracy obtained by using only visible, only thermal and using both

Sensor	J_{zv}	J_{ze}
Only Visible	2.04	2.92
Only Infrared	3.35	3.20
Visible and Infrared (fused)	1.87	2.45

Fig. 6. A pedestrian being tracked in outdoor situation

Since it is a daytime situation with sufficient lighting and temperature difference in the environment, the two sensors are reporting a track similar to the ground truth. Nonetheless, a better result is obtained through data fusion. We haven't shown obvious case of night situation, where visible sensor fails completely and the fused output is according to the infrared sensor only.

7 Conclusion

In this paper, we presented the framework for combining visible and IR for robust object detection and accurate tracking in a surveillance system. The problems that arise in each domain and the potential of combining both modalities in addressing these problems were discussed. Fusion approach for combining information from visible and infrared source at segmentation level and tracking level was discussed in detail. An enhanced object detection strategy is implemented with efficient fusion based approach to handle typical problems of both the domains The following are the contributions of our work. The novelty of our work lies in using Fuzzy logic based-Kalman filtering technique to track objects and obtain fused estimate according to the reliability of the sensors. Suitable measurement parameters are identified to automatically estimate the measurement accuracy of each sensor so that they can be fused in a weighted manner.

References

1. Conaire, C., O. Transfer report-Phd register: Thermal Infrared and Visible Spectrum Fusion for Multi-modal Video Analysis. Dublin City University. (July 28, 2005)
2. Hu, W., Tan, T., Wang, L., and Maybank., S. A survey on visual surveillance of object motion and behaviors. IEEE Transactions on Systems, Man and Cybernetics, 34(3):334-350, August (2004)
3. Cucchiara., R. Multimedia surveillance systems. In VSSN '05: Proceedings of the third ACM international workshop on Video surveillance & sensor networks, New York, NY, USA, pages 3-10 (2005)
4. Bhanu., B., and Han., J. Kinematic-based human motion analysis in infrared sequences. In Proceedings Workshop Applications of Computer Vision, pages 208–212 (2002)
5. Davis, J., and Sharma, V. Robust detection of people in thermal imagery. In Proceedings of International Conference on Pattern Recognition., pages 713–716 (2004)
6. McDaniel, R., Scribner, D., Krebs, W., Warren, P., Ockman, N., McCarley, J. Image fusion for tactical applications. Proceedings of the SPIE - Infrared Technology and Applications XXIV, 3436, 685-695(1998)
7. Torresan, H., Turgeon, B., Ibarra-Castanedo, C., Hébert, P., and Maldague, X. Advanced Surveillance Systems: Combining Video and Thermal Imagery for Pedestrian Detection. In Proceedings of SPIE, Thermosense XXVI, volume 5405 of SPIE, pages 506–515, (2004)
8. Davis, J., and Sharma, V. Fusion-Based Background-Subtraction using Contour Saliency. Computer Vision and Pattern Recognition, 20-26 (June, 2005)
9. Snidaro, L., Niu, R., Varshney, P.K., and Foresti, G.L. Automatic camera selection and fusion for outdoor surveillance under changing weather conditions. IEEE Conference on Advanced Video and Signal based Surveillance, Florida, pp. 364–370 (2003)
10. Escamilla-Ambrosio, P.J., Mort, N. A Hybrid Kalman Filter - Fuzzy Logic Architecture for Multisensor Data Fusion. Proceedings of the 2001 IEEE International Symposium on Intelligent Control , pp. 364-369 (2001)
11. Regazzoni, C., Ramesh, V., and Foresti, G.L. Special issue on video communications, processing, and understanding for third generation surveillance systems. Proceedings of the IEEE, 89(10), 2001.

Dynamic Events as Mixtures of Spatial and Temporal Features

Karteek Alahari* and C.V. Jawahar

Centre for Visual Information Technology,
International Institute of Information Technology,
Gachibowli, Hyderabad 500032, India
`jawahar@iiit.ac.in`

Abstract. Dynamic events comprise of spatiotemporal atomic units. In this paper we model them using a mixture model. Events are represented using a framework based on the Mixture of Factor Analyzers (MFA) model. It is to be noted that our framework is generic and is applicable for any mixture modelling scheme. The MFA, used to demonstrate the novelty of our approach, clusters events into spatially coherent mixtures in a low dimensional space. Based the observations that, (i) events comprise of varying degrees of spatial and temporal characteristics, and (ii) the number of mixtures determines the composition of these features, a method that incorporates models with varying number of mixtures is proposed. For a given event, the relative importance of each model component is estimated, thereby choosing the appropriate feature composition. The capabilities of the proposed framework are demonstrated with an application: recognition of events such as hand gestures, activities.

1 Introduction

Characterization of dynamic events, which are spatiotemporal in nature, has been a problem of great interest in the past few years [1,2,3,4,5,6]. Early methods employ segmentation and tracking of individual parts to model the dynamism in events [2,7]. They are based on identifying moving objects – typically referred to as blobs – constrained by their size or shape. Tracked trajectories of these blobs are used to distinguish events. Naturally, these methods are very sensitive to the quality of segmentation and tracking of blobs. A popular approach has been to represent the dynamism in events as image features [1,5,8]. Typically these approaches, of identifying a fixed feature set (or interesting regions), are applicable to a limited set of events. As observed by Sun *et al.* [9], techniques that learn an optimal set of features from the given event set are of much interest for real life applications. In today's scenario, wherein events can be captured as videos under different conditions, there is also a need to model the variations across videos in a probabilistic framework. Models such as Hidden Markov Models (HMMs) are popular to accomplish this [10]. However, these models fail to capture the events in a low dimensional space. Although there have been attempts to use dimen-

---

* Currently at Oxford Brookes University, UK.

P. Kalra and S. Peleg (Eds.): ICVGIP 2006, LNCS 4338, pp. 540–551, 2006.
© Springer-Verlag Berlin Heidelberg 2006

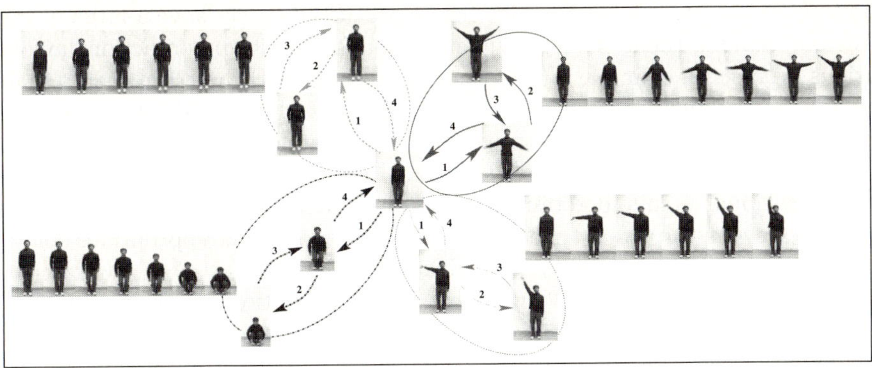

Fig. 1. A sample of events performed by humans (shown as image strips) and action representatives (shown as individual frames). A set of actions constitute an event. Four events and their corresponding actions are shown as distinct groups here (Green (Top Left) - *Jumping*, Red (Top Right) - *Flapping*, Blue (Bottom Left) - *Squatting*, Magenta (Bottom Right) - *Waving*). The arrows denote the temporal transitions between the actions and the number on each arrow denotes the temporal sequencing of the event. Note that the action 'standing' is common to all these events.

sionality reduction methods in combination with these models [9], they fail to be generic. Thus, to characterize events efficiently we need a representation that not only discards the acceptable statistical variability across multiple instances of an event, but also discriminates among different events.

We propose a method to learn a compact representation of events preserving their discriminatory characteristics. An event is modelled as a sequence of atomic spatiotemporal units called *actions*. Actions can be interpreted as subsequences from the event sequence. A probabilistic approach is employed to estimate the actions and the compositional rules for the events, in a low dimensional manifold. This is achieved using a Mixture of Factor Analyzers (MFA) model [11] combined with a probability transition matrix, which encodes the transitions among the action mixtures. The mixtures represent the actions while the transitions represent the compositional rules. In other words, the number of mixtures determines the composition of spatial and temporal features in events. Fixing the number of mixtures for the entire event set is not optimal, as the spatiotemporal characteristics vary among events. A unifying framework which incorporates models with varying number of mixtures (which form the model components) is proposed. For a given event, the relative importance of each model component is estimated from an example set.

The model is based on the observation that events comprise of more fundamental units, *actions*. Similar observations were made in the past in different ways [6,7,8,10,12]. Actions were represented as components of PCA [7], the hidden states of HMMs [10], key frames in the event video, canonical poses, *etc.* It has also been a common practice to analyze the event sequences in a window-based fashion [13] to capture the atomic characteristics in events. In addition to this, we exploit the fact that most of the events have a large degree of overlap among them. This is evident in the form of common actions among various events. An example of this is shown in Figure 1 where the events share the action 'standing'. Furthermore, actions capture the spatial (or the appearance) features in events, while transitions among actions capture the temporal features. The main advantages of the model are: (a) It represents events in a low dimensional manifold retaining their discriminative characteristics, (b) It recognizes events in a real-time fashion, (c) It chooses the appropriate spatial and temporal feature extent by analyzing the event.

Section 2 presents an overview of the event recognition model. It also analyses the dependency of event recognition accuracy on the number of mixtures. Preliminary results on the CMU MoBo database [14] are also presented in this section. The method to combine model components to capture various degrees of appearance and temporal features is described in Section 3. In Section 4 results on human event and Sebastian Marcel Dynamic Hand Posture Database available at [15] are presented along with a discussion. Conclusions are presented in Section 5.

2   Events as Mixture of Actions

Events are represented as a mixture of actions and the transitions among these actions. The representation model consists of an MFA coupled with a probability transition matrix. MFA is essentially a reduced dimension mixture of Gaussians. The model learns action mixtures in a low dimensional space, *i.e.* it accomplishes the task of clustering and estimating a low dimensional representation simultaneously. There are two reasons that argue for action clustering in a subspace representation. Firstly, different actions may be correlated in different ways, and hence the dimensionality reduction metric needs to be different between action mixtures. Secondly, a low dimensional representation may provide better separated mixtures. We choose the MFA model to accomplish this task.

Let the total number of frames from examples of all the events be N and let x_t (of dimension d), $t = 1 \ldots N$, denote the t th frame. Subsequences of x_t form *actions*. For instance, if we consider the event Squatting (which consists of two distinct actions – standing and sitting), the initial few frames represent the action standing and the other frames represent the action sitting (refer Figure 2). The subsequent frames of an action are highly correlated and therefore, for each x_t, a p ($\ll d$) dimensional representation z_t exists. That is, x_t is modelled as $x_t = \Lambda_j z_t + u$, where Λ_j represents the transformation basis for the j th action and u is the associated noise. Multiple such subsequences, occurring across different events, are used to learn Λ_j for each action, and hence the corresponding low dimensional representation.

Consider a generative process for the ensemble of events based on the MFA model. An event, which is captured as a set of frames, is composed of various actions. A typical frame of the event, x_t, can be generated as follows. The action to which it belongs is chosen according to the discrete distribution $P(\omega_j)$,

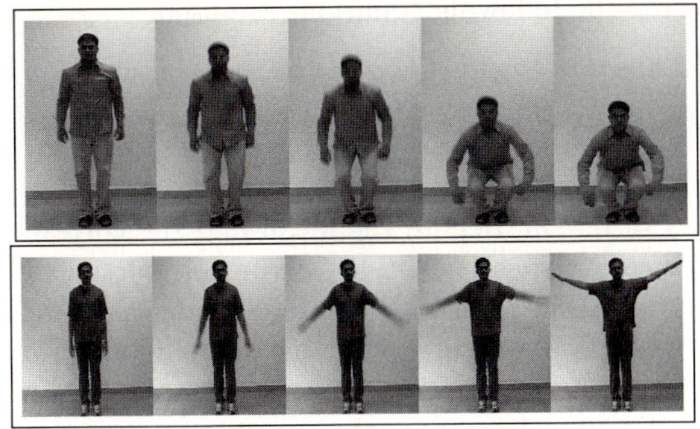

Fig. 2. A few sample frames showing events performed by humans: Squatting (top row), Flapping (bottom row). Note the presence of a common *action* – Standing – between these events. The initial few frames of the event Squatting represent the action standing while the other frames represent the action sitting. The action standing also occurs in the initial few frames of the event Flapping.

$j = 1 \ldots m$. Depending on the chosen action, a continuous subspace representation z_t is generated according to $p(z_t|\omega_j)$. Having learnt z_t and action ω_j, the observation x_t is obtained according to the distribution $p(x_t|z_t, \omega_j)$, *i.e.* x_t is modelled as a "mixture model of actions" according to $p(x_t) = \sum_{j=1}^{m} \int p(x_t|z_t, \omega_j)p(z_t|\omega_j) P(\omega_j)dz_t$, where ω_j, $j = 1 \ldots m$, denotes the j th action. This is a reduced dimension mixture model where the m mixture components are the individual actions. The probability $p(x_t)$ describes the probability of generating a frame given the action which it belongs to, and its corresponding subspace representation. The generative process is to be inverted to learn the parameters of these distributions from the event sequences. This is achieved using an Expectation Maximization (EM) algorithm. It is a general method of finding the maximum-likelihood estimate of the parameters of an underlying distribution from a given data set when the data has missing or unknown values [11]. In this case, the data corresponds to the frames, the unknown values to the low dimensional representations of these frames and the actions to which these frames are associated.

The EM algorithm alternates between inferring the expected values of hidden variables (subspace representation and actions) using observed data (frames), keeping the parameters fixed; and estimating the parameters underlying the distributions of the variables using the inferred values. All the event videos are represented as a sequence of frames and are used for estimating the parameters. The two phases of the EM algorithm – Inference and Learning – are executed sequentially and repeatedly till convergence. The E-step (Inference) proceeds by computing $E[\omega_j|x_t]$, $E[z_t|\omega_j, x_t]$ and $E[z_t z_t^T|\omega_j, x_t]$ for all frames t and actions ω_j [11]. In the M-step (Learning), the parameters π_j, Λ_j, μ_j and Ψ are computed.

During the E-step the following equations are used.

$$E[\omega_j z_t | x_t] = h_{tj}\beta_j(x_t - \mu_j)$$
$$E[\omega_j z_t z_t^T | x_t] = h_{tj}(I - \beta_j\Lambda_j + \Lambda_j(x_t - \mu_j)(x_t - \mu_j)^T\beta_j^T),$$

where $h_{tj} = E[\omega_j | x_t] = \pi_j \mathcal{N}(x_t - \mu_j, \Lambda_j\Lambda_j^T + \Psi)$, $\beta_j = \Lambda_j^T(\Lambda_j\Lambda_j^T)^{-1}$. The parameters μ_j, Λ_j, $j = 1\ldots m$, denote the mean and the corresponding subspace bases of the mixture j respectively. The mixing proportions of actions in the event are denoted by π. The noise in the data is modelled as Ψ. The expectation h_{tj} can be interpreted as a measure of the membership of x_t in the j th action. Interested readers may derive the equations for M-step easily from [11].

Although the MFA model captures the spatial features as actions effectively, it does not account for the temporality in events. As shown by Veeraraghavan *et al.* [16] both spatial and temporal features are important for event recognition. This issue is addressed by modelling the dynamism in events as transitions across the learnt actions $\omega_1, \omega_2, \ldots, \omega_m$. The transition probabilities are computed by observing z_ts across the various actions for each event. After the EM algorithm converges, the action transition matrix $T_k = [\tau_{pq}^k]$, for each event k, is formed as follows.

$$\tau_{pq}^k = \sum_{t=1}^{N-1}[c_t = p][c_{t+1} = q] \quad 1 \leq p, q \leq m, \tag{1}$$

where c_t denotes the class label of the frame x_t and is given by $c_t = \arg\max_j h_{tj}$; $j = 1\ldots m$. Normalizing the entries in the transition matrix gives the corresponding probability transition matrix P_k. Thus, a compact representation of the events by automatically learning the m actions in a low dimensional manifold, and the sequencing information are obtained. The structure of the ensemble of events is contained in the parameters of the actions and the probability transition matrix, *i.e.* $\{(\mu_j, \Lambda_j)_{j=1}^m, \pi, \Psi\}, \{P_k\}_{k=1}^K$.

When recognizing events in a new video sequence, the learnt parameters are used to compute the action mixture (cluster) assignment, c_t for each frame x_t. Let $c_1, c_2, \ldots, c_{N_s}$, denote the action assignments for the respective frames of a N_s frame-long event sequence. The probability that the video frames belong to the k th event, S_k, is given by $S_k = \prod_{t=1}^{N_s-1} P_k[c_t][c_{t+1}]$. The video sequence is assigned to be the event k^*, which maximizes S_k.

This model is validated using the CMU MoBo database [14]. The frames of the video sequence are processed minimally before learning the event-set representation using the EM algorithm described above. The available background images are used to obtain the corresponding silhouette images. The silhouette images, represented as vectors, are used to learn the event representation. After the algorithm converges the sequence probabilities of all the events are computed. The transition probability of a new event video is estimated via the inference step of the EM algorithm, and is labelled following a maximum likelihood approach. Even though the four activities in the database (Slow walk, Fast walk, Incline walk, Walking with a ball) had subtle differences, an average accuracy of 85% is achieved. These results compete with, and also outperform, those reported in [16].

3   Combining Mixture of Actions Models

The relationship between the event recognition accuracy and the number of action mixtures is interesting. Varying the number of actions has minimal influence on the accuracy, beyond a certain limit. For instance, when recognising the event Flapping (of hands) it was observed that beyond 5 mixtures, the accuracy varied negligibly. Low accuracy is observed initially, when the number of actions is small, because the temporal characteristics of the event are not modelled. Similar behaviour was observed for all the events, except that the *optimal* number of actions varied with the event in consideration. Also each of these models captures different characteristics of the events. This argues for an integrated model which learns the appropriate number of actions for each event.

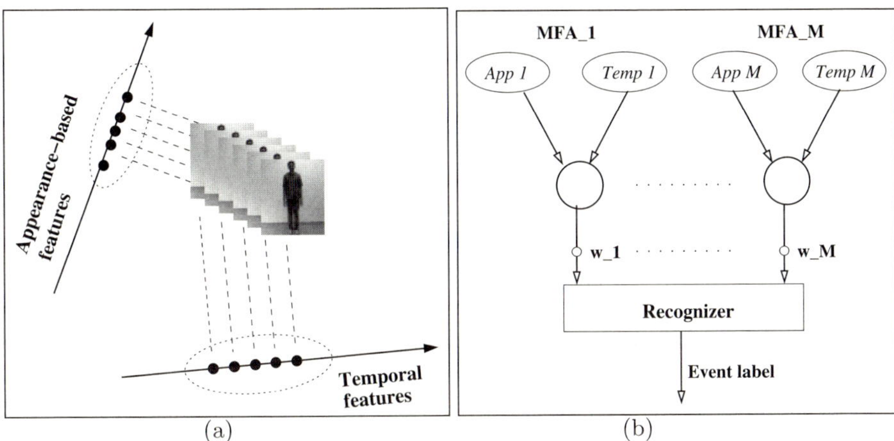

Fig. 3. (a) Event sequences consist of spatial (or appearance) and temporal features. (b) A summary of the proposed appearance and temporal feature integration model: A combination of MFAs (MFA_1 ... MFA_M) is used to have the model choose between appearance (App), temporal (Temp), which are the two extreme cases, and a combination of both features (say, MFA_i) adaptively. The contribution of each of these components in the decision making process is identified by its corresponding weight (w_i).

Varying the number of actions can also be interpreted as varying the appearance and temporal feature content in the event representation. The proposed adaptive scheme chooses the appropriate model component based on the event being recognized. The basic model, *i.e.* mixture of actions model with a transition matrix to capture the temporality in events, is replicated with different number of action mixtures in each of them (see Figure 3). The two ideal extreme cases in this framework are: modelling with (1) a single mixture for each event, and (2) a separate mixture for every frame of an event. In the training phase, the relevance of each component model is also estimated for all the events in the database.

Theoretically, one may define a single mixture for each frame in the event sequence. However, such a scheme is inefficient and impractical due to the possibly large number of transitions between these mixtures. The maximum number of action mixtures is typically decided by the nature of the data set, but is much lower than the total number of frames. Each mixture of actions model, $\mathcal{M}_i, i = 1 \ldots M$, is trained separately with the frames of all the events using an EM algorithm, as described in the previous section. By the end of the mixture model training phase, the parameters of the model – $\{(\mu_j, \Lambda_j)_{j=1}^m, \pi, \Psi\}$, $\{P_k\}_{k=1}^K$ are obtained for each model component.

3.1   Relevance of Each Component

Learning the event representation also involves estimating the relevance of all the component models for any event. This is estimated by optimizing an objective function defined over the training set of N video sequences. The objective function, $J(.)$ is given by

$$J(\Gamma) = \sum_{j=1}^N \sum_{i=1}^M (\gamma_{ij} d_{ij})^2,$$

where $\Gamma \in \mathbb{R}^{MN}$ is a matrix $[\gamma_{ij}]$. γ_{ij} denotes the contribution of the i th mixture of actions model component for the j th video sequence in the data set, and d_{ij} is the distance metric signifying the cost of recognizing the j th sample with the i th model component. The objective function is minimized over the space of γs. This is done by using Lagrange multipliers with the constraint $\sum_{i=1}^M \gamma_{ij} = 1$. The objective function J is formulated so as to minimize the recognition accuracy across all the component models. Given that each component model captures a new composition of temporal and spatial features, this framework provides a unifying scheme to describe events with different compositions of these features.

On observing that the relevance (or weights) for each event sequence are independent, the minimization can be done independently in each column. Thus, the Lagrangian is given by

$$\mathcal{J}(\lambda, \gamma_j) = \sum_{i=1}^M (\gamma_{ij} d_{ij})^2 - \lambda(\sum_{i=1}^M \gamma_{ij} - 1). \tag{2}$$

Differentiating Equation 2 with respect to γ_{pq}, $\gamma_{pq} = \lambda/2(d_{pq})^2$. Using this equation and the constraint $\sum_{r=1}^M \gamma_{rq} = 1$, γ_{pq} can be computed as

$$\gamma_{pq} = 1 \bigg/ (d_{pq})^2 \sum_{r=1}^M (d_{rq})^2 . \tag{3}$$

Equation 3 provides a method to compute the relevance of component models, given the distance metrics d_{ij}. The distance metrics, in this case, are the

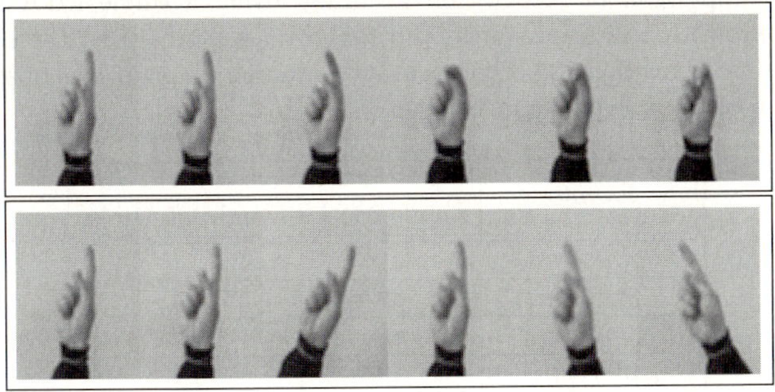

Fig. 4. A few sample frames showing hand gestures [15]: Click (top) and No (bottom)

likelihoods of the mixture of actions model component $\mathcal{M}_i$, which is the probability computed from the corresponding transition matrix. Metrics based on other models such as HMM, SVM, NN, *etc.*, can also be incorporated. Although the framework is generic, we limit the discussion to our mixture of actions model.

3.2   Weighted Measure to Recognize Events

Once the weights $[\gamma_{ij}]$ are identified for all the events, they are used in the recognition framework. Given an un-trained event video sequence, its corresponding low dimensional representation is learnt using each of the model components, $\mathcal{M}_i, i = 1 \ldots M$. The likelihood of the event being recognized as belonging to class j using each of the mixture of actions model components is computed. The decision criteria based on the weighted sum of posterior probabilities (for class j) is given by

$$p_j = \sum_{i=1}^{N} \gamma_{ij} p(j|data, \mathcal{M}_i).$$

The event is labelled as belonging to the class j^*, which maximizes the posterior probability according to $j^* = \arg\max_j p_j$.

4   Recognizing Events

The proposed framework is used to recognise events such as hand gestures and human events. We used hand gesture sequences from Marcel's database [15]. Sample frames of some of the events can be seen in Figures 2 and 4. For the experiment on human events, we used videos of 20 human subjects performing 7 different events for an average duration of 6 seconds. Three samples per subject per event were used. Video sequences of 10 human subjects, *i.e.* $10 \times 7 \times 3$ sequences, and another disjoint set of sequences were used for training and testing respectively. These events occur with the subject either being stationary or indulging in locomotion. In the former category, we consider events Flapping,

Table 1. A comparison of recognition accuracy using a single MFA model (which has a fixed composition of appearance and temporal features) and the combination of MFA models. On an average, 35.35 percentage reduction in error was observed. Sample frames of some of these events can be seen in Figures 2 and 4.

Events	% Accuracy	
	Single MFA	Comb. of MFAs
Hand gestures:		
Click	89	94
No	88	93
StopGraspOk	90	92
Rotate	86	90
Human Activities:		
Flapping	83	88
Jumping	80	86
Squatting	83	90
Waving	82	86
Limping	85	92
Walking	87	93
Hopping	84	90
CMU MoBo database:		
Slow walk	84	92
Fast walk	85	94
Incline walk	86	93
Walk with Ball	85	93

Jumping, Squatting and Waving, while in the latter category (involving locomotion), we consider Limping, Walking and Hopping. All the videos were captured with a Panasonic Digital Video Camera at 24 fps. The model is also validated on the MoBo Database [14] available from the Robotics Institute, Carnegie Mellon University. The database consists of 25 subjects performing 4 different walking activities on a treadmill. Each sequence is 11 seconds long recorded at 30 fps. Data corresponding to one of the view angles (vr03_7 of [14]) is used for experimentation. The training and testing data sequences were disjoint in all the three validations.

Minimal preprocessing is done on the video sequences. In order to retain the visually significant information, background subtraction and normalization is performed on all the frames. The intensity values obtained are used in the process henceforth. For the events involving locomotion, the frames are motion compensated to centre the subject performing the event. Using a set of example videos as the training set, the appropriate composition of appearance and temporal features is learnt, and the parameters that describe them for all the events (refer Section 3). Same training sequences are used in all the component models. To recognize an unlabelled test event, the frame sequence transitions are computed via the inference step of EM algorithm. This results in a set of sequence probabilities computed for each event. The test video is then labelled as the event whose corresponding weighted probability measure is maximum (refer Section 3.2). The recognition accuracy results obtained using the proposed model and an MFA model are presented in Table 1. When compared to the single MFA model, we achieved 35.35 percentage reduction in error on average.

4.1   Discussion

We performed a quantitative analysis of the subspace by reconstructing the original sequences from the learnt representations. Using Λ_j and the low dimensional representation, z_t, the original frames, x_t, $\forall t$, are recovered, thereby generating the entire sequence. The reconstruction error is found to be 0.5%. A comparison of some of the original and recovered frames is shown in Figure 5.

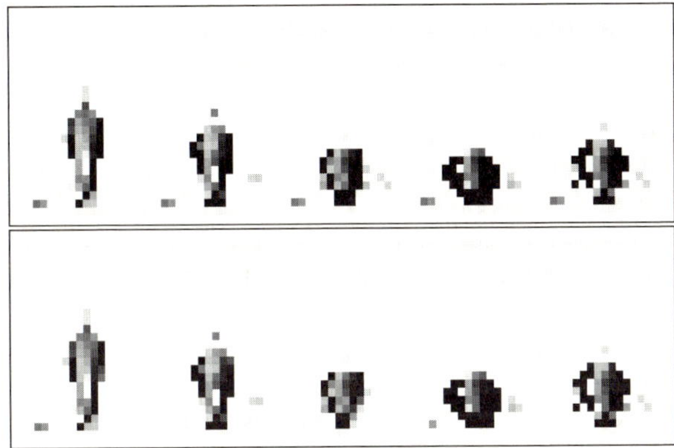

Fig. 5. A comparison of the original (top) and the reconstructed (bottom) frames of the activity Squatting. Even though we achieve 99.94% reduction in size, the reconstruction error is negligible (0.5%).

The recognition process over frames is displayed in Figure 6, as a plot of the log likelihood for each possible activity. The correct activity Squatting – the topmost plot in the figure – is clearly disambiguated within the first few frames (around 5), which shows the ability of the model to obtain all the aspects of the activity quickly and accurately.

The proposed approach differs from various time-series models in many aspects. Our techniques for preprocessing, feature extraction and representation have considerable advantages, as described below.

- In comparison with a standard left-to-right HMM based on [9], the mixture model provides superior recognition. For example, HMM results in 88% accuracy for the hand gesture Click, while the mixture model provides 94% accuracy. Similar improvement (of $6 - 8\%$) is observed in the case of other events.

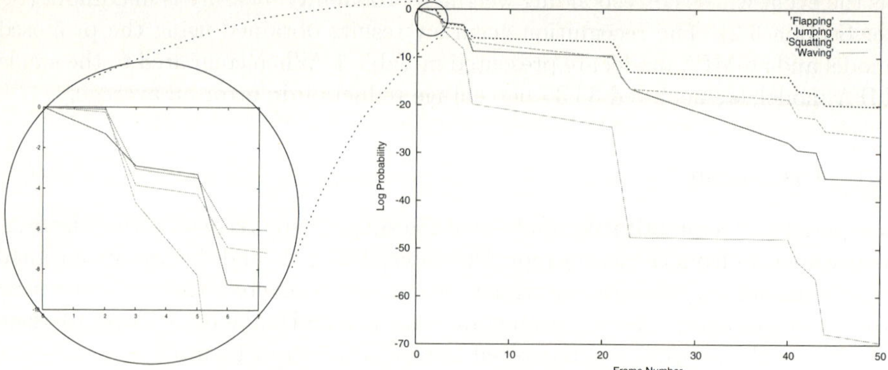

Fig. 6. Cumulative sequence probabilities for the activity Squatting. The horizontal axis represents the frame number and the vertical axis represents the logarithm of sequence probability. The topmost plot (blue dotted line) corresponds to Squatting. A closer view of the graph (shown in inset) indicates that the activity is recognized after observing a few frames – 5 in this case. *Best viewed in pdf*

- The proposed method is related to a standard left-to-right HMM. However, we work at a lower dimension, which is simultaneously obtained while modelling the event structure. Furthermore, a single observation model is used to train all the events in the ensemble unlike HMMs where each event is modelled separately [9].
- Events have been modelled, in the past, using a variety of features [1,7,9]. Most of these methods involve large amount of preprocessing. In contrast, we perform minimal preprocessing and avoid any explicit feature extraction. It is limited to background subtraction and binarization of the individual frames.

5   Conclusion

The mixture model presented in this paper adapts based on the set of events being considered. It learns an optimal combination of various mixture of actions model components. It can also be interpreted as a unifying framework for combining appearance and temporal features in events. The composition of the feature content is controlled by the number of mixtures in the model. The applicability of this framework has been demonstrated using the Mixture of Factor Analyzers model. However, it can easily incorporated in other mixture modelling schemes such as Gaussian Mixture Models. Other video (or event) analysis problems which require a higher level of semantic understanding are yet to explored. Incorporating a discriminant based scheme into this framework is another interesting direction.

Acknowledgments. Karteek Alahari thanks the GE Foundation for financial support through the GE Foundation Scholar-Leaders Program 2003-2005.

References

1. Bobick, A.F., Davis, J.W.: The recognition of human movement using temporal templates. IEEE Trans. on PAMI **23** (2001) 257–267
2. Gavrila, D.M.: The visual analysis of human movement: A survey. Computer Vision and Image Understanding **73** (1999) 82–98
3. Greenspan, H., Goldberger, J., Mayer, A.: A probabilistic framework for spatio-temporal video representation and indexing. In: ECCV. Volume IV. (2002) 461–475
4. Veeraraghavan, A., Chellappa, R., Roy-Chowdhury, A.: The Function Space of an Activity. In: CVPR. Volume 1. (2006) 959–968
5. Wong, S.F., Cipolla, R.: Real-time Interpretation of Hand Motions using a Sparse Bayesian Classifier on Motion Gradient Orientation Images. In: BMVC. Volume 1. (2005) 379–388
6. Sheikh, Y., Sheikh, M., Shah, M.: Exploring the Space of a Human Action. In: ICCV. Volume 1. (2005) 144–149
7. Yacoob, Y., Black, M.J.: Parameterized Modeling and Recognition of Activities. CVIU **73** (1999) 232–247
8. Yilmaz, A., Shah, M.: Actions Sketch: A Novel Action Representation. In: CVPR. Volume 1. (2005) 984–989
9. Sun, X., Chen, C.C., Manjunath, B.S.: Probabilistic Motion Parameter Models for Human Activity Recognition. In: ICPR. Volume 1. (2002) 443–446
10. Brand, M., Kettnaker, V.: Discovery and Segmentation of Activities in Video. IEEE Trans. on PAMI **22** (2000) 844–851
11. Ghahramani, Z., Hinton, G.E.: The EM Algorithm for Mixtures of Factor Analyzers. Technical Report CRG-TR-96-1, University of Toronto, Canada (1996)
12. Robertson, N., Reid, I.: Behaviour understanding in video: a combined method. In: ICCV. Volume 1. (2005) 808–815
13. Zelnik-Manor, L., Irani, M.: Event-Based Analysis of Video. In: CVPR. Volume II. (2001) 123–130
14. Gross, R., Shi, J.: The CMU Motion of Body MoBo Database. Technical Report CMU-RI-TR-01-18, Robotics Institute, CMU, Pittsburgh, PA (2001)
15. Marcel, S.: (Dynamic Hand Posture Database: http://www-prima.inrialpes.fr/ FGnet/data/10-Gesture/dhp_marcel.tar.gz)
16. Veeraraghavan, A., Roy-Chowdhury, A., Chellappa, R.: Role of shape and kinematics in human movement analysis. In: CVPR. Volume 1. (2004) 730–737

Discriminative Actions for Recognising Events

Karteek Alahari* and C.V. Jawahar

Centre for Visual Information Technology,
International Institute of Information Technology, Hyderabad 500032, India
`jawahar@iiit.ac.in`

Abstract. This paper presents an approach to identify the importance of different parts of a video sequence from the recognition point of view. It builds on the observations that: (1) events consist of more fundamental (or atomic) units, and (2) a discriminant-based approach is more appropriate for the recognition task, when compared to the standard modelling techniques, such as PCA, HMM, etc. We introduce *discriminative actions* which describe the usefulness of the fundamental units in distinguishing between events. We first extract actions to capture the fine characteristics of individual parts in the events. These actions are modelled and their usefulness in discriminating between events is estimated as a score. The score highlights the important parts (or actions) of the event from the recognition aspect. Applicability of the approach on different classes of events is demonstrated along with a statistical analysis.

1   Introduction

An event may be considered as a long-term temporally varying object, which typically spans over tens or hundreds of frames [1]. The problem of recognising events has received considerable research attention over the past few years [2,3,4,5,6,7]. It has gained importance because of its immediate applicability to surveillance, gesture recognition, sign language recognition, Human Computer Interaction, etc. [4,8,9]. Many approaches have been proposed in the past to recognise events. Early methods typically employed 2D or 3D tracking to temporally isolate the object performing the event. Subsequent to tracking, the event is recognised by extracting higher-order image features [6,9]. An excellent review of such classical approaches for event recognition can be found in [2]. Owing to the inherent dynamism in events, Hidden Markov Models (HMMs) [10] and Finite State Machines [5] have been popular to address the event recognition problem. Furthermore, models such as HMMs provide elegant ways to incorporate the variability in a large collection of event data.

Another significant direction in event analysis research is to extract static image features from dynamic events [8,11,12]. Bobick and Davis [11] introduced Motion History and Motion Energy Images, which represent the recency and spatial density of motion respectively. In some sense their approach reduces the dimensionality of the event recognition problem from a 3D spatiotemporal space

---

* Currently at Oxford Brookes University, UK.

P. Kalra and S. Peleg (Eds.): ICVGIP 2006, LNCS 4338, pp. 552–563, 2006.
© Springer-Verlag Berlin Heidelberg 2006

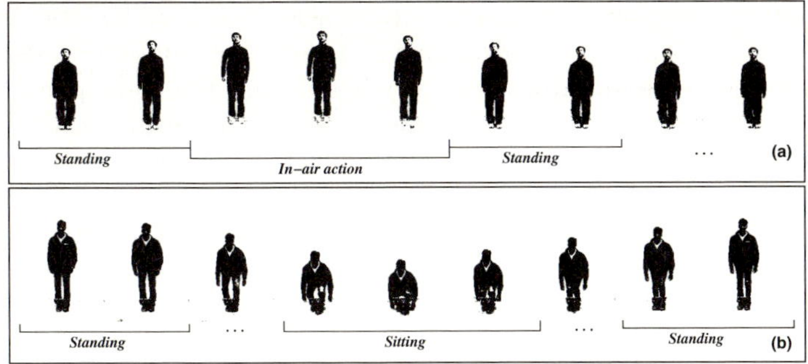

Fig. 1. A few sample processed frames (silhouettes) of the two events: (a) Jumping (first row), and (b) Squatting (second row), showing the constituent actions. Note the presence of a common action – *Standing* – between these events.

to a 2D image space. More recently Yilmaz and Shah [8] proposed a method to generate spatiotemporal volume (STV), in (x, y, t) space, using contours of the subject performing the event. The 3D "objects" are then recognised using differential geometric properties of STV. These methods either analyse the entire video sequence with a single image feature, which fails to capture the fine characteristics in events, or treat all parts of the sequence with equal importance, which leads to confusion in recognising highly similar events.

A method to recognise events using features which have optimal distinguishing characteristics is described in this paper. Our approach is motivated by the following observations.

- Events comprise of more fundamental (or atomic) units, which we refer to as *actions*. They are subsequences of the event sequences, and are a generalisation of the two extremes, namely the individual frames in an event (finest detail) and the entire video (coarsest detail). Analysing a video at the finest detail fails to capture the dynamism in events. On the other hand, analysing a video as a whole does not provide the fine details in various parts of the event sequence. *Actions* provide a natural mechanism to control the coarse-to-fine detail in the analysis.
- Due to the bulky nature of video sequences, it has been common to extract features in a low dimensional space. PCA is a popular modelling technique used to achieve this [2, 4]. However, it has been argued that discriminant techniques are more useful for the recognition task, when compared to modelling techniques [13].
- A direct discriminant analysis of video sequences, analogous to that performed on images, is not meaningful. This is because the relationships between parts of a video sequence are important, unlike the relationships between parts of an image. It is semantically useful to perform such an analysis at the *action* level.

Features, in the form of actions, are extracted to capture the fine characteristics of individual parts in the events. These actions are modelled and their usefulness in discriminating between events is estimated as a corresponding score. The score highlights the important parts (or actions) of the event from the recognition aspect. Using the estimated discriminatory scores and the corresponding action distances, a similarity measure is computed when comparing two events. The main advantages of our approach are as follows: (1) It requires minimal preprocessing of videos. In most situations where the video is recorded using a fixed camera, the background is relatively known, the silhouettes (see Fig. 1) can be extracted easily. (2) It is fast and does not require careful parameter tuning. (3) It is robust to the scheme used to extract actions from the events (Section 4.3).

1.1   Are Events Atomic?

Complex events such as people gesturing when interacting with others [14], playing Tennis [1], doing Aerobics [8], etc., are made up of more fundamental units. In fact, even simpler events such as a person squatting (see Fig. 1b) comprise of fundamental units: *standing* and *sitting*, in this case. Many researchers in the past have made similar observations [1, 3, 5, 15]. The fundamental (or atomic) units of events have been represented in many forms – as states of a stochastic finite automaton [5], components of PCA [15], the hidden states of HMMs [10], key frames in the event video [3], canonical poses [16], etc. There have also been approaches which analyse the event sequences in a window or block based fashion [1] to capture the granularity in the events.

All the above methods constitute a class of approaches which are designed to model the data in an optimal way. They deal with the representational aspects of events. It has been argued that such modelling techniques, suited for efficient representation, need not be the optimal for the classification task [13]. Discriminative models are more appropriate for the recognition task. However, it is not evident how these models can be derived in the context of video sequences.

This paper presents a discriminative model to recognise events effectively. In the past there have been a few attempts to use discriminant techniques for analysing video sequences, but are limited to either tracking [17] or gait-based human recognition [18]. We identify the actions in events, *i.e.* subsequences of the event sequences, which are more useful in discriminating between two events by analysing their statistical characteristics. The individual actions in the event are modelled to compute their discriminatory potential – the relative importance for distinguishing events – following a Fisher-like formulation [19]. To account for the statistical variability in each event, a collection of example event sequences is used. Each action together with its discriminatory potential is called a *discriminative action*. Using the discriminatory potentials (or weights) and the corresponding action distances for individual actions, a statistical distance measure is computed. Action distance denotes the similarity of two corresponding actions. In contrast, Han and Bhanu [18] use discriminant analysis only to extract features for human recognition based on gait. Also, unlike our approach the discriminative characteristics are not explicitly incorporated into the decision making process.

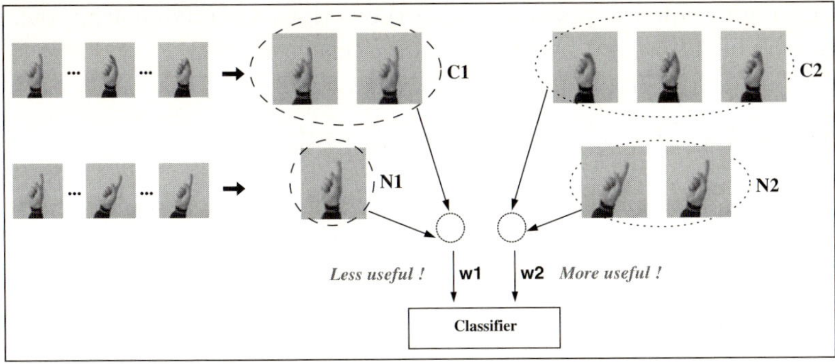

Fig. 2. Sample hand gesture frames showing two parts with different discriminatory potentials. Here the events *Click* (C) and *No* (N), the two events posses similar properties at the beginning of the sequences. The latter frames are more useful in the classification task when compared to the former frames. The individual segments (two shown here) of the video sequences are modelled and their discriminatory potential is combined to compute a similarity score.

The rest of this section discusses the motivation through an example. Section 2 presents the technical background along with an outline of the approach. The algorithm to obtain discriminant-based features for event sequences is given in Section 3. Section 4 presents results on two categories of event videos, namely hand gestures and human activities, along with a statistical analysis. Section 5 provides concluding remarks.

1.2   Motivation

To better appreciate the need for discriminative approaches for event recognition, consider the example illustrated in Fig. 2. It shows sample frames from two hand gesture [14] events: *"Click"*, *"No"*. The high degree of similarity among the gestures establishes the need to select the features which discriminate between the two event classes.

In the *Click* event (see Fig. 2) the subject moves his index finger vertically up and down, while in the *No* event the subject moves his index finger sideways horizontally, as if "saying" no to something. The two events appear to posses similar properties at the beginning of the sequences (where the finger remains in an almost stationary vertical state). As the complete event video sequence begins to appear over time, the distinguishing characteristics unfold, *i.e.* the latter frames of the sequence are more useful for discriminating between the two events when compared to the former frames. Hence, the latter frames should contribute more towards the decision making process. As shown in Fig. 2, the objective is to identify actions **C2** and **N2** which map to a feature space wherein the events are clearly distinguishable. The other parts (**C1** and **N1** in this example) owing to their similarity may not contribute much to the decision criteria. The popular pattern recognition approaches do not allow for such a scheme on video data. They give equal importance to all the actions when comparing two event sequences, which may not be optimal, as in this case.

2   Semantic Discrimination of Events

Distinguishing between different parts of an event sequence, requires the need to "weigh" them appropriately when computing the decision criterion. This is in the spirit of Discriminant Analysis and Statistical Pattern Recognition techniques.

Fisher Discriminant Analysis (FDA) is a popular feature extraction scheme for 2-class problems [19]. It has been used to compute Fisherfaces in the image domain, which are optimal for recognition tasks [13]. FDA finds an optimal direction φ along which the between-class variance is maximised and the within-class variance is minimised. The criterion function $J(.)$ is defined as

$$J(\varphi) = \frac{\varphi^T \mathbf{S_b} \varphi}{\varphi^T \mathbf{S_w} \varphi}, \tag{1}$$

where $\mathbf{S_w}$ and $\mathbf{S_b}$ are the within-class and the between-class scatter matrices. The function $J(.)$ is maximised to compute the optimal φ for discriminating between the patterns. It is shown that any vector φ which maximises the Fisher criterion in Equation 1 satisfies $\mathbf{S_b}\varphi = \lambda \mathbf{S_w}\varphi$ for some constant λ [19]. This can be solved as an eigenvalue problem. Thus, the discriminant vector φ is given by the eigenvector corresponding to the largest eigenvalue of $\mathbf{S_w}^{-1}\mathbf{S_b}$. Extensions of Fisher Discriminant Analysis such as Multiple Discriminant Analysis, Kernel Discriminant Analysis, incremental LDA have also been used in computing discriminant features.

2.1   Event Recognition Using Discriminative Actions

Consider two video sequences $\mathbf{A}$ and $\mathbf{B}$ which belong to events (classes) $\mathcal{A}$ and $\mathcal{B}$ respectively. They represent a sequence of image frames where the corresponding event, like Click, No, etc., is captured.

The similarity between the two video sequences $\mathbf{A}$ and $\mathbf{B}$ can be computed by comparing the sequences directly. If the sequences are of different lengths, say due to variation in frame rate of video capture or duration of the event, a normalisation can be done by resampling. However, this naive comparison of video data frame-by-frame is not valid since the event of interest is macro in nature and cannot be captured from one sample frame. An appropriate intermediate subsequence is chosen for the representation to overcome this problem [1]. The problem we address is identification of the contribution of each of these subsequences (or actions) for the global dissimilarity/discriminative information for the given video sequences.

Let $\mathbf{A}^k$ and $\mathbf{B}^k, k = 1, 2, \ldots, s$ be the s actions extracted from the video sequences $\mathbf{A}$ and $\mathbf{B}$ respectively. Discriminative actions from a collection of event examples are computed as follows. Each action is represented as a corresponding static image by modelling its inherent dynamism. It is then modelled using

Discriminant History Images. This produces s images each for both the events. The discriminatory potentials computed for different parts of the video sequences and the action-action distance metrics are used to compute a weighted decision score when recognising a new video sequence.

Before segmenting the video sequences temporally, to extract the actions, they need to be aligned to account for the difference in frame capture rate. It is assumed that the collection of input video sequences is either already aligned or is captured at a uniform frame rate. A further discussion on the alignment schemes is beyond the scope of this paper. When the video sequences are captured at a uniform frame rate, the sequences are already aligned, and are directly segmented temporally. This process can also be understood as that of analysing the video sequence in a window-based fashion [1]. The number of actions is determined based on the set of events under consideration. For the experiments on videos sequences captured at 25 fps, with about 150 frames each, 6 actions are used, with the assumption that each action is performed in approximately 1 second.

3   Recognition Based on Discriminative Actions

In this section, the technical details of the approach to identify *discriminative actions*, and subsequently use them to recognise events are presented. The separability of the two events is maximised and the variability within the event is minimised to compute these actions.

3.1   Computing Discriminative Actions

Representing Actions: Each action $\mathbf{A}^k$ consists of a set of image frames that describe the inherent dynamism in the action. The action characteristics are modelled using Motion History Images (MHI), which capture the dynamism in events, proposed by Bobick and Davis [11]. Although other modelling techniques are applicable in this context, for the results in this paper MHI features are used. They represent *how* motion is occurring in the actions. Given N_A and N_B instances each for the events $\mathcal{A}$ and $\mathcal{B}$, the MHI of the j th instance of the action $\mathbf{A}^k$ is denoted by $\theta_{\mathcal{A}j}^k$. Similarly, $\theta_{\mathcal{B}j}^k$ for the j th instance of the action $\mathbf{B}^k$. From [11], the intensities at pixels in the history image at time instant t, $H_\tau(t)$, are a function of the temporal history of the motion of the corresponding pixels. It is defined as $H_\tau(t) = \tau$, if $I(t) = \text{foreground}; \max(0, H_\tau(t-1) - 1)$, otherwise, where τ is a pre-determined constant and $I(t) = \text{foreground}$ denotes the set of all pixels belonging to the event-performing subject. History Image features are computed for the last frame of every action. This provides exactly one History Image feature for each action. For instance, if there are p_j^k image frames in the j th instance of the action $\mathbf{A}^k$, $\theta_{\mathcal{A}j}^k = H_\tau(p_j^k)$. MHI features of a few sample video segments are illustrated in Fig. 3a. The motion trails of these actions clearly show how the motion is occurring. To enhance the discriminating characteristics between the two events, the relevance of individual actions for the recognition task is computed.

Computing the Discriminatory potential: The usefulness of a k th action for the recognition task is identified by $\varphi_k, k = 1, 2, \ldots, s$. It is computed such that the action features have optimal distinguishing characteristics along the direction of the vector φ. The within-class scatter (variability within events) is minimised and the between-class scatter (separability of events) is maximised for this. These scatter matrices are defined as

$$\mathbf{S_w} = \sum_{i \in \{\mathcal{A},\mathcal{B}\}} \sum_{j=1}^{N_i} (\theta_{ij} - \bar{\theta}_i)(\theta_{ij} - \bar{\theta}_i)^T,$$

$$\mathbf{S_b} = (\bar{\theta}_\mathcal{A} - \bar{\theta}_\mathcal{B})(\bar{\theta}_\mathcal{A} - \bar{\theta}_\mathcal{B})^T,$$

where the number of instances in class i is denoted by N_i, the symbols without the superscript k denote the sequence features with the action representations (MHIs) computed for each action stacked as rows, and the mean over the instances of a class i is given by $\bar{\theta}_i = \frac{1}{N_i} \sum_{j=1}^{N_i} \theta_{ij}$. Also, $(\theta_{ij} - \bar{\theta}_i)$ is the distance measure defined in the representation space. Here, the $s \times s$ matrices $\mathbf{S_w}$ and $\mathbf{S_b}$ capture the within-class and between-class scatters at the action level. Each entry of $\mathbf{S_b} = \{b_{ij}\}$ represents the variance between actions $\mathbf{A}^i$ and $\mathbf{B}^j$ over the set of all instances. Maximising the objective function in Equation 1 results in a discriminant vector of length s along which the classes possess large discriminating characteristics. Fig. 3b shows the actions and their corresponding discriminatory potentials for the event pair Click vs No. Discriminative actions are computed from a collection of example event video sequences. This constitutes the training phase of the proposed approach which is summarised below.

1. Align all the event video sequences in the training set with respect to a template video sequence, and segment them temporally to obtain s subsequences (or actions) for all the instances in the two classes $\mathcal{A}$ and $\mathcal{B}$. If it is known that the instances are captured at a uniform rate, segment them temporally.
2. Use Motion History Images (MHI) to compute the action representations and obtain the features: $\{\theta^k_{\mathcal{A}j}, \theta^k_{\mathcal{B}j}\}^s_{k=1}$.
3. Compute the discriminant vector φ, whose elements denote the relative importance of each action, by minimising the objective function $J(.)$ according to Equation 1.

3.2 Recognising Events

Let $\mathbf{T}$ be the event sequence which is to be recognised. It is labelled as class i^* according to $i^* = \arg\min_{i \in \{\mathcal{A},\mathcal{B}\}} D_\varphi(\mathbf{T}, i)$, where $D_\varphi(\mathbf{T}, i)$ defines the cost of recognising the sequence $\mathbf{T}$ as the sequence i in the discriminative feature space. The matching cost $D_\varphi(\mathbf{T}, \mathcal{A})$ is given by $D_\varphi(\mathbf{T}, \mathcal{A}) = f(\varphi_1 \ldots \varphi_s, \theta^1_\mathbf{T} \ldots \theta^s_\mathbf{T}, \theta^1_\mathcal{A} \ldots \theta^s_\mathcal{A})$.

The MHI features $\theta^1_\mathbf{T}, \ldots, \theta^s_\mathbf{T}$ of the actions from the test sequence are computed as described before for the training set. The function $f(.)$ models D_φ as a combination of the action level matching costs $d^k(.)$ and the weights φ_k, which discriminate between the actions. In other words, $f(.) = \sum_{k=1}^s \varphi_k d^k(\theta^k_\mathbf{T}, \theta^k_\mathcal{A})$, where $d^k(.)$ is defined as the Euclidean distance between the two MHI feature vectors.

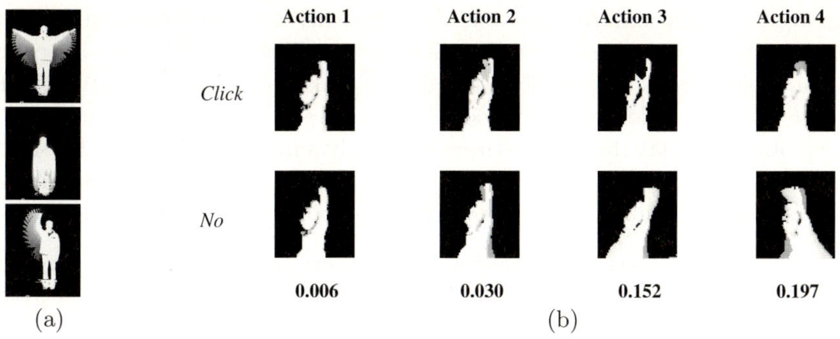

Fig. 3. (a) Motion History Images (MHI) of the events Flapping, Squatting and Waving respectively, clearly illustrating the motion trails. (b) MHI features computed using 4 actions of the events *Click, No,* and their corresponding discriminatory potential (shown in the last row). The first two actions have low discriminatory potential owing to their similarity. The last two actions are more useful for the classification task.

Significance of φ: Along the direction of the vector φ the ratio of between-class scatter and within-class scatter is maximised. When the data points, say, $\Theta_{\mathcal{T}} = [\theta_{\mathcal{T}}^k], k = 1, 2, \ldots, s,$ and $\Theta_{\mathcal{A}} = [\theta_{\mathcal{A}}^k], k = 1, 2, \ldots, s,$ are projected onto this direction as $\varphi^T \Theta_{\mathcal{T}}$ and $\varphi^T \Theta_{\mathcal{A}}$ respectively, each element of φ acts as a weight for the corresponding dimension. In this lower dimension space, the distance between two events $\mathcal{T}$ and $\mathcal{A}$ is expressed as a weighted linear combination of the distances along each dimension. The distance function $f(.)$ defined above can also be written as $f(.) = \varphi^T D(\Theta_{\mathcal{T}}, \Theta_{\mathcal{A}})$, where $D(\Theta_{\mathcal{T}}, \Theta_{\mathcal{A}}) = [d^1(\theta_{\mathcal{T}}^1, \theta_{\mathcal{A}}^1), \ldots, d^s(\theta_{\mathcal{T}}^s, \theta_{\mathcal{A}}^s)]^T$. Assuming that the distance functions are metric, $f(.)$ can be simplified as $f(.) = D(\varphi^T \Theta_{\mathcal{T}}, \varphi^T \Theta_{\mathcal{A}}) = D_\varphi(\mathcal{T}, \mathcal{A})$. Thus, using metric distances the similarity between two events can be computed as a weighted linear combination of the action-level distances and the elements of the discriminant vector.

4   Experiments and Results

Results are presented on two classes of event video sequences – hand gestures and human activities. Both recorded and publicly available videos are used to test the applicability of the model.

4.1   Hand Gestures

Recognising hand gestures has received a lot of attention in the recent past. It finds innumerable applications in HCI, Virtual Reality [4], wherein input to the computer can be regulated through various hand gestures, for instance controlling the visualisation of a CAD model. One of the challenges in hand gesture recognition is the high degree of similarity among the events. Hand gesture videos from Marcel's Dynamic Hand Gesture database [14] are used. It consists of 15 video sequences for each of the 4 dynamic hand gestures, namely Click,

No, StopGraspOk and Rotate. The data was divided into separate train and test sets. Results on three of the possible pairs – Click vs No, StopGraspOk vs Rotate, Rotate vs Click – which have a high degree of similarity between them are discussed. Sample frames of a couple of hand gestures are shown in Fig. 2. It can be observed that the two gestures are highly similar in the initial few frames and their distinguishing characteristics unfold over time in the latter frames. Following is the summary of the experiment conducted on this data set.

1. Minimal preprocessing (background subtraction and subsequent thresholding) is performed to the eliminate the background from the scene. The actions in the events are extracted according to the method discussed in Section 2.1.
2. Discriminative actions are estimated by modelling the actions as MHI features and computing their corresponding discriminatory potential, according to the method described in Section 3.1.
3. Given a new video sequence (of one of the trained categories) to recognise, we perform Step 1, model the actions as MHI features, and then use the estimated discriminant weights to compute the similarity score. The video sequence was labelled as discussed in Section 3.2.

The accuracy results on this data set are illustrated in Table 1. Results are compared to those obtained from a technique which gives equal importance to all parts of the sequence. No resubmission error is observed in the case where an optimally weighted distance measure is used. On average a percentage error reduction of 30.29 on about 200 video sequences is observed. Fig. 3b illustrates the Motion History Image features computed for 4 segments of *Click, No* gestures. It shows that the latter frames of the event sequence are more useful for the classification task.

4.2   Other Activities

Recognition of events involving humans finds many applications in surveillance [2, 6, 11]. Most events performed by humans are marked by a considerable degree of commonality among them (for instance, see Fig. 1). This observation is exploited through the proposed discriminative action based method. For this experiment videos of 4 events, namely Jumping, Squatting, Limping, Walking, performed by 20 different people for an average duration of 6 seconds each, are used. These events occur with the subject either stationary or indulging in locomotion. In the former category, events Jumping and Squatting are considered, while in the latter category, Limping and Walking are considered. The videos are captured with a Panasonic Digital Video Camera at 24 fps. The data set is divided into distinct train and test sets. Minimal preprocessing is done on the video sequences as follows. In order to retain only the visually significant information, background subtraction and normalisation was done on all the frames. Motion compensation is also performed to centre the subject for the events where locomotion is involved. The events are temporally segmented into actions and are modelled using MHI features. The modelled actions are used to estimate the corresponding discriminatory potential. To recognise an unlabelled test event,

Table 1. Recognition accuracy for about 200 video sequences. On an average a 30.29 percentage reduction in error is observed.

Event Pair	% Accuracy	
	Equal weights	Optimal weights
Click vs No	91	93
StopGraspOk vs Rotate	90	92
Rotate vs Click	87	92
Jumping vs Squatting	85	90
Limping vs Walking	87	91

the sequence is preprocessed as above and the similarity measure is computed with respect to the two learnt event representations. The test video is then labelled as the event for which the weighted similarity measure is maximum (refer Section 3.2). The recognition accuracy results on these events are presented in Table 1. On an average, 32.05 percentage reduction in error is achieved.

4.3   Statistical Analysis

The proposed method improves the compactness and the separability of events. Within-event and between-event scatters in the standard and the discriminant-based feature spaces are computed to quantify the performance of the approach. This is done on a set of *Click* and *No* video sequences. Optimality of the feature space is defined in terms of the compactness (low variance within an event) and the separability (high variance between events) of the classes. Low within-event and high between-event scatters shown in Table 2, after transforming the features to a discriminant-based feature space, support our claim that this method identifies an optimal discriminant feature set.

The proposed approach is also not sensitive to the action extraction method used. It is observed that changing the action extraction method leads to negligible change in recognition accuracy. A noticeable change is observed only when the event is modelled as a single action. In the case of *Rotate* vs *Click* video pair, the average recognition accuracy was about 87% when modelled with a single action, and 91% when modelled with two actions. This is due to the fact that, the discriminatory potentials of different parts of the sequence are not exploited in a single action. Similar behaviour is observed on other video sequences.

The recognition scheme presented is applicable in a multiple class scenario as well. There are many ways of combining pairwise classifiers for solving multiple class problems. We use a Directed Acyclic Graph [19] is used to achieve this. The DAG is built following a one-vs-one architecture, where each node is a 2-class classifier. Multiple video sequences of 5 events are used to compute the recognition accuracy. All the 10 possible pairwise combinations of these events are trained to get the corresponding optimal weights. The results of this analysis are presented in Table 3. It shows the accuracy results in the multiclass scenario and certain pairwise combinations of events. The discriminant weight approach shows significant improvement compared to the equal weight approach.

Table 2. Performance of the model in identifying an optimal discriminant feature space. The within-class and the between-class scatters for both the classes (*Click*: Class 1 and *No*: Class 2) in the standard and the proposed discriminant-based feature spaces are shown. The values are computed by considering the events to be comprising of 3 actions. Low within-event and high between-event scatter values indicate that our approach identifies a feature space wherein the classes are compact and well-separated.

Feature Space	Within-class scatter		Between-class scatter	
Standard	Class 1	5.025	Class 1 vs 2	6.174
	Class 2	4.619		
Discriminant-based	Class 1	3.907	Class 1 vs 2	15.958
	Class 2	2.794		

Table 3. Event recognition results for 5 events in a multiclass scenario. The notation x/y denotes x misclassifications for y sequences. Some of the pairwise combination results (among the 10 possible combinations) are also shown. Similar results are observed on other pairs. In all cases the discriminant weight approach outperforms the equal weight approach.

Multiclass classification			Pairwise classification		
Event	No. of misclassifications		Event Pair	No. of misclassifications	
	Equal weights	Optimal weights		Equal wts.	Optimal wts.
1	8/70	5/70	1 vs 2	12/140	5/140
2	6/70	6/70	2 vs 3	14/140	8/140
3	8/70	4/70	3 vs 4	9/140	6/140
4	5/70	4/70	4 vs 5	11/140	7/140
5	5/70	3/70	1 vs 5	10/140	6/140

5   Conclusions

This paper addresses the issue of identifying the importance of different parts of a video sequence from the recognition point of view. It highlights the importance of feature selection for *recognising* rather than just *representing* events. An adaptive technique which chooses the important features from an event sequence is described. It demonstrates that a fixed feature selection scheme may not be appropriate for a wide class of events. This approach: (a) provides a mechanism to identify the video segments (actions) and their importance statistically, (b) is suitable for various domains involving analysis of sequential data such as video event sequences, online handwriting, etc., (c) is straight-forward to implement without requiring careful parameter-tuning, and (d) can be extended on the lines of Multiple Discriminant Analysis and Kernel Discriminant Analysis.

Acknowledgments. Karteek Alahari thanks the GE Foundation for financial support through the GE Foundation Scholar-Leaders Program 2003-2005.

References

1. Zelnik-Manor, L., Irani, M.: Event-Based Analysis of Video. In: Proc. CVPR. Volume II. (2001) 123–130
2. Gavrila, D.M.: The visual analysis of human movement: A survey. CVIU **73** (1999) 82–98
3. Sullivan, J., Carlsson, S.: Recognizing and Tracking Human Action. In: Proc. ECCV. Volume I. (2002) 629–644
4. Buxton, H.: Learning and understanding dynamic scene activity: a review. IVC **21** (2003) 125–136
5. Hongeng, S., Nevatia, R., Bremond, F.: Video-based event recognition: activity representation and probabilistic recognition methods. CVIU **96** (2004) 129–162
6. Haritaoglu, I., Harwood, D., Davis, L.S.: W^4: Real-Time Surveillance of People and Their Activities. IEEE Trans. on PAMI **22** (2000) 809–830
7. Ryoo, M.S., Aggarwal, J.K.: Recog. of Composite Human Activities through Context-Free Grammar based Rep. In: CVPR. Volume 2. (2006) 1709–1718
8. Yilmaz, A., Shah, M.: Actions Sketch: A Novel Action Representation. In: Proc. CVPR. Volume 1. (2005) 984–989
9. Urtasun, R., Fua, P.: Human Motion Models for Characterization and Recognition. In: Automated Face and Gesture Recognition. (2004)
10. Brand, M., Kettnaker, V.: Discovery and Segmentation of Activities in Video. IEEE Trans. on PAMI **22** (2000) 844–851
11. Bobick, A.F., Davis, J.W.: The Recognition of Human Movement Using Temporal Templates. IEEE Trans. on PAMI **23** (2001) 257–267
12. Blank, M., Gorelick, L., Shechtman, E., Irani, M., Basri, R.: Actions as Space-Time Shapes. In: Proc. ICCV. (2005)
13. Belhumeur, P.N., Hespanha, J.P., Kriegman, D.J.: Eigenfaces vs. Fisherfaces: Recognition Using Class Specific Linear Projection. IEEE Trans. on PAMI **19** (1997) 711–720
14. Marcel, S.: (Dynamic Hand Posture Database: http://www-prima.inrialpes.fr/ FGnet/data/10-Gesture/dhp_marcel.tar.gz)
15. Yacoob, Y., Black, M.J.: Parameterized Modeling and Recognition of Activities. CVIU **73** (1999) 232–247
16. E. Ayyappa: Normal human locomotion, part 1: Basic concepts and terminology. Journal of Prosthetics and Orthotics **9** (1997) 10–17
17. Collins, R.T., Liu, Y., Leordeanu, M.: Online Selection of Discriminative Tracking Features. IEEE Trans. on PAMI **27** (2005) 1631–1643
18. Han, J., Bhanu, B.: Statistical Feature Fusion for Gait-based Human Recognition. In: Proc. CVPR. Volume 2. (2004) 842–847
19. Duda, R.O., Hart, P.E., Stork, D.G.: Pattern Classification. John Wiley and Sons, New York (2001)

Continuous Hand Gesture Segmentation and Co-articulation Detection

M.K. Bhuyan[1], D. Ghosh[2], and P.K. Bora[1]

[1] Department of Electronics and Communication Engineering,
Indian Institute of Technology, Guwahati, India
`manas_kb@iitg.ernet.in, prabin@iitg.ernet.in`
[2] Faculty of Engineering and Technology,
Multimedia University, Melaka Campus, Malaysia
`dghosh_iitg@hotmail.com`

Abstract. Gesture segmentation is an extremely difficult task due to both the multitude of possible gesture variations in spatio-temporal space and the co-articulation of successive gestures. In this paper, a robust framework for this problem is proposed which has been used to segment out component gestures from a continuous stream of gestures using finite state machine and motion features in a vision based platform.

1 Introduction

One very interesting field of research in Pattern Recognition that has gained much attention in recent times is Gesture Recognition. Hand gesture recognition from visual images finds applications in areas like human computer interaction, machine vision, virtual reality and so on. Many vision-based gesture recognition systems assume that the input gestures are isolated or segmented. This assumption makes the recognition task easier, but at the same time it limits the naturalness of the interaction between the user and the system, and therefore negatively affects the user's experience. In more natural settings, the gestures of interest are embedded in a continuous stream of motion, and their occurrence has to be detected as part of recognition. This is precisely the goal of gesture spotting *i.e.*, to locate the start point and end point of a gesture pattern, and to classify the gesture as belonging to one of predetermined gesture classes. Another important issue of gesture recognition is co-articulation, which makes the extraction and segmentation of gesture commands even harder in continuous hand movements. Co-articulation is a phenomenon in which one gesture influences the next in a temporal sequence [1]. This happens due to hand movement during transition from one gesture to the next. The problem is very significant in case of fluent sign language. Recognition of co-articulated gestures is one of the difficult tasks in gesture recognition.

Zhao *et al.* calculates velocity, and treats local minima in the velocity as gesture boundaries [2]. However, this method does not produce gestures that are consistent with human perception. The indirect approach uses a state space

P. Kalra and S. Peleg (Eds.): ICVGIP 2006, LNCS 4338, pp. 564–575, 2006.

model of gestures [3]. Lee and Kim proposed a gesture spotting system using a threshold model that calculates the threshold likelihood of a given input sequence as the basis of approving or rejecting the input pattern as a gesture. For gesture spotting, this system detects the end point of a gesture and finds a corresponding start point by searching the Viterbi path from the end point [4]. However, the method has a problem in that the system cannot report the detection of a gesture immediately after the system reaches its end point. Moreover they used heuristic information, such as moving the hand out of the camera range. Such a heuristic is not very natural to humans. Nishimura and Oka also proposed a gesture spotting method using continuous dynamic programming (CDP), which worked on a frame-by-frame basis and matched a sequence of input feature vectors and standard patterns corresponding to each gesture [5]. The matching result is the cumulative distance between cumulative frames and a gesture, and the best match is the result of spotting and recognition. However, this approach is limited to sets of gestures that do not contain any intermediate poses that resemble the start or end poses. In practical applications, this approach of using state-space models for achieving gesture segmentation and recognition severely limits the number of gestures that can be segmented. Vogler and Metaxas used context-dependent HMMs for recognition of continuous gestures [6]. However the context-dependent modelling has some inherent problems. First, it is linguistically implausible, because it fails to model movement epenthesis properly. Second, by using signs as the basic phonetic unit, the number of states used in the HMM recognition network grows roughly with order of $O(W^2)$, where W is the number of signs in the vocabulary, as the number of possible contexts itself grows with order $O(W^2)$.

Though the "segmentation" as well as "co-articulation detection" are the the most important and open research issues for continuous hand gesture recognition, not much vision based approaches are reported till date of this research work. The techniques developed so far for co-articulation detection are not always successful for wide range of gesture vocabulary. Moreover, these algorithms do not address the problems associated with the recognition of continuous hand gestures of different spatio-temporal behavior *viz.*, gestures having only local motions, gestures having only global motions, gestures having both local and global motions, and also fluent finger spelling. Motivating by these facts, we propose a more general and relatively simple model for continuous gesture segmentation by combining good features of state based and motion based approaches. In our method, we first segment the input video stream by detecting gesture boundaries at which the hand pauses for a while during gesticulation. Next, every segment is checked for co-articulation via finite state machine (FSM) matching or by using hand motion information. Thus, co-articulation phases are detected and eliminated from the sequence and we are left with a set of isolated gestures. We proposed to use FSM for segmentation of gestures having only local hand motions, where we used only some selected frames for building up a gesture model. For gestures having both local and global motions, we first determine the co-articulated strokes and subsequently used it for determining gesture boundary.

2 Proposed Scheme for Gesture Spotting and Co-articulation Detection

2.1 Gesture Boundary Detection

Generally a gesture starts and ends with the hand staying in a standstill position for a while. That is, a signer generally starts making a sign from a "pause" state and ends in a "pause" state in case of continuous gesturing. Based on this idea, we propose to use the hand motion information for locating the boundary points of each individual gesture in a continuous stream of gestures. A boundary point is detected whenever the hand pauses during gesturing.

The first step in the proposed method for gesture spotting involves generating the video object plane (VOP) from each input frame in the continuous stream of video. A series of key VOPs are extracted from the generated VOPs, which also gives the duration of each key VOP in terms of the number of frames between each pair of key VOPs [7]. A VOP model diagram showing a portion of a continuous gesture sequence is given in Fig. 1. The diagram shows two gestures in the sequence connected with a co-articulation phase in between them. In the figure, $\text{KVOP}_{m,n}$ represents the nth key VOP in gesture number m and $\text{T}_{m,n}$ is the corresponding time duration, expressed in terms of the number of video frames between $\text{KVOP}_{m,n}$ and $\text{KVOP}_{m,n+1}$

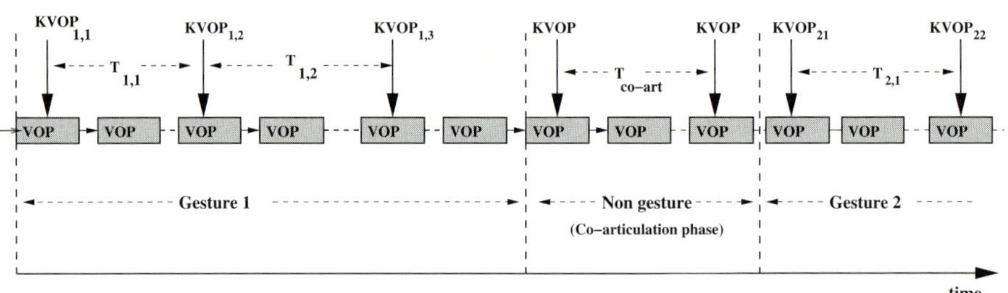

Fig. 1. VOP model for a portion of a continuous gesture sequence showing co-articulation

A key VOP in the sequence corresponds to a particular hand shape and/or position and the key VOP duration indicates the time for which the hand remains more or less fixed in that pose and position. This key VOP information is used in the proposed gesture spotting algorithm as well as for gesture recognition. For gesture spotting, a "pause" in the sequence is detected whenever the duration of a key VOP exceeds or at least equal to the minimum time for which the hand pauses at the starting or ending of a single gesture, as determined during the training session.

In the proposed algorithm, we assume that the camera starts capturing the hand image sometime before the signer starts gesturing. Therefore, the first

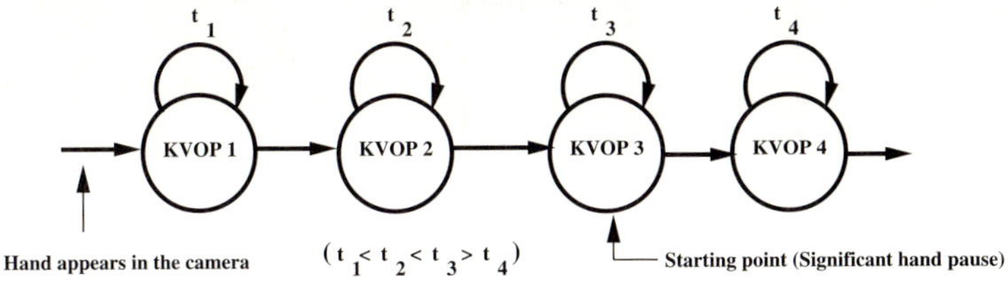

Fig. 2. Gesture sequence starting point detection

"pause" in the video indicates the starting of the first gesture in the sequence, as illustrated in Fig. 2. The gesture may end when the next "pause" in the video stream is spotted. Assuming that there is always some non-gestural movement in between two gestures, the third and fourth "pauses" in the input video will indicate the starting and ending of the second gesture in the sequence respectively and so on. Thus, all the gestures in the input sequence can be conveniently selected out. However, the scheme will fail under certain situations, as listed below, and will result in incorrect spotting of gestures.

1. The assumption that there is always some non-gestural movement of hand in between two gestures may not be always true. For example, if the end position or pose of a gesture is same as the start position or pose of the next gesture then there is generally no extra movement in between these two gestures. In that case, the two gestures are adjoined to each other in the sequence with a common "pause" indicating end of the first gesture and start of the next gesture.

2. In the case of fluent finger spelling, there is generally no motion during the gesturing period while the hand may move in between two gesture poses due to co-articulation. That means, here a "pause" itself in the sequence corresponds to a gesture sign as if the start-point and end-point of the gesture have merged together.

3. In the case of gestures involving global hand motion, there may be some "pauses" within a single gesture. When the hand traverses in space, it makes one or more hand strokes to build up a complete gesture trajectory. Since a hand stroke generally starts from a "pause" and ends in a "pause", a multi-stroke gesture will contain some extra pauses in between. Some examples of ideal gesture trajectories that are made up of one or more gesture strokes are shown in Fig. 3. The first two examples are gestures having global motion only representing "One" and "Square", respectively. As we see in the figure, "One" is a single stroke gesture while "Square" is made up of four strokes. Therefore, the gesture "One" will start from a pause and will end in the next "pause". But, there will be three intermediate "pauses" in the "Square" indicating gesture. The last example is the trajectory of a gesture composed of both local and global motions that represents a sentence in sign language. Here each word in the sentence is signed by a single stroke associated with

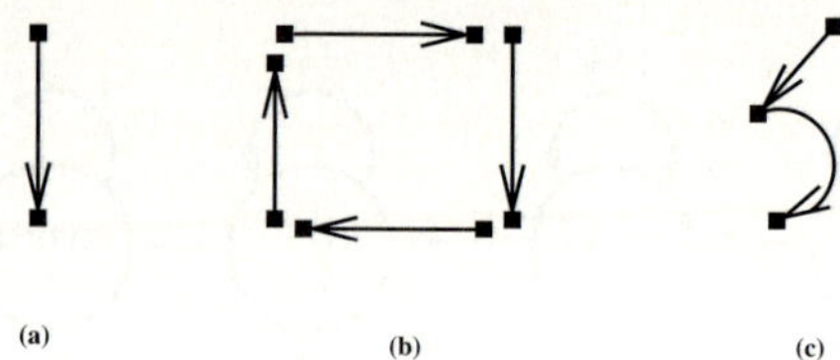

(a)   (b)   (c)

Fig. 3. (a) Single hand stroke for a gesture (b) Multiple hand strokes for a gesture (c) Multiple strokes for a sentence of sign language

changing the hand pose. Hence, the number of strokes in the gesture is equal to the number of words in the sentence. Accordingly, for this example, there will be one extra pause in between.

Hence, it is not always possible to have reliable spotting of gestures only by detecting pauses in an input video. In view of this, we propose to check the nature of hand movement in every video segment in between two "pauses" in the input stream. Assuming that there is no unintentional movement other than co-articulation in between gestures, the proposed gesture spotting method requires to determine the occurrence of co-articulation in the sequence. This is done through FSM matching and/or using motion features, as explained in the next section.

2.2   Co-articulation Detection in Continuous Gestures with Local Motion Only

Following two steps are used for co-articulation detection for gestures having only local hand motions.

Step 1: We assume that after completing a gesture, the signer holds his hand for sometime in the last signed pose in the gesture and then quickly moves it to the starting pose of the next gesture in the sequence. The signer does this by bending his fingers and/or moving his palm in a very short span of time while holding the hand more or less fixed at one position in space. That means, the co-articulation phase is also made up of local hand motions only and hence may be represented by an FSM model. Now since there is fast change in hand shape during co-articulation compared to that during a gesturing phase, the time duration associated with each state of an FSM representing co-articulation will be generally very small than that for an FSM representing a gesture. Therefore, co-articulation in continuous gesturing may be detected if the key VOP durations in between two "pauses" are below a certain threshold. The value of this threshold may be decided during the training session.

Step 2: The co-articulation detected in Step 1 can be verified by representing the KVOPs in the detected co-articulation phase by an FSM. The input video sequence is represented by an FSM and is matched to all the prototype FSMs contained in the database, each prototype FSM representing a local motion gesture in our gesture vocabulary. If no match is obtained then co-articulation is detected.

2.3 Co-articulation Detection in Continuous Gestures Having Global Motion

In the case of gestures having global motion only or gestures having both global and local motions, the gesturing hand traverses in space to form a gesture trajectory. After a gesture trajectory is complete, the hand pauses for a while and then moves with very high velocity to the starting position of the next trajectory. After that, the hand again pauses for a while before starting the next trajectory. Based on this, we now propose to detect co-articulation by observing the motion of the hand between two "pauses" in the input hand motion video.

A gesture phase can be divided into three motion stages – preparation, stroke and retraction, in addition to the starting and ending "pauses" [8]. On the other hand, a co-articulation phase starts from a pause, makes a fast hand stroke and finally ends up in another pause. Therefore, it is possible to distinguish a co-articulation from a gesture stroke if we can determine the behavior of the gesturing hand in between two "pauses". For this, we compute two motion parameters, *viz.*, velocity and acceleration, at every key VOP instant and decide the nature of hand movement at that instant. The proposed scheme for co-articulation detection in the continuous gestures with global hand motions consists of the following two stages.

Step 1: Co-articulation detection by motion features

Acceleration feature for co-articulation detection:

The most important motion parameter that can discriminate a co-articulation phase from a gesture is the change in speed or acceleration. During co-articulation the speed of the hand increases to a very high value from almost zero value and then abruptly comes down to almost zero as illustrated in Fig. 4. That means, the hand moves with very high acceleration (positive or negative) during the co-articulation phase. On the other hand, during gesturing the speed of the hand gradually increases from a pause, may remain constant for sometime and then gradually comes down to almost zero. Therefore, acceleration feature may be a good measure to check for co-articulation.

Velocity feature for co-articulation detection:

The speed of the hand is generally very high while making a stroke. But, that during the preparation and retraction stages is generally very small. That means, the average velocity of the hand during co-articulation is generally very large compared to that during a gesturing phase. Hence, the measure of velocity may serve as an additional feature to detect co-articulation. We now describe how these two motion parameters are used to discriminate between a co-articulation phase and a gesturing phase.

Fuzzy method for co-articulation detection:

We have formulated a scheme to measure the motion behavior in terms of some fuzzy sets and rules to determine whether a particular motion is gesture phase or co-articulation. By observing different gesture samples, we first define four fuzzy sets to denote the different ranges of speed. They are 'Zero' (ZO), 'Positive Small' (PS), 'Positive Medium' (PM) and 'Positive Large' (PL). The corresponding fuzzy membership functions are plotted in Fig. 5. Similarly, we define five fuzzy sets to quantify change in speed in terms of some fuzzy measures. They are 'Negative Medium' (NM), 'Negative Small' (NS), 'Zero' (ZO), 'Positive Small' (PS) and 'Positive Medium' (PM); the corresponding membership functions are shown in Fig. 6. Mathematically these two motion features can be expressed in terms of motion vector (MV_i) as follows.

$$\text{Speed}: \quad S_i = \sqrt{(x_i - x_{i+1})^2 + (y_i - y_{i+1})^2} = MV_i \tag{1}$$

$$\text{Change in speed}: \quad \Delta S_i = S_i - S_{i-1} = MV_i - MV_{i-1} \tag{2}$$

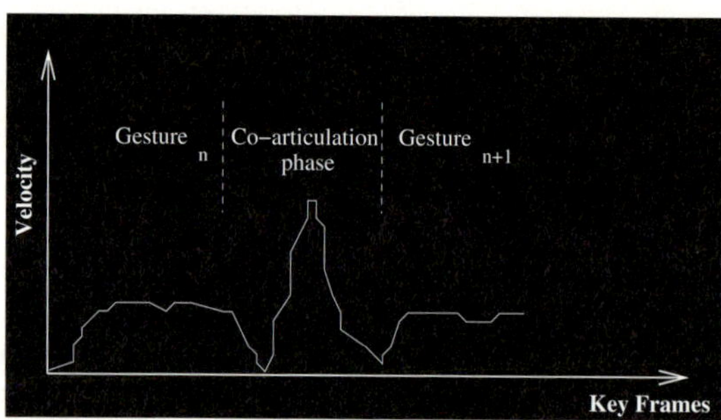

Fig. 4. Example of a typical velocity plot for connected sequentially global motion gestures in a continuous video stream

As given in Algorithm 1, motion vector MV_i for i^{th} video object plane in the gesture sequence is determined from generalized Hausdorff distance measure. Hausdorff tracker can be used to track non–rigid objects in a complex scene [9], [10]. In our algorithm, Hausdorff distance is computed using distance transform algorithm [11]. As explained earlier, a typical gesture can be divided into 5 motion phases. There are three distinct phases: preparation, stroke and end. The stroke is distinguished from the others by the speed and the change of speed. Table 1 shows these 5 motion phases. These two motion parameters are subsequently fuzzified and the motion stage through which the hand is undergoing is determined using some fuzzy rules, as stated below.

Algorithm 1. Estimation of Motion vector

Given $(i-1)^{th}$ VOP O and the ith VOP I and a set of translated vectors **T**
begin
    for $t = (t_x, t_y) \in$ **T**
        Calculate distance transform of edge images O and I.
        Calculate $h_{p,t}(O, I)$.
        Calculate $h_{j,t}(I, O)$.
        Determine $H_t(O, I) = max\{h_p(O, I), h_j(I, O)\}$.
    end.
Find $min\{H_t(O, I)\}$ over $t \in$ **T**.
    Find translation vector $t' = (t'_x, t'_y)$ corresponding to $min\{H(O, I)\}$.
    $MV_i = (t'_x, t'_y)$.
return MV_i
end

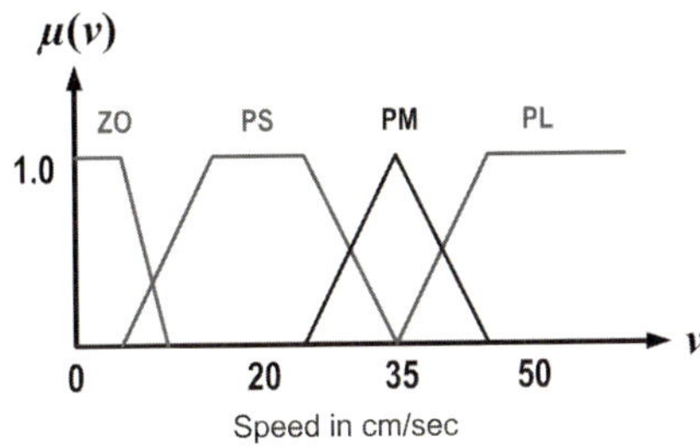

Fig. 5. Fuzzy membership functions defining different ranges of speed

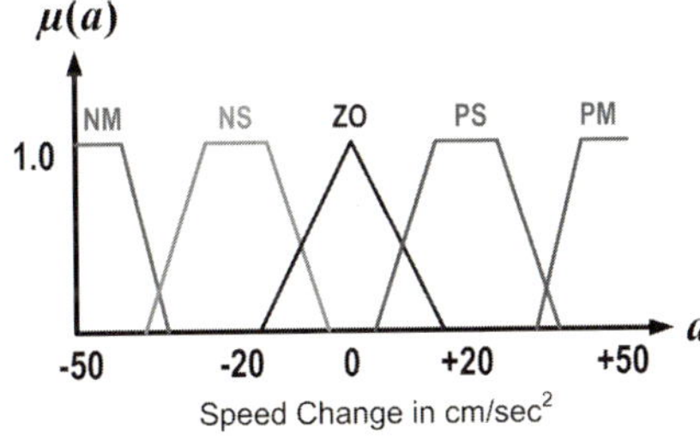

Fig. 6. Fuzzy membership functions defining different ranges of change in speed

From a large set of real gestures we observe that the speed of the hand generally lies within a certain range at every stage in a gesture or co-articulation. So, is the case for change in speed. For example, during the "Preparation" stage the speed is generally 'Positive Small' and the change in speed is either 'Positive Small' or 'Negative Small'. This we can write in the form of a fuzzy rule as

– "IF the speed is Positive Small AND the change in speed is Positive Small OR Negative Small, THEN the hand is in Preparation stage".

Accordingly, if the hand is moving at a speed v and change in speed is a then, using this fuzzy rule and applying min-max method, the degree of certainty by which we can say that the hand is in "Preparation" stage is given as

$$\mu_{\text{Prep}}(v, a) = \min\left[\mu_{\text{PS}}(v), \max\left[\mu_{\text{PS}}(a), \mu_{\text{NS}}(a)\right]\right] \tag{3}$$

The IF-THEN fuzzy rules for all the other three motion phases can be derived in a similar manner and using Table 1 that gives the fuzzy sets for the two motion parameters corresponding to the different stages of hand motion. Using all these fuzzy rules we can compute the degrees of confidence that the hand is doing "Pause", "Preparation", "Stroke" and "Retraction" at a given instant of time. Finally, we decide for the motion stage that has the maximum degree of confidence. In doing so, we are able to find the sequence of hand motion in an input stream of hand gesture video and a motion pattern. If the extracted motion pattern follows the motion phases of Table 1 in order, the video segment is classified as a gesture, otherwise it is labelled as co-articulation.

Table 1. Gesture motion phases and corresponding motion parameters

Motion phase	Speed	Change in Speed
Pause	ZO	ZO, PS, NS
Preparation	PS	PS, NS
Stroke	PL, PM	ZO, PS, NS, PM, NM
Retraction	PS	NS

Step 2: Verification of Co-articulation Using Trajectory Shape

The process of co-articulation detection can be made more reliable and accurate by considering the hand trajectory shape for verification. It is observed that during co-articulation the hand generally moves in a straight path. So, a motion phase is not a co-articulation if the trajectory is not a straight line. Note that a straight-line trajectory does not always indicate co-articulation. It may also represent a valid gesture stroke. The Step I discriminates between co-articulation and such a gesture stroke.

However, the above scheme fails to spot gestures if there is no co-articulation phase between two gestures. In such cases, gesture spotting is done along with recognition. In these types of gestures, every video segment between two "pauses" corresponds to either a gesture stroke in space or a co-articulation phase. Therefore, as a first step towards recognition, it is required to check whether an input segment is a co-articulation or a gesture stroke. If it is a co-articulation then it is discarded and we move on to the next segment. If it is a stroke then we check whether it is a complete gesture trajectory or not by comparing it to all the prototype trajectories contained in the gesture vocabulary database. If not, we then move on to the next segment and check for gesture stroke. This we continue till a valid gesture trajectory is obtained by connecting all these individual hand strokes in a sequential manner.

3   Experimental Results

In a first set of experiments, we considered some sequences of continuous gesturing with local hand motions only. We have used five different gesture sequences taken from Sebastien Marcel's gesture database and Thomas Moeslund's gesture recognition database. The continuous gesture sequences were formed by performing different gesture signs in different orders in such a way that while some gestures were connected to each other in the sequence there were cases where two gestures were separated by a co-articulation phase in between. In our experiments, we achieved an overall recognition accuracy of 90.4%. This high recognition rate confirms that our proposed algorithm for gesture spotting and co-articulation detection was indeed effective in segmenting out meaningful individual gestures in the input sequences accurately and precisely.

In a second set of experiment, we considered some trajectory patterns indicating "One", "Two", "Five", "Seven" and "Three", as shown in the first row of Fig. 7. These gesture signs were performed one after another in different orders to build up different sequences of continuous hand motion gestures with global motion only. The second row of Fig. 7 shows another set of gesture trajectories, *viz.*, "Square", "Circle", "Diamond", "triangle" and "W". These gestures were used in our third set of experiments. As we observe, each gesture in the first row starts from some point at top of the frame and ends somewhere at the bottom. So, in our second set of experiments we always have a co-articulation phase in between two gestures in a sequence. On the other hand, in our third set of experiments the starting and ending of all gestures in a sequence are in the vicinity of each other. That means, here the gestures are generally connected to each other without any co-articulation in between. Fig. 8(a) shows a sample of the continuous gesture sequence without any co-articulation while Fig. 8(b) shows a sequence of gestures connected by co-articulation strokes in between.

In our second set of experiments, we used hand motion information to discriminate the co-articulation phases in the input gesture sequences. Subsequently, all individual gesture patterns in the sequences were segmented out and were identified with an overall accuracy of 90%. This demonstrates the efficiency of our proposed method for co-articulation detection and subsequent trajectory guided recognition. We also observed that the acceleration of the hand was significantly high during co-articulation compared to that during the gesturing phase. Finally, in our third set of experiments, individual gesture patterns in the sequences were segmented out and were identified with an overall accuracy of 94%. This shows that the proposed system is capable of identifying gesture strokes and

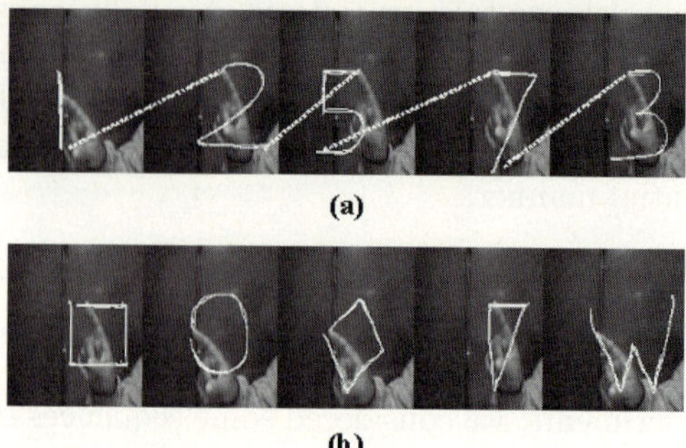

(a)

(b)

Fig. 7. Trajectories of the gestures used in our experiments: (a) Gestures that produce co-articulation, used in our 2nd set of experiments, (b) Gestures that do not produce co-articulation, used in our 3rd set of experiments

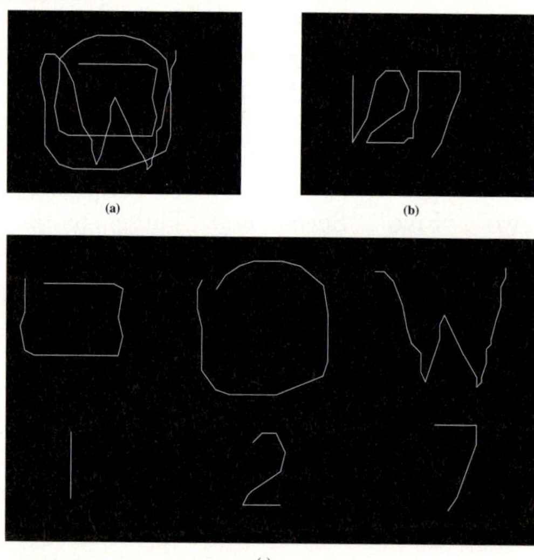

(a)

(b)

(c)

Fig. 8. (a) Continuous motion trajectory without co-articulated stroke (b) Continuous motion trajectory with co-articulated stroke (c) Segmented out trajectory

trajectory patterns with very high accuracy. The segmented out gesture trajectories from the gesture sequence samples in Fig. 8(a) and Fig. 8(b) are shown in Fig. 8(c).

4   Conclusion

Co-articulation is one of the main challenges in continuous gesture recognition. Motion interpretation is a quite ill-posed problem, in which cognitive science and psychological studies need to be combined. That is why, not many vision based approaches for estimating co-articulation have been reported in the literature till date. Most of the proposed algorithms till now have success only for some specific gesture vocabularies, which can not be generalized for all kinds of gestures performed in different contexts. The proposed system for co-articulation detection in a continuous stream of gestures performs well for different types of gesture sequences having different spatio-temporal and motion behaviour in a common vision-based platform. One notable advantage of the proposed method is that finger motion during gesticulation is considered as the shape change of the video object, which can be efficiently quantified using FSM based representation.

References

1. Shamaie, A., Hai, W., Sutherland, A.: Hand gesture recognition for HCI, ERCIM News, http://www.ercim.org/publication/Ercim_News, **46** (2001)
2. Zhao, L.: Synthesis and acquisition of laban movement analysis qualitative parameters for communicative gestures, Ph.D Thesis, CIS, University of Pennsylvania, (2001)
3. Aggarwal, J., Cai, Q.: Human motion analysis: A review, Proc. Nonrigid and Articulated Motion Workshop, (1997) 90–102
4. Lee, H. K., Kim, J. H.: An HMM based threshold model approach for gesture recognition, IEEE Trans. Pattern Analysis and Machine Intelligence, **21(10)** (1999) 961–973
5. Nishimura, T., Oka, R.: Towards the integration of spontaneous speech and gesture based on spotting method, Proc. IEEE/SICE/RSJ International Conf. Multisensor Fusion Integration Intelligent System, (1996) 433–437
6. Vogler, C., Mextaxas, D.: Adapting hidden Markov models for ASL recognition by using three-dimensional computer vision methods, Proc. IEEE International Conf. on Systems, Man and Cybernetics, (1997) 156–161
7. Bhuyan, M.K., Ghosh, D., Bora, P.K.: Key video object plane selection by MPEG-7 visual shape descriptor for summarization and recognition of hand gestures, Proc. 4th Indian Conference on Computer Vision, Graphics and Image Processing (ICVGIP), (2004) 638–643
8. Kendon, A.: Conducting interaction, Cambridge University Press, (1990)
9. Huttenlocher, D.P., Noh, J.J., Rucklidge, W.J.: Tracking non-rigid objects in complex scene, Proc. 4th International Conf. Computer Vision, (1993) 93–101
10. Bhuyan, M.K., Ghosh, D., Bora, P.K.: Estimation of 2D motion trajectories from video object planes and its application in hand gesture recognition, Lecture Notes in Computer Science, Springer-Verlag, **(LNCS 3776)** 509–514
11. Borgefors, G.: Distance transformations in digital images, Computer Vision, Graphics and Image Processing, **34** (1986) 344–371

OBJCUT for Face Detection

Jonathan Rihan, Pushmeet Kohli, and Philip H.S. Torr

Department of Computing
Oxford Brookes University, UK
{jon.rihan, pushmeet.kohli, philiptorr}@brookes.ac.uk
http://cms.brookes.ac.uk/research/visiongroup/

Abstract. This paper proposes a novel, simple and efficient method for face segmentation which works by coupling face detection and segmentation in a single framework. We use the OBJCUT [1] formulation that allows for a smooth combination of object detection and Markov Random Field for segmentation, to produce a real-time face segmentation. It should be noted that our algorithm is extremely efficient and runs in real time.

1   Introduction

Object detection and segmentation are important problems of computer vision and have numerous commercial applications such as pedestrian detection, surveillance and gesture recognition. Image segmentation has been an extremely active area of research in recent years [2,3,4,5,1,6]. In particular segmentation of the face is of great interest due to such applications as Windows Messenger© [7,8].

Until recently the only reliable method for performing segmentation in real time was blue screening. This method imposes strict restrictions on the input data and can only be used for certain specific applications. Recently Kolmogorov *et al.* [9] proposed a robust method for extracting foreground and background layers of a scene from a stereo image pair. Their system ran in real time and used two carefully calibrated cameras for performing segmentation. These cameras were used to obtain disparity information about the scene which was later used in segmenting the scene into foreground and background layers. Although they obtained excellent segmentation results, the need for two calibrated cameras was a drawback of their system.

Shape priors for Segmentation: An orthogonal approach for solving the segmentation problem robustly has been the use of prior knowledge about the object to be segmented. In recent years a number of papers have successfully tried to couple MRFs used for modelling the image segmentation problem with information about the nature and shape of the object to be segmented [3,4,1,10]. The primary challenge in these systems is that of ascertaining what would be a good choice for a prior on the shape. This is because the shape (and pose) of objects in the real world vary with time. To obtain a good shape prior then, there is a need to localize the object in the image and also infer its pose, both of which are extremely difficult problems in themselves.

Kumar *et al.* [1] proposed a solution to these problems by matching a set of exemplars for different parts of the object on to the image. Using these matches they generate a shape model for the object. They model the segmentation problem by combining

P. Kalra and S. Peleg (Eds.): ICVGIP 2006, LNCS 4338, pp. 576–584, 2006.

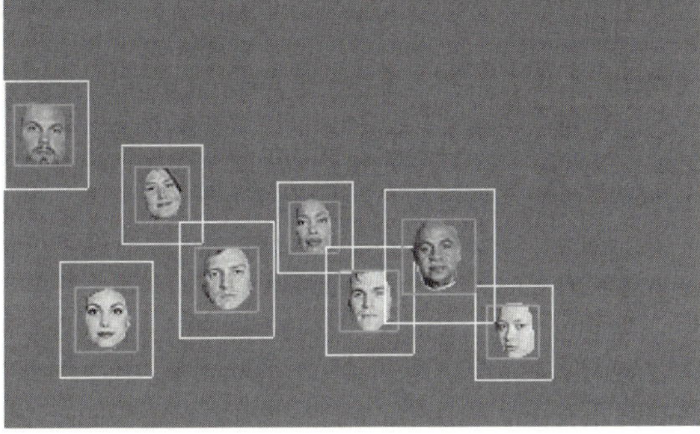

Fig. 1. Real Time Face Segmentation using a face detections. The first image on the first row shows the original image. The second image shows the face detection results. The image on the second row shows the segmentation obtained by using shape priors generated using the detection and localization results.

MRFs with layered pictorial structures (LPS) which provide them with a realistic shape prior described by a set of latent shape parameters. A lot of effort has to be spent to learn the exemplars for different parts of the LPS model.

In their work on simultaneous segmentation and 3D pose estimation of humans, Bray *et al.* [3] proposed the use of a simple 3D stick-man model as a shape prior. Instead of matching exemplars for individual parts of the object, their method followed an iterative algorithm for pose inference and segmentation whose aim was to find the pose corresponding to the human segmentation having the maximum probability (or least energy). Their iterative algorithm was made efficient using the dynamic graph cut algorithm [5]. Their work had the important message that ***rough shape priors were sufficient to obtain accurate segmentation results***. This is an important observation which will be exploited in our work to obtain an accurate segmentation of the face.

Coupling Face Detection and Segmentation: In the methods described above the computational problem is that of localizing the object in the image and inferring its pose. Once a rough estimate of the object pose is obtained, the segmentation can be computed extremely efficiently using graph cuts [2,5,11,12,13]. In this paper we show how an off the shelf face-detector such as the one described in [14] can be coupled with graph cut based segmentation to give accurate segmentation and improved face detection results in real time.

The key idea of this paper is that face localization estimates in an image (obtained from any generic face detector) can be used to generate a rough shape energy. These energies can then be incorporated in to a discriminative MRF framework to obtain robust and accurate face segmentation results as shown in Figure 1. This method is an example of the OBJCUT paradigm for an unarticulated object. We define an uncertainty measure corresponding to each face detection which is based on the energy associated with the face segmentation. It is shown how this uncertainty measure might be used to filter out false face detections thus improving the face detection accuracy.

Organization of the Paper: This paper proposes a method for face segmentation which works by coupling the problems of face detection and segmentation in a single framework. Our method is extremely efficient and runs in real time[1]. The key novelties of the paper include:

- A framework for coupling face detection and segmentation problems together.
- A method for generating rough shape energies from face detection results.
- An uncertainty measure for face segmentation results which can be used to identify and prune false detections.

A summary of the paper follows. In the next section, we briefly discuss the methods for robust face detection and image segmentation. In section 3, we describe how a rough shape energy can be generated using localization results obtained from any face detection algorithm. The procedure for integration of this shape energy in the segmentation framework is given in the same section along with details of the uncertainty measure associated with each face segmentation. We conclude by listing some ideas for future work in section 4.

2   Preliminaries

In this section we give a brief description of the methods used for face detection and image segmentation.

2.1   Face Detection and Localization

Given an image, the aim of a face detection system is to detect the presence of all human faces in the image and to give rough estimates of the positions of all such detected faces. In this paper we use the face detection method proposed by Viola and Jones [14]. This method is extremely efficient and has been shown to give good detection accuracy. A brief description of the algorithm is given next.

The Viola Jones face detector works on features which are similar to Haar filters. The computation of these features is done at multiple scales and is made efficient by using an image representation called the *integral image* [14]. After these features have been extracted, the algorithm constructs a set of classifiers using AdaBoost [15]. Once constructed, successively more complex classifiers are combined in a cascade structure.

---

[1] We have developed a system which uses a single camera and runs in real time.

This dramatically increases the speed of the detector by focussing attention on promising regions of the image. The output of the face detector is a set of rectangular windows in the image where a face has been detected. We will assume that each detection window W_i is parameterized by a vector $\theta_i = \{c_i^x, c_i^y, w_i, h_i\}$ where (c_i^x, c_i^y) is the centre of the detection window and w_i and h_i are its width and height respectively.

2.2 Image Segmentation

Given a vector $\mathbf{y} = \{y_1, y_2, \dots, y_n\}$ where each y_i represents the colour of the pixel i of an image having n pixels, the image segmentation problem is to find the value of the vector $\mathbf{x} = \{x_1, x_2, \dots, x_n\}$ where each x_i represents the label which the pixel i is assigned. Each x_i takes values from the label set $\mathcal{L} = \{l_1, l_2, \dots, l_k\}$. Here the label set $\mathcal{L}$ consists of only two labels i.e. 'face' and 'not face'. The posterior probability for $\mathbf{x}$ given $\mathbf{y}$ can be written as:

$$\Pr(\mathbf{x}|\mathbf{y}) = \frac{\Pr(\mathbf{y}|\mathbf{x})\Pr(\mathbf{x})}{\Pr(\mathbf{y})} \propto \Pr(\mathbf{y}|\mathbf{x})\Pr(\mathbf{x}). \tag{1}$$

We define the energy $E(\mathbf{x})$ of a labelling $\mathbf{x}$ as:

$$E(\mathbf{x}) = -\log\Pr(\mathbf{x}|\mathbf{y}) + \text{constant} = \phi(\mathbf{x}, \mathbf{y}) + \psi(\mathbf{x}) + \text{constant}, \tag{2}$$

where $\phi(\mathbf{x}, \mathbf{y}) = -\log\Pr(\mathbf{y}|\mathbf{x})$ and $\psi(\mathbf{x}) = -\log\Pr(\mathbf{x})$. Given an energy function $E(\mathbf{x})$, the most probable or maximum a posterior (MAP) segmentation solution $\mathbf{x}^*$ can be found as:

$$\mathbf{x}^* = \arg\min_{\mathbf{x}} E(\mathbf{x}). \tag{3}$$

It is typical to formulate the segmentation problem in terms of a Discriminative Markov Random Field [16]. In this framework the likelihood $\phi(\mathbf{x}, \mathbf{y})$ and prior terms $\psi(\mathbf{x})$ of the energy function can be decomposed into unary and pairwise potential functions. In particular this is the contrast dependent MRF [2,5] with energy:

$$E(\mathbf{x}) = \sum_i (\phi(x_i, \mathbf{y}) + \psi(x_i)) + \sum_{(i,j)\in N} (\phi(x_i, x_j, \mathbf{y}) + \psi(x_i, x_j)) + \text{constant}, \tag{4}$$

where N is the neighbourhood system defining the MRF. Typically a 4 or 8 neighbourhood system is used for image segmentation which implies each pixel is connected with 4 or 8 pixels in the graphical model respectively.

Colour and Contrast based Segmentation: The unary likelihood terms $\phi(x_i, \mathbf{y})$ of the energy function are computed using the colour distributions for the different segments in the image [2,1]. For our experiments we built the colour appearance models for the face/background using the pixels lying inside/outside the detection window obtained from the face detector. The pairwise likelihood term $\phi(x_i, x_j, \mathbf{y})$ of the energy function is called the *contrast term* and is *discontinuity preserving* in the sense that it encourages pixels having dissimilar colours to take different labels (see [2,1] for more details). This term takes the form:

$$\phi(x_i, x_j, \mathbf{y}) = \begin{cases} \gamma(i, j) & \text{if } x_i \neq x_j \\ 0 & \text{if } x_i = x_j. \end{cases} \tag{5}$$

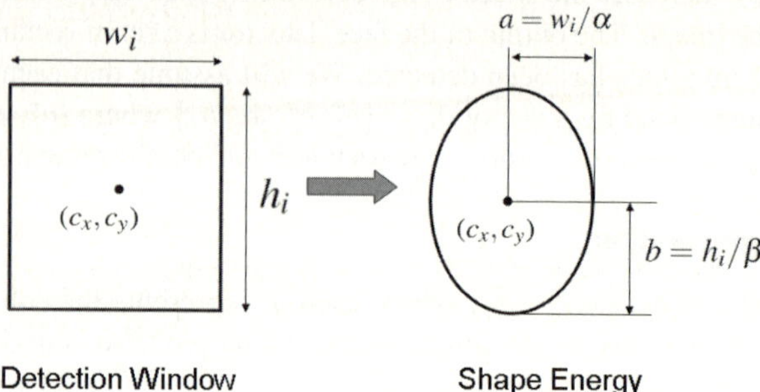

Fig. 2. Generating the face shape energy. The figure shows how a localization result from the face detection stage is used to generate a rough shape energy for the face.

where $\gamma(i,j) = exp\left(\frac{-g^2(i,j)}{2\sigma^2}\right)\frac{1}{\text{dist}(i,j)}$. Here $g^2(i,j)$ measures the difference in the RGB values of pixels i and j and $\text{dist}(i,j)$ gives the spatial distance between i and j.

The pairwise prior terms $\psi(x_i, x_j)$ are defined in terms of a generalized Potts model as:

$$\psi(x_i, x_j) = \begin{cases} K_{ij} & \text{if } x_i \neq x_j, \\ 0 & \text{if } x_i = x_j. \end{cases} \tag{6}$$

and encourage neighbouring pixels in the image[2] to take the same label thus resulting in smoothness in the segmentation solution. In most methods, the value of the unary prior term $\psi(x_i)$ is fixed to a constant. This is equivalent to assuming a uniform prior and does not effect the solution. In the next section we will show how a shape prior derived from a face detection result can be incorporated in the image segmentation framework.

3   Integrating Face Detection and Segmentation

Having given a brief overview of image segmentation and face detection methods, we now show how we couple these two methods in a single framework. Following the OBJCUT paradigm, we start by describing the face energy and then show how it is incorporated in the MRF framework.

The face shape energy: In their work on segmentation and 3D pose estimation of humans, Bray *et al.* [3] show that rough and simple shape energies are adequate to obtain accurate segmentation results. Following their example we use a simple elliptical model for the shape energy for a human face. The model is parameterized in terms of four parameters: the ellipse centre coordinates (c_x, c_y), the semi-minor axis a and the semi-major b (assuming $a < b$). The values of these parameters are computed from the parameters $\theta_k = \{c_k^x, c_k^y, w_k, h_k\}$ of the detection window k obtained from face detector as: $c_x = c_k^x$, $c_y = c_k^y$, $a = w_k/\alpha$ and $b = h_k/\beta$. The values of α and β used in our experiments were set to 2.5 and 2.0 respectively, however these can be computed iteratively in a manner similar to [3]. A detection window and the corresponding shape prior are shown in figure 2.

---

[2] Pixels i and j are neighbours if $(i,j) \in N$.

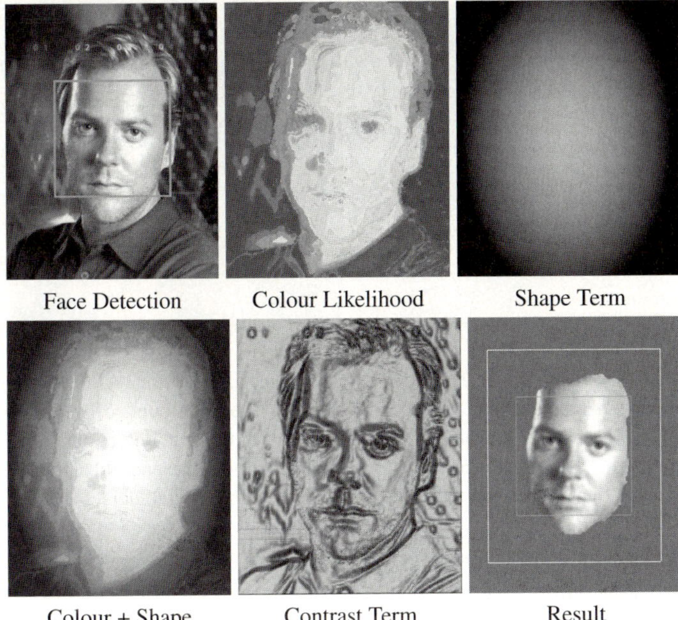

Fig. 3. Different terms of the shape-prior + MRF energy function. The figure shows the different terms of the energy function for a particular face detection and the corresponding image segmentation obtained.

3.1   Incorporating the Shape Energy

For each face detection k, we create a shape energy Θ_k as described above. This energy is integrated in the MRF framework described in section 2.2 using the unary terms $\psi(x_i)$ as:

$$\psi(x_i) = \lambda(x_i|\Theta_k) = -logp(x_i|\Theta_k) \tag{7}$$

where we define $p(x_i|\Theta_k)$ as:

$$p(x_i = \text{`face'}|\Theta_k) = \frac{1}{1 + \exp(\mu * (\frac{(cx_i - c_x^k)^2}{a^{k\,2}} + \frac{(cy_i - c_y^k)^2}{(b^k)^2} - 1))} \tag{8}$$

$$\text{and}\quad p(x_i = \text{`backgound'}|\Theta_k) = 1 - p(x_i = \text{`face'}|\Theta_k) \tag{9}$$

where cx_i and cy_i are the x and y coordinates of the pixel i, $\{c_x^k, c_y^k, a^k, b^k\}$ are parameters of the shape energy Θ_k, and the parameter μ determines how the strength of the shape energy term varies with the distance from the ellipse boundary. The different terms of the energy function and the corresponding segmentation for a particular image are shown in figure 3.

Once the energy function $E(\mathbf{x})$ has been formulated, the most probable segmentation solution $\mathbf{x}^*$ defined in equation (3) can be found by computing the solution of the max-flow problem over the *energy equivalent* graph [13]. The complexity of the max-flow

Fig. 4. The figure shows an image from the INRIA pedestrian data set. After running our algorithm, we obtain four face segmentations, one of which (the one bounded by a black square) is a false detection. The energy-per-pixel values obtained for the true detections were 74, 82 and 83 while that for the false detection was 87. As you can see the energy of false detection is significantly higher than that of the true detections, and can be used to detect and remove it.

algorithm increases with the number of variables involved in the energy function. Recall that the number of random variables is equal to the number of pixels in the image to be segmented. Even for a moderate sized image the number of pixels is in the range of 10^5 to 10^6. This makes the max-flow computation quite time consuming. To overcome this problem we only consider pixels which lie in a window W_k whose dimensions are double of those of the original detection window obtained from the face detector. As pixels outside this window are unlikely to belong to the face (due to the shape term $\psi(x_i)$) we set them to the background. The energy function for each face detection k now becomes:

$$E_k(\mathbf{x}) = \sum_{i \in W_k} \phi(x_i, \mathbf{y}) + \psi(x_i | \Theta_k) + \sum_{j \in W_k, (i,j) \in N} \phi(x_i, x_j, \mathbf{y}) + \psi(x_i, x_j) + \text{constant},$$

$$(10)$$

This energy is then minimized using graph cuts to find the face segmentation $\mathbf{x}_k^*$ for each detection k.

Pruning false detections: The energy $E(\mathbf{x}')$ of any segmentation solution $\mathbf{x}'$ is the negative log of the probability, and can be viewed as a measure of how uncertain that solution is. The higher the energy of a segmentation, the lower the probability that it is a good segmentation. Intuitively, if the face detection given by the detector is correct, then the resulting segmentation obtained from our method should have high probability and hence have low energy compared to the case of a false detections (as can be seen in figure 4). This characteristic of the energy of the segmentation solution can be used to prune false face detections. Alternatively, if the number of people P in the scene is known, then we can choose the top P detections according to the segmentation energy.

3.2   Implementation and Experimental Results

We tested our algorithm on a number of images containing faces. Some detection and segmentation results are shown in figure 6. The time taken for segmenting out the faces

Fig. 5. Effect of smoothing on the contrast term and the final segmentation. The images on the first row correspond to the original noisy image. The images on the second row are obtained after smoothing the image.

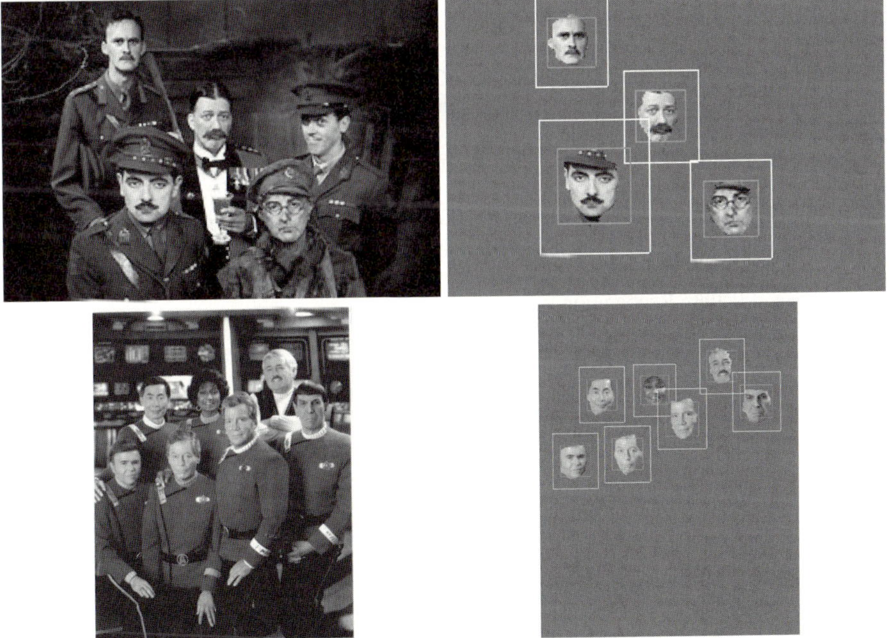

Fig. 6. Some face detection and segmentation results obtained from our algorithm

is of the order of tens of milliseconds. We also implemented a real time system for frontal face detection and segmentation. The system is capable of running at roughly 15 frames per second on images of 320x240 resolution.

Handling Noisy Images: The contrast term of the energy function might become quite bad in noisy images. To avoid this we smooth the image before the computation of this term. The result of this procedure are shown in figure 5.

4   Conclusion and Future Work

In this paper we presented a method for face segmentation which combines face detection and segmentation into a single framework. Our method runs in real time and gives accurate segmentation and improved face detection results.

While segmenting image frames of a video, the use of knowledge of the correct face detections in the previous frames in eliminating errors in the current image frame needs to be explored. Another area for future research is the idea of efficient selective refinement of the shape energy. This procedure could successively refine the shape energy to obtain good segmentations in complicated scenarios. It should be noted that such a procedure could be performed using dynamic graph cuts [5] which would make it computationally efficient.

References

1. Kumar, M., Torr, P., Zisserman, A.: OBJ CUT. In: CVPR. Volume I. (2005) 18–25
2. Boykov, Y., Jolly, M.: Interactive graph cuts for optimal boundary and region segmentation of objects in n-d images. In: ICCV. Volume I. (2001) 105–112
3. Bray, M., Kohli, P., Torr, P.: PoseCut: Simulataneous segmentation and 3d pose estimation of humans using dynamic graph cuts. In: ECCV. (2006) 642–655
4. Freedman, D., Zhang, T.: Interactive graph cut based segmentation with shape priors. In: CVPR. Volume I. (2005) 755–762
5. Kohli, P., Torr, P.: Efficiently solving dynamic markov random fields using graph cuts. In: ICCV. (2005)
6. Rother, C., Kolmogorov, V., Blake, A.: Grabcut: Interactive foreground extraction using iterated graph cuts. ACM Trans. Graph. (2004) 309–314
7. Criminisi, A., G, C., Blake, A., V, K.: Bilayer segmentation of live video. In: IEEE Computer Vision and Pattern Recognition (CVPR). (2006)
8. Sun, I., Zhang, W., Tang, X., Shum, H.: Background cut. In: ECCV. (2006)
9. Kolmogorov, V., Criminisi, A., Blake, A., Cross, G., Rother, C.: Bi-layer segmentation of binocular stereo video. In: CVPR (2). (2005) 407–414
10. Huang, R., Pavlovic, V., Metaxas, D.: A graphical model framework for coupling mrfs and deformable models. In: CVPR. Volume II. (2004) 739–746
11. Boykov, Y., Kolmogorov, V.: An experimental comparison of min-cut/max-flow algorithms for energy minimization in vision. PAMI **26** (2004) 1124–1137
12. Greig, D., Porteous, B., A., S.: Exact maximum a posteriori estimation for binary images. Journal of the Royal Statistical Society **2** (1989) 271–279
13. Kolmogorov, V., Zabih, R.: What energy functions can be minimized via graph cuts? In: ECCV. Volume III. (2002) 65 ff.
14. Viola, P., Jones, M.: Robust real-time object detection. International Journal of Computer Vision (2004)
15. Freund, Y., Schapire, R.E.: A decision-theoretic generalization of on-line learning and an application to boosting. In: Computational Learning Theory: Eurocolt 95. (1995) 23–37
16. Kumar, S., Hebert, M.: Discriminative fields for modeling spatial dependencies in natural images. In: NIPS. (2003)

Selection of Wavelet Subbands Using Genetic Algorithm for Face Recognition

Vinod Pathangay and Sukhendu Das

Visualization and Perception Laboratory
Department of Computer Science and Engineering
Indian Institute of Technology Madras
Chennai - 600 036, India
{vinod@cse, sdas@}iitm.ernet.in

Abstract. In this paper, a novel representation called the *subband face* is proposed for face recognition. The subband face is generated from selected subbands obtained using wavelet decomposition of the original face image. It is surmised that certain subbands contain information that is more significant for discriminating faces than other subbands. The problem of subband selection is cast as a combinatorial optimization problem and genetic algorithm (GA) is used to find the optimum subband combination by maximizing Fisher ratio of the training features. The performance of the GA selected subband face is evaluated using three face databases and compared with other wavelet-based representations.

1   Introduction

The objective of the face recognition task is to determine the identity a person in a given face image. The problem is complicated due to the variations in illumination, pose, facial expression, aging, occlusions such as spectacles, hair, etc. Different techniques proposed for face recognition are surveyed in [1,2,3]. Although the human face is a 3-dimensional structure, only the two-dimensional projection or the 'appearance' of the face is captured by images. In this work, a new representation of the face image based on the wavelet subbands is proposed. The face image is decomposed into subbands using the Discrete Wavelet Transform (DWT) and selected subbands are used to reconstruct the face image. This is based on neurophysiological evidences [4,5] that humans process images similar to multi-resolution, multi-channel processing similar to the wavelet transform. It is therefore surmised that out of all the subbands obtained using DWT, only certain subbands contain the discriminatory information required for face recognition. If such subbands can be identified and the face image is reconstructed from these discriminatory subbands, then the reconstructed *subband face* image can give a better recognition performance. In this paper, GA is used to determine those subbands that contain the discriminatory information for a given population of face images in the presence of illumination variations.

A number of techniques for illumination invariant face recognition have been proposed [6,7,8]. Recently, spherical harmonics based representation has been proposed for illumination invariant recognition [9]. Wavelet-based features have

P. Kalra and S. Peleg (Eds.): ICVGIP 2006, LNCS 4338, pp. 585–596, 2006.
© Springer-Verlag Berlin Heidelberg 2006

been used to obtain a representation for face recognition task in [10,11,12,13]. The use of statistical measures (mean, variance) of fully decomposed wavelet subbands or packets as a feature was reported in [10]. Here, 2D-DWT is used to fully decompose the face image and statistical features such as mean and variance are extracted from the wavelet coefficients, and used as a feature vector for representation. The use of wavelet subbands with kernel associative memory for face recognition was reported in [12]. Here, wavelet decomposed faces are used to build an associative memory model for face images of each person and kernel methods are used to exploit higher order relations which cannot be captured by linear transformations. Different wavelet subbands have been combined at different levels (data level, feature level, classifier level and decision level) for face recognition [13]. In [14], the face image was dyadically decomposed and approximation subbands at different levels were suppressed during reconstruction to obtain an *approximation-suppressed subband face*. In this paper, we explore the suppression of different fully decomposed subbands using GA, for selection of the *optimal subband face*.

Genetic algorithms have been used for selecting the optimal subspace in which the projected data gives a higher recognition accuracy [15,16,17,18,19,20]. In [15], GA has been used to find the Optimal Projection Axes (OPA) for face recognition. The OPA is found by searching through all possible rotations in the whitened PCA subspaces. The fitness function used is a weighted sum of class separation and performance accuracy. It is reported that the OPA selected by the GA yields better performance compared to the eigenspace technique. Face recognition using kernel PCA and GA has been reported in [21], where the input data is transformed to higher dimension using a non-linear transfer function (polynomial function) and GA is used to select the optimal subset of the non-linear principal components with the fitness function taken as the recognition performance. An algorithm for Independent Component Analysis (ICA) is used to represent the face image in terms of non-orthogonal bases in order to capture the higher order statistics [18]. Apart from the optimum subspace selection techniques, selection of optimum non-orthogonal wavelet for representing the face image has also been reported [22]. Here, the GA is used to find optimal basis from a combination of frequencies and orientation angles in the 2D Gabor wavelet transform and entropy is used as the fitness function instead of class separation and performance. In this paper, the face image is fully decomposed to obtain different subbands or wavelet packets and GA is used to select an optimum combination of subbands. The optimal subband face is reconstructed from the selected subbands that contain the desired discriminatory information and suppressing those subbands that contain the similarity information.

The rest of the paper is organized as follows. The proposed subband face representation is described in section 2. Section 3 discusses the use of genetic algorithm for selecting optimal subband combination for generating the subband face. In section 4, the proposed representation is evaluated on three different face databases and the recognition results are compared with other similar techniques. Section 5 concludes the paper and some directions of future work are discussed.

2 Subband Face Representation

A face image of a person contains common (approximation) as well as discriminatory (detail) information with respect to faces of all other persons. The discriminatory information is due to structural variations of the face which are acquired as intensity variations at different locations of the face. The location and degree of intensity variations in a face for an individual are unique features which discriminate one person from the rest of the population. These similarity information and discriminatory information are segregated in different subbands at different levels of decomposition of the face image. Therefore wavelet decomposition can be used to split the features in a face image into different subbands, with 'approximations' containing the common (smooth) parts of the face and 'details', containing the discriminatory (variations) information. Since level-1 decomposition may not be adequate to effectively isolate these pair of visual features, it is necessary to explore different combination of subbands at higher levels to obtain a suitable isolation.

2.1 Wavelet Decomposition

The wavelet transform [23,24] is expressed as an inner product of a signal $f(x)$ with a family of functions which are translations and dilations of a mother wavelet function $\psi(x)$ and the scaling function $\phi(x)$. This is used to split the signal into approximation and detail. For two-dimensional signal or image, the two-dimensional scaling function $\phi(x, y)$ and three two-dimensional wavelet functions $\psi^H(x, y)$, $\psi^V(x, y)$, $\psi^D(x, y)$ are used to produce the approximation and horizontal, vertical, diagonal details respectively. The two-dimensional discrete wavelet transform (2D-DWT) for an image $f(x, y)$ gives the approximations W_ϕ and the details W_ψ^d

$$W_\phi(s_0, m, n) = \frac{1}{\sqrt{MN}} \sum_{x=0}^{M-1} \sum_{y=0}^{N-1} f(x, y)\phi_{s_0,m,n}(x, y) \tag{1}$$

$$W_\psi^d(s, m, n) = \frac{1}{\sqrt{MN}} \sum_{x=0}^{M-1} \sum_{y=0}^{N-1} f(x, y)\psi_{s,m,n}^d(x, y) \tag{2}$$

where $d = \{H, V, D\}$ for horizontal, vertical and diagonal details, $\phi(x, y)$ is the scaling function and $\psi^H(x, y)$, $\psi^V(x, y)$ and $\psi^D(x, y)$ are the three two-dimensional wavelets, s_0 is the starting scale (taken as zero) and $N = M = 2^S$ such that $s = 0, 1, 2, ..., S - 1$ and $m, n = 0, 1, 2, ..., 2^s - 1$. For level-1 decomposition of $f(x, y)$, $s = 0$. Thus the 2D-DWT uses a family of wavelet functions and its associated scaling function to decompose the original image into four subbands, namely the approximation (A), horizontal (H), vertical (V) and diagonal

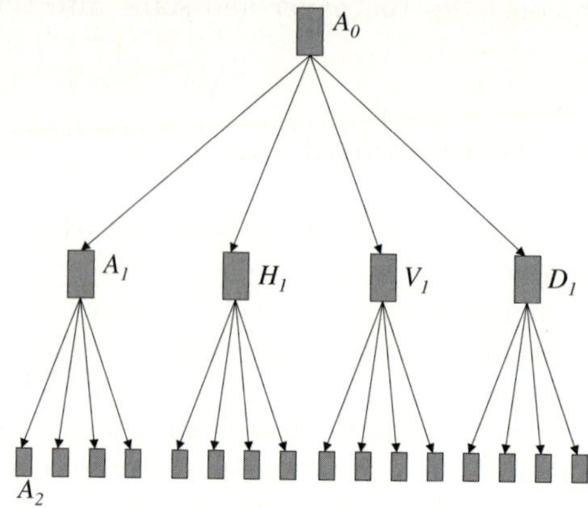

Fig. 1. Wavelet decomposition tree up to level-2. The root node (A_0) represents the original image which is decomposed to A_1, V_1, H_1, D_1. They are in turn decomposed to level-2 subbands which are the leaf nodes.

(D) details. Fig. 1 shows the full level-2 wavelet decomposition tree. The original image A_0 is decomposed to level-1 subbands (A_1, H_1, V_1, D_1) which are in turn decomposed to obtain level-2 subbands. We have used the lifting technique [25] for the 2D-DWT with Haar basis. In the following subsection, the method of reconstructing a subband face using selective wavelet subbands is discussed.

2.2   Reconstruction from Subbands

In order to reconstruct the subband face that contains only the discriminatory information, certain subbands can be selected or retained and others are suppressed during reconstruction. Reconstruction is done using a method similar to inverse DWT. Given the level-1 approximations W_ψ and the details $W_\phi^H, W_\phi^V, W_\phi^D$, the subband image $\hat{f}(x,y)$ is reconstructed using the relation

$$\hat{f}(x,y) = \frac{1}{\sqrt{MN}} \sum_m \sum_n W_\psi(m,n)\psi_{m,n}(x,y)b_A$$

$$+ \frac{1}{\sqrt{MN}} \sum_{d=H,V,D} \sum_m \sum_n W_\phi^d(m,n)\phi_{m,n}^d(x,y)b_d \qquad (3)$$

where b_A, b_H, b_V, b_D are the binary subband selection variables that can be set to zero or one if the subband is to be selected or suppressed respectively. For level-1 subbands, the sequence of four bits $\{b_A, b_H, b_V, b_D\}$ is the *subband code* for generating $\hat{f}(x,y)$. In order to reconstruct the discriminatory subband face from level-l subbands, a 4^l length subband code is to determined. It can be noted that the number of possible subband combinations at level-l is 2^{4^l}. Therefore at higher levels of decomposition, there are a large number of subband combinations. To cater for the search in this large search space, the subband selection problem is cast as a combinatorial optimization problem and a genetic algorithm is used to find an optimum subband code. The following section describes the use of GA and the fitness functions used in selecting a suitable subband code that gives a high recognition accuracy.

3   Subband Selection Using Genetic Algorithm

Due to the exponential increase in the subband combinations with higher levels of decomposition, it is not possible to select an optimum combination using an exhaustive search. Therefore genetic algorithm [26] is used for finding an 'optimal' solution or subband code. GA maintains a population of subband combinations or subband codes and iteratively finds a subband code that has the high fitness value among all subband codes of all generations. The subband code is used as the binary chromosome in the GA. Each subband code has an associated fitness value. Fisher ratio of the training features is used as the fitness function. This is the ratio of the between-class scatter and the total within-class scatter of the training features. This is given by

$$F = \frac{\sum_i \sum_{r \neq i} ||\boldsymbol{\mu}_i - \boldsymbol{\mu}_r||^2}{\sum_i \sum_{j \in C_i} ||\boldsymbol{\mu}_i - \mathbf{x}_j||^2} \tag{4}$$

where i, r are the class indices and j is the feature index, $\boldsymbol{\mu}_i$ mean feature of the class i, $\mathbf{x}_j$ is the jth feature, and C_i is the set of training features of class i. The use of Fisher ratio as the fitness function is motivated by the fact that a large between-class spread and smaller within-class spread will lead to compact clusters with larger separation and thus lesser confusion or overlap between the classes.

The following are the steps involved in the GA used for subband selection:

1. *Initialization*: Start with a random population of subband codes $\mathbf{b}_p$, $p \in [1, P]$ where P is the number of subband codes in the population.
2. *Evaluation*: Evaluate fitness $F(\mathbf{b}_p) \ \forall p$.
3. *Selection*: Select P_s (where $P_s < P$) fittest subband codes for next generation.
4. *Crossover*: From the fittest subband codes selected in the above step, apply crossover on two randomly chosen samples to generate new subband code. This is repeated to obtain P_c (where $P_c \leq P_s$) new subband codes for the next generation.
5. *Mutation*: Apply mutation to randomly selected sample obtained using crossover to generate a new subband code. This is repeated to obtain P_m (where $P_m \leq P_c$) new subband codes.
6. Repeat steps 2-5 (evaluation, selection, crossover and mutation) for each generation until the fitness converges to a high value.

The number of solutions P for each generation is maintained constant by ensuring that $P_s + P_c + P_m = P$. For applying the *crossover* operator on two parent subband codes selected at random, a crossover position is chosen and the bits on the left of the crossover point from one parent and those on the right from the other parent are copied to the child subband code. Thus the child inherits code segments from both parents. For applying the *mutation* operator on a subband code, a bit value is flipped at a randomly chosen location. In this work, a batch GA which has a constant population for all generations is used. The population size is made ten times the length of the chromosome bitstring. This is to have an increased exploration where there are more free parameters. The values for $\frac{P_s}{P}$, $\frac{P_c}{P}$, $\frac{P_m}{P}$ are set to 0.5, 0.3 and 0.2 respectively. In the following section, the experimental results are discussed.

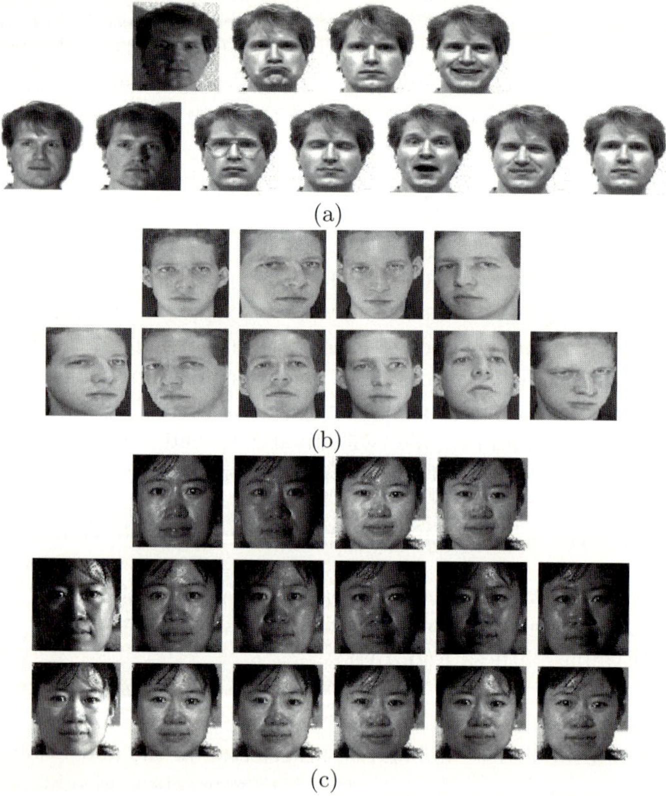

Fig. 2. Face databases used: (a) Yale (b) ORL and (c) PIE. First row shows the training samples and other rows show the testing samples used for experiments.

4   Experiments

In this paper, three face databases are used: Yale, ORL and PIE.

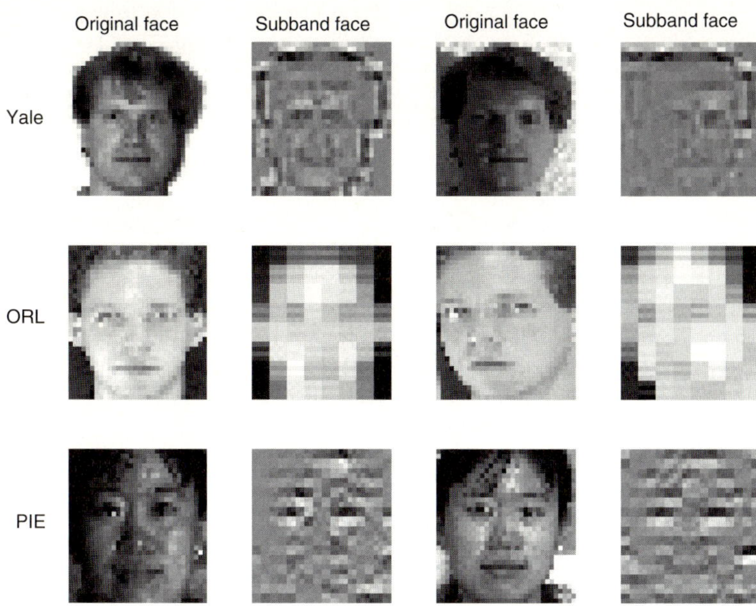

Fig. 3. Original face and the subband face reconstructed from the GA selected subband codes for Yale (top row), ORL (mid row) and PIE (bottom row)

1. The Yale face database (Fig. 2 (a)) has 15 subjects with 11 samples with variations in expression and illumination for each subject. The training sample set contains *rightlight, sad, noglasses, happy* and the testing sample set consists of *centerlight, leftlight, glasses, sleepy, surprised, wink,* and *normal* samples.
2. The ORL face database (Fig. 2 (b)) has 40 subjects with 10 samples for each. There is no change in illumination but there are variations in pose. Training samples used are images numbered 1 to 4 and the rest are used for testing.
3. A subset of the PIE (Pose Illumination and Expression) face database (Fig. 2 (c)) [27] with 60 subjects with only the frontal poses is used. For each subject, 42 samples (flash from 21 different directions with and without the room lights on) are used. Only four samples with flash numbers 12, 13 for both *lights* and *illum* sets are taken for training and the remaining for testing.

The face region is extracted from the background and resized to 32x32 pixels for generating the subband face. The subband face is obtained using the subband code determined by the GA. Fig. 3 shows the original gray-level face image and the subband face generated for sample face images taken from three databases. Although the subband face does not appear similar to the original gray-level face image, it preforms much better than the original face images because it contains only the discriminatory information that is required for a machine to obtain higher recognition accuracy.

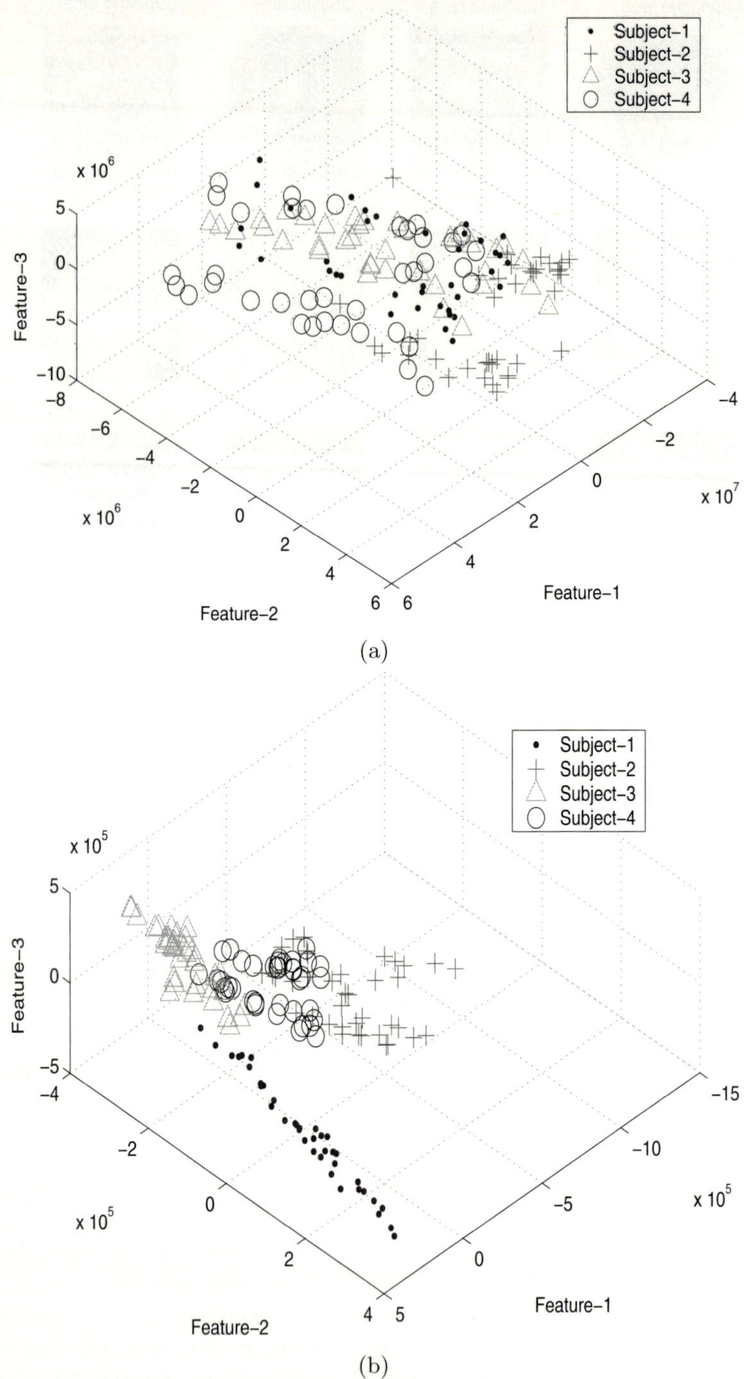

Fig. 4. Features in 3D eigenspace for (a) gray-level and (b) subband faces determined by the GA for four subjects of the PIE database

Table 1. Comparison of the accuracies (%) of face recognition techniques published earlier using wavelet based features. ($A_0 - A_l$ denotes the suppression of approximation A_l during reconstruction of the subband face).

Database	Baseline Eigenface [28]	Approximation suppressed [14]	Best performing subband [13]
Yale	81.9	$(A_0 - A_1)$ 88.6 $(A_0 - A_2)$ 91.4 $(A_0 - A_3)$ 89.5	(D_2) 81.9
ORL	77.1	$(A_0 - A_1)$ 60.0 $(A_0 - A_2)$ 65.0 $(A_0 - A_3)$ 72.5	(A_1) 79.5
PIE	34.3	$(A_0 - A_1)$ 87.1 $(A_0 - A_2)$ 85.3 $(A_0 - A_3)$ 75.4	(H_1) 93.1

Table 2. Accuracy of *subband face* selected by GA using Fisher ratio as the fitness function for PCA features

Database	Decomposition level	Subband code (Hex)	Accuracy (%)
Yale	2	5333	90.5
	3	0354-1040-00CB-0098	87.6
ORL	2	8800	78.5
	3	E888-E084-8004-0000	76.5
PIE	2	5101	88.6
	3	0808-0006-0802-0001	81.1

Fig. 4 (a) shows the projection of the original face images of four subjects of the PIE database in 3D eigenspace. It can be observed that there is a significant overlap of the clusters. Such overlap often leads to misclassification using the nearest-neighbor rule. Fig 4 (b) shows the projection of the subband faces in 3D eigenspace. It can be seen that there is an increase in the separation and compactness of the eigenfeatures of the subband faces generated using the subband code selected by the GA. Therefore there are less chances of misclassification using nearest neighbor rule.

Table 1 shows a comparison of the performance of wavelet-based representations [14,13] against the baseline Eigenface method. Table 2 shows the recognition performance of the GA selected subband face. It can be observed that the performance of the GA selected subband face is comparable to the approximation suppressed subband face and the best performing subbands given in Table 1. It can also be noted that the level-3 subband code found by the GA always gives lesser accuracy compared to level-2. This is due to the sub-optimal determination of the large number of free parameters (64) in level-3 subband code. This is also due to the fact that increase in Fisher ratio of the training features does not guarantee a higher recognition accuracy of test features. It can also be noted from Table 2 that the subband code selected by the GA is dependent on the database. The subband codes determined for Yale and PIE (5333 and 5101 respectively) are very different form that of ORL (8800). This is because ORL has pose variations that are absent in Yale and PIE. The similarity between the subband codes of Yale and PIE is due to the presence of significant lighting changes in the training sets. There is also a similarity between the subband codes selected by the GA and the best performing subbands [13]. Therefore, it can be generalized to a certain extent that, when there is no pose variation and only lighting changes are present, then the level-2 subband code of the form 5*** (which includes the horizontal and diagonal details of level-1 approximation subband) works best. This eliminates the level-2 approximation (A_2) similar to [14]. However, when there are changes in pose, as in the case of ORL database, the level-2 subband code of the form 88** works best. This is because the subband code 88** retains the smoothed approximations of A_1 and H_1 subbands that are invariant to minor pose changes.

5   Conclusion and Future Work

In this paper, we have proposed the subband face as a representation for face recognition. A genetic algorithm is used to select the optimal choice of subbands by using Fisher ratio as the fitness function. It is shown that the GA is able to find the subband codes that contain only the discriminatory information in the face image of different persons of a given population. The performance of the subbands selected by the GA to other wavelet-based representations are compared. The GA selected subbands are also invariant to lighting changes as shown for the PIE database. The subband face is also scalable as the accuracy is consistent with increasing database size (15 to 60 subjects for Yale and PIE respectively). Future work includes exploring the possibility of using class specific subband codes, and use of single training face image for generating virtual training samples with variations in illumination, pose and scale. The use of subband images can also be used for non-face classes.

References

1. Zhao, W., Chellappa, R., Rosenfeld, A., Phillips, P.: Face recognition: A literature survey (2000)
2. Chellappa, R., Wilson, C.L., Sirohey, S.: Human and machine recognition of faces: A survey. Proc. of the IEEE **83** (1995) 705–740
3. Tolba, A.S., El-Baz, A.H., El-Harby, A.A.: Face recognition: A literature review. Int. Journal of Signal Processing **2** (2005) 88–103
4. Kanwisher, N.: Domain specificity in face perception. Nature neuroscience **3** (2000) 759–776
5. Liu, J., Harris, A., Kanwisher, N.: Stages of processing in face perception: an MEG study. Nature neuroscience **5** (2002) 910–916

6. Gross, R., Baker, S., Matthews, I., Kanade, T.: Face recognition across pose and illumination. In Li, S.Z., Jain, A.K., eds.: Handbook of Face Recognition. Springer-Verlag (2004)
7. Lee, J., Machiraju, R., Pfister, H., Moghaddam, B.: Estimation of 3d faces and illumination from single photographs using a bilinear illumination model. In: Proc. Eurographics Symposium on Rendering (EGSR). (2005)
8. Lee, K.C., Moghaddam, B.: A practical face relighting method for directional lighting normalization. In: Int. Workshop on Analysis and Modeling of Faces and Gestures (AMFG). (2005)
9. Zhang, L., Samaras, D.: Face recognition from a single training image under arbitrary unknown lighting using spherical harmonics. IEEE Tran. on Pattern Analysis and Machine Intelligence **28** (2006) 351–363
10. Garcia, C., Zikos, G., Tziritas, G.: Wavelet packet analysis for face recognition. Image and Vision Computing **18** (2000) 289–297
11. Chien, J.T., Wu, C.C.: Discriminant waveletfaces and nearest feature classifier for face recognition. IEEE Tran. on Pattern Analysis and Machine Intelligence **24** (2002) 1644–1649
12. Zhang, B.L., Zhang, H., Ge, S.S.: Face recognition by applying wavelet subband representation and kernel associative memory. IEEE Tran. on Neural Networks **15** (2004) 166–177
13. Ekenel, H.K., Sankur, B.: Multiresolution face recognition. Image and Vision Computing **23** (2005) 469–477
14. Pathangay, V., Das, S.: Exploring the use of selective wavelet subbands for PCA based face recognition. In: Proc. National Conference on Image Processing (NCIP'05), Bangalore, India (2005) 182–185
15. Liu, C., Weschler, H.: Evolution of optimal projection axes (opa) for face recognition. In: Proc. 3rd IEEE Int. Conf. on Automatic Face and Gesture Recognition. (1998) 282–287
16. Liu, C., Weschler, H.: Evolutionary pursuit and its application to face recognition. IEEE Tran. on Pattern Analysis and Machine Intelligence **22** (2000) 570–582
17. Zhang, X., Mersereau, R.M., Broun, C.C.: Visual speech feature extraction for improved speech recognition. In: Proc. of the Int. Conf. on Acoustics Speech and Signal Processing, Orlando, Florida, USA (2002) 1993–1996
18. Yi-qiong, X., Bi-Cheng, L., Bo, W.: Face recognition by fast independent component analysis and genetic algorithms. In: Proc. 4th Int. Conf. on Computer and Information Technology. (2004) 194–198
19. Karungaru, S., Fukumi, M., Akamatsu, N.: Face recognition using genetic algorithm based template matching. In: Proc. Int. Symposium on Communications and Information Technologies. (2004) 1252–1257
20. Zhao, Q., Lu, H., Zhang, D.: A fast evolutionary pursuit algorithm based on linearly combining vectors. Pattern Recognition **39** (2006) 310–312
21. Yankun, Z., Chongqing, L.: Face recognition using kernel principal component analysis and genetic algorithms. In: Proc. 12th IEEE Workshop on Neural Networks for Signal Processing. (2002) 337–343
22. Wang, X., Qi, H.: Face recognition using optimal non-orthogonal wavelet basis evaluated by information complexity. In: Proc. 16th Int. Conf. on Pattern Recognition. Volume 1. (2002) 164–167
23. Mallat, S.G.: A theory for multiresolution signal decomposition: The wavelet representation. IEEE Tran. on Pattern Analysis and Machine Intelligence **11** (1989) 674–693

24. Fliege, N.J.: Multirate Digital Signal Processing. John Wiley and Sons, Ltd. (2004)
25. Jensen, A., Cour-Harbo, A.: Ripples in Mathematics: The Discete Wavelet Transform. Springer-Verlag (2003)
26. David E. Goldberg: Genetic Algorithms in Search, Optimization and Machine Learning. Addison-Wesley (1989)
27. Sim, T., Baker, S., Bsat, M.: The CMU pose, illumination, and expression database. IEEE Tran. on Pattern Analysis and Machine Intelligence **25** (2003) 1615–1618
28. Turk, M.A., Pentland, A.: Face recognition using eigenfaces. In: Proc. 11th Int. Conf. Pattern Recognition. (1991) 586–591

Object Recognition Using Reflex Fuzzy Min-Max Neural Network with Floating Neurons

A.V. Nandedkar and P.K. Biswas

Electronics & Elec. Communication Engg. Department,
Indian Institute of Technology, Kharagpur - 721302, India
{avn, pkb}@ece.iitkgp.ernet.in

Abstract. This paper proposes an object recognition system that is invariant to rotation, translation and scale and can be trained under partial supervision. The system is divided into two sections namely, feature extraction and recognition sections. Feature extraction section uses proposed rotation, translation and scale invariant features. Recognition section consists of a novel Reflex Fuzzy Min-Max Neural Network (RFMN) architecture with "Floating Neurons". RFMN is capable to learn mixture of labeled and unlabeled data which enables training under partial supervision. Learning under partial supervision is of high importance for the practical implementation of pattern recognition systems, as it may not be always feasible to get a fully labeled dataset for training or cost to label all samples is not affordable. The proposed system is tested on shape data-base available online, Marathi and Bengali digits. Results are compared with "General Fuzzy Min-Max Neural Network" proposed by Gabrys and Bargiela.

1   Introduction

Object recognition is an important component in computer vision. Object recognition broadly involves two steps namely, feature extraction and pattern classification. Efficient object recognition demands rotation, translation and scale invariant (RTSI) features. Pattern classification extracts the underlying structure in the data and performs the recognition. Fuzzy interpretation of patterns is very natural in cases where precise partitions of data are not known. Zadeh [1] elaborated the importance of fuzzy logic for pattern classification in his seminal paper. The merge of fuzzy logic and neural network for pattern classification can be found in "Fuzzy Min Max Neural Network" (FMNN) proposed by Simpson [2][3]. Gabrys and Bargilela [4] proposed a merge of FMNN classification and clustering algorithms called as "General Fuzzy Min-max Neural network" (GFMN). This hybridization allowed learning under partial supervision. Semi-supervised learning is of high importance for the practical implementation of pattern recognition systems, as it may not be always feasible to get a fully labeled dataset for training or cost of labeling all the samples is not affordable.

The proposed Object Recognition System (ORS) uses a new set of RTSI features. Recognition is carried out using proposed "Reflex Fuzzy Min-Max Neural Network with Floating Neurons" (RFMN). RFMN is trainable by means of partial supervision.

P. Kalra and S. Peleg (Eds.): ICVGIP 2006, LNCS 4338, pp. 597–609, 2006.

It uses aggregation of fuzzy hyperbox sets (called as hyperbox neurons) [2][3] to represent classes or clusters. A variety of ORS methods are available such as, boundary based analysis via Fourier descriptors [5], neural networks models [6] and invariant moments [7]. However, most of these methods are too computationally expensive or are not invariant under the three types of transformations i.e., rotation, translation and scaling (RTS). An inexpensive ORS was proposed by Torres-Mendez et al [8] based on radial coding technique.

The proposed RFMN with floating neurons exploits use of reflex mechanism inspired from human brain for the pattern classification and clustering. It uses Compensatory Neurons (CN) to overcome the hyperbox overlap and containment problems [9] [10]. CNs are inspired from the reflex system of human brain [11]. CNs maintain the hyperbox dimensions and control the membership in the overlapped region. During the training RFMN tries to label the unlabeled data, thus it is possible to learn from mixture of labeled and unlabeled data. The unlabeled hyperbox neurons created during training are kept floating and are restrained from contributing to the classification. This approach has improved performance of RFMN compared to GFMN [4]. Gabrys and Bargiela advocated the use of a new activation function [4] for FMNN based algorithms. But we observed that their activation function can lead to errors and is discussed in section 3.

The main contribution of this work is development of a new architecture for semi-supervised learning and new set of RTSI features for object recognition. Rest of the paper is organized as follows. Section II elaborates new RTSI features. The proposed new RFMN architecture is explained in section III. Detailed learning algorithm and recall procedure is explained in section IV. Section V shows the experimental results on real datasets. Section VI concludes with summery.

2 RTSI Features

Feature can be defined as quantitative description of input within a lower dimensional space [12]. It plays an important role in object recognition systems (ORS) since the information related to an object is contained within the extracted features. In an ORS, pre-processing is required to extract the features. This may include image enhancement, filtering, segmentation [13] etc. Object segmentation is a must to recognize it. For an invariant ORS feature extraction must be invariant to translation, rotation and scale. Here we propose a new set of RTSI features for object recognition. This includes 1) normalized moment of inertia, 2) max to average ratio, 3) average to max-min difference ratio, 4) radial coding [8] and 5) radial angles.

To extract these features one needs to compute centroid of an object. Here we assume that after segmentation a binary image of the object is available for post processing. The centroid (C_x, C_y) of a two-dimensional object is given by,

$$C_x = \frac{\sum_{i=1}^{N} x_i * f(x_i, y_i)}{N} \quad , \quad C_y = \frac{\sum_{i=1}^{N} y_i * f(x_i, y_i)}{N} \tag{1}$$

$$where \quad f(x_i, y_i) = \begin{cases} 1 & if \quad pixel \quad p(x_i, y_i) \in object \\ 0 & otherwise \end{cases} \tag{2}$$

x_i, y_i : co-ordinate values and N: total number of object pixels.

Once the centroid is computed other features are extracted as follows:

1) Normalized moment of Inertia (NMI)

In general the moment of inertia quantifies the inertia of rotating object by considering its mass distribution. The moment of inertia (MI) is normally calculated by dividing the object into N-small pieces of mass m_1, m_2,...,m_N , each piece is at a distance d_i from the axis of rotation. MI is given by,

$$I = \sum_{i=1..N} m_i d_i^2 \tag{3}$$

In case of object in a binary image, we consider pixel as unit pieces (i.e. $m=1$). Due to the finite resolution of any digitized image, a rotated object may not conserve the number of pixels. So moment of inertia may vary but normalized moment of inertia reduces this problem. Normalized MI is invariant to translation, rotation and scale. This can be observed from Table 1 depicting features for an object shown in Fig. 1(a). The normalized moment of inertia (MI) of an object is [8] computed by,

$$I_N = \frac{1}{N^2} \sum_{i=1}^{N} d_i^2 = \frac{1}{N^2} \sum_{i=1}^{N} ((x_i - C_x)^2 + (y_i - C_y)^2) \tag{4}$$

where (C_x, C_y) are centroid co-ordinates and x_i, y_i are object pixel co-ordinates. d_i pixel distance from centroid.

2) Max to average length ratio (MAR)

MAR is a ratio of maximum (d_{max}) of distance of object pixels from centroid to the average pixel distance (d_{avg}) from centroid.

$$MAR = \frac{d_{max}}{d_{avg}} \tag{5}$$

Note the RTS invariance of this feature from Table 1.

3) Average to Max-Min Difference (AMMD) Ratio

AMMD is a ratio of average pixel distance from centroid d_{avg} to difference between maximum (d_{max}) and minimum (d_{min})of pixel distance from centroid. It is given by,

$$AMMD = \frac{d_{avg}}{(d_{max} - d_{min})} \tag{6}$$

Table 1 indicates AMMD is a RTS invariant feature.

4) Radial Coding (RC) and Radial Angles (RA)

The radial coding features are based on the fact that circle is the only geometrical shape that is naturally and perfectly invariant to rotation. RC is computed by counting the number of intensity changes on circular boundaries of some radius inside the object. This simple coding scheme extracts the topological characteristics of an object

Table 1. NMI, MAR and AMMD for Fig.1(a) with various rotations, translations and scales

Rotation (Degrees)	NMI	MAR	AMMD	Size (%)	NMI	MAR	AMMD
0	0.193	2.161	0.465	120	0.193	2.164	0.466
25	0.193	2.166	0.464	140	0.194	2.154	0.465
55	0.193	2.179	0.463	160	0.193	2.174	0.462
85	0.194	2.176	0.463	180	0.193	2.169	0.463
105	0.194	2.145	0.468	200	0.193	2.171	0.462

regardless of its position orientation and size. The methodology to obtain the radial coding features of an object can be seen in [8]. Along with RC, proposed radial angles (RA) are found out as follows:

1) Obtain the centroid of the object.
2) Generate K equidistant concentric circles C_i around the centroid. The spacing is equal to the distance between centroid and furthest pixel of the object divided by K.
3) For each circular boundary, count the number of intensity changes (zero to one or one to zero) that occur in the image. These are radial coding features.
4) Find the largest angle (θ) between the two successive intensity changes for every circle. These are called as Radial Angles. If $\theta > \pi$ then take θ as $2\pi - \theta$. This is a necessary step to avoid the dependency of angle measurement on reference point or direction of the measurement. If there is no intensity change then take $\theta = 0$.

Fig. 1(b) shows an example of radial coding and angles. Extracted features are shown in Fig.1(c). These features are also rotation, translation and scale invariant and can be noted from Table 2 and 3. We used seven concentric circles to code an object. Thus total feature vector length used in the proposed ORS is 17 (7RC+7RA+ NMI+MAR+AMMD).

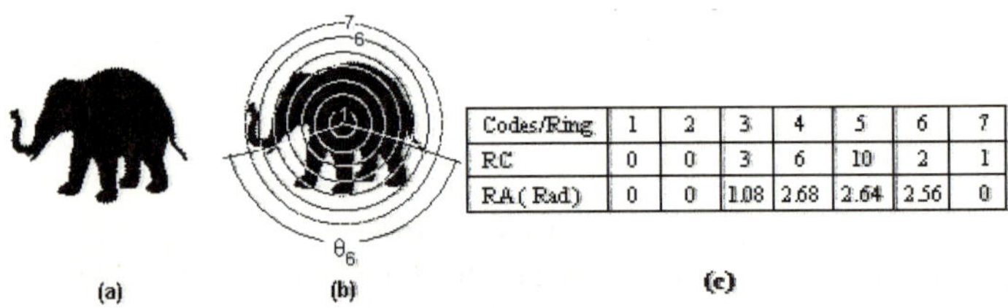

Codes/Ring	1	2	3	4	5	6	7
RC	0	0	3	6	10	2	1
RA (Rad)	0	0	1.08	2.68	2.64	2.56	0

(a)   (b)   (c)

Fig. 1. (a) Object (b) Radial Codes and Angles (c) RC and RA

Table 2. RA for various rotations of Fig 1(a)

Rotation (deg) / Ring	1	2	3	4	5	6	7
0	0	0	1.08	2.68	2.64	2.56	0
25	0	0	1.1	2.78	2.44	2.56	0.06
55	0	0	1.82	2.26	2.02	2.56	0.24
85	0	0	1.82	2.76	2.22	0.46	0
105	0	0	0.74	2.66	2.32	2.56	0

Table 3. RA for various sizes of Fig 1

Size (%)/ Ring	1	2	3	4	5	6	7
120	0	0	1.08	2.6	2.54	2.54	0
140	0	0	1.1	2.7	2.54	2.56	0
160	0	0	1.08	2.7	2.62	2.58	0
180	0	0	1.1	2.7	2.54	2.58	0
200	0	0	1.06	2.7	2.64	2.58	0

3   Reflex Fuzzy Min-Max Neural Network with Floating Neurons

The proposed ORS uses a novel Reflex Fuzzy Min-Max Neural Network (RFMN) with floating neurons for the recognition purpose. RFMN uses aggregation of hyperbox fuzzy sets to represent classes or clusters. It can be trained in two ways i.e. classification (supervised learning) and hybrid mode (semi-supervised learning). During training RFMN tries to accommodate the training samples in the form of hyperbox fuzzy sets. The class overlaps are handled by reflex section. In hybrid mode, RFMN tries to label the unlabeled data using knowledge acquired from available labeled data. After completion of training, many hyperbox fuzzy sets may remain unlabeled due to lack of evidence for these sets. Neurons representing such hyperbox fuzzy sets are restrained from contributing to the output. Such neurons are called as "Floating Neurons". Floating neurons (FN) can be labeled and are allowed to contribute to the output if evidence for a class is found out later on. Since RFMN learns on-line whenever data is made available it can be trained without hampering performance on the earlier acquired knowledge.

3.1   RFMN Architecture

The proposed architecture of Reflex Fuzzy Min-Max Neural Network (RFMN) is shown in Fig. 2.

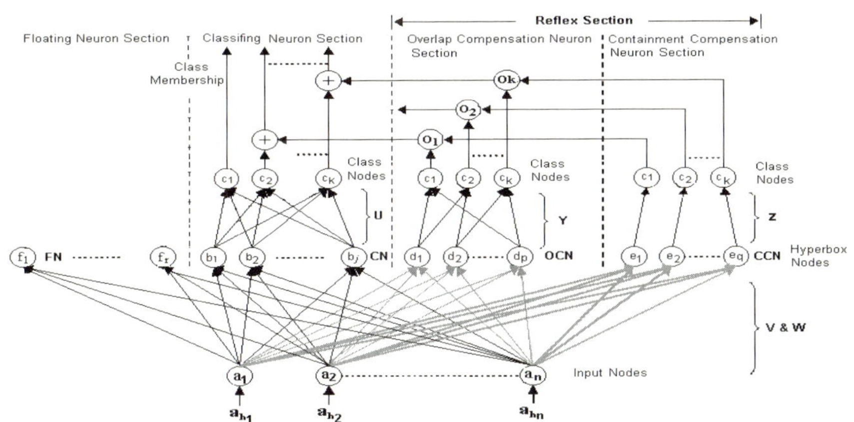

Fig. 2. RFMN Architecture

It is divided into three sections: 1) The classifying neuron section (CL) 2) Reflex section and 3) Floating Neuron section. The classifying section contributes in calculating memberships for different classes. The Reflex section consists of two subsections, Overlap Compensation neuron (OCN) section and Containment Compensation neuron (CCN) section. Reflex section is active whenever a test sample falls in the class overlap area. This action is very similar to the Reflex action of human brain which takes over the control in hazardous conditions. It compensates the output of classifying section and solves the dispute of membership in class overlapped area. Floating neuron section represents hyperbox fuzzy sets whose labels are not confirmed. These neurons are transferred dynamically during training to the classifying neuron section if class evidence is found.

An n-dimensional input $A_h = (a_{h1}, a_{h2}, \ldots a_{hn})$ is applied to the input nodes a_1-a_n. The neurons b_1-b_j are classifying neurons. Classifying section collects output of these neurons at class nodes C_1-C_k. During training hyperboxes belonging different classes do overlap as depicted in Fig3(b), 4(b). These overlaps and containments infer OCNs and CCNs respectively in the reflex section. The nodes d_1-d_p are overlap compensation neurons and e_1-e_q represent the containment compensation neurons. Outputs of OCN & CCN are collected at a class node C_i in respective compensation sections. The output of floating neurons (FNs) f_1 -f_r are not connected to any class node. The activation function of the classifying neuron b_j is given by [3],

$$b_j(A_h, V_j, W_j) = \frac{1}{n}\sum_{i=1}^{n} min\,[(1 - f(a_{hi} - w_{ji}, \gamma)), (1 - f(v_{ji} - a_{hi}, \gamma))] \qquad (7)$$

where V, W: min-max point of the hyperbox b_j. γ: Fuzziness controller, $f(x,y)$ is a two parameter ramp threshold function, n- dimension of data.

$$f(x, y) = \begin{cases} 1 & if\ x\gamma > 1 \\ x\gamma & if\ 0 \le x\gamma \le 1 \\ 0 & if\ x\gamma < 0 \end{cases} \qquad (8)$$

Eq.7 finds membership for a given input as an average of memberships along each dimension. Membership depends on the distance of applied input from hyperbox min and max point along each dimension. Gabrys and Bargiela [4] modified the above activation function and advocated use of their new activation function given by Eq.9 for FMNN based algorithms. It is stated in [4] that Simpson's activation function (Eq.7) [3] offers a large memberships even though very few features are close to the range specified by the hyperbox min-max points. To solve this problem Eq.9 [4] offers a membership based on the minimum of the memberships (match) along each dimension.

$$b_j(A_h, V_j, W_j) = \min_{i=1..n} (min[(1 - f(a_{hi} - w_{ji}, \gamma)), (1 - f(v_{ji} - a_{hi}, \gamma))]) \qquad (9)$$

But we observe that this criterion of offering membership based on minimum membership is not suitable universally. The search for the minimum membership penalizes too heavily and leads to errors in cases where matching of features is more important rather than searching for a minimum match. In case of proposed features for object recognition, the requirement is to see how many features of an input match to the learned patterns, thus we found that Eq.7 is more suitable than Eq.9. This is supported by our results of experiment 1, in Section 5.

As training progresses hyperbox size goes on increasing to accommodate the applied input. The maximum hyperbox size is controlled by the expansion coefficient

$$\Theta \geq \frac{1}{n}\sum_{i=1}^{n}(max\,(w_{ji},a_{hi})-min\,(v_{ji},a_{hi}))$$ (10)

As stated earlier while training the network, hyperboxes representing different classes may overlap, or a hyperbox of one class may contain a hyperbox of another class as depicted in Fig. 3(b), 4(b) respectively. The overlap compensation and containment compensation neurons are trained to handle these situations. Fig. 3(a) depicts the details of overlap compensating neuron (OCN), which represents a hyperbox of size equal to the overlapping region between two hyperboxes. OCN is active only when the test sample falls in the overlap region. The activation function is given by Eq.(11) and (12).

$$d_{j_p}=U(b_j(A_h,V,W)-1)\times(-1+b_{j1}(A_h,V_p,W_p))$$ (11)

$$\text{where }\;b_{j1}(A_h,V_p,W_p)=\frac{1}{n}\sum_{i=1}^{n}max\left(\frac{a_{hi}}{w_{p_{ji}}},\frac{v_{p_{ji}}}{a_{hi}}\right)$$ (12)

$p=1,2.$ d_{j1} and d_{j2} are Class1 and Class2 outputs. V,W: OCN min-max points. V_1,W_1,V_2,W_2: min-max point of overlapping hyperboxes $U(x)$: a unit step function. $b_j()$ is same as Eq.(7).

The unit step function with threshold of '1' allows OCN to be active whenever applied input falls inside the overlap region represented by it. If the test data is outside the OCN region, membership calculated by $b_j()$ is less than one and thus $U(b_j()-1)$ term is zero. This makes compensatory neurons inactive i.e. no compensation is added. Compensation is produced whenever the test data falls inside overlapped region. If data is contained in OCN region (as shown in Fig.3(b)), its membership is calculated for the respective classes depending on its distance from the min max points.The activation function of this neuron is such that it protects the class of the min-max point of the overlapping hyperboxes, which improves the learning accuracy. The output of this neuron is connected to the two class nodes of overlapping classes (OCN section Fig. 1).

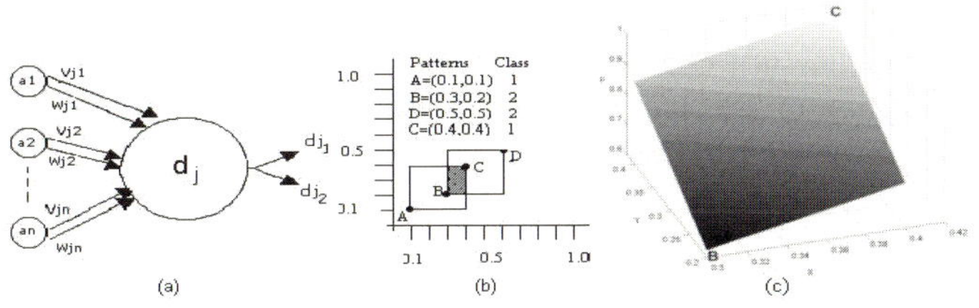

Fig. 3. Overlap Compensatory Neuron

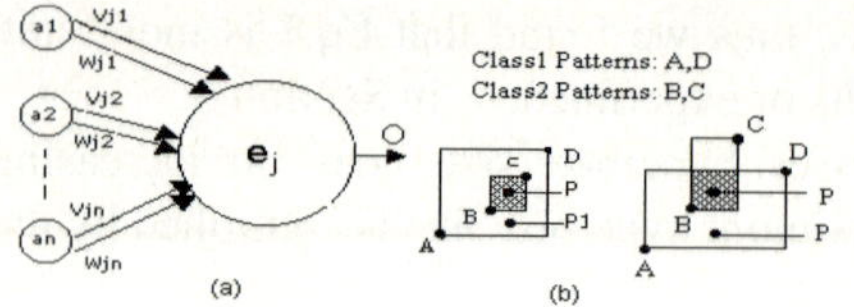

Fig. 4. Containment Compensatory Neuron

Referring to the overlap shown in Fig. 3(b) note that the resulting membership grade after adding compensation decreases gradually from point C to B for class 1 (Fig. 3(c)) and from B to C for class2. Thus activation function tries to give a membership grade for the applied input considering its position in the OCN region.

The containment compensation neuron (CCN) is shown in Fig. 4(a). This represents a hyperbox of size equal to the overlap region between two classes as shown in Fig. 4(b). Similar to OCN activation function the term $U(b_j() -1)$ finds whether the input data falls inside the overlapped region represented by CCN. This neuron is also active only when the test data falls inside the overlapped region. The activation function of CCN is:

$$O_{c_j} = -U(b_j(A_h, V, W) - 1))$$

(13)

where O_{cj}: output, V, W: CCN min-max points, $U(x)$: unit step function, $b_j()$: same as Eq.(7)

This activation function allows a hyperbox of one class to be contained in a hyperbox of different class. The output of CCN is connected to the class that contains the hyperbox of other class (CCN Section Fig.2).

In hybrid mode of learning, there may be generation of hyperboxes without labels due to lack of class evidence. These hyperbox neurons are kept in Floating Neuron section without connection to output and thus are not allowed to contribute to the out put. Floating neurons are brought dynamically into the classifying neuron section if evidence of a class is found.

The number of output layer nodes in CL section is same as the number of classes learned. The number of class nodes in the CCN, OCN section depends on the nature of overlap the network faces during the training process. The final membership calculation is given by,

$$\mu_i = \max_{k=1..j} (b_k u_{ki}) + \min\left(\min_{l=1..p} (d_l y_{li}), \min_{m=1..q} (e_m z_{mi})\right)$$

(14)

where U, Y, Z are the connection matrices for the neurons in the three sections. j, p, q are number of neurons in respective sections.

Eq.(14) takes care of multiple class overlaps. It gives maximum grade to a class from the available grades considering its compensation.

3.2   Comparison of RFMN with GFMN and FMNN

FMNN and GFMN use a process called as contraction to solve the class overlaps. Nandedkar and Biswas [9] [10] pointed out that the contraction process causes errors during training. To overcome this problem, contraction process was removed and a reflex mechanism was added in to the FMNN architecture. It is observed that in case of GFMN hybrid mode of learning, many hyperboxes remain unlabeled after training due to no class evidence for them. Thus any test sample falling in these hyperboxes are not classified. But in situations where we need to take a decision based on existing knowledge, one needs to ignore the output of these neurons. Thus we propose a concept of "Floating Neurons" to overcome this problem. Floating neurons are labeled dynamically and are allowed to contribute to the output if evidence for a class is found.

4   Training Algorithm and Recall Procedure

RFMN Training algorithm creates and expands hyperboxes depending on the demand of the problem. It utilizes the currently learned structure to label the unlabeled data. If there is any overlap, containment created (between hyperboxes of different classes) while expanding labeled hyperboxes, respective compensatory neuron is added to the network. Note that hyperboxes are not contracted in RFMN learning.

a) Training Algorithm
Training algorithm consists of mainly two steps, Data Adaptation and Overlap Test. Assume $\{A_h, C_i\}$ is a training data, $\{b_j, C_j\}$ a hyperbox for class C_j. θ: current hyperbox size θ_{max}: maximum hyperbox size. Initialize the network with b_1 with $V_1=A_h$, $W_1= A_h$ and class C_i for an ordered data pair $\{A_h, C_i\}$, Repeat the following steps 1 and 2 for the all-training samples. Note that for simplicity unlabeled data and hyperboxes are represented by C_0.

STEP 1: Data adaptation
>Find a $\{b_j, C_j\}$ for training sample $\{A_h, C_i\}$ such that $C_j=C_i$ or $C_j=C_0$ offering largest membership, $\theta \leq \theta_{max}$ and is not associated with any OCN or CCN. Adjust the min-max points of hyperbox b_j as:
>$$V_{ji}{}^{new}= min\ (V_{ji}{}^{old},\ A_{hi})\quad W_{ji}{}^{new} = max\ (W_{ji}{}^{old},\ A_{hi})\ \text{where}\ i =1,2...n \qquad (15)$$
>and If $C_j =C_0$ and $C_i \neq C_0$ then $C_j=C_i$. Take a new training sample.
>If no b_j is found, create a new hyperbox with $V_j=W_j=A_h$ and class C_i.

STEP 2: Overlap Test
>Assuming that b_j expanded in previous step is compared with b_k with class label $C_k \neq C_i$.
>
>*a) Isolation Test:*
>>If $(V_{ki}<W_{ki}<V_{ji}<W_{ji})$ or $(V_{ji}<W_{ji}<V_{ki}<W_{ki})$ is true for any i, $(i \in 1..n)$ Then (b_k, b_j) are isolated and Check the following:
>>Case1: if $C_j=C_0$ then assign $C_j=C_k$
>>Case2: if $C_k=C_0$ then assign $C_k=C_j$
>>Case3: if $C_j=C_k=C_0$
>>Stop further expansion of these hyperboxes if any of the above cases is satisfied and go to step1. Else go for Containment test.
>
>*b) Containment Test:*
>>If $(V_{ki}<V_{ji}<W_{ji}<W_{ki})$ or $(V_{ji}<V_{ki}<W_{ki}<W_{ji})$ is true for any i, $(i \in 1.. n)$ then Create a CCN with hyperbox min-max co-ordinates given by,

$$V_{ci}= max(V_{ki}, V_{ji}), \quad W_{ci}=min((W_{ki}, W_{ji}) \text{ for } i =1,2...n \qquad (16)$$

Else hyperboxes are not facing containment problem go to step (c)

c) Overlap compensation neuron creation:

Create a OCN with hyperbox min-max co-ordinates given by,

$$V_{oci}=max(V_{ki}, V_{ji}), \quad W_{oci}=min(W_{ki}, W_{ji}) \text{ for } i=1,2...n \qquad (17)$$

Avoid further expansion of hyperboxes belonging to different classes, which are facing the problem of overlap and containment, in the next expansion cycles.

b) Recall Procedure

The class nodes in each section calculate the class memberships and respective compensations. The summing node in the classifying neuron does the final grade calculation. The membership grade is computed according to Eq. 14 by adding the compensation to the class membership.

5   Experimental Results

The basic aims for the experiments were to verify 1) Effectiveness of change in activation function on the performance of RFMN, 2) To compare performance of proposed set of RTSI features, 3) To verify performance of proposed ORS on various datasets, 4) To check performance of RFMN under partial supervision.

a)   Effect of activation function

Here we used shape database [14] available on line. Fig.5 depicts some examples. It consists of 18 different classes and 12 images for each class, in total 216 images. Proposed RTSI features were extracted and fifty percent samples were selected randomly for training. Performance of RFMN on complete dataset with two different activation functions is compared with GFMN. Results are presented in Table 4.

It is clear from the results that RFMN performance is better than GFMN with activation function Eq.9. But it improves a lot when Eq.7 is used. The reason is that for the proposed RTSI features how many features match to the learned patterns is more important than the mismatches. Hence we recommend using activation functions depending on the nature of features.

Fig. 5. Few Images from Database [14]

Table 4. Activation function comparision

Algorithm	Learning Error (%)	Test Error (%)
RFMN (Eq. 7)	0	1.39
RFMN (Eq. 9)	0	9.26
GFMN	0	19.91

b) Performance on Various Feature Sets

Performance of RFMN, GFMN and K-Nearest Neighbor (KNN) [12] on shape database [14] using various feature sets is compared in Table 5. Training dataset is prepared by selecting 50% samples randomly. Note that a better object recognition is achieved using RFMN and the new set of RTSI features.

Table 5. Feature Set comparison (**LE- Learning Error, TE – Test Error**)

Features	RFMN		GFMN		K-NN (n=1)		K-NN (n=3)	
	LE	TE	LE	TE	LE	TE	LE	TE
New RTSI Features	0	1.39	0	19.91	0	4.62	22.22	20.83
Invariant Moments[13]	0	3.24	0	20.37	0	7.87	15.74	21.29
Radial Coding [8]	0	7.87	0	11.11	0	7.87	22.22	19.90

c) Test for RTS Invariance

To test the RTS invariance performance of proposed ORS rigorously we tested it on Bengali, Marathi digit database and an expanded shape database created from [14].

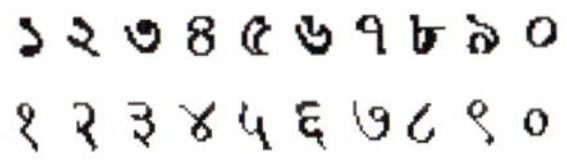

Fig. 6. Bengali (First Row) and Marathi Digits (0-9)

The details of the image database are given in Table 6.

Table 6. Database details

Database	Rotations	Sizes	Classes	Samples /Class	Total
Bengali ,Marathi Digits (0-9)	0, 10 35, 55, 60, 75, 90, 110, 135 Degrees	Font 20,24,28	10	30	300
Expanded Shape Database	0, 45, 90 Degrees	50, 100, 150 % of size in [14]	18	108	1944

For training the system, fifty percent of new RTSI features were selected randomly. Complete dataset is used for the test purpose. Table 7 shows that performance of proposed RFMN classifier is better than GFMN and KNN. A good recognition of proposed ORS i.e. combination of rotation, scale and translation invariance of new RTSI features and RFMN is demonstrated.

d) Semi-Supervised Learning

As stated earlier this mode of learning is suitable for the practical implementation of pattern recognition based systems, since practically it may not be always possible to label every training sample or cost of labeling is very high. To study the performance under partial supervision a mixture of labeled and unlabeled samples is used to train

Table 7. Performances on Bengali, Marathi Digits and Shape Database

Database	RFMN		GFMN		KNN (n=1)		KNN (n=3)	
	LE	TE	LE	LE	LE	TE	LE	TE
Bengali Digits	0	4	0	35.67	0	11	15.33	20
Marathi Digits	0	8	0	35.33	0	12.66	1.33	21
Expanded Shape	0	1.75	0	7.87	0	2.82	4.01	6.79

RFMN and GFMN. RFMN tries to apply the acquired knowledge from the labeled sample to label unlabeled and extract the underlying data structure. In this experiment, fifty percent of shape database and expanded shape database were selected randomly for training. Out of the selected training samples 2/3 samples were unlabeled randomly. This mixture was used to train GFMN and RFMN. Testing was carried out on complete dataset.

Table 8 compares results for RFMN, GFMN and KNN on shape and expanded shape database (Table 6). For training KNN we used available labeled data. RFMN and GFMN expansion coefficients were 0.1 and 0.05 for shape, expanded shape dataset respectively. It is clear that RFMN performance is better than GFMN and KNN. Compared to the hybrid mode learning of RFMN, performance of GFMN is poor due to the problems of unlabeled hyperboxes and its activation function. The interference of unlabeled hyperboxes leads to no classification of the input for GFMN.

Table 8. Semi-Supervised Test Error

Database	RFMN	GFMN	KNN(n=1)	KNN(n=3)
Shape [14]	11.57	48.61	21.29	30.55
Expanded Shape	11.98	45.37	18.10	23.14

6 Conclusion

A new rotation, translation and scale invariant object recognition system along with a novel RFMN architecture with floating neurons is presented. The need to select an activation function for neurons depending on the nature of features is discussed. The problem in GFMN hybrid mode learning is elaborated. The concept of floating neurons has improved the performance of RFMN in hybrid mode of learning. It helped to solve the problem due to unlabeled hyperboxes in GFMN. Experimental results show that the proposed object recognition system with RFMN classifier learns efficiently even with very few labeled samples added to unlabeled data. This is an important consideration for the practical implementation of pattern recognition system. Moreover performance of proposed set of RTSI features is found to be better than radial coding and invariant moments feature.

References

1. Zadeh, L.A.: Fuzzy Sets , Information and control, (1965), Vol. 8, 338-353.
2. Simpson, P.K.: Fuzzy Min-Max Neural Network – Part I: Classification, IEEE Tran. on Neural Networks, Vol.3,no.5, Sep. (1992) 776-786.

3. Simpson, P.K.: Fuzzy Min-Max Neural Network – Part II: Clustering, IEEE Tran. Fuzzy System, Vol.1, no.1, Feb. (1993) 32-45.

4. Gabrys, B., Bargiela, A.: General fuzzy min-max neural network for clustering and classification, IEEE Tran. Neural Network, Vol.11, May (2000) 769-783.

5. Kauppinen H,.Seppanen T, and Pietikamen M.,: An experimental comparison of Autoregressive and Fourier Based Descriptors in 2D shape classification, IEEE Trans. Pattern Analysis, Machine Intelligence, Vol.17, Feb. (1995) 207-210.

6. Perantonis S.J and. Lisboa P. J. G: Translation, rotation and scale invariant pattern recognition by high-order neural networks and moment classifiers, IEEE Trans. Neural Net-works, Vol. 4, July (1993), 276-283.

7. The C.H. and Chin R.T.: On image analysis by the methods of moments, IEEE Trans. Pattern Analysis and Machine Intelligence, Vol. 10, July (1988) 496-513.

8. Torres-Mendez L.A., Ruiz-Suarez J.C., Sucar L.E and Gomez G., "Translation, rotation and scale-invariant object recognition", IEEE Trans. on Systems, Man and Cybernetics, Vol.30, No.1, February (2000) 125-130.

9. Nandedkar, A.V., Biswas, P.K.: A Fuzzy min-max neural network classifier with compensatory neuron architecture, 17th Int. Cnf. on Pattern Recognition (ICPR2004), Cambridge UK , Vol. 4 , Aug (2004) 553-556.

10. Nandedkar A.V., Biswas P.K.: A General fuzzy min max neural network with compensatory neuron architecture, Lecture Notes in Computer Science, Vol. 3683, Aug (2005), 1160-1167.

11. Baitsell, G.A.: Human Biology, second edition, Mc-Graw Hill Book co. inc. NY, (1950).

12. Duda, R.O., Hart, P.E., Stork, D.G.: Pattern classification, 2nd edition, John Wiley &Sons Inc, Singapore (2001).

13. 13.Gonzalez R. C and Woods R. E.: Digital Image Processing, 2nd Edition, Pearson Education Pvt. Ltd., Delhi (2002).

14. T. Sebastian, P. Klein, B. Kimia: Recognition of shapes by editing shock graphs, 18th Int. Cnf. on Computer Vision (ICCV'01), Vol.1, (2001) 755-762.
http://www.lems.brown.edu/vision/researchAreas/SIID/

Extended Fitting Methods of Active Shape Model for the Location of Facial Feature Points

Chunhua Du[1], Jie Yang[1], Qiang Wu[2], Tianhao Zhang[1], Huahua Wang[1], Lu Chen[1], and Zheng Wu[1]

[1] Institute of Image Processing and Pattern Recognition, Shanghai Jiao Tong University, Shanghai, 200240, P.R. China
[2] Department of Computer Systems, University of Technology, Sydney, 2007, Australia

Abstract. In this study, we propose three extended fitting methods to the standard ASM(active shape model). Firstly, profiles are extended from 1D to 2D; Secondly, profiles of different landmarks are constructed individually; Thirdly, length of the profiles is determined adaptively with the change of level during searching, and the displacements in the last level are constrained. Each method and the combination of three methods are tested on the SJTU(Shanghai Jiaotong University) face database. In all cases, compared to the standard ASM, each method improves the accuracy or speed in a way, and the combination of three methods improves the accuracy and speed greatly.

1 Introduction

The location of facial landmarks plays a very important role in face research. Most facial features location methods can be broadly divided into two categories: One is local methods[1],[2],[3]. The other is global methods[4],[5],[6]. Deformable templates, active shape model(ASM) and active appearance model(AAM) all belong to the global methods. Compared to local methods, global methods are more robust, the most important thing is that the number of facial landmarks detected by global methods is greatly more than that of the local methods. ASM has been successfully applied in many areas[7],[8]. However, its drawbacks in accuracy and speed limit its further application. First, standard ASM searches the new position in 1D profile. However, the true new position may not lie in 1D profile, it therefore may bring to some error. Secondly, local structure of each landmark in standard ASM is generated identically. However, all landmarks are characterized by different features. Construct structures alike is unreasonable. Thirdly, length of profiles in different levels equals to each other during searching. In fact, the displacements become to decrease with the increase of the level. Hence length of the profiles in different levels doesn't need to be equal.

This paper presents three methods to address the above problems. Firstly, the 1D profile is extended from 1D to 2D; Secondly, local structures for the different landmarks are constructed according to their characteristic features; Thirdly, we decrease the length of the profiles when it comes to the next level during the fitting. We also constrain the displacements in the last level.

P. Kalra and S. Peleg (Eds.): ICVGIP 2006, LNCS 4338, pp. 610–618, 2006.
© Springer-Verlag Berlin Heidelberg 2006

The rest of the paper is organized as follows. Section 2 introduces the standard ASM. Three extended fitting methods are described in Section 3. Section 4 gives the comparison between the proposed methods and the standard ASM, experimental results are also presented. Section 5 is the conclusion of the paper.

2 Active Shape Models

ASM[4]is a statistic model, which includes the construction and fitting. The parameters used in this paper are listed in Table 1.

Table 1. Parameters of ASM(stand ASM and our methods). Values given between parentheses are used in our experiments.

k	Number of landmarks(60)
n	Number of training images(200)
s	Number of images in the testing set(2069)
t	Number of modes in the shape model(21)
m	Number of points in sub-profile on either side of the landmark (4)
l	Number of points in profile either side of the landmark for searching, length of the profile is 2l+1(11 for the first, second method and single-resolution standard ASM. 11,9 and 7 for different levels of the third method and the combined method)
L	Number of levels(3)
N	Number of iterations(50 for single-resolution scheme,5 for each level of multi-resolution scheme)
T	Threshold of the displacement of the last level for the third method and the combined method(2)

2.1 Construction of the ASM

For each face image in face database, mark k facial landmark $(x_1, y_1),...,(x_k, y_k)$ manually on picture as is shown in Fig. 1. Each landmark with the same index number

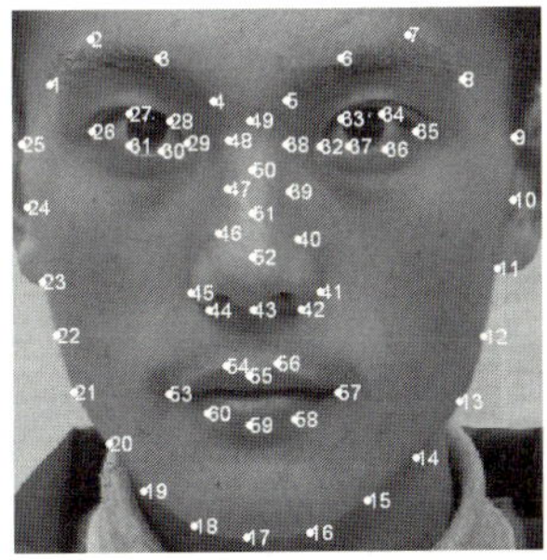

Fig. 1. Facial landmarks

in different images stands for the same feature, and all the landmarks of an image give a shape vector

$$x = (x_1, y_1, x_2, y_2, ..., x_k, y_k) \tag{1}$$

To make the shape model independent of the size, position and orientation, all shape vectors are aligned[4]. Principal component analysis(PCA) is then applied to the aligned shape vectors and we can get the mean shape

$$\bar{x} = \frac{1}{n} \sum_{i=1}^{n} x_i \tag{2}$$

and the covariance

$$S = \frac{1}{n} \sum_{i=1}^{n} (x_i - \bar{x})^T (x_i - \bar{x}) \tag{3}$$

Then the eigenvalues $(\lambda_1, \lambda_2, ..., \lambda_s)$ and the eigenvector $(p_1, p_2, ..., p_s)$ are computed. Select the first t eigenvectors and eigenvalues to satisfy the inequation:

$$\sum_{i=1}^{t} \lambda_i / \sum_{i=1}^{s} \lambda_i \geq 0.95 V_T \tag{4}$$

where V_T is the sum of all the eigenvalues. Then a shape vector can be approximated by

$$x \approx \bar{x} + Pb \tag{5}$$

where b is a vector of weights, computed by

$$b = P^T (x - \bar{x}) \tag{6}$$

In order to find the new positions for facial landmarks, local structure needs to be constructed in advance. As for a landmark (x_i, y_i), sample m pixels on either side then give a profile. Then local structure can be built by using the normalized first derivatives of this profile. Denoting the normalized derivative profiles $g_1, g_2, ..., g_n$, the mean profile $\bar{g}$, covariance matrix S_g, we then can compute the Mahalanobis distance between a new profile g_i and the mean profile

$$f(g_i) = (g_i - \bar{g}) S_g^{-1} (g_i - \bar{g})^T \tag{7}$$

2.2 ASM Fitting

ASM fitting can be realized by two iterative steps:(1)finding a new position for each landmark;(2)updating b and the parameters of the affine transformation.

At first, sample l pixels either side of the landmark and give a profile alike as before, select a sub-profile and compute the Mahalanobis distance. The center of the sub-profile with the minimal Mahalanobis distance is the new position. Find the new position for each landmark and compute the displacement for each landmark to get a displacement vector $dX = (dX_1, dX_2, ..., dX_k)$. Then the following equation is used to update the affine transformation parameters and b:

$$X = M(s, \theta)[x] + X_c \tag{8}$$

According to equation (8), we can get

$$M(s(1+ds), (\theta + d\theta))[x + dx] + (X_c + dX_c) = (X + dX) \tag{9}$$

and

$$M(s(1+ds), (\theta + d\theta))[x + dx] = M(s, \theta)[x] + dX + X_c - (X_c + dX_c) \tag{10}$$

According to equation (5), db is utilized such that $x + dx = \bar{x} + P(b + db)$ and

$db = P^{-1}dx$. Then affine transformation parameters and b are updated as follows:

$$X_c = X_c + w_t dX_c, Y_c = Y_c + w_t dY_c, \theta = \theta + w_\theta d\theta, s = s(1 + w_s ds), b = b + W_b db \tag{11}$$

where w_t, w_θ, w_s, W_b are scalar weights.

3   Extended Fitting Methods of the Active Shape Models

Although there are many ways to refine the standard ASM, we discover that three methods can best improve the accuracy and speed of it.

3.1   Extend the Profile from 1D to 2D

It is well known that there is a key idea in the standard ASM: finding a new position for each landmark. This finding accuracy affects the whole accuracy of ASM directly. In Fig. 2, the target position of the current landmark is point P1, whereas the best position that can be located is point P2. To tackle this problem, we propose to extend profile from1D to 2D as shown in Fig. 3.

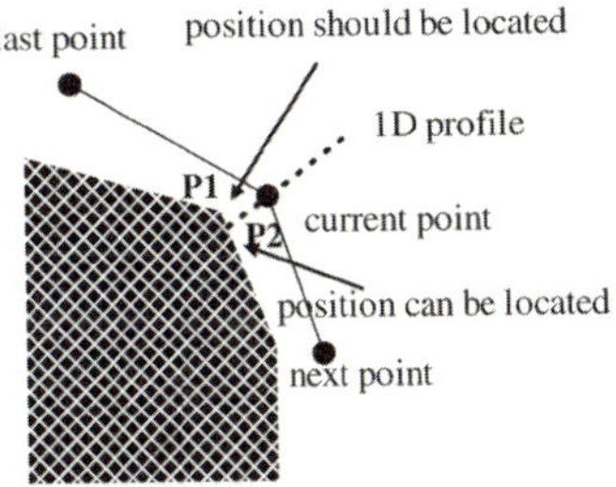

Fig. 2. 1D profile

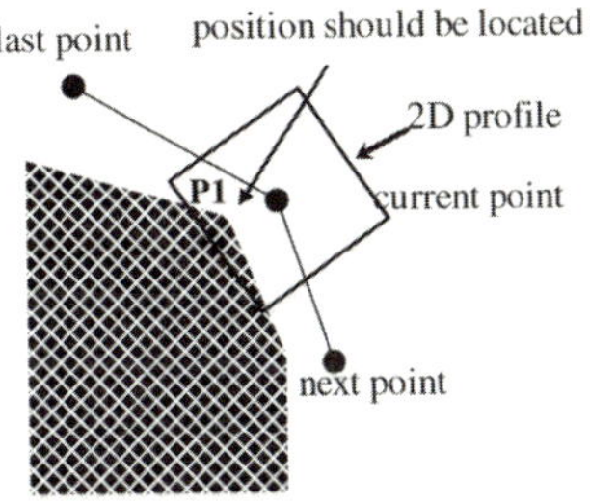

Fig. 3. 2D profile

Since the profile has been extended to 2D, local structure should be constructed in another way: for each landmark, select a square with side length of m and center of current landmark, such that there are n squares, then compute the average gray-scale of each pixel within the square, and get a 2D profile g_o. A square with the side length of l and the center of the current landmark is selected during the fitting. We define a function f_o to replace the Mahalanobis distance:

$$f_o = \frac{1}{m \times m} \sum_{i=1}^{m} \sum_{j=1}^{m} abs(g^{ij}{}_o - temp_o{}^{ij})$$

(12)

where g^{ij}_o is the gray-scale of pixel lies in the ith row, jth column of 2D profile of oth landmark, $temp^{ij}_o$ is counterpart of the sub-profile of the oth landmark, f_o represents the similarity between the 2D profile and the 2D sub-profile. The center of the sub-profile is viewed as the new position for the current landmark if f_o reaches the minimum.

3.2 Construct the Local Structures for Landmarks According to Their Feature

In standard ASM, local structures of all landmarks are constructed identically. However, local structures of landmarks don't express their true feature. Accordingly, the accuracy of location will subject from this kind of local structure. In order to improve the accuracy, we propose to construct the local structures for landmarks individually. For the landmarks around the irises and eyebrows, we construct the local structures not only with profiles, but also with gray-scale information. And a new function is used

$$f(g_i) = gray \times (g_i - \bar{g}) S_g^{-1} (g_i - \bar{g})^T$$

(13)

where $gray$ is the gray-scale of the landmarks. Then for the landmarks on the contour of chin and mouth, we construct their local structures with profiles and edge information, and use another function

$$f(g_i) = -edge \times (g_i - \bar{g}) S_g^{-1} (g_i - \bar{g})^T$$

(14)

where $edge$ is the magnitude of the landmark of the gradient image.

3.3 Adjust the Length of the Profile Adaptively

In the standard ASM, length of the profile in different levels is fixed. Experiments indicate that the displacements of the landmarks in the first level are very large, and the displacements begin to decrease with the increase of the level. Thus we propose to reduce the length of the profile with the increase of the level and constrain the displacements in the last level by setting a threshold T.

4 Comparison and Experiments

To compare the proposed methods with the standard ASM, experiments are conducted on the SJTU face database, which includes 2269 labeled frontal face images and the size of image is 640×480. We divide the SJTU face database into training set and testing set. The former and the latter contain 200 and 2069 images respectively. All experiments are conducted on a P4 2.8GHz machine with Matlab implementations. In order to compare our methods with the standard ASM quantitatively, we first define two functions, average error

$$E_{ave} = \frac{1}{s} \times \frac{1}{k} \sum_{i=1}^{n} \sum_{j=1}^{k} dis(X(i, j) - pos(i, j)) \tag{15}$$

and average computation time

$$ave\_time = \frac{1}{s} \sum_{i=1}^{s} time_i \tag{16}$$

where $X(i, j)$ is the manually marked position of the *jth* landmark of the *ith* image in the testing set, $pos(i, j)$ is the position located by different methods, $dis(X(i, j) - pos(i, j))$ is the Euclidean Distance between $X(i, j)$ and $pos(i, j)$, $time_i$ is the computation time for the fitting of the *ith* face.

At first, we compare the first method with the standard ASM. All other aspects of the two algorithms are identical except the shape of the profiles. Both use 50 iterations for fitting. Since profiles have been extended from 1D to 2D, the corresponding searching spaces are also extended. Therefore, the probability of finding the new positions will be increased and the accuracy of whole fitting will be increased accordingly. We plot the average error against the number of iteration $N=$ 5, 10,…, 50 in Fig. 4, which shows that the average error of the first method is lower than that of the standard ASM during the fitting. Furthermore, it needs less iteration to converge. From Fig. 4 we can also see that the first method has converged after 25 iterations, and the counterpart of the standard ASM is 35. However, on the other hand, the average computation time for two methods is 0.30s and 0.33s. It is not strange because the profile has been extended from 1D to 2D, and the corresponding searching space also be extended form 1D to 2D, it will come down to more pixels and need more computations.

Then for the second method, we construct the local structure for landmark individually. Local structure of the second method has more information. Thus, the new local structure can discriminate the landmarks more efficiently. We plot the average error against the number of the iterations in Fig. 5. It shows that the second method also needs fewer iterations to converge. On the other hand, the second needs more computation since the functions of equation (14) and (15) need a more multiplication operation. The average computation time for the second method and the standard ASM is 0.31s and 0.30s.

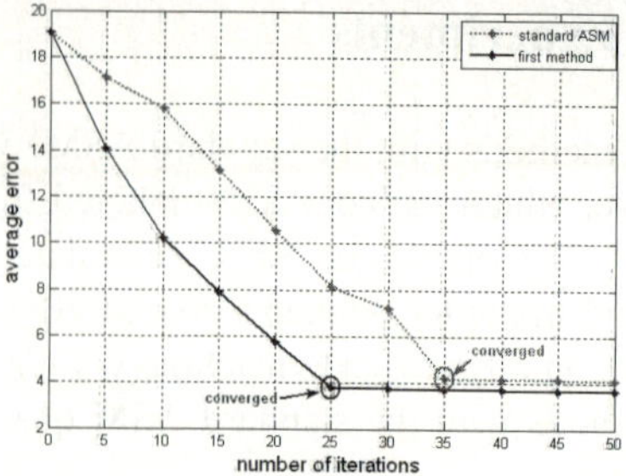

Fig. 4. Average error against the number of iterations

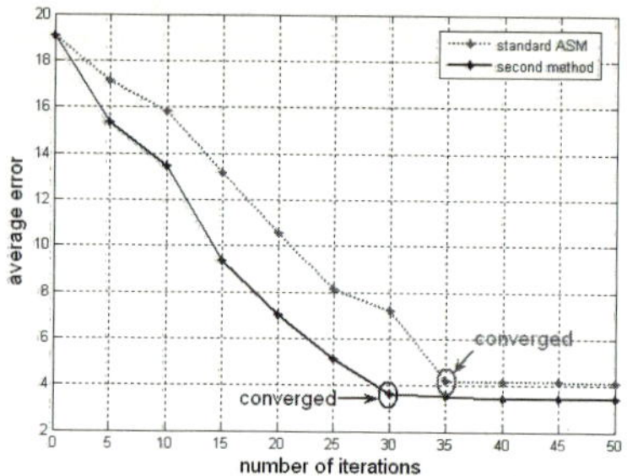

Fig. 5. Average error against the number of iterations

For the third method, the number of pixels each side of the landmark in the first, second and last level is 11, 9 and 7. The displacement threshold T in the last level is 2. For the standard ASM, the number of pixels each side of the current landmark in all levels is 11. For both methods, the number of levels and the iterations of each level is 3 and 5 in turn. We plot the average error against the iterations in Fig. 6, from which we can see that the standard ASM has converged after two levels(1-10 iterations). Fig. 6 also indicates that the average error of the two methods is the same in the first level. When it comes to the second level, we shorten the profiles. As for the third method, the number of iterations for converge is only 8, which is less than that of the standard ASM. The average computation time for the third method and standard ASM is 0.11s and 0.08s

At last, we combine all three methods to give a combined method. Since the profiles are extended to 2D and the local structures of the landmarks are constructed differently, the accuracy of finding the new positions is enhanced, which leads to a great increase in the accuracy of the whole fitting. As the length of the second and third level in the combined method is shortened, the speed for the fitting is reduced. The average computation time of the combined ASM and standard ASM is 0.09s and 0.11s. We also plot the average error against the iterations Fig. 7. It is clear that the combined method needs 7 iterations to fitting.

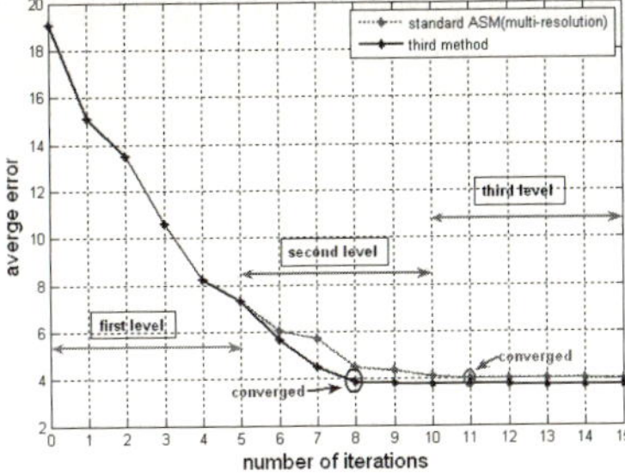

Fig. 6. Average error against the number of iterations

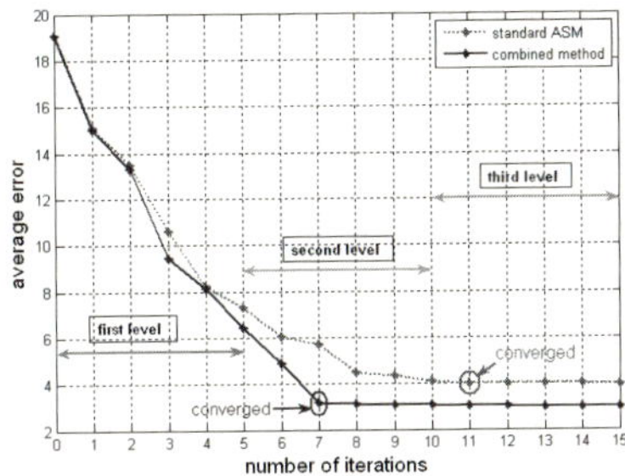

Fig. 7. Average error against the number of iterations

5   Conclusions

In this paper we have presented three methods to the fitting of the standard ASM to locate the facial landmarks. Experimental results demonstrate that each of method can improve the accuracy or speed in a way, and the combined method improves the accuracy and speed greatly, when compared with the standard ASM.

References

1. Zhi-Hua Zhou and Xin Geng, Projection functions for eye detection, Pattern Recognition, vol. 37, no. 5, pp. 1049-1056, 2004.
2. Kawaguchi T and Rizon M, Iris detection using intensity and edge information, Pattern Recognition, vol. 36, no. 2, pp. 549-562, 2003.
3. Shu-Hung Leung, Shi-Lin Wang, and Wing-Hong Lau, Lip image segmentation using fuzzy clustering incorporating an elliptic shape function, IEEE Transactions on Image Processing, vol. 13, no. 1, pp. 51-62, 2004.
4. T.F.Cootes, C.J.Taylor, D.H.Cooper, and J.Graham, Active Shape Models - Their Training and Application, Computer Vision and Image Understanding, vol. 61, no. 1, pp. 38-59, 1995.

5. Alan L.Yuille, Peter W.Hallinan, and David S.Cohen, Feature extraction from faces using deformable templates, International Journal of Computer Vision, vol. 8, no. 2, pp. 99-111, 1992.
6. T.F.Cootes, G. J. Edwards, and C. J. Taylor, Active Appearance Models, IEEE Transactions on Pattern Analysis and Machine Intelligence, vol. 23, no. 6, pp. 681-685, 2001.
7. Christos Davatzikos, Xiaodong Tao, and Dinggang Shen, Hierarchical active shape models, using the wavelet transform, IEEE Transactions on Medical Imaging, vol. 22, no. 3, pp. 414-423, 2003.
8. B. van Ginneken, A. F. Frangi, J. J. Staal, B. M. ter Haar Romeny, and M. A. Viergever, Active shape model segmentation with optimal features, IEEE Transactions on Medical Imaging, vol. 21, no. 8, pp. 924-933, 2002.

Pose Invariant Generic Object Recognition with Orthogonal Axis Manifolds in Linear Subspace

Manisha Kalra, P. Deepti, R. Abhilash, and Sukhendu Das

Visualization and Perception Laboratory
Department of Computer Science and Engineering
Indian Institute of Technology - Madras, Chennai - 600 036, India

Abstract. This paper addresses the problem of pose invariant Generic Object Recognition by modeling the perceptual capability of human beings. We propose a novel framework using a combination of appearance and shape cues to recognize the object class and viewpoint (axis of rotation) as well as determine its pose (angle of view). The appearance model of the object from multiple viewpoints is captured using Linear Subspace Analysis techniques and is used to reduce the search space to a few rank-ordered candidates. We have used a decision-fusion based combination of 2D PCA and ICA to integrate the complementary information of classifiers and improve recognition accuracy. For matching based on shape features, we propose the use of distance transform based correlation. A decision fusion using Sum Rule of 2D PCA and ICA subspace classifiers, and distance transform based correlation is then used to verify the correct object class and determine its viewpoint and pose. Experiments were conducted on COIL-100 and IGOIL (IITM Generic Object Image Library) databases which contain objects with complex appearance and shape characteristics. IGOIL database was captured to analyze the appearance manifolds along two orthogonal axes of rotation.

1   Introduction

Existing object recognition systems [1][2][3][4] focus on recognition of a particular object class as well as its pose only along one axis of rotation. Such systems fail if they are given an object image from an arbitrary viewpoint. It is tough to capture the 3D appearance model of an object using a limited set of 2D views only along a single axis. Also, creation and storage of 3D models of objects poses a problem to the existing 3D model-based recognition systems. The problem we address is not restricted to a single class of objects, say only face recognition or vehicle recognition. Rather, it involves recognition across multiple categories of objects. Content based image retrieval, infant perception and recognition are the potential areas of its application. The goal of this work is to design a framework for generic object recognition (GOR) from arbitrary viewpoints and poses, using a limited set of 2D views of objects along multiple orthogonal axes of rotation. The various approaches for object recognition can be grouped into the following categories based on the type of features and matching strategies used: a) Structural Decomposition: Recognition-by-components [5], 3-D part-based methods;

P. Kalra and S. Peleg (Eds.): ICVGIP 2006, LNCS 4338, pp. 619–630, 2006.

b) Appearance Based Approaches: Principal Component Analysis [1], [2], [6], Support Vector Machines [7], [8]; c) Shape Based Approaches: Shape Context [9], Moment-based methods 4) Model Based Approaches: Geometric Invariants, CAD Model Based approach [10].

Murase and Nayar [1] have addressed the problem of automatically learning object appearance models for recognition and pose estimation using 1D PCA. From the set of 100 objects in COIL database, the authors have picked 20 objects (COIL-20 database) that do not possess pose ambiguities and have reported a recognition rate of 100% on these 20 objects. The object pose estimation is reported to have a mean absolute error of 2.02 degrees and standard deviation of 16.7 degrees. Nagabhushan et al. [2] have experimented the use of 2D Principal Component Analysis (2D PCA) on COIL-20 database for object recognition and have reported that 2D PCA gives a better recognition accuracy than 1D PCA. They also report a 100% recognition rate on the 20 object database for noise-free test samples. However, they did not report their results on COIL-100 database. The existing appearance based techniques (1D and 2D PCA) summarized above try to recognize object class and pose from only one axis of rotation and also do not use any shape cues for verification.

2   Proposed Framework

We propose a two stage framework based on the studies in cognitive psychology where we try to model the 'human visual-pathway' starting with low-level processing like feature extraction (using appearance based cues), to high-level object representation in the human brain, such as perception (using shape cues) and recognition. The flowchart of the overall framework for generic object recognition is shown in Fig. 1. The entire framework can be logically divided into three phases: *(a) Memory, (b) Representation and Classification, (c) Shape Perception*. Below, we describe the three phases.

2.1   Memory : 2D Image Gallery with Multiple Axes Views

The image gallery contains the 2D views of objects from multiple (orthogonal) axis of rotations. These views represent the objects already seen by human beings. This aspect of the framework models the recollection ability of the human beings to retrieve exemplars from the memory on seeing an object and studying its appearance from different poses and viewpoints [11]. A subset of this database is used to train the system, rest of the samples are used for testing.

2.2   Appearance Based Representation and Classification

According to neurological studies, the initial phase of object recognition uses the fact that people might initially characterize the objects using some set of rules or features. The human brain extracts a set of statistical features or cues from images of 3-D objects to represent or recognize it [11][13]. Based on this hypothesis, we propose a method which uses second and higher order statistics

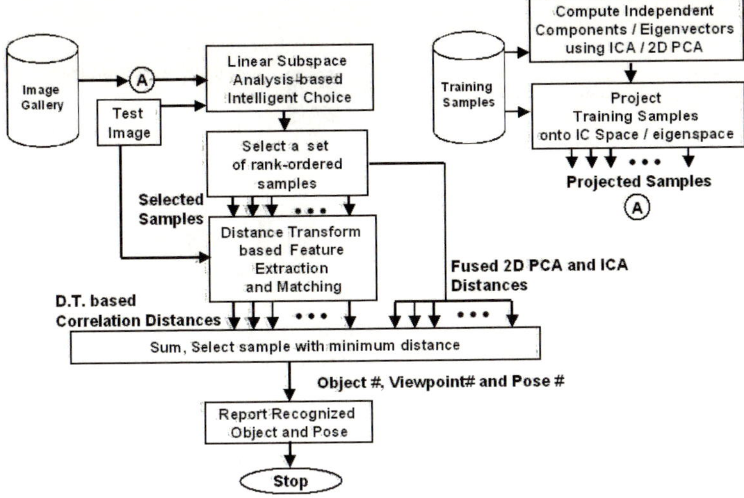

Fig. 1. Flowchart for Generic Object Recognition framework combining appearance (Linear Subspace Analysis) and Shape (DT based matching) cues

[13] to represent objects in a high dimensional space. We use a fusion of two linear subspace analysis based classifiers: 2D PCA [2] and ICA [14] for this task. Both 2D PCA and ICA are shown to capture the appearance manifold of the object from multiple orthogonal axis of rotations. The appearance representation of each object i is defined by a manifold set $M_i = \{o_{ij}|j = 1..K\}$ where o_{ij} is the manifold of the object i captured by rotating the object along the jth orthogonal axis, and K (=2) is the total number of orthogonal axes along which the object is rotated. The manifold curves for an object lie on a manifold surface which is unique for an object. A typical manifold set for an object is shown in Fig. 2. Since consecutive poses (θ) of an object along a particular axis of rotation are close in appearance to each other, they lie close to each other in the manifold.

Decision Fusion of 2D PCA and ICA: Second order statistics (PCA) capture the amplitude spectrum of images but not their phase spectrum. The higher order statistics (ICA) capture the phase spectrum. However, both amplitude and phase spectrum contain important information that drives human perception [14]. The advantages of ICA over PCA have been quoted in [14]. 2D PCA on the other hand, preserves the column-wise or row-wise adjacency of pixels [15]. Each classifier shows different level of performance on different subsets of images, suggesting that different classifiers contribute complementary information to the classification task. A combination scheme involving both 2D PCA and ICA is likely to improve the recognition accuracy.

We use the decision level combination that is more appropriate when the component classifiers use different types of features. We use Sum rule (observed to work the best among all six combination strategies) for combining the two appearance-based object recognition methods : 2D PCA and ICA since it is

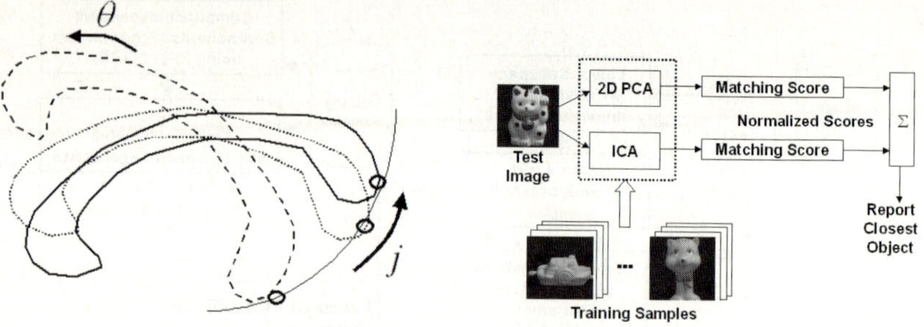

Fig. 2. Expected manifold set for an object in the linear subspace. j represents the axis of rotation (viewpoint), θ represents the pose number.

Fig. 3. Appearance-based Classifier Combination System Framework

the most robust classifier combination strategies [16]. Our combination strategy (shown in Fig. 3) is designed at decision level, utilizing the confidence value, called the matching score provided by each of the two appearance-based recognition schemes. The criterion for appearance-based object recognition is

$$D_{comb} = \frac{D_{2DPCA} + D_{ICA}}{2} \tag{1}$$

where D_{2DPCA} and D_{ICA} are euclidean distances between the test and training features in the 2D PCA Eigenspace and ICA Space respectively. Since each classifier uses its own representation of input patterns, the distances extracted from the patterns are unique to each classifier. Thus, before computing D_{comb}, the matching scores (D_{2DPCA} and D_{ICA}) are normalized using Max normalization, as in [16]. Use of the fused generic classifier helps to reduce the search space for objects, to a few rank ordered similar (in appearance) samples in the gallery. Shape matching is required to verify the object and it helps to improve the recognition accuracy.

2.3   Shape Perception for Verification

Since psychological findings indicate that shape dominates other cues in human object recognition, we suggest a shape perception stage in our framework which tries to imitate the visual similarity detection capability of the human brain. Once a set of rank ordered samples has been selected from the image gallery using appearance cues, the next step is to verify and match it with the test image using shape-based features (distance transform (DT) based matching). As the knowledge about the foreground pixel is stored around it at many positions by the DT, this representation of a bitmap gives the process of matching a high degree of tolerance to noise and discontinuities. DT based features have been preferred over moments and shape context [9] due to reduced computational cost and robustness against noise and discontinuities in edgemaps [17].

Shape Matching using Distance Transform based Correlation: Let $b_{x,y}$ be a bitmap with feature pixels of value 1 and background pixels with value 0. Consider a second bitmap b' and let $d_{x,y}$ be the DT of b'. Let the cross-correlation between DT d and the bitmap b be given as $R(b,d)$. If two samples (test and target shapes) are similar, we obtain small value of correlation indicating a higher degree of match. Instead of using R(b, d) as the distance measure between two bitmaps b and b', we use an average distance of the cross correlations of DT of b with bitmap b' [17]; and that of DT of b' with the bitmap b. Thus the distance measure for choosing the best sample based on the shape of the object is given as

$$DT_{Corr} = \text{avg}(R(T, D(b_i)), R(b_i, D(T)))$$ (2)

where b_i is the edge map of the ith training sample, T is the edge map of the test image and $D(.)$ is the DT function. This criterion works better than just using R as the shape similarity measure, as it is unbiased to T or b_i.

2.4 Combining Appearance-Based Generic Classifier and Shape Perception

The two stage approach (Fig. 1) based on linear subspace analysis (using fusion of 2D PCA and ICA) and DT based correlation attempts to imitate some perceptual properties of the human brain. For each object to be stored in the database, a large set of images from different poses and along multiple orthogonal viewpoints of the object are obtained. The set of images is normalized with respect to scale and projected into the universal linear subspace constructed using 2D PCA and ICA from the set of all object images. Each object is then defined by a manifold set in the universal linear subspace, where each manifold of the object corresponds to a single orthogonal axis of rotation (viewpoint). Given a test image, it is first projected onto the universal linear subspaces (separately for 2D PCA and ICA) and a few rank ordered samples closest to the test sample are selected based on the fused decision given by 2D PCA and ICA classifiers. These objects have overall similarity in appearance with respect to the input test sample. Linear subspace analysis thus acts as a generic classifier to identify such closely appearing objects. Shape matching is then performed using DT based correlation. The object with the minimum value of a sum of (a) appearance based fused ICA and 2D PCA distance (Eq. 1) and, (b) shape (rule as in [16]) cues using DT based matching (Eq. 2) is selected as the best match. The statistical analysis tool represents objects using second and higher order features, and DT based matching takes care of the response of the brain to boundaries of objects and shape features which match the test object with samples in memory. The manifold set of the object captures the perceptual properties of the human brain keeping the images of consecutive poses of objects which are visually similar in appearance, close to each other in the manifolds. The proposed criterion (for detailed flowchart, refer to Fig. 1) is evaluated on the COIL-100 [18] and IGOIL databases, and results are presented in the following section.

3 Experimental Results

We have conducted experiments using our proposed approach on two databases: COIL-100 (Columbia Object Image Library) [17] and IGOIL (IITM Generic Object Image Library) [19]. COIL-100 has been previously used by [1], [2], [7] to test the performance of their appearance based systems. To compare the performance of our proposed approach with the existing state-of-art techniques, we have used COIL-100 Database which contains color images of 100 objects. Images are taken at pose intervals of 5 degrees (72 poses per object). A part of the gallery used has been shown in Fig. 4. However, COIL-100 gallery contains images of objects along only one axis of rotation. To analyze the performance of the proposed methodology for recognition from arbitrary viewpoints, we have generated our own image gallery of objects along two orthogonal axes of rotation. The details of the experimental set up and the results of the application of fused appearance and shape classifier is presented in this section.

IITM Generic Object Image Library (IGOIL): [19] We have captured images of 20 objects along two orthogonal axes of rotation. In general, more than two orthogonal axes of rotation can be used to increase the robustness of the classifier to recognize from arbitrary viewpoints. However, since most of the objects in our gallery have similar appearance along two out of the three axes, we have used only two axes of rotations to capture the object appearances from several viewpoints. Images are taken at pose intervals of 5 degrees along each axis. This corresponds to 144 images per object. The images of objects were taken using a 35mm Sony CCD camera. Ambient light was used to avoid strong shadows. Each object's images along two orthogonal axes of rotation were taken by placing it on a turnable. The images taken by the camera were cropped and size normalized and rescaled to 128×128. The images had uniform black background and there was no occlusion. The 0 degree pose angle views of some objects along two orthogonal axes of rotation is shown in Fig. 5. Experiments

Fig. 4. Sample Objects from COIL-100

Fig. 5. Sample Objects from IGOIL

were conducted separately for both the databases with a part of the gallery chosen for training and the rest for testing. Different experiments were performed with training samples chosen for all objects from each database in the gallery, obtained at increments of every 10, 15, 20, 25 and 30 degrees. The framework was trained (separately for each experimentation) using each of these five training sets. The performance was analyzed using four and eight test samples (4 test samples from each orthogonal axis) per object for COIL-100 (400 test samples) and IGOIL (160 test samples) respectively, selected at random from the rest of the gallery.

3.1   Appearance Based Recognition

Fig. 6 show images of an object from IGOIL database along three orthogonal axes of rotation along with its corresponding manifold set captured using 2D PCA and ICA. For ease of visualization, we have displayed the manifolds using only the first three eigenvectors/ICs. For rest of the experimentation, we have used 10 eigendimensions for 2D PCA on both COIL-100 and IGOIL databases for better separability. We have selected 110 and 45 ICs for ICA on COIL-100 and IGOIL databases respectively. These dimensions was selected empirically by running experiments for 3-20 dimensions with 2D PCA and 10-125 ICs with ICA on both the databases. In order to have control over the number of ICs extracted by the algorithm, we have adopted the method used on face images in [13] for ICA. Given that the two linear subspace analysis based classifiers provide comparable

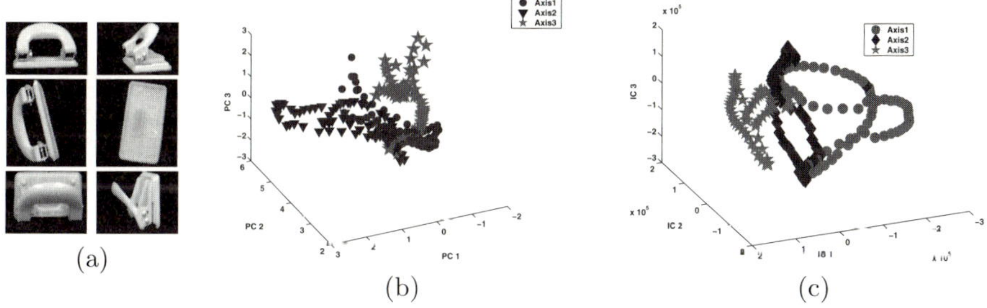

Fig. 6. (a) An object from IGOIL database along three orthogonal axes of rotation (only two views shown for each axis). (b) Parametric Eigenspace (2D PCA) for an object in (a). (c) Parametric IC Space (ICA) for an object in (a). Appearance is represented by a Manifold Set where each manifold corresponds to one axis of rotation.

recognition performances, we examined whether the two representations gave similar patterns of errors on object images. There are objects which only either of the two classifiers are able to recognize. Fig. 7 (a) shows some objects for which 2D PCA worked but ICA failed. Fig. 7 (b) shows a set of objects for which ICA worked but 2D PCA failed. When the two algorithms made errors, however, they did not assign the same incorrect identity. Because the errors made by the two algorithms differed, a combined classifier was employed in which the similarity between a test image and a gallery image was defined by D_{comb} (Eq. 1). The comparison of percentage accuracy of the fused classifier (using D_{comb}), 2D PCA (D_{2DPCA}) and ICA (D_{ICA}) on COIL-100 database has been shown in Fig. 9.

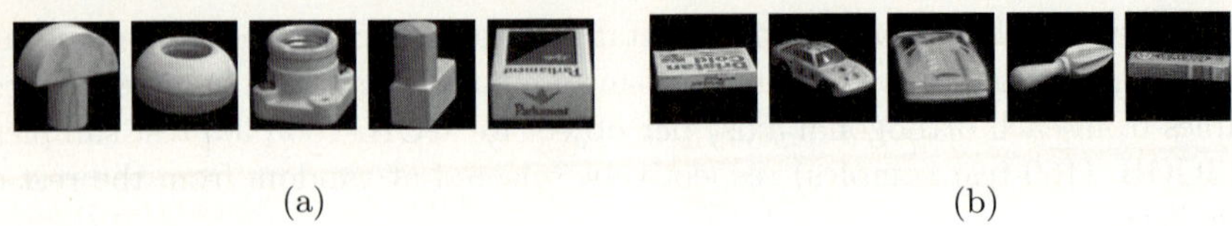

(a)   (b)

Fig. 7. Set of Objects from COIL-100 Database for which (a) 2D PCA succeedes but ICA fails and (b) ICA succeedes but 2D PCA fails

The recognition accuracies using D_{2DPCA}, D_{ICA} and D_{comb} on IGOIL database for 160 test samples (8 test samples per object) are shown in Table 1.

Need for Shape Matching: Linear Subspace analysis techniques (2D PCA and ICA) give good results for objects having distinct appearance and shape characteristics but fail for objects which are similar in appearance, but with minor differences in shape. Fig. 8 (a) and (b) show manifolds of two objects from COIL-100 database generated using (first three eigenvectors) 2D PCA and ICA respectively. The linear subspace techniques show an overlap in the eigenspace/IC space (i.e. both methods fail to discriminate). In such cases, use of shape properties gives an advantage over appearance based schemes to recognize objects from multiple viewpoints. We hence propose the use of shape properties to discriminate such objects and verify the results obtained by 2D PCA/ICA.

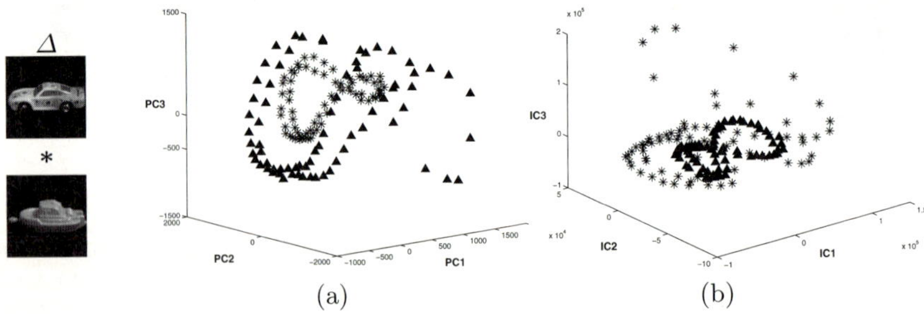

(a)   (b)

Fig. 8. a: Universal Eigenspace (2D PCA) of two objects from COIL-100 database with similar appearance properties; b: IC Space of two objects showing an overlap. Overlap in both 2D PCA and ICA space suggests the use of a shape verification stage.

3.2   Improving Recognition Performance Using Shape Matching

Using linear subspace analysis we first select a set of rank-ordered samples (10 and 3 for COIL-100 and IGOIL respectively) based on their distances in eigenspace / IC Space. Increasing the number of rank-ordered samples does not alter the performance of the system by much, but increases the computational complexity. The number of rank-ordered samples selected is empirically set to approximately 10% of the total number of objects in the database. These samples are then matched with the test object based on shape features and the object with minimum distance of appearance and shape cues is returned as the best match. The criterion for object recognition using combination of 2D PCA and DT based correlation with 2D PCA and ICA are:

$$\mathbf{D}_\xi = D_{2DPCA} + DT_{corr} \quad \mathbf{D}_\rho = D_{ICA} + DT_{corr} \tag{3}$$

The values of D_{2DPCA}, D_{ICA} and DT_{corr} are normalized using Max normalization, before D_ξ and D_ρ are computed. Analysis is also conducted for recognition from arbitrary viewpoints on IGOIL database.

Fusion of combined 2D PCA and ICA system with Shape cues for Recognition: The proposed criterion for object recognition using combination of 2D PCA, ICA and DT based shape cues is

$$D_\lambda = D_{comb} + DT_{corr} \tag{4}$$

where D_{comb} and DT_{corr} are defined in Eq. 1 and 2 respectively. Fig. 10 shows the comparison of recognition accuracies using D_ξ (2DPCA and Shape), D_ρ (ICA and Shape) and D_λ on COIL-100 Database. Table 1 shows the comparison of recognition accuracies of D_ξ, D_ρ and D_λ on IGOIL database for recognition along multiple orthogonal axes. Note (in Fig. 10 and Table 1) that neither D_ξ nor D_ρ performs consistently better than the other. However, D_λ works better than both D_ξ and D_ρ for varying number of training samples given to the classifiers on both COIL-100 and IGOIL databases. The proposed approach gives peak recognition accuracies of 96.375% using 2DPCA, 97.675% with D_ξ, 97% using

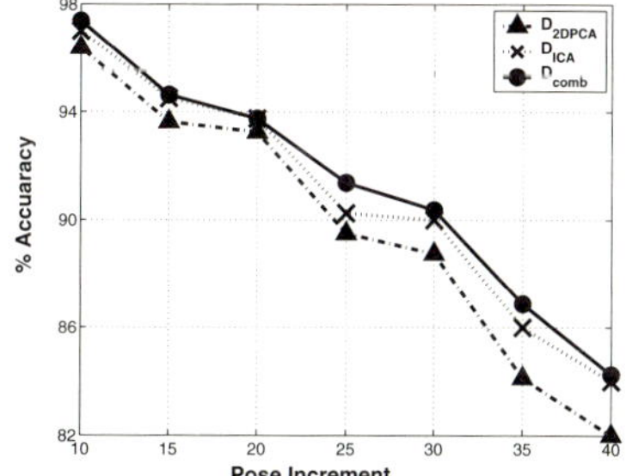

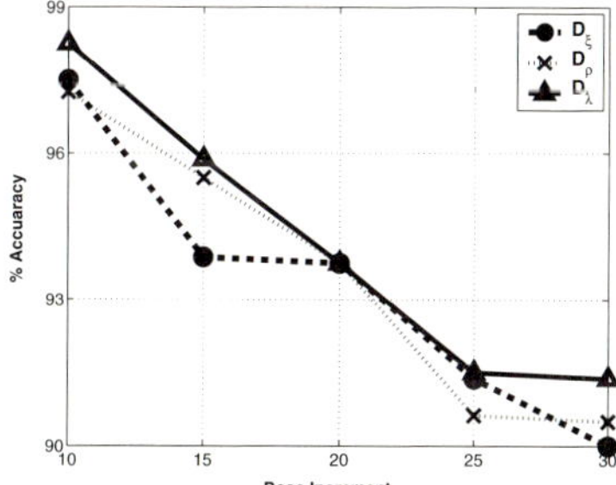

Fig. 9. Comparison of performance of D_{2DPCA} (EigenDimensions=10), D_{ICA} (No. of ICs=110) and D_{comb}. The percentage accuracy is shown as a function of the number of training samples (pose interval).

Fig. 10. Comparison of performance of the proposed method using D_λ , D_ρ and D_ξ on COIL-100 Database in case where the number of Independent Components=110 and Number of eigenvectors=20

ICA, 97.25% using D_ρ and 98.25% using D_λ, when tested with 400 samples on the entire COIL-100 database (pose interval of 10 degrees) containing 100 objects. The method provides a recognition rate of 91.375% with D_λ even when a sparse database was used for training. We compare the performance of our proposed method with that of Murase and Nayar [1] and Nagabhushan [2] as benchmarks which report a 100% recognition performance on 20 objects preselected from the COIL database. Most methods in the literature use only a subset of the 100 objects (typically 20 to 30) from COIL-100 database for experiments. Table 2 shows a comparision of recognition rates of techniques proposed by [1], [2] and [7] with our proposed framework. Our results provide better performance than those reported in [1], [2] and [7], given the fact that we have tested our approach on the entire 100 objects in the COIL database. Fusion of 2D PCA, ICA and DT based shape matching (D_λ) is shown to perform better than all other techniques. The comparison of recognition accuracies of D_{2DPCA}, D_{ICA}, D_ξ, D_ρ and D_λ on IGOIL database is shown in Table 1.

3.3   Results in Cluttered Background

To recognize objects from a cluttered background, we segment the given test image to extract the required object from the cluttered background (selective visual attention) and then recognize it. In segmentation phase, GrabCut [19] is used to extract the required foreground image from background with minimum user interaction. Results are shown in Fig. 11(a) and 11(b) for two different objects with varying background. Failures in segmentation can occur in two cases (i) regions of low contrast at the transition from foreground to background (ii) camouflage, in which the true foreground and background distributions overlap partially in color space (iii) background material inside the user rectangle but not belonging to the object of interest. Recognition is then performed using the technique explained in Fig. 1. The proposed approach gives good results in recognizing objects from highly cluttered backgrounds. We have tested our approach on 10 cluttered scene images. Fig. 11 shows the scenes, the extracted foreground object and the recognized object from the gallery.

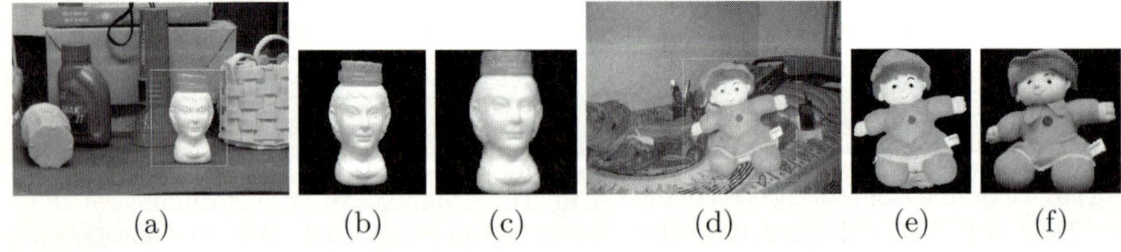

(a)   (b)   (c)   (d)   (e)   (f)

Fig. 11. (a) and (d) Cluttered scenes with user selected ROI. (b) and (e) Extracted object using GrabCut. (c) and (f) Recognized object from IGOIL.

Table 1. Comparison of recognition accuracies of D_{2DPCA}, D_{ICA}, D_{comb}, D_ξ, D_ρ and D_λ on IGOIL database with number of independent components=45 and number of eigenvectors for 2DPCA=15 using 160 test samples (8 test samples per object)

Pose Interval	Recognition Criterion					
	D_{2DPCA}	D_{ICA}	D_{comb}	D_ξ	D_ρ	D_λ
10	98.75	98.75	98.75	99.375	99.375	**99.688**
15	96.25	95.875	96.875	95.938	96.25	**96.875**
20	92.813	95.625	95.625	95.625	96.563	**96.563**
25	91.25	91.875	91.875	92.5	91.875	**92.813**
30	90.625	91.563	91.75	93.438	92.813	**93.75**

Table 2. Comparison of Recognition Rates of 1D PCA, 2D PCA, SVM, ICA and proposed framework (with D_λ as distance measure) on COIL-100 Database with 10 degree pose interval (36 training samples per object for training)

Technique	Reference	No. of Objects	No. of Test Samples	%Accuracy
IDPCA	[1]	20^a	720	100
2DPCA	[2]	20^a	720	100
		100^b	400	96.375
			3600	95.468
SVM	[7]	32^a	1152	96.03
ICA		100^b	400	97
			3600	96.639
Proposed (D_λ)		100	400	**98.25**
			3600	**97.694**

[a]results reported in literature; [b]our implementation

4   Conclusion

We present an efficient framework to Generic Object Recognition from arbitrary viewpoints using a combination of appearance and shape features. We use a fusion of two linear subspace analysis (2D PCA and ICA) techniques to reduce the search space to a few objects and then select the closest match using a sum of distances in linear subspace and DT based shape matching. The proposed method outperforms the recognition accuracy of the existing schemes of using only 1D PCA, 2D PCA and SVM for object recognition and also can capture the appearance manifold set of objects along multiple axes. There is however, a scope for analysis of the performance of the proposed technique for generic object recognition in presence of illumination variance and occlusion.

References

1. Murase, H., Nayar, S.: Visual Learning and recognition of 3-D Objects from Appearance. International Journal of Computer Vision **14** (1995) 5–24
2. Nagabhushan, P., Guru, D., Shekar, B.: Visual Learning and recognition of 3-D Objects from Appearance using two-dimensional principal components analysis : A robust and an efficient approach. Pattern Recognition **39** (2006) 721–725
3. Rosin, P.L., Marshall, D.: Object recognition using local affine frames on distinguished regions. In: Proceedings of the British Machine Vision Conference, London, UK. (2002) 113–122
4. Rothganger, F., Lazebnik, S., Schmid, C., Ponce, J.: 3D Object Modeling and Recognition Using Local Affine-Invariant Image Descriptors and Multi-View Spatial Constraints. International Journal of Computer Vision **66** (2006)
5. Biederman, I.: Recognition by Components: A theory of Human Image Understanding. Psychological Review **94** (1987) 115–147
6. Leonardis, A., Bischof, H.: Robust recognition using eigenimages. Computer Vision and Image Understanding **78** (2000) 99–118
7. Pontil, M., Verri, A.: Support Vector Machines for 3D Object Recognition. IEEE Transactions on Pattern Analysis and Machine Intelligence **20** (1998) 637–646
8. Zhang, H., Berg, A., Mair, M., Malik, J.: SVM-KNN: Discriminative Nearest Neighbor Classification for Visual Category Recognition. In: Computer Vision and Pattern Recognition. Volume 2. (2006) 2126–2136
9. Belongie, Puzicha, J., Malik, J.: Shape Matching and Object Recognition using Shape Contexts. IEEE transactions on Pattern Analysis and Machine Intelligence **24** (2002) 509–522
10. Bohm, J., Bernner, C., Guhring, J., Fritsch, D.: Automated Extraction of features from CAD models for 3-D object recognition. In: International Society for Photogrammetry and Remote Sensing Congress, Amsterdam, Netherlands. Volume 33. (2000)
11. Edelman, S., Buelthoff, H.: Orientation dependence in the recognition of familiar and novel views of three dimensional objects. Vision Research **32** (1992) 2385–2400
12. Kanwisher, N.: Domain Specificity in face perception. Nature Neuroscience **3** (2000) 759–776
13. Hyvarinen, A.: Fast and Robust Fixed-Point Algorithms for Independent Component Analysis. IEEE Trans. on Neural Networks **10** (1999) 626–634
14. Zhang, J.Y., Frangi, A.F., Yang, J.Y.: Two-Dimensional PCA: A New Approach to Appearance-Based Face Representation and Recognition. IEEE Tran. on Pattern Analysis and Machine Intelligence **26** (2004) 131–137
15. Kittler, J., Duin, P., Matas, J.: On Combining Classifiers. IEEE Transactions on Pattern Analysis and Machine Intelligence **20** (1998) 226–239
16. Sanjay, M., Das, S., Yegnanarayana, B.: Robust Template Matching for noisy bitmap images invariant to translation and rotation. In: Indian Conference on Computer Vision, Graphics and Image Processing, New Delhi, India. (1998) 82–84
17. Nene, S.A., Nayar, S.K., Murase, H.: COIL 100 Database (1996) `http://www1.cs.columbia.edu/CAVE/research/softlib/coil-100.html`.
18. Kalra, M., Das, S.: IITM Generic Object Image Library (2006) `http://vplab.cs.iitm.ernet.in/downloads.html`.
19. Rother, C., Kolomogorov, V., Blake, A.: GrabCut- Interactive Foreground extraction using iterated Graph Cuts. ACM transactions on Graphics (SIGGRAPH) (2004) 309–314

A Profilometric Approach to 3D Face Reconstruction and Its Application to Face Recognition

Surath Raj Mitra and K.R. Ramakrishnan

Indian Institute of Science

Abstract. 3D Face Recognition is an active area of research for past several years. For a 3D face recognition system one would like to have an accurate as well as low cost setup for constructing 3D face model. In this paper, we use Profilometry approach to obtain a 3D face model. This method gives a low cost solution to the problem of acquiring 3D data and the 3D face models generated by this method are sufficiently accurate. We also develop an algorithm that can use the 3D face model generated by the above method for the recognition purpose.

1   Introduction

Face Recognition is a very old research problem. For the last 30 years numerous methods have been proposed by the researchers from several different fields to solve this problem [1]. Though a considerable amount of success has been achieved, still there exist a lot of unsolved questions.

A large number of techniques exist for face recognition from still images. In [2], Turk and Pentland have used that Principal Component Analysis for face recognition. Elastic bunch graph matching [3] is another interesting approach. Here each face is represented as a graph and face recognition is based on the graph similarity. In [4], Cootes et al. proposed Active appearance model (AAM) for face recognition. An AAM combines the statistical model of the appearance and shape variation in a shape normalized from.

Recently 3D face recognition has gained a significant attention among the researchers in this field. Intutively a 3D face recognition system should perform better than a 2D face recognition system as face is inherently a 3D object. In [5], Lee and Milios have used Extended Gaussian Image (EGI) based approach for 3D face recognition. Medioni and Waupotitsch [6] proposed to solve the 3D face recognition problem using iterative closest point (ICP) matching of face surfaces. A review of the 3D face recognition systems can be found in [7]. An important problem in a 3D face recognition system is the generation of an accurate 3D model. Generally laser scanners (which are very costly) are used to capture 3D model. On the other hand one can use fringe projection techniques to capture the 3D information.

Fringe projection techniques has been extensively used in industry for the purpose of 3D measurements. One of the popular fringe projection techniques

P. Kalra and S. Peleg (Eds.): ICVGIP 2006, LNCS 4338, pp. 631–640, 2006.

is Fourier Transform Profilometry(FTP) [8]. In FTP, a sinusoidal or rectangular fringe pattern is projected on to the object from an offset angle and the image of the deformed fringe pattern which is phase modulated by the topographical variations of the object surface is captured. Then the phase is extracted from the deformed fringe pattern using Fourier transform analysis. The recovered phase is limited in the interval $[-\pi, \pi]$. This is called the wrapped phase map. Phase unwrapping technique is used to get the natural phase distribution from the wrapped phase. Unwrapping process refers to adding an appropriate integer multiple of 2π to each pixel element of the wrapped phase map. Phase unwrapping should be path independent for a perfect phase map. But, local shadows or low fringe modulation, irregular surface brightness, fringe discontinuities makes phase unwrapping a path dependent problem. One popular approach for phase unwrapping is based on reliability-guided parameter map.A recent review on reliability guided phase unwrapping algorithms can be found in [9]. The unwrapped phase-map so obtained by the phase unwrapping algorithm is proportional to the height variations of the object surface.

In this paper Fourier Transform Profilometry(FTP) [8] method is used to generate a dense depth map of human face to pixel level accuracy as the phase is estimated for each pixel by a Fourier Transform. Then 2D face image estimate (i.e. the image of face without fringe pattern) is generated from the input fringe image. The 3D model of the human face along with the 2D face image estimate is then used for the purpose of the face recognition.

The rest of the paper is organized as follows: In section 2 we describe the basic theory of the Fourier Transform Profilometry(FTP). In this section we also describe the results obtained by the FTP method. In section 3 we describe the Face Recognition algorithm. In section 4 summary and the future work is discussed.

2   3D Face Reconstruction Using Fourier Transform Profilometry

In Fourier Transform Profilometry(FTP) [8],[10],[11] a sinusoidal fringe pattern is projected on a 3D object and resulting image is captured by a CCD camera. The height distribution of the three dimensional object results in phase modulation.The phase contains the information about the object profile. In FTP,Fourier analysis is used to get the phase map from the fringe image. In our experiments, we have used the human face as the three dimensional object. Though the FTP is widely used in industry, it has never been used in human 3D face reconstruction.In the next subsection we will describe the basic theory of FTP.

2.1   Theory of Fourier Transform Profilometry [8]

Takeda et al. introduced FTP in [8]. General optical geometry for Fourier transform profilometry is shown in the figure 1. This is called crossed optical axes geometry. In the figure 1, $E'_p E_p$ is the optical axis of the projector lens and

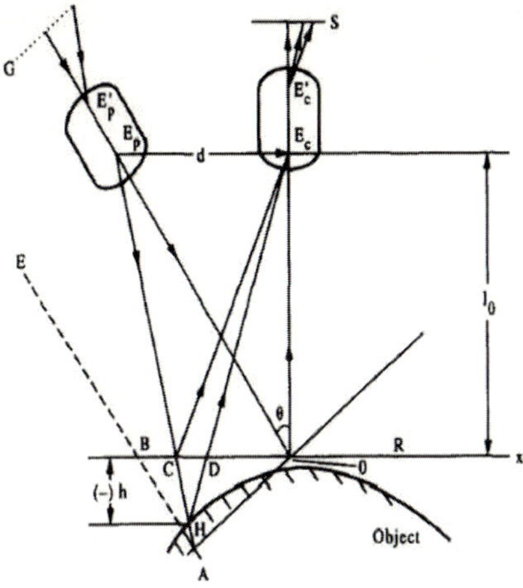

Fig. 1. Optical geometry of FTP[from [8]]

$E'_c E_c$ is the optical axis of the camera lens and R is the reference plane. The reference plane R is a fictitious plane and serves as reference from which object height is measured. The image of a perfectly flat and uniform reference plane (i.e. the height distribution is zero) with fringe pattern projected on it can be expressed as,

$$g_0(x, y) = \sum_{n=-\infty}^{\infty} A_n \exp\{i[2\pi n f_0 x + n\phi_0(x, y)]\} \tag{1}$$

When the measured object (in our case, human face) is put on the reference plane, the deformed fringe pattern observed can be expressed as:

$$g(x, y) = r(x, y) \sum_{n=-\infty}^{\infty} A_n \exp\{i[2\pi n f_o x + n\phi(x, y)]\} \tag{2}$$

where f_0 is the fundamental frequency of the observed fringe image, $\phi(x, y)$ and $\phi_0(x, y)$ are the the phase modulation due to object height distribution and the phase modulation for reference plane (when object height distribution is zero) respectively, r(x, y) and A_n are the non uniform distribution of reflectivity on the object surface and the weighting factors of the Fourier series respectively. $\phi(x, y)$ contains the information about object profile.

In the FTP method, 1D Fourier transform of (2) is calculated. The Fourier spectra obtained is shown in the figure 2. The Fourier transform is calculated with respect to the variable x and the other variable y is treated as a fixed parameter. $r(x, y)$ and $\phi(x, y)$ are assumed to vary very slowly compared to the frequency f_0 of the fringe pattern. Using a suitable filter function only the

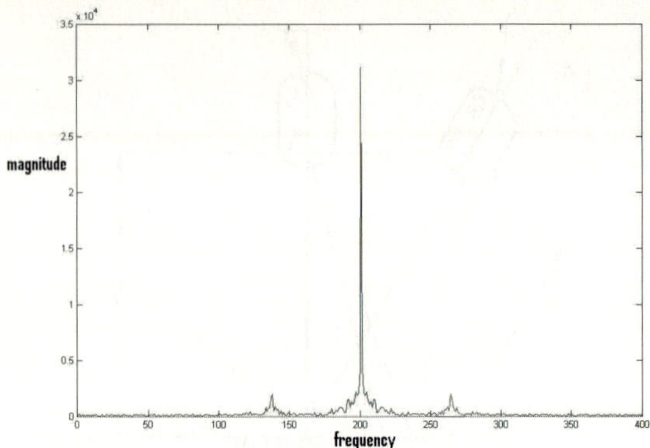

Fig. 2. Spatial frequency spectra of a deformed fringe image for a fixed value of y

fundamental spectrum is selected(shown as red in the figure 2). Applying inverse Fourier transform on the fundamental spectrum,we get,

$$g'(x, y) = A_1 r(x, y) \exp\{i[2\pi f_0 x + \phi(x, y)]\} \tag{3}$$

The same operation on (1) gives,

$$g'_0(x, y) = A_1 \exp\{i[2\pi f_0 x + \phi_0(x, y)]\} \tag{4}$$

Then the phase change ($\triangle\phi(x, y)$) is given by,

$$\triangle\phi(x, y) = \phi(x, y) - \phi_0(x, y) \tag{5}$$

From (3) and (4) $\triangle\phi(x, y)$ is obtained as,

$$\triangle\phi(x, y) = Im(\log(g'(x, y)g'_0{}^*(x, y))) \tag{6}$$

where * denote the conjugate operation.

$\triangle\phi(x, y)$ is approximately proportional to the height variation and thus it is the measure of the object height distribution. The phase calculated here is the wrapped phase. Using phase unwrapping algorithm, we can get the natural phase distribution. In our work we have used zpm [12] algorithm for phase unwrapping.

2.2   Results of FTP

The experimental setup consists of a LCD projector and a CCD camera. Sinusoidal fringe patterns are projected on the face of a subject using the LCD projector and the CCD camera is used to capture the image of the fringe deformation on the face. Figure 3 shows input fringe pattern which is a sinusoidal fringe pattern. The fringe pattern we are using varies only in the vertical direction. So Fourier transform is applied on each column (scan line) of the image. Figure 4 shows different steps in FTP. Figure 4(a) shows the input fringe image. Figure 4(b) shows the wrapped phase map. The gray value at a pixel in the figure 4(b) is proportional to the phase at that pixel. Figure 4(c) shows the unwrapped phase map. Figure 4(d) shows the 3D mesh plot of $\triangle\phi(x, y)$. Figure 5 shows two views of the generated 3D model.

Fig. 3. Input fringe pattern

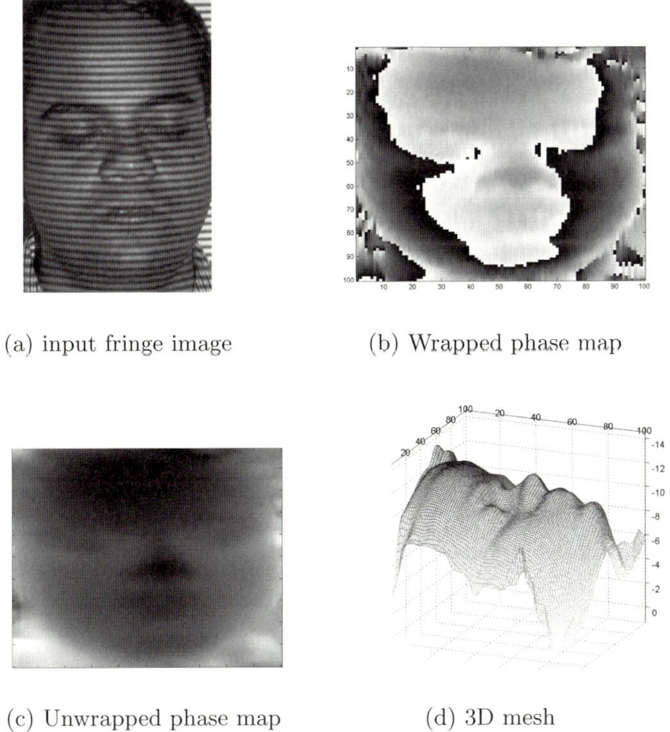

(a) input fringe image   (b) Wrapped phase map

(c) Unwrapped phase map   (d) 3D mesh

Fig. 4. Results of different steps in FTP

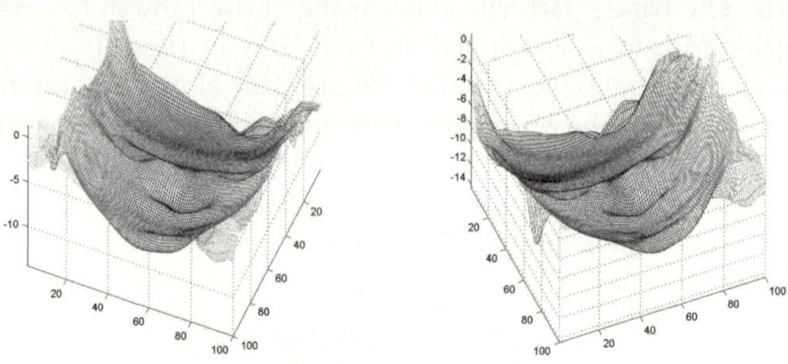

Fig. 5. Two views of generated 3D model

3   A Multimodal(2D+3D) Face Recognition System

The face recognition method we have developed uses both 2D and 3D features. The 3D feature is obtained from the 3D face model that we have generated using FTP. In order to get the 2D feature, we need to generate the 2D face image estimate(i.e. the image of face without fringe pattern) from the input face image with fringe projection. The advantage of generating the 2D image estimate is that the position of the face in the estimated image will be same as that in the 3D model. This will help us in placing the facial grid on both the 3D model and the 2D image estimate which is described latter.

3.1   Estimation of 2D Face Image

For 2D face image estimation we assume that the texture of the face does not have any repetitive patterns comparable to the frequency of the sinusoidal fringe, which in general is true. With this assumption the 2D face image estimate can be done by simple low pass filtering operation. Therefore, we need to separate the low frequency components from the high frequency components those are present in the image after fringe projection. In other words, we need to extract the envelope of the modulated sine wave. This will give us the estimate of the 2D face image. This process is done along each color channel to get a full color estimate of 2D face. Then this is converted to the gray scale as 2D features are extracted from the gray scale image. Figure 6 shows the result of the 2D image estimation.

3.2   Face Recognition Algorithm

The first step in our algorithm is the detection of the nose tip location [13]. Locating nose tip is very easy from the 3D face model. Since our 3D model gives the relative height distribution of the face, the nose tip has always maximum height. So, we just have to find the point with maximum height in the 3D face model. After locating the position of the nose tip the start and the end of the

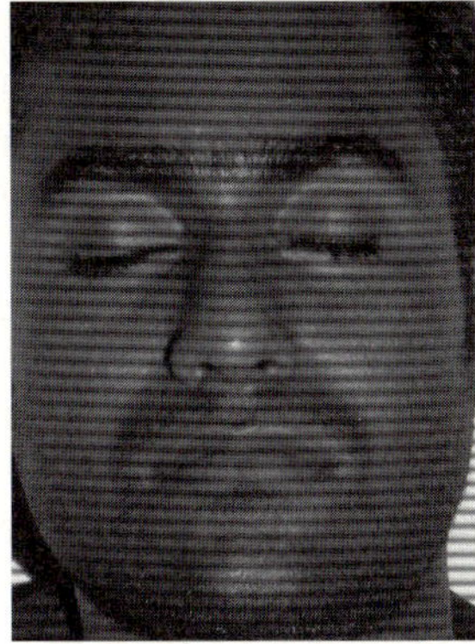 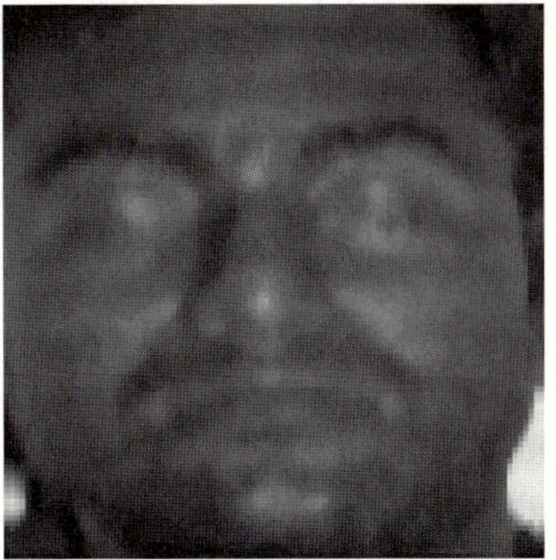

Fig. 6. Result of the 2D image estimation

nose (which approximately points to the eye location and the mouth location respectively) are found. With respect to the nose tip position a facial grid is formed to cover the eye, nose and the mouth portion of the face. Figure 7 shows a subject from our face database with facial grid on the unwrapped phase map as well as on the 2D image estimate.

In order to get the 2D feature, the 2D face image is convolved with the 2D Gabor wavelets [14][3]. The Gabor wavelets (kernels, filters) is defined as follows,

$$\Psi_{\mu,\nu}(z) = (\frac{\parallel k_{\mu,\nu} \parallel^2}{\sigma^2})e^{-(\frac{\parallel k_{\mu,\nu}\parallel^2 \parallel z \parallel^2}{2\sigma^2})}[e^{ik_{\mu,\nu}z} - e^{-(\frac{\sigma^2}{2})}] \tag{7}$$

where μ and ν denote the orientation and scale of the Gabor kernels respectively. $z = (x, y)$, $\parallel \parallel$ denotes the norm operator, and the wave vector $k_{\mu,\nu}$ can be defined as follows,

$$k_{\mu,\nu} = k_\nu e^{i\phi_\mu}$$

where, $k_\nu = \frac{k_{max}}{f^\nu}$, $\phi_\mu = \frac{\pi\mu}{8}$ and f is the the spacing factor between kernels in the frequency domain. The estimated 2D face image is convolved with the Gabor filters.Then for all the points in the facial grid the absolute magnitudes of the complex-valued filter responses are concatenated to form a 2D feature vector (v_t).

In order to get the 3D depth/shape feature, for each point in the facial grid we have considered its eight neighborhood points. Then the mean and the variance of the local height distribution is calculated as,

$$mean = (\frac{1}{8}) \sum_{i=1}^{8}(d_n - d_i) \tag{8}$$

$$variance = (\frac{1}{8}) \sum_{i=1}^{8}(mean - (d_n - d_i))^2 \tag{9}$$

where d_i is the height of a neighborhood point and d_n is the height of the nose tip point. Here by height we mean the value of $\phi(x, y)$ at a facial grid point. So for each facial grid point we have two depth feature. The 3D feature vector (v_d) is obtained by concatenating the mean and variance feature for all the facial grid points.

Given a test 3D face model and its 2D image estimation we form corresponding 2D feature vector (v_t) and 3D feature vector (v_d). Then the nearest neighbor classification rule is applied. In the Nearest neighbor procedure, the closest Euclidean distance match of a test face to the faces in the training set is determined. Then the level of the closest match training face is assigned to the test face. The Euclidean distance between a test face and a training face is given by,

$$D^2 = \alpha \parallel (v_t - (v_t)_k) \parallel^2 + \beta \parallel (v_d - (v_d)_k) \parallel^2 \qquad (10)$$

where $(v_t)_k$ and $(v_d)_k$ are the 2D and the 3D feature vector describing the kth training face and α, β are suitably chosen weights.

3.3   Experiments and Results

In order to test the performance of our face recognition algorithm we have collected a database of 13 persons. Each person has two images on the database, one of which is used for training and other for testing. Each face image is collected after projecting a sinusoidal fringe pattern on the face. Fourier transform analysis is carried out on each of the captured image to get the phase distribution. This phase distribution gives us the estimate of height distribution on the face and hence the 3D model. We have also computed the 2D face image estimation for each of the captured fringe image. Then a facial grid is placed on the 2D image estimate and on the 3D model. The number of facial grid point considered is 160. Then the face recognition algorithm is applied on this database. We have used Gabor wavelets at five different scales, $\nu = \{0, ..., 4\}$ and eight orientations, $\mu = \{0, ..., 7\}$. In our experiment we have used 1 and .1 as the value of α and

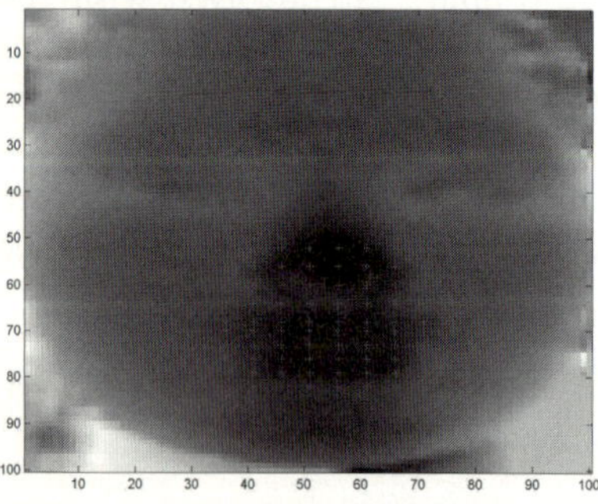

(a)facial grid on unwrapped phase map

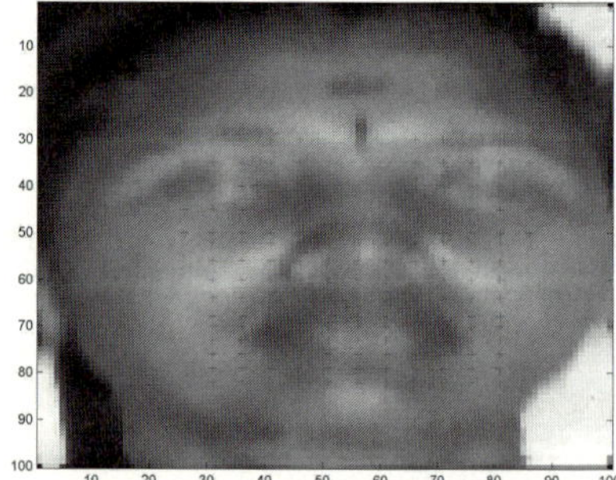

(b)facial grid on 2D image estimate

Fig. 7. A subject with facial grid

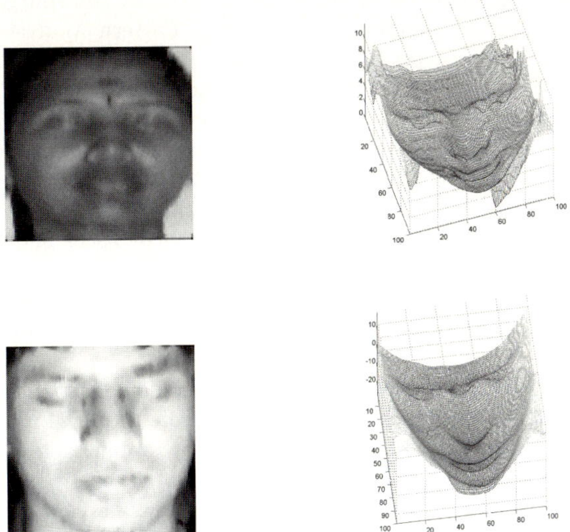

Fig. 8. 2 subjects from the face database

β respectively. An accuracy of more than 90% is obtained in our experiment. Figure 7(a) and 7(b) show a subject from our face database with facial grid on the unwrapped phase map as well as on the 2D image estimate respectively. Figure 8 shows 2 subjects from our database with corresponding 3D models.

4   Summary and Future Work

In this paper we use FTP to construct the 3D model of human face. This method needs only a LCD projector and a CCD camera to acquire the 3D data. These instruments are very cheap and easily available. Thus the FTP approach shows a way to reduce the cost associated with the 3D face data acquisition. In this paper we also propose a multimodal Face Recognition algorithm. However the algorithm is tested only on a small dataset. It needs to be tested on a larger dataset to really bring out the efficacy of this approach for face recognition. So our future work includes collection of a large amount of dataset and testing our approach on that dataset.

References

1. W. Zhao, R. Chellappa, and A. Rosenfeld, Face recognition: a literature survey, ACM Computing Surveys, vol. 35, no. 4, pp. 399-458, December 2003.
2. M. Turk and A. Pentland, Eigenfaces for recognition, Journal of Cognitive Neuroscience, vol. 3, no. 1, pp. 71-86, 1991.

3. L. Wiskott, J.M. Fellous, N. Kruger, and C. von der Malsburg, Face recognition by elastic bunch graph matching, IEEE Trans. Pattern Analysis and Machine Intelligence, vol. 19, no. 7, pp.775-779, 1997.
4. T. F. Cootes, G. J. Edwards and C. J. Taylor, Active appearance models, IEEE Trans. Pattern Analysis and Machine Intelligence 23, pp.681-685, 2001.
5. J. C. Lee and E. Milios, Matching range images of human faces, International Conference on ComputerVision, pp. 722-726, 1990.
6. G. Medioni and R. Waupotitsch, Face recognition and modeling in 3d. IEEE International Workshop on Analysis and Modeling of Faces and Gestures (AMFG 2003), p. 232.233, October 2003.
7. K. W. Bowyer, K. Chang, and P. Flynn. A Survey Of 3D and Multi-Modal 3D+2D Face Recognition, In International Conference on Pattern Recognition (ICPR) 2004.
8. M. Takeda and K. Mouth, Fourier transform profilometry for the automatic measurement of 3-d object shapes, Applied Optics, vol. 22, no. 24, pp. 3977-3982, 1983.
9. X. Su and W. Chen, Reliability guided phase unwrapping algorithm-a review, Opt and Laser Eng, vol. 42, pp. 245-261, 2004.
10. X. Su and W. Chen, Fourier transform profilometry: a review, Opt Laser Eng, vol. 35, pp. 263-284, 2001.
11. J. Li, X. Y. Su, and L. Guo, Improved fourier transform profilometry for the automatic measurement of 3d object shapes, Optical Engineering, vol. 29, no. 12, p. 1439, December 1990.
12. J. Dias and J. Leitao, The zpm algorithm for interferometric image reconstruction in sar/sas, IEEE Transactions on Image processing, vol. 11, no. 4, pp. 408-422, 2002.
13. Y. Lee, T. Yi, 3D face recognition using multiple features for local depth information, 4th EURASIP Conference focused on Video I Imaae Pmcessina and Multimedia Communications, 2-5 July 2003, Zagreb, Croatia
14. C. Liu and H. Wechsler, Independent component analysis of gabor features for face recognition, IEEE Trans. Neural Networks, vol. 14, no. 4, pp. 919-928, July 2003.

Face Recognition Technique Using Symbolic Linear Discriminant Analysis Method

P.S. Hiremath[1] and Prabhakar C.J.[2]

[1] Department of Studies in Computer Science, Gulbarga University,
Gulbarga – 585106, Karnataka, India
`hiremathps@yahoo.co.in`
[2] Department of Studies in Computer Science, Kuvempu University,
Shankaraghatta – 577451, Karnataka, India
`psajjan@yahoo.com`

Abstract. Techniques that can introduce low dimensional feature representation with enhanced discriminatory power are important in face recognition systems. This paper presents one of the symbolic factor analysis method i.e., symbolic Linear Discriminant Analysis (symbolic LDA) method for face representation and recognition. Classical factor analysis methods extract features, which are single valued in nature to represent face images. These single valued variables may not be able to capture variation of each feature in all the images of same subject; this leads to loss of information. The symbolic Linear Discriminant Analysis Algorithm extracts most discriminating interval type features; they optimally discriminate among the classes represented in the training set. The proposed method has been successfully tested for face recognition using two databases, ORL and Yale Face database. The effectiveness of the proposed method is shown in terms of comparative performance against popular classical factor analysis methods such as eigenface method and Linear Discriminant Analysis method. Experimental results show that symbolic LDA outperforms the classical factor analysis methods.

1   Introduction

Feature extraction has been the most fundamental and important in face recognition and other recognition problems. The main objective of research on face recognition problem is to find a technique that can introduce low dimensional feature representation of face objects with enhanced discriminatory power. Among various solutions to this problem, the most successful are those appearance-based approaches [4][5][19][26][27]. Principal Component Analysis (PCA) is a well known appearance based technique, Kirby and Sirovich [14] are among the first who used this technique directly on the characterization of human faces and showed that PCA is an optimal compression scheme that minimizes the mean squared error between the original images and their reconstructions for any given level of compression. Turk and Pentland [22] popularized the use of PCA for face recognition; they used PCA to compute a set of subspace basis vectors (which they called eigenfaces) for a database of face

P. Kalra and S. Peleg (Eds.): ICVGIP 2006, LNCS 4338, pp. 641 – 649, 2006.

images. Grudin [11] showed that the correlation between images of the whole faces is not efficient for satisfactory recognition performance. Illumination normalization is usually necessary for the eigenface approach. Zhao and Yang proposed a new method to compute the covariance matrix using three images each taken in different lighting conditions to account for arbitrary illumination effects. Bartlett et al., [2] proposed using Independent Component Analysis (ICA) for face representation and found that it was better than PCA when cosines were used as the similarity measure. ICA improves upon the PCA scheme by considering higher order statistics and ICA searches for a linear transformation to express a set of random variables as linear combinations of statistically independent source variables. Yang [24] used Kernel PCA for face feature extraction and recognition and showed that the kernel eigenfaces method outperforms the classical eigenfaces method. However, ICA and Kernel PCA are both computationally more expensive than PCA. Swets and Weng [21] present a method to selecting discriminant eigenfeatures using multidimensional linear discriminant analysis (LDA). LDA [25] based algorithms outperform PCA based ones, since the former optimizes the low-dimensional representation of the objects with focus on the Most Discriminant Features (MDFs) extraction while the latter achieves simply object reconstruction. PCA based technique produce a set of Most Expressive Features (MEFs); the features produced are not necessarily good for discriminating among classes defined by the set of samples. The MEFs describe some major variations in the class, such as those due to lighting direction; these variations may well be irrelevant to how the classes are divided. Recently, many appearance-based algorithms have been proposed [9][16][17][18][23][24][27].

The defining characteristic of these classical appearance-based algorithms is that they directly use the pixel intensity values in a face image as the features on which to base the recognition decision. The pixel intensities that are used as features are represented using single valued variables. However, in many situations same face is captured under different orientations, lighting conditions, expressions and backgrounds, which lead to image variations. The corresponding pixel intensities do change because of image variations. The use of single valued variables may not be able to capture the variation of feature values of the images of the same subject. In such a case, we need to consider the symbolic data analysis (SDA) [1][8][15], in which the interval-valued data are analyzed. We have focused our research towards extracting interval type features to represent face images, which are robust to variations due to illumination, orientation and facial expression. In [12], a Symbolic Principal Component Analysis (symbolic PCA) approach for face recognition is presented, in which symbolic PCA is employed to compute a set of subspace basis vectors for symbolic faces and then project the symbolic faces into the compressed subspace. This method requires a small number of features to achieve the same recognition rate as compared to eigenface method. The symbolic PCA technique, however, encodes only for second order statistics, i.e., pixel wise covariance among the pixels, and does not address high-order statistical dependencies such as the relationships among three or more pixels. As these second order statistics provide only partial information on the statistics of both natural images and human faces, it might become necessary to incorporate higher order statistics as well. The kernel PCA [20][24] is capable of deriving low dimensional features that incorporate higher order statistics. Higher order dependencies in an image include nonlinear relations among the pixel intensity values, such as the relationships among three or more pixels in an edge or a curve, which can capture important information for recognition. The kernel PCA is extended to symbolic data analysis as symbolic KPCA [13] for face recognition and the experimental results show improved recognition rate as compared to the symbolic PCA method.

In this paper, symbolic LDA method is presented, which is generalization of the classical linear discriminant analysis to symbolic objects for face recognition. In the first phase, we represent the face images as symbolic objects (symbolic faces) of interval type variables. The representation of face images as symbolic faces accounts for image variations of human faces under different lighting conditions, orientations and facial expressions. It also drastically reduces the dimension of the image space without losing a significant amount of information. Each symbolic face summarizes the variation of feature values through the different images of the same subject. In the second phase, we have applied the proposed symbolic LDA on the symbolic faces and linearly derives low dimensional most discriminant interval type features. Finally, a minimum distance classifier with Minkowsky's symbolic dissimilarity measure proposed by De Carvalho and Diday [1] is employed for classification. The proposed method has been successfully tested using two standard databases ORL and Yale Face database.

The remainder of this paper is organized as follows: the construction of symbolic faces is described in section 2. In section 3, extraction of most discriminant interval type features from symbolic faces is presented. The comparison results are presented in the section 4. Finally, a conclusion is drawn in the section 5.

2 Extraction of Symbolic Faces

Let $\Omega = \{\Gamma_1, \ldots, \Gamma_n\}$ be the collection of n face images of the database, each of size $N \times M$. An image set is a collection of face images of m different subjects (face class) denoted by $E = \{c_1, c_2, \ldots, c_m\}$. We have assumed that images belonging to a face class are arranged from right side view to left side view. The view range of each face class is partitioned into q sub face classes and each sub face class contains r number of images. The feature vector of kth sub face class c_i^k of ith face class c_i, where $k = 1, 2, \ldots, q,$ is described by a vector of p interval variables $Y_1, \ldots, Y_p$, and is of length $p = NM$. The interval variable Y_j of kth sub face class c_i^k of ith face class is described as $Y_j(c_i^k) = [\underline{x}_{ij}^k, \overline{x}_{ij}^k]$, where $\underline{x}_{ij}^k$ and $\overline{x}_{ij}^k$ are minimum and maximum intensity values, respectively, among j^{th} pixels of all the images of sub face class c_i^k. The vector X_i^k of interval variables is recorded for k^{th} sub face class c_i^k of ith face class. This vector is called as *symbolic face*.

We denote

$$X_i^k = \left(Y_1\left(c_i^k\right), ..., Y_p\left(c_i^k\right)\right), i=1,...,m, \ k=1,...,q, \ j=1,...,p.$$ (1)

We represent the qm symbolic faces by a matrix X of size $(p \times qm)$, consisting of column vectors X_i^k, $i=1,...,m, \ k=1,...,q$.

3 Extraction of Most Discriminant Interval Type Features

Let us consider the matrix X containing qm symbolic faces pertaining to the given set Ω of images belonging to m face classes. The centers [6] [7] $x_{ij}^{k^C} \in \Re$ of the intervals $[\underline{x}_{ij}^k, \overline{x}_{ij}^{-k}]$, are given by:

$$x_{ij}^{k^C} = \frac{\overline{x}_{ij}^{k} + \underline{x}_{ij}^{k}}{2}$$ (2)

where $\ i=1,...,m \ \ and \ \ j=1,...,p.$

The $p \times qm$ data matrix X^C containing the centers $x_{ij}^{k^C} \in \Re$ of the intervals for qm symbolic   faces.   The p-dimensional   vectors $X_i^{k^C} = \left(x_{i1}^{k^C}, ..., x_{ip}^{k^C} \right)$, $\underline{X}_i^k = \left(\underline{x}_{i1}^k, ..., \underline{x}_{ip}^k \right)$ and $\overline{X}_i^k = \left(\overline{x}_{i1}^{-k}, ..., \overline{x}_{ip}^{-k} \right)$ represent the centers, lower bounds and upper bounds of the qm symbolic faces X_i^k, respectively. There are m face classes denoted by $E = \{c_1, c_2, ..., c_m\}$, each class c_i contains q_i, $i=1,2,...,m$, number of symbolic faces.

The mean M_i of class c_i is calculated as

$$M_i = \frac{1}{q_i} \sum_{k=1}^{q_i} X_i^{k^C}$$ (3)

where q_i is number of symbolic faces of class c_i.

Similarly the grand mean vector of all qm symbolic faces from all classes is defined as

$$M = \frac{1}{qm} \sum_{L=1}^{qm} X_i^{k^C}, \ for \ \ i=1,...,m, \ \ and \ k=1,...,q.$$ (4)

The within class scatter matrix S_w is defined as

$$S_w = \sum_{i=1}^{m} \sum_{k=1}^{q_i} \left[(X_i^{k^C} - M_i)^T \right]\left[(X_i^{k^C} - M_i) \right]$$ (5)

The between class scatter matrix S_b is defined as

$$S_b = \sum_{i=1}^{m} \left[(M_i - M)^T \right] \left[(M_i - M) \right] \tag{6}$$

where M_i is mean of class c_i $(i = 1, \ldots, m)$.

In discriminant analysis, we want to determine the projection axis W that maximizes the ratio $\dfrac{\det\{S_b\}}{\det\{S_w\}}$. In other words, we want to maximize the between-class scatter matrix while minimizing the within-class scatter matrix. It has been proven (Fisher and Loeve) [10] that this ratio is maximized when the column vectors of projection axis W is the eigenvector of $S_w^{-1} S_b$ associated with the largest eigenvalue.

We need a set of projection axes, $W_1, \ldots, W_d$, which are eigenvectors of $S_w^{-1} S_b$ corresponding to first d largest eigenvalues. The optimal discriminant projection axes, $W_1, \ldots, W_d$ are used for feature extraction.

Since, each symbolic face X_i^k is located between the lower bound symbolic face $\underline{X}_i^k$ and upper bound symbolic face $\overline{X}_i^k$, so it is possible to find most discriminating interval type features $[B_i^k, \overline{B}_i^k]$.

The lower bound features of each symbolic face X_i^k is given by

$$\underline{B}_i^k = W_l^T \underline{X}_i^k \quad , \; l = 1, \, 2, \ldots, \, d \tag{7}$$

for $i = 1, \ldots, m, \; k = 1, \ldots, q$.

Similarly the upper bound features of each symbolic face X_i^k is given by

$$\overline{B}_i^k = W_l^T \overline{X}_i^k \quad , \; l = 1, \, 2, \ldots, \, d \tag{8}$$

Let $c_{test} = [\Gamma_1, \Gamma_2, \ldots, \Gamma_l]$ be the test face class contains face images of same subject with different expression, lighting condition and orientation. The test symbolic face X_{test} is constructed for test face class c_{test} as explained in the section 2. The lower bound test symbolic face of test symbolic face X_{test} is described as $\underline{X}_{test} = \left(\underline{x}_1^{test}, \underline{x}_2^{test}, \ldots, \underline{x}_p^{test} \right)$. Similarly, the upper bound test symbolic face is described as $\overline{X}_{test} = \left(\overline{x}_1^{test}, \overline{x}_2^{test}, \ldots, \overline{x}_p^{test} \right)$.

The interval type features $[\underline{B}^{test}, \overline{B}^{test}]$ of test symbolic face X_{test} are computed as:

$$\underline{B}^{test} = W_l^T \underline{X}_{test}, \tag{9}$$

$$\overline{B}^{test} = W_l^T \overline{X}_{test}, \tag{10}$$

where $l = 1, \, 2, \ldots, \, d$.

3.1 Face Recognition Based on a Minimum Distance Classifier

When test face class c_{test} is presented to the symbolic LDA classifier, low dimensional interval features $[\underline{B}^{test}, \overline{B}^{test}]$ are derived. Let, $[\underline{B}_i^k, \overline{B}_i^k]$, $i = 1,\ldots,m,\ k = 1,\ldots,q$, be the interval features of qm symbolic faces. The classifier applies the minimum distance rule for classification using symbolic dissimilarity measure δ:

$$\delta\left([\underline{B}^{test}, \overline{B}^{test}], [\underline{B}_i^k, \overline{B}_i^k]\right) = \min_i \ \delta\left([\underline{B}^{test}, \overline{B}^{test}], [\underline{B}_i^k, \overline{B}_i^k]\right) \to c_{test} \in c_i \quad (11)$$

The symbolic LDA interval feature vector $[\underline{B}^{test}, \overline{B}^{test}]$ is classified as belonging to the symbolic face, c_i, using appropriate symbolic dissimilarity measure δ.

4 Experimental Results

Face recognition system using symbolic LDA method identify the face by computing nearest face image for a given unknown face images using minimum distance classification rule. If our system is able to recognize given probe image is to same face image in the database then the trial is success, otherwise it is a failure. To show the significance symbolic LDA for dimensionality reduction we have chosen different sized subspaces for experiments. We assess the feasibility and performance of the proposed symbolic LDA on the face recognition task, using ORL and Yale databases, these databases contains frontal face images which were acquired under variable illumination, orientation and facial expressions. The effectiveness of proposed methods is shown in terms of comparative performance against five popular face recognition methods. In particular, we compared our algorithms with eigenfaces [22], fisherfaces [3], symbolic PCA [12], symbolic ICA and symbolic KPCA [13]. The experimentation is done on system with CPU: Pentium 2.5 GHz.

4.1 Experiments Using ORL Database

We assess the feasibility and performance of the proposed symbolic LDA on the face recognition task using ORL database. The ORL face database is composed of 400 images with ten different images for each of the 40 distinct subjects. All the images were taken against a dark homogeneous background with the subjects in an upright, frontal position, with tolerance for some tilting and rotation of up to about 20° from frontal view to left side view and right side view. There is some variation in scale of up to about 10%. The spatial and gray level resolutions of the images are 92×112 and 256, respectively. In our experiments, based on the eye positions, all the face images in the database and the query input are manually cropped to a size of 80×80. All the 400 images from the ORL database are used to evaluate the face recognition performance of proposed methods. We have manually arranged the face images of same subject from right side view to left side view. Six images are randomly chosen from the ten images available for each subject for training, while the remaining images are used to construct the test symbolic face for each trial. Fig.1 shows the some typical images of one subject of ORL database.

Fig. 1. Sample face images belonging to one subject of ORL database

Table 1. Comparison of classification performance of proposed symbolic LDA method using ORL database

Methods	Training time (sec)	Feature Dimension	Recognition Rate (%)
Fisherfaces	98	86	92.8
Eigenfaces	102	189	87.65
Symbolic PCA	38	71	94.85
Symbolic ICA	87	109	89.15
Symbolic KPCA	110	49	95.45
Symbolic LDA	19	28	97.5

Table-1 presents the experimental results for each method corresponding to ORL database. The experimental results show that the proposed method outperforms the classical factor analysis methods. Further, the symbolic LDA method achieves the better recognition rate than symbolic PCA method, symbolic ICA and symbolic KPCA method.

4.2   Experiments on the Yale Face Database

The experiments are conducted using Yale database to evaluate the excellence of the symbolic LDA for the face recognition problem. The Yale Face database consists of a total 165 images obtained from 15 different people, with 11 images from each person. The images contain variations in the following facial expressions or configurations: center-light, with glasses, happy, left light, without glasses, normal, right light, sad, sleepy, surprised and wink. We preprocessed these images by aligning and scaling them so that the distances between the eyes were the same for all images and also ensuring that the eyes occurred in the same co-ordinates of the image. The resulting image was then cropped. The final image was 128×156. The Fig.2 shows some typical images of one subject of Yale Face database.

In our experiments, 9 images are randomly chosen from each class for training, while the remaining two images are used to construct test symbolic face for each trial. The recognition rates, training time and optimal subspace dimension are listed in Table-2. From Table-2, we note that the symbolic LDA method with a smaller number of features outperforms the classical factor analysis methods with a larger number of features.

Fig. 2. Some typical images of one subject of Yale Face database

Table 2. Comparison of classification performance using Yale Face database

Methods	Training time (sec)	Feature Dimension	Recognition Rate (%)
Fisherfaces	59	23	89.85
Eigenfaces	85	110	82.04
Symbolic PCA	35	41	91.15
Symbolic ICA	43	32	92.00
Symbolic KPCA	98	56	94.55
Symbolic LDA	18	13	96.15

5 Conclusion

This paper presents symbolic LDA for face recognition. The feasibility of the symbolic LDA method has been tested successfully using standard databases, ORL and Yale Face database. The experimental results show that the proposed method achieve significantly improved recognition rates as compared to classical factor analysis methods. The proposed symbolic LDA outperforms symbolic PCA, symbolic ICA and symbolic KPCA under variable lighting conditions, orientations and expressions.

The proposed symbolic LDA has many advantages compared to classical factor analysis methods. The drawback of classical factor analysis methods is that in order to recognize a face seen from a particular pose and under a particular illumination, the face must have been previously seen under the same conditions. The symbolic LDA overcomes this limitation by representing the faces by interval type features so that even the faces seen previously in different poses, orientations and illuminations are recognized. Another important merit is that we can use more than one probe images with inherent variability of a face for face recognition. Therefore, symbolic LDA improve the recognition accuracy as compared to classical factor analysis methods at reduced computational cost. This is clearly evident from the experimental results. Further, the symbolic LDA yields significantly better results than other symbolic factor analysis methods.

References

1. Bock, H.H., Diday, E. (Eds.) 2000. Analysis of Symbolic Data. Springer Verlag.
2. Bartlett, Lades, Sejnowski: Independent component representation for face recognition, In: Proc. of the SPIE (1998) 528-539.
3. P. Belhumeur, J. Hespanha, D. Kriegman,1997. Eigenfaces vs. Fisherfaces: Recognition Using Class Specific Linear Projection. IEEE Transaction on PAMI.19 (7): 711-720.

4. Bruneli and Poggio: Face Recognition: Features versus Templates, vol -15. IEEE Trans. Pattern Analysis and Machine Intelligence, (1993)1042-1052.

5. Chellappa, Wilson, Sirohey, 1995. Human and machine recognition of faces: A survey, vol - 83(5). Proc.IEEE) 705-740,

6. Choukria, Diday, Cazes, 1995. Extension of the principal component analysis to interval data. Presented at NTTS'95: New Techniques and Technologies for statistics, Bonn.

7. Choukria, Diday, Cazes, 1998. Vertices Principal Component Analysis with an Improved Factorial Representation. In: A. Rizzi, M.Vichi, H.Bock (eds.): Advances in Data Science and Classification. Pp.397-402, Springer Verlag .

8. Diday, 1993. An Introduction to symbolic data analysis. Tutorial at IV Conf. IFCS.

9. K.Etemad and R.Chellappa, 1997. "Discriminant Analysis for Recognition of Human Face Images", J.Optical Soc. Am. vol-14, pp 1724-1733.

10. Fisher, 1938. The statistical utilization of multiple measurements, Ann. Eugenics, 8, 376-386.

11. M.A.Grudin, 2000. "On internal representations in face recognition systems", Pattern recognition, vol.33, no.7, pp.1161-1177.

12. Hiremath.P.S, Prabhakar.C.J, 2005. "Face Recognition Technique using Symbolic PCA Method", Proc.   Int. Conf. on Pattern Recognition and Machine Intelligence (PreMI'05), Kolkata, 266-271, Springer Verlag.

13. Hiremath.PS, Prabhakar.C.J, "Face Recognition Technique using Symbolic kernel PCA Method", Proc. Int. Conf. on Cognition and Recognition (COGREC'05), Mysore, 801-805, Allied Publishers (2005).

14. Kirby, Sirovich, 1990. Applications of the Karhunen–Loeve procedure for the characterization of human faces, v-12(1). IEEE Trans. Pattern Anal. Machine Intell. 103-108.

15. Lauro, Verde, Palumbo, 1997. Analysis of symbolic data, Bock and Diday (Eds), Springer Verlag.

16. Liu, Wechsler, , 2002. Gabor feature based classification using the enhanced Fisher linear discriminant model for face recognition. IEEE Trans. Image Process. 11(4), 467-476.

17. Liu, Wechsler, 2000: Robust coding schemes for indexing and retrieval from large face databases, IEEE Trans. On image processing 9, 132-137.

18. Liu, Cheng, Yang, 1993. Algebraic feature extraction for image Recognition based on an optimal discriminant criterion, Pattern Recognition, 26, 903-911.

19. A.Pentland, B.Moghaddam and T.Starner, 1994. "View based and modular Eigenfaces for Face Recognition", Proc. Computer Vision and Pattern Recognition, pp.84-91.

20. Scholkopf and A.Smola, and K.Muller, "Nonlinear Component Analysis as a kernel Eigenvalue Problem", Neural Computation, vol.10, pp.1299-1319, 1998.

21. D.Swets, J.Weng, 1996. Using discriminant eigenfeatures for image retrieval. IEEE. Transactions on PAMI,18, 831-836.

22. Turk, Pentland, 1991. Eigenfaces for Recognation, v-3. J Cognitive Neuro Science, 71-86.

23. Yu, Yang, 2001. A Direct LDA algorithm for high dimensional data with application to face recognition, Pattern Recognition, 34(7), 2067-2070.

24. M.H.Yang, "Kernel Eigenfaces vs. Kernel Fisherfaces:Face Recognition using Kernel Methods", Proc. Fifth IEEE Int'l Conf. Automatic Face and Gesture Recognition,pp.215-220,2002.

25. M.H.Yang, N.Ahuja and D.Kriegman, " Face Recognition Using Kernel Eigenfaces", Proc. IEEE Int'l Conf. Image Processing, 2000.

26. Zhao, Chellappa, Phillips, 1999. Subspace linear discriminant analysis for face recognition. Technical Report, CS-TR4009, University of Maryland.

27. Zhao, Chellappa, Phillips, Rosenfeld, 2003. Face Recognition: A literature survey, ACM Comput. Surveys, 35(4), 399-458.

Two-Dimensional Optimal Transform for Appearance Based Object Recognition

B.H. Shekar[1], D.S. Guru[2], and P. Nagabhushan[2]

[1] Department of Computer Science, Mangalore University, Mangalagangotri,
Mangalore, Karnataka, India
[2] Department of Studies in Computer Science, University of Mysore,
Manasagangotri, Mysore, Karnataka, India
bhshekar@yahoo.com, guruds@lycos.com, pnagabhushan@hotmail.com

Abstract. This paper proposes a new method of feature extraction called two-dimensional optimal transform (2D-OPT) useful for appearance based object recognition. The 2D-OPT method provides a better discrimination power between classes by maximizing the distance between class centers. We first argue that the proposed 2D-OPT method works in the row direction of images and subsequently we propose an alternate 2D-OPT which works in the column direction of images. To straighten out the problem of massive memory requirements of the 2D-OPT method and as well the alternate 2D-OPT method, we introduce bi-projection 2D-OPT. The introduced bi-projection 2D-OPT method has the advantage of higher recognition rate, lesser memory requirements and better computing performance than the standard PCA/2D-PCA/Generalized 2D-PCA method, and the same has been revealed through extensive experimentations conducted on COIL-20 dataset and AT&T face dataset.

Keywords: Principal Component Analysis; Optimal Transform; Appearance Based Model; Object Recognition; Face Recognition.

1   Introduction

Appearance based object recognition methods have demonstrated their success in various visual learning and recognition chores such as 3D object recognition, face recognition, ear recognition, palm recognition, and tracking. In particular, principal component analysis (PCA) [5, 7, 8, 9] based methods have been proposed and shown to have good performance. The PCA has also been exploited for accurate identification of faces [2, 10, 13], palms [11], and ears [2]. The drawback of the conventional PCA based approaches is the curse of dimensionality as the size of the covariance matrix is proportional to the size of images. In addition to this, specifically to the application of face recognition, an alternative model, *Fisherfaces* [1], a derivative of Fisher's Linear Discriminant (FLD) has been proposed. The objective of the FLD is to find the optimal projection for the samples such that the discrimination ratio of between-class scatter matrices to within-class scatter matrices reaches its

P. Kalra and S. Peleg (Eds.): ICVGIP 2006, LNCS 4338, pp. 650–661, 2006.

maximum. So far, the FLD method and its variants have been well received by the face recognition community. However, it should be noticed that the PCA/FLD methods [2, 5, 7, 8, 9, 10, 13] are based on the analysis of vectors. When dealing with images, we should firstly tranform the image matrices into vectors. Then based on these vectors, the covariance matrix is calculated and the optimal projection is obtained. As object images are high-dimensional patterns, it is difficult to evaluate the covariance matrix in such a high-dimensional vector-space. To overcome this drawback, Yang et al. [15] proposed a image projection technique called 2D-PCA that is directly based on the analysis of original image matrices. The Generalized 2D-PCA method proposed by Kong et al. [4] overcomes the limitations of 2D-PCA.

On the other hand, we have also seen an evolutionary improvement in the use of PCA based approach for efficient representation and recognition of 3D objects. The major advantage of the approach is that both learning and recognition are performed using just two-dimensional intensity images without any low-level or intermediate-level processing. However, as noticed by many researchers [5, 8, 9, 10] the method in its standard form cannot handle problems such as occlusion, and of varying background. Pentland et al. suggested the use of modular eigenspaces [10] to alleviate the problem of occlusion. Ohba and Ikeuchi [9] proposed the eigen-window method to be able to recognize partially occluded objects. But, due to local windows, these methods lack the global aspect and usually require further processing. To eliminate the effects of varying background, Murase and Nayar [8] introduced the search window, which is the AND area of the object regions of all the images in the training image set. However, the assumption is too restrictive and fails for some class of object models as mentioned in their work itself. Moreover, the target object may be occluded by other target objects which are the images of the training set only, rather than some foreign object. In order to alleviate these problems, Leonardis and Bischof [5] proposed a robust and an efficient approach which is based on multiple eigenspaces. A novel self-organizing framework has been used in their work to construct multiple, low-dimensional eigenspace from a set of training images.

However, it is observed from [3, 12] that the idea of principal component transformaton is based on the reduction of the dimension of original image vectors using some linear mapping such that the resulting feature vectors show pairwise maximum distance. Besides, feature vectors resutling from PCA allow the reconstruction of images with minimal mean quadratic error. If the distribution of features is such that the principal axes of all classes are parallel to each other, the projected features will allow no discrimination of these classes. This problem is called as ADIDAS problem [12] and is illustrated in Fig. 1 considering a 2-D example, where we project the features onto the x-axis. Hence, an alternative objective function is introduced in [3] which eliminates the ADIDAS problem. However, as noticed by many researchers, the computational complexity in the evaluation of covariance matrix still exists in this approach. Motivated by [4, 15], we proposed 2D-OPT and its variants to eliminate the problem of massive memory requirements, higher computational complexity involved in covariance matrix computation, and as well to resolve the ADIDAS problem.

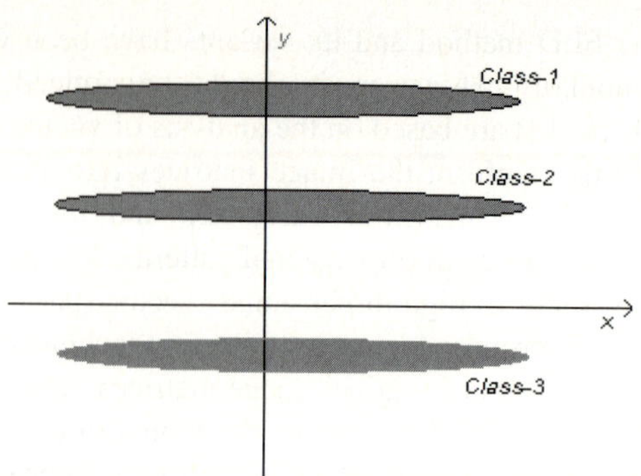

Fig. 1. The 2D-PCA and ADIDAS problem

The rest of the paper is organized as follows. In section 2, we discussed the working model of the 2D-PCA method along with its limitations. In section 3, we propose 2D-OPT transform and establish that the proposed 2D-OPT works in the row direction of images and hence an alternate 2D-OPT which works in the column direction of images is introduced and in sequel a combined model, bi-projection 2D-OPT is proposed. The results of the experiments are presented in section 4 and conclusions are given in section 5.

2 Problems in 2D-PCA

Working model of 2D-PCA: Training is a process of acquiring features from available training images and storing them in a knowledge base for the purpose of recognizing an unknown future scene image. Given a set of samples of each class, the 2D-PCA approach extracts most informative features which could establish a high degree of similarity between samples of the same class and a high degree of dissimilarity between samples of two different classes.

Formally, let there be T number of classes each with k_i, $i=1...T$, number of training images. Therefore, we have totally $N= \sum_{i=1}^{T} k_i$ number of training images. Let A_i^j be an image of size m x n representing the jth sample in the ith class. Let C be the average image of all N training images. In 2D-PCA, the scatter matrix G is computed as follows.

$$G = \frac{1}{N} \sum_{i=1}^{T} \sum_{j=1}^{k_i} (A_i^j - C)^T (A_i^j - C) \tag{1}$$

Once G is computed, it is recommended to find the optimal projection axis X so that the total scatter of the projected samples of the training images is maximized. For this purpose, the criterion used is,

$$J(X) = X^T G X \tag{2}$$

It is a well-known fact that the eigenvector corresponding to the maximum eigenvalue of G is the optimal projection axis which maximizes $J(X)$. Generally, as it is not enough to have only one optimal projection axis, we usually go for d number of projection axes, say $X_1, X_2,..., X_d$, which are the eigenvectors corresponding to the first d largest eigenvalues of G. In 2D-PCA, once these $X_1, X_2,...,X_d$ are computed, each training image A_i^j is then projected onto these X's to obtain the feature matrix W_i^j of size $m \times d$ of the training image A_i^j. So, during training, for each training image A_i^j, a corresponding feature matrix of size $m \times d$, $d<<n$, is constructed and stored in the knowledge base for matching at the time of recognition.

Limitations of 2D-PCA: Albeit the above described 2D-PCA overcomes the limitations of standard PCA based approaches, still it has some shortcomings. As noticed by many researchers, 2D-PCA has massive memory requirements for feature representation and hence consumes much recognition time. Problems occur if the distribution of features is such that the principal axes of all classes are parallel to each other, resulting in ADIDAS problem (see Fig. 1). Hence, the projected features will allow no discrimination of these classes. For this situation, projection on the y-axis would provide discrimination among the classes. Hence, in general, it is necessary to have another plausible optimization criterion, which does not show the disadvantages of 2D-PCA.

3   Two-Dimensional Optimal Transform (2D-OPT)

The scatter matrix introduced in this work is in such a way that the features of the same class have minimum distance and possess maximum distance to other classes. However, knowledge of the classified sample set, like FLD, is required in this case.

3.1   Learning Formulation in 2D-OPT

To devise 2D-OPT, we propose to compute the scatter matrix H_r as follows. Let $\overline{C}_i$ be the average image of all k_i training images of the ith class.

$$H_r = \frac{2}{T(T-1)} \sum_{p=2}^{T} \sum_{q=1}^{p-1} \left(\overline{C}_p - \overline{C}_q\right)^T \left(\overline{C}_p - \overline{C}_q\right) \tag{3}$$

Using this scatter matrix H_r, similar to the original 2D-PCA, in this proposed model also we find the optimal projection axis Y so that the total scatter of the projected samples is maximized using the same criterion introduced in 2D-PCA given by,

$$J(Y) = Y^T H_r Y \tag{4}$$

Thus, the eigenvectors of H_r are computed and then r numbers of eigenvectors corresponding to the first r largest eigenvalues of H_r are chosen. Finally projection of a training image onto these optimal projection axes results with a feature matrix of the respective training image. That is, if Z_i^j represents the feature matrix of A_i^j, then

$$Z_i^j = A_i^j Y \tag{5}$$

It should be noted that the above described scatter matrix (Eq. (3)) in the feature space is equivalent to an optimal transform ψ given by,

$$\psi = \frac{2}{T(T-1)} \sum_{p=2}^{T} \sum_{q=1}^{T-1} (\mu_p - \mu_q)(\mu_p - \mu_q)^T , \tag{6}$$

where μ_i, i=1…T, is the average feature matrix of all feature matrices of the ith class. Hence, using an optimal transform, the distance between the class centers is maximized.

3.2 Recognition

Let I be an image given for recognition. Let I^l be its projected image onto the r number of optimal projection axes computed by $I^l = I Y$. Given two images, say V_{i_1} and V_{i_2} of any object(s)/face(s), represented by feature matrices $Z_1^{i_1} = \left[z_1^{i_1}, z_2^{i_1}, ..., z_q^{i_1} \right]$ and $Z_2^{i_2} = \left[z_1^{i_2}, z_2^{i_2}, ..., z_q^{i_2} \right]$, the similarity $dist(Z_1^{i_1}, Z_2^{i_2})$ is defined as

$$dist(Z_1^{i_1}, Z_2^{i_2}) = \sum_{j=1}^{q} \left\| z_j^{i_1} - z_j^{i_2} \right\|_2 \tag{7}$$

where $\left\| a - b \right\|_2$ denotes the Euclidean distance between the two vectors a and b. If the feature matrices of the training images are Z_1, Z_2, …,Z_N, and each image belongs to some object O_i, then for a given test image I^l, if $dist(I^l, Z_1) = \min_j dist(I^l, Z_j)$ and $Z_1 \in O_i$, then the resulting decision is $I^l \in O_i$.

Theorem 1: The 2D-OPT approach works in the row direction of images.

Proof

Let $\overline{C}_i = \left[\left({}^{(1)}\overline{C}_i \right)^T \left({}^{(2)}\overline{C}_i \right)^T ... \left({}^{(m)}\overline{C}_i \right)^T \right]^T$, where ${}^{(l)}\overline{C}_i$ denotes the lth row vector of $\overline{C}_i$.

The Eq. (3) can be written as

$$H_r = \frac{2}{T(T-1)} \sum_{p=2}^{T} \sum_{q=1}^{p-1} \left(\sum_{k=1}^{m} ({}^{(k)}\overline{C}_p - {}^{(k)}\overline{C}_q)^T ({}^{(k)}\overline{C}_p - {}^{(k)}\overline{C}_q) \right) \tag{8}$$

Equation (8) implies that the image covariance matrix H_r is obtained from the outer product of the row vectors of mean images. Therefore we claim that the 2D-OPT method works in the row direction of images.   □

In the following section, we present a modified version of this 2D-OPT, called alternate 2D-OPT, which works in the column direction of images. It shall be noticed that both the 2D-OPT method and the alternate 2D-OPT method help us in reducing dimension only either in the row direction or in the column direction. Thus, a combined model called bi-projection 2D-OPT which works in both the directions is also presented in the next section. The advantage of this combined approach is that the reduction in dimensionality can be achieved in both row and column directions without any deterioration in recognition performance.

3.3 Alternate 2D-OPT

In alternate 2D-OPT, we propose to compute the scatter matrix H_c as follows.

$$H_c = \frac{2}{T(T-1)} \sum_{p=2}^{T} \sum_{q=1}^{p-1} \left(\overline{C}_p - \overline{C}_q \right)\left(\overline{C}_p - \overline{C}_q \right)^T \tag{9}$$

It shall be observed that H_c in Eq. (9) is obtained in this new formulation as outer products of column vectors unlike H_r (Eq. (3)) in the case of the 2D-OPT. Using this scatter matrix, similar to the original 2D-PCA, in this alternate 2D-OPT model also we find the optimal projection axes V ($m \times s$) so that the total scatter of the projected samples is maximized using the same criterion given by

$$J(V) = VH_c V^T \tag{10}$$

Thus, the eigenvectors of H_c are computed and then s numbers of eigenvectors corresponding to the first s largest eigenvalues of H_c are chosen. Finally projection of a training image onto these optimal projection axes results with a feature matrix of the respective training image. That is if U_i^j represents the feature matrix of A_i^j, then

$$U_i^j = V^T A_i^j \tag{11}$$

Recognition: Let I be an image given for recognition. Let $I^|$ be the feature matrix obtained by projecting I onto V, i.e., $I^| = V^T I$. By using a Euclidean distance based nearest neighbor classifier, the class label of I is obtained as explained in section 3.2.

Theorem 2: The alternate 2D-OPT approach works in the column direction of images.

Proof

Let $\overline{C}_i = \left[\left(^{(1)}\overline{C}_i\right)\left(^{(2)}\overline{C}_i\right)..\left(^{(n)}\overline{C}_i\right) \right]$, where $^{(l)}\overline{C}_i$ denotes the lth column vector of $\overline{C}_i$.

The Eq. (9) can be written as

$$H_c = \frac{2}{T(T-1)} \sum_{p=2}^{T} \sum_{q=1}^{p-1} \left(\sum_{k=1}^{n} (^{(k)}\overline{C}_p - {}^{(k)}\overline{C}_q)(^{(k)}\overline{C}_p - {}^{(k)}\overline{C}_q)^T \right) \tag{12}$$

Equation (12) implies that the image covariance matrix H_c is obtained from the outer product of the column vectors of mean images. Therefore we claim that the alternate 2D-OPT method works in the column direction of images. □

3.4 Bi-projection Two-Dimensional Optimal Transform (B2D-OPT)

In the preceding subsection, we proposed an alternate 2D-OPT concept which works in the column direction capturing information between columns of images. On the other hand, the 2D-OPT works in the row direction capturing information between rows of images. In this subsection, we recommend to project the images on both the directions simultaneously while extracting feature matrices.

Let Y denote n x r optimal projection matrix obtained as explained in the 2D-OPT method (Section 3.1) and let V denote the m x s matrix obtained by the alternate 2D-OPT method (Section 3.3). During training, each training image A_i^j is projected onto both Y and V simultaneously to obtain the respective feature matrix F_i^j which is of dimension s x r as follows.

$$F_i^j = V^T A_i^j Y \tag{13}$$

Recognition: Let I be an image given for recognition. Let I^1 be the feature matrix obtained by projecting I onto V and Y simultaneously, i.e., $I^1 = V^T I Y$. By using a Euclidean distance based nearest neighbor classifier, the class label of I is obtained as explained in section 3.2.

Thus, the B2D-OPT algorithm for training a system is as follows.

Algorithm: B2D-OPT [TRAINING PHASE]

Input: Set of images: $\left\{ A_i^j \mid i = 1...T, \ j = 1...k_i \right\}$

Output: Knowledge base: $\mathcal{F} = \left\{ F_i^j \mid i = 1...T, \ j = 1...k_i \right\}$

Procedure:

    A. **[Computation of optimal projection axes in the row direction: Y]**

        a. Compute the image scatter matrix H_r as explained in section 3.1 (Eq. (3)).

        b. Find the eigenvectors of H_r.

        c. Choose r eigenvectors say $Y_1, Y_2,...,Y_r$ associated with the first r largest eigenvalues of H_r and let $Y = (Y_1, Y_2,...,Y_r)$.

    B. **[Computation of optimal projection axes in the column direction: V]**

        a. Compute the image scatter matrix H_c as explained in section 3.3 (Eq. (9)).

        b. Find the eigenvectors of H_c.

        c. Choose s eigenvectors, say $V_1, V_2,...,V_s$ associated with the first s largest eigenvalues of H_c and let $V = (V_1, V_2,...,V_s)$.

C. [Creation of Knowledge base: $\mathcal{F}$]

$$\text{a.} \qquad \mathcal{F} = \{ F_i^{j} = V^T A_i^{j} Y \mid i = 1...T, \ \ j = 1...k_i \}$$

Algorithm B2D-OPT Training ends.

The corresponding recognition algorithm is as trivial as follows.

Algorithm: B2D-OPT Recognition

Input: Test image, $I\,(m \times n)$
                  Knowledge base, $\mathcal{F}$,
                  Optimal projection axes: Y,
                  Optimal projection axes: V

Output: Class label of I

Procedure:

1. Obtain the feature matrix $I^{|}$ of the input image I using Y and V, $I^{|} = V^T I\,Y$.

2. Find F_p^{q} such that

$$\left\| I^{|} - F_p^{q} \right\|_2 = \arg\ \min \left(\left\| I^{|} - F_i^{j} \right\|_2 , \forall i = 1...T, \ j = 1...k_i \right),$$

where $\left\| \cdot \right\|_2$ denotes Euclidean distance.

3. Classify the test image I as a member of pth class.

Algorithm B2D-OPT Recognition ends.

4 Experimental Results

Experiments on COIL dataset: In this section, we present several experiments conducted to demonstrate the performance of the proposed method for object recognition. We performed all experiments on the standard set of images, COIL-20 [*http://www1.cs.columbia.edu/CAVE/research/softlib/coil-20.html*] which is used by many researchers as a bench mark dataset to verify the validity of their proposed object recognition models. Each object is represented in the database by 72 views obtained by rotating the object in 5° intervals (1440 views in total).

We have conducted a series of experiments to compare the performances of the 2D-OPT, the alternate 2D-OPT, the B2D-OPT and the standard PCA (1D-PCA) [7] methods with varying number of training views. More specifically, we have considered alternate views and tested with the remaining views. Similarly, we have conducted experiments considering 480, 360, 240, 160 and 120 views as training views of the COIL-20 database choosing 24, 18, 12, 8 and 6 views respectively from each object and the recognition performances have been obtained considering the remaining views as test views. The computing time taken by each method (1D-PCA [7], 2D-OPT, alternate 2D-OPT and B2D-OPT) during feature extraction for different training samples is given in Table-1. Table-1 also summarizes the recognition accuracy of each method. It should be noticed that the 2D-OPT method and its variants consume less time when compared to 1D-PCA method for feature extraction and in addition, they have relatively higher recognition rate. As the number of training samples per object set is increased, the relative gain among the 2D-OPT, alternate 2D-OPT, the B2D-OPT and the 1D-PCA becomes more apparent. Figures 2(a), 2(b), 2(c), and 2(d) show respectively the recognition performance of the 1D-PCA, the 2D-OPT, the alternate 2D-OPT and the B2D-OPT methods with varying number of dimensions of feature vector with varying number of training samples. This experiment is conducted to reveal the superiority of the proposed approach over a well accepted method (Murase and Nayar [7]) for 3D object recognition.

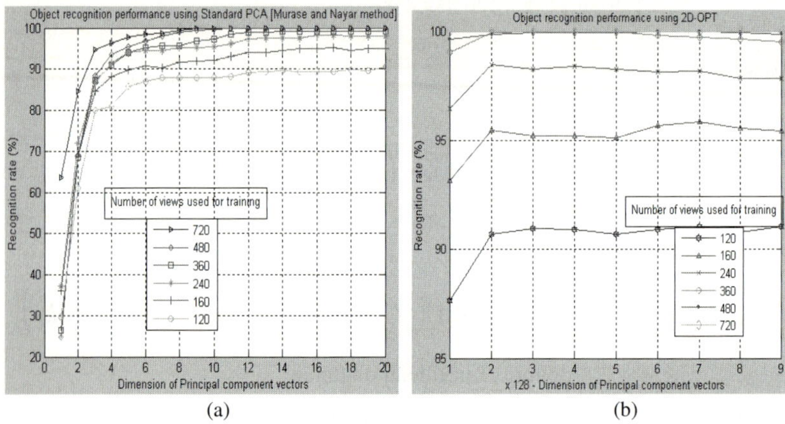

Fig. 2. Recognition performance with varying number of training samples and varying number of principal components- (a) Standard PCA (1D-PCA); (b) 2D-OPT; (c) Alternate 2D-OPT; (d) B2D-OPT, on COIL-20 database

Table 1. Object recognition performance of 1D-PCA, 2D-OPT, alternate 2D-OPT and B2D-OPT

No.of views used to train	No. of views used to test	Computing time for feature extraction (in secs.)				Percentage of recognition			
		1D-PCA (20-D PCs)	2D-OPT (128x10 PCVs)	Alternate 2D-OPT (10x128 PCVs)	B2D-OPT (10x10 PCVs)	1D-PCA (20-D PCVs)	2D-OPT (128x10 PCVs)	Alternate 2D-OPT (10x128 PCVs)	B2D-OPT (10x10 PCVs)
720	720	4080.68	72.578	72.453	67.921	100	100	100	100
480	960	1091.33	48.812	47.296	47.218	99.27	99.79	99.90	100
360	1080	167.98	35.468	35.359	34.421	96.48	99.26	98.98	99.35
240	1200	58.906	23.609	23.765	24.015	94.50	97.42	97.58	98.00
160	1280	35.953	16.281	16.375	17.468	90.86	94.92	94.22	95.08
120	1320	28.766	12.375	12.671	13.609	86.67	90.23	90.83	91.67

Experiments on AT&T dataset: We have also conducted experiments on the standard AT&T face database [*http://www.uk.research.att.com/facedatabase.html*] in order to corroborate the success of the proposed methodology even for face recognition. This face database contains images from 40 individuals, each providing 10 different images of size 112x92. In our experiment, we have considered alternate five samples per class during training and the remaining samples for testing. The recognition performances of the methods 2D-PCA [15], Generalized 2D-CPA [4], 2D-OPT, alternate 2D-OPT and B2D-OPT with varying dimension of feature vectors are given in Fig. 3. The running times of 2D-PCA [15], Generalized 2D-PCA [4], 2D-OPT, alternate 2D-OPT and B2D-OPT with varying dimension of feature vectors are given in Fig. 4. Table-2 gives a comparative analysis of the methods [4, 15] with respect to their running times and dimension of feature vectors. It can be observed from Table-2 that the proposed 2D-OPT and alternate 2D-OPT have better recognition rate with least running time when compared to the 2D-PCA method. The proposed B2D-OPT method achieves the best recognition rate with reduced dimension of feature vector among all the approaches. Nevertheless, it has relatively better running time.

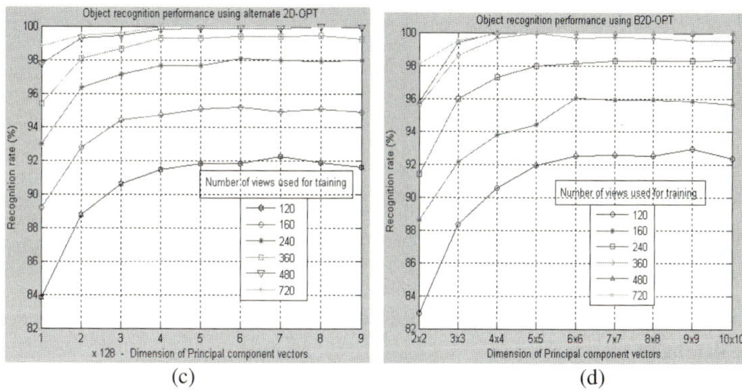

(c)   (d)

Fig. 3. Contd.

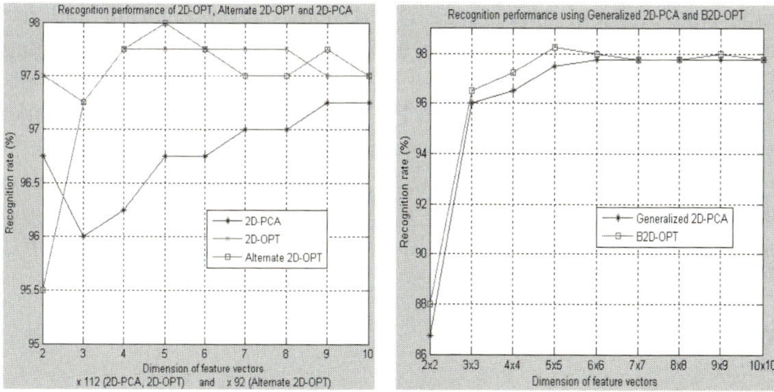

Fig. 4. Recognition performance of different approaches with varying dimension of feature vectors on AT&T face database

Table 2. Running times, Dimension of feature vectors and Recognition rate

Method	Running time (in secs.)	Dimension of feature vector	Best Recognition rate (%)
2DPCA [15]	5.265	112x9	97.25
Generalized 2DPCA [4]	2.719	6x6	97.75
2D-OPT (Proposed method)	**3.766**	**112x4**	**97.75**
Alternate 2D-OPT (Proposed method)	**3.812**	**92x5**	**98.00**
B2D-OPT (Proposed method)	**2.703**	**5x5**	**98.25**

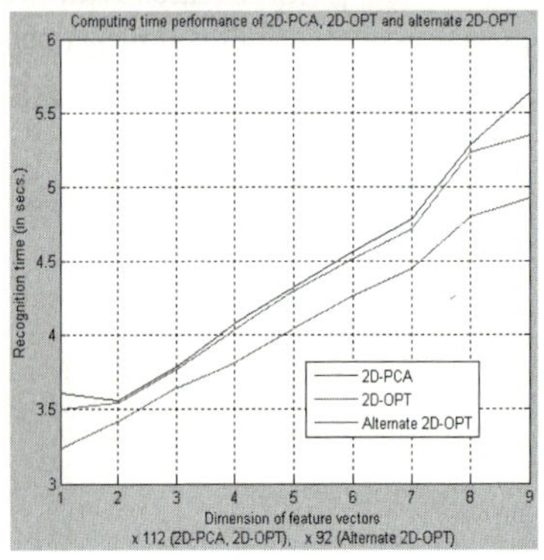

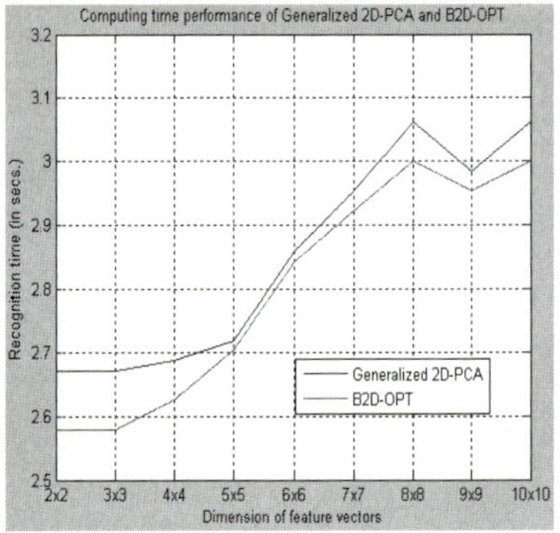

Fig. 5. Running time of different approaches with varying dimension of feature vectors on AT&T face database

5   Conclusions

In this paper, an efficient appearance based object representation and recognition method called 2D-OPT and its variants are introduced. The major advantage of the proposed method, B2D-OPT, is that it requires fewer coefficients for object/face image representation unlike the standard PCA/2D-PCA as it works simultaneously on both row and column directions. Experimental results reveal that the proposed approach is relatively faster and has better recognition rate when compared to the other standard approaches available in the literature for 3D object recognition and face recognition, and, hence, is suitable for real-time recognition applications.

References

1. Belhumeur, P.N., Hespanha, J.P., and Kreigman, D.J. Eigenfaces vs. Fisherfaces: Recognition using class specific linear projection, IEEE Transactions on Pattern Analysis and Machine Intelligence, vol. 19(7), pp. 711-720, July 1997.

2. Chang, K., Bowyer, K.W., Sarkar, S., and Victor, B. Comparison and combination of ear and face images for appearance-based biometrics, IEEE Transactions on Pattern Analysis and Machine Intelligence, vol. 25 (9), pp. 1160-1165, Sept. 2003.
3. Hornegger, J., Niemann, H., and Risack, R. Appearance-based object recognition using optimal feature transforms, Pattern Recognition, vol. 33(2), pp. 209-224, Feb. 2000.
4. Kong, H., Wang, L., Teoh, E.K., Li, X., Wang, J-G., and Venkateswaralu, R. Generalized 2D principal component analysis for face image representation and recognition, Neural Networks, vol. 18(5-6), pp. 585-594, June-July 2005.
5. Leonardis, A., Bischof, H., and Jasna, M. Multiple Eigenspaces, Pattern Recognition, vol. 35(11), pp. 2613-2627, Nov. 2002.
6. Li, M., and Yuan, B. 2D-LDA: A statistical linear discriminant analysis for image matrix, Pattern Recognition Letters, vol. 26(5), 527-532, April 2005.
7. Murase, H., and Nayar, S. K. Visual learning and recognition of 3-D objects from appearance, International Journal of Computer Vision, vol. 14(1), pp. 5-24, Jan. 1995.
8. Murase, H., and Nayar, S. K. Detection of 3D objects in cluttered scenes using hierarchical eigenspace, Pattern Recognition Letters, vol. 18(4), pp. 375-384, Apr. 1997.
9. Ohba, K, and Ikeuchi, K. Detectability, Uniqueness, and Reliability of eigen windows for stable verification of partially occluded objects, IEEE Transactions on Pattern Analysis and Machine Intelligence, vol. 19(9), pp. 1043-1048, Sept. 1997.
10. Pentland, A., Moghaddam, B., and Starner, T. View-based and Modular Eigenspaces for Face Recognition, In Proceedings of the IEEE Conference on Computer Vision and Pattern Recognition, pp. 84-91, 1994.
11. Ribaric, S., and Fratric, I. A biometric identification system based on eigenpalm and eigenfingerprint features, IEEE Transactions on Pattern Analysis and Machine Intelligence, vol. 27(11), pp. 1698-1709, Nov. 2005.
12. Schukat-Talamazzini, E.G. Automatische Spracherkennung, Vieweg, Wiesbaden, 1995.
13. Turk, M. and Pentland, A. Eigenfaces for recognition, Journal of Cognitive Neuroscience, vol. 3(1), pp. 71-86, Mar. 1991.
14. Xiong, H, Swamy, M.N.S., and Ahmad, M.O. Two-dimensional FLD for face recognition, Pattern Recognition, vol. 38(7), pp. 1121-1124, July 2005.
15. Yang, J., Zhang, D., Frangi, A. F., and Yang, J. Two-Dimensional PCA: A new approach to appearance based face representation and recognition, IEEE Transactions on Pattern Analysis and Machine Intelligence, vol. 26(1), pp. 131-137, Jan. 2004.
16. Yang, J., Zhang, D., Yang, X., Yang, J. Two-dimensional discriminant transform for face recognition, Pattern Recognition, vol. 38(7), pp. 1125-1129, July 2005.

Computing Eigen Space from Limited Number of Views for Recognition

Paresh K. Jain, Kartik Rao P.*, and C.V. Jawahar

Centre for Visual Information Technology,
International Institute of Information Technology,
Hyderabad 500032, India
paresh@research.iiit.ac.in, kartikr@kritikalsolutions.com,
jawahar@iiit.ac.in

Abstract. This paper presents a novel approach to construct an eigen space representation from limited number of views, which is equivalent to the one obtained from large number of images captured from multiple view points. This procedure implicitly incorporates a novel view synthesis algorithm in the eigen space construction process. Inherent information in an appearance representation is enhanced using geometric computations. We experimentally verify the performance for orthographic, affine and projective camera models. Recognition results on the COIL and SOIL image database are promising.

1   Introduction

Recognition is an active area of research in computer vision. The problem of view-independent object recognition has received considerable amount of attention in recent years [1,2,3,4,5]. Recognition techniques can be broadly classified into (a) Shape representation based and (b) Appearance based techniques. Shape representation based techniques are popular for specific categories of applications, where the object's structure is more important than the intensity information within its boundaries. Plenoptic function captures object appearance across views and allows to completely model an object. However, estimation of this appearance representation is not a viable intermediate step in recognition. A popular alternative is to model the subspace that will contain all views of the object. Appearance based matching techniques attempt to model this space. Since images are bulky in nature, dimensionality reduction is usually sought to reduce the complexity of the appearance based representation. One of the very popular approaches for this purpose is the eigen image representation [5,6].

Following the successful application of Eigen spaces for face recognition [6], a real-time system [5] was built to recognize hundred objects imaged from multiple view points. This system employed parametric hypersurfaces constructed in the eigenspace, to model the appearance of the objects in different views. View based models are built from a large number of training images in [7]. Correlation between views of an object is exploited to construct the appearance models.

---

* Currently with Kritikal Solutions, New Delhi, India.

P. Kalra and S. Peleg (Eds.): ICVGIP 2006, LNCS 4338, pp. 662–673, 2006.

Performance and applicability of these systems is often limited by the number of views. With reduction in number of views, the parametric representations also become poorer approximations of the real appearance models. A direct method to address this problem is to capture or synthesize additional views of the object and construct the appearance model from these images. When an object is viewed with multiple cameras, there holds some constraints in the geometry of the views [8] which allows the synthesis of novel views.

This paper presents a new approach to solve the view-independent recognition problem from limited number of views. We construct an eigen space, from a limited number views, equivalent to the one obtained from a large number of views. We show that these two are mathematically equivalent, except for the occluded pixels. The following sections have been written with the emphasis on linear Principal Component Analysis (PCA) but it may be extended to nonlinear techniques like Kernel PCA. Note that the output of the proposed technique is a data matrix of new views interpolated in the pose space. A linear PCA, Kernel PCA and many other nonlinear Component Analyses can equally well be applied over this data matrix.

The rest of the paper is organized as follows. Section 2 revisits Principal Component Analysis and introduces the notation used. Section 3 describes the details of the eigen space construction process in the proposed scheme for simple case of orthographic camera projection model. Section 4 discusses its extension to other camera projection models and application to object recognition. In Section 5, we demonstrate that the eigen space constructed from limited views practically approximates the ideal one for orthographic, affine and projective camera models. Performance of recognition is verified on a set of synthetic images and images from the COIL [9] and SOIL [10] databases.

2   Eigen Images for Representation

Eigen space representation is very popular for compression [11] and recognition [5,6]. Eigen space compactly represents the appearance in the presence of variations in instantiation of the object, say human face, due to pose or illumination [6]. A new set of bases vectors (eigenvectors of the covariance matrix) along the direction of maximal variance is employed to build the representation. The decorrelation of features achieved by PCA, allows discarding of features that contribute less to the content of an image, without significant loss of information.

Given a set of images $\{I_1, I_2, \ldots, I_P\}$, each of size $N = h \times w$, the eigen space is obtained as follows: Each image is arranged as a vector by concatenating the pixels in row order. The image vectors are normalized by subtracting the mean vector from each of the images, i.e., $\widetilde{I}_i = I_i - \mu$ where $\mu = \frac{1}{P}\sum_{i=1}^{P} I_i$. These normalized images are arranged to form a data matrix A of dimensions $N \times P$.

$$A = \left[\widetilde{I}_1 \ \widetilde{I}_2 \ \ldots \ \widetilde{I}_P \right] \tag{1}$$

The matrix A is multiplied with its transpose, A^T, to yield the scaled version of the covariance matrix Σ. Eigenvectors corresponding to the larger eigenvalues

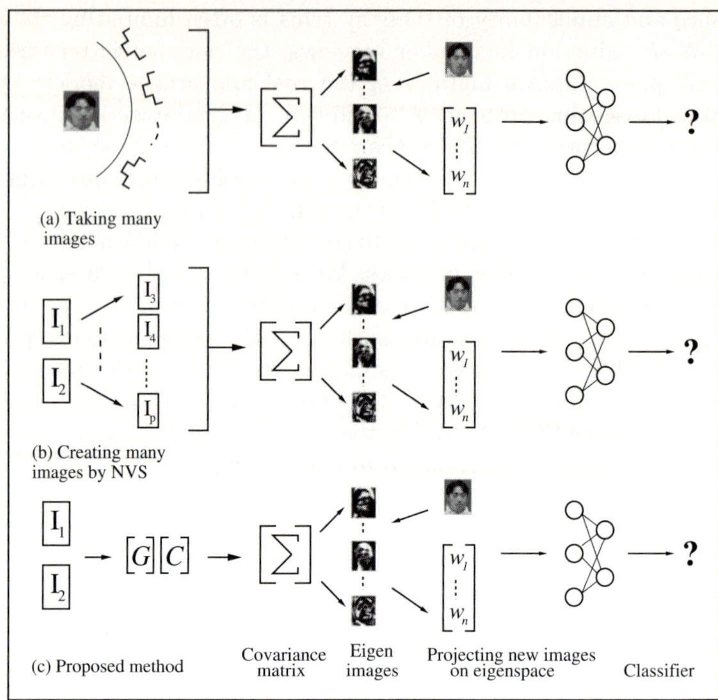

Fig. 1. Three different methods to construct Eigenspace representation. Popular method (a) capture multiple images of the object under different pose. We propose two alternate methods for eigen space construction. Method (b) constructs eigen space by synthesis of many additional images. Method (c) does the same without explicit synthesis of novel views from two views of an object.

act as the basis vectors for the new representation. If the images are not mean centered, we will get a correlation matrix whose eigenvectors are directly related to those of Σ.

To build a view-independent recognition system, a large number of images of an object is needed and the eigenspace is typically constructed [5] from these images. We propose two alternate schemes for constructing high resolution appearance space from limited number of input images. Recent advances in multiview geometry [8] permit us to interpolate or extrapolate from two input views I_1 and I_2 to obtain new views $I_3, \ldots, I_P$. Incorporation of the geometric information into the appearance representation adds the otherwise missing information, which could not be obtained from limited number of images. We propose to construct the eigen space from a set including the synthesized ones. On a closer look, synthesis of novel views seems to be a redundant step in the construction of the eigen space. In the next section, we demonstrate that without the intermediate views, one could directly construct the eigen space and hence carry out recognition from limited views. A conceptual explanation of these alternate procedures is presented in Fig. 1. Although appearance of objects from multiple views can be learnt with method (a) (Fig. 1); it generally requires sophisticated camera(s) and/or light(s) setup. There are a good number of scenarios (for example surveillance) where such freedom is unavailable. Hence there is a need for techniques such as proposed in this paper; which can build a denser eigenspace with limited available views in a computationally efficient manner.

3   Eigenspace Construction for Orthographic Cameras

We start with a simple case, where two orthographic cameras related by a Y-axis rotation provides the input. Let I_1 and I_2 be the input images of size $h \times w$. If x_1 and x_2 are x-coordinates of corresponding points in the two images, then the corresponding point x_3 in a third (novel) image I_3 is given by (see [12])

$$x_3 = ax_1 + bx_2, \tag{2}$$

where a and b depend on the translation and rotation that the camera undergoes to image I_1, I_2 and I_3. The y-coordinate remains the same. Note that it is the coordinates of the corresponding points, which are linearly related, and this does not directly imply anything on the eigenspace constructed from the intensity values. More over, since a and b can be fractional values, x_3 need not be an integer. The intensity at a point in the novel view can be expressed as a linear combination of intensities in its neighborhood, which can be computed from the original image.

Let $G_j^T = \left[I_1(j,1),\ I_1(j,2),\ \dots I_1(j,w) \right]$ denote the intensity values in row j of image I_1. If $C_j^l = \left[y_1\ y_2\ \dots\ y_w \right]$ represents a vector of interpolation coefficients for the lth pixel in the jth row, then the intensity at any point in row j can be expressed as

$$I_3(j,l) = \sum_{k=1}^{w} I_1(j,k) \cdot y_k = G_j^T \cdot C_j^l \tag{3}$$

Let (x_{k_1}, j), (x_{k_2}, j) and (x_{k_3}, j) be corresponding points in I_1, I_2 and the novel view I_3. These are related by Equation (2). To synthesize the digital image, we need to interpolate from the synthesized real coordinates. The point (x_{k_3}, j) contributes to the intensity of $I_3(l,j)$ only if the distance between the two points is less than one unit on the integer grid. The contribution varies inversely with distance. Thus the element y_k, $1 \leq k \leq w$ is given by

$$\begin{matrix} 1 - dist & \text{if} & dist < 1 \\ 0 & \text{if} & dist \geq 1 \end{matrix}' \tag{4}$$

where $dist = |a_i x_{1k} + b_i x_{2k} - l|$. The interpolation vector C_j^l is determined for each pixel in the novel view. Then, the product $G_j^T C_j^l$ is computed for each point (j,l) in the novel view. These products are arranged to obtain the vector form of the novel view I_3. Hence the novel view I_3 is given as

$$[G_1^T C_1^1\ \dots\ G_1^T C_1^w\ \dots G_h^T C_h^1\ \dots\ G_h^T C_h^w]^T$$
$$= \mathcal{G} [C_1^1\ \dots\ C_1^w\ \dots\ C_h^1\ \dots\ C_h^w]^T = \mathcal{G} \mathcal{C}_3,$$

where $\mathcal{G}$ is a $hw \times hw^2$ matrix obtained by appropriately arranging the G_i's and $\mathcal{C}_3$ is a $hw^2 \times 1$ vector obtained by column order concatenation of C_j^l's. Each row of $\mathcal{G}$ can be considered as the concatenation of hw vectors of size $w \times 1$. In each row, $hw - 1$ of these hw vectors are zero. The remaining vector is assigned the value of G_j. It may be noted that $\mathcal{G}$ is highly sparse and the non-zero elements can be efficiently computed.

Novel views can also be generated in a similar manner for different placements of the camera and the corresponding values of a and b. A new variable i is introduced into the notation of the interpolation vector C_j^l to index the novel views. Thus, the view I_i is synthesized using the interpolation vector C_{ij}^l as

$$\mathcal{G}\left[C_{i1}^1 \ldots C_{i1}^w \ldots C_{ih}^1 \ldots C_{ih}^w \right] = \mathcal{G}\mathcal{C}_i \tag{5}$$

Eigen space representation of the set of images involves computation of eigenvectors of AA^T as explained in Section 2. The data matrix A is rearranged as product of two matrices,

$$A = [I_1, I_2, \ldots I_P] = \mathcal{G}[\mathcal{C}_1\mathcal{C}_2 \ldots \mathcal{C}_P] = \mathcal{G}\mathcal{C} \tag{6}$$

where $\mathcal{C}$ is obtained by arranging $\mathcal{C}_1, \ldots, \mathcal{C}_P$ as columns of a matrix. Even though the dimension of these two matrices are huge, the number of operations required to compute the product is small. This is so because both $\mathcal{G}$ and $\mathcal{C}$ are highly sparse.

Since we are considering camera rotation around one axis, let α and θ be the angles between the camera plane for generating I_2 and I_3 from that of I_1. Given these angles, Ullman and Basri [12] show that

$$a = \frac{\sin(\alpha - \theta)}{\sin(\alpha)} \quad \text{and} \quad b = \frac{\sin(\theta)}{\sin(\alpha)}. \tag{7}$$

Given the two input views I_1 and I_2, and the angle α, a and b are computed for different values of θ using Equation (7). The choice of resolution of θ depends on the tradeoff between density of eigenspace needed and the computational effort needed. Let the value of a and b corresponding to $\theta = \theta_i$ be denoted by a_i and b_i respectively. For each pair (a_i, b_i), C_{ij}^l is computed for each pixel in the novel image using Equation (4). From the intensity values of the images and C_{ij}^l, the matrices $\mathcal{G}$ and $\mathcal{C}$ are generated and then the eigenvectors corresponding to A are computed as explained above.

4   Extension to Other Camera Models

Affine Camera The process of construction of eigen space for an object imaged with an affine camera is similar to an object imaged with an orthographic camera. The difference is in the determination of the constants a and b, which is done as follows. We assume that the world is imaged with an affine camera P_1 to generate image I_1. The world is imaged again after transforming P_1 with a transformation

T_1, which is rotation by an angle α, to yield I_2. For a given θ, we compute T_2, the rotation matrix about Y-axis by θ. Now we assume the world is imaged after P_1 is transformed by T_2 to yield I_3. Since Equation (2) holds for corresponding points in the three views, we obtain a system of equations in terms of a, b, P_1, T_1 and T_2. These system of equations can be solved to obtain the values of a and b. Using this procedure, a_i's and b_i's are generated and the remaining steps are followed as for an orthographic camera.

Perspective Camera. The novel view synthesis with general perspective cameras has been explored in [13]. In this technique, trilinear relationships between two views are created and then a tensorial operator is used to create the tensor relating the desired and two initial views. This tensor (say α_k^{ij}) is later used to get the coordinates of a point in new views using the coordinates in the initial view. The relation used is as follows

$$x'' = \frac{x'\alpha_i^{31}p^i - \alpha_i^{11}p^i}{\alpha^{13}p^i - x'\alpha_i^{33}p^i}, y'' = \frac{y'\alpha_i^{32}p^i - \alpha_i^{12}p^i}{\alpha^{13}p^i - y'\alpha_i^{33}p^i}.$$

This relation can be used to modify *dist* as $dist = \sqrt{(x'' - x)^2 + (y'' - y)^2}$, where x'' and y'' are given by above equations. Note that in this case, since the y-coordinate changes as well, the process for creating one pixel would be modified to include the whole image (as raster scanned row vector), instead of just one row as earlier. This would also result in an increase in the coefficient vector of one pixel. This coefficient vector would correspondingly be of $hw \times 1$ size as well. The rest of the process of stacking up pixel to build $\mathcal{G}$ and $\mathcal{C}$ matrices remains the same except for the above change. In this case, the dimensionality of $\mathcal{G}$ and $\mathcal{C}$ would also increase to $hw \times h^2w^2$ and $h^2w^2 \times n$ respectively. However the matrices are still highly sparse and their product can be computed efficiently. It should be noted that perspective novel view synthesis (NVS) relationship is general and is applicable for general motion and not just y-axis rotation as in the previous cases.

4.1   Eigenspace Construction from More Than Two Views

If there are more than two views, even then the eigenspace can be constructed with minor modifications to the algorithm described above. Let there be m views of an object, $I_1 \ldots I_m$, imaged with an orthographic or affine camera. We will get $(m-1)$ pairs of consecutive views. Also, let α_n be the angle between the camera plane for I_n and I_{n+1}, $1 \leq n \leq m-1$. For every pair of consecutive views, the matrices $\mathcal{G}$ and $\mathcal{C}$ are computed. For the nth pair of consecutive views, let these be denoted by $\mathcal{G}_n$ and $\mathcal{C}_n$. The data matrix A will be defined as

$$A = [\mathcal{G}_1\mathcal{C}_1 \ldots \mathcal{G}_{m-1}\mathcal{C}_{m-1}] = \mathcal{G}_1[\mathcal{C}_1, \frac{\mathcal{G}_2}{\mathcal{G}_1}\mathcal{C}_2 \ldots \frac{\mathcal{G}_{m-1}}{\mathcal{G}_1}\mathcal{C}_{m-1}]$$

$$= \mathcal{G}_1[\mathcal{C}_1, \tilde{\mathcal{C}}_2 \ldots \tilde{\mathcal{C}}_{m-1}] = \mathcal{G}\mathcal{C}.$$

Since we want to express the data matrix as the product of two matrices, $\mathcal{G}$ and $\mathcal{C}$, $\mathcal{G}_1$ is brought out as a common factor. After bringing out $\mathcal{G}_1$ as the common factor, we get $\mathcal{G}_n\mathcal{C}_n = \mathcal{G}_1\widetilde{\mathcal{C}}_n$. To compute $\widetilde{\mathcal{C}}_n$, we multiply with the pseudo-transpose of $\mathcal{G}_1$ on both sides of the above equation and compute the matrix $\widetilde{\mathcal{C}}_n$. Having arranged A as a product of the matrices $\mathcal{G}$ and $\mathcal{C}$, the eigenvectors are computed.

4.2   Application to Object Recognition

Suppose there are m objects, that need to be recognized. Also, assume there are at least two views for each object and the angle by which the camera has been rotated for each pair of consecutive views is known. For the nth object, $\mathcal{G}_n$ and $\mathcal{C}_n$, are computed, $1 \leq n \leq m$. The data matrix A is arranged as a product of $\mathcal{C}$ and $\mathcal{G}$, by arranging all the $\mathcal{G}_n$ and $\mathcal{C}_n$, $1 \leq n \leq m$, and then performing the necessary transformations. The eigen subspace for A is constructed by computing its eigenvectors and discarding eigenvectors corresponding to lower eigenvalues. Recognition is performed by projecting a test sample into this space and then classifying.

5   Results and Discussions

To analyze the performance of the proposed formulation, we have considered synthetic and real-images. Synthetic models allow us to conduct the experiments in a controlled manner to systematically study the performance. Real-images are taken from Columbia Object Image Library(COIL) [9] and Surrey Object Image Library (SOIL) [10].

In all the experiments, eigen space is created using the method described in the previous section. Though the eigen space can be constructed from any arbitrary views, for better analysis and understanding, we use input images from cameras rotated around Y axis and separated by α (explained later). We then construct eigen space corresponding to images at θ from the first input image. For example, θ may take values ranging from $-20°$ to $+20°$ at increments of $1°$. This means that the eigen space is created for a $40°$ view cone with a resolution restricted by the $1°$ difference between consecutive views.

5.1   Synthetic Models

The proposed scheme is useful when a reasonably accurate eigenspace is required when there are few input images available for each object. We conducted experiments with synthetic models to test the accuracy of the eigenspace built with the proposed method. We used the eigenspace for recognition problem. Five synthetic objects shown in Fig. 2 (i):(a-e) are considered. These models(O1-O5), were imaged by rotating the camera around the object about the Y-axis. Out of these, two images were taken for construction of the eigen space. From these two images an eigen space corresponding to the images in the range -20 to $+20$ from the first image (out of these two) is constructed. We found that even in the presence of similar objects (Fig. 2(i):(c) and (d)), the eigenspace constructed as per the proposed scheme gives 100% accuracy for a variety of cases (illustrated

α	N	O1	O2	O3	O4	O5	Total(%)
5°	2	100	100	100	100	100	100
10°	2	100	100	100	100	100	100
15°	2	100	100	100	100	96.66	99.33
20°	2	100	100	100	82.22	100	96.44
30°	2	100	100	91.11	77.77	100	93.77
20°	3	100	100	100	100	100	100
30°	3	100	100	100	100	100	100

(i)   (ii)

Fig. 2. (i): The first row (a-e) shows the five synthetic models considered for the experiment. Second row (f-j) shows the novel views of the Policeman(object 1) corresponding to the eigen space representation constructed. Final row (k-o) shows the images which a real-camera could have seen. (ii) Recognition results on objects in (a). As the angle between two views(α) is increased, there is a reduction in performance. But with minimal additional views, this can be compensated. N is the number of views.

in Fig. 2 (ii) and explained in detail below). This experiment underlines the accuracy and utility of the eigenspace created by the proposed scheme.

The test set contained 450 images, 90 images per object. The views ranged from -45^0 to 44° at steps of 1°. These images were obtained by explicitly rotating the camera and capturing the views thus obtained. These test images (Fig. 2(k - o)), in fact, deviate from the synthesized images for the same angle(Fig. 2(f - j)). The test set was projected into the eigenspace and classified using a Nearest Neighbor algorithm. Eigen space is spanned by 15 eigen vectors corresponding to the largest eigen values. The recognition accuracy was equal to or near 100% for the various values of α. The results of some experiments on this set are provided in Table 2. When α is increased to $30°$, the accuracy is found to be above 90% with only two views. When three views were used, 100% accuracy was achieved.

This experiment indicates that for large α the accuracy can be further improved by using additional views. The eigenspace created by using more number of seed views provides a better estimation of the true eigenspace. Although the accuracy with two seed views is high, additional views can be used to improve the performance to suit practical applications.

Interpolated eigenspace Vs Sparse eigenspace. The motivation behind the current work is to capture the information contained in views from different orientation by doing Novel View Synthesis (NVS). In many real life applications very few images per object are available. NVS allows creation of a *denser* set of images from a relatively sparse set. Intuitively such an interpolated eigenspace (created by NVS) would be *closer* to the actual eigenspace of an image (which could be created by exhaustively taking images at various orientation). We validated this intuition by considering a 3D Face model (see Fig. 3 (a)). We considered 48 equally spaced images of this 3D Face model by moving the camera around the model from $-60°$ to $+60°$. It can be assumed that these 48 images make up the *true* eigenspace of this object. N ($\in \{4, 6, 8, 12, 16, 24\}$) equally spaced images

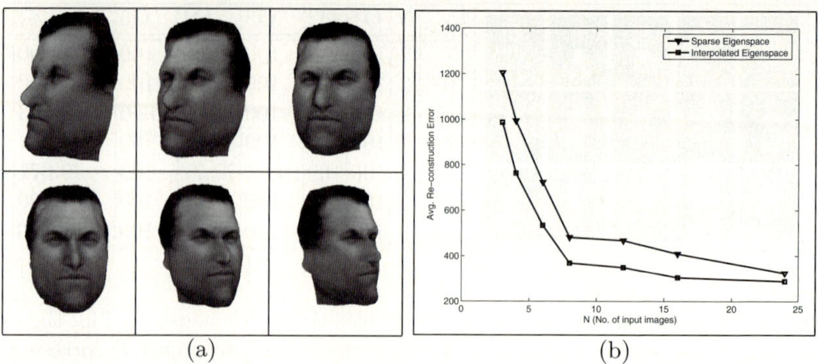

(a)   (b)

Fig. 3. (a) Few images of the 3D Face model used to compare the sparse eigenspace with interpolated eigenspace. (b) A comparison between the average re-construction error per image for sparse eigenspace and interpolated eigenspace.

were selected from this set to create a sparse set of images. Each image was segmented to a uniform size of 70×60 pixels. We built an eigenspace limited to this sparse set and calculated the average re-construction error for each of the 48 original images. We performed NVS on this sparse set and synthesized $25 \times \frac{48}{N}$ new images between every pair of consecutive images in this sparse set. We created an eigenspace with these images and calculated the re-construction error for this *interpolated* eigenspace. In both cases top eigenvectors corresponding to energy factor $k = 0.99$ ($k = \sum_i^k \sigma_i / \sum_i^T \sigma_i$, where σ_is are the eigenvalues and T is the total number of eigenvalues) were picked. For the intermediate set of $N = 6$ initial images the error with interpolated images was 534.4 while with sparse eigenspace, it was 723.3. This error is over a total of $60 \times 70 = 4200$ pixels. In Fig. 3 (b) more detailed comparison of the re-construction errors between sparse and interpolated eigenspaces is shown. Clearly, the interpolated eigenspace represents the appearance of objects better than the sparse eigenspace.

5.2   Application to Recognition

We conducted recognition experiments on two datasets (e.g. COIL-20 [9], SOIL-47 [10]) to show the applicability of the proposed eigenspace in the context of object recognition. Good performance with recognition accuracy in the range of $> 90\%$ was achieved.

Experiments on COIL images. We verified the performance of the proposed scheme on COIL [9] images (Fig. 4 (a)). The Columbia Object Image Library was developed for conducting experiments on object recognition [5]. This database has been widely used by researchers for verification of object recognition algorithms. This library provides images of objects rotated about the Y-axis at intervals of $5°$.

The training set consisted of 180 images, with views ranging from $-20°$ to $20°$ (inclusive) at steps of $5°$. In fact, only two images per object are used for

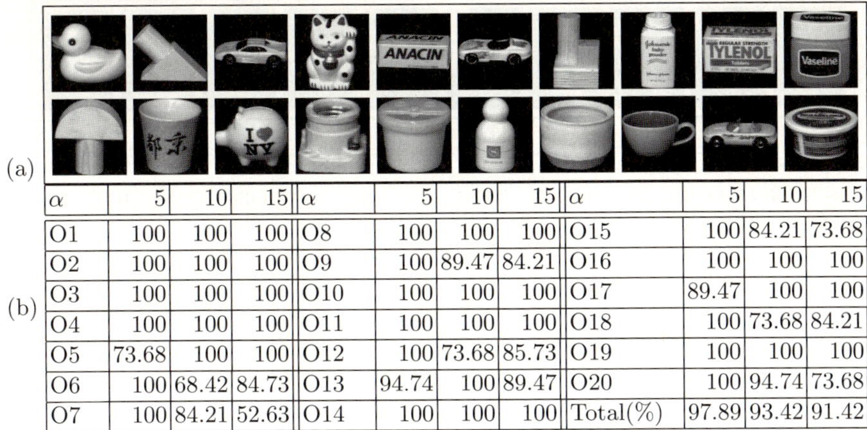

α	5	10	15	α	5	10	15	α	5	10	15
O1	100	100	100	O8	100	100	100	O15	100	84.21	73.68
O2	100	100	100	O9	100	89.47	84.21	O16	100	100	100
O3	100	100	100	O10	100	100	100	O17	89.47	100	100
O4	100	100	100	O11	100	100	100	O18	100	73.68	84.21
O5	73.68	100	100	O12	100	73.68	85.73	O19	100	100	100
O6	100	68.42	84.73	O13	94.74	100	89.47	O20	100	94.74	73.68
O7	100	84.21	52.63	O14	100	100	100	Total(%)	97.89	93.42	91.42

Fig. 4. (a)All COIL-20 Objects used for the recognition experiment. (b) Recognition results on COIL images. With only two images, most of the images in 90° view cone can be recognized with good accuracies. With minimal increase in the number of images, 100% accuracy is achieved. See text for details.

constructing the eigen space. i.e., in reality only 40 images were used to get an effective representation, which we could have computed from all the 180. The test set consisted of 380 images, 19 images for each object at increments of 5° from -45° to 45° (inclusive). The results of the experiment on the real world images are provided in Fig. 4 (b).

The recognition accuracy ranging from 88% to 95%, is achieved by using two images per object. This outperforms the direct methods for recognition by explicitly constructing eigen spaces. Crowley [14] achieved around 90% recognition from four views. Their results were verified only for a smaller view cone, compared to that of ours. Additionally, we have exhaustively tested images beyond the scope of the training images. i.e., even if we construct the eigen space for $-20°$ to $+20°$, applicability was verified for $-45°$ to $+45°$. In general, the proposed method is found to give good results even for such test images. Additionally the recognition accuracy is found to improve if the number of initial seed images is increased.

Experiments on SOIL images. The Surrey Object Image Library (SOIL [10]) consists of 25 planar and 22 complex shaped objects (some of which are shown in Fig. 5 (a)). This dataset is also widely used for testing recognition performance in literature along with COIL-20. There are 2 sets, SOIL-47A and SOIL-47B which differ in overall illumination. We conducted our experiments on SOIL-47A. There are 20 images per object taken at approximately 9° intervals spanning 180°.

We considered 2 images of all 47 objects in the 90° middle sector. Here we varied initial angle α as 9° and 18° and generated 18 $(2\alpha, \alpha = 9)$ and 36$(2\alpha, \alpha = 18)$ images respectively per object, separated at 1° intervals spanning the central

(a)

(b)

α	9	18	α	9	18	α	9	18	α	9	18
O1	83.66	83.66	O13	100	83.33	O25	100	83.33	O37	100	100
O2	66.67	66.67	O14	83.33	100	O26	100	100	O38	100	100
O3	100	83.33	O15	100	83.33	O27	100	100	O39	100	100
O4	100	100	O16	66.67	83.33	O28	66.67	83.33	O40	100	100
O5	100	100	O17	100	83.33	O29	100	100	O41	100	100
O6	66.67	83.33	O18	83.33	83.33	O30	100	100	O42	100	100
O7	83.33	66.67	O19	100	100	O31	100	100	O43	66.67	83.33
O8	100	83.33	O20	83.33	83.33	O32	100	100	O44	100	100
O9	100	100	O21	83.33	66.67	O33	100	100	O45	100	100
O10	83.33	66.67	O22	83.33	83.33	O34	66.67	83.33	O46	100	100
O11	66.67	100	O23	83.33	83.33	O35	66.67	83.33	O47	100	100
O12	83.33	100	O24	100	83.33	O36	100	100	Total(%)	90.43	90.07

Fig. 5. (a) Few images taken from the SOIL-47 database. (b) Recognition results on SOIL-47 images. With only two images, most of the images in the 90° cone are recognized. See text for details.

2α section. These ($47 \times 18 = 846$, $47 \times 36 = 1692$) images were taken as the training set. The testing set consisted of images in the range -2α to 2α (5 and 7 images respectively per object for 47 objects). Recognition accuracies above 90% validate the use of the proposed technique. More detailed results are in Fig. 5 (b). The recognition experiments show that the eigenspace estimated from view in a limited range can be used to recognize the views outside the range. It is evident that the multi-view relationships can be used to enhance appearance models to enable view independent recognition of objects.

6   Conclusion

The major contribution of this work is in construction of eigenspace from limited number of views. The algorithms proposed for the construction of eigenspace involve matrices that are very sparse. Efficient algorithms for performing operations on sparse matrices are used for implementation. A detailed analysis of the computational complexity of these algorithms is beyond the scope of the current work. The reconstruction error per pixel for various camera models are found to be less than 1%, validating the correctness of eigenspace construction process. Further, the recognition experiments conducted on both synthetic and real world data ascertain that the approach presented can be used to build view independent recognition systems. Future work would focus on the applicability of this for accurate pose estimation from limited views for deformable objects.

Acknowledgments

One of the authors, Paresh K. Jain, would like to acknowledge the financial support provided by GE (through the GE Foundation Scholar-Leaders Program 2004-06) while carrying out this work.

References

1. Wang, Y., Chua, C.S.: Face Recognition Across Views From 2D and 3D Images. Asian Conference on Computer Vision **2** (2004) 730–735
2. Mori, G., Malik, J.: Recognizing Objects in Adversial Clutter: Breaking a visual CAPTCHA. IEEE Conference on Computer Vision and Pattern Recognition **1** (2003) 134–144
3. Liu, X., Srivastava, A., Gallivan, K.: Optimal Linear Representation of Images for Object Recognition. IEEE Conference on Computer Vision and Pattern Recognition **1** (2003) 229–234
4. Pentland, A., Moghaddam, B., Starner, T.: View-based and modular eigenspaces for face recognition. IEEE Conference on Computer Vision and Pattern Recognition (1994) 84–91
5. Nayar, S.K., Nene, S.A., Murase, H.: Real Time 100 Object Recognition System. IEEE Int'l Conference on Robotics and Automation **3** (1996) 2321–2325
6. Turk, M., Pentland, A.: Face Recognition Using Eigenfaces. IEEE Conference on Computer Vision and Pattern Recognition (1991) 586 – 591
7. Cootes, T., Wheeler, G., Walker, K., Taylor, C.: Coupled View Active Appearance Models. British Machine Vision Conference **1** (2000) 52–61
8. Hartley, R., Zisserman, A.: Multiple View Geometry in Computer Vision. Cambridge University Press (2000)
9. Nene, S.A., Nayar, S.K., Murase, H.: Columbia Object Image Library(COIL-20). Technical Report CUCS-005-96 (1996)
10. J. Burianek, A. Ahmadyfard, J. Kittler: SOIL-47, The Surrey Object Image Library, Centre for Vision, Speach and Signal processing, Univerisity of Surrey. (at http://www.ee.surrey.ac.uk/Research/VSSP/demos/colour/soil47/)
11. Chatterjee, S., Banerjee, S., Biswas, K.K.: Reconstruction of Local Features for Facial Video Compression. Int'l Conf. on Image Processing **2** (2000) 211–214
12. S.Ulmann, R.Basri: Recognition by Linear Combination of Models. IEEE Trans. Pattern Anal. Machine Intell. **13** (1991) 992–1006
13. Avidan, S., Shashua, A.: Novel view synthesis by cascading trilinear tensors. IEEE Transactions on Visualization and Computer Graphics **4** (1998) 293–306
14. de Verdiere, V.C., Crowley, J.L.: Visual Recognition Using Local Appearance. European Conference on Computer Vision **1** (1998) 640–654

Face Recognition from Images with High Pose Variations by Transform Vector Quantization

Amitava Das, Manoj Balwani[1], Rahul Thota[1], and Prasanta Ghosh[2]

Microsoft Research India. Bangalore, India
amitavd@microsoft.com

Abstract. Pose and illumination variations are the most dominating and persistent challenges haunting face recognition, leading to various highly-complex 2D and 3D model based solutions. We present a novel transform vector quantization (TVQ) method which is fast and accurate and yet significantly less complex than conventional methods. TVQ offers a flexible and customizable way to capture the pose variations. Use of transform such as DCT helps compressing the image data to a small feature vector and judicious use of vector quantization helps to capture the various poses into compact codebooks. A confidence measure based sequence analysis allows the proposed TVQ method to accurately recognize a person in only 3-9 frames (less than ½ a second) from a video sequence of images with wide pose variations.

1   Introduction

Pose and illumination variations are the most dominating challenges in face recognition and have been the focus of many studies in the past [3][9][8][7]. Holistic face recognition methods such as the PCA-based Eigenface method [6] perform nicely for image sets where pose variation is minimal and performs rather poorly when there are wide variations of pose (e.g. the MSRI-V1 database shown in Fig. 1).

Even if the pose variation is minimal, e.g. for frontal images as shown in Fig. 2, there may still be a wide variation of expressions, which also limits the performance of several traditional face recognition approaches such as PCA. To overcome the challenges of pose and expression variations, several 2D and 3-D pose-normalization methods have been proposed, as nicely surveyed in [3]. However, in the same survey, it has been noted that most of these methods (which can handle pose variations) are quite complex in terms of computation complexity and memory usage.

Several recent studies [5][11][4][12][13] have shown that face recognition performance improves dramatically if a face video, or a sequence of face images of a person, is used for recognition, as opposed to using a single image. Several spatial-temporal methods such as [10], also reported good results. A good review can be found in [3]. Once again, due to the complex modeling employed to handle pose variations, these methods also require high computational complexity and the processing of a reasonably large sets of image frames, before reaching a decision.

---

1) IIT-Madras MTech & 2) IISc-Bangalore MS students, doing internship at MSR-India.

P. Kalra and S. Peleg (Eds.): ICVGIP 2006, LNCS 4338, pp. 674–685, 2006.

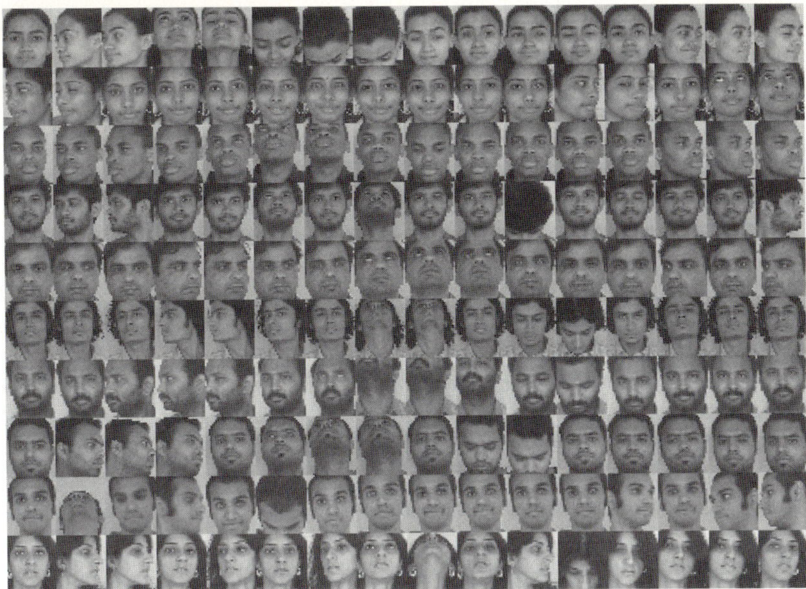

Fig. 1. Pose Variations in the MSRI-V1 Face Database

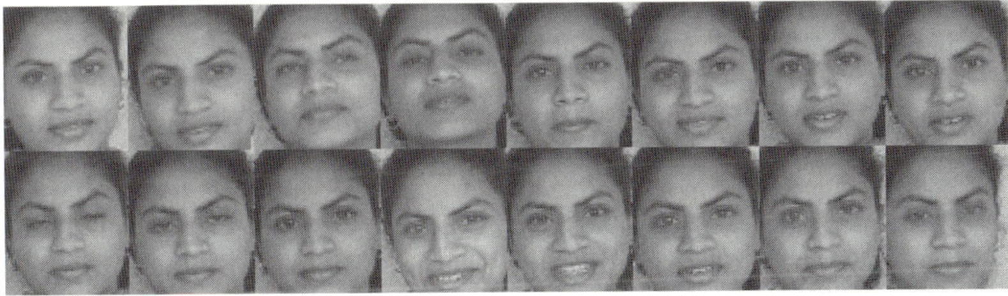

Fig. 2. Example of expression variations (MSRI V2 database of frontal face images)

We present a novel low-complexity transform vector quantization (TVQ) based face recognition method which handles pose variation quite efficiently and to some extent can handle illumination variation as well. The use of Discrete Cosine Transform [2] in our feature extraction delivers a significant amount of dimensionality reduction at much lower complexity than PCA. Our main contribution however is the application of vector quantization [1] in the transform domain, which allows the TVQ system to capture the pose variations of a person very effectively as multiple code vectors of a person-specific codebook (see Fig. 6). The proposed TVQ method gives a customizable platform, which can be tailored to work well with any kind of face data – with or without pose variations. For image data with little pose variation, TVQ demonstrates 100% identification accuracy with a very small codebook (size 4 and dimension 15) per person, compared to the 93% identification accuracy offered by PCA, using a 416 dimension feature vector per person. We also present a confidence-measure based fast face recognition from video, which delivers 100% accurate results with high confidence very quickly [processing only 3-9 frames or in about 400 ms]. Finally, a set of illumination-variation trials indicate that the proposed TVQ is also quite robust to illumination variation. The computational complexity and memory requirements of TVQ is significantly less than traditional PCA based methods [6][7].

2 Face Recognition by Transform Vector Quantization

The proposed Transform vector quantization (TVQ) face recognition method exploits the de-correlating property of the Discrete Cosine Transform [2] to extract a low-dimension feature vector from the input face image. For classification, we use a Vector Quantization [1] based scheme. A confidence-measure based fast-selection process further reduces the complexity and speeds up the face recognition process, while guaranteeing 100% accuracy. Details of the pre-processing, feature extraction and classification steps are presented next.

2.1 Preprocessing, Feature Extraction and Face-Transform Space in TVQ

The input images frames $<X_1, X_2,.. X_k, .. X_M>$ from the video are converted into gray images. From each frame, a N1 x N2 size image is cut (in our experiments we kept N1=136 and N2 = 120) from the region of interest (ROI) to create images $<I_1, I_2,.. I_k, .. I_M>$. The ROI is automatically extracted by tracking the face contour in the image using vertical and horizontal projections of selected areas of the image. Figure 2 shows the pre-processing step and resulting processed gray images.

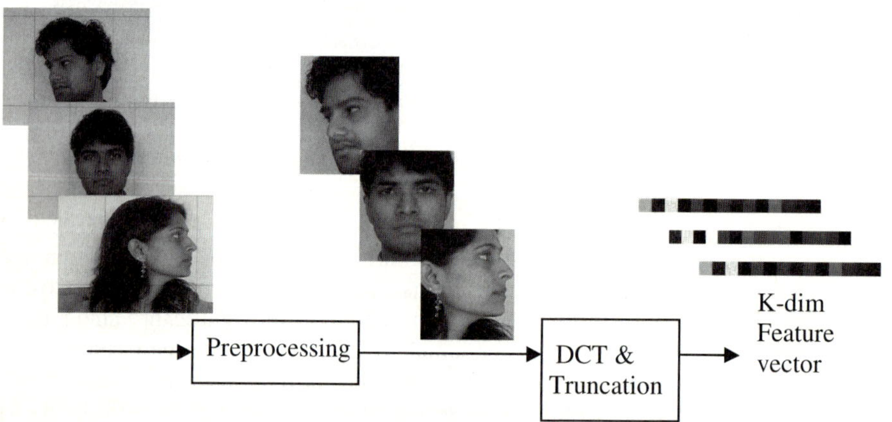

Fig. 3. Preprocessing and feature vector extraction in the proposed TVQ method

A 2-D DCT is then applied to the gray image I_k and the coefficients of the top left **m x m** corner of the transform coefficient matrix **C** is selected to form a feature vector F_k of size $K=(m^2-1)$. Note that all the components, except the 1st one (which is the DC coefficient $C(0,0)$), are chosen. Removal of the DC coefficient makes the proposed TVQ method somewhat immune to illumination variation.

This way a large amount of the face image information is stored into a significantly low dimension feature vector. In our experiment, our input image size was 280x320 or 89600 pixels and we used feature vectors having dimensions ranging from 9 to 63. Fig. 4 shows images reconstructed after such truncation of DCT coefficients for various values of K. Note that here the objective is not to preserve the quality of the input image but to pack important discerning attributes of the face image into a small feature vector. Thus the images reconstructed from the truncated DCT coefficients (our feature vector) do not represent as much spatial detail as the original image, but as we will see later, they are quite successful in differentiating the face images of different persons. This feature vector dimension $\mathbf{K} = (\mathbf{m}^2 - 1)$ will be a system parameter in the proposed TVQ face recognition method.

Original   K=15   K=35   K=63

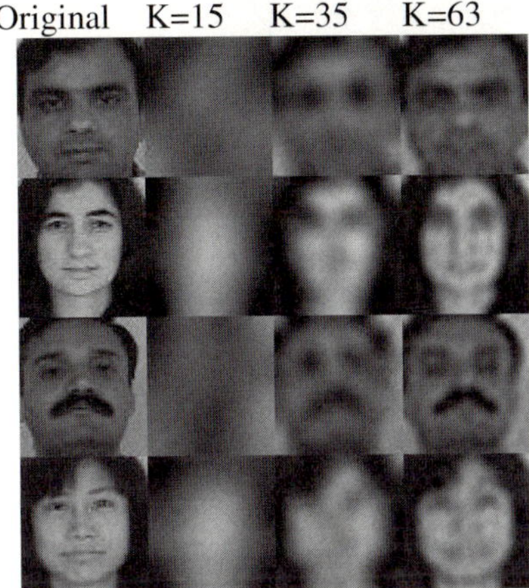

Fig. 4. Impact of the size of K in reconstructing back the image

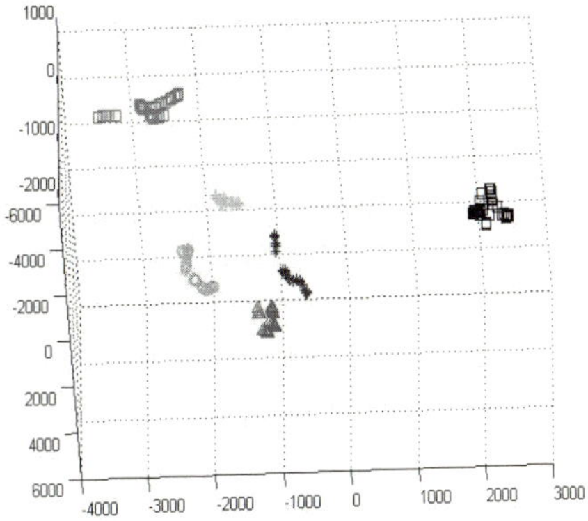

Fig. 5. Person clusters in the face transform space (K=3, 6 person system)

2.2 Recognition of Face by Transform Vector Quantization

In the TVQ method, the input face images are converted into the K-dimension feature vectors comprising of DCT coefficients. This can be interpreted as follows. The face images of all the T persons to be recognized, P_1, P_2, to P_T, are now lying in this K-dimension "face-transform" space. The face images (various poses) of each person will be occupying a certain "region" of this face-transform space. Vector quantization [1] can now be used to design a person-specific codebook, which by a proper Voronoi tessellations of this K-dimension face-transform space, will be able to capture and define the regions of various persons. Fig. 5 shows the results of a toy example, in which TVQ is applied to the face images of 6 different persons. Here K is chosen to be only 3 so that we can plot the "person regions" in the 3-D face transform space. Six distinct clusters, one for each person, are clearly seen in Fig. 5.

All the various face images of the i-th person, P_i , will now be lying within the i-th region in the face-transform space and can be represented by an N-size VQ codebook, $\mathbf{CB_i} = [\mathbf{C_{i1}}, \mathbf{C_{i2}}, ..., \mathbf{C_{ij}}, ... \mathbf{C_{iN}}]$, each $\mathbf{C_{ij}}$, being a K-dimensional code vector. The

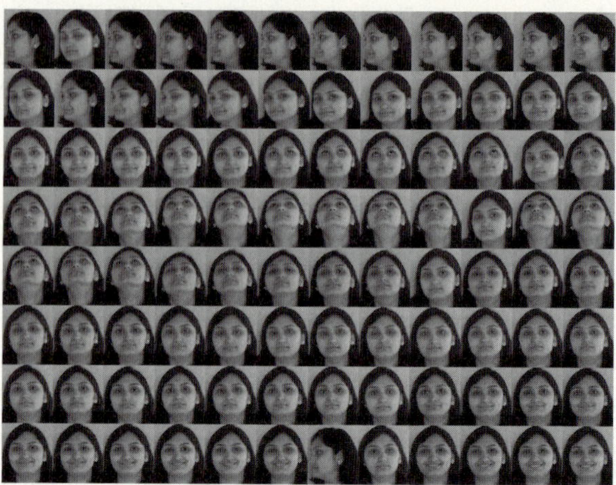

Input set of face images of various pose

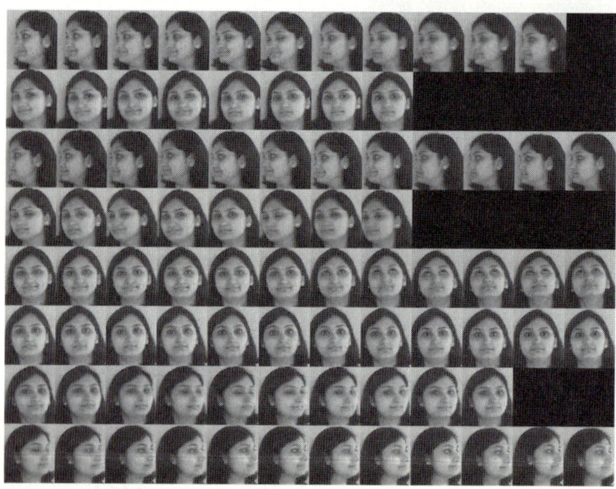

Same images encoded & clustered by TVQ

Fig. 6. Capture of the various poses of a person's face by the TVQ codebook. When a set of face images of various poses of a person (shown at the top collage) is encoded by the TVQ codebook of the same person, the different poses get automatically clustered as shown on the bottom collage. In the bottom collage, all the images in the i-th row is closest to the i-th vector of the TVQ codebook of the person. K=15 and N=8 are the codebook parameters for this example. This demonstrates that in TVQ, the different code-vectors of a person do capture the different poses of the person. Note that in the bottom collage, a maximum of 12 images per row is shown, i.e. some code-vectors (e.g. 5,6 and 8) has more than 12 images closest to them.

various poses of the i-th person will be captured by the various code vectors of this codebook C as shown in Figure 6. Here, the face images, which are "closest" to each of the 8 code vectors of the codebook of a certain speaker are shown. As seen here, the different code vectors do capture the pose variations of the same person. Such codebooks, one for each person, can be designed by any VQ training algorithm such as LBG [1]. A large number of pose variations can be captured by a reasonably-sized codebook. Thus, representation of each person, in our proposed TVQ method, is much more "richer" than traditional PCA based approach [6] in which only one representative face data, the M-dimensional weight vector, represents the person.

Given an input face image, the recognition task by TVQ then becomes the search for the best codebook, $\mathbf{CB_{j*}}$, which is "closest" to the feature vector $\mathbf{F}$, extracted from the input image. We present 3 TVQ algorithms next: a) person identification from a single face image, b) person verification from a single image, and c) person identification from a video.

Algorithm 1: Person Identification by TVQ

a) Given an input image $\mathbf{X}$, extract the transform feature vector $\mathbf{F}$.
b) For each person, P_i, find D_i the closest distance of its codebook $\mathbf{CB_i}$ from the input feature vector $\mathbf{F}$:
D_i = minimum of D_{ij}, where $D_{ij} = \|\mathbf{F} - \mathbf{C_{ij}}\|^2$, j=1,2,…,N, $\mathbf{C_{ij}}$ being the code vector of the codebook $\mathbf{CB_i}$
c) The identified person is person P_k, where D_k is the minimum of all D_i, i=1,2,3…T.

Algorithm 2: Person Verification by TVQ From a Single Image

For person verification, a face image $\mathbf{X}$ is presented along with an "identity claim" k. The task is now to verify whether the image belongs to the k-th person P_k, or not. The TVQ verification algorithm is given below:

1) Given an input face image $\mathbf{X}$, extract the transform feature vector $\mathbf{F}$.
b) Given the identity claim, k, compute two distances, d_trgt & d_bkgr, as follows:
d_trgt = minimum distance of the input feature vector from the codebook $\mathbf{CB_k}$ of claimed person P_k; In other words, d_trgt = minimum of D_{ij}, where $D_{ij} = \|\mathbf{F} - \mathbf{C_{ij}}\|^2$, j=1,2,…,N, $\mathbf{C_{ij}}$ being the code vector of the codebook $\mathbf{CB_k}$ of the target person P_k.
d_bkgr = minimum distance of the input feature vector from the collection of all codebooks of all other persons except person P_k. In other words, d_bkgr = minimum of D_{ij}, where $D_{ij} = \|\mathbf{F} - \mathbf{C_{ij}}\|^2$, j=1,2,…,N; i=1,2,3,..T ; i not equal to k, where $\mathbf{C_{ij}}$ is the i-th code vectors of j-th codebook.
c) Compute a confidence measure λ = d_trgt/d_bkgr, and if $\lambda < \theta$ (θ being a predetermined threshold during training) then the presented identity claim is accepted as person P_k; else it is rejected.

Algorithm 3: Person Identification by TVQ from a Video

In contrast to earlier methods of face recognition from video, which require processing of a reasonably large set of such frames before making a decision, TVQ offers a much faster and less complex method as described below:
a) Given input image sequence $\mathbf{X_1}$, $\mathbf{X_2}$,…$\mathbf{X_M}$, extract feature vectors, $\mathbf{F_1}$, $\mathbf{F_2}$,…$\mathbf{F_M}$
b) At each k-th sequence, for each person, P_i, compute an accumulated distance (AD) A_i as follows:

$A_i(k) = D_i(1) + D_i(2) + D_i(3) + \ldots + D_i(k)$, where $D_i(k)$ is the minimum distance of the feature vector $\mathbf{F_k}$ to the codebook $\mathbf{CB_i}$ of person P_i

c) If $\mathbf{A_j}$ is the least among all j=1,2,...T, then compute a confidence measure β_j, which is the difference $(\mathbf{A_j} - \mathbf{A_m})$ between the best candidate $\mathbf{A_j}$ and the next best candidate (say $\mathbf{A_m}$). If this confidence measure β_j is greater than a pre-determined threshold τ_j (learned during training), then the j-th person is chosen as the identified person. τ_j is calculated by computing the histogram of β_j with the training data and then setting τ_j as a fraction of the mean value of β_j .

We call the number of frames TVQ takes to detect a person as the Time-of-Detection or ToD, which is used later in our trials as a performance metric.

3   Face Recognition Tasks, Databases and Description of Trials

At Microsoft Research India, we created our own Biometric Person Recognition Database called the MSRI database by recording face video as well speech from a wide set of people of various nationalities. For face recognition, we used two subsets (Table 1) of the MSRI database: a) MSRI-V1, consisting of face images with various pose variations (Fig. 1) and b) MSRI-V2, with only frontal face images (Fig. 2).

Table 1. Details of the MSRI-V1 & MSRI-V2 Face Databases

	MSRI-V1	MSRI-V2
No of Person in the database	65	52
Average no of Images/Person for Training	324	55
Average no of Images/Person for Testing	325	83
Total number of test trials	16884	5414

The performance metrics used for the tasks of identification, verification and verification from video are Percentage of Accuracy, Equal Error Rate (EER) and Time to Detect (ToD) respectively. Two system parameters, N (codebook size) and K (code-vector dimension), are varied during trials. The PCA based Eigenface [6] method was also ran for comparison and the dimension M of the pattern weight vector Ω was varied as the system parameter.

4   Results and Discussions

The results, shown in Table 2&3 for MSRI-V1 and MSRI-V2 respectively, clearly shows the proposed TVQ method outperforms conventional PCA based method significantly when there is high pose variation.

Table 2. Identification accuracy of the TVQ and PCA based face recognition methods on the MSRI-V1 database having face images with high pose variations

		K=15	K=35	K=63		M=416	M=240	M=60
	N=4	83.7	86.2	87.0				
TVQ	N=8	92.4	94.3	94.7	PCA	68.8	68.7	67.6
	N=16	96.9	96.8	97.1				
	N=32	98.8	99.1	99.4				

Table 3. Identification accuracy of the TVQ and PCA based face recognition methods on the MSRI-V2 database having only frontal face images

		K=15		M=260	M=60	M=30	M=15
	N=1	90.9					
TVQ	N=2	99.0	PCA	93.9	92.8	90.4	85.7
	N=4	100.0					

The performance of TVQ increases dramatically if we increase N (number of code-vectors) as opposed to increasing K (feature dimension) as evident in these tables. For only frontal images, TVQ delivers 100% accuracy at N=4 and K=15 or storage of only 60 data points per person and 60*T multiply-add operations, as opposed to 93.9% performance by PCA which requires 260 data points to store per person, requiring 260*T multiply-add operations. The feature extraction process of TVQ is also much simpler (2*P*K multiply-add for a PxP image and K-dim TVQ) than PCA (P*P*M multiply add for a PxP image and M dimension PCA weight vector).

4.2 Person Verification

As seen in Table 4, TVQ is offering an EER of 2.1% for MSRI-V1, which is much better than the PCA figure of 48%. For the MSRI-V2 database, TVQ (N=16;K=15) delivered 1.5% EER. We did not run PCA for this trial.

Table 4. Performance comparison (in terms of Equal Error Rate) of the TVQ and PCA based face recognition methods on the MSRI-V1 database having high pose variations

		K=15	K=63		M=416
TVQ	N=4	5.2	4.4	PCA	48%
	N=16	2.1	2.0		

4.3 Person Recognition from Video

We ran these experiments only on the MSRI-V1 database, as for MSRI-V2 we are always getting the correct detection in the first frame itself.

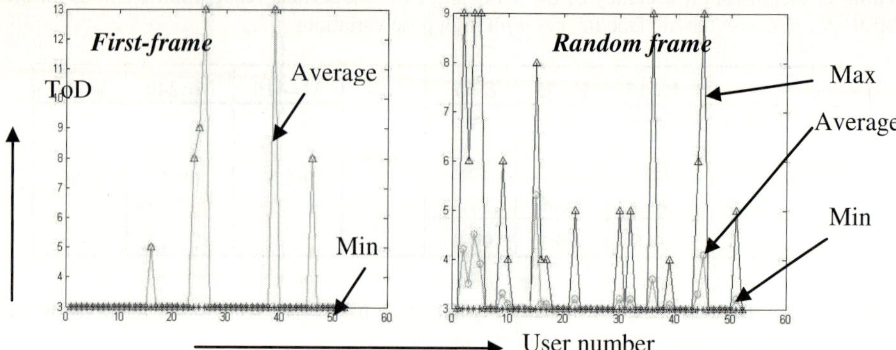

Fig. 7. Time to Detect Statistics of TVQ (n=16 K=15) for MSRI-V1

The goal is to determine how many frames (Time of detection or ToD) does TVQ need to recognize a person with total confidence. We ran two experiments: a) FIRST-FRAME, where the 1st frame is always the starting frame (this was ran 1 time per speaker), and b) RANDOM, here the starting frame is chosen at random, thereby allowing the processing to start from any pose variations (this trial is ran 10 times for each speaker) The results are shown in Fig. 7.

In case of FIRST-FRAME, the worst-case detection time is 13 frames or approx. 400 mill-second, although most persons were detected in 3 frames only (90 ms). For the RANDOM trial it was found that on average (green circle) the detection time is approximately 5 frames or 150 ms, where as the worst case was found to be 9 frames or 270 ms.

4.4   Illumination Variation Trials

In this experiment, we artificially changed the illumination of the test images from 80% to 120% in 3 different ways (as shown in Figure 8) : a) L-X: Change only left half (multiply by X%), b) C-X: change entire image, c) R-X: Change only right half (X=80% or 120%). This reflects somewhat what can happen in a real life situation.

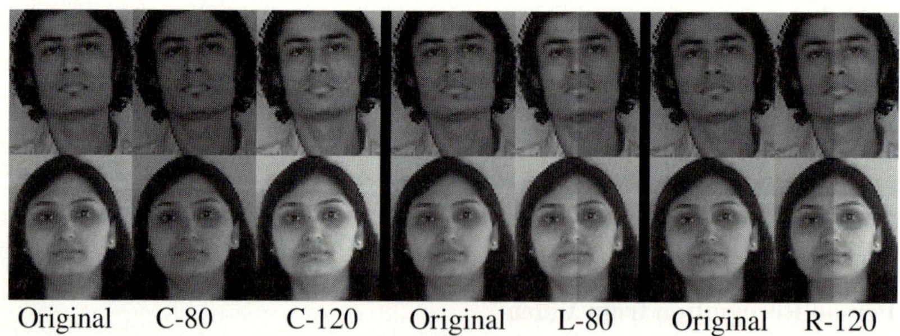

Fig. 8. Example images with 3 types of artificially-created illumination variation

Table 5 shows the performance figures (Identification Accuracy) for various illumination variations and Figure 7 shows the ToD figures for the L-80. For PCA the performance dropped from 68.8% (original) to 63% for R-120.

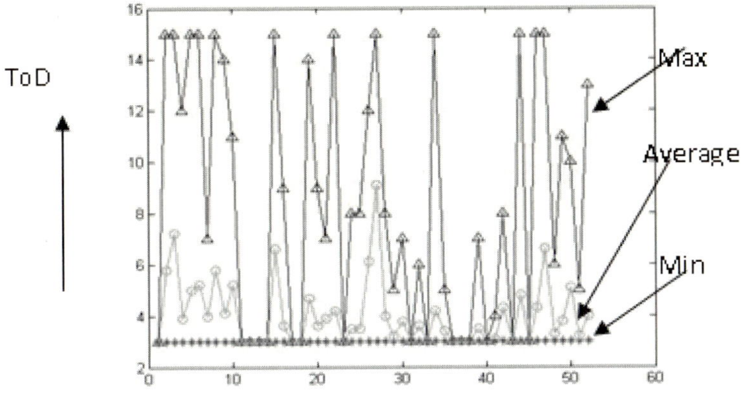

Fig. 9. Time to Detect results for the L-80 illumination variation trial (N=16; K=15)

Table 5. Identification accuracy of TVQ for various illumination-variation trials

	Left			Center			Right		
N x K	L80	Orig	L120	C80	Orig	C120	R80	Orig	R120
4 x 15	74	83.7	80	78	83.7	81	73	83.7	74
16 x 15	89	96.9	96	90	96.9	97	84	96.9	88

As seen in Fig. 9 and Table 5, illumination variation is impacting the identification accuracy of TVQ to some extent but not to a great extent and especially the ToD results are quite good. On average, people are getting detected in less than 7 frame (210 ms) and the worst case detection time is 15 frames or 450 ms for the L-80 condition.

5   Conclusions

We presented a novel transform vector quantization (TVQ) face recognition method which can be tailored to provide high performance for various extents of pose and illumination variations. Use of transform such as DCT in TVQ helps compressing the image data to a small feature vector and judicious use of vector quantization helps to capture the various poses into compact codebooks. The computational complexity of TVQ is significantly less than a conventional PCA based method as shown in Table 6.

Table 6. Comparison of TVQ with PCA for face images with high pose variation

	TVQ	PCA
	N=32;k=15	M=416
System Parameters		
Identification-Accuracy for MSRI-V1	98.80%	68.80%
EER for MSRI-V1	2.10%	48%
ToD for MSRI-V1-average value	3 frames	-
Feature extraction complexity - 160x160 image	4800	10649600
Classification complexity / per person	480	416
Overall Detection Complexity / per person	5280	10650016
Memory/user(float number to store) / per person	480	416

In the proposed TVQ method, high extent of pose variation can be handled by having more number of code vectors, while more image precision can be obtained by increasing the feature vector dimension. A confidence measure based sequence analysis allows the proposed TVQ method to accurately recognize a person in only 3-9 frames (less than ½ a second) from a video sequence of images with wide pose variations.

References

1. Gersho A. and Gray R.: Vector Quantization and Signal Compression. Kluwer Academic Publishers. (1992)
2. Rao K. and Yip P.: Discrete Cosine Transform – Algorithms, Advantages, Applications. Academic Publisher. (1990)
3. Zhao W., Chellappa R., Rosenfeld A., and Phillips P.J.: Face recognition: A literature survey. ACM Computing Surveys. Vol. 35. (2003) 399 – 458
4. Zhou, S., Krueger V., Chellappa R.: Probabilistic recognition of human faces from video. Computer Vision and Image Understanding. Vol. 91. (2003) 214 – 245
5. 5. Kuang-Chih Lee Ho, Ming-Hsuan Yang J., Kriegman, D.: Video-based face recognition using probabilistic appearance manifolds. Proc. IEEE CVPR (2003) 313 – 320
6. Turk M. and Pentland A.: Eigenfaces for recognition. Journal of Cognitive Neuroscience, 3(1). (1991) 71 – 86
7. Moghaddam B. and Pentland A. : Face recognition using view-based and modular eigenspaces. In : Automatic Systems for the Identification and Inspection of Humans, Vol. 2277. SPIE. (1994)
8. Phillips P., Grother P., Micheals R., Blackburn D., Tabassi E., and Bone J.: Face recognition vendor test 2002: Evaluation report. Technical Report NISTIR 6965, http://www.frvt.org (2003)
9. Yang M., Kriegman D., Ahuja N.: Detecting Faces in Images : A Survey. IEEE Trans. PAMI, vol. 24. (2002) 34 – 58
10. Li Y., Gong S., Liddell H. : Video-based face recognition using identity surfaces. Technical report, Queen Mary, University of London (2001)
11. Biuk Z. and Loncaric S.: Face Recognition from Multi-Pose Image Sequence. In: Proceedings of 2nd Intl. Symposium on Image and Signal Processing (2001) 319 – 324

12. Krueger V. and S. Zhou S.: Exemplar-based face recognition from video. In: Proc. ECCV (2002) 732–746
13. Aggarwal G., Roy-Chowdhury A., and Chellappa R.: A system identification approach for video-based face recognition. In: Proc. ICPR (2004) 23 – 26
14. Gong S., Psarrou A., Katsouli I., and Palavouzis P.: Tracking and Recognition of Face Sequences. In: European Workshop on Combined Real and Synthetic Image Processing for Broadcast and Video Production (1994)
15. Hafed Z. and Levine M.: Face recognition using the discrete cosine transform. Int. J. Comput. Vision Vol. 43(3) (2001) 167 – 188
16. Howell A. and Buxton H.: Towards unconstrained face recognition from image sequences. In: Proc. Intl. Conf. on Automatic Face Recognition (1996) 224 – 229

An Integrated Approach for Downscaling MPEG Video

Sudhir Porwal[1] and Jayanta Mukherjee[2]

[1] Image Analysis Center
Defence Electronics Applications Laboratory
Dehradun, India 248001
[2] Dept. of Computer Science
Indian Institute of Technology
Kharagpur, India 721302

Abstract. Digital video databases are widely available in compressed format. In many applications such as video browsing, picture in picture, video conferencing etc. data transfer at lower bit rate is required. This requires downscaling of the video before transmission. The conventional spatial domain approach for downscaling video is computationally very expensive. The computation can greatly be reduced if downscaling and inverse motion compensation (IMC) are performed in Discrete Cosine Transform (DCT) domain. There are many algorithms in the literature to perform IMC in the DCT domain. In this paper, we propose an efficient integrated technique to perform IMC and downscaling in DCT domain. This new approach results in significant improvement in computational complexity.

1 Introduction

Due to the day to day advancement in multi-media based applications, more and more video data are available in digital formats. A digital video is typically stored in the compressed form to reduce storage space and transmission time. International Organization for Standardization (ISO) has proposed MPEG standards [1] for video compression. According to MPEG standard, a video stream consists of a number of GOPs and each GOP is a pre-specified sequence of different kinds of frames. There are three such different types of frames, namely, I, P and B. The I frames are intra coded frame and they are followed by P and B kinds of frames which are known as inter coded frames. They are also called motion compensated frames. There are quite a few good review papers [2] [3] [4] dealing with this standard.

There are applications as video browsing, picture in picture, video conferencing which requires video to be transcoded at lower bit rates and of reduced frame size. A straightforward method to perform this transcoding is to decode each frame in the input video, downscale each frame spatially and re-encode at a lower bit rate. This technique is known as spatial domain downscaling. But the spatial domain technique is very time consuming and computationally inefficient to meet the requirement of real time applications. The DCT/IDCT

P. Kalra and S. Peleg (Eds.): ICVGIP 2006, LNCS 4338, pp. 686–695, 2006.
© Springer-Verlag Berlin Heidelberg 2006

operations and motion estimation during re-encoding of downscaled video are main bottlenecks of this approach. The computation time can greatly be reduced if we perform downscaling in the DCT domain itself, which eliminates the requirement of costly IDCT operation. There exists many algorithms [5] [6] [7] [8] [9] [10] [11] that provide different approaches for image/video downscaling in the DCT domain. As stated earlier, many frames in an MPEG stream (MPEG-1, MPEG-2) are motion compensated to achieve higher degree of compression. One has to reconstruct these motion compensated frames using inverse motion compensation(IMC) techniques before downscaling. This problem of inverse motion compensation (IMC) in DCT domain was studied in the work of Chang and Messerschmit [9], and subsequently in [12], [13], [14], [15]. Merhav[12] has proposed an excellent scheme to perform IMC in the DCT domain. He has also proposed an efficient computational model for performing this task with the help of factorization of the DCT and IDCT matrices that correspond to fast eight point winograd DCT/IDCT [16]. In [14], the shared information in a macroblock is used to speed up the process of IMC. It shows about 19% and 13.5% improvement over the method presented in [12], [13] respectively. In [15], a Macroblockwise Inverse Motion Compensation (MBIMC) scheme is presented to predict a complete macroblock in single step. This work is extension to the work of Merhav [12]. The method presented in [15] has shown 27% improvement over the Merhav approach.

In this paper, we propose a different approach for video downscaling by combining the downscaling and IMC as a composite operation. This approach is extention of our previous work [15] reported as Macroblockwise Inverse Motion Compensation (MBIMC) scheme. This work formulate a single expression for downscaling and inverse motion compensation. This reduces the computational complexity. We have computed the complexities in terms of multiplication and addition operations. Since multiplication operation is always costlier than addition operation, we assume in our work that a single multiplication is equivalent to 3 machine instructions and addition as a single machine instruction (as considered in [17]). The results are recorded using video stream containing I and P frames only (n=3, m=1 GOP structure is used). However the proposed approach can easily be extended to videos containing B frames also. In the next section (section II), we discuss in brief about MBIMC scheme [15]. In the section III, the integrated approach for downscaling a video with IMC is discussed. Subsequently, results are presented and discussed in section IV.

2   Conversion of a P Frame to an I Frame

In an MPEG video stream, motion compensated frame (P) can be converted to an intra (I) frame by performing the IMC operation. In motion compensation, each macroblock M in current frame is predicted from the previous encoded frame. If predicted macroblock is M' then error E is computed as $E = M - M'$ and finally this error block E is encoded in the video stream. A motion compensated frame is called inter coded frame. The inverse motion compensation is required to convert an inter coded frame (P-frames) to an intra coded frame (I-frames).

During motion compensation, the best matching reference macroblock M' may not be aligned to any macroblock of its reference frame. In general, the predicted macroblock M' may intersect with nine 8×8 blocks (see Figure 2). Our aim is to compute $DCT(M)$ of current macroblock using the fact $M = M' + E$. As $DCT(E)$ is available directly from the compressed stream, we have to compute $DCT(M')$.

In [15], the MBIMC scheme is presented to perform IMC for a macroblock. We discuss the MBIMC scheme here for the sake of completeness.

2.1 Macroblockwise Inverse Motion Compensation (MBIMC)

In MPEG video stream, motion estimation and compensation are performed for each macroblock. A macroblock contains four 8×8 DCT blocks. A motion vector is generated for each macroblock and each 8×8 block in the macroblock shares the same motion vector.

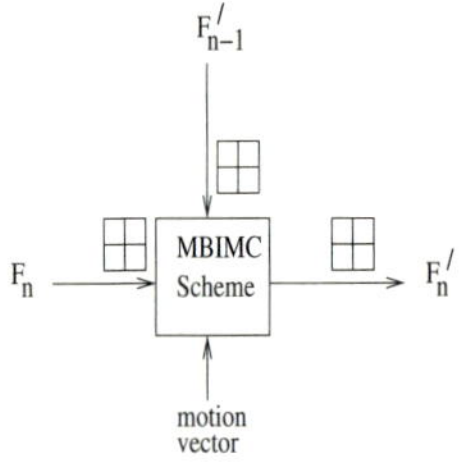

Fig. 1. Block diagram of MBIMC scheme

The functionality of MBIMC scheme is shown in Figure 1. The F'_{n-1} represents the $(n-1)^{th}$ intra/reference frame. F_n is the nth motion compensated inter frame in the video sequence. The MBIMC scheme uses the motion vector and macroblocks from reference and current (inter) frames to perform the IMC for complete macroblock. The IMC operation converts an inter macroblock in to Intra macroblock which can easily be downscaled by any downscaling algorithm.

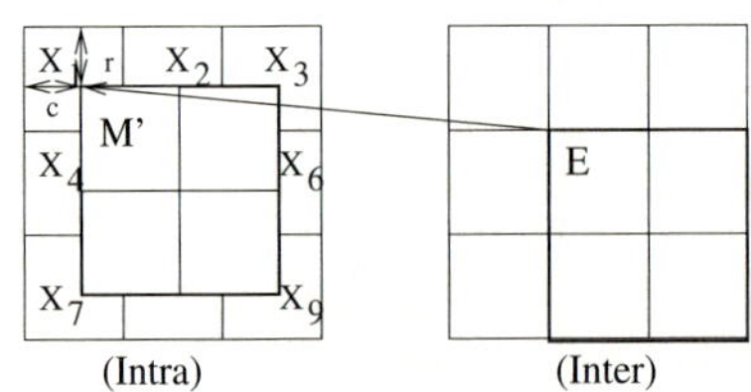

Fig. 2. Macroblockwise inverse motion compensation (MBIMC)

As shown in Figure 2, M' is the predicted macroblock in the reference frame which starts from the location (r, c). Macroblock M' does not always align with the block boundaries and intersects with nine 8×8 DCT blocks in general. In MBIMC scheme, the M' is computed from the nine 8×8 DCT blocks. If $x_1, x_2, x_3, x_4, x_5, x_6, x_7, x_8, x_9$ are the adjacent blocks in spatial domain then a 16×16 block from the 24×24 block can be extracted using the Eq. (1).

$$m' = c_r \begin{bmatrix} x_1 & x_2 & x_3 \\ x_4 & x_5 & x_6 \\ x_7 & x_8 & x_9 \end{bmatrix} c_c \tag{1}$$

Where m' is the predicted macroblock in spatial domain and c_r is a 16×24 matrix, c_c is 24×16 matrix. These matrices are different for different values of r and c (refer Figure 2). Since $1 \leq r \leq 8$ and $1 \leq c \leq 8$, there can be eight different c_r and c_c matrices which can be pre-computed and stored.

Since we have DCT blocks $X_1, X_2, X_3, X_4, X_5, X_6, X_7, X_8, X_9$ and we have to extract macroblock M' from these nine DCT blocks. The macroblock M' is a group of four adjacent 8×8 DCT blocks. To achieve this, Eq. (1) is expressed in the DCT domain as follows:

$$\mathbf{M'} = \begin{pmatrix} S_8 & 0 \\ 0 & S_8 \end{pmatrix} \left\{ c_r \begin{bmatrix} S_8^t & 0 & 0 \\ 0 & S_8^t & 0 \\ 0 & 0 & S_8^t \end{bmatrix} \begin{bmatrix} X_1 & X_2 & X_3 \\ X_4 & X_5 & X_6 \\ X_7 & X_8 & X_9 \end{bmatrix} \begin{bmatrix} S_8 & 0 & 0 \\ 0 & S_8 & 0 \\ 0 & 0 & S_8 \end{bmatrix} c_c \right\} \begin{pmatrix} S_8^t & 0 \\ 0 & S_8^t \end{pmatrix} \tag{2}$$

Here $'0'$ represents a 8×8 matrix of zeros. The matrix multiplication inside the curly braces results in a 16×16 matrix, which represent the spatial domain block. The premultiplication of $\begin{pmatrix} S_8 & 0 \\ 0 & S_8 \end{pmatrix}$ and post multiplication of $\begin{pmatrix} S_8^t & 0 \\ 0 & S_8^t \end{pmatrix}$ results in a 16×16 macroblock containing four 8×8 DCT blocks. Let us define $\mathbf{S}$ and $\mathbf{S^t}$ as shown below.

$$\mathbf{S} = \begin{bmatrix} S_8 & 0 & 0 \\ 0 & S_8 & 0 \\ 0 & 0 & S_8 \end{bmatrix} \text{ and } \mathbf{S^t} = \begin{bmatrix} S_8^t & 0 & 0 \\ 0 & S_8^t & 0 \\ 0 & 0 & S_8^t \end{bmatrix}$$

Then $\mathbf{S^t}$ can be written using the well known factorization of 8 point DCT matrix S as shown in Eq. (3).

$$S_8 = DPB_1B_2MA_1A_2A_3 \tag{3}$$

Here D is a diagonal matrix, P is a permutation matrix, B_1, B_2, A_1, A_2, A_3 are sparse matrices of zeros and ones and M is sparse matrix of real numbers. The details can be seen in [16].

$$\mathbf{S^t} = \underbrace{\begin{bmatrix} (MA_1A_2A_3)^t & 0 & 0 \\ 0 & (MA_1A_2A_3)^t & 0 \\ 0 & 0 & (MA_1A_2A_3)^t \end{bmatrix}}_{\mathbf{Q^t}} \underbrace{\begin{bmatrix} B_2^t & 0 & 0 \\ 0 & B_2^t & 0 \\ 0 & 0 & B_2^t \end{bmatrix}}_{\mathbf{B2^t}} \underbrace{\begin{bmatrix} B_1^t & 0 & 0 \\ 0 & B_1^t & 0 \\ 0 & 0 & B_1^t \end{bmatrix}}_{\mathbf{B1^t}} \underbrace{\begin{bmatrix} P^t & 0 & 0 \\ 0 & P^t & 0 \\ 0 & 0 & P^t \end{bmatrix}}_{\mathbf{P^t}} \underbrace{\begin{bmatrix} D^t & 0 & 0 \\ 0 & D^t & 0 \\ 0 & 0 & D^t \end{bmatrix}}_{\mathbf{D^t}}$$

Similarly, equation for $\mathbf{S}$ is factorized also.

Using the above mentioned notations, we can rewrite Eq. (2) as given below.

$$\mathbf{M'} = \begin{pmatrix} S_8 & 0 \\ 0 & S_8 \end{pmatrix} \left\{ \mathbf{c_r Q^t B2^t B1^t P^t D^t} \begin{bmatrix} X_1 & X_2 & X_3 \\ X_4 & X_5 & X_6 \\ X_7 & X_8 & X_9 \end{bmatrix} \mathbf{DPB1B2Q c_c} \right\} \begin{pmatrix} S_8^t & 0 \\ 0 & S_8^t \end{pmatrix} \tag{4}$$

The Eq. (4) is used to perform IMC for a macroblock in MBIMC scheme. The MBIMC scheme can be referred in detail in [15].

3   Video Downscaling and IMC : Integrated Scheme

Interestingly, the IMC in the DCT domain and downscaling can also be clubbed together in to a single step. The functionality of integrated scheme is described in Figure 3. F'_{n-1} is $(n-1)^{th}$ downscaled reference frame and F_n is next inter frame in the video sequence. Each downscaled reference frame (F'_{n-1}) is upscaled (using [5]) by a factor of two, to reconstruct the next frame (F_n) in the video sequence. The $(n-1)^{th}$ upscaled frame is represented as F''_{n-1}. It may be noted that the upsampling of I frames is not required as it is already available from the compressed video stream. The integrated scheme takes the four 8×8 blocks from F_n and F''_{n-1}, performs IMC and downscaling and generate 8×8 downscaled intra block F'_n.

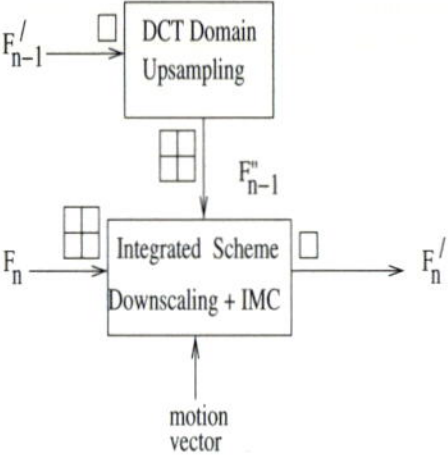

Fig. 3. Integrated scheme for downscaling+IMC

An equation can be derived to perform IMC and downscaling operations simultaneously. But in the integrated approach, we have to perform upsampling of the downscaled frame to convert next inter frame in the video sequence in to intra frame. This upsampling requires additional computation. if we combine the downscaling operation with inverse motion compensation, the Eq. (4) can be written as

$$\mathbf{X'} = \begin{pmatrix} S_8 & 0 \\ 0 & S_8 \end{pmatrix} \left\{ \mathbf{d} \left\{ \mathbf{c_r Q^t B2^t B1^t P^t D^t} \begin{bmatrix} X_1 & X_2 & X_3 \\ X_4 & X_5 & X_6 \\ X_7 & X_8 & X_9 \end{bmatrix} \mathbf{DPB1B2Qc_c} \right\} \mathbf{d^t} \right\} \begin{pmatrix} S_8^t & 0 \\ 0 & S_8^t \end{pmatrix} \tag{5}$$

where $\mathbf{d}$ is a downscaling filter as shown in Eq. (6).

$$\mathbf{d} = 0.5 \begin{bmatrix} 1 & 1 & 0 & 0 & 0 & 0 & 0 & 0 & 0 & 0 & 0 & 0 & 0 & 0 & 0 & 0 \\ 0 & 0 & 1 & 1 & 0 & 0 & 0 & 0 & 0 & 0 & 0 & 0 & 0 & 0 & 0 & 0 \\ 0 & 0 & 0 & 0 & 1 & 1 & 0 & 0 & 0 & 0 & 0 & 0 & 0 & 0 & 0 & 0 \\ 0 & 0 & 0 & 0 & 0 & 0 & 1 & 1 & 0 & 0 & 0 & 0 & 0 & 0 & 0 & 0 \\ 0 & 0 & 0 & 0 & 0 & 0 & 0 & 0 & 1 & 1 & 0 & 0 & 0 & 0 & 0 & 0 \\ 0 & 0 & 0 & 0 & 0 & 0 & 0 & 0 & 0 & 0 & 1 & 1 & 0 & 0 & 0 & 0 \\ 0 & 0 & 0 & 0 & 0 & 0 & 0 & 0 & 0 & 0 & 0 & 0 & 1 & 1 & 0 & 0 \\ 0 & 0 & 0 & 0 & 0 & 0 & 0 & 0 & 0 & 0 & 0 & 0 & 0 & 0 & 1 & 1 \end{bmatrix}_{8 \times 16} \tag{6}$$

The $\mathbf{d}$ and $\mathbf{d^t}$ matrix multiplication with internal 16×16 IMC block, will yield the 8×8 block. Here DCT represent the 8-point DCT of the resultant block. $\mathbf{X'}$ is the IMC and downscaled version of the actual reference macroblock which can directly be added to downscaled error macroblock $\mathbf{E}$ to get the desired downscaled intra macroblock. An efficient scheme is derived to perform matrix multiplication as given in Eq. (5).

Let us represent

$$\mathbf{J_r} = \mathbf{dc_r Q^t} \qquad 1 \le r \le 8$$
$$\mathbf{K_c} = \mathbf{Qc_c d^t} \qquad 1 \le c \le 8$$

$(\mathbf{dc_r})$ and $(\mathbf{c_c d^t})$ multiplication will generate matrices of size 8×24 and 24×8, which can be calculated a priory (16 such matrices). The sizes of the $\mathbf{J_r}$ and $\mathbf{K_c}$ will be 8×24 and 24×8. Since $\mathbf{J_r}$ and $\mathbf{K_c}$ have similar structure, both require same number of operations to perform matrix multiplication with an arbitrary matrix of size 24×24.

It is observed that $\mathbf{J_r}$ has two different structures depending on whether $\mathbf{r}$ is even or odd (similarly it is true for $\mathbf{K_c}$). We will consider two cases when $\mathbf{r = 2}$ and $\mathbf{r = 5}$, to present our efficient computation model to perform the matrix multiplication of $\mathbf{J_r}$ matrices with an arbitrary matrix. The matrix $\mathbf{J_2}$ is computed and given below.

$$\mathbf{J_2} = \begin{bmatrix}
2 & -2 & 0 & 0 & D & 2A & E & 0 & 0 & 0 & 0 & 0 & 0 & 0 & 0 & 0 & 0 & 0 & 0 & 0 & 0 & 0 & 0 & 0 \\
2 & 2 & -2A & -2 & 0 & 0 & 0 & 0 & 0 & 0 & 0 & 0 & 0 & 0 & 0 & 0 & 0 & 0 & 0 & 0 & 0 & 0 & 0 & 0 \\
2 & -2 & 0 & 0 & -D & -2A & -E & 0 & 0 & 0 & 0 & 0 & 0 & 0 & 0 & 0 & 0 & 0 & 0 & 0 & 0 & 0 & 0 & 0 \\
1 & 1 & A & 1 & C & 0 & -B & -1 & 1 & 1 & A & 1 & C & 0 & B & 1 & 0 & 0 & 0 & 0 & 0 & 0 & 0 & 0 \\
0 & 0 & 0 & 0 & 0 & 0 & 0 & 0 & 2 & -2 & 0 & 0 & D & 2A & E & 0 & 0 & 0 & 0 & 0 & 0 & 0 & 0 & 0 \\
0 & 0 & 0 & 0 & 0 & 0 & 0 & 0 & 2 & 2 & -2A & -2 & 0 & 0 & 0 & 0 & 0 & 0 & 0 & 0 & 0 & 0 & 0 & 0 \\
0 & 0 & 0 & 0 & 0 & 0 & 0 & 0 & 2 & -2 & 0 & 0 & -D & -2A & -E & 0 & 0 & 0 & 0 & 0 & 0 & 0 & 0 & 0 \\
0 & 0 & 0 & 0 & 0 & 0 & 0 & 0 & 1 & 1 & A & 1 & C & 0 & -B & -1 & 1 & 1 & A & 1 & -C & 0 & B & 1
\end{bmatrix}$$

Where A = 0.7071, B = 0.9239, C = 0.3827, D = .5412 and E = 1.3066

For computing $\mathbf{u} = \mathbf{J_2 v}$ where $\mathbf{u} = (u_1, \ldots u_8)^t$ and $\mathbf{v} = (v_1, \ldots v_{24})^t$, an efficient an efficient scheme is provided below. (Here $'$ and $''$ are used to represents variables. It does not represent derivatives.)

$Y_1 = v_1 + v_2$	$Y_1' = v_9 + v_{10}$	$Y_1'' = v_{17} + v_{18}$
$Y_2 = v_1 - v_2$	$Y_2' = v_9 - v_{10}$	$Y_2'' = v_{17} - v_{18}$
$Y_3 = Av_3$	$Y_3' = Av_{11}$	$Y_3'' = Av_{19}$
$Y_4 = Dv_5$	$Y_4' = Dv_{13}$	$Y_4'' = Dv_{21}$
$Y_5 = Ev_7$	$Y_5' = Ev_{15}$	$Y_5'' = Ev_{23}$
$Y_6 = Cv_5$	$Y_6' = Cv_{13}$	$Y_6'' = Cv_{21}$
$Y_7 = Bv_7$	$Y_7' = Bv_{15}$	$Y_7'' = Bv_{23}$
$Y_8 = Av_6$	$Y_8' = Av_{14}$	$Y_8'' = Av_{22}$
$Y_9 = Y_6 - Y_7$	$Y_9' = Y_6' - Y_7'$	$Y_9'' = Y_6'' - Y_7''$

$$u_1 = 2Y_2 + Y_4 + 2Y_8 + Y_5$$
$$u_2 = 2Y_1 - 2Y_3 - 2v_4$$
$$u_3 = 2Y_2 - Y_4 - 2Y_8 - Y_5$$
$$u_4 = Y_1 + Y_3 + v_4 + Y_9 - v_8 + Y_1' + Y_3' + v_{12} - Y_9' + v_{16}$$
$$u_5 = 2Y_2' + Y_4' + 2Y_8' + Y_5'$$
$$u_6 = 2Y_1' - 2Y_3' - 2v_{12}$$
$$u_7 = 2Y_2' - Y_4' - 2Y_8' - Y_5'$$
$$u_8 = Y_1' + Y_3' + v_{12} + Y_9' - v_{16} + Y_1'' + Y_3'' + v_{20} - Y_9'' + v_{24}$$

Similar exercise could be carried out for J_4, J_6 and J_8 matrices. For $\mathbf{r = 5}$, $\mathbf{J_5}$ matrix is given below.

$$J_5 = \begin{bmatrix}
2 & 0 & -2A & -1 & -2B & -A & -2C & 0 & 0 & 0 & 0 & 0 & 0 & 0 & 0 & 0 & 0 & 0 & 0 & 0 & 0 & 0 & 0 & 0 \\
2 & 0 & 2A & 1 & 2C & -A & -2B & -1 & 0 & 0 & 0 & 0 & 0 & 0 & 0 & 0 & 0 & 0 & 0 & 0 & 0 & 0 & 0 & 0 \\
0 & 0 & 0 & 0 & 0 & 0 & 0 & 2 & 0 & 2A & 1 & -2C & A & 2B & 1 & 0 & 0 & 0 & 0 & 0 & 0 & 0 & 0 & 0 \\
0 & 0 & 0 & 0 & 0 & 0 & 0 & 2 & 0 & -2A & -1 & 2B & A & 2C & 0 & 0 & 0 & 0 & 0 & 0 & 0 & 0 & 0 & 0 \\
0 & 0 & 0 & 0 & 0 & 0 & 0 & 2 & 0 & -2A & -1 & -2B & -A & -2C & 0 & 0 & 0 & 0 & 0 & 0 & 0 & 0 & 0 & 0 \\
0 & 0 & 0 & 0 & 0 & 0 & 0 & 2 & 0 & 2A & 1 & 2C & -A & -2B & -1 & 0 & 0 & 0 & 0 & 0 & 0 & 0 & 0 & 0 \\
0 & 0 & 0 & 0 & 0 & 0 & 0 & 0 & 0 & 0 & 0 & 0 & 0 & 0 & 0 & 2 & 0 & 2A & 1 & -2C & A & 2B & 1 \\
0 & 0 & 0 & 0 & 0 & 0 & 0 & 0 & 0 & 0 & 0 & 0 & 0 & 0 & 0 & 2 & 0 & -2A & -1 & -2B & A & 2C & 0
\end{bmatrix}$$

Where A = 0.7071, B = 0.9239 and C = 0.3827.

To compute $\mathbf{u} = \mathbf{J_5 v}$, we calculate according to following steps. (Here also $'$ and $''$ are used to represents variables. It does not represent derivatives.)

$Y_1 = 2Av_3 + v_4$	$Y_1' = 2Av_{11} + v_{12}$	$Y_1'' = 2Av_{19} + v_{20}$
$Y_2 = 2(B+C)(v_5 + v_7)$	$Y_2' = 2(B+C)(v_{13} + v_{15})$	$Y_2'' = 2(B+C)(v_{21} + v_{23})$
$Y_3 = 2Cv_5$	$Y_3' = 2Cv_{13}$	$Y_3'' = 2Cv_{21}$
$Y_4 = 2Bv_7$	$Y_4' = 2Bv_{15}$	$Y_4'' = 2Bv_{23}$
$Y_5 = Av_6$	$Y_5' = Av_{14}$	$Y_5'' = Av_{22}$
$Y_6 = Y_2 - Y_3 - Y_4$	$Y_6' = Y_2' - Y_3' - Y_4'$	$Y_6'' = Y_2'' - Y_3'' - Y_4''$
$Y_7 = Y_5 + v_8$	$Y_7' = Y_5' + v_{16}$	$Y_7'' = Y_5'' + v_{24}$
$Y_8 = Y_3 - Y_4 - Y_7$	$Y_8' = Y_3' - Y_4' - Y_7'$	$Y_8'' = Y_3'' - Y_4'' - Y_7''$

$$u_1 = 2v_1 - Y_1 - Y_6 - Y_5$$
$$u_2 = 2v_1 + Y_1 + Y_8$$
$$u_3 = 2v_9 + Y_1' - Y_8'$$
$$u_4 = 2v_9 - Y_1' + Y_6' + Y_5'$$
$$u_5 = 2v_9 - Y_1' - Y_6' - Y_5'$$
$$u_6 = 2v_9 + Y_1' + Y_8'$$
$$u_7 = 2v_{17} + Y_1'' - Y_8''$$
$$u_8 = 2v_{17} - Y_1'' + Y_6'' + Y_5''$$

Similar exercise can be done for J_1, J_3 and J_7 matrices. By developing similar implementation schemes of matrix multiplication, the number of operations required to perform matrix multiplication of J_i matrices with an arbitrary matrix of size 24×24 are computed and shown in Table 1. The K_c matrices will also require same number of operations to perform matrix multiplication due to similar structures.

Table 1. Multiplication complexities of $\mathbf{J_i}$ matrices in integrated scheme

Matrix	Computations/column
J_1	10m + 34a
J_2	17m + 44a
J_3	14m + 38a
J_4	16m + 43a
J_5	15m + 41a
J_6	17m + 44a
J_7	14m + 38a
J_8	15m + 44a

Let us now compute the total computational complexity for Inverse Motion Compensation and downscaling of a block. Consider a case when $\mathbf{r} = \mathbf{c} = \mathbf{6}$ in Eq. (5). This requires maximum number of computations to perform IMC and downscaling (refer Table 1). It is considered for finding the computational requirements in the worst case. Total operations required to perform IMC and downscaling (when $\mathbf{r} = \mathbf{c} = \mathbf{6}$) using Eq. (5) for each macroblock are 856m + 3496a. It requires 3.34 multiplications and 13.65 additions operations per pixel

Table 2. Computational complexities for downscaling a P frame from CIF resolution to QCIF resolution

Function	Complexity			
	Mults.	Adds	Shifts	Total Cost
Spatial Domain based downscaling				
Input CIF frame processing				
Inverse Quant. + IDCT (144m, 464a per 8 × 8 block)	228096	734976		
Inverse Motion Compensation (256a per 16 × 16 block)		101376		
Output QCIF frame processing				
Downscale by 2 (3a, 1s per pixel)		76032	25344	
Full search ME (±15 pels, 738048a per 16 × 16 block)		73066752		
Motion Compensation (256a per 16 × 16 block)		25344		
DCT + Quant. (144m, 464a per 8 × 8 block)	57024	183744		
Total	285120	74188224	25344	
Total Operation count (Add = 1 op, shift = 1 op, Mult. = 3ops)				**75068928**
DCT domain based downscaling (Using MBIMC)				
Input CIF frame processing				
Inverse Quant. (64m per 8 × 8 block)	101376			
IMC using MBIMC ((3.43m, 20.5a per pixel)	347720	2078208		
Output QCIF frame processing				
DCT Downscale by 2 (1.25m, 1,25a per pixel)	126720	126720		
AMVR (9m, 30a, 1shift per 16 × 16 block)	891	2970	99	
DCT domain MC (3.43m, 20.5a per pixel)	86930	519552		
Quant. (64m per 8 × 8 block)	25344			
Total	688981	2727450	99	
Total Operation count (Add = 1 op, shift = 1 op, Mult. = 3ops)				**4794492**
DCT domain based downscaling (Using Integrated Scheme)				
Input CIF frame processing				
Inverse Quant. (64m per 8 × 8 block)	101376			
IMC using Integrated Scheme ((3.34m, 13.65a per pixel)	338595	1383782		
DCT Upscale by 2 for intermediate frame processing (1.25m, 1,25a per pixel)	126720	126720		
Output QCIF frame processing				
AMVR (9m, 30a, 1shift per 16 × 16 block)	891	2970	99	
DCT domain MC (3.43m, 20.5a per pixel)	86930	519552		
Quant. (64m per 8 × 8 block)	25344			
Total	679856	2033024	99	
Total Operation count (Add = 1 op, shift = 1 op, Mult. = 3ops)				**4072592**

of the input video frame. The computations required per pixel in the integrated approach is less than the MBIMC scheme [15]. In the integrated approach, we have to upsample the resulting downscaled frame to reconstruct the next inter frame in the video sequence. This requirement will add extra computational cost to the integrated scheme. We have used the Dugad and Ahuja [5] approach for upsampling of the frames which requires 1.25 multiplications and 1.25 additions per pixel of the upsampled frame. If we assume that one multiplication is equivalent to three machine instructions and one addition is one machine instruction (refer [17]), the video downscaling using the integrated scheme shows 23% improvement over the MBIMC scheme (The method presented in [5] is used for downscaling with MBIMC scheme).

4   Results

We have implemented the MBIMC scheme presented in [15] and integrated scheme to perform IMC and used Dugad and Ahuja's approach for downscaling/upscaling wherever required. The integrated scheme discussed above performs downscaling and IMC in DCT domain and convert each interframe (P-frame) in to an intraframe (I-frame). We have compared the spatial domain video downscaling system with DCT domain based video downscaling system using the MBIMC scheme and Integrated scheme. The computational comparison of these schemes are shown in Table 2. In the DCT domain based video downscaling methods the AMVR [17] method is used for motion vector re-estimation. The

Table 3. Comparison of Different Technique

	PSNR (dB)								
	Spatial Domain			MBIMC Scheme			Integrated Scheme		
video	Y	U	V	Y	U	V	Y	U	V
Coastguard	25.17	32.54	32.55	26.84	42.69	44.07	26.68	42.38	43.78
Foreman	28.61	32.20	32.08	31.45	40.84	42.45	30.89	40.38	41.80
Container	25.76	32.49	32.78	27.03	40.95	40.46	26.49	39.88	39.20
Tennis	24.98	32.36	31.58	26.82	40.55	41.88	26.19	39.41	40.19

four different MPEG video streams with only I and P frames are used to record the results. These video streams are downscaled to QCIF resolution (at 500 kbps) from CIF resolution (at 1.5 mbps). To compute the PSNR, each frame from downscaled QCIF video stream is upsampled to CIF resolution and then compared with the original video frame. In spatial domain technique, frames are upsampled using 'bilinear' technique and in other DCT domain based techniques, frames are upsampled in DCT domain using Dugad and Ahuja's technique [5]. The average PSNR values for different video streams are shown in the Table 3.

In Table 3, we can observe that average PSNR values of Integrated approach are much higher than the spatial domain approach and very close to MBIMC scheme. It is obvious from Table2 that the MBIMC scheme is approximately 15 times faster than the spatial domain technique, however the integrated scheme shows 23% improvement over the MBIMC scheme.

5   Conclusion

In this paper, we propose a integrated scheme to perform inverse motion compensation (IMC) and downscaling directly on DCT blocks of an MPEG video stream. This scheme performs IMC and downscaling over a complete macroblock in a single step. It also uses the factorization of the DCT/IDCT matrices to reduce computational complexity of the IMC operation. A fast mathematical model is proposed to perform the computations efficiently. The integrated scheme shows 23% improvement for downscaling operation over the MBIMC scheme.

References

1. Coding of Moving Pictures and Associated Audio for Digital Storage Media up to 1.5 bits/s, ISO/IEC JTC1 CD 11172, 1992.
2. Coding of Moving and Associated Audio. Committee Draft of Standard ISO 11172: ISO/MPEG 90/176, Dec. 1990.
3. Video Codec for Audio Visual Services at px64 Kbits/s. CCITT Recommendation H. 261, 1990.
4. D. le Gall, MPEG : A video compression standard for multimedia applications, Commun. ACM, vol. 34, no. 4, pp. 47-58, Apr, 1991.
5. R Dugad and N. Ahuja, A fast scheme for image size change in the compressed domain, IEEE Trans. Circuits Syst. Video Technology, vol. 11, pp. 461-474, Apr. 2001.

6. Jayanta Mukherjee, Sanjit K. Mitra, Image resizing in the compressed domain using subband DCT, IEEE Trans. Circuits Syst. Video Technology, vol 12, No. 7, July 2002.

7. Jayanta Mukherjee, S. K. Mitra, Resizing of images in the DCT space by arbitrary factors, IEEE Int. Conf. on Image Processing (ICIP), Singapore, 2004, pp. 2801-2804.

8. Jayanta Mukherjee, S. K. Mitra, Arbitrary resizing of images in DCT space, Communicated to IEE Proc. Vis. Image Signal Process.

9. S. F. Chang and D. G. Messerschmitt, Manipulation and compositing of MC-DCT compress video, IEEE J. Select. Areas Commun., vol. 13, pp. 1-11, Jan. 1995.

10. B. C. Smith and L. Rowe, Algorithms for manipulating compressed images, IEEE Comput. Grap. Applicat. Mag., vol. 13, pp. 34-42, Sept. 1993.

11. Q. Hu and S. Panchanathan, Image/video spatial scalability in compressed domain, IEEE Trans. Ind. Electron., vol. 45, pp. 23-31, Feb. 1998.

12. N. Merhav and V. Bhaskaran, Fast algorithms for DCT-domain image downsampling and for inverse motion compensation, IEEE Trans. Circuits Syst. Video Technology, vol. 7, pp. 468-476, June 1997.

13. P. A. A. Assuncao and M. Ghanbari, "Transcoding of MPEG-2 video in the frequency domain," in ICASSP 1997, 1997, pp. 2633-2636.

14. Junehwa Song, Boon-Lock Yeo, "A Fast Algorithm for DCT-Domain Inverse Motion Compensation Based on Shared Information in a Macroblock," IEEE Trans. on Circuits and Systems for Video Technology, vol. 10, No. 5, Aug. 2000.

15. Sudhir Porwal, Jayanta Mukhopadhyay, "A Fast DCT Domain Based Video Downscaling System," IEEE Int. Conf. on Acoustics, Speech and Signal Processing (ICASSP), Toulouse, France, 2006, pp. 885-888.

16. Y. Arai, T. Agui, and M. Nakajima, A fast DCT-SQ scheme for images, Trans. IEICE, vol. E 71, no. 11, p. 1095, Nov. 1998.

17. Bo Shen, Ishwar K. Sethi, Bhaskaran Vasudev, Adaptive Motion Vector Resampling for Compressed Video Downscaling, IEEE Trans. Circuits Syst. Video Technology, Vol. 9, No. 6, Sept., 1999.

DCT Domain Transcoding of H.264/AVC Video into MPEG-2 Video

Vasant Patil[1,2], Tummala Kalyani[1], Atul Bhartia[1], Rajeev Kumar[1],
and Jayanta Mukherjee[1]

[1] Computer Science and Engineering Department,
Indian Institute of Technology Kharagpur, WB 721 302, India
[2] Institute for Systems Studies and Analyses, Delhi 110 054, India

Abstract. As the number of different video compression standards increase, there is a growing need for conversion between video formats coded in different standards. H.264/AVC is a newly emerging video coding standard which achieves better video quality at reduced bit rate than other standards. The standalone media players that are available in the market do not support H.264 video playback. In this paper, we present novel techniques that can achieve conversion of pre-coded video in H.264/AVC standard to MPEG-2 standard directly in the compressed domain. Experimental results show that the proposed approach can produce transcoded video with quality comparable to the pixel-domain approach at significantly reduced cost.

1 Introduction

Video transcoding deals with converting a previously compressed video signal into another one with different format, such as different bit rate, frame rate, frame size, or even compression standard. Due to the diversity of multimedia applications and present communication infrastructure comprising of different underlying networks and protocols, there has been a growing need for inter-network multimedia communication over heterogeneous networks. Besides the problem of channel characteristics and capacities, different end devices used in today's communication also introduce some problems. For example, people like to use small handheld devices, such as cellular phones, handheld computers, etc., for video communication and Internet access. Most current handheld devices only have limited computing and display capabilities, which are not suitable for high quality video decoding and display. In this case, precoded high quality video may need to be converted into a lower quality one for displaying on handheld devices.

There are applications such as video on demand, video browsing, picture in picture and video conferencing which require video to be transcoded at lower bit rates, reduced frame size and to different codec formats. H.264/AVC is a new generation video codec that has been replacing all previous standards. But it consumes enormous computing and storage resources. So there is a need for transcoding H.264/AVC bitstream to other formats. In this paper, we consider

P. Kalra and S. Peleg (Eds.): ICVGIP 2006, LNCS 4338, pp. 696–707, 2006.

a problem of converting a bitstream coded in H.264/AVC format to MPEG-2 one. A straightforward approach to achieve this is to completely decode the H.264/AVC video into pixel domain and re-encode the decoded frames into MPEG-2 video by performing full-scale motion estimation (FSME) and motion compensation (MC). However, FSME and MC being computationally the most expensive part of the overall encoding process, this approach is not suitable for real time applications. We propose an approach that converts the pre-coded video in H.264/AVC format to MPEG-2 one directly in the DCT domain. The proposed approach obtains the motion compensated residual errors, required to code the transcoded video, directly in the DCT domain and incorporates the motion vector re-estimation techniques to obtain outgoing motion vectors. The experimental results show that the proposed approach significantly reduces the computations while achieving quality comparable to the much costlier pixel-domain approach.

The rest of the paper is organized as follows. Transform domain transcoding of H.264 video is briefly discussed in Section 2. The proposed techniques to obtain motion compensated residual errors in transcoding of I slice and P slice of H.264 video are discussed in Sub-sections 2.1 and 2.2, respectively. Experimental results are presented in Section 3, before we conclude in Section 4.

2   Transcoding in Transform Domain

A picture or frame is a collection of one or more slices in H.264/AVC coding standard. Each slice can be coded using different coding types such as I slice, P slice, B slice, SP slice and SI slice. However, baseline profile uses only two slice coding types, that is, I slice and P slice. In an I slice all macroblocks of the slice are encoded using intra prediction. In a P slice, in addition to the coding types of the I slice, some macroblocks can also be coded using inter prediction with at most one motion vector for prediction macroblock partition [1]; refer [2] for issues in H.264 to MPEG-2 transcoding.

2.1   Transcoding an I Slice

Unlike H.264/AVC, the MPEG-2 video does not support intra frame prediction. To transcode H.264 to MPEG-2 the intra predicted macroblocks in I picture must be converted to intra macroblocks without prediction. Conversion of an I frame of H.264 to equivalent I frame in MPEG-2 in the compressed domain is a two step process. First intra prediction is removed and then 8×8 DCT blocks are computed from four adjacent 4×4 integer transform blocks.

Removing intra prediction: The H.264/AVC comprises of two intra coding modes denoted as $Intra_{4\times4}$ or $Intra_{16\times16}$ together with chroma prediction and I_{PCM} prediction modes; see [3] for further details. In $Intra_{4\times4}$ and $Intra_{16\times16}$ macroblock, the predicted block can be obtained in transform domain by using appropriate transformation matrices. For example, the predicted block for modes 0 and 1 is obtained by Eqn. (1) and Eqn. (2) as follows:

Mode 0 (Horizontal prediction):

$$DCT\begin{pmatrix} x & x & x & I \\ x & x & x & J \\ x & x & x & K \\ x & x & x & L \end{pmatrix} DCT\begin{pmatrix} 0 & 0 & 0 & 0 \\ 0 & 0 & 0 & 0 \\ 0 & 0 & 0 & 0 \\ 1 & 1 & 1 & 1 \end{pmatrix} = DCT\begin{pmatrix} I & I & I & I \\ J & J & J & J \\ K & K & K & K \\ L & L & L & L \end{pmatrix} \tag{1}$$

Mode 1 (Vertical prediction):

$$DCT\begin{pmatrix} 0 & 0 & 0 & 1 \\ 0 & 0 & 0 & 1 \\ 0 & 0 & 0 & 1 \\ 0 & 0 & 0 & 1 \end{pmatrix} DCT\begin{pmatrix} x & x & x & x \\ x & x & x & x \\ x & x & x & x \\ A & B & C & D \end{pmatrix} = DCT\begin{pmatrix} A & B & C & D \\ A & B & C & D \\ A & B & C & D \\ A & B & C & D \end{pmatrix} \tag{2}$$

Mode 2 (DC prediction): It is the average of all the neighboring pixels in upper and left neighboring blocks. To get a predicted block for prediction mode 2 in DCT domain, the upper block is pre-multiplied by $DCT\begin{pmatrix} 0 & 0 & 0 & 1 \\ 0 & 0 & 0 & 1 \\ 0 & 0 & 0 & 1 \\ 0 & 0 & 0 & 1 \end{pmatrix}$ and post-multiplied by $DCT\begin{pmatrix} 1 & 1 & 1 & 1 \\ 1 & 1 & 1 & 1 \\ 1 & 1 & 1 & 1 \\ 1 & 1 & 1 & 1 \end{pmatrix}$. Similarly, the left block is pre-multiplied by $DCT\begin{pmatrix} 1 & 1 & 1 & 1 \\ 1 & 1 & 1 & 1 \\ 1 & 1 & 1 & 1 \\ 1 & 1 & 1 & 1 \end{pmatrix}$ and post-multiplied by $DCT\begin{pmatrix} 0 & 0 & 0 & 0 \\ 0 & 0 & 0 & 0 \\ 0 & 0 & 0 & 0 \\ 1 & 1 & 1 & 1 \end{pmatrix}$. The resultant blocks are then summed up and averaged. Since, the transformation matrices are sparse and their transform is also sparse, intra prediction for these modes in DCT domain requires less computation than pixel domain computation. Similarly, proper transformation matrices for other macroblocks are obtained. The transform domain residual is then added to the predicted blocks so obtained. Table 1 shows the comparison of the intra prediction techniques with pixel domain processing. In this table, a, s and d denote addition, shift and division operations, respectively. It is found that transcoding I picture in transform domain is three times faster as compared to pixel domain transcoding.

Table 1. Computational complexity of transcoding an I slice

Functions	Pixel Domain	Transform Domain		
		Mode 0	Mode 1	Mode 2
IDCT	$16a+24s$	0	0	0
Computing a predicted block	0 for mode 0 and 1 $128a+16d$ for mode 2	$12a+16s$	$12a+16s$	$40a+40s+16d$
Adding residual	$16a$	$16a$	$16a$	$16a$
forward DCT	$16a+24s$	0	0	0
Total	$48a+32s+16s$ for mode 0 and 1 $176a+32s+16s+16d$ for mode 2	$28a+16s$	$28a+16s$	$56a+40s+16d$

Transform and block size conversion: Four 4×4 adjacent blocks of H.264 bitstream are converted into one single 8×8 block as follows:

$$X' = [S_8] \left\{ \begin{bmatrix} I_4^t & 0 \\ 0 & I_4^t \end{bmatrix} \begin{bmatrix} X_1 & X_2 \\ X_3 & X_4 \end{bmatrix} \begin{bmatrix} I_4 & 0 \\ 0 & I_4 \end{bmatrix} \right\} [S_8^t] \tag{3}$$

where, $'t'$ denotes transposition operation, S_8 is an 8×8 real $2D$ DCT matrix and $X_1 \ldots X_4$ are 4×4 transform coefficient blocks of H.264/AVC bitstream. I_4 is a 4×4 integer transform matrix given as:

$$\begin{bmatrix} 1 & 1 & 1 & 1 \\ 2 & 1 & -1 & -2 \\ 1 & -1 & -1 & 1 \\ 1 & -2 & 2 & -1 \end{bmatrix}$$

Let $T = \begin{bmatrix} S_8 \end{bmatrix} \begin{bmatrix} I_4^t & 0 \\ 0 & I_4^t \end{bmatrix}$ and $T^t = \begin{bmatrix} I_4 & 0 \\ 0 & I_4 \end{bmatrix} \begin{bmatrix} S_8^t \end{bmatrix}$. The matrix T is given as:

$$\begin{pmatrix} a & 0 & 0 & 0 & a & 0 & 0 & 0 \\ b & f & -l & p & -b & f & l & p \\ 0 & g & 0 & j & 0 & -g & 0 & -j \\ -c & h & m & -q & c & h & -m & -q \\ 0 & 0 & a & 0 & 0 & 0 & a & 0 \\ d & -i & n & r & -d & -i & -n & r \\ 0 & -j & 0 & g & 0 & j & 0 & -g \\ -e & k & -o & s & e & k & o & s \end{pmatrix} \tag{4}$$

where $a = 1.4142$, $b = 1.2815$, $f = 0.4618$, $l = 0.1056$, $p = 0.0585$, $g = 1.1152$, $j = 0.0793$, $c = 0.4500$, $h = 0.8899$, $m = 0.7259$, $q = 0.0461$, $d = 0.3007$, $i = 0.4319$, $n = 1.0864$, $r = 0.5190$, $e = 0.2549$, $k = 0.2412$, $o = 0.5308$, $s = 0.9875$. It can be pre-computed and stored. Since, this matrix is sparse and symmetric it can be computed as similar to the method suggested by [4]. It needs a total of 704 operations. The pixel domain approach needs 256 multiplications and 416 additions for $\mathrm{DCT}(S_8)$. According to [3], each inverse transform (I_4) needs 8 shifts and 32 additions giving a total of 32 shifts and 128 additions for four I_4. The overall computation requirement of the pixel domain processing is 256 multiplications, 32 shifts, 544 additions, for a total of 832 operations. Hence, the DCT domain approach with fast transform implementation saves 128 operations for an 8×8 block, saving about 15% of the computation.

2.2 Transcoding a P Slice

Motion estimation (ME) is the most compute intensive process in video encoding. The ME component is more complex in H.264 because it uses motion vectors that can point to areas outside the picture boundary. The H.264 coding also supports a number of different macroblock partition shapes and sizes for each macroblock resulting in a maximum of sixteen motion vectors [3]. It also uses multiple reference frames and quarter-pixel motion vector resolution increasing the search range thereby the complexity.

To transcode H.264 to MPEG-2, the multi-frame references have to be collapsed to a single-frame reference and motion vectors have to be displaced based on the macroblock partition size used in H.264 as MPEG-2 does not support as many macroblock partition sizes for motion compensation. Note that, in this case of transcoding H.264 to MPEG-2, we have considered only baseline profile video which uses single reference frame only. Transcoding inter frames involves three step. First, all the P slices of H.264/AVC are converted into I slices by inverse motion compensation in 4×4 DCT domain. Next, these I slices are converted to an equivalent I frames in MPEG-2 using 8×8 block DCT and then finally, converted to P frames by forward motion compensation in DCT domain.

Converting a P frame to an I frame: A P frame can be converted to an intra (I) frame by performing the Inverse Motion Compensation (IMC) operation. The DCT domain IMC was first studied in Chang $et\ al.$ [5] and subsequently in Merhav $et\ al.$ [5], Liu $et\ al.$ [6] and Assuncao $et\ al.$ [7]. Their techniques compute a predicted block in DCT domain. A reference block B_{ref} may intersect with four neighboring blocks as shown in Fig. 1. The h and w represent vertical

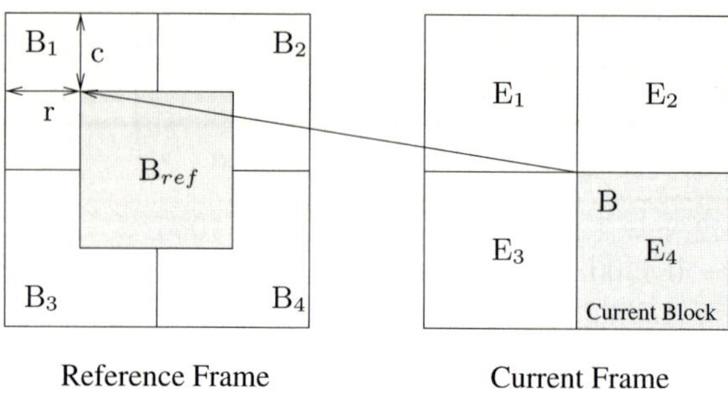

Fig. 1. Single blockwise inverse motion compensation

and horizontal components of the motion vector respectively. If B_1, B_2, B_3, B_4 represent the four neighboring blocks in the spatial domain, then block B_{ref} can be represented by Eqn. (5) as below:

$$B_{ref} = \sum_{i=1}^{4} c_{i1} B_i c_{i2} \tag{5}$$

For a 4×4 block, c_{ij} , $i = 1\ldots 4$ and $j = 1, 2$ are 4×4 sparse matrices of 0 and 1 that perform window and shift operations accordingly. From Eqn. (5), we have

$$DCT(B_{ref}) = S_4 \left(\sum_{i=1}^{4} c_{i1} S_4^t S_4 B_i S_4^t S_4 c_{i2} \right) S_4^t \tag{6}$$

where, S_4 represents a 4-point DCT matrix. Since, DCT is an unitary orthogonal transformation and is guaranteed to be distributive to matrix multiplications, above equation can be re-written as:

$$DCT(B_{ref}) = \sum_{i=1}^{4} DCT(c_{i1}) DCT(B_i) DCT(c_{i2}) \tag{7}$$

The DCT of the inverse motion compensated block from the current error residual block E is then given as:

$$DCT(B) = DCT(B_{ref}) + DCT(E) \qquad (8)$$

Using the approach presented in [5] and [6] to compute the 4×4 DCT block from the reference frame, we require sixteen iterations to completely predict a macroblock of partition size 16×16. In the proposed approach, we extend these schemes to compute the macroblock partition block in one step. We also extend it to include half-pixel interpolation using 6-tap FIR filter. We present IMC for an 8×8 macroblock partition. The extension to the other partitions is straightforward.

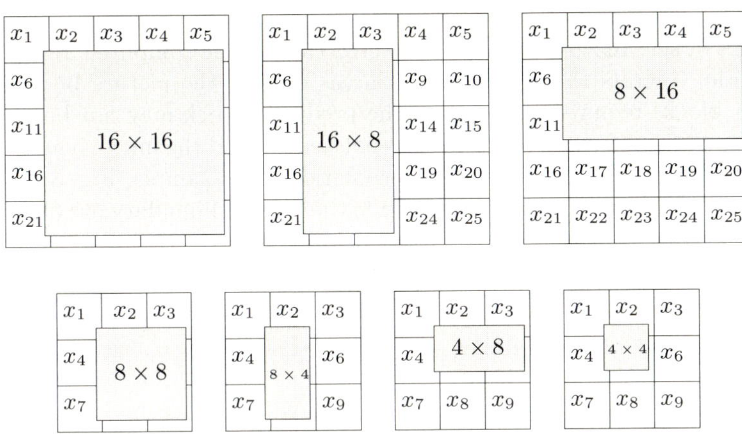

Fig. 2. Macroblock partition wise inverse motion compensation

As shown in Fig. 2, X' is the predicted macroblock in the reference frame which starts from the location (r, c) with reference to the first block in the array of adjacent blocks. If $x_1 \ldots x_9$ are the adjacent blocks in spatial domain then an 8×8 macroblock partition block from the 12×12 block can be extracted as follows:

$$x' = L_r \begin{pmatrix} x_1 & x_2 & x_3 \\ x_4 & x_5 & x_6 \\ x_7 & x_8 & x_9 \end{pmatrix} R_c \qquad (9)$$

where, x' is the predicted macroblock in spatial domain, L_r is an 8×12 matrix and R_c is a 12×8 matrix. These matrices are different for different values of r and c (refer Fig. 1). Since $1 \leq r \leq 4$ and $1 \leq c \leq 4$, there can be four different L_r and R_c matrices which can be pre-computed and stored. The structure of L_r matrix is given as:

$$L_r = \begin{bmatrix} 0_{8 \times r-1} & I_8 & 0_{8 \times 4-r+1} \end{bmatrix}_{8 \times 12}$$

where, I_8 is an identity matrix of length 8 and '0' represents a matrix of zero elements. Similarly, we can derive R_c matrices. Let us define 12×12 matrices $\overline{S}, \overline{S}^t$ and A as follows:

$$\overline{S} = \begin{pmatrix} I_4 & 0 & 0 \\ 0 & I_4 & 0 \\ 0 & 0 & I_4 \end{pmatrix} , \quad \overline{S}^t = \begin{pmatrix} I_4^t & 0 & 0 \\ 0 & I_4^t & 0 \\ 0 & 0 & I_4^t \end{pmatrix} \text{ and } A = \begin{pmatrix} X_1 & X_2 & X_3 \\ X_4 & X_5 & X_6 \\ X_7 & X_8 & X_9 \end{pmatrix}$$

where, I_4 is a 4×4 forward integer transform matrix, 't' denotes matrix transposition. I_4^t is a 4×4 inverse integer transform matrix of H.264/AVC and $X_i = DCT(x_i)$. Assuming that we have obtained X_1 to X_9 by partial decoding, Eqn. (9) can be re-written to extract macroblock X' in DCT domain as:

$$X' = \begin{pmatrix} S_4 & 0 \\ 0 & S_4 \end{pmatrix} \left\{ L_r \times \overline{S}^t \times A \times \overline{S} \times R_c \right\} \begin{pmatrix} S_4^t & 0 \\ 0 & S_4^t \end{pmatrix} \tag{10}$$

The matrix multiplication inside the curly braces results in an 8×8 spatial domain block. The pre-multiplication of $\begin{pmatrix} S_4 & 0 \\ 0 & S_4 \end{pmatrix}$ and post-multiplication of $\begin{pmatrix} S_4^t & 0 \\ 0 & S_4^t \end{pmatrix}$ result in an 8×8 macroblock partition. With the above procedure, macroblock partitions of size 16×16, 16×8, 8×16 etc., can also be computed. Since, H.264 uses motion vectors that can point to areas outside the picture boundary, all adjacent blocks required to compute the predicted block may not be available. In that case, the reference frame is extrapolated beyond the image boundaries by repeating the edge samples before interpolation. For example, Fig. 3 illustrates the need for expansion. The blocks outside the picture boundary are obtained by

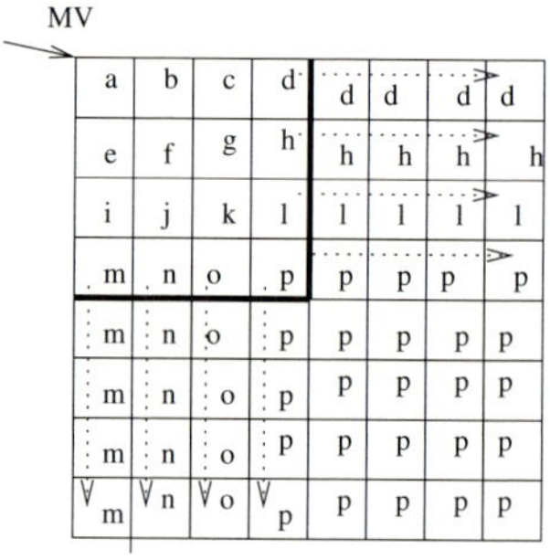

MV

a	b	c	d	d	d	d	d
e	f	g	h	h	h	h	h
i	j	k	l	l	l	l	l
m	n	o	p	p	p	p	p
m	n	o	p	p	p	p	p
m	n	o	p	p	p	p	p
m	n	o	p	p	p	p	p
m	n	o	p	p	p	p	p

Fig. 3. Motion vectors pointing outside object boundary

copying the boundary row or column pixels. This is achieved by pre-multiplying the collected adjacent block matrices x_1 to x_9 in Eqn. (9) for up and down directions and post-multiplying them for left and right directions with proper matrices. It is found that total sixteen type of expansion matrices are required. Eqn. (10) may be re-written to consider expansion matrices as follows:

$$X' = \begin{pmatrix} S_4 & 0 \\ 0 & S_4 \end{pmatrix} \left\{ L_r \times e_r \times \overline{S}^t \times A \times \overline{S} \times e_c \times R_c \right\} \begin{pmatrix} S_4^t & 0 \\ 0 & S_4^t \end{pmatrix} \tag{11}$$

where, e_r and e_c are row and column wise expansion matrices.

Half-pixel and quarter-pixel inverse motion compensation: H.264/AVC uses quarter-pixel accurate motion vectors with 6-tap FIR filter. The motion vectors in MPEG-2 are half-pixel accurate and the half-pixel samples are obtained by bilinear interpolation of the neighboring four samples. In inverse motion compensation using fractional sample accuracy, the 6-tap FIR filter should be used to obtain luma half-pixel samples, bilinear interpolation to obtain quarter-pixel luma samples and weighted bilinear interpolation to obtain $\frac{1}{8}^{th}$ pixel accurate chroma samples. The fractional pixel predicted luma block is computed by applying 6-tap FIR filter in horizontal direction only, vertical direction only, horizontal first and then vertical direction, vertical first and then horizontal direction. This is achieved by modifying the L_r and R_c matrices in Eqn. (9) and Eqn. (10) to include the 6-tap FIR filter. For example, L_r and R_c matrices for 4×4 macroblock partition using horizontal direction only half samples when $r = 3$ and $c = 3$ are given below:

$$
L_r = \begin{bmatrix}
0 & 0 & 1 & -5 & 20 & 20 & -5 & 1 & 0 & 0 & 0 & 0 \\
0 & 0 & 0 & 1 & -5 & 20 & 20 & -5 & 1 & 0 & 0 & 0 \\
0 & 0 & 0 & 0 & 1 & -5 & 20 & 20 & -5 & 1 & 0 & 0 \\
0 & 0 & 0 & 0 & 0 & 1 & -5 & 20 & 20 & -5 & 1 & 0
\end{bmatrix}
\begin{array}{l}
\\ 2 \ \text{column} \qquad\qquad 9 \ \text{column} \qquad\qquad 1 \ \text{column}
\end{array}
$$

and

$$
R_c = \begin{bmatrix}
0 & 0 & 1 & 0 & 0 & 0 & 0 & 0 & 0 & 0 & 0 & 0 \\
0 & 0 & 0 & 1 & 0 & 0 & 0 & 0 & 0 & 0 & 0 & 0 \\
0 & 0 & 0 & 0 & 1 & 0 & 0 & 0 & 0 & 0 & 0 & 0 \\
0 & 0 & 0 & 0 & 0 & 1 & 0 & 0 & 0 & 0 & 0 & 0
\end{bmatrix}^t
$$

Similarly, L_r and R_c matrices for vertical direction only half samples are obtained.

Chroma sub-pixel interpolation in transform domain: Chroma $\frac{1}{8}^{th}$ pixel samples are obtained using L_r and R_c matrices. For $r = 3$ and $c = 3$, we have

$$
L_r = \begin{bmatrix}
0 & 0 & jf0 & jf1 & 0 & 0 & 0 & 0 & 0 & 0 & 0 & 0 \\
0 & 0 & 0 & jf0 & jf1 & 0 & 0 & 0 & 0 & 0 & 0 & 0 \\
0 & 0 & 0 & 0 & jf0 & jf1 & 0 & 0 & 0 & 0 & 0 & 0 \\
0 & 0 & 0 & 0 & 0 & jf0 & jf1 & 0 & 0 & 0 & 0 & 0
\end{bmatrix}
\begin{array}{l}
\\ 2 \ \text{column} \qquad 5 \ \text{column} \qquad 5 \ \text{column}
\end{array}
$$

and

$$
R_c = \begin{bmatrix}
0 & 0 & if0 & if1 & 0 & 0 & 0 & 0 & 0 & 0 & 0 & 0 \\
0 & 0 & 0 & if0 & if1 & 0 & 0 & 0 & 0 & 0 & 0 & 0 \\
0 & 0 & 0 & 0 & if0 & if1 & 0 & 0 & 0 & 0 & 0 & 0 \\
0 & 0 & 0 & 0 & 0 & if0 & if1 & 0 & 0 & 0 & 0 & 0
\end{bmatrix}^t
$$

where, $if0 = xFrac$, $if1 = 8 - xFrac$, $jf0 = yFrac$, $jf1 = 8 - yFrac$. The $xFrac$ and $yFrac$ denote fractional part of x and y component of a motion vector, respectively. Similar, matrices can be derived for other values of r and c.

In this way, a P frame in H.264 is converted to an I frame without intra prediction. This I frame consists of DCT blocks of size 4×4. The transform block size and kernel is converted by using the conversion transform kernel in Eqn. (4). The I frames are then converted back to the P frames in MPEG-2 as discussed in the following section.

Conversion of an *I* frame in MPEG-2 into a *P* frame in MPEG-2: A *P* frame is obtained by performing motion estimation and then motion compensation. In this case, the motion vectors can be re-estimated by AMVR method [8]. Motion compensation in DCT domain is done using the similar approach discussed in Section 2.2. The predicted macroblock (16×16) is obtained by applying Merhav's scheme [5] for the whole macroblock at once as follows:

$$X' = \begin{pmatrix} S_8 & 0 \\ 0 & S_8 \end{pmatrix} \left\{ L_r \times \widehat{S}^t \times A \times \widehat{S} \times R_c \right\} \begin{pmatrix} S_8^t & 0 \\ 0 & S_8^t \end{pmatrix} \tag{12}$$

where, S_8 is forward DCT matrix of size 8×8. L_r and R_c are row and column transformation matrices, respectively, as explained in Sect. 2.2. $\widehat{S}$, $\widehat{S}^t$ and A denote 32×32 matrices given as $\widehat{S} = \begin{pmatrix} S_8 & 0 & 0 \\ 0 & S_8 & 0 \\ 0 & 0 & S_8 \end{pmatrix}$, $\widehat{S}^t = \begin{pmatrix} S_8^t & 0 & 0 \\ 0 & S_8^t & 0 \\ 0 & 0 & S_8^t \end{pmatrix}$ and $A = \begin{pmatrix} X_1 & X_2 & X_3 \\ X_4 & X_5 & X_6 \\ X_7 & X_8 & X_9 \end{pmatrix}$. An 8-point DCT matrix is factorized as $S_8 = DPB_1B_2MA_1A_2A_3$ where, D is an 8×8 diagonal matrix and P is an 8×8 permutation matrix. B_1, B_2, A_1, A_2, A_3 are 8×8 sparse matrices of 1, 0 and -1. M is an 8×8 sparse matrix of real numbers. Refer [5] for exact entries of D, P, B_1, B_2, A_1, A_2, A_3 and M matrices.

Then, $\widehat{S}^t$ can be re-written using the above factorization as follows:

$$\widehat{S}^t = \underbrace{\begin{bmatrix} Q^t & 0 & 0 \\ 0 & Q^t & 0 \\ 0 & 0 & Q^t \end{bmatrix}}_{\widehat{Q}^t} \underbrace{\begin{bmatrix} B_2^t & 0 & 0 \\ 0 & B_2^t & 0 \\ 0 & 0 & B_2^t \end{bmatrix}}_{\widehat{B}_2^t} \underbrace{\begin{bmatrix} B_1^t & 0 & 0 \\ 0 & B_1^t & 0 \\ 0 & 0 & B_1^t \end{bmatrix}}_{\widehat{B}_1^t} \underbrace{\begin{bmatrix} P^t & 0 & 0 \\ 0 & P^t & 0 \\ 0 & 0 & P^t \end{bmatrix}}_{\widehat{P}^t} \underbrace{\begin{bmatrix} D^t & 0 & 0 \\ 0 & D^t & 0 \\ 0 & 0 & D^t \end{bmatrix}}_{\widehat{D}^t} \tag{13}$$

where $Q^t = (MA_1A_2A_3)^t$ given as:

$$Q^t = \begin{bmatrix} 1 & 1 & a & 1 & -c & 0 & b & 1 \\ 1 & -1 & a & 0 & -c & a & b & 0 \\ 1 & -1 & -a & 0 & b & a & c & 0 \\ 1 & 1 & -a & -1 & b & 0 & c & 0 \\ 1 & 1 & -a & -1 & -b & 0 & -c & 0 \\ 1 & -1 & -a & 0 & -b & -a & -c & 0 \\ 1 & -1 & a & 0 & c & -a & -b & 0 \\ 1 & 1 & a & 1 & c & 0 & -b & 1 \end{bmatrix}$$

$a = 0.7071$, $b = 0.9239$, and $c = 0.3827$. Note that, $\widehat{D}^t$, $\widehat{P}^t$, $\widehat{B}_1^t$, $\widehat{B}_2^t$ and $\widehat{Q}^t$ denote matrices of size 24×24. Similarly, $\widehat{S}$ can also be factorized as $\widehat{S} = \widehat{D}\widehat{P}\widehat{B}_1\widehat{B}_2\widehat{Q}$. The Eqn. (12) can be re-written as:

$$M' = \begin{pmatrix} S_8 & 0 \\ 0 & S_8 \end{pmatrix} \left\{ L_r \times \widehat{Q}^t\widehat{B}_2^t\widehat{B}_1^t\widehat{P}^t\widehat{D}^t \times A \times \widehat{D}\widehat{P}\widehat{B}_1\widehat{B}_2\widehat{Q} \times R_c \right\} \begin{pmatrix} S_8^t & 0 \\ 0 & S_8^t \end{pmatrix} \tag{14}$$

The multiplication by $\widehat{Q}^t(\widehat{Q})$, $\widehat{B}_2^t(\widehat{B}_2)$, $\widehat{B}_1^t(\widehat{B}_1)$, $\widehat{P}^t(\widehat{P})$ and $\widehat{D}^t(\widehat{D})$ can be realized by performing multiplication with corresponding 8×8 component matrices

$Q^t(Q)$, $B_2^t(B_2)$, $B_1^t(B_1)$, $P^t(P)$ and $D^t(D)$, respectively. When counting the operations, multiplication by P^t and P can be ignored as they cause only changes in the order of the components. The multiplications by D^t and D can also be ignored while counting the operations because these can be absorbed in the quantizer and dequantizer [5]. The multiplication of $\widehat{B}_1(\widehat{B}_1^t)$ and $\widehat{B}_2(\widehat{B}_2^t)$ matrices with another 24×24 arbitrary matrix requires 288 addition operations. Let $J_r = L_r \times Q^t$ and $K_c = Q \times R_c$. The J_r and K_c matrices are sparse having similar kind of structure. We adopt a similar strategy as suggested in [5] to perform multiplication with J_r and K_c matrices. This in worst case ($r = c = 5$) requires $880m + 5248a$ operations, where 'a' denotes addition and 'm' denotes multiplication operation. This means $3.59m + 23.06a$ operations per pixel to extract a 16×16 macroblock. By assuming one multiplication to be equivalent to three machine instructions and one addition to be equivalent to one machine instruction this is 23.52% improvement over 8×8 block based approach of Merhav et al. [5].

Half-precision motion vectors: With half-pixel precision motion vectors, either two or four pixels are needed to calculate the actual prediction of single pixel. This means, in worst case, we need to apply Eqn. (14) four times to extract M' with half-pixel precision motion vectors along both the directions as:

$$M' = \begin{pmatrix} S_8 & 0 \\ 0 & S_8 \end{pmatrix} \left\{ \overline{L}_r \times \widehat{Q}^t \widehat{B}_2^t \widehat{B}_1^t \widehat{P}^t \widehat{D}^t \times A \times \widehat{D}\widehat{P}\widehat{B}_1\widehat{B}_2\widehat{Q} \times \overline{R}_c \right\} \begin{pmatrix} S_8^t & 0 \\ 0 & S_8^t \end{pmatrix} \qquad (15)$$

where, $\overline{L}_r = \frac{1}{2}(L_r + L_{r+1})$ and $\overline{R}_c = \frac{1}{2}(R_c + R_{c+1})$. Multiplication by $\overline{L}_r$ and $\overline{R}_c$ require 384 multiplications and 384 addition operations each. This means $6.09m + 19.38a$ operations per pixel to extract a 16×16 macroblock with half-pixel precision motion vectors along both the directions. By assuming one multiplication to be equivalent to three machine instructions and one addition to be equivalent to one machine instruction this is 79.42% improvement over the brute-force approach of Merhav *et al.* [5].

3   Experimental Results

The experimental results are based on our transcoding implementation using JM reference software version 10.2. To present the results we use *Foreman* and *Container* test sequences. The first 150 frames of these sequences in SIF (352×288) format are encoded using the baseline profile with I and P frames. Table 2 shows the computation comparison of the proposed DCT domain approach with the pixel domain approach. To obtain the outgoing motion vectors in transform domain approach, we have used AMVR method [8]. It is assumed that only 50% of the 4×4 transform block has non zero coefficients. It is observed that about 80% of the inter frame blocks have diagonal mode of interpolation. Fig. 4(a) and (b), show the PSNRs (dB) for individual frames of *Foreman* and *Container* sequences, respectively. As it can be seen, the proposed DCT domain approach produces the transcoded video with quality comparable with the pixel-domain approach at substantially reduced computations.

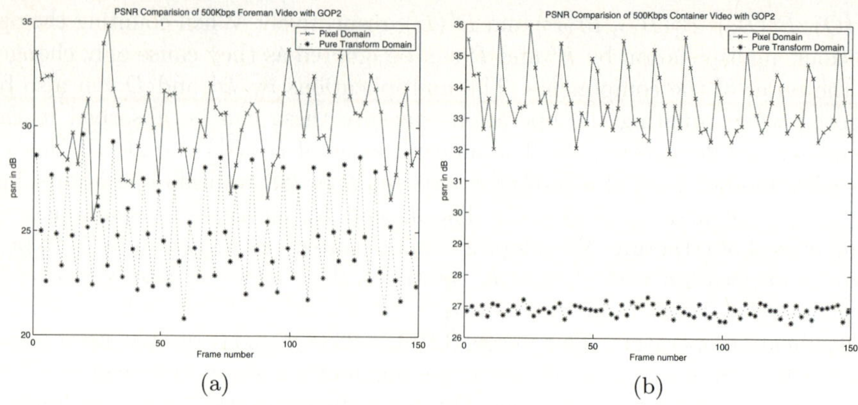

(a)   (b)

Fig. 4. Experimental results: (a) *Foreman* (b) *Container*

Table 2. Computational complexity

Approach	Functions	Complexities		
		Mults.	Adds.	Shifts
Pixel-Domain	IDCT ($32a+8s$ per $4x4$ block)		512	128
	IMC interpolation ($192m+192a$ per $4x4$ block)	3072	3072	
	AMVR ($36m+50a$ per Macroblock)	36	50	
	FDCT ($256m+461a$ per $8x8$ block)	1024	1844	
	Total	4132	5478	128
DCT-Domain	MPIMC interpolation($24a+94s$ per $4x4$ block)		384	1504
	8×8 DCT conversion ($352m+352a$ per $8x8$ block)	1408	1408	
	AMVR ($36m+50a$ per Macroblock)	36	50	
	MC ($3.59m+23.06a$ or $6.09m+19.38a$ per pixel)	879	5248	
	Total	2323	7090	1504

4   Conclusions

We have presented a transform domain approach to convert the H.264/AVC video to MPEG-2 video. In this, we have presented novel techniques to convert I and P slice in H.264/AVC video to MPEG-2 frames, directly in the DCT domain. As compared with the pixel domain approach, the proposed approach significantly reduces the computational requirement. Our experimental results using baseline profile show that the proposed approach produces MPEG-2 video with PSNR comparable to the pixel domain approach.

References

1. Sullivan, G., Topiwala, P., Luthra, A.: The H.264/AVC advanced video coding standard: Overview and introduction to fidelity range extensions. SPIE Conference on Applications of Digital Image Processing XXVII Special Session on Advances in the New Emerging Standard: H.264/AVC (2004)

2. Kalva, H.: Issues in H.254/MPEG-2 video transcoding. In: First IEEE Consumer Communications and Networking Conference. (2004) 657–659
3. Weigand, T., Sullivan, T.: Draft ITU-T recommendation and final draft international standard of joint video specification. ITU-T Rec. H.264 — ISO/IEC 14496-10 AVC (2003)
4. Xin, J., Vetro, A., Sun, H.: Converting DCT coefficients to H.264/AVC transform coefficients. In: IEEE Pacific-Rim Conference on Multimedia (PCM), Lecure Notes in Computer Science. (2004)
5. Merhav, N., Bhaskaran, V.: Fast algorithms for DCT-Domain image down-sampling and for inverse motion compensation. IEEE Transactions on Circuits and Systems for Video Technology **7** (1997) 468–474
6. Koc, U.V., Liu, K.J.R.: Motion compensation on DCT domain. EURASIP Journal on Applied Signal Processing (2001) 147–162
7. Assuncao, P.A.A., Ghanbari, M.: A frequency-domain video transcoder for dynamic bitrate reduction of MPEG-2 bit streams. IEEE Transactions on Circuits and Systems for Video Technology **8** (1998) 953–967
8. Shen, B., Ishwar, I.K., Bhaskaran, V.: Adaptive motion-vector re-sampling for compressed video downscaling. IEEE Transactions on Circuits and Systems for Video Technology **9** (1999) 929–936

Adaptive Scalable Wavelet Difference Reduction Method for Efficient Image Transmission

Bindulal T.S. and M.R. Kaimal

Department of Computer Science, University of Kerala
Trivandrum 695 581, Kerala, India
bindulalts@yahoo.com, mrkaimal@yahoo.com

Abstract. This paper presents a scalable image transmission scheme based on the wavelet-based coding technique supporting region of interest properties. The proposed scheme scalable WDR (SWDR), is based on the wavelet difference reduction scheme, progresses adaptively to get different resolution images at any bit rate required and is supported with the spatial and SNR scalability. The method is developed for the limited bandwidth network where the image quality and data compression are mopst important. Simulations are performed on the medical images, satellite images and Standard test images like Barbara, fingerprint images. The simulation results show that the proposed scheme is up to 20-40% better than other famous scalable schemes like scalable SPIHT coding schemes in terms of signal to noise ratio values (dB) and reduces execution time around 40% in various resolutions. Thus, the proposed scalable coding scheme becomes increasingly important.

1 Introduction

The multimedia images are coded efficiently using the wavelet transform based traditional coding techniques. Due to the popularity of multimedia applications, the scalable image compression and transmissions are necessary through the heterogeneous networks with different processing capabilities and network access bandwidths. The images like medical images and satellite images are focussed on efficient use of compressed data without causing the quality of outputted data. Hence, the code scheme should be controlled adaptively to provide flexible bit streams so as to support the scalable image processing [1].

Compression of different types of images with various imaging models like real time transmission, image library archival, limited buffer and bandwidth resources etc are designed using image compression standard JPEG2000. Now a days, the object based coding scheme have much attention due to the ROI based functionalities of JPEG2000 [7]. JPEG2000 utilizes two types of wavelet filter. Daubechies 9/7 floating point wavelet filter provides lossy compression. Biorthogonal 5/3 integer wavelet filter supports lossless compression at the cost of higher compression bit rate. Here, the reverse integer filter is used to produce a scalable bit stream for medical images and biorthogonal 9/7 filter for satellite images and standard test images like Barbara, fingerprint images etc. which builds up scalable quality image representation.

P. Kalra and S. Peleg (Eds.): ICVGIP 2006, LNCS 4338, pp. 708–717, 2006.

The multi-resolution signal representation using wavelet transform is used in most famous embedded coding algorithms like EZW [10] and SPIHT [2] algorithms. Danyali and Mertins proposed a SPIHT [6] algorithm which supports the spatial resolution scalability in spite of its SNR scalability. But some times, the zero tree coding methods are computationally very complex. The wavelet difference reduction method of Tian and Well [3] is one of the major alternatives of the SPIHT algorithm which is quite useful for fast reconstruction using the idea of run-length coding technique for coding images. The WDR algorithm has been improved by various authors. Among them, ASWDR of Walker and Nguan [4] and context-modeling with WDR (CMWDR) method by Yuan and Mandal [5] offer better performances than SPIHT algorithm even without entropy coding.

The proposed scalable coding scheme is based on the wavelet difference reduction method and incorporates the scalability property. Compression of multimedia images like medical images, satellite images etc. and its transmission offers better utilization of available bit rate such that high fidelity is maintained for relatively small regions rather than for the entire image. The wavelet coefficients of regions of interest are re-arranged using the zero tree concepts in accordance with a priority so that the run length coding performance can be increased.

The paper is organized as follows: the extraction of region and the scalability concept is presented in the section 2, the proposed scalable WDR algorithm is presented in section 3, the experimental results are discussed in section 4 and conclusion in section 5.

2   Region Extraction and Scalability Concepts

The traditional coding techniques follow the multi-resolution form of the image. The wavelet transform is one mathematical tool for viewing or processing the image at multiple resolutions. In addition to being an efficient, highly intuitively framework for the representation and storage of multi-resolution images, the DWT provides powerful insight into the spatial and frequency characteristics of the images. Even if the wavelet transform is applied to the image, each and every subband maintains not only its frequency domain characteristics but its time domain characteristics also. So, here we are considering both time and frequency characteristics for locating the wavelet coefficients inside the textured regions and edges accurately and remove the back ground noise part.

Consider the multiresolution form of the image, I as

$$I = \begin{bmatrix} LL_i & HL_i \\ LH_i & HH_i \end{bmatrix} \tag{1}$$

The most significant coefficients are clustered in some areas of each subband. The corners and textures are to be re-arranged for coding efficiently with proper priority assigned to each component. So we applied eigen value analysis to the subbands to get the textured regions. Consider the subband B, any one from set $\{HL_i, LH_i, HH_i\}$ at level 'i', for eigen value analysis. Apply linear transformation to the subband B to get subband L_B which has spatial resolution dependency with the subband LL_i. The linearly transformed subband L_B is divided into fixed size window w for labelling content feature inside the subband B. Before starting the eigenspace analysis, the subband gradient calculations are carried out, so that the most textured regions can be seperated in terms of edges and corners more accurately. $L_B(i)$ is the linearly transformed wavelet coefficient value in 2-D window w which has the spatial domain dependency with the LL_i. $\nabla L_B(i)$ is the gradient at each point i in w.

$$\nabla L_B(i) = \left(L_{Bx}(i), L_{By}(i) \right)^T ,\tag{2}$$

where $L_{Bx}(i) = \partial L_B / \partial x$ and $L_{By}(i) = \partial L_B / \partial y$ and the autocorrelation matrix is formed as,

$$C = \begin{bmatrix} \sum L^2{}_{Bx}(i) & \sum L_{Bx}(i)L_{By}(i) \\ \sum L_{Bx}(i)L_{By}(i) & \sum L^2{}_{By}(i) \end{bmatrix}\tag{3}$$

The singular value decomposition is performed on the 2x2 symmetric autocorrelation matrix C in equation (3) , so that we get the normal equation $C = UDU^T$, where U is the orthonormal column vector and D is the diagonal matrix $diag(e_1, e_2), e_1 \geq e_2$, where e_i are the eigen values of the autocorrelation matrix C.

Based on the meaning of Us and e's , there are three different cases regarding the visual content of the images.

1. If e_1 is small, $L_B(i)$ in w corresponds to smooth regions in w.
2. If e_1 is of predominant magnitude, or equivalently e_2 is of extremely small magnitude, then there will be edge(s) in w.
3. If e_2 is significant, there remains considerable frequency gradients and regular patterns and textures in the window w.

Considering these three typoes of conditions, we can apply particular threshold value on eigen values (e_1, e_2) of L_B so that edges and textures area of B are located and extracted [9]. Examples of such extracted texture area of Barbara image, MRI head image and satellite image are shown in figure 1 Meaningful extracted areas can be obtained by selecting appropriate values for the eigen values above. After the region extraction process, we consider the processed subband B for applying the zero tree concept. Each textured block in B has four child blocks in the next level of subband decomposition and all such child blocks are collected from parent node to lowest level child blocks. Moreover, the processed subband block B has the mirror image on all other subbands of the same level. Hence, we get the texture regions on the wavelet coefficients in all subbands in a single eigen value analysis and this can be encoded as fast as possible from lowest frequency to highest frequency.

The scalable coding technique codes different resolution subbands independently one by one in each bit plane. The resolution level of the image is identified from the number of wavelet decompositions performed. Let the image be decomposed into N levels, the image has the (N+1) levels of spatial resolution subbands [6]. We can also represent the spatial resolution with original resolution as $(1/2^{L-1})$, where L is the level of resolution. Each level of the subband consists of three parts HL_L, LH_L and HH_L. The scalable algorithm considers each subband level as coded separately allowing the decoder or encoder to reconstruct different spatial resolution images.

Consider the subband level L, the subbands are grouped as $\lambda_L = [HL_L, LH_L, HH_L]$. The algorithm progresses through each level of suband groups from $(N+1) \le L \le 1$ so that a flexible stream of bits will be generated. The general structure of scalable encoder bit stream is shown in figure 2.

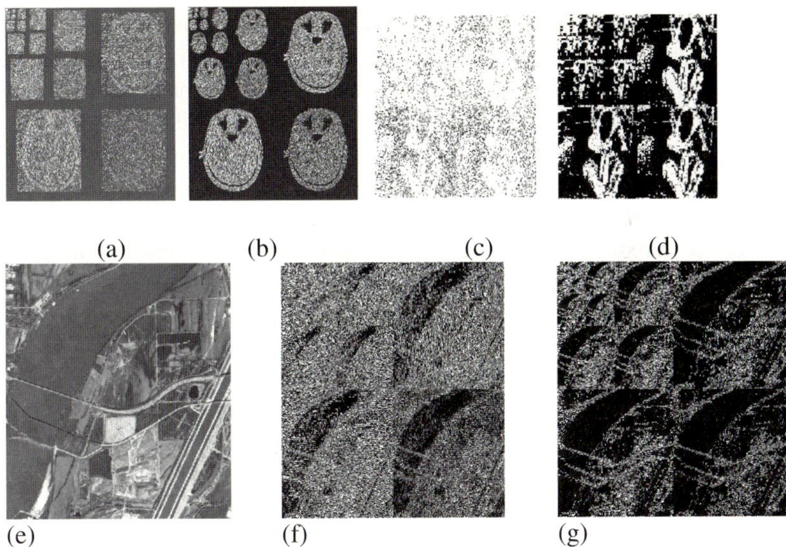

(a)   (b)   (c)   (d)

(e)   (f)   (g)

Fig. 1. (a) Multi resolution form of MRI images. (b) Region extraction of MRI images. (c) Multi resolution form of Barbara image. (d) Region extraction of Barbara image. (e) Satellite image (f) multi resolution form of satellite image (g) Region extraction of satellite image.

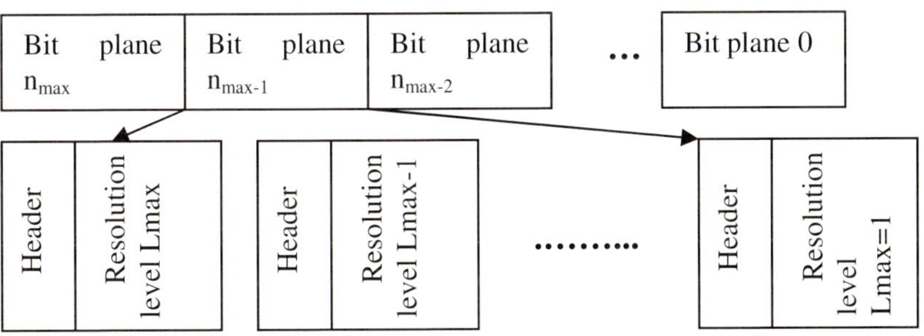

Fig. 2. Scalable bit stream structure with progressive quality

3 Scalable Wavelet Difference Reduction Method

The proposed algorithm is a modification of wavelet difference reduction method (WDR) [5, 6] incorporating the scalability property. The scalability properties are incorporated through multiple resolution dependent lists. The scalable WDR (SWDR) coding scheme uses the data structures *RGE* (coefficients that are collected during the adaptive scanning process in Region Growing manner), *SNS* (Significant Neighbour Sub-array, *SPS* (Significant Parent Sub-array), *LIP* (List of Insignificant Pixels), *LSP* (List of Significant Pixels), *TPS* (Temporary Set of Significant coefficients) to divide the wavelet coefficients and code efficiently and get good compression results.

For each spatial subband group λ_L , the lists are ordered as RGE_L, SNS_L, SPS_L, LIP_L so that L will be L_{max}, L-1,----1 where L_{max} is the maximum number of spatial resolution level supported by the encoder or decoder. During the processing of wavelet coefficients from the subband level λ_L , coefficients from outside the subband will be included in the next level of list at $(L$-$1)$ level. Scalable WDR bit stream can easily be reordered for multi resolution decoding at any desired bit rate. The total number of bits belonging to a particular bit plane is the same for original scheme and its scalable version, but they are re-arranged in accordance with their spatial resolution dependency. The definitions of sets, symbols and functions are listed below.

(i, j) $\qquad$ = $\qquad$ Pixel coordinates.

w_{ij} $\qquad$ = $\qquad$ Wavelet coefficient at pixel location (i, j)

n $\quad$ = $\quad \left\lfloor \log_2 \left(\max_{(i,j) \in I} |w_{ij}| \right) \right\rfloor$, maximum number of bit planes.

t_n $\qquad$ = Threshold value at bit-plane n

(m, n) = Pixel coordinate generated from (i, j)

L_{max} $\qquad$ = maximum level of spatial scalability to be supported by the bit stream $(1<=L_{max}<=N+1)$, where N is he number of wavelet decomposition levels applied to the image.

$$\lambda_L \quad = \quad \begin{cases} \{LL_{L-1}\} & ifL = N+1 \\ \{HL_L, LH_L, HH_L\} & 1 <= L <= N \end{cases}$$

$$\sigma(w_{ij}, t_n) = \begin{cases} 1 & : \quad |w_{ij}| \geq t_n \quad \text{Significant test of a coordinates} \\ 0 & : \quad |w_{ij}| < t \qquad\qquad (i,j) \text{ at bitplane } n \end{cases}$$

$$Sign(w_{ij}) = \begin{cases} + & : \quad w_{ij} \geq 0 \\ - & : \quad w_{ij} < 0 \end{cases}$$

Neighborhood functions
1. *cluster* $(w_{ij}, t_n) = \{(m,n)\}$, when

　　1. $(i-1) \leq m \leq (i+1), (j-1) \leq n \leq (j+1)$

　　2 $(m,n) \in \lambda_L \ \& \ (i,j) \in \lambda_L$

2. *child* $(w_{ij}, t_n) = \{(m,n)\}$, when

$$1. \quad (m,n) \in \left\{ \begin{array}{l} (2i,2j),(2i,2j+1) \\ (2i+1,2j),(2i+1,2j+1) \end{array} \right\}$$

$$2. \quad (m,n) \in \lambda_{L-1} \ \& \ (i,j) \in \lambda_L$$

Encoding Procedure is outlined below.

1. Initialization

$$LSP_L = \phi \quad , TSP_L = \phi \quad \forall L \quad ,1 \le L \le L_{max}$$

$$LIP_L = \left\{ \begin{array}{l} \phi \quad , \quad \forall L \quad ,1 \le L \le L_{max} \quad such \quad that \\ RGE_L = \phi, SNS_L = \phi, SPS_L = \phi \end{array} \right.$$

$$t_{n-1} = 2^{n+1} , t_n = t_{n-1}/2$$

L=Lmax;

2. Sorting pass

If $LIP_L \left(\sigma \left(w_{ij}, t_{n-1} \right) = 0 \right)$

$\quad$ {If $LIP_L \left(\sigma \left(w_{ij}, t_n \right) = 1 \right)$ {Coding (w_{ij}, L) ;}}

If $\lambda_L \ne \phi$

$\quad$ {If $\sigma \left(w_{ij}, t_{n-1} \right) = 0$ {If $\sigma \left(w_{ij}, t_n \right) = 1$

$\quad\quad$ {Coding (w_{ij}, L); $RGE_L = cluster \left(w_{ij}, t_n \right)$;

$\quad\quad$ Do {If $RGE_L \ne \phi$

$\quad\quad\quad$ {If $RGE_L \left(\sigma \left(w_{ij}, t_{n-1} \right) \right) = 0$ { {If $RGE_L \left(\sigma \left(w_{ij}, t_n \right) \right) = 1$

$\quad\quad\quad\quad$ Coding (w_{ij}, L); $RGE_L = cluster \left(w_{ij}, t_n \right)$ }}

$\quad\quad\quad\quad$ } while (End (RGE$_L$)! =True) ;}}}

Function coding (w_{ij}, L)

{   Output distance 'd' from previous significant
    Send binary representation of 'd' without leading
    MSB '1'.Send sign information of w_{ij}, Sign $\left(w_{ij} \right)$

    Add w_{ij} into TPS$_L$.

}

3 Index updating pass:

If $TPS_L \ne \phi$ {

$\quad$ $SNS_L = cluster \left(w_{ij}, t_n \right)$; $\quad \forall (i,j) \in TPS_L$

$\quad$ $SPS_{L-1} = child \left(w_{ij}, t_n \right)$; $\quad \forall (i,j) \in TPS_L$ }

$LIP_L = RGE_L + SNS_L + SPS_L$

4 Refinement Pass:

$\quad$ If $LSP_L \ne \phi$ { If $LSP_L \left(\sigma \left(w_{ij}, t_{n-1} \right) = 1 \right)$

$\quad\quad$ {Add nth MSB of $LSP_L \left(w_{ij} \right)$.}}

$\quad$ $LSP_L = LSP_L + TPS_L.; TPS_L = \phi$;

5 Resolution scale updates:
$\quad$ Send Header Information;

```
    If (L > 1) L=L-1; Goto step 2.
    Else L=Lmax;
  6 Threshold update:
```

$$If\ t_n >1 t_{n-1} = t_n \qquad \& \qquad t_n = t_n /2$$

```
      Goto step 2.
    End
```

The above encoder steps are recapitulated in the decoder side for producing a quantization output. The algorithm produces four symbols: +, -, 1, 0. These symbols are coded as in CM-WDR [5] algorithm using 2 bits as 11 for +, 10 for -, 01 for 1 and 00 for 0. The proposed algorithm Scalable WDR coding scheme also avoids the arithmetic coding.

4 Experimental Results

The proposed scheme is compared with original SPIHT and its scalable version. The simulations were done on 8-bit images like Barbara, Fingerprint etc with size 512x512, satellite images and 8-bit MRI images of 512x512. 10 classes of medical images with 100 frames in each class are also considered for the simulation. The original resolutions of these images were (512x512) pixels. The wavelet decomposition is based on the bi-orthogonal 5/3 integer wavelet filter and 9/7-tap bi-orthogonal Daubechies filter with symmetric extension at the image boundary [8]. Six levels of wavelet decomposition were first applied to each test image, then the scalable WDR encoder was set to encode the coefficients from bitplane$_{max}$ to bitpane$_0$ supporting maximum spatial scalability levels as 7.

The bit stream for each spatial resolution at different rates and the fidelity was measured by the peak signal to noise ratio defined as,

$$PSNR = 10\ \log_{10}\left(\frac{max^2}{MSE}\right)\ dB\ ,\qquad (4)$$

where MSE is mean squared error between the original and the reconstructed image; *max* is the maximum possible magnitude of a pixel inside the image. The integer wavelet decomposition produced the *max* value is 255. and the *max* value for biorthogoanl 9/7 wavelet filter is 255 for an 8 bits/pixel original image (level-1) and $255*2^{L-1}$ for resolution level L This is done by considering the fact that the resolution level L is obtained from the original image after applying (L-1) levels of 2-D wavelet decomposition with filters having a DC amplification of $\sqrt{2}$. The bit rates for all levels were calculated according to the number of pixels in the original full size image [6].

All the results for SPIHT, scalable SPIHT and scalable WDR were obtained by decoding the binary bit streams without considering the arithmetic coding. The simulation results obtained using bi-orthogonal 5/3 integer wavelet filter performed on medical images are given in Table 1 and the results obtained using bi-orthogonal 9/7 wavelet filter performed on standard test images and satellite images are given in

Table 2. The reconstructed images at different resolution level are shown in figure 3. The simulation results show that the proposed coding scheme is much better than the existing SPIHT and its scalable version. The performance gain for full resolution is meaningless, because both encoders, original and its scalable version, produce almost the same number of bit streams. For full resolution MRI image reconstruction, the performance gain is from 0.30 dB to 0.40 dB for various bit rates using bi-orthogonal 5/3 integer wavelet filter. For full resolution reconstruction, the standard test images Barbara, fingerprint images and satellite images have from 0.35 to 0.50 db coding gain in various bit rates.

Table 1. Scalable coding results of MRI using biorthogonal 5/3 tap Integer wavelet transform

Test Image	Bit rate	Full Resolution (512x512)		(1/2 Resolution) 256x256		
		SPIHT	SWDR	SPIHT	SSPIHT	SWDR
MRI	0.0313	23.47	23.99	23.29	23.30	23.79
	0.0625	27.41	27.54	27.16	27.36	27.43
	0.125	29.10	29.52	28.99	29.28	30.97
	0.25	33.77	34.13	33.85	37.16	38.29
	0.5	39.08	39.35	39.36	45.84	46.20
	1	43.99	44.40	-	-	-

Table 2. Scalable coding results of standard test images and satellite image using biorthogonal 9/7 tap wavelet transform

Image	Bit rate	Full Resolution (512x512)		(1/2 Resolution) 256x256		
		SPIHT	SWDR	SPIHT	SSPIHT	SWDR
Finger-print	0.125	21.92	22.27	22.67	22.68	23.04
	0.25	24.65	25.14	25.67	25.90	26.26
	0.5	28.12	28.74	30.18	30.90	31.33
	0.75	30.48	30.91	34.24	36.07	36.41
	1	32.04	32.56	35.88	41.80	41.95
Barbara	0.125	24.89	25.21	28.56	30.11	30.30
	0.25	27.64	28.20	31.46	34.64	34.95
	0.5	31.62	32.09	36.02	41.39	41.82
	0.75	34.49	34.92	38.82	46.87	47.11
	1	36.80	37.23	41.68	51.57	51.69
Satellite Image	0.125	23.49	23.71	25.61	25.71	25.91
	0.25	25.69	25.89	28.68	29.54	29.85
	0.5	28.55	28.98	31.86	35.93	36.26
	0.75	30.97	31.29	35.54	42.05	42.21
	1	32.96	33.42	37.09	47.88	47.95

But, the performance of coding in PSNR value (in dB) increases when the resolution scale decreases. For resolution level 2 of medical images MRI, i.e. 256x256, the performance gains of SWDR are from 0.26dB to 6.84 dB compared to the normal SPIHT and from 0.36 dB to 1.68 dB compared to the scalable SPIHT for various bit rates using 5/3 integer wavelet filter shown in table 1. Similar experimental results are obtained for the various resolutions for satellite images and standard test images like Barbara, Fingerprint images etc. Moreover, around 40% of time is saved for proposed scheme as compared to the zero tree coding scheme.

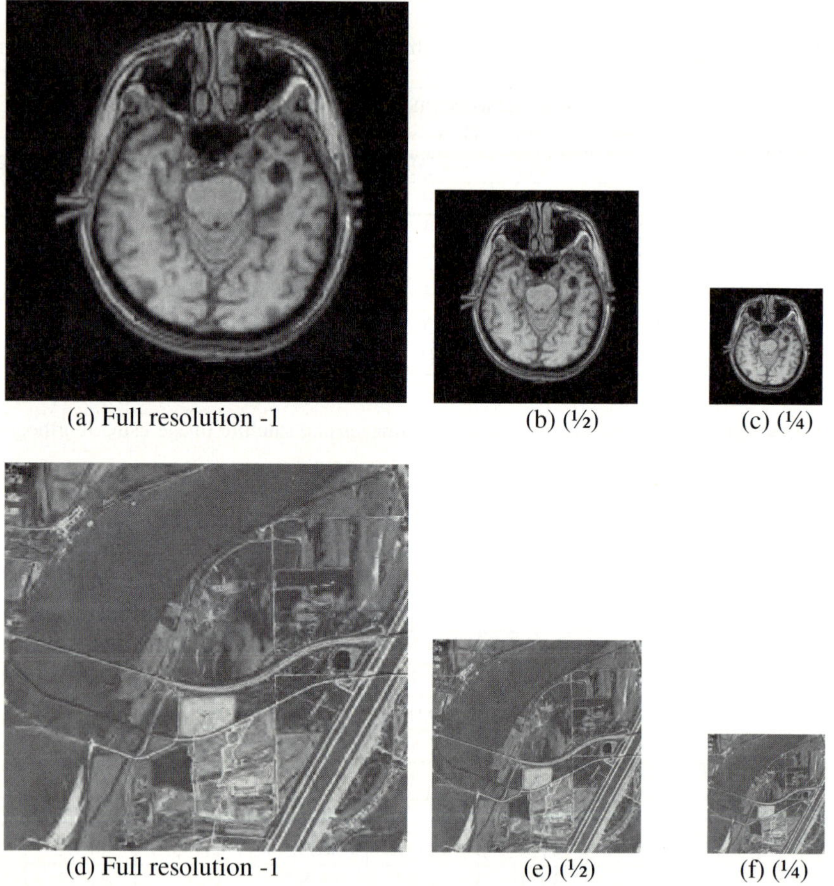

(a) Full resolution -1   (b) (½)   (c) (¼)

(d) Full resolution -1   (e) (½)   (f) (¼)

Fig. 3. Scalable image reconstruction at bit rate 0.0625 (a, b, c) MRI image, (d, e, f) satellite image

The original decoder decodes the whole image at each bit rate and then the requested spatial resolutions are reconstructed. The scalable decoder obtained the proper bit streams tailored by the parser for each resolution level. All bits in the reordered scalable bit stream for a particular resolution belong only to that resolution; while in the original coding scheme stream bits that belong to different resolution levels are interwoven. The performance expected is much better than the existing methods for resolution level greater than one. The difference between scalable and non scalable methods becomes more and more significant, when the resolution levels increases.

5   Conclusion

We propose a scalable WDR coding method which supports spatial and SNR scalability. The flexible bit stream generated by the encoder can be decoded adaptively to get any level of spatial resolution images. The scalable WDR is 20 - 40 % better than the scalable SPIHT and original SPIHT at any bit rate in scalable properties and is of low complexity than the zero tree coding techniques. The proposed coding scheme is applied to the medical images, satellite images and standard test images like Barbara, Fingerprint images. The scalability features of proposed method have interesting perspectives for numerous visual communications applications. Extensions of this work to video coding, and particularly to efficient frame-rate adaptive methods, are worth investigating for potential solutions to adaptive video delivery scenarios.

References

1. Liang, J.: Highly scalable image coding for multimedia applications, *Proc. ACM Multimedia* (1997) 11-19.
2. A. Said, W. A. Pearlman.: A new fast and efficient image codec based on set portioning in hierarchical trees, *IEEE Trans. Circuits Syst. Video Technol.*, 6 (1996) 243-250.
3. J. Tian, Jr. R. O. Wells.: Embedded image coding using wavelet difference reduction, *Wavelet image and video compression*, P. Topiwala, Ed. Norwell, MA: Kluwer, (1998) 289-302.
4. James S. Walker, Truong Q. Nguyen,: Lossy image codec based on adaptively scanned wavelet difference reduction, *Optical Engineering* 39, (2000) 1891 1897.
5. Yufei Yuan, Mrinal K. Mandal.: Novel embedded image coding algorithms based on wavelet difference reduction, *In Proc. of IEE*, 152 (2005) 9-19.
6. H. Danyali, A. Mertins.: Flexible, highly scalable, object-based wavelet image compression algorithm for network applications, *IEE proceedings Vis. Image Signal Process.*, 151, (2004) 498-510.
7. C. Christopoulos, J. Askelof, M. Larsson.: Efficient methods for encoding regions of integer in upcoming JPEG2000 still image coding standards, *IEEE Signal Processing letters*,7 (2000) 247-249.
8. Strang, G., T. Nguyen.: Wavelets and filter banks, *Wellesley-Cambridge Press*, (1996).
9. Jie Wei, "Video Content Classification Based on 3-D Eigen Analysis", IEEE Trans. On Image Processing, 14 (2005) 662-73.
10. J.M. Shapiro, "Embedded image coding using zero trees of wavelets coefficients", IEEE Trans. Signal Process. 41 (1993) 3445-3462.

GAP-RBF Based NR Image Quality Measurement for JPEG Coded Images

R. Venkatesh Babu[1] and S. Suresh[2]

[1] Department of Electrical Engineering
Indian Institute of Science, Bangalore, India
venkatesh.babu@gmail.com
[2] School of EEE,
Nanyang Technological University, Singapore
suresh99@gmail.com

Abstract. In this paper, we present a growing and pruning radial basis function based no-reference (NR) image quality model for JPEG-coded images. The quality of the images are estimated without referring to their original images. The features for predicting the perceived image quality are extracted by considering key human visual sensitivity factors such as edge amplitude, edge length, background activity and background luminance. Image quality estimation involves computation of functional relationship between HVS features and subjective test scores. Here, the problem of quality estimation is transformed to a function approximation problem and solved using GAP-RBF network. GAP-RBF network uses sequential learning algorithm to approximate the functional relationship. The computational complexity and memory requirement are less in GAP-RBF algorithm compared to other batch learning algorithms. Also, the GAP-RBF algorithm finds a compact image quality model and does not require retraining when the new image samples are presented. Experimental results prove that the GAP-RBF image quality model does emulate the mean opinion score (MOS). The subjective test results of the proposed metric are compared with JPEG no-reference image quality index as well as full-reference structural similarity image quality index and it is observed to outperform both.

1   Introduction

The main objective of image/video quality assessment metrics is to provide an automatic and efficient system to evaluate visual quality. It is imperative that these measures exhibit good correlation with perception by the human visual system (HVS). The most widely used objective image quality metrics, namely mean square error (MSE) and peak signal to noise ratio (PSNR), as widely observed do not correlate well with human perception [1] besides requiring the original reference image to compute distortion. Most images on the Internet and in multimedia databases are only available in compressed form, and hence inaccessibility of the original reference image, makes it difficult to measure the

P. Kalra and S. Peleg (Eds.): ICVGIP 2006, LNCS 4338, pp. 718–727, 2006.
© Springer-Verlag Berlin Heidelberg 2006

image quality. Therefore, there is an unquestionable need to develop metrics that closely correlate with human perception without needing the reference image.

Considerable volume of research has gone into developing objective image/ video quality metrics that incorporate perceived quality measurement with due consideration for HVS characteristics. However, most of the proposed metrics based on HVS characteristics require the original image as reference [2,3,4,5]. Though it is easy to assess the image quality without any reference by manual observations, developing a no-reference (NR) quality metric is a difficult task. To develop NR metrics, it is essential to have *apriori* knowledge about the nature of artifacts. Currently, NR quality metrics are the subject of considerable attention by the research community, visibly so, with the emergence of video quality experts group (VQEG) [6], which is in the process of standardizing NR and reduced-reference (RR) video quality assessment methods.

In recent years, neural networks have emerged as powerful mathematical tools for solving problems as diverse as pattern classification/recognition, medical imaging, speech recognition etc. The increasing popularity of neural networks is due to their ability to construct good approximation of functional relationship between the known set of input and output data. In neural networks, the choice of learning algorithm, number of hidden neurons and weight initialization are important factors in the learning performance. In particular, the choice of learning algorithm determines the rate of convergence, computational cost, and the optimality of the solution. The choice of number of hidden neurons determines the learning and generalization ability of the network. Another important problem is that the re-training process involved in the architectures, whenever we receive a new set of observations (images). Sometimes, the new set of observations may change complexity of the input-output relationship (complexity of the model) and in-turn affects the approximation ability of the neural network model. The process of developing the new neural model with the current training set may leads to increase in computational time. Sequential learning algorithms, which do not require retraining whenever new observation is received, helps to overcome the afore mentioned problems faced by neural network.

In this work, problem of image quality estimation without reference image is reduced to a function approximation problem using GAP-RBF networks. The unknown functional relationship between the HVS features and MOS is captured by the leaning phase of GAP-RBF network. The GAP-RBF quality model is developed with set of 20 source images and its 134 compressed images. The generalization performance of the quality model is evaluated using a new set of 9 source images and its 70 compressed images. The results show that the proposed GAP-RBF model could emulate the MOS effectively compared to the existing techniques.

The paper is organized as follows: Section 2 presents the concepts underlying feature extraction based on various HVS criteria. The basics of GAP-RBFN Image Quality Model are dealt with, in section 3. Subjective test results and discussions are presented in Section 4. Finally Section 5 concludes the paper.

2 HVS-Based Feature Extraction

It is easily deducible that most of the distortion in image/video is due to block DCT-based compression. The most popular and widely used image format, on Internet and digital cameras, happens to be, JPEG [7]. Since JPEG uses block-based DCT transform for coding, to achieve compression, the major artifact that JPEG-compressed images suffer, is blockiness. In JPEG coding, non-overlapping 8×8 pixel blocks are coded independently using DCT transform. The compression (bit-rate) and image quality are mainly determined by the degree of quantization of these DCT coefficients. The undesirable consequences of quantization manifest as blockiness, ringing and blurring artifacts in the JPEG coded image. It turns out that the subjective data for all these artifacts are highly correlated [8]. Hence, measuring the blockiness in-turn indicates the overall image quality.

The proposed NR metric is designed to take into consideration the various human visual criteria while quantifying the blocking artifact. These blocking artifacts would appear as horizontal and vertical edge distortions at the boundaries of 8×8 blocks. The visual sensitivity to these edges is affected by the following parameters [2]: i) Edge Amplitude ii) Edge Length iii) Background Activity and iv) Background Luminance.

The objective of the proposed metric is to integrate the afore-mentioned human visual factors to measure the quality of the JPEG-compressed images. First, we obtain the edges along horizontal and vertical directions using the corresponding 'prewitt' edge operators. Activity along, as well as, on either sides of the horizontal and vertical edges, is captured by high-pass filtering. The final binary activity mask is obtained by hard thresholding the activity measure. This mask only permits regions with lower activity to be considered for blockiness measurements. The background luminance weights are obtained based on the model proposed by Karunasekera et al., [2]. Here darker regions (0 to 127) are given less weight and brighter regions (128 to 255) are given higher weights. Each pixel of the edges that belong to the activity mask is multiplied by the corresponding luminance weight, in order to obtain the obtain final horizontal and vertical edge maps. The horizontal and vertical edge profiles are computed from these weighted edge maps. These profiles indicate the edge strength along each row and column of the weighted edge map. Since the effect of blockiness is seen only at block boundaries, every eighth location of the horizontal and vertical profiles is considered for measuring blockiness. The measure of deviation at every eighth location from the average value of the neighborhood of both (horizontal and vertical) profiles is used for extracting the features. For detailed explanation of feature extraction refer [9].

Since image quality is a subjective phenomenon, the human observer plays a major role in testing image quality metric. The subjective test designates the opinion of a viewer (opinion score) on a given image based on how it is perceived. The mean opinion score (MOS) is the average opinion score over all subjects. The aim of any quality metric is to predict the quality as close as possible to MOS. Hence, the objective here is to find the functional relationship between extracted HSV features and MOS to quantify image quality. In the next section we explain the network architecture and learning algorithm used for quantifying image quality.

3   GAP-RBFN Image Quality Model

In recent years, many sequential learning algorithms have been developed to overcome the problems encountered in neural networks [10,11,12]. Here, radial basis function network (RBF) is used to approximate the functional relationship. These sequential learning algorithms perform better than the batch learning algorithms as they do not require retraining whenever new observations are received. In sequential learning algorithms, the training samples are presented only once to capture the functional relationship whereas in batch learning algorithms, the samples are presented many times. Hence, the sequential learning algorithms require less computational effort and memory requirement than the batch learning algorithms.

Most of the sequential learning algorithms employ some strategy to obtain a compact network to represent input-output relationship. Recently Huang et al., [12] proposed a new sequential learning algorithm called 'growing and pruning radial-basis function (GAP-RBF) network. In this algorithm, the criteria for growing/pruning of hidden neurons is based on the significance of the neurons to the network output. The algorithm updates only the parameters of the nearest neuron to minimize the error. Hence this method is economical from computational as we as memory requirement point of view. Here, we use 'growing and pruning radial-basis function network' to approximate the functional relationship between HVS-based features and MOS. Also, we show that the GAP-RBF based image quality model adapts its features when new image sets are presented. Finally, we compare the performance of the proposed GAP-RBF model with the existing NR and FR image quality metrics [1,13].

The GAP-RBF image quality model is shown in Fig. 1. The basic building block for GAP-RBF is the radial basis function network. In general, a radial-basis function network consists of three layers of processing elements. The first layer linear and only distributes the input signal, while the next layer is nonlinear and uses Gaussian functions. The third layer linearly combines the Gaussian outputs. In a GAP-RBF quality model, the inputs are the extracted HVS features (U) of a given image while the output is the approximated image quality ($\hat{Q}$). The objective is to find a the compact model to approximate the MOS using HVS-based features. The learning algorithm uses 'growing and pruning' strategy to decide on the significance of a neuron towards realizing a compact model. The network parameters such as center vectors, connection weights and widths of hidden neurons are tuned using extended Kalman filter (EKF) algorithm [12].

The output of an GAP-RBF quality model with K Gaussian neurons has the following form:

$$\hat{Q} = \sum_{i-1}^{K} \alpha_i exp \left(-\frac{1}{\sigma_i^2} \|U - \mu_i\| \right) \tag{1}$$

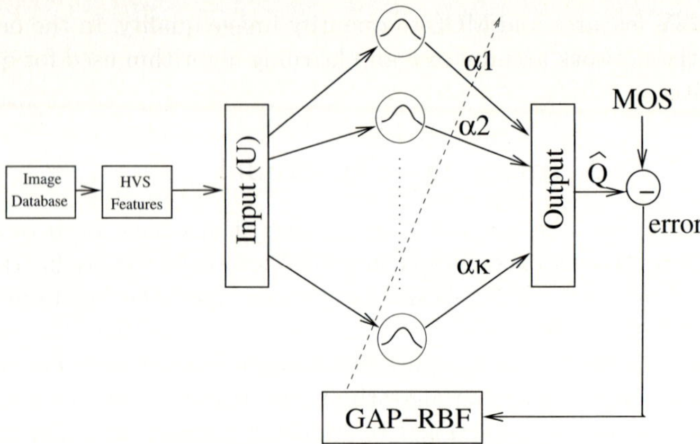

Fig. 1. Overview of the proposed image quality estimation algorithm

where U is the HVS-based feature input vector, α_i is the weight connecting the ith Gaussian neuron to the output neuron, μ_i is the center vector of ith Gaussian neuron and σ_i is the width of the Gaussian neuron.

GAP-RBF is initialized with zero hidden neurons. As new images are received sequentially, the HVS-based features (inputs) are extracted and the network builds up based on a 'growth and pruning' criterion. The algorithm adds/prunes hidden neurons and also tunes the network parameters. Detailed description of the the algorithms can be found in [12]. The following are the steps involved in obtaining a compact network.

3.1 Growing and Pruning Algorithm

Given an approximation error e_{min}, for each observation (U_n, MOS_n), where $U_n \in R$, and assuming the number of neurons developed using previous $n-1$ images to be K, the following steps are used to develop the model:

Step 1 **Compute** the estimated image quality for a given image using equation (1)

Step 2 **Growth criterion**: Compute the criterion using the specified parameters

$$\epsilon_n = max\left\{\epsilon_{max}\gamma^n, \epsilon_{min}\right\}$$
$$e_n = \hat{Q}_n - Q_n \tag{2}$$

Step 3 **Adding neuron** based on growth criterion and other conditions
IF $\|U_n - \mu_{nr}\| > \epsilon_n$ and $(1.8.\kappa\|U_n - \mu_{nr}\|)\,|e_n|/S(U) > e_{min}$ then
Allocate $(K+1)$th hidden neuron with

$$\alpha_{K+1} = e_n$$
$$\mu_{K+1} = U_n$$
$$\sigma_{K+1} = \kappa\|U_n - \mu_{nr}\| \tag{3}$$

    ELSE
    Update the network parameters α_{nr}, μ_{nr} and σ_{nr} for the nearest neuron only, using EKF algorithm [12].
    Criterion for **pruning** the hidden neurons:
    IF $|(1.8\sigma_{nr})^l \alpha_{nr}/S(U)| < e_{min}$, where $S(U)$ is the estimated size of the range where the training samples are drawn from,
    remove the nrth hidden neuron
    reduce the dimensionality by EKF method
    END IF
    END IF

The parameters of the growing and pruning algorithm ϵ_{min}, ϵ_{max}, $S(X)$, γ and κ critically depends on the functional relationship to be approximated and also on the specified minimum approximation error (e_{min}).

4   Experiments and Discussions

In our simulations, we have used the live image quality assessment database [14]. Here, 29 JPEG images are used to generate a database of 204 JPEG images with different compression rates. including the original images, we have 233

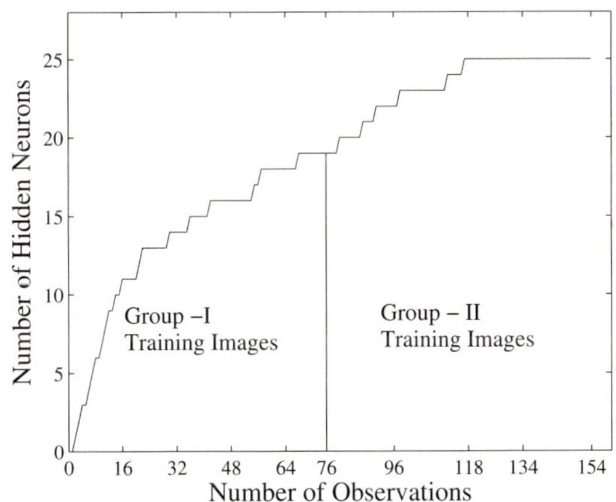

Fig. 2. Hidden neuron development

JPEG images for image quality estimation. First, the study was conducted in two sessions (first session 116 images with 20 subjects and the next session 117 images with 13 subjects). Each observer was shown the images randomly and asked to mark the perception quality on a continuous linear scale that was divided into five equal regions marked with adjectives bad, poor, fair, good and excellent. The scale was then linearly transformed to $1-10$ range. The resulting MOS was used to develop the GAP-RBF model to predict the image quality.

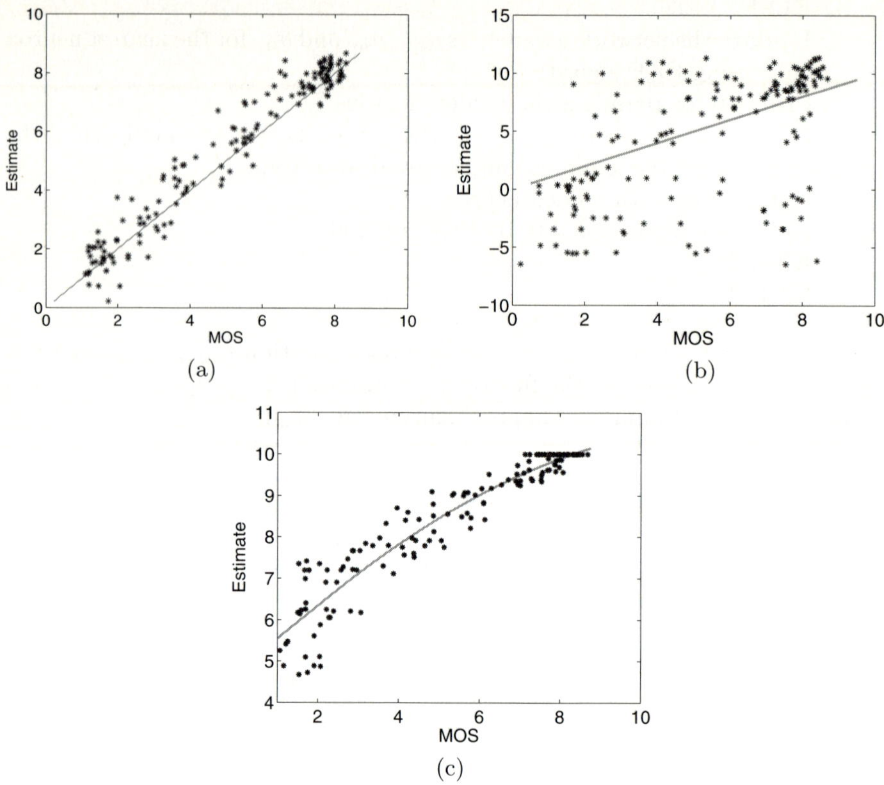

Fig. 3. Image quality prediction by (a) proposed GAP-RBF method (b) Wang-Bovik method and (c) SSIM score for 154 training images

To develop the GAP-RBF image quality model, we have selected two disjoint sets of images for training and testing. The training set images and its compressed versions are not used in testing set. Out of 29 source images, 20 images were used for training and the remaining 9 source images were used for testing. Totally 154 images were used for training (20 original and its 134 compressed versions) and 79 images for testing (9 original and its 70 compressed versions). First, we presented 154 training images sequentially to the GAP-RBF algorithm to develop the model. In our simulations, we set the following network parameters: $\epsilon_{min} = 0.001$, $\epsilon_{max} = 0.05$, $s(x) = 1$, $\gamma = 0.999$ and $\kappa = 0.1$. The expected minimum accuracy selected for our modeling is 0.0001. The GAP-RBF network initialized with zero hidden neuron, builds the network based on the 'growing and pruning' strategy mentioned earlier. The neuron history (Fig. 2) shows that 25 neurons are required to approximate the functional relationship. From Fig. 2, we see that the neuron growth saturates at 25 after the 117th training image sample. The developed GAP-RBF network model is tested with the 79 test images. The correlation between MOS and GAP-RBF based image quality metric

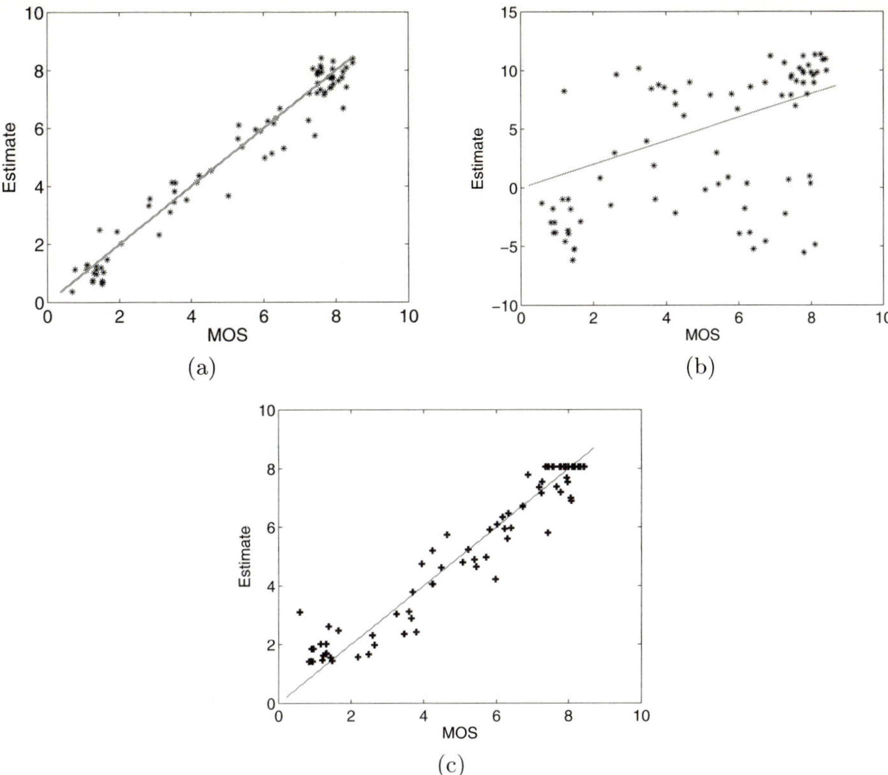

Fig. 4. Image quality prediction by (a) proposed GAP-RBF method (b) Wang-Bovik method and (c) SSIM score for 79 test images

for training and test images are shown in Figs. 3 (a) and 4 (a). Similar study is carried out using wang's NR quality metric (see Figs. 3 (b) and 4 (b)) [15] and full-reference SSIM index (Figs. 3 (c) and 4 (c)) (the SSIM index results are shown after fitting non-linear logistic function) [13]. The results clearly show that the proposed GAP-RBF model predicts the image quality better than the others. This can also be deduced from the quantitative performance analysis. The root mean square error (RMSE) deviation from MOS for image quality metric using different methods are given in table 1. From the table, it can be inferred that the proposed GAP-RBF model predicts image quality better than the other models.

Table 1. RMSE between MOS and Prediction

Metric	Testing	Training
GAP-RBF	0.46	0.61
Wang's	4.32	5.12
SSIM	0.67	0.62

5 Conclusions

In this paper, we have presented a system for predicting image quality using GAP-RBF network, considering various human visual characteristics. The functional relationship between the extracted HVS features and MOS is modeled by GAP-RBF network. Since sequential learning algorithm is used, GAP-RBF network does not require retraining when presented with a new data set. This helps us improve the model over time, receiving new sets of subjective results with minimal computational and memory requirements. The performance of the proposed metric is found to be better than other previously reported NR/FR image quality metrics.

Acknowledgment

The authors would like to thank Prof. Bovik and his lab members for providing the JPEG image quality assessment database to test our metric.

References

1. Wang, Z., Sheikh, H.R., Bovik, A.C.: No-reference perceptual quality assessment of JPEG compressed images. In: Proc. ICIP'02. Volume 1. (2002) 477–480
2. S. A. Karunasekera and N.G. Kingsbury: A distortion measure for blocking artifacts in images based on human visual sensitivity. IEEE Transactions on Image Processing **4** (1995) 713–724
3. Wu, H.R., Yuen, M.: A generalized block-edge impairment metric for video coding. IEEE Signal Processing Letters **70** (1998) 247–278
4. Suthaharan, S.: A perceptually significant block-edge impairment metric for digital video coding. In: Proc. ICASSP'2003. Volume 3., Hong Kong (2003) 681–684
5. Gao, W., Mermer, C., Kim, Y.: A de-blocking algorithm and a blockiness metric for highly compressed images. IEEE Transactions on Circuits and Systems for Video Technology **12** (2002) 1150–1159
6. Video Quality Experts Group (VQEG): (website: http://www.vqeg.org)
7. JPEG official site: (http://www.jpeg.org/)
8. Meesters, L., Martens, J.B.: A single-ended blockiness measure for JPEG-coded images. Signal Processing **82** (2002) 369–387
9. Babu, V., Perkis, A.: An HVS-based no-reference perceptual quality assessment of JPEG coded images using neural networks. In: Proc. Int. Conf. on Image Processing (ICIP'05). Volume 1., Genova, Italy (2005) 433–436
10. Karayiannis, N.B., Mi, G.W.: Growing radial basis neural networks: Merging supervised and unsupervised learning with network growth techniques. IEEE Trans. on Neural Networks **8** (1997) 1492–1506
11. Yingwei, L., Sundararajan, N., Saratchandran, P.: A sequential learning scheme for function approximation using minimal radial basis function (RBF) neural networks. Neural Computation **9** (1997) 461–478
12. G.-B. Huang, P.S., Sundararajan, N.: An efficient sequential learning algorithm for growing and pruning RBF (GAP-RBF) networks. IEEE Trans. on Systems, Man and Cybernautics: Part-B Cybernautics **34** (2004) 2284–2292

13. Wang, Z., Bovik, A.C., Sheikh, H.R., Simoncelli, E.P.: Image quality assessment: From error visibility to structural similarity. IEEE Trans. Image Processing **3** (2004) 600–612
14. Sheikh, H.R., Wang, Z., Cormack, L., Bovik, A.C.: (Live image quality assessment database) http://live.ece.utexas.edu/research/quality.
15. Z. Wang and A. C. Bovik and L. Lu : Why is image quality assessment so difficult? In: Proc. ICASSP'02. Volume 4. (2002) 3313–3316

A Novel Error Resilient Temporal Adjacency Based Adaptive Multiple State Video Coding over Error Prone Channels

Ragunathan M. and Mala C.

National Institute of Technology (Deemed University, Govt. of India),
Department of Computer Science and Engineering,
Tiruchirappalli, Tamil Nadu, India. Pin Code – 620 015
mragunathan@gmail.com, mala@nitt.edu

Abstract. Video streaming applications have been gaining interest rapidly in various perspectives from entertainment to e-learning. Practically, these applications suffer from inevitable loss in the transmission channels. Hence it is a challenging task to improve the quality of video streaming over the error prone channels. Multiple Description Coding (MDC) is a promising error resilient coding scheme which sends two or more descriptions of the source to the receiver to improve the quality of video streaming over error prone channels. Depending on the number of descriptions received, the reconstruction-distortion gets reduced at the receiver. Multiple State Video Coding (MSVC) is a MDC scheme based on frame-wise splitting of the video sequence into two or more sub-sequences. Each of these sub-sequences is encoded separately to generate descriptions, which can be decoded independently on reception. Basic MSVC is based on the separation of frames in a video into odd and even frames and sending each part over a different path. The drawbacks or certain subtleties of the basic MSVC such as lack of meaningful basis behind the frame wise splitting, inability to support adaptive streaming effectively, less error resiliency are brought out and discussed. Thus to overcome them and to improve the quality of video streaming, the design of a novel MSVC scheme based on the temporal adjacency between video frames is proposed in this paper. This temporal adjacency based splitting of the video stream into N sub-sequences also enables the proposed scheme to adapt to varying bandwidths in heterogeneous environments effectively. The simulation results show that the proposed scheme also outperforms Single State Video Coding (SSVC) scheme in terms of the sensitivity of perception of the reconstructed video sequence, under various loss scenarios.

1   Introduction

The demand for good quality Multimedia services over networks has been growing. Particularly Video streaming applications have been gaining interest rapidly in various perspectives from entertainment to e-learning. In these applications, since video data are voluminous it requires high compression before transmission using various encoding schemes. The transmission systems of the video streaming

P. Kalra and S. Peleg (Eds.): ICVGIP 2006, LNCS 4338, pp. 728 – 737, 2006.

applications rely on the reliability of the networks and impose stringent timing requirements as they deal with time based media. But all real networks are unreliable despite wired or wireless. Hence practically errors are inevitable and these applications suffer from inevitable loss in the transmission channels. This lossy transmission affects the quality of the reconstructed video. There exist conventional methods for resolving these packet losses and improving the quality of streaming such as Retransmission [11] and Forward Error Correction (FEC) [9]. However, if the transmission system was not able to afford an additional back-channel, or if the additional Round Trip Time (RTT) delay was not bearable, then the Retransmission cannot be employed. Also FEC approaches are designed to be effective only for losses less than a threshold. Obviously this cannot be guaranteed due to the highly dynamic nature of the networks. Since it is almost impossible to guess the threshold value, the scheme proves to be inefficient. Thus the demand for an Error resilient coding scheme naturally increases. MDC [6] is a promising error resilient coding scheme which sends two or more descriptions of the source to the receiver to improve the quality of video streaming over error prone channels. Depending on the number of descriptions received, the reconstruction-distortion gets reduced at the receiver. MSVC is a MDC scheme based on frame-wise splitting of the video sequence into two or more sub-sequences. Each one of these sub-sequences can be encoded separately to generate descriptions, which can then be decoded independently on reception. The advantages of MSVC are that the streams are independently decodable and they provide bi-directional data, that is, certain past and future frames are known appropriate to any instant of time. This helps in effective reconstruction as the received independent frames can recover the state of corrupted streams. The basic MSVC scheme [2] suggests the splitting of the given sequence into two sub-sequences. The original sequence is split frame-wise into two groups. One consisting of the odd frames and the other consisting of the even frames. Each of these two groups is separately encoded to form two descriptions or sub-sequences, one containing the odd and the other containing the even frames. Then these two sub-sequences arc sent to the destination through diverse paths. Due to the diverse paths maintained, the reception would be experiencing only the average behavior of all the channels through which the descriptions are sent. Naturally this improves the performance of the system. The improvement in performance can be justified by the argument that the probability that all of the multiple paths will be congested simultaneously is less than the probability that the single path is congested.

Our goal in this paper is to propose a novel Multiple State Video Coding scheme. The novelty of the proposed scheme is the way by which the given video sequence is split into sub-sequences. In the basic MSVC scheme suggested in [2], [4] the basis of splitting the video frames is thze frame number i.e. whether they are odd or even. Obviously these subsequences alone or together can provide an acceptable quality of reconstruction despite losses. However the notion behind the scheme is purely mathematical. Almost the same effect can be got by splitting the video into three sub-sequences, where one containing the frames which are divisible by 3, the other containing the frames divisible by 2, and the third sub-sequences that are not divisible by both 2 and 3. Thus the absence of a meaningful notion behind the splitting of the video frames place no boundary on, the basis of splitting and the number of sub-sequences to be generated. The proposed scheme overcomes these subtleties with a meaningful notion as its basis. The notion behind the proposed MSVC scheme is the *summary* and *non-summary* frames. The summary frames are the snapshots or relatively a small number of frames of the original complete video sequence which provide the summary of the video content. Naturally the frames that are not summary frames are non-summary frames. In short the summary frames are those frames which are temporally adjacent, that is they are visually dissimilar or their content difference is large. The interesting aspect of this notion is that the summary and non-summary frames alone / together can provide a comprehendible reconstructed video. This aspect is interesting since it holds despite the fact that the summary frames contain a relatively small number of frames of the original video, whereas the non-summary frames contain relatively large number of frames. This is due to the characteristics of the summary frames, that they can summarize the whole content with relatively small number of frames but they are substitutable by the non-summary frames. Through the reception of summary frames we can ensure a comprehendible video, however their loss are substitutable by the non-summary frames, thereby increasing the error resiliency. Also the transmission of summary frames requires less bandwidth compared to that of non-summary frames / original sequence, thereby increasing the adaptive nature when streaming to heterogeneous clients. Thus a novel error resilient temporal adjacency based adaptive MSVC scheme is proposed. Then the performance of the proposed scheme is compared with the SSVC scheme, in terms of the sensitivity of perception of the reconstructed video sequence. The performance analysis is done *shot wise* under various loss scenarios such as single and burst error, when the channel losses are independent and dependent. Finally a discussion on the ability of the scheme to adapt to the varying bandwidths is presented. Further the discussion investigates the application of the proposed scheme in the context of adaptive streaming to heterogeneous clients.

The remainder of the paper is organized as follows. Section 2 discusses the existing schemes, MDC and basic MSVC. In Section 3, the design of the proposed scheme is presented. The performance analysis over SSVC is presented in Section 4. This is followed by Section 5, where the effectiveness of the proposed scheme over the basic MSVC scheme [2] is discussed. Section 6 concludes the paper.

2   Existing Schemes

Multiple Description Coding (MDC) has emerged as a power framework for robust coding and transmission of the video data over lossy networks. The two main problems of the real networks [5] are the limited bandwidth and the packet losses. Limitation on bandwidth is natural and can be resolved by duly considering it. The conventional methods of resolving packet losses such as retransmission and FEC cannot be employed effectively as mention in Section 1. MDC is a promising error resilient coding scheme. MDC was invented in Bell Labs primarily for telephone conversations. But it is used for image, video/audio transmission. Multiple Description Coding *"represents a single information source with several chunks of data (i.e. descriptions) so that the source can be approximated from any subset of chunks"* [3]. MDC is applied to some major coding techniques such as scalar quantization, vector quantization of motion vectors [10], correlating transforms, or quantized frame expansions. A summary of the state-of-the-art system designs can be found in [3]. High rates, low latency requirements, and error drift are however the main problems encountered in MDC schemes for video streaming due to possible desynchronization of encoders and decoders [4].

MSVC is a MDC scheme which is inspired by the frame-wise splitting of the video stream into sub-sequences. Each of these sub-sequences can be independently decodable. Thus MSVC is a kind of MDC with the novelty of the additional state recovery capability [1]. The MSVC scheme is less complex than MDC. The other advantages of MSVC include low delay property, nil error propagation, and the bi-directional information the streams provide. The goal of MSVC is to combine the high compression and the high error resilience. The advantage of MSVC over SSVC schemes is that in MSVC the streams received provide bi-directional information, that is the information about the future and the past frames received through multiple descriptions, which help in increasing the state recovery property during reconstruction. Whereas in SSVC when a previously decoded frame is lost the quality degrades until the state is refreshed by the next I-frame. Basic MSVC is based on the separation of video frames into odd and even frames in a stream and sending each part over a different path. Here the path diversity is maintained in transmitting the two descriptions. This is to achieve a better reconstruction quality since the independent loss patterns in the two channels results in only the average path behavior. However the basic MSVC have certain drawbacks such as lack of meaningful basis behind the frame wise splitting, inability to support adaptive streaming effectively and less error resiliency. To overcome them and to improve the quality of video streaming, the design of a novel MSVC scheme based on the temporal adjacency between video frames is proposed in the next section. Complete information about the basic MSVC scheme can be found in [1].

3   The Proposed MSVC Scheme

This section first introduces the basic idea of summary and non-summary frames behind the proposed MSVC scheme. The aspects of the proposed scheme's basic notion which increases the error resilience capability and adaptive nature of the coding scheme are then discussed. The algorithm for selecting the summary frames from a given video stream is presented. This is followed by the design of a two-state MSVC following the proposed scheme. Then the necessary details about extending this novel MSVC scheme to N states are presented.

The inspiration for the notion of summary and non-summary frames is got from [8], where the summary and non-summary frames were introduced and used for developing a disruption tolerant content aware video coding. The proposed scheme incorporates the notion of summary and non-summary frames with subtle changes into the context of MSVC.

The 'summary frames' in short are the snapshots or relatively a small number of frames of the original complete video sequence which provide a summary of the video content. As the name suggests, by viewing the summary frames of a video the user can comprehend the content of the video. Naturally, if a set of frames are summary frames of a video, then the frames that are not summary frames are the set of 'non-summary frames'. It can be well perceived that the non-summary frames can provide a video of quality very close to the original complete sequence. Since only a relatively small number of frames of the original sequence form the summary frames, the video is not much altered without them.

The interesting aspect of this notion is that the summary and non-summary frames alone/together can provide a comprehendible reconstructed video. This aspect is interesting since it holds despite the fact that the summary frames contain relatively small number of frames of the original video, whereas the non-summary frames contain relatively large number of frames that are not summary frames. This is due to the characteristics of the summary frames, that they can summarize the whole content with relatively small number of frames but they are substitutable by the non-summary frames. This follows that the reception of summary frames ensures the comprehension of the video, however their loss are substitutable by the non-summary frames, thereby increasing the error resiliency of the scheme. Also the transmission of summary frames requires less bandwidth compared to that of non-summary frames/ original sequence, thereby increasing the adaptive nature of the scheme when streaming to heterogeneous clients.

3.1   Algorithm - For Selecting the Summary Frames of a Given Video Sequence

The algorithm for generating two sets of frames i.e. the summary frames and non-summary frames from a given video sequence is given below.

Let F be the set containing all the frames in the given sequence. Let Fs denote the summary frames set and Fns denote the non-summary frame set. Let L be a list built of all the frames in the set F and f_i denote the frame i in the list L. Let D be a two dimensional array containing the content difference of the frames in the list L. For example $D(i,j)$ contains the content difference of the frames $L(i)$ and $L(j)$.

```
Initially the set F_s contains all the frames of the
video and the set F_ns has no frames i.e. empty.

1. Find the minimum content difference D(i,j)in the
array D and delete the frame f_i if the frames f_i and its
predecessor are less temporally adjacent than that of
f_j and its successor. Else delete the frame f_j from the
set F_ns.

2. Include f_i or f_j to the set F_s depending on whether
the frame f_i or f_j of is deleted, respectively.

3. Update the D array with the content difference
between the frame deleted and its adjacent frame.

4. Repeat steps 1 and 2 until there is no frames in F_s
or when the number of frames in F_ns is equal to R.
```

The variable R can be defined as the ratio between the total number of frames present in the original video to the number of summary frames required. Naturally with this variable the number of summary frames and how densely are they required to be spaced can be controlled. A basic interpretation may be - if R is large the summary frames will be too sparsely spaced and vice versa.

3.2 Design of a Two-State MSVC Based on the Proposed Scheme

For the video sequence to be transmitted two subsequences are generated – one containing 'the summary frames' and the other containing 'the non-summary frames'. This can be done by processing the given video sequence with the above algorithm to generate two sets of frames F_s and F_{ns} .These two sets of frames are encoded separately to form two sub-sequences or descriptions that are independently decodable. These two subsequences are transmitted to the destination following two different paths. When at the reception the summary frame sequence alone is received, it can provide the summary of the video. If the non-summary frames sequence alone is received it can also provide the video sequence of quality nearly equal to the original sequence as said before. If both are received with some losses then they can be decoded and combined to get an optimum quality video. Thus we have two descriptions of the video and thereby a two state MSVC. Since the proposed notion of summary and non-summary frames is used, this forms the design of a two-state MSVC based on the proposed scheme.

3.3 Extending the Design to N Descriptions or State

In the above algorithm for a video sequence two sets of frames F_s and F_{ns} are got as output. Each of these two sets of frames is encoded to generate a description. Thus we have two descriptions and hence the two state MSVC. To extend it to more than two states say 'n', 'n' descriptions have to be generated. To generate 'n' descriptions, 'n' set of frames are necessary as it was two sets F_s and F_{ns} for n=2 i.e. in two state MSVC. This can be done by applying the above discussed algorithm again with F_{ns1} (let Fns1 be the non-summary frames got by applying the algorithm for the first time on the original sequence) as F. By this two sets of frames F_{s2} and F_{ns2} can again be got. This is continued (n-1) times to get 'n' sets: $F_{n(1)}$, $F_{n(2)}$, $F_{n(3)}$...$F_{n(n-1)}$ and $F_{ns(n-1)}$. Thus we have n-1 summary frame sets and 1 non-summary frame set, totally 'n' sets. From these 'n' sets 'n' descriptions can be generated and thereby this leads to an 'n' state MSVC technique.

4 Performance Analysis over SSVC

This section provides the results of performance analysis of the proposed MSVC scheme over the SSVC scheme. A 3-state MSVC codec based on the proposed scheme is developed using C-Language. The encoder encodes the given video sequence into three sub-sequences namely ns, s1 and s2. Where s1 is the sub-sequence got by summarizing the given video with the summarizing ratio R1 and let ns' be the resulting non-summary frames. s2 and ns are the summary frames and non-summary frames got by further summarizing the non-summary frames ns' with the summarizing ratio R2. The error patterns while transmitting the sub-sequences to the destination through diverse paths are simulated. The error pattern simulation is done for various scenarios.

The comparison is done in terms of Sensitivity Of Perception (SOP), which is a number signifying the sensitivity perceived by the user when a transition from one frame to the other takes place while streaming a video. The decoder accepts the frames transmitted after error simulation is done manually and it decodes them independently. The lost frames are reconstructed by inserting *black frames* in order to improve the sensitivity of perception and thereby making the performance analysis clearer.

When the sub-sequences are transmitted via three diverse paths, the losses in the three channels may be independent or dependent. The loss patterns of the three channels will be independent if they do not have any partial common path. But the losses will be dependent if two or three of them have partial common paths. Now the performance is analyzed for both the cases of independent and dependent channel losses. And in each of these two cases both the single frame loss and burst frame losses are considered. Thus an analysis of SSVC over proposed MSVC is done for four scenarios.

For this a reference video sequence that has 110 frames and 4 shots is considered. However our analysis is confined to the first shot which consists of frames 0-38. The summary ratios R1 and R2 used are 4 and 2 respectively.

The graphs got by simulation are given in Fig.1 and Fig.2. Fig 1 corresponds to the Scenario 1- Single frame loss in two channels (independent) and Fig 2 corresponds to the Scenario 2- Burst frame loss in two channels (dependent).

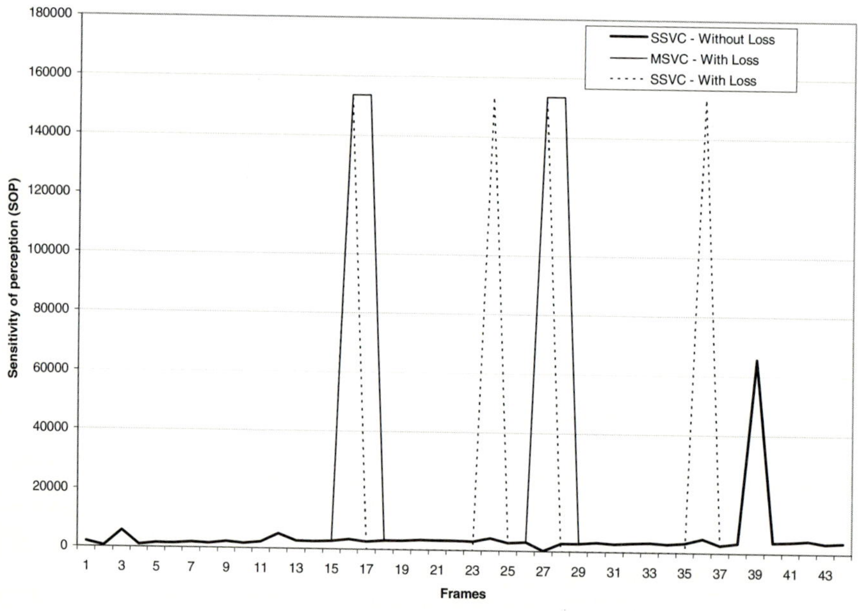

Fig. 1. Scenario-Single frame loss in two channels (independent)

Scenario 1: In this scenario frame 27 is lost in channel s1. And frame 16 is lost in channel s2. The dark thick line corresponds to a streaming of the normal lossless video. The dotted line corresponds to the streaming of the reconstructed SSVC – with loss. The normal dark line corresponds to that of MSVC. It can be seen that both the SSVC (dotted) and MSVC (normal) are getting deviated at the frame number 16, since it is lost (to improve the SOP this frame is replaced by black frame for analysis sake). The MSVC returns to normal streaming at frame 17 but the SSVC returns to the normal streaming only after the state is refreshed by the next I-frame (frame 24) received. Thus the viewer is subjected to a bad SOP for long time in SSVC, whereas it is not so in MSVC. The same argument holds for the loss of frame 27 in channel s2.

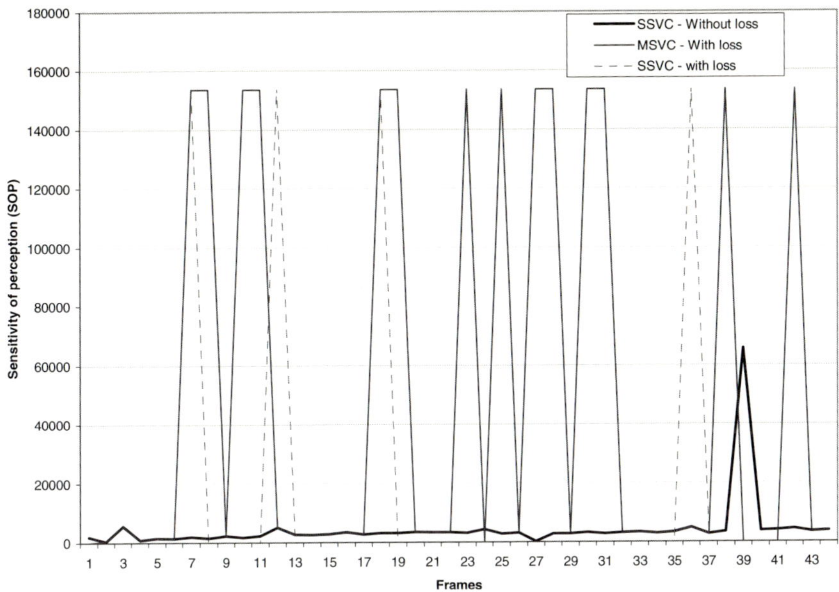

Fig. 2. Scenario-Burst frame loss in two channels (dependent)

Scenario 2: In this scenario frames 7, 10, 27 are lost in channel s1 and frames 18 23 24 30 38 are lost in channel us. Here too the viewer is subjected to a bad SOP for long time in SSVC, whereas it is not so in MSVC. This can be seen from the graph of Fig.2.

5   Effectiveness of the Proposed Scheme over the Basic MSVC Scheme

The effectiveness issues apart from those mentioned in the introduction part of this paper is presented in this section.

The performance improvement of the basic MSVC over SSVC is justified by the argument that the probability that all of the multiple paths will be congested simultaneously is less than the probability that the single path is congested [7]. Following the same argument the proposed scheme extends the two states to N states to improve the performance further since the probability that all of the N paths will be congested simultaneously is less than the probability that the two paths are simultaneously congested. Also the loss of frames in either of the channel where the odd / even frames sub-sequences are sent will just mean loss of frames. Nothing can be inferred about the reconstruction quality from the knowledge of losses in these channels before transmission by any of the channel look up techniques. But the knowledge about the loss of frames in any of the channels through which the summary or non-summary sub-sequences are sent convey meaning. Suppose the loss is only in the non-summary frames implies that we can have a quality of video that is comprehendible. Similarly the loss of frames only in the channel through which the summary frames sub-sequence is sent implies that they can be substituted by the non-summary frames that are receive, thereby implying an acceptable quality of reconstruction.

6 Conclusions

The work presented in this paper explored the subtleties of the MSVC scheme proposed in [2], [1]. The exploration resulted in the conclusion that the basis of frame-splitting is purely mathematical. Thus the absence of a meaningful notion behind the splitting of the video frames in the basic MSVC [1], [4] placed no boundary on the basis of splitting and the number of sub-sequences to be generated. Also a drawback of the basic MSVC, that it does not possess effective adaptive streaming capability is opened up. To overcome the drawbacks a novel MSVC scheme is proposed. The scheme is based on the notion of summary and non-summary frames. The justification for the better performance of the proposed MSVC scheme over the basic MSVC scheme, due to its meaningful notion behind splitting the video frames is presented. The performance is better in terms of quality of the video streaming over error prone channels and the effectiveness of adaptation when streaming to heterogeneous clients. The codec for the proposed MSVC is developed and the various loss scenarios when the encoded video stream is transmitted are simulated. The simulation results concluded that the proposed MSVC scheme outperformed the SSVC, in terms of the Sensitivity Of Perception (SOP).

References

1. Vorgelegt von, Diplom Ingenieurin, Siila Ekmekciaus, Frankfurt am Main. "Multi-State Video Coding over Error Prone Channels", Thesis,Technical University Berlin, December 2004.
2. J. G. Apostolopoulos. "Reliable video communication over lossy packet networks using multiple state encoding and path diversity", Visual Communications and Image Processing, Proceedings of SPIE, vol. 4310, pp.392–409, 2001.
3. V. K. Goyal. "Multiple description coding: compression meets the network", IEEE Signal Processing Magazine, vol. 18, no. 5, pp. 74–93, 2001.
4. Sila Ekmekci, Thomas Sikora. "Unbalanced Quantized Multiple State Video Coding". EURASIP Journal on Applied Signal Processing, Article ID 14694, pp.1–10, 2006.
5. Fisichee Naturali, Notes on "Networked Multimedia Systems - error detection and control schemes", Università degli Studi di Verona, 2001.
6. Raman Venkataramani. "Multiple Description Coding with Many Channels". DIMACS workshop on network information theory, Harvard University, Cambridge, MA, 2003.

7. Sila Ekmekci, Thomas Sikora. "Multi-State vs. Single-State Video Coding over Error-Prone Channels", in the Thirty-Seventh Asilomar Conference on Signals, Systems and Computers, vol.2, pp.1544-47, Nov. 2003.

8. Tiecheng Liu and Srihari Nelakuditi. "Disruption-Tolerant Content Aware Video Streaming", Proceedings of the 12th annual ACM International Multimedia Conference, pp. 420 – 423, 2004.

9. R. Puri, K. Ramchandran, K.W. Lee and V. Bharghavan. "Forward error correction (FEC) codes based multiple description coding for Internet video streaming and multicast", Signal Processing: Image Communication, vol. 16, no. 8, pp. 745–762, 2001.

10. C.S. Kim and S.U. Lee. "Multiple description motion coding algorithm for robust video transmission", Proceedings of IEEE International Symposium on Circuits and Systems, vol. 4, pp. 717–720, Geneva, Switzerland, May 2000.

11. Injong Rhee and Srinath R. Joshi. "Error Recovery for Interactive Video Transmission over the Internet", IEEE Journal on Selected Areas in Communication, vol.18, no.6, pp. 1033-1049, June 2000.

Adaptive Data Hiding in Compressed Video Domain

Arijit Sur and Jayanta Mukherjee

Department of Computer Science and Engineering,
Indian Institute of Technology, Kharagpur
{arijits, jay}@cse.iitkgp.ernet.in

Abstract. In this paper we propose a new adaptive block based compressed domain data hiding scheme which can embed relatively large number of secret bits without significant perceptual distortion in video domain. Macro blocks are selected for embedding on the basis of low inter frame velocity. From this subset, the blocks with high prediction error are selected for embedding. The embedding is done by modifying the quantized DCT AC coefficients in the compressed domain. The number of coefficients (both zero and non zero) used in embedding is adaptively determined using relative strength of the prediction error block. Experimental results show that this blind scheme can embed a relatively large number of bits without degrading significant video quality with respect to Human Visual System (HVS).

1 Introduction

With the enormous advancement of the multimedia technology such as High definition television (HDTV), Video on Demand (VOD), Video telephony etc, multimedia security becomes a significant issue nowadays. Video watermarking is one of possible countermeasure defending the world wide video piracy. Again secret communication through video stream is another interesting field in most modern era of information hiding. So data hiding in streaming media become an important research aspect today. There are number of video watermarking techniques are proposed in the recent literature. Three major trends can be classified such as extension of still image watermarking scheme, exploiting another temporal dimension such as motion and using standard video compression techniques such as MPEG standards. The extension of still image watermarking schemes are mostly based on spatial domain embedding which is computationally intensive and suffers from lack of robustness due to the inherent lossy nature of the video compression. According to the recent literature of compressed domain video watermarking, embedding is generally done either by modifying motion vector information or using prediction error. The motion vector based video watermarking is first proposed by *F. Jordan et al* [1] where motion vector of MPEG 4 video stream is slightly modified to embed secret message. Some improved version of the motion vector based watermarking schemes are proposed in [2-5]. These schemes are robust but suffer from lack of payload. Only high value

P. Kalra and S. Peleg (Eds.): ICVGIP 2006, LNCS 4338, pp. 738–748, 2006.

motion vectors can be modified to embed secret message without significant visual distortion. Prediction error based embedding schemes are not very robust as secret message is truncated during the quantization process especially when bit rate is very low. In this paper we propose a new prediction error based adaptive data hiding scheme that can embed relatively large number of bits without significant visual distortion. This blind scheme is relatively robust with respect of the quantization error because embedding is done after quantization. From a pschyco-visual heuristic, the visual distion for injecting slight noise to the block with relatively less inter frame velocity is not very perceptually significant. In proposed scheme, the macro-blocks with less inter frame velocity and with high prediction error are selected for embedding such that embedding distortion may not be visually perceptible. The strength of the error block can be tracked by the quantized DC coefficient of the block. Number of quantized AC coefficients of the prediction error block, which are used for embedding, is adaptively selected on the basis of relative strength of the error block i.e. more numnber of coefficients of the block having higher quantized DC value are used for embedding. Selected number of quantized AC coefficients of prediction error block are modified to embed the secret bits. The experimental result reveals that much more secret bits can be embedded with this proposed scheme than the motion vector based scheme proposed in [5] without significant visual distortion. The visual quality performance comparison is made by compairing PSNR and Watson Metric[6]. Watson Metric which is designed on the basis of characteristics of human visual system, measures the total perceptual error based on frequency sensitivity, luminance sensitivity and contrast masking. The rest of the paper is organized as follows, in section 2 we experimentally shows that more bits can be embedded into error blocks with higher energy (i.e., blocks with larger DC coefficients in transformed domain) without significant perceptual distortion. The details of embedding and extracting schemes are discussed in the section 3. Experimental results will be given in the section 4 and section 5 contains conclusion and future research.

2   Impact of Embedding in the Prediction Error Block

The effect of bit embedding in the quantized DCT error blocks are discussed in this section. The main notion of our proposed scheme depends on the following two observations:

- The quantized error blocks with relatively large DC value are more noise tolerant with respect to the Human Visual system (HVS).
- The total perceptual error is directly proportional to the number of secret bits being embedded. So more the bits are embedded, larger is the perceptual error.

In these experimentations, 8x8 quantization matrix is used for inverse quantization where all matrix elements are sixteen[1](16). 8x8 IDCT matrix (defined in

---

[1] As specified for the default quantization table of prediction error used in MPEG 1 standard.

MATLAB) is used for inverse DCT. The secret bits which are to be embedded
are binary random bit stream.

2.1 Relationship of DC Value and Total Perceptual Error of Prediction Error Block Due to Embedding with Fixed Payload

In this subsection, we are trying to show that for a fixed embedding change i.e.
payload[2], the total perceptual error (due to the embedding) of the blocks with
relatively higher DC value is lesser than the blocks with relatively lower DC
value. To show the above observation experimentally, we collect large number
of 8×8 quantized prediction error blocks of a test video sequence. Now for a
fixed embedding change (payload), we calculate the total perceptual error with
different DC value for each of the block. The average TPE (total perceptual
error) of all the blocks for the different DC value with fixed payload is plotted
in figure 1.

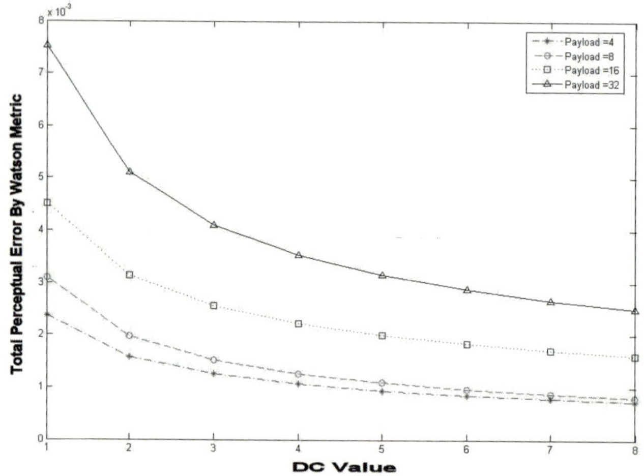

Fig. 1. Relationship between Total Perceptual Error and DC value with fixed Payload

The expermental result shows that the total perceptual error of the block is
gradually decreasing with increas of DC value of the block when payload is fixed.

2.2 Relationship of Payload and Total Perceptual Error of Prediction Error Block Due to Embedding with Fixed DC Value

In this subsection, we are trying to show that for a fixed DC value, total perceptual error is gradually increasing with increase of embedding change i.e. payload.

---

[2] Since secret bit stream is random binary sequence, then the payload i.e. number of
bits to be embedded is generally doubled of the number of embedding change.

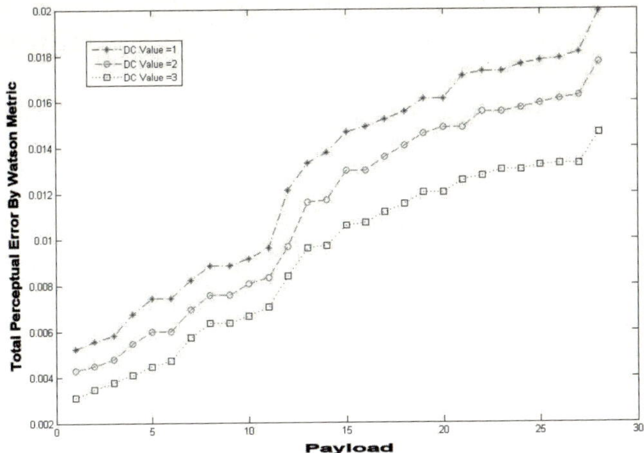

Fig. 2. Relationship between Total Perceptual Error and Payload with fixed DC value

To show this argument experimentally, we collect large number of prediction error blocks of a test video sequence. Now for a fixed DC value, we calculate different total perceptual error of the blocks on different payload. The average total perceptual error of all the blocks for different payload with fixed DC value is plotted in figure 2.

The experimental result shows that the total perceptual error is gradually increasing with increase of payload when DC value is fixed. From the above observations, payload of a block can be adaptively determined by the equation 1 such that we can control the payload depending on given perceptual error tolerance.

$$payload = \begin{cases} 0 & \text{if } dc \leq 0 \\ \min\left(\left\lceil \frac{2 \times dc - 2}{\lambda} \right\rceil, 32\right) & \text{if } dc > 0 \end{cases} \tag{1}$$

where λ is a constant and $\lceil \bullet \rceil$ is the Ceiling operator. A small λ leads to a large *payload* so that more data can be embedded with greater total perceptual error to the cover, and vice versa.

3   Embedding and Extraction Scheme

3.1   Embedding Scheme

In embedding process, the macro-blocks with less inter frame velocity and with high prediction error are selected for embedding such that embedding distortion may not be visually perceptible. The strength of the error block can be tracked by the quantized DC coefficient of the prediction error block. Number of quantized AC coefficients of the prediction error block, which are used for embedding, is adaptively selected on the basis of relative strength of the error block i.e. more numnber of coefficients, of the block having higher quantized DC value, are used for embedding. Selected number of quantized AC coefficients of prediction error block are modified to embed the secret bits. The step by step embedding algorithm is given below:

1. Let the motion vector information of the ith macro block[3] (B[i]) of a P frame in a video sequence is

$$MV[i], \ 0 < i < MB \tag{2}$$

   where MB=total number of macro blocks presents in the frame.
2. Calculate the magnitude of the motion vector

$$|MV[i]| = abs(H[i]) + abs(V[i]) \tag{3}$$

   where, H[i] is the horizontal component of motion vector in the ith macroblock; V[i] is the vertical component of motion vector in the ith macroblock of the frame.
3. Given threshold ϵ, select the macroblocks for watermark embedding,

$$S[i] = F[i] \times B[i] \tag{4}$$

   where $B[i] = i^{th}$ macro block of the current frame, S=selected macroblocks and $F[i]$ is defined as follows:

$$F[i] = \begin{cases} 1 & \text{if } |MV[i]| \leq \epsilon \\ 0 & \text{if } |MV[i]| > \epsilon \end{cases} \quad 0 < i < MB$$

   A large ϵ implies the selection of macro blocks with higher motion vector magnitude for embedding. That leads to greater perceptual distortion.
4. Let $dc(j)$ is the DC coefficient of jth block among four 8×8 blocks in the selected macroblock, the number of coefficients $N(j)$ which are modified during embedding is calculated as

$$N(j) = \begin{cases} 0 & \text{if } dc(j) \leq 0 \\ \min\left(\left\lceil \frac{2 \times dc(j) + 2}{\lambda} \right\rceil, 32\right) & \text{if } dc(j) > 0 \end{cases} \tag{5}$$

   where λ is a constant and $\lceil \bullet \rceil$ is the Ceiling operator. A small λ leads to a large $N(j)$ so that more data can be embedded with greater perceptual error to the cover, and vice versa. Blocks with quantized DC value equal to zero is not used for embedding.

5. Scan the selected error block for $N(j)$ number of quantized AC coefficients in zig zag scan order and embed the current secret bit with the current coefficient in scan order by equation 6. Only quantized AC coefficients are to be modified during embedding. Quantized DC value is kept unchanged. Secret bits are asuumed as random binary digits.

$$C'_j(m,n) = \begin{cases} C_j(m,n) & \text{if } mod(|C_j(m,n)|, 2) = E \\ C_j(m,n) + 1 & \text{if } mod(|C_j(m,n)|, 2) \neq E \end{cases} \tag{6}$$

---

[3] Size of macro block is 16×16.

where $C_j(m, n)$ is coefficient positioned in m^{th} row and n^{th} coloum of jth error block where $1 \leq m, n \leq 8$. $C'_j(m, n)$ is corresponding modified coefficient after embedding. E is the current binary secret bit to be embedded.

3.2   Extracting Scheme

Extraction scheme is very simple. The step by step extraction algorithm is given below to extract the hidden bits at the decoder side.

1. The macro blocks are selected at the decoder end by the same equations (3 and 4) as discussed in embedding scheme.
2. The number of modified coefficients can be determined from the unalterd DC value by the same way using equation 5 as in encoder.
3. Scan these coefficients in the same zig zag order as in embedding and determine the secret bits using equation 7 as

$$E' = Mod(C'_j(m, n), 2) \tag{7}$$

where $C'_j(m, n)$ is modified coefficients in j^{th} block in a selected macro block and E' is secret bit extracted.

By above extraction method, we can extract all hidden bits without any error.

4   Expermental Result

In this section, we will give the experimental results which show that our proposed scheme can embed relatively large number of secret bits without significant visual distortion. In these experimentations we have used 84 frames of *suzie*, *Miss America* and *salesman* test video sequences with fixed bit rate of 1.152

Table 1. Payload of Our Scheme and Scheme proposed in [5]

Scheme	suzie	miss america	salesman
Our Scheme	20414 bits	18714 bits	20346 bits
Scheme in [5]	3434 bits	963 bits	423 bits

Mbps, frame rate of 25 frames/sec, PAL video format, 176x144 frame size for testing. The relative payload of our scheme with respect to the scheme proposed in [5] is given in table 1. The comparison plot of PSNR and total perceptual error (by Watson Metric) of Cover [4], Stego[5] by our proposed scheme and Stego by scheme proposed in [5] for is given in figure 3. The comparison between our

---

[4] Innocent video frame without any embedded data.
[5] Video frame after embedding secret bits.

scheme and scheme proposed in [5] are given using another 7 video quality metrics[7] such as NMSE(Normalized Mean Square Error), SC(Structural Content), AAD(Absolute Average Difference), CQ(Correlation Quality), NCC(Normalized Cross-Correlation), PMSE (Pulse Mean Square Error)and IF (Image Fidelity). Results shows that our scheme can embed relatively large amount of data maintaining almost same visual quality as proposed in [5] with respect to the above video quality metrics. The comparison plot of NMSE and SC is given in figure 4, comparison plot of AAD and CQ is given in figure 5, comparison plot of NCC and PMSE is given in figure 6 and comparison plot of IF is given in figure 7.

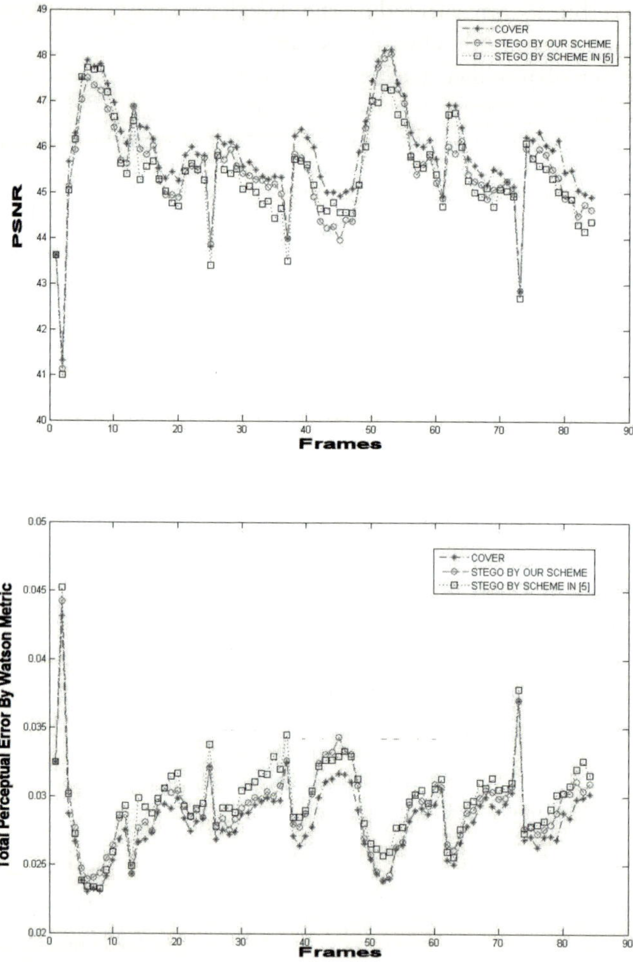

Fig. 3. The PSNR and Total Perceptual Error Plot for Cover, Stego by Our scheme and Stego by schme in [5]

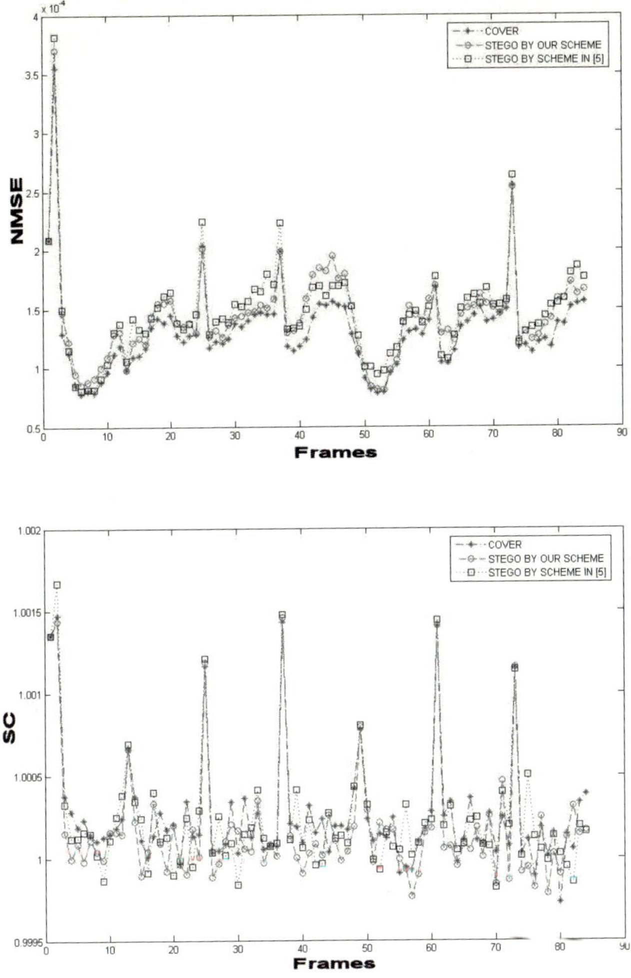

Fig. 4. The Normalized mean square error(NMSE) and Structural Content(SC) Plot for Cover, Stego by Our scheme and Stego by schme in [5]

5   Conclusion and Future Research

In this paper we have proposed a new adaptive block based compressed domain data hiding scheme which can embed relatively large number of secret bits without significant perceptual distortion in video domain. Macro blocks are selected for embedding on the basis of low inter frame velocity and high prediction error. The embedding is done by modifying the quantized DCT AC coefficients in the compressed domain. The number of coefficients (both zero and non zero) used in embedding is adaptively determined using relative strength of the

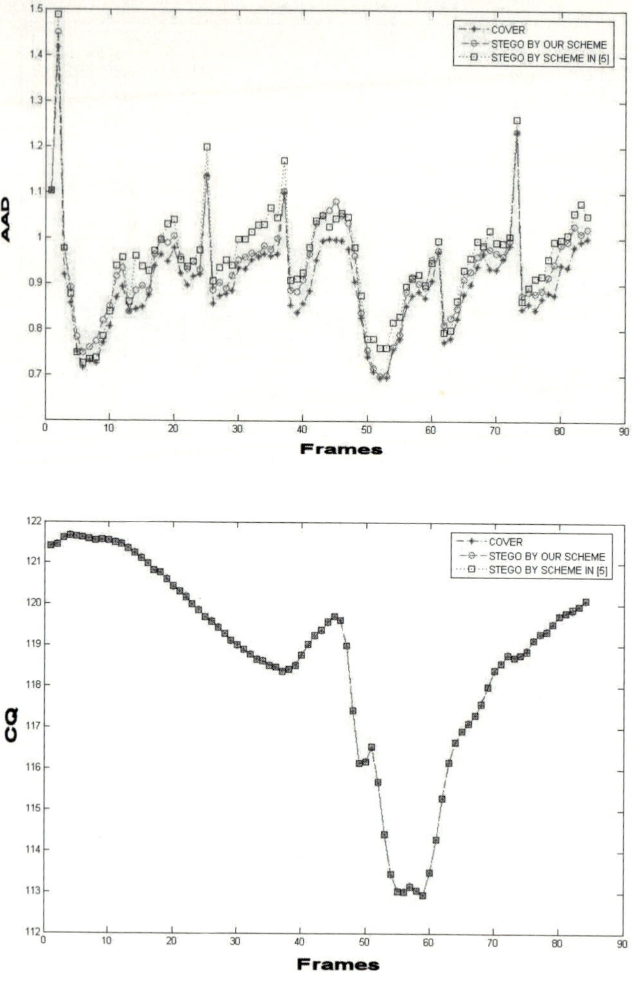

Fig. 5. The Absolute Average Difference(AAD) and Corellation Quality(CQ) Plot for Cover, Stego by Our scheme and Stego by schme in [5]

prediction error block. This blind scheme is relatively more robust with respect of the quantization error because embedding is done after quantization. There may be slightly degradation in visual quality in case of low fixed bit rate video. The proposed scheme is suitable for blind video watermarking where higher payload is necessary and can be used as video steganography as well. In these experimentation, we find that some zone of error block are more noise tolerant so more suitable for embedding. In future, we will concentrate on the problem of adaptive zone selection such that perceptual error due to embedding can be minimized.

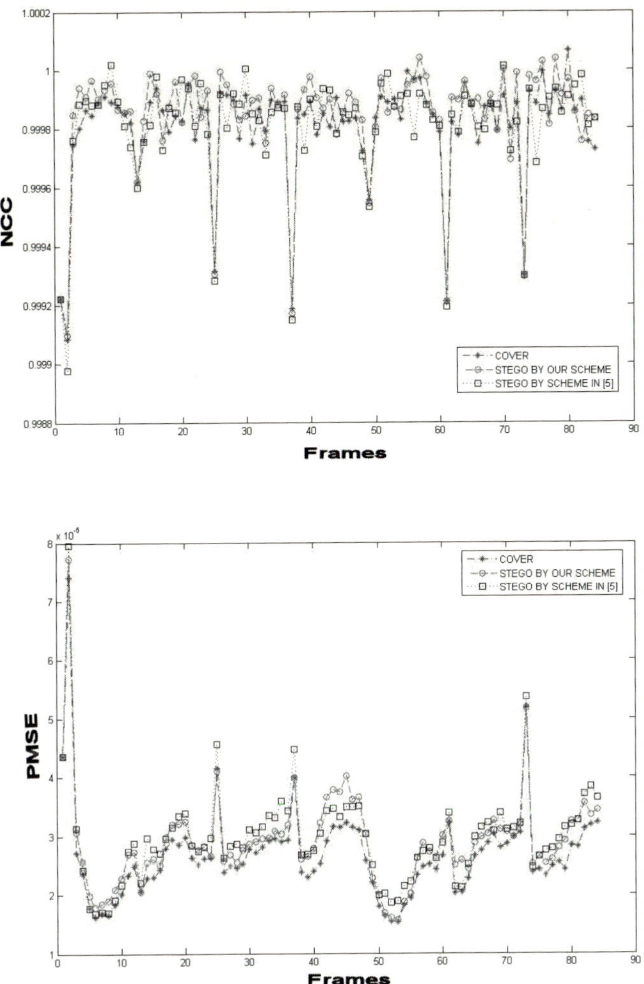

Fig. 6. The Normalized Cross-Corellation(NCC) and Peak Mean Square Error(PMSE) Plot for Cover, Stego by Our scheme and Stego by schme in [5]

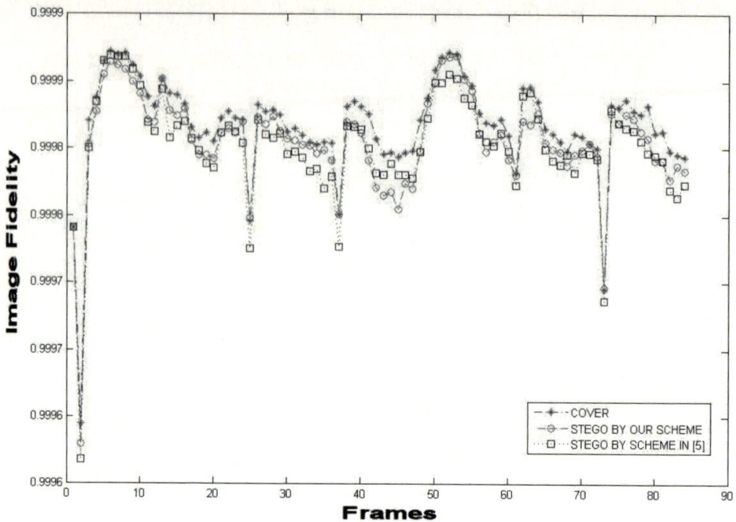

Fig. 7. The Image Fidelity(IF) for Cover, Stego by Our scheme and Stego by schme in [5]

References

1. Kutter M., Jordan F. and Ebrahimi T.: Proposal of a watermarking technique for hiding/retriving data in compressed and decompressed video, Technical reportM2881, ISO/IEC document, JTC1/Sc29/WG11,1997
2. Jun, Z., Jiegu, L., Ling, Z.: Video Watermark technique in motion vector, Proceeding of XIV Brazilian Symposium on Computer graphics and Image Processing, pp. 179-182, 2001.
3. Zhu, Z.,Jiang, G.,Yu, M.,Wu X.: New algorithm for video watermarking, Signal Processing, 2002 6th International Conference on Volume 1, 26-30 Aug. 2002.
4. Liu, L., Liang, H., Niu, X., Yang, Y.: A robust video watermarking in motion vectors, Signal Processing, 2004. Proceedings. ICSP '04. 2004 7th International Conference on Volume 3, 31 Aug.-4 Sept. 2004
5. Zhang, J.,Maitre, H.,Li, J.,Zhang, L.: Embedding watermark in MPEG video sequence, Multimedia Signal Processing, 2001 IEEE Fourth Workshop on 3-5 Oct. 2001
6. Mayache, A., Eude, T., Cherifi, H.: A comparison of image quality models and metrics based on human visual sensitivity, Image Processing, 1998. ICIP 98. Proceedings. 1998 International Conference on 4-7 Oct. 1998.
7. Hazem, M., A., -O.: Evaluation of reconstruction quality in image vector quantisation using existing and new measures, IEE Proc.-Vis. Image Signal Process, Vol. 145, No. 5, October 1998

Learning Segmentation of Documents with Complex Scripts

K.S. Sesh Kumar, Anoop M. Namboodiri, and C.V. Jawahar

Centre for Visual Information Technology,
International Institute of Information Technology, Hyderabad, India

Abstract. Most of the state-of-the-art segmentation algorithms are designed to handle complex document layouts and backgrounds, while assuming a simple script structure such as in Roman script. They perform poorly when used with Indian languages, where the components are not strictly collinear. In this paper, we propose a document segmentation algorithm that can handle the complexity of Indian scripts in large document image collections. Segmentation is posed as a graph cut problem that incorporates the apriori information from script structure in the objective function of the cut. We show that this information can be learned automatically and be adapted within a collection of documents (a book) and across collections to achieve accurate segmentation. We show the results on Indian language documents in Telugu script. The approach is also applicable to other languages with complex scripts such as Bangla, Kannada, Malayalam, and Urdu.

1   Introduction

Document image understanding algorithms are expected to work with a document, irrespective of its layout, script, font, color, etc. Segmentation aims to partition a document image into various homogeneous regions such as text blocks, image blocks, lines, words etc. [1]. Page segmentation algorithms can be broadly classified into three categories: bottom-up [2,3], top-down [4,5], and hybrid [6] algorithms. The classification is based on the order in which the regions in a document are identified and labeled. The layout of the document is represented by a hierarchy of regions: *page, image* or *text blocks, lines, words, components,* and *pixels.* The traditional document segmentation algorithms give good results on most documents with complex layouts but assume the script in the document to be simple as in English. These algorithms fail to give good results on the documents with complex scripts such as African, Persian and Indian scripts.

1.1   Challenges in Segmentation of Indian Language Documents

In the recent past, the number of document images available for Indian languages has grown drastically with the establishment of Digital Library of India [7]. The digital library documents originate from a variety of sources, and vary considerably in their structure, script, font, size, quality, etc. Of these, the variations in the structure of the script are the most taxing to any segmentation algorithm.

P. Kalra and S. Peleg (Eds.): ICVGIP 2006, LNCS 4338, pp. 749–760, 2006.

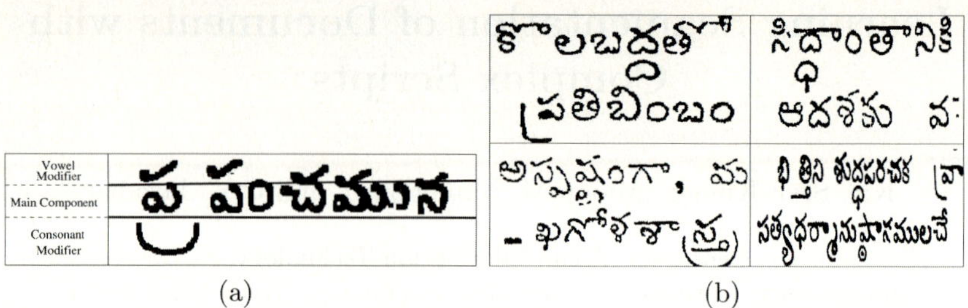

Fig. 1. Complexities of Telugu Script: (a) spatial distribution of connected components, (b) Non-uniform spacing between lines and components

In this paper we deal with documents in Indian languages such as Telugu, Tamil, Bangla, and Malayalam, which have similar script structure. The complexity of these scripts lie in the spatial distribution of the connected components. Unlike English, most characters in Indian scripts are made up of more than one connected component. These connected components do not form meaningful characters by themselves, but when grouped together, form different characters in the alphabet. The components of a character can be classified into:

Main Component: It is either a vowel, a consonant or a truncated consonant. The main components of characters within a line are nearly collinear.

Consonant Modifier: In the above scripts, a character could be composed of two consonants, the main component and a *consonant modifier* or *half consonant*. Spatially, the consonant modifier could be to the left, right or bottom of the main component, and hence lie within a line, or below it.

Vowel Modifier: A character also can have a vowel modifier, which modifies the consonant. When the vowel modifier does not touch the main component, it forms separate component, which lies above the main component.

Figure 1(a) shows the spatial distribution of components in Telugu script. Due to variations in spatial distribution of the components within a the line structure is non-uniform. This is the primary reason for the failure of many traditional segmentation algorithms. Due to the positional variation of a modifier component, the task of assigning it to a line above it or below it is ambiguous. Heuristics such as assigning a component to its nearest line might fail because the distances between the components vary depending on the font style, font size and typeset as shown in figure 1(b).

Variations in scanned books are also introduced due to the change in writing style of certain character over time, which need to be taken into account while segmenting a document. Most of the old books are typeset by human and not machine and hence it is difficult to specify a consistent distance between the components. We introduce a *Spatial Language Model* that encapsulates the local variations in component distribution and use it to perform segmentation.

2   Document Segmentation Using Graph Cuts

Segmentation is the process of partitioning an image into regions with homogeneous properties. Ideally, pixels forming a semantically meaningful object should be grouped together. Traditional image segmentation approaches usually group pixels using low level cues such as brightness, color, texture, and motion. However, the end goal is to have segments that correspond to a particular object, which is often measured using mid and high level cues such as symmetry of objects and object models. This warrants a framework, where both low level cues and high level cues are integrated to segment an image. For document images, this would mean the use of higher level structure of the document in determining the grouping of connected components to form characters, words, and lines.

Segmentation can thus be posed as an optimization problem, where low level cues are used to group the pixels into regions that represent an object, which can be analyzed using high level cues. A variety of methods have been proposed that pose segmentation as an optimization problem. Graph cuts is one of the methods used to perform image segmentation. It promises a near optimal solution; i.e., a solution at a known distance from the global optimum. To apply graph cuts to document images, a graph is built using either the pixels or the connected components of the image as nodes, which are linked to its neighbors through edges. During segmentation, a cut is defined on the graph, which labels the pixels or components on either side of the cut as belonging to different segments. Boykov *et al.* [8] proved that minimizing an energy function is equivalent to minimizing the cost of cut on the graph.

Graph cuts form an effective combination of top-down and bottom-up approaches for the segmentation [9,10] problem. They also provide a framework for learning the shape priors [11] and use them to perform effective segmentation. The traditional page segmentation algorithms do not provide the ability to learn from or adapt to the nature of images, given a large collection of data. We pose the page segmentation problem as an optimization problem, which minimizes the energy calculated using graph cuts. This provides the ability to learn the layout parameters in an incremental fashion.

We propose a segmentation algorithm that partitions a document with complex scripts. We initially assume that the layout not very complex, contains only text, and the document is skew corrected [12,13]. Later, we show how to extend the algorithm to work with complex layouts also.

Each connected component forms a node that is linked to its k nearest neighbors, where the nearest neighbors are calculated using the Euclidean distance between the centers of their bounding boxes. The value of k is selected such that each component is connected to all the components surrounding it spatially. For Telugu, the value of k that yielded the best results was 8. Once the neighbors are identified, a graph is constructed, and an initial estimate of the lines is obtained using the horizontal projection profile. The initial cut ensures that a majority of the components that belong to a particular line remain connected. Later we replace the projection profile based method with simple heuristics on components to arrive at a robust initial segmentation of documents with complex layouts.

2.1   Energy Function

Our goal is to assign a line number (label) to every connected component within a document. All the connected components that belong to a document ($\mathcal{C}$) need to be partitioned into mutually exclusive and collective exhaustive subsets, $\mathcal{C}_i$, where i denotes the line number. The goal is to find a labeling f that labels each component $c \in \mathcal{C}$ a label $f_p \in \mathcal{L}$, where $\mathcal{L}$ denotes the label set (here the line numbers). The labeling should be done in such a way that it is piecewise smooth. In this framework, a labeling f is computed so as to minimize the total energy:

$$E(f) = E_{smooth}(f) + E_{data}(f), \tag{1}$$

where E_{smooth} gives the measure of the smoothness of the labeling, while E_{data} gives a measures of the consistency of labeling with the observed data.

Smoothness Term: If a component along with k nearest neighbors belong to a single line, the labeling is considered extremely smooth and the contribution due to the component to the E_{smooth} term decreases.

$$E_{smooth}(f) = \sum_{(c,c') \in \mathcal{N}} V_{(c,c')}(c, c'), \tag{2}$$

where $\mathcal{N}$ denotes the set of neighboring connected components within a document. We will require the term $V_{c,c'}$ to be a metric for the expansion algorithm to give near optimal solution using the graph cut.

Data Term: The data term is one of the most important measure in the calculating the energy of the segmentation algorithm. This term enables the improvement of the segmentation algorithm by using apriori information, which is available in the form of *spatial language models*. This term gives a measure of disagreement of labeling of a connected component to a line above it or to the one below it.

$$E_{data}(f) = \sum_{c \in \mathcal{C}} D(f(c)) \tag{3}$$

The calculation of $D(f(c))$ denotes the disagreement of the observed data and the apriori information available. For instance if a particular type of connected component, according to the apriori information available through the spatial language model, belongs to the line above it in spite of being nearer to the line below it, the Disagreement of labeling the connected component to the line above it is less than the labeling of the connected component to the line below it. Thus we attain better segmentation with the availability of good spatial language models of the document. However, if the E_{data} term is a constant function for any assignment of labels to a connected component c, the graph cut is same as a distance based heuristic, i.e., assign the connected component to the line that it is nearest to.

2.2   Graph Construction

The problem of segmenting a text block into lines can be viewed as the grouping of connected components into clusters. Each of the cluster of connected components define a line. Hence, the first and the foremost step is to find the number of clusters. The number of lines within a text block can be calculated using the projection profile formed by the horizontal projection of foreground pixels. The number of peaks within the profile gives the number of lines, n_l into which the text block is to be segmented.

Graph cuts need an initial labeling of the connected components. The text block is first segmented into n_l lines using the projection profile based approach. There exist connected components that lie between two lines. All these components are assigned to the lines that lie below it. Thus the text blocks are segmented into lines, where there are chances that some of the component assignments could be wrong. However, an initial labeling of the components is achieved through this process. Now the cost of graph cuts could be used to perform changes of labeling such that the cut is minimal and the energy calculated using the labeling is minimized.

We start with the initial set of labels for all the connected components computed from the projection-based cut. A graph is constructed using these initial set of labels. We know all the components that belong to two consecutive lines. A graph is constructed for every pair of consecutive lines with two extra nodes, (α, β), representing the labels of the nodes. Every pair of nodes that represent neighboring components (c, c') are linked by and edge, $e(c, c')$ with the weight $V_{(c,c')}(c, c')$, a metric in the label space (i.e. the distance defined between the labels of the two components). It follows a Potts model defined by:

$$V(\alpha, \beta) = K.T(\alpha \neq \beta) \tag{4}$$

where $T(.)$ is 1 if its argument is true, and 0 otherwise.

Each of the components is also linked to one the two nodes, α, and β, which represent the labels of the lines. The weights of these edges, denoted by t_c^α and t_c^β, are calculated using the following equation:

$$t_c^\alpha = D_c(\alpha) + \sum_{q \in \mathcal{N}_p; q P_{\alpha\beta}} V(\alpha, f_c), \tag{5}$$

where $D_c(\alpha)$ is the distance of the connected component to the nearest component of the line with the label α, which is calculated using the spatial language models. t_c^β is also calculated in a similar manner.

Now we have a graph that is constructed using the connected components as nodes, along with two extra nodes with labels of the two lines. The α-β swap algorithm, proposed by Boykov *et al.* [8], is used to perform the graph cut. If the cut separates the node representing the component c with the node α, it given the label α, which specifies the line it belongs to. The $\alpha - \beta$ swap algorithm tries to swap the labels of the nodes in such a way that the energy calculated using

Fig. 2. Zones of a Connected Component

the configuration of the graph is minimum. This graph cut algorithm iteratively swaps the labels in such a way that the local minima of the energy function calculated using equation 1 attained for the particular labeling.

3   Spatial Language Models

A large number of document collections are available in the digital library of India that belong to the different Indian languages. There is no ground truth available for these documents. Most of the documents available are from a large number of books that are scanned. The books with same script that are published by a same publisher may have same font size, font style and similar typeset. Hence the Spatial Language Models of all these books will be the same. There could be Spatial Language Models that could be built for a book, a publisher, etc.

Each component can be classified into one of the classes: main component, vowel modifier and consonant modifier. The main component falls within a line, the vowel modifier falls above a line, and the consonant falls below a line. Hence a vowel modifier has higher affinity towards the line below it and a consonant modifier has higher affinity to the line above it. The affinities can be changed appropriately by changing the metric (distance between two components), such that the a vowel modifier falls into a line below it and the consonant modifier falls into a line above it even if they are farther from the line to which they belong.

The region surrounding a component is divided into 8 equi-angular regions labeled in a clockwise direction as shown in the Figure 2. The affinities between two components is represented by an $n \times n \times 8$ matrix denoted by $\mathbf{K}$, where n is the number of classes of the component recognition system. The prior information is fed into the system by initializing the matrix based on language information. As noted before, the n classes have three types of components: the main components, the vowel modifier and the consonant modifier. The affinities that belong to the classes of the main components are initialized to 1. However if the components are vowel modifiers, they have higher affinity to lines below it. Hence the zones 5,6,7 and 8 of the particular vowel modifier has lower values. If the component is a consonant modifier, it has higher affinity to lines above it. Hence the zones 1,2,3 and 4 of the consonant modifier are initialized to lower values.

$$\mathbf{K}^k_{i,j} = \begin{cases} 0.75 & \text{if } i \text{ is a vowel modifier and} \\ & j \text{ takes all values from 1 to n and } k \text{ ranges from 5 to 8} \\ 0.75 & \text{if } i \text{ is a consonant modifier} \\ & \text{and } j \text{ takes all values from 1 to n and } k \text{ ranges from 1 to 4} \\ 1 & \text{remaining } i,j \text{ and } k \end{cases} \tag{6}$$

3.1   Distance Based Graph

The connected components attained by connected component labeling are first classified using a naive classifier. We define a metric to calculate the distance between two components based on the affinity between them as follows.

$$w_{ij} = \mathbf{K}^k_{i,j} * d_{ij}, \tag{7}$$

where d_{ij} denotes the nearest distance between the components, i denotes the class the first component belongs to, j denotes the class the second component belongs to and k denotes the zone of the first component through which the line joining both the component passes through.

A graph is created with the components as the nodes the distance between the components as the weight of the edge joining the components. The distance between the components is calculated using the equation 7. The components that belong to a line are within a particular distance threshold. Thus line segmentation of the document image is performed.

3.2   Learning to Segment

The matrix $\mathbf{K}$ denotes affinity of a particular component to another component in a particular direction. In a particular book a modifier component are generally placed at a constant distance from a particular main component in the complete book. When a component that belongs to a particular line is encountered, which is still at a large distance from the main component, we reduce the distance between the components by reducing the value of $\mathbf{K}^k_{i,j}$. Here, i denotes the class label of the main component, j denotes the class label of the modifier component, and k is the zone of the main component, where the second component lies.

The segmentation of the documents can be learnt over time across documents. The values of the matrix $\mathbf{K}$ are initialized as shown in Equation 6. A graph is built using the components in the document image as shown in section 3.1. The line segmentation is performed using graph cut proposed in section 2 and the quality of segmentation is calculated using the segmentation quality metric equation 8 proposed in [14].

$$J_l(.) = \frac{1}{1 + \sigma_1} + \frac{1}{1 + \sigma_2} - BLD + ILD, \tag{8}$$

where σ_1 denotes the variance of height of the lines, σ_2 denotes the variance of distance between the lines, BLD density of black/foreground pixels between two lines and ILD the density of black/foreground pixels within a line. $J_l(.)$ takes values between $\{-1, 3\}$.

This gives an estimate of the performance of line segmentation. If the performance is low i.e the value of $J(.)$ calculated is less than 2 then we perform the line segmentation . The segmentation is projection profile based, and has a tunable set of parameters. The best segmentation results are achieved by learning the best set of values for the parameters using the segmentation quality metric in equation 8.

The line segmentation algorithm detects line boundaries that gives the set of edges in the graph that cross the line boundaries. The weights of all such edges are increased by changing the values of $\mathbf{K}_{i,j}^{k_1}$ and $\mathbf{K}_{j,i}^{k_2}$ as shown in equation 9. The weights of all the missing edges within a line are reduced by changing the values of $\mathbf{K}_{i,j}^{k_1}$ and $\mathbf{K}_{j,i}^{k_2}$ as shown in equation 10.

$$\mathbf{K}_{i,j}^{k_1} = \mathbf{K}_{i,j}^{k_1} + 0.05; \qquad\qquad \mathbf{K}_{j,i}^{k_2} = \mathbf{K}_{j,i}^{k_2} + 0.05 \qquad (9)$$

$$\mathbf{K}_{i,j}^{k_1} = \mathbf{K}_{i,j}^{k_1} - 0.10; \qquad\qquad \mathbf{K}_{j,i}^{k_2} = \mathbf{K}_{j,i}^{k_2} - 0.10, \qquad (10)$$

where i and j gives the class labels of the components, k_1 denotes the zone that component j belongs to with respect to i, and k_2 denotes the zone that the component i belongs to with respect to j. The weights of the graph are recalculated using the above equation and the lines segmentation is again performed as suggested in section 3.1. The segmentation quality metric is then recalculated. This is performed iteratively until the segmentation quality metric improves to an acceptable value. This gives the learning phase of the document, where the corrections made by a segmentation algorithm automatically is learnt and stored in the form of the matrix $\mathbf{K}$. The procedure to perform segmentation iteratively on a document is give in Algorithm 1. To improve the performance across documents the $\mathbf{K}$ is retained for further documents.

Algorithm 1. Learning Spatial Language Models and Segmentation.

1: Initialize the Spatial Language Models $\mathbf{K}$
2: **while** Change in $\mathbf{K}$ **do**
3:     Find components with ambiguous Orientation(TOP/BOTTOM)
       and initialize with arbitrary orientation
4:     Calculate the distances between components using $\mathbf{K}$
5:     Create a graph and calculate the edges of the graph using the distances and
       initial labels
6:     Perform Graph Cut to give new labels to the components
7:     **if** Errors in segmentation **then**
8:        Correct them and update $\mathbf{K}$
9:     **end if**
10: **end while**

---

4   Results and Discussions

There are large number of Indian language documents available at the Digital Library of India. In this work, we used the documents that were scanned from a Telugu book titled "Aadarsam", which was printed in the year 1973 and contains 256 pages. The goal is to learn the spatial language model of a particular book from a few initial pages and use it to segment the remaining pages in the book. There are two important steps involved in the process: i) adaptation of segmentation to a single document, and ii) learning the spatial language model from the sample documents.

Adaptation. We take a sample page from the above mentioned book. This sample page is segmented without using any apriori information. This leads to poor results of segmentation. When the segmentation is corrected either manually, or using ground truth, or using another segmentation algorithm, the spatial language models that belong to the particular page are updated. On segmenting the same page with the updated spatial language models, it is observed that the performance of the segmentation is improved. This is done iteratively to improve the accuracy of the segmentation.

Figure 3 shows that the segmentation of the document improves over iterations because spatial language models are adapted to the document with iterations. The components marked by the oval are the dangling components that need to be assigned an appropriate line number. It can be observed that all the similar looking components that were assigned a wrong line initially, are assigned to the correct lines over iterations. The affinity of a component in a particular direction is learnt during segmentation correction of the previous iterations. Figure 4(a) shows the improvement in performance of segmentation on a particular document over iterations. The performance of segmentation is calculated using the Equation 8. From Figure 4(b) it can also be observed that the number of corrections that need to be made on the document decreases over iterations.

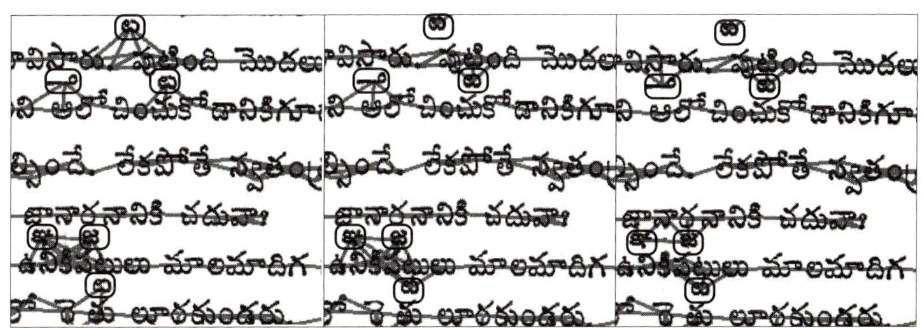

Fig. 3. Segmentation of a single document after 1st, 24th and final iterations

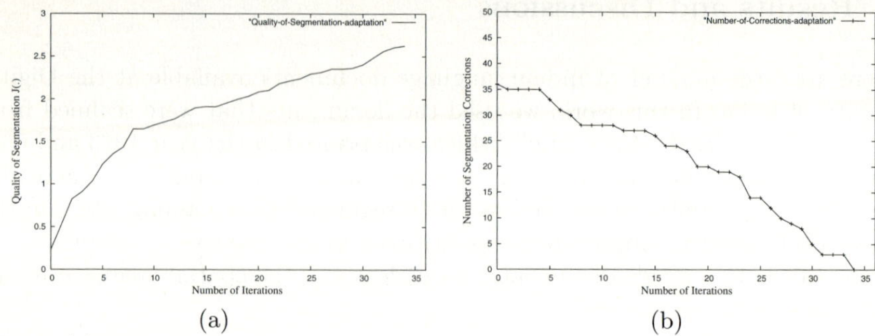

(a)   (b)

Fig. 4. (a):Performance of segmentation on a particular document over iterations, (b): Number of corrections made after each segmentation

Learning: We take all the pages of the book and perform segmentation on each page iteratively adapting the spatial language models to the initial pages of the book. After a few pages, there is no necessity to adapt the documents because the spatial language models have completely learnt the characteristics of the book and it can be used directly to perform segmentation on the remaining pages of the book. Figure 5 shows that the algorithm can learn the spatial language model of documents with different styles and give good results on segmentation.

Figure 6(a) shows that the performance of the segmentation eventually improves on every page as information gathered from every page is used to perform segmentation on later pages of the book. Figure 6(b) shows that the number of segmentation corrections that need to be made on a new page is close to zero after adapting to the first 44 pages of the book. The remaining 212 pages could be segmented without any errors for the book under consideration.

The algorithm can also handle text with arbitrarily complex layouts as long as an initial estimate of lines can be found. We use the component classifier to identify the main components and use it to find an initial assignment of components to lines. Performance of segmentation on a wavy text can be seen in Figure 7 and semi-circular text in Figure 8.

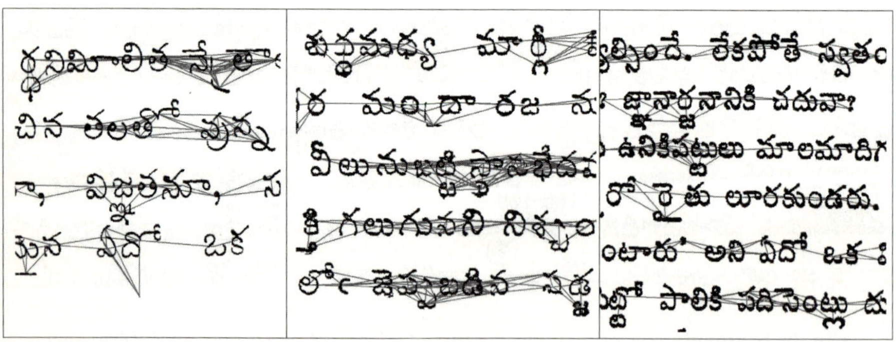

Fig. 5. Segmentation results on three documents of different styles

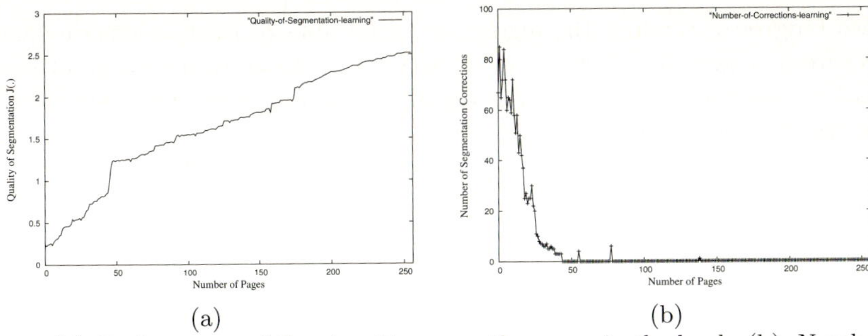

(a) (b)

Fig. 6. (a): Performance of the algorithm over the pages in the book, (b): Number of segmentation corrections made for each document

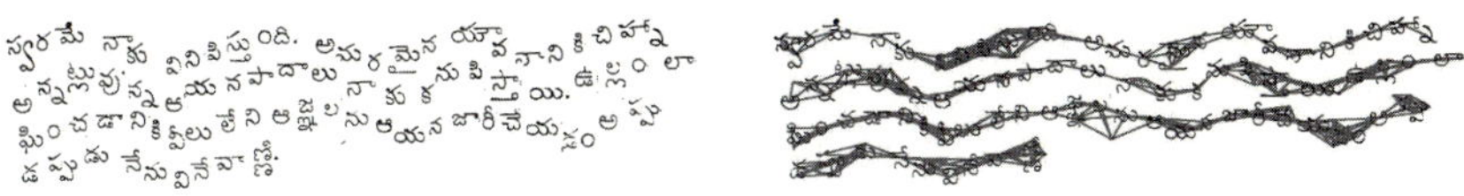

Fig. 7. Segmentation results on a page with *wavy* layout

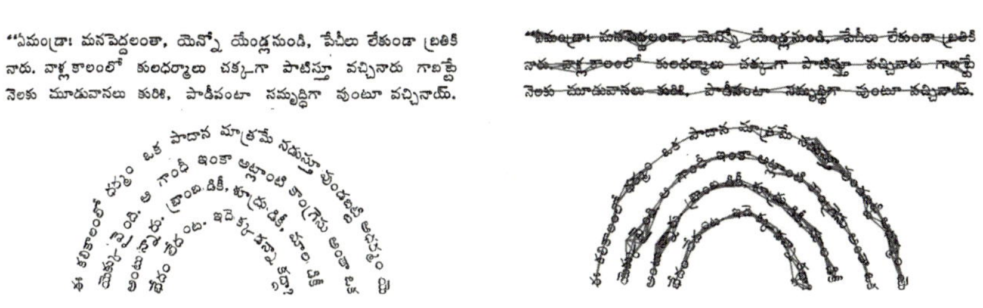

Fig. 8. Segmentation results on a page with *semi-circular* layout

The algorithm is also fast in practice, since the graphs that are formed using the k-nearest neighbor algorithm are sparse. However, if the graph is completely connected, the time complexity can rise up to $O(n^2)$. To segment a document with around 1200 components and 25 lines, the graph cuts takes an average time of 0.268 seconds on a PC with 512 MB RAM and 3GHz single core processor.

5   Conclusions and Future Work

We have presented a graph cut based framework for segmentation of document images that contain complex scripts such as in Indian languages. The framework enables learning of the spatial distribution of the components of a specific script and can adapt to a specific document collection, such as a book. Moreover, we are able to use both corrections made by the user as well as any segmentation quality metric to improve the quality of the segmentation. We have demonstrated, albeit on a limited set of examples, the ability of the framework to work with complex scripts, where the traditional algorithms fail completely. Currently, we are working on extending the algorithm to be able to learn a generic spatial model from a varying collection of documents to so as to give a good initial guess for a specific script. Moreover, the algorithm also needs to be extended to other region types such as words, paragraphs, etc.

References

1. Shafait, F., Keysers, D., Breuel, T.M.: Performance comparison of six algorithms for page segmentation. In: Proceedings of the Seventh IAPR Workshop on Document Analysis Systems (LNCS 3872), Nelson, New Zealand (2006) 368–379
2. O'Gorman, L.: The Document Spectrum for Page Layout Analysis. IEEE Transactions on Pattern Analysis and Machine Intelligence **15** (1993) 1162–1173
3. Kise, K., Sato, A., Iwata, M.: Segmentation of Page Images Using the Area Voronoi Diagram. Computer Vision and Image Understanding **70** (1998) 370–382
4. Nagy, G., Seth, S., Viswanathan, M.: A Prototype Document Image Analysis System for Technical Journals. Computer **25** (1992) 10–22
5. H.S.Baird, S.E.Jones, S.J.Fortune: Image segmentation by shape-directed covers. In: Proceedings of International Conference on Pattern Recognition(ICPR). (1990) 820–825
6. T.Pavlidis, J.Zhou: Page Segmentation and Classification. Graphical Models and Image Processing **54** (1992) 484–496
7. Ambati, V., N.Balakrishnan, Reddy, R., Pratha, L., Jawahar, C.V.: The Digital Library of India Project: Process, Policies and Architecture. In: Second International Conference on Digital Libraries(ICDL). (2006)
8. Boykov, Y., Veksler, O., Zabih, R.: Fast approximate energy minimization via graph cuts. IEEE Transaction on Pattern Analysis and Machine Intelligence **23** (2001) 1222–1239
9. Shi, J., Malik, J.: Normalized cuts and image segmentation. IEEE Transactions on Pattern Analysis and Machine Intelligence **22** (2000) 888–905
10. Shental, N., Zomet, A., Hertz, T., Weiss, Y.: Learning and inferring image segmentations using the GBP typical cut algorithm. In: International Conference in Computer Vision. (2003) 1243–1250
11. Kumar, M.P., Torr, P.H.S., Zisserman, A.: OBJ CUT. In: Proceedings of the IEEE Conference on Computer Vision and Pattern Recognition, San Diego. (2005) 18–25
12. Baird, H.S.: The skew angle of printed documents. In: Document Image Analysis. IEEE Computer Society Press, Los Alamitos, CA, USA (1995) 204–208
13. Yan, H.: Skew correction of document images using interline cross-correlation. CVGIP: Graphical Models Image Processing **55** (1993) 538–543
14. Kumar, K.S.S., Namboodiri, A.M., Jawahar, C.V.: Learning to segment document images. In: Proceedings of the First International Conference on Pattern Recognition and Machine Intelligence (PReMI). (2005) 471–476

Machine Learning for Signature Verification

Harish Srinivasan[1], Sargur N. Srihari[1], and Matthew J. Beal

Department of Computer Science and Engineering
University at Buffalo, The State University of New York, Buffalo NY, USA
[1]Center of Excellence for Document Analysis and Recognition (CEDAR), Buffalo NY

Abstract. Signature verification is a common task in forensic document analysis. It is one of determining whether a questioned signature matches known signature samples. From the viewpoint of automating the task it can be viewed as one that involves machine learning from a population of signatures. There are two types of learning to be accomplished. In the first, the training set consists of genuines and forgeries from a general population. In the second there are genuine signatures in a given case. The two learning tasks are called person-independent (or general) learning and person-dependent (or special) learning. General learning is from a population of genuine and forged signatures of several individuals, where the differences between genuines and forgeries across all individuals are learnt. The general learning model allows a questioned signature to be compared to a single genuine signature. In special learning, a person's signature is learnt from multiple samples of only that person's signature– where within-person similarities are learnt. When a sufficient number of samples are available, special learning performs better than general learning (5% higher accuracy). With special learning, verification accuracy increases with the number of samples.

Keywords: machine learning, forensic signature examination, biometrics, signature verification, digital document processing.

1 Introduction

The most common task in the field of forensic document analysis [1, 2, 3, 4, 5] is that of authenticating signatures. The problem most frequently brought to a document examiner is the question relating to the authenticity of a signature: *Does this questioned signature (Q) match the known, true signatures (K) of this subject?* [6] A forensic document examiner– also known as a questioned document (QD) examiner–uses years of training in examining signatures in making a decision in case work.

The training of a document examiner involves years of learning from signatures that are both genuine and forged. In case-work, exemplars are usually only available for genuine signatures of a particular individual, from which the characteristics of the genuine signature are learnt.

Algorithms for visual signature verification are considered in this paper. The performance task of signature verification is one of determining whether a questioned signature is genuine or not.

P. Kalra and S. Peleg (Eds.): ICVGIP 2006, LNCS 4338, pp. 761–775, 2006.

Visual signature verification is naturally formulated as a machine learning task. A program is said to exhibit machine learning capability in performing a task if it is able to learn from exemplars, improve as the number of exemplars increase, etc. [7]. Paralleling the learning tasks of the human questioned document examiner, the machine learning tasks can be stated as *general learning* (which is person-independent) or *special learning* (which is person-dependent) [8].

In the case of general learning the goal is to learn from a large population of genuine and forged signature samples. The focus is on differentiating between genuine-genuine differences and genuine-forgery differences. The learning problem is stated as learning a two-class classification problem where the input consists of the difference between a pair of signatures. The verification task is performed by comparing the questioned signature against each known signature. The general learning problem can be viewed as one where learning takes place with near misses as counter-examples [9].

Special learning focuses on learning from genuine samples of a particular person. The focus is on learning the differences between members of the class of genuines. The verification task is essentially a one-class problem of determining whether the questioned signature belongs to that class or not.

There is scattered literature on automatic methods of signature verification [10, 11, 12, 13, 14]. Automatic methods of writer verification– which is the task of determining whether a sample of handwriting, not necessarily a signature, was written by a given individual– are also relevant [15]. Identification is the task of determining as to who among a given set of individuals might have written the questioned writing. The handwriting verification and identification tasks parallel those of biometric verification and identification for which there is a large literature. The use of a machine learning paradigm for biometrics has been proposed recently [16].

The rest of this paper is organized as follows. Section 2 describes feature extraction in general. Section 3 describes the two methods of learning. Section 4 deals with how the learnt knowledge is used in evaluating a questioned signature (called the performance task). A comparison of the accuracies of the two strategies on a database of genuines and forgeries, along with the particular feature description is described in Section 5. Section 6 is a paper summary.

2   Feature Extraction and Similarity Computation

Signatures are relied upon for identification due to the fact that each person develops unique habits of pen movement which serve to represent his or her signature. Thus at the heart of any automatic signature verification system are two algorithms: one for extracting features and the other for determining the similarities of two signatures based on the features. Features are elements that capture the uniqueness. In the QD literature such elements are termed *discriminating elements* or *elements of comparison*. A given person's samples can have a (possibly variable) number of elements and the combination of elements have greater discriminating power.

A human document examiner uses a chart of elemental characteristics [6]. Such elements are ticks, smoothness of curves, smoothness of pressure changes, placement, expansion and spacing, top of writing, base of writing, angulation/slant, overall pressure, pressure change patterns, gross forms, variations, connective forms and micro-forms. Using the elemental characteristics such as speed, proportion, pressure and design are determined. These in turn allow rhythm and form and their balance are determined.

Automatic signature verification methods described in the literature use an entirely different set of features. Some are based on image texture such as wavelets while others focus on geometry and topology of the signature image. Types of features used for signature verification are wavelet descriptors [17], projection distribution functions [18,14,19], extended shadow code [18] and geometric features [20].

The features are considered representative characteristics of the signature. In order to compare two signatures and to quantify their similarity, a similarity measure or a distance measure is used to compute a score that signifies the strength of match between the features of the two samples. Eventually, irrespective of the method used, one can arrive at a distance space representation of the data that characterizes the strength of match between two signatures. It is usefull to note here that, the learning strategies that ensue are general and are applicable not just to signature veriication but to any bio-metric. As long, as there exist a similarity measure that maps the feature values between a pair of samples, to a score, the below mentioned learning strategies can be used. The particular set of features used for signature verification are described in detail in the experiment and result section 5.

3   Learning Strategies

Person-independent or general learning is a one-step approach that learns from a large population of genuine and forged samples. On the other hand person-dependent(person specific) learning focuses on learning from the genuine samples of a specific individual.

3.1   Person-Independent (General) Learning

The general learning approach uses two sets of signature pairs: genuine-genuine and genuine-forgery. Forgeries in forensic document examination can be either simulated or traced. In this sense task is analogous to learning from near misses in the machine learning literature.

Features are extracted for each pair of signatures and a similarity measure is used to compute the distance between each pair. Let D_S denote the vector of distances between all pairs in set *one*, which represents the distribution of distances when samples truly came from the same person. Similarly let D_D denote the vector of distances between all pairs in set *two*, which represents the distribution of distances when samples truly came from different persons. These distributions can be modeled using known distributions such as Gaussian or gamma. The Gaussian assigns non-zero probabilities to negative values of distance although such values are never encountered. Since this problem in not there with the gamma it is to be preferred. The probability density function of the gamma distributions is as follows: $Gamma(x) = \frac{x^{\alpha-1}\exp^{(-x/\beta)}}{(\Gamma(\alpha))\beta^\alpha}$ Here α and β are gamma parameters which can be evaluated from the mean and variance as follows $\alpha = \mu^2/\sigma^2$ and $\beta = \sigma^2/\mu$. 'α' is called the shape parameter and 'β' is the scale parameter. The parameters that need to be learnt for such a model are typically derived from the sufficient statistics of the distribution, and are namely μ (mean) and σ (variance) for a Gaussian, or α (shape) and β (width) for a gamma. These distributions are referred to as genuine-genuine and genuine-impostor distributions in the domain of biometrics.

3.2   Person-Dependent Learning (Person Specific Learning)

In questioned document case work there are typically multiple genuine signatures available. They can be used to learn the variation across them– so as to determine whether the questioned signature is within the range of variation. First, pairs of known samples are compared using a similarity measure to obtain a distribution over distances between features of samples — this represents the distribution of the variation/similarities amongst samples — for the individual. The corresponding classification method involves comparing the questioned sample against all available known samples to obtain another distribution in distance space. The Kolmogorov-Smirnov test, KL-divergence and other information-theoretic methods can be used to obtain a probability of similarity of the two distributions, which is the probability of the questioned sample belonging to the ensemble of knowns. These methods are discussed below.

Within-person distribution. If a given person has N samples, $\binom{N}{2}$ defined as $\frac{N!}{N!(N-r)!}$ pairs of samples can be compared as shown in Figure 1. In each comparison, the distance between the features is computed. This calculation maps feature space to distance space. The result of all $\binom{N}{2}$ comparisons is a $\{\binom{N}{2}\times 1\}$ distance vector. This vector is the distribution in distance space for a given person. For example, in the signature verification problem this vector is the distribution in distance space for the ensemble of genuine known signatures for that writer. A key advantage of mapping from feature space to distance space is that the number of data points in the distribution is $\binom{N}{2}$ as compared to N for a distribution in feature space alone. Also the calculation of the distance between every pair of samples gives a measure of the variation in samples for that writer. In essence the distribution in distance space for a given known person captures the similarities and variation amongst the samples for that person. Let N be the total number of samples and $N_{WD} = \binom{N}{2}$ be the total number of comparisons that can be made which also equals the length of the within-person distribution vector. The within-person distribution can be written as

$$D_W = (d_1, d_2, \ldots, d_{N_{WD}})^\top \tag{1}$$

where $\top$ denotes the transpose operation and d_j is the distance between the pair of samples taken at the jth comparison, $j \in \{1, \ldots, N_{WD}\}$.

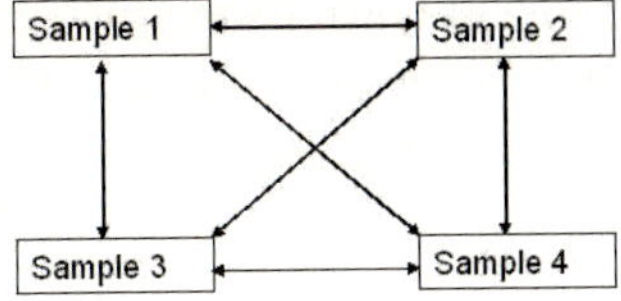

Fig. 1. Person-dependent (special) learning involves comparing all possible genuine-genuine pairs, as shown for four genuine samples, to form the vector $\boldsymbol{D_W}$, which in this example is of length $N_{WD} = \binom{4}{2} = 6$ comparisons

4 Performance Task

The performance task of signature verification is to answer the question whether or not a questioned signature belongs to the genuine signature set. The person-independent method uses knowledge from a general population to determine whether two samples, one a questioned and the other a genuine, belong to the same person. This task is called 1:1 verification. Person-dependent classification tasks involves matching one questioned sample against multiple known samples from the person. Details of the two performance algorithms are given below.

4.1 Person-Independent Classification

The process of $1:1$ verification(one input sample compared with one known sample) starts with feature extraction and then computing the distance d between the features using a similarity measure. From the learning described in Section 3.1, the likelihood ratio defined as $\frac{P(D_S|d)}{P(D_D|d)}$ can be calculated, where $P(D_S|d)$ is the probability density function value under the D_S distribution at the distance d and $P(D_D|d)$ is the probability density function value under the D_D distribution at the distance d. If the likelihood ratio is greater than 1, then the classification answer is that the two samples do belong the same person and if the ratio is less than 1, they belong to different persons. If there are a total of N known samples from a person, then for one questioned sample N, $1:1$ verifications can be performed and the likelihood ratios multiplied. In these circumstances it is convenient to deal with log likelihood-ratios rather than with just likelihood ratios. The log-likelihood-ratio (LLR) is given by $\log P(D_S|d) - \log P(D_D|d)$. The decision of same-person is favored if $\log P(D_S|d) - \log P(D_D|d) > 0$, and the decision of different-person chosen if $\log P(D_S|d) - \log P(D_D|d) < 0$. When N of these 1:1 verifications are performed these LLR's are summed and then the decision is taken.

4.2 Person-Dependent Classification

When multiple genuines are available then the within-person distribution is obtained in accordance with equation 1. A questioned can be compared against the ensemble of knowns for verification. The classification process consists of two steps.

(i) obtaining questioned *vs* known distribution; and

(ii) comparison of two distributions: questioned *vs* known distribution and within-person distribution.

Questioned vs *Known Distribution.* In Section 3.2 and with equation 1 the within-person distribution is obtained by comparing every possible pair of samples from within the given persons samples. Analogous to this, the questioned sample can be compared with every one of the N knowns in a similar way to obtain the questioned vs known distribution. The questioned vs known distribution is given by

$$D_{QK} = (d_1, d_2, \ldots, d_N)^\top ,\qquad (2)$$

where d_j is the distance between the questioned sample and the jth known sample, $j \in \{1, \ldots, N\}$.

Comparing Distributions. Once the two distributions are obtained, namely the within-person distribution, denoted D_w (Section 3.2, equation 1), and the Questioned Vs Known distribution, D_{QK} (Section 4.2, equation 2), the task now is to compare the two distributions to obtain a probability of similarity. The intuition is that if the questioned sample did indeed belong to the ensemble of the knowns, then the two distributions must be the same (to within some sampling noise). There are various ways of comparing two distributions and these are described in the following sections.

Kolmogorov-Smirnov Test. The Kolmogorov-Smirnov (KS) test can be applied to obtain a probability of similarity between two distributions. The KS test is applicable to unbinned distributions that are functions of a single independent variable, that is, to data sets where each data point can be associated with a single number [21]. The test first obtains the cumulative distribution function of each of the two distributions to be compared, and then computes the statistic, D, which is a particularly simple measure: it is defined as the maximum value of the absolute difference between the two cumulative distribution functions. Therefore, if comparing two different cumulative distribution functions $S_{N1}(x)$ and $S_{N2}(x)$, the KS statistic D is given by $D = \max_{-\infty < x < \infty} |S_{N1}(x) - S_{N2}(x)|$. The statistic D is then mapped to a probability of similarity, P, according to equation 3

$$P_{KS} = Q_{KS}\left(\sqrt{N_e} + 0.12 + (0.11/\sqrt{N_e})D\right) ,\qquad (3)$$

where the $Q_{KS}(\cdot)$ function is given by (see [21] for details):

$$Q_{KS}(\lambda) = 2\sum_{j=1}^{\infty}(-1)^{j-1}e^{-2j^2\lambda^2} ,\text{ such that} : Q_{KS}(0) = 1 , Q_{KS}(\infty) = 0 ,\qquad (4)$$

and N_e is the effective number of data points, $N_e = N_1 N_2 (N_1 + N_2)^{-1}$, where N_1 is the number of data points in the first distribution and N_2 the number in the second. The following sections discuss other methods of comparing two distributions.

Kullback-Leibler Divergence and other methods. The Kullback-Leibler (KL) divergence is a measure that can be used to compare two binned distributions. The KL divergence measure between two distributions is measured in bits or nats. An information theoretic interpretation is that it represents the average number of bits that are wasted by encoding events from a distribution P with a code which is optimal for a distribution Q (i.e. using codewords of length $-\log q_i$ instead of $-\log p_i$). Jensen's inequality can be used to show that $D_{KL} = KL(P\|Q) \geq 0$ for all probability distributions P and Q, and $D_{KL} = KL(P\|Q) = 0$ iff $P = Q$. Strictly speaking, the KL measure is a *divergence* between distributions and not a distance, since it is neither symmetric nor satisfies the triangle equality). The KL divergence so obtained can be converted to represent a probability by $\exp(-\zeta D_{KL})$ (for the sake of simplicity we set $\zeta = 1$ in this article). If the divergence D_{KL} is 0, then the probability is 1 signifying that the two distributions are the same. In order to use this method and other methods discussed in the following sections it is first necessary to convert the two unbinned distributions to binned distributions with a probability associated with each bin. The KL divergence between two distributions is given in equation 5 below, where B is the total number of bins, P_b and Q_b are the probabilities of the bth bin of two distributions respectively. P_{KL} denotes the probability that the two distributions are the same. Other related measures between distributions P and Q that we will examine are given in equations 6, 7 and 8

$$\text{Kullback-Leibler:} \quad D_{KL} = \sum_{b=1}^{B} P_b \, \log(\frac{P_b}{Q_b}) \quad P_{KL} = e^{-\zeta D_{KL}} \tag{5}$$

$$\text{Reverse KL:} D_{RKL} = KL(Q\|P) = \sum_{b=1}^{B} Q_b \, \log(\frac{Q_b}{P_b}) P_{RKL} = e^{-\zeta D_{RKL}} \tag{6}$$

$$\text{Symmetric KL:} \quad D_{HKL} = \frac{1}{2} KL(P\|Q) + \frac{1}{2} KL(Q\|P) - \frac{D_{KL} + D_{RKL}}{2} \quad P_{HKL} = e^{-\zeta D_{HKL}}$$

$$\tag{7}$$

$$\text{Jensen-Shannon KL:} \quad D_{JS} = \frac{1}{2} KL\left(P \left\| \frac{P+Q}{2} \right. \right) + \frac{1}{2} KL\left(Q \left\| \frac{P+Q}{2} \right. \right) \quad P_{JS} = e^{-\zeta D_{JS}}$$

$$\tag{8}$$

Combined KL and KS measure. A combination of the Kolmogorov-Smirnov and Kullback-Leibler measure, denoted KLKS, has been found to outperform the individual measures as will be analyzed in the performance evaluation section following this. The method to combine is very simple and is obtained by averaging the probabilities defined in equations 3 and 5.

$$P_{KLKS} = \frac{P_{KL} + P_{KS}}{2} \tag{9}$$

5   Performance Evaluation

The particular set of features used for signature verification are mentioned below.

5.1   Multiresolution Features

A quasi-multiresolution approach for features are the Gradient, Structural and Concavity, or GSC, features [22, 23]. Gradient features measure the local scale characteristics (obtained from the two-dimensional gradient of the image), structural features measure the intermediate scale ones (representing strokes), and concavity can measure the characteristics over the scale of whole image (representing concavities and topology). Following this philosophy, three types of feature maps are drawn and the corresponding local histograms of each cell is quantized into binary features. Fig. 2(a) shows an example of a signature, which has a 4x8 grid imposed on it for extracting GSC features; rows and columns of the grid are drawn based on the black pixel distributions along the horizontal and vertical directions. A large number of binary features have been extracted from these, as shown in Fig. 2(b), which are *global word shape features* [24]; there are 1024 bits which are obtained by concatenating 384 gradient bits, 384 structural bits and 256 concavity bits.

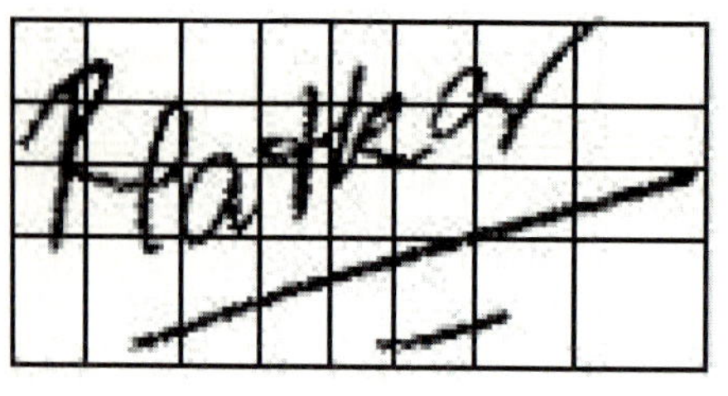

(a) Variable size grid   (b) 1024-bit binary feature vector

Fig. 2. Signature feature computation using a grid: (a) variable size 4x8 grid, and (b) binary feature vector representing gradient, structural and concavity features

A similarity or distance measure is used to compute a score that signifies the strength of match between two signatures. The similarity measure converts the pairwise data from feature space to *distance* space.

Several similarity measures can be used with binary vectors, including the well-known Hamming distance. Much experimentation with binary-valued GSC features, has led to the *correlation* measure of distance as yielding the best asccuracy in matching handwriting shapes [25]. It is defined as follows. Let S_{ij} $(i, j \in \{0, 1\})$ be the number of occurrences of matches with i in the first vector and j in the second vector at the corresponding positions, the dissimilarity D between the two feature vectors X and Y is given by the formula:

$$D(X,Y) = \frac{1}{2} - \frac{S_{11}S_{00} - S_{10}S_{01}}{2\sqrt{(S_{10} + S_{11})(S_{01} + S_{00})(S_{11} + S_{01})(S_{00} + S_{10})}}$$

It can be observed that the range of $D(X,Y)$ has been normalized to $[0,1]$. That is, when $X = Y$, $D(X,Y) = 0$, and when they are completely different, $D(X,Y) = 1$.

A refined method to compute the features and obtain the distance values is discussed in [26].

5.2   Experiments

A database of off-line signatures was prepared as a test-bed [13]. Each of 55 individuals contributed 24 signatures thereby creating 1320 genuine signatures. Some were asked to forge three other writers' signatures, eight times per subject, thus creating 1320 forgeries. One example of each of 55 genuines are shown in Figure 3. Ten examples of genuines of one subject (subject no. 21) and ten forgeries of that subject are shown in Figure 4. Each signature was scanned at 300 dpi gray-scale and binarized using a gray-scale histogram. Salt pepper noise removal and slant normalization were two steps involved in image preprocessing. The database had 24 genuines and 24 forgeries available for each writer as in Figure 4. For each test case a writer was chosen and N genuine samples of that writer's signature were used for learning. The remaining $24 - N$ genuine samples were used for testing. Also 24 forged signatures of this writer were used for testing. Figure (Fig. 5) shows the image of a questioned signature is matched against multiple images of known signatures in figure.

Fig. 3. Genuine signature samples

Fig. 4. Samples for one writer: (a) genuines and (b) forgeries

Two different error types can be defined for any biometric person identification problem. False reject rate (Type 1) is the fraction of samples classified as not belonging to the person when truly there were from that person. False acceptance rate (Type 2) is the fraction of samples classified as belonging to the person when truly the samples were not from that person. In the domain of signatures, Type 1 is the fraction of samples classified as forgeries when truly they were genuine and Type 2 the fraction of samples classified as genuine when truly they were forgeries.

5.3   Person-Independent (General) Method

The classification decision boundary discussed in Section 4.1 is given by the sign of the log likelihood-ratio, LLR, $\log P(D_S|d) - \log P(D_D|d)$. A modified decision boundary can be constructed using a threshold α, such that $\log P(D_S|d) - \log P(D_D|d) > \alpha$. When α is varied, we can plot ROC curves as shown in Figure 6. The different subplots in the figure correspond to the ROC curves as the number of known samples is increased from 5 to 20. For each plot, the total error rate defined as (False acceptance+False reject)/2 is minimum at a particular value of α. This is the best setting of α for the specified number of known samples, denoted the *operating point*, and is indicated with an asterix '*'. When 20 samples are used for learning the error rate is approximately 79%. Figure 7 shows the distribution of LLRs when the questioned samples were genuine and when they were forgeries. A larger region of overlap indicates a higher error rate.

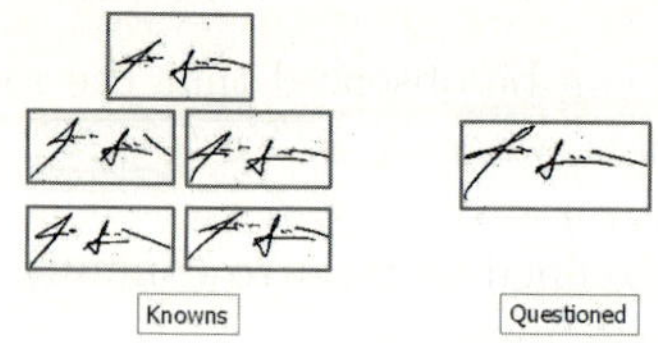

Fig. 5. Signature verification with multiple knowns

5.4   Person-Dependent Method

The person-dependent classification discussed in Section 4.1 mentioned six different statistics for comparing the two distributions to obtain a probability of

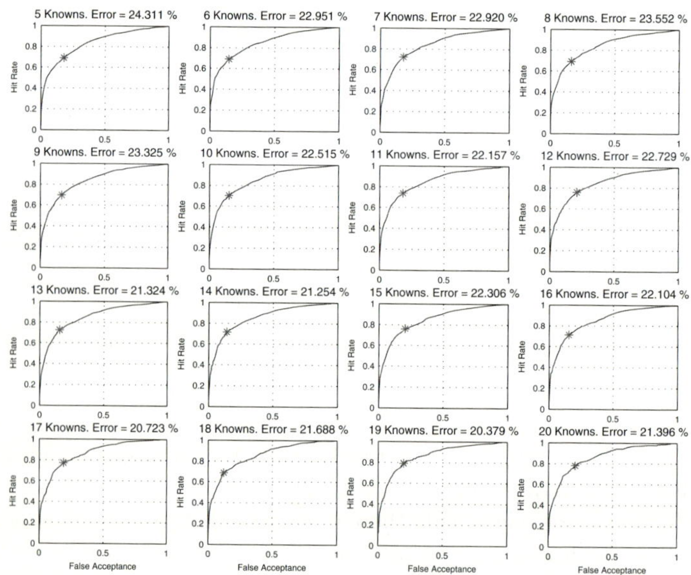

Fig. 6. ROC curves parameterized by α is varied. Each subplot is titled with the number of knowns used for training and the optimum error rate that is possible. The asterix '*' denotes the optimal operating point α for that model.

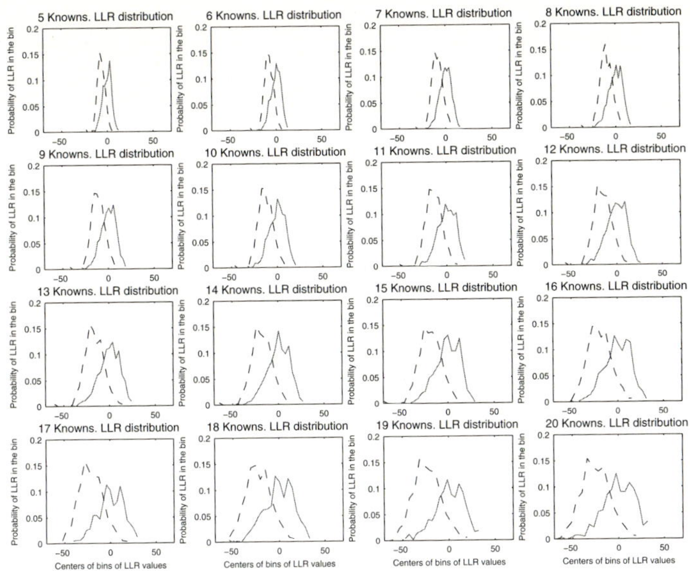

Fig. 7. LLR's obtained from each test case plotted as histograms. The probability (y-axis) that the LLR falls into a range of LLR values (x-axis) is shown for the results of truly genuine (solid) and forgery cases (dotted). Each subplot corresponds to training on a different number of knowns.

Table 1. Error rates for signature verification. Measures are Kolmogorov-Smirnov (**KS**), Kullback-Leibler (**KL**), reverse KL (**RKL**), symmetrized KL (**HKL**), Jensen-Shannon (**JS**), and combined KL and KS (**KL and KS**). These are graphed in Figure 8(a).

No. of Knowns	KS	KL	RKL	HKL	JS	KL and KS
5	25.88	24.70	25.61	24.96	25.26	23.87
6	23.54	25.10	25.40	24.57	24.60	22.52
7	22.71	23.35	23.83	23.57	23.31	21.54
8	21.67	23.76	24.60	23.58	23.30	21.20
9	22.17	23.31	24.01	23.03	23.03	20.94
10	21.36	21.93	22.79	21.94	21.63	20.58
11	19.27	20.74	20.96	20.28	20.18	19.02
12	21.13	20.96	21.71	20.42	20.10	19.58
13	20.14	21.73	20.81	21.25	20.78	19.72
14	19.06	20.03	20.84	19.46	19.33	18.41
15	18.28	18.88	19.15	18.10	17.76	17.32
16	19.27	19.08	20.08	18.50	18.38	17.56
17	17.37	17.28	17.36	16.68	16.43	16.07
18	17.79	17.88	18.31	17.58	17.52	17.17
19	17.39	18.09	18.42	17.75	17.37	16.97
20	17.31	17.15	18.58	16.90	17.23	16.40

match between the questioned sample and the ensemble of knowns. In order to measure error rates for this classificaton technique, once again a decision needs to be made based on the probability of whether or not the questioned sample belongs to the ensemble of knowns. If the probability of match $> \alpha$, then the decision is in favour of the questioned signature to be genuine, and if the probability

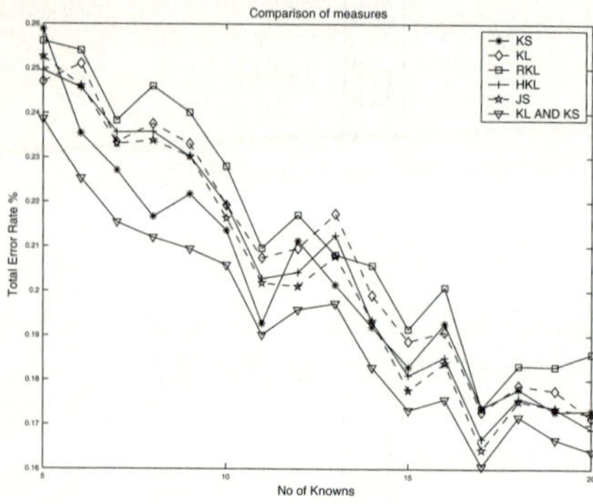

(a) Comparison of measures. The total error rate is plotted for the different measures as the number of knowns used for training is increased. The combined KL and KS measure (lowest trace) outperforms other measures (see text).

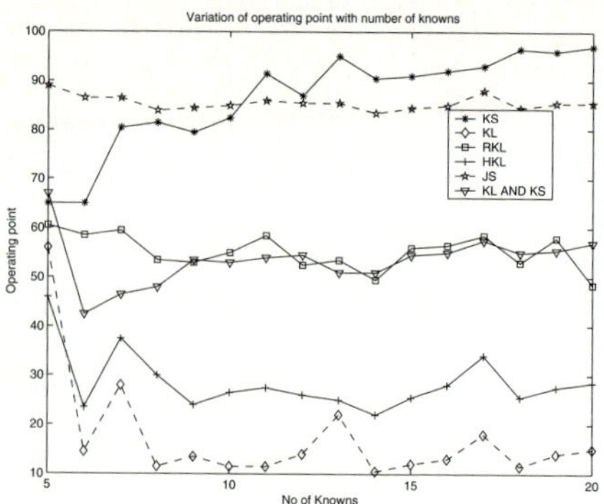

(b) Variation of operating point of the different measures, as a function of the number of knowns used for training. Operating point correponds to the best setting of the decision boundary (probability) for classifying samples as genuine or forgery.

Fig. 8.

of match $< \alpha$, the decision is in favor of a forgery (this α should not be confused with that used in the person-independent method). By varying the parameter α, once again ROC curves (False Accept vs. False Reject) can be plotted for each of the six measures. The best setting of α is termed as the *operating point*. This setting of α corresponds to the least total error rate possible. Note that the ROC curves are plotted for the test data set and the operating point determined on them. These test data set can be considered as a validation set that helps to determine the operating point. In the curve, the operating point is the point closest to the origin. Table 1 shows the least total error rate possible when different number of known samples were used for training for each of the 6 different measures. Figure 8(a) shows the same table as a graph comparing the different measures and it can be seen that the combined KL and KS measure performs the best. The reason for this can be intutively explained by the fact that KS statistic has low false accept rates whereas the KL statistic has low false reject rates. The combination of these two in the KL and KS measure works the best.

Figure 8(b) shows how the operating point (best setting of α) varies with the number of known samples used. It can be seen that in order to obtain the least total error rate, the value of α changes with the number of knowns for certain measures. The value of α explains a lot about what each statistic learns from the known samples. For example, the high value of α for the KS statistic when large numbers of known samples were used explains that the KS statistic focuses on learning the variation amongst the known samples. Presence of large known samples accounts for greater variation amongst them. Hence if KS focuses on

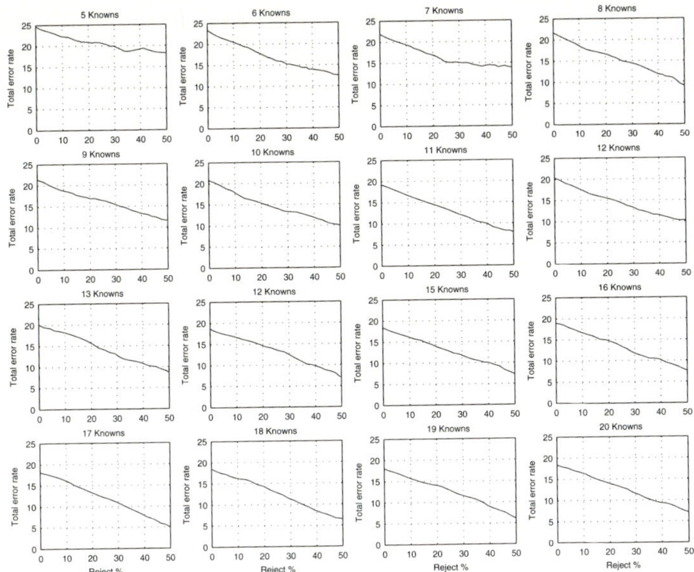

Fig. 9. Error rates as the percentage of allowed rejected (no decision) cases increases. The rejection rate is indirectly controlled by varying the β which assigns the probability region $50 - \beta$ and $50 + \beta$ where no decisions are made and considered as rejects. The different subplots show the plots for different number of knowns used for learning. We have plotted only the trend for the combined KL and KS measure.

learning the variation, then almost every questioned sample ends up receiving a high probability of match as the majority of questioned samples (genuines and forgeries) invariably fall within the variation. Thus by setting a high value of α the decision that a sample is truly genuine is made only if probability is really high. In simple terms this means that when more samples are used for training the KS statistic will declare a sample as genuine only if the probability of match is really high. In contrast to this measure the KL measure captures the similarities amongst the known samples a lot. This is evident by the low value of α for large number of knowns. Presence of large number of samples accounts for observing more similarities. The KL measure focuses on learning the similarities amongst the samples and it returns a high probability of match very rarely and only when every similarity that is learnt amongst the known samples is present in the questioned sample. Hence the majority of questioned sample receive a low probability of match by the KL measure. To counter this a low value of α ensures that the KL measure will declare a sample as forgery only if the probability of match is really low. Similar comments can be made about other measures and it is important to note that those measures for which the operating point does not vary with the number of knowns and those which are around the 50% mark can be a useful property. This basically shows that irrespective of the number of knowns used for training, one can make a decision using the same operating point, and also if the operating point is around the 50% mark there is an equal range of probabilties across which the two different decisions fall. And it is also intuitive that the combined KL KS measure has this fine property. It can be seen that the operating point for the combined KL and KS measure is closest to the 50% mark amongst other measure and is also independent of the number of known samples to some extent. Proceeding with the conclusion that the combined KL KS measure has a few desired properties and also outperforms other measures in terms total error rate, we can now consider allowing rejections to reduce the error rates even further. Consider probabilities between $.5 - \beta$ and $.5 + \beta$ for some $\beta > 0$ as the region for reject probabilities. No decision is made if $.5 - \beta < Probability < .5 + \beta$. This can significantly reduce the total error rate. Figure 9 shows the total error rate as it the rejection percentage is changed by changing the value of β. This analysis enables the operator to select a value of β that will induce a certain rejection rate and in turn result in a certain desired error rate. For example, in order to obtain a error rate of 10% with 20 knowns in this data set one should set β to .15 and that accounts for 35% reject rate. Similarly for an error rate of 5% for 20 knowns, β needs be set to .30 which accounts for 62% reject rate.

6   Summary and Discussion

Automatic signature verification is a task where machine learning can be used as a natural part of the process. Two different machine learning approaches, one involving genuines and forgeries in a general set and another involving only genuines for a particular case were described. The first approach is analogous to using counter-examples with near misses in the learning process. Both approaches involve using a similarity measure to compute a distance between features of two signatures. Special learning outperforms general learning particularly as the number of genuines increases. General learning is useful when the number of genuines is very small (less than four). A refined method of extracting features for signatures was also discussed which can further increase verification accuracy. Future work should consider combining the two types of learning to improve performance.

Acknowledgments. This work was supported in part by the National Institute of Justice grant 2004-IJ-CX-K030

References

1. Osborn, A.: Questioned Documents. Nelson Hall Pub (1929)
2. Robertson, E.W.: Fundamentals of Document Examination. Nelson-Hall (1991)
3. Bradford, R.R., Bradford, R.: Introduction to Handwriting Examination and Identification. Nelson-Hall (1992)
4. Hilton, O.: Scientific Examination of Questioned Documents. CRC Press (1993)
5. Huber, R., Headrick, A.: Handwriting Identification: Facts and Fundamentals. CRC Press (1999)
6. Slyter, S.A.: Forensic Signature Examination. Charles C. Thomas Pub (1995)
7. Mitchell, T.M.: Machine Learning. McGraw-Hill (1997)

8. Srihari, S.N., Xu, A., Kalera, M.K.: Learning strategies and classification methods for off-line signature verification, Proceedings of the Seventh International Workshop on Frontiers in Handwriting Recognition(IWHR), IEEE Computer Society Press (2004) 161–166

9. Winston, P.: Learning structural descriptions from examples. In Winston, P., ed.: The Psychology of Computer Vision. McGraw-Hill (1975) 157–210

10. Leclerc, F., Plamondon, R.: Automatic signature verification: the state of the art, 1989-1993. International Journal of Pattern Recognition and Artificial Intelligence **8** (1994) 643–660

11. Guo, J.K., Doermann, D., Rosenfield, A.: Local correspondences for detecting random forgeries, Proceedings of the International Conference on Document Analysis and Recognition (1997) 319–323

12. Plamondon, R., Srihari, S.N.: On-line and off-line handwriting recognition: A comprehensive survey. IEEE Transactions on Pattern Analysis and Machine Intelligence **22** (2000) 63–84

13. Kalera, M.K., Zhang, B., Srihari, S.N.: Off-line signature verification and identification using distance statistics. International Journal of Pattern Recognition and Artificial Intelligence **18** (2004) 1339–1360

14. Fang, B., Leung, C.H., Tang, Y.Y., Tse, K.W., Kwok, P.C.K., Wong, Y.K.: Off-line signature verification by the tracking of feature and stroke positions. Pattern Recognition **36** (2003) 91–101

15. Srihari, S.N., Cha, S., Arora, H., Lee, S.: Individuality of handwriting. Journal of Forensic Sciences (2002) 856–872

16. Srinivasan, H., Beal, M., Srihari, S.N.: Machine learning approaches for person verification and identification. Volume 5778., Proceedings of SPIE: Sensors, and Command, Control, Communications, and Intelligence Technologies for Homeland Security (2005) 574–586

17. Deng, P.S., Liao, H.Y., Ho, C., Tyan, H.R.: Wavelet-base off-line handwritten signature verification. Computer Vision Image Understanding **76** (1999) 173–190

18. Sabourin, R.: Off-line signature verification: Recent advances and perspectives. BSDIA (1997) 84–98

19. Coetzer, J., B.M.Herbst, du Preez, J.: Off-line signature verification using the discrete radon transform and a hidden markov model. Journal on Applied Signal Processing **4** (2004) 559–571

20. Ferrer, M.A., Alonso, J.B., Travieso, C.M.: Off-line geometric parameters for automatic signature verification using fixed-point arithmetic. IEEE Transactions on Pattern Analysis and Machine Intelligence **27** (2005) 993–997

21. Press, W.H., Flannery, B.P., Teukolsky, S.A., Vetterling, W.T.: Numerical Recipes in C: The Art of Scientific Computing. Cambridge University Press (1992)

22. Srikantan, G., Lam, S., Srihari, S.: Gradient based contour encoding for character recognition. Pattern Recognition **7** (1996) 1147–1160

23. Zhang, B., Srihari, S.N.: Analysis of handwriting individuality using handwritten words, Proceedings of the Seventh International Conference on Document Analysis and Recognition, IEEE Computer Society Press (2003) 1142–1146

24. Zhang, B., Srihari, S.N., Huang, C.: Word image retrieval using binary features. In Smith, E.H.B., Hu, J., Allan, J., eds.: SPIE. Volume 5296. (2004) 45–53

25. Zhang, B., Srihari, S.: Properties of binary vector dissimilarity measures. Cary, North Carolina (September, 2003)

26. Chen, S., Srihari, S.N.: A new off-line signature verification method based on graph matching, Proc. International Conference on Pattern Recognition (ICPR 2006) (August 2006)

Text Localization and Extraction from Complex Gray Images

Farshad Nourbakhsh*, Peeta Basa Pati, and A.G. Ramakrishnan

MILE Laboratory, Department of EE,
Indian Institute of Science, Bangalore, India – 560012
farshad@ragashri.ee.iisc.ernet.in

Abstract. We propose two texture-based approaches, one involving Gabor filters and the other employing log-polar wavelets, for separating text from non-text elements in a document image. Both the proposed algorithms compute local energy at some information-rich points, which are marked by Harris' corner detector. The advantage of this approach is that the algorithm calculates the local energy at selected points and not throughout the image, thus saving a lot of computational time. The algorithm has been tested on a large set of scanned text pages and the results have been seen to be better than the results from the existing algorithms. Among the proposed schemes, the Gabor filter based scheme marginally outperforms the wavelet based scheme.

1 Introduction

The advancement in science and technology has increased the need for information from the document images. Automatic conversion of paper into electronic document simplifies storage, retrieval, interpretation and updating processes. However, prior to such a conversion , we need to separate the text and non-text regions of the page. This enables proper conversion and interpretation of a document image. Besides, such separation of text and non-text regions, finds many other useful applications in document processing [1]. Moreover, the performance of a document understanding system, such as an optical character recognizer, greatly depends on this separation task.

Numerous approaches on text localization have been reported in the literature. Smith [2] uses vertical edge information for localizing caption text in images. Jung [3] used a neural network based filtering scheme to classify the pixels of input image as belonging to text or non-text regions. Jiang et al. [4] have applied merging bounding blocks, which are using special color features, edge features and morphology operator. These features are used to eliminate the false text candidates. However, this method is script dependent and is reported to be working well for Chinese documents. Yuan & Tan [5] have used edge information to extract textual blocks in Manhattan layout. Messelodi et. al. [6] extract connected components (CC) to characterize text objects in book cover

---

* Corresponding author.

P. Kalra and S. Peleg (Eds.): ICVGIP 2006, LNCS 4338, pp. 776–785, 2006.

color images. This is based on the (i) size information of the connected blocks, (ii) geometrical features of a single component, and (iii) spatial relationship of the connected block with other such connected components. Jain and Yu [7] extract a set of images by analyzing the color spaces of the input image. They employ connected component analysis (CCA) on each of the derived images to locate possible text regions. Finally, they merge the information so obtained to locate text regions in the original image. Strouthpoulos et. al. [8] have proposed a technique to separate text from non-text elements based on the optimal number of color components present in the input image. In the first step, an unsupervised neural network clusters the color regions. Subsequently, using a tree-search procedure and split-and-merge conditions, they decide whether color classes must be split or merged. They use a page layout analysis technique, on each of the obtained optimal color images. Finally, they merge the information obtained from each of the optimal color images to extract the text regions. Sabari *et. al.* [9] have employed a multi-channel Gabor filter bank approach for separating text from non-text elements in gray images. In the first level, they separate the obviously non-text objects by a statistical analysis of the connected components of the text page. Following this, they extract a Gabor feature vector at each pixel position. Based on these feature vectors, they decide if the pixel belongs to a text region. Antani *et. al.* [10] and Jung *et. al.* [11] present two comprehensive surveys for text separation and its information extraction in document images and videos.

2   System Description

Here, we propose a texture based text extraction scheme. Figure 1 demonstrates a schematic block representation of the scheme. It is assumed that text regions of an image contain more of abrupt changes in the gray values, in various directions. This makes such regions rich in edge information. An ideal feature to discriminate between text and non-text areas should invariably involve directional frequency. So, the idea of this paper is to separate text areas by applying some direction selective functions. Gabor function based filters are well known for their direction-frequency selectivity. Log-polar wavelet energy signature has also been widely used for texture classification tasks [12]. So it is proposed to

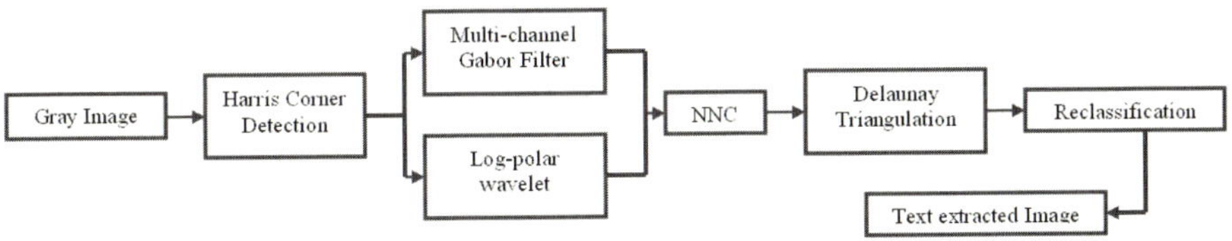

Fig. 1. Figure demonstrating a schematic representation of the proposed text separation algorithms. One of the approaches uses Gabor filters for local energy evaluation while the other uses log-polar wavelets.

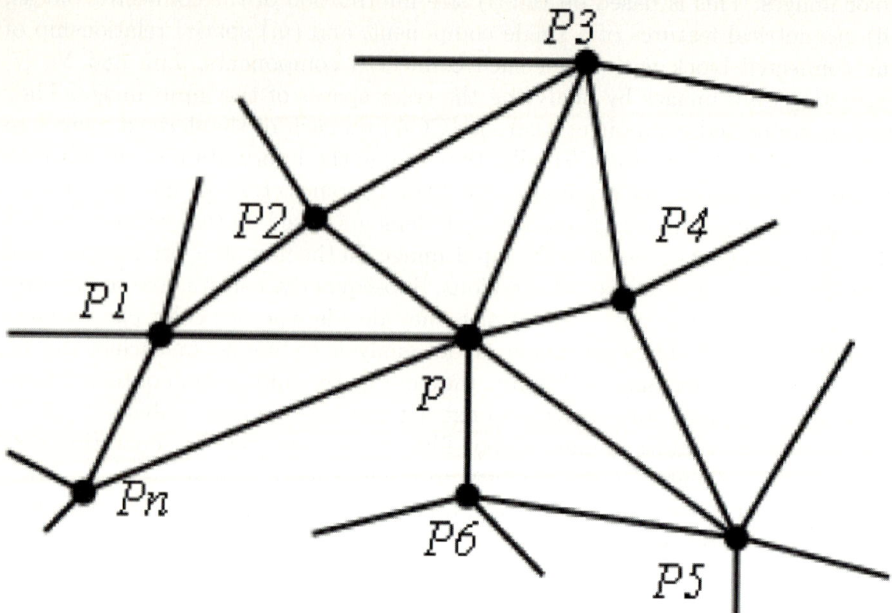

Fig. 2. Figure demonstrating a point p and its neighbors the number of neighbors are n and the Figure shows the connectivity between point p and its neighbors

test its efficacy in distinguishing text and non-text regions of a document image and compare it against that of the Gabor functions.

Previously reported works have used the above mentioned texture descriptors in the following ways: (i) extract the local energy signatures at a pixel level throughout the image, (ii) divide the image into smaller uniform blocks and apply the technique at such a block level. The local energy computation is done uniformly throughout the image in both of the above mentioned ways. However, in the present work, we propose to apply these texture descriptors in a non-uniform fashion, *i.e.*, in some selected information rich points of the image. Such information rich locations are marked by Harris' corner detector [13]. Each of this information rich Harris' corner points are classified as either a text point or non-text point by a Nearest Neighbor classifier (NNC)in the feature domain. The database consists of two classes, text and non-text, formed from english document images. The size of each class is 2000. The extraction of the features at selected points, for text/non-text separation, reduces the computational complexity of the algorithm by many times.

Subsequently, Delaunay triangles are formed using these labeled corner points in the image domain. Lets consider a corner point P in the image, as shown in figure 2. A number of triangles originate from P. Thus, P is associated with a number of other such corner points, P1, P2 $\cdots$ Pn, by the Delaunay triangles. All such points, P1, P2, $\cdots$ Pn are connected to the point P by the Delaunay triangles are said to be the neighbor points of the point P. All these points are already labeled as text/non-text points. For any given P, the labels of all such neighbor points are considered. For any P, if 75% of the neighboring corner points have a different label, the label of P is altered. Finally, a windowed portion of the original image is retained around all the points which have text label. The rest portions of the image are suppressed to the background.

2.1 Harris Corner Detector

The Harris corners [13] are located as follows:

1. For each pixel located at (x, y) in the image, I, calculate the autocorrelation matrix M.

$$\mathbf{M(x,y)} = \mathbf{G}_\sigma * \begin{pmatrix} (\frac{\partial \mathbf{I}}{\partial x})^2 & (\frac{\partial \mathbf{I}}{\partial x})(\frac{\partial \mathbf{I}}{\partial y}) \\ (\frac{\partial \mathbf{I}}{\partial x})(\frac{\partial \mathbf{I}}{\partial y}) & (\frac{\partial \mathbf{I}}{\partial x})^2 \end{pmatrix} \tag{1}$$

where $\mathbf{G}$ is a Gaussian blurring function with variance σ.
2. Construct a cornerness $\mathbf{C}(x, y)$

$$\mathbf{C}(x,y) = \mathrm{Det}(\mathbf{M}) - k * \mathrm{Trace}(\mathbf{M})^2 \tag{2}$$

Here k is a constant (i.e 0.4-0.6).
3. Threshold the cornerness map $\mathbf{C}(x, y)$ – set all values in $\mathbf{C}(x, y)$ below a threshold T to zero. Here, the threshold T is taken to be 10 percent of the maximum corner response.
4. Perform non-maximal suppression to find local maxima.
All non-zero points that remain after step 4 are declared as the corners.

2.2 Multi-channel Gabor Filtering

Sabari *et. al.* [9] have used Gabor filter banks for text localization and extraction. The technique involves multi-channel filtering with Gabor function based filters, for page layout analysis. Such a method is reported to detect text regardless of the type of script, size of font or the layout the text is embedded in. It is also claimed to be more robust than other kinds of feature detection models. The bank of Gabor filters reported by Sabari et al. [9], with minor changes to the parameters, is used for the presented work. Here, we are using 8 orientations and 5 different radial frequencies.

2.3 Delaunay Triangulation

The definition of the Delaunay Triangulation [14] is based on the Voronoi diagram through the principle of duality. Given a set of points, the plane can be split in domains for which the first point is closest; the second point is closest, etc. Such a partition is called a Voronoi diagram. If one draws a line between any two points whose Voronoi domains touch, a set of triangles is obtained, known as the Delaunay triangles. Generally, this triangulation is unique. One of its properties of this triangulation rule is that the enclosing circle of a Delaunay triangle does not contain another point. This is demonstrated in figure 3.

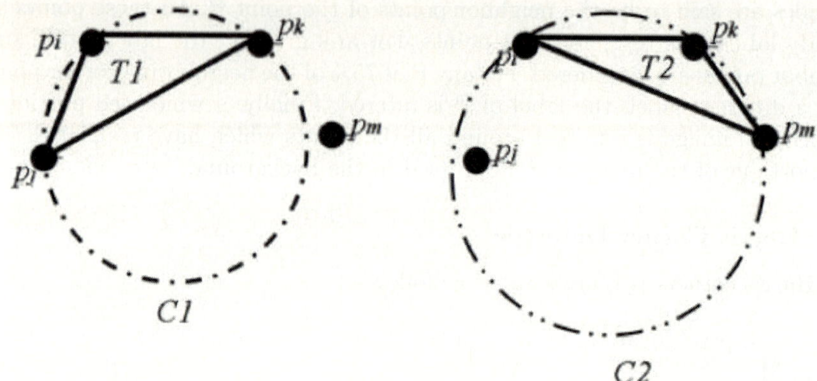

Fig. 3. Figure demonstrating the definition of the Delaunay triangulation between the 3 points pi, pj, pk. Here, the triangle T1 is a Delaunay triangle while the triangle T2 is not because the point Pj lies inside enclosing circle C2. This violates the Delaunay triangulation criteria.

2.4   Log-Polar Wavelet Energy Signature

Pun and Lee [12] have proposed log-polar wavelet energy signatures for rotation and scale invariant texture classification. Their scheme applies a log-polar transform to attain rotation and scale invariance. This produces a row shifted log-polar image which is then passed to an adaptive row shift invariant wavelet packet transform. This is done to eliminate the row shift effects. Thus, the output wavelet coefficients are both rotation and scale invariant. A feature vector consisting of the most dominant log-polar wavelet energy signatures, extracted from each sub-band of wavelet coefficients, is constructed. This feature vector is used for texture classification. We use 25 most significant coefficients to form the feature vector at each point for text/non-text separation.

3   Experimental Results

Document images are scanned using (a) Hewlett Packard Scanjet 2200c, and (b) UMAX ASTRA 5400 scanners and stored with Windows Device Independence Bitmap (BMP) format. The database contains about 100 such scanned document images. The images have variation in document layout and scripts (3 scripts Persian, English and Kannada) and have been taken from newspapers, journals and books. Some images are downloaded from the www net. The input to all the algorithms are gray images. However, we have presented the results with the corresponding color images for better visibility.

Figure 4 shows the outputs of the proposed algorithm at various stages. The colored version of the original input image is presented in (a). The output of the Harris' corner detection algorithm is presented in (b). Here, the detected corner points are marked on the original image. Each of these corner points are classified as either text or non-text points, using a nearest neighbor classifier (NNC)

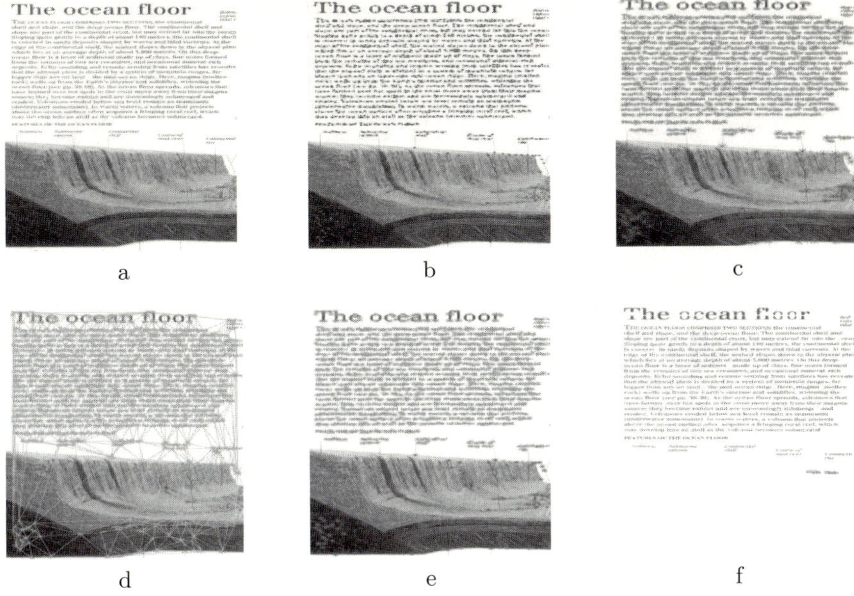

Fig. 4. Figure demonstrating the various stages of the proposed algorithms. (a) Original input image, (b) output of the Harris' corner detection algorithm, (c) labeled text/non-text points - labeling done by NNC on either the Gabor features, (d) Delaunay triangulation using the Harris corner points, (e) classification of the document page using the Delaunay triangles, and (f) the final output.

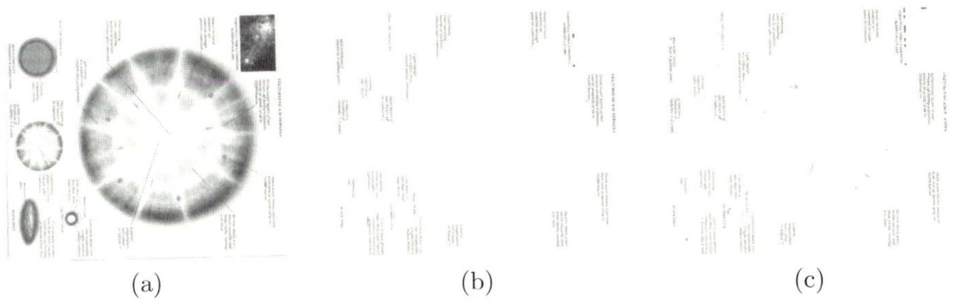

Fig. 5. Comparison of results of the algorithm using the Gabor features (b) and the log-polar wavelet features (c) for the input image (a)

on either the Gabor features or the log-polar wavelet features. Here, this classification task has employed Gabor features and the results are presented in (c). (d) presents the Delaunnay triangulation using the corner points. (e) demonstrates the results of re-classifying the corner points after the Delaunay triangulation and class label consideration of the neighboring corner points. Finally, the output of the proposed algorithm, with the detected text areas, is presented in (f).

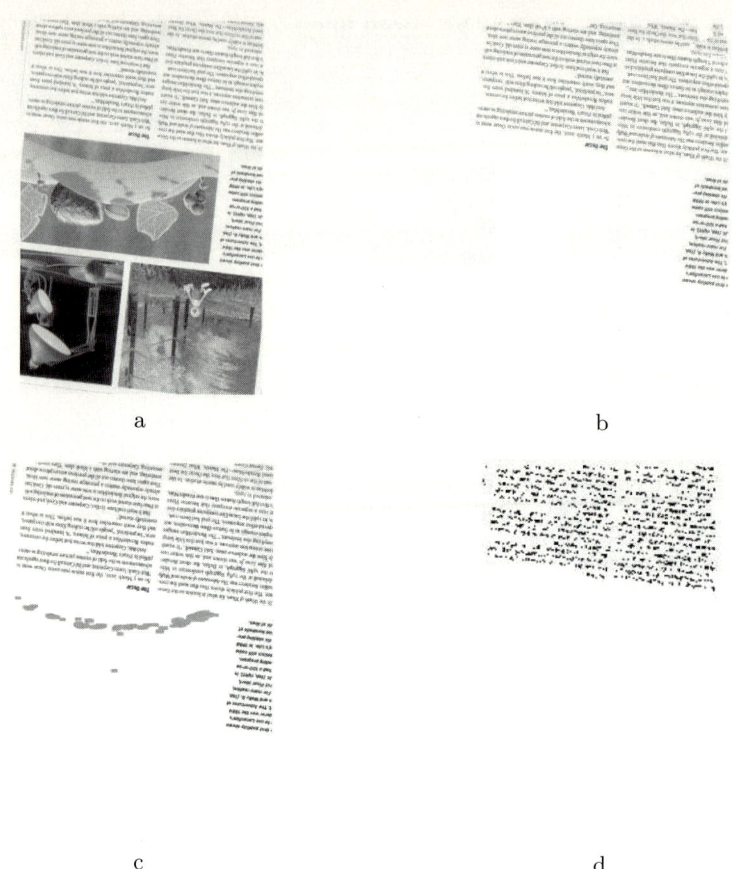

Fig. 6. Figure demonstrating the comparison between result of the algorithm and two previously existing techniques.(a) Original image, (b) the output of the proposed scheme, (c) output of scheme proposed by Sabari *et. al.*, and (d) output of scheme proposed by Xiao *et. al.*

A comparison of the results generated by use of (a) the Gabor features and (b) the Log-polar wavelet features has been demonstrated in figure 5. The above mentioned features have been extracted at the corner points and a near-neighbor classifier has been employed to classify such points to text and non-text points, as has been described in the section 2. Here, it could be observed that the result of employing the Gabor feature has yielded a better output than the ones employing the wavelet features. This has been observed with consistency when tested on other images as well. So, we have used Gabor features for generating the output of our proposed algorithm, in all cases of reported results.

The comparison of the results of the proposed algorithm with those two of the previously proposed algorithms have been demonstrated in figure 6. The two previously proposed algorithms are: (i) page layout analysis using Delaunay Tesselations [15], and (ii) the layout analysis technique proposed by Sabari *et. al.* in [9].

a

b

c

d

Fig. 7. Figure demonstrating the result of the algorithm for different documents. (a) input image with text in Kannada script, (b) output of the input image in (a), (c) web text image of Persian script and (d) the output of (c).

In this figure, (a) shows the original input image. The output of the proposed algorithm, using the Gabor features, has been presented in (b). (c) and (d) represent the output of the text analysis schemes proposed by Sabari *et. al.* and Xiao *et. al.*, respectively. It could be noted that the result of the proposed algorithm has generated output, which is better than the results generated by the other two techniques.

Figure 7 presents the results of our proposed algorithm, using Gabor features, on some more images. The right column of each row of the figure shows the output of the algorithm for the input image, shown in the left column of the same row.

4   Conclusion and Discussion

The proposed algorithm has been tested on a large set of images. Such images have a lot of variation in the non-text elements present in them. They also have variations in font style, size and script used in the document image. The results have also been verified against two other existing algorithms and the results, in all cases, have either been found to be better than the existing algorithms or as good as their output. Thus, it can be concluded that the proposed algorithm works fine for separation of text from non-text elements in a document image.

A comparison of the results generated by use of Gabor features with those generated by the use of Log-polar wavelet features, has also been done. Here, it is observed that the results of employing Gabor features generates better text/non-text separation in most cases. In some other cases, it is as good as the ones generated using the wavelet features. We never came across a case where result of the wavelet feature was substantially better than the one of Gabor features. This result substantiates the claim made by Sabari *et. al.* that the Gabor functions generate the optimal feature set for text/non-text separation.

The major advantages of the algorithm are:

  (i) handles multi-scripted documents,
 (ii) invariant to any arbitrary skew,
(iii) accommodates complex layout, and non-Manhattan documents,
(iv) works on poor quality images with acceptable result, and
 (v) computationally more efficient than the other proposed techniques.

References

1. K. C. Fan, L. S. Wang and Y. K. Wang, "page segmentation and identification for intelligent signal processing", Signal Processing, 45:329-346, 1995.
2. Smith, M.A., Kanade, T.: "Video skimming for quick browsing based on audio and image characterization", CMU-CS-95-186, Technical report, Carnegie Mellon University, 1995.
3. Jung, K., "Neural network-based text location in color images", Pattern Recognition Letters 22:1503-1515, 2001.
4. Jiang Wu, Shao-Lin Qu, Qing Zhuo, Wen-Yuan Wang, "Automatic text detection in complex color images", Proc. of Intl. Conf. on Machine Learning and Cybernetics, 2002.

5. Yuan, Q., Tan, C. L., "Text Extraction from Gray Scale Document Images Using Edge Information", Proc. of Sixth Intl. Conf. on Document Analysis and Recognition, 2001.
6. Messelodi, S., Modena, C.M., "Automatic identification and skew estimation of text lines in real scene images", Pattern Recognition, 32:791-810, 1999.
7. Jain, A.K., Yu, B., " Automatic text location in images and video frames", Pattern Recognition, 31:2055-2076, 1998.
8. C.Strouthpoulos, N.Papamarkos, Atsalakis, A.E., "Text extraction in complex color Document", Pattern Recognition, 35:1743-1758, 2002.
9. S. Sabari Raju, P.B. Pati, and A.G. Ramakrishnan, "Text Localization and Extraction from Complex Color Images", Int. Sym. on Visual Computing, LNCS – 3804:486-493, 2005.
10. R. Jain, S. Antani and R. Kasturi, "A survey on the use of pattern recognition methods for abstraction, indexing and retrieval of images and video", Pattern Recognition, 35(4):945-965, 2002.
11. K. Jung, K. I. Kim and A. K. Jain, "Text Information Extraction in Images and Video: A Survey", Pattern Recognition, 37(5): 977-997, 2004.
12. C.M. Pun and M.C. Lee, "Log-polar wavelet energy signature for rotation and scale invariant texture classification", IEEE Trans. PAMI 25(5):590-603, 2003.
13. C. Harris and M. Stephens, "A combined corner and edge detector", proc. 4th Alvey Vision Conf., 147-151, 1988.
14. F. Davoine, et al., "Fractal images compression based on Delaunay triangulation and vector quantization", IEEE Trans. on Image Processing, 5(2):338-346, 1996.
15. Y. Xiao and H. Yan, "Text region extraction in a document image based on the Delaunay tessellation", Pattern Recognition, 36:799-809, 2003.

OCR of Printed Telugu Text with High Recognition Accuracies

C. Vasantha Lakshmi, Ritu Jain, and C. Patvardhan

Dayalbagh Educational Institute
Agra – 282005, India
cvasantha@rediff.com, rituritu2006@rediff.com,
cpatvardhan@hotmail.com

Abstract. Telugu is one of the oldest and popular languages of India spoken by more than 66 million people especially in South India. Development of Optical Character Recognition systems for Telugu text is an area of current research.

OCR of Indian scripts is much more complicated than the OCR of Roman script because of the use of huge number of combinations of characters and modifiers. Basic Symbols are identified as the unit of recognition in Telugu script. Edge Histograms are used for a feature based recognition scheme for these basic symbols. During recognition, it is observed that, in many cases, the recognizer incorrectly outputs a very similar looking symbol. Special logic and algorithms are developed using simple structural features for improving recognition accuracies considerably without too much additional computational effort. It is shown that recognition accuracies of 98.5 % can be achieved on laser quality prints with such a procedure.

1 Introduction

During the past few decades, substantial research efforts have been devoted to Optical Character Recognition (OCR) [1,2]. The object of OCR is automatic reading of optically sensed document text materials to translate human-readable characters into machine-readable codes. Research in OCR is popular for its application potential in banks, post-offices and defense organizations. Other applications involve reading-aid for the blind, library automation, language processing and multi-media design [3].

Commercial OCR packages are already available for languages like English. Considerable work has also been done for languages like Japanese and Chinese [1]. Recently, work has been done for development of OCR systems for Indian languages. This includes work on recognition of Devanagari characters [4], Bengali characters [5], Kannada characters [6] and Tamil characters [7]. Some more recent work on Indian languages is also reported [8,9,10,11,12].

Telugu is one of the popular languages of India that is spoken by more than 66 million people especially in South India. Work on Telugu character recognition is not substantial [13,14]. Vasantha Lakshmi et al. [17] have recently reported the development of a Telugu OCR System for Printed text (TOSP) based on identification of symbols defined as Basic Symbols by them. A Basic Symbol is a single connected entity in Telugu script and is treated as the unit of segmentation. The system works in three steps as described. Recognition rates of over 97% have been reported over a wide variety of fonts and sizes. Their approach is essentially a feature based approach where features of all the basic symbols in several different fonts and sizes are stored and symbols of same fonts but different sizes are recognized on the basis of these features. The features used by them are the local gradients at various pixels called the Radial Direction Features [17, 18].

Recent work in the context of MPEG-7 features has shown the utility of Edge Histograms to aid the recognition in various image processing applications [22]. These are utilized in this work. Further improvement in recognition accuracies is achieved by identifying pairs of symbols that are frequently confused for each other. The logic for determining the correct basic symbol and the results of OCR before and after incorporation of this logic are given.

The sets of symbols that are confused for each other are a characteristic property of the script. They are confused for each other because they are similar. These sets remain more or less same irrespective of the feature extractor and recognizer that operates over the whole set of Basic Symbols. Therefore, many of the ideas presented in this paper could be used with advantage in improving the recognition accuracy with any OCR system for Telugu. Another important point is that Confusion Logic is called into play only when one of the confusing symbols is recognized in order to verify or contradict it. Further, simple features are used to resolve the confusion. Therefore, this does not add substantially to the computational requirements.

The rest of the paper is organized as follows. The approach adopted in this work is presented briefly in section 2. In section 3, the Confusion Table is presented. Detailed logic for resolving the confusion in each set is presented in section 4. Results of OCR after incorporation of additional logic are presented in section 5. Some conclusions and pointers toward future work are highlighted in section 6.

2 Recognition of Printed Telugu Text

The recognition works by isolating and recognizing Basic Symbols. Basic Symbols are connected regions in the image. If a modifier is physically attached to the character it modifies, they together constitute a single basic symbol. It has been shown [17] that such an approach is extremely useful in reducing the number of symbols that the recognizer has to deal with to manageable levels (around 400) from the lakhs of combinations of characters and modifiers possible. Therefore, the task in segmentation is to isolate such basic symbols.

The processing starts with the conversion of the gray scale image of a page of text into a binary image using thresholding. Any small blobs introduced due to scanning noise are removed to clean the image.

The actual basic symbol is represented by black pixels and background is represented by white pixels. Any skew in the image is detected and removed using a modified Hough transform method adapted for Telugu text [19].

Table 1. Steps in recognition of printed Telugu text

1. Conversion of a gray scale image of input text to binary image.
2. Image rectification
3. Skew detection and its removal
4. Separation of text into lines, words, and basic symbols.
5. Preliminary classification using size property for each basic symbol.
6. Computation of Edge Histogram Features for each basic symbol.
7. Recognition by means of Nearest Neighbour (NN) classifier.
8. Output.

Table 2. Confusion Table depicting Symbols that are confused for each other

S. No.	Element 1 of Confusion Set		Other Element(s) of Confusion Set	
	Phonetic English	Telugu symbol	Telugu symbol	Phonetic English
1	/pa/	ప	స	/sa/
2	/va/	వ	న	/na/
3	/gha/	ఘ	ను	/su/
4	/ma/	మ	ను	/nu/
5	/ra/	ర	ల	/la/
6	/la/	ల	ట	/Ta/
7	/lu/	లు	ట	/Ta/
	/lU/	లూ	టూ	/TA/
8	/cha/	చ	వ	/va/
9	/vA/	వా	హా	/ha/
10	/da/	ద	డ	/u/
			డ	/Da/
11	/ri/	ఋ	ి	/imatra/
12	/lu/	లు	యు	/yi/

Profiling is used to segment the text image into lines and words. This is done taking advantage of the spacing between lines and between words. In every word, each basic symbol is identified by determining connected components. For each basic symbol, a preliminary classification scheme is implemented on the basis of the relative sizes of the symbols. All the symbols are converted to size corresponding to 36 columns and the row sizes for this column size is used to classify the basic symbols into 14 different sets.

The features used are the Edge Histogram features. The database is created with three popular fonts i.e. Harshapriya, Godavari and Hemalatha [21] and three different sizes i.e. 25, 30 and 35. The feature vectors are divided into 14 sets as described above and stored in the database. The algorithm for feature extraction is represented succinctly in the following pseudo-code.

1. For each word in every line of a scanned printed page of Telugu text,
2. Isolate the next basic symbol from the word as given above.
   Repeat steps 3 to 10 for each basic symbol.
3. Obtain the bounding box eliminating the blank surrounding space.
4. Partition the bounding box into N1 x N2 blocks. In this work N1 and N2 are taken as 4 each.
5. Determine the edges of the symbol using the Canny edge operator.
6. Calculate the gradient magnitude and direction at each pixel location on the edges within each block.
7. Quantize the edge directions into K ranges. K=9 in this work i.e. 0-20, 20-40,…, 160-180. Directions 180-360 are mapped again onto 0-180 range of directions.
8. Calculate the adaptive threshold of gradient magnitude and perform thresholding to obtain the new threshold gradient direction at each pixel location.
9. Calculate the relative edge histogram by dividing the edge direction values in Step 6 by total number of pixels in that block.
10. Concatenate the feature vectors from all the partitions to obtain the complete feature vector.

The OCR of a text page begins with the scanned image. The segmentation steps described above are performed on this image to isolate the image of each basic symbol. The feature vector of the symbol to be recognized is computed as given above. This is then provided to the recognizer. The recognizer uses a preliminary classification scheme and a Nearest Neighbour (NN) classifier scheme on the feature vectors stored in the database to identify the basic symbol.

The preliminary classification classifies a basic symbol based on its height into one of the 14 different sets. The classifier considers only the basic symbols in the set identified by the preliminary classification scheme. This results in a considerable saving in the computational expense. However, it does not result in a degradation of the recognition performance. The process is repeated till all the basic symbols are recognized.

This approach has been implemented and tested over a variety of images with different fonts i.e. Harshapriya, Hemalatha and Godavari and sizes 15, 18, 20, 23, 25, 28, 30, 32, 35. Recognition accuracy by directly using the above scheme is 95.4 % as presented in Tables 3, 4, and 5. This recognition accuracy needs to be improved further for actual use.

In computing this recognition accuracy, if a particular basic symbol appears three times in the text and it is mis-recognized all the three times it is taken as three errors

Table 3. Raw and improved results on DS1 to DS9 with Hemalatha font

Data Set #	Type	Size	# of BS	NN	
				Initial Recognition Ratio	Recognition ratio with additional logic
DS1	Hm	15	127	0.937	0.976
DS2		18	127	0.969	0.992
DS3		20	127	0.969	1.000
DS4		23	127	0.969	0.992
DS5		25	127	0.953	0.976
DS6		28	127	0.945	0.992
DS7		30	127	0.937	0.961
DS8		32	127	0.945	0.992
DS9		35	127	0.953	0.984
	TOTAL		**1143**	**0.953**	**0.985**

Table 4. Raw and improved results on DS10 to DS18 with Harshapriya font

Data Set #	Type	Size	# of BS	NN	
				Initial Recognition ratio	Recognition ratio with additional logic
DS10	Hr	15	127	0.921	0.976
DS11		18	127	0.945	0.992
DS12		20	127	0.969	1.000
DS13		23	127	0.929	0.992
DS14		25	127	0.945	0.984
DS15		28	127	0.961	0.992
DS16		30	127	0.969	1.000
DS17		32	127	0.969	1.000
DS18		35	129	0.946	0.969
	TOTAL		**1145**	**0.950**	**0.990**

and not one. So actual misrecognized symbols are even lesser than what this number indicates. This also provides the motivation for deeper analysis into why a particular symbol is misrecognized every time it appears because if logic can be found to rectify this then at one stroke several of the errors could be eliminated. Such an effort is made in the next section.

3   The Confusion Table

As mentioned above, an analysis of the results shows that some symbols are often recognized incorrectly. The reason for mistakes in recognition can be scanning noise, defect in the paper where the symbol is printed that leads to extra dark pixels, spread of ink on the paper etc. These are, however, random causes and cannot be the reason

Table 5. Raw and improved results on DS19 to DS27 with Godavari fon

Data Set #	Type	Size	# of BS	NN classifier	
				Initial Recognition ratio	Recognition ratio with additional logic
DS19	Go	15	126	0.976	0.984
DS20		18	127	0.961	0.984
DS21		20	128	0.961	0.984
DS22		23	129	0.938	0.977
DS23		25	127	0.953	0.984
DS24		28	127	0.976	0.984
DS25		30	127	0.969	0.984
DS26		32	127	0.945	0.969
DS27		35	127	0.953	0.984
TOTAL			**1145**	**0.959**	**0.982**

for consistent wrong recognition of a particular symbol as another symbol. It is observed that, in many cases, a symbol is recognized erroneously because the recognizer incorrectly outputs a very similar looking basic symbol. The low level features that are used in the recognition process are not able to distinguish between the two. Recourse is taken, therefore, to higher level structural features that can provide the distinction.

The sets of similar symbols are arranged in the form of a table with each row corresponding to a set. This is referred to as the Confusion Table [Table 2]. Though the symbols in each set of the Confusion Table look very similar, on closer observation, it is seen that each basic symbol has some unique feature that distinguishes it from the other(s) in the set. This feature is identified and made use of in correctly identifying it.

4   Resolution of Confusions

In this section, an attempt is made to identify a distinguishing feature that can be used to distinguish between the elements of each set. This is non-trivial because the distinction may be very fine, especially for the smaller sized characters.

4.1.1   Confusions 1 to 4

The confusion among the first four row entries in the Table 2 are resolved using a similar logic. This is possible because there is no possibility of confusion across sets reported in different rows. It is observed from column 3 of the table for all these 4 entries that there is a small closed loop at the bottom near the left end for these symbols. However, as is seen in column 4 for the corresponding entries, the characters with which they are confused are open near the bottom left end. An algorithm is designed to detect the presence or absence of the closed loop. Care is taken to ensure that the logic works for a variety of fonts and sizes.

Figure 1 shows the images of two Telugu characters /pa/ and /sa/. Long lines in these figures divide each of the images into two halves i.e. the top half and the bottom half therefore, only the bottom half of the image is considered for resolving the confusion. The figure also shows a short line inside the loop of /pa/. The ends of this line, denoted by 'a' and 'b', indicate the beginning and end of the possible loop in the image. The point 'a' is the left most pixel found in the bottom half of the image. The logic for determining the existence of loop is given succinctly in Algorithm 1.

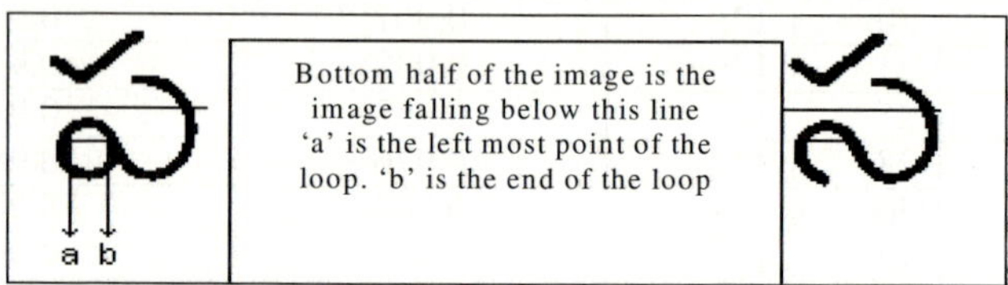

Fig. 1. Images of Telugu characters /pa/ and /sa/

Although the algorithm is explained for the pairs reported in the table only, the same can also be used for resolving confusion among the pairs generated by attaching same modifier symbols.

Algorithm 1

1. Split the image into two halves. Consider only the bottom half of the image for further processing.
2. Find the left most pixel position 'a'. Let 'i' denote its row number and 'j' the column number.
3. By moving along the row 'i' to the right from the pixel 'a' identify the pixel at position 'b' as shown in Figure 1.
4. For each of the pixels between 'a' and 'b' scan down to the bottom row of the image starting from row 'i'. In this process, if for any column, a foreground pixel is not encountered at all, the element belongs to column 4 of Table 2. A single gap is sufficient as the characters are thick enough.
5. If no gap is found for any column, the symbol belongs to column 3 of the same Table.

4.1.2 Confusion Between /ra/ and /la/ Families of Consonants

These form the fifth row of Table 4. The /ra/ and /la/ families are quite similar because attaching modifiers to each of these, i.e., /ra/ and /la/, results in similar compound characters. The concept of Zero Crossings (ZC) is made use of in differentiating between these two basic symbol families. A ZC is a transition from a character or foreground pixel to a background pixel or vice-versa. The images of /ra/ and /la/ consonants are identical near the bottom and differ near their top ends. /la/ has a loop at the top left end whereas /ra/ has a tick mark. The images of /la/ and /ra/ are shown in Figures 2(ii) and 2 (iii) respectively.

For differentiating between these two or any pairs in their families, the bottom most pixel of the image, labeled as 'a' in Figure 2 (i) is taken as the starting point.

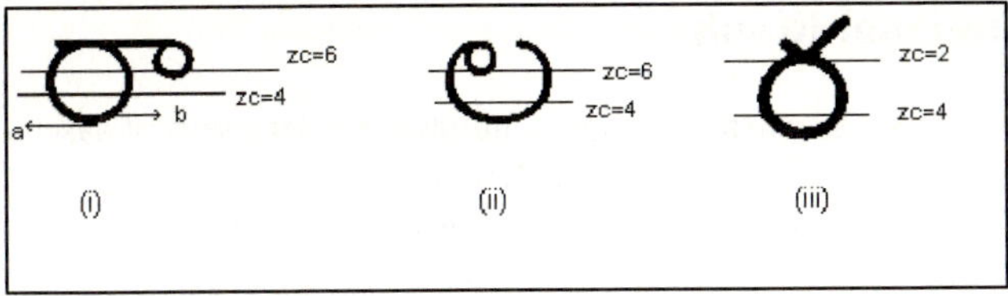

Fig. 2. Images of basic symbols (i) rA (ii) la

The thickness of the character starting from the bottom most point is avoided in searching for ZC. For this purpose, the pixel labeled as 'b' in Figure 2 (i) is identified by scanning up in the same column as 'a' and stopping at the last foreground pixel among the continuous foreground pixels. From here onwards a count of ZC is noted for every row starting with the row above this row. The ZC count for both the consonants /ra/ and /la/ is 4 for all the rows in the beginning. This is clearly indicated by the line ZC=4 in Figure 2. The ZC count for consonant /la/ increases to 6 and that for /ra/ decreases to 2, as the rows above 'b' are scanned.

The same logic is also applicable for the members of the two consonant families generated by attaching the vowel modifiers of /i/, /I/, /e/, /E/, /AW/ on the two consonants. However, this algorithm does not work as such for the members of /ra/ and /la/ families that are formed by attaching the vowel modifiers of /A/, /o/ and /O/. These compound characters assume shapes that contradict the logic given above.

Consider the image of consonant /ra/ modified by the vowel modifier of /A/ shown in Figure 2(i). For this image a loop is encountered and the corresponding ZC count is 6. Therefore, as per the above logic, it will be treated as /lA/ and not /rA/, as the ZC count is greater than 4. However, it is observed that in this case the ZC count increases because of the loop in the right portion of the compound character and not because of a loop in the left portion as in /la/. Similar is the case with modifiers of /o/ and /O/. Therefore, the logic given above is suitably modified to work for pairs of symbols generated by all the vowel modifiers. The ZC count is not taken for all the columns. Only, the columns in which the left side loop is possibly encountered are considered. With this modification the above logic is useful for distinguishing between all the members of the two families. Since noise has already been removed for small specks and isolated larger ones would be recognized as separate characters, zero crossings do not create any problem.

Algorithm 2

1.   Find the bottom most pixel 'a' of the image, as shown in Figure 2(i).
2.   Find the pixel marked as 'b' in the same figure that is in the same column as 'a'.
3.   Let startrow be the row above the row in which 'b' is located.
4.   Consider the left portion of the image from startrow upwards.
5.   For startrow, find ZC. Store it as previous ZC.
6.   For each row above startrow, find ZC.
         if ZC >previous ZC, id=/la/ else if ZC<prevZC, id=/ra/ else continue.
7.   end.

Similarly, logic based structural differences is designed for distinguishing between the rest of the sets of basic symbols.

5   Computational Results

OCR experiments were carried out on a number of data sets of laser quality prints containing text in three fonts and nine different sizes. Results of OCR experiments on 27 data sets DS1 to DS27 without additional improvement logic for Confusing Symbols were analyzed and the correction logic incorporated for rectifying the commonly occurring errors. An important point to be noted is that the correction logic for a particular pair of confusing symbols is executed only when the recognizer recognizes one of the symbols in the set as being present in the image under consideration. Thus, the computational burden is not enhanced too much with the inclusion of this logic. Still, the correction of the commonly occurring errors enhances the recognition rate. Results of OCR experiments are presented on the same data sets DS1 to DS27 in Tables 3 to 5 but this time with the incorporation of the logic described above for the correction of errors due to the presence of confusing symbols. Edge Histogram features are still used. Recognition accuracies are enhanced in all cases going up to 99 % in the case of Harshapriya font. Overall recognition accuracy in the case of all the fonts is improved from 95.4% to 98.5 %.

6   Conclusion

This paper is concerned with achieving better recognition rates in OCR of printed Telugu text by use of Edge histogram features and additional logic for resolving confusion among similar symbols. Simple structural features are utilized to improve recognition accuracies. Incorporation of this logic does not add too much to the computational requirements. This is in direct to contrast to the more computationally intensive dictionary matching schemes. But, still, recognition accuracies show considerable improvement. The logic presented in this paper can be incorporated to improve recognition accuracy with any OCR system for Telugu, as it is quite general and works with different fonts and sizes i.e. the structural features used to aid resolution of confusion are font independent. The approach is novel as it utilizes simple structural features instead of commonly employed complicated dictionary matching procedures towards the same result.

Work is being pursued in improving the recognition accuracies further by incorporation of additional post-processing logic based on the frequency of association of symbols that are found together in the text. For example, it is known that the some modifiers occur very frequently with some characters and some modifiers occur very infrequently. Development of better feature sets by better choice of features is also another direction being pursued.

References

[1] G. Nagy, Twenty years of Document Image Analysis in PAMI, IEEE Transactions on Pattern Analysis and Machine Intelligence, 2000, 22(1), pp 38-63.
[2] S. Mori, C. Y. Suen, K. Yamamoto, Historical review of OCR Research and Development, Proc. of the IEEE, 1992, pp 1029 - 1058.

[3]   V.K. Govindan, A.P Shivaprasad., Character recognition -- A review, Pattern Recognition, 1990, 23(7), pp. 671-683.

[4]   V. Bansal, R. M.K Sinha, A survey of OCR in Indian Languages and a Devanagari OCR scheme, in Proceedings of the STRANS – 01, IIT, Kanpur, 2001.

[5]   B.B. Chaudhuri, U.Pal, A complete printed Bangla OCR system, Pattern Recognition, 1998, 31, pp 531-549.

[6]   P. Nagabhushan, A. Radhika, Improved region decomposition method for the recognition of non-uniform sized characters, in Proceedings of the International Conference on Cognitive science, ICCS-97, New Delhi, 1997, Vol. 1, pp. 36-42.

[7]   S. Anna Durai, et al., Tamil character recognition using multilayer neural network, in Indian Conference on Pattern Recognition, Image Processing and Computer Vision (ICPIC), 1995., pp. 155-160.

[8]   A. Bishnu, B. Chaudhuri, Segmentation of Bangla Handwritten text into characters by recursive contour following, in Proceedings of the Fifth International Conference on Document Analysis and Recognition, ICDAR'99, pp 402 – 405.

[9]   U. Pal, B. Chaudhuri, Script line separation from Indian Multi-Script Documents, in Proceedings of the Fifth International Conference on Document Analysis and Recognition, ICDAR'99, 1999, pp 406 – 409.

[10] V. Bansal, R. Sinha, On how to describe shapes of Devanagari Characters and use them for Recognition, in Proceedings of ICDAR'99, 1999, pp 410 – 413.

[11] S. Anatani, L. Agnihotri, Gujarati Character Recognition, in Proceedings of ICDAR'99, 1999, pp 418 – 421.

[12] C. Sundaresan, S. Keerthi, A study of representation for Pen based Handwriting recognition of Tamil Characters, in Proceedings of ICDAR'99, 1999, pp 422 – 425.

[13] M.B. Sukhaswami, Seetharamulu, A.K Pujari, Recognition of Telugu characters using Neural Networks, Int. Journal of Neural Systems, September, 1995, 6(3), page 317 – 357.

[14] A. Negi, et al., An OCR system for Telugu, in Proceedings of International Conference on Document Analysis and Recognition, ICDAR – 2001, Seattle, USA.

[15] C. Vasantha Lakshmi, C. Patvardhan, Ranjit Singh, "A novel basic symbol approach for Telugu OCR with neural networks", Journal of the Computer Society of India, March, 2003, pp 31-39.

[16] C. Vasantha Lakshmi, C. Patvardhan, "Recognition of basic symbols in Telugu by Neural networks", STRANS-2002, March, 15 – 17, 2002, IIT Kanpur, Kanpur.

[17] C. Vasantha Lakshmi, C. Patvardhan, "An OCR system for Telugu text: A basic symbol approach", Int. Jl. on Pattern Analysis and Applications, July, 2004, pp 190 - 204.

[18] C. Vasantha Lakshmi, Unpublished Ph.D. Thesis, Dayalbagh Educational Institute, Agra, India, 2003.

[19] M. Sonka, V. Hlavac, R. Boyle, Image processing, Analysis, and Machine Vision, Second Edition, Brooks/Cole Publishing Company, 1998.

[20] G. Srikanthan, S. W. Lam, and S.N. Srihari, Gradient based contour encoding for character recognition, Pattern Recognition, 1996, 29(7), pp 1147 - 1160.

[21] LEAP, Indian language software, CDAC, Pune, India.

[22] Manjunath B.S., Salembier, P., and Sikora, T. (Eds.), Introduction to MPEG-7, John Wiley & Sons, 2002.

A MLP Classifier for Both Printed and Handwritten Bangla Numeral Recognition

A. Majumdar and B.B. Chaudhuri

Pricewaterhouse Coopers, Pvt. Ltd, India.
CVPR Unit, Indian Statistical Institute, Kolkata – 700108, India
angshul@gmail.com,
bbc@isical.ac.in

Abstract. This paper concerns automatic recognition of both printed and handwritten Bangla numerals. Such mixed numerals may appear in documents like application forms, postal mail, bank checks etc. Some pixel-based and shape-based features are chosen for the purpose of recognition. The pixel-based features are normalized pixel density over 4 X 4 blocks in which the numeral bounding-box is partitioned. The shape-based features are normalized position of holes, end-points, intersections and radius of curvature of strokes found in each block. A multi-layer neural network architecture was chosen as classifier of the mixed class of handwritten and printed numerals. For the mixture of twenty three different fonts of printed numerals of various sizes and 10,500 handwritten numerals, an overall recognition accuracy of 97.2% has been achieved.

1 Introduction

Recognizing handwritten numerals is an important area of research because of its various application potentials. Automating bank cheque processing, postal mail sorting, job application form sorting and other applications where numeral recognition is necessary. Impressive research has been done on the recognition of Roman, Arabic and Chinese numerals which is excellently reviewed in[1]. Le Cun et al [2] has developed an algorithm for identifying Arabic numerals, which has a high recognition rate that.

Limited amount of research has been done in the recognition of Indian numerals. In this paper, we concentrate on the recognition of Bangla numerals. Bangla is the second most popular language in India and is the fifth most popular in the world. We are considering recognition of both Handwritten and Printed Bangla numerals. Mixture of these two types of scripts may appear in a single document. A typical example is as shown in figure 1. To get an idea of the variability of Indian numerals, 10 sets of printed fonts and 10 sets of handwritten characters are shown in Figure 2.a and 2.b.

Till now to the best of our knowledge effort had been on the recognition of either handwritten Bangla numerals only [3-6] or printed fonts. But, in the actual world forms, checks and mailing addresses are encountered where there are both

P. Kalra and S. Peleg (Eds.): ICVGIP 2006, LNCS 4338, pp. 796 – 804, 2006.

handwritten as well as printed numerals. For example a person may write a cheque by hand, but when an organisation pays its employees by cheque, the salary amount is printed on the cheque. A similar situation might arise for postal addresses also. A typical form where both handwritten and printed numerals may be encountered is provided in Figure 1. In this paper, the concentration will be on the recognition of both handwritten and printed numerals by a single system.

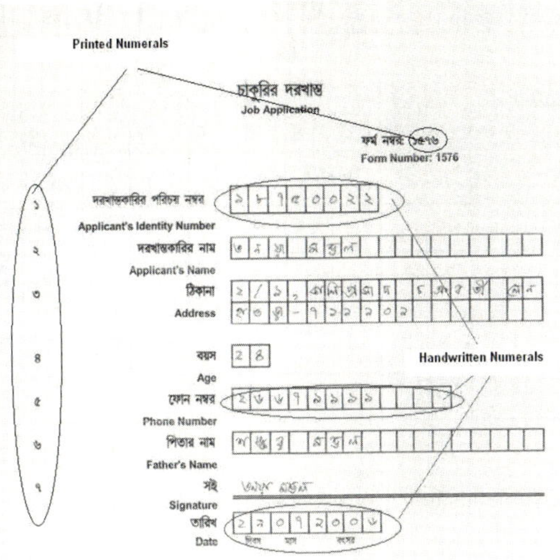

Fig. 1. Sample form

Neural Networks had been one of the most widely used approaches for numeral recognition. It has been used both for the recognition of non-Indian [2, 7-9] as well as Indian [3-6, 10, 11] digits. In this paper, a multi-layer neural network will be employed for the recognition of Bangla numerals. Here we concentrate only on isolated numerals.

The rest of the paper is organized as follows. The data sets used for the training and testing of the neural networks is described in the following section. In section 3 the preprocessing required for optical character recognition will be discussed. This will be followed by section 4 that will describe in detail the feature selection techniques. In section 5 the discussion will be on Neural Network implementation. Section 6 will present the results obtained from the experiments and in the final section, 7, conclusions and future scope of work will be discussed.

2   Data Set

Neural Networks had been one of the most widely used approaches for numeral recognition. It has been used both for the recognition of non-Indian [2, 7-9] as well as Indian [3-6, 10, 11] digits. In this paper, a multi-layer neural network will be

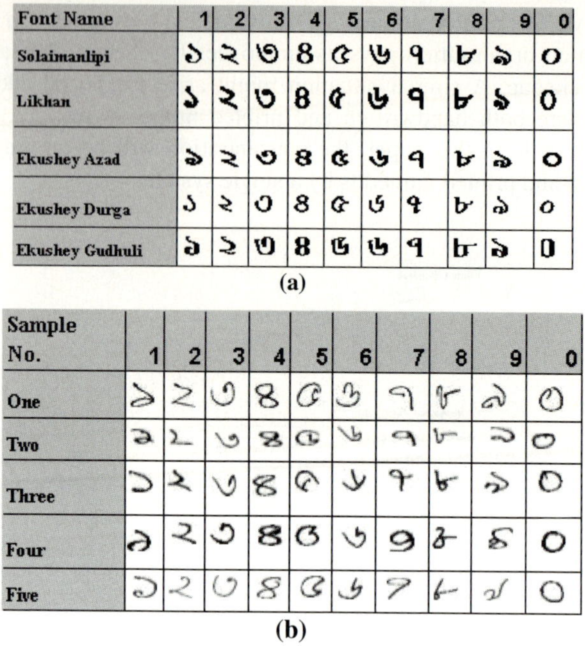

Font Name	1	2	3	4	5	6	7	8	9	0
Solaimanlipi	১	২	৩	৪	৫	৬	৭	৮	৯	০
Likhan	১	২	৩	৪	৫	৬	৭	৮	৯	০
Ekushey Azad	১	২	৩	৪	৫	৬	৭	৮	৯	০
Ekushey Durga	১	২	৩	৪	৫	৬	৭	৮	৯	০
Ekushey Gudhuli	১	২	৩	৪	৫	৬	৭	৮	৯	০

(a)

Sample No.	1	2	3	4	5	6	7	8	9	0
One										
Two										
Three										
Four										
Five										

(b)

Fig. 2. (a) Numerals in various printed fonts.(b) Handwriting examples.

employed for the recognition of Bangla numerals. Here we concentrate only on isolated numerals.

The rest of the paper is organized as folows. The data sets used for the training and testing of the neural networks is described in the following section. In section 3 the preprocessing required for optical character recognition will be discussed. This will be followed by section 4 that will describe in detail the Neural Network implementation. Section 5 will present the results obtained from the experiments and in the final section, 6, conclusions and future scope of work will be discussed.

Handwritings of 105, each having written 0-9 ten times comprises the handwritten numeral dataset. The writers were mostly university students and employees in a private software company. Only a few samples belonged to shopkeepers, children, domestic maid and peons. The majority of the writers were male. There was no restriction on the type of pen used and its ink colour or the paper sheet on which the wrtings were taken.

23 fonts were considered for training and testing the neural network. The fonts considered here are: 1. SolaimanLipi, 2. Aakash, 3. Bangla, 4. Likhan, 5. Amar Bangla, 6. Ekushey Azad, 7. Ekushey Durga, 8. Ekushey Godhuli, 9. Ekushey Mohua, 10. Ekushey Puja, 11. Ekushey Punarbhaba, 12. Ekushey Saraswati, 13. Ekushey Sharifa, 14. Ekushey Sumit, 15. Mukti Narrow, 16. Rupali and 17. BN TT Durga 18. Ekushey Lohit 19. Sagar 20. Mitra Mono 21. Aharoni 22. Bangla Samay 23. Bangla Digital. For, the printed numerals, font-sizes 10, 12, 14, 18, 24, 32, 40, 48, 60 and 72 points were used for training and testing. All the digits of the seventeen fonts were printed on A4 size papers and scanned at 300 dpi.

3   Preprocessing

The first step in pre-processing was to normalize the images to a suitable size. All the digit-images were normalized to 24 X 24 pixels using Bicubic resizing. After normalizing the input, the image was binarised using the Otsu Algorithm [12]. However for noisy images Niblac Algorithm [13] could be used.

While writing it sometimes occurs that a hole is not completed as in an '8' (Bangla 'Four') or '0' or '9' (Bangla 'Seven'). Some examples of handwritten numerals with gaps are provided below

$\mathcal{O}$ (zero) $\mathcal{C}$ (five) $\mathcal{q}$ (seven)

After binarisation, a morphological bridging operation was carried out to connect previously unconnected pixels. Black pixels which were separated by at most two pixel positions were bridged. For example certain regions having the form

0 1 1		0 1 1
0 1 1	were converted to	0 0 0
1 1 0		1 1 0

Another irregularity that is noticeable in handwritten numeral is that certain strokes are not ended at points where they are intended to. They continue as spurs. As is seen in the following examples

Pixels in a certain region of the form

1 1 1 1		1 1 1 1
1 1 0 1	was converted to	1 1 1 1
0 0 1 1		0 0 1 1
0 0 1 1		0 0 1 1.

The morphological bridging and spur removing operation had been implemented in the Matlab Image Processing Toolbox function reference. Help was taken of these built in functions to perform these operations.

4   Feature Selection

A list of structural features like the position of holes, intersection points, terminal points etc. were used to identify a numeral. A major work in Bangla handwritten numeral recognition has already been done [6], where Bangla handwritten numerals were classified by certain topological and structural features like loops, junctions, positions of terminal nodes, etc. and then recognized by Multi Layer Perceptron networks. By using such a scheme, correct recognition rate of 93.26% was achieved.

4.1   Hole Position

Any enclosed area will be considered as a hole. There are certain numerals that have very distinct hole positions, as in the numerals below:

$\bigcirc$ (Zero) ∂ (One) $\mathcal{8}$ (Four) $\mathcal{G}$(Five) $\mathcal{7}$ (Seven) $\mathcal{6}$ (Eight).

Zero and Five have holes that encompass the entire image. One has a whole that is either in the bottom left corner or in the bottom half of the figure, and similar is the case for Eight. For Seven, the position of hole is on the upper half of the image.

There can be seven positions in the image where there can be a hole. A hole can encompass the entire image, or it can be in the top or bottom half, or it can be in any of the four quadrants (upper-right, upper-left, bottom-left, or bottom-right).

4.2 Position of Terminating and Intersecting Points

The terminating and intersecting points also play an important part in identification of Bangla numerals. It can be seen from the figures above that Zero $\bigcirc$ has no terminating or intersecting point. One $\mathcal{S}$ has 1 terminating point in the upper left corner and two terminating points in the bottom half. Five $\mathcal{G}$ has three terminating points along the right side. Similarly the other numerals (not shown here) can be seen to have distinct terminating points.

4.3 Curves

Each digit can be considered to be composed of a number of curves, having specific starting - ending points and radius of curvature. The curves were extracted from the image based on the curve detection technique proposed by He and Hung [13]. The start and end points of the detected curves, and their radius of curvature were extracted and provided as inputs to the neural network. The start points of the curves

detected in Two is  .

4.4 Block-Wise Proportion

The entire image was divided into 16 blocks of 4 rows and 4 columns (as shown in Figure 3). The proportion of black pixels (pixels pertaining to the foreground, i.e. the digit) falling in each of the blocks were calculated. Values of these proportions were provided as inputs to the neural network.

4.5 Block-Wise Corner Position

Position of intersecting and terminating points were found earlier. In the previous sub section it was discussed how the entire image was divided into 16 blocks. Number of terminating and intersecting points falling in each block was calculated. And these numbers were also provided as inputs to the neural network.

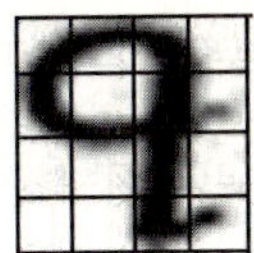

Fig. 3. Bangla numeral Seven divided in blocks

5   Neural Network Implementation

This section will be containing four sub-sections. In the first sub-section the inputs to the neural network will be discussed; in the second, the discussion will be on the neural network architecture, on the third section the training algorithm will be discussed in brief and finally the logic for deciding the output from the neural network will be discussed in the fourth sub-section.

5.1   Network Architecture

The neural network consists of One Input Layer, Two intermediate Hidden Layers and One Output layer (marked in the figure).

There is no theoretical development based on which, the optimal number of hidden layers and the number of neurons in the hidden layer can be determined. The number of hidden layers required for a particular problem is determined experimentally. It is best to start the training process with a single hidden layer and if the network does not perform suitably, extra hidden layers are added [15]. With two hidden layers we obtained the least classification error. Similar results were also observed in [16, 17]. A plausible reason behind this has been provided by Chester [18]. He explained that the problem with a single hidden layer was that the neurons interacted with each other globally, making it difficult to improve an approximation at one point without worsening it elsewhere. With two hidden layers, the effects of the neurons are isolated and the approximations in different regions can be adjusted independently of each other, much as is done in the Finite Element Method for solving partial differential equations or the spline technique for fitting curves.

5.2   Training Algorithm

As discussed before the neural network architecture used here consists of two hidden layers. In such a case the Neural Network remains ill-conditioned initially [21].In

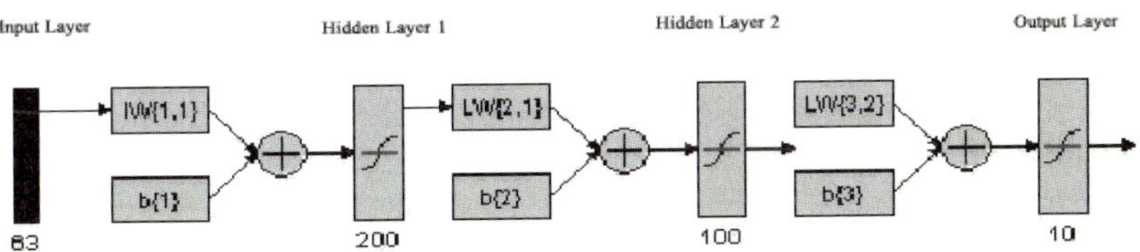

Fig. 4. Neural Network Architecture

such a case algorithms that use only first-order information, such as steepest descent and standard Backpropagation, are notoriously slow for ill-conditioned problems. In such a case, the more use an algorithm makes use of second-order information, the better it will behave under ill-conditioning. Algorithms like steepest descent, conjugate gradients, quasi-Newton, Gauss-Newton and Newton-Raphson, makes use of second order information. Of these, the conjugate gradient algorithms were the best in terms of speed of operation and memory utilization. We used the Scaled Conjugate Gradient [22] training algorithm which converged in the least number of iterations.

5.3 Output

When the neural network is used for testing a particular digit, a transfer function obtains the output vector from the output layer of the neural network. All the elements from the output vector are checked and the element with the highest value is decided to be the winner. However, before declaring upon the output, it is checked if the winner is greater than a pre-determined threshold. If the value of the winner falls below this threshold the input numeral remains unrecognized. Otherwise, if the winner crosses this threshold, the winner is declared to be the recognized character.

	0	1	2	3	4	5	6	7	8	9
0	**97.31**	0.45	0.3	0.23	0.18	0.57	0.19	0.21	0.37	0.19
1	0.42	**97.24**	0.16	0.33	0.4	0.18	0.23	0.16	0.37	0.51
2	0.51	0.47	**96.93**	0.35	0.23	0.35	0.14	0.38	0.36	0.28
3	0.28	0.3	0.16	**97.37**	0.22	0.44	0.31	0.39	0.27	0.26
4	0.56	0.4	0.26	0.3	**97.27**	0.27	0.33	0.24	0.12	0.25
5	0.42	0.51	0.32	0.21	0.17	**97.25**	0.38	0.14	0.27	0.33
6	0.21	0.33	0.23	0.3	0.32	0.67	**96.96**	0.3	0.52	0.16
7	0.25	0.27	0.24	0.31	0.45	0.16	0.22	**97.42**	0.37	0.31
8	0.33	0.29	0.22	0.21	0.44	0.24	0.25	0.31	**97.34**	0.37
9	0.33	0.71	0.35	0.24	0.19	0.32	0.34	0.48	0.13	**96.91**

Fig. 5. Confusion Matrix

6 Results

Our entire dataset consisted of 10,500 samples of handwritten numerals and 2300 samples of printed numerals belonging to 23 different fonts, each of 10 different font-sizes. In each of the experiments, the training set comprised of an even mix of printed and handwritten numerals, so that the network did not become biased towards handwritten numerals. But as the data set corresponding to printed numerals is smaller than the handwritten one, the training set comprised of duplicate instances of printed numerals.

The network was trained with 8,000 samples of Handwritten numerals and 16 different fonts. 500 samples of handwritten numerals and three fonts were for validating the training of the neural network, so that the network did not overfit the training data. The network was tested with 2000 samples of handwritten numerals and

4 different fonts. The combined accuracy of the network classifier was 97.2%. The confusion matrix is provided below.

It can be seen that One has been repeatedly misidentified as Nine, also Nine had been mis-identified as one. The reason behind this is, handwritten Nine of one person can be mistakenly identified as One of somebody else's. For example ⟋ (nine) of one person is much like ⟋ (one) of another person. Similar confusion may arise between ⟳ (three) and ⟲ (zero) as also between ⟨ (five) and ⟲ (zero).

7 Conclusion

The aim of this work was to identify handwritten and printed Bangla numerals. We have achieved a maximum accuracy of 95.7% for handwritten numerals and an accuracy of 99.2% for identifying printed numerals. To the best of our knowledge such a block based approach was not used for identification of Bangla numerals. The approach is new, and the recognition accuracy may be increased by extracting more features from each of the blocks.

References

1. R. Plamondon and S. N. Srihari, "On-line and off-line handwritten character recognition: A comprehensive survey", IEEE Transactions on Pattern Analysis and Machine Intelligence, Vol. 22, pp 62-84, 2000.
2. Y. Le Cun, B. Boser, J. S. Denker, R. E. Howard, W. Habbard, L. D. Jackel and D. Henderson, "Handwritten digit recognition with a back-propagation network", Advances in neural information processing systems, 1990, p. – 396 to 404.
3. U. Pal and B.B. Chaudhuri, "Automatic Recognition of Unconstrained Off-Line Bangla Handwritten Numerals", Advances in Multimodal Interfaces - ICMI 2000: Third International Conference, Beijing, China, October 2000. Proceedings, p. 371
4. U. Bhattacharya, B.B Chaudhuri, "A majority voting scheme for multiresolution recognition of handprinted numerals", International Conference on Document Analysis and Recognition, 2003. Vol. 1, p. – 16
5. U. Bhattacharya, T. K. Das, A. Datta, S. K. Parui, B. B. Chaudhuri, N. R. Pal, S. Pal, "A hybrid scheme for handprinted numeral recognition based on a self-organizing network and MLP classifiers", International Journal for Pattern Recognition and Artificial Intelligence, 16(7), 2002, 845-864.
6. "On the choice of training set, architecture and combination rule of multiple MLP classifiers for multiresolution recognition of handwritten characters", Frontiers in Handwriting Recognition, 2004. IWFHR-9 2004. p. - 419- 424.
7. S. Knerr, L. Personnaz and G Dreyfus, "Handwritten digit recognition by neural networks with single-layer training", IEEE Transactions on Neural Networks, Nov 1992, Vol. 3, Issue 6, p. – 962 to 968.
8. Y. Lee, "Handwritten digit recognition using K nearest-neighbor, radial-basis function, and backpropagation neural networks", 1991, Neural Computation, Vol. 3, Issue 3, p. – 440.
9. S. Lee, "Off-Line Recognition of Totally Unconstrained Handwritten Numerals Using Multilayer Cluster Neural Network", IEEE Transactions on Pattern Analysis and machine Intelligence, June 1996 (Vol. 18, No. 6) pp. 648-652.

10. R. Bajaj, L. Dey and S. Chaudhury, "Devnagari numeral recognition by combining decision of multiple connectionist classifiers", Sadhana Vol. 27, Part 1, February 2002, pp. 59–72.

11. S. Basu, C. Chaudhuri., M. Kundu, M. Nasipuri, D. K. Basu, N. R. Pal, N. Kasabov, R.L Mudi, S. Pal and S.K. Parui "A two-pass approach to pattern classification", ICONIP 2003, vol. 3316, pp. 781-786

12. N. Otsu, "A Threshold Selection Method from Gray-Level Histograms," IEEE Transactions on Systems, Man, and Cybernetics, vol. 9, no. 1, pp. 62-66, 1979.

13. W. Niblack, "An Introduction to Digital Image Processing", pp. 115-116, Prentice Hall, 1986.

14. X.C He, and N.H.C Yung, "Curvature scale space corner detector with adaptive threshold and dynamic region of support", Proceedings of the 17th International Conference on Pattern Recognition, 2004. ICPR 2004. Volume 2, 23-26 Aug. 2004 Page(s):791 - 794Y. Y. Tang, H. D. Cheng, & C. Y. Suen, "Transformation-Ring-Projection (TRP) Algorithm and Its VLSI Implementation", Character & Handwriting Recognition: Expanding Frontiers, 1991, World Scientific Publishing Co. Pte. Ltd., Singapore.

15. K. Hornik, M. Stinchombe and H. White, "Neural Networks", 2, 359, 1990.

16. J. Heaton, "Introduction to Neural Networks with Java", Chapter 5, Heaton Research Inc.

17. http://www.willamette.edu/~gorr/classes/cs449/multilayer.html

18. D. L. Chester "Why Two Hidden Layers are Better than One", *IJCNN-90-WASH-DC*, Lawrence Erlbaum, 1990, volume 1, pp265-268.

19. D. Ostafe, "Neural Network Hidden Layer Number Determination Using Pattern Recognition Techniques". 2nd Romanian-Hungarian Joint Symposium on Applied Computational Intelligence, SACI 2005.

20. B. Verma, "A Contour Code Feature Based Segmentation For Handwriting Recognition", Proceedings of the Seventh International Conference on Document Analysis and Recognition (ICDAR 2003)

21. S. Saarinen, R. Bramley, and G. Cybenko, "Ill-conditioning in neural network training problems," Siam J. of Scientific Computing, 14, 693-714, 1993.

22. Moller, M. F., "A scaled conjugate gradient algorithm for fast supervised learning," Neural Networks, vol. 6, pp. 525-533, 1993

Recognition of Off-Line Handwritten Devnagari Characters Using Quadratic Classifier

N. Sharma, U. Pal*, F. Kimura**, and S. Pal

Computer Vision and Pattern Recognition Unit, Indian Statistical Institute
203 B T Road, Kolkata-700108, India
*umapada@isical.ac.in
** Graduate School of Engineering, Mie University 1577 Kurimamachiya-cho
TSU, Mie 514-8507, Japan

Abstract. Recognition of handwritten characters is a challenging task because of the variability involved in the writing styles of different individuals. In this paper we propose a quadratic classifier based scheme for the recognition of off-line Devnagari handwritten characters. The features used in the classifier are obtained from the directional chain code information of the contour points of the characters. The bounding box of a character is segmented into blocks and the chain code histogram is computed in each of the blocks. Based on the chain code histogram, here we have used 64 dimensional features for recognition. These chain code features are fed to the quadratic classifier for recognition. From the proposed scheme we obtained 98.86% and 80.36% recognition accuracy on Devnagari numerals and characters, respectively. We used five-fold cross-validation technique for result computation.

1 Introduction

Recognition of handwritten characters has been a popular research area for many years because of its various application potentials. Some of its potential application areas are Postal Automation, Bank cheque processing, automatic data entry, etc. There are many pieces of work towards handwritten recognition of Roman, Japanese, Chinese and Arabic scripts, and various approaches have been proposed by the researchers towards handwritten character recognition [1, 6-11]. Although there are many script and languages in India but not much research is done for the recognition of handwritten Indian characters. In this paper, we propose a system towards the recognition of unconstrained off-line handwritten Devnagari characters.

Many pieces of work have been done towards the recognition of Indian printed characters and at present OCR systems are commercially available for some of the printed Indian scripts [3]. Although several pieces of research work exist on Indian printed characters but only a few attempts have been made towards the recognition of Indian off-line handwritten characters [2]. Among off-line handwritten work of

P. Kalra and S. Peleg (Eds.): ICVGIP 2006, LNCS 4338, pp. 805 – 816, 2006.

Indian scripts, maximum research has been done for Bangla. Systems are available for unconstrained off-line Bangla isolated numerals and characters. Also some systems have been developed for unconstrained Bangla handwritten word recognition for Indian postal recognition [19, 21]. Although first research report on handwritten Devnagari characters was published in 1977 [17] but not much research work is done after that. At present researchers have started to work on handwritten Devnagari characters and few research reports are published recently. Hanmandlu and Murthy [13] proposed a Fuzzy model based recognition of handwritten Hindi numerals and they obtained 92.67% accuracy. Ramteke et al [14] proposed an isolated Marathi handwritten numeral scheme based on invariant moments. They employed a Gaussian Distribution Function for classification and obtained only 87% accuracy. Bajaj et al [15] employed three different kinds of features namely, density features, moment features and descriptive component features for classification of Devnagari Numerals. They proposed a multi-classifier connectionist architecture for increasing the recognition reliability and they obtained 89.6% accuracy. Kumar and Singh [16] proposed a Zernike moment feature based approach for Devnagari handwritten character recognition. They used an artificial neural network for classification. Sethi and Chatterjee [17] proposed a decision tree based approach for recognition of constrained hand printed Devnagari characters using primitive features. Bhattacharaya et al [18] proposed a Multi-Layer Perceptron (MLP) neural network based classification approach for the recognition of Devnagari handwritten numerals and obtained 91.28% results. They considered a multi-resolution features based on wavelet transform in their proposed system.

In this paper, we propose a scheme for unconstrained off-line handwritten Devnagari numeral and character recognition using quadratic classifier, based on the feature obtained from chain code histogram. Here the bounding box of a character is segmented into blocks and chain code histogram is computed in each blocks. This chain code features are then fed to the classifier for recognition.

Rest of the paper is organized as follows. In Section 2 we discuss about Devnagari language, its character set and the preprocessing of the data used for the proposed scheme. Feature extraction procedure is presented in Section 3. Section 4 details the classifier used for the recognition. The experimental results are discussed in Section 5. Conclusion on the paper is given in Section 6.

2 Devnagari Language and Data Collection

Devnagari is the most popular script in India and the most popular Indian language Hindi is written in Devnagari script. Nepali, Sanskrit and Marathi are also written in Devnagari script. Moreover, Hindi is the national language of India and Hindi is the third most popular language in the world [2]. Thus, the work on Devnagari script is very useful for the country.

The alphabet of the modern Devnagari script consists of 14 vowels and 37 consonants. These characters may be called *basic characters*. The basic characters of Devnagari script are shown in Fig.1. Writing style in Devnagari script is from left to right. The concept of upper/lower case is absent in Devnagari script. In Devnagari script a vowel following a consonant takes a modified shape. Depending on the vowel, its modified shape is placed at the left, right (or both) or bottom of the consonant. These modified shapes are called *modified characters*. A consonant or vowel following a consonant sometimes takes a compound orthographic shape, which we call as *compound character*. Compound characters can be combinations of two consonants as well as a consonant and a vowel. Compounding of three or four characters also exists in these two scripts. There are about 280 compound characters in Devnagari [2].

A Devnagari text line can be partitioned into three zones. The *upper-zone* denotes the portion above the head-line, the *middle zone* covers the portion between head-line and base-line, the *lower-zone* is the portion below base-line.

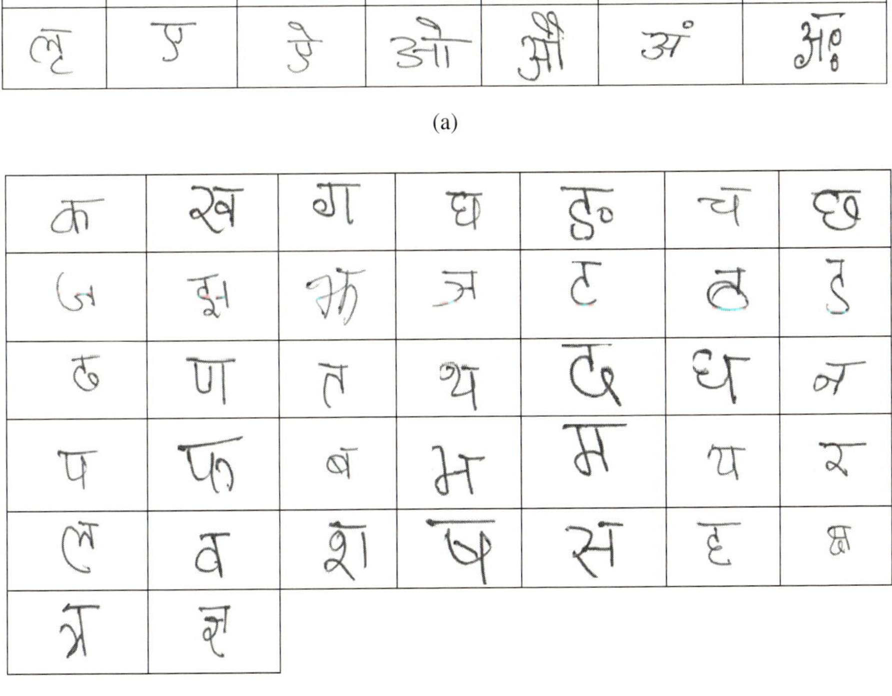

Fig. 1. Samples of handwritten Devnagari basic characters (a) Vowels, (b) Consonants

Because of the writing styles of different individuals, characters can have different shapes. As a result recognition of unconstrained handwritten characters becomes a difficult task. To get an idea about such shape difference between printed and handwritten text, printed Devnagari numerals and their coresponding handwritten samples are shown in Table 1.

Table 1. Examples of printed and handwritten Devnagari numerals

Numeral	Printed Devnagari numeral	Handwritten Devnagari numeral				
0	०	०	०	०	०	०
1	१	१	१	१	१	१
2	२	२	२	२	२	२
3	३	३	३	३	३	३
4	४	४	४	४	४	४
5	५	५	५	५	५	५
6	६	६	६	६	६	६
7	७	७	७	७	७	७
8	८	८	८	८	८	८
9	९	९	९	९	९	९

In this work we are concerned with the recognition of Devnagari numerals and basic characters only and data used in the present work has been collected from different individuals. For numeral recognition we considered the data discussed in the paper [20]. For the experiment of Devnagari character recognition we collected 11270 samples of vowels and consonants (at least 210 samples of each vowels and consonants). A flat bed scanner was used for digitization. Digitized images are in gray tone with 300 dpi and stored as TIF format. We have used a histogram based global binarizing algorithm to convert them to two-tone (0 and 1) images (Here '1'represents object point and '0'represents background point). For removing noises from the images, we have used a method discussed in [3].

3   Feature Extraction

Histograms of direction chain code of the contour points of the characters are used as feature for recognition [12]. Here we use 64 dimensional features for our recognition purpose. The feature extraction techniques are described below.

3.1   64 Dimensional Feature Extraction

Given a two-tone image, we first find the contour points of the image by the following algorithm. For all object points in the image, consider a 3 x 3 window surrounded to the object point. If any one of the four neighboring points (as shown in Fig.2(a)) is a background point then this object point (P) is considered as contour point. Otherwise it is a non-contour point.

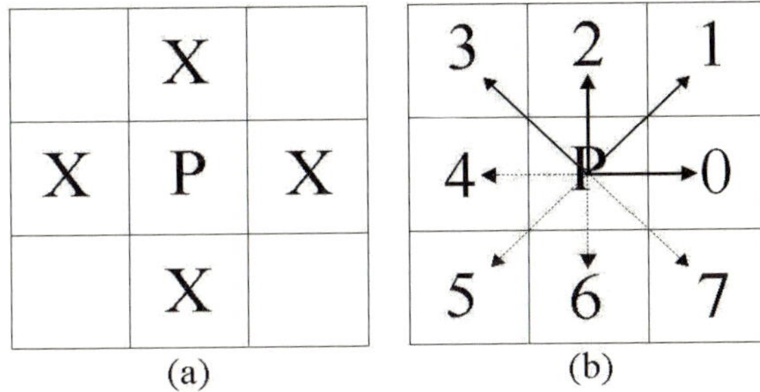

(a)   (b)

Fig. 2. (a) For a point P and its four neighbors are shown by 'X', (b) For a point P the direction codes for its eight neighboring points are shown

The bounding box (minimum rectangle containing the character shown in Fig. 3(b)) of an input character is then divided into 7 x 7 blocks (as shown in Fig.3(c)). In each of these blocks, the direction chain code for each contour point is noted and the frequency of the direction codes is computed. Here we use chain code of four directions only [directions 0 (horizontal), 1 (45 degree slanted), 2(vertical) and 3 (135 degree slanted)]. See Fig.2(b) for illustration of four chain code directions. We assume chain code of direction 0 and 4, 1 and 5, 2 and 6, 3 and 7, are same. Thus, in each block we get an array of four integer values representing the frequencies and those frequency values are used as feature. Histogram of the values of these four direction codes in each block of a Devnagari numeral is shown in Fig.3(e) . Thus, for 7 x 7 blocks we get 7 x 7 x 4= 196 features. To reduce the feature dimension, after the histogram calculation in 7 x 7 blocks, the blocks are down sampled with a Gaussian filter into 4x4 blocks. As a result we have 4 x 4 x 4 = 64 features for recognition. Histogram of all the direction obtained after down sampling is shown in Fig.3(f). Example of feature extraction process on a Devnagari character is shown in Fig.4. To normalize the features we compute maximum value of the histograms from all the blocks. We divide each of the above features by this maximum value to get the feature values between 0 and 1.

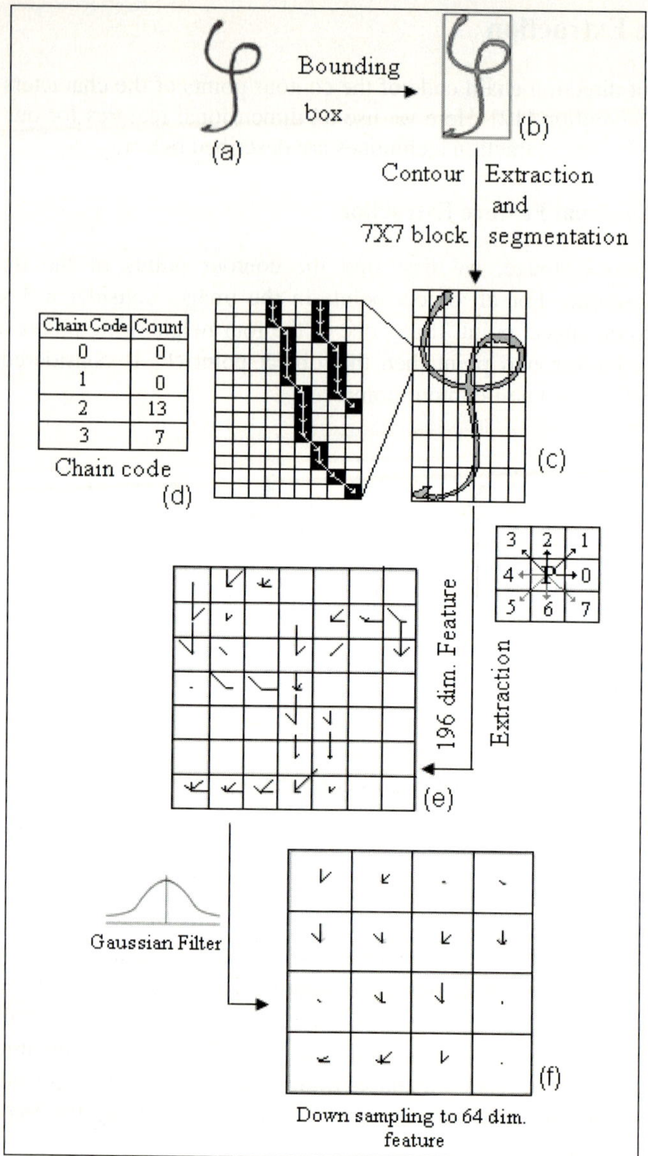

Fig. 3. Pictorial representation of the 64 dimensional feature extraction process for a sample Devnagari numeral. (a) Two tone image of a Devnagari numeral 'five', (b) Bounding box of the numeral. (c) Contour of the numeral shown in black color and the bounding box is segmented into 7 X 7 blocks. (d) Chain code of a block shown in zoomed version. (e) 196 dimensional Chain code features of each block. (f) 64 dimensional features obtained after down sampling using a Gaussian filter.

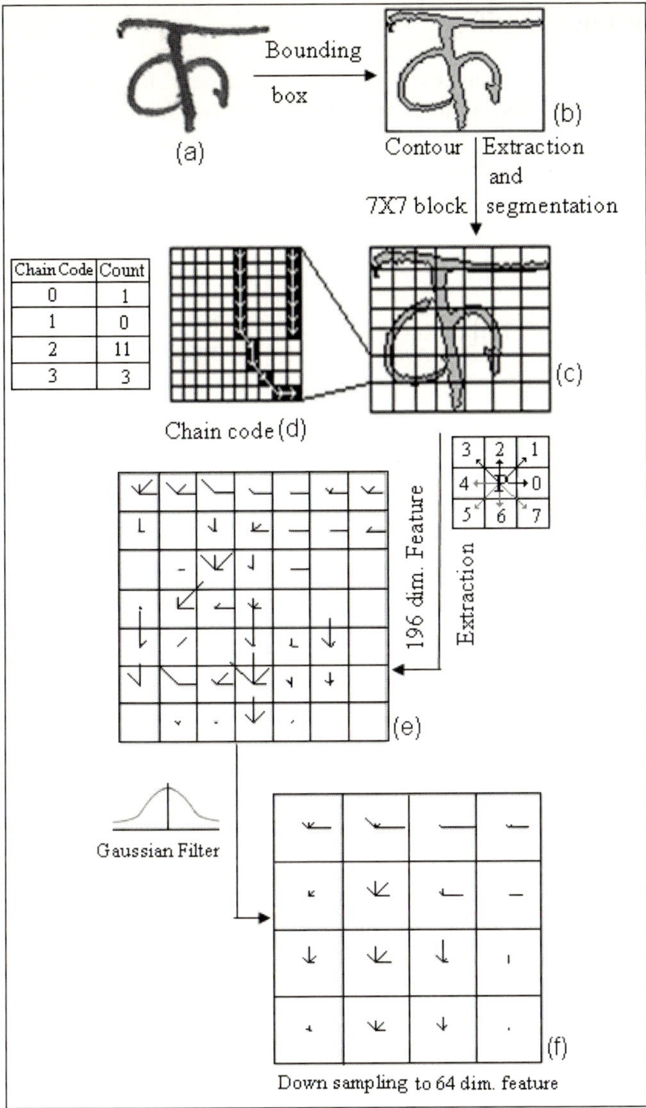

Fig. 4. Pictorial representation of the 64 dimensional feature extraction process for a sample Devnagari character. (a) Two tone image of a Devnagari character, (b) Bounding box of the character. (c) Contour of the character shown in black color and the bounding box is segmented into 7 X 7 blocks. (d) Chain code of a block shown in zoomed version. (e) 196 dimensional Chain code features of each block. (f) 64 dimensional features obtained after down sampling using a Gaussian filter.

4 Recognition Classifier

Many classifiers have been used by the researchers for handwritten character recognition. Here we used a quadratic classifier for our recognition purpose because we noted from the work [12] that this classifier gives better results than other classifiers like Bayes classifier, subspace method etc. Descriptions of the quadratic classifier used for our recognition purpose are given below.

A Modified Quadratic Discriminant function (MQDF) is used by the quadratic classifier [12] which is defined by,

$$g(X) = (N + N_0 - n - 1)\ln\left[1 + \frac{1}{N_o\sigma^2}\left[\| X - M \|^2 - \sum_{i=1}^{k}\frac{\lambda_i}{\lambda_i + \frac{N_o}{N}\sigma^2}\{\Phi_i^T(X - M)\}^2\right]\right]$$

$$+ \sum_{i=1}^{k}\ln(\lambda_i + \frac{N_o}{N}\sigma^2)$$

Where, X is the feature vector of an input character, M is a mean vector of samples, Φ_i^T is the ith eigen vector of the sample covariance matrix, λ_i is the ith eigen value of the sample covariance matrix, n is the feature size, σ^2 is the average variance of all classes, N is the average sample of all classes, and N_0 is selected experimentally and we consider $N_0 = 3N/7$ for 64 dimensional feature. We do not use all eigen values and their respective eigen vectors for the classification. We sort the eigen values in descending order and take first 20 eigen values and their respective eigen vectors for classification. Rejection in the system is done if for a character the difference of 1st and 2nd value of g(X) is smaller than a threshold.

5 Result and Discussion

Data used for the present work was collected from different individuals. We digitized 11270 samples of Devnagari characters (vowels as well as consonants) for the experiment of the proposed work. For the experiment of Devnagari numerals we consider the data discussed in [20] and this dataset contains 22,556 handwritten samples.

From experiments we noted that the overall recognition accuracy of the proposed scheme for numerals is 98.86% and for characters is 80.36% with zero percent rejection. 99.80% accuracy was obtained if we consider first two top choices of the recognition results for numerals and 90.56% accuracy was obtained considering the first two top choices for characters. The detail recognition results with different top choices are given in Table 2. Here we have used five-fold cross validation scheme for recognition result calculation. Here database is divided into 5 subsets and testing is done on each subset using rest of the subsets for learning. The recognition rates for all the subsets are averaged to get accuracy.

From the experiment we noticed that for Devnagari numeral recognition, we can achieve 99.73% accuracy when we reject 4.25% of the numeral samples. Also from the experiment we noticed that for Devnagari character recognition we obtained 86.41% accuracy when we reject 7% samples.

We computed accuracy of the individual Devnagari numerals and their accuracy is given in Table 3. From the experiment we noted the maximum accuracy of 99.81% was achieved for the Devnagari numeral O (zero). The next highest accuracy of about 99.66% was achieved for the numeral ४ (four). We also noted that the lowest accuracy of 97.15% was achieved for numeral ३ (three).

The accuracy of individual Devnagari characters was also computed. Maximum accuracy of 90.48% was achieved for the Devnagari characters ई and this is because of its unique shape. The next highest accuracy of about 90.13% was achieved for the character ऑ.

We also noticed the main confusing pairs of Devnagari characters and their error rates are shown in Table 4. The characters ध and घ confused the most, having an error rate of 0.62%. The next most confusing pair is य and प, having an error of about 0.35%. From the experiments we noticed that mainly similar shaped characters are confused by the system at higher rate.

Table 2. Recognition results for Devnagari numerals and characters based on different choices from top (without any rejection)

Top choices	Accuracy for Numerals	Accuracy for Characters
1	98.86%	80.36%
2	99.80%	90.56%
3	99.92%	94.28%
4	99.96%	96.17%
5	99.98%	97.77%

Table 3. Recognition results of individual numerals

Numeral	Accuracy	Numeral	Accuracy
1	99.49%	2	98.21%
3	97.15%	4	99.66%
5	98.57%	6	98.69%
7	98.79%	8	99.63%
9	98.77%	0	99.81%

Table 4. Main Confusing pairs among Devnagari characters

Class	Classified as	% of error
थ	छ	0.62%
श	य	0.35%
रू	रू	0.34%
भ	भ	0.23%
व	व	0.22%

We compared our results with the existing pieces of work on off-line handwritten Devnagari numerals and characters. To the best of our knowledge, Hanmandlu and Murthy [13] reports the highest recognition accuracy of about 92.67% for numerals. But we have obtained an accuracy of about 98.86%, which is 6.19% better than the results reported by Hanmandlu and Murthy [13]. For Devnagari characters we obtained 80.36% accuracy using 11270 samples of data, but Kumar and Singh [16] reported 80% accuracy and they tested only 200 data samples. The details about the comparison results on Devnagari numerals and characters are given in Table 5 and Table 6, respectively.

Table 5. Comparison results for Devnagari Numerals

Sl. No.	Method proposed by	Accuracy obtained
1.	Hanmandlu and Ramana Murthy [13]	92.67%
2.	Ramteke et al. [14]	87%
3.	Bajaj et al. [15]	89.6%
4.	Bhattacharaya et al.[18]	91.28%
5.	Our proposed method	**98.86%**

Table 6. Comparison results for Devnagari Characters

Sl. No.	Method proposed by	Data size	Accuracy obtained
1.	Kumar and Singh [16]	200	80%
2.	Proposed method	11270	**80.36%**

6 Conclusion

India is a multi-lingual and multi-script country comprising of twelve different scripts. But not much work has been done towards off-line handwriting recognition. In this paper we present a quadratic classifier based system for the recognition of unconstrained off-line Devnagari handwritten characters. Dimension of the feature vector was 64, and the features are obtained based on the directional chain codes of the contour of the character. From the experiment we obtained encouraging results. This work will be helpful for the research towards the recognition of other Indian script characters.

References

1. R. Plamondon and S. N. Srihari, "On-Line and off-line handwritten recognition: A comprehensive survey", IEEE Trans on PAMI, Vol.22, pp.62-84, 2000.
2. U. Pal and B.B. Chaudhuri, "Indian script character recognition: A Survey", Pattern Recognition, Vol. 37, pp. 1887-1899, 2004.
3. B. B. Chaudhuri and U. Pal, "A complete printed Bangla OCR system", Pattern Recognition, vol. 31, pp. 531-549, 1998.
4. K. G. Aparna, A. G. Ramakrishnan: A Complete Tamil Optical Character Recognition System. Proc. in the 5th Intl workshop on Document Analysis and Systems , pp. 53-57, 2002
5. Veena Bansal and R.M.K. Sinha, "Integrating Knowledge Sources in Devanagari Text Recognition", IEEE Transaction on Systems, Man and Cybernetics, Vol. 30, 4, 2000.
6. D. Yu and H. Yan, "Reconstruction of broken handwritten digits based on structural morphological features", Pattern Recognition, Vol.34, No.2, pp.235-254, 2001.
7. J.Cai and Z.Q.Liu, "Integration of structural and statistical information for unconstrained handwritten character recognition", IEEE PAMI, Vol. 21, pp.263-270, 1999.
8. H.Byan and S.W. Lee, "A Survey on pattern recognition application of support vector machines", IJPRAI 17, 459-486, 2003.
9. P. Wunsch and A.F. Laine, "Wavelet Descriptors for Multi resolution Recognition of Hand-printed Digits", Pattern Recognition, Vol.28, pp.56-66, 1995.
10. Z.Chin and H. Yan, "A handwritten character recognition using self-organizing maps and fuzzy rules", Pattern Recognition, Vol.22, pp. 923-937, 2000.
11. K.Kim and S.Y. Bang, "A handwritten character classification using tolerant Rough set", IEEE Trans. on PAMI, Vol.22, pp.923-937, 2000.
12. T. Wakabayashi, S. Tsuruoka, F. Kimura and Y. Miyake, "Increasing the Feature size in handwritten Numeral Recognition to improve accuracy, System and Computers in Japan, Vol.26, No.8, pp.35-44, 1995.
13. M. Hanmandlu and O.V. Ramana Murthy, "Fuzzy Model Based Recognition of Handwritten Hindi Numerals", Intl.Conf. on Cognition and Recognition, pp. 490-496, 2005.
14. R.J. Ramteke, P.D.Borkar, S.C. Mehrotra, "Recognition of Marathi Handwritten Numerals: An Invariant Moments Approach", Intl.Conf. on Cognition and Recognition, pp. 482-489, 2005.

15. Reena Bajaj, Lipika Dey, and S. Chaudhury, "Devnagari numeral recognition by combining decision of multiple connectionist classifiers", Sadhana, Vol.27, part. 1, pp.-59-72, 2002.
16. Satish Kumar and Chandan Singh, "A Study of Zernike Moments and its use in Devnagari Handwritten Character Recognition", Intl.Conf. on Cognition and Recognition, pp. 514-520, 2005.
17. I.K. Sethi and B. Chatterjee, "Machine Recognition of constrained Hand printed Devnagari", Pattern Recognition, Vol. 9, pp. 69-75, 1977.
18. U. Bhattacharya, B. B. Chaudhuri, R. Ghosh and M. Ghosh, "On Recognition of Handwritten Devnagari Numerals", In Proc. of the Workshop on Learning Algorithms for Pattern Recognition (in conjunction with the 18th Australian Joint Conference on Artificial Intelligence), Sydney, pp.1-7, 2005.
19. K. Roy, U. Pal and F. Kimura, "Recognition of Handwritten Bangla Characters", In Proc. 2nd International Conference on Machine Intelligence (ICMI), pp.480-485, 2005.
20. U. Bhattacharya and B. B. Chaudhuri, "Databases for research on recognition of handwritten characters of Indian scripts" In Proc. 8th ICDAR, pp.789-793, 2005.
21. U. Pal, K. Roy and F. Kimura, "A Lexicon Driven Method for Unconstrained Bangla Handwritten Word Recognition", In 10th International Workshop on Frontiers in Handwriting Recognition , 2006 (accepted).

On Recognition of Handwritten Bangla Characters

U. Bhattacharya[1], M. Shridhar[2], and S.K. Parui[1]

[1] Computer Vision and Pattern Recognition Unit,
Indian Statistical Institute, Kolkata, India
{ujjwal, swapan}@isical.ac.in
[2] Department of Electrical and Computer Engineering,
University of Michigan-Dearborn, USA
mals@engin.umd.umich.edu

Abstract. Recently, a few works on recognition of handwritten Bangla characters have been reported in the literature. However, there is scope for further research in this area. In the present article, results of our recent study on recognition of handwritten Bangla basic characters will be reported. This is a 50 class problem since the alphabet of Bangla has 50 basic characters. In this study, features are obtained by computing local chain code histograms of input character shape. Comparative recognition results are obtained between computation of the above feature based on the contour and one-pixel skeletal representations of the input character image. Also, the classification results are obtained after down sampling the histogram feature by applying Gaussian filter in both these cases. Multilayer perceptrons (MLP) trained by backpropagation (BP) algorithm are used as classifiers in the present study. Near exhaustive studies are done for selection of its hidden layer size. An analysis of the misclassified samples shows an interesting error pattern and this has been used for further improvement in the recognition results. Final recognition accuracies on the training and the test sets are respectively 94.65% and 92.14%.

1 Introduction

India is a multilingual country of more than 1 billion population with 18 constitutional languages and 10 different scripts. Bangla is its second most popular script next to Devanagari. It is the script of two other Indian languages, *viz.*, Assamese and Manipuri. On the other hand, Bangla is the official language and script of Bangladesh, a neighbour of India. Thus, handwritten character recognition research for Bangla script has a lot of significance.

Significant research works on optical character recognition (OCR) for printed Indian scripts including Bangla [1] are found in the literature. A survey of Indian script character recognition research can be found in [2]. However, not much research work towards recognition of handwritten characters of Indian scripts is available. The technology of printed OCR cannot unfortunately be extended to

P. Kalra and S. Peleg (Eds.): ICVGIP 2006, LNCS 4338, pp. 817–828, 2006.

recognition of handwritten characters due to the enormous variability in people's handwriting styles. However, if a suitable technology for off-line recognition of handwritten characters of Indian scripts can be developed, automatic processing of hand-filled-in forms can be done in the Indian scenario.

Only a few studies [3,4,5,6] on off-line recognition of handwritten Bangla characters are available in the literature. However, there are several works on off-line recognition of handwritten Bangla numerals which include [7,8,9,10]. Also, there exists research work on recognition of handwritten Devanagari [11], Telugu [12], Tamil [13] and Oriya [14] characters.

Many diverse algorithms/schemes for handwritten character recognition [15,16] exist and each of these has its own merits and demerits. Possibly the most important aspect of a handwriting recognition scheme is the selection of an appropriate feature set which is reasonably invariant with respect to shape variations caused by various writing styles. A large number of feature extraction methods are available in the literature [17].

In the present article, a study on recognition of handwritten Bangla basic characters is presented. This study is based on a large database of real-life handwritten samples. Local chain code histogram features are computed based on both contour and skeletal representations of the input character image. During simulation it has been observed that the chain code histogram feature computed from the character contour provides better recognition results compared to the same corresponding to the character skeleton. This is justified by the fact that contour provides more information about a character shape than its skeleton. Classification results are also obtained after down sampling chain code histogram features in each of the above cases using Gaussian filter. MLP classifiers are used for classification purpose. In each of the above classification attempts, all the fifty classes are considered and not in a single case satisfactory recognition performance is achieved. However, an analysis of the misclassified samples show that most of the misclassifications occur within several subgroups of character classes. So, for each of these subgroups separate classifiers (for fewer classes) are trained and each sample is classified for the second time by a smaller MLP classifier according to the result of initial sub-grouping by the 50 class MLP classifier.

The rest of this article is organized as follows. In Section 2, the database used for training and test of the proposed recognition methods has been described. Recognition methodology is described in Section 3. Some details of our experimental results are provided in Section 4. Section 5 concludes the article.

2   Handwritten Bangla Character Database

All major Indian scripts including Bangla are mixtures of syllabic and alphabetic scripts. They are varied in character and form. Like most of the Indian languages the script of Bangla came from the ancient Indian script, Brahmi. This script runfrom left to right and has no equivalent to capital letters of Latin scripts.

The difficulty in automatic recognition of these handwritten Bangla characters arises from the facts that this is a moderately large symbol set, shapes are usually extremely cursive even when written separately and there exist quite a few groups of almost similar shape characters in their handwritten forms. Basic characters of Bangla alphabet consist of 11 vowels and 40 consonants. However, the shapes of two consonant characters are the same. Thus, there are 50 different shapes in the Bangla basic character set. Shapes of Bangla basic characters are shown in Fig. 1.

Most of the existing off-line recognition studies on handwritten characters of Indian scripts are based on different databases collected either in laboratory environment or from smaller groups of the concerned population. However, it is an accepted fact that any genuine research work in this area primarily needs at least one representative database. In the present work, we have used a moderately large representative database of handwritten Bangla basic characters.

2.1   Data Collection

Samples of the present database were collected by distributing several standard application forms among different groups of population of the state of West Bengal in India. Subjects were asked to fill-up these forms in Bangla. Since data collected through such forms are not evenly distributed among the character classes, another specially designed form consisting of 2-dimensional array of rectangular boxes had been used for data collection purpose. Subjects were requested to write one single character of Bangla alphabet per box. No other restriction was imposed on the writers. The purpose of data collection was not disclosed to them so that they could produce samples reflecting their natural handwriting styles. In approximately 60% cases, the same subject was asked to write on both types of forms on two different occasions using his/her own writing instrument. In case writing instrument was not available with the subject, it was supplied at random from a set of different types of such instruments. All the above forms were printed on papers of different brands and the samples have been collected over a span of more than two years.

2.2   Data Preparation

The above filled-in forms were scanned at 300 d.p.i. resolution using a state-of-the-art HP flatbed scanner. These are stored as grayscale images using 1 byte per pixel. A software was used for extraction of isolated characters from individual boxes. Since such a software is bound to produce some erroneous results, all the TIF files of isolated character images were checked manually through their thumbnail view and manual extraction (using an image editor) was done whenever certain error in automatic extraction was detected.

2.3   Database Statistics

The present database of Bangla handwritten basic characters consists of 20187 isolated basic character images unevenly distributed over different classes. The main reason of this uneven distribution is that a major part of the data was collected using several standard forms in which entries are proper nouns and there are several characters in the Bangla alphabet which are rarely used in proper nouns. However, this problem could only be partially tackled by using the specially designed form described above. The distribution of samples in 50 classes of this database is shown in Fig. 1.

Shape		Shape		Shape		Shape		Shape		Shape	
(A)	500	(R)	260	(NYA)	496	(NA)	500	(SHA)	476	(KHAND)	321
(AA)	497	(KA)	500	(TTA)	320	(PA)	500	(SSA)	500		
(I)	379	(KHA)	302	(TTHA)	268	(PHA)	473	(SA)	500		
(II)	344	(GA)	443	(DDA)	344	(BA)	500	(HA)	430		
(U)	500	(GHA)	500	(DDHA)	500	(BHA)	500	(RRA)	270		
(UU)	364	(NGA)	272	(NNA)	370	(MA)	314	(DHRA)	378		
(E)	343	(CA)	415	(TA)	500	(YA)	326	(YYA)	500		
(AI)	274	(CHA)	358	(THA)	448	(RA)	500	(ANUS)	260		
(O)	378	(JA)	336	(DA)	500	(LA)	500	(VISARG)	320		
(AU)	285	(JHA)	500	(DHA)	329	(BA)	*	(BINDU)	294		

Fig. 1. Number of samples against each basic character shape is shown; within parentheses pronunciations are shown in English; * indicates that this shape occurred before

A small sample set consisting of a few handwritten basic character images from the present database is shown in Fig. 2.

This image database is divided into training and test sets. The training set for Bangla basic characters is composed of 200 samples taken randomly from each of the 50 classes. Thus the total size of the training set for basic characters is 10,000. The remaining 10187 samples form the test set of Bangla basic characters and the minimum number of samples in a class of this test set is 60.

3   Recognition Methodology

3.1   Smoothing and Binarization

The first step of the present recognition scheme is smoothing of the graylevel character image. This is a common preprocessing operation of any character recognition approach for the purpose of removing possible artifacts present in a character image. In the present work, we consider a restricted mean filtering

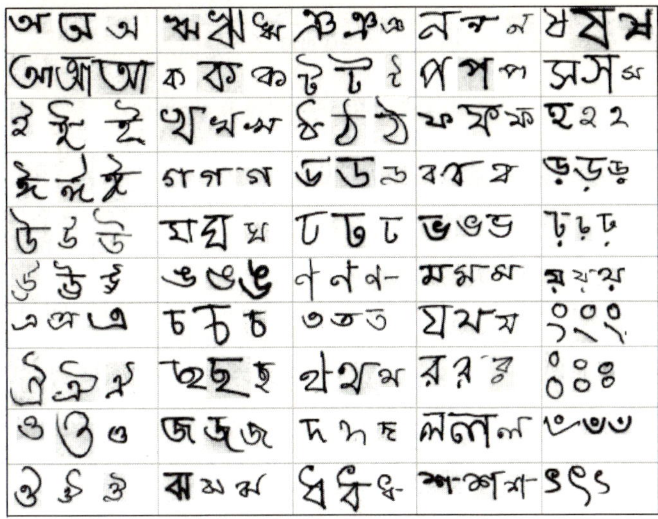

Fig. 2. Samples from the present database of handwritten Bangla characters; three samples in each category are shown

approach for the above purpose. Use of the ordinary mean filter may often connect two disjoint components of a character like ড় causing significant loss in shape information. However, in the restricted mean filter approach, a pixel value is changed by the usual mean provided this does not result in joining two disjoint components existing in the binarized image before smoothing. In Fig. 3, an example of this situation has been shown. After smoothing of the input image it is binarized using Otsu's global thresholding technique [18].

(a) (b)

Fig. 3. (a) Ordinary mean filtering joins two disconnected components; (b) Restricted mean filtering does not join originally disconnected components

3.2   Removal of Extra Long Headline

Many Bangla alphabetic characters in their printed/ideal form have a horizontal line (called matra or headline) at the upper part of the symbol; a few characters have a curve-like extension above the headline and several other characters do not have any part above it. Examples of both these cases are shown in Fig. 4.

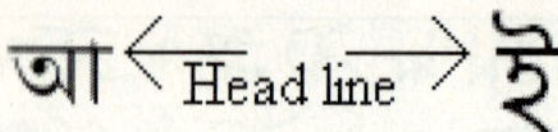

Fig. 4. Headline or matra is shown

Detection of the headline in a handwritten Bangla character is often found crucial whenever it is elongated enough (such as in Fig. 5) increasing the width of the character image substantially. In such situations, normalization of subsequent feature values gets affected. So, before computation of features, headlines are detected using simple heuristics. Example of successful removal of extra long headline according to these heuristics is shown in Fig. 5(a). Also, a situation when our heuristics failed to remove extra long headline is shown in Fig. 5(b).

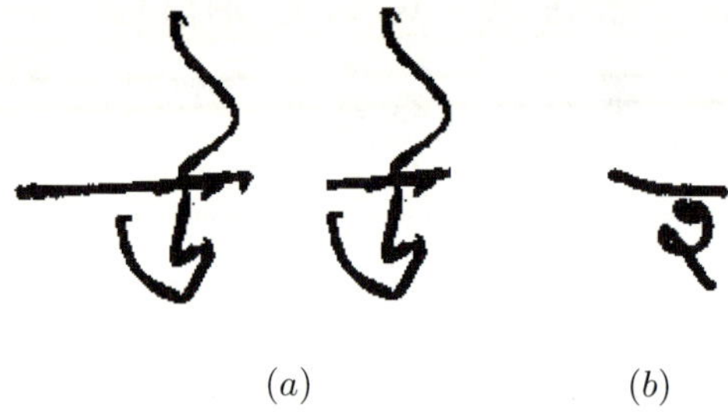

(a) (b)

Fig. 5. (a) Removal of headline or matra is shown; (b) Headline cannot be removed

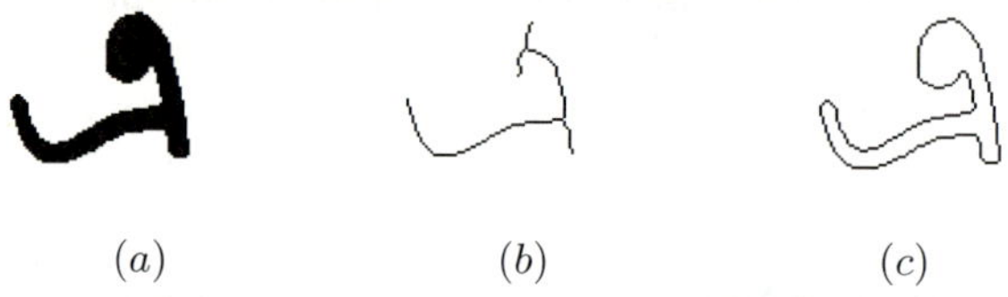

(a) (b) (c)

Fig. 6. Shape representations of character image: (a) An input character image (binarized); (b) skeletal representation of the character image; (c) contour representation of the character image

3.3   Feature Extraction

In the present study chain code histogram features of an input character image have been computed from its both the skeletal (thinning as in [19]) and contour representations. The skeletal and contour representations of a character image are shown in Fig. 6. From this example, it is seen that the skeletal representation are often affected by the presence of hair(s) removal of which is usually difficult.

Chaincode Representation of the shape of an input character image is obtained by using Freeman codes [20] while tracing its skeleton or contour. The scheme of Freeman's chain code and the shape representation following this scheme are shown in Fig. 7.

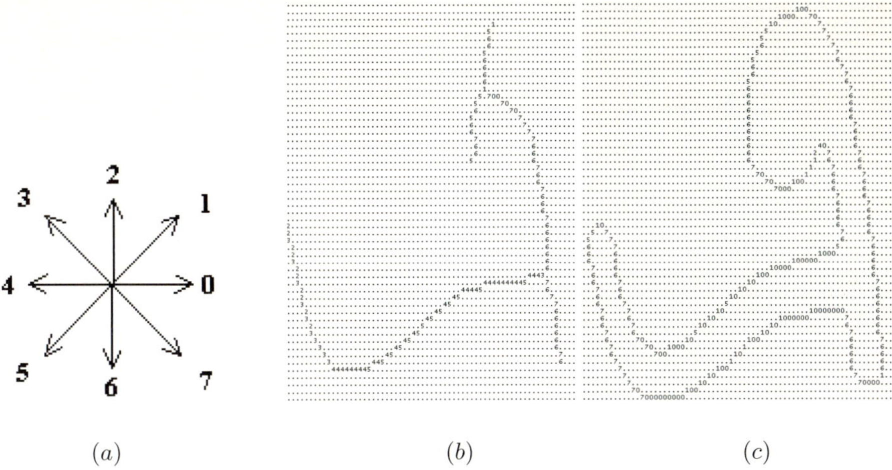

(a)   (b)   (c)

Fig. 7. (*a*) Scheme for chaincodes; (*b*) chain code representation of the shape in Fig. 6(*b*); *c*) chain code representation of the shape in Fig. 6(*c*)

Chaincode Histogram Features [21] are the main features used in the present recognition task and these are obtained as follows. The smallest rectangular frame (bounding box) enclosing the character skeleton or its contour is computed and this is divided into 5 or 7 equal horizontal and vertical strips. If any of the number of rows or columns of the above rectangular frame is not a multiple of 5 or 7, the rightmost vertical or bottommost horizontal strip should have fewer number of rows or columns respectively. Thus, the said frame is divided into 25 or 49 rectangular blocks (Fig. 8) of equal areas save for a few possible extreme blocks with less areas. In each block, a local histogram of the chain codes is calculated. Since the directions along the skeleton or contour should be effectively quantized into one of 4 possible values, *viz.* 0 or 4, 1 or 5, 2 or 6 and 3 or 7, the histogram of each block has four components. The feature vector is composed of these local histograms computed either from the skeletal or contour representation of the input image. Thus, the feature vector has either $4 \times 5 \times 5 = 100$ or $4 \times 7 \times 7 = 196$ components. For size normalization, each component of the feature is divided by the sum of the height and width of the bounding box of the skeleton or contour of input character image depending upon the particular case. In the present study, we also considered feature vector by down sampling the above 7×7 blocks into 4×4 blocks using Gaussian filter.

3.4   Designing Classifier

Multilayer Perceptrons (MLPs) have been chosen as the classifiers of the present study of recognition of handwritten Bangla basic characters. The well known backpropagation (BP) algorithm [22] is used for the training of MLP classifiers. However, in many applications like the present one, the proper training of an MLP largely depends on the choice of the parameter (learning rate and

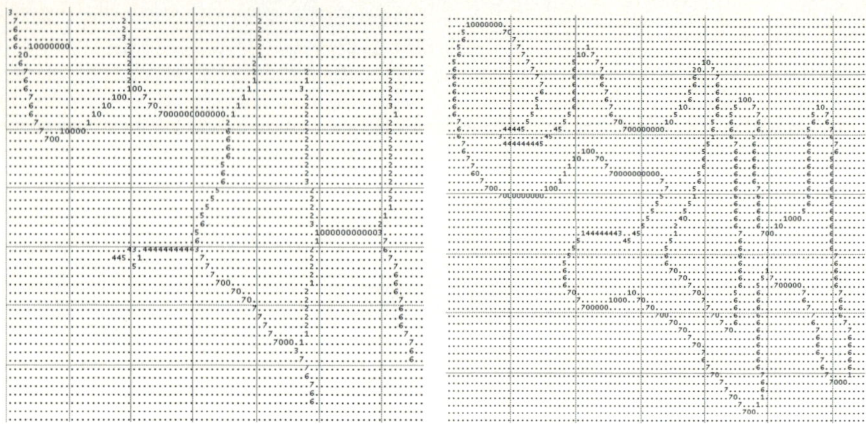

Fig. 8. Division of rectangular frame into 7×7 rectangular zones

momentum factor) values and also it often converges too slowly. There exist a number of modified BP algorithms which take care of these problems of the original BP algorithm. In the present classification task, we considered a modified BP algorithm [23] using self-adaptive learning rate values.

Another issue associated with the use of an MLP classifier is the choice of the size of its hidden layer(s). In fact, it is difficult to get an idea of an optimal size of the hidden layer(s). We experimented with several different choices of hidden layer size in each case and classification results will be reported in the next section corresponding to the best among these choices.

Finally, the strategic selection of the point of termination of the iterative learning of BP algorithm is another important issue. Often a validation set of samples is used to avoid overtraining, and thus a better generalization performance of the network is ensured. Usually, during the initial stages of training of an MLP using BP training algorithm, it gradually decreases the system error [22] on both the training and validation sets. However, after a certain amount of training, this error further decreases on the training set while it starts increasing on the validation set (as shown in Fig.9). The point of time when the error on the validation set increases for at least three consecutive sweeps for the first instance is noted and the weight values before the error starts increasing, are stored.

Since the present database described in the previous section does not exclusively provide any validation set, we have synthetically generated a validation set consisting of 150 samples from each class. These samples have been generated by taking 50 random samples of each class from the training set. These samples are randomly rotated between $-10°$ to $+10°$. Gaussian blurring kernel (standard deviation 2) has been applied on these rotated samples and finally these are binarized using three different threshold values.

An Analysis of Misclassifications after the above first stage of the present recognition scheme, shows that a significant percentage of misclassifications

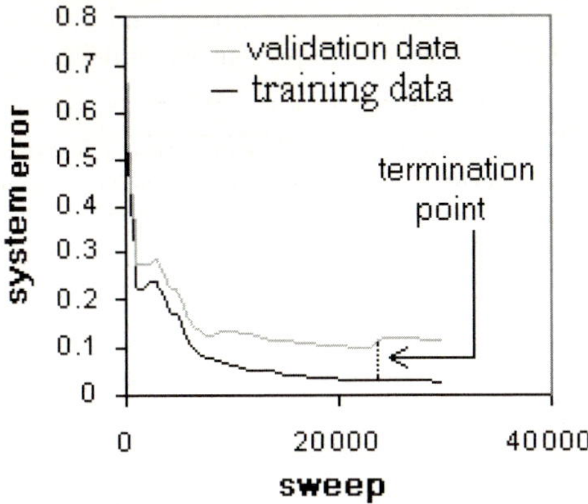

Fig. 9. Increase in error on validation set indicates termination of learning; here, system error is the mean square error between the target and computed output vectors

occurred within several small groups of character classes. In Table 1, these groups of Bangla basic characters corresponding to the recognition results based on chain code histogram features (7×7 blocks down sampled into 4×4 blocks) computed from contour representations of their handwritten shapes are listed. The above situation provided the best recognition performance among our various other choices.

For each of these sub-groups, a distinct MLP classifier with fewer hidden nodes was trained. Samples initially classified as a member of such a group is presented to the relevant smaller MLP architecture for its classification in the second stage. Contour representation based chain code histogram features computed on the 7×7 blocks after their down sampling (with Gaussian filter) to 4×4 blocks had been used in our simulation as the feature vector of the second stage of the present recognition scheme. This second stage of classification, improves the recognition accuracy of the first stage.

In the above context, it is apparent that if an input sample in the first stage of its classification is misclassified in a group other than its own (as shown in Table 1), then the second stage of classification cannot do any help for its correct classification. Only if an input sample is misclassified as a character of its own group, then it gets a second chance of being properly classified by the second stage of classification.

4   Experimental Results

We used six different but related feature sets for the present recognition study of handwritten Bangla basic characters. These are chain code histogram features on 5×5 blocks, 7×7 blocks and histogram on 7×7 blocks down sampled (with Gaussian filter) to 4×4 blocks. Each of the above three sets of features was computed using both skeleton (obtained by thinning) and contour representations of the input character image.

Table 1. Recognition results (best situation) within and outside groups of confusing character shapes after the 1st stage of the present recognition approach

Group No.	Basic characters	Total no. of samples in the Group		Misclassification(%) within group		Misclassification(%) outside the group		Misclassification (%) (Total)	
		Training	Test	Training	Test	Training	Test	Training	Test
1	অ আ ত	600	897	0.45	0.52	0.42	0.41	0.87	0.93
2	ই ঈ	400	323	0.26	0.26	0.28	0.36	0.54	0.62
3	উ ঊ ও ঔ	800	727	0.32	0.50	0.30	0.32	0.62	0.82
4	ক ঝ ধ ফ ব র	1200	1602	0.16	0.31	0.40	0.41	0.56	0.72
5	খ ঘ	400	402	0.70	1.14	0.52	0.76	1.22	1.90
6	গ ন প ল শ	1000	1419	0.25	0.52	0.21	0.33	0.46	0.85
7	ঙ ড ভ ড়	800	586	0.31	0.38	0.47	0.68	0.78	1.06
8	চ ট ঢ	600	693	0.25	0.41	0.33	0.38	0.58	0.79
9	থ য ষ য়	800	974	0.51	0.77	0.51	0.74	1.02	1.51
10	ম স	400	414	0.49	0.85	0.39	0.52	0.88	1.37
11	Others (15)	3000	3688	0.14	0.19	0.22	0.29	0.36	0.48
	Total	10000	11725	3.84	5.85	4.05	5.20	7.89	11.05

Table 2. Comparative recognition performance (1st stage) of six feature sets (chain code histogram based) on the present database

Shape representation	Block size	Feature size	No. of hidden nodes	Recognition Accuracy	
				Training	Test
Skeleton	5 X 5	100	55	70.76	68.24
	7 X 7	196	75	77.22	74.65
	7 X 7 down sampled to 4 X 4	64	40	89.42	86.16
Contour	5 X 5	100	55	75.45	71.86
	7 X 7	196	75	80.86	76.12
	7 X 7 down sampled to 4 X 4	64	40	92.11	88.95

Different MLP classifiers were trained using the above six feature vectors. In each case, the near optimal size of the hidden layer was obtained by extensive simulations and these are shown in Table 2. The best results obtained by the first stage of our classification scheme correspond to the feature vector consisting of histogram values on 7×7 blocks computed from the contour representation of an input character followed by its down sampling to 4×4 blocks.

We simulated a second stage of classification for all the eleven groups of characters as shown in Table 1. After the second stage of classification, the final recognition accuracy corresponding to the best situation of the first stage was 92.14% on the test set and 94.65% on the training set.

5   Conclusions

In the present recognition study, we observed that if chain code histogram features are used for recognition of handwritten basic characters, then acceptable recognition performance may be obtained by computing these features using a division of character contour into 7×7 blocks followed by down sampling the resulting feature components into 4×4 blocks.

Based on the above recognition results, we identified a few groups of characters within which misclassifications are significant. Further classifications within each such group improved the final recognition accuracy.

In future, we plan to study similar recognition performance by using a different feature vector in the second stage for further improvement of the classification accuracy.

References

1. Chaudhuri, B. B., Pal, U.: A Complete Printed Bangla OCR System. Pattern Recognition, Vol. 31. (1998) 531-549
2. Pal, U., Chaudhuri, B. B.: Indian Script Character Recognition: A Survey: Pattern Recognition, Vol. 37 (2004) 1887-1899.
3. Bhattacharya, U., Parui, S. K., Sridhar, M., Kimura, F.: Two-stage Recognition of Handwritten Bangla Alphanumeric Characters using Neural Classifiers, CD Proc. IICAI (2005) 1357-1376
4. Bhowmik, T. K., Bhattacharya, U., Parui, S. K.: Recognition of Bangla Handwritten Characters Using an MLP Classifier Based on Stroke Features, Proc. ICONIP, (2004) 814-819.
5. Rahman, F. R., Rahman, R., Fairhurst, M. C.: Recognition of Handwritten Bengali Characters: A Novel Multistage Approach. Pattern Recognition, Vol. 35 (2002) 997-1006
6. Datta, A., Chaudhury, S.: Bengali alpha-numeric character recognition using curvature features. Pattern Recognition, Vol. 26 (1993) 1757-1770.
7. Bhattacharya, U., Chaudhuri, B.B.: Fusion of Combination Rules of an Ensemble of MLP Classifiers for Improved Recognition Accuracy of Handprinted Bangla Numerals, Proc. of ICDAR, Seoul (2005) 322-326.
8. Bhattacharya, U., Das, T. K., Datta, A., Parui, S. K. Chaudhuri, B. B.: A hybrid scheme for handprinted numeral recognition based on a self-organizing network and MLP classifiers. International Journal for Pattern Recognition and Artificial Intelligence, Vol. 16 (2002) 845-864
9. Bhattacharya, U., Das, T. K., Chaudhuri, B. B.: A cascaded scheme for recognition of handprinted numerals. Proceedings of the third Indian Conference on Computer Vision, Graphics and Image Processing, Ahmedabad, India (2002) 137 - 142
10. Pal, U., Chaudhuri, B. B.: Automatic Recognition of unconstrained off-line Bangla hand-written numerals, Advances in Multimodal Interfaces, Springer Verlag Lecture Notes on Computer Science (LNCS-1948), Eds. T. Tan, Y. Shi and W. Gao. (2000) 371-378.

11. Ramakrishnan, K. R., Srinivasan, S. H., Bhagavathy, S. The independent components of characters are 'Strokes', Proc. of the 5th ICDAR (1999) 414-417.
12. Sukhaswami, M. B., Seetharamulu, P., Pujari, A. K.: Recognition of Telugu characters using neural networks, Int. J. Neural Syst., Vol. 6 (1995) 317-357.
13. Suresh, R. M., Ganesan, L.: Recognition of Printed and Handwritten Tamil Characters Using Fuzzy Approach, Proc. of Sixth ICCIMA'05 (2005) 286-291.
14. Mohanti, S.: Pattern recognition in alphabets of Oriya Language using Kohonen Neural Network, IJPRAI, vol. 12 (1998) 1007-1015.
15. Plamondon, R., Srihari, S. N.: On-Line and Off-Line Handwriting Recognition: A Comprehensive Survey. IEEE Trans. Patt. Anal. and Mach. Intell., Vol. 22 (2000) 63-84
16. Arica, N., Yarman-Vural, F.: An Overview of Character Recognition Focused on Off-line Handwriting. IEEE Transactions on Systems, Man, and Cybernetics, Part C: Applications and Reviews, Vol. 31 (2001) 216 - 233
17. Trier, O. D., Jain, A. K. and Taxt, T.: Feature Extraction Methods for Character Recognition - A Survey. Pattern Recognition, Vol. 29 (1996) 641 - 662
18. Otsu, N.: A Threshold Selection Method from Grey-Level Histograms. IEEE Trans. Systems, Man, and Cybernetics, Vol. 9 (1979) 377-393
19. Datta, A., Parui, S. K.: A robust parallel thinning algorithm for binary images. Pattern Recognition, Vol. 27 (1994) 1181-1192
20. Freeman, H.: Computer processing of Line-drawing Images. ACM Computing Surveys, Vol. 6 (1974) 57-97
21. Kimura, F., Miyake, Y., Sridhar, M.: Handwritten ZIP Code Recognition using Lexicon Free word Recognition Algorithm. Proc. Int. Conf. Document Analysis and Recognition, Vol. II, Motreal, Canada (1995) 906 - 910
22. Rumelhart, D. E., Hinton, G. E., Williams, R. J. Learning internal representations by error propagation. Institute for Cognitive Science Report 8506, San Diego: University of California (1985)
23. Bhattacharya, U., Parui, S. K.: Self-adaptive learning rates in backpropagation algorithm improve its function approximation performance. Proc. of the IEEE International Conference on Neural Networks, Australia (1995) 2784-2788

Evaluation Framework for Video OCR

Padmanabhan Soundararajan[1], Matthew Boonstra[1], Vasant Manohar[1],
Valentina Korzhova[1], Dmitry Goldgof[1], Rangachar Kasturi[1], Shubha Prasad[2],
Harish Raju[2], Rachel Bowers[3], and John Garofolo[3]

[1] Computer Science and Engineering, University of South Florida, Tampa, FL, USA
{psoundar, boonstra, vmanohar, korzhova, r1k, goldgof}@cse.usf.edu
[2] VideoMining Corporation, State College, PA, USA
{hraju, sprasad}@videomining.com
[3] National Institute of Standards and Technology (NIST), Information Technology
Lab - Information Access Division, Speech Group
{john.garofolo, rachel.bowers}@nist.gov

Abstract. In this work, we present a recently developed evaluation
framework for video OCR specifically for English Text but could well
be generalized for other languages as well. Earlier works include the development of an evaluation strategy for text detection and tracking in
video, this work is a natural extension. We sucessfully port and use the
ASR metrics used in the speech community here in the video domain.
Further, we also show results on a small pilot corpus which involves 25
clips. Results obtained are promising and we believe that this is a good
baseline and will encourage future participation in such evaluations.

1 Introduction

The importance of indexing and retrieval technologies in video is poised for a big
leap. There is an ever growing need to do search, based on the text appearing
in video. There are more systems coming out with algorithms specifically recognizing text in video content. Evaluating this is equally important to check the
progress and also give developers feedback on what scenarios they have difficulties in the transcription.

In this work, we present an evaluation framework specifically designed for
evaluating English text recognition in video. While detection and tracking are
necessary, they are not evaluated here. Please refer to [1] for a similar evaluation
scenario involving detection and tracking text in video. The contributors of the
system output were only scored on the recognition performance. For the system
to recognize text mean that they are also able to detect the words spatially in
the video frame and potentially track them across frames.

2 Text Recognition Task

The goal of the text recognition task is to recognize text objects in a video
sequence. This task does not require the system to track these text blocks in a

P. Kalra and S. Peleg (Eds.): ICVGIP 2006, LNCS 4338, pp. 829–836, 2006.

video frame; that part of the task is relegated to the text detection and tracking task. The text will be annotated at the word level according to the annotation guidelines.

The performance of the task is scored at the frame level and be based on how accurate the system recognizes the characters in each word in the frame. The system input and output tags are pre-determined earlier. The text is transcribed at the word level. Text which is annotated as unevaluable by the evaluators and annotators will not be evaluated. To keep things simple in this initial phase, only alpha-numeric characters will be considered, capitalization and word-external punctuation will be filtered from both the system output and reference transcripts. Word-internal punctuations such as hyphens and apostrophes are not filtered. Also, line breaks constitute word boundaries, so wrapped words are treated as separate text tokens. At a higher level, special cases which are not evaluated are:

1. Scrolling text.
2. Dynamic Text
3. Reference Text with Readability Levels Greater Than 1. (See Section 3

For this particular task, annotation tags will include:

1. Video Filename.
2. Object id (unique for the frame).
3. BBox location parameters upper left corner, height, width and rotation attributes for each word.
4. The transcription of each word (each BBox contents).

3   Ground Truth Annotations

For any evaluation, it is important and highly critical to have good quality annotations. There are many ways to annotate a text object and one of the standard method to do so in the OCR community: each text word is bounded by a rectangular box. If the words are occluded then the boxes are approximated and also the specific attributes are marked as occluded so that they can be removed from evaluations if necessary. Additionally as required each individual word box is transcribed so that the error rates can be computed.

There are many free and commercially available tools which can be used for ground truthing videos such as Anvil, VideoAnnex, ViPER [2] and many others. In our case, we used ViPER [1] (Video Performance Evaluation Resource), a ground truth authoring tool developed by the University of Maryland.

Fig 1 shows a sample annotation using ViPER for text in a broadcast news segment. Observe that each word is enclosed in a Bounding box and further, the actual annotations have a unique ID for each box along with their transcriptions.

---

[1] http://viper-toolkit.sourceforge.net

Fig. 1. Sample Annotation Frame showing Word boundaries in a Broadcast News Clip

3.1   Annotation Guidelines

To ensure quality in-terms of these annotations, a well defined set of guidelines are established which are strictly enforced and adhered by each annotator. Further, some of the clips are doubly annotated (two different annotators annotate the same clip) and their performances compared visually as well as being subjected to rigorous software checks. The software checks are too detailed to list here but essentially the philosophy is that all attributes are compared (each object ID has many attributes) and any inconsistencies are ironed out by fine-tuning the annotation guidelines. This process by itself undergoes numerous iterations.

Every new text area is marked with a box when it appears in the video. Moving and scaling the selection box tracks the text as it moves in succeeding frames. This process is done at the line level (with offsets specified for word boundaries) until the text disappears from the frame.

There are two types of text:

- Graphic text is anything overlaid onto the picture. Example, the "CNN" logo in Fig 1.
- Scene text is anything in the background/foreground of what is actually being filmed.

Text readability consists of three levels. Completely unreadable text is signified by READABILITY = 0 and is defined as text in which no character is identifiable. Partially readable text is given READABILITY = 1 and contains characters that are both identifiable and non-identifiable. Clearly readable text is assigned READABILITY = 2 and is used for text in which all letters are identifiable.

The OCCLUSION attribute is set to TRUE when the text is cut off by the bounds of the frame or by another object. The LOGO attribute is set to TRUE when the text region being marked is a company logo imprinted in stylish fonts. Example, the text "CNN" in Fig 1.

Of all the objects of interest in video, text is particularly difficult to be uniformly bound. For this reason, text regions are marked meticulously based on a comprehensive set of rules, namely,

- All text within a selected block (word) must contain the same readability level and type.
- Blocks of text (word) must contain the same size and font. Two allowances are given to this rule. A different font or size may be included in the case of a unique single character and the font color may vary among text in a group.
- The bounding box should be tight to the extent that there is no space between the box and text. The maximum distance from the box to the edge of bounded text may not exceed half the height of the characters when Readability = 2 (clearly readable). When Readability = 0 or 1 the box should be kept tight but does not require separate blocks for partial lines in a paragraph.
- Text boxes may not overlap other text boxes unless the characters themselves are specifically transposed atop one another.

The additional set of attributes described above is used in deciding whether a particular text region should be evaluated. The specific settings for evaluating a text region used in this evaluation are - TEXT-TYPE = Graphic, READABILITY = 2, OCCLUSION = FALSE and LOGO = FALSE.

All other regions are treated as "Don't Care" where the system output is neither penalized for missing nor given credit for detecting. It has to be noted that each of these attributes can be selectively specified to be included in evaluation through the scoring tool that we have developed.

4   Performance Measures

The performance measure for the recognition task is based on insertion, deletion and substitutions errors at the word level. The measure requires a unique one-to-one mapping of ground truth and detected text object using some optimization (see Section 4.1). The mapping will be performed using spatial information and also WER (Word Error Rate) score obtained. Both of these have equal weighting in the internal matching algorithm. By this strategy, we make sure that the system generated and the reference words are closest to each other both in the spatial sense and also in the language sense. The Word Error Rate is defined as:

$$WER(t) = \frac{(Insertion + Substitution + Deletion)}{(Total\ Reference\ Words)} \tag{1}$$

where t indicates the particular frame. The WER(t) is then averaged for the full clip and on the whole dataset to obtain the Word Error Rate (WER).

On each mapped word, we also compute the Character Error Rate (CER). The true CER is then averaged out for the entire set of words in the whole dataset. The WER and CER are both standard error metrics in the Speech Recognition Evaluations [3]. Fig 2 shows an example explaining the impact on WER measure resulting from Insertion, Substitution and Deletion errors.

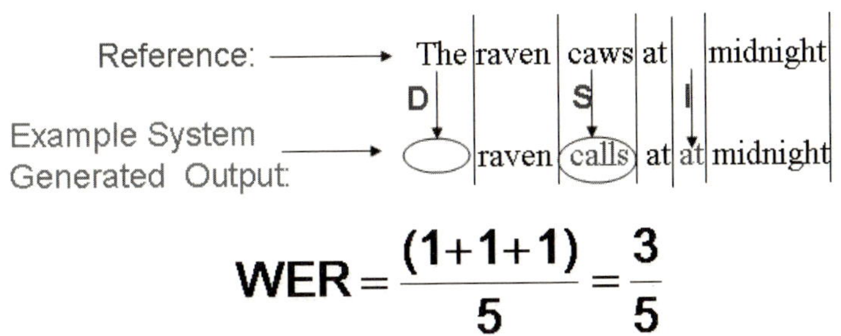

$$WER = \frac{(1+1+1)}{5} = \frac{3}{5}$$

Fig. 2. Example WER Computation on different system generated errors

4.1   Matching Strategies

The maximal scoring is obtained for the *optimal* ground-truth and system output pairs. Potential strategies to solve this assignment problem are the weighted bipartite graph matching [4] and the Hungarian algorithm [5].

	DT_1 DT_2 ... DT_M
GT_1	x
GT_2	x
$\vdots$	
GT_N	x

Assume that there are N ground truth (GT) objects and M detected (DT) objects. A brute force algorithm would have an exponential complexity, a result of having to try out all possible combination of matches (n!). However, this is a standard optimization problem and there are standard techniques to get the optimal match. The matching is generated with the constraint that the sum of the chosen function of the matched pairs is minimized or maximized as the case may be. In usual assignment problems, the number of objects in both cases are equal, i.e, when $N = M$. However, this is not a requirement and unequal number of objects can also be matched.

There are many variations of the basic Hungarian strategy most of which exploit constraints from specific problem domains they deal with. The algorithm has a series of steps which is followed iteratively and has a polynomial time complexity, specifically some implementations have $O(N^3)$. Faster implementations have been known to exist and have the current best bound to be at

$O(N^2 logN + NM)$ [6]. In our case, we take advantage of the fact that the matrix is mostly sparse by implementing a hash function for mapping sub-inputs from the whole set of inputs.

5   Results and Conclusions

The results are obtained on 25 clips in the Broadcast News domain. These clips contain both CNN and ABC newsfeeds. The total time of video evaluated is about 62 minutes. The total number of word objects that occurred in this entire dataset is 4178. The total number of word frame instances is 68,738. Since this is a pilot study, we had only one participant (anonymized here). This is helpful in setting a baseline for this task before beginning a formal evaluation.

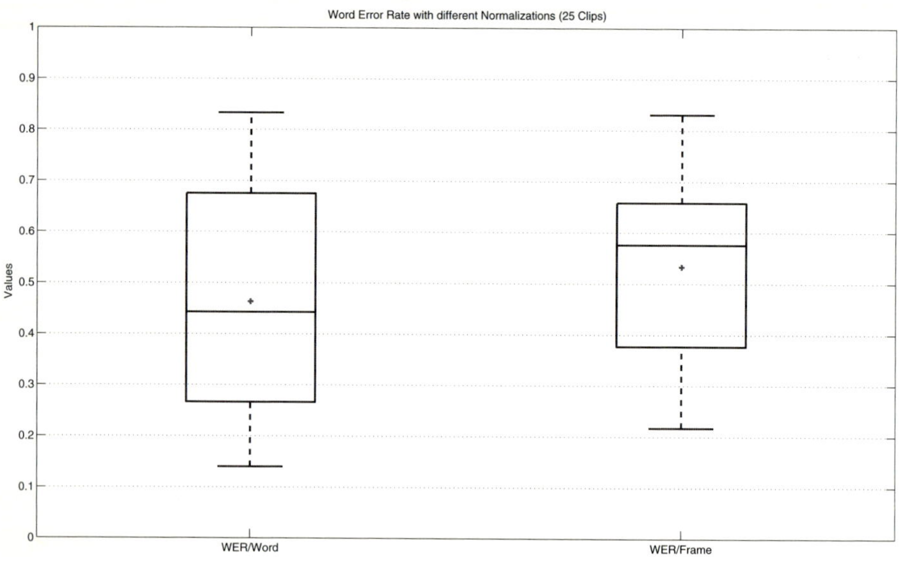

Fig. 3. WER Score Distribution on all 25 Clips (with different normalizations) '+' indicates the mean value

The WER obtained over the entire dataset is 0.423 and the CER is 0.282. Fig 3 shows the boxplots of the WER obtained using different normalizations. We can infact compute the error rates with respect to the total number of words occuring in a particular clip: the distribution of which is shown in the first boxplot. The second boxplot shows the scores obtained after normalizing with respect to the total number of frames in the entire clip.

We should also note that some of these errors could potentially occur due to the system locating the word at a wrong location (since detection is inherently assumed). We could re-evaluate the performance by giving prior knowledge of

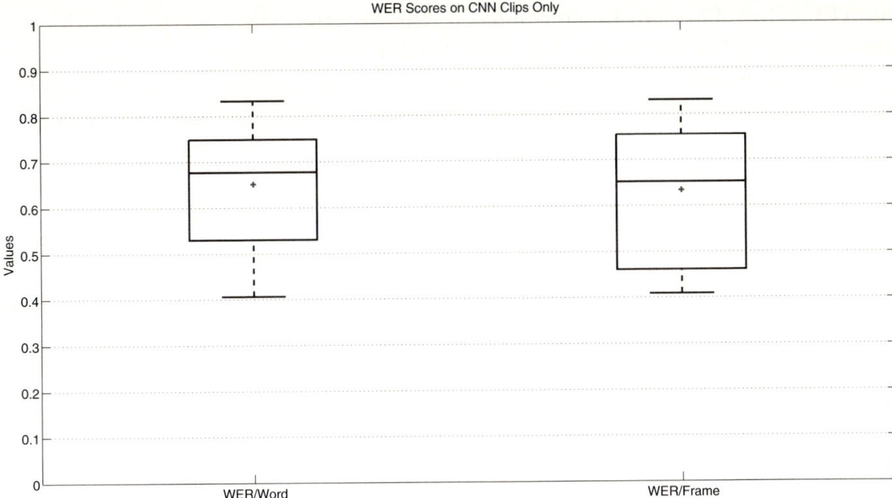

Fig. 4. WER Score Distribution on only the CNN Clips (12 clips) '+' indicates the mean value

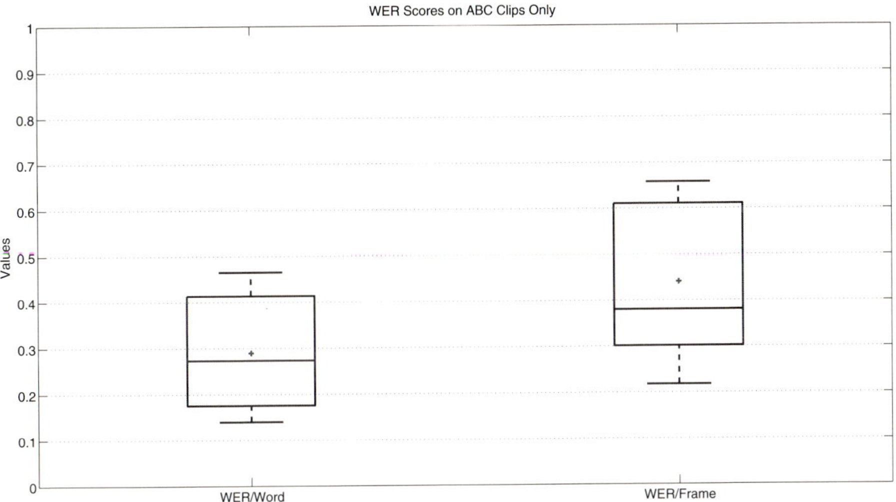

Fig. 5. WER Score Distribution on only the ABC Clips (13 clips) '+' indicates the mean value

the word locations and get the recognition error rates. Nevertheless, we again re-iterate that the scores obtained here are good baselines that can be improved.

Figs 4 and 5 shows the performance based on the CNN and ABC newsfeeds. As can be seen, the performance on CNN clips is worse than the performance on ABC clips. This can be attributed to the fact that there are less captions in the ABC newsfeeds compared to the CNN for this dataset.

We have shown a practical OCR evaluation framework in video. Useful annotations and metrics have resulted in making this evaluation framework possible. In future, more challenging forms of text including other languages can also be evaluated. We could also include harder to read as well as dynamic and scrolling text. Further, we could also extend the evaluation to include semantic knowledge where a system has to include a knowledge model for better performance. Challenges arise in the form of defining newer metrics, refine the annotations and also the interpretations of the systems for scoring.

References

1. Manohar, V., Soundararajan, P., Boonstra, M., Raju, H., Goldgof, D., Kasturi, R., Garofolo, J.: Performance Evaluation of Text Detection and Tracking in Video. In: 7_{th} IAPR Workshop on Document Analysis Systems (DAS). Volume 3872. (2006) 576–587
2. Doermann, D., Mihalcik, D.: Tools and Techniques for Video Performance Evaluation. In: ICPR. Volume 4. (2000) 167–170
3. McCowan, I., Moore, D., Dines, J., Gatica-Perez, D., Flynn, M., Wellner, P., Bourlard, H.: "on the use of information retrieval measures for speech recognition evaluation". Technical report, IAIDP (2005)
4. Papadimitriou, C.H., Steiglitz, K.: Combinatorial optimization: algorithms and complexity. Prentice-Hall, Inc., Upper Saddle River, NJ, USA (1982)
5. Munkres, J.R.: Algorithms for the Assignment and Transportation Problems. J. SIAM **5** (1957) 32–38
6. Fredman, M.L., Tarjan, R.E.: Fibonacci Heaps and their uses in Improved Network Optimization Algorithms. Journal of ACM **34** (1987) 596–615

Enabling Search over Large Collections of Telugu Document Images – An Automatic Annotation Based Approach

Pramod Sankar K. and C.V. Jawahar

Centre for Visual Information Technology,
International Institute of Information Technology, Hyderabad, India
`jawahar@iiit.ac.in`

Abstract. For the first time, search is enabled over a massive collection of 21 Million word images from digitized document images. This work advances the state-of-the-art on multiple fronts: i) *Indian language document images* are made searchable by textual queries, ii) *interactive* content-level access is provided to document *images* for search and retrieval, iii) a novel *recognition-free* approach, that does not require an OCR, is adapted and validated iv) a suite of image processing and pattern classification algorithms are proposed to efficiently *automate* the process and v) the scalability of the solution is demonstrated over a *large collection* of 500 digitised books consisting of 75,000 pages.

Character recognition based approaches yield poor results for developing search engines for Indian language document images, due to the complexity of the script and the poor quality of the documents. Recognition free approaches, based on word-spotting, are not directly scalable to large collections, due to the computational complexity of matching images in the feature space. For example, if it requires 1 mSec to match two images, the retrieval of documents to a single query, from a large collection like ours, would require close to a day's time. In this paper we propose a novel automatic annotation based approach to provide textual description of document images. With a one time, offline computational effort, we are able to build a text-based retrieval system, over annotated images. This system has an interactive response time of about 0.01 second. However, we pay the price in the form of massive offline computation, which is performed on a cluster of 35 computers, for about a month. Our procedure is highly automatic, requiring minimal human intervention.

1   Introduction

Large collections of document images are being created from the various digitisation projects across the globe. These include the Universal Digital Library (UDL) [1], Digital Library of India (DLI) [2], Google Books, etc. [3]. Much effort is being put into the digitisation of massive quantities of documents. The popularity of these digital libraries will depend on their usability, especially through

P. Kalra and S. Peleg (Eds.): ICVGIP 2006, LNCS 4338, pp. 837–848, 2006.
© Springer-Verlag Berlin Heidelberg 2006

content level search. For printed-document images, content level access was traditionally provided by using Optical Character Recognition (OCR) [4,5], to recognise the text. A text retrieval system would then be built over the recognised text. This approach produced satisfactory systems for the English language [6]. However, despite considerable effort, robust OCRs are not available for many Indian, Arabic and African languages. This is mostly becasue of the inherent complexity of the language owing to an extended character set, writing style and printing variations. Besides, the accuracy of OCRs reduces rapidly with degradations [5], which are common in scanned documents. The obtained text is thereby, not well-suited for indexing and retrieval.

On the other hand, recently proposed recognition free approaches, avoid explicit character recognition [7,8,9,10,11] by performing *Word Spotting* of a query in the image collection. The retrieval time using this approach is large since image matching in feature space is computationally intensive. If N is the number of documents, and M is the number of words in each document, then, the computations required for retrieving a single query would be of $O(N \cdot M \cdot l^2)$ (l is length of feature vector for each word). If we assume that matching a pair of images requires 0.01 second, the retrieval time for each query, from a collection of 21 million images would be three days. Thus, a purely recognition-free approach is not scalable to large collections of images and queries.

The drawbacks of the previous approaches can be overcome by an *Annotation* based approach. Annotation is the process of assigning relevant keywords to a given image. With an annotated collection, an image can be represented in the text domain, enabling us to build an efficient retrieval system. Conventionally, annotation is performed by analysing a given image to identify the keywords that annotate it. *It can be observed that recognising the text using an OCR corresponds to annotating the image with the obtained text.* In this paper, we propose a novel approach called *Reverse Annotation*, where we analyse each word and find the corresponding images that it could annotate. Textual words are converted to the image domain and the generated images are matched with the words in the document. The matched documents are annotated by the textual keyword.

However, to annotate images, accurate image matching is required, which is computationally intensive. These computations need to be performed for every pair of generated and real word images. Given a vocabulary of k words the order of comparisons would be $O(k \cdot N \cdot M)$. To make annotation feasible, we employ the clustering technique. In text-retrieval, clustering is used to arrange the documents in a manner that facilitates immediate retrieval. Similarly, we arrange the images such that the image matching could be performed in a hierarchy of increasing complexity and decreasing number. Images are first clustered using a coarse feature representation and a matching algorithm. These clusters are then used to index the word images for quick annotation. With this scheme, the complexity of annotation reduces to approximately $O(log(N \cdot M) \cdot log k)$.

The significance of our work is that we provide an interactive content level access to a massive collection of document images. Our approach is recognition-free, where images are accessed in the text domain through the proposed *Reverse*

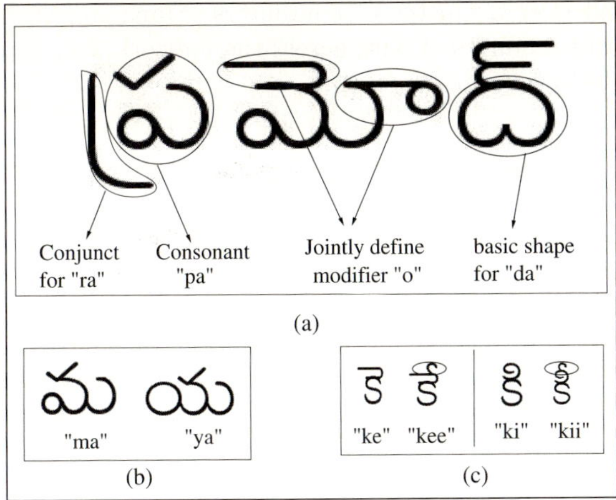

Fig. 1. Examples demonstrating the subtleness of the Telugu language. In (a) the consonant modifier is shown to be displaced from the consonant in different ways (b) the two characters *ma* and *ya* are distinguished only by the relative size of the circle (c) the small stroke at the top changes the vowel that modifies the consonant.

Annotation framework. The annotation is made computationally feasible by employing efficient clustering techniques. We demonstrate the power and scalability of our solution by creating a search engine over 500 books of Telugu language document images. The collection contained 75,000 pages with 21 million words. The search engine that was built searches the document collection in a mere 0.01 seconds.

2   The Challenges Faced

Language-specific Issues. Telugu, like most Indian languages, has a complex script, where the consonant could be modified by a vowel, consonant and/or a diacritic. A snippet of the complexity is demonstrated in Figure 1. Due to this inherent complexity of the language's script and writing style, accurate segmentation and matching of words (and characters) is a very difficult task [12].

Issues in Scanning. Scanned document images contain a large number of artifacts, which are cleaned on a large scale using a a semi-automatic process [3], by using various image processing operations. Owing to the variation in quality across the images, a single setup of image processing parameters would not be suitable for all. Consequently, the overall quality of the processed images is poor, thereby matching and recognising such words is very difficult.

Scalability. The massiveness of the digital library collections, is a serious challenge for automation of the processes. Due to this magnitude, even the quick image processing routines require large amounts of time. Despite considerable optimisations, the computation required is enormous, and the processing has to be distributed over a cluster of computers. Managing such a cluster and transfering of large amounts of data across the network were some of the major bottlenecks in the system development.

3   Reverse Annotation

Content based image retrieval (CBIR) systems have thus far focused on enabling search and retrieval over relatively small image collections. With the massive increase in image collections, the scalability, performance and computational complexity issues need to be further addressed. In traditional CBIR, image matching is performed online to retrieve similar images to a given query. This online matching of queries results in large retrieval time and is thus not scalable. Indexing in the image feature space was explored in literature [13,14]. The indexing structures, such as k-d trees, are not scalable to large number of features and images. On the other hand, users are accustomed to sub-second retrieval of web pages by commercial search engines. The performance of text retrieval could be replicated for images, only by having a text-based system at this stage. This requires a textual representation for each image, which corresponds to an annotation of the images with text [15].

In the early years of image retrieval systems, images were annotated manually. For automatic annotation, the images are analysed to identify the annotation keywords, by performing image segmentation, object recognition, scene analysis etc. In recent years, cross-media relevance models have been used to annotate images based on co-occurrence of features and associated textual descriptions [16,17]. Annotations could also be learned from user feedbacks [18] or from search results over the Internet [19]. However, these techniques are not easily applicable to the domain of document images.

In our approach, instead of identifying the keywords for a given image, we identify the images that correspond to a given keyword. This scheme is called *Reverse Annotation*. In reverse annotation, we built an example image for a given keyword, and identify the images in the collection that are visually similar to it. When there is a match, the keyword is used to annotate the matched image.

This scheme is especially suitable for document images, where the knowledge of the vocabulary provides us with the possible annotations (in contrast to generic images, where annotations depend on subjectivity). For the document images, an exact keyword has to be identified for a given word image. This circumvents the problems of *synonymy* and *polysemy*, and semantic annotations which are required in the case of generic images.

3.1   Image Matching for Annotation

The reverse annotation problem can be stated as *"given a set of word images, identify all the word images that match a given keyword image"*. The correspondence between word- and keyword-images can be established by computing a similarity measure between each such pair. An accurate feature description and similarity measure is used for this purpose and the word is annotated with the keyword whenever there is considerable match between the two. However, any accurate matching procedure is a computationally intensive process. If it requires about 0.05 seconds to compute the similarity between two word images, the annotation of a collection of 21 million words with a set of 30,000 keywords would require close to a thousand years. This is impractical and infeasible. To make this process feasible, we use an efficient solution derived from text retrieval, which is described in the next section.

4   Clustering for Annotation

In a text retrieval system, documents are indexed with the words present in them. Given a query, the documents are immediately read out of the index. It can be seen that the documents are clustered by the indexing procedure, based on the words in them. Following this strategy, we index the large collection of word images, such that similar words belong to one cluster.

At the finest level, the clusters would contain all instances of a given word in the collection, with all the variations in font type, style and size. At a coarse level, a large number of *similar-looking* words would be present in the same cluster. The feature description and similarity measure should be chosen such that they are invariant to font type, style and size changes, while being able to quickly cluster the images. Accordingly, word profile features were chosen, since they have been very useful for clustering word images [10]. The features used here are the upper word profile, lower word profile, projection profile and transition profile. The features are normalised to provide invariance to font size. Features are compared using a Dynamic Time Warping (DTW) approach since it inherently handles font type and style variations [7]. DTW is essentially a dynamic programming technique, that calculates a distance between two feature vectors, by accumulating local distances $d(i,j)$ between the i th and j th features of the two vectors, using the following formula:

$$D(i,j) = \min \begin{cases} D(i\ \ 1, j-1) \\ D(i-1, j) \\ D(i, j-1) \end{cases} + d(i,j)$$

Hierarchical Clustering. The feature representation and similarity computations between images yield non-metric pairwise distances. In such cases, the popular choice of clustering is the Hierarchical Agglomerative Clustering (HAC). HAC begins with individual clusters for each point and proceeds by merging the closest clusters until a stopping-criterion is met. However, this would require the computation of similarity between every pair of words, which is $O(N^2)$. To quicken the clustering, we only cluster those points that were not previously clustered. With such a technique, the pairwise distances need to be computed for only those words that have not yet been clustered. This results in a $O(N \cdot logN)$ algorithm, and the running time depends on the size of the clusters. With a large cluster size, we obtain coarse clusters *quickly*, since the number of points to be clustered decreases rapidly at each iteration. With smaller cluster size, the time

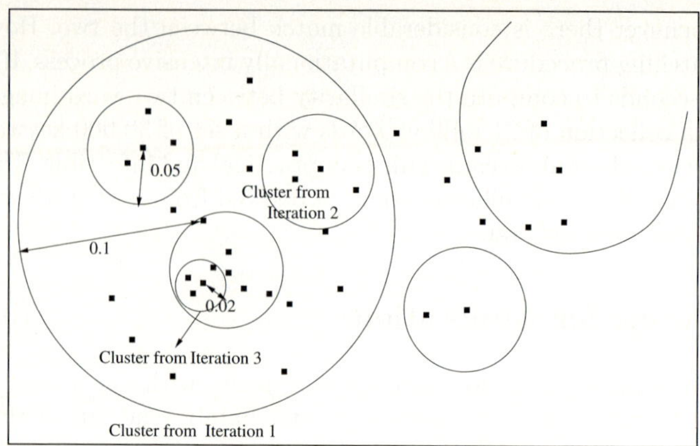

Fig. 2. Depiction of Clustering Procedure. In the first iteration, the data is partitioned to large clusters, quickly. Smaller clusters are then found within the larger clusters. A hierarchy of three levels of fine-ness is shown in the figure.

increases rapidly. To obtain good clusters quickly, the points are first clustered (or partitioned) coarsely and then refined to finer clusters. The assumption is that, two points cannot be found in a fine cluster, if they do not belong to a coarse cluster. The clustering is depicted in Figure 2. The cluster centroid is defined as the word with the least sum distance from the other points in the cluster.

By clustering at multiple levels, a hierarchy of clusters are built, where the number of points in the clusters reduces at each level, while the number of clusters increases. This is depicted in Figure 4. With such a hierarchy, we could identify the clusters relevant to a given keyword, and match for exact annotation within the cluster. By clustering, we eliminate a large number of comparisons which would not yield a match, thereby remarkably speeding up the annotation process. With this scheme, the number of comparisons for annotation are of $O(logk \cdot logN)$ (K being number of keywords and N the number of words). The annotation of 21 million words can now be performed in about 260 days (instead of the 1000 years required otherwise).

About 500 random clusters were manually evaluated to estimate the accuracy of clustering and the results are presented in Table 1.

Table 1. Precision-Recall of the clustering procedure, evaluated manually from 500 randomly picked clusters

Width of centroid word (in pixels)	30 - 500	500 - 1000	1000 - 1500	1500 - 2000	Total
Precision	92.54%	73.91%	73.76%	68.53%	72.66%
Recall	62.72%	76.69%	80.44%	72.39%	75.45%

5   Building the System

In this section we describe the stages involved in building the search system using the approach described above.

Data Collection. The data for our project was obtained from the digitisation under the Digital Library of India project. The books are available for free access at [20]. The books are digitised on a large scale at a resolution of 600dpi. Our collection consists of 500 books of the Telugu language, with 76, 425 page images.

Segmentation. The document images are segmented using the *docstrum* [21] algorithm. The large number of segmentation errors are corrected using the techniques described in Section 5.1.

Feature Extraction. Coarse features are extracted from each of the word segments. These features are the profile and transition features, which are described in Section 4.1

Clustering. Words are clustered using the hierarchical agglomerative clustering procedure detailed in Section 4.1. The time for clustering increases quadratically with the number of points to be clustered. To ensure that the clustering is tractable, we perform clustering over each individual book, which on an average, contains 50K words.

Merging Clusters. The clusters from different books are merged by comparing the cluster centroids of the respective books.

Annotation. The obtained clusters are annotated by finding the closest word match the cluster centroid, as elaborated in Section 5.2.

Search Index Building. Annotations for the clusters are used to identify the documents that correspond to each keyword. The search index is built using this correspondence. The details of the search system are described in Section 5.3.

5.1   Segmentation

To annotate each word, we require a segmentation of the document at word level. Due to the writing pattern of Telugu, as described in Section 2, the segmentation algorithms that work well on English documents, yield very poor results. An example is shown in Figure 3 (a), where the vowel modifiers are segmented separately from the word they belong to. In general, about 25% extra segments arise due to noise and the displaced vowel modifiers. Manual correction of these segmentation errors is infeasible, taking about three minutes per page.

The error patterns that occur in the segmentation are handled using an automatic correction scheme as

- In cases where the vowel modifier is displaced, intra-word segments occur, which generally overlap or are closer to each other than inter-word segments. The segmentation correction scheme identifies adjacent segments and merges

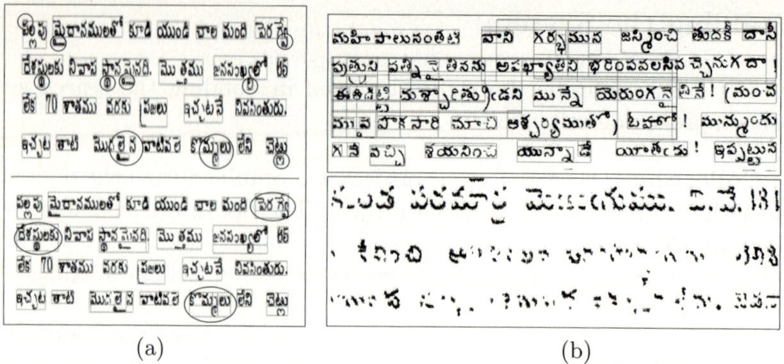

(a)   (b)

Fig. 3. (a) Example of segmentation errors (above) and corrected segmentation (below). The errors are encircled and some of the corrected ones are highlighted below, (b) Over correction of poor segmentation (above), Sample page image with heavy degradations (below).

those that are closer than the average distance. An example is shown in Figure 3 (above).

– Segments from noise are considerably small in size. Accordingly all segments with dimensions less than 30 pixels are removed, which corresponds to one-twentieth of an inch, when scanned at 600 dpi.
– Segments from illustrations are generally larger than the average word size. Segments greater than 2000 pixels (three-and-half inches at 600 dpi) are, therefore, removed.

However, in some pages, due to the close proximity between successive words/ lines of text, the scheme *over-corrects*, as shown in Figure 3 (b). The outliers from incorrect segmentation, increase the computation required, but, the improvement in segmentation accuracy justifies this additional expense.

5.2   Annotation

For Reverse Annotation, we begin with the words of the language that are present in the document collection. These words are used to build the templates that shall be used for annotation. However, the document images do not have a parallel text. A text corpus is used to identify the words and proper nouns that are generally present in the documents of the given language. Moreover, it is well known in the information retrieval (IR) domain, that the frequency of word occurrence is roughly inversely proportional to its rank in terms of frequency, i.e., the frequency of the k-th most frequent word would have a frequency f_0/k, where f_0 is the frequency of the most frequent term. This is called the Zipf's law [22]. The index terms should be taken from the middle of this distribution. Highly frequent words are *stop words* and low frequency are not queried for often. With an appropriate set of words, a considerable percentage of the text and queries would be covered. Accordingly, we obtain words that are found in the

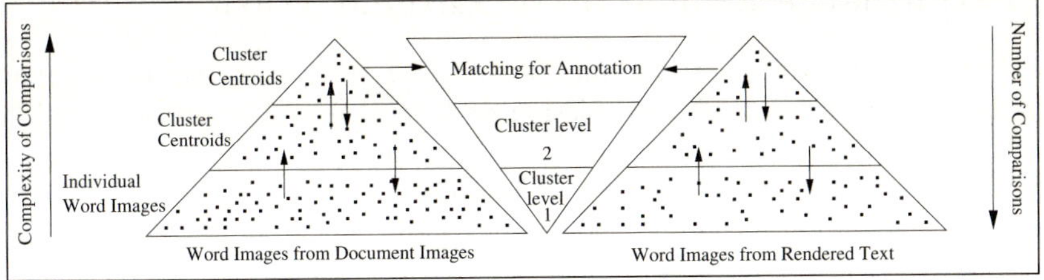

Fig. 4. Depiction of Annotation built above the clustering procedure

frequency range 10 to 200. The obtained set of keywords are rendered to form word images using the Eenadu font. These keyword images are also clustered using the profile features and DTW distance.

To annotate the word images, a hierarchy of comparisons are performed between the keyword- and word-images. Firstly, the cluster centroids of the word images are matched with the cluster centroids of the keyword images. The closest keyword-centroid is assigned to each word-centroid. This is performed for the two levels of hierarchy of word image and keyword clusters. We now have a correspondence between a keyword cluster and a word image cluster. An exact comparison of images can now be performed to identify the appropriate annotation for each word image. The procedure is depicted in Figure 4.

5.3   The Search Engine

From the word annotation, the documents that contain a given keyword can be obtained by identifying the words that are annotated by the keyword. This allows us to build the search index for the document collection. The index would contain the keywords that were used for annotation. A query is searched for in this index file and the documents containing the keyword are retrieved for the user. Since the search is in the text domain, the matching of query and index term is very quick. The system allows for querying using a transliteration scheme called *omtrans*, where the Telugu language query is entered in a Roman format. The search system has a response time of about 0.01 seconds per query. The relevant document images are retrieved for the user. Since the delivery is in the image format, the delivery of the image requires close to 3.4 seconds.

5.4   Computing Resources

The clustering and annotation phases require large computation resources. To make the process feasible, we distributed the computation over a cluster of 35 machines. Each machine was assigned a set of books, which were processed in a semi-automatic manner, with minimal manual intervention. One of the major challenges in this project was the handling of large amounts of data, and transferring the data across different machines.

6   Performance Evaluation on Ground Truth

The system built using the techniques described in this paper, was tested against a ground truth of five books, consisting of 1030 pages. The ground truth was created by manually typesetting the content of each page. The number of words in the text were 100,000, consisting of 50,000 unique words. The segmentation algorithm yielded more than 211,000 words. Following the merging of segments for segmentation-correction, the word count was 300,000. These words were clustered to 16,000 clusters. The number of words in a cluster indicates the number of words similar to the centroid in all the documents, which ideally corresponds to the word occurrence frequency in the text documents. The clusters were matched against the frequency of occurrence of each individual word in the text. The percentage of match was found to be 58.77 %.

The annotation performance was tested against the real text documents. The accuracy of annotation was calculated as the number of matching words divided by the total number of words in the given document, averaged over all documents. The accuracy of annotation was found to be 48.63%, while 24.75% of the words were annotated with a word form variation of the actual word. This is allowable, since the retrieval system would perform stemming and index a word by only its stem word. The search systems built separately over text documents and the annotated images. In case of the ground truth collection, all words were indexed, ensuring a near-perfect precision-recall. The two search engines were evaluated against 20 queries picked randomly from the keyword set. The retreival results are evaluated using the R-precision measure, which is the precision of the system at R documents retrieved, R being the number of known relevant documents for the given query in the collection. R is obtained from the result of the groundtruth search system. The top 20 results were evaluated for retreival performance and the overlap in the retrieved documents was found to be about 77.38%. Thus the annotated documents are able to replciate text retrieval perfcormance to upto an accuracy of 77%. *The difference between the accuracies of the two systems comes from the inaccuracies in the image processing domain.* The errors in segmentation, clustering and annotation propogate from one stage to the next and contribute to this mismatch in the performance between purely-text based and annotated image based systems.

7   Related Work

Our work is similar to many of the feature indexing methods [14] and especially [7,10]. However, we annotate each of the clusters, instead of directly using them to build the index. An attempt at manual annotation of word image clusters was reported in [23], which is generally un-affordable. The motivation to use an annotation based approach comes from recent interest in automatic annotation [16,17,15]. Especially [15] uses an annotation based approach for images and videos using their textual content. Our work improves upon existing image matching systems and provides a scheme for building practical search systems for image collections.

8 Conclusion and Future Directions

We have demonstrated the power and effectiveness of an annotation based approach toward building search systems for document images. We tested our approach on the Indian language – Telugu, which is considered one of the most challenging to build a search system on (using conventional approaches). We built a system on 75,000 page images consisting of 21 million words, which is the largest test set used thus far in the known literature. The retrieval performance was found to be satisfactory. The approach is scalable to large collections, as is shown by our work, with the annotation time increasing linearly with the collection, while the retrieval time remains unchanged.

Since the system depends heavily on word image matching, robust and quick techniques could speed up the process. Better features and similarity measures could improve the performance of clustering, and thus of the entire system. Efficient clustering and indexing schemes could be further explored for speeding up the process. The applicability of the techniques could be tested for document images of other languages. The scalability of the approach to large digital libraries of tens of thousands of books needs to be evaluated. Finally, the results of annotation could be used to refine the segmentation of the page at word level, which could be used to learn better segmentation techniques.

References

1. Universal Library at: http://www.ulib.org.
2. Ambati, V., N.Balakrishnan, Reddy, R., Pratha, L., Jawahar, C.V.: The digital library of india project: Process, policies and architecture. In: 2nd International Conference on Digital Libraries(ICDL). (2006)
3. Pramod Sankar, K., Vamshi Ambati, Lakshmi Pratha, Jawahar, C. V.: Digitizing a million books: Challenges for document analysis. In: 7th International Workshop on Document Analysis Systems, DAS, LNCS, Springer-Verlag (2006) 425–436
4. Mitra, M., Chaudhuri, B.B.: Information retrieval from documents: A survey. Inf. Retr. **2** (2000) 141–163
5. Doermann, D.: The indexing and retrieval of document images: A survey. In: Computer Vision and Image Understanding (CVIU) 70. (1998) 287–298
6. Taghva, K., Borsack, J., Condit, A.: Evaluation of model-based retrieval effectiveness with ocr text. ACM Trans. Inf. Syst. **14** (1996) 64–93
7. Rath, T., Manmatha, R.: Word image matching using dynamic time warping. Proc. Computer Vision and Pattern Recognition (CVPR) **2** (2003) 521–527
8. Marinai, S., Marino, E., Soda, G.: Font adaptive word indexing of modern printed documents. IEEE Trans. Pattern Anal. Mach. Intell. **28** (Aug., 2006) 1187–1199
9. Harit, G., Chaudhury, S., Ghosh, H.: Managing document images in a digital library: An ontology guided approach. In: DIAL '04: Proc. of the First International Workshop on Document Image Analysis for Libraries. (2004) 64
10. Jawahar, C.V., Million Meshesha, Balasubramanian, A.: Searching in document images. In: 4th Indian Conference on Computer Vision, Graphics and Image Processing (ICVGIP). (2004) 622–627
11. Srihari, S.N., Huang, C., Srinivasan, H.: Search engine for handwritten documents. Document Recognition and Retrieval **SPIE, Vol. 5676** (2005) 66–75

12. Pal, U., Chaudhuri, B.B.: Indian script character recognition: a survey. Pattern Recognition **37** (2004) 1887–1899
13. Schmid, C., Mohr, R.: Local grayvalue invariants for image retrieval. IEEE Transactions on Pattern Analysis & Machine Intelligence **19** (1997) 530–534
14. Sivic, J., Zisserman, A.: Video Google: A text retrieval approach to object matching in videos. In: Proc. ICCV. Volume 2. (2003) 1470–1477
15. Pramod Sankar K., Meshesha, M., Jawahar, C.V.: Annotation of images and videos based on textual content without OCR. In: Proc. ECCV Workshop on Computation Intensive Methods in Computer Vision. (2006)
16. Duygulu, P., Barnard, K., de Freitas, N., Forsyth, D.: Object recognition as machine translation: Learning a lexicon for a fixed image vocabulary. In: European Conference on Computer Vision. (2002) 97–112
17. Jeon, J., Lavrenko, V., Manmatha, R.: Automatic image annotation and retrieval using cross-media relevance models. In: ACM SIGIR. (2003) 119–126
18. Wenyin, L., Dumais, S., Sun, Y., Zhang, H., Czerwinski, M., Field, B.: Semi-automatic image annotation. In: Proc. of Interact: Conference on HCI. (2001) 326–333
19. Wang, X., Zhang, L., Jing, F., Ma, W.Y.: Annosearch: Image auto-annotation by search. In: Proc. CVPR, New York, USA (June, 2006) 1483–1490
20. Digital Library of India at: http://dli.iiit.ac.in.
21. O'Gorman, L.: The document spectrum for page layout analysis. IEEE Trans. Pattern Anal. Mach. Intell. **15** (1993) 1162–1173
22. Zipf, G.: Human Behaviour and the Principle of Least Effort. Addison-Wesley, Cambridge, MA (1949)
23. Balasubramanian, A., Million Meshesha, Jawahar, C.V.: Retrieval from document image collections. In: 7th International Workshop on Document Analysis Systems, DAS, LNCS, Springer-Verlag (2006) 1–12

Retrieving Images for Remote Sensing Applications

Neela Sawant, Sharat Chandran, and B. Krishna Mohan

Department of Computer Science and Engineering
Indian Institute of Technology Bombay
http://www.cse.iitb.ac.in/~{neela, sharat}
http://www.csre.iitb.ac.in/bkmohan

Abstract. A unique way in which content based image retrieval (CBIR) for remote sensing differs widely from traditional CBIR is the widespread occurrences of *weak textures*. The task of representing the weak textures becomes even more challenging especially if image properties like scale, illumination or the viewing geometry are not known.

In this work, we have proposed the use of a new feature *'texton histogram'* to capture the weak-textured nature of remote sensing images. Combined with an automatic classifier, our texton histograms are robust to variations in scale, orientation and illumination conditions as illustrated experimentally. The classification accuracy is further improved using additional image driven features obtained by the application of a feature selection procedure.

1   Introduction

For many years, information extracted from remote sensing image archives has been exploited for specialized applications like monitoring land cover and land usage, identifying cases of floods or fires, urbanization, deforestation, and so on. Building such applications have been relatively easy with existing domain knowledge and readily available information about image properties like scale, orientation, and illumination conditions. This scenario is changing rapidly as technological advances such as Google Earth demand a generic framework to satisfy unpredictable 'casual' user queries with possibly unknown image properties.

Remote sensing images are essentially textured images with lands, grass, forests, mountain ranges, water, clouds, snow, buildings, and the like. Majority of these categories exhibit weak textures and a highly irregular structure. Hence the focus of remote sensing CBIR systems should be on identifying the texture features correctly. In the past, many CBIR systems have tried capturing characteristic textures using features like local texture patterns [1], Gabor multiscale features [2,3,4], Markov random field (MRF) textures [5,6], Gibbs Markov models [7], and wavelet features [8,9]. The SIMPLIcity (Semantics-Sensitive Integrated Matching for Picture Libraries) [10] system uses a combination of texture and color features.

P. Kalra and S. Peleg (Eds.): ICVGIP 2006, LNCS 4338, pp. 849–860, 2006.
© Springer-Verlag Berlin Heidelberg 2006

Based on our experiments, we find that the success of these methods limited owing to the problems in handling unknown imaging conditions and the inability to capture weak textures effectively. Gabor features for example, respond well to strong textures but are not able to capture the weak textures effectively. Multi-scale filter based techniques, like Gabor or wavelet based approaches, extract features at multiple scales and try to find the best match across them. Considering the weak-textured nature of remote sensing images, it is often difficult to get distinguished texture readings across scales. Moreover, features from different texture categories at different scales may falsely appear similar, thus limiting the classification accuracy further. MRF features represent weak textures well, but they are not scale independent.

A classic problem faced by most of the existing systems is the *misleading image appearances*. The color and texture appearances of the same surface vary significantly with the changes in illumination and camera angle properties. Fig. 1 shows an example where water appears green in one image and blue in another. To a human observer, there is no confusion regarding the presence of water. However this similarity will not be detected if only low level features are used.

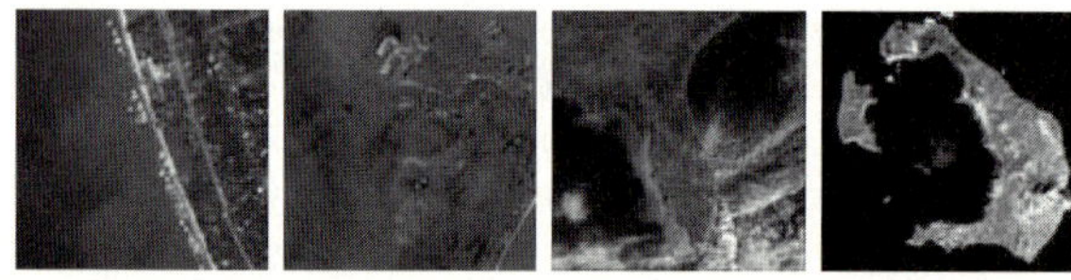

Fig. 1. The color of ocean water exhibits a spectrum from green to dark blue

The effect of imaging condition on textures is explained in [11,12,13] using the CUReT textures database. Different textures might appear very similar resulting in large inter-class similarities or the same surface might exhibit different textures leading to large intra-class variations. Misleading image appearances is a common problem for remote sensing applications as the illumination varies with the time and season. The pose of camera does not vary much for the satellite images taken from great heights but it plays a significant role for aerial images taken from surveillance helicopters.

1.1   Our Contributions

1. We propose a new texture feature, the *'texton histogram'* to represent the characteristic weak textures of remote sensing images. We have shown that this feature is largely robust to the problems of unknown scaling, orientation, and global illumination.
2. We develop a classifier system to identify image contents semantically, using the texton histogram as the base feature. The accuracy of semantic classification is further improved using additional features obtained from an extensive feature selection procedure. We show that our system can handle the problems of misleading image appearances as well as that of unknown image properties.

3. We develop an efficient end-to-end system that retrieves results containing similar semantic contents in about 100ms (Matlab based, database size of 400 images).

1.2   Proposed Approach

The problem of similarity retrieval is posed as a semantic matching problem where an image is represented as a composition of high level concepts. We use six frequent remote sensing categories, viz., *bushes (forest), clouds, plains, snow, urban, and water* as the high level concepts. The application of a semantic approach helps in identifying image contents independent of the scale, orientation conditions as well as the intra-class feature variations and the inter-class feature similarities.

The mapping from low-level features to high-level concepts is done by Support Vector Machine (SVM) classifiers trained using multiple-instance learning approach. A feature selection technique, the *gain-ratio* method is used to choose concept-specific selective low-level features from the feature-space of color and texture features.

1.3   Organization of Paper

The paper is organized as follows. Sec. 2 discusses the features chosen to represent remote sensing imagery. The focus of this section is on the construction of the texton histogram, followed by a discussion of its ability to detect weak textures, irrespective of illumination, scale and orientation conditions. Sec. 3 discusses our semantic learning approach. The overall system architecture is described in Sec. 4. Experimental results are given in Sec. 5 followed by concluding remarks in the last section.

2   Features

The accuracy of a CBIR system can only be as good as the features used to represent images. If only gray-scale texture features are used, water and snow covers might be indistinguishable. Similarly, if only color is used, snow and clouds might appear indistinguishable. Hence, it is better to use a combination of carefully chosen multiple features to distinguish a category from another. In our experiments, we selected category-specific features from a feature-space of color, weak textures and strong texture features and used them to train a single SVM classifier for that category.

2.1   Texton Histogram

Textons are the putative units of preattentive human texture perception [14]. Different definitions are given in different works to compute textons. [15] gives an operational definition where textons are computed as the frequently co-occurring combinations of oriented linear filter responses. [13] defines textons as the joint distribution of intensity values over extremely compact neighborhoods. Our definition of textons is inspired by the work in [13]. Our design is equally focused on local property that is a function of a 3 x 3 neighborhood *and* the *texton histogram* which is more global in nature. Based on an extensive set of experiments with one thousand seven hundred 128 x 128 image tiles, a *texton dictionary* is learned using an unsupervised process. Each item in the dictionary (a texton) is a pixel label computed from a large number of 3 x 3 local neighborhoods of various pixels. The process is summarized in Fig. 2 and Fig. 3.

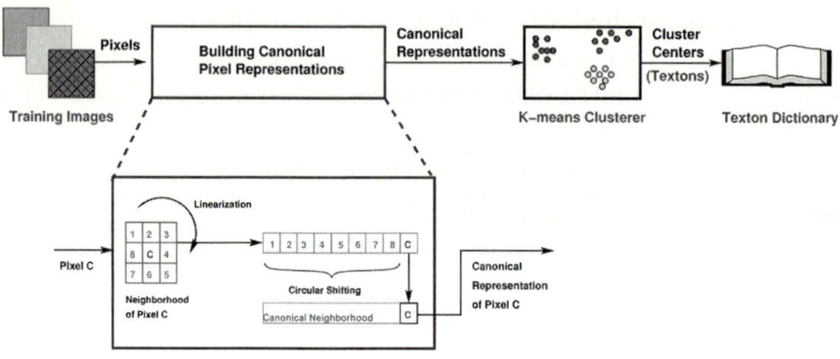

Fig. 2. Constructing a texton dictionary

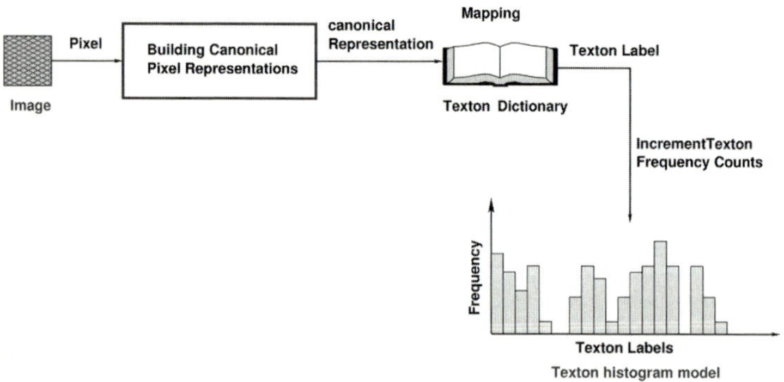

Fig. 3. Constructing a texton histogram. A texton histogram captures the local property of weak texture, but is also invariant to various effects.

Details. For a pixel p under consideration, the 3 x 3 local neighborhood without p is linearized to form an 8-element string representation s. This string is circularly shifted to yield a canonical form $\overline{S}$. The canonical representation satisfies two properties:

1. For any string representation s' of the same neighborhood, $\overline{S}$ is lexicographically smaller than or equal to s'.
2. The left and right neighbors for every element in $\overline{S}$ are the same as in s, under circular shift condition.

Pixel p is then appended at the end to form a 9 element vector for the next step.

The canonical representations for a large number of pixels are clustered using the K-means algorithm, where K is found automatically. The cluster centers are chosen as the representative textons to form the dictionary. Each texton is thus a 9-element array of tuples (mean, variance) corresponding to each of the 9 dimensions of the 3 x 3 local neighborhood. The textons in the dictionary are identified by a unique identifier, the texton-id. This procedure is depicted in Fig. 2. It is performed offline, and done exactly once in the system.

To summarize the weak textures for any candidate image, we build a probabilistic model, the texton histogram. After an image is intensity normalized, each image pixel is labeled with the closest item in the texton dictionary. The texton histogram feature is computed as the fraction of the total number of image pixels assigned per texton. The procedure for computing the texton histogram is shown in Fig. 3.

2.2   Texton Histogram Properties

1. **Invariance to global illumination changes:** Preprocessing images using *mean-center intensity normalization* makes the process more robust to illumination effects.
2. **Invariance to local neighborhood orientations:** Using a canonical form to represent a pixel neighborhood ensures that any orientation of the 3 x 3 neighborhood still maps to the same texton. Strictly speaking, we must scan convert a circle and use a circular neighborhood. The 3 x 3 neighborhood we use is simply a practical measure that works well.
3. **Invariance to noise in local neighborhoods:** Clustering ensures that the textons are well separated from each other in space. By binning pixel neighborhoods to closest textons, the problem arising from small noise and intensity fluctuations is overcome. Even if some pixels are mapped to the wrong textons, it does not have a significant effect on the final texton histogram representation.
4. **Invariance to scale:** Combining a local representation with an unsupervised voting process enables scale tolerance. Unlike ours, the texton histogram feature described in [13] is capable of resolving the misleading texture problem; however, it is not scale-independent. The scale associated with a remote sensing image is quasi-global [16]. This global nature is captured in a histogram model whereas the basic unit texton captures the local textures. Experimental proof for this appears in Fig. 4 which shows the behavior of texton histogram feature for a sample image under scaling. The plots show the behavior of texton histograms at zoom-in factors 1.5, 2.0 and 2.5 and 3.0 of the original image size. Observe that the overall shape of the texton histogram remains similar under scaling, and especially note that the peak positions match nicely. Fig. 5 demonstrates the behavior of texton histogram for the same image at a zoom factor of 0.2 marking its robust nature under zoom-out situations. After observing a similar behavior for a large number of images we conclude that the texton histogram feature is robust to image scaling to a large extent.

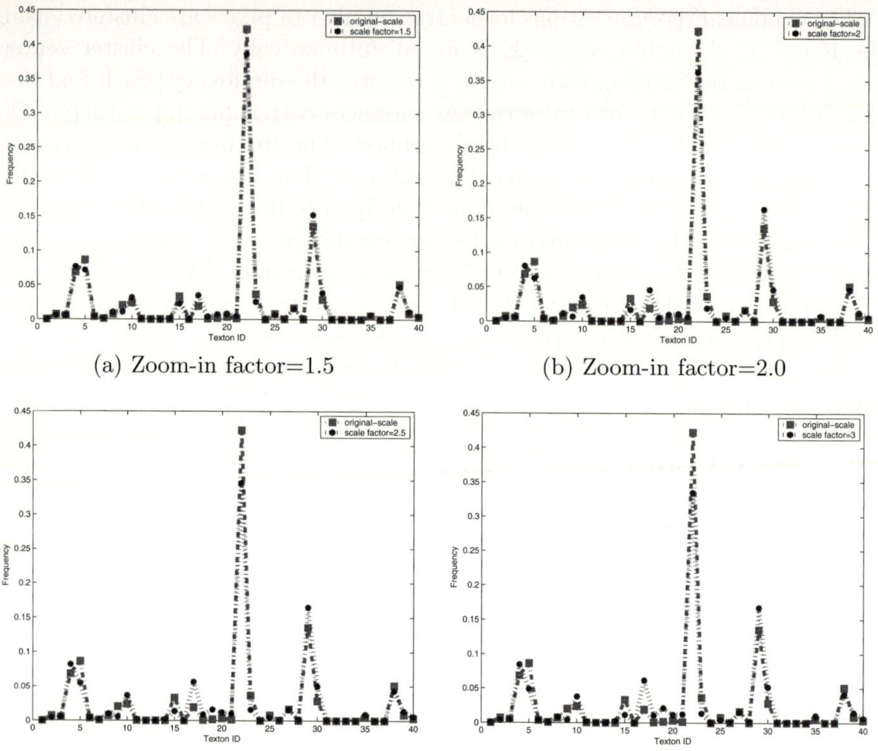

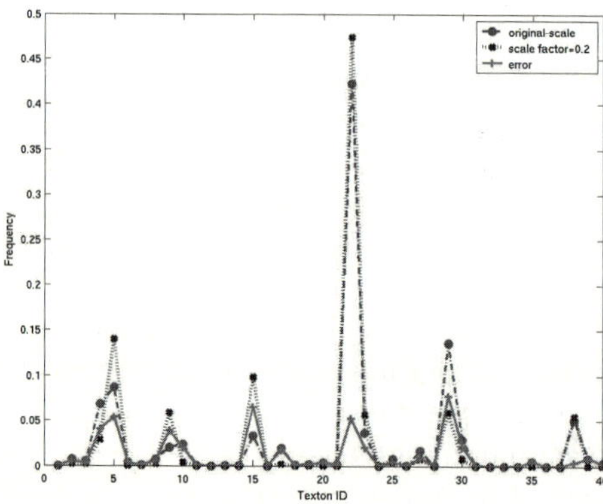

Fig. 4. Effect of scaling on texton histograms. The red and blue colors correspond to the texton histograms at the original scale and at the zoom factor respectively.

Fig. 5. Effect on texton histogram under "zoom-out" (factor=0.2)

2.3   Color and Strong Texture Features

To boost the identification of categories, we selected additional features from a feature-space encompassing color and strong texture features. In addition to the texton histogram (termed TH), we chose six color features, the dominant Y, Cb, Cr (DY, DCb, DCr) and the average Y, Cb, Cr (AY, ACb, ACr) values. The choice of YCbCr color space over RGB and HSV was made experimentally. We computed the strong texture features using a thresholded response of pixels to Sobel masks corresponding to the edges in directions 0, 45, 90, 135 degrees (termed EH0, EH45, EH90, EH135).

3   Learning Semantics

The association of distinguishing low level features to semantic categories is learned using a multiple instance learning (MIL) approach [17].

3.1   Multiple Instance Learning

In the multiple instance learning approach, an image is labeled positive for all the categories present in it. For a category, the task of learning distinguishing features reduces to identifying features which are common to the positively labeled images and absent from the negative images along with their relative weights. We use the 'gain-ratio' attribute selection [18] procedure to select an initial subset of useful features for each category. The gain-ratio method returns a ranking of all features for their discriminative capacity for the dataset under consideration. The SVM classifiers are tuned using a greedy selection [19] for these feature subsets . A binary SVM classifier is learned using the dominant features for each category. The final classifier package consists of 6 SVMs, one for each category.

For our experiments, we annotated 1700 image tiles of size 128 x 128 with positive/negative labels for each of the 6 categories. Full feature vectors and the corresponding labels were input to the feature selection process. The final feature dimensions selected for each concept are given in Table 1.

We observed that the inaccuracies in classification were mainly caused due to the variations in appearances of categories. The accuracy for clouds category is

Table 1. Table of concept-wise dominant features-set and classification accuracy

Concept	Dominant feature dimensions	Accuracy
bushes(forest)	TH,AY,ACb,ACr,DY	96.18
clouds	TH,DY,AY,ACr,DCb	87.19
plains	TH,ACr,ACb,DCr,DCb	90.11
snow	TH,DY	98.47
urban	TH,ACb,EH0,EH90,ACr	92.81
water	TH,ACb,ACr,AY,DY,DCr	93.23

relatively low, owing to the occasional sparse cloud nature where cloud detection is difficult and the occasional dense nature where it is confused with snow.

4   System Architecture

Fig. 6 shows the overall block diagram of the proposed retrieval system. The system can be explained in terms of three main modules: a) Learning module, b) Semantic profiles generation module and c) Query retrieval module.

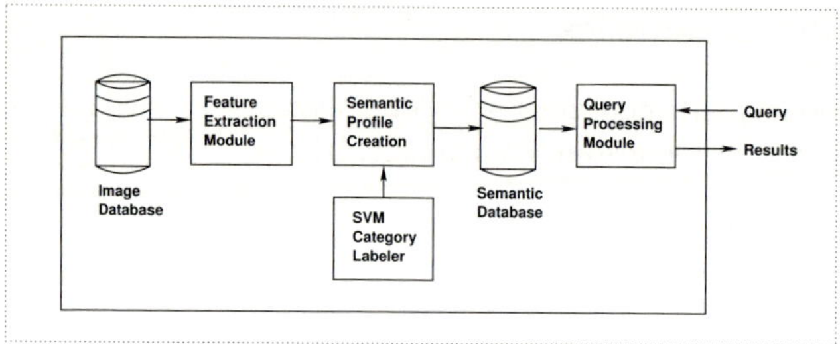

Fig. 6. Block diagram of the proposed system

Learning Module: The job of the learning module (not explicitly shown in Fig. 6) is to build the texton dictionary and the SVM category classifiers through learning. Both these tasks are done offline. The quality of texton dictionary and SVM classifier play a decisive role in assuring high quality results for the task of image classification and retrieval.

Semantic Profiles Generation: An image is divided in tiles of size 128 x 128 pixels. Features are computed for each tile and input to the SVM classifier package containing classifiers for the selected semantic categories. The output (i.e., label '1' if semantic concept is detected, '0' otherwise) of all the six classifiers is put together to construct a 6-element semantic profile for the tile. The semantic profile of the entire image is a 6-element vector where each element corresponds to the fraction of tiles voting positive for a concept. For example, if 3 out of 10 tiles vote for water and 8 out of 10 tiles contribute to land, then the semantic profile of image is {0.3 water, 0.8 land}. A tile may vote for any number of categories under consideration. A similar approach is described in [20] where an image is divided in 10 x 10 regions, each voting for a single category. Our framework differs in this aspect from [20], as for large sized images, a region is bound to contain more than one category. Hence it makes more sense to detect all of them and not restrict a region to a single label.

Query Retrieval Module: The semantic profiles for all the database images are stored in a semantic profile database. Given a user query, its semantic profile is constructed. The results are ordered based on the Euclidean distance between the semantic profiles of the query and the candidate database image. Our approach also enables us to develop a framework for fuzzy queries, e.g., 'retrieve images containing largely water' or 'do not retrieve images containing any cloud cover'.

5   Experimental Setup and Results

To test the proposed technique, we developed a heterogeneous image database consisting of images from different on-line resources. Images showing none, one or more of the selected concepts were downloaded from the freely available image galleries of commercial satellite companies like Orbimage and Spaceimaging, and government organizations NRSA (India) and US-based NASA's 'Earth Observatory. The image database consists of 400 natural color satellite images, which are stored in JPEG format with sizes varying from 500 x 500 up to 25000 x 25000. The image resolutions vary from a few inches per pixel to a few meters per pixel. The images have been taken from across the globe, at different times of the day and across seasons making the illumination properties different. We have kept no metadata information about resolution, scale or orientation.

We evaluated the performance of the proposed system in two ways. First we computed the system performance statistically giving precision values. We also compared the retrieved results with the results of 'SIMPLIicity' system using the same underlying image database. Like in most region-based retrieval systems, in SIMPLIicity, an image is represented by a set of regions, roughly corresponding to objects, which are characterized by color, texture, shape, and location. This system classifies images into semantic categories such as textured-nontextured, city-landscape, and so on. It uses a wavelet-based approach for feature extraction and an integrated region matching technique to match the image regions.

5.1   Performance of Query Retrieval

To provide numerical results, we asked 5 human annotators to manually check the relevance of results for 18 randomly chosen sample query images. For the same images, relevance of results given by SIMPLIcity is also evaluated by the same annotators. The top ten results are considered for evaluation and the precision is computed as the fraction of images retrieved correctly as per human judgment. For each of the eighteen query images, the average precision of results given by both systems are plotted in Fig. 7. We find that on an average, the precision of the proposed system is greater than that of SIMPLIcity by 0.342.

5.2   Query Comparison

Fig. 8 shows the comparison of results between the proposed system and the SIMPLIcity for a query image in which water appears green. The top row shows our experimental results and the bottom row shows retrieval results of SIMPLIcity. The leftmost image in each row is the query image. Due to the limitation of

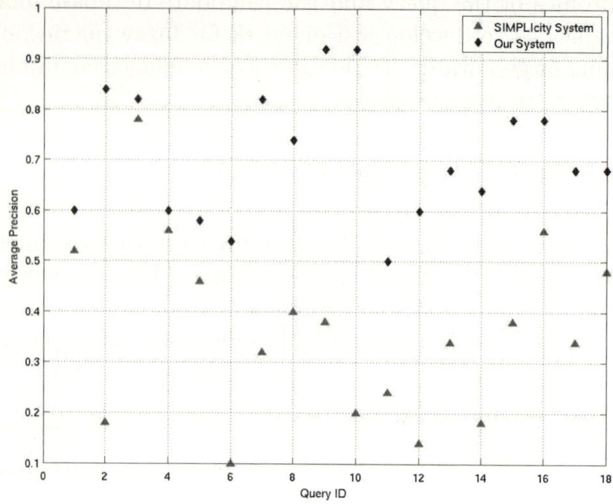

Fig. 7. Comparison of average precision values (best seen in color)

space, we have shown only top 10 matches for each query comparison. Our system has successfully identified that the query contains water and corresponding images involving water are returned irrespective of the intra-class variations in appearances.

More (favorable) results of the comparison do not appear in this version due to space limitations but are available at our website.

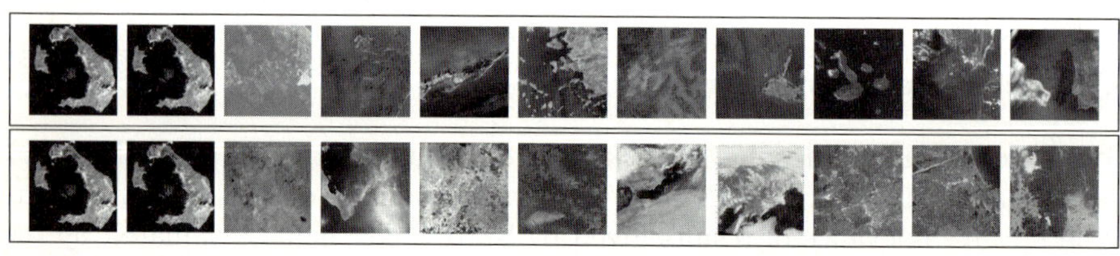

Fig. 8. Using semantic retrieval to overcome intra-class differences in appearances of a concept. The top row shows the first ten results of our system and the bottom row shows the results obtained using SIMPLIcity technique.

6   Concluding Remarks

Texton histogram is a robust feature capable of capturing the weak textured nature of remote sensing images in a scale, orientation and illumination independent manner. This feature along with other features can effectively learn the high level concepts present in remote sensing domain. Using such a semantic approach effectively counters the intra-class image variations and inter-class image similarities. Hence, the proposed framework is able to characterize remote sensing images in a generic manner. However it should be noted that our framework does not handle spatial adjacency constraints.

Acknowledgments

We thank Appu Shaji and Vinay Namboodiri for the cafeteria-based brainstorming sessions, and Aniruddha Joshi for his inputs on the intricacies of training SVMs. We thank J. Z. Wang who enabled comparisons by providing the SIMPLIcity executable, and data.

References

1. Kitamoto, A.: Digital typhoon: Near real-time aggregation, recombination and delivery of typhoon-related information. In: Fourth International Symposium on Digital Earth. (2005) (CD–ROM)
2. Puzicha, J., Hofmann, T., Buhmann, J.: Non-parametric similarity measures for unsupervised texture segmentation and image retrieval. In: Computer Vision and Pattern Recognition (CVPR '97), Washington, DC, USA, IEEE Computer Society (1997) 267
3. Newsam, S., Wang, L., Bhagavathy, S., Manjunath, B.S.: Using texture to annotate remote sensed datasets. In: 3rd International Symposium on Image and Signal Processing and Analysis (ISPA). (2003)
4. Newsam, S., Wang, L., Bhagavathy, S., Manjunath, B.S.: Using texture to analyze and manage large collections of remote sensed image and video data. Journal of Applied Optics: Information Processing **43** (2004) 210–217
5. Wang, L., Liu, J.: Texture classification using multiresolution markov random field models. Pattern Recogn. Lett. **20** (1999) 171–182
6. Valeriano, M.I., Escada, S.: Mining patterns of change in remote sensing image databases. In: Fifth IEEE International Conference on Data Mining (ICDM'05). (2005) 362–369
7. Schroder, M., Rehrauer, H., Seidel, K., Datcu, M.: Spatial information retrieval from remote- sensing images - part 2: Gibbs-markov random fields. IEEE Trans. Geosci. Remote Sensing (1998) 1446–1455
8. Unser, M.: Texture classification and segmentation using wavelet frames. Image Processing, IEEE Transactions on **4** (1995) 1549–1560
9. Wang, J.Z., Wiederhold, G., Firschein, O., Wei, S.X.: Content-based image indexing and searching using daubechies' wavelets. International Journal on Digital Libraries **1** (1997) 311–328
10. Wang, J., Li, J., Wiederhold, G.: SIMPLIcity: Semantics-sensitive integrated matching for picture LIbraries. IEEE Transactions on Pattern Analysis and Machine Intelligence **23** (2001) 947–963
11. Varma, M., Zisserman, A.: Classifying images of materials: Achieving viewpoint and illumination independence. In: ECCV (3). (2002) 255–271
12. Varma, M., Zisserman, A.: Statistical approaches to material classification. In: Second Indian Conference on Computer Vision, Graphics and Image Processing. (2002) 167–172

13. Varma, M., Zisserman, A.: Texture classification: Are filter banks necessary? In: International Conference on Computer Vision and Pattern recognition. (2003) 691–698
14. Julesz, B.: Textons, the elements of texture perception, and their interactions. Nature **290** (1981) 91–97
15. Malik, J., Belongie, S., Shi, J., Leung, T.K.: Textons, contours and regions: Cue integration in image segmentation. In: ICCV (2). (1999) 918–925
16. Gilles, S.: Robust description and matching of images. Technical report, University of Oxford (1998) Ph.D. Thesis.
17. Yang, C., Lozano-Perez, T.: Image database retrieval with multiple-instance learning techniques. In: Proc. International Conference on Data Engineering. (2000) 233–243
18. Quinlan, J.R.: Induction of decision trees. In Shavlik, J., Dietterich, T., eds.: Readings in Machine Learning. Morgan Kaufmann (1990) Originally published in *Machine Learning*1:81–106, 1986.
19. John, G.H., Kohavi, R., Pfleger, K.: Irrelevant features and the subset selection problem. In: International Conference on Machine Learning. (1994) 121–129
20. Vogel, J., Schiele, B.: Natural scene retrieval based on a semantic modeling step. International Conference on Image and Video Retrieval CIVR 2004, Dublin, Ireland, LNCS **3115** (2004)

Content-Based Image Retrieval Using Wavelet Packets and Fuzzy Spatial Relations

Minakshi Banerjee and Malay K. Kundu

Machine Intelligence Unit, Indian Statistical Institute
203, B.T. Road, Kolkata 700 108, India
{minakshi_r, malay}@isical.ac.in

Abstract. This paper proposes a region based approach for image retrieval. We develop an algorithm to segment an image into fuzzy regions based on coefficients of multiscale wavelet packet transform. The wavelet based features are clustered using fuzzy C-means algorithm. The final cluster centroids which are the representative points, signify the color and texture properties of the preassigned number of classes. Fuzzy Topological relationships are computed from the final fuzzy partition matrix. The color and texture properties as indicated by centroids and spatial relations between the segmented regions are used together to provide overall characterization of an image. The closeness between two images are estimated from these properties. The performance of the system is demonstrated using different set of examples from general purpose image database to prove that, our algorithm can be used to generate meaningful descriptions about the contents of the images.

1 Introduction

Effective searching of relevant images using information derived from the visual contents (color, texture, shape etc.) is the focus of interest for most research on image databases. In the recent past, Content-Based Image Retrieval (CBIR) techniques became popular [1], [2], [3], [4],[5], [6], [7], [8] for retrieving relevant images from an image database by measuring similarity between the automatically derived features (color, texture, shape etc.) of the query image and the images stored in the database [5]. But even with the most sophisticated design, it is often not possible to achieve satisfactory results, because the image features may convey different meanings under different context (semantic gap). There are ongoing efforts by the researchers for bridging the gap between human intuitive understanding and information derived from image features.

Apparently different set of features are suitable for different purposes. For example, shape related features are not suitable to extract textured pictures only. The features like color, texture, shape as well as the spatial relationship between the individual regions play a significant role in depicting the overall meaning associated with the scene. The properties of individual regions can be coupled with spatial relationships between them, to provide more realistic matching between two images. Methodologies to compute spatial relationships of the objects have

P. Kalra and S. Peleg (Eds.): ICVGIP 2006, LNCS 4338, pp. 861–871, 2006.

been proposed by [9], [10], [11]. However the methods mostly deal with the geometric attributes of a region like (area, shape adjacency, surroundedness etc.). Fuzzy similarity measure between regions have been introduced in FIRM [12] where the properties of all regions are integrated by a family of fuzzy features. The geometric relationships between the regions are not considered.

Extracting significant features using wavelets have been proved to be promising [13]. Wavelet transform provides a suitable framework for analysis and characterization of images at different scales [14], [15]. As significant texture information requires over complete decomposition, wavelet packet frames which comprise of all possible combinations of subband tree decomposition, can serve better representation of textural analysis than standard dyadic wavelets. Not all the bases are equally important. Hence finding out computationally efficient optimal basis based on the some statistical criteria becomes important [13].

In this paper, we propose a simple technique to identify uniform color textured regions. The approximate boundary regions are also extracted for detecting the differences of textures in adjacent regions. We use Fuzzy C- means algorithm for assigning multiclass membership values to each pixel, for approximate segmentation into homogeneous regions. We use wavelet packet frames to extract features for segmentation, and obtain the best basis based on entropy measure. The centroids of the segmented regions depict the color and textural properties. To estimate the intersection between the fuzzy partitions a property namely Index of fuzziness [16] is computed. Fuzzy Topological relation known as, shape distance [17] is computed between the fuzzy regions of the segmented image. The proposed algorithm shows fairly promising performance in case of retrieving perceptually similar images from benchmark databases. The performance is compared with other approaches like (a) Color, texture histogram similar to [18] (b) gabor texture features, to prove the efficiency of the proposed scheme.

The remaining sections are organized as follows. The segmentation algorithm and the feature extraction process is described in section 2. The Experimental results and comparative studies are made in section 3. The paper is concluded in section 4.

2 Integrating Wavelet Features for Extraction of Colored Textures

Features extracted from different frequency bands of wavelet coefficients are shown to be effective for representing texture properties [15]. This can be explained from the fact that coefficients in different frequency band show variation in different scales and directions. An input color image can be looked as a 3-D energy function $E(x, y, \lambda)$ where (x,y) denotes the spatial coordinates and λ denotes the wavelength of light energy. The local spatial frequency characteristics of $E(u, v, \lambda)$ can be used to capture texture characteristics. The properties can be combined in the wavelet domain by convolution with a wavelet filter in the spatial domain with the independent color channels [19].

$$\hat{M}(u,v,\lambda) = h(u,v) * \int E(u,v,\lambda)d\lambda \qquad (1)$$

The filter bank $h(u,v)$ is a set of band pass filters with frequency selective properties. The original image is available in RGB format. The RGB values encode the color information. Each of the individual components are transformed separately. The discrete normalized scaling and wavelet basis functions are defined as [13],

$$\begin{aligned}
\phi_{i,k}(l) &= 2^{i/2}h_i(2^i l - k)\\
\psi_{i,k}(l) &= 2^{i/2}g_i(2^i l - k)
\end{aligned} \qquad (2)$$

where i and k are the dilation and translation parameters and h_i and g_i are respectively the sequence of lowpass and bandpass filters of increasing width indexed by i. The full discrete wavelet expansion of a signal that forms an orthonormal basis for $L^2(R^2)$ is given as,

$$x(l) = \sum_{k\in z} c_{(d_0)}(k)\phi_{d_0,k} + \sum_{i=1}^{d_0}\sum_{k\in z} d_{(i)}(k)\psi_{i,k} \qquad (3)$$

$d_{(i)}$ are the wavelet coefficients and $c_{(d_0)}$ are the expansion coefficients of the coarser signal approximation $x_{(d_0)}$. The $c_{(d_0)}$ and $d_{(i)}$ can be interpreted in terms of simple filtering and down sampling operations. The 2-D DWT is computed by applying a separable filter bank to the image where $c_i(x,y)$ corresponds to low frequencies (LL) $d_i^1(x,y)$ corresponds to the vertical high frequencies (horizontal edges, LH), $d_i^2(x,y)$ horizontal high frequencies(vertical edges, HL), $d_i^3(x,y)$ the high frequencies in both directions (the corners, HH). The image $I(x,y)$ is represented at several scales by { cd_0, $d_i^n(x,y)$, n= 1,2,3, i=1,..., d_0 }. The 2D-DWT transform of an $2^i \times 2^i$ image is represented as a set of shifted and dilated wavelet function resulting into subbabnd images,each of size $2^{i-1} \times 2^{i-1}$. The standard dyadic transform are not suitable for analysis of high frequency signals with relatively narrow band because the subband decomposition is applied on the low pass component plane of the input image. To obtain efficient texture properties, multiscale overcomplete packet transform is necessary. Wavelet packets comprises all possible combinations of subband decomposition applied recursively to the lowpass and high pass filter results of the previous wavelet transform step. As a result, it is possible to create arbitrary tree structures that generates various combinations of orthonormal bases [20]. As an example, a 2-level decomposition on the orthogonal subspaces generates bases, $P_{2,i,k}(l)$, i= 0,1,2,3 $p_{1,1,k}(l)=1/2\psi(l/2-k)$, $p_{2,0,k}(l)=1/4\psi(l/4-k)$, $p_{2,1,k}(l)=1/4\psi(l/4-k)$ forms orthogonal sets. The significant nodes are computed and the optimal basis is obtained based on entropy minimized tree, where the entropy function is computed between a parent and quad child. Only those nodes are considered for which the entropy exceeds the predefined threshold. The entropy minimized tree forms a nested sequence of subspaces, $V_1 \subset V_2 \subset ...V_n$.

2.1   Multiresolution Feature Extraction

Having obtained the entropy minimized tree, multiresolution analysis is performed considering the spatial similarities across subbands. In general there are spatial similarities across subbands [20]. The pixels in each subband are linked to the pixels of the adjacent subband at the next lower level. Each pixel (x, y) from the former set of subbands acts as the root of pixels $(2x, 2y)$, $(2x + 1, 2y)$, $(2x, 2y + 1)$, $(2x + 1, 2y + 1)$. For a (n) level decomposition the same rule links the pixels of the adjacent subbabnds starting from LHn, HLn, HHn, respectively. The selected bases V_n are interpolated by factor (n), to ensure the identity to the sampling spaces. This approach is computationally effective. It helps in reducing blockyness arising in case of the block based methods and the computational cost involved in pixel wise segmentation. The local features of the filter output (wavelet domain) around each (x,y) th pixel is estimated from the selected bases. The moments of the wavelet coefficients of various frequency bands have proven effective for discriminating textures [21]. To obtain the moments a Daubechies-4 wavelet transform is applied. Around the (x,y) pixels of a certain subband a $W \times W$ window is centered. The raw moments m00,m10,m01,m20,m02,m11 are computed. From which the centralized moments $\mu20,\mu02,\mu11$ are computed on each window, [22], as follows.

$$\mu20 = m20 - \frac{m10^2}{m00}$$
$$\mu02 = m02 - \frac{m01^2}{m00} \qquad (4)$$
$$\mu11 = m11 - \frac{m10*m01}{m00}$$

For a color input image, the moments computed along the individual channels are represented as, $F_k\lambda =[\mu20,\mu02,\mu11]$ The feature computed along the three channels are considered as linearly independent and represented as,

$$F_k(x, y) = \sum F_{k\lambda} \qquad (5)$$

The segmentation obtained with the moments are shown in Figs.1(b), 2(b), 3(b).

   Apart from $\mu20,\mu02,\mu11$, the variance of the coefficients of the selected window is computed from the (R) plane across the dimension of rows. Classifying these features we approximately segment the boundaries between the homogeneous region as shown in Figs.1(c), 2(c).

$$F_k(x, y)var = (\sum_{x=1}^{W} \sum_{y=1}^{W} w_k(x, y) - \bar{F}_k(x, y))^2 \qquad (6)$$

where $\bar{F}_k(x, y)$ is the local mean and $w_k(x, y)$ is the coefficients at different scales k. The size of the window is an important parameter. Accurate texture measurement demands larger window size and better localization of region boundaries require smaller window size. The extracted features are integrated in the feature space to produce approximate segmentation into homogeneous regions. The features need to be clustered into different categories. We have used the standard fuzzy C- means algorithm [23]for pattern classification. Let $X= \{x_1, x_2, ..,x_N\}$

be a finite subset of n dimensional vector space R^n where x_i is a feature vector for a pixel in the image. For an integer $C, 2 \leq C \leq N$, a $C \times N$ matrix $U = [u_{ik}]$ is called the fuzzy C partition of X whenever the entries U satisfies the following conditions. $u_{ij} \in [0, 1]$ for all i and j, u_{ij} is the degree of membership of x_i in the cluster j, $\sum_{i=1}^{C} u_{ij} = 1$ for all j and $0 \leq \sum_{j=1}^{N} u_{ij} \leq N$ for all i.

2.2   Attributes of Fuzzy Sets on Segmented Image

Index of fuzziness : From fuzzy C-means clustering of $F_k(x, y)$, or $F_k(x, y) var$ a fuzzy partition matrix U of size C by N is obtained, where C is number of clusters and N is number of data points. The feature vector usually belongs to multiple regions with different degrees of memberships as opposed to classical region representation in which the feature vector belongs to exactly one region. The measure of fuzziness between the C fuzzy partitions of X, as obtained from the fuzzy C-means clustering is considered. Let the fuzzy partitions $(u_1, u_2, ..\ u_C)$ on X be defined by the set of C menbership functions, $\mu u_j(x)$ for all $x \in X$ and $j = 1, 2, ...C$. The intersection between two fuzzy partitions u_m and u_j , $(m \neq j)$ from the C collections is defined from [16]

$$I(u_j \cap u_m) = \frac{1}{|X|} \sum_{x \in X} [min(\mu u_j(x), \mu u_m(x))] \tag{7}$$

Shape distance : The pixels of the fuzzy partition are assigned distinct class label for which the membership is maximum. As a result, we obtain the segmented image. Each segmented region can be looked upon a bounded fuzzy set where the membership is zero outside the region. We consider the shape properties of the fuzzy regions of the segmented image, as proposed in [17],

If $\mu(x, y)$ is the membership of the fuzzy set μ at the point (x, y) in R^2, the center of gravity of μ is the point (x_0, y_0) where $x_0 = \frac{\int_s x \mu(x, y) ds}{A(S)}$ and $y_0 = \frac{\int_s y \mu(x, y) ds}{A(S)}$ where $A(S) = \int_s u(x, y) ds$. The dissimilarity between two fuzzy sets u and v is defined as,

$$D_1(u, v) = \int_s |u - v| ds \tag{8}$$

The shape distance between two fuzzy sets u and v (here u and v corresponds to individual segmented regions) are defined as,

$$D_3 = min[D_1(u, v_{\alpha 1 - \alpha 2}), D_1(u, v_{\alpha 1 - \alpha 2 + \pi})] \tag{9}$$

where $\alpha 1$ and $\alpha 2$ are the orientations defined as the angles that the major axis of u and v make with the x axis. $D_1(u, v_\alpha)$ is the dissimilarity with respect to rotation of v by angle α. The major and minor axes are perpendicular to each other and passes through the center of gravity. D_3 is the smaller of the D_1 values in these two orientations. The orientation θ of a fuzzy set can be obtained from the relation as follows,

$$tan2\theta = \frac{2\int_s(x-x_0)(y-y_0)\mu(x,y)\,ds}{\int_s(x-x_0)^2\mu(x,y)\,ds - \int_s(y-y_0)^2\mu(x,y)\,ds} \qquad (10)$$

It can be proved that D_3 is a metric. This metric can be used in pattern recognition and matching problems in a fuzzy framework. We have not considered the relations like left to , above etc. as the segmented regions may not represent the image at object levels. The feature representation of the segmented image can be looked as a collection of features $[F_1, F_2, ...F_C]$ representing the variance of the centroids where C represents the number of classes. The index of fuzziness I_{mj} for $m \neq j$ between any two partitions of the C separable classes are considered. Also the shape distance S_{m1m2} between any two segmented fuzzy regions (m1, m2) are computed to generate the effective characterization of an image. In order to compute feature similarities between two images, Euclidean distance metric is used to compute the dissimilarity value between the centroids. If $X = [x_1, x_2, \cdots, x_i]$ and $Y = [y_1, y_2, \cdots, y_i]$ are two feature vectors then the Euclidean distance metric between X,Y is given by,

$$E_d = \sqrt{\sum(x_i - y_i)^2} \qquad (11)$$

The intuitive similarity between two regions are computed from shape distance. The rank is computed as follows. The similarity is performed on each type of features separately. Finally the rank obtained from each individual set of features are combined to get the final result. The rank obtained from matching the centroids and index of fuzziness features are decided by measuring Euclidean distance between the features of the query and the target images. The total similarity is calculated as follows :

$$d_{qt} = \sum_{k=1}^{n}(r_{tk})/n \qquad (12)$$

where d_{qt} is the similarity distance of the query image q to image t. n is the total number of features r_{tk} is the rank of the image t in feature k.

3   Experimental Steps

We test our algorithm on a database consisting of 1000 images with 100 images from ten different categories down loaded http://wang.ist.psu.edu/docs/related. The experimental results are shown from Figs. 1 to Fig. 6. We grossly partition the image into three meaningful classes to analyze the region attributes and spatial relations between these regions. Fixing the number of classes may not effectively partition all database images at individual object level. It is expected that similar partitions will be generated for images with similar semantics for use in computing overall image to image similarity. If the segmentation becomes

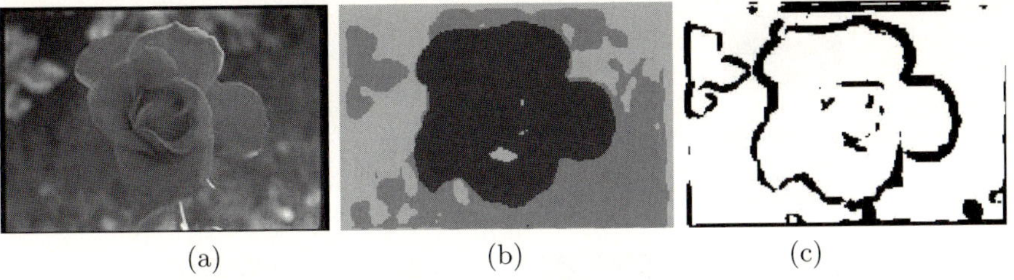

(a)   (b)   (c)

Fig. 1. (a) original image (b) segmented output (3 regions) (c) segmented output (3 class, boundaries assigned a common black label)

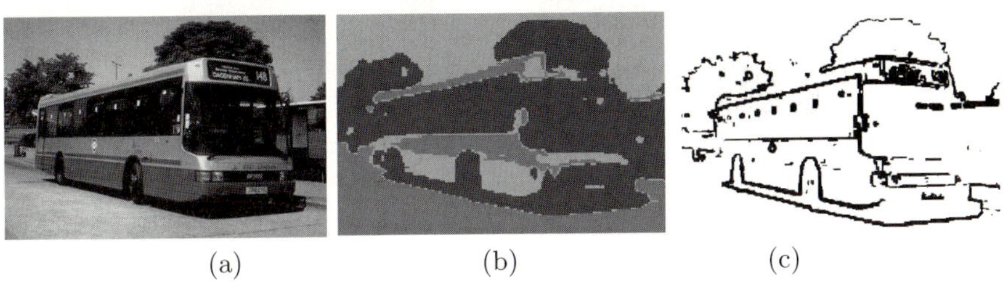

(a)   (b)   (c)

Fig. 2. (a) original image (b) segmented output (3 regions) (c) segmented output (3 class, boundaries assigned a common black label)

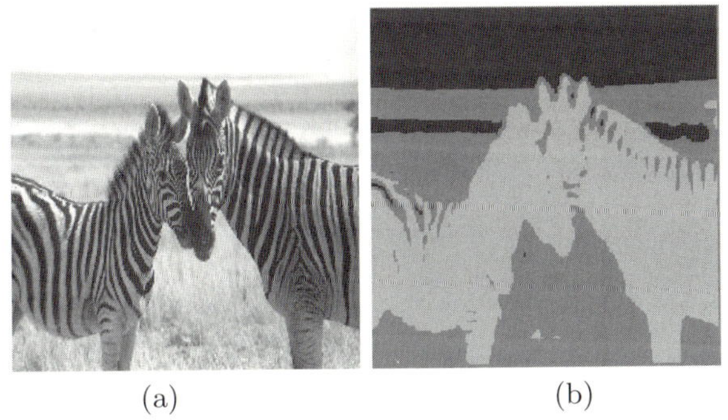

(a)   (b)

Fig. 3. (a) original image (b) segmented output (3 regions)

finer, the uncertainty in characterizing the perceptual contents increases due to detailed classifications within regions. This degrades the overall impression of the object nature. The segmentation results are shown from Figs. 1 to Fig. 3. The image shown as Fig. 1(b) is the segmented output of Fig.1(a) into three regions. Individual regions are characterized with different gray values. Fig.1(c) is the segmented output which broadly classifies the boundary between the regions using the features obtained from (6). The regions boundaries are assigned a common class label (plotted as dark boundary pixels). The segmented output of Fig. 2(a) is shown in Fig. 2(b) using the features computed from (4). The classified

Fig. 4. Retrieval results. With top left image as the query image.

Fig. 5. Retrieval results. With top left image as the query image.

regions boundaries plotted as dark pixels are shown in Fig. 2(c). Similarly the segmented output for Fig. 3(a) is shown in Fig. 3(b). The segmentation results shown are quite satisfactory in classifying the images into the assigned regions. By intelligent selection of the basis the number of features have been reduced for the desired segmentation. In our problem the description of the entire image is used in querying rather than taking the attribute of individual regions. We have taken query examples from all categories of images and tested the performance with the proposed features. We try two explain the results obtained on

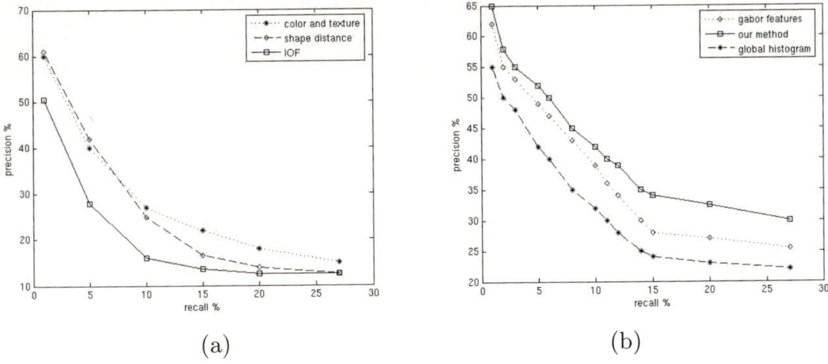

Fig. 6. (a) Recall, Precision curve from results with individual features (b) Comparative results

images with some distinctive properties. Images in Fig. 4 are constituting of a significant object with some background object. The main object almost occupies the major portion of the scene. We have tested the results considering the features (centroids) and other two spatial features separately. The combined result is shown in Fig. 4 with the top left image as as the query. The results obtained from the combined features outer performed the the individual feature retrieval. It has been found that shape distance and index of fuzziness provides a better attribute in such case. Intuitively the shape of the object itself is more meaningful than the color or texture information in the example. This provides evidence that our approach for computing relations between the regions is effective for such cases. In the second example, both the background and object arc important. The object region has quite a common color and texture. The centroid features which carry the region attributes in terms of color and texture provide a better index than the shape distance. In this case the color and texture carried most of the useful information. Combining shape distance did not make significant difference to the query results. The retrieval results after combining all the features together is shown in Fig. 5 with top left image as the query. The final similarity of the combined features is found better than each of the individual feature ranking.

With each test set image as the query, the average precision and recall for individual feature retrieval is shown in the Fig. 6(a). If the system retrieves r images that belongs to the same class $C1$ as the query ($r \leq n$). If there are N_{c1} images in the class $C1$ of the query, then $P=r/n$ is the precision and $R = r/N_{c1}$ the recall for this query. We found that the similarity as obtained from index of fuzziness alone is not satisfactory. Intuitively this feature measures the fuzziness in clustering and indirectly captures dissimilarity between the regions. However the combined results improves the precision. We benchmark our results with retrieval algorithms using global color texture histograms as used in [18]. Color is represented using a 2D histogram over the HS coordinates of the HSV space. Texture is represented by two histograms (coarseness and directionality), of the image. The similarity distance between two color histograms is computed by histogram intersection. The similarity between two textures of the whole image is determined by a weighted sum of the Euclidean distance. We also provide a comparison in retrieval results with Gabor features computed around randomly selected points. We tested the results in almost all categories of images as shown in Fig.6(b). Histogram gave satisfactory results for images objects having significant objects with quite a common color and texture. In case case of general scenes our algorithm generated better results. This proves that the proposed features captures additional spatial information of the segmented regions.

The experiment is performed in (SUN microsytems Ultra 60) system using MATLAB package. The average cputime time required for computing the feature vector is 10 seconds.

4   Conclusion

In this work we have developed an image segmentation algorithm using wavelet packet based features and the fuzzy C- means statistical clustering algorithm. The color and texture attributes of the fuzzy regions are unified with the topological features effective in capturing spatial relation between the regions. However we have not incorporated the topological properties extracted from the region boundaries in retrieval. Using these features we intend to incorporate some more spatial relation properties in order to capture crucial semantic details.

Acknowledgment. Minakshi Banerjee is grateful to the Department of Science and Technology, New Delhi, India, for providing her research fellowship under women Scientist scheme, vide, grant (no.SR-WOS A/ET-111/2003).

References

1. Smith, J.R., Chang, S.F.: VisualSEEK a fully automated content-based image query system. Proc. ACM Multimedia (1996) 87–98
2. Carson, C., Thomas, M., .Belongie, S., Hellerstein, J., J.Malik: Blobworld a system for region - based image indexing and retrieval. Proceedings of Visual Information Systems (1999) 509–516
3. Ma, W.Y., Manjunath, M.: NeTra :a toolbox for navigating large image databases. Proc. IEEE International Conference on Image Processing (1997) 568–571
4. Laaksonen, J., Koskela, M., Oja, E.: PicSOM :self organising maps for content based image retrieval. Proc. on International joint Conference on Neural Networks **75** (1999) 150–164
5. Smeulders, A.W.M., Worring, M., Santini, S., Gupta, A., Jain, R.: Content-based image retrieval at the end of the early years. IEEE Transactions on Pattern Analysis and Machine Intelligence **22(12)** (2000) 1349–1380
6. Gevers, T., Smeulders., A.W.M.: Combining color and shape invariant features for image retrieval. Image and Vision computing. **17(7)** (1999) 475–488
7. Krishnapuram, R., Medasani, S., Jung, S.H., Choi, Y.S., Balasubramaniam, R.: Content-based image retrieval based on a fuzzy approach. IEEE Transactions on Knowledge and Data Engineering **16(10)** (2004) 1185–1199

8. Bracamonte, J., Ansorge, M., Pellandini, F., Farine, P.A.: Efficient compressed domain target image search and retrieval. 4th International Conference on Image and Video Retrieval, Singapore (2005) 154–163

9. Freeman, J.: The modeling of spatial relations. Computer Graphics and Image Processing **4** (1975) 156–171

10. Pal, S.K.: Fuzziness, image information and scene analysis. In Yager, R.R., zadeh, L.A., eds.: An Introduction to Fuzzy Logic Applications in Intelligent Systems. Kluwer Academic, Norwell (1992) 147–184

11. Krishnapuram, R., Keller, J.M., Ma, Y.: Quantitative analysis of properties and spatial relations of fuzzy image regions. IEEE Transactions on Fuzzy Systems **1(3)** (1993) 222–233

12. Chen, Y., Z.Wang, J., Li, J.: A region-based fuzzy feature approach to content-based image retrieval. IEEE Transactions on Pattern Analysis and Machine Intelligence **24(9)** (2002) 1–16

13. Mallat, S.: A theory for multiresolution signal decomposition. IEEE Transactions on Pattern Analysis and Machine Intelligence **11(7)** (1989) 674–693

14. M.Acharya, kundu, M.K.: Robust texture calssification using wavelet frames. Image Processing and communications **5(2)** (1999) 19–37

15. M.Acharya, kundu, M.K.: An adaptive approach to unsupervised texture segmentation using m-band wavelet transform. Signal Processing **81** (2001) 1337–1356

16. Pal, S.K., Majumder, D.D.: Fuzzy mathematical Approach to Pattern Recognition. Willey Eastern Limited, New York (1985)

17. Chaudhuri, B.B.: Fuzzy geometry and shape relations in image spaces. IETE Journal of Research **44(4-5)** (1998) 161–175

18. Ortega, M., Rui, Y., Chakrabarti, K., Mehrotra, S., Huang, T.S.: Supporting similarity queries in mars. In Proceedings of the 5th ACM International Multimedia Conference, Seattle, Washington **403-413** (1997)

19. Hoang, M.A., Geusebroek, J.M., Smeulders, A.W.M.: Color texture measurement and segmentation. Signal Processing **85** (2005) 265–275

20. Rao, R.M., Bopardikar, A.S.: Wavelet Transforms Introduction to Theory and Applications. Pearson Education, Asia (Singapore) (2002)

21. Unser, M.: Texture classification and segmentation using wavelet frames. IEEE Transactions on Image Processing **4(11)** (1995) 1549–1560

22. Gonzalez, R.C., Woods, R.E.: Digital Image Processing. Wiley, New York (1985)

23. Bezdek, J.: Pattern Recognition with Fuzzy Objective Function Algorithms. New York, Plenium Press (1981)

Content Based Image Retrieval Using Region Labelling

J. Naveen Kumar Reddy, Chakravarthy Bhagvati, S. Bapi Raju,
Arun K. Pujari, and B.L. Deekshatulu

Dept. of Computer and Information Sciences
University of Hyderabad, Hyderabad 500046

Abstract. This paper proposes a content based image retrieval system
that uses semantic labels for determining image similarity. Thus, it aims
to bridge the semantic gap between human perception and low-level features. Our approach works in two stages. Image segments, obtained from
a subset of images in the database by an adaptive k-means clustering algorithm, are labelled manually during the training stage. The training
information is used to label all the images in the database during the
second stage. When a query is given, it is also segmented and each segment is labelled using the information available from the training stage.
Similarity score between the query and a database image is based on the
labels associated with the two images. Our results on two test databases
show that region labelling helps in increasing the retrieval precision when
compared to feature-based matching.

1   Introduction

Research in Content Based Image Retrieval (CBIR) steadily gained momentum
in recent years consequent to the dramatic increase in the volume of digital images. Image databases containing thousands and sometimes millions of images
are available in many fields such as remote sensing, medical imaging and biometrics (e.g., fingerprints). The main difference between data retrieval from a
conventional database and CBIR is that the former is based on predefined keywords (or keys) associated with each stored record, while the latter utilises visual
cues. A good survey of CBIR field may be found in the review paper by Sameer
Antani, Rangachar Kasturi and Ramesh Jain[1].

CBIR systems mainly use colour[2,3,4,5], texture[6,7,8], shape[9,10,11] and
other low-level features to assess similarity while human beings rely on high-
level symbolic (e.g., chair, Taj Mahal) and abstract (e.g., war, happy occasions)
concepts. Such a difference between computer and human perception of similarity, often called the *semantic gap*, led researchers into exploring methods that
fall broadly into three categories: relevance feedback, modeling human perception and linguistic indexing.

Relevance feedback is an on-line learning strategy where user provides feedback on the retrieved images which adapts the response from the CBIR system.
Usually, the user responses are used either to modify the query or the similarity measures[12,13]. Several attempts have been made to incorporate human

P. Kalra and S. Peleg (Eds.): ICVGIP 2006, LNCS 4338, pp. 872–881, 2006.

perception into CBIR systems by developing computational models for early human vision[14,15,16] or similarity functions consistent with human perception [17,18,19]. In lingusitic indexing, images are categorized into different types and annotated (or labelled) by using a trained classifier. The problem of CBIR is thus reduced to the problem of text-based retrieval. Examples of such work are found in the paper by Chen and Wang[20].

There are two major approaches to linguistic indexing. The first is region-based and initially segments images into regions. If the segmentation process is ideal each region is treated as a semantically meaningful object and retrieval is based on similarity between regions. UCSB NeTra[7], Berkeley's Blobworld[21] and Stanford's SIMPLIcity[22] are examples of such systems. Integrated Region Matching (IRM) [23] (and used in [22]) and its enhancement using fuzzy membership functions for more perceptual segmentation and region matching[24] illustrate how sophisticated region-based similarity measures may be defined for CBIR applications.

The second approach is to organize the digital library in a semantically meaningful manner using image classification. Such classification is also useful to index images automatically. Unfortunately, there is no effective method yet to obtain good semantic categorization from low-level features. A compromise is manual annotations, which are potentially subjective and ambiguous and sometimes difficult because image data is rich in detail. In specific domains, however, classification provides a powerful set of semantic features for CBIR.

In this paper, we describe a CBIR system based on semi-automatic region labelling for remote sensing images. Remote sensing images have the advantage that their classification is well-researched, and well-defined with several standard schemes in existence. We also used the same method on a miscellaneous database containing different categories of objects such as flowers, aeroplanes, flags, etc. Our results indicate that region-labelling, even though it is sometimes incorrect, leads to improved precision in retrieving images.

The rest of the paper is organized as follows. Section 2 describes feature extraction and segmentation. Section 3 describes the two-stage segment labelling process and subsequent query processing. Section 4 illustrates the results on two test databases and Section 5 concludes the paper.

2 Feature Extraction and Segmentation

Our system segments images using an adaptive k-means algorithm based on colour and texture features. We follow the same approach described in [22] and [23]. An image is divided into 4×4 blocks from which three colour and three texture features are computed. The colour features are the average L, U and V components where LUV colour space is used for its perceptually uniform properties. The three texture features are obtained from Daubechies-4 wavelet transform on the L component. The 4×4 block is decomposed into four 2×2 frequency bands after a one level wavelet transform. The HL texture feature f_{HL} is then given by

$$f_{HL}(k,l) = \left(\frac{1}{4} \sum_{i=0}^{1} \sum_{j=0}^{1} C^2_{k+i,j+l} \right)^{\frac{1}{2}}$$

where C_{00}, C_{01}, C_{10} and C_{11} are the four values in each 2×2 block. The HH and LH band features are similarly calculated.

k-means algorithm is used for segmenting the images by clustering the feature vectors. If the number of 4×4 blocks in the image is B, the goal of k-means algorithm is to partition the set of feature vectors $f_i, 1 \leq i \leq B$ into k groups with means $\overline{f}_1, \overline{f}_2, \ldots, \overline{f}_k$ such that

$$D(k) = \sum_{i=1}^{L} \min_{1 \leq j \leq k} (f_i - \overline{f}_j)^2$$

is minimized.

We adaptively choose the number of clusters by starting with $k = 2$ and increasing it until one of the following three criteria is met: $D(k)$ is below a specified threshold indicating that the clusters are tight; change in $D(k)$ between consecutive iterations is below a threshold indicating convergence; and, k exceeds an upper bound indicating too large a number of clusters.

3   Region Labelling

Region labelling step assigns a semantic label to each segment obtained from k-means clustering. The labelling is done in two stages. A subset of images from the database that illustrate the semantic concepts important in querying is chosen in the first, manual or training, stage. The different segments in the images are shown to the trainer and are assigned labels manually. As there exist many regions that have identical labels, the average feature vector of such regions along with the associated label are stored in a label database. Some sample regions and labels are shown in Figure 1 from a test database of approximately 1200 low-resolution remote sensing images obtained from the National Remote Sensing Agency (NRSA), Hyderabad. An example of a segmented image that is labelled manually is shown in Figure 2.

In the second stage, all the segmented images in the database are automatically assigned labels utilizing the label database created in the training stage. The feature vector corresponding to an unlabelled segment is compared with the mean feature vectors in the label database. The label associated with the nearest feature vector in the label database is assigned to the unlabelled region. An example of automatic labelling is shown in Figure 3. It may be noticed that the labelling is not fully correct in that snowy regions are labelled as a *water body*. Such inaccuracies have an impact on the precision and recall values of the CBIR system as we shall see in the next section.

When a query image is given, it is segmented and automatically labelled using the approach described above. Image similarity is measured on the labels and not

Color Name	Color	Interpretation
Dark Red		Dense Vegetation
Red		Normal Vegetation
Light Red		Sparse Vegetation
Pure Black		Pure Water Body
Black		Water Body with less sediments
Gray		Water Body with less sediments
Dark Blue		Water Body with some sediments
Blue		Water Body with some sediments
Grayish Blue		Water body with more sediments
Cyan		Water Body with more sediments

Fig. 1. Image segments and associated labels

on the feature vectors leading to retrieval using semantics rather than low-level characteristics. Similarity score is given by

$$S = \frac{n_m}{n}$$

where n is the number of regions in the query image and n_m is the number of identical labels between the query and the database images. S ranges from 0 to 1.0. Many variants of the above similarity score exist in literature[25] although they have not been tried yet by us.

4   Experimental Results

We initially experimented with a database of remote sensing images from NRSA, Hyderabad. The retrieved results for a query image showing waterbody along with some clouds are shown in Figure 4. Similarity score is based on the labels automatically assigned to the images (as explained in the previous section). It may be seen that all the top eight images are relevant. However, several of the images contain clouds while there are many other images in the database that are not cloudy.

More sophisticated queries allowed by our system specify the *location*, *extent* or *absence* of a class in conjunction with a query image. In this case, additional

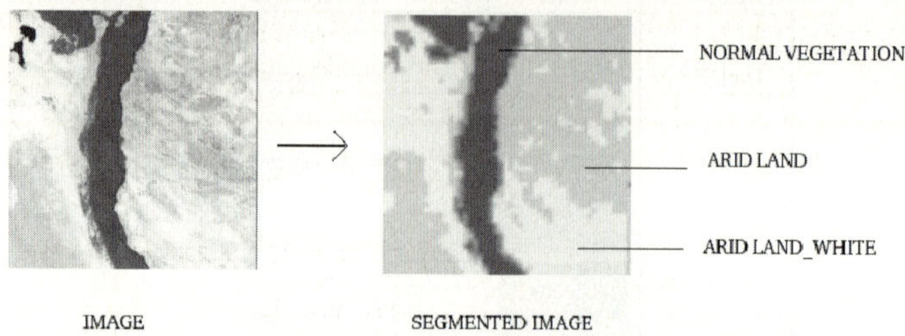

Fig. 2. Example of a segmented image that is manually labelled

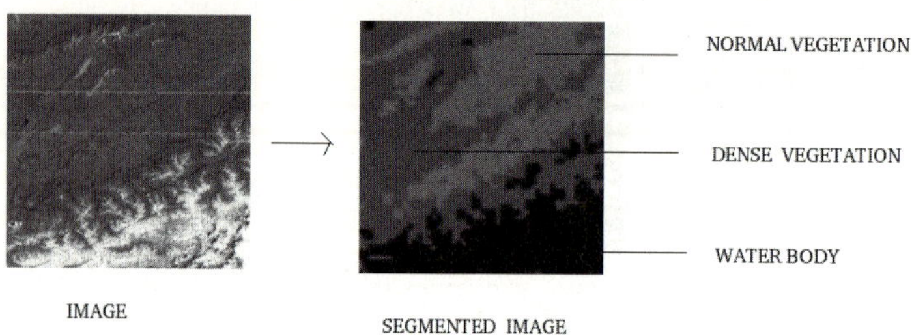

Fig. 3. Example of a segmented image that is automatically labelled

information about the bounding box and area of the segment is included along with the similarity measure. One example of such queries is extremely useful to NRSA and involves retrieving *cloud-free* images similar to a given query. Figure 5 shows the results for the same query image of Figure 4 but with the additional condition that the results do not contain cloudy regions. It may now be noticed that the query image is not the first image to be retrieved but the third. The first two images are less cloudy leading to higher similarity score than for the query image itself because its cloudy regions lower the similarity with the query. Overall, the resulting images are of better quality than the earlier set but some of them still contain clouds. The reason is that the wispy clouds seen are misclassified as water bodies with sedimentation and are hence retrieved.

We also experimented with a much larger and more varied database containing approximately 8000 images. These show objects such as flowers, aeroplanes, sunsets, fireworks and others. Figure 6 shows an example query image of fireworks and the retrieved images. Again, all the top eight images are relevant. We compared our results against the Integrated Region Matching (IRM) method proposed in [23]. The results from the IRM method are shown in Figure 7. It may be seen that three of the images do not show fireworks and are therefore irrelevant.

A more detailed comparison of the performance of the region-labelling method and IRM is shown in Figure 8. We took 10 query images each from seven categories — remote sensing (C1), flags (C2), flowers (C3), landscapes (C4),

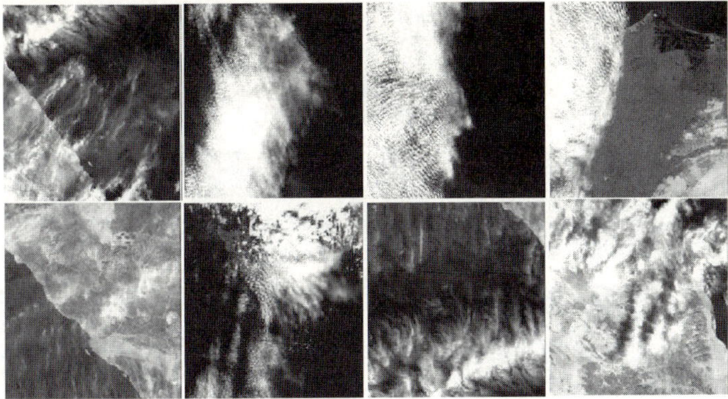

Fig. 4. Retrieved images for *waterbody* class using region-labelling method. Query is the first image.

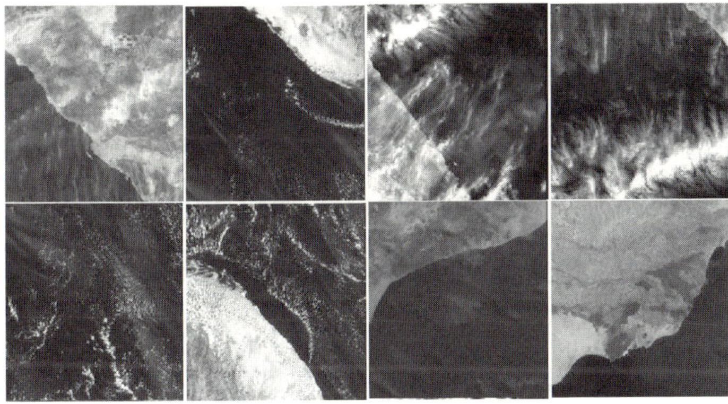

Fig. 5. Retrieved images when an additional *cloud-free* constraint is specified. Query is the same as in Figure 4.

Fig. 6. Query results using region-labelling for the fireworks image shown at the top

Fig. 7. Query results for the same query image as in Figure 6 using IRM method

automobiles (C5), aeroplanes (C6), and fruits and vegetables (C7) — and computed the average precision for each category. We first used region-labelling and then the IRM method. From the Figure 8 it may be seen that for Category *C1*, the average precision for region-labelling method (identified as *labelling* in the figure) is approximately 0.9 while it is about 0.8 for IRM. The average precision for all categories (except *C4*, i.e., landscape images) is higher than 0.7 indicating good overall performance.

It may also be seen that for all categories except *C3*, i.e. flower images, region-labelling results in a higher average precision than IRM.

Finally, we show a recall-precision graph (Figure 9) that compares the performance of the region-labelling approach with IRM and its fuzzy extension UFM in retrieving remote sensing images. It may be seen that the region-labelling approach is better than both IRM and UFM.

An image contains many colours and regions, but a human user generally focusses on only a few high level concepts while ignoring the finer details. Consequently, in our system, we restricted the maximum number of segments in an image to six. The performance of our system on low-resolution remote sensing images and on images containing flags, fireworks and other such easily distinguishable objects justifies the choice of a small value for the number of segments. We noticed that our system gives consistently high precision and recall when the images contain one or two dominant objects.

We used simple colour and texture features in our approach. They may not be adequate to distinguish between certain semantic classes. An example is Figure 5 where images containing clouds are present in the results even though the query specified otherwise. The 6 features are not capable of distinguishing between water containing large levels of sedimentation and clouds, both of which are greyish white in colour and contain no texture.

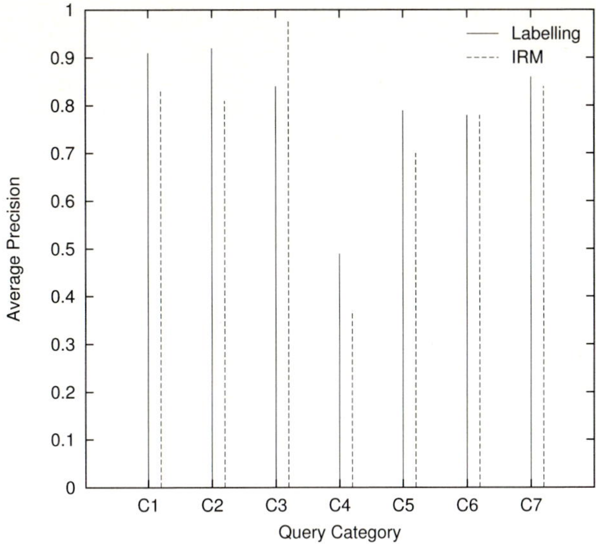

Fig. 8. Comparison of average precision between region labelling and IRM methods over 7 categories of images

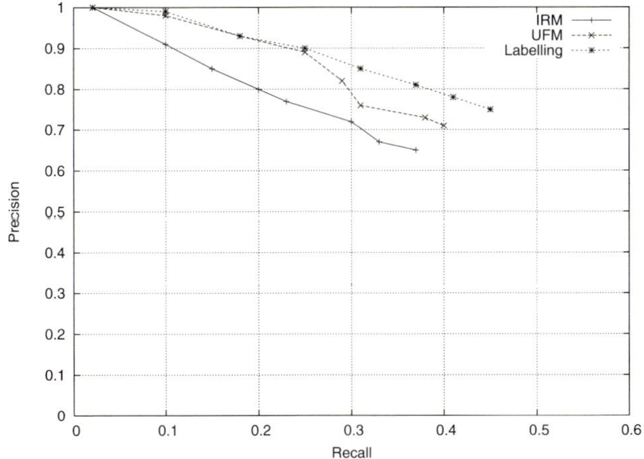

Fig. 9. Recall-precision graph comparing region labelling with IRM and UFM

Sometimes, however, it is not easy to label the segments in an image. For example, *landscapes* are particularly difficult if they involve a panoramic view of the countryside with few dominant features. There are two problems with such images: there are more than 6 semantically meaningful segments, and it is not easy to associate a label with low-level features. The latter problem causes our classification method based on nearest neighbour approach to fail.

To summarise, our proposed CBIR system based on supervised classification gives higher precision in retrieval when images contain a small number of meaningful segments and a few dominant objects. In other cases, either the segmentation or the labelling becomes inaccurate. Inaccuracy in segmentation does not seriously affect the performance as the similarity measure is based mainly on labelling and not on region properties. However, poor segmentation can lead to inaccurate labelling. Labelling has a direct impact on precision and good classification algorithms should be used.

5 Conclusion

In the paper, we presented a CBIR system that retrieves images based on high-level semantics that are assigned using a trained classifier. The results indicate that even our simple approach based on only 6 colour and texture features in conjunction with a supervised nearest neighbour classification scheme can lead to higher precision in retrieving several types of images. Our approach, demonstrated on remote sensing images, may be extended to querying other image databases provided that the images contain a small number of regions and distinct features that act as cues for matching.

References

1. Antani, S., Kasturi, R., Jain, R.: A Survey on the Use of Pattern Recognition Methods for Abstraction, Indexing and Retrieval of Images and Video. Pattern Recognition **35** (2002) 945–965
2. Fuertes, J.M., Lucena, M., Blanca, N.P.d.l., Chamorro-Martinez, J.: A Scheme of Colour Image Retrieval from Databases. Pattern Recognition Letters **22** (2001) 323–337
3. Kankanhalli, M.S., Mehtre, B.M., Huang, H.Y.: Colour and Spatial Feature for Content-Based Image Retrieval. Pattern Recognition Letters **20** (1999) 109–118
4. Pass, G., Zabih, R., Miller, J.: Comparing Images Using Color Coherence Vectors. In: Proc. of the ACM Multimedia'96 Conference. (1996) 65–73
5. Prasad, B.G., Gupta, S.K., Biswas, K.K.: Region-Based Image Retrieval Using Integrated Color Shape and Location Index. Computer Vision and Image Processing **94** (2004) 193–233
6. Li, M., Chen, Z., Zhang, H.J.: Statistical Correlation Analysis in Image Retrieval. Pattern Recognition **35** (2002) 2687–2693
7. Ma, W.Y., Manjunath, B.S.: NETRA: A toolbox for navigating large image databases. In: Proc. IEEE Int. Conf. on Image Processing, Santa Barbara, California (1997) 568–571
8. Unser, M.: Texture Classification and Segmentation Using Wavelet Frames. IEEE Trans. on Image Processing **4** (1995)
9. Zhang, J., Zhang, X., Krim, H., Walker, G.G.: Object Representation and Recognition in Shape Spaces. Pattern Recognition **36** (2003) 1143–1154
10. Badawy, O.E., Kamel, M.: Shape based image retrieval applied to Trademark images. Int. J. of Graphics and Image Processing **2** (2002) 1–19

11. Jain, A.K., Vailaya, A.: Shape-Based Retrieval: A Case Study with Trademark Image Databases. Pattern Recognition **31** (1998) 1369–1390
12. I.J.Cox, M.L.Miller, T.P.Minka, T.V.Papathomas, Yianilos: The bayesian image retrieval system, PicHunter: theory,implementation and psychophysical experiments. IEEE Trans. Image Processing **9** (2000) 20–37
13. Kherfi, M.L., Ziou, D., Bernardi, A.: Learning from Negative Example in Relevance Feedback. IEEE Trans. on Image Processing (2002)
14. Lu, G., Phillips, J.: Using perceptually weighted histograms for colour-based image retrieval. In: Proc. Fourth Int. Conf. on Signal Processing. (1998)
15. Mojsilovic, A., Kovacevic, J., Hu, J., Safranek, R.J., Ganapathy, S.K.: Matching and retrieval based on the vocabulary and grammar of color patterns. IEEE Trans. on Image Processing **9** (2000)
16. Nathalie, G., Heve, L.B., Jeanny, H., Anne, G.D.: Towards the introduction of human perception in natural scene classification system. IEEE Trans. on Neural Networks and Signal Processing (2002)
17. Rubner, Y., Tomasi, C.: Perceptual Metrics for Image Database Navigation. Kluwer Academic Publishers (2001)
18. Celebi, M.E., Aslandogan, Y.A.: Content-based image retrieval incorporating models of human perception. IEEE Trans. on Computers and Communication **2** (2004)
19. Frese, T., Boumann, C.A., Allenbach, J.P.: A methodology for designing image similarity metrics based on human visual system models. In: Proc. of SPIE/IS&T Conf. on Human Vision and Electronic Imaging II. (2002)
20. Chen, Y., Wang, J.Z.: Image categorization by learning and reasoning with regions. J. of Machine Learning Research (2004)
21. C.Carson, M.Thomas, S.Belongie, J.M.Hellerstein, J.Malik: Blobworld, A system for region-based image indexing and retrieval. In: Third Int. Conf. on Visual Information and Information Systems (VISUAL 99). (1999)
22. Wang, J.Z., Li, J., Wiederhold, G.: ”simplicity: Semantics sensitive integrated matching for picture libraries ”. IEEE Trans. Pattern Analysis and Machine Intelligence (2001)
23. Li, J., Wang, J.Z., Wiederhold, G.: IRM: Integrated Region Matching for Image Retrieval. In: Proc. of 8th ACM Int. Conf. on Multimedia, Los Angeles, California (2000) 147–156
24. Chen, Y., Wang, J.Z.: A region-based fuzzy feature matching approachto content based image retrieval. IEEE Trans. on Pattern Analysis and Machine Intelligence (2002)
25. Tubbs, J.D.: A Note on Binary Template Matching. Pattern Recognition **22** (1989) 359–365

Using Strong Shape Priors for Stereo

Yunda Sun, Pushmeet Kohli, Matthieu Bray, and Philip H.S. Torr

Department of Computing,
Oxford Brookes University, UK
samy.sun@mail.edu.cn,
{pushmeet.kohli, philiptorr}@brookes.ac.uk
http://cms.brookes.ac.uk/research/visiongroup/

Abstract. This paper addresses the problem of obtaining an accurate 3D reconstruction from multiple views. Taking inspiration from the recent successes of using strong prior knowledge for image segmentation, we propose a framework for 3D reconstruction which uses such priors to overcome the ambiguity inherent in this problem. Our framework is based on an object-specific Markov Random Field (MRF)[10]. It uses a volumetric scene representation and integrates conventional reconstruction measures such as photo-consistency, surface smoothness and visual hull membership with a strong object-specific prior. Simple parametric models of objects will be used as strong priors in our framework. We will show how parameters of these models can be efficiently estimated by performing inference on the MRF using dynamic graph cuts [7]. This procedure not only gives an accurate object reconstruction, but also provides us with information regarding the pose or state of the object being reconstructed. We will show the results of our method in reconstructing deformable and articulated objects.

1 Introduction

Obtaining 3D reconstructions of objects from multiple images is a fundamental problem in computer vision. Reflecting the importance of the problem, a number of methods have been proposed for its solution. These range from methods such as shape from silhouettes [14] and space carving [11] to image based methods [12]. However, the problem of obtaining accurate reconstructions from sparse multiple views still remains far from being solved. The primary problem afflicting reconstruction methods is the inherent ambiguity in the problem (as shown in figure 1(a)) which arises from the many-one nature of the mapping that relates 3D objects and their images.

Intuitively the ambiguity in the object reconstruction can be overcome by using prior knowledge. Researchers have long understood this fact and weak priors such as surface smoothness have been used in a number of methods [8,13,15]. Such priors help in recovering from the errors caused by noisy data. Although they improve results, they are weak and do not carry enough information to guarantee a unique solution. At this point, the question to be asked is: *Can we make use of stronger prior knowledge?* A possible source for a strong prior could be *the knowledge of the shape of the object we are trying to reconstruct*. In other words, if we know which object we are trying to reconstruct, we can use a strong *object-specific* prior to force the reconstruction to look like that object.

P. Kalra and S. Peleg (Eds.): ICVGIP 2006, LNCS 4338, pp. 882–893, 2006.

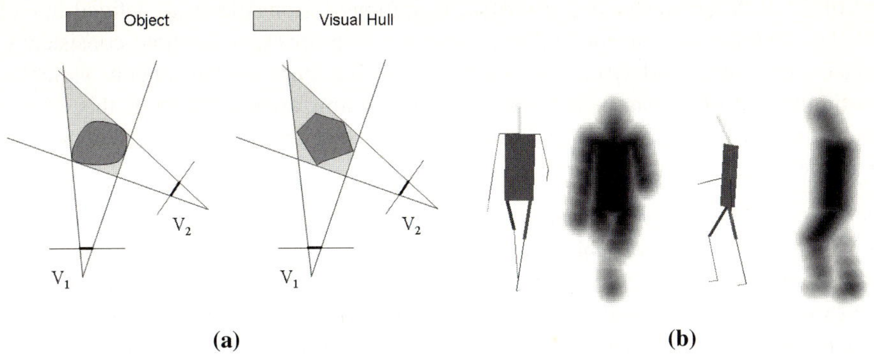

Fig. 1. a) Ambiguity in object reconstruction from sparse multiple views. The figure shows how two completely different objects can have the same visual hull. Further, if both objects have the same colour, the photo hull and their projections on multiple viewpoints would also be the same. b) Example of an articulated model. The figure shows a simple stick-model of a human in different poses and the corresponding priors as its 3D distance transforms used to set up our energy described in Section 2.

Strong Object-Specific Priors. Kumar *et al.* [10] proposed a method for using strong priors for solving image segmentation. They introduced the "Object-Specific Markov Random Field" model which combined Markov Random Fields (MRFs) with an *object-specific* shape prior. This shape-prior was defined by a Layered Pictorial Structures (LPS) model. The LPS model provided them with a strong prior able to model shape variations parameterized by a set of latent shape parameters. They obtained good object localization and segmentation results using their approach. However, their method required a large library of exemplars for different parts for the LPS model. Bray *et al.* [4] suggested using a simple articulated model. This makes the problem easier to solve computationally while still giving excellent segmentation results.

Parametric Models of Strong Prior Knowledge. In this work we will investigate the use of parametric models of objects as strong priors on the reconstruction, together with the weak prior of surface smoothness. The models are parameterized by a set of latent shape parameters which inherently characterize the state of the object to be reconstructed. Specifically we illustrate our ideas in terms of two model categories: articulated and deformable. Models belonging to the first category are used as strong priors for reconstructing articulated objects such as humans. They are parameterized by a set of pose parameters which characterize the pose of the object. Figure 1(b) shows an example of an articulated human model. Models belonging to the second category are used as strong priors on active-shape or deformable objects. The individual instances of these objects might be different from each other but they can be described by a common high-level parametrization. For example, objects like chairs can be parameterized in terms of parameters like height, width of seat etc. A deformable model for a vase is shown in figure 3(a).

Framework for Integrating Strong Prior Knowledge. A Bayesian approach to solve the 3D stereo reconstruction problem would typically be to formulate it in terms of a MRF.

This offers us the advantage of a seamless integration of strong priors (as defined above) with data, in this case conventional reconstruction measures such as photo-consistency, surface smoothness and visual hull membership. Inference on the random variables constituting the MRF can be seen as an energy minimization problem. If this energy function is *regular* (explained in Section 3) then its solution can be obtained in polynomial time using efficient graph-cut algorithms [9].

Inference of Model Shape Parameters. To guarantee an object-like reconstruction, our prior should have latent variables that model the shape variability of our object of interest. Then we optimize the energy of the *object-specific* MRF with respect to all these latent variables. Thus obtaining at the same time an accurate reconstruction as well as an estimate of the latent parameters. As explained in section 3, such an optimization procedure is extremely computationally expensive since it requires a graph cut to be computed multiple number of times. While performing this inference procedure, we make the observation that as we optimize over the model parameters, the energy function of the MRF we were trying to minimize changes minimally. This motivates us to use the recently proposed dynamic graph cut algorithm [7], which enables fast minimization of regular energy functions which change minimally from one instance to the next.

Organization of the Paper. The outline of the paper is as follows. We start by describing the object-specific MRF which forms the basis of this work. We explain how recently proposed methods for reconstruction can be explained in terms of this framework. The details of the efficient algorithm for performing inference over this MRF is given in section 3. In section 4, we will illustrate the use of this framework in reconstructing deformable and articulated objects, and provide results of experiments performed on real data. The conclusions and directions for future research are given in section 5.

2   Bayesian Framework

Within this section we provide a Bayesian formulation of the object reconstruction problem. This framework allows for the integration of strong object-specific priors with widely used data based terms such as photo-consistency and visual hull membership. We will also show how existing methods for object reconstruction such as [8,13,15] can be explained in this framework.

Object-Specific Markov Random Field for Reconstruction. A MRF comprises of a set of discrete random variables $\{X_1, X_2, \ldots, X_n\}$ defined on the index set $\mathcal{V}$, such that each variable X_v takes a value x_v from the label set $\mathcal{X} = \{\mathcal{X}_1, \mathcal{X}_2, \ldots, \mathcal{X}_l\}$ of all possible labels. We represent the set of all variables $x_v, \forall v \in \mathcal{V}$ by the vector $\mathbf{x}$. Unless noted otherwise, we use symbols i and j to denote values in $\mathcal{V}$. Further, we use $\mathcal{N}_v$ to denote the set consisting of indices of all variables which are neighbours of the random variable x_v in the graphical model.

   For the reconstruction problem, the set $\mathcal{V}$ corresponds to the set of all voxels in the volume of interest, $\mathcal{N}$ is a neighbourhood defined on this set[1], the binary variable

---

[1] In this paper, we have used the standard 6-neighbourhood i.e. each voxel is connected to the 6 voxels surrounding it.

x_v denotes the labeling of the voxel $v \in \mathcal{V}$, and the set $\mathcal{X}$ comprises of two labels ('obj','empty') representing whether the voxel belongs to the empty space or not. We will use $\mathcal{H}$ to denote the set of all voxels present in the visual hull obtained from object silhouettes. Every configuration $\mathbf{x}$ of such an MRF defines a 3D object reconstruction.

Given a set of images $\mathbf{I}$ and (or) a visual hull $\mathbf{H}$ (obtained using silhouettes), collectively constituting the data $\mathbf{D}$, $\mathbf{D}$ could be images, measurements and it could also include the result of some other algorithm e.g. a visual hull, we wish to reconstruct a known object. This can be done by labelling each voxel v in the volume of interest $\mathcal{V}$ as belonging to the object reconstruction, or belonging to the scene. Taking a Bayesian perspective, the optimal labels for the voxels are those which maximize the posterior probability $p(\mathbf{x}|\mathbf{D})$, which can be written in terms of a Gibbs distribution as:

$$p(\mathbf{x}|\mathbf{D}) = \frac{p(\mathbf{D}|\mathbf{x})p(\mathbf{x})}{p(\mathbf{D})} = \frac{1}{Z_{\mathbf{x}}} \exp(-\Psi(\mathbf{x})), \tag{1}$$

where $\Psi(\mathbf{x})$ is the energy of the configuration $\mathbf{x}$ of the MRF. The most probable or maximum a posteriori (MAP) reconstruction solution can be found by computing the least energy configuration $\mathbf{x}^* = \arg\min_{\mathbf{x}} \Psi(\mathbf{x})$. The energy $\Psi(\mathbf{x})$ corresponding to the configuration $\mathbf{x}$ consists of likelihood and prior terms. These can be written in terms of individual and pairwise interaction functions as:

$$\Psi(\mathbf{x}) = \sum_{i \in \mathcal{V}} (\psi(x_i) + \phi(\mathbf{D}|x_i)) + \sum_j (\psi(x_i, x_j) + \phi(\mathbf{D}|x_i, x_j))) + \text{const.} \tag{2}$$

Specifying the Likelihood Terms. Given the data $\mathbf{D}$, the unary likelihood term $\phi(\mathbf{D}|x_i)$ specifies the penalty (or cost) for assigning the label x_i to the voxel v_i. Assuming $\mathbf{D} = \mathbf{H}$, we can define $\phi(\mathbf{D}|x_i)$ in terms of the visual hull as:

$$\phi(\mathbf{D}|x_i = \text{'obj'}) = \begin{cases} \alpha & \text{if } i \in \mathcal{H}, \\ \beta & \text{otherwise,} \end{cases} \tag{3}$$

where α and β are arbitrary constants and satisfy the property $\alpha < \beta$. Snow *et al.* [13] used raw images along with their binary segmentations to develop a generalized version of these terms. Their likelihood function incorporated the absolute difference in the intensities of the pixels which intersected at a voxel. Their approach can be viewed as using a visual hull where each voxel has an associated confidence value. In contrast to the above approach, Kolmogorov *et al.* [8] only used image information and assumed the segmentation to be unknown. They took $(\mathbf{D} = \mathbf{I})$ and used an image based photo-consistency measure to define $\phi(\mathbf{D}|x_i)$ as: $\phi(\mathbf{D}|x_i = \text{'obj'}) = \min\{0, (I_p - I_q)^2 - K\}$ where p and q are pixels in the images, which lie near the projection of the voxel i, and I_p and I_q are their intensities.

In their recent work on multi-view stereo, Vogiatzis *et al.* [15] took $\mathbf{D} = \{\mathbf{I} \text{ and } \mathbf{H}\}$ i.e. they used both the visual hull $\mathbf{H}$ and object images $\mathbf{I}$ as the data $\mathbf{D}$. They used a photo-'consistency term that was obtained from the images. Further, instead of using the entire volume of interest, they only performed inference on the labels of voxels between two specific surfaces S_{base} and S_{in}. They defined S_{base} as the surface of the visual hull, and defined S_{in} as the locus of voxels which are located at a specific distance d_{in} inside S_{base}. This is equivalent to using the unary likelihood term:

$$\phi(\mathbf{D}|x_i = \text{`obj'}) = \begin{cases} -\infty & \text{if} & i \in \mathcal{H}^-, \\ +\infty & \text{if} & i \notin \mathcal{H}, \\ 0 & \text{otherwise}, \end{cases} \tag{4}$$

where $\mathcal{H}^-$ is the volume enclose by S_{in} and is in effect a contraction of the actual visual hull $\mathcal{H}$. Although the use of various measures for the unary likelihood have been investigated, the pairwise likelihood $\phi(\mathbf{D}|x_i, x_j)$ has remained relatively ignored by researchers. This term reflects the compatibility of two neighbouring latent variables in the MRF, and has been shown to be extremely useful in the context for the image segmentation problem, where it is called the contrast term [3,10]. We define this term as:

$$\phi(\mathbf{D}|x_i, x_j) = \lambda \exp\left(\frac{-g^2(i,j)}{2\sigma^2}\right)\frac{1}{dist(i,j)} \tag{5}$$

where $g^2(i,j)$ measures the difference in the estimated intensity values of the voxels i and j and $dist(i,j)$ gives the spatial distance between i and j. Such as estimate can be obtained either by using voxel colouring methods or directly from the object images in a manner analogous to the photo-consistency term. The effect of this term will be to favour discontinuities aligning with the object surface.

2.1   Incorporating Priors

We now describe how weak and strong prior information can be incorporated in our MRF framework.

Surface Smoothness as a Weak Prior. The pairwise interaction term $\psi(x_i, x_j)$ has been used in a number of methods as a weak prior to encourage smoothness in the reconstruction surface [8,13]. This is done by penalizing dissimilar label assignments in neighbouring voxels. The pairwise prior term takes the form of a Generalized Potts model:

$$\psi(x_i, x_j) = \begin{cases} K_{ij} & \text{if } x_i \neq x_j, \\ 0 & \text{if } x_i = x_j. \end{cases} \tag{6}$$

Parametric Models as Strong Priors. Suppose we know the object we are trying to reconstruct. Such information could be used to constrain the reconstruction result to look like the object and intuitively improve the reconstruction. However, we face two key problems at this juncture: (1) It is difficult to know what should be an appropriate representation for such knowledge. (2) How could we integrated such information in our Bayesian framework for the reconstruction problem? Our solution to the first problem is the use of generative parametric models to represent knowledge about the object. These models are parameterized by a set of parameters θ, which define the state of the object. The MRF formulation is shown in the graphical model shown in figure 2.

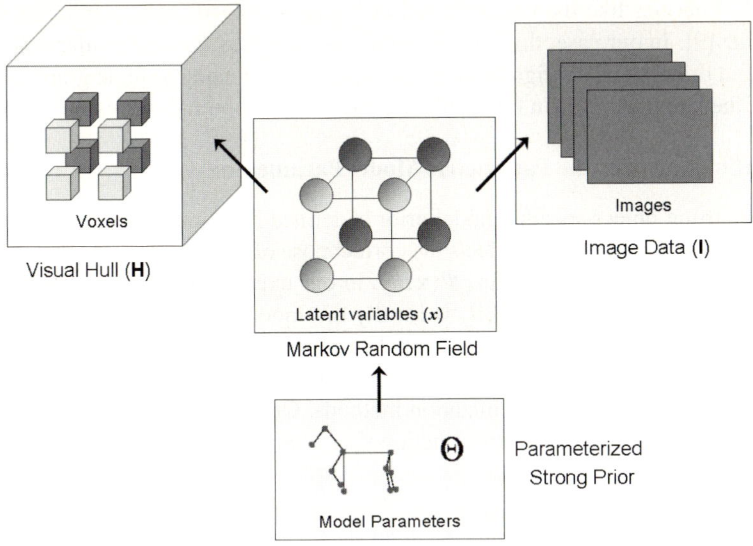

Fig. 2. The Bayesian framework for Object Reconstruction

In this framework the parameters of the object model are considered as latent (or hidden) variables. The energy function of the MRF is:

$$\Psi(\mathbf{x}, \theta) = \sum_{i \in \mathcal{V}} (\psi(x_i|\theta) + \phi(\mathbf{D}|x_i) + \sum_{j} (\psi(x_i, x_j) + \phi(\mathbf{D}|x_i, x_j))). \qquad (7)$$

For a particular value of θ, the model could be used to generate a coarse reconstruction of the object. This reconstruction is used to define the unary prior term $\psi(x_i|\theta)$. The function $\psi(x_i|\theta)$ is chosen such that given an estimate of the location and shape of the object, voxels near to that shape are more likely to be included in the reconstruction, the term used by us is: $\psi(x_i|\theta) = -\log p(x_i|\theta)$ where $p(x_i|\theta)$ is defined as:

$$p(x_i = \text{`obj'}|\theta) = \frac{1}{1 + \exp(\mu * (d(i, \theta) - d_{sur}))} \qquad (8)$$

where $d(i, \theta)$ is the distance of a voxel i from the surface generated by the parametric model and d_{sur} is the average distance from the model surface to the surface voxels in the true object reconstruction. The distance for all the voxels in the volume of interest is efficiently computed by performing a 3D distance transform [5]. An example of a 3D distance transform is shown in figure 1(b). The parameter μ determines the ratio of the magnitude of the penalty that points outside the shape prior have compared with points inside the shape.

3   MAP-MRF Inference Using Dynamic Graph Cuts

We next describe how to find the optimal configuration of the object specific MRF. As stated earlier this problem can be solved by minimizing the energy function defined by the MRF. Energies like the one defined in (7) can be solved using graph cuts if they are *regular* [9]. In our case, this is indeed the case and thus for a particular value of θ, we can find the optimal configuration $\mathbf{x}^* = \min_{\mathbf{x}} \Psi(\mathbf{x}, \theta)$ using a single graph cut. The labels of the latent variable in this configuration give the optimal reconstruction.

3.1   Optimizing over the Parametric Model Parameters

Since our strong object-specific model prior is defined in terms of latent variables, we would like to make sure that it reflects the correct pose of the object. To do this we solve the problem: $\theta_{opt} = \arg\min_{\theta} \min_{\mathbf{x}} \Psi(\mathbf{x}, \theta)$. In our experiments we observed that the energy function projection $\Psi(\mathbf{x}^*, \theta)$ is locally uni-modal and can be optimized using standard techniques like gradient descent. The plots of this projection can be seen in figure 5(i). Our algorithm starts with an initial guess of the latent variables pose and optimizes it using standard minimization methods. Once an estimate of θ_{opt} has been found we can find the optimal reconstruction $\mathbf{x}_{opt} = \arg\min_{\mathbf{x}} \Psi(\mathbf{x}, \theta_{opt})$ using a single graph cut.

Minimizing Energies using Dynamic Graph Cuts. The minimization procedure for estimating θ_{opt} involves computing the value of $\min_{\mathbf{x}} \Psi(\mathbf{x}, \theta)$ for different values of θ. Each such computation requires a graph cut to be computed and if the time taken for computing this cut is high, it would make our optimization algorithm quite slow. Here we make the following observation: Between different iterations of the optimization algorithm, the change in the value of θ is small. This is reflected in the change in the energy function we are required to minimize, which is small as well. For such a sequence of energies, the graph cut computation can be made significantly faster by using the dynamic graph cut algorithm recently proposed in [7]. This algorithm works by using the solution of the previous graph cut computation for solving the new instance of the problem. In our experiments, we found that the dynamic algorithm was 15-25 times faster than the algorithm proposed in [2], which recomputes the st-mincut from scratch and has been shown to be the fastest algorithm for graphs commonly used in computer vision problems.

4   Applications

Within this section, we will show some results obtained by using the Bayesian framework defined in section 2. We apply our approach on two object categories to show how strong object-specific priors can help in obtaining accurate reconstructions from ambiguous and noisy data.

4.1   Deformable Models

Deformable models as the name suggests can alter their shape and in the process generate different instances of the object. These can be used while reconstructing objects with high intra class variability. The latent variables θ characterizing these models dictate the exact shape that the model takes. We illustrate their use in obtaining 3D reconstructions of a vase, from a few images shown in figure 3(b).

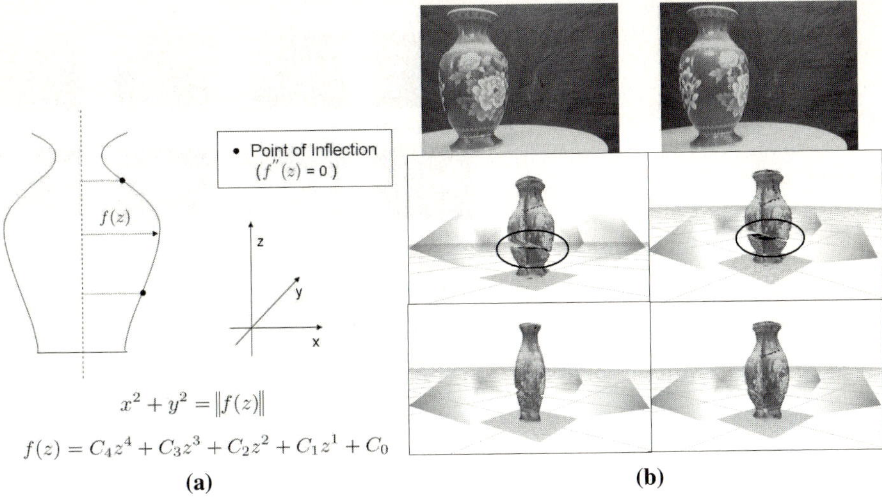

(a)   **(b)**

Fig. 3. a) The Parametric Deformable Vase Model. b) Object Reconstruction using Deformable Models. The images used for reconstruction are shown in row 1. The second row shows two views of the visual hull obtained using noisy silhouettes of the vase. In the third row, we show the results obtained by our method before/after optimizing the parameters of the deformable model. It should be noted here that the reconstruction results obtained by our method are smoother and do not suffer from discontinuities such as the cut seen in the visual hull.

The Parametric Vase Model. We use a rotationally symmetric model (shown in figure 3(a)) for the vase. The model is described in terms of circles in the horizontal plane as: $x^2 + y^2 = \|f(z)\|$ where $f(z)$ is a n-degree polynomial. In our experiments, we bound the degree of $f(z)$ to four, making it take the form:

$$f(z) = C_4 z^4 + C_3 z^3 + C_2 z^2 + C_1 z + C_0. \tag{9}$$

The coefficients $\{C_0, \ldots, C_4\}$ of the function constitute the set of latent parameters θ characterizing the shape of the model. We optimize over the values of these coefficients (as explained in section 3) to obtain a shape that acts as a coarse reconstruction of the actual object. The model can be strengthened by making it more object-specific. It can be observed that the vase surface has two inflection points. This constraint can be incorporated in our model by making sure that the second derivative of $f(z)$, which is defined as $f''(z) = 12C_4 z^2 + 6C_3 z + 2C_2$ has two unequal real roots. This gives us the constraint: $36C_3^2 - 96C_4 C_2 > 0$.

Experiments. We use the images and silhouettes of the vase as data. These are obtained from four cameras which are uniformly distributed around the object as shown in figure 3(b). We quantize the volume of interest into 3×10^5 voxels. The *object-specific* MRF formulated for the reconstruction problem has 1.5×10^5 binary latent variables. The energy $\Psi(\mathbf{x}^*, \theta)$ of this MRF is constructed as described in section 2. We then minimize it with respect to the shape model parameters θ to obtain an estimate of θ_{opt}. The results from the experiment are shown in figure 3(b).

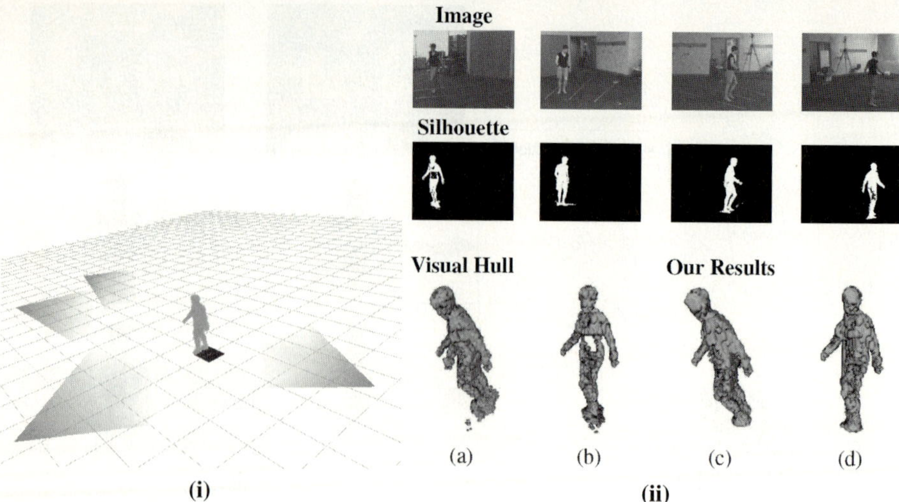

Fig. 4. i) Camera Positions and Reconstruction. The figure show the position and orientations of the four cameras which were used to obtain the images which constituted the data-set for our first experiment. We also see the reconstruction result generated by our method. ii) 3D Object Reconstruction using Strong Object-Specific priors. The first and second rows show the images and silhouettes used as the data. Two views of the visual hull generated using the data are shown in the first two columns of the bottom row ((a) and (b)). The visual hull is noisy and contain artifacts like the spurious third arm caused by the ambiguity in the problem. We are able to overcome such problems by using strong prior knowledge. The reconstructions obtained by our method are shown in column 3 and 4 ((c) and (d)).

4.2   Articulated Models

Articulated models not only help in reconstructing the object, but also provide information about its pose. In this section, we will use an articulated stick-man model to solve the challenging problem of reconstructing and estimating the shape (and pose) of humans. The problem is especially hard because humans have many joint angles and thus the parametric model needed to describe them will have a high number of latent variables.

The Stick-man model.   We use a simple articulated stick-man model (shown in figure 1(b)) in our experiments to generate a rough pose-specific prior on the reconstruction of the human. The model is parameterized by a 26 dimensional pose vector θ that describes absolute position and orientation of the torso, and various other joint angle values. There are no constraints or joint-limits incorporated in our model.

Experiments.   We use real and synthetic video sequences of humans as data. The data-set for our first experiment consists of videos sequences of four views of a human subject walking in a circle. This data-set is used in [1]. It comes with silhouettes of the human subject obtained using pixel-wise background intensity modeling. The cameras position and orientations with respect to the object are shown in the figure 4(i).

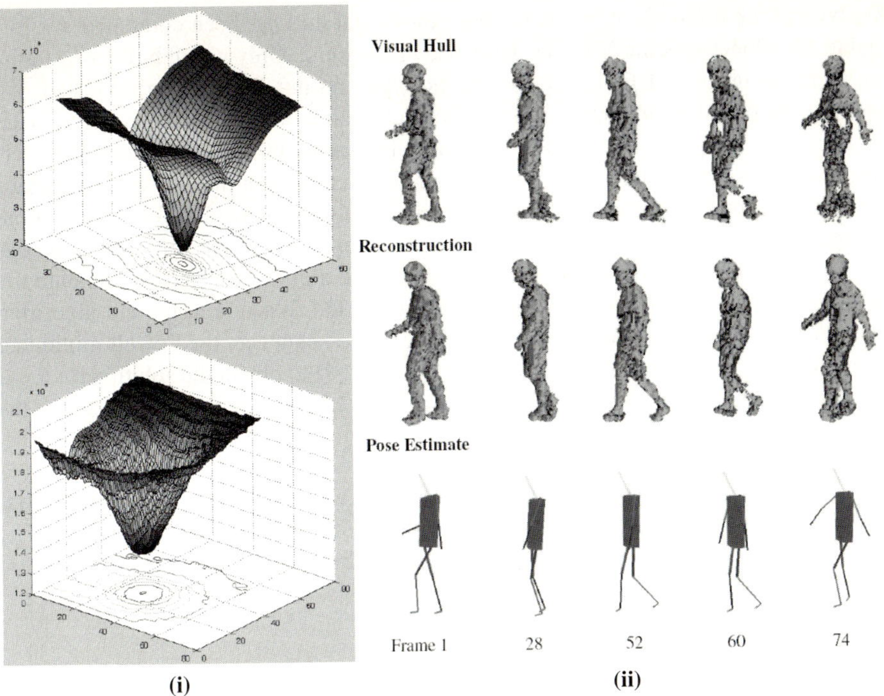

Fig. 5. i) The plots shows how the value of $\min_{\mathbf{x}} \Psi(\mathbf{x}, \theta)$ is affected by changes in the pose parameters of the stick model used to generate the reconstruction prior. The first plot shows the values obtained by varying the global translation and rotation parameters of the stick-man model in the x-axis. The second plot shows the values while varying the joint angles of the left shoulder in x and z axes. Observe that the effect of changing the joint angles of the left shoulder is less than the effect caused by changes in the global translation and rotation parameters. ii) Pose Inference and 3D Object Reconstruction results. The data-set is the same as used in [1] and consists of 4 views of a human subject walking in a circular path. Middle row: Reconstruction result. Bottom row: Pose estimate. Observe that we are able to get excellent reconstruction and pose estimation results even when the visual hull contains large errors (as seen in frame 60 and 74).

The first step in our method is the computation of the visual hull. The procedure starts with the quantization of the volume of interest as a grid of cubical voxels of equal size. Once this is done, each voxel center is projected into the input images. If any of the projections falls outside the silhouette, then the voxel is discarded. All remaining voxels constitute the visual hull. Some visual hull results are illustrated in figure 4(ii). It can be observed that because of the skewed distribution of cameras, the visual hull is quite different from the true object reconstruction. Further, as object segmentations are not accurate, it has large errors. The prominent defects in the visual hull results include: (i) The presence of holes because of segmentation errors in the object silhouettes (bottom row (b)), (ii) the presence of auxiliary parts caused by shadows, (iii) the *third-arm effect* resulting from self-occlusion and ambiguity in the reconstruction due to small number of views (bottom row (a)). It can be seen that our reconstruction results do not suffer from these errors (bottom row (c) and (d)).

Analysis of the Inference Algorithm. Once the visual hull has been computed, we formulate the object-specific MRF as described in section 2. Only visual hull based terms are included in the MRF energy construction, and no image based term is used. We estimate the optimal parameters θ_{opt} for the stick-man model by minimizing the MRF energy given in equation (7). Figure 5(i) shows how $\min_{\mathbf{x}} \Psi(\mathbf{x}, \theta)$ changes with different parameters of the stick-man model. It can be clearly seen that the energy surface is locally uni-modal. We use the Powell minimization [6] algorithm for optimization. The graph constructed for the energy minimization procedure has a million nodes connected in a 6 neighbourhood. The time taken by the algorithm of [2] to compute the st-mincut in this graph is 0.3 seconds. In contrast, the dynamic graph cut algorithm only takes 0.01 seconds. For each frame of the video sequence, the Powell minimizer needs roughly 500 function evaluations of $\min_{\mathbf{x}} \Psi(\mathbf{x}, \theta)$ to obtain the solution for $\theta_{\mathbf{opt}}$. Further, as each function evaluation takes roughly 0.15 seconds, we are able to get the pose and reconstruction results in a minute.

Results. Our method is able to obtain accurate object reconstruction results. Additionally, we also obtain an accurate estimate of the pose parameters of the subject. The reconstruction and pose estimation results for a few frames are shown in figure 5(ii).

5   Conclusions

This paper sets out a Bayesian framework for 3D object reconstruction which allows for the integration of 'strong' object-specific and 'weak' smoothness priors with a data based likelihood term. We showed how simple deformable and articulated models can be used as strong priors to overcome the ambiguity plaguing the reconstruction problem. The results of our experiments show that this formulation is not only able to obtain good reconstruction results from noisy data, but also provides us with an accurate estimate of the state of the object, which is quite useful in applications such as human pose inference.

References

1. S. Bhatia, L. Sigal, M. Isard, and M.J. Black. 3d human limb detection using space carving and multi-view eigen models. In *ANM Workshop*, volume I, page 17, 2004.
2. Y. Boykov and V. Kolmogorov. An experimental comparison of min-cut/max-flow algorithms for energy minimization in vision. *PAMI*, 26(9):1124–1137, September 2004.
3. Y.Y. Boykov and M.P. Jolly. Interactive graph cuts for optimal boundary and region segmentation of objects in n-d images. In *ICCV*, pages 105–112, 2001.
4. M. Bray, P. Kohli, and P.H.S. Torr. Posecut: Simulataneous segmentation and 3d pose estimation of humans using dynamic graph cuts. In *ECCV*, pages 642–655, 2006.
5. Meijster et al. A general algorithm for computing distance transforms in linear time. *MMAIS-Processing*, pages 331–340, 2000.
6. Press et al. *Numerical recipes in C*. Cambridge Uni. Press, 1988.
7. P. Kohli and P. Torr. Efficiently solving dynamic markov random fields using graph cuts. In *ICCV*, 2005.
8. V. Kolmogorov and R. Zabih. Multi-camera scene reconstruction via graph cuts. In *ECCV*, volume III, page 82 ff., 2002.

9. V. Kolmogorov and R. Zabih. What energy functions can be minimized via graph cuts? In *ECCV*, volume III, page 65 ff., 2002.
10. M.P. Kumar, P.H.S. Torr, and A. Zisserman. Obj cut. In *CVPR*, volume I, pages 18–25, 2005.
11. K.N. Kutulakos and M. Seitz. A theory of shape by space carving. *IJCV*, 38(3), 2000.
12. D. Scharstein and R. Szeliski. A taxonomy and evaluation of dense two-frame stereo correspondence algorithms. *IJCV*, 47(1-3):7–42, 2002.
13. D. Snow, P. Viola, and R. Zabih. Exact voxel occupancy with graph cuts. In *CVPR*, 2000.
14. R. Szeliski. Rapid octree construction from image sequences. *CVGIP*, 58:23–32, 1993.
15. G. Vogiatzis, P.H.S. Torr, and R. Cipolla. Multi-view stereo via volumetric graph-cuts. In *CVPR*, volume II, pages 391–398, 2005.

An Efficient Adaptive Window Based Disparity Map Computation Algorithm by Dense Two Frame Stereo Correspondence

Narendra Kumar Shukla, Vivek Rathi, and Vijaykumar Chakka

Dhirubhai Ambani Institute of Information and Communication Technology,
Gandhinagar, India

Abstract. This paper presents an efficient algorithm for disparity map computation with an adaptive window by establishing two frame stereo correspondence. Adaptive window based approach has a clear advantage of producing dense depth maps from stereo images. In recent years there has not been much research on adaptive window based approach due its high complexity and large computation time. Adaptive window based method selects an appropriate rectangular window by evaluating the local variation of the intensity and the disparity. Ideally the window need not be rectangular but to reduce algorithmic complexity and hence computation time, rectangular window is taken. There is a need for correction of errors introduced due to the rectangular window which is not dealt by the existing algorithm. To reduce this error, a method has been proposed which not only improves the disparity maps but also has a lesser computational complexity. To demonstrate the effectiveness of the algorithm the experimental results from synthetic and real image pairs (provided by middlebury research group) including ones with ground-truth values for quantitative comparison with the other methods are presented. The proposed algorithm outperforms most of the existing algorithms evaluated in the taxonomy of dense two frame stereo algorithms. The implementation has been done in C++. The algorithm has been tested with the standard stereo pairs which are used as benchmark for comparison of algorithms in the taxonomy implementation.

1 Introduction

Stereo correspondence for obtaining dense disparity map in two frame stereo is a classical problem in computer vision. Various algorithms have been proposed for the disparity map computation in past whose taxonomy was very well presented by Scharstein and Szeliski [3]. Most of these techniques utilize intensity variation to compute disparity map. The most common amongst them are SSD (Sum of Squared Intensity Difference) based, which compute the window with minimum SSD to estimate the disparity. One Common problem these algorithms face is the computation of support region or window size. Each pixel has neighborhood (support region/window) with different intensity and disparity variations. So selecting an efficient window becomes a difficult task. The region enclosed by

P. Kalra and S. Peleg (Eds.): ICVGIP 2006, LNCS 4338, pp. 894–905, 2006.
© Springer-Verlag Berlin Heidelberg 2006

window must be large enough to include enough intensity variations and small enough to avoid the effect of projective distortion. We need to adaptively compute the window dimensions for each pixel based on the intensity and disparity variations around the pixel.

The algorithms gaining popularity now-a-days are Graph cut based [4]. These are global algorithms which make explicit smoothness assumptions.

2   Adaptive Window Algorithm

M. Okutomi and T. Kanade [1] proposed a method to compute adaptive window for each pixel which iteratively updates window size and disparity estimate in each run. Adaptive Windows can be considered a form of local segmentation, as they divide the image into logical units to be considered separately. Here the logical unit is an image area with enough visual interest for a good match but not too much depth variation. The major problem in computing a locally

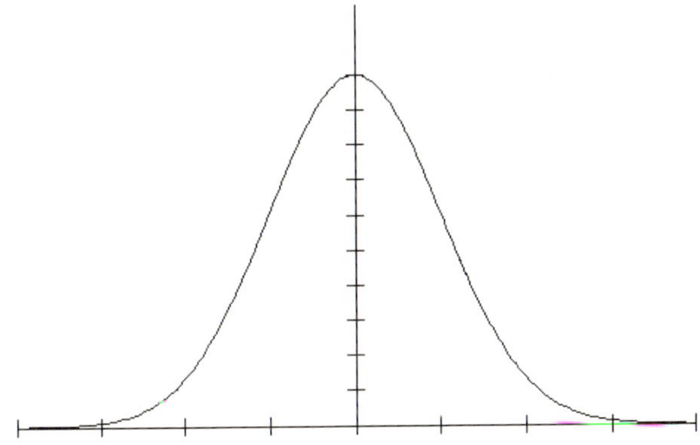

Fig. 1. Gaussian Distribution of Certainty in Disparity Estimation

adaptive window is in computing and using disparity variances. All we can measure directly is intensity variation. Two major algorithms proposed so far are based on rectangular window [1] and arbitrary shaped window [2]. The algorithm with arbitrary shaped window requires a higher computation time in comparison to the former. [1] employed a statistical model of the disparity distribution within the window with the assumption that difference of disparity at a point in the window from the center point $(0,0)$ has a zero-mean Gaussian distribution with variance proportional to the distance between these points as shown in Figure (1). As we move farther from the center pixel, the uncertainty of disparity estimate as compared to that of center pixel increases. The Disparity estimate and its uncertainty for a given window W can be calculated by:

$$\hat{\Delta d} = \frac{\sum_{i,j\in W} \frac{(f_1(\xi_i,\eta_j)-f_2(\xi_i+d_0(0,0),\eta_j))\frac{\partial}{\partial\xi}f_2(\xi_i+d_0(0,0),\eta_j)}{2\sigma_n^2+\alpha_f\alpha_d\sqrt{\xi_i^2+\eta_j^2}}}{\sum_{i,j\in W} \frac{(\frac{\partial}{\partial\xi}f_2(\xi_i+d_0(0,0),\eta_j))^2}{2\sigma_n^2+\alpha_f\alpha_d\sqrt{\xi_i^2+\eta_j^2}}} \tag{1}$$

$$\sigma^2_{\Delta d} = \frac{1}{\sum_{i,j\in W} \frac{(\frac{\partial}{\partial\xi}f_2(\xi_i+d_0(0,0),\eta_j))^2}{2\sigma_n^2+\alpha_f\alpha_d\sqrt{\xi_i^2+\eta_j^2}}} \tag{2}$$

where, $f_1(x,y)$ and $f_2(x,y)$ are the intensity functions of reference and matching image respectively, $d_0(x,y)$ is the initial disparity estimate, σ_n^2 is the power of noise of error per image. The parameters α_f and α_d represents the disparity and intensity fluctuation respectively. We can compute the values of α_f and α_d within the window as:

$$\alpha_d = \frac{1}{N_w}\sum_{i,j\in W}\frac{(d_0(\xi_i,\eta_j)-d_0(0,0))^2}{\sqrt{\xi_i^2+\eta_j^2}} \tag{3}$$

$$\alpha_f = \frac{1}{N_w}\sum_{i,j\in W}(\frac{\partial}{\partial\xi}f_2(\xi_i+d_0(0,0),\eta_j))^2 \tag{4}$$

where N_w is the number of samples within the window. Therefore given all the required parameters, equations 1 - 4 will enable to calculate a better estimate of disparity at the center of the window as $d_0(x,y) + \Delta d$ with the minimum uncertainty. So we can improve the disparity estimate given initial estimate by minimizing its uncertainty and simultaneously replacing the new disparity estimate by incrementing the current disparity estimate by $\hat{\Delta d}$.

2.1   The Algorithm

Let us go through the algorithmic approach given by [1] for computing better disparity estimates, given the input stereo pair and their initial disparity estimate:

1. Start with an initial disparity estimate $d_0(x,y)$.
2. For each pixel (x,y) in f_1,
    (a) Place a 3 x 3 Window centered at x,y and compute uncertainty by using equation 2.
    (b) Expand the window by one pixel in one direction, e.g., to the right $x+$, for trial, and compute the uncertainty for the expanded window. If the expansion increases the uncertainty, the direction is prohibited from further expansions. Repeat the same process for each of the other three directions $x-, y+$, and $y-$ (excluding the already prohibited ones).
    (c) Compare the uncertainties for all the directions tried and choose the direction which produces the minimum uncertainty.
    (d) Expand the window by one pixel in the chosen direction.

(e) Iterate steps (b) to (d) until all directions become prohibited from expansion or until the window size reaches a limit that is previously set.

(f) Update the disparity $d_0(x, y)$ by adding Δd computed by equation 1 for the modified window.

3. Iterate the above process until the disparity estimate $d(x, y)$ converges, or up to a certain maximum number of iterations.

The algorithm truly justifies its approach. Flat surfaces have very less disparity variation but taking large window may blur the edges. In contrast, a smaller window gives sharper disparity edges at the cost of noisy surfaces. The adaptive window algorithm takes care of flat surfaces as well as sharp edges, however, there are two major problems with the above algorithm:

1. When window size is increased by a row or a column, the new row or column might have some pixels, although in lesser quantity, which increase the uncertainty of the disparity estimate. This causes errors in disparity estimation.

2. The above algorithm requires a lot of computation especially when there is a large area of flatness in the image.

Although researchers have tried to solve the first problem by taking arbitrary shaped (non-rectangular) window, but computation of such windows increases the computation time even more and hence makes the second problem even worse. Also applying the above algorithm till convergence of disparity makes it unsuitable for real-time applications.The next section solves these problems of the adaptive window.

3   The Proposed Efficient Adaptive Window Algorithm

On the basis of major pitfalls identified for the algorithm described above, the new approach is categorized into two parts viz. Reducing the errors in disparity estimate and Reducing the computation time, although the solution to the first one also reduces the computation time. Then the approach is compiled into an algorithm succeeding the two sections. Thereafter the results of the improved algorithm are compared and analyzed with the existing algorithms.

3.1   Reducing the Errors in Disparity Estimate

The errors introduced by rectangular window tend to be large specially when image contains less flat surfaces or more curved surfaces. This is because, when the optimum rectangular window is computed, it may consist of pixels which have less intensity correspondence but other pixels in the row or column nullify its effect leading to errors in disparity estimation. This my introduce error in prediction up to three-four pixels. Therefore, there is a need for correction of this error. A new method to correct the error is proposed.

For each pixel take the optimized adaptive window as computed by the adaptive window algorithm. Now, for this window compute SSD by shifting the window in the range $-d$ to $+d$ around the disparity predicted by the above algorithm.d may be 0, 1, 2, 3, 4... . Let d_i be the value between $-d$ and $+d$ at which SSD comes out to be minimum. Now update the new value of disparity as:

$$d_r(x, y) = d_r(x, y) + d_i$$

This value is the new value of the disparity of pixel of interest. By shifting the window over the range $-d$ to $+d$ we compute the disparity which further reduces the error as by doing the above process we compute the best possible match of the pixel in the reference image with the matching image within the neighborhood of the disparity estimate. Thus the disparity estimate computation by this algorithm will converge faster as compared to adaptive window algorithm of [1]. Hence it also reduces the computation time and increases convergence rate. The next section deals with reducing the computation time of the optimum window for the pixels in image.

3.2   Reducing the Computation Time

In the adaptive algorithm of [1] we take the initial window of size 3 x 3 and increase the size of the window in the direction of minimum uncertainty. And then for the next pixel we again start from 3 x 3. By the property of disparity smoothness for most of the region in the image, we can start with the window size averaged over the surrounding left, upper-left and diagonal-left, diagonal-right, i.e., the window size of surrounding pixels which are already computed.

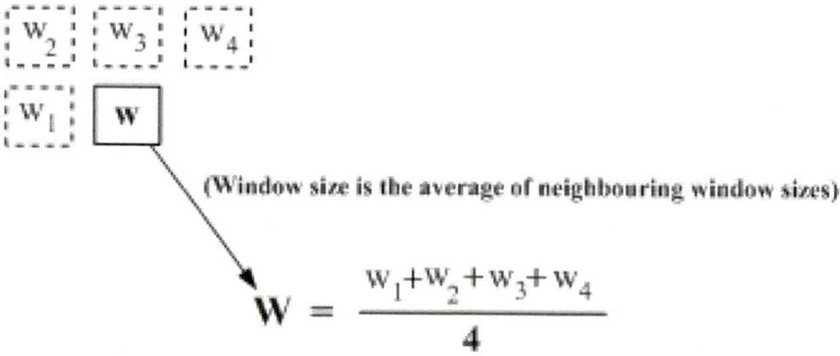

Fig. 2. Initial window estimate: Direction-wise Average of already computed neighboring window sizes

Now taking this window size contract the window by one pixel in each direction and check if the uncertainty decreases for any direction. If for a direction the uncertainty $\sigma^2_{\Delta d}$ decreases then from next iteration start contracting in that direction(i.e. reduce the window size in that direction) otherwise start expanding in that direction. This approach applies to all the directions. After this, if at a particular iteration, the uncertainty does not decrease, then that direction is prohibited from further expansion/contraction.

3.3   The Proposed Algorithm

Given below is the complete algorithm for the improved adaptive window approach described in the previous two sections:

1. Start with an initial disparity estimate $d_0(x, y)$.
2. Make label for all the pixel as 'NW'.
3. For each pixel (x, y) in f_1,

   (a) Place a Window centered at x, y of dimensions average of windows of all the neighboring pixels having label 'W' and compute uncertainty by using equation 2. If all the neighboring pixels have label NW then take the initial window size as 3 x 3, label all the edges of this window as 'E' and skip the next step.

   (b) Contract the one of window edge by one pixel and compute the uncertainty. If it decreases the uncertainty then label the edge as 'C' else label the edge as 'E'. Repeat the process for all the edges.

   (c) Expand/Contract the edge by one pixel (Depending on whether label associated with it is 'E' or 'C') in one direction, e.g., to the right $x+$, for trial, and compute the uncertainty for the expanded/contracted window. If the expansion/contraction increases the uncertainty, the direction is prohibited from further expansions and label the edge as 'P'. Repeat the same process for each of the other three directions $x-, y+$, and $y-$ (excluding the edges with 'P' label).

   (d) Compare the uncertainties for all the directions tried and choose the direction which produces the minimum uncertainty.

   (e) Expand/Contract the window by one pixel in the chosen direction.

   (f) Iterate steps (c) to (e) until all the edges become prohibited with label 'P' or until the window size reaches a limit that is previously set.

   (g) Store the final window size and label the pixel as 'W'.

   (h) Update the disparity $d_0(x, y)$ by adding Δd computed by equation 1 for the modified window.

   (i) Compute the SSD for the disparity set $\{d_0(x, y) - d, d_0(x, y) + d\}$ (d is the maximum disparity error to be rectified) and update $d_0(x, y)$ with the disparity with minimum SSD.

4. Iterate the above process until the disparity estimate $d(x, y)$ converges, or up to a certain maximum number of iterations.

The above algorithm computes the new disparity map in much less time. This is because, in general, the window sizes comes out to be nearly same to the neighboring window sizes. Also as in each step, the disparity is also improved by computing disparity corresponding to minimum SSD, the algorithm converges in less number of iterations. The results which top each category are shown in bold face. This algorithm converges faster for the images with large planar or textured surfaces. The results of the proposed algorithm are examined in the next section.

4 Experiment and Results

The evaluation criteria used for the experiments is based on the propositions given in [3]. B_O stands for occluded pixels, $B_{\bar{O}}$ stands for non occluded pixels, B_T stands for textured pixels, $B_{\bar{T}}$ stands for non-textured pixels and B_D stands for pixels at discontinuity. For complete description of evaluation criteria, refer [3]. In all of the experiments, the window size threshold has been kept as 16, due to increased time complexity. The value of d (Range of disparity for correction) is taken as 6 for all the results. For a complete set of input images, please refer [5]. The section proceeds with the results of the algorithms on images followed by the comparison with other existing algorithms.

4.1 Improvement in Results

Results with Tsukuba Image: Tsukuba image contains non-planar surfaces with occlusions. So the window sizes computed comes out to be lower. Figure 3 show the ground truth image, disparity image computed with SSD 9x9 window, disparity image of adaptive window algorithm using initial disparity estimate of the ground truth image, and disparity image of proposed algorithm. Clearly the proposed algorithm outperforms the other two algorithms as clear with the data shown in the Table 1 and 2.

The result shown in Table 1 and 2 are tested with value of d = 3 and only two iterations are performed. Obviously, the proposed improved adaptive algorithm will converge faster than the existing adaptive window algorithm. Clearly, the edges of the objects have sharpened and errors textured and non-textured have

Table 1. Root mean square error comparison of simple SSD 9x9 window algorithm, adaptive window algorithm and the Proposed Adaptive Window Algorithm of tsukuba image based on several parameters. The results which top each category are shown in bold face.

Algorithm	Iterations	B_O	$B_{\bar{O}}$	B_T	$B_{\bar{T}}$	B_D	All
SSD 9x9 Window	-	5.06	1.67	1.72	1.60	3.27	1.84
Adaptive Window	2	5.06	1.60	1.69	1.46	3.18	1.77
Proposed Adaptive Window	**2**	**4.96**	**1.43**	**1.57**	**1.21**	**2.96**	**1.62**

Table 2. Bad pixel percentage (with disparity error greater than 1 pixel) comparison of simple SSD 9x9 window algorithm, adaptive window algorithm and the Proposed Adaptive Window Algorithm of tsukuba image based on several parameters. The results which top each category are shown in bold face.

Algorithm	Iterations	B_O	$B_{\bar{O}}$	B_T	$B_{\bar{T}}$	B_D	All
SSD 9x9 Window	-	87.95%	9.88%	9.55%	10.33%	37.25%	11.89%
Adaptive Window	2	88.49%	9.12%	8.59%	9.85%	34.56%	11.17%
Proposed Algorithm	**2**	**83.53%**	**7.25%**	**7.15%**	**7.38%**	**30.84%**	**9.21%**

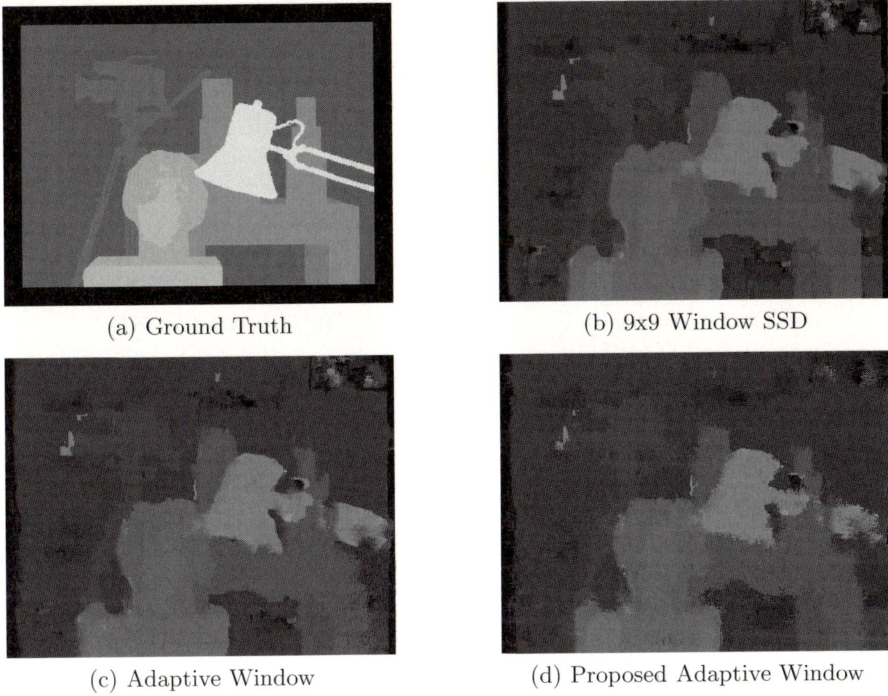

(a) Ground Truth

(b) 9x9 Window SSD

(c) Adaptive Window

(d) Proposed Adaptive Window

Fig. 3. Result of image tsukuba with Proposed Adaptive window Algorithm (2 Iterations)

improved a lot. This is because the errors are expected to be in the vicinity of the current estimation. So even if correct result is not predicted in the first iteration, it is likely to converge in the second iteration. Further the bad pixel percentage have decreased in all the areas. If the initial estimate was better, the new estimate could have been much better.

Results with Venus Image: Venus image contains planar surfaces with occlusions. It has 5 planes, some slant, untextured regions and one crease. Figure 4 show the ground truth image, disparity image computed with SSD 9 x 9 window, disparity image of adaptive window algorithm using initial disparity estimate of the ground truth image, and disparity image of the proposed algorithm.

The result shown in Table 3 and 4 are tested with value of d = 3 and only two iterations are performed. Although, with this image, the proposed algorithm does not perform so well in the occluded regions, but it performs considerably well in textured as well as non textured region. As we can see from Figure 4(a), the algorithm has improve the results considerably in the top right region of the image, which is textured region. Obviously the proposed algorithm outperforms the other two algorithms, as it is clear with the data shown in the succeeding tables.

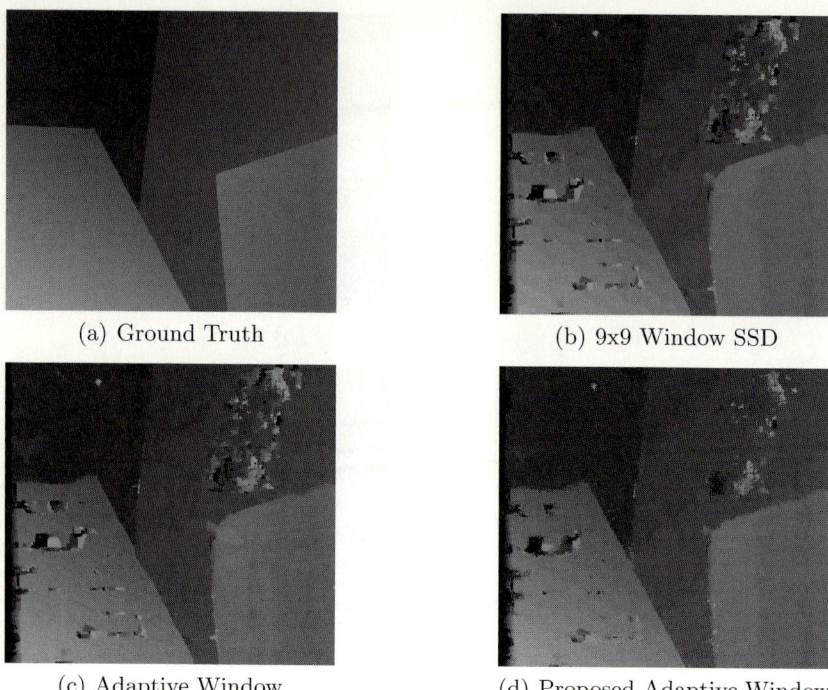

(a) Ground Truth

(b) 9x9 Window SSD

(c) Adaptive Window

(d) Proposed Adaptive Window

Fig. 4. Result of image venus with Proposed Adaptive window Algorithm (1 Iteration)

Table 3. Root mean square error comparison of simple SSD 9x9 window algorithm, adaptive window algorithm and the Proposed Adaptive Window Algorithm of Venus image based on several parameters.The results which top each category are shown in bold face.

Algorithm	Iterations	B_O	$B_{\bar{O}}$	B_T	$B_{\bar{T}}$	B_D	All
SSD 9x9 Window	-	6.81	2.31	1.65	3.27	1.70	2.47
Adaptive Window	1	7.73	2.01	1.43	2.84	3.01	2.25
Proposed Adaptive Window	**1**	**8.18**	**1.71**	**1.27**	**2.36**	**2.21**	**2.02**

4.2   Time Complexity Analysis

As proposed in section 3.2, the time analysis has been done for the four image sets viz. Map, Sawtooth, Tsukuba, Venus. Table 5 shows the computation time taken for the four images including the initial disparity estimation time. The experiments have been performed on 2.6 GHz, Pentium 4 computer running windows XP operating system.

Table 5 clearly shows the large reduction in computation time. Note that it does not include SSD optimization as proposed in section 3.1, because at each iteration SSD has its own computation time at the same time helps the results

Table 4. Bad pixel percentage (with disparity error greater than 1 pixel) comparison of simple SSD 9x9 window algorithm, adaptive window algorithm and the Proposed Adaptive Window Algorithm of Venus image based on several parameters. The results which top each category are shown in bold face.

Algorithm	Iterations	B_O	$B_{\bar{O}}$	B_T	$B_{\bar{T}}$	B_D	All
SSD 9x9 Window	-	85.95%	14.11%	6.96%	28.70%	10.24%	15.43%
Adaptive Window	1	93.75%	11.13%	6.35%	20.88%	40.68%	12.65%
Proposed Algorithm	1	**92.42%**	**7.36%**	**4.54%**	**13.12%**	**24.44%**	**8.93%**

Table 5. Time Taken to compute disparity estimate without ssd optimization including initial disparity estimation time

Image	Computation Time of existing algorithm (in secs.)	Computation Time of Proposed algorithm (in secs.)
Map	86.387	13.343
Sawtooth	338.25	51.248
Tsukuba	229.474	21.234
Venus	345.312	52.232

converge faster then existing adaptive window algorithm. So SSD reduces overall time but increases the iteration time. As iteration time and overall time are not related in the direct way, therefore analysis has been done without SSD optimization. Also note that the window size has been limited to 16 x 16 so the optimization gives errors at some point. It is intended to improve this in the future. Although the time has considerably reduced with the proposed approach, further optimizations are required to make the algorithm work for real-time applications.

4.3   Comparison with Other Algorithms

An important feature of adaptive window algorithm proposed by [1] is that it is completely local and does not include any global optimization. Also, the algorithm does not use any post-processing smoothing, but smooth surfaces are recovered as smooth while sharp disparity edges are retained. Therefore, it performs better in most of the region than existing algorithms. A comparison of proposed algorithm has been done with the other algorithms based on the results given in [3]. The parameters used are $B_{\bar{O}}$ (RMS Error in non occlude pixels), $B_{\bar{T}}$ (RMS Error for non textured pixels) and B_D (RMS error at discontinuity).The proposed algorithm with reduced computation time has not been compared with existing algorithm due to unavailability of computation results of other algorithms. Figure 5 show the comparison of proposed algorithm with other algorithms. The results of the proposed algorithm are underlined. Clearly the algorithm outperforms most of the algorithms, given that a good initial disparity estimate is taken. The correctness of this comparison is subject to the

	Tsukuba			Sawtooth			Venus			Map	
	$B_{\bar{O}}$	$B_{\bar{T}}$	B_D	$B_{\bar{O}}$	$B_{\bar{T}}$	B_D	$B_{\bar{O}}$	$B_{\bar{T}}$	B_D	$B_{\bar{O}}$	B_D
SSD Window	*1.67*	*1.67*	*3.27*	*1.47*	*1.32*	*3.53*	*2.31*	*3.27*	*1.71*	*2.84*	*9.36*
Adaptive Window	*1.60*	*1.46*	*3.18*	*1.42*	*1.27*	*3.43*	*1.99*	*2.84*	*3.01*	*2.82*	*9.30*
New. Adaptive W.	*1.43*	*1.21*	*2.96*	*1.17*	*0.90*	*2.59*	*1.81*	*2.46*	*2.61*	*2.81*	*9.29*
20 Layered	1.58 (3)	1.06 (4)	8.82 (3)	0.34 (1)	0.00 (1)	3.35 (1)	1.52 (3)	2.96 (10)	2.62 (2)	0.37 (6)	5.24 (6)
*4 Graph cuts	1.94 (5)	1.09 (5)	9.49 (5)	1.30 (6)	0.06 (3)	6.34 (6)	1.79 (7)	2.61 (8)	6.91 (4)	0.31 (4)	3.88 (4)
19 Belief prop.	1.15 (1)	0.42 (1)	6.31 (1)	0.98 (5)	0.30 (5)	4.83 (5)	1.00 (2)	0.76 (2)	9.13 (6)	0.84 (10)	5.27 (7)
11 GC+occl.	1.27 (2)	0.43 (2)	6.90 (2)	0.36 (2)	0.00 (1)	3.65 (2)	2.79 (12)	5.39 (13)	2.54 (1)	1.79 (13)	10.08 (12)
10 Graph cuts	1.86 (4)	1.00 (3)	9.35 (4)	0.42 (3)	0.14 (4)	3.76 (3)	1.69 (6)	2.30 (6)	5.40 (3)	2.39 (16)	9.35 (10)
8 Multiw. cut	8.08 (17)	6.53 (14)	25.33 (18)	0.61 (4)	0.46 (8)	4.60 (4)	0.53 (1)	0.31 (1)	8.06 (5)	0.26 (3)	3.27 (3)
12 Compact win.	3.36 (8)	3.54 (8)	12.91 (9)	1.61 (9)	0.45 (7)	7.87 (7)	1.67 (5)	2.18 (4)	13.24 (9)	0.33 (5)	3.94 (5)
14 Realtime	4.25 (12)	4.47 (12)	15.05 (13)	1.32 (7)	0.35 (6)	9.21 (8)	1.53 (4)	1.80 (3)	12.33 (7)	0.81 (9)	11.35 (15)
*5 Bay. diff.	6.49 (16)	11.62 (19)	12.29 (7)	1.45 (8)	0.72 (9)	9.29 (9)	4.00 (14)	7.21 (16)	18.39 (13)	0.20 (1)	2.49 (2)
9 Cooperative	3.49 (9)	3.65 (9)	14.77 (11)	2.03 (10)	2.29 (14)	13.41 (13)	2.57 (11)	3.52 (11)	26.38 (17)	0.22 (2)	2.37 (1)
*1 SSD+MF	5.23 (15)	3.80 (10)	24.66 (17)	2.21 (11)	0.72 (10)	13.97 (15)	3.74 (13)	6.82 (15)	12.94 (8)	0.66 (8)	9.35 (10)
15 Stoch. diff.	3.95 (10)	4.08 (11)	15.49 (15)	2.45 (14)	0.90 (11)	10.58 (10)	2.45 (9)	2.41 (7)	21.84 (15)	1.31 (12)	7.79 (9)
13 Genetic	2.96 (6)	2.66 (7)	14.97 (12)	2.21 (12)	2.76 (16)	13.96 (14)	2.49 (10)	2.89 (9)	23.04 (16)	1.04 (11)	10.91 (14)
7 Pix-to-pix	5.12 (14)	7.06 (17)	14.62 (10)	2.31 (13)	1.79 (12)	14.93 (17)	6.30 (17)	11.37 (18)	14.57 (10)	0.50 (7)	6.83 (8)
6 Max flow	2.98 (7)	2.00 (6)	15.10 (14)	3.47 (15)	3.00 (17)	14.19 (16)	2.16 (8)	2.24 (5)	21.73 (14)	3.13 (17)	15.98 (18)
*3 Scanl. opt.	5.08 (13)	6.78 (15)	11.94 (6)	4.06 (16)	2.64 (15)	11.90 (11)	9.44 (19)	14.59 (19)	18.20 (12)	1.84 (14)	10.22 (13)
*2 Dyn. prog.	4.12 (11)	4.63 (13)	12.34 (8)	4.84 (19)	3.71 (19)	13.26 (12)	10.10 (20)	15.01 (20)	17.12 (11)	3.33 (18)	14.04 (17)
17 Shao	9.67 (18)	7.04 (16)	35.63 (19)	4.25 (17)	3.19 (18)	30.14 (20)	6.01 (16)	6.70 (14)	43.91 (20)	2.36 (15)	33.01 (20)
16 Fast Correl.	9.76 (19)	13.85 (20)	24.39 (16)	4.76 (18)	1.87 (13)	22.49 (18)	6.48 (18)	10.36 (17)	31.29 (18)	8.42 (20)	12.68 (16)
18 Max surf.	11.10 (20)	10.70 (18)	41.99 (20)	5.51 (20)	5.56 (20)	27.39 (19)	4.36 (15)	4.78 (12)	41.13 (19)	4.17 (19)	27.88 (19)

Fig. 5. Initial window estimate: Direction-wise Average of already computed neighboring window sizes

data of other algorithms given in [3]. The algorithm is performing a bit worse at discontinuity in Venus image due to slanted regions, but overall it is better. After a set of experiments most of the stereo pairs gave best results with minimum limiting window size of 16 x 16 and value of d as 6, however, the value of d must be decreased with the number of iterations, as the disparity error reduce in each iteration.

5   Conclusion

We have presented an improved and efficient iterative stereo matching algorithm using adaptive window in this paper. The algorithm selects a window adaptively computed by the algorithm proposed by [1] and performs WTA for SSD around each pixel to reduce disparity errors introduced by usage of rectangular window and floating point disparity errors. The proposed algorithm helps improving the disparity estimate at each iteration over the image which in turn helps the disparity estimate to converge faster. The adaptive window algorithm proposed by [1] has been taken because, it is completely local and does not include any global optimization. Also, the algorithm does not use any post-processing smoothing, but smooth surfaces are recovered as smooth while sharp disparity edges are retained. Given a good initial disparity estimate, the proposed algorithm will reduce the disparity errors. However, the number of iterations and computation time depends on the algorithmic parameters. The experimental results demonstrate a clear advantage of the proposed algorithm over the algorithms with a fixed window size and existing adaptive window based algorithm for standard stereo pairs. Also the proposed algorithm improves the computational complexity by a large factor. We are working towards further reducing the computation for the real-time applications.

References

1. Takeo Kanade and Masatoshi Okutomi, A stereo matching algorithm with an adaptive window: Theory and Experiment, IEEE Transactions on Pattern Analysis and Machine Intelligence, 16(9):920 932, September 1994.
2. O Veksler, Stereo correspondence with compact windows via minimum ratio cycle, IEEE Transactions on Pattern Analysis and Machine Intelligence, 24(12):1654-1660, December 2002.
3. Daniel Scharstein and Richard Szeliski, A Taxonomy and Evaluaion of Dense Two-Frame Stereo Correspondence Algorithms, International Journal of Computer Vision, Vol. 47, Numbers 1-3, pages 7-42, April 2002.
4. V. Kolmogorov, Graph Based Algorithms for Scene Reconstruction from Two or More Views. PhD thesis, Cornell University, 2004.
5. http://cat.middlebury.edu/stereo/, Middlebury Stereo data and basic implementation.

Robust Homography-Based Control for Camera Positioning in Piecewise Planar Environments

D. Santosh Kumar and C.V. Jawahar

Center for Visual Information Technology
International Institute of Information Technology
Hyderabad 500032, India
{santosh@students., jawahar@}iiit.ac.in

Abstract. This paper presents a vision-based control for positioning a camera with respect to an unknown piecewise planar object. We introduce a novel homography-based approach that integrates information from multiple homographies to reliably estimate the relative displacement of the camera. This approach is robust to image measurement errors and provides a stable estimate of the camera motion that is free from degeneracies in the task space. We also develop a new control formulation that meets the contradictory requirements of producing a decoupled camera trajectory and ensuring object visibility by only utilizing the homography relating the two views. Experimental results validate the efficiency and robustness of our approach and demonstrate its applicability.

1 Robotic Vision

The use of computer vision techniques to control robotic systems has received great popularity in recent times [1]. Images captured by cameras attached to a robot provide ample information about its surroundings that assists it in efficiently navigating the environment. This field, known as *Visual Servoing* [2], has gained recent prominence due to the widespread availability of high quality cameras and low cost microprocessors. In addition to robotics, visual servoing algorithms also find interesting applications for interactive vision systems such as video conferencing, tracking, active vision, augmented reality etc. The visual feedback increases the accuracy of the overall vision system and relaxes the requirement of high precision accessories.

Many servoing techniques have been proposed and extensively studied in literature. In [3], optical flow is used to control the pose of the camera in conjunction with a Jacobian-based adaptive controller. In [4], $3D$ object pose is estimated and utilized to regulate the camera pose error. The class of algorithms similar to the former method constitute the popular *Image-based* Visual Servoing techniques while the latter pertain to *Position-based* approaches. For the relative merits and demerits of the above techniques, the reader may refer to [2]. Recently, a new group of algorithms have been proposed [5,6,7] that exploit a combination of the above methods to estimate the camera displacement between the desired and the current pose. They combine the traditional Jacobian-based control with

P. Kalra and S. Peleg (Eds.): ICVGIP 2006, LNCS 4338, pp. 906–918, 2006.

other techniques to form the class of *Hybrid Visual Servoing* algorithms. These methods yield a decoupled, straight-line camera trajectory and possess a large singularity-free task space.

Hybrid algorithms can essentially be classified into two primary categories. Algorithms in the first category are generally based on the computation of the essential matrix relating the two camera views [7,8]. Although the relative camera displacement can be obtained even for unknown (non-planar) scenes, a problem with epipolar geometry is that, it degenerates in certain critical cases (for example, when the target is planar or when the relative displacement is a pure rotation) and hence is not suitable for servoing. Note that a positioning task is accomplished only when the current and the desired images of the scene are similar, which corresponds to the degenerate case. The second class of algorithms determine the relative camera displacement by computing the homography induced by a scene plane relating the two views. However, a major drawback of these methods is the implicit assumption of the planarity of the scene, which prevents their application to real world scenarios as the world is often made up of non-planar regions. It must be emphasized that in either cases, the degeneracies critically affect the convergence and predictability of the system. Thus dealing with such degeneracies is of vital importance in the design of a stable system.

In summary, the desirable characteristics of a *hybrid* visual-control algorithm are

- Absence of degeneracies in its task space
- Applicability to both planar and non-planar environments
- Robustness to image measurement errors
- Continuity in velocity instruction and smooth convergence behavior
- Independence from prior knowledge of the object model and initialization of parameters

In this paper, we propose a new homography-based servoing algorithm that achieves the above features. Our method integrates homographies induced by multiple scene planes using geometric and subspace constraints to efficiently estimate the motion and structure parameters (Fig. 1). Another contribution of this paper is the development of a modified control law that provides the

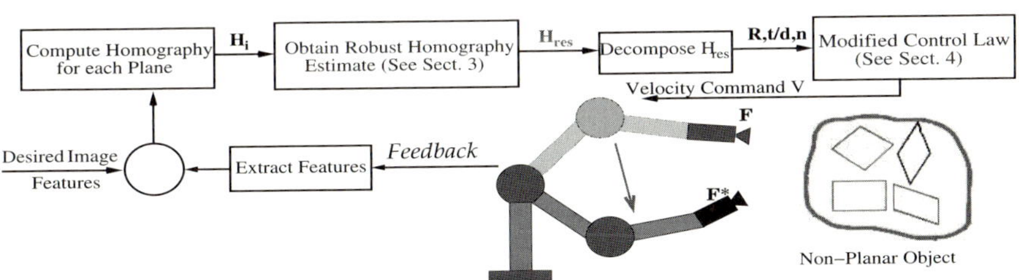

Fig. 1. Visual-feedback control: Multiple homographies are integrated to obtain a robust homography, which is used in the modified control law to gain superior performance

complementary characteristics of producing a decoupled camera trajectory and ensuring object visibility by only using the homography transformation relating the two camera poses.

2 Homography-Based Visual Control

A visual servo control compares the current image of a target with the desired image and the difference (or 'error') is used to drive the camera towards the goal position. Often the task is not just to regulate the image error but also to ensure a realizable camera trajectory. In such scenarios, homography-based control acts as a convenient option as it regulates the error in camera pose by estimating the $3D$ motion parameters only using image information.

If all the object points lie on a $3D$ plane, their coordinates in the current image I and the goal image I^* are related by a 'collineation' [9]. Assume that a point P lies on a plane whose normal vector is n as shown in Fig. 2. The point

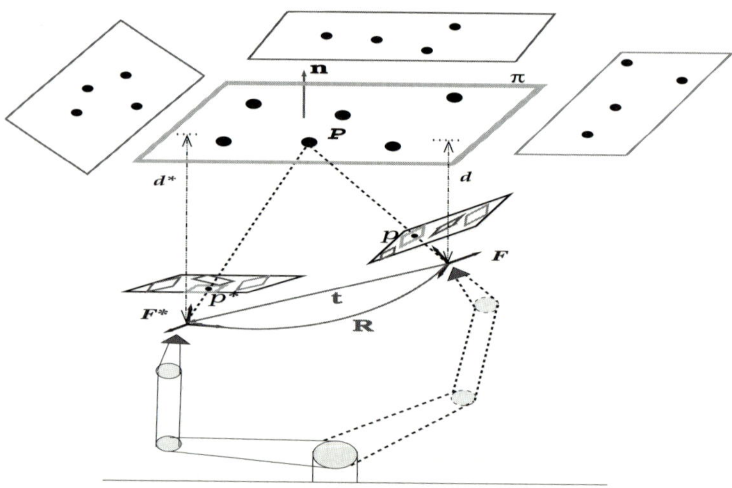

Fig. 2. Homography-based Visual Servoing

expressed in current camera frame $\mathcal{F}$ is related to goal camera frame $\mathcal{F}^*$ by a rotation matrix R and translation vector t as

$$P^* = R\,P + t = (R + t\frac{n^T}{d})P, \tag{1}$$

where $d = n^T P$ is the distance of the plane π from the current camera center. Assuming the camera intrinsic parameters are known, the image coordinates of the $3D$ points are given by $p = \frac{P}{Z}$ and $p^* = \frac{P^*}{Z^*}$ respectively. This transforms (1) to

$$\frac{Z^*}{Z}p^* = (R + t\frac{n^T}{d})p, \tag{2}$$

which can be rewritten as $\alpha p^* = Hp$ where $H_{3\times3} = R + t\frac{n^T}{d}$ is called the 'homography' matrix up to a scale factor α [9].

The recovered homography can be decomposed to obtain the rotation matrix R, the scaled translation vector $\frac{t}{d}$ and the plane normal n using the procedure described in [10]. Unfortunately, in the most general case the decomposition of H yields four different solutions (two of them being the 'opposites' of the other). They can be reduced to two solutions by applying the visibility constraint (*i.e.*, all the features must lie within the camera field of view). Further ambiguity can be resolved by decomposing an additional homography induced by another scene plane. Two pairs of solutions (S_1, S_2) and (S_1', S_2') are obtained respectively and a compatible pair (S_i, S_j') among them is found, *i.e.*, a pair with common motion $(R, \frac{t}{d})$. In general, there is only one compatible pair, and hence the unique solution can be obtained. Thus using information from multiple planes, H can be decomposed unambiguously to obtain the motion and structure parameters. These parameters are used in the control law to generate the optimal velocity instruction.

2.1   Degenerate Configurations and the Use of Multiple Planes

Some of the limitations of the existing *hybrid* techniques to estimate the relative camera displacement were reviewed in Sect. 1. Recently, another method was proposed by Malis *et al.* [6] to compute the relative orientation between the two camera views for a non-planar object using the concept of 'virtual parallax' [11]. By defining a plane using three arbitrary points on the object, they estimate the homography using this virtual plane and perform the positioning task.

A single homography estimate is not sufficient when a camera has to undergo large displacements in visual servoing as the control can be affected by degenerate configurations. Degeneracies in the task space can result either due to occlusion of the feature points, the camera center approaching the world (virtual) plane, the camera centers and the feature points arriving in a singular configuration [9] or due to singular homographies. In either of the cases, when a degeneracy is reached, the plane in consideration is switched *i.e.*, the points used to define the virtual plane are changed and a new plane using three different points is defined. This switching causes a discontinuity in the velocity command and leads to the instability of the control system. In Fig. 3, the effect of switching is demonstrated, where a positioning task with respect to a piecewise planar object was studied.

The other drawbacks in defining a non-planar object using arbitrary planes include

- **Unfavorable for planar scenes.** The methods using virtual parallax are theoretically inefficient to deal with planar objects as the epipolar geometry degenerates in this case [6].
- **Initialization of plane parameters.** In order to resolve the ambiguity in homography decomposition, *a priori* information about the normal vector of the virtual plane is required.
- **Assumption of point features.** Point correspondences are not available in many practical situations or could be noisy. Since the virtual plane is defined

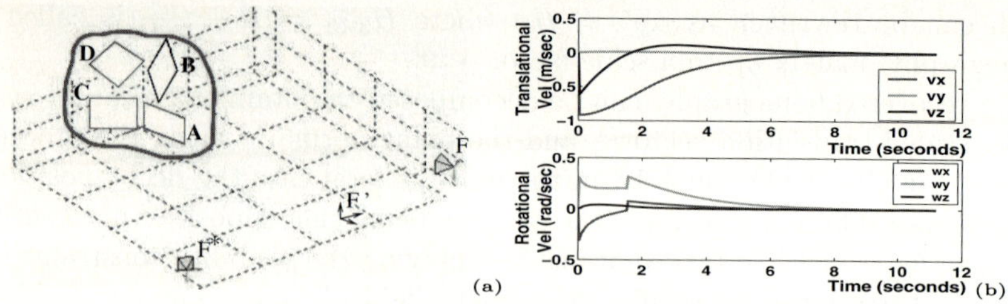

Fig. 3. Velocity Screw using virtual parallax algorithm: (a) Servoing begun using plane A reaches a degeneracy at F' whose origin intersects the plane (b) Discontinuity in the velocity screw is due to the switching of planes (A to C) at F'

explicitly using the non-coplanar points on the object, these methods may not be applicable when such features are not available.

- **Effect of measurement errors.** Homography estimation is affected due to measurement errors (*'drift'*) in the correspondences. By choosing a different set of points (that are error-free) to define the virtual plane, one can obtain better results.

It must be emphasized that the above limitations are caused by the fact that only information from a single plane is being utilized to perform the positioning task. The bottleneck has been the fact that there exists no single homography relating the two camera views that can be absolutely relied upon. Nevertheless, by selectively exploiting the information available from multiple planes, one can avoid the above drawbacks and achieve superior performance.

3   Homography Estimation Using Multiple Planes

The objective of the servoing task is to drive the disparity between the current and the desired camera configurations to zero. The homographies relating the two camera poses induced by different planar regions are used to guide the positioning task.

Our approach proceeds initially by partially tessellating the non-planar scene into piecewise planar patches. This is done by a simple partitioning of the image features into homogeneous planar regions (See Fig. 6(a)). Interest regions are detected and the regions subject to planarity constraint form a set of matching regions [12]. The seed regions act as a 'driver' to guide the evolution of planar patches in the image. Any interest region detector with the ability to detect robust and stable regions can be employed here. For each pair of matching regions, a plane-induced homography is calculated.

Even though a single homography is sufficient to determine the motion parameters (*rigidity constraint*), information from multiple homographies can be combined to obtain a reliable estimate of the camera displacement. However, to avoid the estimation of multiple homographies at each instant, the constraints on homographies can be exploited to reduce the computations. Recall from (2) that any H induced by a $3D$ scene plane is described by $H_{3\times3} \approx R+tn^T$. Given a homography matrix H_π induced by some $3D$ plane π, all other homographies H_i can be described as $\lambda_i H_\pi + tn_i^T$ for a fixed pair of cameras [9]. This observation results from the fact that all the homographies differ only in their scale λ_i and plane n_i parameters. Consider k homography matrices $H_1, H_2, \ldots, H_k$, each expressed as a column vector in a $9 \times k$ matrix. The rank of this matrix is known to be utmost four [13]. Hence the space of all homographies between two fixed camera views is embedded in a 4-dimensional linear subspace of $\Re^9$. This observation follows the fundamental fact that multiple planar patches in the scene share the common global camera geometry (*i.e.*, R, t).

3.1   Computation of the Reliable Homography

Given the rank-4 constraint, any new homography can be computed as a weighted combination of four linearly independent homographies. The four homographies are in general selected such that they are induced by planes that possess largest area and best visibility (if the centroid of the features in a planar region is within a threshold distance from the nearest image boundary, then it satisfies the visibility constraint) since they are the most reliable.

The resultant homography H_{res} is defined as

$$H_{res} = \lambda_1 H_1 + \lambda_2 H_2 + \lambda_3 H_3 + \lambda_4 H_4, \tag{3}$$

where the weights λ_i are assigned such that good homographies receive higher weights while the degenerate or errored estimates are given low priority. By appropriately choosing the λ_i's, a reliable homography can be deduced. Recall that, in general, any homography in the subspace can be expressed as a linear combination of four base homographies. In our case, H_{res} is one such 'valid' homography possessing certain desired characteristics.

The principle behind the weight assignment is to prefer valid homographies and reject singular ones in order to prevent abrupt switching of planes during a degeneracy. It must be emphasized that most of the degeneracies are not arbitrary changes and in general, can be predicted in advance. For instance, distance between a camera and a (virtual) plane gradually regresses to zero. Likewise, occlusion of planes can be anticipated by the persistent decrease in area of the planar region (or the number of features). Other degenerate cases can also be predicted in a similar manner and thus homographies that are likely to confront a degenerate configuration can be rejected.

Assignment of weights. Let us define the constraints to assign the weights and hence the parameter λ_i that is used in the computation of H_{res}.

- **Re-projection Error.** This constraint measures the accuracy of the estimated homography. A high error in re-projection indicates a poor estimate and such H should receive less weight as parameters obtained from it will be unreliable. Thus the weights are set inversely proportional to the re-projection error. This ensures that planar regions that are affected by the cumulative tracking errors ('*drift error*') are avoided and thereby guaranteeing the robustness of H_{res} to image measurement errors. The exact weight λ_i^e is defined by first calculating the re-projection error *i.e.,* $e = \sum_k d(p_k^*, Hp_k) = \sum_k \left\| \frac{p_k^*}{\|p_k^*\|} - \frac{H*p_k}{\|H*p_k\|} \right\|$ and then assigning it using a one-sided Normal distribution $N(e_{thres}, \sigma_e)$ where e_{thres} is the tolerable re-projection error and σ_e is the variance.

- **Homography Determinant.** This quantity signifies the 'goodness' of a homography estimate. If the determinant is tending toward zero, it suggests the arrival of a degeneracy and hence such a homography should acquire low weight. Therefore the weights are set directly proportional to the value of the determinant D. This constraint ascertains the resultant homography to be free of singularities. Here again, the weights λ_i^D are set using a one-sided Normal density function $N(D_{thres}, \sigma_D)$ where D_{thres} is the minimum acceptable determinant.
- **Area of the Plane.** Occlusion of a plane can be detected by measuring the gradient of the plane area dA. If the area of the planar region decreases drastically, then it indicates a possible occlusion of this plane in the near future. Thus the λ_i's are to be set inversely proportional to the value of dA. More precisely, the weight λ_i^{dA} is set using a one-sided Normal distribution $N(dA_{thres}, \sigma_{dA})$ where dA_{thres} is the minimum acceptable gradient.

These weights are normalized and summed together to obtain the resultant weight λ_i. The final expression for H_{res} is calculated as

$$H_{res} = \sum_{i=1}^{4} \lambda_i H_i, \quad \text{where} \quad \sum_i \lambda_i = 1.$$

Hence a judicious assignment of weights using the above constraints helps in deducing a 'virtual' homography with the desirable characteristics. A change of bases might be required in case one of the H_i degenerate. However, the degenerate homography would automatically procure a low λ value and its replacement does not affect the stability of the system. This approach is applicable even if the scene consists of less than four planar regions. In such a case, the unavailable homographies in (3) acquire zero weight. It must be emphasized that the method utilizes additional homographies to obtain a reliable homography estimate rather than computing the optimal estimate. The parameters obtained from decomposition of H_{res} are used in the modified control law to compute the camera trajectory.

4   Modified Control Design

Given the stable estimate of the motion and structure parameters, our focus is to design a robust control that not only produces a decoupled camera trajectory but also guarantees feature visibility. Classical approaches such as the $3D$ control algorithms compute an optimal camera trajectory but very often violate the visibility criteria. $2D$ controls ensure the features to remain in the camera field of view, although they suffer from non-optimal trajectory, computational complexity of calculating the Jacobian pseudo-inverse and the demand for $3D$ depth estimates. Note that providing the contradictory requirements of either controls poses a daunting challenge in the design of an optimum control scheme. Though a few attempts in this direction have been made [5,6,14], the devised controls do not satisfy all the above requirements.

Much of the information that is required for performing the positioning task is readily available from the homography transformation. The presence of multiple planes in the scene further compliments this fact. We exploit this result to fulfill the requirements of the desired optimal control.

Proposed Control. We first introduce the Cartesian ($3D$) control law and then proceed to derive the robust control. Given the parameters obtained from homography decomposition, the translational velocity to go directly to the goal is determined as $-\lambda_v(\frac{t}{d})\,d$, where λ_v is a gain factor and d is the distance to the plane (See Fig. 2). The rotational velocity is computed as $-\lambda_\omega u\theta$, where λ_ω is again a gain factor and u,θ denote the rotation axis and angle that are obtained using the Rodriguez formula for the rotation matrix R as $\theta = \arccos(\frac{1}{2}(tr(R)-1))$ and $[\mathbf{u}]_\times = \frac{R-R^T}{2\,\mathrm{sinc}(\theta)}$ [4].

However, a direct control in the Cartesian space might result in the features leaving the camera field of view. To enforce the visibility constraint, we use a single image point to control two axes of rotation (around x and y) and the final axis of rotation is controlled directly using the rotation matrix. This is done as follows: We know from the image-based visual servoing control [2]

$$\begin{bmatrix} u - u^* \\ v - v^* \end{bmatrix}_{2\times 1} = \underbrace{\begin{bmatrix} -\frac{1}{Z} & 0 & \frac{u}{Z} \end{bmatrix}}_{L_\nu}\;\underbrace{\begin{bmatrix} uv & -(1+u^2) \end{bmatrix}}_{L_{\omega xy}}\;\underbrace{\begin{bmatrix} v \\ -u \end{bmatrix}}_{L_{\omega z}} \begin{bmatrix} \nu_{3\times 1} \\ \omega_{3\times 1} \end{bmatrix}_{6\times 1}, \quad (4)$$

where $p = [u\ v\ 1]^T = [x\ 1]^T$, $p^* = [u^*\ v^*\ 1]^T = [x^*\ 1]^T$, $Z = \mathbf{Z}(P)$ (See Fig. 2) and $[\nu\ \omega]^T$ denotes the camera velocity. Equation (4) relates the motion of image features $i.e.$, $x - x^*$ to the camera motion using the 2×6 Jacobian matrix L. It can be rewritten as $x - x^* = [L_\nu\ L_{\omega xy}\ L_{\omega z}][\nu\ \omega_{xy}\ \omega_z]^T$. Observe that a simple rearrangement of terms yields

$$\omega_{xy} = L_{\omega xy}^{-1}[(x - x^*) - L_\nu\nu - L_{\omega z}\omega_z], \quad (5)$$

where $\nu = (\frac{t}{d})\hat{d}$ and $\omega_z = \mathbf{u_z}\theta$. In (5), the rotational motion ω_{xy} is controlled not only to minimize the differences between the current and the goal image features but also to compensate the effects caused by translation on the image. This ensures a straight-line feature trajectory in the image and thereby guarantees object visibility. Estimates of the values Z and d are required in (4) that can be obtained as follows: Firstly, observe that

$$det(H) = det(R + \frac{tn^T}{d}) = det(R + \frac{t(n^{*T}R)}{d}) \quad (6)$$

$$= det(I + \frac{tn^{*T}}{d})det(R) = \frac{d + n^{*T}t}{d} \tag{7}$$

where (6) uses the fact that $n^* = Rn$ (See Fig. 2). Equation (7) can be further simplified using the result $d^* - d = n^{*T}P^* - n^T P = n^{*T}(P^* - RP) = n^{*T}t$. Hence we have $\hat{d} = \frac{\hat{d^*}}{det(H)}$. Using (7), Z can be calculated as

$$\frac{Z}{d^*} = \frac{Z}{d^*}\frac{d}{n^T P} = \frac{1}{n^T p}\frac{1}{det(H)}. \tag{8}$$

Thus we have $\hat{Z} = \frac{\hat{d^*}}{n^T p}\frac{1}{det(H)}$, where $\hat{d^*}$ is an estimate of the constant distance to the plane in the desired camera frame. In general, this quantity is considered as a gain ratio [6] and a coarse estimate obtained from a simple stereo technique is adequate. Consequently, all the parameters required for the control are now available directly from the homography decomposition.

In summary, the resultant expression for the velocity $\mathbf{v}$ is given as

$$\mathbf{v} = \begin{bmatrix} -\lambda_v I_{3\times3} & 0_{3\times2} & 0_{3\times1} \\ 0_{2\times3} & -\lambda_{\omega_{xy}} I_{2\times2} & 0_{2\times1} \\ 0_{1\times3} & 0_{1\times2} & -\lambda_{\omega_z} I_{1\times1} \end{bmatrix} \begin{bmatrix} \nu \\ \omega_{xy} \\ \omega_z \end{bmatrix} \left(= \begin{bmatrix} L_{\omega_{xy}}^{-1}[(x - x^*) - L_\nu \nu - L_{\omega_z}\omega_z] \\ \mathbf{u_z}\theta \end{bmatrix} \right) \tag{9}$$

Equation (9) has only one singularity that occurs at $Z = 0$ (See expression for L_ν). However, as discussed in the earlier section, this degenerate configuration is avoided by the reliable homography computation algorithm. Thus by incorporating image features into the $3D$ control, an efficient control offering the complimentary features of object visibility and decoupled trajectory has been developed.

5   Experimental Results

In our experiments, we constructed an arbitrary configuration of planes as shown in Fig. 4(a). The projection of points belonging to these planar regions onto the image were considered as features. A perspective camera projection model was assumed. The basic implementation of the proposed algorithm given below was used to perform the positioning task.

1. Extract features from the current image and partition them into piecewise planar regions
2. Compute homography H_i induced by each region
3. Select four independent homographies induced by the regions that have the largest areas and best visibility (Only the selected regions need to be tracked in the successive iterations)
4. Determine the weights using the geometric constraints and compute the normalized weight λ_i for the selected homographies (Sect. 3.1)
5. Determine the robust homography H_{res} using (3)
6. Decompose H_{res} to obtain the motion and structure parameters (Resolve ambiguity using an additional homography)

7. Use the control law to obtain the velocity instruction $\mathbf{v}$ (See (9))
8. Repeat above steps until convergence

We analyzed the performance of our algorithm by generating several random initial camera configurations and then moving the camera to a fixed desired pose in a multi-plane scenario as shown in Fig. 4(a). Observe that a camera can frequently encounter degenerate cases during the positioning task in such a scene. However, in almost all the cases, the proposed algorithm was uninfluenced by degeneracies. In Fig. 4(c), the velocity command generated by the proposed approach for the particular scenario as tested in Fig. 3(a) is shown. Fig. 4(b) shows the variation in weights corresponding to the homographies. Observe that the weight corresponding to degenerate H tends towards the minimum value as the camera approaches the degeneracy. The smooth velocity screw in Fig. 4(c) demonstrates the stable behavior of the algorithm unlike in Fig. 3(b). Fig. 4(d) displays the camera trajectory. Note that the expression for Z in (8) requires at

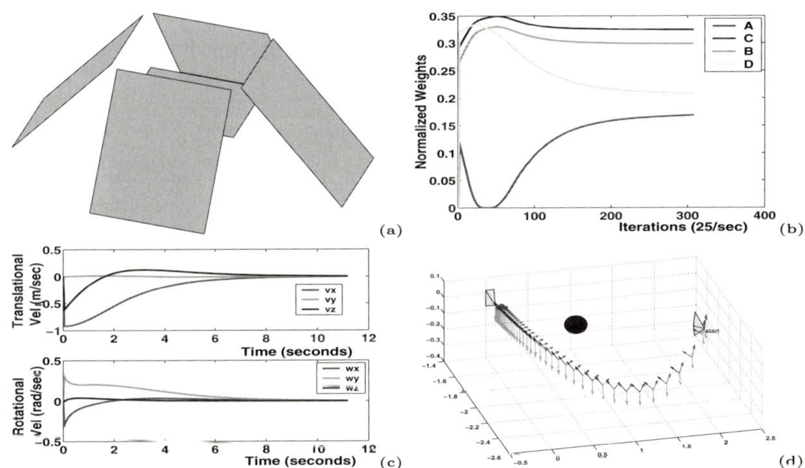

Fig. 4. (a) Non-Planar scene considered in the experiments. (b) Normalized weight values (c) Velocity Screw and (d) Camera Trajectory obtained for the scenario described in Fig. 3(a) . Smooth convergence even in presence of degeneracies confirms the stable behavior of the proposed approach.

least one feature p belonging to the planar region. However as a virtual homography is being used in our case, it might not correspond to any physical plane in the scene. In our method, we obtained this feature by finding the intersection of the plane inducing the virtual homography H_{res} with other scene planes as described in [15].

Analysis of the Control Law. The performance of the control law was analyzed in simulation. Fig. 5 shows the velocity screw and the image feature trajectory obtained during a positioning task using the proposed, $3D$ and the

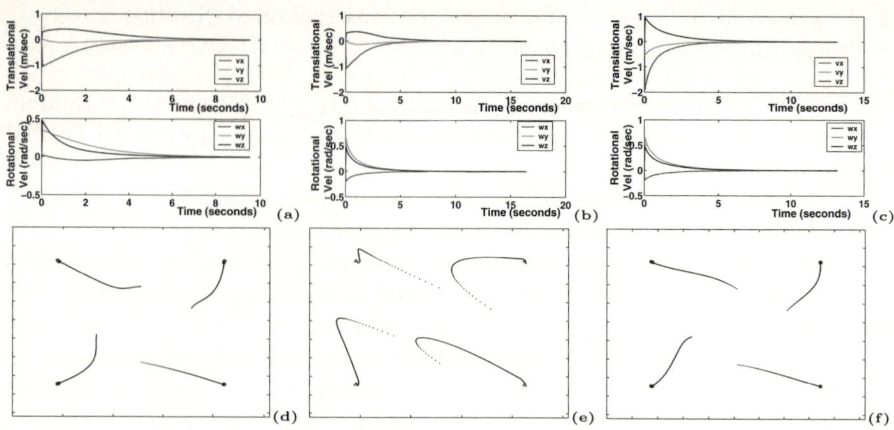

Fig. 5. Analysis of proposed control: Fig.(a),(b),(c) show the velocity screw obtained in case of proposed, $3D$ and $21/2D$ controls respectively while (d),(e),(f) display the feature trajectory. Similarity of velocity screws in (a) and (b) confirms the optimal trajectory behavior of the proposed control while near straight-line image feature trajectory in (d) ascertains the feature visibility.

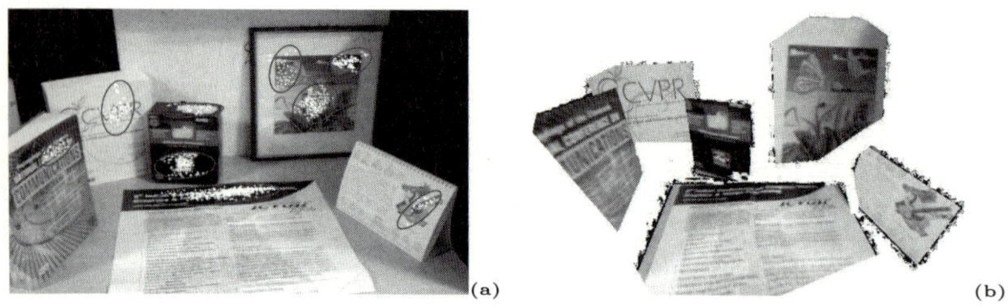

Fig. 6. Planar scene reconstruction using inter-image homographies: (a) A sample frame along with the detected interest regions on the scene planes (b) Reconstruction result

$21/2D$ [6] controls respectively. The velocity screw obtained using the proposed control is very similar to the one obtained using the $3D$ control. Further, the feature trajectory almost follows a straight line. These two observations ascertain our claims of decoupled (straight-line) camera trajectory and object visibility using the proposed control. Inter-image homographies are an interesting tool for reconstruction of planar surfaces. The decomposition of homographies provide the $3D$ plane parameters required to reconstruct the scene. By considering a common feature belonging to two planes n_i and n, a relationship could be derived between their distances using (8) as

$$Z = \frac{d_i}{n_i^T p} \frac{1}{det(H)} = \frac{d}{n^T p} \frac{1}{det(H)} \quad i.e., \quad d_i = \frac{n_i^T p}{n^T p} d, \qquad (10)$$

where p denotes the common image feature. Thus given the plane normals n_i, the $3D$ scene could be reconstructed up to a scale factor d (See Fig. 6(b)). Given an estimate of d, the exact scene can be reconstructed.

6   Conclusion

A novel homography-based control capable of positioning a camera even in presence of non-planar objects has been developed for the first time in this paper. A robust homography estimate was efficiently computed using multiple homographies by employing geometric and subspace constraints. This homography estimate was used in a modified control law to compute the optimal camera trajectory. The method performed better in comparison to existing servoing algorithms and avoided their critical drawbacks. In future, we plan to investigate further the utility of multi-plane homography-based formulations for efficiently solving other classical computer vision problems.

References

1. DeSouza, G., Kak, A.: Vision for mobile robot navigation: A survey. IEEE Transactions on Pattern Analysis and Machine Intelligence **24** (2002) 237–267
2. Hutchinson, S.A., Hager, G.D., Corke, P.I.: A tutorial on visual servo control. IEEE Transactions on Robotics and Automation **12** (1996) 651–670
3. Chaumette, F., Espiau, B.: A new approach to visual servoing in robotics. IEEE Transactions on Robotics and Automation **8** (1992) 313–327
4. Wilson, W.J., Hulls, C.C.W., Bell, G.S.: Relative end effector control using cartesian position based visual sovoing. IEEE Transactions on Robotics and Automation **12** (1996) 684–696
5. Taylor, C.J., Ostrowski, J.P., Jung, S.H.: Robust visual servoing based on relative orientation. IEEE Computer Society Conference on Computer Vision and Pattern Recognition **2** (1999) 574–580
6. Malis, E., Chaumette, F.: 2 1/2D visual servoing with respect to unknown objects through a new estimation scheme of camera displacement. International Journal of Computer Vision **37** (2000) 79–97
7. Rives, P.: Visual servoing based on epipolar geometry. IEEE/RSJ International Conference on Intelligent Robots and Systems **1** (2000) 602–607
8. Basri, R., Rivlin, E., Shimshoni, I.: Visual homing: surfing on the epipoles. IEEE International Conference on Computer Vision (1998) 863–869
9. Hartley, R., Zisserman, A.: Multiple view geometry in computer vision. Cambridge University Press (2003)
10. Faugeras, O., Lustman, F.: Motion and strucutre from motion in a piecewise planar environment. International Journal of Pattern Recognition and Artificial Intelligence **2** (1988) 485–508
11. Boufama, B., Mohr, R.: Epipole and fundamental matrix estimation using the virtual parallax property. IEEE International Conference on Computer Vision (1995) 1030–1036
12. Fraundorfer, F., Bischof, H.: Detecting distinguished regions by saliency. Scandinavian Conference on Image Analysis (2003) 208–215

13. Shashua, A., Avidan, S.: The rank-4 constraint in multiple view geometry. European Conference on Computer Vision **2** (1996) 196–206
14. Deguchi, K.: Optimal motion control for image-based visual servoing by decoupling translation and rotation. IEEE/RSJ International Conference on Intelligent Robots and Systems **2** (1998) 705–711
15. Johansson, B.: View synthesis and 3D reconstruction of piecewise planar scenes using intersection lines between the planes. IEEE International Conference on Computer Vision **1** (1999) 54–59

Direct Estimation of Homogeneous Vectors: An Ill-Solved Problem in Computer Vision

Matthew Harker and Paul O'Leary

Institute for Automation, University of Leoben, A-8700 Leoben, Austria
matthew.harker@stud.unileoben.ac.at
http://automation.unileoben.ac.at

Abstract. Computer Vision theory is firmly rooted in Projective Geometry, whereby geometric objects can be effectively modeled by homogeneous vectors. We begin from Gauss's 200 year old theorem of least squares to derive a generic algorithm for the direct estimation of homogeneous vectors. We uncover the common link of previous methods, showing that direct estimation is not an ill-conditioned problem as is the popular belief, but has merely been an ill-solved problem. Results show improvements in goodness-of-fit and numerical stability, and demonstrate that "data normalization" is unnecessary for a well-founded algorithm.

1 Introduction

Geometric objects which can be modeled by homogeneous vectors range from implicit curves and surfaces, to the fundamental matrix describing epipolar geometry, and projective transformations such as camera matrices and homographies. Metric Vision tasks have real-time constraints, so it is critical to have fast and robust techniques for the estimation of homogeneous vectors. The basis of this paper is a plethora of seemingly unrelated techniques for the direct (i.e. non-iterative) estimation of homogeneous vectors. Direct estimation techniques have several advantages, namely, that the minimization yields the global minimum of the cost function, and they are computed in a finite number of steps. Three of the most commonly encountered methods for direct estimation are:

1. **Normalization:** The algorithm proceeds by normalizing the data, followed by minimization of the algebraic error subject to a unit norm constraint [1]. While the method has the advantage of simplicity, Hartley notes that without normalization, the algorithm is guaranteed to perform extremely poorly, which indicates the algorithm is poorly founded, not ill-conditioned. The unit norm constraint is typically justified by the homogeneity of the vector; however, we show that it is rarely a mathematically justifiable constraint. Specifically, for linear geometric models, the algorithm returns meaningless results. An algorithm that cannot handle linear models clearly cannot suffice for a generic methodology.

2. **Invariant Fitting:** This entails the least-squares minimization of algebraic error subject to a geometrically invariant constraint. Invariant fitting was originally proposed by Bookstein [2] to fit conics independent of the chosen

P. Kalra and S. Peleg (Eds.): ICVGIP 2006, LNCS 4338, pp. 919–930, 2006.

coordinate frame, and was later adapted to fundamental matrix estimation by Torr [3]. Other variations include fitting conics of specific types [4]. At this point in time, algorithms are limited to these applications, since viable invariant constraints must be quadratic [5]. This too corresponds to minimizing an algebraic distance, however, the results differ from the normalization scheme because a different constraint is imposed.

3. **Gradient-Weighted Fitting:** Sampson [6] proposed that the so-called algebraic distance weighted by its gradient would provide an improved metric for fitting conics, although his approach to attempt to minimize said cost function was iterative. Taubin [7] showed that an approximation to the minimum of the cost function can be found directly by generalized eigenvectors, which is often referred to as Gradient-Weighted Fitting. Here we show that while it has the potential to provide a better approximation, the algorithm is fundamentally unstable from a numerical point of view; in fact, it is far too unstable to yield useful results in Computer Vision applications (i.e. with pixel coordinates). Introducing data normalization alleviates, but does not rectify this instability.

In the present work, we derive a generic algorithm for the direct estimation of homogeneous vectors which (i) has the goodness-of-fit properties of gradient weighted fitting, however, with immeasurably improved stability, (ii) is largely invariant to the choice of coordinate frame and (iii) circumvents the need for data normalization. Simply put, it amalgamates the desirable properties of the most relied-upon techniques for the direct estimation of homogeneous vectors.

2   Gauss's Theorem of Least Squares

We hearken back to a two hundred year old theorem, Gauss's theorem of least-squares [8], which is central to estimation in the presence of uncertainty. Sadly, we find that it is largely misused, and the original theorem all but forgotten, save in a handful of Numerical Analysis literature. Gauss proposed various models for errors in measurements; the most fruitful was exponential-based, providing a realistic model that can be treated analytically. A measurement error is modeled as a random n-vector, δ, which behaves according to the probability distribution

$$P(\delta) = ((2\pi)^n |\Lambda|)^{-\frac{1}{2}} \exp -\frac{1}{2}\delta^{\mathrm{T}}\Lambda^{-1}\delta, \tag{1}$$

where Λ is the $n \times n$ covariance matrix [9,10]. This has come to be known as a Gaussian distribution.

Least Squares as a Maximum Likelihood Criterion. Gauss begins with a set of observations (i.e. measurements), which should conform to a linear model,

$$\begin{bmatrix} x_{11} & x_{12} & \cdots & x_{1n} \\ \vdots & \vdots & \vdots & \vdots \\ x_{m1} & x_{m2} & \cdots & x_{mn} \end{bmatrix} \begin{bmatrix} a_1 \\ a_2 \\ \vdots \\ a_n \end{bmatrix} = \begin{bmatrix} e_1 \\ \vdots \\ e_n \end{bmatrix}. \tag{2}$$

Each error, e_i, is assumed to be an independent random variable that follows the Gaussian distribution, $\psi(e_i) = h\pi^{-\frac{1}{2}}\exp{-h^2 e_i^2}$, where h is a positive constant; this assumes that all errors are mean-free and have the same variance. The function Ω is proposed, $\Omega = \prod_{i=1}^{n}\psi(e_i)$, the motivation being that for a normal distribution, the smallest error is the most probable: the function Ω should therefore be maximized. This function gives rise to the principle of maximum likelihood. Under the above assumptions, we have,

$$\Omega = h^n \pi^{-\frac{1}{2}n}\exp{-h^2\left(e_1^2 + e_2^2 + \ldots + e_n^2\right)}. \tag{3}$$

Hence, to maximize the likelihood, Ω, we must minimize,

$$\epsilon \triangleq e_1^2 + e_2^2 + \ldots + e_n^2 = \sum_{i=1}^{n} e_i^2, \tag{4}$$

the sum of squared errors. Gauss later proved that if the variances of the errors are all scaled to unity, then the least squares solution is such that the estimation errors have minimal variance. Summarizing the postulates:

1. Errors in measurements behave according to Gaussian distributions.
2. The errors are mean-free and scaled such that they have a unit variance.

The significance of the two postulates is clear. If the errors are not mean-free and normally distributed with equal variances, the least-squares solution is no longer a maximizer of the likelihood function Ω.

3   Linear Models

Linear models of geometric objects in two, three, and n dimensions, are respectively lines, planes, and hyperplanes. The following theory applies generally to these models, but for simplicity and visualization, we specifically address lines in the plane. The homogeneous equation of a line in the plane is given as,

$$\mathbf{p}^{\mathrm{T}}\mathbf{z} = ax + by + c = 0, \tag{5}$$

where

$$\mathbf{p} = \begin{bmatrix} x & y & 1 \end{bmatrix}^{\mathrm{T}} \qquad \text{and} \qquad \mathbf{z} = \begin{bmatrix} a & b & c \end{bmatrix}^{\mathrm{T}}. \tag{6}$$

In practice, we measure points $(\hat{x}, \hat{y})$, which do not lay on the line, but deviate by some error which we model as the random variables (δ_x, δ_y), such that

$$(\hat{x}, \hat{y}) = (x + \delta_x, y + \delta_y). \tag{7}$$

For mathematical convenience, we model the random coordinate pair $\delta = (\delta_x, \delta_y)$ as mean-free and correlated according to the Gaussian distribution,

$$P(\delta_x, \delta_y) = \frac{1}{2\pi}\left(\left|\begin{bmatrix}\sigma_{xx} & \sigma_{xy}\\ \sigma_{xy} & \sigma_{yy}\end{bmatrix}\right|\right)^{-\frac{1}{2}}\exp{-\frac{1}{2}\begin{bmatrix}\delta_x & \delta_y\end{bmatrix}\begin{bmatrix}\sigma_{xx} & \sigma_{xy}\\ \sigma_{xy} & \sigma_{yy}\end{bmatrix}^{-1}\begin{bmatrix}\delta_x\\ \delta_y\end{bmatrix}}, \tag{8}$$

defined by the covariance matrix, Λ. Since the ideal point (x, y) fits the model, we may write,

$$a(\hat{x} - \delta_x) + b(\hat{y} - \delta_y) + c = 0. \tag{9}$$

Rearranging yields,

$$a\hat{x} + b\hat{y} + c = a\delta_x + b\delta_y. \tag{10}$$

The left hand side is the familiar algebraic residual error associated with a point and a line, which we denote as, r_a, such that

$$r_\mathrm{a}(\hat{x}, \hat{y}, \mathbf{z}) \triangleq a\hat{x} + b\hat{y} + c. \tag{11}$$

The right hand side tells us how the error in the algebraic residual behaves according to the random errors in the point coordinates (δ_x, δ_y); we denote the right hand side as r_s, the stochastic form of the residual, such that

$$r_\mathrm{s}(\delta_x, \delta_y, \mathbf{z}) \triangleq a\delta_x + b\delta_y. \tag{12}$$

Since we have assumed a mathematical model for the error (δ_x, δ_y), we may analytically compute the expected value and variance of the error [9],

$$E[r] = \int_{-\infty}^{\infty} \int_{-\infty}^{\infty} P(\delta_x, \delta_y) r_\mathrm{s}(\delta_x, \delta_y, \mathbf{z}) \mathrm{d}\delta_x \mathrm{d}\delta_y = 0, \tag{13}$$

and

$$\mathrm{Var}\,(r) = \int_{-\infty}^{\infty} \int_{-\infty}^{\infty} P(\delta_x, \delta_y)(r_\mathrm{s}(\delta_x, \delta_y, \mathbf{z}) - E[r])^2 \mathrm{d}\delta_x \mathrm{d}\delta_y \tag{14}$$

$$= a^2 \sigma_{xx} + 2ab\sigma_{xy} + b^2 \sigma_{yy}. \tag{15}$$

There are a few important points to note:

1. The stochastic form of the residual is independent of the constant term, c, hence so are the mean and variance. In the case of some linearized models, such as homographies or camera matrices, there are multiple constant terms.
2. The variance is clearly a quadratic form in the statistically dependent coefficients, which will always be the case since variance is quadratic.

In light of these facts, we first partition the vector of unknowns into its statistically dependent and independent terms as

$$\mathbf{z} = \begin{bmatrix} \mathbf{z}_A \\ \mathbf{z}_B \end{bmatrix} \quad \text{where for the line,} \quad \mathbf{z}_A = \begin{bmatrix} a \\ b \end{bmatrix} \quad \text{and} \quad \mathbf{z}_B = c. \tag{16}$$

As will be seen, this partitioning is critical, although it is largely ignored in the literature. We may therefore write the variance of the error, r, as the quadratic form, $\mathrm{Var}\,(r) = \mathbf{z}_A^\mathrm{T} \Lambda \mathbf{z}_A$. Now, if we are to properly implement a least-squares solution, each error should be weighted such that it has unit variance. We hence write the ith error as,

$$\breve{e}_i = \frac{r_i}{\sqrt{\mathrm{Var}\,(r_i)}} = \frac{\mathbf{p}_i^\mathrm{T} \mathbf{z}}{\sqrt{\mathbf{z}_A^\mathrm{T} \Lambda_i \mathbf{z}_A}}, \tag{17}$$

where the notation $\breve{e}$, is to stress the fact that $\breve{e} \neq e$, but is however an error with unit variance[1]. We may now use the least-squares criterion; the cost function is

$$\epsilon(\mathbf{z}_A, \mathbf{z}_B) = \sum_{i=1}^{n} \breve{e}_i^2 = \sum_{i=1}^{n} \frac{\left(\mathbf{p}_i^{\mathrm{T}} \mathbf{z}\right)^2}{\mathbf{z}_A^{\mathrm{T}} \Lambda_i \mathbf{z}_A} \tag{18}$$

The function ϵ is now in appropriate form such that minimizing ϵ corresponds to maximizing Ω.

On the Unit Norm Constraint. For argument's sake, if we assume each error has the identity matrix as covariance matrix, i.e., $\Lambda = \mathsf{I}$, then the variance of each residual is $\mathrm{Var}\,(r) = a^2 + b^2$. The variance is clearly a function of the line direction; to ensure that the variance of the errors is independent of the line direction, we impose the constraint, $a^2 + b^2 = \alpha^2 = \text{constant}$. The resulting variances of the residuals are constant with respect to the direction of the line. This uncovers the first fault in imposing a unit norm constraint on a homogeneous vector. For the line, this would mean $a^2 + b^2 + c^2 = 1$. The resulting variance of each residual would be, $\mathrm{Var}\,(r) = 1 - c^2$; since c is the scaled distance of the line to the origin, this means that the variance of the error is functionally dependent on the position of the point in the plane, which is preposterous.

3.1   Minimizing the Least-Squares Cost Function

For convenience of manipulation, the cost function ϵ in Equation (18) can be written in matrix form, namely, as the squared 2-norm of a residual vector, i.e.,

$$\epsilon(\mathbf{z}_A, \mathbf{z}_B) = \|\mathsf{W}_A \mathsf{D}_A \mathbf{z}_A + \mathsf{W}_A \mathsf{D}_B \mathbf{z}_B\|_2^2, \tag{19}$$

where

$$\mathsf{W}_A = \mathrm{diag}\left(\left(\mathbf{z}_A^{\mathrm{T}} \Lambda_1 \mathbf{z}_A\right)^{-\frac{1}{2}}, \ldots, \left(\mathbf{z}_A^{\mathrm{T}} \Lambda_n \mathbf{z}_A\right)^{-\frac{1}{2}}\right), \tag{20}$$

and the subscript indicates the functional dependence $\mathsf{W}_A = \mathsf{W}_A(\mathbf{z}_A)$. For the case of the line, we have

$$\mathsf{D}_A = \begin{bmatrix} \hat{x}_1 & \hat{y}_1 \\ \vdots & \vdots \\ \hat{x}_n & \hat{y}_n \end{bmatrix} \quad \text{and} \quad \mathsf{D}_B = \begin{bmatrix} 1 \\ \vdots \\ 1 \end{bmatrix}. \tag{21}$$

The residual vector is linear in $\mathbf{z}_B$, hence, ϵ is minimal when,

$$\mathbf{z}_B = -\left(\mathsf{W}_A \mathsf{D}_B\right)^{+} \mathsf{W}_A \mathsf{D}_A \mathbf{z}_A, \tag{22}$$

where $\left(\mathsf{W}_A \mathsf{D}_B\right)^{+}$ is the Moore-Penrose pseudo-inverse [11]. Substituting Equation (22) into the cost function, it takes the general form,

---

[1] This variance weighted error is also known as the Mahalanobis distance from the point to the line, plane, or hyperplane.

$$\epsilon(\mathbf{z}_A) = \left\| \mathsf{W}_A \mathsf{D}_A \mathbf{z}_A - \mathsf{W}_A \mathsf{D}_B \left(\mathsf{W}_A \mathsf{D}_B \right)^+ \mathsf{W}_A \mathsf{D}_A \mathbf{z}_A \right\|_2^2. \tag{23}$$

Note the functional dependence of the cost function; this reduction corresponds to an oblique form of the Eckart-Young projection onto the constrained portion of the residual vector [12]. The reduced cost function corresponds to the Variable Projection (or VARPRO) method, whereby proof that $\mathbf{z}_A^*$ attaining the global minimum of $\epsilon(\mathbf{z}_A)$ with $\mathbf{z}_B$ given as in Equation (22) is equivalent to finding the global minimum of the function $\epsilon(\mathbf{z}_A, \mathbf{z}_B)$ can be found in [13]. Minimizing the cost function depends on the nature of the covariance matrices; we enumerate the three special cases as follows:

Identical Covariance Matrices. If all covariance matrices are identical, then the weighting matrix W_A can be written as $\mathsf{W}_A = \left(\mathbf{z}_A^{\mathsf{T}} \Lambda \mathbf{z}_A \right)^{-\frac{1}{2}} \mathsf{I}$. The cost function simplifies to,

$$\epsilon = \frac{\left\| \mathsf{D}_A \mathbf{z}_A - \mathsf{D}_B \mathsf{D}_B^+ \mathsf{D}_A \mathbf{z}_A \right\|_2^2}{\mathbf{z}_A^{\mathsf{T}} \Lambda \mathbf{z}_A} = \frac{\mathbf{z}_A^{\mathsf{T}} \mathsf{D}_A^{\mathsf{T}} \left(\mathsf{I} - \mathsf{D}_B \mathsf{D}_B^+ \right) \mathsf{D}_A \mathbf{z}_A}{\mathbf{z}_A^{\mathsf{T}} \Lambda \mathbf{z}_A}, \tag{24}$$

If we define the matrix $\mathsf{S} \triangleq \mathsf{D}_A^{\mathsf{T}} \left(\mathsf{I} - \mathsf{D}_B \mathsf{D}_B^+ \right) \mathsf{D}_A$, then the cost function takes the form

$$\epsilon = \frac{\mathbf{z}_A^{\mathsf{T}} \mathsf{S} \mathbf{z}_A}{\mathbf{z}_A^{\mathsf{T}} \Lambda \mathbf{z}_A}, \tag{25}$$

which is known as the Rayleigh quotient [11]. Indeed, we are interested in the extrema of this quotient, which in turn will yield the global minimum of the cost function. The extrema are, in fact, the eigenvalues and eigenvectors of the corresponding generalized eigenvalue problem,

$$\left(\mathsf{S} - \epsilon \Lambda \right) \mathbf{z}_A = \mathbf{0}. \tag{26}$$

The global minimum is attained with the generalized eigenvector, $\mathbf{z}_A^*$, corresponding to the minimum eigenvalue, ϵ. Previously, to solve this problem it was recommended to apply an affine transformation to the data such that the covariance matrices were identity matrices, then perform a geometric minimization [9]. Clearly, this solution is algorithmically simpler and more direct.

Approximately Equal Covariance Matrices. In the ideal case, the variance of each residual is unity, which poses difficulty when each covariance matrix is unique. We may, however, impose the constraint that on average, this is the case. This amounts to the assumption that $\Lambda_i \approx E[\Lambda]$ for $i = 1, \ldots, n$. Given the variance of the ith residual, we compute the mean variance to be

$$E[\mathrm{Var}\,(r)] = \frac{1}{n} \sum_{i=1}^{n} \mathbf{z}_A^{\mathsf{T}} \Lambda_i \mathbf{z}_A = \mathbf{z}_A^{\mathsf{T}} \left(\frac{1}{n} \sum_{i=1}^{n} \Lambda_i \right) \mathbf{z}_A, \tag{27}$$

by which we define, $\Lambda_{\mathrm{m}} \triangleq E[\Lambda] = \frac{1}{n} \sum_{i=1}^{n} \Lambda_i$. Solving the eigenvalue problem in Equation (26) with $\Lambda = \Lambda_{\mathrm{m}}$, will, on average, weight each error correctly.

This minimization can be justified as an approximate solution to the global minimum by the fact that it yields the exact global minimum when all covariance matrices are the same. The bias of this solution can be calculated along with the solution, since each covariance matrix deviates from the mean by $\delta\Lambda = \Lambda_m - \Lambda_i$, and therefore the bias, β_i, of an estimate $\mathbf{z}_A$ is,

$$\beta_i = \frac{\mathbf{z}_A^T \left(\Lambda_m - \Lambda_i\right) \mathbf{z}_A}{\mathbf{z}_A^T \Lambda_m \mathbf{z}_A} = 1 - \frac{\mathbf{z}_A^T \Lambda_i \mathbf{z}_A}{\mathbf{z}_A^T \Lambda_m \mathbf{z}_A}. \tag{28}$$

If $\Lambda_i \approx \Lambda_m$, then clearly $\beta_i \approx 0$.

Unique Covariance Matrices. It may be that each covariance matrix varies dramatically and the bias will be large. This case requires a non-linear algorithm to find the true global minimum of the cost function $\epsilon(\mathbf{z}_A)$. The formulation of the cost function in Equation (23) enables the use of Gauss-Newton minimization.

4   Linearized Models

We investigate the estimation of homogeneous vectors of linearized models using the example of a circle, since it is equivalently a plane fitting problem in three dimensions. Geometrically speaking, fitting a linearized model is in general a hyperplane fitting problem. The homogeneous equation of a circle is given as

$$a\left(x^2 + y^2\right) + bx + cy + d = 0. \tag{29}$$

Substituting the model coordinates $(x, y) = (\hat{x} - \delta_x, \hat{y} - \delta_y)$ and rearranging,

$$a\left(\hat{x}^2 + \hat{y}^2\right) + b\hat{x} + c\hat{y} + d = -a\delta_x^2 - a\delta_y^2 + a\hat{x}\delta_x + a\hat{y}\delta_y + b\delta_x + c\delta_y. \tag{30}$$

That is, the functional dependence of the algebraic residual on the random variables δ_x and δ_y is described as,

$$r_s(\delta_x, \delta_y, \hat{x}, \hat{y}, \mathbf{z}) \triangleq -a\delta_x^2 - a\delta_y^2 + a\hat{x}\delta_x + a\hat{y}\delta_y + b\delta_x + c\delta_y. \tag{31}$$

For simplicity, we assume that the errors in the point coordinates behave with covariance matrices, $\Lambda = \sigma^2 I$, although general covariance matrices may also be used. The mean value and variance of the residual error are,

$$E[r] = -2a\sigma^2 \tag{32}$$

and

$$\text{Var}\,(r) = \mathbf{z}_A^T C \mathbf{z}_A = \begin{bmatrix} a\ b\ c \end{bmatrix} \begin{bmatrix} 4\sigma^4 + \sigma^2\left(\hat{x}^2 + \hat{y}^2\right) & 2\sigma^2\hat{x} & 2\sigma^2\hat{y} \\ 2\sigma^2\hat{x} & \sigma^2 & 0 \\ 2\sigma^2\hat{y} & 0 & \sigma^2 \end{bmatrix} \begin{bmatrix} a \\ b \\ c \end{bmatrix}. \tag{33}$$

The following are artifacts of linearizing non-linear problems, all of which undermine Gauss's least-squares theorem:

1. The variance of the residual is dependent on the measured point $(\hat{x}, \hat{y})$. That is to say, the variance of the residual depends not only on the error in the measured quantity, but also on measured quantity itself.
2. The random variables δ_x and δ_y follow Gaussian distributions, but the terms δ_x^2 and δ_y^2 in Equation (31) do not. Specifically they behave according to the Bessel function of the second kind, K_0 [10].
3. The residuals are not mean-free; this is an artifact of the non-Gaussian terms δ_x^2 and δ_y^2.

It is these effects which link the common direct estimation techniques to Gaussian Least Squares:

Relation to "Normalization". Hartley's argument for normalization was that it improves the conditioning of the design matrix [1], which is indeed true; however, this is not the true problem at hand. From a statistical point of view, normalization improves the error structure of the statistically dependent portion of the design matrix, D_A. In consequence, the problem which normalization aims to correct (unbeknownst to its propenents) is the dependence of the variances of the residuals on the measured point. For argument's sake, say we apply normalization to the circle fitting problem. We transform the data such that the centroid is the origin, and $\frac{1}{n}\sum_{i=1}^{n}(\hat{x}_i^2 + \hat{y}_i^2) = \sqrt{2}$. If we solve the minimization with the unit norm constraint, $\mathbf{z}^T\mathbf{z} = 1$, then the average variance of the residuals behaves according to the quadratic form, $E[\mathrm{Var}\,(r)] = \mathbf{z}^T C'\mathbf{z}$, with

$$C' = \mathrm{diag}\left(4\sigma^4 + 4\sqrt{2}\sigma^2, \sigma^2, \sigma^2, 0\right) \tag{34}$$

The average variance of the residuals is consequently bounded by the eigenvalues of the matrix C', which are $\lambda(C') = 0, \sigma^2, \sigma^2, 4\sigma^2(\sigma^2 + \sqrt{2})$. The bound on the average variance is therefore

$$0 \leq E[\mathrm{Var}\,(r)] \leq 4\sigma^2(\sigma^2 + \sqrt{2}). \tag{35}$$

Normalization, hence bounds the average variance of the residuals to values close to the actual noise level of the data. By this argument, circle fitting would be better implemented with data normalization followed by partitioning the statistically dependent and independent portions, which would correspond to the method of Nievergelt [14]. This would make the error behaviour of the residuals closer to an isotropic distribution; however, Equation (35) reveals the problem that the result quality would be dependent on the choice of the scaling factor.

Relation to "Invariant Fitting". The methods of Bookstein [2], Torr and Fitzgibbon [3], and Harker et al. [4] effectively partition quadratic terms from the linear and constant terms. That is, they effectively partition the non-Gaussian errors from the Gaussian and error free portions of the residual vectors. However, what is not treated is the fact that each residual depends on the measured point itself. This means that the residuals are each weighted irregularly (i.e. by some weighting not related to its variance), which is why the methods often lead to inappropriate fits. Effectively, the algorithm circumvents the normalization step, but is still minimizing an algebraic error.

Relation to "Gradient Weighted Fitting". To weight each algebraic error by the local gradient is equivalent to weighting each error by the first order Taylor approximation to its variance under the assumption of isotropic errors in the coordinates. Hence, the Gradient-Weighting scheme minimizes the algebraic error subject to the constraint that the average first order approximation to the variance is equal to unity. There is, however, an important caveat: the gradient constraint is degenerate because the derivative of the constant term is zero. This leads to gross numerical instability in the generalized eigenvectors [11], making the results heavily dependent on the conditioning and configuration of the data. This instability produces unusable results even in cases when the data exactly fits the model. Taubin himself noted that the method would yield useless results in some cases, but obviously did not correctly identify the cause as poor problem formulation [15].

5   Stable Direct Statistical Fitting

We previously showed that with "data normalization," the average variance of the residuals is bounded, but not constrained. In a manner analogous to fitting lines to heteroscedastic data (Section 3), we may perform the minimization subject to the constraint that the average variance is unity. This assumes that each individual covariance matrix is well approximated by the average covariance matrix. This corresponds to solving the minimization with

$$
\mathsf{D}_A = \begin{bmatrix} \hat{x}_1^2 + \hat{y}_1^2 & \hat{x}_1 & \hat{y}_1 \\ \vdots & \vdots & \vdots \\ \hat{x}_n^2 + \hat{y}_n^2 & \hat{x}_n & \hat{y}_n \end{bmatrix} \quad \text{and} \quad \mathsf{D}_B = \begin{bmatrix} 1 \\ \vdots \\ 1 \end{bmatrix} \triangleq \mathbf{1}, \tag{36}
$$

with the constraint matrix

$$
\mathsf{C} = \frac{1}{n} \sum_{i=1}^{n} \begin{bmatrix} 4\sigma^4 + 4\sigma^2\left(\hat{x}_i^2 + \hat{y}_i^2\right) & 2\sigma^2\hat{x}_i & 2\sigma^2\hat{y}_i \\ 2\sigma^2\hat{x}_i & \sigma^2 & 0 \\ 2\sigma^2\hat{y}_i & 0 & \sigma^2 \end{bmatrix}. \tag{37}
$$

The related eigenvalue problem[2] is

$$
\mathsf{D}_A^{\mathsf{T}} \left(\mathsf{I} - \mathbf{1}\mathbf{1}^{+}\right) \mathsf{D}_A \mathbf{z}_A = \epsilon \mathsf{C} \mathbf{z}_A. \tag{38}
$$

This approach is numerically stable in comparison to the standard Gradient Weighting scheme by the following reasoning: For the case of a circle, some manipulation shows that, $\det \mathsf{C} = 4\sigma^6 \left(\sigma^2 + \mathrm{Var}\left(\hat{x}\right) + \mathrm{Var}\left(\hat{y}\right)\right)$. This shows that the constraint is, analytically speaking, not degenerate unless the data itself is ill-conditioned (i.e. very "point-like"). With the Gradient Weighting scheme, in contrast, the constraint is always degenerate making the eigenvectors always unstable. Worse yet, is if the data fits the model then both matrices are degenerate. This means that the algorithm is most unstable for best-case data sets, which is hardly desirable.

---

[2] This should be solved using the GSVD, but space limitations preclude just discussion.

Summary of the Algorithm. The algorithm can be summarized as follows, whereby steps 1 and 2 are undertaken once, offline, whereas steps 3 and 4 are the online portion of the fitting algorithm.

1. Formulate the linearized model of the geometric object, $\mathbf{d}^T\mathbf{z} = 0$.
2. Partition the coefficient vector into its statistically dependent and independent portions, $\mathbf{d}_A^T\mathbf{z}_A + \mathbf{d}_B^T\mathbf{z}_B = 0$, such that the analytic expression for the variance of the ith residual can be written as the quadratic form, $\text{Var}\,(r_i) = \mathbf{z}_A^T\mathsf{C}_i\mathbf{z}_A$.
3. Compute the average covariance matrix, C_m, and solve the generalized eigenvalue problem,

$$\mathsf{D}_A^T\left(\mathsf{I} - \mathsf{D}_B\mathsf{D}_B^+\right)\mathsf{D}_A\mathbf{z}_A = \epsilon\mathsf{C}_m\mathbf{z}_A. \tag{39}$$

4. Backsubstitute the minimizing eigenvector to find $\mathbf{z}_B = -\mathsf{D}_B^+\mathsf{D}_A\mathbf{z}_A$.

6   Numerical Testing

To test the new algorithm, we have applied it to the Metric Vision task of material tracking and measurement. Metric calibration of the planar scene is accomplished with circular targets to determine the homography. Figure 1 shows the scene, and the results of circle fitting. The gradient-weighted circle fit is useless due to the aforementioned numerical instability.

The position, orientation and dimensions of the steel plate can be determined by fitting a fourth order curve, or quartic. In Figure 2, the left hand images show the results of each algorithm to the edge data obtained with a contouring algorithm. The right hand images show the quartic fits after perturbing the data with a small amount of Gaussian noise ($\sigma = 1\,\text{pixel}$). This test shows

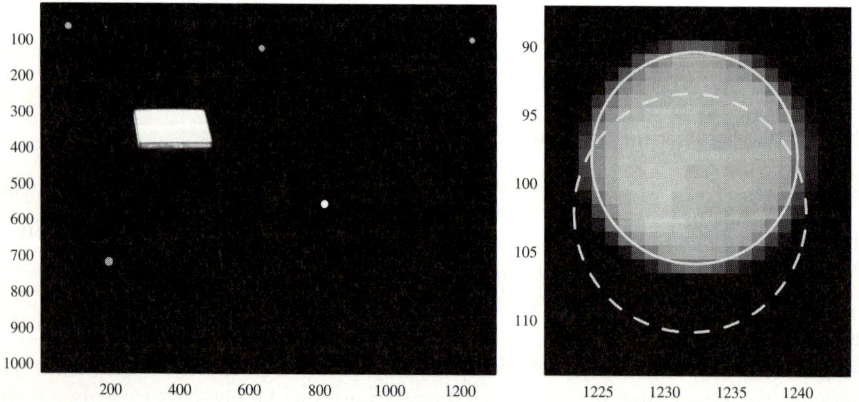

Fig. 1. (LEFT) The Metric Vision task of material tracking and measurement in a steel mill. (RIGHT) Circle fitting to a calibration target. The Gradient-Weighted solution $(--)$ is nonsense due to numerical instability. All other algorithms $(-)$, including a non-linear geometric fit, return the same circle.

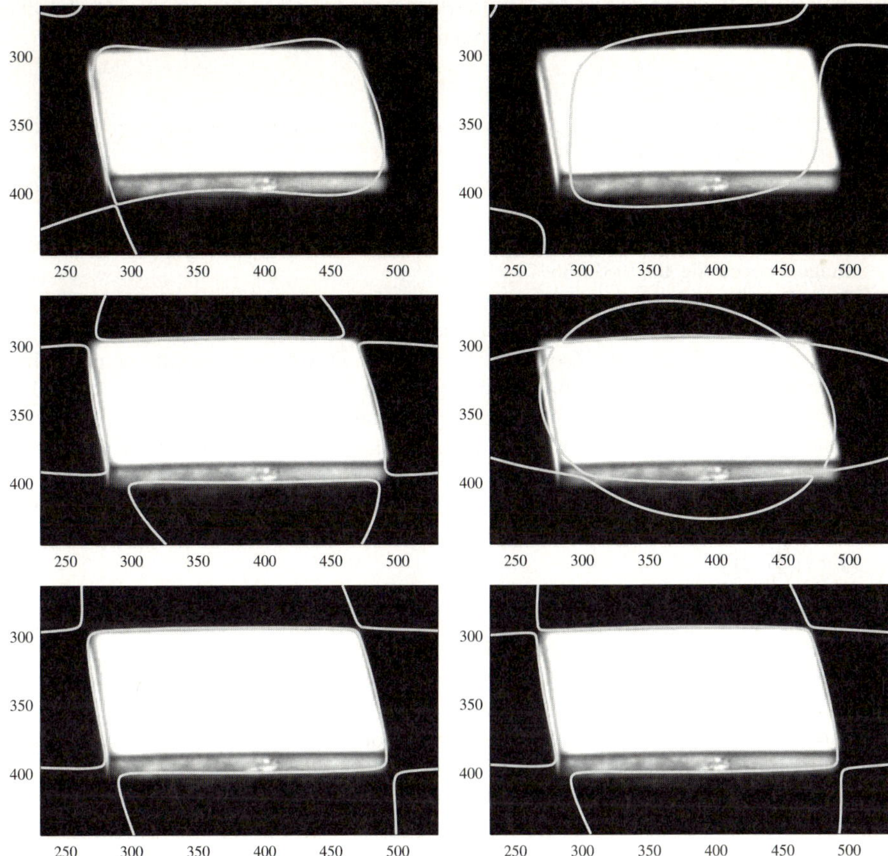

Fig. 2. Fitting quartic curves to determine the position, orientation, and dimensions of steel plates. Row-wise are the solutions obtained with "Gradient-Weighting", "Normalization", and the New Method. In the left column the curves are fitted to the edge data obtained by contouring. In the right column, a small amount of Gaussian noise ($\sigma = 1$ pixel) is added to demonstrate the sensitivity of each solution.

that the gradient-weighting and normalization solutions are very sensitive to perturbations in the data, which indicates instability of the solution vector. The new algorithm is not only insensitive to the large values and offsets of the image coordinates, but it is also relatively insensitive to Gaussian noise perturbing the coordinates.

7   Conclusion

We have proposed a generalized approach to the direct estimation of homogeneous vectors which has improved goodness-of-fit properties and numerical stability, whilst circumventing data normalization. The normal vector of the hyperplane fit is constrained to a hyperellipsoid, which is aimed at statistically regularizing the error metric in the space of linearized models.

References

1. Hartley, R.: In defense of the eight-point algorithm. IEEE Trans. Pattern Analysis and Machine Intelligence **19** (1997) 580–593
2. Bookstein, F.: Fitting conic sections to scattered data. Computer Graphics and Image Processing **9** (1987) 56–71
3. Torr, P., Fitzgibbon, A.: Invariant fitting of two view geometry. IEEE Trans. Pattern Analysis and Machine Intelligence **26** (2004) 648–650
4. Harker, M., O'Leary, P., Zsombor-Murray, P.: Direct type-specific conic fitting and eigenvalue bias correction. Submitted to Image and Vision Computing: 2004 British Machine Vision Conference Special Issue (2005) 17
5. Gander, W.: Least squares with a quadratic constraint. Numer. Math. **36** (1981) 291–307
6. Sampson, P.: Fitting conic sections to "very scattered" data: An iterative refinement of the Bookstein algorithm. Computer Graphics and Image Processing **18** (1982) 97–108
7. Taubin, G.: Estimation of planar curves, surfaces and nonplanar space curves defined by implicit equations with applications to edge and range image segmentation. IEEE Trans. on Pattern Analysis and Machine Intelligence **13** (1991)
8. Gauss, C.: Méthode des moindres carrés. Mémoires sur la combinaison des observations. Mallet-Bachelier, Paris (1855)
9. Hartley, R., Zisserman, A.: Multiple View Geometry in Computer Vision. Second edn. Cambridge University Press, Cambridge (2003)
10. Förstner, W.: Uncertainty and projective geometry. In Bayro Corrochano, E., ed.: Handbook of Geometric Computing. Springer (2005) 493–535
11. Golub, G., Van Loan, C.: Matrix Computations. Third edn. John Hopkins University Press, Baltimore (1996)
12. Golub, G., Hoffman, A., Stewart, G.: A generalization of the Eckart-Young-Mirsky matrix approximation theorem. Lin. Alg. and its Applic. **88/89** (1987) 317–327
13. Golub, G., Pereyra, V.: The differentiation of pseudoinverses and nonlinear least squares problems whose variables separate. SIAM J. Num. Anal. **10** (1973) 413–432
14. Nievergelt, Y.: Hyperspheres and hyperplanes fitted seamlessly by algebraic constrained total least-squares. Linear Algebra and its Applications **331** (2001) 43–59
15. Taubin, G.: An improved algorithm for algebraic curve and surface fitting. In: International Conference on Computer Vision, Berlin, Germany (1993) 658–665

Fingerprint Matching Based on Octantal Nearest-Neighbor Structure and Core Points

Li-min Yang[1], Jie Yang[1], and Hong-tao Wu[2]

[1] Institute of Image Processing and Pattern Recognition, Shanghai JiaoTong University (SJTU),
Shanghai, 200240, P.R. China
[2] School of Computer Science and Software, Hebei University of Technology,
Tianjin, 300130, P.R. China
{ylm, jieyang}@sjtu.edu.cn, wht_121@163.com

Abstract. In this paper, we propose a novel Octantal Nearest-neighbor Structure and core points based fingerprint matching scheme. A novel fingerprint feature named the octantal nearest-neighbor structure (ONNS) is defined. Based on the ONNS, the minutiae pairing algorithm is conducted to find the corresponding minutiae pairs, and a novel algorithm is developed to evaluate the translational and rotational parameters between the input and the template fingerprints. Core point based orientation pairing is performed thereafter. Matching score is calculated. Experimental results on the FVC2004 fingerprint databases show the good performance of the proposed algorithm.

Keywords: Core point; Corresponding minutia pair; Fingerprint alignment; Fingerprint matching.

1 Introduction

Most of the fingerprint matching approaches introduced in the last four decades are minutia based [1]. However, minutiae matching faces a series of challenges such as the location and orientation errors of detected minutiae, as well as the presence of spurious minutiae and the absence of genuine minutiae. One of the most difficult problems to overcome is the nonlinear distortion introduced when the three-dimensional surface of the finger is mapped onto a two-dimensional surface by the fingerprint acquisition technique.

Many researchers have tried to address the problem of nonlinear distortion to make the minutiae matching method more robust [2-10]. In [2], a minutiae matching method based on both the local and global structures is proposed. The local structure of a central minutia is used to find the correspondence of two minutiae sets. The best matching pair is then selected and used for registering the input and the template fingerprints. The global structure is used to enforce the result of local matching and a final score is computed to determine the uniqueness of a fingerprint. Similarly in [5], the defined local topological structure (LTS) includes the minutiae circled around the central minutia within r radius.

Different from the above two methods, a fingerprint feature named the adjacent feature vector (AFV) is proposed for fingerprint matching in [3]. For a central

P. Kalra and S. Peleg (Eds.): ICVGIP 2006, LNCS 4338, pp. 931–940, 2006.

minutia, its four adjacent points with the same distance '*ADis*' to the central minutia are selected to compute four adjacent relative orientations and six ridge counts, which are rotation and translation invariant. It is worth to notice that *ADis* is also a constant. If *ADis* is small, the orientation field in a small region becomes less discriminable. Even two different small regions may have the similar AFV. If *ADis* is large, the nonlinear distortion can severely impact the distance between two AFVs. In such case, the same central minutia in different impressions may not be considered as a genuine minutia pair.

In this paper, we propose a novel fingerprint matching scheme, which is based on the octantal nearest-neighbor structure (ONNS) and core points. For each central minutia, the nearest neighboring minutia (NNM) in each octant is extracted to construct the local feature structure. Based on the ONNS, the minutiae pairing algorithm is conducted to find the corresponding minutiae pairs. To reduce alignment error, a novel algorithm is developed to evaluate the translational and rotational parameters between the input and template fingerprints. The core points are used to register the orientation fields of input and template fingerprint images. The final matching score measures both the similarity level of two sets of minutiae and two orientation fields. It helps to decrease both the false acceptance rate (FAR) and the false reject rate (FRR). This paper is organized as follows. Section 2 describes the proposed ONNS in detail. Section 3 presents the novel fingerprint matching algorithm. The experimental results are reported in Section 4. Section 5 concludes this paper.

2 Octantal Nearest-Neighbor Structure

Let $\{M_i = (x_i, y_i, \theta_i, q_i)\}_{i=1,2,...,N}$ denote the extracted minutiae from the given fingerprint, where (x_i, y_i) is its coordinate, θ_i is the local ridge orientation, and the quality q_i has the range $[1,100]$: $q = 100$ implies the neighborhood of the minutia has higher possible quality while $q = 1$ represents the lowest possible quality. Although the ridge orientation has the range $[0,180°)$, the minutia can be directed into the range $[0,360°)$ to increase its discrimination [2].

To simplify the description of the ONNS, the difference between two angles θ_i and θ_k is defined by a function $d(\theta_i, \theta_k)$:

$$d(\theta_i, \theta_k) = \begin{cases} \theta_i - \theta_k, & if \quad -180° \leq \theta_i - \theta_k < 180° \\ 360° - \theta_i + \theta_k, & if \quad \theta_i - \theta_k \geq 180° \\ 360° + \theta_i - \theta_k, & if \quad \theta_i - \theta_k < -180° \end{cases} \tag{1}$$

For a minutia $M_i = (x_i, y_i, \theta_i, q_i)$, its octant is defined as follows:

$$\left\{ [\theta_i + (j-1) \times 45°, \theta_i + j \times 45°) \right\}_{j=1}^{8}$$

Denote $f(\theta_i, j)$ as the j th octant of M_i. Let $\beta = \theta_i + (j-1) \times 45°$, then $f(\theta_i, j) = [\beta, \beta + 45°)$. Because β and $\beta + 45°$ may be bigger than $360°$, $f(\theta_i, j)$ should be modulated as follows:

$$f(\theta_i, j) = \begin{cases} [\beta, \beta + 45°), & if \quad \beta + 45° < 360° \\ [\beta, 360°) \cup [0°, \beta + 45° - 360°), & if \quad \beta < 360° \le \beta + 45° \\ [\beta - 360°, \beta + 45° - 360°), & if \quad \beta \ge 360° \end{cases} \quad (2)$$

For the central minutia M_i, its j th NNM "P_{ij}" within $f(\theta_i, j)$ is defined as follows:

$$P_{ij} = \min_{M_k \in f(\theta_i, j)} D_{M_i M_k}, \quad j = 1, 2, \cdots, 8 \quad (3)$$

where $D_{M_i M_k}$ denotes the distance between the central minutia M_i and minutia M_k.

The definition of the novel feature structure named the ONNS is given as follows:

$$F_{M_i} = \{(D_{M_i P_{ij}}, C_{M_i P_{ij}}, d(\theta_i, \alpha_{ij}), d(\theta_i, \theta_j), h(q_i, q_j))\}_{j=1,2,\ldots,8} \quad (4)$$

where $D_{M_i P_{ij}}$ denotes the distance between central minutia M_i and minutia P_{ij}, $C_{M_i P_{ij}}$ denotes the ridge-counts between M_i and P_{ij}, α_{ij} denotes the direction of the directed line segment $\overrightarrow{M_i P_{ij}}$, and $h(q_i, q_j)$ denotes the joint quality between the quality q_i of M_i and that of P_{ij}. Refer to Fig.1 for clarification.

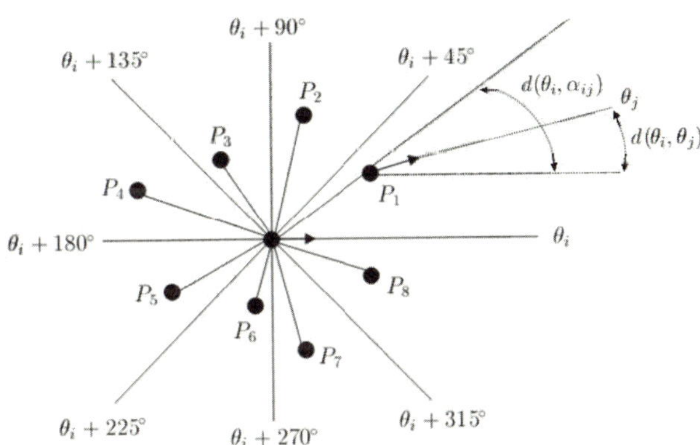

Fig. 1. Illustration of octantal nearest-neighbor structure

The number of ridges between two minutiae and the quality of each minutia should be calculated in the minutiae detection phase. In this work, the joint quality between q_i and q_j is calculated by $h(q_i, q_j) = q_i \times q_j$.

3 Fingerprint Matching

Using the proposed ONNS, we develop a new fingerprint matching algorithm making use of both fingerprint minutiae and core points.

3.1 Corresponding Minutiae Pairs Identification

To identify whether two minutiae are corresponding minutia pair, we need to calculate the similarity level between their ONNSs first:

Suppose $F_{M_i}^I$ and $F_{M_j}^T$ are the ONNS of minutia M_i^I from the input fingerprint and that of minutia M_j^T from the template fingerprint, respectively. The following algorithm is used to calculate the similarity level $S(M_i^I, M_j^T)$ between M_i^I and M_j^T.

Step 1: Compute the similarity level $S_k(M_i^I, M_j^T)$ at the k th octant between M_i^I and M_j^T:

If the k th NNM P_{ik}^I and P_{jk}^T both exist and the following conditions are satisfied:

$$D_{ijk} = |D_{M_i^I P_{ik}^I} - D_{M_j^T P_{jk}^T}| < T_D \tag{5}$$

$$C_{ijk} = |C_{M_i^I P_{ik}^I} - C_{M_j^T P_{jk}^T}| < T_C \tag{6}$$

$$\gamma_{ijk} = |d(d(\theta_i^I, \alpha_{ik}^I), d(\theta_j^T, \alpha_{jk}^T))| < T_\theta \tag{7}$$

$$\eta_{ijk} = |d(d(\theta_i^I, \theta_k^I), d(\theta_j^T, \theta_k^T))| < T_\theta \tag{8}$$

then the similarity level $S_k(M_i^I, M_j^T)$ is calculated as follows:

$$S_k\left(M_{ik}^I, M_{jk}^T\right) = h\left(h\left(q_i^I, q_k^I\right), h\left(q_j^T, q_k^T\right)\right)\left(1 - \frac{\left(\dfrac{w_D D_{ijk}}{T_D} + \dfrac{w_C C_{ijk}}{T_C} + \dfrac{w_\theta\left(\gamma_{ijk} + \eta_{ijk}\right)}{T_\theta}\right)}{w_D + w_C + 2w_\theta}\right) \tag{9}$$

If P_{ik}^I or P_{jk}^T does not exist, or the conditions Equation(5)-(8) are not all satisfied, $S_k(M_i^I, M_j^T)$ should be set to zero. The coefficients (i.e., w_D、w_C and w_θ) specify the weights associated with the corresponding component of the ONNS. The three thresholds(i.e., T_D、T_C and T_θ) are the size of matching box, which change according to the distance D_{ijk}, as described in [5]. For example:

$$T_D = \begin{cases} T_{DL}, & if \quad D_{ijk} < T_L \\ T_{DH}, & if \quad D_{ijk} > T_H \\ T_{DL} + \dfrac{T_{DH} - T_{DL}}{T_H - T_L}(D_{ijk} - T_L), & otherwise \end{cases}$$

Here, T_L, T_H, T_{DL} and T_{DH} are four pre-established parameters.

Step 2: Calculate the similarity level $S(M_i^I, M_j^T)$ between M_i^I and M_j^T:

$$S(M_i^I, M_j^T) = h\left(q_i^I, q_j^T\right) \sum_{k=1}^{8} S_k(M_i^I, M_j^T) \tag{10}$$

The similarity level $S(M_i^I, M_j^T)$ describes a matching certainty level of an ONNS pair instead of simply matched or not. $S(M_i^I, M_j^T) = 1$ implies a perfect match while $S(M_i^I, M_j^T) = 0$ represents a total mismatch. From Fig.2 to Fig.4, we show an example of the proposed ONNS.

Fig. 2. A fingerprint image named "33 6.tif" from FVC2004 DB1A.

Fig. 3. Extracted minutiae and their directions of the image "33 6.tif"

Fig. 4. An example of the ONNS: the NNM of the central minutia in each octant all exists

Fig. 5. Another example of the ONNS: there is not a NNM in the 1st and 7th octants of the central minutia

If $S(M_i^I, M_j^T) > T_s$ (T_s is a threshold), M_i and M_k are considered a corresponding minutiae pair. Let $\{(M_{p_j}^I, M_{q_j}^T): j = 1, 2, \ldots, L\}$ ($L \leq K$) denote the detected corresponding minutiae pairs.

3.2 Translational and Rotational Parameters Estimation

After the corresponding minutiae pairs are identified, the global translational and rotational parameters between the input and the template fingerprints can be evaluated as follows:

1) Calculate the mass center of the corresponding minutiae:

$$\begin{bmatrix} x_0^I \\ y_0^I \end{bmatrix} = \frac{1}{L} \begin{bmatrix} \sum_{j=1}^{L} x_{p_j}^I \\ \sum_{j=1}^{L} y_{p_j}^I \end{bmatrix}, \quad \begin{bmatrix} x_0^T \\ y_0^T \end{bmatrix} = \frac{1}{L} \begin{bmatrix} \sum_{j=1}^{L} x_{q_j}^I \\ \sum_{j=1}^{L} y_{q_j}^I \end{bmatrix}$$

2) Compute the translational parameters Δx and Δy :

$$\begin{bmatrix} \Delta x \\ \Delta y \end{bmatrix} = \begin{bmatrix} x_0^T - x_0^I \\ y_0^T - y_0^I \end{bmatrix}$$

3) Evaluate the rotational parameter $\Delta\theta$:

$$\Delta\theta = \max_{\theta} \sum_{|d(\theta,\theta_0)| \le \alpha_0} (\alpha_0 + 1 - |d(\theta,\theta_0)|) S_\theta$$

where α_0 is a parameter(in this work $\alpha_0 = 15°$), and

$$\theta_0 = d(\theta_{p_j}^I, \theta_{q_j}^T), \quad S_\theta = \sum_{\theta=\theta_0, j=1,2,\dots,L} S(M_{p_j}^I, M_{q_j}^T)$$

After obtaining the translational and rotational parameters $(\Delta x, \Delta y, \Delta\theta)$, the new location (x_i^I, y_i^I) for minutia M_i^I , $i = 1, 2, \cdots, K_0$,   can be calculated as follows:

$$\begin{bmatrix} x_i^{I'} \\ y_i^{I'} \end{bmatrix} = \begin{bmatrix} \cos(\Delta\theta) & \sin(\Delta\theta) \\ -\sin(\Delta\theta) & \cos(\Delta\theta) \end{bmatrix} \begin{bmatrix} x_i^I - x_0^I \\ y_i^I - y_0^I \end{bmatrix} + \begin{bmatrix} x_i^I + \Delta x \\ y_i^I + \Delta y \end{bmatrix}$$

The direction of each minutia of the input fingerprint is also aligned:

$$\theta_i^{I'} = \theta_i^I + \Delta\theta$$

Let $M_i^{I'} = \{x_i^{I'}, y_i^{I'}, \theta_i^{I'}, q_i^{I'}\}$ denote the new minutia of the input fingerprint after transformation with the estimated translation and rotation parameters.

3.3 ONNS Based Pairing

For the transformed minutiae set $\{M_i^{I'}\}_{i=1,2,\cdots,K_0}$, we re-compute the ONNS of each minutia. Using the improved algorithm described above, we find the corresponding minutiae pairs between the transformed minutiae set $\{M_i^{I'}\}_{i=1,2,\cdots,K_0}$ and the originally extracted minutiae set $\{M_j^{T}\}_{j=1,2,\cdots,K_1}$. $\{M_{c_k}^{I'}, M_{c_k}^{T}\}_{k=1,2,\ldots,K'}$, $K' \leq \min(K_0, K_1)$, denote the corresponding minutiae pairs.

3.4 Core Point Based Orientation Pairing

A core is defined as a point in the orientation field where the orientation in a small local neighborhood around the point presents semi-circular tendency. It is a salient feature in a fingerprint image. In this work, the Poincaré index introduced by [13] is used to extract core points. Fig. 6 shows example of an extracted core point.

Notice that there may be one or two core point(s) in one fingerprint image, we discuss the one core point cases first.

Fig. 6. An extracted core point

Assume $Core^{I}(x^{I}, y^{I}, \theta^{I})$ and $Core^{T}(x^{T}, y^{T}, \theta^{T})$ are core points from input fingerprint and template fingerprint, respectively. Calculate the translational and rotational parameters $(\Delta x_c, \Delta y_c, \Delta \theta_c)$ as follows:

$$\begin{bmatrix} \Delta x_c \\ \Delta y_c \\ \Delta \theta_c \end{bmatrix} = \begin{bmatrix} x^{T} - x^{I} \\ y^{T} - y^{I} \\ \theta^{T} - \theta^{I} \end{bmatrix}$$

By translating and rotating the input fingerprint image according to parameter $(\Delta x_c, \Delta y_c, \Delta \theta_c)$, a new transformed input fingerprint image is obtained.

Divide the transformed input fingerprint image and the template fingerprint image into a number of sub-blocks, then calculate the orientation of each sub-block[11]. Let (B_i^{I}, B_i^{T}) denote the corresponding orientation block pair, block B_i^{I} from the transformed input fingerprint, block B_i^{T} from the template fingerprint, respectively, $i = 1, 2, \cdots, N_B$, N_B is the number of blocks in one image. The similarity level $S(B_i^{I}, B_i^{T})$ of the two blocks B_i^{I} and B_i^{T} is calculated as follows:

$$S(B_i^{I'}, B_i^T) = \begin{cases} \dfrac{T_B - \left|O(B_i^{I'}) - O(B_i^T)\right|}{T_B} & if \ \left|O(B_i^{I'}) - O(B_i^T)\right| < T_B, \\ 0 & otherwise. \end{cases} \quad (11)$$

where T_B is a threshold, and $O(\bullet)$ denotes the orientation of a block.

If there are two core points in the input image or template image, or two core points in both fingerprint images, each core point in one image would pair with all the core point(s) in the other image to get a set of transform parameters. Repeat the pairing procedure described above. The core point pair with the maximal summatory similarity level is considered as the corresponding core point pair.

3.5 Matching Score Computation

The final matching score Ms between input and template fingerprints can be determined by minutia matching score M_m and core point based matching score M_c. The minutia matching score M_m can be calculated according to the following equation:

$$M_m = \sum_{k=1}^{K'} S(M_{c_k}^{I'}, M_{c_k}^T)$$

where $(M_{c_k}^{I'}, M_{c_k}^T)$ is the corresponding minutiae pair, one from the transformed input fingerprint and another from the original template fingerprint, respectively.

The core point based matching score M_c is defined by

$$M_c = \sum_{i=1}^{N_B} S(B_i^{I'}, B_i^T)$$

where $(B_i^{I'}, B_i^T)$ is the corresponding orientation pair, one from the transformed input fingerprint and another from the original template fingerprint, respectively.

If there are no core points or over two core points detected in input or template fingerprint due to poor quality or other reasons, M_c should be set to zero.

The final matching score Ms is computed as follows:

$$Ms = \alpha_m M_m + \alpha_c M_c \quad (12)$$

where α_m and α_c are weights, and $\alpha_m = 1 - \alpha_c$ (in this work, if $M_c = 0$, then $\alpha_c = 0$ otherwise $\alpha_c = 0.4$).

4 Results

The proposed scheme has been evaluated by applying to DB1A and DB3A of FVC2004, because the distortion between some fingerprints from the same finger in these two databases is large. The fingerprints of DB1A are acquired through

CrossMatch "V300" optical sensor, and each fingerprint is with 640×480 pixels and 500 dpi. The fingerprints of DB3A are acquired through thermal sweeping sensor "FingerChip FCD4B14CB" by Atmel, and each fingerprint is with 300×480 pixels and 512 dpi. Both databases contain 800 fingerprints captured from 100 different fingers, eight impressions for each finger.

Table 1. Comparison of the proposed scheme with algorithm P026 on FVC2004 DB1A

Algorithm	EER	FMR 100	FMR 1000	Average enroll time	Average match time
Our scheme	5.36%	7.44%	12.40%	2.11s	2.32s
P026	5.54%	9.25%	19.11%	2.60s	3.56s

Table 2. Comparison of the proposed scheme with algorithm P004 on FVC2004 DB3A

Algorithm	EER	FMR 100	FMR 1000	Average enroll time	Average match time
Our scheme	1.86%	2.25%	5.23%	0.84s	1.02s
P004	1.89%	2.61%	7.14%	0.76s	0.80s

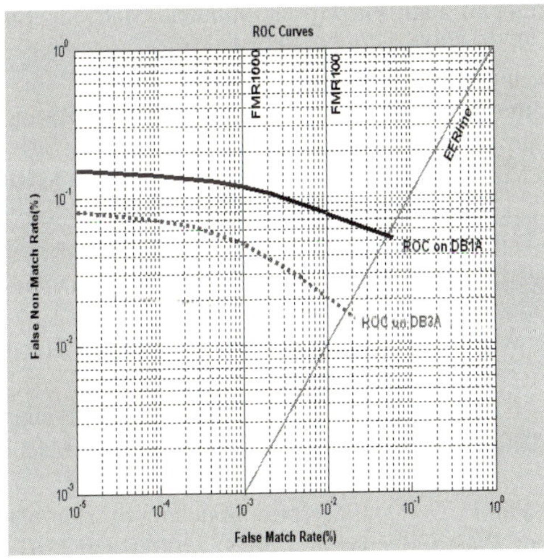

Fig. 7. The ROC curves obtained by the proposed scheme on FVC2004 DB1A and DB3A

In Table 1 and Table 2, We compare the results of the proposed scheme on DB1A with that of the algorithm called "P026", and compare the results of the proposed scheme on DB3A with that of the algorithm called "P004", which have been participated in FVC2004, and ranked the ninth and the sixth places respectively. According to the ranking rule in terms of EER in FVC2004, the proposed scheme is better than the two algorithms, which means a good performance both for the DB1a and DB3a. In FVC2004, the maximum time cost for each enrollment and each matching is 10 seconds and 5 seconds, respectively[12]. Table 1 and Table 2 show that the time cost of the proposed scheme satisfies the conditions of the open category on FVC2004. The receiver operating characteristic (ROC) curves obtained by the proposed scheme on FVC2004 DB1A and DB3A are illustrated in Fig.7.

5 Conclusions

In this paper, we propose an ONNS and core point based fingerprint matching scheme. A novel feature structure ONNS is defined, which is translation and rotation invariant. Based on ONNS and core points, fingerprint matching is performed. Because both minutiae information and core points information are used in this work, it is more robust than minutiae-based methods. The usefulness of our proposed approach is confirmed in the experiments conducted, which show good performance. However, there are still some difficulties to be overcome in the future, such as how to locate minutiae and core points in poor quality fingerprints more reliably, and how to solve the problems introduced by nonlinear distortion. Those would be our future directions.

References

1. Davide Maltoni, Dario Maio, Anil K. Jain, and Salil Prabhakar: Handbook of Fingerprint Recognition. Springer-Verlag, New-York (2003)
2. Xudong Jiang, Wei-Yun Yau: Fingerprint Minutiae Matching Based on the Local and Global Structures. *ICPR 2000*, 2, (2000)1042-1045
3. Xifeng Tong, Jianhua Huang, Xianglong Tang, Daming Shi: Fingerprint Minutiae Matching Using the Adjacent Feature Vector. Pattern Recognition Letters, 26(9), (2004)1337-1345
4. En Zhu, Jiangping Yin, Guomin Zhang: Fingerprint Matching based on Global Alignment of Multiple Reference Minutiae. Pattern Recognition, 38(10), (2005)1685-1694
5. Xinjian Chen, Jie Tian, Xin Yang: A New Algorithm for Distorted Fingerprint Matching Based on Normalized Fuzzy Similarity Measure. IEEE translations on Image Processing, 15(3), (2006)767-776
6. Jin Qi, Yangsheng Wang: A Robust Fingerprint Matching Method. Pattern Recognition, 38(10), (2005)1665-1671
7. Arun Ross, Sarat C. Dass, Anil K. Jain: Fingerprint Warping Using Ridge Curve Correspondences. IEEE transactions on Pattern Analysis and Machine Intelligence, 28(1), (2006)19-30
8. Asker M. Bazen, Sabih H. Gerez: Fingerprint Matching by Thin-plate Spline Modelling of Elastic Deformations. Pattern Recognition, 36(8), (2003)1859-1867
9. Arun Ross, Sarat C. Dass, Anil K. Jain: A Deformable Model for Fingerprint Matching. Pattern Recognition, 38(1), (2005)95-103
10. Neil Yager, Adnan Admin: Nonparametric Fingerprint Deformation Modelling. CAIP 2005, LNCS 3691, (2005)73-80
11. Anil K. Jain, Lin Hong, and Ruud Bolle: On-Line Fingerprint Verification. IEEE Transactions on Pattern Analysis and Machine Intelligence, 19(4), 302-314 (1997)
12. Biometric Systems Lab., Pattern Recognition and Image Processing Lab., Biometric Test Center., [Online] Available: http://bias.csr.unibo.it/fvc2004/
13. Kawagoe, M., Tojo, A.: Fingerprint pattern classification. Pattern Recognition 17 (3), (1984)295-303

Dempster-Shafer Theory Based Classifier Fusion for Improved Fingerprint Verification Performance

Richa Singh[1], Mayank Vatsa[1], Afzel Noore[1], and Sanjay K. Singh[2]

[1] West Virginia University, Morgantown, WV - 26506, USA
{richas, mayankv, noore}@csee.wvu.edu
[2] Institute of Engineering and Technology, Jaunpur, UP 222001, India
sksiet@yahoo.com

Abstract. This paper presents a Dempster Shafer theory based classifier fusion algorithm to improve the performance of fingerprint verification. The proposed fusion algorithm combines decision induced match scores of minutiae, ridge, fingercode and pore based fingerprint verification algorithms and provides an improvement of at least 8.1% in the verification accuracy compared to the individual algorithms. Further, proposed fusion algorithm outperforms by at least 2.52% when compared with existing fusion algorithms. We also found that the use of Dempster's rule of conditioning reduces the training time by approximately 191 seconds.

1 Introduction

Fingerprint verification systems are widely based on minutiae and ridge information [1], [2]. Some algorithms use pattern information to recognize an individual [3]. Forensic experts rely on level-3 information such as pores and high level ridge information [4] for making a comparison. Further, many researchers have combined the outputs of two or more classifiers to improve the performance compared to a single classifier [5], [6], [7], [8]. The output of different classifiers can be fused at different levels such as image level, feature level, match score level, and decision level. However, fusing the output of different classifiers at match score level or at decision level makes the output independent of the type of classifier used.

Several different techniques such as sum rule [5], [6] and kernel based technique [8] have been proposed for biometric information fusion at match score or decision level. Most of these techniques rely on heuristic information extracted from the training data. Generally, these techniques do not update the priors regularly with the presence of new evidences, i.e. these techniques do not update the prior every time a new data is added in the database which is not pragmatic in high security applications. Another technique which is widely studied in classical classifier fusion but less addressed in biometrics is Dempster-Shafer (DS) theory [9], [10]. DS theory is a powerful method of combining accumulative evidences or for changing priors in the presence of new evidences. In [7], a match score fusion

P. Kalra and S. Peleg (Eds.): ICVGIP 2006, LNCS 4338, pp. 941–949, 2006.
© Springer-Verlag Berlin Heidelberg 2006

algorithm is presented to fuse the information of face and voice using theoretic evidence of k-NN classifiers based on DS theory. Although authors have used DS theory, they did not use the conditioning scheme to regularly update the system based on new data. In this paper, four fingerprint verification algorithms; minutiae based [1], ridge based [2], fingercode based [3] and pores based [4] algorithms are used as different classifiers. Proposed Dempster-Shafer theory based fusion algorithm fuses decision induced match scores obtained from fingerprint verification algorithms. Further, conditioning algorithm is used to update the priors when new data is added in the database. On a fingerprint database obtained from different law enforcement agencies, experimental results show that the proposed algorithm is at least 2.52% better than the existing fusion algorithms. Section 2 presents an overview of DS theory and Section 3 presents the proposed classifier fusion algorithm. Section 4 shows the experimental results followed by conclusion in Section 5.

2   Overview of Dempster-Shafer Theory

Let Θ be a finite set of mutually exclusive and exhaustive proposition or commonly known as frame of discernment. The power set 2^{Θ} is the set of all subsets of Θ including itself and null set $\emptyset$. Each subset in the power set is called focal element. A value between $[0, 1]$ is assigned to each focal element which is based on the evidence. 0 shows no belief and 1 shows total belief. Basic belief assignment (bba), in DS theory, is assigned to the individual proposition which is also known as mass of the individual proposition. It is assigned to every subset of the power set. If bba of an individual proposition A is $m(A)$ then,

$$\sum_{A \subset \Theta} m(A) = 1 \tag{1}$$

Also, bba of a null set is zero, i.e.

$$m(\emptyset) = 0 \tag{2}$$

Ignorance is represented by assigning the complementary probability to $m(\Theta)$. Measure of total belief committed to A, $Bel(A)$, is computed using Equation 3.

$$Bel(A) = \sum_{B \subset A} m(B) \tag{3}$$

According to Smets [10], formal notation of Bel is given as,

$$Bel_{Y,t}^{\Theta,\Re}[E_{Y,t}](\omega_o \in A) = x \tag{4}$$

This equation denotes the degree of belief x of the classifier Y at time t when ω_o belongs to set A, where A is the subset of Θ and $A \in \Re$; $\Re$ is a Boolean algebra of Θ. Belief is based on the evidential corpus $E_{Y,t}$ held by Y at time t where

$E_{Y,t}$ represents all what Y knows at time t. For simplicity $Bel_{Y,t}^{\Theta,\Re}[E_{Y,t}](\omega_o \in A)$ can be written as $Bel[E](A)$ or $Bel(A)$.

Plausibility function of A is defined as,

$$Pl(A) = 1 - Bel(\neg A) = \sum_{B \cap A \neq \emptyset} m(B) \tag{5}$$

$Bel(A)$ represents the lower limit of probability and $Pl(A)$ represents the upper limit. The difference between belief function and plausibility function represents the ignorance and $Bel(\Theta) = 1$, $Pl(\Theta) = 1$.

In most of the cases, it is required to update the belief based on new evidences or data. Let $E \subset \Theta$ and E_v be the evidence which states that the actual world is not in $\neg E$. Now suppose that the new data or evidence provides the exact value of E_v. Belief function is revised using the Dempster's rule of conditioning,

$$Bel[E_v](A) = Bel(A \cup \neg E) - Bel(\neg E) \tag{6}$$

Further, multiple evidences can be combined using Dempster's rule of combination. Let A and B be used for computing new belief function for the focal element C, Dempster's rule of combination is written as

$$m(C) = \frac{\sum_{A \cap B = C} m(A)m(B)}{1 - \sum_{A \cap B = \emptyset} m(A)m(B)} \tag{7}$$

3   DS Theory Based Classifier Fusion

In the proposed classifier fusion algorithm, DS theory [9], [10] is applied to combine the output of individual fingerprint verification algorithms to improve the verification performance shown in Figure 1. Minutiae based fingerprint verification algorithm [1], ridge based verification algorithm [2], fingercode based

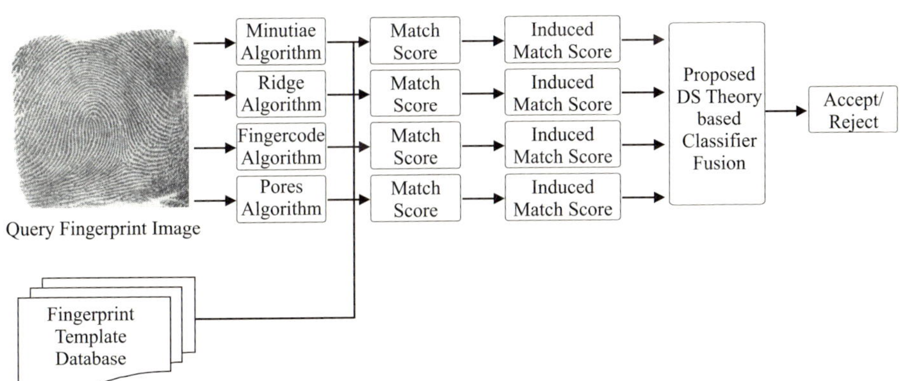

Fig. 1. Fusing the outputs of four fingerprint verification algorithms using proposed DS Theory based classifier fusion algorithm

verification algorithm [3] and pores based verification algorithm [4] are used as the primary classifiers. For every input fingerprint image, each classifier assigns a label true or 1 to proposition i, $i \in \Theta$ and the remaining classes are labeled as false or 0. Thus there are two focal elements for each fingerprint verification algorithm i and $\neg i = \Theta - i$. i is for confirming and $\neg i$ is for denying a single proposition for mass assignment in the DS theory. For every verification algorithm, we compute the respective predictive rates which are used to assign their bba. For a c class problem, let us assume that an input pattern belonging to class j $(j \in c)$ be classified as one of the k $(k \in c + 1)$ classes including the rejection class, i.e. $(c+1)^{th}$ class. So, the predictive rate of a classifier P_k for an output class k is the ratio of the number of input patterns classified correctly to the total number of patterns classified as class k where input patterns belonging to all classes is presented to the classifier.

In the proposed approach, when the jth fingerprint verification algorithm classifies the result $k \in (c + 1)$ over the normalized matching score S_j, it is considered that for all instances the likelihood of k being the actual class is P_k and the likelihood of k not being the correct class is $(1 - P_k)$. For the jth fingerprint verification algorithm, first the decision induced match score is computed by multiplying P_{kj} with the respective normalized match score S_j. This score is then used as the basic belief assignment or mass $m_j(k)$ (Equation 8).

$$m_j(k) = P_{kj} \cdot S_j \tag{8}$$

where $j = 1, 2, 3, 4$, corresponds to the four fingerprint verification algorithms. Similarly disbelief is assigned to $m_j(\neg k)$; with $m(\Theta) = 1$. Further, mass of each evidence or classifier is combined recursively using Equation 9,

$$m_{final} = m_1 \oplus m_2 \oplus m_3 \oplus m_4 \tag{9}$$

where $\oplus$ shows the Dempster rule of combination. Since we are dealing with two class problem (true, false), we do not have to deal with the increasing computational complexity of DS theory [9]. Final result is obtained by applying threshold t to m_{final},

$$Result = \begin{cases} Accept, & if \quad m_{final} \geq t \\ Reject, & otherwise \end{cases} \tag{10}$$

Finally, the Dempster rule of conditioning given in Equation 6 is used to update the belief assignment associated with each fingerprint algorithm as and when required. With this rule, only new or updated bba is used for modification. This rule makes the update process easy as it is not required to train the complete classification algorithm when a new training data is added.

4   Experimental Results

Proposed DS theory based classifier fusion algorithm is validated using a fingerprint database obtained from different law enforcement agencies. The database contains five rolled fingerprints and five slap fingerprints from 500 different classes. All the fingerprints are scanned at 1000 ppi. From each class, two rolled fingerprint images are randomly selected as training data. Rest of the images from each class are used as the test data. As stated earlier, minutiae based algorithm [1], ridge based algorithm [2], fingercode based algorithm [3] and pores based algorithm [4] are used as the primary classifiers. In the experiments, we compute the verification accuracy of all the algorithms at 0.001% false accept rate (FAR). Experimental results are divided into four subsections. In the first subsection, we compute the verification accuracies when test image is rolled fingerprint image, i.e. matching a rolled fingerprint with rolled fingerprint. In the next experiment, explained in Section 4.2, we compute the verification accuracies with slap fingerprints as the test images, i.e. matching rolled fingerprint with slap fingerprint. There are approximately 20 - 25 minutiae in a slap fingerprint which is less than the number of minutiae in rolled fingerprints (60 - 80 minutiae). Thus this experiment evaluates the performance when limited amount of information is present. The third experiment, which is the comparison of proposed fusion algorithm with existing fusion algorithms, is presented in Section 4.3. Finally, Section 4.4 presents the advantage of using Dempster rule of conditioning to reduce the training time.

4.1   Matching Rolled Fingerprints

For matching two rolled fingerprints using the four individual fingerprint verification algorithms, the best performance of 90.04% is obtained from minutiae based verification algorithm followed by 88.45% accuracy from pores based algorithm. Ridge and fingercode based algorithms give an accuracy of 84.61% and 85.39% respectively. Figure 2 shows the ROC plot of this experiment. It also shows that the verification accuracy of 98.14% is obtained when outputs of all the four verification algorithms are fused using the proposed DS theory based classifier fusion algorithm. Thus, the fingerprint verification performance is improved by 8.1%. Further, the verification accuracy of all the combinations of individual verification algorithms is computed by fusing the outputs of different verification algorithms using proposed fusion algorithm. Results are shown in Table 1. It shows that any combination with minutiae and pores based algorithms give better accuracy in comparison with other combinations.

4.2   Matching Rolled Fingerprint with Slap Fingerprint

In this experiment, the database images are rolled fingerprints and the testing dataset consists of slap fingerprints. Verification performance is computed for all combinations of four verification algorithms. Results of this experiment are shown in Table 2. It shows that the verification accuracy for all the combinations decreases by 2 - 3% in comparison to the verification accuracy of matching rolled to rolled fingerprints. In this experiment, fusion of outputs of all the four verification algorithms gives best result with 97.34% followed by fusion of minutiae and pores based algorithms with 95.85%.

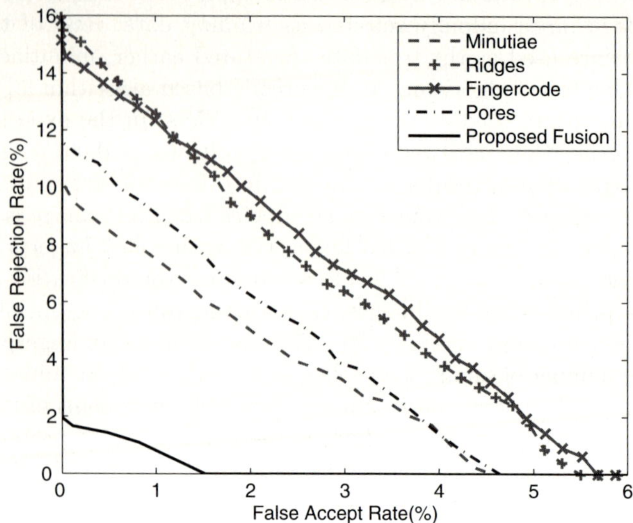

Fig. 2. ROC plot showing the performance of proposed fusion algorithm and individual fingerprint verification algorithms

Table 1. Verification accuracies of possible combinations using proposed fusion algorithm at 0.001% FAR (Matching rolled fingerprints)

Fusion Combination	Verification Accuracy
Minutiae + Ridges	94.70 %
Minutiae + Fingercode	94.66 %
Minutiae + Pores	96.43 %
Ridge + Fingercode	92.78 %
Ridge + Pores	93.89 %
Fingercode + Pores	93.56 %
Minutiae + Ridges + Fingercode	94.74 %
Minutiae + Ridges + Pores	96.07 %
Minutiae + Fingercode + Pores	95.69 %
Ridges + Fingercode + Pores	95.15 %
Minutiae + Ridges + Fingercode + Pores	**98.14 %**

Further, we cropped the testing fingerprint images (slap fingerprints) such that no minutiae is present in the image with the constraint that the size of input testing image is 64 × 64. Using these images as testing images, we found that only pores based algorithm gives best performance with 87.93% whereas other verification algorithms give 0% accuracy. When the outputs are fused, any combination which includes the output of pores based algorithm give an accuracy of 87.93% and rest of the combinations give 0% verification accuracy. This experiment shows that with limited information pores based algorithm

Table 2. Verification accuracies of possible combinations using proposed fusion algorithm at 0.001% FAR with slap fingerprint images (Matching rolled fingerprints with slap fingerprints)

Fusion Combination	Verification Accuracy
Minutiae + Ridges	92.62 %
Minutiae + Fingercode	92.23 %
Minutiae + Pores	95.85 %
Ridge + Fingercode	90.46 %
Ridge + Pores	91.27 %
Fingercode + Pores	90.91 %
Minutiae + Ridges + Fingercode	93.12 %
Minutiae + Ridges + Pores	94.76 %
Minutiae + Fingercode + Pores	93.51 %
Ridges + Fingercode + Pores	94.08 %
Minutiae + Ridges + Fingercode + Pores	**97.34 %**

is more useful and the proposed fusion algorithm is able to correctly fuse the outputs without compromising the verification performance.

4.3   Comparison with Existing Fusion Algorithms

In this experiment, a comparison of the proposed DS theory based classifier fusion algorithm with existing fusion algorithms is performed. For comparison, rolled fingerprint images are used as both training and testing images and fusion is performed with the outputs of minutiae and pores based algorithms only. Existing algorithms which are used for comparison are: Min/Max rule [5], Product rule [5], Sum rule [5], [6], and SVM fusion [8]. Figure 3 shows the ROC plot of this experiment. In this experiment, we found that Min/Max rule gives verification accuracy of 91.17%, product rule gives 92.01%, sum rule gives 92.76%, SVM fusion gives 93.91% whereas the proposed fusion algorithm outperforms these four fusion algorithms by at least 2.52% and gives an accuracy of 96.43%. This shows that the proposed fusion algorithm leads to greater improvement in performance compared to the other fusion algorithms.

4.4   Experiments with Dempster Rule of Conditioning

Another advantage of the proposed classifier fusion algorithm is low time complexity due to the Dempster's rule of conditioning. With this rule, the training time is reduced by splitting large dataset into smaller parts and updating mass assignments using the conditioning rule. Table 3 shows that when database size is 100, training time with and without conditioning rule is 245 seconds. This includes the time taken by four fingerprint verification algorithms and the proposed classifier fusion algorithm. When conditioning rule is not used, time required for training increases significantly with the increase in database size. However, the increment in time taken to train the database is much less when the conditioning

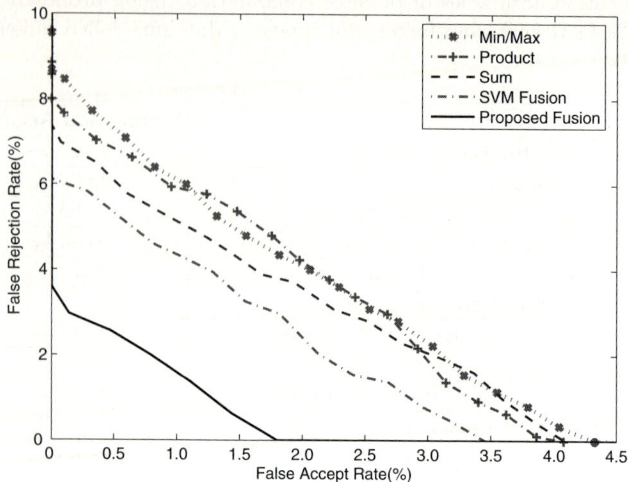

Fig. 3. ROC plot showing the performance comparison of proposed fusion algorithm with existing fusion algorithms

Table 3. Reducing training time of proposed fusion algorithm using Dempster's rule of conditioning

Database Size	Training time of fusion without conditioning (seconds)	Training time of fusion with conditioning (seconds)
100	245	245
200	459	392
300	631	538
400	829	685
500	1022	831

rule is used and is in the range of 146 - 147 seconds. This experiment shows that the use of conditioning algorithm can reduce the time complexity of fusion algorithm.

5   Conclusion

Improving the performance of fingerprint recognition algorithms is of paramount interest. In this paper, we proposed Dempster-Shafer theory based classifier fusion algorithm for improving fingerprint verification performance. Decision induced match scores of individual classifiers are used to compute the belief function in the DS theory based fusion algorithm. Further, multiple evidences are fused using Dempster's rule of combination. Four fingerprint algorithms are used as primary classifiers. Using a fingerprint database obtained from law enforcement agencies, verification accuracies of individual algorithms range from 84.61%

to 90.04%, whereas the proposed fusion algorithm gives an accuracy of 98.14% which is an improvement of around 8%. Further, performance of the proposed fusion algorithm is evaluated when limited information is presented and experimental results show that the proposed fusion algorithm is able to give consistent performance. A comparison of proposed fusion algorithm with existing fusion techniques is also performed, which demonstrates that the proposed fusion algorithm gives best results with 96.43% verification accuracy followed by SVM based fusion algorithm [8] with 93.91% accuracy. Finally, Dempster's rule of conditioning is used to reduce the time taken for training the database. Using this rule, time taken for training the database is reduced by approximately 191 seconds. This level of results shows the usefulness of proposed fusion algorithm for fingerprint recognition systems.

Acknowledgment

This research is supported in part through a grant (Award No. 2003-RC-CX-K001) from the Office of Science and Technology, National Institute of Justice, Office of Justice Programs, United States Department of Justice.

References

1. Jain, A. K., Hong, L., Bolle, R.: On-line fingerprint verification. IEEE Transactions on PAMI. **19(4)** (1997) 302–314
2. Marana, A. N., Jain, A. K.: Ridge-based fingerprint matching using hough transform. Proceedings of Brazilian Symposium on Computer Graphics and Image Processing. (2005) 112–119
3. Jain, A. K., Prabhakar, S., Hong, L., Pankanti, S.: FingerCode: a filterbank for fingerprint representation and matching. Proccodings of IEEE Conference on CVPR. **2** (1999) 187–193
4. Kryszczuk, K., Drygajlo, A., Morier, P.: Extraction of level 2 and level 3 features for fragmentary fingerprints. Proceedings of the 2nd COST275 Workshop. (2004) 83–88
5. Kittler, J., Hatef, M., Duin, R. P., Matas, J. G.: On combining classifiers. IEEE Transactions on PAMI. **20(3)** (1998) 226–239
6. Ross, A., Jain, A. K.: Information fusion in biometrics. Pattern Recognition Letters. **24(13)** (2003) 2115–2125
7. Teoh, A., Samad, S. A., Hussain, A.: Nearest neighborhood classifiers in a bimodal biometric verification system fusion decision scheme. Journal of Research and Practice in Information Technology. **36(1)** (2004) 47–62
8. Aguilar, J. F., Garcia, J. O., Rodriguez, J. G., Bigun, J.: Kernel-based multimodal biometric verification using quality signals. Proceedings of SPIE Biometric Technology for Human Identification. **5404** (2004) 544–554
9. Shafer, G.: A mathematical theory of evidence. Princeton University Press 1976
10. Smets, P.: Decision making in a context where uncertainty is represented by belief functions. Belief Functions in Business Decisions (Srivastava, R., Mock, T. J. (ed.)) Physica-Verlag (2002) 17–61

Fingerprint Image Enhancement Using Decimation Free Directional Adaptive Mean Filtering

Muhammad Talal Ibrahim[1], Imtiaz A. Taj[2], M. Khalid Khan[3],
and M. Aurangzeb Khan[3]

[1] Department of Computer Engineering,
Center for Advanced Studies in Engineering, Islamabad, Pakistan
mtalal@gmail.com
[2] Department of Computer Engineering,
Center for Advanced Studies in Engineering, Islamabad, Pakistan
imtiaz@carepvtltd.com
[3] Department of Electrical Engineering,
COMSATS Institute of Information technology, Islamabad, Pakistan
khalid_aurangzeb@yahoo.com

Abstract. In this paper we proposed a new enhancement technique that is based on the integration of Decimation Free Directional responses of the Decimation Free Directional Filter Banks (DDFB), adaptive mean filtering and the eigen decomposition of the Hessian matrix. By decomposing the input fingerprint image into decimation free directional images, it is easy to remove the noise directionally by means of adaptive mean filtering and further eigen decomposition of the Hessian matrix was used for the segmentation purpose. As the input fingerprint image is not uniformly illuminated so we have used the bandpass filter for the elimination of non-uniform illumination and for the creation of frequency ridge image before giving it to DDFB. The final enhanced result is constructed on a block-by-block basis by comparing energy of all the directional images and picking one that provides maximum energy.

1   Introduction

Fingerprint is the first biometric system adopted by law enforcement agencies, and now is also the most widely used system. A fingerprint is believed to be unique to each person. Fingerprints of even identical twins are different thats why they have gained so much popularity for the identification purpose. Any fingerprint identification system highly depends on the quality of the fingerprint image. As the fingerprint images are corrupted by different kinds of noise so the need of enhancement is always there. Several techniques have been proposed in the literature for fingerprint image enhancement but there is still need of improvement.

Researchers in recent years have used different methods for the enhancement of the fingerprint. In a recent study[1] fingerprint enhancement, feature extraction and matching [2] has been proposed using directional filter banks. One most

P. Kalra and S. Peleg (Eds.): ICVGIP 2006, LNCS 4338, pp. 950–961, 2006.
© Springer-Verlag Berlin Heidelberg 2006

commonly used directional filter for fingerprint enhancement and matching is a Gabor filter [3,4]. They have both frequency-selective and orientation-selective properties and have optimal joint resolution in both spatial and frequency domains. They have been used in [5], where the gradient direction of the pixels have been identified and then the image is being filtered according to the gradient direction and combined to get an enhanced image. The use of the second directional derivatives has been proposed in [6] where the positive second directional derivative was used to detect the ridges in the image.

In this paper we have used DDFB for the directional analysis of the input image and then adaptive mean filtering was used for the noise removal. After applying adaptive mean filtering on each of the directional image as an output of DDFB, the eigen decomposition of the Hessian matrix was computed at each image pixel. Rest of the paper is organized as follows: in Section II, the proposed system is discussed whereas reconstruction of the enhanced image, some of the experimental results and a comparison is presented in Section III.

2 Fingerprint Image Enhancement

The proposed system takes the fingerprint as an input for the enhancement as shown in Fig. 1. The main steps involved in the proposed system are described below in a sequential order.

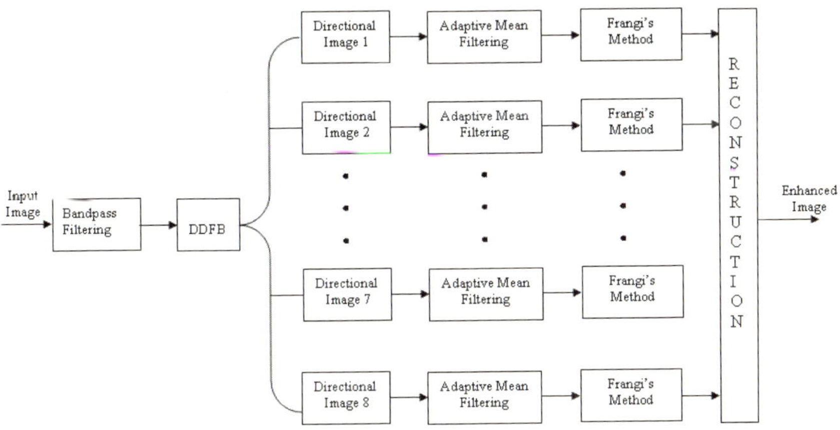

Fig. 1. Proposed Fingerprint Image Enhancement System

2.1 Illumination Adjustment and Creation of Ridge Frequency Image

The fingerprint can be approximated by a two-dimensional sinusoidal of different orientations as proposed in [7,5]. It is shown in Fig. 3, that a periodic sinusoid of a particular orientation in the spatial domain is represented by two points in

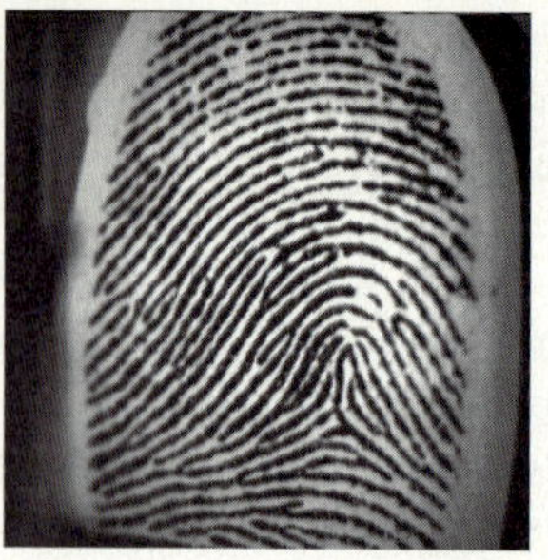

Fig. 2. Fingerprint Test Image

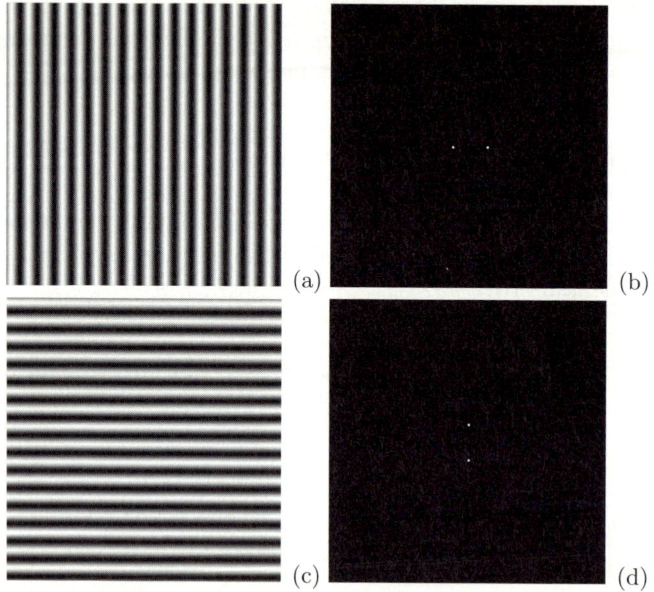

Fig. 3. a,c) Periodic Sinusoidal of a particular direction in Spatial Domain b,d) Periodic Sinusoidal represented by two points in frequency Domain

the frequency domain. As the fingerprint image is a two dimensional sinusoids of different orientations, so the ridge frequencies are represented by the points in a circular region in the frequency domain as show in in Fig. 4. As we are interested in the enhancement of the ridges only rather than the background, we have used the bandpass filter whose passband allows the ridge frequencies represented by the circular region in the frequency domain to pass through it. The bandpass filter not only allows us to have a ridge frequency image but also helps in the removal of non-uniform illumination. As the non-uniform illumination is present as low frequency content in the frequency domain, so we have applied the non-ideal butterworth bandpass filter. It is filtered out by the lower stop-band region

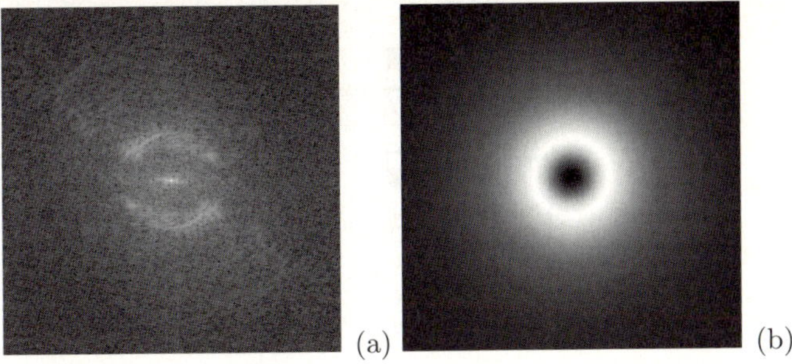

Fig. 4. a) Representation of image in Frequency Domain. b) Frequency Response of Bandpass Filter.

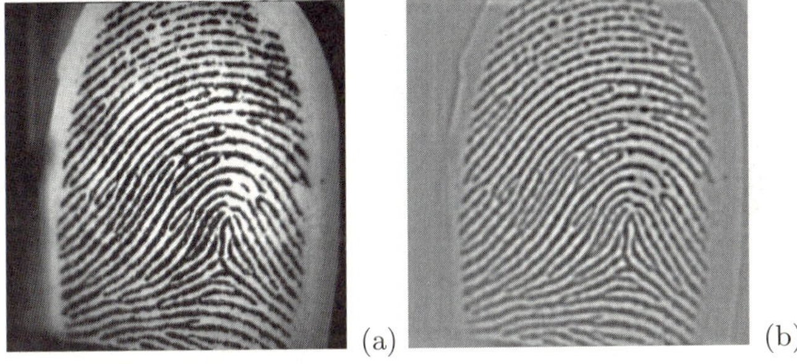

Fig. 5. Illumination Adjustment: a) Non-uniformly illuminated image. b) Simply processed to eliminate the effects of non-uniform illumination and having ridge frequencies only.

of the bandpass filter. High frequency noise is treated by the upper stop-band region of the bandpass filter. The equation of the bandpass filter is given below

$$H(u,v) = \begin{cases} 1 \text{ if } D(u,v) < D_0 - \frac{W}{2} \\ 0 \text{ if } D_0 - \frac{W}{2} \le D(u,v) \le D_0 + \frac{W}{2} \\ 1 \text{ if } D(u,v) > D_0 + \frac{W}{2} \end{cases} \qquad (1)$$

where $D(u,v)$ is a radial distance from the origin., W is the width of the band, and D_0 is the radial center. The bandpass filter was applied by taking the discrete fourier transform (DFT) of the input image as shown in Fig. 4. After filtering the image, inverse DFT has been applied to transform the filtered image from fourier domain back to spatial domain. Finally we got a uniformly illuminated image having the ridge frequencies only as shown in Fig. 5. One important benefit of using bandpass filtering is that the segmentation of Fig. 5.b in order to find the fingerprint area is easier as compared to the original image and we can use the local variance to segment the image. We used the bandpass filter whose passband is designed in such a way that only the ridge frequencies can pass through it as shown in Fig. 4.

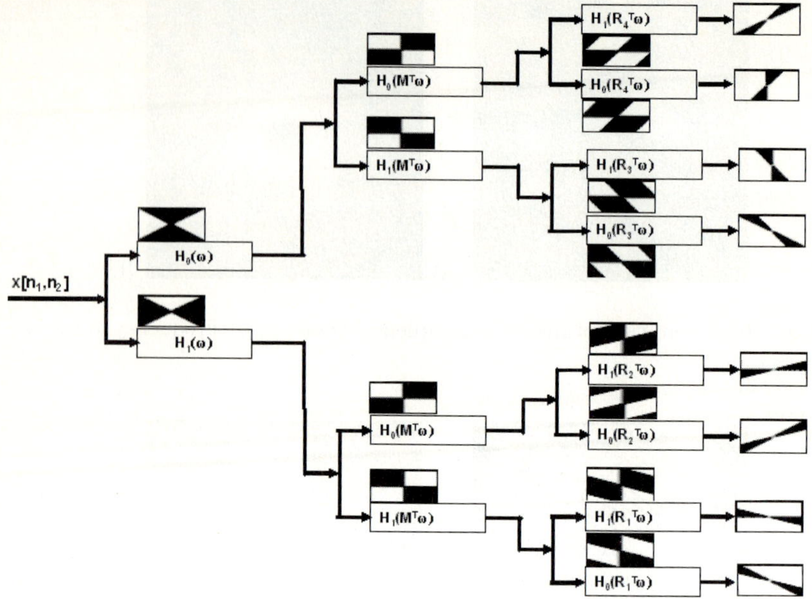

Fig. 6. Schematic Diagram of DDFB

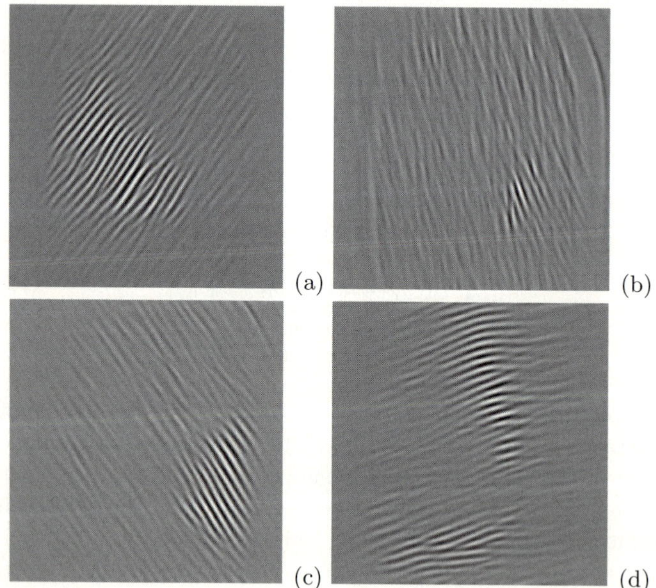

Fig. 7. Four out of eight Directional Images

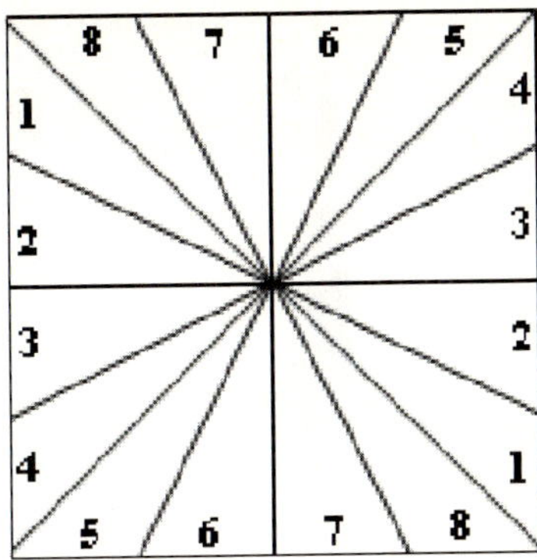

Fig. 8. Frequency partition map for 8-band DFB

2.2   Creation of Decimation-Free Directional Images

We have used the Decimation Free Directional Filter Banks (DDFB) for the directional analysis of the input image as proposed in [1]. The reason for using the DDFB rather than the Directional Filter banks(DFB), is that the output of the DDFB is of the same size as of the input image, so we can avoid extra step of interpolation which was required for the output of DFB for the enhancement purpose. DDFB decomposes the spectral region of the input image into wedge-shaped passband regions shown in Fig. 8. It is easily shown that these wedge-shaped regions correspond to directional components of an image. The filters related to wedge-shaped regions are commonly referred to as fan filters [8]. The block diagram of DDFB structure is shown in Fig. 6. Four out of eight directional images are shown in Fig. 7.

2.3   Noise Removal Using Adaptive Mean Filtering

We have used the adaptive mean filtering [9] for the removal of the gaussian noise in each of the eight directional outputs of the DDFB as shown in Fig. 9. As noise is a random variable, so it can be measured statistically by using its mean and variance which are closely related to the appearance of an image. The average gray level is represented by the mean in the local region S_{xy} over which it is computed, and variance gives the measure of average contrast in that local region S_{xy}. The equation of adaptive mean filter is given below

$$output = g(x,y) - \frac{\sigma_\eta^2}{\sigma_L^2}[g(x,y) - m_L], \tag{2}$$

Our filter operates locally in a region, S_{xy}. The response of the filter at any point (x,y) on which the region is centered is to be based on four quantities:

1. $g(x,y)$, the value of the noisy image at (x,y).

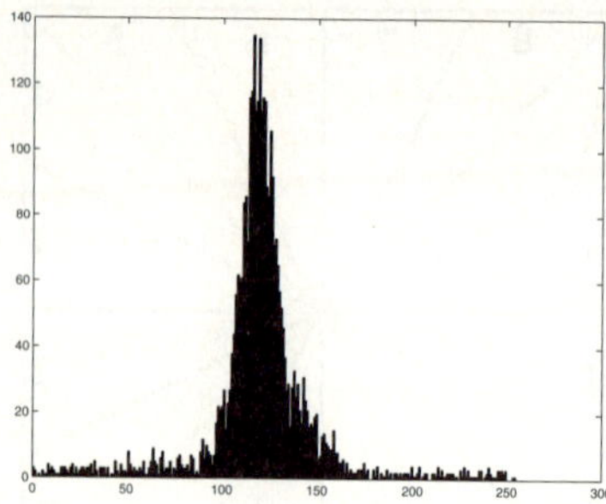

Fig. 9. Noise represented by Gaussian Distribution

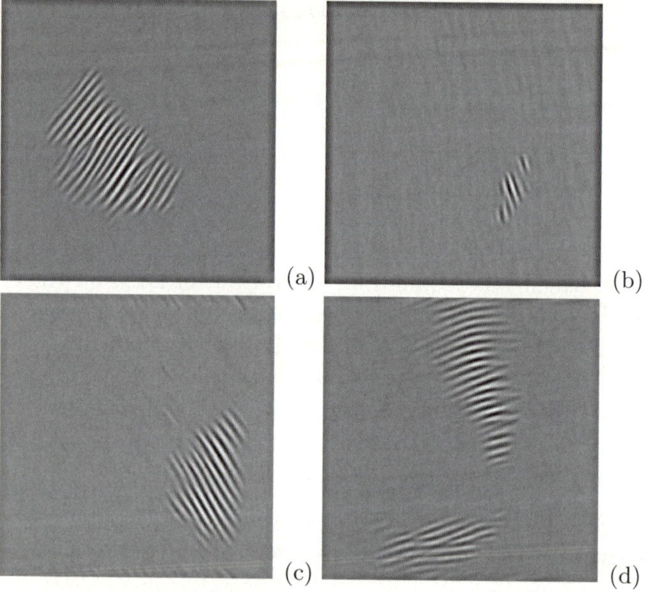

Fig. 10. Creation of noise-free images: (a) Noise-free image of Fig. 7. a, (b) Noise-free image of Fig. 7 b, (c) Noise-free image of Fig. 7. c, (d) Noise-free image of Fig. 7. d

2. σ_η^2, the variance of the noise corrupting f(x,y) to form g(x,y)) and can be calculated as

$$\sigma_\eta^2 = \sum_{z_i \varepsilon S_{xy}} (z_i - \mu_\eta)^2 p(z_i) \tag{3}$$

μ can be calculated as

$$\mu_\eta = \sum_{z_i \varepsilon S_{xy}} (z_i) p(z_i) \tag{4}$$

3. m_L, the local mean of the pixels in S_{xy}.
4. σ_L^2, the local variance of the pixels in S_{xy}.

where z_i is the value of the gray level in S_{xy} and $p(z_i)$ is the probability of each gray level in S_{xy}. The results after applying the adaptive mean filtering is shown in Fig. 10. It can be seen that the filter has removed the noise directionally.

2.4   Segmentation of Decimation Free Directional Images

In this section, noise-free images obtained as an output of DDFB are segmented in a way that whole ridge structure can easily be discriminated from the background.

In recent years there has been a fair amount of research on fingerprint and vessel enhancement. One popular way is to use eigen decomposition of the Hessian computed at each image pixel [10], [11], [12], [13], [14]. We proved that this enhancement which was initially used for detecting blood vessels in the medical images can be successfully used to enhance ridges. Eigenvalues are used in rules to decide if a particular location is a ridge pixel or not. When a pixel passes this test, the eigenvector corresponding to the smaller (in absolute value) eigenvalue points along the vessel. The signs of the eigenvalues determine bright or dark structures. Vesselness measures are defined in [11]and [12]. Frangi et al. [11]

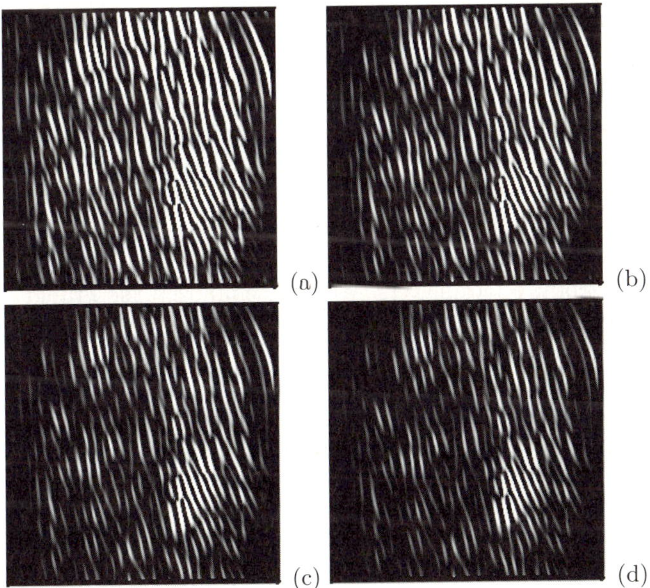

Fig. 11. Results obtained by applying Frangi's method on Fig. 7 at different values of β_2 but at constant β_1. (a) Segmented image of Fig. 10. b with $\beta_1 = 2$ and $\beta_2 = 4$, (b) Segmented image of Fig. 10 b with $\beta_1 = 2$ and $\beta_2 = 6$, (c) Segmented image of Fig. 10. b with $\beta_1 = 2$ and $\beta_2 = 8$. (d) Segmented image of Fig. 10. b with $\beta_1 = 2$ and $\beta_2 = 10$.It is clear from all the results that by increasing the value of β_2 we have managed to reduce noise but on expense of low-contrast ridges which also diminished along with noise. Where β_1 and β_2 are thresholds which control the sensitivity of the measures R_A and R_B.

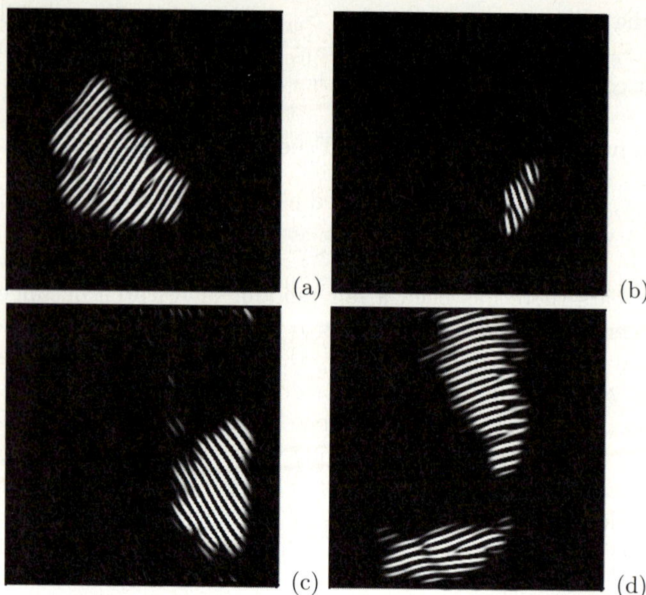

Fig. 12. (a) Segmented image of Fig. 10. a, (b) Segmented image of Fig. 10 b, (c) Segmented image of Fig. 10. c, (d) Segmented image of Fig. 10. d.

proposed using ratios of the eigenvalues $|\lambda_1| \leq |\lambda_2| \leq |\lambda_3|$ to determine scores $R_B = |\lambda|/|\lambda_2\lambda_3|$ and $R_A = |\lambda_2|/|\lambda_3|$ and computing the Frobenius norm, S, of Hessian to measure overall strength. For tube-like structures, including vessels, R_B should be low and R_A should be high. Since there is an involvement of second order derivatives the presence of noise is significant. For eliminating noise Frangi et. al. introduce parameters. We have employed the Frangi's method on the directional images obtained as an output of the previous step as shown in Fig. 12. We also implemented the Frangi's method direct to the input image as shown in Fig. 11, it is clear from the Fig. 11 that for the fingerprint image enhancement we cant use the Frangi's method directly, we need to remove the noise directionally, so we can say that the noise present in the fingerprint image was a directional noise which needs to be removed directionally by means of adaptive mean filtering.

3   Reconstruction of Enhanced Image

We have used directional energy of the cleaned directional images for construction of enhanced image. In DDFB we can compare energy estimates for samples which correspond to the same spatial regions due to the same size of directional images. Overlapping block-by-block directional energy is computed for each directional image by using the formula given below:

$$D^i_{energy}(x, y) = \Sigma(\Sigma(|D^i_{image}(x : x + B(1), y : y + B(2)) - m_B|)), \qquad (5)$$

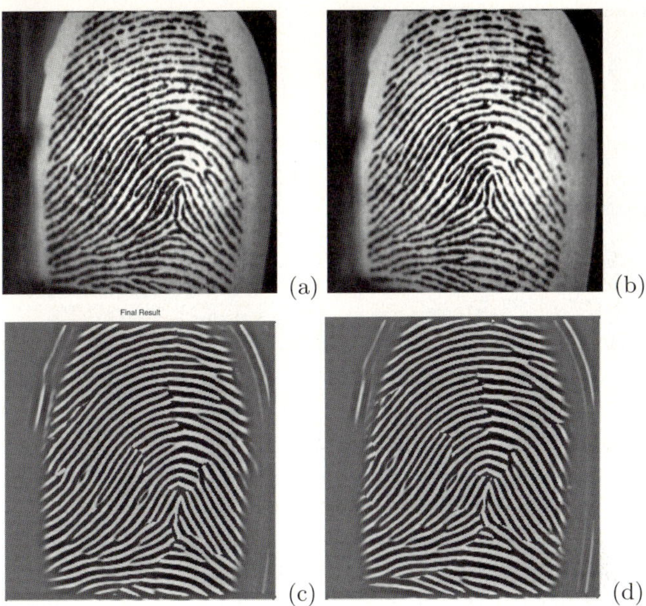

(a)   (b)

(c)   (d)

Fig. 13. (a),(b) Images of the same subject from the FVC2002 Database.(c),(d) Enhanced Images of (a),(b).

where B is a vector which defines the block size $B(1) \times B(2)$ for which the energy is to be calculated, and (x, y) represents pixel positions in an integer image lattice. $D^i_{image}(x : x + B(1), y : y + B(2))$ represents block from directional image i and m_B represents the mean of that block. Here m_B is subtracted from each block to remove the effect of local non-uniform illumination. In this manner we will have eight directional energy images D^i_{energy} $(i = 1, 2, 3, 4, 5, 6, 7, 8)$, where each directional energy image correspond to one of the eight directional images.

Energy equation used in this paper gives the rate of change among pixel values. Enhanced image H_{enh} can be constructed from the directional energy images by using following steps.

1. For each pixel (x, y) find the energy image having maximum directional energy. For example, for pixel position (x, y), we would find maximum $(max(D^i_{energy}(x, y)))$ in all D^i_{energy} images. Here (x, y) are pixel positions in an image lattice. Mathematically we can say that,

$$[m, ind] = max(D^i_{energy}(x, y)) \tag{6}$$

   where i = 1,2,3,4,5,6,7,8.

where m is the value of maximum energy for a particular pixel position (x, y) and ind is the index of D_{energy} image from which pixel (x, y) is declared as maximum. After calculating maximum energy for each pixel we form a new image E_{image} having only maximum energies. This E_{image} is the final enhanced fingerprint.

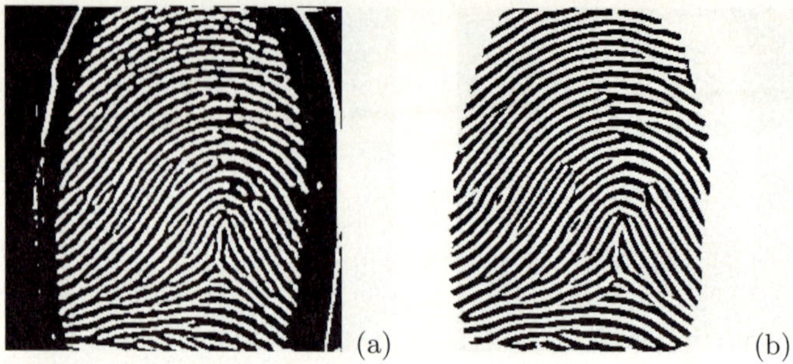

(a)   (b)

Fig. 14. (a) Result of Binarization of original image. (b) Result of Binarization of enhanced image.

The final enhanced fingerprint image E_{image} obtained is shown in Fig. 13c. Comparing the result with the original image shown in Fig. 2 reveals that all the ridge structure is intact while the spatial noise has been cleaned substantially. Fig. 14 show the results of binarization of the original image and that of the enhanced image respectively. We see that enhanced fingerprint image results in a binary image with clear ridges and valleys. The quality of the fingerprint image enhancement system depends on how it enhances the fingerprint images of the same person. We have tested our proposed approach on the fingerprint images from FVC2002 and the comparison between Fig. 13c,d with the images shown in Fig. 13a,b reveals that the proposed system has enhanced both the images in the same manner which is the requirement of any fingerprint recognizing system for the identification.

References

1. M. Khalid Khan Mohammad A.U. Khan and M. Aurangzeb Khan, "Fingerprint image enhancement using decimation free directional filter banks," *Information Technology Journal*, vol. 4, no. 4, pp. 16–20, 2005.
2. C. H. Park, J. J. Lee, M. J. T. Smith, S. Park, and K. J. Park, "Directional filter bank-based fingerprint feature extraction and matching," *IEEE. Trans. on Circuits and Systems for Video Technology*, vol. 14, no. 1, pp. 74–85, Jan. 2004.
3. A. K. Jain and F. Farrokhnia, "Unsupervised texture segmentation using gabor filters," *Pattern Recog*, vol. 24, pp. 1167–1186, 1991.
4. L. Hong S. Pankanti A. K. Jain, S. Prabhakar, "Filterbank-based fingerprint matching," *IEEE Transactions on Image Processing*, vol. 9, no. 5, pp. 846–859, 2000.
5. Y. Wan L. Hong and A. K. Jain, "Fingerprint image enhancement: algorithm and performance evaluation," *EEE Transactions on Pattern Analysis and Machine Intelligence*, vol. 20, no. 8, pp. 777–789, 1998.
6. V. Onnia M. Tico and P. Huosmanen, "Fingerprint image enhancement based on second directional derivative of the digital image," *EURASIP Journal on Applied Signal Processing*, , no. 10, pp. 1135–1144, 2002.
7. *Handbook of Image and Video Processing editor Al-Bovik*, Academic Press., 2000.
8. R. Ansari, "Efficient iir and fir fan filters," *IEEE Trans. Circuits Syst.*, vol. CAS-34, pp. 941–945, Aug. 1987.

9. Rafael C. Gonzalez and Richard E. Woods, *Digital Image Processing (2nd Edition)*, Pearson Education, Inc., 2002.

10. S. Aylward and E. Bullitt, "Initialization, noise, singularities, and scale in height-ridge traversal for tubular object centerline extraction," *IEEE Trans. Medical Imaging*, vol. 21, pp. 61–75, 2002.

11. A. Frangi, W. J. Niessen, K. L. Vincken, and M. A. Viergever, "Multiscale vessel enhancement filtering," in *1st International Conference of Medical Image Computing and Computer-Assisted Intervention (MICCAI 1998)*, 1998, pp. 130–137.

12. T. Lindeberg, "Edge detection and ridge detection with automatic scale selection," *International Journal of Computer Vision*, vol. 30, pp. 117–156, Nov. 1998.

13. T. Lindeberg, "Feature detection with automatic scale selection," *International Journal of Computer Vision*, vol. 30, pp. 79–116, Nov. 1998.

14. Y. Sato, S. Nakajima, H. Atsumi, T. Koller, G. Gerig, S. Yoshida, and R. Kikinis, "3d multi-scale line filter for segmentation and visualization of curvilinear structures in medical images.," in *First Joint Conference Computer Vision, Virtual Reality and Robotics in Medicine and Medial Robotics and Computer-Assisted Surgery*, Grenoble, France, June 1997, pp. 213–222.

4. Link, [illegible], and Kachian, K. Witch[illegible], Perfor[illegible] [illegible] Plan[illegible] Char[illegible] Machine[illegible]
   Post[illegible] Symposium, New York, [illegible]
5. [illegible] and [illegible] Turner. [illegible] vaporization in a [illegible] enhance in heat [illegible]
   [illegible]

Author Index

Printing: Mercedes-Druck, Berlin
Binding: Stein+Lehmann, Berlin